Simply Visual Basic® 2008

Third Edition

Deitel® Series Page

Simply Series

Simply C++: An Application-Driven Tutorial Approach
Simply C#: An Application-Driven Tutorial Approach
Simply Java™ Programming: An Application-Driven Tutorial Approach
Simply Visual Basic® 2005, 2/E: An Application-Driven Tutorial Approach

How to Program Series

Internet & World Wide Web How to Program, 4/E
Java How to Program, 7/E
C++ How to Program, 6/E
C How to Program, 5/E
Visual Basic® 2005 How to Program, 3/E
Visual C#® 2005 How to Program, 2/E
Small Java™ How to Program, 6/E
Small C++ How to Program, 5/E
Advanced Java™ 2 Platform How to Program
XML How to Program
Visual C++® 2008 How to Program, 2/E
Perl How to Program
Python How to Program

Also Available

SafariX Web Books
`www.deitel.com/books/SafariX.html`
C++ How to Program, 5/E & 6/E
Java How to Program, 6/E & 7/E
Simply C++: An Application-Driven Tutorial Approach
Simply Visual Basic 2005: An Application-Driven Tutorial Approach, 2/E
Small C++ How to Program, 5/E
Small Java How to Program, 6/E
Visual Basic 2005 How to Program, 3/E
Visual C# 2005 How to Program, 2/E

To follow the Deitel publishing program, please register for the free *DEITEL® BUZZ ONLINE* e-mail newsletter at:

`www.deitel.com/newsletter/subscribe.html`

To communicate with the authors, send e-mail to:

`deitel@deitel.com`

For information on corporate on-site seminars offered by Deitel & Associates, Inc. worldwide, visit:

`www.deitel.com/training/`

or write to:

`deitel@deitel.com`

For continuing updates on Prentice Hall/Deitel publications visit:

`www.deitel.com`,
`www.prenhall.com/deitel`

Check out our Resource Centers for valuable web resources that will help you master Visual Basic, other important programming languages, software and Web 2.0 topics:

`www.deitel.com/ResourceCenters.html`

Simply Visual Basic® 2008

Third Edition

P. J. Deitel
Deitel & Associates, Inc.

H. M. Deitel
Deitel & Associates, Inc.

G. J. Ayer

Upper Saddle River, NJ 07458

Library of Congress Cataloging-in-Publication Data

On file

Vice President and Editorial Director, ECS: ***Marcia J. Horton***
Associate Editor: ***Carole Snyder***
Supervisor/Editorial Assistant: ***Dolores Mars***
Director of Team-Based Project Management: ***Vince O'Brien***
Senior Managing Editor: ***Scott Disanno***
Managing Editor: ***Robert Engelhardt***
Production Editor: ***Marta Samsel***
A/V Production Editor: ***Greg Dulles***
Art Studio: ***Artworks, York, PA***
Art Director: ***Kristine Carney***
Cover Design: ***Abbey S. Deitel, Harvey M. Deitel, Francesco Santalucia, Kristine Carney***
Interior Design: ***Harvey M. Deitel, Kristine Carney***
Manufacturing Manager: ***Alan Fischer***
Manufacturing Buyer: ***Lisa McDowell***
Director of Marketing: ***Margaret Waples***

Printed in the United States of America

10 9 8 7 6 5 4 3 2

ISBN 0-13-605303-3

Pearson Education Ltd., *London*

Pearson Education Australia Pty. Ltd., *Sydney*

Pearson Education Singapore, Pte. Ltd.

Pearson Education North Asia Ltd., *Hong Kong*

Pearson Education Canada, Inc., *Toronto*

Pearson Educación de Mexico, S.A. de C.V.

Pearson Education–Japan, *Tokyo*

Pearson Education Malaysia, Pte. Ltd.

Pearson Education, Inc., *Upper Saddle River, New Jersey*

To Carole Snyder of Prentice Hall:

Thank you for the extraordinary job you've done over the years recruiting and managing, under demanding time constraints, the academic and industry teams that review our books.

Paul and Harvey

To my father:

You've sacrificed more for me than I'll ever know,
And done more for me than you'll ever know.
I love you Dad.

Greg

Trademarks:

Deitel Resource Centers

Our Resource Centers focus on the vast amounts of free content available online. Find resources, downloads, tutorials, documentation, books, e-books, journals, articles, blogs, RSS feeds and more on many of today's hottest programming and technology topics. For the most up-to-date list of our Resource Centers, visit:

`www.deitel.com/ResourceCenters.html`

Let us know what other Resource Centers you'd like to see! Also, please register for the free *DEITEL® BUZZ ONLINE* e-mail newsletter at:

`www.deitel.com/newsletter/subscribe.html`

Dive Into Web 2.0 eBook

Computer Science
Regular Expressions
Games and Game Programming

Computer Game Programming
Computer Games
Mobile Gaming
Sudoku

Programming
ADO.NET
Adobe Flex
Ajax
Amazon Web Services
Apex
ASP.NET
ASP.NET 3.5
ASP.NET Ajax
C
C++
C++ Boost Libraries
C++ Game Programming
C#
Cloud Computing
Code Search Engines and Code Sites
Computer Game Programming
CSS 2.1
Dojo
Facebook Developer Platform
Flash 9
Java
Java Certification and Assessment Testing
Java Design Patterns
Java EE 5
Java SE 6
Java SE 7 (Dolphin) Resource Center
JavaFX
JavaScript
JSON
Microsoft LINQ
Microsoft Popfly
MySpace Developer Platform
.NET
.NET 3.0
.NET 3.5
OpenGL
OpenSocial
Perl
PHP
Programming Projects
Python
Regular Expressions
Refactoring
REST Web Services
Ruby
Ruby on Rails
Service-Oriented Architecture (SOA)
Silverlight
Visual Basic
Visual Basic 2008
Visual C++
Visual C# 2008 and C# 3.0
Visual Studio Team System
Web 3D Technologies
Web Services
Windows Presentation Foundation
XHTML
XML

Internet Business
Affiliate Programs
Competitive Analysis
Facebook Social Ads
Google AdSense
Google Analytics
Google Services
Internet Advertising
Internet Business Initiative
Internet Public Relations
Link Building
Location-Based Services
Online Lead Generation
Podcasting
Search Engine Optimization
Selling Digital Content
Sitemaps
Web Analytics
Website Monetization
YouTube and AdSense

Java
Java
Java Certification and Assessment Testing
Java Design Patterns
Java EE 5
Java SE 6
Java SE 7 (Dolphin) Resource Center
JavaFX

Microsoft
ADO.NET
ASP.NET
ASP.NET 3.5
ASP.NET Ajax
DotNetNuke (DNN)
Internet Explorer 7 (IE7)
Microsoft LINQ
Microsoft Popfly
.NET
.NET 3.0
.NET 3.5
SharePoint
Silverlight
Silverlight 2.0
SQL Server 2008
Visual Basic
Visual Basic 2008
Visual C++
Visual C# 2008 and C# 3.0
Visual Studio Team System
Windows Communication Foundation
Windows Presentation Foundation
Windows Vista

Open Source & LAMP Stack
Apache
DotNetNuke (DNN)
Eclipse
Firefox
Linux
MySQL
Open Source
Perl
PHP
Python
Ruby

Software
Apache
DotNetNuke (DNN)
Eclipse
Firefox
Internet Explorer 7 (IE7)
Linux
MySQL
Open Source
Search Engines
SharePoint
Skype
Web Servers
Wikis
Windows Vista

Web 2.0
Avatars
Alert Services
KNOL
Attention Economy
Blogging
Building Web Communities
Community Generated Content
Facebook Developer Platform
Facebook Social Ads
Google Base
Google Video
Google Web Toolkit (GWT)
Internet Video
Joost
Location-Based Services
Mashups
Microformats
Recommender Systems
RSS
Social Graph
Social Media
Social Networking
Software as a Service (SaaS)
Virtual Worlds
Web 2.0
Web 3.0
Widgets

Other Topics
Computer Games
Computing Jobs
Gadgets and Gizmos
Ring Tones
Sudoku

Brief Table of Contents

Simply
a can opener

ONTENTS

PREFACE

Welcome to the Visual Basic® 2008 programming language and the world of Microsoft® Windows®, and Internet and web programming with Microsoft's .NET 3.5 platform! At Deitel & Associates, we write programming language textbooks and professional books for Prentice Hall, deliver corporate training courses worldwide and develop Web 2.0 Internet businesses. This book, which is part of our *Simply* series, has been updated based on Visual Studio 2008 and .NET 3.5. Our goal was to write a book that focuses on core concepts and features while keeping the discussion as simple as possible. The book is intended for readers using Windows Vista® or Windows® XP.

To achieve this goal, we implemented an innovative teaching methodology. We present the core concepts of leading-edge computing technologies using the tutorial-based, APPLICATION-DRIVEN approach, combined with the DEITEL® signature LIVE-CODE approach of teaching programming using complete, working, real-world applications. We merged the notion of a lab manual with that of a conventional textbook, creating a book that works well in a traditional classroom setting or with students sitting at computers and building each example application as they read the tutorials. The book is also appropriate for online distance learning courses.

As students work through the tutorials, they learn about visual programming, graphical-user-interface (GUI) components, file processing, database processing and web-based applications development. Most sections are followed by self-review questions with answers, so that students receive immediate feedback.

All of this has been carefully reviewed by distinguished academics, industry developers and Microsoft Visual Basic team members who worked with us on *Simply Visual Basic 2008®, Third Edition.*

We believe that this book and its support materials provide students and professionals with an informative, interesting, challenging and entertaining Visual Basic educational experience. We provide a suite of ancillary materials that help instructors maximize their students' learning experience.

As you read the book, if you have questions, send an e-mail to

`deitel@deitel.com`

and we'll respond promptly. For updates on this book and its supporting Visual Basic software, visit

`www.deitel.com/books/SimplyVB2008/`

Sign up for the free *DEITEL® BUZZ ONLINE* e-mail newsletter at

`www.deitel.com/newsletter/subscribe.html`

and check out our growing list of Visual Basic and related Resource Centers at

`www.deitel.com/ResourceCenters.html`

Each week we announce our latest Resource Centers in the newsletter.

New and Updated Features in *Simply Visual Basic 2008, Third Edition*

Here are some of our key updates to the third edition of *Simply Visual Basic 2008*:

- ***LINQ.*** Many Microsoft technical evangelists say that LINQ (Language-Integrated Query) is the single most important new feature in Visual Basic 2008 and Visual C# 2008. LINQ provides a uniform syntax for querying data, and it enables insert, update and delete operations. Strong typing enables Visual Studio to provide *IntelliSense* support for LINQ operations and results. LINQ can be used on different types of data sources, including collections (LINQ to Objects, Tutorials 20, 21and 23), databases (LINQ to SQL, Tutorials 24 and 30) and XML (LINQ to XML, Tutorial 32). Many of the new Visual Basic language features we cover were introduced to support LINQ.
- ***Databases.*** We use real-world applications to teach the fundamentals of database programming using the free Microsoft SQL Server Express Edition. Tutorials 24 and 30 discuss database and LINQ to SQL fundamentals, presented in the context of an address-book desktop application and a web-based bookstore application, respectively. Tutorial 24 also demonstrates using the Visual Studio tools to build a GUI that uses LINQ to SQL to access the database.
- ***Windows Presentation Foundation (WPF) GUI and Graphics.*** Graphics make applications fun to create and use. In our introduction to graphics, Tutorial 26, we discuss Graphical Device Interface (GDI+)—the Windows service that provides the graphical features used by Windows `Forms` applications in Visual Studio 2008—to teach students to print a personalized bank check. We extend our coverage of GUI and graphics (in Tutorial 27) with an introduction to Windows Presentation Foundation (WPF)—Microsoft's new framework that integrates GUI, graphics and multimedia capabilities. We present a WPF-based painting application to demonstrate WPF GUI and graphics capabilities.
- ***ASP.NET 3.5 and ASP.NET AJAX Case Study.*** We present a sequence of four tutorials in which the student builds a web-based bookstore application, complete with AJAX functionality. Tutorial 28 discusses the ASP.NET Development Server (which enables you to test your web applications on your local computer), multitier architecture and simple web transactions. Tutorials 29–31 use ASP.NET 3.5 and LINQ to build an application that retrieves information from a database and displays it in a web page. We use the new `LinqDataSource` from a web application to manipulate a database. We use ASP.NET AJAX controls to add AJAX functionality to web applications to improve their responsiveness—in particular, we use the `UpdatePanel` control to perform partial page updates.
- ***Silverlight.*** In Tutorial 32, we introduce Silverlight, Microsoft's technology for building Rich Internet Applications (RIA). Silverlight, a competitor to Adobe's Flash and Flex technologies, allows programmers to create visually stunning user interfaces for web applications using .NET languages such as Visual Basic. Silverlight is a subset of WPF that runs in a web browser using a plug-in. Many large media companies have begun to use Silverlight because it can stream high-definition video.
- ***XML Axis Properties.*** Visual Basic 2008 has many new features that integrate XML with the language. In Tutorial 32, we use so-called XML axis properties to manipulate the XML returned from a web service.
- ***Conditional `If` Expressions.*** Visual Basic provides a new conditional `If` expression (introduced in Tutorial 7), which consists of a condition, a true expression and a false expression. It tests its condition, then evaluates to its

true or false expression based on the truth or falsity of the condition. This can be used as shorthand notation for some `If...Then...Else` statements.

- ***Local Type Inference.*** When you initialize a local variable in its declaration, you can now omit the variable's type—the compiler infers it from the variable's initializer value (introduced in Tutorial 11).
- ***Optional Parameters.*** You can specify method parameters with default values—if a corresponding method argument is not provided in the method call, the compiler inserts the optional parameter's default value in the call (introduced in Tutorial 13).
- ***Object Initializers.*** When creating a new object, you can use the new object initializer syntax to assign values to the new object's properties (introduced in Tutorial 23).
- ***"Quick Fix" Window.*** The IDE now provides an **Error Correction Options** window that enables you to quickly fix certain common programming errors (introduced in Tutorial 5).

Pedagogic Features in Simply Visual Basic 2008, Third Edition

This book is loaded with pedagogic features, including:

- ***APPLICATION-DRIVEN Tutorial Approach.*** Each tutorial uses a contemporary, real-world application to teach programming concepts. The examples and exercises are up-to-the-minute with common desktop, Internet and web applications. An alphabetical list of these applications appears in Fig. 1. Most examples have a business, home or personal focus. At the beginning of each tutorial, students "test-drive" the completed application so they can see how it works. Then they build the application by following detailed, step-by-step instructions. The book concentrates on the principles of good software engineering and stresses program clarity.
- ***LIVE-CODE Approach.*** This book emphasises LIVE-CODE examples. Each tutorial ends with the complete, working program code, and the students can run the application that they just created. We call this method of teaching and writing the ***LIVE-CODE Approach***.
- ***Real-World Technologies.*** This text incorporates contemporary technologies to develop useful applications. For example, we use the Unified Modeling Language™ (UML) to replace flowcharts—an older standard. The UML has become the preferred graphical modeling language for designing object-oriented applications. In *Simply Visual Basic 2008, 3/e* we use the UML to show the flow of control for several control statements, so students gain practice reading the type of diagrams that are used in industry.
- ***Visual Programming and Graphical User Interfaces (GUIs).*** From the first tutorial, we immerse students in visual programming techniques, which students use to create and modify GUI-based programs quickly and easily. The early tutorials provide students with a foundation for designing GUIs—concepts that they'll apply throughout the book as we teach core programming concepts. Many tutorials contain GUI Design Tips that are summarized at the end of the tutorial for easy reference. Appendix C compiles all the GUI Design Tips.
- ***Windows Forms vs. Windows Presentation Foundation (WPF).*** Microsoft recommends that developers use Windows `Forms` rather than WPF for line-of-business applications, which is the primary market for students and professionals reading this book. We implement most of our GUIs with Windows `Forms`, but we also introduce WPF, which Microsoft recommends for more advanced GUI, graphics and multimedia applications.

Applications in *Simply Visual Basic 2008*		
Account Information	Dvorak Keyboard	Photo Album
Address Book	Encryption	Pig Latin
Address Book GUI	Enhanced Dental Payment	Present Value Calculator
Advanced Painter	Factorial	Prime Numbers
Airline Reservation	Fee Calculator	Quiz Average
Alarm	File Scrape	Radio GUI
Alarm Clock GUI	Flag Quiz	Restaurant Bill
Anagram Game	Food Survey	Road Sign Test
Arithmetic Calculator	Form Painter	Salary Survey
Average Three Numbers	Fund Raiser	Sales Commission
Birthday Saver	Fuzzy Dice Order Form	Sales Report
Bookstore	Gas Pump	Savings Calculator
Bouncing Ball Game	Grade Calculator	Schedule Book
Cafeteria Survey	Guess the Number	Screen Saver
Calculator GUI	Income Tax Calculator	Screen Scraping
Car Payment Calculator	Interest Calculator	Security Panel
Car Reservation	Inventory	Shipping Hub
Cash Register	Inventory Enhancement	Shipping Time
"Cat and Mouse" Painter	Length/Distance Converter	Sibling Survey
Cell Phone GUI	Letterhead Designer	Simple Calculator
Check Writer	Line Length	Simple Encryption
Circle Painter	Lottery Picker	Stock Portfolio
Class Average	Maximum	Student Grades
Company Logo Designer	Microwave Oven	Supply Cost Calculator
Compound Interest	Microwave Oven GUI	Task List
Counter	Miles Per Gallon	Temperature Converter
Craps Game	Monitor Invoice GUI	Ticket Information
Currency Converter	Mortgage Calculator	To-Do List
Charge Account Analyzer	Multiplication Teacher	Typing Tutor
Dental Payment	Odd Numbers	US State Facts
Dice Simulator	Office Supplies	Vending Machine GUI
Digit Extraction	Password GUI	Wage Calculator
Discount Calculator	Pay Raise Calculator	Weather Viewer
Display Square	Phone Book	Welcome

Figure 1 Applications in Simply Visual Basic 2008.

- ***Full-Color Presentation.*** This book is in full color so that students can see sample outputs as they would appear on a screen. Key terms are presented in **bold blue**. Also, we syntax color the Visual Basic code, similar to the way Visual Studio 2008 colors the code in its editor window, so students can match what they see in the book with what they see on their screens. Our syntax-coloring conventions are as follows:

```
comments appear in green
keywords appear in dark blue
literal values appear in light blue
text, class, method, variable and property names appear in black
errors and scripting delimiters appear in red
```

- ***Object-Oriented Programming.*** Object-oriented programming is the most widely employed technique for developing robust, reusable software, and Visual Basic 2008 offers substantial object-oriented programming features. This book introduces students to defining classes and using objects, laying a foundation for more advanced programming courses.
- ***Visual Studio 2008 Debugger.*** Debuggers are software tools that help programmers find and correct logic errors in program code. Visual Studio 2008 contains a powerful debugger that allows programmers to analyze their programs line-by-line as they execute. Throughout the book, we teach the Visual Studio 2008 Debugger; we explain how to use its key features and offer many debugging exercises.

To the Instructor

Focus of the Book

Simply Visual Basic 2008, 3/e is intended for introductory-level courses and course sequences in computer programming for students with little or no programming experience. This book teaches computer programming principles and the Visual Basic 2008 language, including data types, control statements, object-oriented programming, .NET Framework Class Library classes, GUI concepts, event-driven programming, database and web applications development, and more. After mastering the material in this book, students will be able to program in Visual Basic 2008 and to employ many key capabilities of the .NET 3.5 platform.

The book is up-to-date with Microsoft's latest release of Visual Studio—Visual Studio 2008, which includes Visual Basic 2008. We rebuilt every application in the book using the 2008 software. All applications and solutions have been fully tested and run on this new platform.

A Note Regarding Software for the Book

We use Microsoft Visual Studio 2008 development tools, including the free Visual Basic® 2008 Express Edition and the free Visual Web Developer™ 2008 Express Edition. Per Microsoft's website, Microsoft Express Editions are "lightweight, easy-to-use and easy-to-learn tools for the hobbyist, novice and student developer." The Express Editions provide rich functionality and can be used to build robust .NET applications. They are appropriate for academic courses and for professionals who do not have access to a complete version of Visual Studio 2008.

You may use the Express Editions to compile and execute all the example programs and solve all the exercises in the book (with the exception of Tutorial 32, whose software requirements are presented below in the *Other Software Requirements* section). You may also use the full Visual Studio product to build and run the examples and exercises. All of the features supported by the Express Editions are also available in the complete Visual Studio 2008 editions.

This book includes the Microsoft® Visual Studio® 2008 Express Editions All-in-One DVD, which contains Visual Basic 2008 Express Edition, Visual Web Developer 2008 Express Edition and SQL Server 2005 Express Edition. (SQL Server 2008 Express Edition was not available at the time of this writing.) You can also download these from:

`www.microsoft.com/express/`

When you install the software (discussed in the Before You Begin section that follows this Preface), you also should install the help documentation and SQL Server 2005 Express. Microsoft provides a dedicated forum for help using the Express Editions at:

`forums.microsoft.com/msdn/ShowForum.aspx?siteid=1&ForumID=24`

When SQL Server 2008 Express Edition becomes available, we'll add information on using it with this book at `www.deitel.com/books/SimplyVB2008`.

Windows Vista vs. Windows XP

Readers of this book can use either Windows Vista or Windows XP. We used Windows Vista while developing this book, but the steps in Windows XP should be identical. When they're not, we point out the Windows XP-specific steps in the text. Throughout the book, we use the Windows Vista Segoe UI font in the graphical user interfaces. If any Windows XP-specific issues arise after the book is published, we'll post them with appropriate instructions at `www.deitel.com/books/SimplyVB2008`. If you encounter any problems, write to us at `deitel@deitel.com`, and we'll respond promptly.

Other Software Requirements

For Tutorial 24 and for the case study in Tutorials 28–31, you'll need the SQL Server 2005 Express Edition. Tutorials 28–31 require Visual Web Developer 2008 Express (or a full Visual Studio 2008 edition).

We present Microsoft Silverlight in Tutorial 32. At the time of this writing Silverlight 2 was in beta and the tools for developing Silverlight applications were available only for Visual Studio 2008 (not Express Editions); tools for developing Silverlight applications with the Express Editions will be available soon. When the final tools become available, we'll post updates at `www.deitel.com/books/SimplyVB2008`.

For updates on the software used in this book, subscribe to our free e-mail newsletter at `www.deitel.com/newsletter/subscribe.html` and visit the book's website at `www.deitel.com/books/SimplyVB2008/`. Also, be sure to visit our Visual Basic 2008 resource center (`www.deitel.com/VisualBasic2008/`) frequently for new Visual Basic 2008 resources.

A Note Regarding Terminology Used in the Book

In Tutorial 13, we discuss methods as `Sub` procedures (sometimes called subroutines) and `Function` procedures (sometimes called functions). We use this terminology for two reasons. First, the keywords `Sub` and `Function` are used in procedure and method definitions, so this naming is logical for students. Second, Visual Basic professionals have used this terminology for years and will continue to do so. We also use the term "function" at certain points in this text to refer to Visual Basic 6 `Function` procedures that remain in Visual Basic 2008 (such as `Val` and `Pmt`). When we introduce object-oriented programming concepts in Tutorial 19, we discuss the difference between procedures and methods and indicate that the procedures defined throughout the text are, in fact, methods.

Objectives

Each tutorial begins with objectives that inform students of what to expect and give them an opportunity, after reading the tutorial, to determine whether they have met the intended goals.

Outline

The tutorial outline enables students to approach the material in top-down fashion. Along with the tutorial objectives, the outline helps students anticipate topics and set an appropriate learning pace.

Example Applications (with Outputs)

We present Visual Basic 2008 features in the context of complete, working programs. We call this our LIVE-CODE approach. All examples are available as downloads from:

```
www.deitel.com/books/SimplyVB2008
```

Illustrations/Figures/"ACE" Tables

Abundant charts, line drawings and application outputs are included. The control-statements discussion, for example, features carefully drawn UML activity diagrams. [*Note:* We do not teach UML diagramming as an application-development tool, but we do use UML diagrams to explain the precise operation Visual Basic 2008's control statements.] Most tutorials include our "ACE" tables that list the actions, controls and events that are crucial to implementing the tutorial applications.

Programming Tips

Hundreds of programming tips help students focus on important aspects of application development. These tips and practices represent the best the authors have gleaned from a combined seven decades of programming and teaching experience.

Good Programming Practice

Good Programming Practices call attention to techniques that will help you produce programs that are clearer, more understandable and more maintainable.

Common Programming Error

Students tend to make certain errors frequently. Pointing out these *Common Programming Errors* reduces the likelihood that you'll make the same mistakes.

Error-Prevention Tip

These tips contain suggestions for exposing bugs and removing them from your programs; many describe aspects of Visual Basic 2008 that prevent bugs from getting into programs in the first place.

Portability Tip

We include *Portability Tips* to help you write code that will run on a variety of platforms and to explain how Visual Basic 2008 achieves its high degree of portability among .NET 3.5 platforms.

Software Design Tip

The *Software Design Tips* highlight architectural and design issues that affect the construction of software systems.

GUI Design Tip

The *GUI Design Tips* highlight graphical-user-interface conventions to help students design attractive, intuitive, user-friendly GUIs. Appendix C compiles the *GUI Design Tips.*

Skills Summary

Each tutorial includes a bullet-list-style summary of the new programming concepts presented. This reinforces key actions taken to build the application in each tutorial.

Key Terms

Each tutorial includes a list of important terms defined in the tutorial. These terms and definitions also appear in the index and in a bookwide glossary, so the student can locate terms and their definitions quickly.

Self-Review Questions and Answers

Self-review multiple-choice questions and answers are included after most sections to build students' confidence with the material and prepare them for the regular exercises. Students should be encouraged to attempt all the self-review exercises and check their answers.

Exercises (Solutions in Instructor Solutions Manual)

Each tutorial concludes with exercises. Typical exercise sections include 10 multiple-choice questions, a "What does this code do?" exercise, a "What's wrong with this code?" exercise, three programming exercises and a programming challenge. [*Note:* In the "What does this code do?" and "What's wrong with this code?" exercises, we show only portions of the code in the text.]

The questions involve simple recall of important terminology and concepts, writing individual Visual Basic 2008 statements, writing small portions of Visual Basic 2008 applications and writing complete Visual Basic 2008 methods, classes and applications. Every programming exercise uses a step-by-step methodology to suggest how to solve the problems. The solutions for the exercises are *available only to instructors* through their Prentice-Hall representatives.

[*NOTE:* Please do not write to us requesting access to the Prentice Hall Instructor's Resource Center, which contains the exercise solutions and the book's ancillaries. Access is limited strictly to college instructors teaching from the book. Instructors may obtain access only through their Prentice Hall representatives.]

GUI Design Guidelines

Consistent and proper graphical-user-interface design is crucial to visual programming. In each tutorial, we summarize the GUI design guidelines that were introduced. Appendix C presents a cumulative list of these GUI design guidelines for easy reference.

Controls, Events, Properties & Methods Summaries

Each tutorial includes a summary of the controls, events, properties and methods covered in the tutorial. The summary includes a picture of each control, shows the control "in action" and lists the control's properties, events and methods that were discussed up to and including that tutorial.

Thousands of Index Entries

We have included an extensive index which is especially useful when you use the book as a reference.

"Double Indexing" of Visual Basic 2008 Code Examples

For every source-code program in the book, we index the figure caption both alphabetically and as a subindex item under "Examples." This makes it easier to find examples using particular features.

Microsoft Developer Network Academic Alliance (MSDNAA) and Microsoft DreamSpark

Microsoft Developer Network Academic Alliance (MSDNAA)— Free Microsoft Software for Academic and Research Purposes

The MSDNAA provides free software for academic and research purposes. For software direct to faculty, visit `www.microsoft.com/faculty`. For software for your department, visit `www.msdnaa.com`.

Microsoft DreamSpark— Professional Developer and Designer Tools for Students

Microsoft provides many of its developer tools to students for free via a program called DreamSpark (`downloads.channel8.msdn.com/`). At the time of this writing, the DreamSpark website states that students in 11 countries (United States, the

United Kingdom, Canada, China, Germany, France, Finland, Spain, Sweden, Switzerland and Belgium) can obtain this software after being verified as a student.

Instructor Resources for Simply Visual Basic 2008, Third Edition

Simply Visual Basic 2008, 3/e has extensive instructor resources. The Prentice Hall *Instructor's Resource Center* contains the *Instructor Solutions Manual* with solutions to the end-of-chapter exercises, a *Test Item File* of multiple-choice questions (approximately two per section) and PowerPoint® slides containing the code and figures in the text, plus bulleted summaries of key points in the text. Instructors can customize the slides. If you are not already a registered faculty member, contact your Prentice Hall representative or visit `vig.prenhall.com/replocator/`.

[*NOTE:* Please do not write to us requesting access to the Prentice Hall Instructor's Resource Center, which contains the exercise solutions and the book's ancillaries. Access is limited strictly to college instructors teaching from the book. Instructors may obtain access only through their Prentice Hall representatives.]

DEITEL BUZZ® ONLINE *Free E-mail Newsletter*

Each week, the *DEITEL® BUZZ ONLINE* newsletter announces our latest Resource Center(s) and includes commentary on industry trends and developments, links to free articles and resources from our published books and upcoming publications, product-release schedules, errata, challenges, anecdotes, information on our corporate instructor-led training courses and more. It's also a good way for you to keep posted about issues related to *Simply Visual Basic 2008, 3/e*. To subscribe, visit

`www.deitel.com/newsletter/subscribe.html`

The Deitel Online Resource Centers

Our website `www.deitel.com` provides more than 100 Resource Centers on various topics including programming languages, software, Web 2.0, Internet business and open source projects—see the complete list of Resource Centers in the first few pages of this book. The Resource Centers evolved out of the research we've done to support our books and business endeavors. We've found many exceptional resources online, including tutorials, documentation, software downloads, articles, blogs, podcasts, videos, code samples, books, e-books and more—most of them are free. Each week we announce our latest Resource Centers in our newsletter, the *DEITEL® BUZZ ONLINE* (`www.deitel.com/newsletter/subscribe.html`). The following Resource Centers may be of interest to you as you study *Simply Visual Basic 2008, 3/e*:

- ADO.NET
- ASP.NET 3.5
- ASP.NET AJAX
- LINQ
- Microsoft Popfly
- .NET 3.5
- Silverlight 2.0
- SQL Server 2008
- Visual Basic 2008
- Visual Studio Team System
- Windows Communication Foundation
- Windows Presentation Foundation
- Windows Workflow Foundation
- Windows Vista

Acknowledgments

It's a pleasure to acknowledge the efforts of people whose names do not appear on the cover, but whose hard work, cooperation, friendship and understanding were crucial to the book's production. Many people at Deitel & Associates, Inc. devoted long hours to this project—thanks especially to Abbey Deitel and Barbara Deitel.

We are fortunate to have worked on this project with the talented and dedicated team of publishing professionals at Prentice Hall. We appreciate the extraordinary efforts of Marcia Horton, Editorial Director of Prentice Hall's Engineering and Computer Science Division. Carole Snyder and Dolores Mars did an extraordinary job recruiting the book's review team and managing the review process. Francesco Santalucia (an independent artist) and Kristine Carney of Prentice Hall did a wonderful job designing the book's cover—we provided the concept, and they made it happen. Scott Disanno, Robert Engelhardt and Marta Samsel did a marvelous job managing the book's production. Our marketing manager Chris Kelly and his boss Margaret Waples did a great job marketing the book through academic channels.

Simply Visual Basic 2008, Third Edition *Reviewers*

We wish to acknowledge the efforts of our reviewers. Adhering to a tight time schedule, they scrutinized the text and the programs, providing countless suggestions for improving the accuracy and completeness of the presentation.

Microsoft reviewers: Adrian "Spotty" Bowles (Microsoft Corporation), Marcelo Guerra Hahn (Microsoft Corporation), Huanhui Hu (Microsoft Corporation), Timothy Ng (Microsoft Corporation), Akira Onishi (Microsoft Corporation), April Reagan (Microsoft Corporation), Steve Stein (Microsoft Corporation) and Scott Wisniewski (Microsoft Corporation). ***Academic reviewers:*** Douglas B. Bock (Southern Illinois University Edwardsville), Edward Hunter (Chapman University College), Christopher J. Olson (Dakota State University) and Josh Pauli (Dakota State University). ***Industry reviewers:*** Jeff Certain (Colorado CustomWare, Inc.), Matthew Kleinwaks (Abby Rating Systems, Inc.; Microsoft Visual Basic MVP), Éric Moreau (Moer, Inc.; Microsoft Visual Basic MVP), José Antonio González Seco (Parliament of Andalusia), Rod Stephens (President, Rocky Mountain Computer Consulting, Inc.) and Chris Williams (Magenic; Microsoft Visual Basic MVP).

Well, there you have it! Visual Basic 2008 is a powerful programming language that will help you write programs quickly and effectively. It scales nicely into the realm of enterprise systems development to help organizations build their business-critical and mission-critical information systems. As you read the book, we would sincerely appreciate your comments, criticisms, corrections and suggestions for improvement. Please address all correspondence to:

`deitel@deitel.com`

We'll respond promptly, and we'll post corrections and clarifications on the book's website:

`www.deitel.com/books/SimplyVB2008/`

We hope you enjoy reading *Simply Visual Basic 2008, Third Edition* as much as we enjoyed writing it!

Paul J. Deitel
Dr. Harvey M. Deitel
Greg J. Ayer

About the Authors

Paul J. Deitel, CEO and Chief Technical Officer of Deitel & Associates, Inc., is a graduate of MIT's Sloan School of Management, where he studied Information Technology. He holds the Java Certified Programmer and Java Certified Developer certifications, and has been designated by Sun Microsystems as a Java Champion. Through Deitel & Associates, Inc., he has delivered Visual Basic, C#, C++, C and Java courses to industry clients, including Cisco, IBM, Sun Microsystems, Dell, Lucent Technologies, Fidelity, NASA at the Kennedy Space Center, White Sands Missile Range, the National Severe Storm Laboratory, Rogue Wave Software, Boeing, Stratus, Hyperion Software, Adra Systems, Entergy, CableData Systems, Nortel Networks, Puma, iRobot, Invensys and many more. He has also lectured on Java and C++ for the Boston Chapter of the Association for Computing Machinery. He and his father, Dr. Harvey M. Deitel, are the world's best-selling programming language textbook authors.

Dr. Harvey M. Deitel, Chairman and Chief Strategy Officer of Deitel & Associates, Inc., has 47 years of experience in the computer field. Dr. Deitel earned B.S. and M.S. degrees from MIT and a Ph.D. from Boston University. He has extensive college teaching experience, including earning tenure and serving as the Chairman of the Computer Science Department at Boston College before founding Deitel & Associates, Inc., with his son, Paul J. Deitel. He and Paul are the co-authors of several dozen books and multimedia packages and they are writing many more. The Deitels' texts have earned international recognition with translations published in Japanese, German, Russian, Spanish, Traditional Chinese, Simplified Chinese, Korean, French, Polish, Italian, Portuguese, Greek, Urdu and Turkish. Dr. Deitel has delivered hundreds of professional seminars to major corporations, academic institutions, government organizations and the military.

Greg Ayer is a junior at Northeastern University completing a B.S. in Computer Science. His industry experience includes freelance web development, game programming, consulting and technical writing. Through the Northeastern Co-Op program, he worked at Deitel & Associates for two six-month co-ops. He continues consulting with Deitel & Associates. His course work includes database development, computational theory, operating systems, networking and a variety of programming languages.

About Deitel & Associates, Inc.

Deitel & Associates, Inc., is an internationally recognized corporate training and content-creation organization specializing in computer programming languages, Internet and web software technology, object technology education and Internet business development through its Web 2.0 Internet Business Initiative. The company provides instructor-led courses on major programming languages and platforms, such as Visual Basic, C#, Visual C++, C++, Java, C, XML, Perl, object technology, Internet and web programming, and a growing list of additional programming and software-development related courses. The founders of Deitel & Associates, Inc., are Paul J. Deitel and Dr. Harvey M. Deitel. The company's clients include many of the world's largest companies, government agencies, branches of the military, and academic institutions. Through its 32-year publishing partnership with Prentice Hall, Deitel & Associates, Inc. publishes leading-edge programming textbooks, professional books, interactive multimedia *Cyber Classrooms*, *LiveLessons* DVD-based and web-based video courses, and e-content for popular course management systems. Deitel & Associates, Inc., and the authors can be reached via e-mail at:

`deitel@deitel.com`

To learn more about Deitel & Associates, Inc., its publications and its worldwide *Dive Into*® Series Corporate Training curriculum, visit:

```
www.deitel.com
www.deitel.com/books/
www.deitel.com/training/
```

and subscribe to the free *DEITEL® BUZZ ONLINE* e-mail newsletter at:

`www.deitel.com/newsletter/subscribe.html`

Check out the growing list of Deitel Resource Centers at:

`www.deitel.com/resourcecenters.html`

Individuals wishing to purchase Deitel publications can do so through `Amazon.com` and `Informit.com` by visiting our website:

`www.deitel.com`

Bulk orders by corporations, the government, the military and academic institutions should be placed directly with Prentice Hall. For more information, visit

`www.prenhall.com/mischtm/support.html#order`

BEFORE YOU BEGIN

This section contains information you should review before using this book and instructions to ensure that your computer is set up properly for use with this book. We'll keep the latest version of this Before You Begin section on the book's website at `www.deitel.com/books/SimplyVB2008/`.

Font and Naming Conventions

We use fonts to distinguish between features, such as menu names, menu items, and other elements that appear in the program development environment. Our convention is to emphasize IDE features in a sans-serif bold **Helvetica** font (for example, **Properties** window) and to emphasize program text in a sans-serif `Lucida` font (for example, `Private x As Boolean = True`).

A Note Regarding Software for the Book

This textbook includes a DVD which contains the Microsoft® Visual Studio® 2008 Express Edition integrated development environments for Visual Basic 2008, Visual C# 2008, Visual C++ 2008, Visual Web Developer 2008 and SQL Server 2005. These are also downloadable from `www.microsoft.com/express`. The Express Editions are fully functional, and there is no time limit for using the software. We discuss the setup of this software shortly. You do not need Visual C# or Visual C++ for use with this book.

Hardware and Software Requirements for the Visual Studio 2008 Express Editions

To install and run the Visual Studio 2008 Express Editions, Microsoft recommends these minimum requirements:

- **Operating System:** Windows XP Service Pack 2 (or above), Windows Server 2003 Service Pack 1 (or above), Windows Server 2003 R2 (or above), Windows Vista or Windows Server 2008.
- **Processor:** Computer with a 1.6 GHz or faster processor (2.2 GHz or higher recommended—2.4 GHz on Vista).
- **RAM minimum:** 192 MB, but Microsoft recommends 384 MB (768 MB on Vista).
- **Hard Drive:** 1.3 GB for complete install.
- **Display:** 1024 x 768 (1280 x 1024 recommended).
- To test and build the examples in Tutorial 24 and 28–31, **you must install Microsoft's SQL Server 2005 Express**, which is an option during the installation of each Express Edition.

Display Settings

Simply Visual Basic® 2008, 3/e includes hundreds of screenshots of applications. Your screen's display settings may need to be adjusted so that the screenshots in the book match what you see on your computer screen as you develop each application. Follow these steps to configure your screen correctly:

- **Windows Vista**
  1. Right click the desktop, then click **Personalize**.
  2. Click the **Adjust font size (DPI)** item on the left side of the dialog.
  3. Make sure **Default scale (96 DPI)** is selected. [*Note:* If you already have this setting, you do not need to do anything else.]
  4. Click **Apply**.
- **Windows XP**
  1. Right click the desktop, then click **Properties**.
  2. Click the **Settings** tab.
  3. Click the **Advanced** button.
  4. In the **General** tab, make sure **Normal size (96 DPI)** is selected. [*Note:* If you already have this setting, you do not need to do anything else.]
  5. Click **OK**, then click **OK** again to complete the changes.

If you choose to use different settings, the `Size` and `Location` that we specify for each GUI control (such as a `Button` or `Label`) might not be the same on your screen.

Desktop Theme Settings for Windows Vista Users

If you are using Windows Vista, we assume that your theme is set to **Windows Vista**. Follow these steps to set Windows Vista as your desktop theme:

1. Right click the desktop, then click **Personalize**.
2. Click the **Theme** item. Select **Windows Vista** from the **Theme:** drop-down list.
3. Click **Apply** to save the settings.

Desktop Theme Settings for Windows XP Users

If you are using Windows XP, the windows you see on the screen will look slightly different from the screen captures in the book. We assume that your theme is set to **Windows XP**. Follow these steps to set Windows XP as your desktop theme:

1. Right click the desktop, then click **Properties**.
2. Click the **Themes** tab. Select **Windows XP** from the **Theme:** drop-down list.
3. Click **OK** to save the settings.

Viewing File Extensions

Several screenshots in *Simply Visual Basic 2008, 3/e* display file names on a user's system, including the file-name extension (e.g., `.txt`, `.vb` or `.png`). Your settings may need to be adjusted to display file-name extensions. Follow these steps to configure your computer:

1. In the **Start** menu, select **All Programs**, then **Accessories**, then **Windows Explorer**.
2. In Windows Vista, press *Alt* to display the menu bar, then select **Folder Options...** from **Windows Explorer**'s **Tools** menu. In Windows XP, simply select **Folder Options...** from **Windows Explorer**'s **Tools** menu.
3. In the dialog that appears, select the **View** tab.
4. In the **Advanced settings:** pane, uncheck the box to the left of the text **Hide extensions for known file types**. [*Note*: If this item is already unchecked, no action needs to be taken.]

Notes to Windows XP Users Regarding the Segoe UI Font Used in Our Applications

As part of Windows Vista, Microsoft has released a new font called Segoe UI, which all of the applications in Tutorials 1–27 use. This font is not available by default on Windows XP, but you can get it by installing Windows Live Mail—a free download from get.live.com/wlmail/overview.

You must also enable ClearType on your system; otherwise, the font will not display correctly. ClearType is a technology for smoothing the edges of fonts displayed on the screen. To enable ClearType, perform the following steps:

1. Right click your desktop and select **Properties...** from the popup menu to view the **Display Properties** dialog.
2. In the dialog, click the **Appearance** tab, then click the **Effects...** button to display the **Effects** dialog.
3. In the **Effects** dialog, ensure that the **Use the following method to smooth edges of screen fonts** checkbox is checked, then select **ClearType** from the combobox below the checkbox.
4. Click **OK** to close the **Effects** dialog, then click **OK** to close the **Display Properties** dialog.

Obtaining the Code Examples

The examples for *Simply Visual Basic 2008, 3/e* are available for download at

www.deitel.com/books/SimplyVB2008

Follow the steps in the box below to download the examples and to create the Examples directory on your hard drive. Screenshots in this box might differ slightly from what you see on your computer, depending on your version of Windows. We used Windows Vista to prepare the screenshots for this book.

Downloading the Book Examples from the Deitel Website

1. ***Registering at www.deitel.com.*** If you are not already registered at our website, go to www.deitel.com and click the **Register** link below our logo in the upper-left corner of the page; otherwise, proceed to *Step 2*. Fill in your information. There is no charge to register, and we do not share your information with anyone. We send you only account management e-mails unless you register separately for our free e-mail newsletter at www.deitel.com/newsletter/subscribe.html. After registering, you'll receive a confirmation e-mail with your verification code. You need this code to sign in at www.deitel.com for the first time.
2. ***Downloading the book's code examples.*** In your web browser, go to www.deitel.com and sign in using the **Login** link below our logo in the upper-left corner of the page. Next, go to www.deitel.com/books/SimplyVB2008. Click the **Examples** link to download the Examples.zip file to your computer. Write down the location where you choose to save the file on your computer. Next, Windows Vista users should perform *Step 3*; Windows XP users should perform *Step 4*.
3. ***Extracting Examples.zip on Windows Vista.*** We assume the examples are located in the C:\Examples directory on your computer. To place the examples in this location, perform the following steps (these may differ if you have your own ZIP extraction tool installed):
   - Locate the Examples.zip folder in Windows Explorer.
   - Right click Examples.zip and select **Extract All...** to display the **Extract Compressed (Zipped) Folders** dialog.
   - Type C:\ in the **Files will be extracted to this folder** textbox.
   - Click the **Extract** button. The C:\Examples folder is created for you.

(cont.)

[*Note:* Some people are not allowed to place files directly in `C:\` or prefer to place their files elsewhere. If you choose a different location in which to extract the files, you must substitute that location in the tutorial steps that refer to the location `C:\Examples`.]

4. ***Extracting `Examples.zip` on Windows XP.*** We assume the examples are located in the `C:\Examples` directory on your computer. To place the examples in this location, perform the following steps:

   - Locate the `Examples.zip` folder in Windows Explorer.
   - Right click `Examples.zip` and select **Extract All...** to display the **Extraction Wizard** dialog.
   - Click the **Next >** button.
   - Type `C:\` in the **Files will be extracted to this directory** textbox. The extraction tool will create a folder named `Examples` on your `C:` drive.
   - Click the **Next >** button.
   - Click the **Finish** button. The `C:\Examples` folder is created for you.

   [*Note:* Some people are not allowed to place files directly in `C:\` or prefer to place their files elsewhere. If you choose a different location in which to extract the files, you must substitute that location in the tutorial steps that refer to the location `C:\Examples`.]

Creating Your Working Directory

In the following box, you create a directory on your `C:` drive in which you'll save the applications you create. Throughout the book, we assume the folder you'll use is `C:\SimplyVB2008`. If you choose a different location for your working directory, you must substitute that location in tutorial steps that refer to `C:\SimplyVB2008`.

Creating a Working Directory on Windows Vista

1. ***Selecting the drive.*** Open the **Start** menu and select **Computer** to access a list of your computer drives (Fig. 1). Double click **Local Disk (C:)**. The contents of the `C:` drive are displayed in the window.

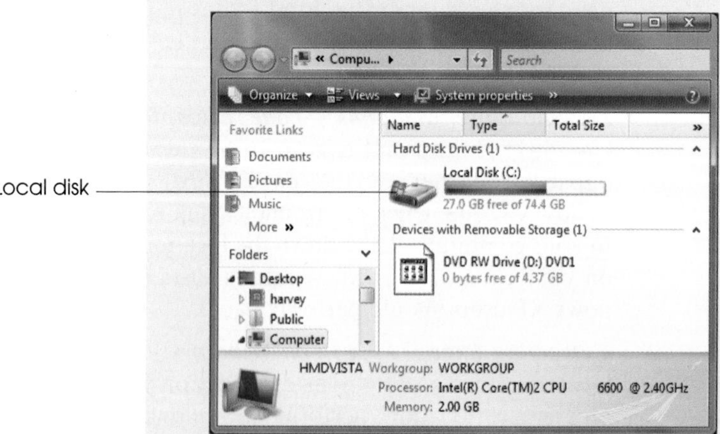

Figure 1 Computer drives listed under **Computer**.

2. ***Creating a new directory.*** Click the **Organize** button and select **New Folder** (Fig. 2). A new, empty directory appears on your `C:` drive (Fig. 3).

(cont.)

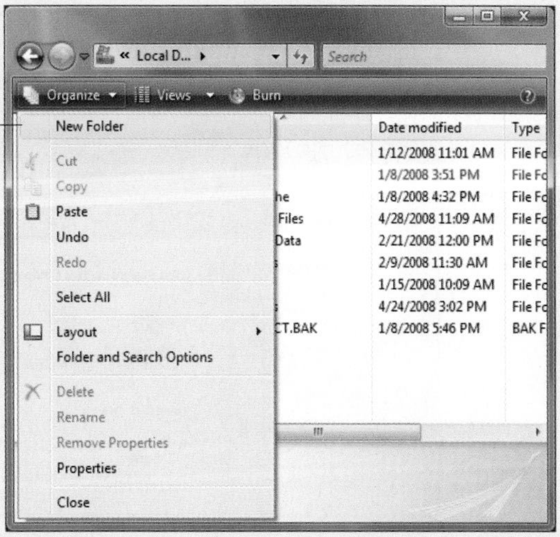

New folder option (selected)

Figure 2 Creating a new directory.

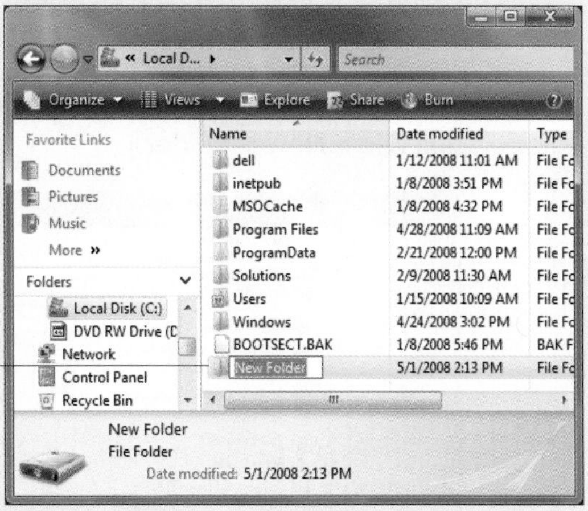

New directory

Figure 3 New directory appears on the `C:` drive.

3. ***Naming the directory.*** Enter a name for the directory. We suggest that you choose a name that you recognize and remember. We named the directory `SimplyVB2008` (Fig. 4) and use this name in the steps throughout the book.

Newly created working directory

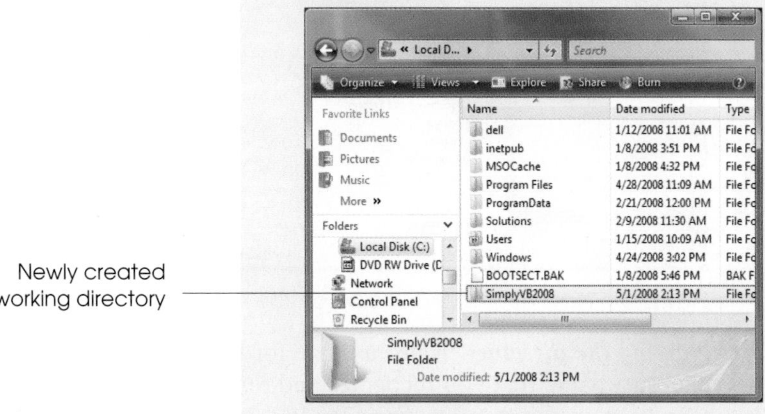

Figure 4 New working directory on the `C:` drive.

Creating a Working Directory on Windows XP

1. ***Selecting the drive.*** Open the **Start** menu and select **My Computer** to access a list of your computer drives (Fig. 5). Double click the `C:` drive. The contents of the `C:` drive are displayed in the window.

Figure 5 Computer drives listed under **My Computer**.

2. ***Creating a new directory.*** Select the **File** menu. Under the **New** submenu, select **Folder** (Fig. 6). A new, empty directory appears on your `C:` drive (Fig. 7). [*Note:* From now on, we use the > character to indicate the selection of a menu command. For example, to perform this step, we'd use the notation **File > New > Folder**.]

Figure 6 Creating a new directory.

Figure 7 New directory appears on the `C:` drive.

3. ***Naming the directory.*** Enter a name for the directory. We suggest that you choose a name that you recognize and remember. We chose `SimplyVB2008` (Fig. 8). You can use this directory to save your own applications and your exercise solutions.

(cont.)

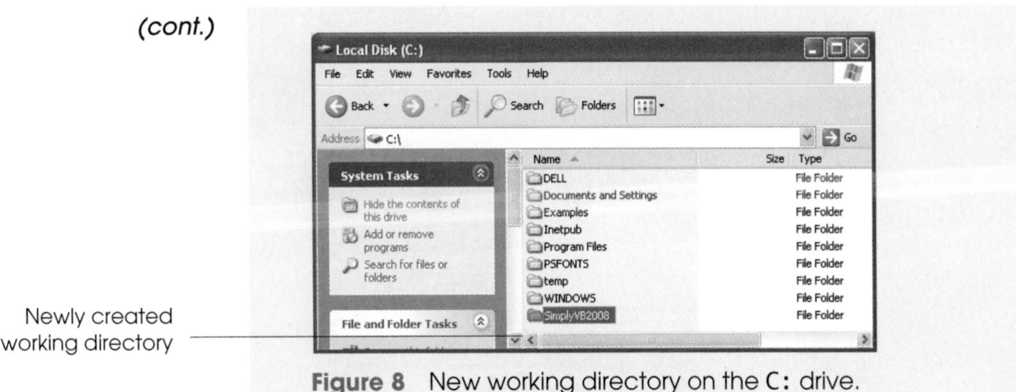

Figure 8 New working directory on the C: drive.

Installing the Software

Before you can run the applications in *Simply Visual Basic 2008, 3/e* or build your own applications, you must install a development environment. We used the free Microsoft's Visual Basic 2008 Express Edition in the examples for Tutorials 1–27 and Visual Web Developer 2008 Express Edition for Tutorials 28–31. Tutorials 24 and 28–31 also require SQL Server 2005 Express Edition. (SQL Server 2008 Express Edition was not available at the time of this writing.) Tutorial 32 currently requires a full Visual Studio 2008 edition. All of the Visual Studio Express Editions are included on a DVD bundled with this book and can be downloaded from:

`www.microsoft.com/express/`

In the following box, you install the Express Edition software.

Installing Visual Basic 2008 Express Edition and Visual Web Developer 2008 Express Edition

1. ***Launching the Express Editions installer.*** Insert the DVD that accompanies this book into your computer's DVD drive to launch the software installer (Fig. 9). If the **Visual Studio 2008 Express Editions Setup** window does not appear, use Windows Explorer to view the contents of the DVD drive and double click `Setup.hta` to launch the installer

Figure 9 **Visual Studio 2008 Express Editions Setup** window.

2. ***Launching the Visual Basic 2008 Express Edition installer.*** In the **Visual Studio 2008 Express Editions Setup** window, click **Visual Basic 2008 Express Edition** to display the **Visual Basic 2008 Express Edition Setup** window (Fig. 10), then click **Next >**.

(cont.)

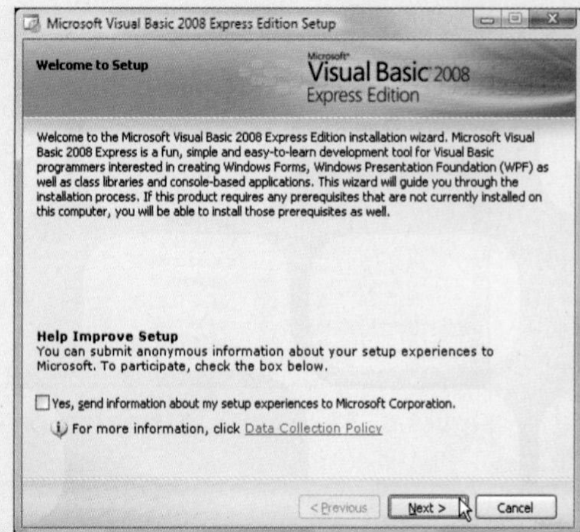

Figure 10 **Visual Basic 2008 Express Edition Setup** window.

3. ***Accepting the license agreement.*** Carefully read the license agreement (Fig. 11). Click the **I have read and accept the license terms** radio button to agree to the terms, then click **Next >**. [*Note:* If you do not choose to accept the license agreement, the software will not install and you will not be able to create or execute Visual Basic applications.]

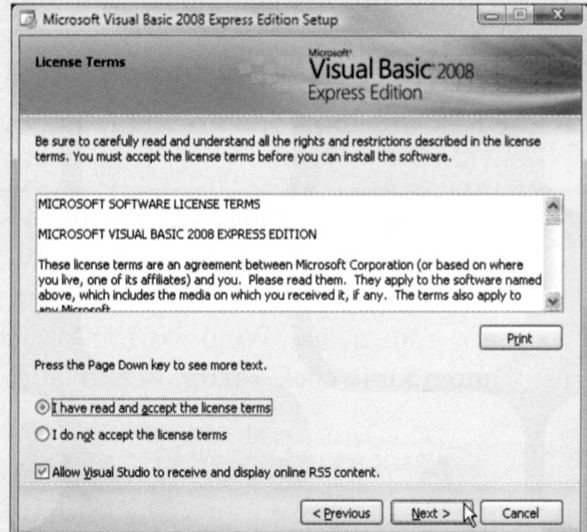

Figure 11 Accepting the license agreement.

4. ***Selecting the installation options.*** Select the **MSDN Express Library for Visual Studio 2008**, **Microsoft SQL Server 2005 Express Edition (x86)** and **Microsoft Silverlight Runtime** options to install (Fig. 12). Click **Next >**. [*Note:* Installing the MSDN documentation is not required but is highly recommended.]

5. ***Continuing and finishing the installation.*** Click **Next >**, then click **Finish >** to continue with the installation. The installer will now begin copying the files required by Visual Basic 2008 Express Edition and SQL Server 2005 Express Edition (Fig. 13). Wait for the installation to complete before proceeding—the installation process can be quite lengthy. When the installation completes, click **Exit**.

6. ***Launching the Visual Web Developer 2008 Express Edition installer.*** In the **Visual Studio 2008 Express Editions Setup** window, click **Visual Web Developer 2008 Express Edition** to display the **Visual Web Developer 2008 Express Edition Setup** window, then click **Next >**.

(cont.)

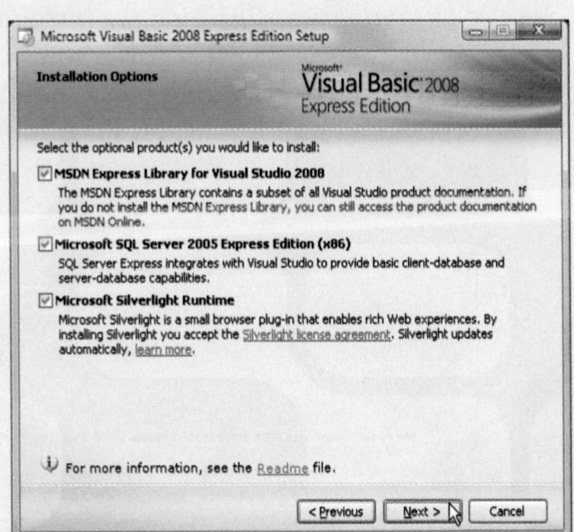

Figure 12 Installation options dialog.

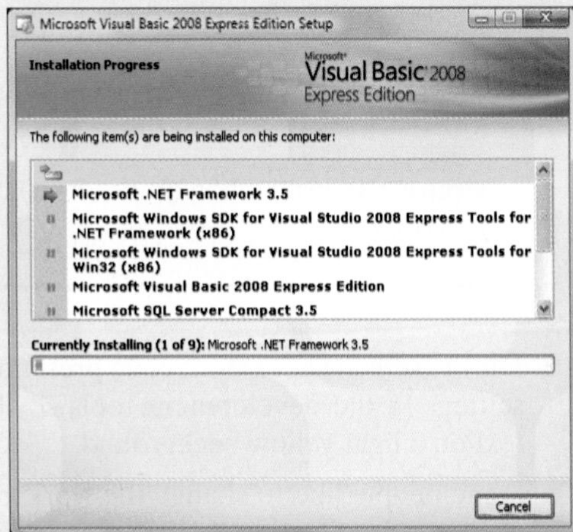

Figure 13 Installation (in progress) of Visual Basic 2008 Express Edition.

7. ***Accepting the license agreement.*** Carefully read the license agreement (Fig. 14). Click the **I have read and accept the license terms** radio button to agree to the terms, then click **Next >**. [*Note:* If you do not choose to accept the license agreement, the software will not install and you will not be able to create or execute web applications with Visual Web Developer.]

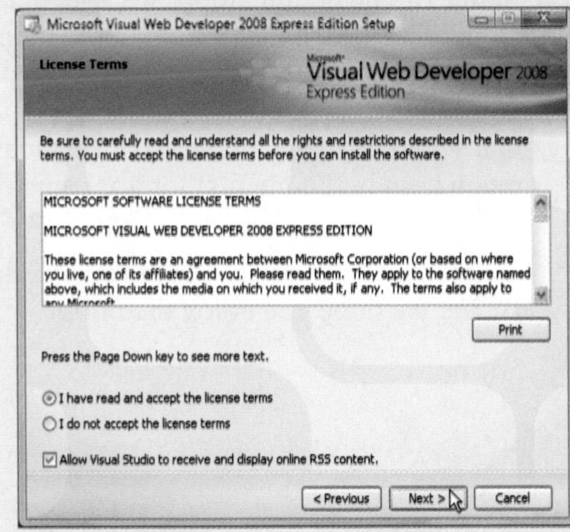

Figure 14 Accepting the license agreement.

(cont.)

8. ***Continuing and finishing the installation.*** Click **Install >** to continue with the installation. The installer will now begin copying the files required by Visual Web Developer 2008 Express Edition (Fig. 15). This portion of the install process should be much faster, since you've already installed most of the supporting software and files required by Visual Web Developer. When the installation completes, click **Exit**.

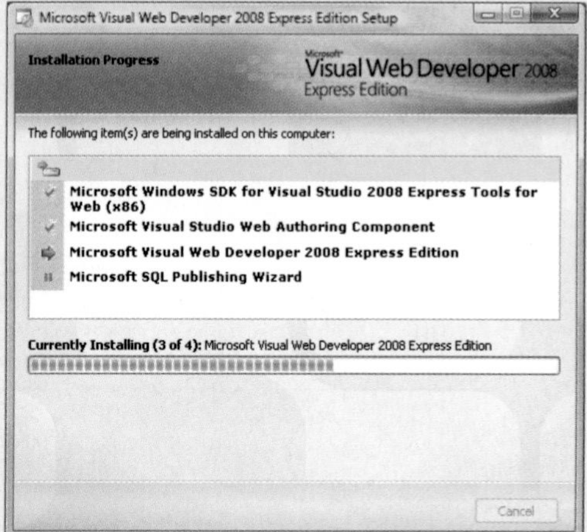

Figure 15 Installation (in progress) of Visual Web Developer 2008 Express Edition.

Miscellaneous Notes

- For the screen captures of code presented in this book, we changed the color settings in the development tools so that selected text appears with black text on a light yellow background.
- Some people like to change the workspace layout in the development tools. You can return the tools to their default layouts by selecting **Window > Reset Window Layout**.
- There are differences between the full Visual Studio 2008 products and the Express Edition products we use in this book, such as additional menu items. One key difference is that the **Database Explorer** window we refer to in Tutorials 24, 31 and 32 is called the **Server Explorer** window in the full Visual Studio 2008 products.
- Many of the menu items we use in the book have corresponding icons (shown with each menu item in the menus) on one of the toolbars at the top of the develoment environment. As you become familiar with these icons, you can use the toolbars to help speed up your development time. Similarly, many of the menu items have keyboard shortcuts (also shown with each menu item in the menus) for accessing commands quickly.

You are now ready to begin your Visual Basic studies with *Simply Visual Basic 2008, 3/e*. We hope you enjoy the book!

TUTORIAL 1

Advanced Painter Application

Introducing Computers, the Internet and Visual Basic

Objectives

In this tutorial, you learn to:

- Identify the characteristics of low-level and high-level programming languages.
- Apply the basics of object-oriented programming.
- Run your first Visual Basic application.
- Locate additional .NET and Visual Basic information.

Outline

Welcome to Visual Basic 2008! This book uses a straightforward, step-by-step tutorial approach to teach the fundamentals of Visual Basic programming. We hope that you'll be informed and entertained as you learn Visual Basic.

The core of the book teaches Visual Basic using our **application-driven approach**, which provides step-by-step instructions for creating and interacting with useful, real-world computer applications. With this approach and our signature **live-code approach**, which shows dozens of complete, working Visual Basic applications and depicts their outputs, you learn the basic skills that underlie good programming. You'll study bonus tutorials on graphics, multimedia and web programming. All of the book's program examples are available on our website, `www.deitel.com/books/simplyVB2008`.

Computer use is increasing in almost every field. In an era of rising costs, computing costs are actually decreasing dramatically because of rapid developments in both hardware and software technology. Silicon-chip technology has made computing so economical that more than a billion general-purpose computers are in use worldwide, helping people in business, industry, government and their personal lives.

This text will start you on a challenging and rewarding educational path. If you'd like to communicate with us, send an e-mail to `deitel@deitel.com`, and we'll respond promptly. For more information, visit `www.deitel.com`.

1.1 What Is a Computer?

A **computer** is a device that can perform calculations and make logical decisions millions, billions and even trillions of times faster than humans can. For example, many of today's personal computers can perform billions of additions per second. A person operating a desk calculator might require a lifetime to complete the same number of calculations that a powerful personal computer can perform in one second. Today's fastest **supercomputers** are already performing trillions of additions per second!

Computers process **data**, using sets of instructions called **computer programs**. These programs guide computers through orderly sets of actions that are specified by people known as **computer programmers**. In this book, we generally use the term "application" instead of "program." An application is a program that does something particularly useful. Each tutorial in this book, on average, presents five applications—one in the main example and often four in the exercises—for a total of more than 100 applications in the book.

A computer is composed of various devices (such as the keyboard, screen, mouse, hard drives, memory, DVD drives, printer and processing units) known as **hardware**. The programs that run on a computer are referred to as **software**. Object-oriented programming (which models real-world objects with software counterparts), available in Visual Basic and other programming languages, is a significant breakthrough that can greatly enhance your productivity.

SELF-REVIEW

1. Computers process data, using sets of instructions called _________.

a) hardware | b) computer programs
c) processing units | d) programmers

2. The devices that make up a computer are called _________.

a) hardware | b) software
c) programs | d) programmers

Answers: 1) b. 2) a.

1.2 Computer Organization

Computers can be thought of as being divided into six units:

1. **Input unit.** This "receiving" section of the computer obtains information (data and computer programs) from various **input devices**, such as the keyboard and the mouse. Other input devices include microphones (for recording speech to the computer), scanners (for scanning images) and digital cameras (for taking photographs and making videos).
2. **Output unit.** This "shipping" section of the computer takes information that the computer has processed and places it on various **output devices**, making the information available for use outside the computer. Output can be displayed on screens, printed on paper, played on audio/video devices, transmitted over the Internet, etc. Output also can be used to control other devices, such as robots used in manufacturing.
3. **Memory unit.** This rapid-access, relatively low-capacity "warehouse" section of the computer stores data temporarily while an application is running. The memory unit retains information that has been entered through input devices, so that information is immediately available for processing. To be executed, computer programs must be in memory. The memory unit also retains processed information until it can be sent to output devices on which it is made available to users. Often, the memory unit is called either **memory** or **primary memory**. **Random-access memory (RAM)** is an example of primary memory. Primary memory is usually **volatile**, which means that it is erased when the machine is powered off.
4. **Central processing unit (CPU).** The CPU serves as the "administrative" section of the computer, supervising the operation of the other sections. The CPU alerts the input unit when information should be read into the memory unit, instructs the ALU when to use information from the memory unit in calculations and tells the output unit when to send information from the memory unit to certain output devices. Many of today's more powerful desktop computers have several CPUs.
5. **Arithmetic and logic unit (ALU).** The ALU (a part of the CPU) is the "manufacturing" section of the computer. It performs calculations such

as addition, subtraction, multiplication and division. It also makes decisions, allowing the computer to perform such tasks as determining whether two items stored in memory are equal.

6. **Secondary storage unit.** This unit is the long-term, high-capacity "warehousing" section of the computer. Secondary storage devices, such as hard drives, CD-ROM drives, DVD drives, and USB memory sticks, normally hold programs or data that other units are not actively using. The computer can retrieve this information when it is needed—immediately or possibly hours, days, months or even years later. Information in secondary storage takes much longer to access than information in primary memory. However, secondary storage is much less expensive than primary memory. Secondary storage is nonvolatile, retaining information even when the computer is powered off.

SELF-REVIEW

1. The _________ is responsible for performing calculations and contains decision-making mechanisms.
   a) central processing unit
   b) memory unit
   c) arithmetic and logic unit
   d) output unit
2. Information stored in _________ is normally erased when the computer is turned off.
   a) primary memory
   b) secondary storage
   c) CD-ROM drives
   d) hard drives

Answers: 1) c. 2) a.

1.3 Machine Languages, Assembly Languages and High-Level Languages

Programmers write instructions in various programming languages. Some of these are directly understandable by computers, and others require intermediate translation steps. Although hundreds of computer languages are in use today, they can be divided into three general types:

1. Machine languages
2. Assembly languages
3. High-level languages

A computer can directly understand only its own **machine language**. As the "natural language" of a particular computer, machine language is defined by the computer's hardware design. Machine languages generally consist of streams of numbers (ultimately reduced to 1s and 0s) that instruct computers how to perform their most elementary operations. You normally work in the decimal number system with digits in the range 0–9. The number system with only 1s and 0s is called the binary number system. Machine language programs are sometimes called "binaries" for that reason. Machine languages are machine dependent, which means that a particular machine language can be used on only one type of computer. The following section of a machine-language program, which adds *overtime pay* to *base pay* and stores the result in *gross pay*, demonstrates the incomprehensibility of machine language to humans:

```
+1300042774
+1400593419
+1200274027
```

As the popularity of computers increased, machine-language programming proved to be slow and error prone. Instead of using the strings of numbers that computers could directly understand, programmers began using English-like abbreviations to represent the computer's basic operations. These abbreviations formed the basis of **assembly languages**. **Translator programs** called **assemblers** convert assembly-language programs to machine language at computer speeds. The following section of an assembly-language program also adds *overtime pay* to *base pay* and stores the result in *gross pay*, but the steps are somewhat clearer to human readers than in the machine-language example:

```
LOAD   BASEPAY
ADD    OVERPAY
STORE  GROSSPAY
```

Although it is clearer to humans, computers cannot understand assembly-language code until it is translated into machine language by an assembler program.

The speed at which programmers could write programs increased rapidly with the creation of assembly languages, but these languages still require many instructions to accomplish even the simplest tasks. To speed up the programming process, **high-level languages** (in which single program statements accomplish more substantial tasks) were developed. Translator programs called **compilers** convert high-level-language programs into machine language. High-level languages enable programmers to write instructions that look almost like everyday English and contain common mathematical notations. For example, a payroll application written in a high-level language might contain a statement such as

```
grossPay = basePay + overTimePay
```

From these examples, it is clear why programmers prefer high-level languages to either machine languages or assembly languages. Visual Basic is one of the world's most popular high-level programming languages. In the next section, you learn about Microsoft's latest version of this language, called Visual Basic 2008.

SELF-REVIEW

1. The only programming language that a computer can directly understand is its own _________.

   a) high-level language b) assembly language
   c) machine language d) English

2. Programs that translate high-level language programs into machine language are called _________.

   a) assemblers b) compilers
   c) programmers d) converters

Answers: 1) c. 2) b.

1.4 Visual Basic

Visual Basic evolved from **BASIC** (Beginner's All-purpose Symbolic Instruction Code), developed in the mid-1960s by Professors John Kemeny and Thomas Kurtz of Dartmouth College as a language for writing simple programs quickly and easily. BASIC's primary purpose was to teach novices fundamental programming techniques.

When Bill Gates founded Microsoft Corporation in the 1970s, he implemented BASIC on several early personal computers. In the late 1980s and the early 1990s, Microsoft developed the Microsoft® Windows® **graphical user interface (GUI)**—the visual part of the operating system with which users interact. With the creation of the Windows GUI, the natural evolution of BASIC was to **Visual Basic**, introduced by Microsoft in 1991 to make programming Windows applications easier.

Until Visual Basic appeared, developing Microsoft Windows-based applications was a difficult process. Visual Basic is now a so-called object-oriented, event-driven visual programming language in which programs are created with the use of a software tool called an **Integrated Development Environment (IDE)**. With

Microsoft's **Visual Studio** IDE, you can write, run, test and debug Visual Basic programs quickly and conveniently.

The latest versions of Visual Basic are fully object oriented—you'll learn some basics of object technology shortly and will study a rich treatment in the remainder of the book. Visual Basic is event driven—you'll write programs that respond to user-initiated **events** such as mouse clicks, keystrokes and timers. It is a visual programming language—in addition to writing program statements to build portions of your applications, you'll also use Visual Studio's graphical user interface to conveniently drag and drop predefined objects like buttons and textboxes into place on your screen, and label and resize them. Visual Studio will write much of the GUI code for you.

Microsoft introduced its .NET (pronounced "dot-net") strategy in 2000. The **.NET platform**—the set of software components that enables .NET programs to run—allows applications to be distributed to a variety of devices (such as cell phones) as well as to desktop computers. The .NET platform offers a programming model that allows software components created in different programming languages (such as Visual Basic and C#) to communicate with one another. We discuss .NET in more detail in Section 1.9.

SELF-REVIEW

1. Microsoft created ________ in 1991 to make it easier to program Windows applications.
   a) Windows b) BASIC
   c) Visual Basic d) C#
2. Visual Basic evolved from ________, which was created as a language for writing simple programs quickly and easily.
   a) .NET b) Windows
   c) Java d) BASIC

Answers: 1) c. 2) d.

1.5 Other High-Level Languages

Although hundreds of high-level languages have been developed, only a few have achieved broad acceptance. IBM Corporation developed **Fortran** (Formula Translator) in the mid-1950s to create scientific and engineering applications that require complex mathematical computations. Fortran is still widely used.

COBOL was developed in the late 1950s by a group of computer manufacturers in conjunction with government and industrial computer users. COBOL is used primarily for business applications that require the manipulation of large amounts of data. A considerable portion of today's business software is still programmed in COBOL.

The C language, which Dennis Ritchie developed at Bell Laboratories in the early 1970s, gained widespread recognition as a development language of the UNIX operating system. C++, an extension of C, was developed by Bjarne Stroustrup in the early 1980s at Bell Laboratories. C++ provides capabilities for **object-oriented programming (OOP)**. Many of today's major operating systems (such as Microsoft Windows) are written in C or C++.

Objects are reusable software **components** that model items in the real world. Object-oriented programs are often easier to understand, correct and modify than programs developed with previous techniques. Visual Basic 2008 provides full object-oriented programming capabilities.

In the early 1990s, many organizations, including Sun Microsystems, predicted that intelligent consumer-electronic devices would be the next major market in which **microprocessors**—the chips that make computers work—would have a profound impact. But the marketplace did not develop as quickly as Sun had anticipated. When the World Wide Web exploded in popularity in 1993, Sun saw the potential for using its new **Java** programming language to create interactive animated content for web pages. Sun announced Java in 1995, grabbing the attention of the business community because of the widespread interest in the web. Developers now use Java to create web pages with dynamic content (content that is generated in response to user interactions), to build large-scale enterprise applications, to enhance the functionality of web servers (the computers that provide the content distributed to your web browser when you browse websites), to provide applications for consumer devices (for example, cell phones, pagers and PDAs) and for many other purposes.

In 2000, Microsoft announced **C#** (pronounced "C-Sharp") at the same time that it announced its .NET strategy. The C# programming language was designed specifically for the .NET platform. It has roots in C, C++ and Java, adapting the best features of each. Like Visual Basic, C# is object oriented and has access to .NET's powerful library of prebuilt components, enabling you to develop applications quickly. C#, Java and Visual Basic have comparable capabilities, so learning Visual Basic may create many career opportunities for you.

SELF-REVIEW

1. _________ is an extension of C and offers object-oriented capabilities.
   a) Visual Basic b) C++
   c) assembly language d) Windows

2. _________ is a programming language originally developed for Microsoft's .NET platform.
   a) C# b) Java
   c) C++ d) Visual Basic

3. _________, developed in the late 1950s, is still used to program a considerable portion of today's business software.
   a) COBOL b) Fortran
   c) Java d) C

4. _________, developed in the 1950s, is still used to create scientific and engineering applications that require complex mathematical computations.
   a) Visual Basic b) Fortran
   c) COBOL d) C#

Answers: 1) b. 2) a. 3) a. 4) b.

1.6 Structured Programming

During the 1960s, software-development efforts often ran behind schedule, costs greatly exceeded budgets and the finished products were unreliable. People began to realize that software development was a far more complex activity than they had imagined. Research activity intended to address these issues resulted in the evolution of **structured programming**—a disciplined approach to creating programs that are clear, correct and easy to modify.

One result of this research was the development of the **Pascal** programming language in 1971. Pascal, named after the 17th-century mathematician and philosopher Blaise Pascal, was designed for teaching structured programming and rapidly became the preferred introductory programming language in most colleges. Unfortunately, the language lacked many features needed to make it useful in commercial, industrial and government applications. By contrast, C, which also arose from research on structured programming, did not have the limitations of Pascal, and professional programmers quickly adopted it.

The **Ada** programming language, based on Pascal, was developed under the sponsorship of the U.S. Department of Defense (DOD) during the 1970s and early 1980s. The language was named after Ada Byron, Lady Lovelace, daughter of the poet Lord Byron. Lady Lovelace is generally acknowledged as the world's first computer programmer, having written an application in the early 1800s for Charles Babbage's Analytical Engine mechanical computing device.

SELF-REVIEW

1. During the 1960s and 1970s, research to address such software development problems as running behind schedule, exceeding budgets and creating unreliable products led to the evolution of ________.

   a) multithreading
   b) object-oriented programming
   c) Ada
   d) structured programming

2. ________ was designed to teach structured programming in academic environments.

   a) C++
   b) C
   c) Java
   d) Pascal

Answers: 1) d. 2) d.

1.7 Key Software Trend: Object Technology

As the benefits of structured programming were realized in the 1970s, improved software technology began to appear. Not until object-oriented programming became widely used in the 1980s and 1990s, however, did software developers feel they had the tools to dramatically improve the software-development process.

What are objects, and why are they special? **Object technology** is a packaging scheme for creating meaningful software units. There are date objects, time objects, paycheck objects, invoice objects, automobile objects, people objects, audio objects, video objects, file objects, record objects and so on. In fact, almost any noun can be reasonably represented as a software object. Objects have **properties** (also called **attributes**), such as color, size and weight; and perform **actions** (also called **behaviors** or **methods**), such as moving, sleeping or drawing. **Classes** are types of related objects. For example, all cars belong to the "car" class, even though individual cars vary in make, model, color and options packages. A class specifies the general format of its objects, and the properties and actions available to an object depend on its class. An object is related to its class in much the same way as a building is related to its blueprint from which the building is constructed. Contractors can build many buildings from the same blueprint; programmers can instantiate (create) many objects from the same class.

Before object-oriented languages appeared, **procedural programming languages** (such as Fortran, Pascal, BASIC and C) focused on actions (verbs) rather than things or objects (nouns). This made programming a bit awkward. However, using today's popular object-oriented languages, such as Visual Basic, C++, Java and C#, you can program in an object-oriented manner that more naturally reflects the way in which you perceive the world. This has resulted in significant productivity gains.

With object technology, properly designed classes can be reused on future projects. Using libraries of classes can greatly reduce the amount of effort required to implement new systems. Some organizations report that the key benefit they get from object-oriented programming is not, in fact, software reusability. Rather, it is the producting of software that is more understandable because it is better organized and has fewer maintenance requirements.

Object orientation allows you to focus on the "big picture." Instead of worrying about the minute details of how reusable objects are implemented, you can focus on the behaviors and interactions of objects. A road map that showed every tree, house and driveway would be difficult, if not impossible, to read. When such details are removed and only the essential information (roads) remains, the map becomes easier to understand. In the same way, an application that is divided into objects is easy to understand, modify and update because it hides much of the detail.

It is clear that object-oriented programming will be the key programming methodology for the next several decades. Visual Basic is one of the world's most widely used object-oriented languages.

SELF-REVIEW

1. _________ focuses on actions (verbs) rather than things (nouns).

   a) C# b) Object-oriented programming
   c) Visual Basic d) Procedural programming

2. In object-oriented programming, _________, which are in a sense like blueprints, are types of related objects.

   a) classes b) attributes
   c) behaviors d) properties

Answers: 1) d. 2) a.

1.8 The Internet and the World Wide Web

In the late 1960s, ARPA—the Advanced Research Projects Agency of the Department of Defense—rolled out plans to network the main computer systems of approximately a dozen ARPA-funded universities and research institutions. The computers were to be connected with communications lines operating at a then-stunning 56 Kbps (1 Kbps is equal to 1,024 bits per second), at a time when most people (of the few who even had networking access) were connecting over telephone lines to computers at a rate of 110 bits per second. Academic research was about to take a giant leap forward. ARPA proceeded to implement what quickly became known as the **ARPAnet**, the grandparent of today's **Internet**.

Things worked out differently from the original plan. Although the ARPAnet enabled researchers to network their computers, its main benefit proved to be the capability for quick and easy communication via what came to be known as **electronic mail (e-mail)**. This is true even on today's Internet, with e-mail, instant messaging and file transfer allowing more than a billion people worldwide to communicate with each other.

The protocol (in other words, the set of rules) for communicating over the ARPAnet became known as the **Transmission Control Protocol (TCP)**. TCP ensured that messages, consisting of pieces called "packets," were properly routed from sender to receiver, arrived intact and were assembled in the correct order.

In parallel with the early evolution of the Internet, organizations worldwide were implementing their own networks for both intraorganization (that is, within an organization) and interorganization (that is, between organizations) communication. A huge variety of networking hardware and software appeared. One challenge was to enable these different networks to communicate with each other. ARPA accomplished this by developing the **Internet Protocol (IP)**, which created a true "network of networks," the current architecture of the Internet. The combined set of protocols is now called **TCP/IP**.

Businesses rapidly realized that by using the Internet, they could improve their operations and offer new and better services to their clients. Companies started spending large amounts of money to develop and enhance their Internet presence. This generated fierce competition among communications carriers and hardware and software suppliers to meet the increased infrastructure demand. As a result, **bandwidth**—the information-carrying capacity of communications lines—on the Internet has increased tremendously, while hardware costs have plummeted.

The **World Wide Web** is a collection of hardware and software associated with the Internet that allows computer users to locate and view multimedia-based documents (documents with various combinations of text, graphics, animations, audios and videos) on almost any subject. Even though the Internet was developed more than three decades ago, the introduction of the World Wide Web (WWW) was a relatively recent event. In 1989, Tim Berners-Lee of CERN (the European Organization for Nuclear Research) began to develop a technology for sharing information via "hyperlinked" text documents. Berners-Lee called his invention the **HyperText Markup Language (HTML)**. He also wrote communication protocols such as **HyperText Transfer Protocol (HTTP)** to form the backbone of his new hypertext information system, which he referred to as the World Wide Web.

In October 1994, Berners-Lee founded an organization, called the **World Wide Web Consortium** (**W3C**, `www.w3.org`), devoted to developing technologies for the World Wide Web. One of the W3C's primary goals is to make the web universally accessible to everyone regardless of disabilities, language or culture.

The Internet and the web will surely be listed among the most important creations of humankind. In the past, most computer applications ran on "stand-alone" computers (computers that were not connected to one another). Today's applications can be written with the aim of communicating among the world's computers. In fact, as you'll see, this is the focus of Microsoft's .NET strategy. The Internet and the World Wide Web make information instantly and conveniently accessible to large numbers of people, enabling even individuals and small businesses to achieve worldwide exposure. They are profoundly changing the way we do business and conduct our personal lives. To highlight the importance of Internet and web programming, we include four tutorials at the end of the book in which you'll actually build and run a web-based bookstore application.

SELF-REVIEW

1. Today's Internet evolved from the ________, which was a Department of Defense project.

   a) ARPAnet　　b) HTML
   c) CERN　　d) WWW

2. The combined set of protocols for communicating over the Internet is called ________.

   a) HTML　　b) TCP/IP
   c) ARPA　　d) TCP

Answers: 1) a. 2) b.

1.9 Introduction to Microsoft .NET

In June 2000, Microsoft announced its **.NET initiative** (`www.microsoft.com/net`), a broad new vision for using the Internet and the web in the development, engineering, distribution and use of software. Rather than forcing developers to use a single programming language, the .NET initiative permits developers to create .NET applications in any .NET-compatible language (such as Visual Basic, Visual C++, Visual C# and others). Part of the initiative includes Microsoft's **ASP.NET** technology, which allows you to create web applications. You use ASP.NET 3.5 (the current version) to build the web-based bookstore application later in the book.

The .NET strategy extends the idea of **software reuse** to the Internet by allowing programmers to concentrate on their specialties without having to implement every component of every application. Visual programming (which you'll learn throughout this book) has become popular because it enables programmers to create Windows and web applications easily, using such prepackaged graphical components as **buttons**, **textboxes** and **scrollbars**.

The Microsoft **.NET Framework** is at the heart of the .NET strategy. This framework executes applications and web services, contains a class library (called the **Framework Class Library**) and provides many other programming capabilities that you'll use to build Visual Basic applications. In this book, you'll develop .NET software with Visual Basic. Steve Ballmer, Microsoft's CEO, has stated that Microsoft was "betting the company" on .NET. Such a dramatic commitment surely indicates a bright future for Visual Basic 2008 programmers.

SELF-REVIEW

1. _________ is a technology specifically designed for the .NET platform and intended for programmers to create web-based applications.

   a) Visual Basic b) C++
   c) HTML d) ASP.NET

2. Programmers use the _________, a part of the .NET Framework, to build Visual Basic 2008 applications.

   a) Visual Basic Library b) Framework Class Library
   c) Microsoft Class Library d) Visual Basic Framework

Answers: 1) d. 2) b.

1.10 Test-Driving the Visual Basic Advanced Painter Application

In each tutorial, you are given a chance to "test-drive" that tutorial's featured application. You'll actually run and interact with the completed application. Then, you'll learn the Visual Basic features you need to build the application. Finally, you'll "put it all together," creating your own working version of the application. You begin here in Tutorial 1 by running an existing application that allows the user to draw with "brushes" of four different colors and three different sizes. You'll actually build a part of this application in Tutorial 27, then finish the application in the Tutorial 27 exercises.

The following box, *Test-Driving the* **Advanced Painter** *Application*, will show you how the application allows the user to draw with different brush styles. The elements and functionality you see in this application are typical of what you'll learn to program in this text. [*Note:* We use fonts to distinguish between IDE features (such as menu names and menu items) and other elements that appear in the IDE. Our convention is to emphasize IDE features (such as the **File** menu) in a semibold **sans-serif Helvetica** font and to emphasize other elements, such as file names (for example, `Form1.cs`), in a `sans-serif Lucida` font. Each term that is being defined is set in **bold blue text**.]

Test-Driving the Advanced Painter Application

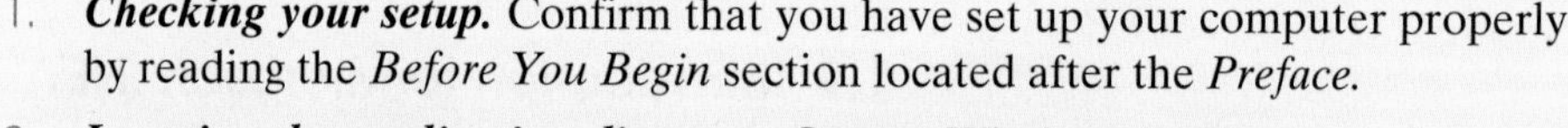

1. ***Checking your setup.*** Confirm that you have set up your computer properly by reading the *Before You Begin* section located after the *Preface.*

2. ***Locating the application directory.*** Open a Windows Explorer window and navigate to the `C:\Examples\Tutorial01` directory (Fig. 1.1).

Double click this file to run the application

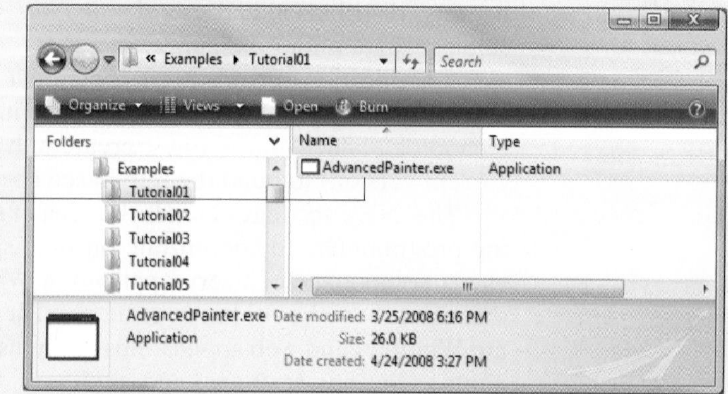

Figure 1.1 Contents of `C:\Examples\Tutorial01`.

3. ***Running the*** **Advanced Painter** ***application.*** Now that you are in the proper directory, double click the file name `AdvancedPainter.exe` (Fig. 1.1) to run the application (Fig. 1.2).

(cont.)

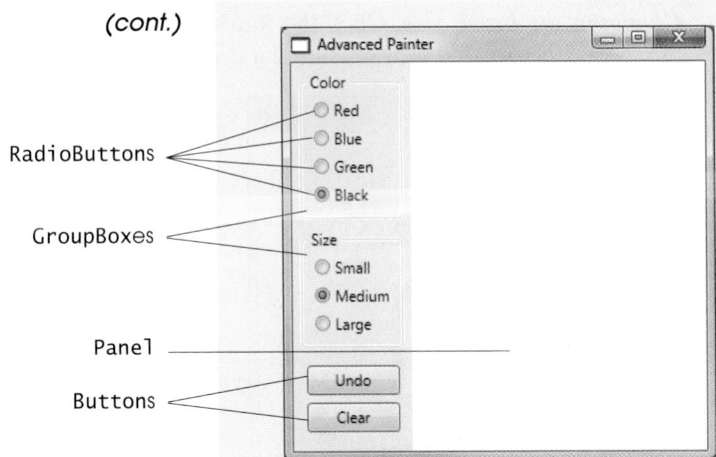

Figure 1.2 Visual Basic **Advanced Painter** application.

In Fig. 1.2, several graphical elements—called **controls**—are labeled. The controls include `GroupBoxes`, `RadioButtons`, a `Panel` and `Buttons` (these controls are discussed in depth later in the text). The application allows you to draw with a red, blue, green or black brush of small, medium or large size. You'll explore these options in this test-drive. You can also undo your previous operation or clear the drawing to start from scratch.

By using existing controls—which are objects—you can create powerful applications in Visual Basic much faster than if you had to write all the code yourself. In this text, you'll learn how to use many preexisting controls, as well as how to write your own program code to customize your applications.

The brush's properties, selected in the `RadioButtons` labeled **Black** and **Medium**, are default settings—the initial settings you see when you first run the application. You include default settings to provide visual cues for users to choose their own settings. Now you'll choose your own settings.

4. ***Changing the brush color.*** Click the `RadioButton` labeled **Red** to change the color of the brush and **Small** to change the size of the brush. ClickPosition the mouse over the white `Panel`, the press and hold down the left mouse button to draw with the brush. Draw flower petals, as shown in Fig. 1.3. Then click the `RadioButton` labeled **Green** to change the color of the brush again.

Figure 1.3 Drawing with a new brush color.

(cont.)

5. ***Changing the brush size.*** Click the `RadioButton` labeled **Large** to change the size of the brush. Draw grass and a flower stem, as shown in Fig. 1.4.

Figure 1.4 Drawing with a new brush size.

6. ***Finishing the drawing.*** Click the `RadioButton` labeled **Blue**. Then click the `RadioButton` labeled **Medium**. Draw raindrops, as shown in Fig. 1.5, to complete the drawing.

Figure 1.5 Finishing the drawing.

7. ***Closing the application.*** Close your running application by clicking its **close box**, (Fig. 1.5).

1.11 Web Resources

The Internet and the web are extraordinary resources. This section includes links to interesting and informative websites. Reference sections like this one are included throughout the book where appropriate.

`www.deitel.com/visualbasic2008/`
Our Visual Basic Resource Center focuses on the enormous amount of Visual Basic content available online. Search for resources, downloads, tutorials, documentation, books, e-books, journals, articles, blogs and more that will help you develop Visual Basic applications.

`www.deitel.com`
Visit this site for code downloads, updates, corrections and additional resources for Deitel & Associates publications, including *Simply Visual Basic 2008* errata, Frequently Asked Questions (FAQs), hot links and code downloads.

`www.prenhall.com/deitel`
The Deitel & Associates page on the Prentice Hall website contains information about our publications and code downloads for this book.

`msdn.microsoft.com/vbasic`
This is Microsoft's Visual Basic website with links to code samples, starter kits, tutorials, blogs, webcasts and other valuable resources.

`www.softlord.com/comp`
Visit this site to learn more about the history of computers.

`www.elsop.com/wrc/h_comput.htm`
This site presents the history of computing. It includes content about famous people in the computer field, the evolution of programming languages and the development of operating systems.

`www.w3.org/History.html`
Visit this site for the history of the web.

`www.netvalley.com/intval/07262/main.htm?sdf=1`
This site presents the history of the Internet.

1.12 Wrap-Up

In this tutorial, you learned how computers are organized. You studied the levels of programming languages and which kinds of languages, including Visual Basic, require translators. You became familiar with some of the most popular programming languages. You learned the importance of structured programming and object-oriented programming. You studied a brief history of the Internet and the web, were introduced to Microsoft's .NET initiative and learned some key aspects of .NET.

You took a working Visual Basic application out for a "test-drive." In the process of doing this, you learned that Visual Basic provides lots of prebuilt controls that perform useful functions, and that by familiarizing yourself with the capabilities of these controls, you can develop powerful applications much faster than if you tried to build them completely yourself. You were encouraged to explore several websites with additional information on this book, computers, the Internet, the web, .NET and Visual Basic.

In the next tutorial, you'll learn about the Visual Basic 2008 Integrated Development Environment (IDE). This will help you prepare to create your own Visual Basic applications. You'll continue to learn with our application-driven approach, in which you'll see Visual Basic features in useful applications and will

1. study the user requirements for an application,
2. test-drive a working version of the application,
3. learn the technologies you'll need to build the application yourself, and
4. build your own version of the application.

As you work through the book, if you have any questions about Visual Basic 2008, just send an e-mail to `deitel@deitel.com`, and we'll respond promptly. We sincerely hope you enjoy learning the latest version of Microsoft's powerful Visual Basic language—one of the most widely used programming languages in the world—with *Simply Visual Basic 2008, Third Edition*. Good luck!

KEY TERMS

Ada—A programming language, named after Lady Ada Lovelace, that was developed under the sponsorship of the U.S. Department of Defense (DOD) in the 1970s and early 1980s.

arithmetic and logic unit (ALU)—The "manufacturing" section of the computer. The ALU performs calculations and makes decisions.

ARPAnet—The grandfather of today's Internet.

ASP.NET—.NET software that helps you create web applications.

assembler—A translator program that converts assembly-language programs to machine language at computer speeds.

assembly language—A type of programming language that uses English-like abbreviations to represent the fundamental operations on the computer.

attribute—Another name for a property of an object.

bandwidth—The information-carrying capacity of communications lines.

BASIC (Beginner's All-purpose Symbolic Instruction Code)—A programming language for writing simple programs. Developed in the mid-1960s by Professors John Kemeny and Thomas Kurtz of Dartmouth College. Its primary purpose was to familiarize novices with programming techniques.

Central Processing Unit (CPU)—The part of the computer's hardware that is responsible for supervising the operation of the other sections of the computer.

class—The type of a group of related objects. A class specifies the general format of its objects; the properties and actions available to an object depend on its class. An object is to its class much as a house is to the blueprint from which a house is constructed.

COBOL (COmmon Business Oriented Language)—A programming language that was developed in the late 1950s by a group of computer manufacturers in conjunction with government and industrial computer users. This language is used primarily for business applications that manipulate large amounts of data.

compiler—A translator program that converts high-level-language programs into machine language.

computer—A device capable that can perform computations and make logical decisions millions, billions and even trillions of times faster than human beings can carry out the same tasks.

computer program—A set of instructions that guides a computer through an orderly series of actions.

computer programmer—A person who writes computer programs.

control—A reusable GUI component, such as a `GroupBox`, `RadioButton`, `Button` or `Label`.

C#—A programming language that was designed specifically for the .NET platform. It has roots in C, C++ and Java, adapting the best features of each. Like Visual Basic, C# is object oriented and has access to .NET's powerful library of prebuilt components, enabling you to develop applications quickly.

event-driven program—A program that responds to user-initiated events, such as mouse clicks and keystrokes.

Fortran (Formula Translator)—A programming language developed by IBM Corporation in the mid-1950s (and still widely used) to create scientific and engineering applications that require complex mathematical computations.

Framework Class Library—.NET's collection of "prepackaged" classes and methods for performing mathematical calculations, string manipulations, character manipulations, input/output operations, error checking and many other useful operations.

graphical user interface (GUI)—The visual part of an application with which users interact.

hardware—The various devices that make up a computer, including the keyboard, screen, mouse, hard drive, memory, CD-ROM, DVD, printer and processing units.

high-level language—A type of programming language in which a single program statement accomplishes a substantial task. High-level languages use instructions that look almost like everyday English and contain common mathematical notations.

HyperText Markup Language (HTML)—A language for marking up information to share over the web via hyperlinked text documents.

HyperText Transfer Protocol (HTTP)—The protocol that enables HTML files to be transmitted over the web.

input device—Devices that are used to interact with a computer, such as keyboards, mice, microphones, scanners and digital cameras.

input unit—The "receiving" section of the computer that obtains information (data and computer programs) from various input devices, such as keyboards, mice, microphones, scanners and digital cameras.

Integrated Development Environment (IDE)—A software tool that enables you to write, run, test and debug programs quickly and conveniently.

Internet—A worldwide computer network. Most people today access the Internet through the web.

Java—A popular programming language that is used to create web pages with dynamic content , to build large-scale enterprise applications, to enhance the functionality of web servers, to provide applications for consumer devices and for many other purposes.

machine language—A computer's natural language, generally consisting of streams of numbers that instruct the computer how to perform its most elementary operations.

memory—Another name for the memory unit.

memory unit—The rapid-access, relatively low-capacity "warehouse" section of the computer, which stores data temporarily while an application is running.

method—A portion of a class that performs a task and possibly returns information when it completes the task.

microprocessor—The chip that makes a computer work (that is, the "brain" of the computer).

.NET Framework—Microsoft-provided software that executes applications, provides the Framework Class Library and supplies many other programming capabilities.

.NET Framework Class Library—.NET's collection of "prepackaged" classes and methods for performing mathematical calculations, string manipulations, character manipulations, input/output operations, error checking and many other useful operations.

.NET Initiative—Microsoft's vision for using the Internet and the web in the development, engineering, distribution and use of software.

.NET Platform—The set of software components that enables .NET programs to run—allows applications to be distributed to a variety of devices as well as to desktop computers. Offers a programming model that allows software components created in different programming languages (such as Visual Basic and C#) to communicate with one another.

objects—Software components that model items in the real world.

object-oriented programming (OOP)—Models real-world objects with software counterparts.

object technology—A packaging scheme for creating meaningful software units. The units are large and are focused on particular application areas. There are date objects, time objects, paycheck objects, file objects and the like.

output device—A device to which information that is processed by the computer can be sent.

output unit—The section of the computer that takes information the computer has processed and places it on various output devices, making the information available for use outside the computer.

Pascal—A programming language designed for teaching structured programming, named after the 17th-century mathematician and philosopher Blaise Pascal.

primary memory—Another name for the memory unit.

procedural programming language—A programming language (such as Fortran, Pascal, BASIC and C) that focuses on actions (verbs) rather than things or objects (nouns).

properties—Object attributes, such as size, color and weight.

random-access memory (RAM)—An example of primary memory.

secondary storage unit—The long-term, high-capacity "warehouse" section of the computer.

software—The set of applications that run on computers.

software reuse—The reuse of existing pieces of software, an approach that enables you to avoid "reinventing the wheel," helping you to develop applications faster.

structured programming—A disciplined approach to creating programs that are clear, correct and easy to modify.

translator program—Converts assembly-language programs to machine languag.

Transmission Control Protocol/Internet Protocol (TCP/IP)—The combined set of communications protocols for the Internet.

Visual Basic—Programming language introduced by Microsoft in 1991 to make programming Windows applications easier.

visual programming with Visual Basic—You use Visual Studio's graphical user interface to conveniently drag and drop predefined controls into place on the screen, and to label and resize them. Visual Studio writes much of the Visual Basic code, saving you considerable effort.

Visual Studio—Integrate development environment (IDE) for developing applications using Visual Basic (and other languages).

volatile memory—Memory that is erased when the machine is powered off.

World Wide Web (WWW)—A communications system that allows computer users to locate and view multimedia documents (such as documents with text, graphics, animations, audios and videos).

World Wide Web Consortium (W3C)—A forum through which qualified individuals and companies cooperate to develop and standardize technologies for the web.

MULTIPLE-CHOICE QUESTIONS

1.1 The web was developed _________.

a) by ARPA
b) at CERN by Tim Berners-Lee
c) before the Internet
d) as a replacement for the Internet

1.2 Microsoft's _________ initiative integrates the Internet and the web into software development.

a) .NET
b) BASIC
c) Windows
d) W3C

1.3 `TextBox`es, `Button`s and `RadioButton`s are examples of _________.

a) platforms
b) high-level languages
c) IDEs
d) controls

1.4 _________ is an example of primary memory.

a) TCP
b) RAM
c) ALU
d) CD-ROM

1.5 Visual Basic is an example of a(n) _________ language, in which single program statements accomplish substantial tasks.

a) machine
b) intermediate-level
c) high-level
d) assembly

1.6 Which protocol is primarily intended to create a "network of networks"?

a) TCP
b) IP
c) OOP
d) None of the above

1.7 A major benefit of _________ programming is that the software it produces is more understandable and better organized than software produced with earlier techniques.

a) object-oriented
b) centralized
c) procedural
d) HTML

1.8 .NET's collection of prepackaged classes and methods is called the _________.

a) NCL
b) WCL
c) .NET Framework Class Library
d) PPCM

1.9 The information-carrying capacity of communications lines is called _________.

a) networking
b) secondary storage
c) traffic
d) bandwidth

1.10 Which of these programming languages was specifically created for .NET?

a) C#
b) C++
c) BASIC
d) Visual Basic

EXERCISES

1.11 Categorize each of the following items as either hardware or software:

a) CPU
b) Compiler
c) Input unit
d) A word-processor program
e) A Visual Basic program

1.12 Translator programs, such as assemblers and compilers, convert programs from one language (referred to as the source language) to another language (referred to as the target language). Determine which of the following statements are *true* and which are *false*:

a) A compiler translates high-level-language programs into target-language programs.
b) An assembler translates source-language programs into machine-language programs.
c) A compiler translates source-language programs into target-language programs.
d) High-level languages are generally machine dependent.
e) A machine-language program requires translation before it can run on a computer.

1.13 Computers can be thought of as being divided into six units.

a) Which unit can be thought of as the "boss" of the other units?
b) Which unit is the high-capacity "warehouse" and retains information even when the computer is powered off?
c) Which unit might determine whether two items stored in memory are identical?
d) Which unit obtains information from devices like the keyboard and the mouse?

1.14 Expand each of the following acronyms:

a) W3C
b) TCP/IP
c) OOP
d) HTML

1.15 What are the advantages to using object-oriented programming techniques?

2 TUTORIAL

Objectives

In this tutorial, you learn to:

- Navigate Visual Studio 2008's **Start Page**.
- Create a Visual Basic project.
- Use the IDE's menus and toolbars.
- Manipulate windows in the Visual Basic 2008 Express Edition IDE.
- Use the auto-hide feature.
- Use the Visual Basic 2008 Express Edition IDE's help features.
- Close a Visual Basic project.

Outline

Welcome Application

Introducing the Visual Basic 2008 Express Edition IDE

Visual Studio® 2008 is Microsoft's **integrated development environment (IDE)** for creating, running and debugging applications written in a variety of .NET programming languages. The IDE allows you to create applications by dragging and dropping existing building blocks into place—a technique called **visual programming**—greatly simplifying application development. In this tutorial, you learn the Visual Studio 2008 IDE features that you need to begin creating your own Visual Basic applications.

2.1 Test-Driving the Welcome Application

In this section, you continue learning with our application-driven approach as you prepare to build an application that displays a welcome message and a picture. This application must meet the following requirements:

Application Requirements

A software company (Deitel & Associates) has asked you to develop a Visual Basic application that displays the message "Welcome to Visual Basic 2008!" and a picture of the company's bug mascot.

In this tutorial, you familiarize yourself with the Visual Basic 2008 Express Edition IDE and begin to develop the Welcome application. Then, in Tutorial 3, you "put it all together" and create the working **Welcome** application by following our step-by-step boxes. [*Note*: Our convention is to display application names in the **Helvetica** font.] You begin by test-driving the completed application. Then you learn the Visual Basic capabilities you need to create your own version of this application.

Test-Driving the Welcome Application

1. ***Checking your setup.*** Confirm that you have set up your computer properly by reading the *Before You Begin* tutorial at the beginning of this book just after the *Preface.*

2. ***Locating the application directory.*** Open Windows Explorer and navigate to the `C:\Examples\Tutorial02` directory (Fig. 2.1).

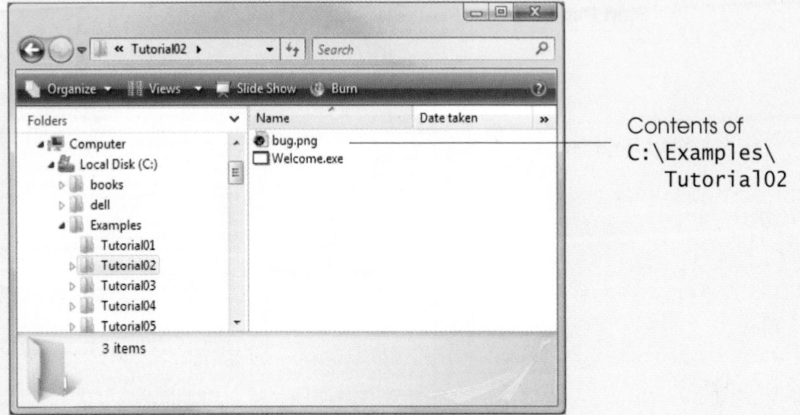

Figure 2.1 `C:\Examples\Tutorial02`

3. ***Running the Welcome application.*** Double click `Welcome.exe` (Fig. 2.1) to run the application (Fig. 2.2).

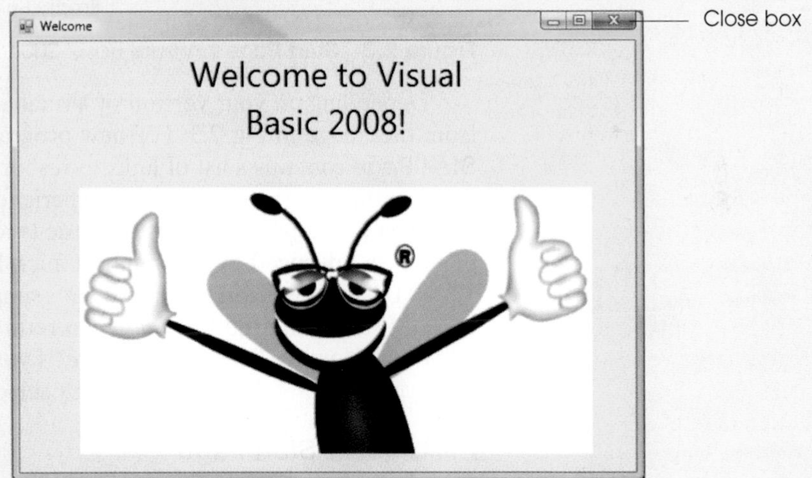

Figure 2.2 **Welcome** application executing.

4. ***Closing the application.*** Close your running application by clicking its close box, ![X].

2.2 Overview of the Visual Basic 2008 Express Edition IDE

Many versions of Visual Studio are available. The examples in this book are based on the *Microsoft Visual Basic 2008 Express Edition*, which supports only the Visual Basic programming language. You can also purchase a full version of Visual Studio 2008, which includes support for other languages in addition to Visual Basic, such as Visual C# and Visual C++. Our screen captures and discussions focus on the IDE of the Visual Basic 2008 Express Edition. We assume that you have some familiarity with Microsoft Windows.

This section introduces you to the Visual Basic 2008 Express Edition IDE. To start the IDE, select **Start > All Programs > Microsoft Visual Basic 2008 Express**

Edition. We use the > character to indicate the selection of a menu command from a menu. For example, we use the notation **File > Open File** to indicate that you should select the **Open File** command from the **File** menu. Once the Express Edition begins execution, the **Start Page** displays (Fig. 2.3).

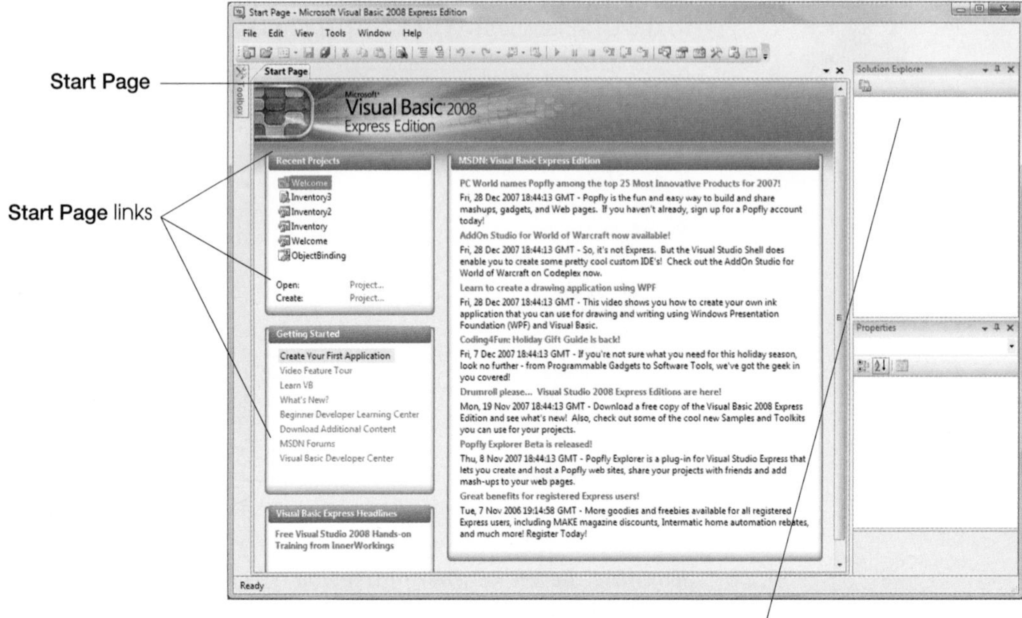

Figure 2.3 **Start Page** in Visual Basic 2008 Express Edition with an empty project list.

Depending on your version of Visual Studio, the **Start Page** may look different from the image in Fig. 2.3. For new programmers unfamiliar with Visual Basic, the **Start Page** contains a list of links to resources in the Visual Basic 2008 Express Edition IDE and on the Internet. For experienced developers, this page provides links to the latest developments in Visual Basic (such as updates and bug fixes) and to information on advanced programming topics. From this point forward, we refer to the Visual Basic 2008 Express Edition IDE simply as "Visual Basic" or "the IDE." Once you start exploring the IDE, you can return to the **Start Page** by selecting **View > Other Windows > Start Page**. [*Note:* If you change the layout of the windows in the IDE, you can reset the IDE's layout by selecting **Window > Reset Window Layout**.]

Links on the Start Page

The **Start Page** links are organized into sections—**Recent Projects**, **Getting Started**, **Visual Basic Express Headlines** and **MSDN: Visual Basic Express Edition**—that contain links to helpful programming resources. Clicking any link on the **Start Page** displays relevant information associated with that link. We refer to single clicking with the left mouse button as selecting, or clicking; we refer to double clicking with the left mouse button simply as double clicking.

The **Recent Projects** section contains information on projects you have recently created or modified. You can also open existing projects or create new ones by clicking the links in this section. The **Getting Started** section focuses on using the IDE for creating programs, learning Visual Basic, connecting to the Visual Basic developer community (i.e., other software developers with whom you can communicate through newsgroups and web sites) and providing various development tools.

If you are connected to the Internet, the **Visual Basic Express Headlines** and **MSDN: Visual Basic Express Edition** sections provide links to information about programming in Visual Basic, including online courses and the latest news about Visual Basic. To access more extensive information on Visual Studio, you can browse the MSDN (Microsoft Developer Network) online library at msdn2.microsoft.com/library. The MSDN site contains articles, downloads and tutorials on technologies of interest to Visual Basic developers. You can also browse the web from the IDE using Internet Explorer (also called the **internal web browser** in the IDE). To request a web page, type its URL into the **location bar** (Fig. 2.4) and press the *Enter* key—your computer, of course, must be connected to the Internet. (If the location bar is not already displayed, select **View > Other Windows > Web Browser**.) The web page that you wish to view appears as another **tab**, which you can select, inside the Visual Basic IDE (Fig. 2.4). Other windows appear in the IDE in addition to the **Start Page** and the internal web browser; we discuss several of them later in this tutorial.

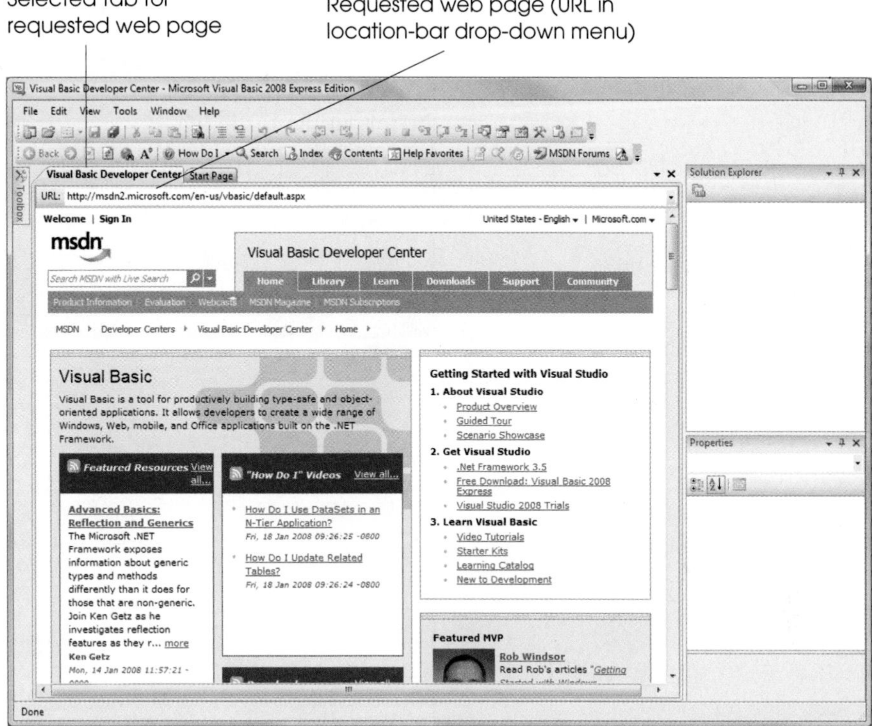

Figure 2.4 Displaying a web page in the Visual Basic 2008 Express Edition IDE.

SELF-REVIEW

1. When you first open the Visual Basic 2008 Express Edition, the ________ displays.
   a) **What's New Page** b) **Start Page**
   c) **Welcome Page** d) None of the above.

2. The ________ section in the **Start Page** contains a listing of projects opened or created in Visual Basic.
   a) **MSDN** b) **Getting Started**
   c) **Recent Projects** d) **Visual Basic Express Headlines**

Answers: 1) b. 2) c.

2.3 Creating a Project for the Welcome Application

In this section, you create a simple Visual Basic **Windows Forms application**. Visual Basic organizes applications into **projects** and **solutions**. A project is a group of related files, such as the Visual Basic code and any images that might make up a program. Solutions contain one or more projects. In this book, every application consists of one solution. Large-scale applications can contain many projects, in which each project performs a single well-defined task. In this book, each application you build contains only one project.

Creating a Project for the Welcome Application

1. ***Creating a new project.*** If you have not already done so, start Visual Basic. There are several ways to create a new project or open an existing one, including:

   - Select either **File > New Project...**, which creates a new project, or **File > Open Project...**, which opens an existing project.
   - From the **Start Page**, under the **Recent Projects** section, click the link **Create: Project...** or **Open: Project...**.
   - Click either the **New Project** `Button` (Fig. 2.5), causing the **New Project** dialog to display (Fig. 2.6), or the **Open File** `Button` (Fig. 2.5), which displays the **Open File** dialog.

   Dialogs are windows that can display information for, and gather information from, the application's user. Like other windows, dialogs are identified by the text in their **title bar**.

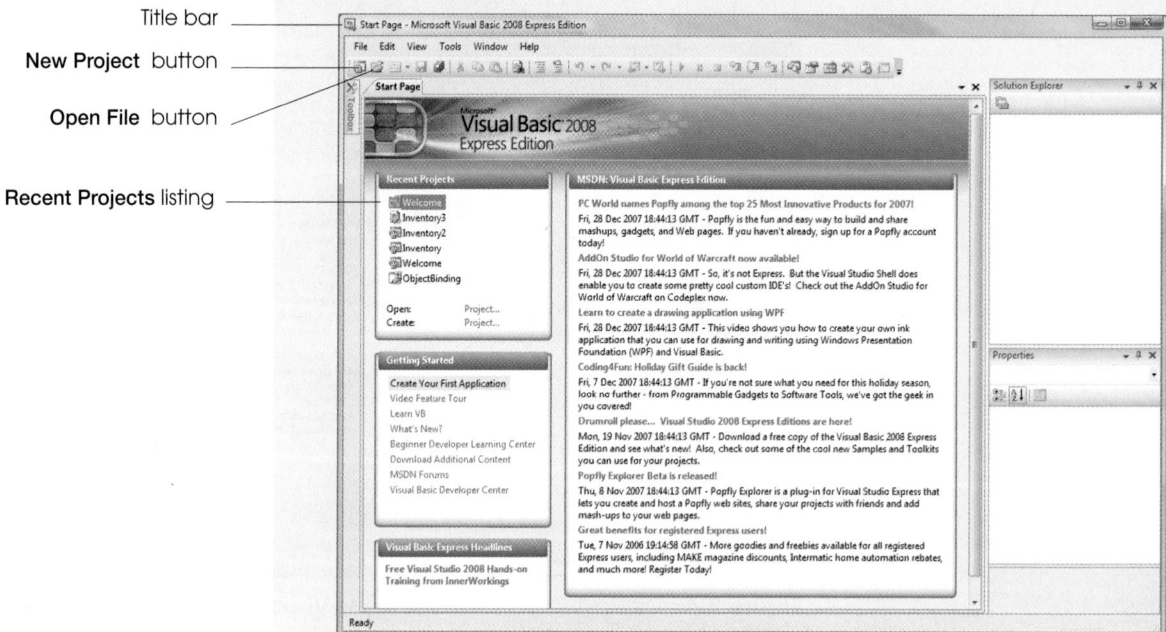

Figure 2.5 **New Project** button and **Recent Projects** listing.

2. ***Selecting the project type.*** Visual Basic provides templates for a variety of projects (Fig. 2.6). **Templates** are the project types you can create in Visual Basic—Windows Forms applications, console applications and others (you mainly use Windows Forms applications in this textbook). You can also create your own custom application templates. [*Note*: Depending on your version of Visual Studio, the names and number of items shown in the **Templates:** pane could differ.]

3. ***Selecting the template.*** Select **Windows Forms Application** (Fig. 2.7), which is an application that executes within a Windows operating system (e.g., Windows XP or Vista) and has a **graphical user interface (GUI)**—the visual part of the application with which the user interacts. Windows applications include Microsoft software products like Microsoft Word, Internet Explorer and Visual Studio; software products created by other vendors; and customized software that you and other programmers create.

(cont.)

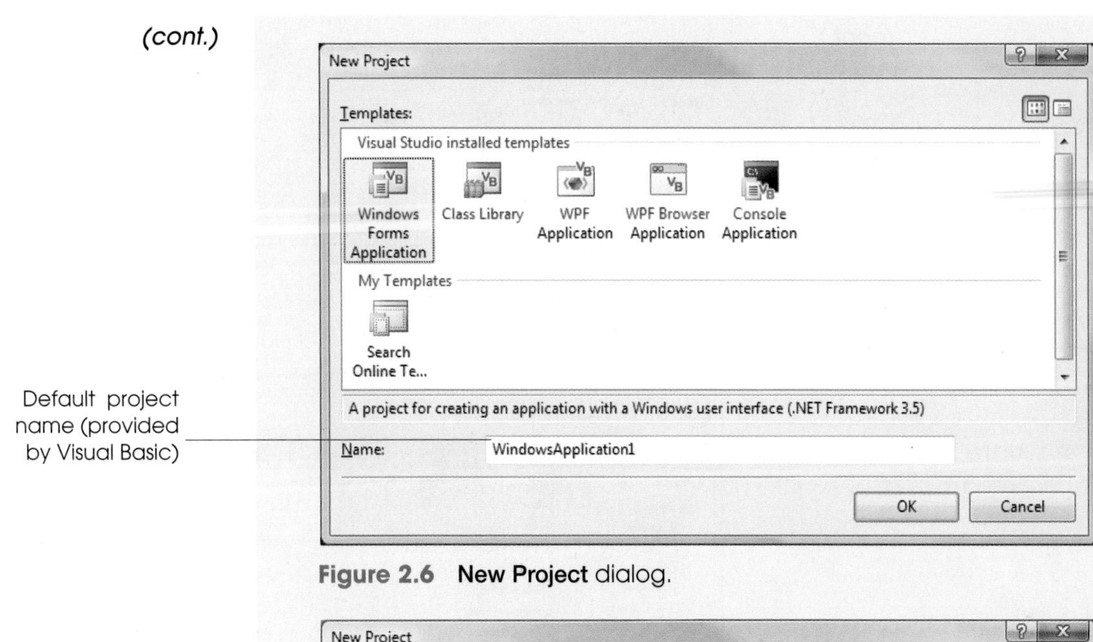

Figure 2.6 **New Project** dialog.

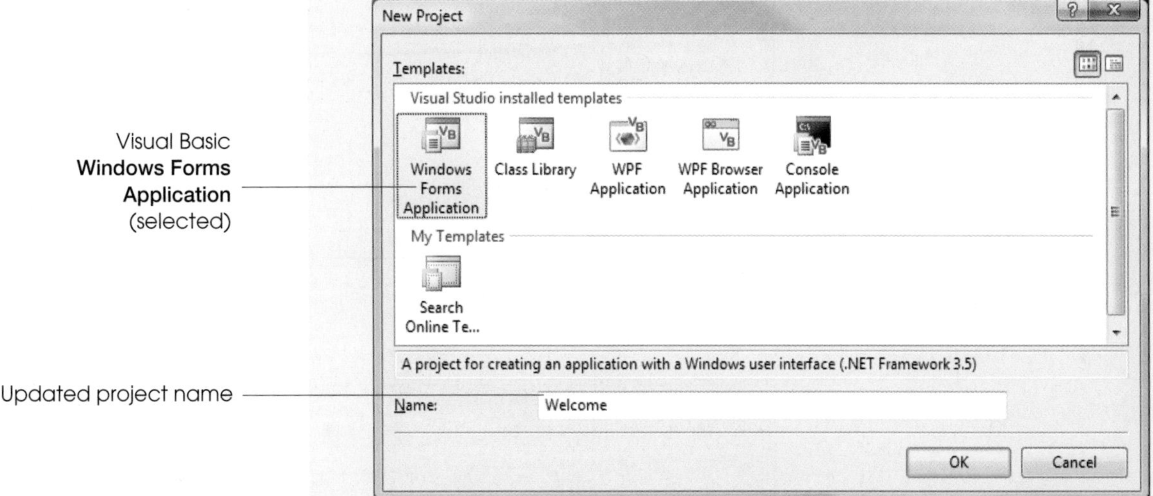

Figure 2.7 **New Project** dialog with updated project information.

4. ***Changing the name of the project.*** By default, Visual Basic assigns the name **WindowsApplication1** to the project (Fig. 2.6) and places these files in a directory named `WindowsApplication1`. To rename the project, type `Welcome` in the **Name:** `TextBox` (Fig. 2.7). Then click **OK**. Changing the project's name to `Welcome` also changes its folder's name to `Welcome`.

5. ***Changing the location of the project.*** Save this project in your `C:\SimplyVB2008` directory. To change the project's location, select **File > Save All**, which causes the **Save Project** dialog to appear (Fig. 2.8). In this dialog, use the **Browse...** `Button` to locate your `SimplyVB2008` directory, and click **Select Folder** (Fig. 2.9). [*Note:* If you are using Windows XP click **Open**]. After providing the project's name and location in the **Save Project** dialog, click **Save**. This displays the IDE in **Design view** (Fig. 2.10), which contains the features you need to begin creating a Windows application. Note that your screen may look slightly different—some windows, such as the **Solution Explorer**, may not immediately appear. We demonstrate how to open these windows shortly.

(cont.)

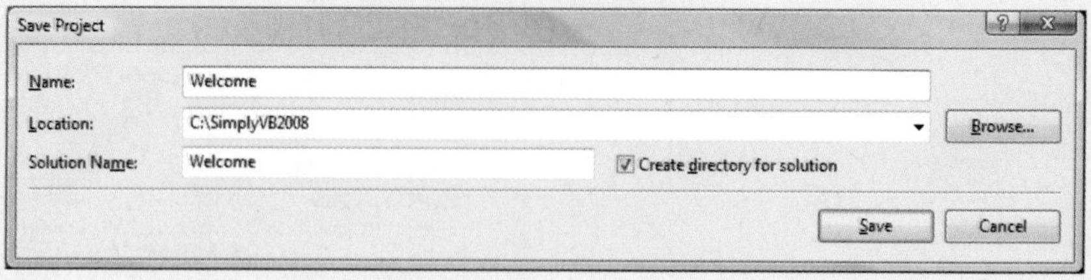

Save Project

Name: Welcome

Location: C:\SimplyVB2008 Browse...

Solution Name: Welcome ☑ Create directory for solution

Save Cancel

Figure 2.8 **Save Project** dialog.

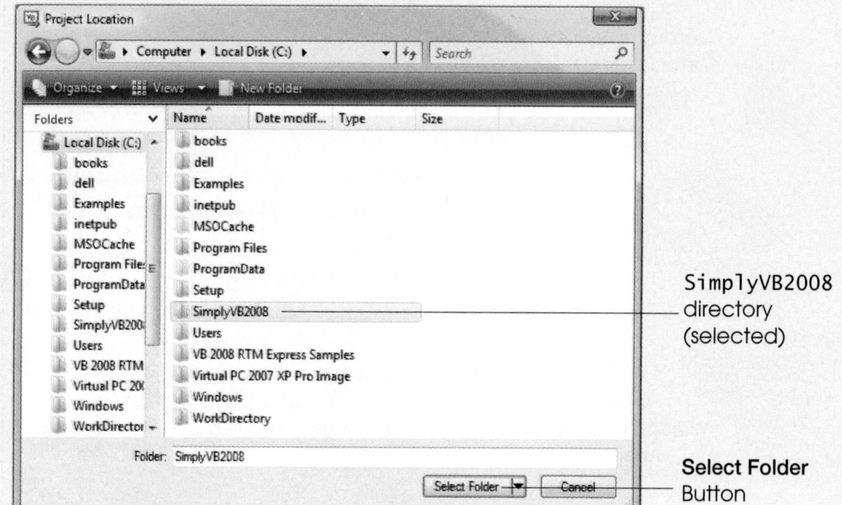

Figure 2.9 **Project Location** dialog.

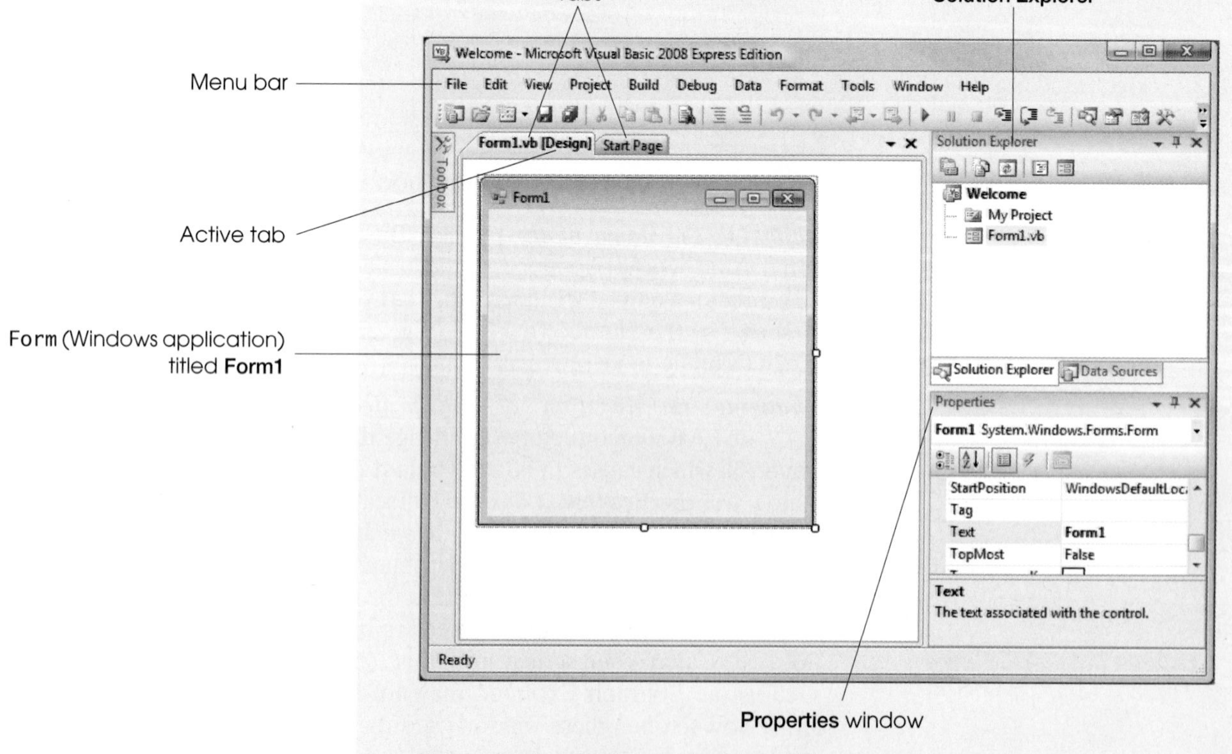

Figure 2.10 **Design** view of the IDE.

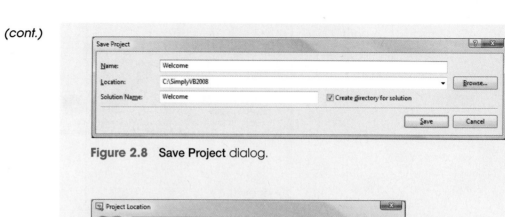

The name of each open file is listed on a **tab** (**Form1.vb [Design]** and **Start Page** in Fig. 2.10). To view a file, click its tab. Tabs provide easy access to multiple files. The **active tab** is displayed in bold text (**Form1.vb [Design]** in Fig. 2.10).

The content of the **Form1.vb [Design]** tab, which includes the gray rectangle (called a `Form`), is the **Windows Form Designer**. The `Form` (titled **Form1**) represents the main window of the Windows Forms application that you are creating. `Form`s can be enhanced by adding controls (i.e., reusable components), such as `Button`s. Collectively, the `Form` and controls make up the application's GUI. Users enter data (**inputs**) into the application by typing at the keyboard, by clicking the mouse buttons and in a variety of other ways. Applications display instructions and other information (**outputs**) for users to read in the GUI. For example, the **New Project** dialog in Fig. 2.6 is a GUI in which users click the mouse to select project types and input project names from the keyboard.

GUI controls (such as buttons) aid both in data entry by users and in formatting and presenting data outputs to users. For example, Internet Explorer (Fig. 2.11) displays web pages requested by users. Internet Explorer's GUI has a menu bar that contains six menus: **File**, **Edit**, **View**, **Favorites**, **Tools** and **Help**. These menus allow users to print files, save files and more. Below the menu bar is a **toolbar** that contains buttons. Each button contains an image (called an **icon**) that identifies the button. When clicked, toolbar buttons execute tasks (such as printing and searching). Above the menu bar is a `ComboBox` in which users can type the locations of web sites to visit. Users also can click the `ComboBox`'s drop-down arrow to select web sites they've visited previously. At the top of the window is the title of the web page the user is visiting. The menus, buttons and `Label` are part of Internet Explorer's GUI; they allow users to interact with the Internet Explorer application. Using Visual Basic, you can create your own applications that have all the GUI controls shown in Fig. 2.11 and many more.

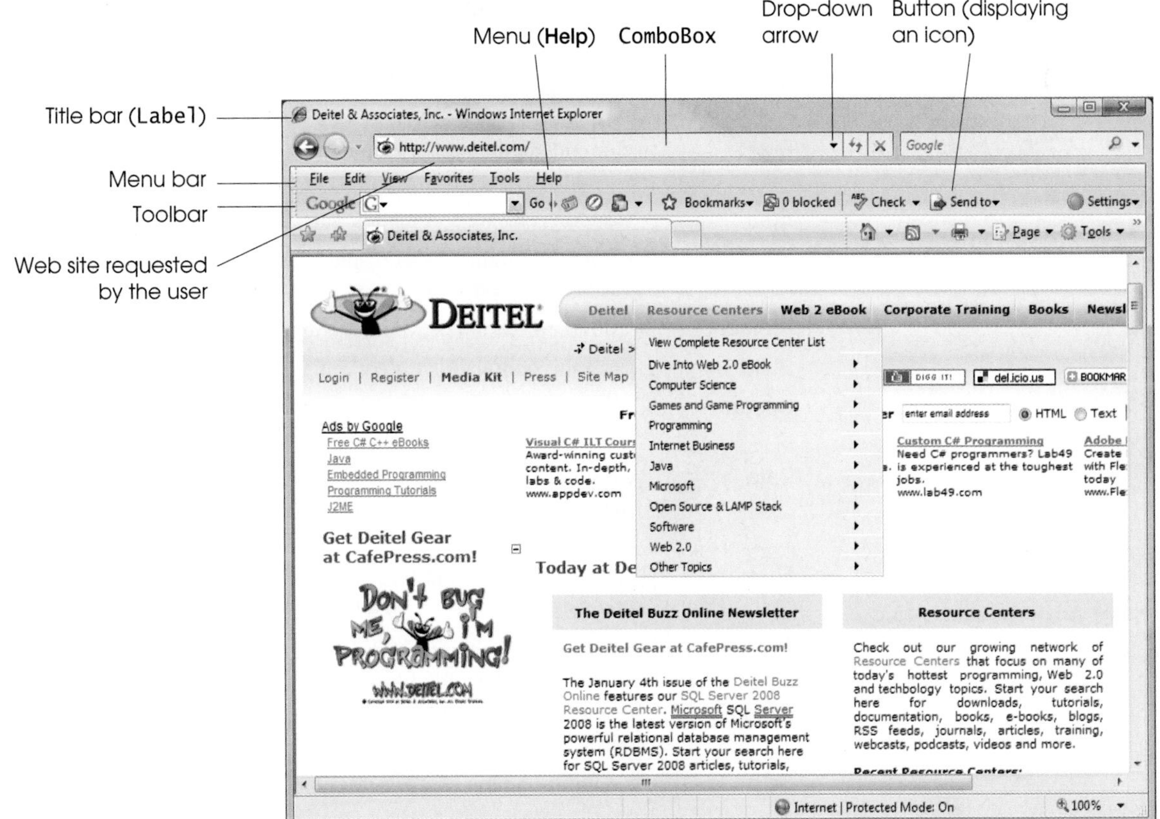

Figure 2.11 Internet Explorer window with GUI controls labeled. (Web site content courtesy of Deitel & Associates, Inc.)

SELF-REVIEW

1. The visual part of the application with which users interact is the application's ________.
   a) graphical user interface b) project
   c) solution d) title bar

2. A ________ contains one or more projects that collectively form an application.
   a) dialog b) `Form`
   c) solution d) GUI

Answers: 1) a. 2) c.

2.4 Menu Bar and Toolbar

Visual Basic programmers use **menus** (located on the Visual Basic IDE **menu bar** shown in Fig. 2.12) that contain commands for managing the IDE and for developing and executing applications. The set of menus displayed depends on what you are currently doing in the IDE.

File Edit View Project Build Debug Data Format Tools Window Help

Figure 2.12 Visual Basic 2008 IDE menu bar.

Each menu has a group of related **commands** (also called **menu items**) that, when selected, cause the IDE to perform specific actions, such as opening windows, saving files, printing files and executing applications. For example, to display the **Toolbox** window, select **View > Toolbox**. The menus in Fig. 2.12 are summarized in Fig. 2.13—you'll learn to use many of these menus throughout the book. [*Note:* The menus that actually appear depend on what you're doing—for example, some menus are visible only if a project is loaded.] In Tutorial 21, **Typing** Application (Introducing Keyboard Events, Menus and Dialogs), you learn how to create and add your own menus and menu items to your applications.

Menu	Description
File	Contains commands for opening, closing, adding and saving projects, as well as printing project data and exiting Visual Studio.
Edit	Contains editing commands, such as **Cut**, **Paste** and **Undo**.
View	Contains commands for displaying IDE windows (e.g., **Solution Explorer**, **Toolbox**, **Properties** window) and toolbars.
Project	Contains commands for managing projects and their files.
Build	Contains commands for compiling Visual Basic applications.
Debug	Contains commands for debugging (i.e., identifying and correcting problems in applications) and running applications.
Data	Contains commands for interacting with **databases**, which store the data that an application processes. [*Note*: You learn database concepts in Tutorial 24, **Address Book** Application.]
Format	Contains commands for aligning and modifying a `Form`'s controls. This menu appears only when a GUI component is selected in **Design** view.
Tools	Contains commands for accessing additional IDE tools and options that enable customization of the IDE.
Window	Contains commands for hiding, opening, closing and displaying IDE windows.
Help	Contains commands for accessing the IDE's help features.

Figure 2.13 Visual Basic IDE menu summary.

Rather than navigate the menus from the menu bar, you can access many of the more common commands from the IDE toolbar (Fig. 2.14), which contains icons that graphically represent commands. To execute a command via the IDE toolbar, simply click its icon. Some icons have associated down arrows that, when clicked, display additional commands.

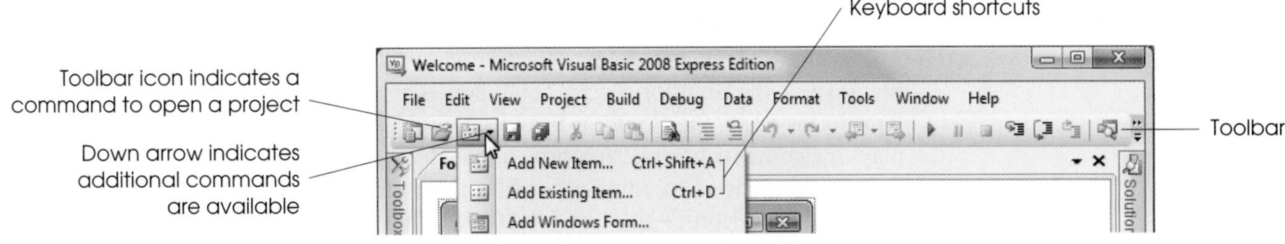

Figure 2.14 IDE toolbar.

It is difficult to remember what each of the icons on the toolbar represents. Positioning the mouse pointer over an icon highlights it and, after a brief pause, displays a description of the icon called a **tooltip** (Fig. 2.15). Tooltips help you become familiar with the IDE's features.

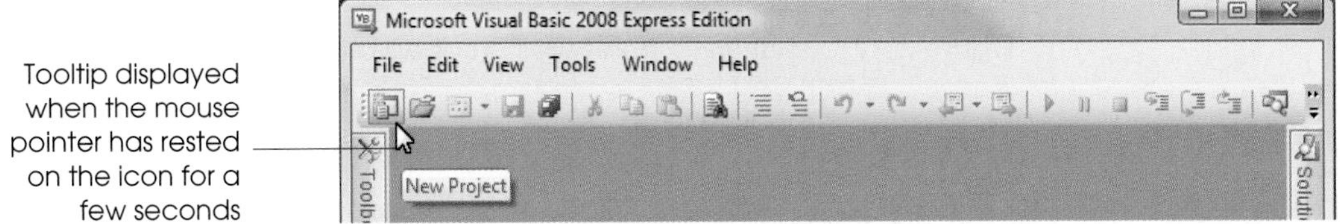

Figure 2.15 Tooltip demonstration.

SELF-REVIEW

1. ________ contain groups of related commands.

a) Menu items b) Menus
c) Tooltips d) None of the above

2. When the mouse pointer is positioned over an IDE toolbar icon for a few seconds, a ________ is displayed.

a) toolbox b) toolbar
c) menu d) tooltip

Answers: 1) b. 2) d.

2.5 Visual Basic 2008 Express Edition IDE Windows

The IDE provides windows for accessing project files and for customizing forms and controls by changing their attributes (names, colors, etc.). These windows provide visual aids for common programming tasks, such as managing files in a project. In this section, you become familiar with several windows—**Solution Explorer**, **Properties** and **Toolbox**—that are essential for creating Visual Basic applications. You can access these windows by using the IDE toolbar icons (Fig. 2.16) or by selecting the window name, using the **View** menu. [*Note*: These icons may not appear if the IDE window is too narrow. If you cannot view the icons shown in Fig. 2.16, widen the IDE window.]

Figure 2.16 Toolbar icons for four Visual Basic IDE windows.

Solution Explorer

The **Solution Explorer** window (normally located on the right side of the IDE, as shown in Fig. 2.10) provides access to solution files. This window allows you to manage files visually. The **Solution Explorer** window displays a list of the files in a project and the projects in a solution. (In this book you create only single-project applications, but remember that a solution can contain one or more projects.) If the **Solution Explorer** window is not shown in the IDE, you can display it by clicking the **Solution Explorer** icon in the IDE (Fig. 2.16), by selecting **View > Solution Explorer**. When the IDE is first loaded, the **Solution Explorer** window is empty; there are no files to display. Once a project is open, the **Solution Explorer** window displays its contents. Figure 2.17 displays the contents for the **Welcome** application. By default, the IDE displays only files that you may need to edit—other files generated by the IDE are hidden. Click the **Show All Files** icon to display all the files in the solution, including those generated by the IDE (Fig. 2.18).

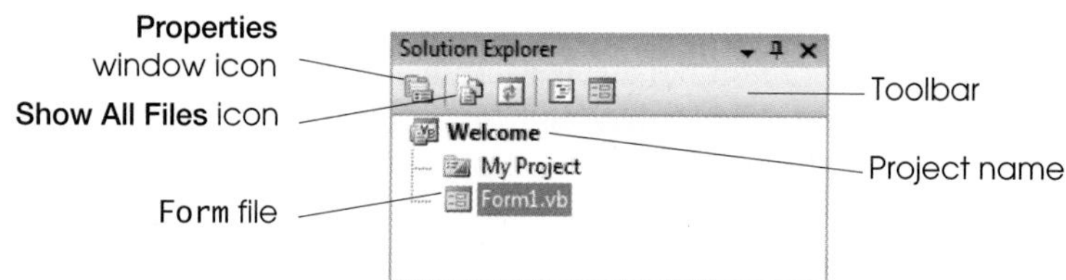

Figure 2.17 **Solution Explorer** with an open project.

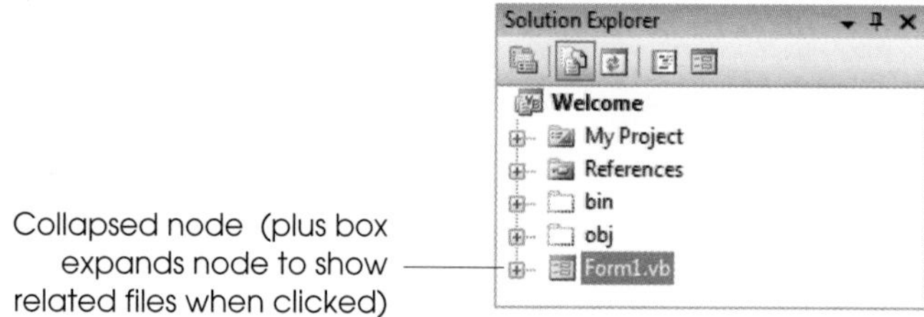

Figure 2.18 Using the **Show All Files** icon to display all the files in a solution.

For your single-project solution, **Welcome** is the only project. The file, which corresponds to the `Form` shown in Fig. 2.10, is named `Form1.vb`. (Visual Basic `Form` files use the `.vb` file-name extension, which is short for "Visual Basic.")

The **plus** and **minus** boxes to the left of the **My Project**, **References**, **bin**, **obj** and **Form1.vb** items are called **nodes**. The plus and minus boxes expand and collapse information, respectively.

Navigating a Project with the Solution Explorer

1. ***Expanding a node.*** After clicking the **Show All Files** icon (Fig. 2.18), click the plus box to the left of the **My Project** folder to expand the node. The **Solution Explorer** window should look like Fig. 2.19.

Expanded node (minus box)

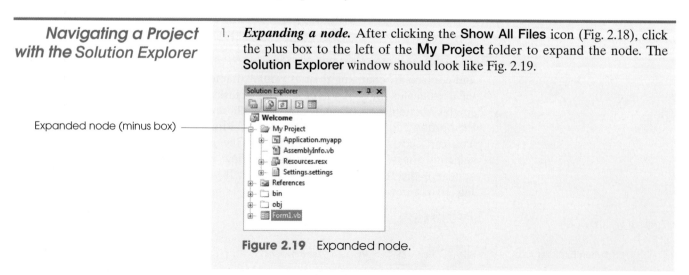

Figure 2.19 Expanded node.

(cont.)

2. ***Collapsing a node.*** Click the minus box to the left of the **My Project** folder (Fig. 2.19) to collapse the node. The minus box now becomes a plus box as in Fig. 2.20.

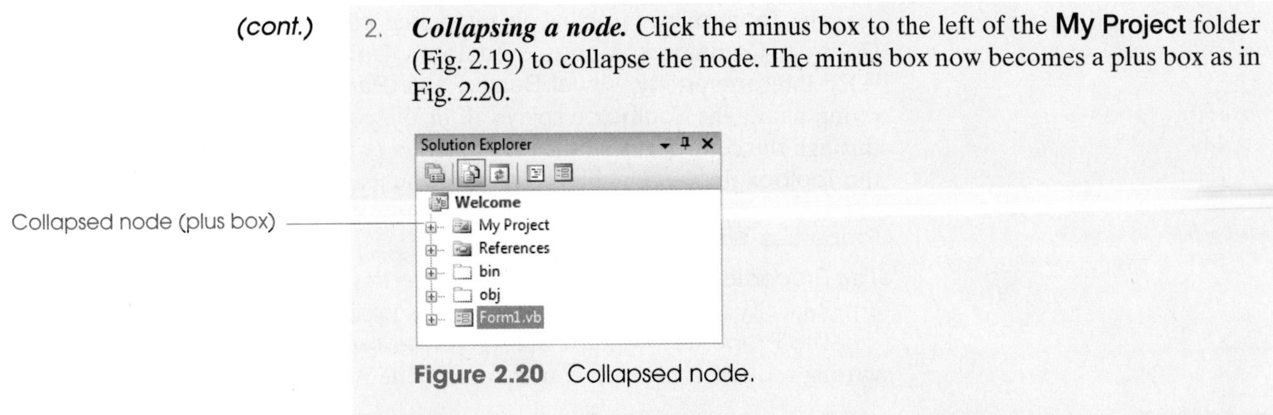

Figure 2.20 Collapsed node.

Toolbox

Using visual programming, you can "drag and drop" controls onto the `Form` quickly and easily instead of building them from scratch, which is a slow and complex process. Just as you do not need to know how to build an engine to drive a car, you do not need to know how to build controls to create effective GUIs. The **Toolbox** (Fig. 2.21) contains a wide variety of controls for building GUIs. You'll use the **Toolbox** as you finish creating the **Welcome** application in Tutorial 3. If the **Toolbox** is not visible, select **View > Toolbox**.

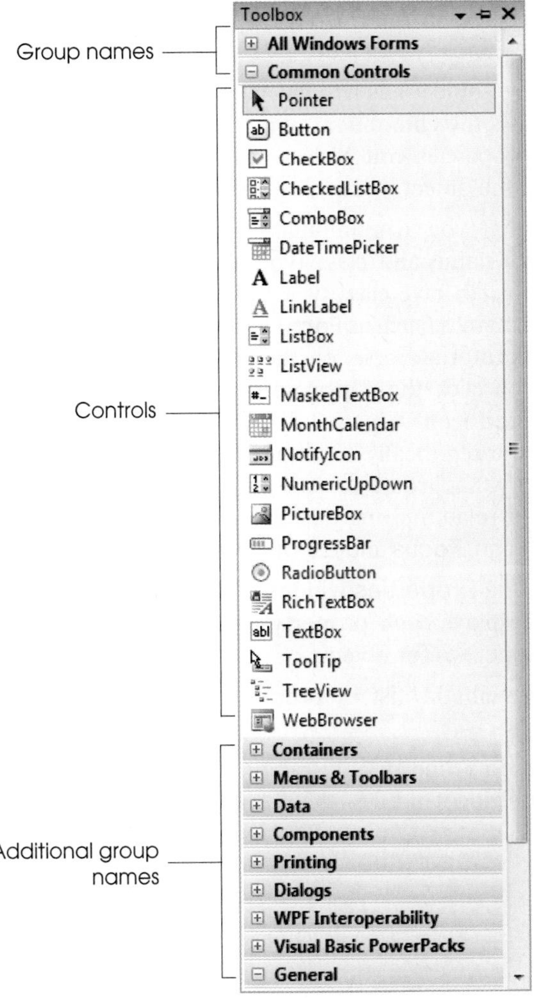

Figure 2.21 **Toolbox** displaying the contents of the **Common Controls** tab.

The **Toolbox** groups controls into categories—**All Windows Forms**, **Common Controls**, **Containers**, **Menus & Toolbars**, **Data**, **Components**, **Printing**, **Dialogs**, **WPF Interoperability**, **Visual Basic PowerPacks** and **General**. When you click a group name, the **Toolbox** displays all of the controls in that group. You can scroll through the controls using the **scroll arrows** (when they are present) to the right of the **Toolbox**. In the remaining tutorials, you use dozens of the **Toolbox**'s controls.

Properties **Window**

The **Properties** window displays the **properties** for `Form` and control objects. Properties specify an object's attributes, such as its size, color and position.

The **Properties** window allows you to set object properties visually without writing code. This provides a number of benefits:

- You can see a brief description of the selected property that helps you understand the property's purpose.
- You can set a property quickly.
- You can see which properties can be modified and, in many cases, you can learn the acceptable values for a given property. Property values that you modify are displayed in bold.
- You do not have to remember or search the Visual Basic documentation (see Section 2.7) for a property's settings.

These features are designed to help ensure that settings are correct and consistent throughout the project. If the **Properties** window is not visible, select **View > Properties Window** (or press *F4*). Figure 2.22 shows a `Form`'s **Properties** window:

- Each `Form` or control object has its own set of properties. At the top of the **Properties** window is the **component object box**, which allows you to select the object whose properties you wish to display in the **Properties** window. You can also select the object by clicking on it in the Form Designer.
- You can confirm that you're manipulating the correct object's properties because the object's name and class type are displayed in the component object box. `Form` objects have class type `System.Windows.Forms.Form` and are assigned generic names (such as `Form1`). You learn about the class types for controls in the next tutorial. Icons on the toolbar sort the properties either alphabetically (if you click the **Alphabetical icon**) or categorically (if you click the **Categorized icon**). Figure 2.22 shows the **Properties** window with its properties sorted categorically. Each gray horizontal bar to the left of the scrollbar is a category that groups related properties. For example, the **Design** category groups four related properties. The categories visible in Fig. 2.22 are **Behavior**, **Data**, **Design**, **Focus** and **Layout**. Note that each category is a node.
- The left column of the **Properties** window lists the object's property names; the right column displays each property's value. In the next tutorial, you learn how to set properties for objects.
- You can scroll through the list of properties by dragging the scrollbar's scrollbox up or down.
- Whenever you select a property, a description of the property displays at the bottom of the **Properties** window—the property `Text` is selected in Fig. 2.22.

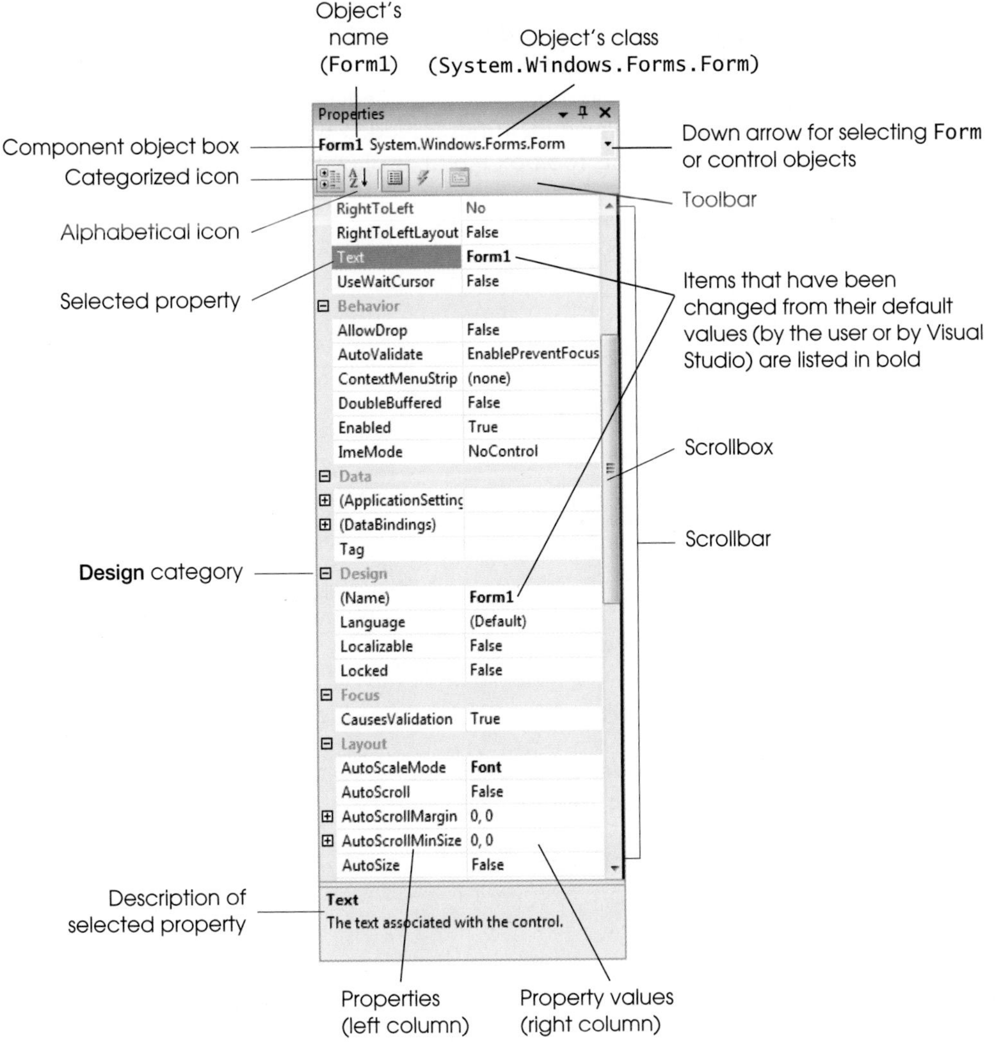

Figure 2.22 **Properties** window displaying a `Form`'s properties.

SELF-REVIEW

1. The _________ allows you to add controls to the `Form` in a visual manner.
   a) **Solution Explorer** b) **Properties** window
   c) **Toolbox** d) **Dynamic Help** window

2. The _________ window allows you to view a solution's files.
   a) **Properties** b) **Solution Explorer**
   c) **Toolbox** d) None of the above

Answers: 1) c. 2) b.

2.6 Auto-Hide

Visual Basic provides a space-saving feature called **auto-hide** that allows you to hide or show certain windows of the Visual Basic IDE, such as the **Toolbox**, **Solution Explorer** and **Properties** window. When auto-hide is enabled for these windows, tabs representing the hidden windows appear along an edge of the IDE window.

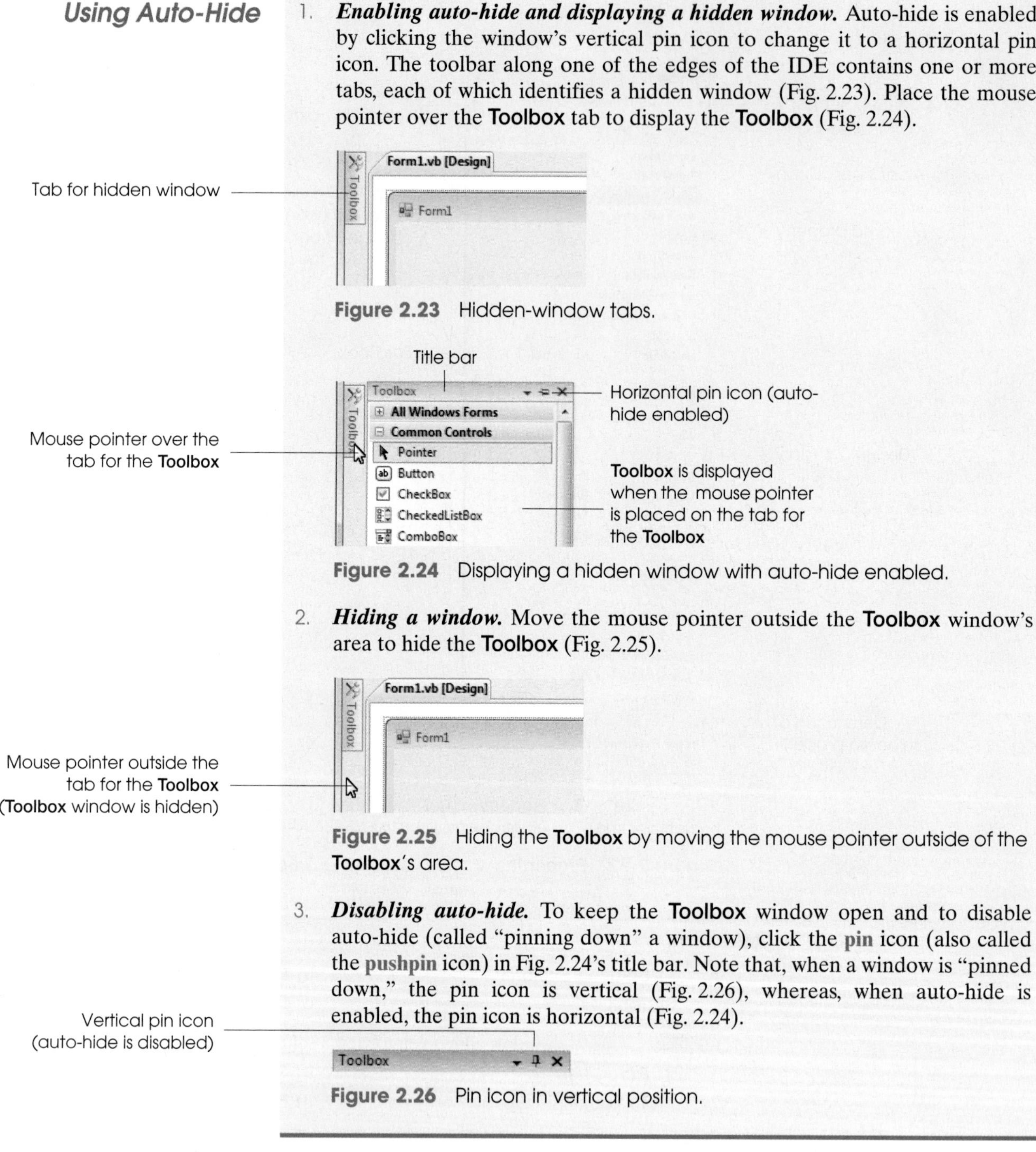

Using Auto-Hide

1. ***Enabling auto-hide and displaying a hidden window.*** Auto-hide is enabled by clicking the window's vertical pin icon to change it to a horizontal pin icon. The toolbar along one of the edges of the IDE contains one or more tabs, each of which identifies a hidden window (Fig. 2.23). Place the mouse pointer over the **Toolbox** tab to display the **Toolbox** (Fig. 2.24).

Figure 2.23 Hidden-window tabs.

Figure 2.24 Displaying a hidden window with auto-hide enabled.

2. ***Hiding a window.*** Move the mouse pointer outside the **Toolbox** window's area to hide the **Toolbox** (Fig. 2.25).

Figure 2.25 Hiding the **Toolbox** by moving the mouse pointer outside of the **Toolbox**'s area.

3. ***Disabling auto-hide.*** To keep the **Toolbox** window open and to disable auto-hide (called "pinning down" a window), click the **pin** icon (also called the **pushpin** icon) in Fig. 2.24's title bar. Note that, when a window is "pinned down," the pin icon is vertical (Fig. 2.26), whereas, when auto-hide is enabled, the pin icon is horizontal (Fig. 2.24).

Figure 2.26 Pin icon in vertical position.

SELF-REVIEW

1. Visual Basic provides a space-saving feature called _________.

   a) auto-close b) hide
   c) collapse d) auto-hide

2. When auto-hide is enabled, its pin icon is _________.

   a) horizontal b) vertical
   c) down d) diagonal

Answers: 1) d. 2) a.

2.7 Using Help

Visual Basic provides extensive help features. The **Help** menu commands are summarized in Fig. 2.27. Using **Help** is an excellent way to get information quickly about the IDE and its features. It provides a list of articles pertaining to the "current content" (i.e., the items around the location of the mouse cursor). Visual Basic also provides **context-sensitive help**, which displays relevant help articles rather than a generalized list of articles (Fig. 2.28). To use context-sensitive help, click an item, such as the form, then press the *F1* key. The help window provides help topics, code samples and "Getting Started" information. There is also a toolbar that provides access to the **How Do I**, **Search**, **Index** and **Contents** help features. To return to the IDE, either close the help window or select the icon for the IDE in your Windows task bar.

Command	Description
How Do I?	Contains links to relevant topics, including how to upgrade applications and learn more about web services, architecture and design, files, data and more.
Search	Finds help articles based on search keywords.
Index	Displays an alphabetized list of topics which you can browse.
Contents	Displays a categorized table of contents in which help articles are organized by topic.

Figure 2.27 **Help** menu commands.

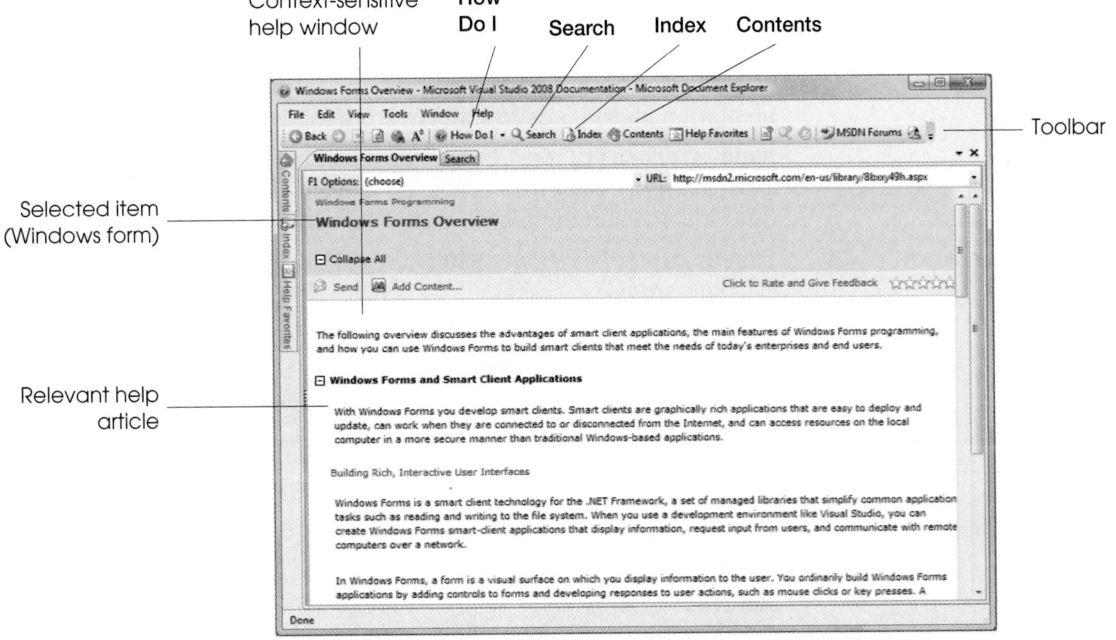

Figure 2.28 Context-sensitive help window.

SELF-REVIEW 1. ________ displays relevant help articles, based on the selected object.

a) Internal help
b) Context-sensitive help
c) External help
d) Context-driven help

2. **Help** command _________ displays an alphabetized list of topics through which you can browse.

a) **Search** b) **Browse**
c) **Contents** d) **Index**

Answers: 1) b. 2) d.

2.8 Saving and Closing Projects in Visual Basic

Once you're finished with a project, you should save the project's files and close the project.

Closing the Project for the Welcome Application

1. ***Saving the project's files.*** Before closing the project for the **Welcome** application, you should save its files, ensuring that any changes made to the project are not lost. Although you did not make any changes to the project's files for this particular tutorial, you'll be making such changes in most of the tutorials, so for practice, save your project files by selecting **File > Save All**.
2. ***Closing the project.*** Select **File > Close Project**.

2.9 Web Resources

Please take a moment to visit each of these sites briefly.

`www.deitel.com/VisualBasic2008/`
This site lists many of the key web resources we used as we were preparing to write *Simply Visual Basic 2008: An Application-Driven Tutorial Approach*. There's lots of great stuff here to help you become familiar with the world of Visual Basic 2008.

`msdn.microsoft.com/vstudio`
This site is the home page for Microsoft Visual Studio. The site includes news, documentation, downloads and other resources.

`msdn.microsoft.com/vbasic/default.aspx`
This site provides information on the newest release of Visual Basic, including downloads, community information and resources.

`forums.microsoft.com/MSDN/default.aspx?ForumGroupID=10&SiteID=1`
This site provides access to the Microsoft Visual Basic forums, which you can use to get your Visual Basic language and IDE questions answered.

`msdn.microsoft.com/msdnmag/`
This is the *Microsoft Developer Network Magazine* site. This site provides articles and code on many Visual Basic and .NET programming topics. There is also an archive of past issues.

`www.vbi.org`
This site has Visual Basic articles, reviews of books and software, documentation, downloads, links and more.

`www.vbcity.com`
This site provides Visual Basic articles, tutorials, FAQs and more. Submit your Visual Basic code to be reviewed and rated by other developers. Includes polls on Visual Basic topics.

2.10 Wrap-Up

This tutorial introduced the Visual Basic 2008 Express Edition integrated development environment (IDE). You learned key features, including tabs, menus, menu bars, toolbars, icons, auto-hide and more.

You created a Visual Basic Windows Forms application that contained a `Form` object named `Form1.vb`. Controls placed on a `Form` represent the application's graphical user interface (GUI).

You worked with the **Solution Explorer**, **Toolbox** and **Properties** windows, all of which are essential to developing Visual Basic applications. The **Solution Explorer** window allows you to manage your solution's files visually. The **Toolbox** window contains a rich collection of controls (organized in groups) that allow you to create GUIs. The **Properties** window allows you to set the attributes of the `Form` and its controls.

You explored Visual Basic's help features, including the **Help** window, the **Help** menu and context-sensitive help. The **Help** window displays links related to the item you select with the mouse pointer. You learned about web sites that provide additional Visual Basic information.

In the next tutorial, you begin creating Visual Basic applications. You follow step-by-step instructions for completing the **Welcome** application by using visual programming and the IDE features you learned in this tutorial.

SKILLS SUMMARY

Creating a New Project

- Select **File > New Project...** or **File > Open Project...** .
- Click the links **Create: Project...** or **Open: Project...** (from the **Start Page**, under the **Recent Projects** section).
- Select **Windows Forms Application** in the **Templates:** pane.
- Provide the project's name in the **Name:** `TextBox`.
- Click the **OK** `Button`.

Saving a Project

- Select **File > Save All**.
- Provide the project's name in the **Name:** `TextBox`.
- Provide the project's directory information in the **Location:** `TextBox`.

Viewing a Tooltip for a Visual Basic Icon

- Place the mouse pointer on the icon, and keep it there until the tooltip appears.

Collapsing a Node in the Solution Explorer

- Click the node's minus box.

Expanding a Node in the Solution Explorer

- Click the node's plus box.

Scrolling Through the List of Controls in the Toolbox

- Click the scroll arrows.

Viewing the Properties Window

- Select **View > Properties Window** or press *F4*.

Viewing the Solution Explorer

- Select **View > Solution Explorer**.

Viewing the Toolbox

- Select **View > Toolbox**.

Displaying a Hidden Window

- Place the mouse pointer over the hidden window's tab.

Disabling Auto-Hide and "Pinning Down" a Window

- Click the window's horizontal pin icon to change it to a vertical pin icon.

Enabling Auto-Hide

- Click the window's vertical pin icon to change it to a horizontal pin icon.

Opening the Help Window

- Select **Help > How Do I**, **Help > Search**, **Help > Contents** or **Help > Index**.
- Select an item on which you want help and press the *F1* key.

KEY TERMS

active tab—The tab of the document displayed in the IDE.

Alphabetical icon—The icon in the **Properties** window that, when clicked, sorts properties alphabetically.

auto-hide—A space-saving IDE feature used for windows such as **Toolbox**, **Properties** and **Solution Explorer** that hides a window until the mouse pointer is placed on the hidden window's tab.

Categorized icon—The icon in the **Properties** window that, when clicked, sorts properties categorically.

component object box—The `ComboBox` at the top of the **Properties** window that allows you to select the `Form` or control object whose properties you want set.

context-sensitive help—A help option (launched by pressing *F1*) that provides links to articles that apply to the current content (that is, the item selected with the mouse pointer).

Contents command—The command that displays a categorized table of contents in which help articles are organized by topic.

database—Stores information for access by applications.

Data menu—The menu of the IDE that contains commands for interacting with databases.

Debug menu—The menu of the IDE that contains commands for debugging and running an application.

Design view—The IDE view that contains the Windows Forms designer to allow you to layout controls in a Windows Forms application.

dialog—A window that can display and gather information.

`Form`—The object that represents the Windows application's graphical user interface (GUI).

graphical user interface (GUI)—The visual part of the application with which the user interacts.

icon—The graphical representation of commands in the Visual Studio 2008 IDE.

Integrated Development Environment (IDE)—The software used to create, document, run and debug applications.

input—Data that the user enters into an application.

internal web browser—The web browser (Internet Explorer) included in Visual Basic 2008 Express, with which you can browse the web.

location bar—The `ComboBox` in Visual Basic's internal web browser where you can enter the name of a web site to visit.

menu—A group of related commands that, when selected, cause the IDE to perform specific actions, such as opening windows, saving files, printing files and executing applications.

menu bar—Contains the menus for a window.

menu item (or command)—A command located in a menu that, when selected, causes an application to perform a specific action.

Microsoft Developer Network (MSDN)—An online library that contains articles, downloads and tutorials on technologies of interest to Visual Basic developers.

minus box—An icon that, when clicked, collapses a node.

New Project dialog—A dialog that allows you to choose what type of application you wish to create.

output—The results of an application.

pin (or pushpin) icon—An icon that enables or disables the auto-hide feature.

plus box—An icon that, when clicked, expands a node.

project—A group of related files that compose an application.

Properties window—The window that displays the properties for a `Form` or control object.

property—Specifies a control or `Form` object's attributes, such as size, color and position.

scroll arrows—Arrows at the ends of a scrollbar that enable you to scroll through items.

solution—Contains one or more projects.

Solution Explorer—A window that provides access to all the projects and their files in a solution.

Start Page—The initial page displayed when Visual Studio 2008 is opened.

templates—Starting points for the projects you create in Visual Basic.

title bar—The top of a window in which the title of the window is displayed.

toolbar—A bar that contains buttons that, when clicked, execute commands.

toolbar icon—A picture on a toolbar button.

Toolbox—A window that contains controls used to build and customize `Forms`.

Tools menu—A menu of the IDE that contains commands for accessing additional IDE tools and options that enable customization of the IDE.

tooltip—The description of an icon that appears when the mouse pointer is held over that icon for a few seconds.

Visual Studio—Microsoft's integrated development environment (IDE), which allows developers to create applications in a variety of .NET programming languages.

Windows Forms application—An application that executes on a Windows operating system (e.g., Windows XP or Vista) and has a graphical user interface (GUI)—the visual part of the application with which the user interacts.

Windows Form Designer—Used to design the GUI of a Windows Forms application.

MULTIPLE-CHOICE QUESTIONS

2.1 The _________ integrated development environment is used for creating applications written in programming languages such as Visual Basic.

a) **Solution Explorer**　　b) Gates
c) Visual Studio　　d) Microsoft

2.2 The `.vb` file-name extension indicates a _________.

a) Visual Basic file　　b) dynamic help file
c) help file　　d) very big file

2.3 The pictures on toolbar buttons are called _________.

a) prototypes　　b) icons
c) tooltips　　d) tabs

2.4 The _________ allows programmers to configure controls visually, without writing code.

a) **Properties** window　　b) **Solution Explorer**
c) menu bar　　d) **Toolbox**

2.5 The _________ hides the **Toolbox** when the mouse pointer is moved outside the **Toolbox**'s area.

a) component-selection feature　　b) auto-hide feature
c) pinned command　　d) minimize command

2.6 A _________ appears when the mouse pointer is positioned over an IDE toolbar icon for a few seconds.

a) drop-down list　　b) menu
c) tooltip　　d) down arrow

2.7 The Visual Basic IDE provides _________.

a) help documentation　　b) toolbars
c) windows for accessing project files　　d) All of the above

2.8 The _________ contains a list of helpful links, such as **Getting Started** and **Visual Basic Express Headlines**.

a) **Solution Explorer** window　　b) **Properties** window
c) **Start Page**　　d) **Toolbox** link

2.9 The **Properties** window contains _________.

a) the component object box
b) a **Solution Explorer**
c) menus
d) a menu bar

2.10 A _________ can be enhanced by adding reusable components such as `Buttons`.

a) control
b) `Form`
c) tab
d) property

2.11 For web browsing, Visual Basic includes _________.

a) Web View
b) Excel
c) a **Web** tab
d) Internet Explorer

2.12 An application's GUI can include _________.

a) toolbars
b) icons
c) menus
d) All of the above

2.13 The _________ does not contain a pin icon.

a) **Properties** window
b) **Solution Explorer** window
c) **Toolbox** window
d) active tab

2.14 When clicked, _________ in the **Solution Explorer** window will expand nodes and _________ will collapse nodes.

a) minus boxes; plus boxes
b) plus boxes; minus boxes
c) up arrows; down arrows
d) left arrows; right arrows

2.15 `Form` _________ specify attributes such as size and position.

a) nodes
b) inputs
c) properties
d) title bars

EXERCISES

2.16 ***(Closing and Opening the Start Page)*** In this exercise, you learn how to close and reopen the **Start Page**. To accomplish this task, perform the following steps:

a) Close Visual Basic if it is open by selecting **File > Exit** or by clicking its close box.
b) Start Visual Basic 2008 Express Edition.
c) Close the **Start Page** by clicking its close box (Fig. 2.29).
d) Select **View > Other Windows > Start Page** to display the **Start Page**.

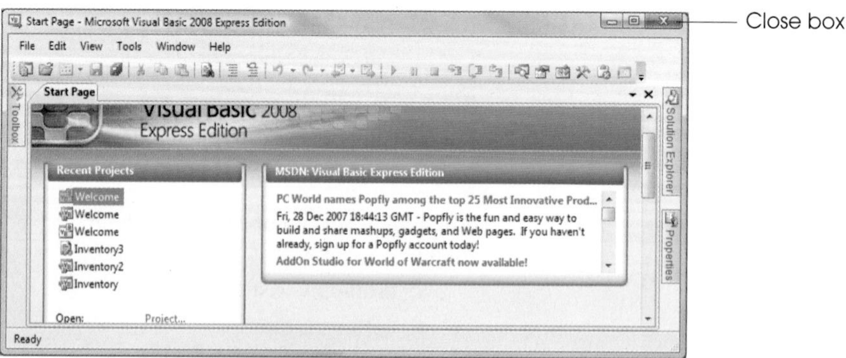

Figure 2.29 Closing the **Start Page**.

2.17 ***(Enabling Auto-Hide for the Solution Explorer Window)*** In this exercise, you learn how to use the **Solution Explorer** window's auto-hide feature by performing the following steps:

a) Open the **Start Page**.
b) In the **Start Page**, click the **Open Project** `Button` to display the **Open Project** dialog. You can skip to *Step e* if the **Welcome** application is already open.

c) In the **Open Project** dialog, navigate to `C:\SimplyVB2008\Welcome`, and click **Open**.

d) In the **Open Project** dialog, select `Welcome` (this might display as `Welcome.sln`), and click **Open**.

e) Position the mouse pointer on the vertical pin icon in the **Solution Explorer** window's title bar (Fig. 2.30).

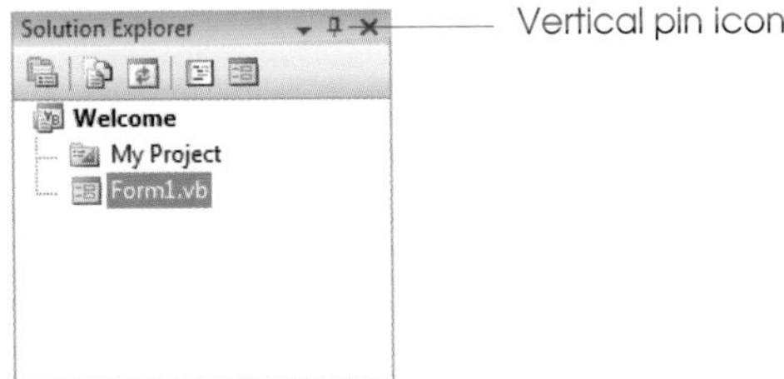

Figure 2.30 Enabling auto-hide.

f) Click the vertical pin icon. This action causes a **Solution Explorer** tab to appear on the right side of the IDE and changes the vertical pin icon to a horizontal pin icon (Fig. 2.31). Auto-hide has now been enabled for the **Solution Explorer** window.

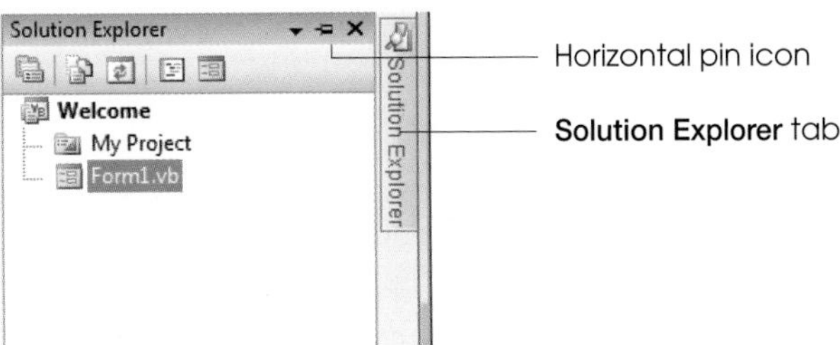

Figure 2.31 **Solution Explorer** window with auto-hide enabled.

g) Position the mouse pointer on the **Solution Explorer** tab to view the **Solution Explorer** window.

2.18 ***(Sorting Properties Alphabetically in the Properties Window)*** In this exercise, you learn how to sort the **Properties** window's properties alphabetically by performing the following steps:

a) Open the **Welcome** application by performing steps a) through d) of Exercise 2.17. If the **Welcome** application is already open, you can skip this step.

b) Locate the **Properties** window. If it is not visible, display it by selecting **View > Properties Window.**

c) Click the `Form`.

d) To sort properties alphabetically, click the **Properties** window's **Alphabetical** icon (Fig. 2.32). The properties display in alphabetic order.

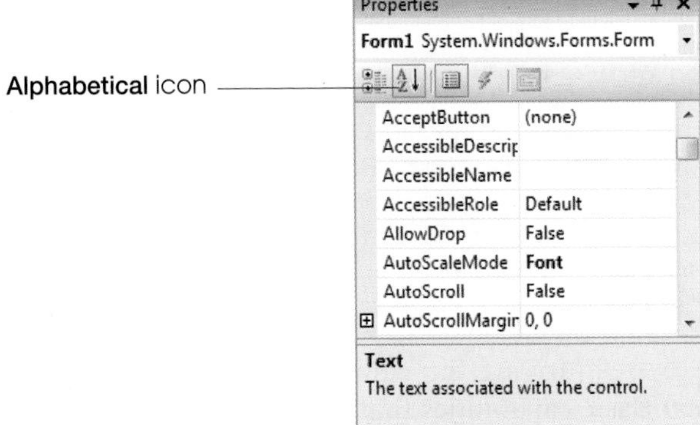

Figure 2.32 Sorting properties alphabetically.

3 TUTORIAL

Welcome Application

Introduction to Visual Programming

Objectives

In this tutorial, you will learn to:

- Set the text in the `Form`'s title bar.
- Change the `Form`'s background color.
- Place a `Label` control on the `Form`.
- Display text in a `Label` control.
- Place a `PictureBox` control on the `Form`.
- Display an image in a `PictureBox` control.
- Execute an application.

Outline

Today, users prefer software with interactive graphical user interfaces (GUIs) that respond to actions such as `Button` clicks, data input and much more. As a result, the vast majority of Windows applications, such as Microsoft Word and Internet Explorer, are GUI based. With Visual Basic, you can create Windows applications that input and output information in a variety of ways, which you learn throughout the book.

In this tutorial, you use visual programming to complete the **Welcome** application you began creating in Tutorial 2. You build the application's GUI by placing two controls—a `Label` and a `PictureBox`—on the `Form`. You use the `Label` control to display text and the `PictureBox` control to display an image. You customize the appearance of the `Form`, `Label` and `PictureBox` objects by setting values in the **Properties** window. You set many property values, including the `Form`'s background color, the `PictureBox`'s image and the `Label`'s text. You also learn how to execute your application in the Visual Basic 2008 IDE.

3.1 Test-Driving the Welcome Application

The last tutorial introduced you to the Visual Basic 2008 IDE. In this tutorial, you use Visual Basic to build the **Welcome** application you started in Tutorial 2. This application must meet the following requirements:

> ***Application Requirements***
>
> *Recall that a software company (Deitel & Associates) has asked you to develop a simple* ***Welcome*** *application that includes the greeting "Welcome to Visual Basic 2008!" and a picture of the company's bug mascot. Now that you're familiar with the Visual Basic IDE, your task is to develop this application to satisfy the company's request.*

You begin by test-driving the completed application. Then you learn the additional Visual Basic capabilities that you need to create your own version of this application.

Test-Driving the Welcome Application

1. ***Opening the completed application.*** Start Visual Basic and select **File > Open Project...** (Fig. 3.1) to display the **Open Project** dialog (Fig. 3.2). Select the `C:\Examples\Tutorial03\CompletedApplication\Welcome` directory. Select the **Welcome** solution file (`Welcome.sln`) and click the **Open** `Button`.

Open Project... command (selected) opens an existing project

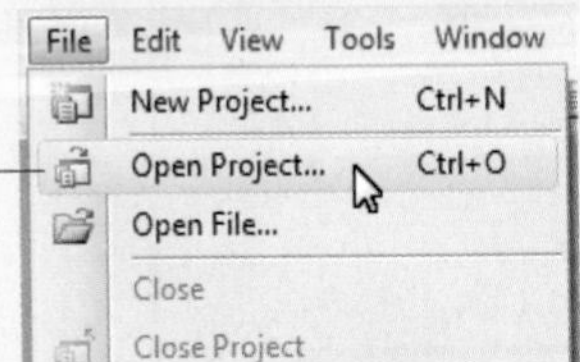

Figure 3.1 Opening an existing project with the **File** menu's **Open Project...** command.

Open Project dialog

Welcome solution file

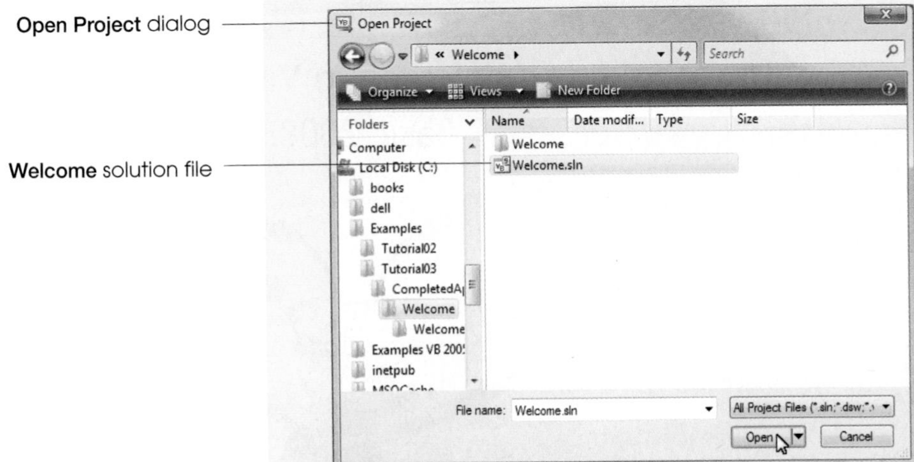

Figure 3.2 **Open Project** dialog displaying the contents of the **Welcome** solution.

2. ***Opening the Form in Design view.*** Double click `Welcome.vb` in the **Solution Explorer** to open the **Welcome** application's `Form` in **Design** view (Fig. 3.3).

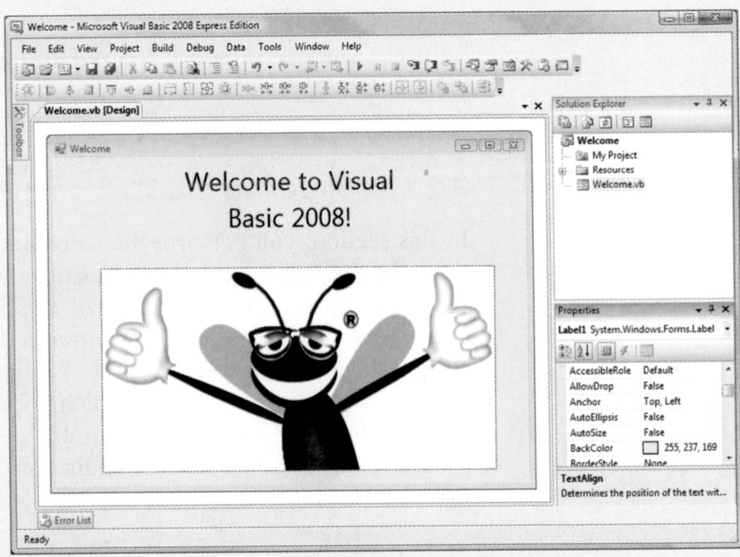

Figure 3.3 **Welcome** application's `Form` in **Design** view.

(cont.)

3. ***Running the Welcome application.*** Select **Debug > Start Debugging** (Fig. 3.4). The **Start Debugging** command runs the application. The **Welcome** `Form` shown in Fig. 3.5 appears.

Start Debugging command (selected) runs the application

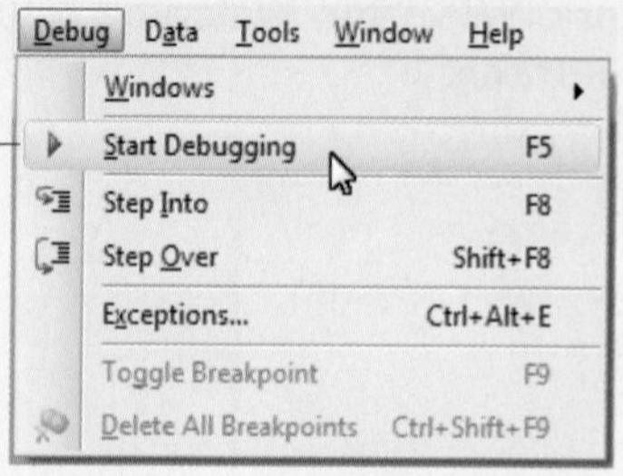

Debug Data Tools Window Help
Windows
Start Debugging F5
Step Into F8
Step Over Shift+F8
Exceptions... Ctrl+Alt+E
Toggle Breakpoint F9
Delete All Breakpoints Ctrl+Shift+F9

Figure 3.4 Running the **Welcome** application using the **Debug** menu's **Start Debugging** command.

Close box

Figure 3.5 **Welcome** application running.

4. ***Closing the application.*** Close the running application by clicking its close box ( ).

5. ***Closing the project.*** Close the project by selecting **File > Close Project.**

3.2 Constructing the Welcome Application

In this section, you perform the steps necessary to develop the **Welcome** application. The application consists of a single `Form` that uses a `Label` control and a `PictureBox` control. A **`Label`** control displays text that the user cannot change. A **`PictureBox`** control displays an image that the user cannot change. You do not write a single line of code to create this application. Instead, you use the technique called **visual programming**, in which Visual Basic processes your actions (such as clicking, dragging and dropping controls) and writes the program for you! The following box shows you how to begin constructing the **Welcome** application, using the solution you created in Tutorial 2 as a starting point.

Changing the Form's File Name and Title Bar Text

1. ***Opening the Welcome application's project.*** Double click the `C:\SimplyVB2008\Welcome\Welcome.sln` file that you created in Tutorial 2 to open your application. Double click `Form1.vb` in the **Solution Explorer** window to display the blank `Form`. Figure 3.6 shows the **Welcome** application open in the IDE.

Figure 3.6 Blank `Form`.

2. ***Changing the Form's file name.*** When a Windows application is created, Visual Basic names the `Form` file `Form1.vb`. Select `Form1.vb` in the **Solution Explorer** window (Fig. 3.6) to display the file's properties in the **Properties** window (the window on the left in Fig. 3.7). If either window is not visible, you can select **View > Properties Window** or **View > Solution Explorer** to display the appropriate window. Double click the field to the right of the **`File Name`** property's box to select the current file name, and type `Welcome.vb` (Fig. 3.7). Press the *Enter* key to update the `Form`'s file name. Note that the file name changes in the **Solution Explorer** window (the window on the right in Fig. 3.7) and in the **Properties** window.

Good Programming Practice

Change your application's `Form` file name (`Form1.vb`) to a name that describes the application's purpose.

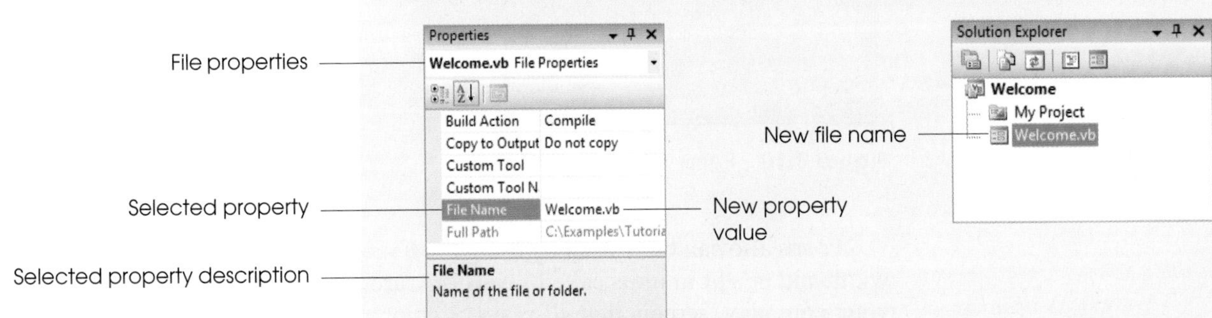

Figure 3.7 Changing the `Form`'s file name.

GUI Design Tip

Choose short, descriptive `Form` titles. Capitalize words that are not articles, prepositions or conjunctions. Do not use punctuation.

3. ***Setting the text in the Form's title bar.*** The title bar is the top portion of the window that contains the window's title. To change the text in the `Form`'s title bar from **Form1** to **Welcome**, use the **Properties** window (Fig. 3.8). Click the gray area in the `Form`. As in Fig. 3.7, double click the field to the right of the **`Text`** property in the **Properties** window to select the current text, and type `Welcome`. Press the *Enter* key to update the `Form`'s title bar (Fig. 3.9).

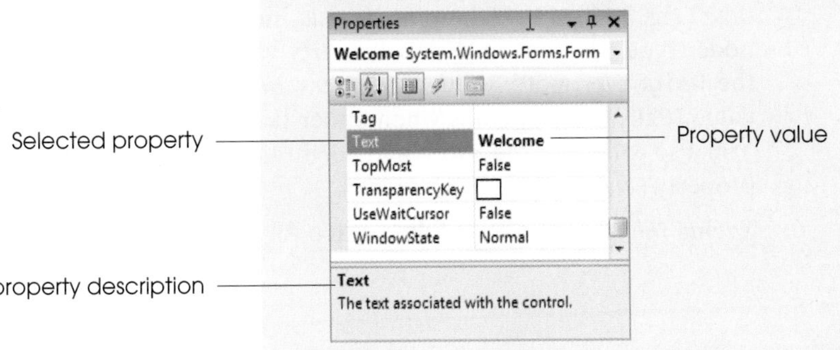

Figure 3.8 Setting the `Form`'s `Text` property.

(cont.)

Figure 3.9 Title bar for the **Welcome** application.

4. ***Saving the project.*** Select **File > Save All** to save your modified project.

There are several ways to resize the `Form`. If the resizing does not have to be precise, you can click and drag one of the `Form`'s enabled **sizing handles** (the small white squares that appear around the `Form`, as shown in Fig. 3.10). The mouse cursor, when moved over an enabled sizing handle, changes to a pointer with two arrows indicating the directions in which you can drag the handle to resize the `Form`.

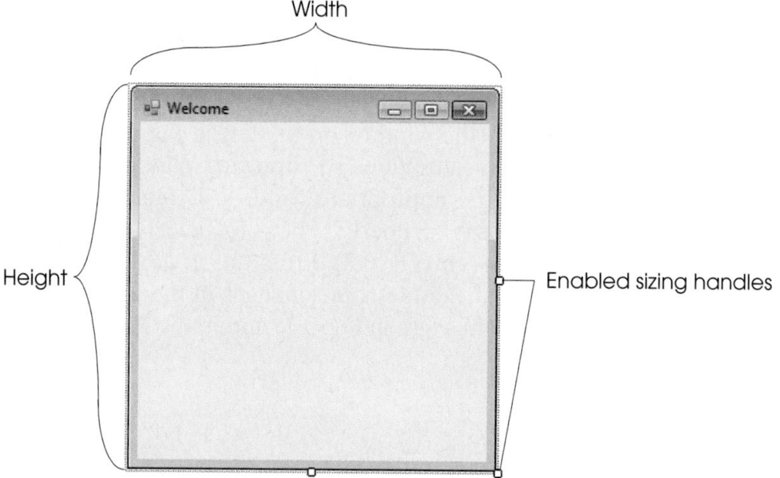

Figure 3.10 `Form` with sizing handles.

`Forms` also can be resized by using the **`Size`** property, which specifies the `Form`'s width and height in units called **pixels** (*pic*ture *el*ements). A pixel is a tiny point on your computer screen that displays a color. The `Size` property has two members—the **`Width`** and **`Height`** properties. The `Width` property indicates the width of the `Form` in pixels, and the `Height` property specifies the height in pixels. Next, you learn how to set the `Form`'s width and height.

Setting the Form's `Size` Property

1. ***Setting the Form's width and height.*** For your **Welcome** application GUI to look exactly like Fig. 3.5, you need to resize the `Form` and its controls. Click the `Form` to select it. Locate the `Form`'s `Size` property in the **Properties** window (Fig. 3.11). Click the plus box, ⊞, next to this property to expand the node. Type `616` for the `Width` property value and press *Enter*. Type `440` for the `Height` property value and press *Enter*. Note that the `Size` property value `(616, 440)` updates when either the `Width` or the `Height` is changed. You also can enter the width and height (separated by a comma) in the `Size` property's value field.
2. ***Saving the project.*** Select **File > Save All** to save your modified project.

(cont.)

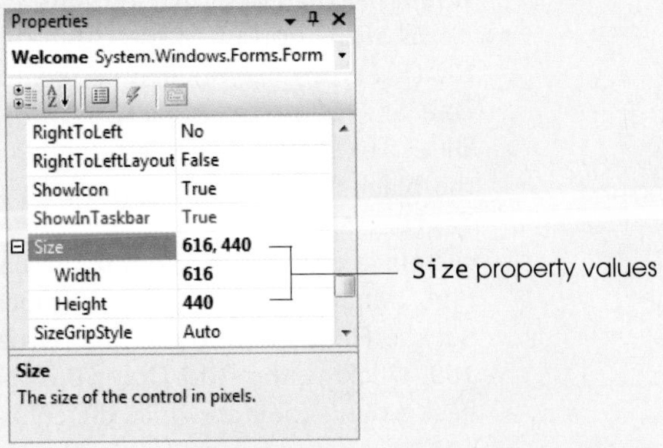

Figure 3.11 **Size** property values for the `Form`.

Now that you have set the `Form`'s size, you customize the `Form` further by changing its background color from gray to yellow.

Setting the Form's Background Color

1. ***Exploring the available colors.*** Click the `Form` to display its properties in the **Properties** window. The **`BackColor`** property specifies an object's background color. When you click the **BackColor** property's value in the **Properties** window, a down-arrow (▾) `Button` appears (Fig. 3.12). When clicked, the down-arrow `Button` displays three tabs: **System** (the default), **Web** and **Custom**. Each tab offers a series of colors called a **palette**. The **System** tab displays a palette containing the colors used in the Microsoft Windows GUI. This palette includes the colors for Windows controls and the Windows desktop. The **System** tab's colors are based on the Windows color settings. The **Web** tab displays a palette of **web-safe colors**—colors that display the same on different computers. The **Custom** tab palette allows you to choose from a series of predefined colors or to create your own color. Click the **Custom** tab to display its palette as shown in Fig. 3.12.

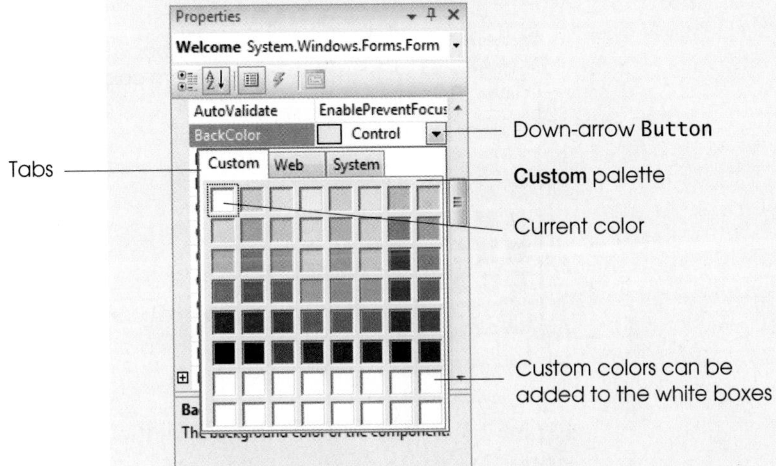

Figure 3.12 Viewing the **Custom** palette in the `Form`'s `BackColor` property value field.

(cont.)

GUI Design Tip

Use colors in your applications, but not to the point of distracting the user.

2. ***Changing the Form's background color.*** Right click any one of the 16 white boxes at the bottom of the **Custom** palette to display the **Define Color** dialog (Fig. 3.13). Colors can be created by entering three values in the **Hue:**, **Sat:** and **Lum:** `TextBox`es, by providing values for the **Red:**, **Green:** and **Blue:** `TextBox`es or by selecting a color in the rainbow window and sliding the black arrow up and down. The values for the **Red:**, **Green:** and **Blue:** `TextBox`es describe the amount of red, green and blue needed to create the custom color and are commonly called **RGB values**. Each red, green and blue value is in the range `0–255`, inclusive. We use RGB values in this book. Set the **Red:** value to `255`, the **Green:** value to `237` and the **Blue:** value to `169`. Clicking the **Add Color** `Button` closes the dialog, changes the `Form`'s background color and adds the color to the **Custom** palette (Fig. 3.14).

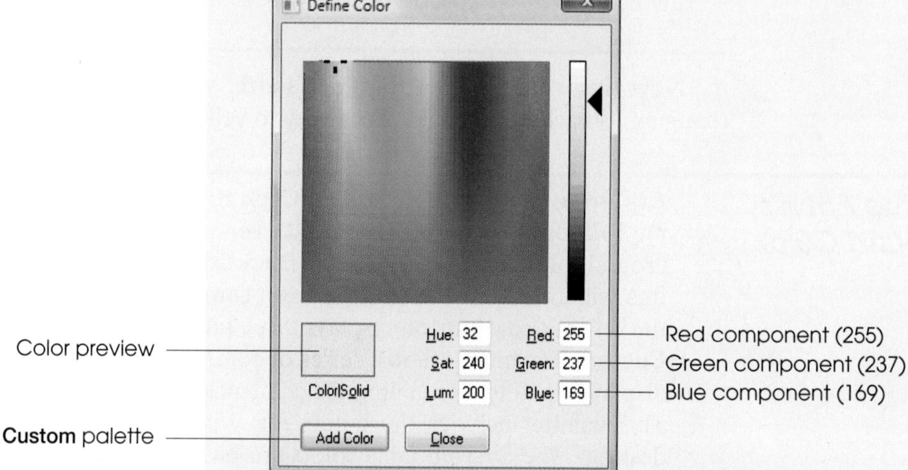

Figure 3.13 Adding a color to the **Custom** palette.

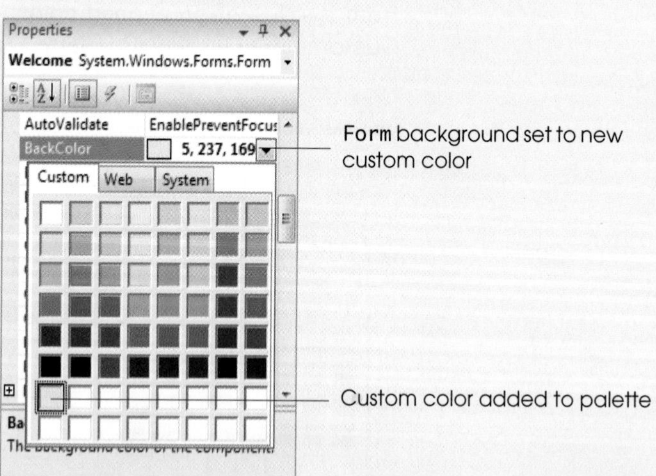

Figure 3.14 **Properties** window after the new custom color has been added.

3. ***Saving the project.*** Select **File > Save All** to save your modified project.

Now that you've finished customizing the `Form`, you can add a control to the `Form`—a customized `Label` that displays a greeting.

Adding a `Label` to the `Form`

Use `Label`s to display text that users cannot change.

1. ***Adding a `Label` control to the `Form`.*** Click the **Common Controls** group in the **Toolbox** (Fig. 3.15) if it is not already expanded. If the **Toolbox** is not visible, select **View > Toolbox**. Double click the `Label` control in the **Toolbox**. A `Label` appears in the upper-left corner of the `Form` (Fig. 3.16). You can also drag the `Label` from the **Toolbox** and drop it on the `Form`. You use this `Label` control to display the welcome message. The `Label` displays the text **Label1** by default.

   Note that the `Label`'s background color is the same as the `Form`'s background color. When a `Label` control is added to the `Form`, the IDE initially sets the control's `BackColor` property value to the `Form`'s `BackColor` property value.

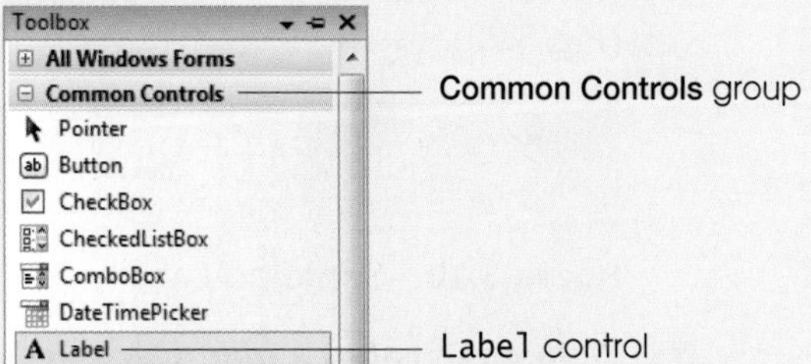

Figure 3.15 Clicking the **Common Controls** tab in the **Toolbox**.

2. ***Setting the `Label`'s `AutoSize` property.*** Click the `Label` to select it. Notice that the `Label`'s properties now appear in the **Properties** window. Visual Basic by default does not provide sizing handles (Fig. 3.16) for you to resize a `Label`. If the `Label`'s `AutoSize` property is `True`, the `Label` expands or contracts to accommodate the value in the `Label`'s `Text` property. To enable manual resizing, you must set the `Label`'s `AutoSize` property to `False` (Fig. 3.17). You can do this by double clicking this property's value or by selecting `False` from the drop-down list.

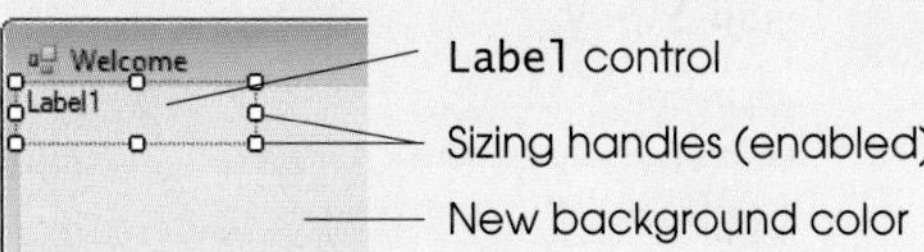

Figure 3.16 Adding a `Label` to the `Form`.

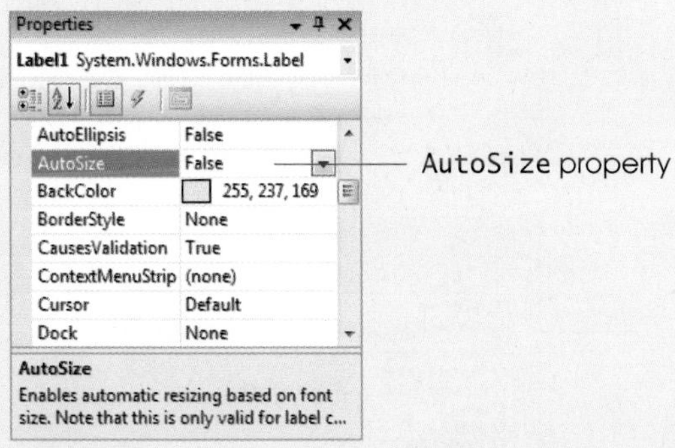

Figure 3.17 Setting a Label's `AutoSize` property to `False`.

Ensure that all `Label` controls are large enough to display their text.

3. ***Customizing the `Label`'s appearance.*** The `Label`'s `Text` property specifies the text (**Label1**) that the `Label` displays. Type `Welcome to Visual Basic 2008!` for the `Label`'s `Text` property value and press *Enter*. Note that this text does not fit in the `Label` (Fig. 3.18). Use the sizing handles to enlarge the `Label` so all the text is displayed (Fig. 3.19)

(cont.)

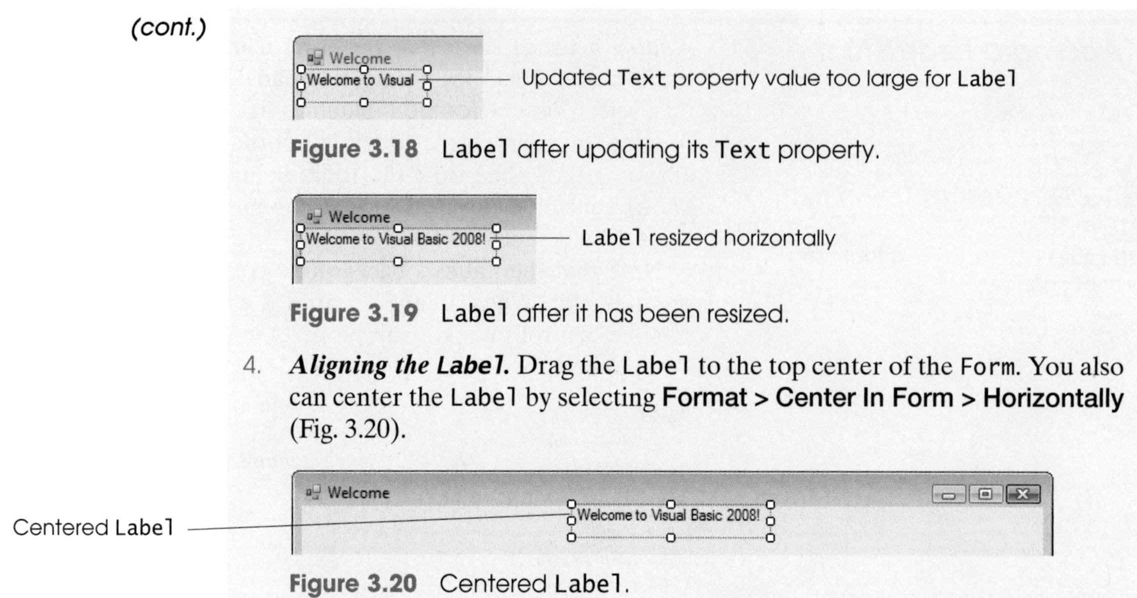

Figure 3.18 `Label` after updating its `Text` property.

Figure 3.19 `Label` after it has been resized.

4. ***Aligning the*** `Label`***.*** Drag the `Label` to the top center of the `Form`. You also can center the `Label` by selecting **Format > Center In Form > Horizontally** (Fig. 3.20).

Figure 3.20 Centered `Label`.

GUI Design Tip

Use 9pt `Segoe UI` font to improve readability for controls that display text.

5. ***Setting the*** `Label`***'s font.*** Click the value of the `Font` property to cause an ellipsis `Button` to appear (Fig. 3.21). Click the ellipsis `Button` to display the `Font` dialog (Fig. 3.22). The ellipsis is a convention used for each property that displays a dialog to help you set the property's value. In this dialog, you can select the font name (**Segoe UI**, **Times New Roman**, etc.), font style (**Regular**, **Italic**, etc.) and font size (**16**, **18**, etc.) in points (one point equals 1/72 of an inch). The text in the **Sample** `Label` displays the selected font. Under the **Size:** category, select **24** points. Under the **Font** category, select **Segoe UI**, and click **OK**. If the `Label`'s text does not fit on a single line, it wraps to the next line. Use the sizing handles to enlarge the `Label` vertically so that the text appears on two lines, then center the `Label` again as in *Step 4*.

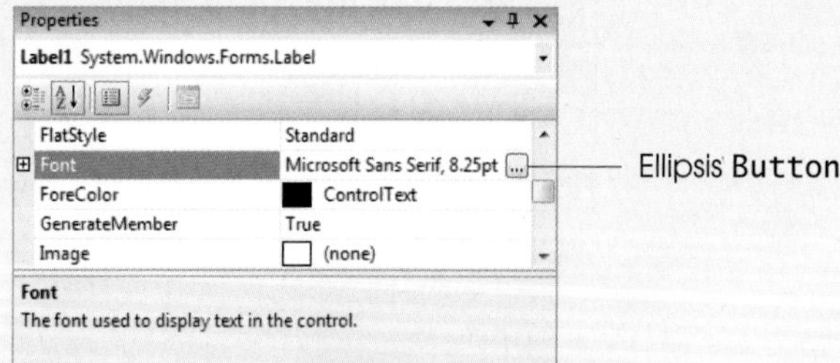

Figure 3.21 **Properties** window displaying the `Label`'s properties.

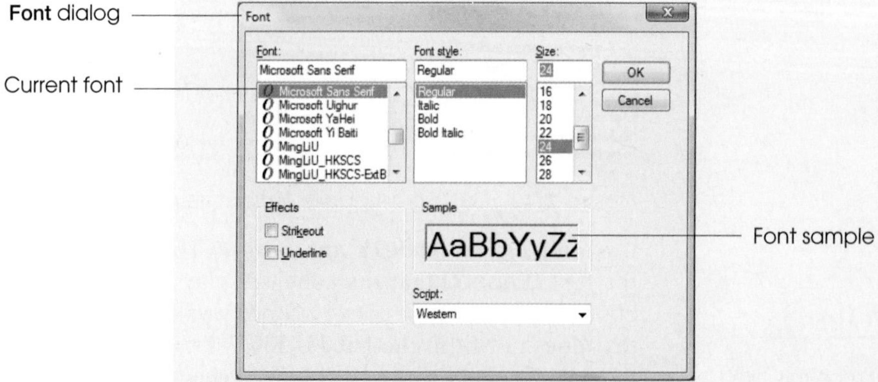

Figure 3.22 **Font** dialog for selecting fonts, styles and sizes.

(cont.)

6. ***Aligning the Label's text.*** To align text inside a Label, use the Label's TextAlign property. Clicking the TextAlign property displays a down-arrow Button. Click the down-arrow Button to display a three-by-three grid of Buttons (Fig. 3.23). The position of each Button shows where the text appears in the Label. Click the middle-center Button in the three-by-three grid to align the text at the middle-center position in the Label. The value MiddleCenter is assigned to property TextAlign. You may also set this property's value by repeatedly double clicking the property value to the right of the property's name. This enables you to cycle through all the allowed TextAlign property values. This technique works for any property that provides a set of options via a down arrow to the right of the property value in the **Properties** window.

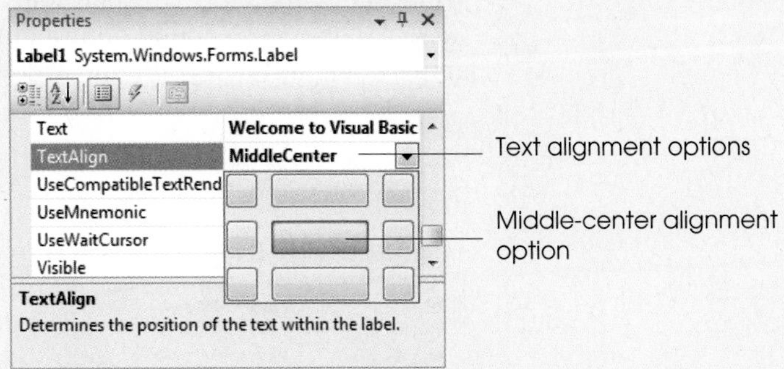

Figure 3.23 Centering the Label's text.

7. ***Saving the project.*** Select **File > Save All** to save your modified project.

To finish this first Visual Basic Windows application, you need to insert an image and execute the application. We use a PictureBox control to add an image to the Form before running the application. The following box guides you step by step through the process of adding an image to your Form.

Inserting an Image and Running the Welcome Application

1. ***Adding a PictureBox control to the Form.*** The PictureBox allows you to display an image. To add a PictureBox control to the Form, double click the PictureBox control icon

PictureBox

in the ToolBox. When the PictureBox appears, drag it below the Label and center it on the Form (Fig. 3.24).

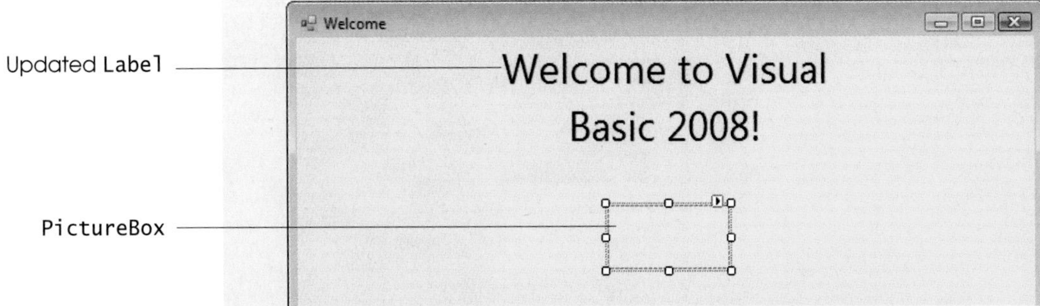

Figure 3.24 Inserting and aligning the PictureBox.

(cont.)

GUI Design Tip

Use `PictureBox`es to enhance GUIs with graphics that users cannot change.

2. ***Setting the Image property.*** Click the `PictureBox` to display its properties in the **Properties** window. Locate the **Image** property, which displays a preview of the image (if one exists). No picture has yet been assigned to the `Image` property, so its value is `(none)` (Fig. 3.25) and an empty white box appears to the left of `(none)`. You can use any of several popular image formats, including *PNG* (*Portable Network Graphics*), *GIF* (*Graphic Interchange Format*), *JPEG* (*Joint Photographic Experts Group*) and *BMP* (*Windows Bitmap*).

   For this application, you use a PNG-format image. Creating new images requires image-editing software, such as Adobe® Photoshop® (`www.adobe.com`), Corel® Paint Shop Pro® Photo X2™ (`www.corel.com`), Adobe® Fireworks® (`www.adobe.com`), Microsoft® Paint (provided with Windows), Paint.NET™ (open source from `www.getpaint.net`) and Picnik (`www.picnik.com`; online photo-editing service). You do not create images in this book; instead, you're provided with the images used in the tutorials.

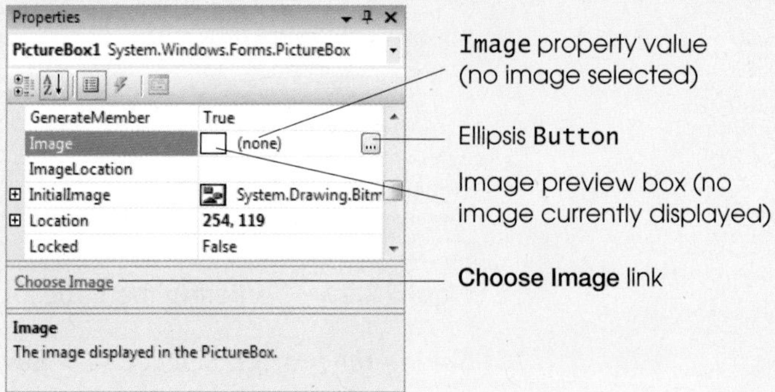

Figure 3.25 `Image` property of the `PictureBox`.

3. ***Displaying an image.*** In the **Properties** window, click the value of the `PictureBox`'s `Image` property to display an ellipsis `Button` (Fig. 3.25). Click the ellipsis `Button` to display the **Select Resource dialog** (Fig. 3.26). You can also display the dialog by clicking the **Choose Image** link in the property description (Fig. 3.25) or by right clicking the `PictureBox` control. The **Select Resource** dialog is used to import files, such as images, to any application. Click the **Import...** `Button` to browse for an image to insert. In our case, the picture is `bug.png`. In the **Open** dialog that appears, navigate to the `C:\Examples\Tutorial03\CompletedApplication` directory. Select the file `bug.png` and click the **Open** `Button`. (Fig. 3.27). The image is previewed in the **Select Resource** dialog (Fig. 3.28). Click **OK** to place the image in your application. Note that the `PictureBox` does not display the entire image (Fig. 3.29). You solve this problem in the next step.

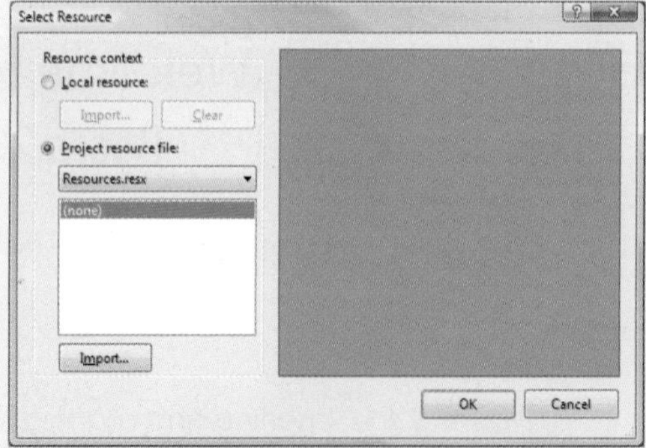

Figure 3.26 **Select Resource** dialog to select an image for the `PictureBox`.

(cont.)

`bug.png` file (may display `bug` depending on whether your computer is set to display file-name extensions)

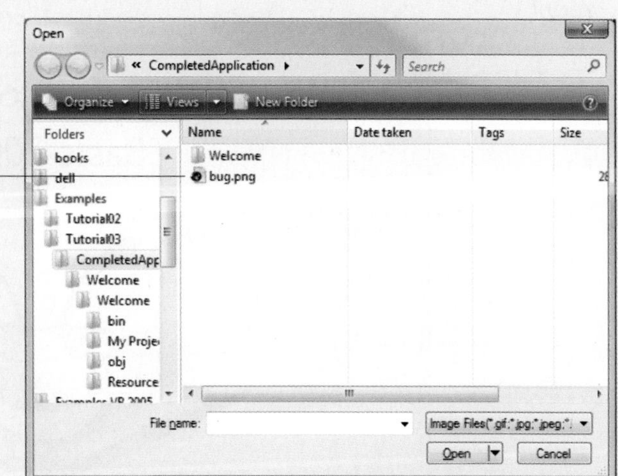

Figure 3.27 **Open** dialog used to browse for a `PictureBox` image.

Figure 3.28 **Select Resource** dialog displaying a preview of selected image.

4. ***Sizing the image to fit the*** **`PictureBox`*.*** We want the image to fit in the `PictureBox`. `PictureBox` property **`SizeMode`** specifies how an image is displayed in a `PictureBox`. To size the image to fit in the `PictureBox`, change the `SizeMode` property to **`StretchImage`**, which **scales** the image (changes its width and height) to the size of the `PictureBox`. To resize the `PictureBox`, double click the `Size` property and enter `500, 250`. Center the image horizontally by clicking the `PictureBox` and selecting **Format > Center in Form > Horizontally**. The `Form` should now look like Fig. 3.30. [*Note*: You may need to move the `PictureBox` up or down at this point to make your `Form` appear as it does in Fig. 3.30. To do this, you can simply click the `PictureBox`, then use the up- and down-arrow keys.]

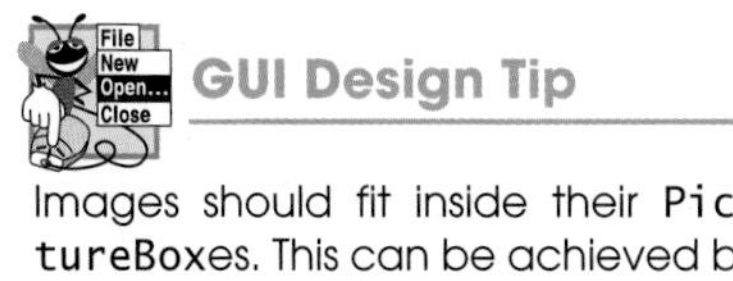

GUI Design Tip

Images should fit inside their `PictureBoxes`. This can be achieved by setting `PictureBox` property `SizeMode` to `StretchImage`.

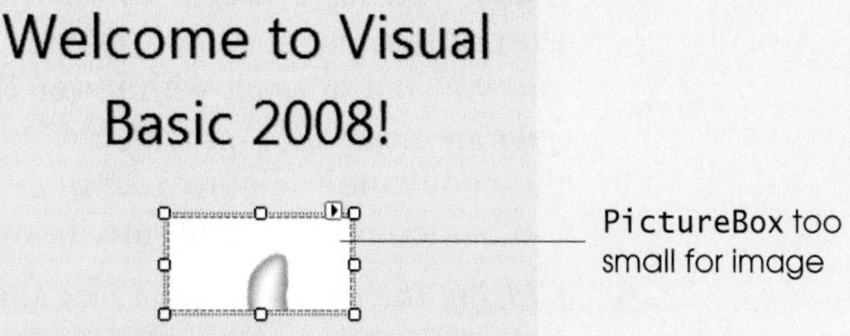

`PictureBox` too small for image

Figure 3.29 Newly inserted image.

(cont.)

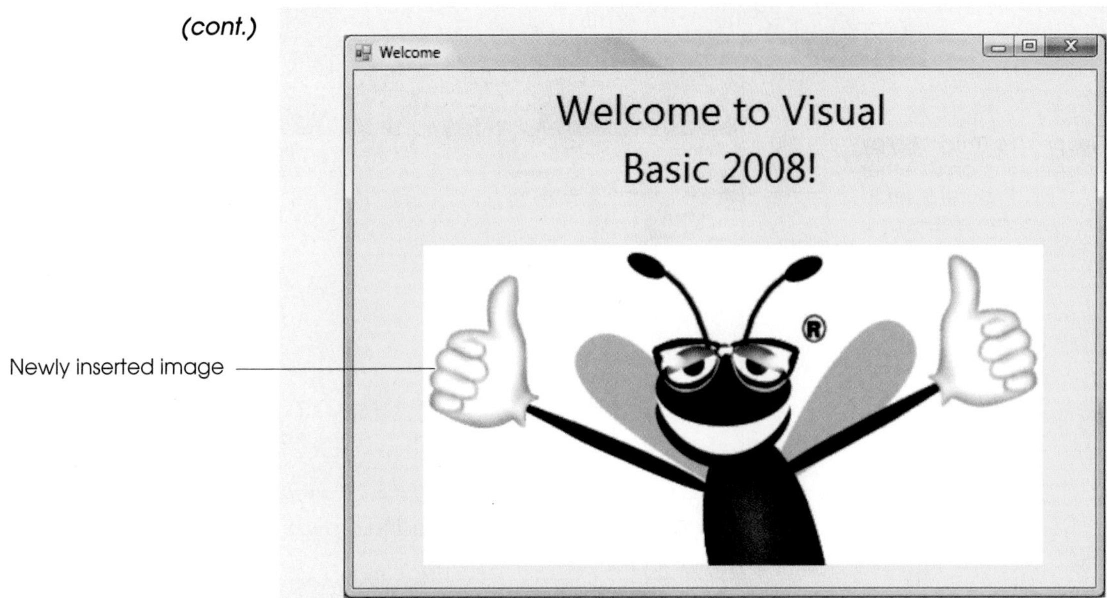

Figure 3.30 `PictureBox` displaying an image.

5. ***Locking the Form controls.*** Often, programmers accidentally alter the size and location of controls on the `Form`. To ensure that the controls remain in position, select **Format > Lock Controls** (Fig. 3.31). This locks all the controls on the `Form`. You can lock individual controls by setting the control's `Locked` property to `True`. Additional capabilities are available by right clicking the `Form` in **Design** view.

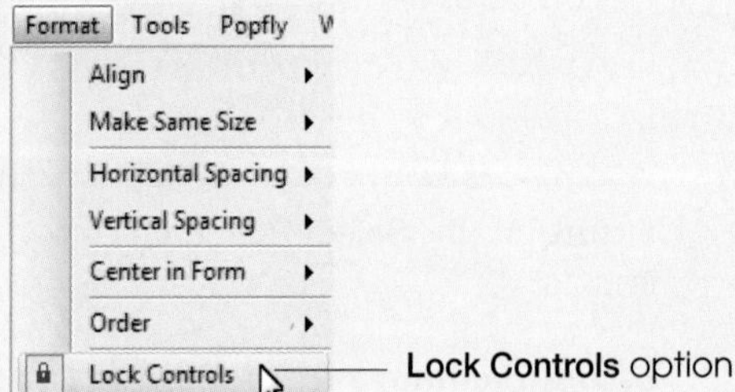

Figure 3.31 Locking controls by using the **Format** menu.

6. ***Saving the project.*** Select **File > Save All** to save your modified project. You should save your files to your `C:\SimplyVB2008` directory frequently. Note, however, that it's not necessary to save project files if you're about to run the application. When a Visual Basic application is run in the IDE, the project files are automatically saved for you.

7. ***Running the application.*** The text **Welcome.vb [Design]** at the top of the design area indicates that we've been working in the IDE **design mode**. (That is, the application being created is not executing.) While in design mode, you have access to all the IDE windows (for example, **Toolbox**, **Properties**), menus and toolbars. In **run mode**, the application is running, and you can interact with fewer IDE features. Features that are not available are disabled ("grayed out"). Select **Debug > Start Debugging** to run the application. Figure 3.32 shows the IDE in run mode. Note that many toolbar icons and menus are disabled.

8. ***Closing the application.*** Close the running application by clicking its close box, ![X]. This action returns the IDE to design mode.

9. ***Closing the IDE.*** Close the IDE by clicking its close box.

(cont.)

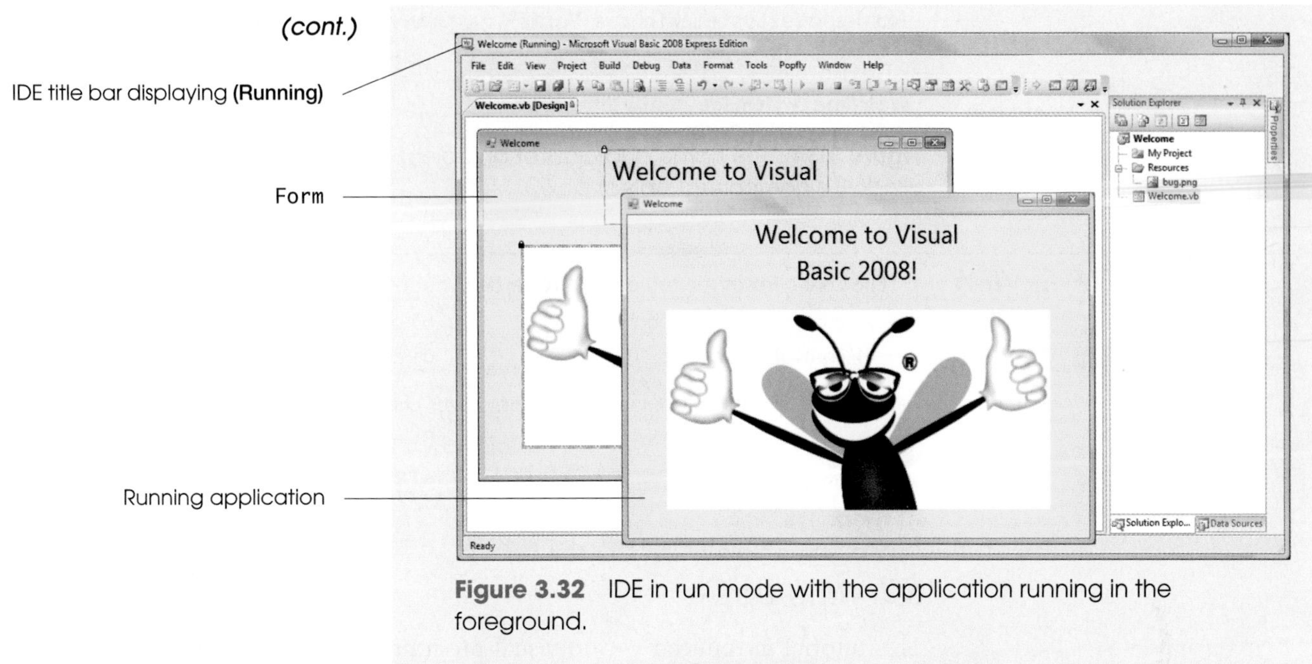

Figure 3.32 IDE in run mode with the application running in the foreground.

SELF-REVIEW

1. The Form's ________ property specifies the text that is displayed in the Form's title bar.
   a) Title b) Text
   c) (Name) d) Name

2. Property ________ specifies how text is aligned within a Label's boundaries.
   a) Alignment b) AlignText
   c) Align d) TextAlign

Answers: 1) b. 2) d.

3.3 Objects Used in the Welcome Application

In Tutorials 1 and 2, you learned that controls are reusable software components called objects. The **Welcome** application used a Form object, a Label object and a PictureBox object to create a GUI that displayed text and an image. Each of these objects is an instance of a class defined in the .NET Framework Class Library. The Form object was created by the Visual Basic IDE. The Label and PictureBox objects were created when you double clicked their respective icons in the **Toolbox**.

We used the **Properties** window to set the properties (attributes) for each object. Recall that the ComboBox at the top of the **Properties** window—also called the component object box— displays the names and class types of Form and control objects (Fig. 3.33). In Fig. 3.34, the component object box displays the name (Welcome) and class type (Form) of the Form object. In the .NET Framework Class Library, classes are organized by functionality into directory-like entities called **namespaces**. The class types used in this application have namespace System.Windows.Forms. This namespace contains control classes and the Form class. You'll be introduced to additional namespaces in later tutorials.

Figure 3.33 Component object box expanded to show the **Welcome** application's objects.

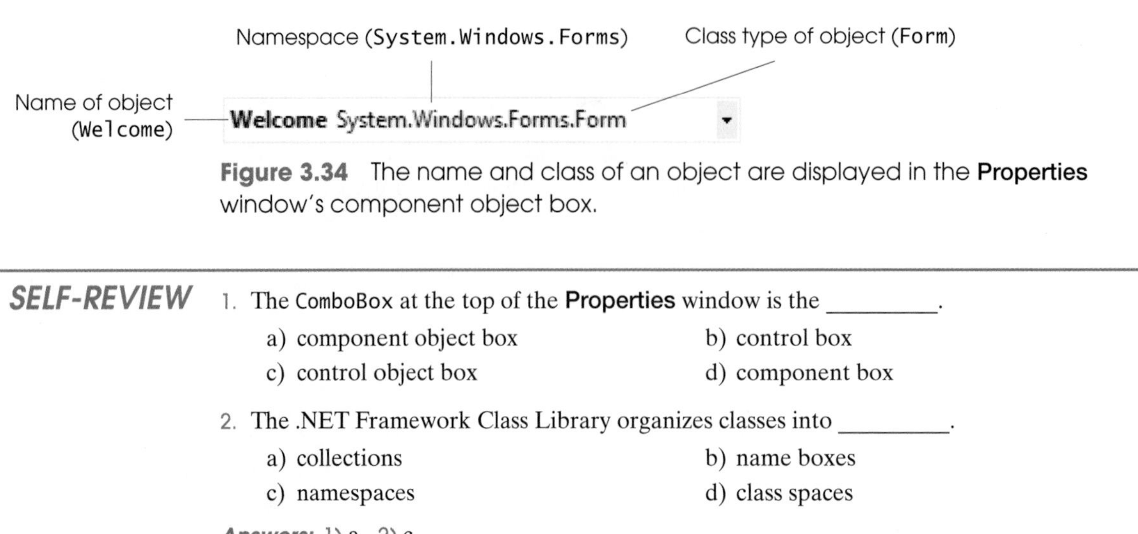

Figure 3.34 The name and class of an object are displayed in the **Properties** window's component object box.

SELF-REVIEW

1. The ComboBox at the top of the **Properties** window is the ________.
   a) component object box
   b) control box
   c) control object box
   d) component box

2. The .NET Framework Class Library organizes classes into ________.
   a) collections
   b) name boxes
   c) namespaces
   d) class spaces

Answers: 1) a. 2) c.

3.4 Wrap-Up

This tutorial introduced you to visual programming in Visual Basic. You learned that visual programming helps you to design and create the graphical user interface portions of applications quickly and easily, by dragging and dropping controls onto Forms.

In creating your **Welcome** application, you used the **Properties** window to set the Form's title-bar text, size (width and height) and background color using properties Text, Size and BackColor, respectively. You learned that Labels are controls that display text and that PictureBoxes are controls that display images. You displayed text in a Label by setting its Text and TextAlign properties, and you displayed an image by setting a PictureBox control's Image and SizeMode properties.

You also examined the relationship between controls and classes. You learned that .NET Framework Class Library classes are grouped into directory-like entities called namespaces and that controls are instances (objects) of .NET Framework Class Library classes. The .NET Framework Class Library classes used in this tutorial (Form, Label and PictureBox) belong to namespace System.Windows.Forms. You used the **Properties** window's component object box to view an object's name, namespace and class type.

In the next tutorial, you continue learning visual programming. In particular, you'll create an application with controls that are designed to accept user input.

SKILLS SUMMARY

Creating GUIs Quickly and Efficiently

- Use visual programming techniques.

Placing a Control on the Form

- Double click the control in the **Toolbox** to place the control in the upper-left corner of the Form, or drag the control from the **Toolbox** onto the Form.

Aligning Controls

- Use the **Format** menu's commands.

Resizing the Form or Control with Sizing Handles

- Click and drag one of the object's enabled sizing handles.

Setting the Dimensions of the Form or Control by Using Property Size

- Use the **Properties** window to enter the width and height of the Form or control in the Size field.

Setting the Width and Height of the Form or Control

- Use the **Properties** window to enter values in the Width and Height property fields (or use the Size property field).

Setting the Form's Background Color

- Use the **Properties** window to set the Form's BackColor property.

Adding a Label Control to the Form

- Double click the Label control in the **Toolbox** to place the control in the upper-left corner of the Form, or drag the Label from the **Toolbox** onto the Form.

Setting a Label's Text Property

- Use the **Properties** window to set the Label's Text property.

Setting a Label's Font Property

- Click the value of the Font property in the **Properties** window, which causes an ellipsis Button to appear next to the value. Click the ellipsis Button to display the **Font** dialog. Change the font name, style and size of the Label's text.

Aligning Text in a Label

- Use the **Properties** window to set the Label's TextAlign property.

Resizing a Label

- Use the **Properties** window to set the AutoSize property to False, then use the sizing handles in the Form Designer.

Adding an Image to the Form

- Use a PictureBox control to display the image. In the **Properties** window, click the ellipsis Button next to the PictureBox Image property's value or the **Choose Image** link in the property description to browse for an image to insert using the **Select Resource** dialog.
- Scale the image to the size of the PictureBox by setting property SizeMode to value StretchImage.

Displaying a Form or Control's Properties in the Properties Window

- Click the Form or a control on the Form.

KEY TERMS

AutoSize property of a Label—Determines whether a Label is automatically sized based on its content.

BackColor property—Specifies the background color of the Form or a control.

design mode—IDE mode that allows you to create applications using Visual Studio 2008's windows, toolbars and menu bar.

File Name property—Specifies the name of a source code file.

Font property—Specifies the font name, style and size of any displayed text in the Form or one of its controls.

Height property—This property, a member of property Size, indicates the height of the Form or one of its controls in pixels.

Image property—Indicates the file name of the image displayed in a PictureBox.

Label—Control that displays text the user can't modify.

Locked property—Prevents a control from being moved or resized.

namespace—Classes in the .NET Framework Class Library are organized by functionality into these directory-like entities.

palette—A set of colors.

PictureBox—Control that displays an image.

pixel—A tiny point on your computer screen that displays a color.

RGB value—The amount of red, green and blue needed to create a color.

run mode—IDE mode indicating that the application is executing.

Select Resource dialog—Used to import files, such as images, to any application.

Size property—Property that specifies the height and width, in pixels, of the Form or one of its controls.

SizeMode property—Property that specifies how an image is displayed in a PictureBox.

sizing handle—Square that, when enabled, can be used to resize the Form or one of its controls.

StretchImage—Value of PictureBox property SizeMode that scales an image to fill the PictureBox.

Text property—Specifies the text displayed by the Form or a Label.

TextAlign property—Specifies how text is aligned within a Label.

visual programming—Technique in which Visual Basic processes your actions (such as clicking, dragging and dropping controls) and writes code for you.

web-safe colors—Colors that display the same on different computers.

Width property—This setting, a member of property Size, indicates the width of the Form or one of its controls, in pixels.

GUI DESIGN GUIDELINES

Overall Design

- Use colors in your applications, but not to the point of distracting the user.

Forms

- Choose short, descriptive Form titles. Capitalize words that are not articles, prepositions or conjunctions. Do not use punctuation.
- Use 9pt Segoe UI font to improve readability for controls that display text.

Labels

- Use Labels to display text that users cannot change.
- Ensure that all Label controls are large enough to display their text. You can do this by setting AutoSize to True, or by setting AutoSize to False and resizing the Label manually.

PictureBoxes

- Use PictureBoxes to enhance GUIs with graphics that users cannot change.
- Images should fit inside their PictureBoxes. This can be achieved by setting PictureBox property SizeMode to StretchImage.

CONTROLS, EVENTS, PROPERTIES & METHODS

Label A Label This control displays on the Form text that the user can't modify.

- *In action*

Welcome to Visual
Basic 2008!

- *Properties*

Text—Specifies the text displayed in the Label.

Font—Specifies the font name, style and size of the text displayed in the Label.

TextAlign—Determines how the text is aligned in the Label.

AutoSize—Allows for automatic resizing of the Label to fit its text.

PictureBox PictureBox This control displays an image on the Form.

- *In action*

- *Properties*

Image—Specifies the image that is displayed in the PictureBox.

SizeMode—Specifies how the image is displayed in the PictureBox.

Size—Specifies the width and height (in pixels) of the PictureBox.

`Form` Represents the main window of a GUI application.

- ***In action***

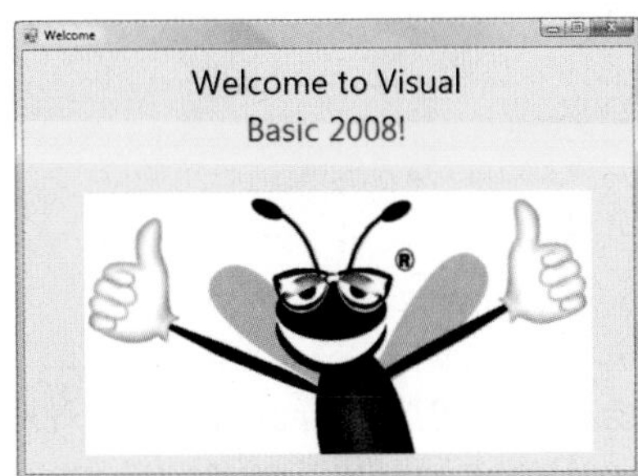

- ***Properties***

  `BackColor`—Specifies the background color of the `Form`.

  `Font`—Specifies the font name, style and size of any displayed text in the `Form`. The `Form`'s controls use this font by default.

  `Size`—Specifies the width and height (in pixels) of the `Form`.

  `Text`—Specifies the text displayed in the title bar of a `Form`.

MULTIPLE-CHOICE QUESTIONS

3.1 Property _________ determines the `Form`'s background color.

a) `BackColor` b) `BackgroundColor`
c) `RGB` d) `Color`

3.2 To save all the project's files, select _________.

a) **Save > Solution > Save Files** b) **File > Save**
c) **File > Save All** d) **File > Save As...**

3.3 When the ellipsis `Button` to the right of the **Font** property value is clicked, the _________ is displayed.

a) **Font Property** dialog b) **New Font** dialog
c) **Font Settings** dialog d) **Font** dialog

3.4 `PictureBox` property _________ contains a preview of the image displayed in the `PictureBox`.

a) `Picture` b) `ImageName`
c) `Image` d) `PictureName`

3.5 When setting the `BackColor` property, the _________ tab allows you to create your own color.

a) **Custom** b) **Web**
c) **System** d) **User**

3.6 `PictureBox` property _________ specifies how an image is displayed in a `PictureBox`.

a) `Size` b) `Height`
c) `Width` d) `SizeMode`

3.7 A `Label` control displays the text specified by property _________.

a) `Caption` b) `Data`
c) `Text` d) `Name`

3.8 In _________ mode, the application is executing.

a) start b) run
c) break d) design

3.9 The _________ command prevents programmers from accidentally altering the size and location of the Form's controls.

a) **Lock Controls**
b) **Anchor Controls**
c) **Lock**
d) **Bind Controls**

3.10 Pixels are _________.

a) picture elements
b) controls in the **Toolbox**
c) a set of fonts
d) a set of colors on the **Web** tab

EXERCISES

*For Exercises 3.11–3.16, you are asked to create the GUI shown in each exercise. You use the visual programming techniques presented in this tutorial to create a variety of GUIs. You are creating only GUIs, therefore your applications are not fully operational. For example, the **Calculator** GUI in Exercise 3.11 does not behave like a calculator when its `Buttons` are clicked. You learn how to make your applications fully operational in later tutorials. Create each application as a separate project. If you accidentally double click a control in **Design** view, the IDE displays the `Form's` source code. To return to **Design** view, select **View > Designer**.*

3.11 ***(Calculator GUI)*** Create the GUI for the calculator shown in Fig. 3.35.

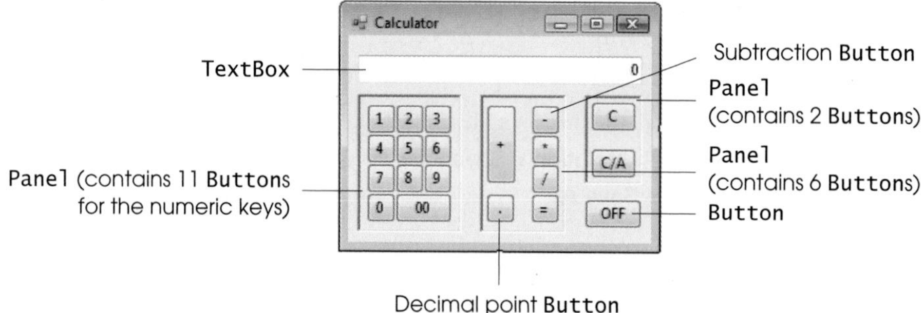

Figure 3.35 **Calculator** GUI.

a) ***Creating a new project.*** Create a new **Windows Forms Application** named `Calculator`.

b) ***Renaming the Form file.*** Name the `Form` file `Calculator.vb`.

c) ***Manipulating the Form's properties.*** Change the `Text` property of the `Form` to `Calculator`. Change the `Font` property to 9pt `Segoe UI`. Change the `Size` property of the `Form` to `272, 204`. Note that Visual Studio resizes a `Form` when you change its font size. *Be sure to set the font size before setting the `Form's` size.*

d) ***Adding a TextBox to the Form.*** Add a `TextBox` control by double clicking it in the **Toolbox**. A `TextBox` control enables the user to enter input into applications. Set the `TextBox's Text` property to `0`. Change the `Size` property to `240, 23`. [*Note:* You cannot change the height of a single-line `TextBox`. You'll learn how to create multiline `TextBoxes` in Tutorial 11.] Set the `TextAlign` property to `Right`; this right aligns text displayed in the `TextBox`. Finally, set the `TextBox's Location` property to `8, 16`—this property specifies where the upper-left corner of the control is placed on the form.

e) ***Adding the first Panel to the Form.*** `Panel` controls are used to group other controls. Double click the `Panel` icon (Panel) in the **Containers** category of the **Toolbox** to add a `Panel` to the `Form`. Change the `Panel's BorderStyle` property to `Fixed3D` to make the inside of the `Panel` appear recessed. Change the `Size` property to `88, 112`. Finally, set the `Location` property to `8, 48`. This `Panel` will contain the calculator's numeric keys.

f) ***Adding the second Panel to the Form.*** Click the `Form`. Double click the `Panel` icon in the **Toolbox** to add another `Panel` to the `Form`. Change the `Panel's BorderStyle` property to `Fixed3D`. Change the `Size` property to `72, 112`. Finally, set the `Location` property to `112, 48`. This `Panel` will contain the calculator's operator keys.

g) ***Adding the third (and last)* Panel *to the Form.*** Click the Form. Double click the Panel icon in the **Toolbox** to add another Panel to the Form. Change the Panel's BorderStyle property to Fixed3D. Change the Size property to 48, 72. Finally, set the Location property to 200, 48. This Panel will contain the calculator's **C** (clear) and **C/A** (clear all) keys.

h) ***Adding* Buttons *to the Form.*** There are 20 Buttons on the calculator. To add a Button to a Panel, drag a Button (Button) from the **Toolbox** and drop it on the appropriate Panel. Change the Text property of each Button to the calculator key it represents. The value you enter in the Text property appears on the face of the Button. Finally, resize the Buttons, using their Size properties. Each Button labeled 0–9, *, /, -, = and . (decimal point) should have a size of 24, 24. The **00** and **OFF** Buttons have size 48, 24. The **+** Button is sized 24, 64. The **C** (clear) and **C/A** (clear all) Buttons are sized 38, 24. To align the numeric Buttons as they appear in Fig. 3.35, select the **1** Button and set its Location property to 6, 6 and its Lock property to True. Place the **2** and **3** Buttons to the right of the **1** Button. Select the three Buttons in the top row (**1**, **2** and **3**) by clicking the **1** Button, then holding the shift key while you select the **2** and **3** Buttons. The formatting you do next is based on the Button you selected first (that is, the **1** Button). Use the **Format > Horizontal Spacing > Remove** option to place the Buttons directly next to each other. Use the **Format > Align > Middles** option to place them in a straight row. Repeat the process to vertically align Buttons **1**, **4**, **7** and **0** using the **Format > Vertical Spacing > Remove** and **Format > Align > Centers** options. You can drag and drop the rest of the numeric Buttons into position—the IDE "snaps" each Button into alignment with those around it. The **Format** menu contains many useful options. [*Note:* You can display many of the **Format** menu options in a Visual Studio toolbar—right click the toolbar in the IDE and select **Layout**.]

i) ***Saving and closing the project.*** Select **File > Save All** to save your changes. Then select **File > Close Project** to close the project for this application.

3.12 *(Alarm Clock GUI)* Create the GUI for the alarm clock in Fig. 3.36.

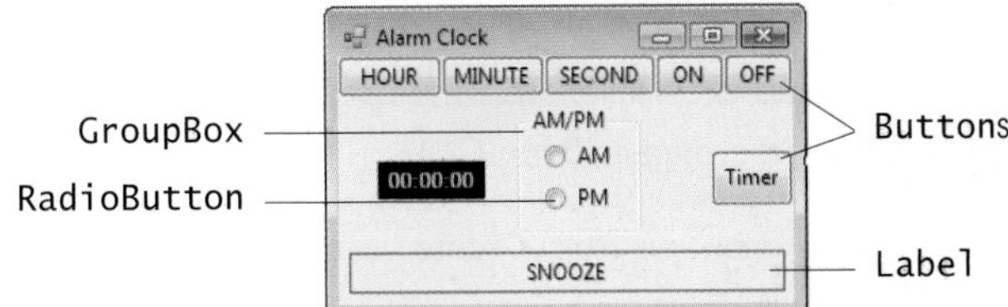

Figure 3.36 **Alarm Clock** GUI.

a) ***Creating a new project.*** Create a new **Windows Forms Application** named AlarmClock.

b) ***Renaming the Form file.*** Name the Form file AlarmClock.vb.

c) ***Manipulating the Form's properties.*** Change the Font property of the Form to 9pt Segoe UI. Change the Text property to Alarm Clock. Change the Size property of the Form to 281, 176. Remember to change the Font property's size before you set the Form's Size property.

d) ***Adding* Buttons *to the Form.*** Add six Buttons to the Form. Change the Text property of each Button to the appropriate text. Change the Size properties of the **Hour**, **Minute** Buttons to 60, 23. Change the Size of the **Second** Button to 65, 23. Change the Size of the **ON** and **OFF** Buttons to 40, 23. The **Timer** Button gets size 48, 32. Use the **Format > Horizontal Spacing > Remove** option to align the Buttons in the top row so the Buttons appear as shown in Fig. 3.36.

e) ***Adding a* Label *to the Form.*** Add a Label to the Form. Change the Text property to **SNOOZE**. Set its AutoSize property to False and its Size to 254, 23. Set the Label's TextAlign property to MiddleCenter. Finally, to draw a border around the edge of the **SNOOZE** Label, change the BorderStyle property of the **SNOOZE** Label to FixedSingle.

f) ***Adding a GroupBox to the Form. GroupBoxes*** are like Panels, except that GroupBoxes can display a title. To add a GroupBox to the Form, double click the GroupBox control

(GroupBox) in the **Container** tab of the **Toolbox**. Change the `Text` property to `AM/PM`, and set the `Size` property to `72, 72`. To place the `GroupBox` in the correct location on the `Form`, set the `Location` property to `104, 29`.

g) ***Adding AM/PM*** **`RadioButtons`** ***to the*** **`GroupBox`**. Add two `RadioButtons` to the `Form` by dragging the `RadioButton` control (RadioButton) in the **Toolbox** and dropping it onto the `GroupBox` twice. Change the `Text` property of one `RadioButton` to `AM` and the other to `PM`. Then place the `RadioButtons` as shown in Fig. 3.36 by setting the `Location` of the **AM** `RadioButton` to `16, 16` and that of the **PM** `RadioButton` to `16, 40`. Set the `AutoSize` property to `False` and set their `Size` properties to `48, 24`.

h) ***Adding the time*** **`Label`** ***to the*** **`Form`**. Add a `Label` to the `Form` and change its `Text` property to `00:00:00`. Change the `BorderStyle` property to `Fixed3D` and the `BackColor` to `Black`. Set the `AutoSize` property to `False` and set the `Size` property to `64, 23`. Use the `Font` property to make the time bold. Change the `ForeColor` to `Silver` (located in the **Web** tab) to make the time stand out against the black background. Set `TextAlign` to `MiddleCenter` to center the text in the `Label`. Position the `Label` as shown in Fig. 3.36.

i) ***Saving and closing the project.*** Select **File > Save All** to save your changes. Then select **File > Close Project** to close the project for this application.

3.13 ***(Microwave Oven GUI)*** Create the GUI for the microwave oven shown in Fig. 3.37.

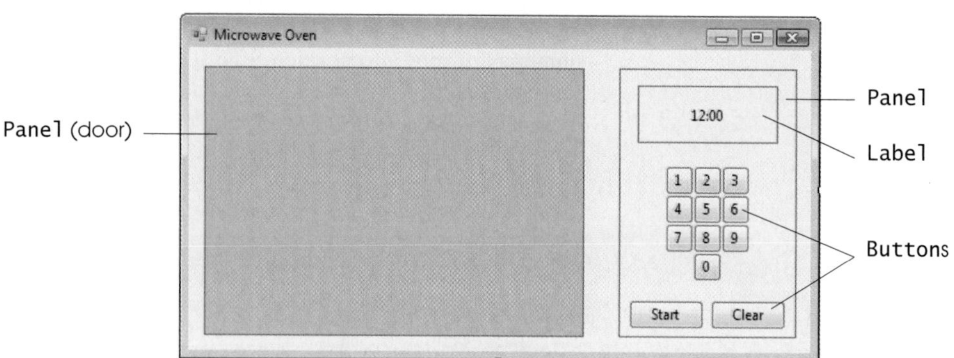

Figure 3.37 Microwave Oven GUI.

a) ***Creating a new project.*** Create a new **Windows Forms Application** named `Microwave`.

b) ***Renaming the*** **`Form`** ***file.*** Name the `Form` file `Microwave.vb`.

c) ***Manipulating the*** **`Form`**'***s properties.*** Change the `Form`'s `Font` property to 9pt `Segoe UI` and the `Text` property to `Microwave Oven`. Change the `Size` property to `552, 288`.

d) ***Adding the microwave oven door.*** Add a `Panel` to the `Form` by double clicking the `Panel` control (Panel) in the **Toolbox**. Select the `Panel` and change the `BackColor` property to `Silver` (located in the **Web** tab) in the **Properties** window. Then change the `Size` to `328, 224`. Next, change the `BorderStyle` property to `FixedSingle`. Position the `Panel` as shown in Fig. 3.37 by using the four-way arrow icon ( ) in the upper-left corner of the selected `Panel`.

e) ***Adding another*** **`Panel`**. Add another `Panel` and change its `Size` to `152, 224` and its `BorderStyle` to `FixedSingle`. Place the `Panel` to the right of the door `Panel`, as shown in Fig. 3.37.

f) ***Adding the microwave oven clock.*** Add a `Label` to the right `Panel` by clicking the `Label` in the **Toolbox** once, then clicking once inside the right `Panel`. Change the `Label`'s `Text` to `12:00`, `BorderStyle` to `FixedSingle`, `AutoSize` to `False` and `Size` to `120, 48`. Change `TextAlign` to `MiddleCenter`. Place the clock as shown in Fig. 3.37.

g) ***Adding a keypad to the microwave oven.*** Place a `Button` in the right `Panel` by clicking the `Button` control in the `Toolbox` once, then clicking inside the `Panel`. Change the `Text` to `1` and the `Size` to `24, 24`. Repeat this process for nine more `Buttons`, changing the `Text` property in each to the next number in the keypad. Then add the

Start and **Clear** Buttons, each of Size 64, 24. Don't forget to set the Text properties for each of these Buttons. Finally, arrange the Buttons as shown in Fig. 3.37. The **1** Button is located at 39, 80 and the **Start** Button is located at 8, 192.

h) ***Saving and closing the project.*** Select **File > Save All** to save your changes. Then select **File > Close Project** to close the project for this application.

3.14 *(Cell Phone GUI)* Create the GUI for the cell phone shown in Fig. 3.38.

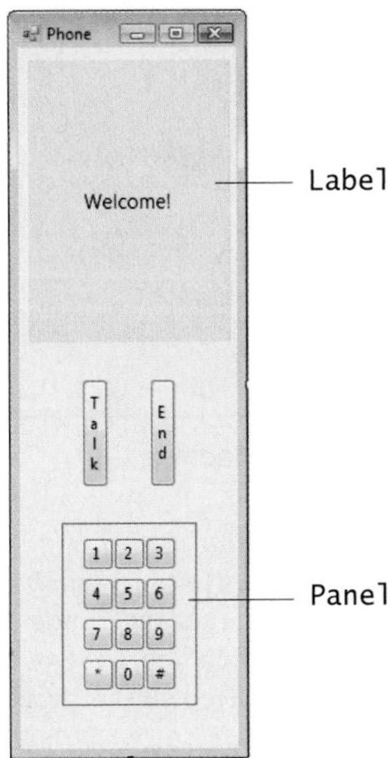

Figure 3.38 **Cell Phone** GUI.

a) ***Creating a new project.*** Create a new **Windows Forms Application** named Phone.

b) ***Renaming the Form file.*** Name the Form file Phone.vb.

c) ***Manipulating the Form's properties.*** Change the Form's Font property to 9pt Segoe UI. Change the Text property to Phone and the Size to 184, 558.

d) ***Adding the display Label.*** Add a Label to the Form. Change its BackColor property to NavajoWhite (in the **Web** tab palette), the Text to Welcome!, AutoSize to False and the Size to 156, 210. Change the TextAlign property to MiddleCenter. Then place the Label as shown in Fig. 3.38.

e) ***Adding the keypad Panel.*** Add a Panel to the Form. Change its BorderStyle property to FixedSingle and its Size to 104, 136.

f) ***Adding the keypad Buttons.*** Add the keypad Buttons to the Form (12 Buttons in all). Each Button on the number pad should be of Size 24, 24 and should be placed in the Panel. Change the Text property of each Button such that numbers 0-9, the pound (#) and the star (*) keys are represented. Then add the final two Buttons such that the Text property for one is Talk and for the other is End. Change the Size of each Button to 20, 80, and notice how the small Size causes the Text to align vertically.

g) ***Placing the controls.*** Arrange all the controls so that your GUI looks like Fig. 3.38.

h) ***Saving and closing the project.*** Select **File > Save All** to save your changes. Then select **File > Close Project** to close the project for this application.

3.15 *(Vending Machine GUI)* Create the GUI for the vending machine in Fig. 3.39.

a) ***Creating a new project.*** Create a new **Windows Forms Application** named VendingMachine.

b) ***Renaming the Form file.*** Name the Form file VendingMachine.vb.

c) ***Manipulating the Form's properties.*** Set the Font property of the Form to 9pt Segoe UI, the Text property to Vending Machine and the Size to 560, 488.

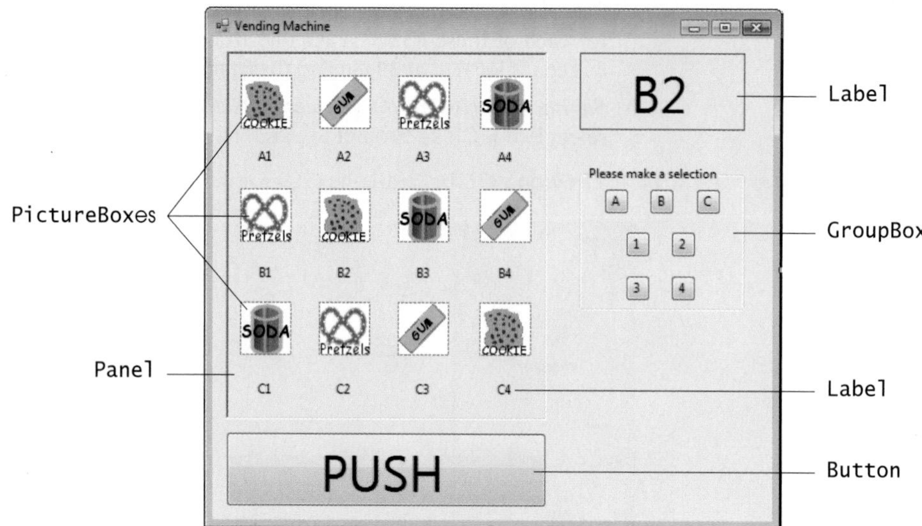

Figure 3.39 **Vending Machine** GUI.

d) ***Adding the food-selection*** **`Panel`*.*** Add a `Panel` to the `Form`, and change its `Size` to `312, 344` and `BorderStyle` to `Fixed3D`. Add a `PictureBox` to the `Panel`, and change its `Size` to `50, 50`. Then set the `Image` property by clicking the **Choose Image** link and choosing a file from the `C:\Examples\Tutorial03\ExerciseImages\VendingMachine` directory. Repeat this process for 11 more `PictureBoxes`.

e) ***Adding*** **`Labels`** ***for each vending item.*** Add a `Label` under the first `PictureBox`. Change the `Text` property of the `Label` to `A1`, the `TextAlign` property to `MiddleCenter`, `AutoSize` to `False` and `Size` to `50, 16`. Place the `Label` so that it's located as in Fig. 3.39. Repeat this process for `A2` through `C4` (11 `Labels`).

f) ***Creating the vending machine door (as a*** **`Button`*).*** Add a `Button` to the `Form` by dragging the `Button` control in the **Toolbox** and dropping it below the `Panel`. Change the `Button`'s `Text` property to `PUSH`, its `Font Size` to `36` and its `Size` to `312, 56`. Then place the `Button` on the `Form` as shown in Fig. 3.39.

g) ***Adding the selection-display*** **`Label`*.*** Add a `Label` to the `Form`, and change the `Text` property to `B2`, `BorderStyle` to `FixedSingle`, `Font Size` to `36`, `TextAlign` to `MiddleCenter`, `AutoSize` to `False` and `Size` to `160, 72`.

h) ***Grouping the input*** **`Buttons`*.*** Add a `GroupBox` below the `Label`, and change the `Text` property to `Please make a selection` and the `Size` to `160, 136`.

i) ***Adding the input*** **`Buttons`*.*** Finally, add `Buttons` to the `GroupBox`. For the seven `Buttons`, change the `Size` property to `24, 24`. Then change the `Text` property of the `Buttons` such that each `Button` has one of the values `A`, `B`, `C`, `1`, `2`, `3` or `4`, as shown in Fig. 3.39. When you are done, move the controls on the `Form` so that they are aligned as shown in the figure.

j) ***Saving and closing the project.*** Select **File > Save All** to save your changes. Then select **File > Close Project** to close the project for this application.

Programming Challenge

3.16 ***(Radio GUI)*** Create the GUI for the radio in Fig. 3.40. [*Note:* All colors used in this exercise are from the **Web** palette.] In this exercise, you create this GUI on your own. Feel free to experiment with different control properties. For the image in the `PictureBox`, use the file (`MusicNote.gif`) found in the `C:\Examples\Tutorial03\ExerciseImages\Radio` directory.

a) ***Creating a new project.*** Create a new **Windows Forms Application** named `Radio`.

b) ***Renaming the Form file.*** Name the `Form` file `Radio.vb`.

c) ***Manipulating the Form's properties.*** Change the `Form`'s `Font` property to 9pt `Segoe UI`, the `Text` property to `Radio` and the `Size` to `576, 240`. Set `BackColor` to `PeachPuff`.

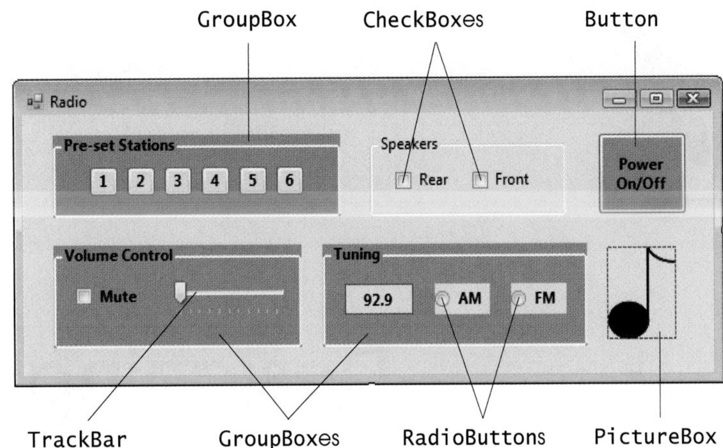

Figure 3.40 Radio GUI.

d) ***Adding the Pre-set Stations GroupBox and Buttons.*** Add a GroupBox to the Form. Set its Size to 232, 64, its Text to Pre-set Stations, its ForeColor to Black and its BackColor to RosyBrown. Change its Font to bold. Finally, set its Location to 24, 16. Add six Buttons to the GroupBox. Set each BackColor to PeachPuff and each Size to 24, 24. Change the Buttons' Text properties to 1, 2, 3, 4, 5, 6, respectively.

e) ***Adding the Speakers GroupBox and CheckBoxes.*** Add a GroupBox to the Form. Set its Size to 160, 64, its Text to Speakers and its ForeColor to Black. Set its Location to 280, 16. Add two CheckBoxes to the Form. Set each CheckBox's AutoSize property to False and Size to 56, 24. Set the Text properties for the CheckBoxes to Rear and Front.

f) ***Adding the Power On/Off Button.*** Add a Button to the Form. Set its Text to Power On/Off, its BackColor to RosyBrown, its ForeColor to Black and its Size to 72, 64. Change its Font style to Bold.

g) ***Adding the Volume Control GroupBox, the Mute CheckBox and the Volume TrackBar.*** Add a GroupBox to the Form. Set its Text to Volume Control, its BackColor to RosyBrown, its ForeColor to Black and its Size to 200, 80. Set its Font style to Bold. Add a CheckBox to the GroupBox. Set its Text to Mute and its Size to 56, 19. Add a TrackBar (TrackBar)—found in the **All Windows Forms** category—to the GroupBox.

h) ***Adding the Tuning GroupBox, the radio station Label and the AM/FM RadioButtons.*** Add a GroupBox to the Form. Set its Text to Tuning, its ForeColor to Black and its BackColor to RosyBrown. Set its Font style to Bold and its Size to 216, 80. Add a Label to the GroupBox. Set its BackColor to PeachPuff, its BorderStyle to FixedSingle, its TextAlign to MiddleCenter and its Size to 56, 24. Set its Text to 92.9. Place the Label as shown in Fig. 3.40. Add two RadioButtons to the GroupBox. Change the BackColor to PeachPuff and change the Size to 45,24. Set one's Text to AM and the other's Text to FM.

i) ***Adding the image.*** Add a PictureBox to the Form. Set its BackColor to Transparent, its SizeMode to StretchImage and its Size to 56, 72. Set its Image property to C:\Examples\Tutorial03\ExerciseImages\Radio\MusicNote.gif.

j) ***Saving and closing the project.*** Select **File > Save All** to save your changes. Then select **File > Close Project** to close the project for this application.

TUTORIAL

Designing the Inventory Application

Introducing TextBoxes and Buttons

Objectives

In this tutorial, you learn to:

- Visually program, using GUI design guidelines.
- Rename the Form.
- Add TextBoxes and a Button to the Form.
- Use the BorderStyle property for Labels.

Outline

This tutorial introduces you to GUI design. You design the graphical user interface for a simple inventory application. Through each set of steps, you enhance the application's user interface by adding controls. You design a Form on which you place Labels, TextBoxes and a Button. You learn new properties for Labels and TextBoxes. At the end of the tutorial, you find a list of new GUI design guidelines to help you create appealing and easy-to-use graphical user interfaces.

4.1 Test-Driving the Inventory Application

In this tutorial, you create an inventory application that calculates the number of textbooks received by a college bookstore. This application must meet the following requirements:

Application Requirements

A college bookstore receives cartons of textbooks. In each shipment, all cartons contain the same number of textbooks. The inventory manager wants to use a computer to calculate the total number of textbooks arriving at the bookstore for each shipment. The inventory manager will enter the number of cartons received and the fixed number of textbooks in each carton for each shipment; then the application will calculate the total number of textbooks in the shipment.

This application performs a simple calculation. The user (the inventory manager) inputs into TextBoxes the number of cartons and the number of items in each carton. The user then clicks a Button, which causes the application to multiply the two numbers and display the result—the total number of textbooks received. You begin by test-driving the completed application. Then you learn the additional Visual Basic capabilities needed to create your own version of this application.

Test-Driving the Inventory Application

1. ***Opening the completed application.*** Open the directory `C:\Examples\Tutorial04\CompletedApplication\Inventory` to locate the **Inventory** application. Double click `Inventory.sln` to open the application in the Visual Basic IDE. Depending on your system configuration, you may not see the `.sln` file-name extension. In this case, double click the file named `Inventory` that contains a solution file icon, .

2. ***Running the Inventory application.*** Select **Debug > Start Debugging** to run the application. The **Inventory** `Form` shown in Fig. 4.1 will appear.

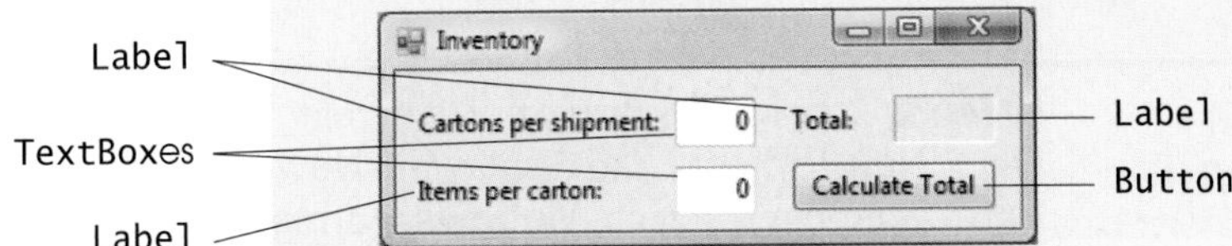

Figure 4.1 **Inventory** `Form` with default data displayed by the application.

Note that there are two controls that you did not use in the **Welcome** application—the `TextBox` and `Button` controls. A **`TextBox`** is a control that the user can enter data into from the keyboard and that can display data to the user. A **`Button`** is a control that causes the application to perform an action when clicked.

3. ***Entering quantities in the application.*** Some controls (such as `TextBoxes`) do not display self-descriptive text—we refer to these controls by using the `Labels` that identify them. For example, we refer to the `TextBox` to the right of the **Cartons per shipment:** `Label` as the **Cartons per shipment:** `TextBox`. Enter `3` in the **Cartons per shipment:** `TextBox`. Enter `15` in the **Items per carton:** `TextBox`. Figure 4.2 shows the `Form` after these values have been entered.

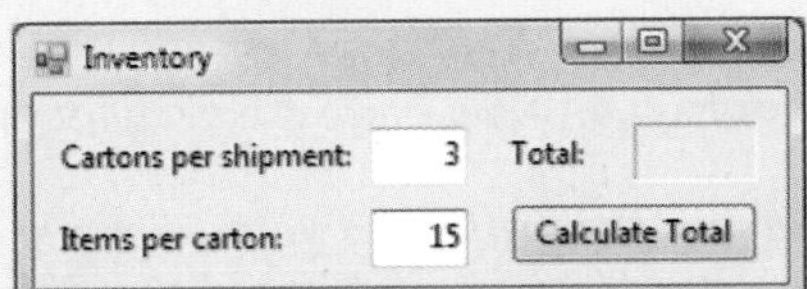

Figure 4.2 **Inventory** application with new quantities entered.

4. ***Calculating the total number of items received.*** Click the **Calculate Total** `Button`. This causes the application to multiply the two numbers you entered and to display the result (`45`) in the `Label` to the right of **Total:** (Fig. 4.3).

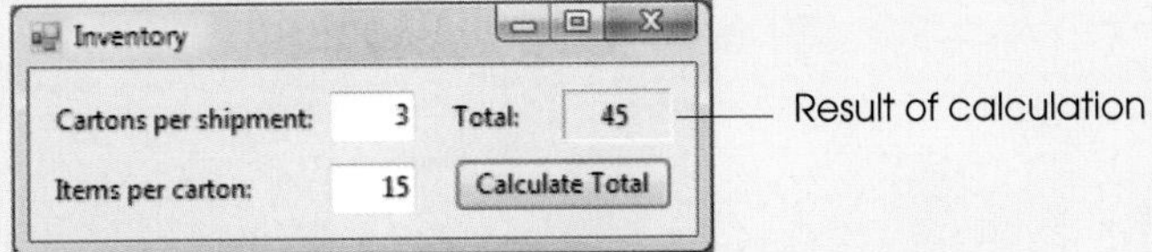

Figure 4.3 Result of clicking the **Calculate Total** `Button` in the **Inventory** application.

5. ***Closing the application.*** Close your running application by clicking its close box.

6. ***Closing the project.*** Select **File > Close Project**.

4.2 Constructing the Inventory Application

Now that you have test-driven the completed application, you begin creating your own version of the application. You'll create a new project that contains the Form on which you place the controls required for the **Inventory** application. Then you save the solution containing the Form to your working directory, C:\SimplyVB2008. [*Note:* We assume you have created this directory as per the instructions in the *Before You Begin* section. If you chose to use a different directory, save the solution to that directory.] Finally, the initial steps conclude with instructions for renaming the Form.

Creating a New Application

1. ***Creating the new project.*** To create a Windows application, select **File > New Project...**, to display the **New Project** dialog (Fig. 4.4). From the list of templates, select **Windows Forms Application**. Type Inventory in the **Name:** Textbox, and click the **OK** Button.

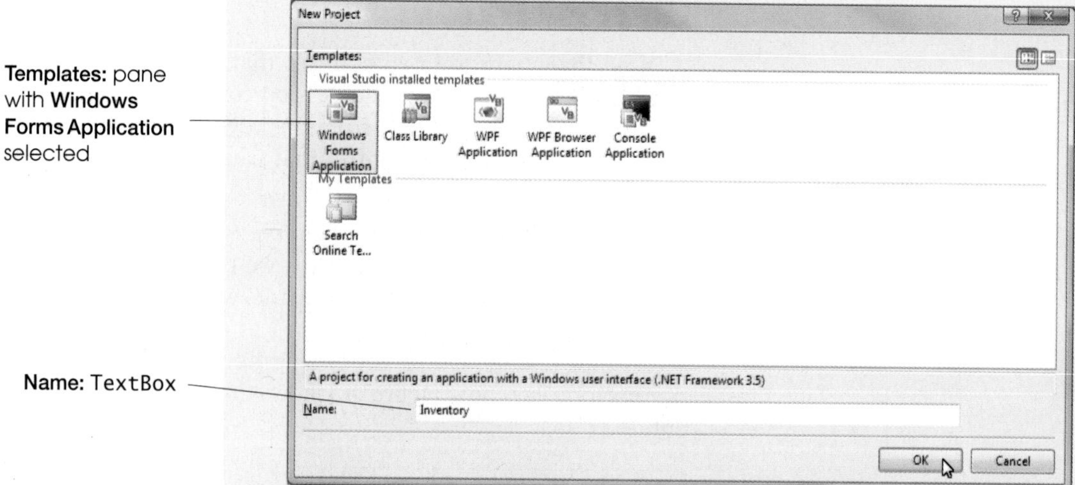

Figure 4.4 **New Project** dialog for creating new applications.

2. ***Saving the project to your working directory.*** Now that a blank workspace has loaded, select **File > Save All,** to display the **Save Project** dialog (Fig. 4.5). Click the **Browse...** Button, and the **Project Location** dialog appears (Fig. 4.6). Because you already created the SimplyVB2008 directory, navigate to C:\SimplyVB2008. Click **Select Folder** to select the directory and dismiss the dialog. The selected directory then appears in the **Location:** TextBox.

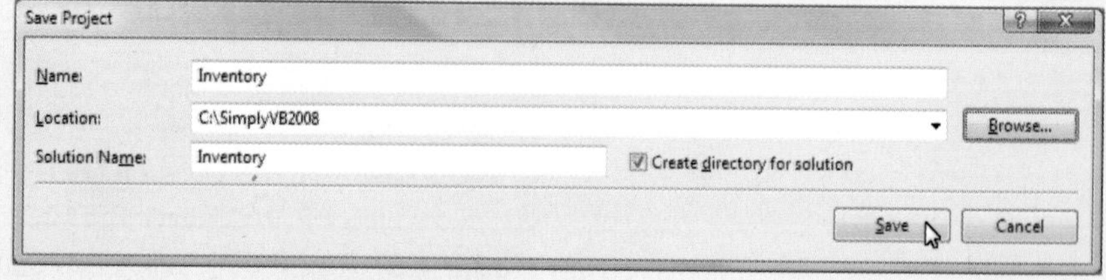

Figure 4.5 **Save Project** dialog for saving the newly created application

3. ***Viewing the Form.*** Click the **Save** Button (Fig. 4.5) to close the **Save Project** dialog. The IDE then returns to the application, containing a Form named **Form1** (Fig. 4.7). If the Form does not appear as in Fig. 4.7, select **View > Designer**. Then click the Form in the IDE to select it.

(cont.)

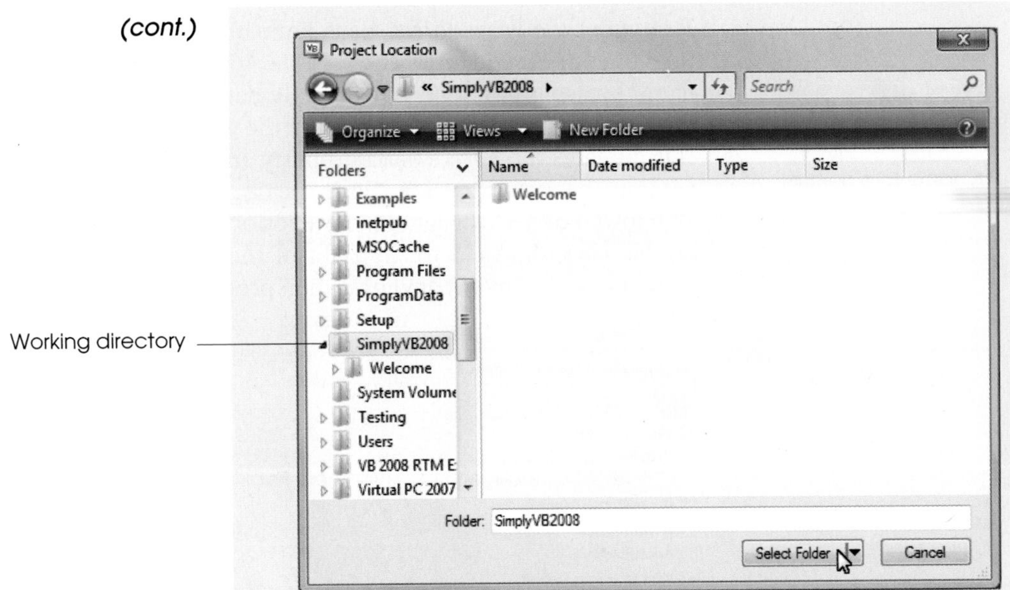

Figure 4.6 **Project Location** dialog used to specify the directory in which the project files reside.

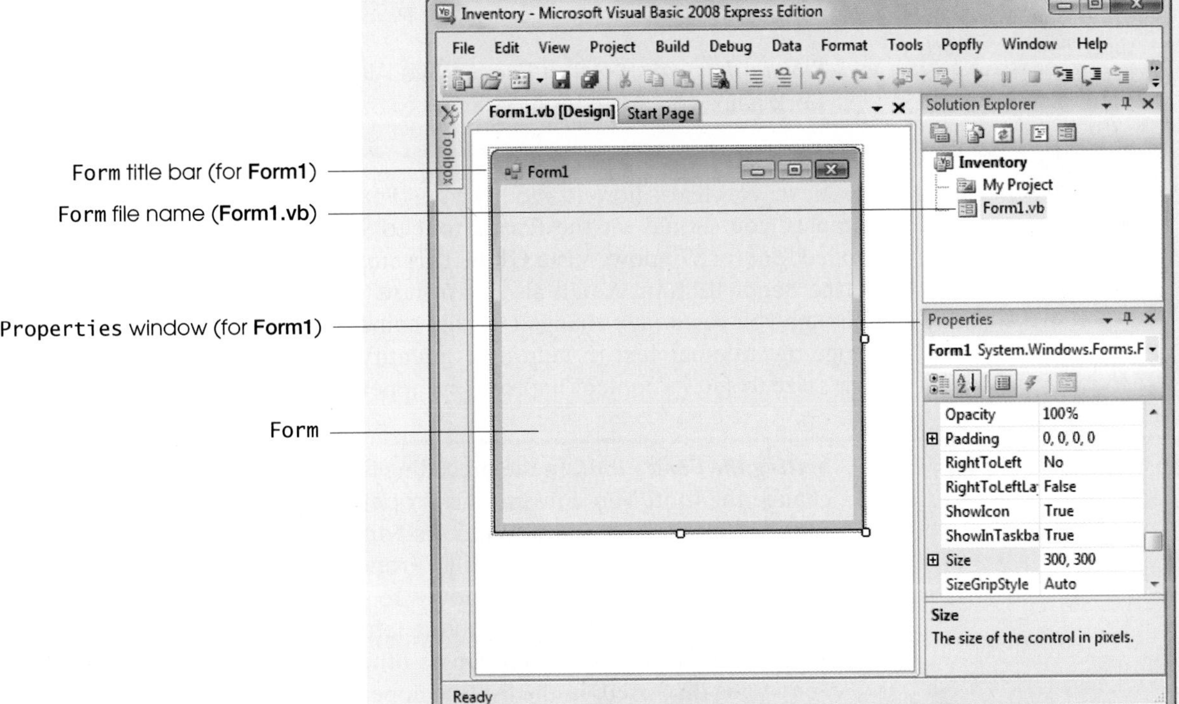

Figure 4.7 New Windows application in Visual Studio.

4. ***Renaming the* Form *file.*** It's a good practice to change the `Form`'s file name to a name more meaningful for your application. To do so, click the `Form`'s file name (`Form1.vb`) in the **Solution Explorer**. Then select `File Name` in the **Properties** window, and type `Inventory.vb` in the field to the right. Press *Enter* to update the file name. Unless otherwise noted, you need to press *Enter*, or select another property, for changes made in the **Properties** window to take effect.

(cont.)

Good Programming Practice

Change the Form name to a unique and meaningful name for easy identification.

5. ***Renaming the Form object.*** Each Form object needs a unique and meaningful name for easy identification. In the Visual Basic IDE, you set the Form's name by using the **Name** property. By default, the Visual Basic IDE names the Form Form1. When you change the Form's file name, the Visual Basic IDE updates the Form's Name property automatically to the name of the file without the .vb extension—in this case, Inventory. Click the Form in the Windows Form Designer. In the **Properties** window (Fig. 4.8), locate and double click the field to the right of the Name property, listed as (Name). Type the name InventoryForm, then press *Enter* to update the name.

Figure 4.8 Renaming a Form in the **Properties** windows.

Good Programming Practice

Use standard suffixes for names of objects (controls and Forms) so that you can easily tell them apart. Append the suffix Form to Form names. Capitalize the first letter of the Form name because Form is a class. Objects (such as controls) should begin with lowercase letters.

6. ***Saving the project.*** Select **File > Save All** to save your changes. Saving your work helps you avoid losing changes to the application.

GUI Design Tip

Change the Form's font to 9pt Segoe UI to be consistent with Microsoft's recommended font for Windows Vista.

Next, you learn how to modify your Form by setting its font. As in all our examples, you should set the Form's font to 9pt Segoe UI, the Microsoft-recommended font for Windows Vista GUIs. This ensures that controls added to the Form use the Segoe UI font. You'll also learn how to change the Form's title and size. Although you've already changed the file name to Inventory.vb, you still need to change the title-bar text to help users identify the Form's purpose. Changing the Form's size to suit its content improves its appearance.

Customizing the Form

1. ***Setting the Form's font.*** In the preceding tutorial, you used the **Font** dialog to change the font. You now use the **Properties** window to change the Form's font. Select the Form in the Windows Form Designer. If the **Properties** window is not already open, click the **Properties** icon in the IDE toolbar or select **View > Properties Window**. To change the Form's font to 9pt Segoe UI, click the plus box ⊞ to the left of the Font property in the **Properties** window (Fig. 4.9). This causes other properties related to the Form's Font to be displayed. In the list that appears, select the font's Name property, then click the down arrow to the right of the property value. In the list that appears, select Segoe UI. [*Note*: The list may contain fonts other than those shown in Fig. 4.9, depending on the fonts that are installed on your system.] Then set the font's Size property to 9.

   Notice that several properties, such as Font, have a plus box ⊞ next to the property name to indicate that additional properties are available for this node. For example, when you expand the Font node, you'll see that the Name, Size and Bold properties of a Font each have their own listings in the **Properties** window.

(cont.)

Click plus box to display `Font` properties

`Name` property

Click down arrow to display drop-down list

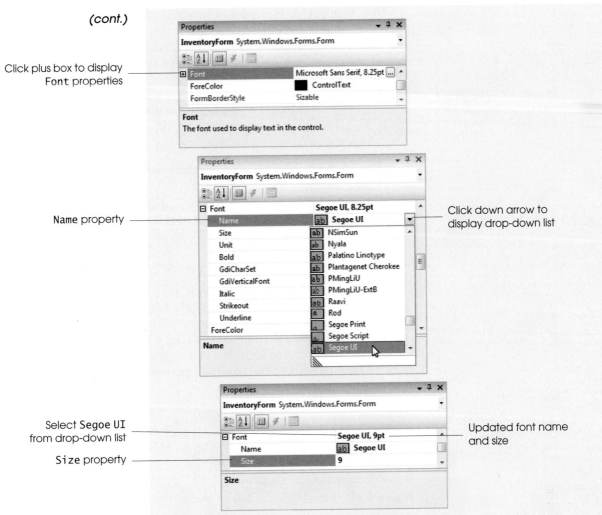

Select `Segoe UI` from drop-down list

`Size` property

Updated font name and size

Figure 4.9 Setting a `Form`'s font to 9pt `Segoe UI`.

GUI Design Tip

Changing the `Form`'s title allows users to identify the `Form`'s purpose.

GUI Design Tip

`Form` titles should use book-title capitalization.

2. ***Setting the text in the Form's title bar.*** The text in the `Form`'s title bar is determined by the `Form`'s **`Text`** property. To display the `Form`'s properties in the **Properties** window, click the `Form` in the Windows `Form` Designer. Double click the field to the right of the `Text` property in the **Properties** window, type `Inventory` and press *Enter*. `Form` titles should use book-title capitalization. **Book-title capitalization** is a style that capitalizes the first letter of each significant word in the text and does not end with any punctuation (for example, *Capitalization in a Book Title*). The updated title bar is shown in Fig. 4.10.

Title-bar text set to **Inventory**

Figure 4.10 Resized `Form` displaying new title-bar text.

3. ***Resizing the Form.*** Double click the field to the right of the `Size` property in the **Properties** window, then enter `320, 112` and press *Enter* (Fig. 4.10). Note that the `Form` is now the same size as the completed application you test-drove at the beginning of the tutorial.
4. ***Saving the project.*** Select **File > Save All** to save your changes.

Now that you've created and modified the Form, you'll add controls to the GUI. Labels describe the purpose of controls on the Form and can be used to display results of calculations. In the next section, you learn how to add Label controls and set each Label's name, text and position on the Form.

SELF-REVIEW

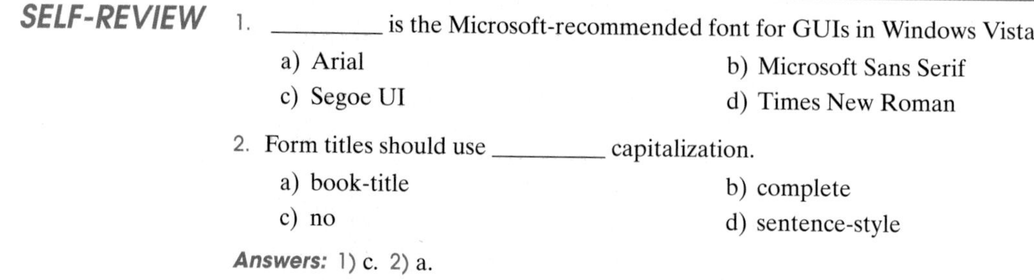

1. ________ is the Microsoft-recommended font for GUIs in Windows Vista.
   a) Arial b) Microsoft Sans Serif
   c) Segoe UI d) Times New Roman

2. Form titles should use ________ capitalization.
   a) book-title b) complete
   c) no d) sentence-style

Answers: 1) c. 2) a.

4.3 Adding Labels to the Inventory Application

Although you might not have noticed it, there are four Labels in this application. You can easily recognize three of the Labels from the application you designed in Tutorial 3. The fourth Label, however, has a border and contains no text until the user clicks the **Calculate Total** Button (Fig. 4.11). As the control's name indicates, Labels are often used to identify other controls on the Form. **Descriptive Labels** help the user understand each control's purpose and **output Labels** are used to display program output.

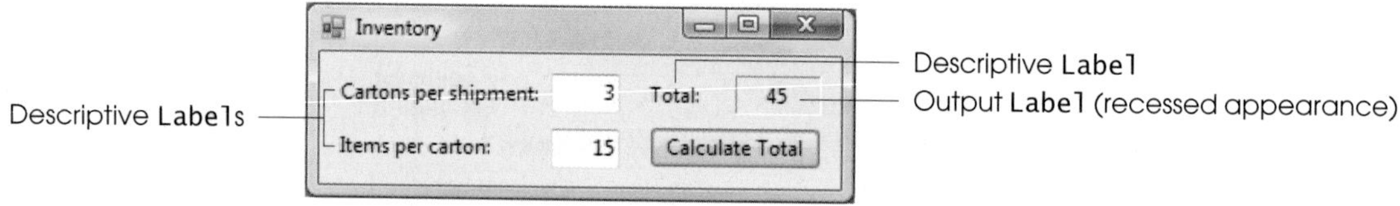

Figure 4.11 Labels used in the **Inventory** application.

Adding Labels to the Form

1. ***Adding a Label control to the Form.*** Click the **All Windows Forms** group in the **Toolbox**. Then, double click the Label control in the **Toolbox** to place a Label on the Form (Fig. 4.12).

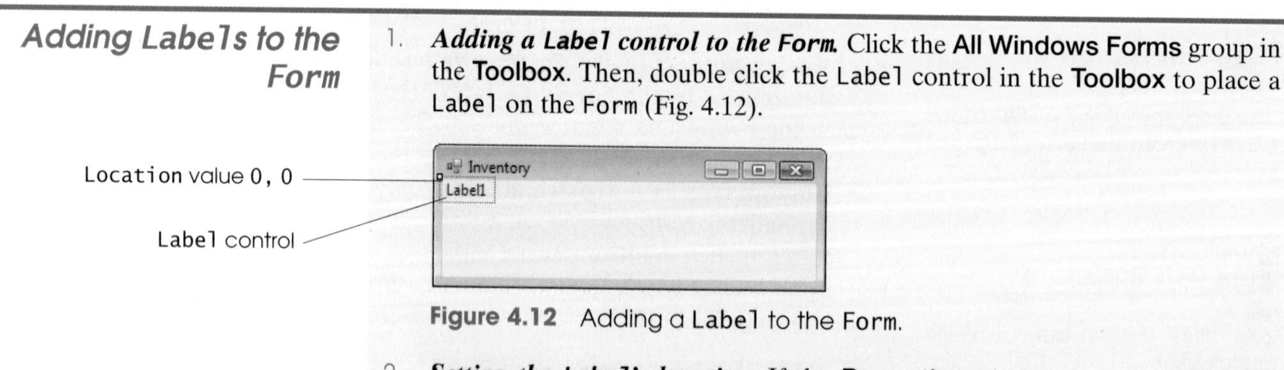

Figure 4.12 Adding a Label to the Form.

2. ***Setting the Label's location.*** If the **Properties** window is not open, select **View > Properties Window**. In the **Properties** window, set the Label's Location property to 9, 15. Using these numbers provides adequate space between the Label and the edges of the Form. As you learned in the preceding tutorial, you can drag a control from the **Toolbox** onto the Form. You can also fine tune a control's position by selecting it and using the arrow keys to move it.

GUI Design Tip

Leave space between the edges of the Form and its controls.

(cont.)

GUI Design Tip

The `Location` property can be used to specify a control's precise position on the `Form`.

The `Label`'s **`Location`** property specifies the position of the upper-left corner of the control on the `Form`. The IDE assigns the value `0, 0` to the top-left corner of the `Form`, not including the title bar (Fig. 4.12). A control's `Location` property is set according to its distance from that point on the `Form`. As the first number (the *x*-coordinate) of the `Location` property increases, the control moves to the right. As the second number (the *y*-coordinate) of the `Location` property increases, the control moves toward the bottom of the `Form`. In this case, the value `9, 15` indicates that the `Label` is placed 9 pixels to the right of the `Form`'s top-left corner and 15 pixels down from the top-left corner. The `Location 16, 48` would indicate that the `Label` is placed 16 pixels to the right of the top-left corner and 48 pixels down from the top-left corner.

Good Programming Practice

Append the `Label` suffix to all `Label` control names.

3. ***Setting the Label's Name and Text properties.*** In the **Properties** window, double click the field to the right of the `Text` property, then type `Cartons per shipment:`. Set the `Name` property to `cartonsLabel`.

   When entering values for a `Label`'s `Text` property, you should use sentence-style capitalization. **Sentence-style capitalization** means that you capitalize the first letter of the first word in the text. Every other letter in the text is lowercase unless it is the first letter of a proper noun (for example, *Deitel*).

GUI Design Tip

A `Label` used to describe the purpose of a control should use sentence-style capitalization and end with a colon. This is called a descriptive `Label`.

4. ***Modifying the Label's text alignment.*** Select the `TextAlign` property in the **Properties** window; then, in the field to the right, click the down arrow (Fig. 4.13). Property `TextAlign` sets the alignment of text within a control such as a `Label`. Clicking the down arrow opens a window in which you can select the alignment of the text in the `Label` (Fig. 4.13). In this window, select the middle-left rectangle, which indicates that the `Label`'s text aligns to the middle, vertically, and to the left, horizontally, in the control. The value of the property changes to `MiddleLeft`. Figure 4.14 displays the `Label` after you set its properties.

GUI Design Tip

The `TextAlign` property of a descriptive `Label` should be set to `MiddleLeft`. This ensures that text within groups of `Label`s align.

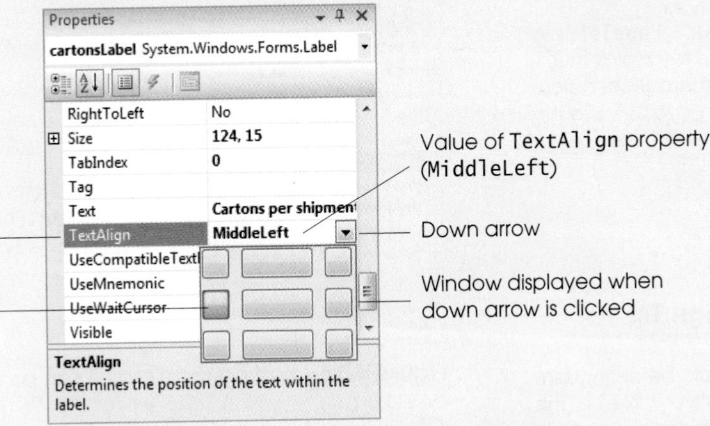

Figure 4.13 Changing the `TextAlign` property of a `Label`.

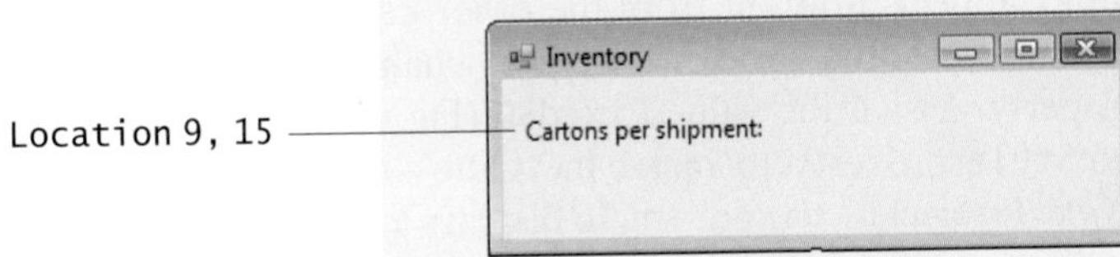

Figure 4.14 GUI after the `Label` has been customized.

5. ***Saving the project.*** Select **File > Save All** to save your changes.

Now you'll add the remaining Labels to the Form. They help the user understand what inputs to provide and interpret the application's output. These Labels identify the controls that you'll add to the Form later.

Placing Additional Labels on the Form

GUI Design Tip

Align the left or right sides of a group of descriptive Labels if the Labels are arranged vertically.

1. ***Adding a second descriptive Label.*** Double click the Label control on the **Toolbox** to add a second Label. Set the Label's Location property to 9, 46. Set the Label's Text property to Items per carton:, and change the Name property of this Label to itemsLabel. Then set the Label's TextAlign property to MiddleLeft.

2. ***Adding a third descriptive Label.*** Double click the Label control on the **Toolbox** to add a third Label. Set the Label's Location property to 190, 15. Set the Label's Text property to Total: and change the Name property of this Label to totalLabel. Then set the Label's TextAlign property to MiddleLeft.

GUI Design Tip

Use a descriptive Label to identify an output Label.

GUI Design Tip

Place an application's output below and/or to the right of the Form's input controls.

3. ***Adding an output Label.*** To add the fourth Label, double click the Label control on the **Toolbox**. Set the Label's AutoSize property to False. Then, set the Label's Size property to 50, 23 and the Label's Location property to 243, 11. Note that these settings cause the text in the output label to align with the text in its corresponding descriptive label. Then name this Label totalResultLabel. Set the Label's TextAlign property to MiddleCenter. For the previous Labels, you set this property to MiddleLeft. To select value MiddleCenter, follow the same actions as in *Step 2*, but select the center rectangle shown in Fig. 4.15. You should use MiddleCenter text alignment to display results of calculations because it distinguishes the value in the output Label from the values in the descriptive Labels (whose TextAlign property is set to MiddleLeft).

GUI Design Tip

If several output Labels are arranged vertically to display numbers used in a mathematical calculation (such as in an invoice), use the MiddleRight value for the TextAlign property.

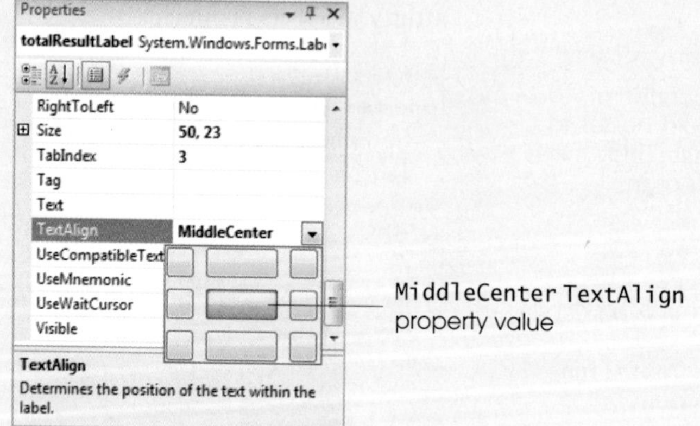

Figure 4.15 Setting the TextAlign property to MiddleCenter.

GUI Design Tip

Output Labels should be distinguishable from descriptive Labels. This can be done by setting the BorderStyle property of an output Label to Fixed3D.

4. ***Changing a Label's BorderStyle property.*** The totalResultLabel displays the result of the application's calculation; therefore, you should make this Label appear different from the other Labels. To do this, you'll change the appearance of the Label's border by changing the value of the **BorderStyle** property. Assign the value Fixed3D (Fig. 4.16) to totalResultLabel's BorderStyle property to make the Label seem three-dimensional (Fig. 4.17). [*Note*: If selected, FixedSingle displays a single dark line as a border.]

Good Programming Practice

Clear the an output Label's value initially or provide a default value. When the application performs the calculation for that value, the Label's Text property should be updated to the new value. You'll learn how to do this in the next tutorial.

(cont.)

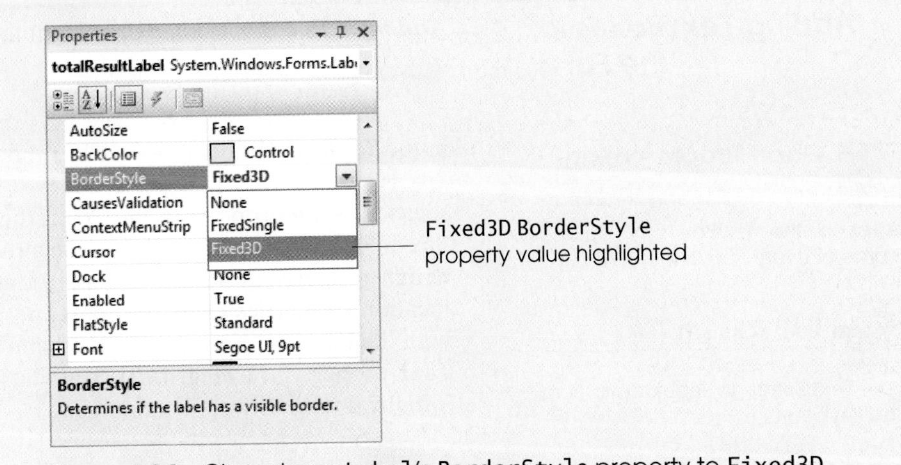

Figure 4.16 Changing a `Label`'s `BorderStyle` property to `Fixed3D`.

5. ***Clearing a `Label`'s `Text` property.*** When a `Label` is added to a `Form`, the `Text` property is assigned the default name of the `Label`. In this case, you should clear the text of the `Label`, because you will not be adding meaningful text to `totalResultLabel` until later. To do this, delete the text to the right of the `Text` property in the **Properties** window and press *Enter*. Figure 4.17 displays the GUI with all `Label`s added.

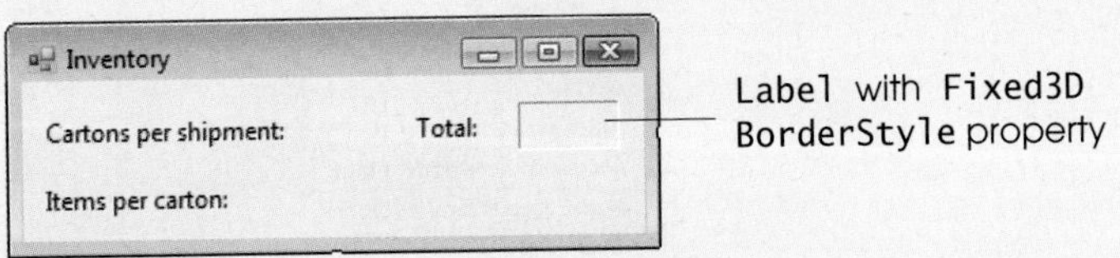

Figure 4.17 GUI with all `Label`s added.

6. ***Saving the project.*** Select **File > Save All** to save your changes.

SELF-REVIEW

1. The value ________ for the `Location` property indicates the top-left corner (not including the title bar) of the `Form`.
   a) `1, 1` b) `0, 0`
   c) `1, 0` d) `0, 1`

2. An output `Label` should ________.
   a) be distinguishable from other `Label`s
   b) initially have an empty `Text` property or a default value (e.g., 0)
   c) use `Fixed3D` for the `BorderStyle` property
   d) All of the above

Answers: 1) b. 2) d.

4.4 Adding TextBoxes and a Button to the Form

The **Inventory** application requires user input to calculate the total number of textbooks that have arrived per shipment. Specifically, the user types in the number of cartons and the fixed number of books per carton. Because data of this type is entered from the keyboard, you use a `TextBox` control. Next, you'll learn how to add `TextBox`es to your `Form` and set their properties. Then, you'll add a `Button` control to complete your GUI.

Adding TextBoxes to the Form

Good Programming Practice

Append the TextBox suffix to the name of every TextBox control.

GUI Design Tip

Use TextBoxes to input data from the keyboard.

1. ***Adding a TextBox to the Form.*** Double click the TextBox control,

   abl TextBox

   in the **Toolbox** to add a TextBox to the Form. Setting properties for a TextBox is similar to setting the properties for a Label. To name the TextBox, select its Name property in the **Properties** window, and enter cartonsTextBox in the field to the right of the property (Fig. 4.18). Set the TextBox's Width property to 40 and Location property to 136, 12. These size and location properties cause the baseline of the text in the TextBox to align with the baseline of the text in the Label that describes it. Set the TextBox's Text property to 0 (Fig. 4.19). This causes the value for your TextBox to be initially 0 when the application runs.

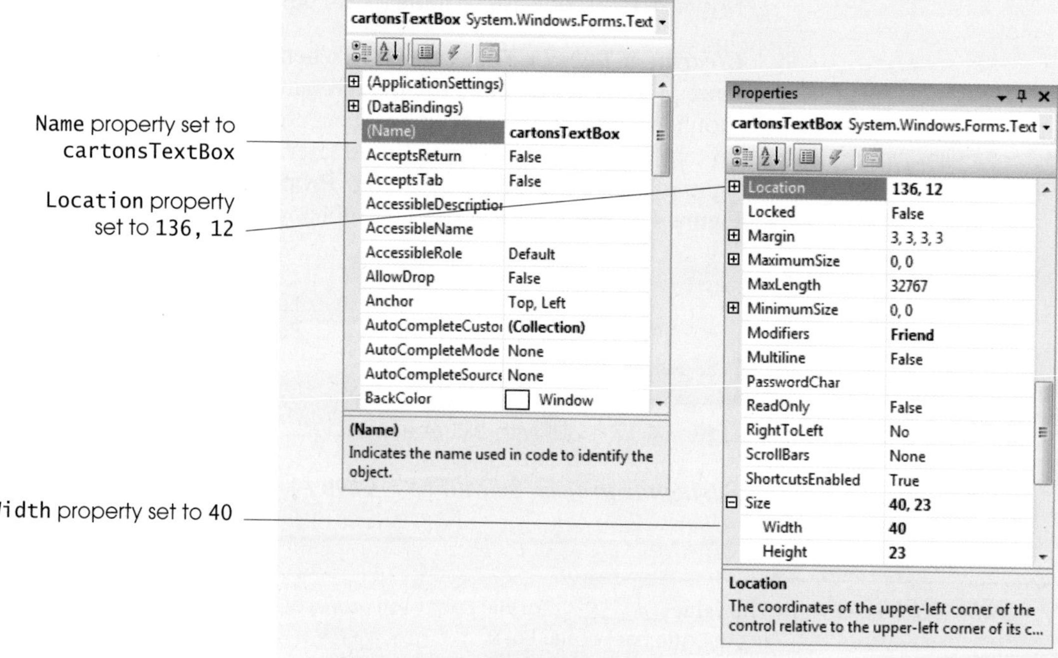

Figure 4.18 **Properties** window for the cartonsTextBox TextBox.

GUI Design Tip

Each TextBox should have a descriptive Label indicating the input expected from the user.

2. ***Changing the TextAlign property of a TextBox.*** Change cartonsTextBox's TextAlign property to Right. Note that, when you click the down arrow to the right of this property, the window in Fig. 4.13 does not appear. This is because TextBoxes have fewer TextAlign options, which are displayed simply as a list. Select Right from this list (Fig. 4.19). Generally, when multiple TextBoxes used for numeric input are stacked vertically, their text should be right aligned.

GUI Design Tip

Place each descriptive Label either above or to the left of the control (for instance, a TextBox) that it identifies.

3. ***Adding a second TextBox to the Form.*** Double click the TextBox control in the **Toolbox**. Name the TextBox itemsTextBox. Set the Width property to 40 and the Location property to 136, 43. These settings ensure that the left sides of the two TextBoxes align. The settings also align the baseline of the text in the TextBox and the baseline of the text in the Label that describes it. Set the Text property to 0 and the TextAlign property to Right. Figure 4.20 shows the Form after the TextBoxes have been added and their properties have been set.

(cont.)

Notice that many of the second `TextBox`'s properties match those of the first `TextBox` (e.g., `Width`, `Text` and `TextAlign`). When creating multiple controls of the same type with many of the same property values, it's often easier to copy the original control. To do this, select the control you wish to copy and press *Ctrl* + *C*. Then press *Ctrl* + *V* to paste it onto the `Form`. Reposition the new control and adjust its properties as needed.

GUI Design Tip

Make `TextBoxes` wide enough for their expected inputs.

GUI Design Tip

A descriptive `Label` and the control it identifies should be aligned on the left if they are arranged vertically.

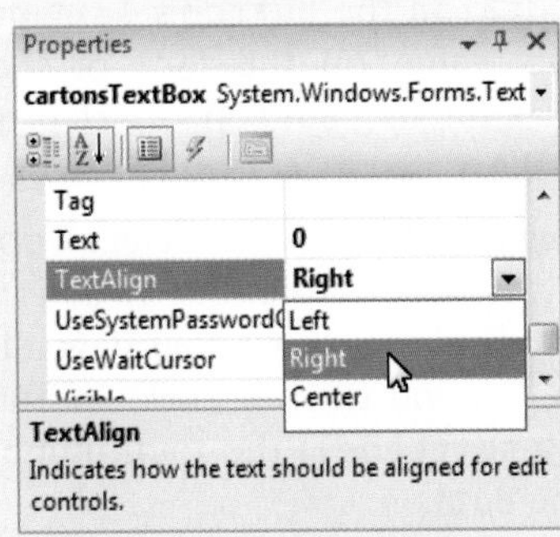

Figure 4.19 Selecting value `Right` of the `TextAlign` property of a `TextBox` control.

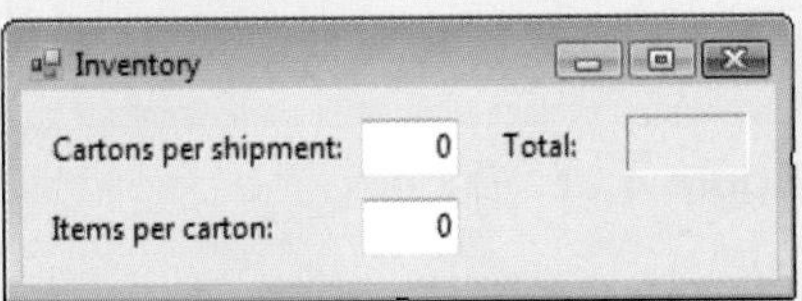

Figure 4.20 GUI after `TextBoxes` have been added and modified.

4. ***Saving the project.*** Select **File > Save All** to save your changes.

GUI Design Tip

The text in a descriptive `Label` and the text in the control it identifies should be aligned on the bottom if they are arranged horizontally.

Note that your controls align horizontally and vertically. In general, you should place each descriptive `Label` above or to the left of the control it describes (for instance, a `TextBox`). If you are arranging your controls on the same line, the text of the descriptive `Label` and the text of the control it describes should be aligned. However, if you arrange your controls vertically, the `Label` should be placed above the control it describes and the left sides of the controls should align. Following these simple guidelines will make your applications more appealing visually and easier to use by making the controls on the application less crowded.

Now that the user can enter data using a `TextBox`, you need a way for the user to command the application to perform the calculation and display the result. The most common way for a user to do this is by clicking a `Button`. The following box explains how to add a `Button` to the **Inventory** application.

Adding a `Button` to the Form

GUI Design Tip

`Buttons` are often stacked downward from the top right of a `Form` or arranged on the same line starting from the bottom right of a `Form`.

1. ***Adding a `Button` to the Form.*** Add a `Button` to the `Form` by double clicking the `Button` control,

   Button

   in the **Toolbox**. Setting the properties for a `Button` is similar to setting the properties for a `Label` or a `TextBox`. Enter `calculateButton` in the `Button`'s `Name` property.

(cont.)

Set the Button's Size to 100, 24 and Location to 193, 42. Note that these settings cause the left and right sides of the Button to align with the Labels above it (Fig. 4.21). You also can accomplish this by aligning the left side of the Button with the Label above it. Then drag the sizing handle on the right side of the Button until the blue snapline appears to indicate that the Button is aligned with the right side of the Label above it. Enter Calculate Total in the Button's Text property. A Button's Text property displays its value on the face of the Button. You should use book-title capitalization in a Button's Text property. When labeling Buttons, keep the text as short as possible while still clearly indicating the Button's function.

Good Programming Practice

Append the Button suffix to Button control names.

2. ***Running the application.*** Select **Debug > Start Debugging** to run the application (Fig. 4.21). Note that no action occurs if you click the **Calculate Total** Button. This is because you haven't written code that tells the application how to respond to your click. In Tutorial 5, you'll write code to display (in totalResultLabel) the total number of books in the shipment when you click the Button.

GUI Design Tip

As you drag controls, the IDE displays blue and purple lines called snaplines. The blue lines help you position controls relative to one another. The purple lines help you position controls relative to the control text.

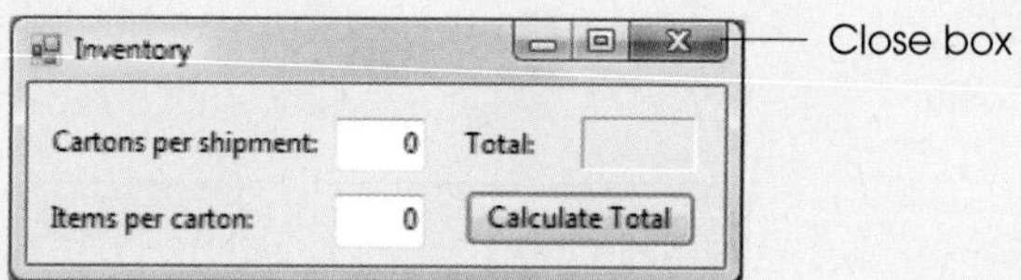

Figure 4.21 Running the application after completing its design.

GUI Design Tip

Buttons are labeled using their Text property. These labels should use book-title capitalization and be as short as possible while still being meaningful to the user.

3. ***Closing the application.*** Close your running application by clicking its close box.

4. ***Closing the IDE.*** Close the Visual Basic IDE by clicking its close box.

SELF-REVIEW

1. A Button's ________ property sets the text on the face of the Button.

   a) Name b) Text
   c) Title d) Face

2. Buttons are often ________ of the Form.

   a) on the same line, from the bottom right b) aligned with the title bar text
   c) stacked from the top left d) Either a or c

Answers: 1) b. 2) d.

4.5 Wrap-Up

In this tutorial, you began constructing your **Inventory** application by designing its graphical user interface. You learned how to use Labels to describe controls and how to set a Label's TextAlign and BorderStyle properties. You used these properties to distinguish between descriptive and output Labels.

After labeling your Form, you added TextBoxes to allow users to input data from the keyboard. Finally, you added a Button to the **Inventory** application, allowing a user to signal the application to perform an action (in this case, to multiply two numbers and display the result). While adding controls to the Form, you also learned some GUI design tips to help you create appealing and intuitive graphical user interfaces.

The next tutorial teaches you to program code in Visual Basic that runs when the user clicks the **Calculate Total** Button. When the Button is clicked, the application receives a signal called an event. You'll learn how to program your application to respond to that event by performing the multiplication calculation and displaying the result.

SKILLS SUMMARY

Creating a New Project

- Select **File > New Project...** to create a project.
- In the **New Project** dialog, select the **Windows Forms Application** and provide a descriptive name in the **Name:** TextBox.
- Select **File > Save All** to save a project to your working directory (C:\SimplyVB2008) by selecting it from the **Project Location** dialog.

Setting the Application's Font to Segoe UI

- Select Segoe UI from the Font Name property ComboBox in the Form's **Properties** window. Set the Font Size property to 9.

Creating a Descriptive Label

- Add a Label to your Form, then change the TextAlign property to MiddleLeft.
- Use sentence-style capitalization in the label and end the label's text with a colon (:).

Creating an Output Label

- Add a Label to your Form, and change the BorderStyle property to Fixed3D and the TextAlign property to MiddleCenter.

Enabling User Input from the Keyboard

- Add a TextBox control to your Form.

Signaling That the Application Should Perform an Action

- Add a Button to the Form, and write program code to perform that action. (You'll learn how to add program code in Tutorial 5.)

KEY TERMS

book-title capitalization—A style that capitalizes the first letter of the each word in the text (for example, **Calculate Total**).

BorderStyle property—Specifies the appearance of a Label's border, which allows you to distinguish one control from another visually. The BorderStyle property can be set to None (no border), FixedSingle (a single dark line as a border), or Fixed3D (giving the Label a "sunken" appearance).

Button control—When clicked, commands the application to perform an action.

descriptive Label—A Label used to describe another control on the Form. This helps users understand a control's purpose.

Location property—Specifies the location (*x*- and *y*-coordinates) of the upper-left corner of a control. This property is used to place a control on the Form precisely.

Name property—Assigns a unique and meaningful name to a control for easy identification.

output Label—A Label used to display results.

sentence-style capitalization—A style that capitalizes the first letter of the first word in the text. Every other letter in the text is lowercase, unless it is the first letter of a proper noun (for example, **Cartons per shipment**).

Segoe UI font—The Microsoft-recommended font for use in Windows Vista applications.

Text property—Sets the text displayed on a control.

TextBox control—Retrieves user input from the keyboard.

GUI DESIGN GUIDELINES

Overall Design

- Leave space between the edges of the Form and its controls.
- Although you can drag a Label control to a location on the Form, the Location property can be used to specify a precise position.
- Place an application's output below and/or to the right of the Form's input controls.

- As you drag controls, the IDE displays blue and purple lines called snaplines. The blue lines help you position controls relative to one another. The purple lines help you position controls relative to the control text.

Buttons

- Buttons are labeled using their Text property. These labels should use book-title capitalization and be as short as possible while still being meaningful to the user.
- Buttons should be stacked downward from the top right of a Form or arranged on the same line starting from the bottom right of a Form.

Forms

- Changing the Form's title allows users to identify the Form's purpose.
- Form titles should use book-title capitalization.
- Change the Form font to 9pt Segoe UI to be consistent with Microsoft's recommended font for Windows Vista.

Labels

- A Label used to describe the purpose of a control should use sentence-style capitalization and end with a colon. These types of Labels are called descriptive Labels.
- The TextAlign property of a descriptive Label should be set to MiddleLeft. This ensures that text within groups of Labels aligns.
- Place each descriptive Label above or to the left of the control (for instance, a TextBox) that it identifies.
- Align the left or right sides of a group of descriptive Labels if the Labels are arranged vertically.
- Use a descriptive Label to identify an output Label.
- Output Labels should be distinguishable from descriptive Labels. This can be done by setting the BorderStyle property of an output Label to Fixed3D.
- If several output Labels are arranged vertically to display numbers used in a mathematical calculation (such as in an invoice), use the MiddleRight value for the TextAlign property.
- A descriptive Label and the control it identifies should be aligned on the left if they are arranged vertically.
- The text in a descriptive Label and the text in the control it identifies should be aligned if they are arranged horizontally.

TextBoxes

- Use TextBoxes to input data from the keyboard.
- Each TextBox should have a descriptive Label indicating the input expected from the user.
- Make TextBoxes wide enough for their expected inputs.

CONTROLS, EVENTS, PROPERTIES & METHODS

Button [ab] Button When clicked, commands the application to perform an action.

- *In action*

Calculate Total

- *Properties*

Location—Specifies the location of the Button on the Form relative to the Form's top-left corner.

Name—Specifies the name used to identify the Button. The name should include the Button suffix.

Size—Specifies the width and height (in pixels) of the Button.

Text—Specifies the text displayed on the Button.

`Form` Represents the main window of a GUI application.

- ***In action***

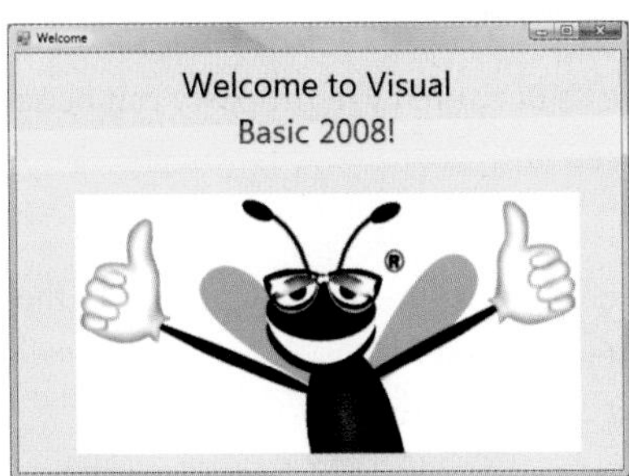

- ***Properties***

  `BackColor`—Specifies the background color of the `Form`.

  `Font`—Specifies the font name, style and size of any displayed text in the `Form`. The `Form`'s controls use this font by default.

  `Name`—Specifies the name used to identify the `Form`. The name should include the `Form` suffix.

  `Size`—Specifies the width and height (in pixels) of the `Form`.

  `Text`—Specifies the text displayed in the title bar of a `Form`.

`Label` A Label This control displays text that the user cannot modify.

- ***In action***

- ***Properties***

  `AutoSize`—Allows for automatic resizing of the `Label` to fit its contents.

  `BorderStyle`—Specifies the appearance of the `Label`'s border.

  `Font`—Specifies the font name, style and size of the text displayed in the `Label`.

  `Location`—Specifies the location of the `Label` on the `Form` relative to the `Form`'s top-left corner.

  `Name`—Specifies the name used to identify the `Label`. The name should include the `Label` suffix.

  `Size`—Specifies the width and height (in pixels) of the `Label`.

  `Text`—Specifies the text displayed in the `Label`.

  `TextAlign`—Determines how the text is aligned within the `Label`.

`TextBox` abl TextBox This control allows the user to input data from the keyboard.

- ***In action***

- ***Properties***

  `Location`—Specifies the location of the `TextBox` on the `Form` relative to the `Form`'s top-left corner.

  `Name`—Specifies the name used to identify the `TextBox`. The name should include the `TextBox` suffix.

  `Size`—Specifies the width and height (in pixels) of the `TextBox`.

  `Text`—Specifies the initial text displayed in the `TextBox`.

  `TextAlign`—Specifies how the text is aligned within the `TextBox`.

  `Width`—Specifies the width (in pixels) of the `TextBox`.

MULTIPLE-CHOICE QUESTIONS

4.1 A new Windows application is created by selecting ________ from the **File** menu.

a) **New Program** b) **New File...**
c) **New Project...** d) **New Application**

4.2 A Label's BorderStyle property can be set to ________.

a) Fixed3D b) Single
c) 3D d) All of the above

4.3 When creating a Label, you can specify the Label's ________.

a) text alignment b) border style
c) size d) All of the above

4.4 Changing the value stored in the ________ property changes the name of the Form's file.

a) Name b) File
c) File Name d) Full Path

4.5 ________ should be appended as a suffix to all TextBox names.

a) Text Box b) Text
c) Box d) TextBox

4.6 A(n) ________ helps the user understand a control's purpose.

a) Button b) descriptive Label
c) output Label d) title bar

4.7 A ________ is a control in which the user can enter data from a keyboard.

a) Button b) TextBox
c) Label d) PictureBox

4.8 A descriptive Label uses ________.

a) sentence-style capitalization b) book-title capitalization
c) a colon at the end of its text d) Both a and c

4.9 You should use the ________ font in your Windows Vista applications.

a) Segoe UI b) MS Sans Serif
c) Times d) Palatino

4.10 ________ should be appended as a suffix to all Button names.

a) Press b) Label
c) Click d) Button

EXERCISES

At the end of each tutorial, you'll find a summary of new GUI design tips listed in the GUI Design Guidelines section. A cumulative list of GUI design guidelines, organized by control, appears in Appendix C. In these exercises, you'll find Visual Basic Forms that do not follow the GUI design guidelines presented in this tutorial. For each exercise, modify control properties so that your end result is consistent with the guidelines presented in the tutorial. Note that these applications do not provide any functionality.

4.11 ***(Address Book GUI)*** In this exercise, you apply the GUI design guidelines you've learned to a graphical user interface for an address book (Fig. 4.22).

a) ***Copying the template to your working directory.*** Copy the directory C:\Examples\Tutorial04\Exercises\AddressBook to your C:\SimplyVB2008 directory.

b) ***Opening the application's template file.*** Double click AddressBook.sln in the AddressBook directory to open the application.

c) ***Applying GUI design guidelines.*** Rearrange the controls and modify properties so that the GUI conforms to the design guidelines you've learned.

d) ***Saving the project.*** Select **File > Save All** to save your changes.

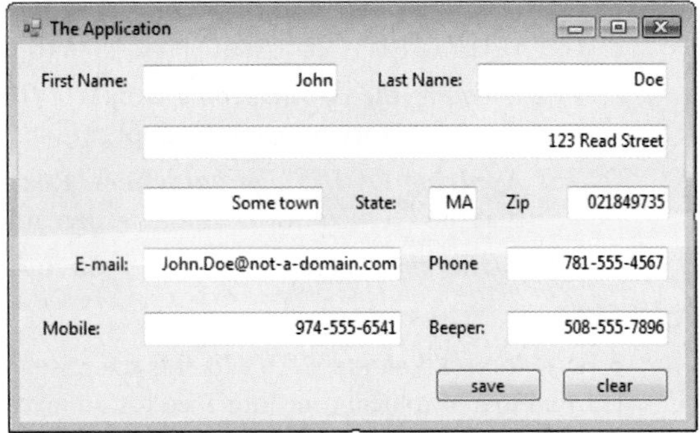

Figure 4.22 **Address Book** application without GUI design guidelines applied.

4.12 ***(Mortgage Calculator GUI)*** In this exercise, you apply the GUI design guidelines you've learned to a graphical user interface for a mortgage calculator (Fig. 4.23).

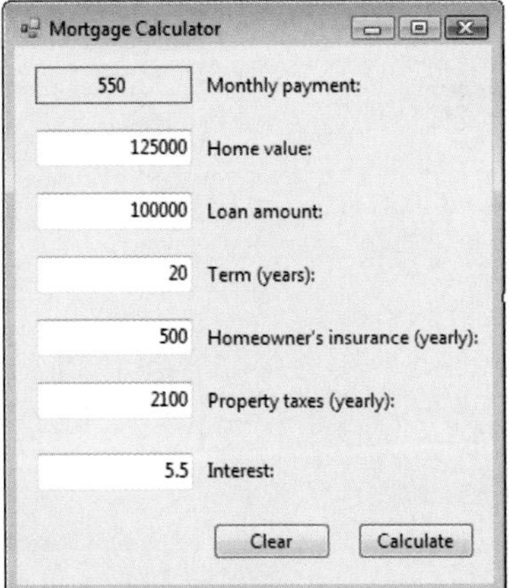

Figure 4.23 **Mortgage Calculator** application without GUI design guidelines applied.

a) ***Copying the template to your working directory.*** Copy the directory `C:\Examples\Tutorial04\Exercises\MortgageCalculator` to your `C:\SimplyVB2008` directory.

b) ***Opening the application's template file.*** Double click `MortgageCalculator.sln` in the `MortgageCalculator` directory to open the application.

c) ***Applying GUI design guidelines.*** Rearrange the controls and modify properties so that the GUI conforms to the design guidelines you've learned.

d) ***Saving the project.*** Select **File > Save All** to save your changes.

4.13 ***(Password GUI)*** In this exercise, you apply the GUI design guidelines you've learned to a graphical user interface for a password-protected message application (Fig. 4.24).

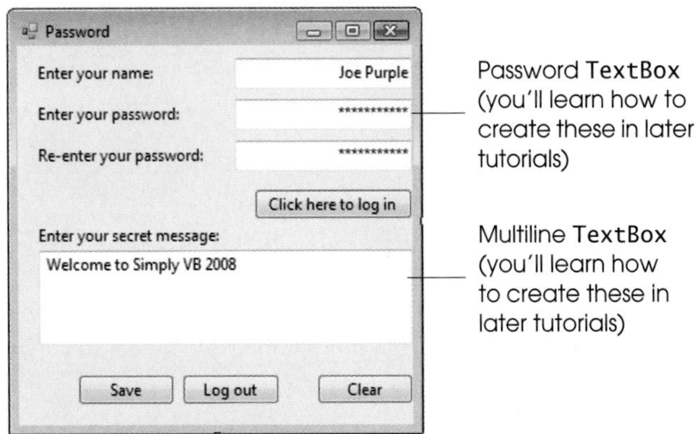

Figure 4.24 **Password** application without GUI design guidelines applied.

a) ***Copying the template to your working directory.*** Copy the directory `C:\Examples\Tutorial04\Exercises\Password` to your `C:\SimplyVB2008` directory.

b) ***Opening the application's template file.*** Double click `Password.sln` in the `Password` directory to open the application.

c) ***Applying GUI design guidelines.*** Rearrange the controls and modify properties so that the GUI conforms to the design guidelines you've learned.

d) ***Saving the project.*** Select **File > Save All** to save your changes.

Programming Challenge

4.14 ***(Monitor Invoice GUI)*** In this exercise, you apply the GUI design guidelines you've learned to a graphical user interface for an invoice application (Fig. 4.25).

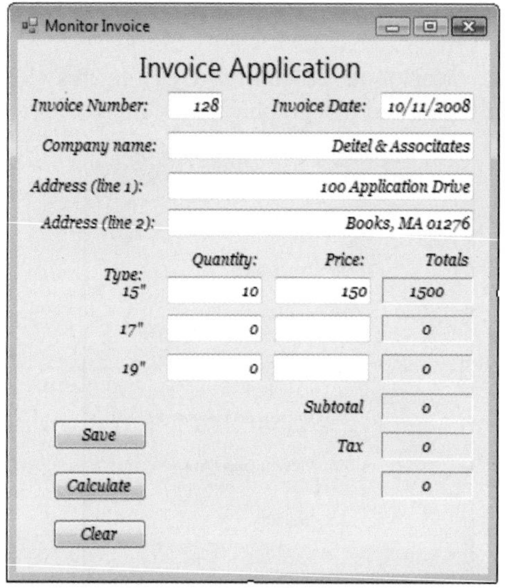

Figure 4.25 **Invoice** application without GUI design guidelines applied.

a) ***Copying the template to your working directory.*** Copy the directory `C:\Examples\Tutorial04\Exercises\MonitorInvoice` to your `C:\SimplyVB2008` directory.

b) ***Opening the application's template file.*** Double click the `MonitorInvoice.sln` file to open the application.

c) ***Applying GUI design guidelines.*** Rearrange the controls and modify properties so that the GUI conforms to the design guidelines you've learned.

d) ***Saving the project.*** Select **File > Save All** to save your changes.

TUTORIAL 5

Completing the Inventory Application

Introducing Programming

Objectives

In this tutorial, you learn to:

- Add an event handler for a `Button` control.
- Insert code into an event handler.
- Access a property's value by using Visual Basic code.
- Use the assignment and multiplication operators.
- Use the Visual Basic IDE to fix compilation errors.

Outline

This tutorial introduces fundamentals of programming to create an application with which users can interact. You'll learn these concepts as you add functionality (with Visual Basic code) to the **Inventory** application you designed in Tutorial 4. The term **functionality** describes the actions an application can execute. In this tutorial, you'll examine GUI **events**, which represent user actions, such as clicking a `Button` or altering a value in a `TextBox`, and **event handlers**, which are pieces of code that execute when such events occur (that is, when the events are "raised"). You'll learn why events and event handlers are crucial to programming Windows applications.

5.1 Test-Driving the Inventory Application

In this tutorial, you'll complete the **Inventory** application you designed in Tutorial 4. Recall that the application must meet the following requirements:

> ***Application Requirements***
>
> *A college bookstore receives cartons of textbooks. In each shipment, all cartons contain the same number of textbooks. The inventory manager wants to use a computer to calculate the total number of textbooks arriving at the bookstore for each shipment. The inventory manager will enter the number of cartons received and the fixed number of textbooks in each carton for each shipment; then the application will calculate the total number of textbooks in the shipment.*

The inventory manager has reviewed and approved your design. Now you must add code that, when the user clicks a `Button`, makes the application multiply the number of cartons by the number of textbooks per carton and display the result—the total number of textbooks received. You'll begin by test-driving the completed application. Then you learn the additional Visual Basic capabilities needed to create your own version of this application.

Test-Driving the Inventory Application

1. ***Opening the completed application.*** Open the directory `C:\Examples\Tutorial05\CompletedApplication\Inventory2` to locate the **Inventory** application. Double click `Inventory2.sln` to open the application in the Visual Basic IDE.

2. ***Running the* Inventory *application.*** Select **Debug > Start Debugging** to run the application (Fig. 5.1). Enter 3 in the **Cartons per shipment:** `TextBox`. Enter 15 in the **Items per carton:** `TextBox`. Figure 5.1 shows the `Form` after these values have been entered.

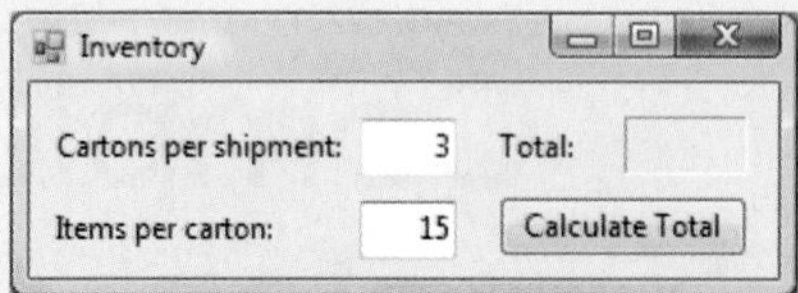

Figure 5.1 **Inventory** application with quantities entered.

3. ***Calculating the total number of items received.*** Click the **Calculate Total** `Button`. The application multiplies the two numbers you entered and displays the result (45) in the `Label` to the right of **Total:** (Fig. 5.2).

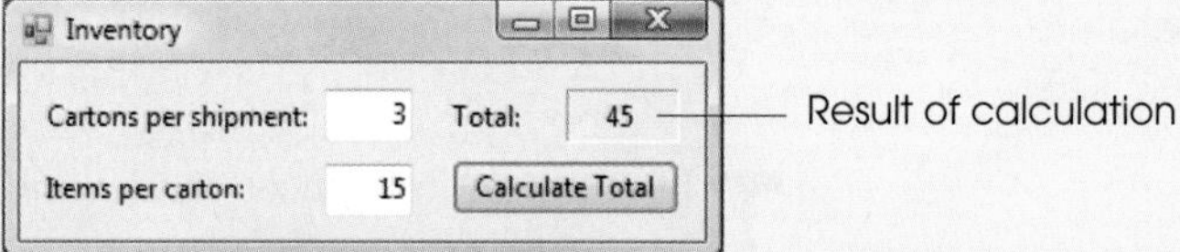

Figure 5.2 Result of clicking the **Calculate Total** `Button` in the **Inventory** application.

4. ***Closing the application.*** Close your running application by clicking its close box.

5. ***Closing the IDE.*** Select **File > Exit**.

5.2 Introduction to Visual Basic Code

In Tutorial 3 and Tutorial 4, you were introduced to a concept called visual programming, which allows you to create GUIs without writing any program code. In this section, you combine visual programming with conventional programming techniques to enhance the **Inventory** application.

Before you begin to view and edit code, you should customize the way the IDE displays and formats your code. In the following box, you open the template application and change the display and format settings to make it easy for you to work with code and follow our discussions. Adding line numbers, adjusting tab sizes and setting fonts and colors help you to navigate your code more easily.

Customizing the IDE

1. ***Copying the template to your working directory.*** Copy the `C:\Examples\Tutorial05\TemplateApplication\Inventory2` directory to your `C:\SimplyVB2008` directory. This directory contains the application created by following the steps in Tutorial 4.

2. ***Opening the* Inventory *application's template file.*** Double click `Inventory2.sln` in the `Inventory2` directory to open the application in the Visual Basic IDE. If an error occurs when you try to copy or modify the template, please consult your system administrator to ensure that you have proper privileges to edit these applications.

(cont.)

3. ***Displaying line numbers.*** In our programming discussions, we refer to specific code elements by line number. To help you locate where to insert code in the examples, you need to enable the IDE's capability to show line numbers in your code. Select **Tools > Options...**, and, in the **Options** dialog that appears (Fig. 5.3), expand the **Text Editor Basic** category by clicking the triangle next to it. [*Note:* Make sure the **Show all settings** CheckBox is *not* selected—otherwise the dialog displays different categories.] Select the **Editor** category that subsequently appears (Fig. 5.4) and locate the **Interaction** group of CheckBoxes in this category. If the CheckBox next to **Line numbers** is not checked, click inside the box to add a checkmark. If the box is already checked, you need not do anything; however, do not close the dialog.

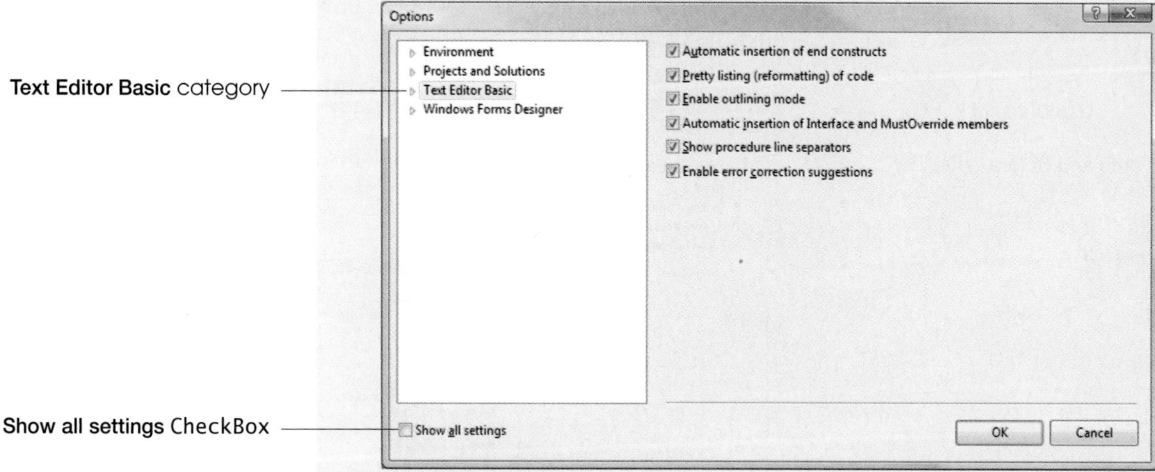

Figure 5.3 **Options** dialog.

4. ***Setting the tab size.*** Just as you indent the first line of each paragraph when writing a letter, it is important to use proper spacing when writing code. Indenting code improves program readability. You can control indents with tabs. In the **Options** dialog that you opened in the preceding step (Fig. 5.4), enter 3 for both the tab size and indent size fields.

   The tab size setting indicates the number of spaces each tab character represents. The **Indent size:** setting determines the number of spaces each indent inserted by the Visual Basic IDE represents. The IDE inserts three spaces for you if you are using the **Smart** indenting feature (Fig. 5.4)—you can insert them yourself with one keystroke by pressing the *Tab* key.

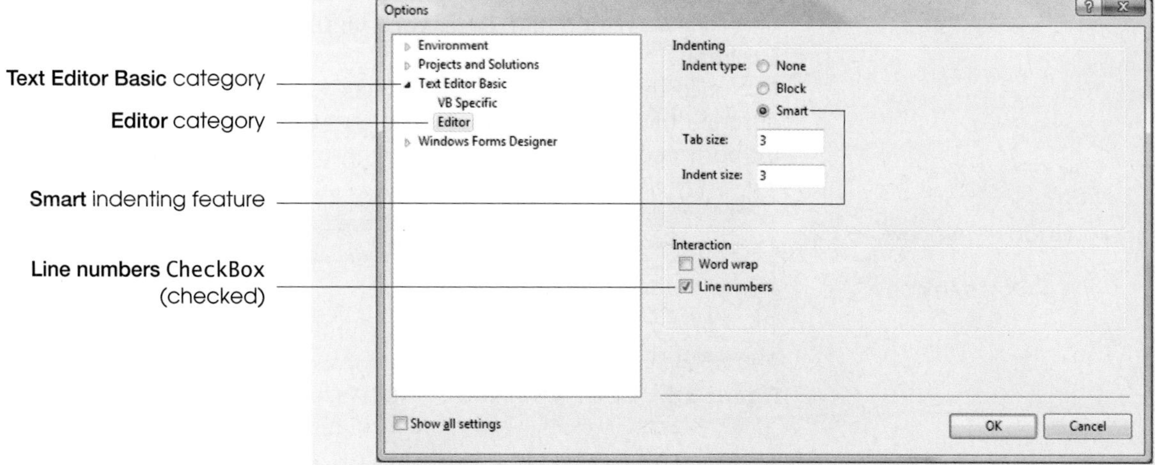

Figure 5.4 **General** settings page for Visual Basic text editor.

(cont.)

Good Programming Practice

You can change the font and color settings if you prefer a different appearance for your code. To remain consistent with this book, however, we recommend that you not change the default font and color settings.

5. ***Exploring fonts and colors.*** Click the triangle next to the **Environment** category; then click the **Fonts and Colors** category that appears. The subsequent screen allows you to customize fonts and colors used to display code. The Visual Basic IDE can apply colors and fonts to make it easier for you to read and edit code. Note that, if your settings are not consistent with the default settings, what you see on your screen will appear different from what is presented in this book. If you need to reset your settings to the default for fonts and colors, click the **Use Defaults** `Button` (Fig. 5.5).

   In the book's examples, you will see code with the **Selected Text** background set to yellow for emphasis. The default setting for **Selected Text** is a blue background. You should use the default settings on your machine.

6. ***Applying your changes.*** Click the **OK** `Button` to apply your changes and dismiss the **Options** dialog.

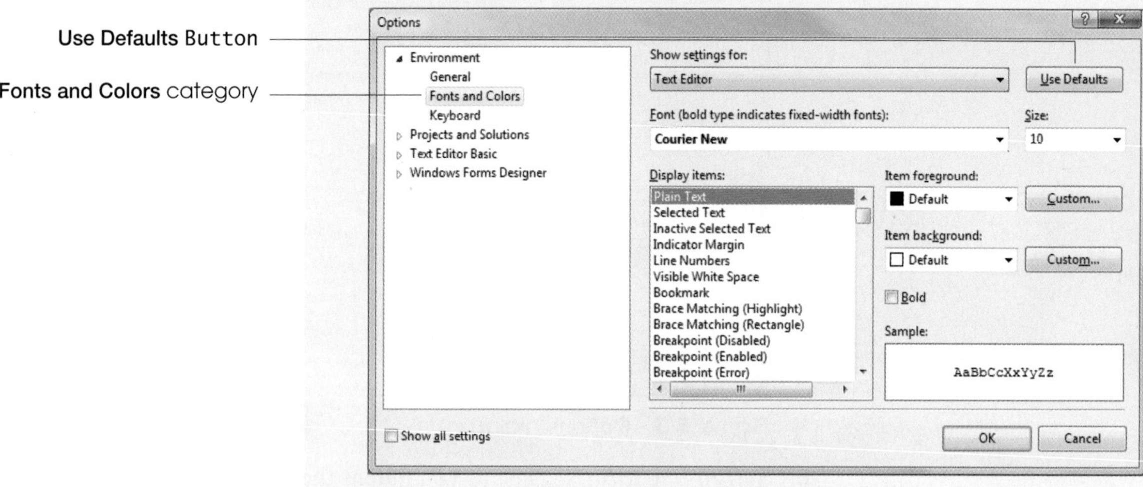

Figure 5.5 Examining the **Fonts and Colors** page.

Next, you will take your first peek at Visual Basic code.

Introducing Visual Basic Code

1. ***Viewing application code.*** If the Windows `Form` Designer is not open, double click the `Inventory.vb` file in the **Solution Explorer** window. Then switch to **Code view** (where the application's code is displayed in an editor window) by selecting **View > Code** or pressing *F7*. The tabbed window (`Inventory.vb`) in Fig. 5.6, also called a **code editor**, appears. Note that when you are asked to select **View > Code**, the `Inventory.vb` file must be selected in the **Solution Explorer**.

   Notice that the IDE through which we present code to you may appear different than your IDE. To improve readability, we show only the code editor portion of the IDE and the tabbed windows.

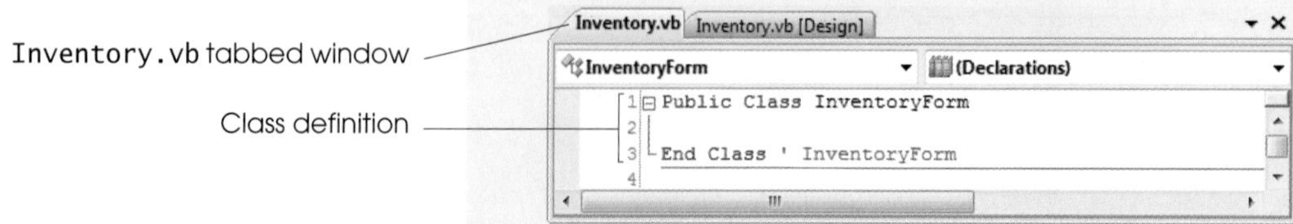

Figure 5.6 IDE showing code for the **Inventory** application.

(cont.)

Most Visual Basic programs consist of pieces called classes, which simplify application organization. Recall from Tutorial 1 that classes contain groups of code statements that perform tasks and return information when the tasks are completed. The code in this application defines your **Inventory** application class. (These lines collectively are called a **class definition**.) Most Visual Basic applications consist of a combination of code written by programmers (like you) and preexisting classes written and provided by Microsoft in the .NET Framework Class Library. Again, the key to successful Visual Basic application development is achieving the right mix of the two. You'll learn how to use both techniques in your programs.

2. ***Examining class definitions.*** Line 1 (Fig. 5.6) begins the class definition. The **`Class` keyword** introduces a class definition in Visual Basic and is immediately followed by the **class name** (`InventoryForm` in this application, the value you entered in the `Form`'s `Name` property).

The name of the class is an **identifier**, which is a series of characters consisting of letters, digits and underscores (_). Identifiers cannot begin with a digit and cannot contain spaces. Examples of valid identifiers are `value1`, `label_Value` and `exitButton`. The name `7welcome` is not a valid identifier, because it begins with a digit, and the name `input field` is not a valid identifier, because it contains a space. The class definition ends at line 3 with the keywords **`End Class`**. **Keywords** (or reserved words) are reserved for use by Visual Basic (you'll learn the various keywords throughout the text). Note that keywords appear in blue by default in the IDE. A complete list of Visual Basic keywords can be found in Appendix E, Keyword Chart.

The `Class` keyword is preceded by the `Public` keyword. The code for every `Form` you design in the Visual Basic IDE begins with the `Public` keyword. You'll learn about this keyword in Tutorial 19.

Visual Basic keywords and identifiers are not **case sensitive**. This means that uppercase and lowercase letters are considered to be identical in identifiers; this practice causes `InventoryForm` and `inventoryform` to be understood by Visual Basic as the same identifier. Although the first letter of every keyword is capitalized, keywords are nevertheless not case sensitive. The IDE applies the correct case to each letter of a keyword and identifier, so when you type `clasS`, it changes to `Class` when you press the *Enter* key.

Good Programming Practice

Capitalize the first letter of each class identifier, such as the `Form` name.

SELF-REVIEW

1. Identifiers ________.
   a) can begin with any character, but cannot contain spaces
   b) must begin with a digit, but cannot contain spaces
   c) cannot begin with a digit or contain spaces
   d) cannot begin with a digit, but can contain spaces

2. Visual Basic keywords are ________.
   a) case sensitive
   b) comments
   c) not reserved words
   d) not case sensitive

Answers: 1) c. 2) d.

5.3 Inserting an Event Handler

Now that you've finalized the GUI, you are ready to modify the application to respond to user input. You'll do this by inserting code manually. Most of the Visual Basic applications in this book provide functionality in the form of event handlers. Recall that an event handler executes when an event occurs, such as clicking a `Button`. The next box shows you how to add an event handler to your application.

Adding a Button's Click Event Handler

1. ***Adding an event handler for the Button.*** In this step, you use the Windows Form Designer to create an event handler and enter **Code** view. Begin by clicking the Inventory.vb [Design] tab to view the Windows Form Designer. Then double click the Form's **Calculate Total** Button to enter **Code** view. Note that the code for the application, which now includes the new event handler in lines 3–5 of Fig. 5.7, is displayed.

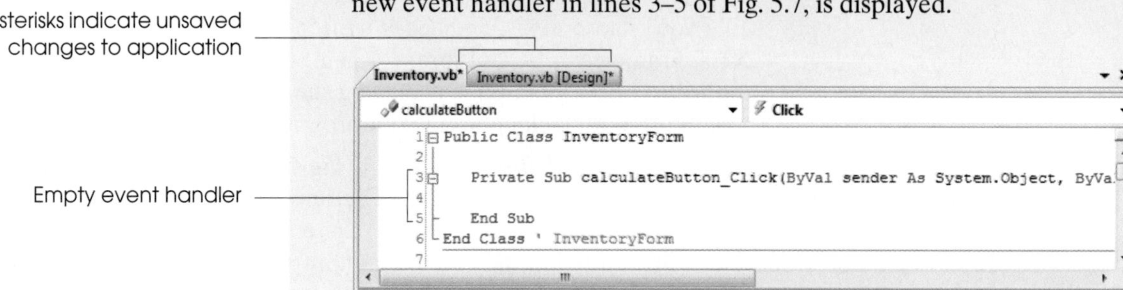
Asterisks indicate unsaved changes to application
Empty event handler
Inventory.vb*
Inventory.vb [Design]*
calculateButton
Click
1 Public Class InventoryForm
2
3 Private Sub calculateButton_Click(ByVal sender As System.Object, ByVa
4
5 End Sub
6 End Class ' InventoryForm
7

Figure 5.7 Event handler calculateButton_Click before you add your program code.

Double clicking the **Calculate Total** Button in **Design** view caused the Visual Basic IDE to generate the Button's **Click** event handler—the code that executes when the user clicks the **Calculate Total** Button. When you double click a control, the IDE inserts an event handler for that control (or displays the event handler, if it already exists). [*Note:* If you accidentally create an event handler, you can simply delete the generated code.] The type of event that is handled differs based on the control. For instance, double clicking a Button control creates a Click event handler. Double clicking other controls generates other types of event handlers. Each control has a default type of event handler that is generated when you double click the control in **Design** view.

At the end of each event handler's first line, Visual Basic inserts a Handles clause. Scroll to the right in **Code** view to see the Handles clause for the **Calculate Total** Button's Click event handler (line 3)

```
Handles calculateButton.Click
```

This **Handles clause** indicates that the event handler is called when the calculateButton's Click event occurs.

In Visual Basic, event handlers by convention follow the naming scheme *controlName_eventName*. This convention mimics the event handler's Handles clause. The word *controlName* refers to the name of the control provided in its Name property (in this case, calculateButton). The word *eventName* represents the name of the event (in this case, Click) raised by the control. When event *eventName* occurs on the control *controlName*, event handler *controlName_eventName* executes. In this application, calculateButton_Click handles the **Calculate Total** Button's Click events—in other words, the code in calculateButton_Click executes when the user clicks the **Calculate Total** Button.

2. ***Running the application.*** Select **Debug > Start Debugging** to run the application (Fig. 5.8). The IDE automatically saves your work before running the application. Click the **Calculate Total** Button.

(cont.)

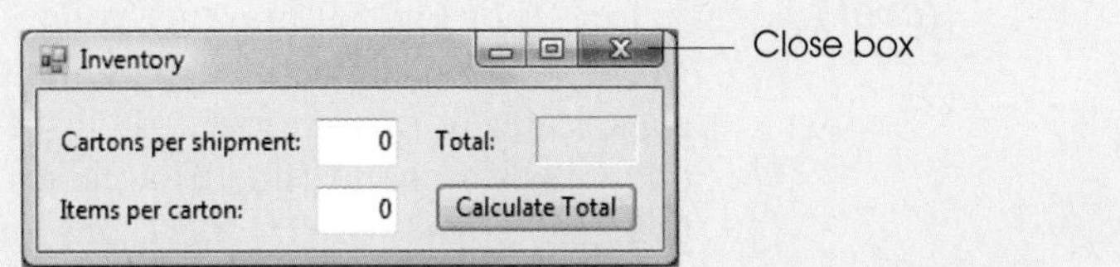

Figure 5.8 Running the application without functionality.

Although you've added an event handler for the `Button`'s `Click` event, no action occurs when you click the `Button` because you have not yet added any code to the event handler. In the next box, you add code to the event handler so that, when a user clicks the `Button`, text displays in the output `Label` (`totalResultLabel`).

3. ***Closing the application.*** Close the running application by clicking its close box—you cannot edit the application's code while it is running.

Now that you've created an event handler for the **Calculate Total** `Button`, you need to insert code to perform an action. Specifically, you need to make the application multiply the number of cartons in a shipment by the fixed number of items per carton when a user clicks the **Calculate Total** `Button`. You write your first Visual Basic statement in the following box.

Adding Code to an Empty Event Handler

1. ***Changing to* Code *view.*** If you are not already in **Code** view, select **View > Code** to view the application's code.

2. ***Adding code to the event handler.*** In the event handler, insert lines 5–6 of Fig. 5.9 by typing the text on the screen. Add the comment in line 7 following the keywords `End Sub`.

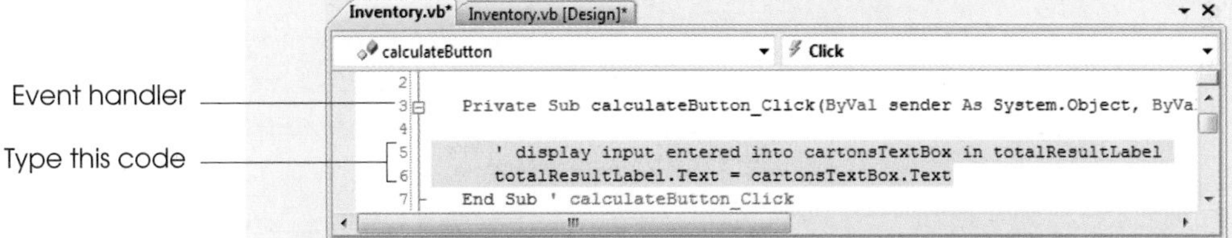

Figure 5.9 Code added to the **Calculate Total** `Button`'s event handler.

Line 5 of Fig. 5.9 begins with a **single-quote character** (`'`), which indicates that the remainder of the line is a **comment**. You insert comments in programs to improve the readability of your code. These comments explain the code so that other programmers who need to work with the application can understand it more easily. By default, comments are displayed in green.

Comments also help you read your own code, especially when you haven't looked at it for a while. Comments can be placed either on their own lines (these are called "full-line comments") or at the end of a line of Visual Basic code (these are called "end-of-line comments").

The Visual Basic compiler ignores comments—they do not cause the computer to perform any actions when your applications run. The comment in line 5 simply indicates that the next line displays the value entered into the **Cartons per shipment:** `TextBox` in the **Total:** `Label`. Comments appear in green when displayed in the code editor of the Visual Basic IDE.

Good Programming Practice

Comments written at the end of a line should be preceded by a space, to enhance program readability.

(cont.)

Line 6 of Fig. 5.9 presents your first executable Visual Basic **statement**, which performs an action. By default, statements end when the current line ends. Later in this tutorial, you'll see how to continue a statement past one line. This statement (line 6) accesses the `Text` properties of `cartonsTextBox` and `totalResultLabel`. In Visual Basic, properties are accessed in code by placing a period between the control name (for example, `totalResultLabel`) and property name (for example, `Text`). This period, which is placed to the right of the control name, is called the **member-access operator** (`.`), or the **dot operator**. When the control name and member-access operator are typed, a window appears listing that object's members (Fig. 5.10). This convenience feature, known as ***IntelliSense***, displays items that are available in the program and can be used in the current context, such as all the members in an object. The *IntelliSense* window can also be opened by pressing *Ctrl* + *Space*. You scroll to the member you are interested in and select it. You also can continue typing to narrow down the choices. Click the member name once to display a description of that member; double click it to add the member's name to your application. You can also press *Enter* or *Tab* to insert the member—*Tab* inserts the member, *Enter* inserts the member and a new line. *IntelliSense* can be useful in discovering a class's members and their purpose. Note that the *IntelliSense* window in Fig. 5.10 shows two tabs—**Common** and **All**. The **Common** tab shows the most commonly used members that can appear to the right of the dot operator. The **All** tab shows every member that can appear to the right of the dot operator. You can close the *IntelliSense* window by pressing *Esc*.

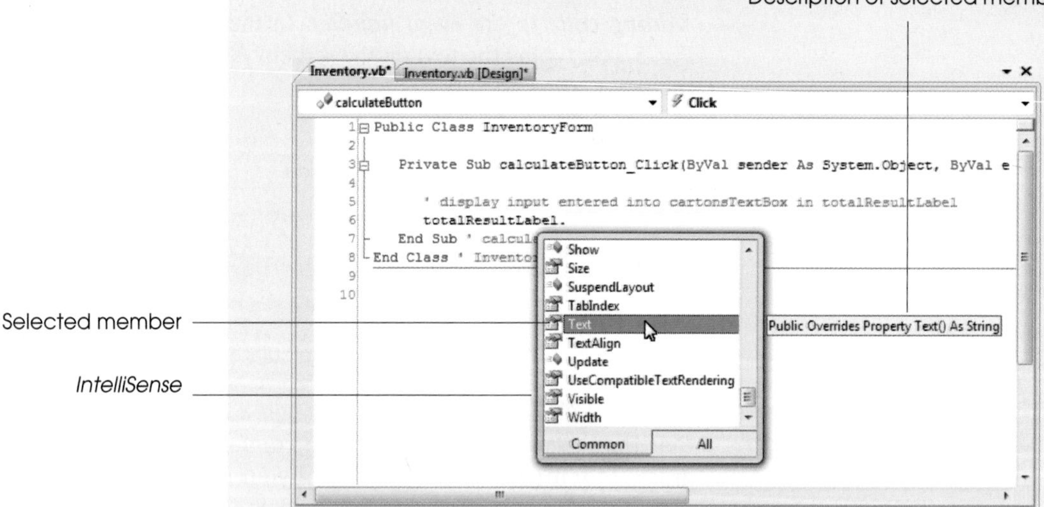

Figure 5.10 *IntelliSense* activating while entering code.

Let's examine line 6 of Fig. 5.9 more closely. Reading the line from left to right, we see `totalResultLabel`'s `Text` property, followed by an "equals" sign (=), followed by `cartonsTextBox`'s `Text` property value. The "=" symbol, as used here, is known as the **assignment operator**. The expressions on either side of the assignment operator are referred to as its **operands**. This assignment operator assigns the value on the right of the operator (the **right operand**) to the variable on the left of the operator (the **left operand**). The assignment operator is known as a **binary operator** because it has two operands—`totalResultLabel.Text` and `cartonsTextBox.Text`.

(cont.)

The entire statement is called an **assignment statement** because it assigns a value to the left operand. In this example, you are assigning the value of `cartonsTextBox`'s `Text` property to `totalResultLabel`'s `Text` property. The statement is read as, "The `Text` property of `totalResultLabel` *gets* the value of `cartonTextBox`'s `Text` property." Note that the right operand is unchanged by the assignment statement.

When the user clicks the **Calculate Total** `Button`, the event handler executes, displaying the value the user entered in the **Cartons per shipment:** `TextBox` in the output `Label` `totalResultLabel`. Clearly, this is not the correct result—the correct result is the number of items per carton times the number of cartons per shipment. In the box *Completing the* **Inventory** *Application*, you correct this error. Note that we've added a comment in line 7 of Fig. 5.9, indicating the end of our event handler.

Good Programming Practice

Add comments following the `End Sub` keywords to indicate the end of an event handler.

3. ***Running the application.*** Select **Debug > Start Debugging** to run the application (Fig. 5.11). Type `5` into the **Cartons per shipment:** `TextBox` and `10` into the **Items per carton:** `TextBox`, then click the **Calculate Total** `Button`. The text of `totalResultLabel` now incorrectly displays the data, `5`, that was entered into the **Cartons per shipment:** `TextBox`, rather than the correct result, `50`. You'll fix this in the next box.

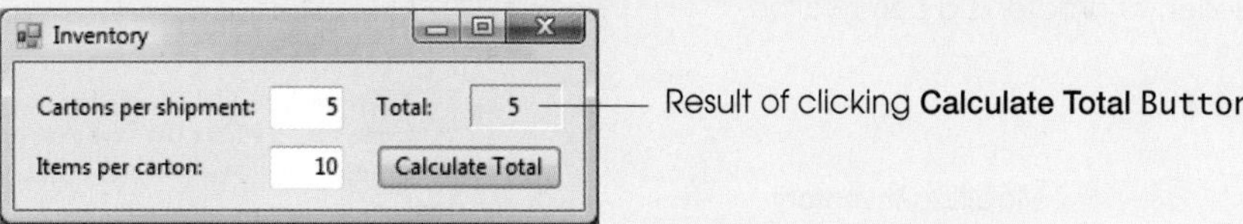

Figure 5.11 Running the application with the event handler.

4. ***Closing the application.*** Close the running application by clicking its close box.

SELF-REVIEW

1. Event handlers generated by the Visual Basic IDE follow the naming convention ________.

a) *controlName_eventName* b) *eventName_controlName*
c) *eventNameControlName* d) *controlNameEventName*

2. The expressions on either side of the assignment operator are referred to as its ________.

a) operator values b) results
c) operands d) arguments

Answers: 1) a. 2) c.

5.4 Performing a Calculation and Displaying the Result

Now that you're familiar with displaying output in a `Label`, you'll complete the **Inventory** application by displaying the product of the number of cartons per shipment and the number of items per carton. In the following box, you'll learn how to perform mathematical operations in Visual Basic.

Completing the Inventory Application

Good Programming Practice

A lengthy statement may be spread over several lines. If a single statement must be split across lines, choose breaking points that make sense, such as after an operator. If a statement is split across two or more lines, indent all subsequent lines with one "level" of indentation.

Common Programming Error

Splitting a statement over several lines without including the line-continuation character is a compilation error.

Common Programming Error

Placing non-whitespace characters, including comments, to the right of a line-continuation character is a compilation error. Compilation errors are introduced in the box, *Using the IDE to Eliminate Compilation Errors* in Section 5.5.

1. ***Changing the event handler.*** If you are not already in **Code** view, select **View > Code** or click the `Inventory.vb` tab. Insert underscore (_) characters preceded by at least one space as shown at the right of lines 3–4 in Fig. 5.12. Indent lines 4–5. The underscore character is known as the **line-continuation character**. This character indicates that the next line is a continuation of the previous line. A single statement can contain as many line-continuation characters as necessary. However, at least one space character must precede each line-continuation character and only whitespace characters may appear to the right of a line-continuation character. A **whitespace character** is a space, tab or newline (the character inserted by pressing the *Enter* key). You use the line-continuation character in lines 3–4 to split the first line of the event handler into three lines—this enables all the program code to fit in the window. The line-continuation character has no effect when placed at the end of a comment.

   Replace the body of `calculateButton_Click` with the code in lines 7–9. The comment in line 7 indicates that you'll be multiplying the two values input by the user and displaying the result in a `Label`.

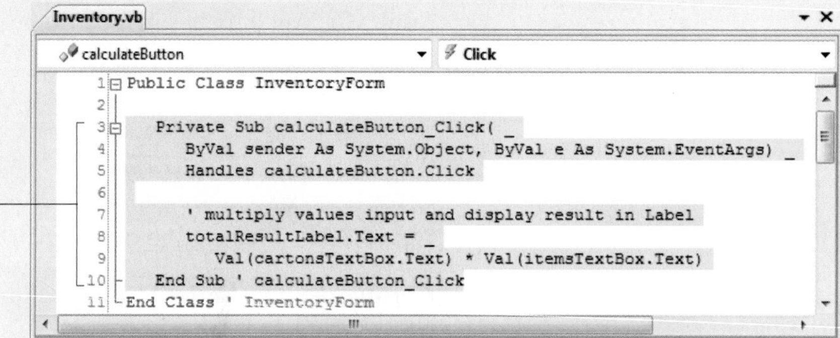

Modified Inventory application code
Inventory.vb
calculateButton
Click
1 Public Class InventoryForm
2
3 Private Sub calculateButton_Click(_
4 ByVal sender As System.Object, ByVal e As System.EventArgs) _
5 Handles calculateButton.Click
6
7 ' multiply values input and display result in Label
8 totalResultLabel.Text = _
9 Val(cartonsTextBox.Text) * Val(itemsTextBox.Text)
10 End Sub ' calculateButton_Click
11 End Class ' InventoryForm

Figure 5.12 Using multiplication in the **Inventory** application.

2. ***Adding multiline code.*** Lines 8–9 perform the multiplication and assignment. You again use the assignment operator to assign a value to `totalResultLabel.Text` in line 8. The line-continuation character in line 8 indicates that the statement has been continued past the current line, so look to the next line for the assignment operator's right operand.

   The assignment operator in line 8 assigns the result of multiplying the numbers input by the user to `totalResultLabel.Text`. In line 9, the expression `Val(cartonsTextBox.Text)` is followed by an asterisk (*) then the expression `Val(itemsTextBox.Text)`. The asterisk is known as the **multiplication operator**—the operator's left and right operands are multiplied together.

   Your **Inventory** application cannot prevent users from accidentally entering nonnumeric input, such as letters and special characters like $ and @. Line 9 uses the **`Val` function** to prevent inputs like this from terminating the application. A function is a piece of code that performs a task when called (executed) and sends, or returns, a value to the location from which it was called. In this case, the values returned by `Val` become the values used in the multiplication expression (line 9). You call functions (as in line 9) by typing their name followed by parentheses. Any values inside the parentheses (for example, `cartonsTextBox.Text`) are known as function **arguments**. Arguments are inputs to the function that provide information the function needs to perform its task. In this case, the argument specifies which value you want to send to function `Val`. You'll learn how to create your own functions in Tutorial 13.

(cont.)

Function `Val` obtains a value from a string of characters (keyboard input). The value obtained is guaranteed to be a number. We use `Val` because this application is not intended to perform arithmetic calculations with characters that are not numbers. `Val` reads its argument one character at a time until it encounters a character that is not a number. Once a nonnumeric character is read, `Val` returns the number it has read up to that point. `Val` ignores whitespace characters (for example, `"33 5"` will be converted to `335`). Figure 5.13 presents samples of `Val` calls and their results. `Val` recognizes the decimal point as a numeric character, and the plus and minus signs when they appear at the beginning of the string (to indicate that a number is positive or negative). `Val` does not recognize such symbols as commas and dollar signs. If function `Val` receives an argument that cannot be converted to a number (for example, `"b35"`, which begins with a nonnumeric character), it returns `0`. The result of the calculation is assigned to `totalResultLabel.Text` (line 8), to display the result to the user.

Be careful when using `Val`—although the value returned is a number, it is not always the value the user intended (see Fig. 5.13). If incorrect data is entered by the user, `Val` makes no indication of the error. The function returns a value (usually not the value intended by the user) and the application continues, possibly using the incorrect input in calculations. For example, someone entering a monetary amount may enter the text `$10.23`, which `Val` evaluates to `0`. Note how a common mistake causes an application to execute incorrectly. Visual Basic provides two ways to handle invalid input. One way is to use Visual Basic's string-processing capabilities to examine input. You'll learn about such capabilities as you read this book. The other form of handling invalid input is called exception handling, where you write code to handle errors that may be raised as the application executes. You'll learn about exception handling in Tutorial 25.

3. ***Running the application.*** Select **Debug > Start Debugging** to run your application. Now the user can enter data in both `TextBoxes`. When the **Calculate Total** `Button` is clicked, the application multiplies the two numbers entered and displays the result in `totalResultLabel`.

4. ***Closing the application.*** Close the running application by clicking its close box.

5. ***Saving the project.*** Select **File > Save All** to save your modified code.

`Val` Function call examples	Results
`Val("16")`	`16`
`Val("-3")`	`-3`
`Val("1.5")`	`1.5`
`Val("67a4")`	`67`
`Val("8+5")`	`8`
`Val("14 Main St.")`	`14`
`Val("+1 2 3 4 5")`	`12345`
`Val("hello")`	`0`

Figure 5.13 `Val` function call examples.

Figure 5.14 presents the **Inventory** application's code. The lines of code that contain new programming concepts you learned in this tutorial are highlighted.

```
Public Class InventoryForm

   Private Sub calculateButton_Click( _
      ByVal sender As System.Object, ByVal e As System.EventArgs) _
      Handles calculateButton.Click

      ' multiply values input and display result in Label
      totalResultLabel.Text = _
         Val(cartonsTextBox.Text) * Val(itemsTextBox.Text)
   End Sub ' calculateButton_Click
End Class ' InventoryForm
```

Figure 5.14 **Inventory** application code.

SELF-REVIEW

1. ________ provide information that functions need to perform their tasks.

   a) Comments　　b) Arguments

   c) Outputs　　d) Both a and b

2. What is the result of `Val("%5")`?

   a) `5`　　b) `0`

   c) `500`　　d) `0.05`

Answers: 1) d. 2) b.

5.5 Using the IDE to Eliminate Compilation Errors

So far in this book, you've executed applications by selecting **Debug > Start Debugging**. This compiles and runs the application. If you do not write your code correctly, errors appear in a window known as the **Error List**. **Debugging** is the process of fixing errors in an application. There are two types of errors—compilation errors and logic errors.

Compilation errors occur when code statements violate the grammatical rules of the programming language or when code statements are simply incorrect in the current context. Examples of compilation errors include misspellings of keywords or identifiers, failure to use the line-continuation character when splitting a statement across multiple lines or using an identifier in the wrong context. An application cannot be executed until all of its compilation errors are corrected. A subset of compilation errors are known as **syntax errors**. These are specifically the errors that violate the grammatical rules of the programming language, such as failure to use the line-continuation character when splitting a statement across multiple lines.

Logic errors do not prevent the application from compiling successfully, but do cause the application to produce erroneous results. The Visual Basic IDE contains a **debugger** that allows you to analyze the behavior of your application to determine whether it is executing correctly.

You can compile an application without executing it by selecting **Build > Build** [*Project Name*], where project name appears as the name of your current project. Programmers frequently do this when they wish to determine whether there are any compilation errors in their code. Using either **Debug > Start Debugging** or **Build > Build** [*Project Name*] will display any compilation errors in the **Error List** window. The **Output** window displays the result of the compilation. If this window is not visible, select **Debug > Windows > Output** to view it while debugging. Figure 5.15 displays the output window for an application with no errors.

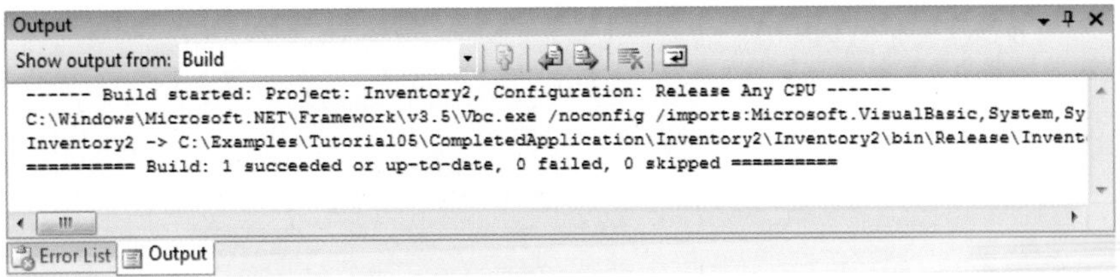

Figure 5.15 Results of successful build in the **Output** window.

In the Visual Basic IDE, compilation errors appear in the **Error List** window along with a description of each error. Figure 5.16 displays the error that appears when the line-continuation character is left out of a multiple-line statement. Double click the error in the **Error List** window to go the location of the error in the code. For additional information on a compilation error, right click the error statement in the **Error List** window, and select **Show Error Help**. This displays a help page explaining the error message and suggests corrections. Next, you'll create compilation errors, view the results and fix the errors.

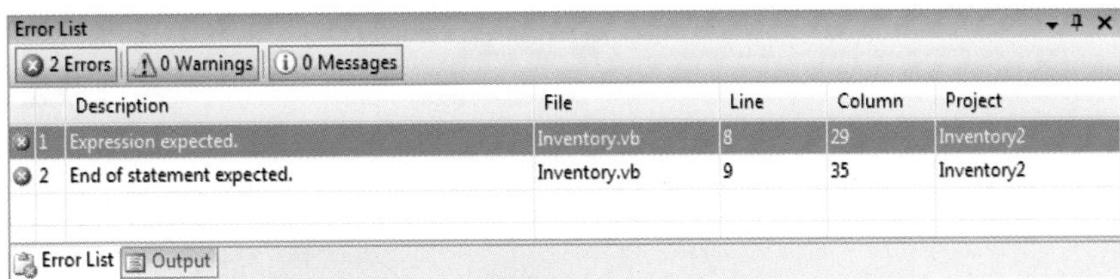

Figure 5.16 **Error List** lists compilation errors.

Using the IDE to Eliminate Compilation Errors

1. ***Opening the completed application.*** If the **Inventory** application is not currently open, locate the `Inventory2.sln` file, then double click it to load your application in the IDE.
2. ***Creating your own compilation errors.*** Now you'll create your own compilation errors, for demonstration purposes. If you're not in **Code** view, select **View > Code**. Open the **Error List** window by selecting **View > Error List**. Insert an additional character (`"s"`) in `Label totalResultLabel` on line 8 and delete the right parenthesis at the end of the assignment statement in line 9. Note the changes to the IDE (Fig. 5.17).

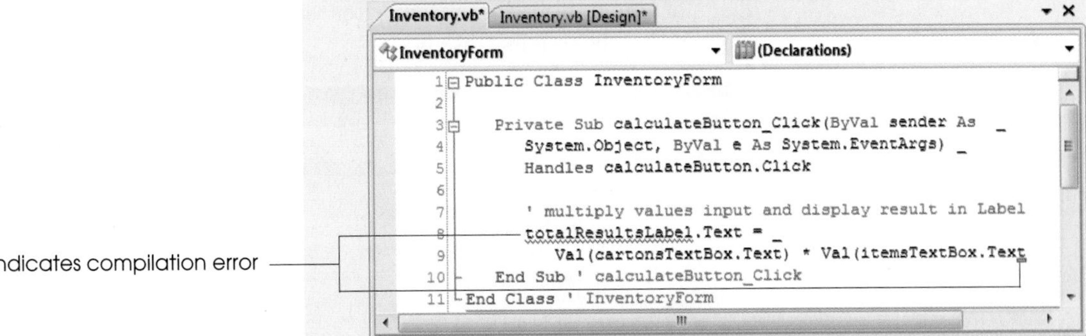

Figure 5.17 IDE with compilation errors.

The Visual Basic IDE provides **real-time error checking**. While manipulating the code in the code editor, you may have noticed that compilation errors are immediately reported in the **Error List**. The precise location of the error in your code is also emphasized by a blue jagged line. Unrecognized identifier `totalResultsLabel` and the missing parenthesis are reported in the **Error List** (Fig. 5.18).

(cont.)

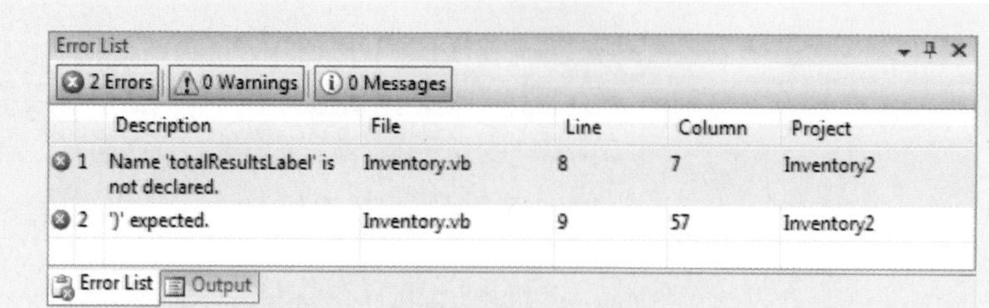

Figure 5.18 **Error List** displaying the compilation errors.

These features notify you of possible errors and give you a chance to fix them before compiling the application. The IDE refuses to run your modified application until *all* compilation errors have been corrected.

3. ***Locating the compilation errors.*** Double clicking an error in the **Error List** window selects the code containing that error. Double click the first error to highlight the error in line 8 (Fig. 5.19). Placing the cursor over the compilation error displays the error message.

Highlighted compilation error

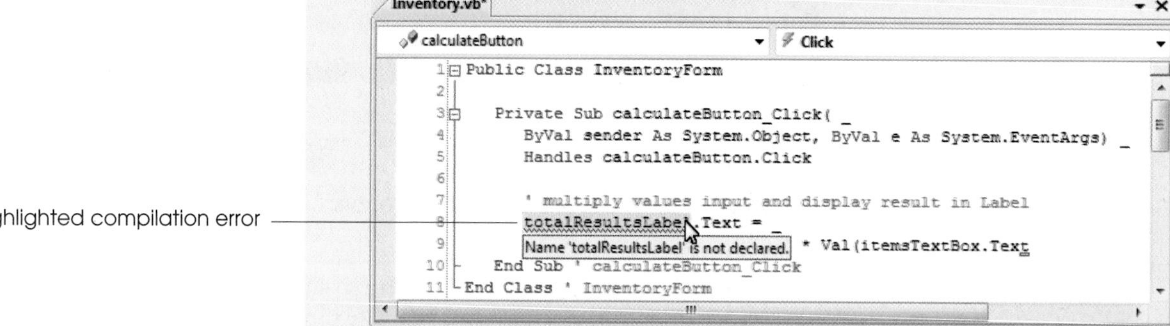

Figure 5.19 Highlighting the code where a compilation error occurs.

4. ***Getting additional help.*** Additional help regarding the compilation error is also available through the **Error List** item's context menu, which you can access by right clicking an item. Right click the **Name 'totalResultsLabel' is not declared** error message from the **Error List**, and select **Show Error Help** (Fig. 5.20). This displays a reference page with information regarding the general form of the compilation error, possible solutions and links to other documentation (Fig. 5.21). After viewing this information, close the help page by clicking its close box.

Context help

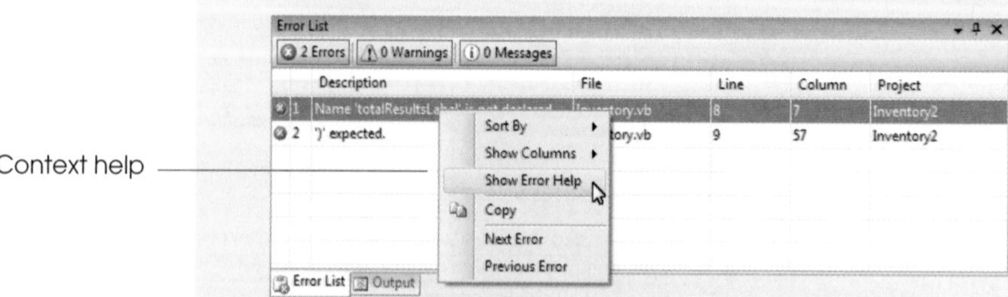

Figure 5.20 Getting additional help.

(cont.)

Name '<name>' is not declared - Microsoft Visual Studio 2008 Documentation - Microsoft Document Explorer

File Edit View Tools Window Help

Back | How Do I | Search | Index | Contents | Help Favorites | MSDN Forums

Name '<name>' is not declared | Search

F1 Options: (choose) URL: http://msdn2.microsoft.com/en-us/library/d3xk5aeb.aspx

Visual Basic Reference: Error Messages

Name '<name>' is not declared

Collapse All

Send | Add Content... | Click to Rate and Give Feedback

A statement refers to a programming element, but the compiler cannot find an element with that exact name.

Error ID: BC30451

To correct this error

1. Check the spelling of the name in the referring statement. Visual Basic is case-insensitive, but any other variation in the spelling is regarded as a completely different name. Note that the underscore (_) is part of the name and therefore part of the spelling.

2. Check that you have the member access operator (.) between an object and its member. For example, if you have a TextBox control named TextBox1, to access its Text property you should type TextBox1.Text. If instead you type TextBox1Text, you have created a different name.

Done

Suggested solutions to misspelled identifier (note that the debugger interprets the misspelling as a new, undeclared identifier)

Figure 5.21 **Error Help** window.

5. ***Fixing the compilation errors.*** Now that you know how to locate and fix the compilation error, go back to **Code** view and correct the two errors you created in *Step 2*. Remove the extra character you added to the `totalResultLabel` identifier. When you correct the error, note that the jagged line does not disappear immediately. However, when you move the cursor to another line, the IDE rechecks the code for errors, removes the jagged underline for the corrected compilation error and removes the error from the **Error List** window. To fix the second compilation error, hover over the small red rectangle located where the missing parenthesis should be. The **Error Correction Options** icon ( ) appears. Click this icon to open the **Error Correction Options** window (Fig. 5.22). The blue text toward the top of this window provides possible corrections for the compilation error. In this case, the IDE indicates that inserting the missing parenthesis will fix the compilation error. Click the suggested correction—**Insert the missing ')'**—to apply the correction.

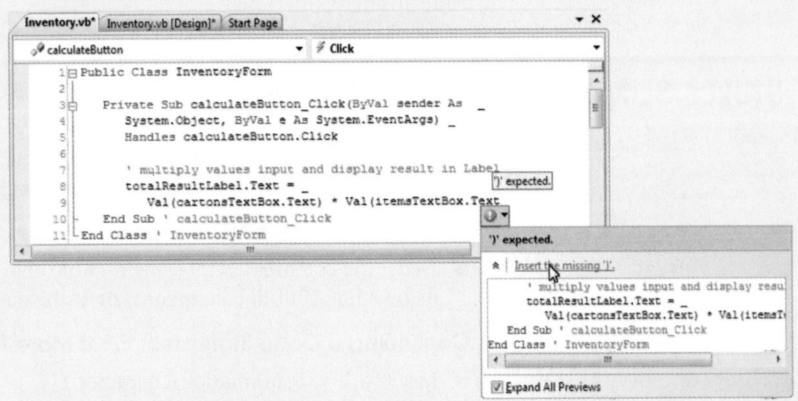
Inventory.vb* | Inventory.vb [Design]* | Start Page
calculateButton
Click
Public Class InventoryForm
Private Sub calculateButton_Click(ByVal sender As _
System.Object, ByVal e As System.EventArgs) _
Handles calculateButton.Click
' multiply values input and display result in Label
totalResultLabel.Text = _
Val(cartonsTextBox.Text) * Val(itemsTextBox.Text
End Sub ' calculateButton_Click
End Class ' InventoryForm
')' expected.
')' expected.
Insert the missing ')'.
Expand All Previews

Figure 5.22 Using the **Error Correction** window to fix a compilation error.

6. ***Saving the project.*** Select **File > Save All** to save your modified code. The application is now ready to be compiled and executed.

7. ***Closing the IDE.*** Close the Visual Basic IDE by clicking its close box.

In this section, you learned about compilation errors and how to find and correct them. In later tutorials, you'll learn to detect and remove logic errors by using the Visual Basic IDE runtime debugger.

SELF-REVIEW

1. If there are compilation errors in an application, they appear in a window known as the ________.

   a) **Task List** b) **Output**
   c) **Properties** d) **Error List**

2. A compilation error occurs when ________.

   a) a keyword is spelled incorrectly b) a parenthesis is omitted
   c) a statement breaks over several lines without line-continuation characters d) All of the above

Answers: 1) d. 2) d.

5.6 Wrap-Up

In this tutorial, you were introduced to Visual Basic programming. You learned how to use a `TextBox` control to allow users to input data and how to use a `Button` control to signal to your running application that it is to perform a particular action. You learned that a key to good programming is to achieve the right balance between employing visual programming (in which the IDE writes code for you) and writing your own code.

After learning about operators in Visual Basic, you wrote a few lines of code as you added an event handler to your application to perform a simple multiplication calculation. You used the `Val` function obtain a value from the user input and used that value in the calculation. You then displayed the result to the user by assigning it to a `Label`'s `Text` property. You also used comments to improve the readability of your code. You learned that placing code in an event handler allows an application to respond to that type of event, such as clicking a `Button`.

Finally, you learned about compilation errors and how to use the Visual Basic IDE to locate and fix them. In the next tutorial, you continue developing your **Inventory** application by using identifiers to create variables. You also enhance your **Inventory** application by using the `TextChanged` event, which is raised when the user changes the value in a `TextBox`. After applying your knowledge of variables, you use the debugger while an application runs to remove a logic error from that application.

SKILLS SUMMARY

Accessing a Property's Value by Using Visual Basic Code

- To access a control's property, place the property name after the control name and the member-access operator (`.`). For example, to access the `Text` property of a `TextBox` named `cartonsTextBox`, use `cartonsTextBox.Text`.

Inserting Visual Basic Comments in Code

- Begin the comment with a single-quote character (`'`). A comment can be placed either on its own line (full-line comment) or at the end of a line of code (end-of-line comment).

Continuing a Code Statement Over More Than One Line

- Insert a line-continuation character (_), preceded by one or more space characters, to indicate that the next line is a continuation of the preceding line. Only whitespace characters may follow a line-continuation character.

Naming an Event Handler

- Use the format for an event handler, *controlName_eventName*, where *controlName* is the name of the control that the event is related to and *eventName* is the name of the event.

Inserting an Event Handler for a Button Control's Click Event

- Double click the Button in **Design** view to create an empty event handler; then insert the code that executes when the event occurs.

Using an Assignment Statement

- Use the = ("equals" sign) to assign the value of its right operand to its left operand.

Using the Multiplication Operator

- Use an asterisk (*) between the two expressions to be multiplied. The operator multiplies the right and left operands if both operands contain numeric values. It is a compilation error to use the multiplication operator on values of nonnumeric data types.

Obtaining a Numeric Value from a TextBox

- Pass the value of the TextBox's Text property to function Val.

Finding a Compilation Error

- Double click the error message in the **Error List** window.

Obtaining Help for a Compilation Error

- Right click the error message in the **Error List** window, and select **Show Error Help** from the context menu.

KEY TERMS

argument—Inputs to a function that provide information the function needs to perform its task.

assignment operator—The "=" symbol used to assign values in an assignment statement.

assignment statement—A statement that copies one value to another. An assignment statement contains an "equals" sign (=) operator that causes the value of its right operand to be copied to its left operand.

binary operator—An operator that requires two operands.

case sensitive—The instance where two words that are spelled identically are treated differently if the capitalization of the two words differs.

class definition—The code that belongs to a class, beginning with keywords Public Class and ending with keywords End Class.

class name—The identifier used to identify the name of a class in code.

Class keyword—The keyword that begins a class definition.

Click event—An event raised when a user clicks a control.

code editor—A window where a user can create, view or edit an application's code.

Code view—A mode of the Visual Basic IDE where the application's code is displayed in an editor window.

comment—Text that follows a single-quote character (') and is inserted to improve an application's readability.

compilation error—An error that occurs when program statements violate the grammatical rules of a programming language or when statements are simply incorrect in the current context.

debugger—A tool that allows you to analyze the behavior of your application to determine whether it is executing correctly.

debugging—The process of fixing errors in an application.

dot operator—See member-access operator.

End Class keywords—Mark the end of a class definition.

Error List window—A window which displays compilation errors in your code.

event—A user action that can trigger an event handler.

event handler—A section of code that is executed (called) when a certain event is raised (occurs).

functionality—The actions an application can execute.

Handles clause—Specifies the event handled by an event handler and the object to which the event corresponds.

identifier—A series of characters consisting of letters, digits and underscores used to name program units such as classes, controls and variables.

IntelliSense—Visual Basic IDE feature that aids you during development by providing windows that list program items that are available in the current context.

keyword—A word in code reserved by the compiler for a specific purpose. By default, these words appear in blue in the IDE and cannot be used as identifiers.

left operand—The expression on the left side of a binary operator.

line-continuation character—An underscore character (_) preceded by one or more space characters, used to continue a statement to the next line of code.

logic error—An error that does not prevent the application from compiling successfully, but does cause the application to produce erroneous results.

member-access operator—Also known as the dot operator (.). Allows you to access a control's properties using code.

multiplication operator—The asterisk (*) used to multiply two operands, producing their product as a result.

operand—An expression on which an operator performs its task.

Output window—A window which displays the result of the compilation.

real-time error checking—Feature of the Visual Basic IDE that provides immediate notification of possible errors in your code. For example, unrecognized identifier errors are indicated by blue, jagged underlines in code.

right operand—The expression on the right side of a binary operator.

reserved words (keywords)—Words that are reserved by the Visual Basic compiler.

single-quote character(')—Indicates the beginning of a code comment.

statement—A unit of code that, when compiled and executed, performs an action.

syntax error—An error that occurs when program statements violate the grammatical rules of a programming language. Syntax errors are a subset of compilation errors.

`Val` function—Filters a number from its argument if possible. This avoids errors introduced by entering nonnumeric data when only numbers are expected. However, the result of the `Val` function is not always what you intended.

whitespace character—A space, tab or newline character.

CONTROLS, EVENTS, PROPERTIES & METHODS

`Button` [ab] Button This control allows the user to raise an action or event.

- ***In action***

Calculate Total

- ***Event***

`Click`—Raised when the user clicks the `Button`.

- ***Properties***

`Location`—Specifies the location of the `Button` on the `Form` relative to the `Form`'s top-left corner.

`Name`—Specifies the name used to identify the `Button`. The name should include the `Button` suffix.

`Size`—Specifies the width and height (in pixels) of the `Button`.

`Text`—Specifies the text displayed on the `Button`.

MULTIPLE-CHOICE QUESTIONS

5.1 A(n) _________ represents a user action, such as clicking a `Button`.

a) statement
b) event
c) application
d) function

5.2 To switch to **Code** view, select _________.

a) **Code > View**
b) **Design > Code**
c) **View > Code**
d) **View > File Code**

5.3 Code that performs the functionality of an application ________.

a) normally is provided by the programmer
b) can never be in the form of an event handler
c) always creates a graphical user interface
d) is always generated by the IDE

5.4 Comments ________.

a) help improve program readability
b) are preceded by the single-quote character
c) are ignored by the compiler
d) All of the above

5.5 The ________ allows a statement to continue past one line (when that character is preceded by one or more space characters).

a) single-quote (`'`) character
b) hyphen (`-`) character
c) underscore (`_`) character
d) plus (`+`) character

5.6 A(n) ________ causes an application to produce erroneous results.

a) logic error
b) event
c) assignment statement
d) compilation error

5.7 A(n) ________ is a portion of code that performs a specific task and returns a value.

a) variable
b) function
c) operand
d) identifier

5.8 Visual Basic keywords are ________.

a) identifiers
b) reserved words
c) case sensitive
d) properties

5.9 The Visual Basic IDE refuses to run your application until all ________ errors are corrected.

a) logical
b) serious
c) compilation
d) runtime

5.10 An example of a whitespace character is a ________ character.

a) space
b) tab
c) newline
d) All of the above

EXERCISES

5.11 ***(Inventory Enhancement)*** Extend the **Inventory** application to include a `TextBox` in which the user can enter the number of shipments received in a week. Assume that every shipment has the same number of cartons (each of which has the same number of items). Then modify the code so that the **Inventory** application uses that value in its calculation.

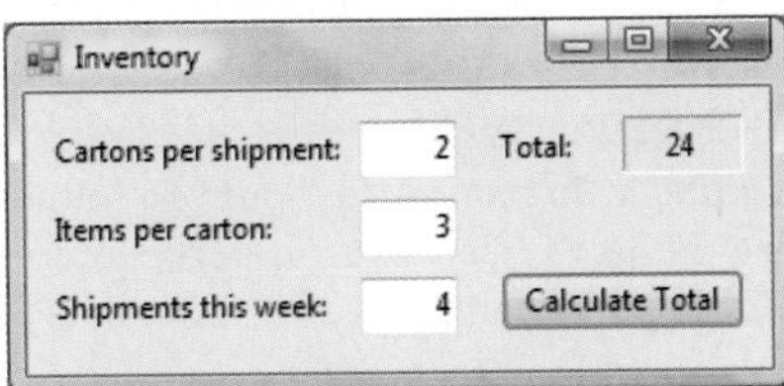

Figure 5.23 Enhanced **Inventory** application GUI.

a) ***Copying the template application to your working directory.*** Copy the directory `C:\Examples\Tutorial05\Exercises\InventoryEnhancement` to your `C:\SimplyVB2008` directory.

b) ***Opening the application's template file.*** Double click `InventoryEnhancment.sln` in the `InventoryEnhancement` directory to open the application.

c) ***Resizing the Form.*** Resize the Form you used in this tutorial by setting the Size property to 320, 147. Move the Button toward the bottom of the Form, as shown in Fig. 5.23. Its new location should be 193, 72.

d) ***Adding a Label.*** Add a Label to the Form and change the Text property to Shipments this week:. Set the Location property to 9, 77. Set the Label's Name property to shipmentsLabel.

e) ***Adding a TextBox.*** Add a TextBox to the right of the Label. Set its Text property to 0 and the Location property to 136, 74. Set the TextAlign and Size properties to the same values as for the other TextBoxes in this tutorial's example. Set the TextBox's Name property to shipmentsTextBox.

f) ***Modifying the code.*** Modify the **Calculate Total** Button's Click event handler so that it multiplies the number of shipments per week with the product of the number of cartons in a shipment and the number of items in a carton.

g) ***Running the application.*** Select **Debug > Start Debugging** to run your application. Enter values for the number of cartons per shipment, items per carton and shipments in the current week. Click the **Calculate Total** Button and verify that the total displayed is equal to the result when the three values entered are multiplied together. Enter a few sets of input and verify the total each time.

h) ***Closing the application.*** Close your running application by clicking its close box.

i) ***Closing the IDE.*** Close the Visual Basic IDE by clicking its close box.

5.12 ***(Counter Application)*** Create a counter application that consists of a Label and Button on the Form. The Label initially displays 0, but, each time a user clicks the Button, the value in the Label is increased by 1. When incrementing the Label, you need to write a statement such as totalLabel.Text = Val(totalLabel.Text) + 1.

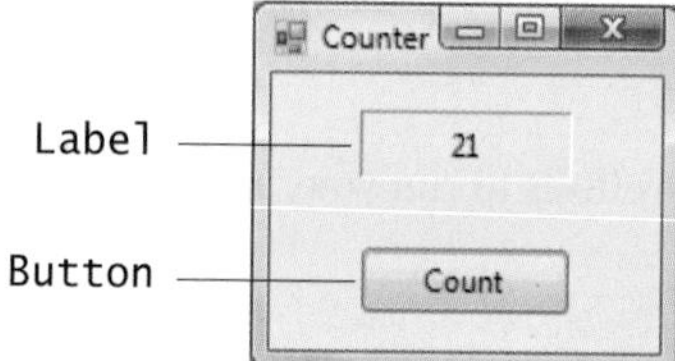

Figure 5.24 **Counter** GUI.

a) ***Creating the application.*** Create a new project named Counter.

b) ***Changing the name of the Form file.*** Change the name of Form1.vb to Counter.vb.

c) ***Modifying the Form.*** Change your Form's Font property to 9pt Segoe UI and the Size property to 176, 144. Modify the Form so that the title reads **Counter**. Change the name of the Form to CounterForm.

d) ***Adding a Label.*** Add a Label to the Form, and place it as shown in Fig. 5.24. Make sure that the Label's Text property is set to 0 and that TextAlign property is set so that any text will appear in the middle (both horizontally and vertically) of the Label. This can be done by using the TextAlign property's MiddleCenter value. Set the BorderStyle property to Fixed3D. Set the Label's Name property to countTotalLabel.

e) ***Adding a Button.*** Add a Button to the Form so that it appears as shown in Fig. 5.24. Set the Button's Text property to contain the text **Count**. Set the Button's Name property to countButton.

f) ***Creating an event handler.*** Add an event handler to the **Count** Button such that the value in the Label increases by 1 each time the user clicks the **Count** Button.

g) ***Running the application.*** Select **Debug > Start Debugging** to run your application. Click the **Count** Button several times and verify that the output value is incremented each time.

h) ***Closing the application.*** Close your running application by clicking its close box.

i) ***Closing the IDE.*** Close the Visual Basic IDE by clicking its close box.

5.13 ***(Account Information Application)*** Create an application that allows a user to input a name, account number and deposit amount. The user then clicks the **Enter** `Button`, which causes the name and account number to be copied and displayed in two output `Label`s. The deposit amount entered will be added to the balance amount displayed in another output `Label`. The result is displayed in the same output `Label`. Every time the **Enter** `Button` is clicked, the deposit amount entered is added to the balance amount displayed in the output `Label`, keeping a cumulative total. When updating the `Label`, you need to write a statement such as `depositsLabel.Text = Val(depositsLabel.Text) + Val(depositAmountTextBox.Text)`.

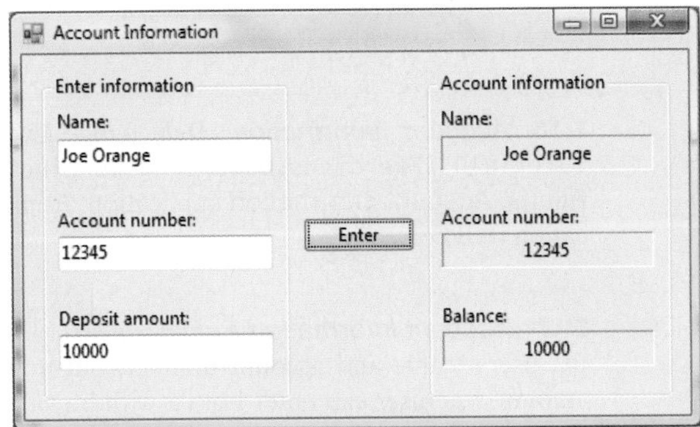

Figure 5.25 **Account Information** GUI.

a) ***Copying the template application to your working directory.*** Copy the directory `C:\Examples\Tutorial05\Exercises\AccountInformation` to your `C:\SimplyVB2008` directory.

b) ***Opening the application's template file.*** Double click `AccountInformation.sln` in the `AccountInformation` directory to open the application.

c) ***Creating an event handler.*** Add an event handler for the **Enter** `Button`'s `Click` event.

d) ***Coding the event handler.*** Code the event handler to copy information from the **Name:** and **Account number:** `TextBox`es to their corresponding output `Label`s. Then add the value in the **Deposit amount:** `TextBox` to the **Balance:** output `Label`, and display the result in the **Balance:** output `Label`.

e) ***Running the application.*** Select **Debug > Start Debugging** to run your application. Enter the values in Fig. 5.25 and click the **Enter** `Button`. Verify that the account information is displayed in the `Label`s on the right. Enter varying deposit amounts and click the **Enter** `Button` after each. Verify that the balance amount on the right has the new values added.

f) ***Closing the application.*** Close your running application by clicking its close box.

g) ***Closing the IDE.*** Close the Visual Basic IDE by clicking its close box.

What does this code do?

5.14 After entering `10` in `priceTextBox` and `1.05` in `taxTextBox`, a user clicks the `Button` named `enterButton`. What is the result of the click, given the following code?

```
Private Sub enterButton_Click(ByVal sender As _
   System.Object, ByVal e As System.EventArgs) _
   Handles enterButton.Click

   outputLabel.Text = Val(priceTextBox.Text) * Val(taxTextBox.Text)
End Sub ' enterButton_Click
```

What's wrong with this code?

5.15 The following event handler should execute when the user clicks a **Calculate** `Button`. Identify the error(s) in its code.

```
Private Sub calculateButton_Click(ByVal sender As
   System.Object, ByVal e As System.EventArgs) _ ' second line
   Handles calculateButton.Click

   resultLabel.Text = priceTextBox.Text * taxTextBox.Text
End Sub ' calculateButton_Click
```

Using the Debugger

5.16 ***(Account Information Debugging Exercise)*** Copy the directory `C:\Examples\Tutorial05\Exercises\DebuggingExercise` to your `C:\SimplyVB2008` directory, then run the **Account Information** application. Remove any compilation errors, so that the application runs correctly.

Programming Challenge

5.17 ***(Account Information Enhancement)*** Modify Exercise 5.13 so that it no longer asks for the user's name and account number, but now asks the user for a withdrawal or deposit amount. The user can enter both a withdrawal and deposit amount at the same time. When the **Enter** `Button` is clicked, the balance is updated appropriately.

a) ***Copying the template application to your working directory.*** If you have not already done so, copy the `C:\Examples\Tutorial05\Exercises\AccountInformation` directory to your `C:\SimplyVB2008` directory.

b) ***Opening the application's template file.*** Double click `AccountInformation.sln` in the `AccountInformation` directory to open the application.

c) ***Modifying the GUI.*** Modify the GUI so that it appears as in Fig. 5.26.

d) ***Setting the default values.*** Set the default name and account number to the values shown in Fig. 5.26 using the **Properties** window.

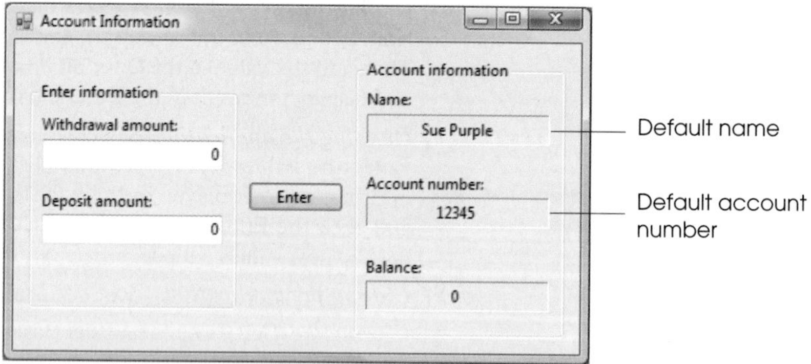

Figure 5.26 Enhanced **Account Information** GUI.

e) ***Writing code to add functionality.*** Update the account balance for every withdrawal (which decreases the balance) and every deposit (which increases the balance). When the balance is updated, reset the `TextBox`es to `"0"`.

f) ***Running the application.*** Select **Debug > Start Debugging** to run your application. Enter various withdrawal and deposit amounts; click the **Enter** `Button` after each. Verify that the balance on the right of the application is updated appropriately after each click of the **Enter** `Button`.

g) ***Closing the application.*** Close your running application by clicking its close box.

h) ***Closing the IDE.*** Close the Visual Basic IDE by clicking its close box.

TUTORIAL

Enhancing the Inventory Application

Introducing Variables, Memory Concepts and Arithmetic

Objectives

In this tutorial, you learn to:

- Create variables.
- Handle the `TextChanged` event.
- Apply basic memory concepts using variables.
- Understand the precedence rules of arithmetic operators.
- Set breakpoints to debug applications.

Outline

In the previous tutorial, you developed an **Inventory** application that used multiplication to calculate the number of items received into inventory. You learned how to create `TextBoxes` to read user input from the keyboard. You also added a `Button` to a `Form` and programmed that `Button` to respond to a user's click. In this tutorial, you'll enhance your **Inventory** application using additional programming concepts, including variables, events and arithmetic.

6.1 Test-Driving the Enhanced Inventory Application

In this tutorial, you'll enhance the previous tutorial's **Inventory** application by inserting code rather than dragging and dropping Visual Basic controls. You'll use variables to perform arithmetic in Visual Basic, and you'll study memory concepts to help you understand how applications run on computers. Recall that your **Inventory** application from Tutorial 5 calculated the number of items received from information supplied by the user—the number of cartons and the number of textbooks per carton. The enhanced application must meet the following requirements:

Application Requirements

The inventory manager notices a flaw in your ***Inventory*** *application. Although the application calculates the correct result, that result continues to display even after new data is entered. The only time the output changes is when the inventory manager clicks the* ***Calculate Total*** *`Button` again. You need to alter the* ***Inventory*** *application to clear the result as soon as the user enters new information into either of the `TextBoxes`, to avoid any confusion over the accuracy of your calculated result.*

You'll begin by test-driving the completed application. Then you'll learn the additional Visual Basic technologies needed to create your own version of this application. At first glance, the application does not seem to operate any differently from the application in the previous tutorial. However, you should notice that the **Total:** `Label` clears when you enter new data into either of the `TextBoxes`.

Test-Driving the Enhanced Inventory Application

1. ***Opening the completed application.*** Open the `C:\Examples\Tutorial06\CompletedApplication\Inventory3` directory to locate the enhanced **Inventory** application. Double click `Inventory3.sln` to open the application in the Visual Basic IDE.

2. ***Running the Inventory application.*** Select **Debug > Start Debugging** to run the application (Fig. 6.1).

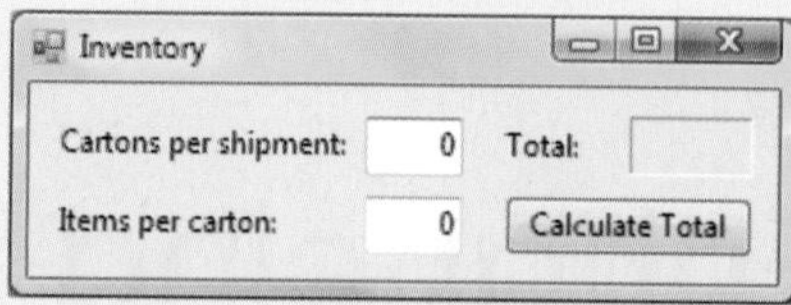

Figure 6.1 **Inventory** application GUI displayed when the application runs.

3. ***Calculating the number of items in the shipment.*** Enter `5` in the **Cartons per shipment:** `TextBox` and `6` in the **Items per carton:** `TextBox`. Click the **Calculate Total** `Button`. The result (`30`) displays in the **Total:** output `Label` (Fig. 6.2).

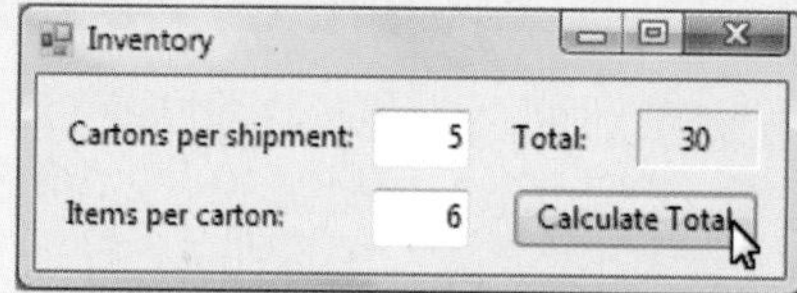

Figure 6.2 Running the **Inventory** application.

4. ***Entering new quantities.*** After you modify the application, the result displayed in the **Total:** `Label` will be removed when the user enters a new quantity in either `TextBox`. Enter `13` as the new number of cartons—the last calculation's result is cleared (Fig. 6.3). This is explained later in this tutorial.

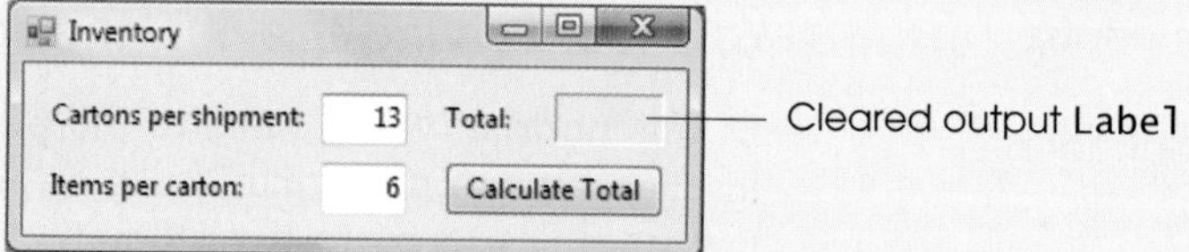

Figure 6.3 Enhanced **Inventory** application clears output `Label` after new input.

5. ***Closing the application.*** Close your running application by clicking its close box.

6. ***Closing the IDE.*** Close the Visual Basic IDE by clicking its close box.

6.2 Variables

A **variable** holds data for your application, much as the `Text` property of a `Label` holds the text to be displayed to the user. Unlike the `Text` property of a `Label`, however, variable values are not shown to the user by default. Using variables in an application allows you to store and manipulate data without necessarily showing the data to the user and to store data without adding or using controls. Variables store data such as numbers, the date, the time and so on. However, each variable used in Visual Basic corresponds to exactly one type of information. For example, a variable of a numeric data type cannot be used to store text.

In Visual Basic, all variables must be **declared**, or reported, to the compiler by using program code. All **declarations** that you'll make within event handlers begin with the keyword **`Dim`**. Recall that keywords are reserved for use by Visual Basic. (A complete list of Visual Basic keywords is presented in Appendix E.)

The following box introduces programming with variables. A variable name can be any valid identifier, which, as you learned in Tutorial 5, is a name that the compiler can recognize (and is not a keyword). As you also learned in the last tutorial, there are many valid characters for identifiers.

Using Variables in the Inventory Application

1. ***Copying the template to your working directory.*** Copy the `C:\Examples\Tutorial06\TemplateApplication\Inventory3` directory to your `C:\SimplyVB2008` directory.

2. ***Opening the* Inventory *application's template file.*** Double click `Inventory3.sln` in the `Inventory3` directory to open the application in the Visual Basic IDE.

3. ***Adding variable declarations to event handler `calculateButton_Click`.*** If you are in **Design** view, enter **Code** view by selecting **View > Code**. Add lines 7–10 of Fig. 6.4 to event handler `calculateButton_Click`. Lines 8–10 are declarations, which begin with keyword `Dim`. Note that, when you type the word `Dim`, as with all keywords, the IDE colors it blue by default. The words `cartons`, `items` and `result` are variable names. Lines 8–10 declare that variables `cartons`, `items` and `result` store data of type `Integer`, using the `As` keyword. The `As` keyword indicates that the following word (in this case `Integer`) is the variable type. `Integer` variables store **integer** values (whole numbers such as 919, 0 and –11). Notice that the IDE initially underlines the variables to indicate that they have not been used in the application. This is to safeguard against including any unnecessary variables in your application.

Good Programming Practice

Use only letters and digits as characters for your variable names.

Good Programming Practice

Typically, variable-name identifiers begin with a lowercase letter. Every word in the name after the first word should begin with a capital letter—for example, `firstNumber`. This is often called camel case.

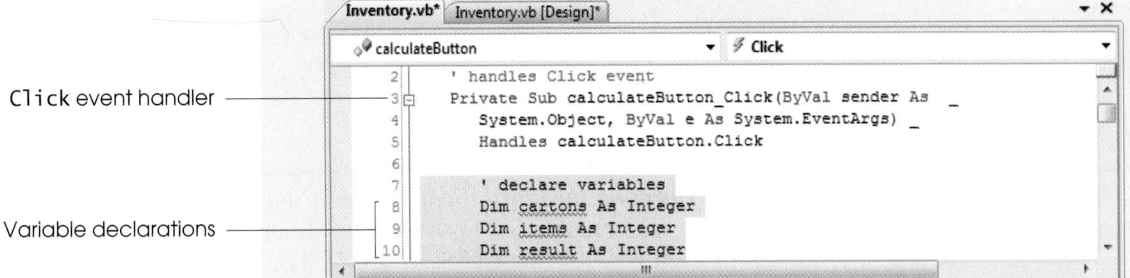
Inventory.vb* Inventory.vb [Design]*
calculateButton
Click
2 ' handles Click event
3 Private Sub calculateButton_Click(ByVal sender As _
4 System.Object, ByVal e As System.EventArgs) _
5 Handles calculateButton.Click
6
7 ' declare variables
8 Dim cartons As Integer
9 Dim items As Integer
10 Dim result As Integer
Click event handler
Variable declarations

Figure 6.4 Declaring variables in event handler `calculateButton_Click`.

4. ***Retrieving input from TextBoxes.*** Skip one line after the variable declarations, and add lines 12–14 of Fig. 6.5 in event handler `calculateButton_Click`. Once the user enters numbers and clicks **Calculate Total**, the values found in the `Text` property of each `TextBox` control are converted to numerical values by the `Val` function. Then the numbers are assigned to variables `cartons` (line 13) and `items` (line 14) with the assignment operator, =. Line 13 is read as "`cartons` *gets* the result of the `Val` function applied to `cartonsTextBox.Text`."

5. ***Saving the project.*** Select **File > Save All** to save your modified code.

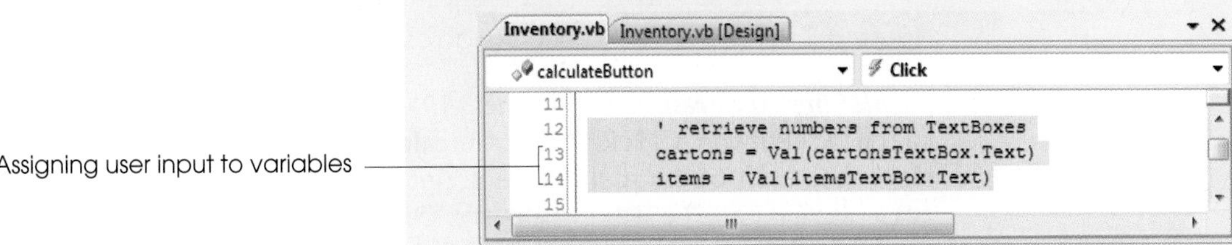
Inventory.vb Inventory.vb [Design]
calculateButton
Click
11
12 ' retrieve numbers from TextBoxes
13 cartons = Val(cartonsTextBox.Text)
14 items = Val(itemsTextBox.Text)
15
Assigning user input to variables

Figure 6.5 Retrieving numerical input from `TextBoxes`.

The `Val` function returns a numerical value as data type **`Double`** when converting a value retrieved from a `TextBox`'s `Text` property. Data type `Double` is used to store both whole and fractional numbers. Normally, `Double`s store floating-point numbers, which are numbers with decimal points such as 2.3456 and –845.4680. Variables of data type `Double` can hold much larger (and much smaller) values than variables of data type `Integer`.

After `Val` converts the two values input by the user to `Double`s, lines 13–14 implicitly convert the `Double`s to `Integer` values. The integer value obtained by converting the `Double` in line 13 is assigned to variable `cartons`, which is of type `Integer`. Likewise, the integer value obtained by converting the `Double` in line 14 is assigned to variable `items`. Because `Double`s and `Integer`s are different types, Visual Basic performs a conversion from one type to the other. This process is called **implicit conversion** because the conversion is performed by Visual Basic without any additional code. Implicit conversions from `Double` to `Integer` are generally considered poor programming practice due to the potential loss of information. In Tutorial 15, you'll learn how to perform explicit conversions. Now that you've assigned values to your new variables, use the variables to calculate the number of textbooks received.

Visual Basic defines 15 **primitive data types** (listed in Fig. 6.6), such as `Integer`. Primitive data type names are also keywords. In addition to the primitive types, Visual Basic also defines the type `Object`. Together, the primitive data types and type `Object` are known as **built-in data types**. You'll use some of these data types throughout the book. Appendix F lists the primitive types and their value ranges.

Built-in (primitive) data types				
`Boolean`	`Date`	`Integer`	`Long`	`Short`
`Byte`	`Decimal`	`Single`	`Char`	`Double`
`SByte`	`String`	`UInteger`	`ULong`	`UShort`

Figure 6.6 Visual Basic built-in data types.

Using Variables in a Calculation

1. ***Performing the multiplication operation.*** Skip one line from the end of the last statement you inserted and insert lines 16–17 in event handler `calculateButton_Click` (Fig. 6.7). The statement in line 17 multiplies the `Integer` variable `cartons` by `items` and assigns the result to variable `result`, using the assignment operator `=`. The statement is read as, "`result` *gets* the value of `cartons * items`." (Most calculations are performed in assignment statements.)

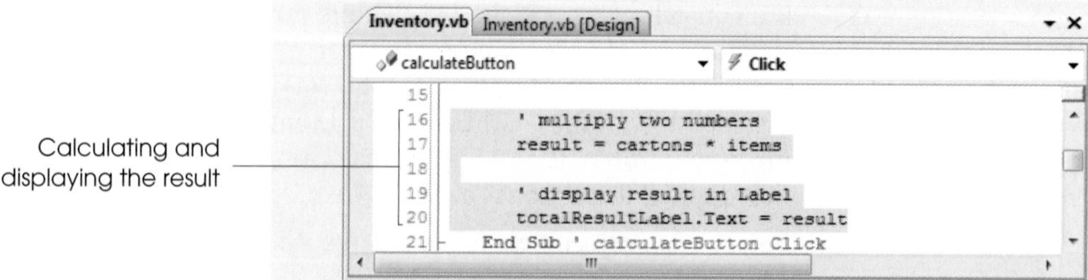
Calculating and displaying the result
Inventory.vb
Inventory.vb [Design]
calculateButton
Click
15
16 ' multiply two numbers
17 result = cartons * items
18
19 ' display result in Label
20 totalResultLabel.Text = result
21 End Sub ' calculateButton_Click

Figure 6.7 Multiplication, using variables in `calculateButton_Click`.

2. ***Displaying the result.*** Add lines 19–20 of Fig. 6.7 to event handler `calculateButton_Click`. After the calculation is completed, line 20 displays the result of the multiplication operation. The number is assigned to `totalResultLabel`'s `Text` property. Once the property is updated, the `Label` displays the result of the multiplication operation (Fig. 6.8).

(cont.)

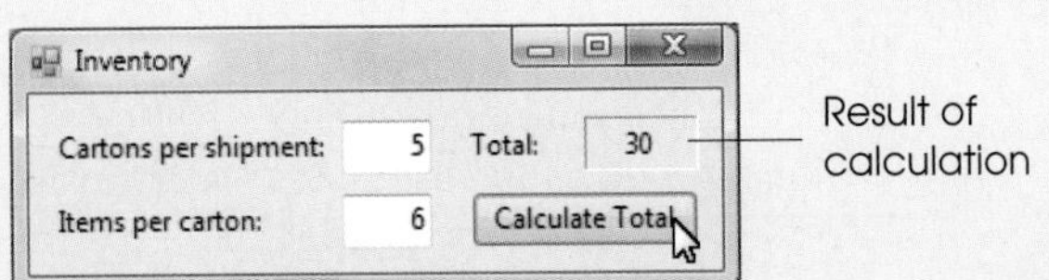

Figure 6.8 Displaying the multiplication result using variables.

3. ***Running the application.*** Select **Debug > Start Debugging** to run your application. Enter `5` in the **Cartons per shipment:** `TextBox` and `6` in the **Items per carton:** `TextBox`. Then click the **Calculate Total** `Button` to test your application.

4. ***Closing the application.*** Close your running application by clicking its close box.

SELF-REVIEW

1. When Visual Basic converts a `Double` to an `Integer` without requiring any code, this is referred to as a(n) ________.

   a) explicit conversion b) implicit conversion
   c) data-type change d) transformation

2. Data types already defined in Visual Basic, such as `Integer`, are known as ________ data types.

   a) provided b) existing
   c) defined d) built-in

Answers: 1) b. 2) d.

6.3 Handling the TextChanged Event

You may have noticed that the flaw, or **bug**, mentioned in the application requirements at the beginning of this tutorial remains in your application. Although `totalResultLabel` displays the current result, once you enter a new number into a `TextBox`, that result is no longer valid—the result displayed does not change again until you click the **Calculate Total** `Button`, potentially confusing the application user. In the next box, you'll add event handlers to clear the output whenever new data is entered.

Handling the TextChanged Event

Good Programming Practice

If a statement is wider than the code editor window, use the line-continuation character to continue it on the next line.

1. ***Adding an event handler for `cartonsTextBox`'s `TextChanged` event.*** Switch to the IDE's **Design** view and double click the **Cartons per shipment:** `TextBox` to generate an event handler for the **TextChanged** event, which is raised when the `TextBox`'s text changes. This is the default event for `TextBoxes`. The IDE generates an event handler with an empty body (no additional code) and places the cursor in the body. Insert line 28 of Fig. 6.9 into your code. Note that we've added line-continuation characters (_) at the ends of lines 24–25 of this code, as well as a comment in line 23, before the event handler. Recall from Tutorial 5 that using line-continuation characters increases code readability by avoiding long lines that don't fit in the window.

   According to the application requirements for this tutorial, the application should clear the value in `totalResultLabel` every time users change the text in either `TextBox`. Line 28 clears the value in `totalResultLabel`. The notation `""` (side-by-side double quotes) in line 28 is called an **empty string**, which is a value that does not contain any characters. This empty string replaces whatever is stored in `totalResultLabel.Text`. Note that you can also represent an empty string as `String.Empty`.

(cont.)

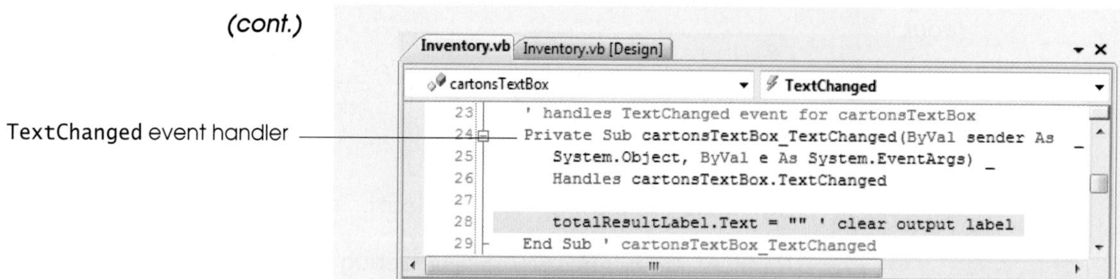

Figure 6.9 `TextChanged` event handler for **Cartons per shipment:** `TextBox`.

2. ***Adding an event handler for `itemsTextBox`'s `TextChanged` event.*** You want the result cleared regardless of which `TextBox` changes value first. Return to **Design** view by clicking the **Inventory.vb [Design]** tab. Then double click the **Items per carton:** `TextBox`, and insert line 36 from Fig. 6.10 into the new event handler. Note that these lines perform the same task as line 28—you want the same action to occur, namely, clearing a `TextBox`.

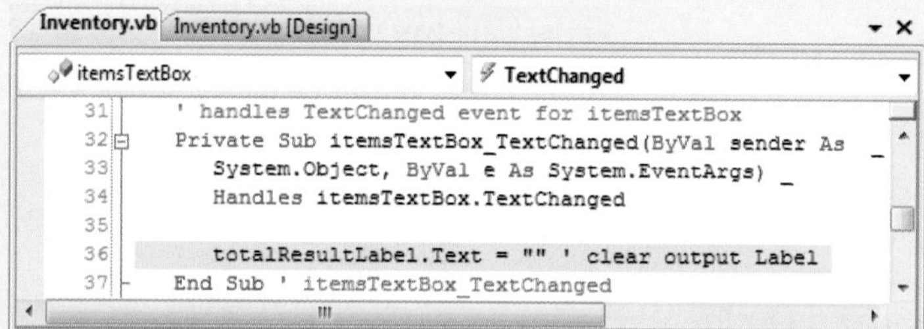

Figure 6.10 `TextChanged` event handler for **Items per carton:** `TextBox`.

3. ***Running the application.*** Select **Debug > Start Debugging** to run your application. To test the application, enter 8 in the **Cartons per shipment:** `TextBox` and 7 in the **Items per carton:** `TextBox`. When you click the **Calculate Total** `Button`, the number `56` should appear in the output `Label`. Then enter 9 in the **Items per carton:** `TextBox` to ensure that the `TextChanged` event handler clears the output `Label`.

4. ***Closing the application.*** Close your running application by clicking its close box.

Figure 6.11 presents the source code for the enhanced **Inventory** application. The lines of code that contain new programming concepts you learned in this tutorial are highlighted.

Use keyword `Dim` to declare variables inside an event handler

```
Public Class InventoryForm
   ' handles Click event
   Private Sub calculateButton_Click(ByVal sender As _
      System.Object, ByVal e As System.EventArgs) _
      Handles calculateButtton.Click

      ' declare variables
      Dim cartons As Integer
      Dim items As Integer
      Dim result As Integer

```

Figure 6.11 **Inventory** application code. (Part 1 of 2.)

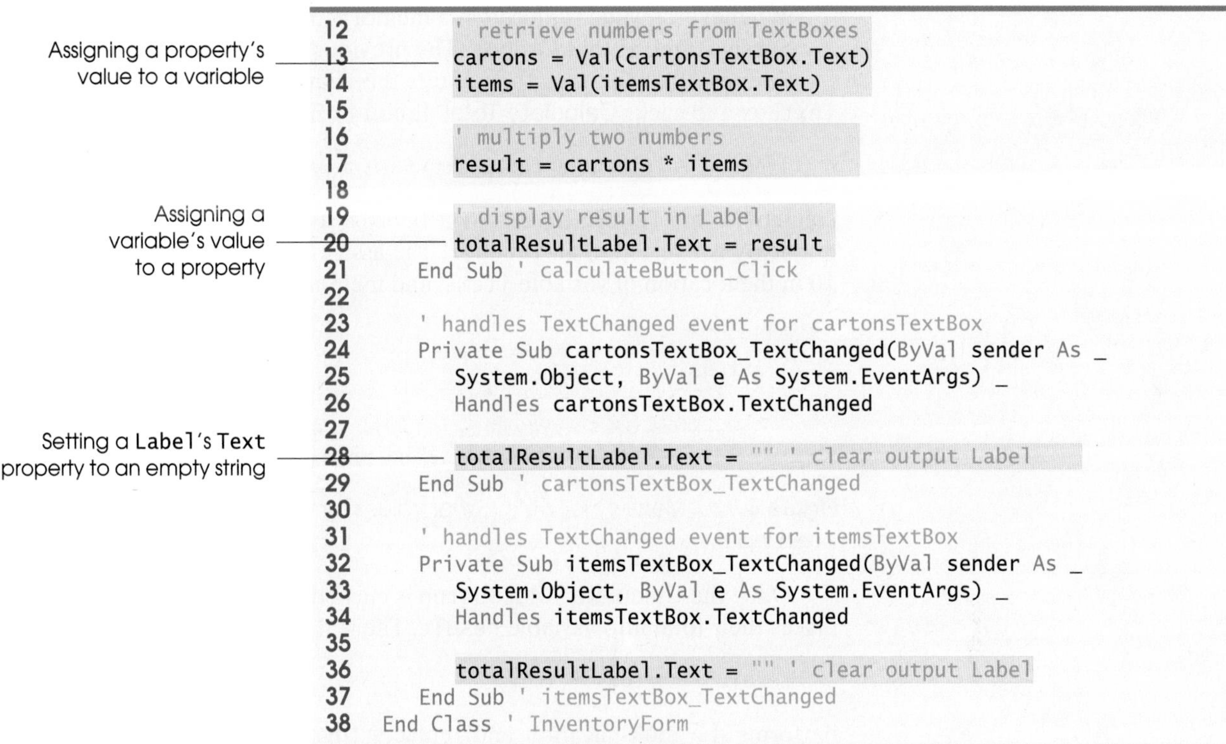


```
12         ' retrieve numbers from TextBoxes
13         cartons = Val(cartonsTextBox.Text)
14         items = Val(itemsTextBox.Text)
15
16         ' multiply two numbers
17         result = cartons * items
18
19         ' display result in Label
20         totalResultLabel.Text = result
21      End Sub ' calculateButton_Click
22
23      ' handles TextChanged event for cartonsTextBox
24      Private Sub cartonsTextBox_TextChanged(ByVal sender As _
25         System.Object, ByVal e As System.EventArgs) _
26         Handles cartonsTextBox.TextChanged
27
28         totalResultLabel.Text = "" ' clear output Label
29      End Sub ' cartonsTextBox_TextChanged
30
31      ' handles TextChanged event for itemsTextBox
32      Private Sub itemsTextBox_TextChanged(ByVal sender As _
33         System.Object, ByVal e As System.EventArgs) _
34         Handles itemsTextBox.TextChanged
35
36         totalResultLabel.Text = "" ' clear output Label
37      End Sub ' itemsTextBox_TextChanged
38   End Class ' InventoryForm
```

Figure 6.11 **Inventory** application code. (Part 2 of 2.)

SELF-REVIEW

1. The ________ is represented by "" in Visual Basic.
   a) empty character
   b) empty string
   c) empty value
   d) None of the above

2. Use the ________ property to remove any text displayed in a `TextBox`.
   a) `ClearText`
   b) `Remove`
   c) `Display`
   d) `Text`

Answers: 1) b. 2) d.

6.4 Memory Concepts

Variable names—such as `cartons`, `items` and `result`—correspond to actual locations in the computer's memory. Every variable has a **name**, **type**, **size** and **value**. In the **Inventory** application code listing in Fig. 6.11, when the statement (line 13)

```
cartons = Val(cartonsTextBox.Text)
```

executes, the user input stored in `cartonsTextBox.Text` is implicitly converted to an `Integer`. Suppose that the user enters the characters `12` in the **Cartons per shipment:** `TextBox`. This input is stored in `cartonsTextBox.Text`. When the user clicks **Calculate Total**, line 13 converts the user input to a `Double` using `Val`, then the `Double` value is implicitly converted to an `Integer`. The assignment then places the `Integer` value 12 in the location for variable `cartons`, as shown in Fig. 6.12.

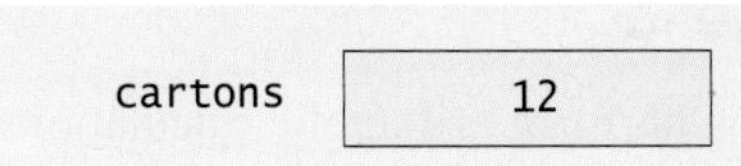

Figure 6.12 Memory location showing name and value of variable `cartons`.

Whenever a value is placed in a memory location, this value replaces the value previously stored in that location. The previous value is overwritten (lost).

Suppose that the user then enters the characters `10` in the **Items per carton:** `TextBox` and clicks **Calculate Total.** Line 14 of Fig. 6.11

```
items = Val(itemsTextBox.Text)
```

converts `itemsTextBox.Text` to a `Double` using `Val`; then the `Double` value is implicitly converted to an `Integer`. The assignment then places the `Integer` value `10` in the location of variable `items`, and memory appears as shown in Fig. 6.13.

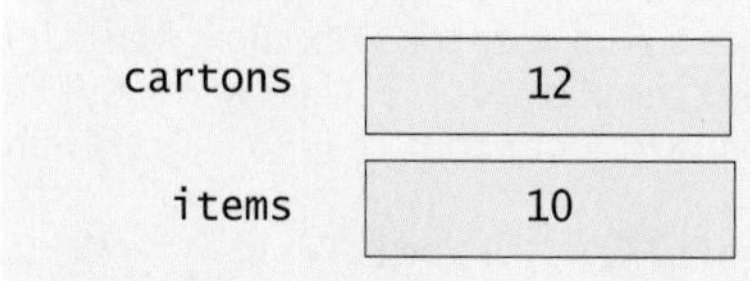

Figure 6.13 Memory locations after values for variables `cartons` and `items` have been input.

Once the **Calculate Total** `Button` is clicked, line 17 multiplies these values and places their total into variable `result`. The statement

```
result = cartons * items
```

performs the multiplication and replaces (that is, overwrites) `result`'s previous value. After `result` is calculated, the memory appears as shown in Fig. 6.14. Note that the values of `cartons` and `items` appear exactly as they did before they were used in the calculation of `result`. Although these values were used when the computer performed the calculation, they were not destroyed. This illustrates that when a value is read from a memory location, the process is **nondestructive** (meaning that the value is not overwritten).

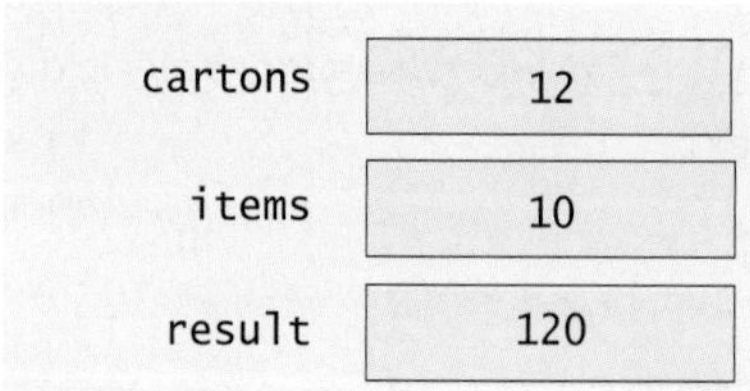

Figure 6.14 Memory locations after a multiplication operation.

SELF-REVIEW

1. When a value is placed into a memory location, the value _________ the previous value in that location.
   a) copies
   b) replaces
   c) adds itself to
   d) moves

2. When a value is read from memory, that value is _________.
   a) overwritten
   b) replaced with a new value
   c) moved to a new location in memory
   d) not overwritten

Answers: 1) b. 2) d.

6.5 Arithmetic

Most programs perform arithmetic calculations. In the last tutorial, you performed the arithmetic operation multiplication by using the multiplication operator (*). The **arithmetic operators** are summarized in Fig. 6.15. Note the use of various special symbols not used in algebra. For example, the **asterisk** (*) indicates multiplication, the keyword Mod represents the **modulus operator**, the **backslash** (\) represents integer division and the **caret** (^) represents exponentiation. Most of the arithmetic operators in Fig. 6.15 are **binary operators**, each requiring two operands.

Visual Basic .NET operation	Arithmetic operator	Algebraic expression	Visual Basic 2008 expression
Addition	+	$f+7$	`f + 7`
Subtraction	–	$p-c$	`p - c`
Multiplication	*	bm	`b * m`
Division (float)	/	x / y or $\frac{x}{y}$ or $x \div y$	`x / y`
Division (integer)	\	none	`v \ u`
Modulus	Mod	$r \bmod s$	`r Mod s`
Exponentiation	^	q^p	`q ^ p`
Unary Negative	-	$-e$	`-e`
Unary Positive	+	$+g$	`+g`

Figure 6.15 Arithmetic operators.

For example, the expression sum + value contains the binary operator + and the two operands sum and value. Visual Basic also provides **unary operators**, which are operators that take only one operand. For example, unary versions of plus (+) and minus (-) are provided so that programmers can write expressions such as +9 (a positive number) and -19 (a negative number).

Visual Basic has separate operators for **integer division** (the backslash, \) and **floating-point division** (the forward slash, /). Floating-point division divides two numbers (whole or fractional) and returns a floating-point number (a number with a decimal point). The operator for integer division treats its operands as integers and returns an integer result. When floating-point numbers (numbers with decimal points) are used with the integer-division operator, the numbers are first rounded as follows:

- numbers ending in .5 are rounded to the nearest *even* integer—for example, 6.5 rounds *down* to 6 and 7.5 rounds *up* to 8
- all other floating-point numbers are rounded to the nearest integer—for example, 7.1 rounds *down* to 7 and 7.7 rounds *up* to 8

then divided. This means that, although 4.5 \ 2 evaluates to 2 as expected, the statement 5.5 \ 2 evaluates to 3, because 5.5 is rounded to 6 *before* the division occurs. Similarly, although 7.1 \ 4 evaluates to 1 as expected, the statement 7.7 \ 4 evaluates to 2, because 7.7 is rounded to 8 *before* the division occurs. Note that any fractional part in the integer division result simply is discarded (also called truncated)—no rounding occurs. Neither division operator allows division by zero. If your code divides by zero, a runtime error known as an "exception" occurs. By default, this error terminates the application. You learn about exception handling in Tutorial 25.

Attempting to divide by zero is a **runtime error** (that is, an error that has its effect while the application executes). Dividing by zero terminates an application.

The modulus operator, Mod, yields the remainder after division. The expression x Mod y yields the remainder after x is divided by y. Thus, 7 Mod 4 yields 3, and 17 Mod 5 yields 2. This operator is used most commonly with Integer operands, but also can be used with other types. The modulus operator can be applied to several interesting problems, such as discovering whether one number is a multiple of another. If a and b are numbers, a Mod b yields 0 if a is a multiple of b. 8 Mod 3 yields 2, so 8 is not a multiple of 3. But 8 Mod 2 and 8 Mod 4 each yield 0, because 8 is a multiple both of 2 and of 4.

Arithmetic expressions in Visual Basic must be written in **straight-line form** so that you can type them into a computer. For example, the division of `7.1` by `4.3` cannot be written

$$\frac{7.1}{4.3}$$

but is written in straight-line form as `7.1 / 4.3`. Raising 3 to the second power cannot be written as 3^2 but is written in straight-line form as `3 ^ 2`.

Parentheses are used in Visual Basic expressions to group operations in the same manner as in algebraic expressions. To multiply *a* times the quantity *b* + *c*, you write

```
a * ( b + c )
```

Visual Basic applies the operators in arithmetic expressions in a precise sequence, determined by the **rules of operator precedence**, which are generally the same as those followed in algebra. These rules enable Visual Basic to apply operators in the correct order.

Rules of Operator Precedence

1. ***Operators in expressions contained within a pair of parentheses are evaluated first.*** Thus, *parentheses can be used to force the order of evaluation to occur in any sequence you desire.* Parentheses are at the highest level of precedence. With **nested** (or **embedded**) parentheses, the operators contained in the innermost pair of parentheses are applied first.
2. ***Exponentiation is applied next.*** If an expression contains several exponentiation operations, operators are applied from left to right.
3. ***Unary positive and negative, + and -, are applied next.*** If an expression contains several sign operations, operators are applied from left to right.
4. ***Multiplication and floating-point division operations are applied next.*** If an expression contains several multiplication and floating-point division operations, operators are applied from left to right.
5. ***Integer division is applied next.*** If an expression contains several `Integer` division operations, operators are applied from left to right.
6. ***Modulus operations are applied next.*** If an expression contains several modulus operations, operators are applied from left to right.
7. ***Addition and subtraction operations are applied last.*** If an expression contains several addition and subtraction operations, operators are applied from left to right.

Note that we mention nested parentheses. Not all expressions with several pairs of parentheses contain nested parentheses. For example, although the expression

```
a * ( b + c ) + c * ( d + e )
```

contains multiple pairs of parentheses, none of the parentheses are nested. These sets of parentheses are referred to as being "on the same level" and are evaluated from left to right.

Let's consider several expressions in light of the rules of operator precedence. Each example lists an algebraic expression and its Visual Basic equivalent.

The following calculates the average of three numbers:

Algebra: $m = \frac{(a + b + c)}{3}$

Visual Basic: `m = ( a + b + c ) / 3`

The parentheses are required because floating-point division has higher precedence than addition. The entire quantity (a + b + c) is to be divided by 3. If the parentheses are omitted, erroneously, we obtain a + b + c / 3, which evaluates as

$$a + b + \frac{c}{3}$$

The following is the equation of a straight line:

Algebra: $y = mx + b$

Visual Basic: `y = m * x + b`

No parentheses are required. The multiplication is applied first, because multiplication has a higher precedence than addition. The assignment occurs last because it has a lower precedence than multiplication and addition.

To develop a better understanding of the rules of operator precedence, consider how the expression $y = ax^2 + bx + c$ is evaluated:

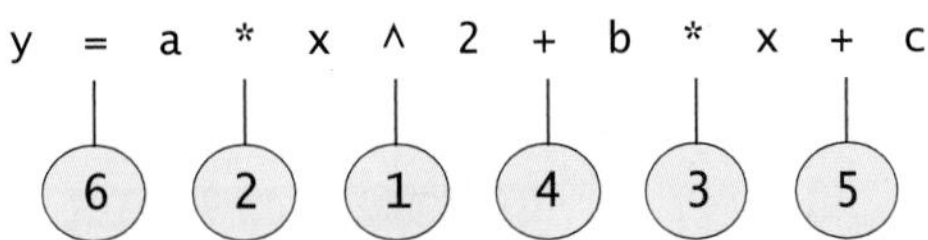

The circled numbers under the statement indicate the order in which Visual Basic applies the operators. Remember that in Visual Basic x^2 is represented as x ^ 2. Also, note that the assignment operator is applied last because it has a lower precedence than any of the arithmetic operators.

Using redundant parentheses in complex arithmetic expressions can make the expressions easier to read.

As in algebra, it is acceptable to place unnecessary parentheses in an expression to make the expression easier to read—these are called **redundant parentheses**. For example, the preceding assignment statement might use redundant parentheses to emphasize terms:

```
y = ( a * ( x ^ 2 ) ) + ( b * x ) + c
```

SELF-REVIEW

1. Arithmetic expressions in Visual Basic must be written ________ to facilitate entering applications into the computer.
   a) using parentheses b) on multiple lines
   c) in straight-line form d) None of the above

2. The expression to the right of the assignment operator (=) is always evaluated ________ the assignment occurs.
   a) before b) after
   c) at the same time d) None of the above

Answers: 1) c. 2) a.

6.6 Using the Debugger: Breakpoints

The debugger will be one of your most important tools in developing applications, once you become familiar with its features. You were introduced to the debugger in Tutorial 5, where you used it to locate and eliminate syntax errors. In this tutorial, you continue your study of the debugger, learning about breakpoints, which allow you to examine what your application is doing while it is running. A **breakpoint** is a marker that can be set at any executable line of code. When application execution reaches a breakpoint, execution pauses, allowing you to peek inside your application and ensure that there are no logic errors, such as an incorrect calculation. In the next box, *Using the Debugger: Breakpoints*, you learn how to use breakpoints in the Visual Basic IDE debugger.

Using the Debugger: Breakpoints

1. ***Inserting breakpoints in the Visual Basic IDE.*** Ensure that the `Inventory3` project is open in the IDE's **Code** view. To insert a breakpoint in the IDE, either click inside the **margin indicator bar** (the gray margin indicator at the left of the code window, Fig. 6.16) next to the line of code at which you wish to break, or right click that line of code and select **Breakpoint > Insert Breakpoint**. You can set as many breakpoints as necessary. Set breakpoints at lines 17 and 20 of your code. A solid circle appears where you clicked, indicating that a breakpoint has been set (Fig. 6.16). When the application runs, it suspends execution at any line that contains a breakpoint. The application is said to be in **break mode** when the debugger pauses the application's execution. Breakpoints can be set during design mode, break mode and run mode.

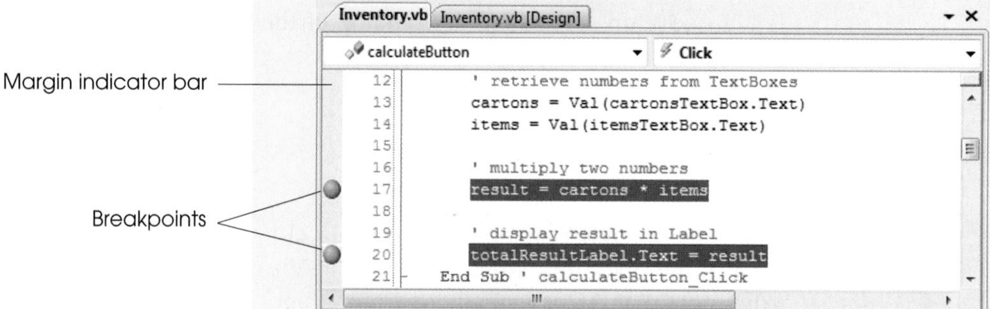

Figure 6.16 Setting two breakpoints.

2. ***Beginning the debugging process.*** After setting breakpoints in the code editor, select **Debug > Start Debugging** to begin the debugging process. During debugging of a Windows application, the application window appears (Fig. 6.17), allowing application interaction (input and output). Enter 10 and 7 into the `Textboxes` and click **Calculate Total** to continue. The title bar of the IDE displays **(Debugging)** (Fig. 6.18), indicating that the IDE is in break mode.

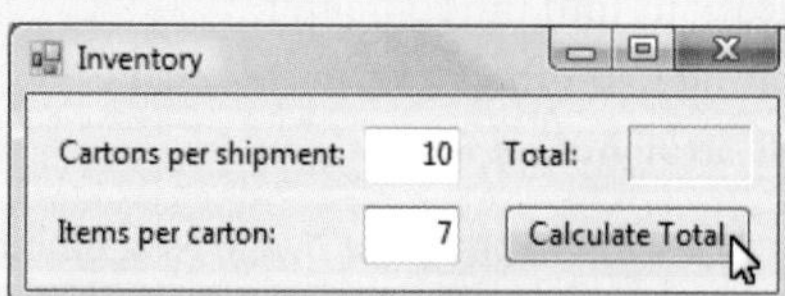

Figure 6.17 **Inventory** application running.

Title bar displays **(Debugging)**

Inventory3 (Debugging) - Microsoft Visual Basic 2008 Express Edition

File Edit View Project Build Debug Tools Window Help

Figure 6.18 Title bar of the IDE displaying **(Debugging)**.

3. ***Examining application execution.*** Application execution suspends at the first breakpoint, and the IDE becomes the **active window** (Fig. 6.19). The yellow arrow to the left of line 17 indicates that this line contains the next statement to execute.

(cont.)

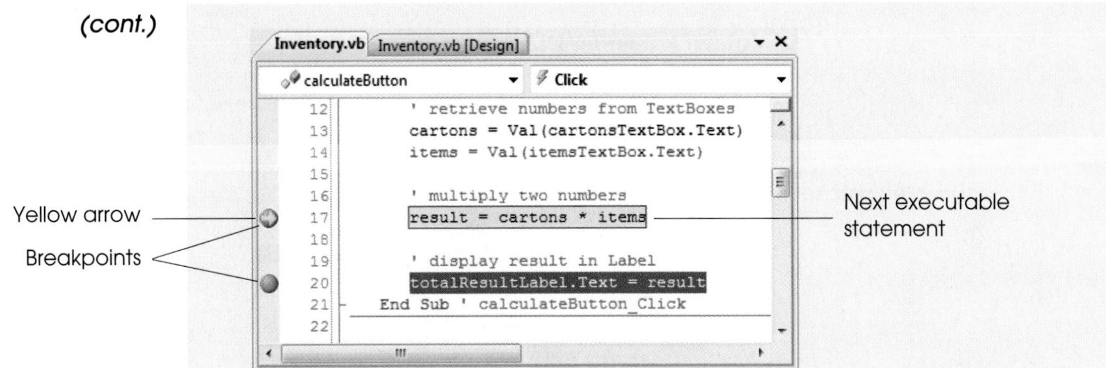

Figure 6.19 Application execution suspended at the first breakpoint.

4. ***Using the Continue command to resume execution.*** To resume execution, select **Debug > Continue** (or press *F5*). The application executes until it stops at the next breakpoint, in line 20. Note that when you place your mouse pointer over the variable name `result`, the value that the variable stores is displayed in a ***Quick Info*** box (Fig. 6.20). In a sense, you are peeking inside the computer at the value of one of your variables. As you'll see, this can help you spot logic errors in your applications.

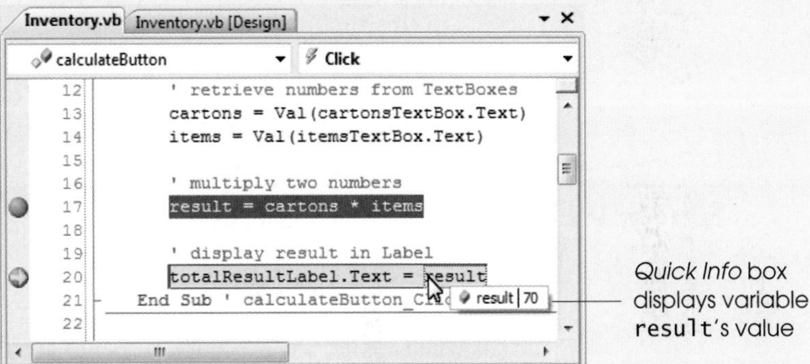

Figure 6.20 Displaying a variable value by placing the mouse pointer over a variable name.

5. ***Finishing application execution.*** Use the **Debug > Continue** command to complete the application execution. When there are no more breakpoints at which to suspend execution, the application executes to completion and the output appears in the **Total:** `Label` (Fig. 6.21).

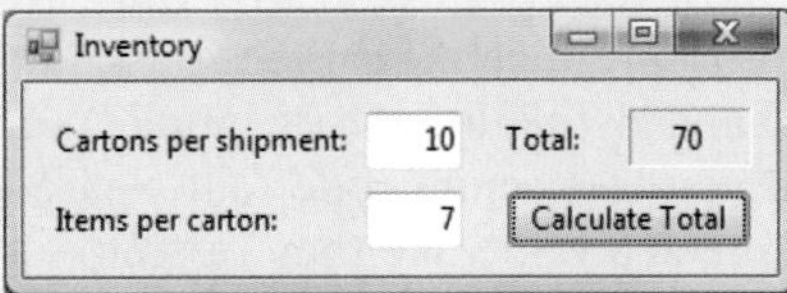

Figure 6.21 Application output.

6. ***Closing the application.*** Close your running application by clicking its close box.

7. ***Disabling a breakpoint.*** To disable a breakpoint, right click a line of code in which a breakpoint has been set, and select **Breakpoint > Disable Breakpoint**. The disabled breakpoint is indicated by a hollow maroon circle (Fig. 6.22). Disabling rather than removing a breakpoint allows you to re-enable the breakpoint (by clicking inside the hollow circle) in an application. This also can be done by right clicking the line marked by the hollow maroon circle and selecting **Breakpoint > Enable Breakpoint**.

(cont.)

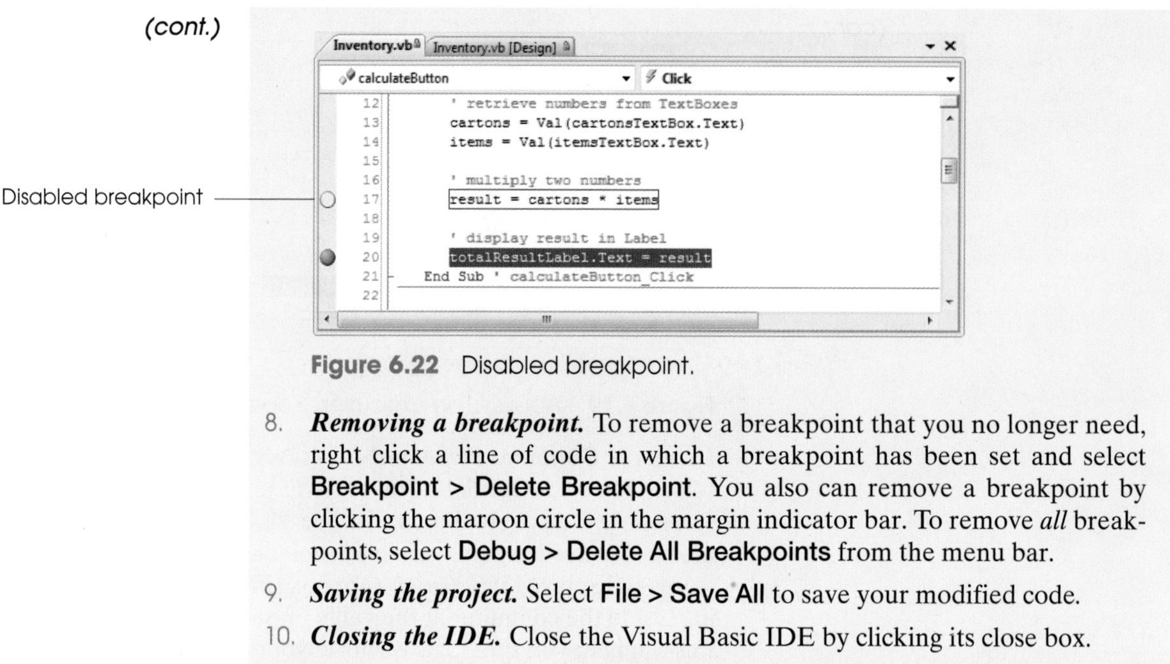

Figure 6.22 Disabled breakpoint.

8. ***Removing a breakpoint.*** To remove a breakpoint that you no longer need, right click a line of code in which a breakpoint has been set and select **Breakpoint > Delete Breakpoint**. You also can remove a breakpoint by clicking the maroon circle in the margin indicator bar. To remove *all* breakpoints, select **Debug > Delete All Breakpoints** from the menu bar.
9. ***Saving the project.*** Select **File > Save All** to save your modified code.
10. ***Closing the IDE.*** Close the Visual Basic IDE by clicking its close box.

In this section, you learned how to use the debugger to set breakpoints so that you can examine the results of code while an application is running. You also learned how to continue execution after an application suspends execution at a breakpoint and how to disable and remove breakpoints.

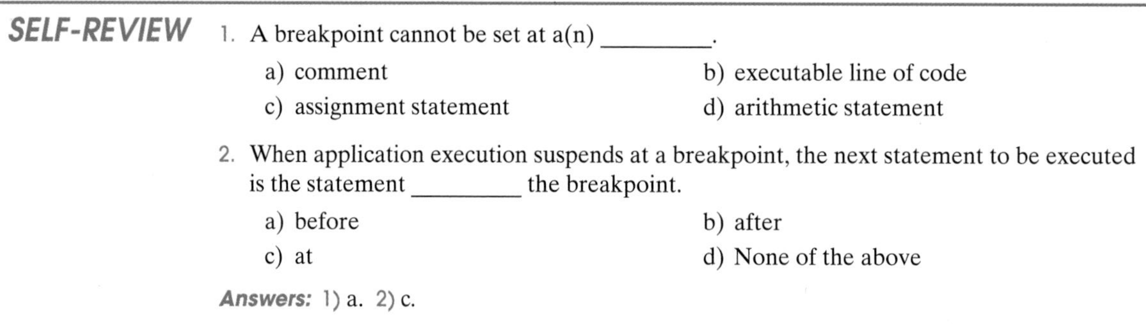

SELF-REVIEW

1. A breakpoint cannot be set at a(n) ________.

a) comment b) executable line of code
c) assignment statement d) arithmetic statement

2. When application execution suspends at a breakpoint, the next statement to be executed is the statement ________ the breakpoint.

a) before b) after
c) at d) None of the above

Answers: 1) a. 2) c.

6.7 Wrap-Up

You've now added variables to your **Inventory** application. You began by using variables to produce the same results as your previous **Inventory** application. Then you enhanced the **Inventory** application, using the `TextChanged` event, which allowed you to execute code that cleared the value in the output `Label` when the user changed a value in either `TextBox`.

You learned about memory concepts, including how variables are read and written. You'll apply these concepts to the applications that you build in later tutorials, which rely heavily on variables. You learned how to perform arithmetic in Visual Basic, and you studied the rules of operator precedence to evaluate mathematical expressions correctly. Finally, you learned how to insert breakpoints in the debugger. Breakpoints allow you to pause application execution and examine variable values. This capability will prove useful to you in finding and fixing logic errors.

In the next tutorial, you'll design a graphical user interface and write code to create a wage calculator. You'll use pseudocode, an informal language that helps you design the application. You'll learn to use the debugger's **Watch** window, another useful tool that helps you remove logic errors.

SKILLS SUMMARY

Declaring a Variable

- Use the keyword `Dim`.
- Use a valid identifier as a variable name.
- Use the keyword `As` to indicate that the following word specifies the variable's data type.
- Specify a type such as `Integer` or `Double`.

Handling a TextBox's TextChanged Event

- Double click a `TextBox` on a `Form` to generate an empty `TextChanged` event handler.
- Insert code into the event handler that executes when the text in a `TextBox` changes.

Reading a Value from a Memory Location

- Use the variable's name (as declared in the variable's `Dim` statement) at the point in the code where the variable's value is needed.

Replacing a Value in a Memory Location

- Use the variable name, followed by the assignment operator (=), followed by an expression giving the new value.

Representing Positive and Negative Numbers

- Use the unary versions of plus (+) and minus (-).

Performing Arithmetic Operations

- Write arithmetic expressions in straight-line form.
- Use the operator precedence rules to determine the order in which operators are applied.
- Use operator + to perform addition.
- Use operator - to perform subtraction.
- Use operator * to perform multiplication.
- Use operator / to perform floating-point division.
- Use operator \ (backslash) to perform integer division, which treats the operands as `Integer`s and returns an `Integer` result.
- Use operator ^ to perform exponentiation.
- Use the modulus operator, `Mod`, to report the remainder after division.
- Use parentheses to manage the order of operations and to clarify expressions.

Setting a Breakpoint

- Click the margin indicator bar (the gray margin indicator at the left of the code window) next to the line at which you wish to break, or right click a line of code and select **Breakpoint > Insert Breakpoint**.

Resuming Application Execution after Entering Break Mode During Debugging

- Select **Debug > Continue**.

Disabling a Breakpoint

- Right click a line of code containing a breakpoint, and select **Breakpoint > Disable Breakpoint**.

Enabling a Breakpoint

- Enable a disabled breakpoint by clicking inside the hollow circle in the margin indicator bar.
- You also can enable a disabled breakpoint by right clicking the line marked by the hollow maroon circle and selecting **Breakpoint > Enable Breakpoint**.

Removing a Breakpoint

- Right click a line of code containing a breakpoint, and select **Breakpoint > Delete Breakpoint**.
- You also can remove a breakpoint by clicking the maroon circle in the margin indicator bar.

KEY TERMS

active window—The frontmost window on your screen.

arithmetic operators—The operators +, -, *, /, \, ^ and Mod.

As keyword—Used in variable declarations. Indicates that the following word (such as Integer) is the variable type.

asterisk (*)—Multiplication operator. The operator's left and right operands are multiplied together.

backslash (\)—Integer division operator. The operator divides its left operand by its right and returns an Integer result.

binary operators—An operator that takes two operands.

break mode—The IDE mode when application execution is suspended. This mode is entered through the debugger.

breakpoint—A location where execution is to suspend, indicated by a solid maroon circle.

bug—A flaw in a program that prevents it from executing correctly.

built-in data type—A data type already defined in Visual Basic, such as an Integer.

caret (^)—Exponentiation operator. This operator raises its left operand to a power specified by the right operand.

declaration—The reporting of a new variable to the compiler. The variable can then be used in the Visual Basic code.

declare a variable—Report the name and type of a variable to the compiler.

Dim keyword—Indicates the declaration of a variable.

Double data type—Stores both whole and fractional numbers. Normally, Doubles store floating-point numbers.

embedded parentheses—Another term for nested parentheses.

empty string—A string that does not contain any characters.

exponentiation operator (^)—This operator raises its left operand to a power specified by the right operand.

floating-point division—Divides two numbers (whole or fractional) and returns a floating-point number.

implicit conversion—A conversion from one data type to another performed by Visual Basic.

integer—A whole number, such as 919, -11, 0 and 138624.

Integer data type—Stores integer values.

integer division—Integer division takes two Integer operands and yields an Integer result. The fractional portion of the result is discarded.

margin indicator bar—A margin in the IDE where breakpoints are displayed.

Mod (modulus operator)—The modulus operator yields the remainder after division.

name of a variable—The identifier used in an application to access or modify a variable's value.

nested parentheses—These occur when an expression in parentheses is found within another expression surrounded by parentheses. With nested parentheses, the operators contained in the innermost pair of parentheses are applied first.

nondestructive memory operation —A process that does not overwrite a value in memory.

primitive data type—A data type already defined in Visual Basic, such as Integer.

***Quick Info* box**—Displays the value of a variable during debugging.

redundant parentheses—Unnecessary parentheses used in an expression to make it easier to read.

rules of operator precedence—Rules that determine the precise order in which operators are applied in an expression.

runtime error—An error that has its effect at execution time.

size of a variable—The number of bytes required to store a value of the variable's type.

straight-line form—The manner in which arithmetic expressions must be written to be represented in Visual Basic code.

TextChanged event—Occurs when the text in a TextBox changes.

type of a variable—Specifies the kind of data that can be stored in a variable and the range of values that can be stored.

unary operator—An operator that takes only one operand.

value of a variable—The piece of data that is stored in a variable's location in memory.

variable—A location in the computer's memory where a value can be stored.

CONTROLS, EVENTS, PROPERTIES & METHODS

TextBox abl TextBox This control allows the user to input data from the keyboard.

- *In action*

0

- *Event*

TextChanged—Raised when the text in the TextBox is changed.

- *Properties*

Location—Specifies the location of the TextBox on the Form relative to the Form's top-left corner.

Name—Specifies the name used to identify the TextBox. The name should include the TextBox suffix.

Size—Specifies the width and height (in pixels) of the TextBox.

Text—Specifies the initial text displayed in the TextBox.

TextAlign—Specifies how the text is aligned within the TextBox.

MULTIPLE-CHOICE QUESTIONS

6.1 Parentheses added to an expression simply to make it easier to read are known as _________ parentheses.

a) necessary b) redundant
c) embedded d) nested

6.2 The _________ operator performs integer division.

a) \ b) +
c) Mod d) ^

6.3 Every variable has a _________.

a) name b) value
c) type d) All of the above

6.4 In Visual Basic, arithmetic expressions must be written in _________ form.

a) straight-line b) top-bottom
c) left-right d) right-left

6.5 Arithmetic expressions are evaluated _________.

a) from right to left b) from left to right
c) according to the rules of operator precedence
d) Both b and c

6.6 Variable declarations in event handlers begin with the keyword _________.

a) Declare b) Dim
c) Sub d) Integer

6.7 Entering a value in a TextBox raises the _________ event.

a) TextAltered b) ValueChanged
c) ValueEntered d) TextChanged

6.8 The _________ function converts user input from a TextBox to a value of type Double.

a) Convert b) MakeDouble
c) Val d) WriteDouble

6.9 Variables that store integer values should be declared as an _________.

a) `Integer` b) `Int`
c) `IntVariable` d) None of the above

6.10 The data type in a variable declaration is immediately preceded by keyword _________.

a) `IsA` b) `Type`
c) `Dim` d) `As`

EXERCISES

6.11 ***(Simple Encryption Application)*** This application uses a simple technique to encrypt a number. Encryption is the process of modifying data so that only those intended to receive the data can undo the changes and view the original data. The user enters the data to be encrypted via a `TextBox`. The application then multiplies the number by 7 and adds 5. The application displays the encrypted number in a `Label` as shown in Fig. 6.23.

Figure 6.23 Result of completed **Simple Encryption** application.

a) ***Copying the template to your working directory.*** Copy the directory `C:\Examples\Tutorial06\Exercises\SimpleEncryption` to your `C:\SimplyVB2008` directory.

b) ***Opening the application's template file.*** Double click `SimpleEncryption.sln` in the `SimpleEncryption` directory to open the application.

c) ***Coding the `Click` event handler.*** Encrypt the number in the `Click` event handler for the **Encrypt** `Button` by using the preceding technique. The user input should be stored in an `Integer` variable (`number`) before it's encrypted. The event handler then should display the encrypted number.

d) ***Clearing the result.*** Add an event handler for the **Enter number to encrypt:** `Text-Box`'s `TextChanged` event. This event handler should clear the **Encrypted number:** output `Label` whenever the user enters new input.

e) ***Running the application.*** Select **Debug > Start Debugging** to run your application. Enter the value `25` into the **Enter number to encrypt:** `TextBox` and click the **Encrypt** `Button`. Verify that the value `180` is displayed in the **Encrypted number:** output `Label`. Enter other values and click the **Encrypt** `Button` after each. Verify that the appropriate encrypted value is displayed each time.

f) ***Closing the application.*** Close your running application by clicking its close box.

g) ***Closing the IDE.*** Close the Visual Basic IDE by clicking its close box.

6.12 ***(Temperature Converter Application)*** Write an application that converts a Celsius temperature, *C*, to its equivalent Fahrenheit temperature, *F*. Figure 6.24 displays the completed application. Use the following formula:

$$F = \frac{9}{5}C + 32$$

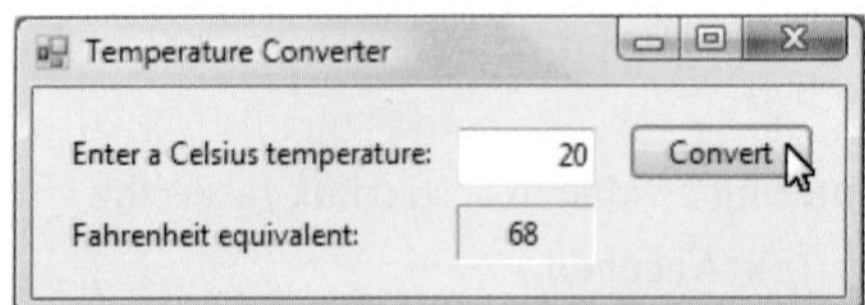

Figure 6.24 Completed **Temperature Converter**.

a) ***Copying the template to your working directory.*** Copy the directory `C:\Examples\Tutorial06\Exercises\TemperatureConversion` to your `C:\SimplyVB2008` directory.

b) ***Opening the application's template file.*** Double click TemperatureConversion.sln in the TemperatureConversion directory to open the application.

c) ***Coding the Click event handler.*** Perform the conversion in the **Convert** Button's Click event handler. Define Integer variables to store the user-input Celsius temperature and the result of the conversion. Display the Fahrenheit equivalent of the Celsius temperature.

d) ***Clearing user input.*** Clear the result in the **Enter a Celsius temperature:** TextBox's TextChanged event.

e) ***Running the application.*** Select **Debug > Start Debugging** to run your application. Enter the value 20 into the **Enter a Celsius temperature:** TextBox and click the **Convert** Button. Verify that the value 68 is displayed in the output Label. Enter other Celsius temperatures; click the **Convert** Button after each. Use the formula provided above to verify that the proper Fahrenheit equivalent is displayed each time.

f) ***Closing the application.*** Close your running application by clicking its close box.

g) ***Closing the IDE.*** Close the Visual Basic IDE by clicking its close box.

6.13 ***(Simple Calculator Application)*** In this exercise, you'll add functionality to a simple calculator application. The calculator allows a user to enter two numbers in the TextBoxes. There are four Buttons labeled +, -, / and *. When the user clicks the Button labeled as addition, subtraction, multiplication or division, the application performs that operation on the numbers in the TextBoxes and displays the result. The calculator also should clear the calculation result when the user enters new input. Figure 6.25 displays the completed calculator.

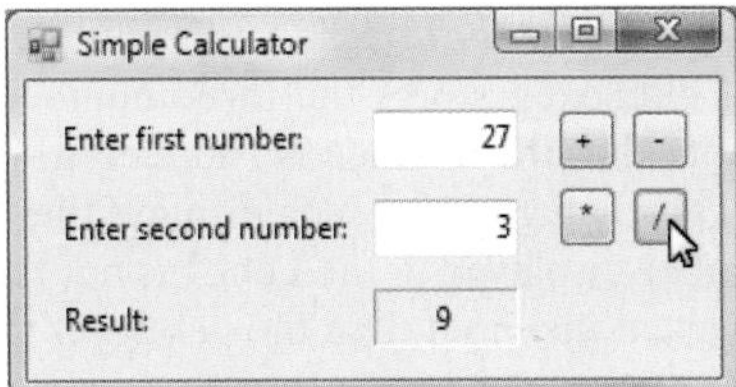

Figure 6.25 Result of **Calculator** application.

a) ***Copying the template to your working directory.*** Copy the directory C:\Examples\Tutorial06\Exercises\SimpleCalculator to your C:\SimplyVB2008 directory.

b) ***Opening the application's template file.*** Double click SimpleCalculator.sln in the SimpleCalculator directory to open the application.

c) ***Coding the addition Click event handler.*** This event handler should add the two numbers and display the result.

d) ***Coding the subtraction Click event handler.*** This event handler should subtract the second number from the first number and display the result.

e) ***Coding the multiplication Click event handler.*** This event handler should multiply the two numbers and display the result.

f) ***Coding the division Click event handler.*** This event handler should divide the first number by the second number and display the result.

g) ***Clearing the result.*** Write event handlers for the TextBoxes' TextChanged events. Write code to clear resultLabel after the user enters new input into either TextBox.

h) ***Running the application.*** Select **Debug > Start Debugging** to run your application. Enter a first number and a second number, then verify that each of the Buttons works by clicking each and viewing the output. Repeat this process with two new values and again verify that the proper output is displayed based on which Button is clicked.

i) ***Closing the application.*** Close your running application by clicking its close box.

j) ***Closing the IDE.*** Close the Visual Basic IDE by clicking its close box.

What does this code do?

6.14 This code modifies variables `number1`, `number2` and `result`. What are the final values of these variables?

```
Dim number1 As Integer
Dim number2 As Integer
Dim result As Integer

number1 = 5 * (4 + 6)
number2 = 2 ^ 2
result = number1 \ number2
```

What's wrong with this code?

6.15 Find the error(s) in the following code, which uses variables to perform a calculation.

```
Dim number1 As Integer
Dim number2 As Integer
Dim result As Integer

number1 = (4 * 6 ^ 4) / (10 Mod 4 - 2)
number2 = (16 \ 3) ^ 2 * 6 + 1
result = number1 - number2
```

Using the Debugger

6.16 ***(Average Three Numbers)*** You've just written an application that takes three numbers as input in `TextBoxes`, stores the three numbers in variables, then finds the average of the numbers (note that the average is rounded to the nearest integer value). The output is displayed in a `Label` (Fig. 6.26, which displays the incorrect output). You soon realize, however, that the number displayed in the `Label` is not the average, but rather a number that does not make sense given the input. Use the debugger to help locate and remove this error.

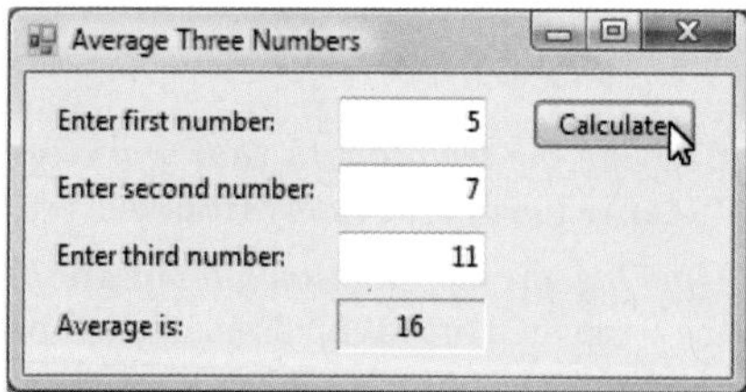

Figure 6.26 **Average Three Numbers** application.

a) ***Copying the template to your working directory.*** Copy the directory `C:\Examples\Tutorial06\Exercises\AverageDebugging` to your `C:\SimplyVB2008` directory.

b) ***Opening the application's template file.*** Double click `AverageDebugging.sln` in the `AverageDebugging` directory to open the application.

c) ***Running the application.*** Select **Debug > Start Debugging** to run your application. View the output to observe that the output is incorrect.

d) ***Closing the application.*** Close the application, and view the `Average.vb` file in **Code** view.

e) ***Setting breakpoints.*** Set a breakpoint in the `calculateButton_Click` event handler. Run the application again, and use the debugger to help find the error(s).

f) ***Finding and correcting the error(s).*** Once you have found the error(s), modify the application so that it correctly calculates the average of three numbers.

g) ***Running the application.*** Select **Debug > Start Debugging** to run your application. Enter the three values from Fig. 6.26 into the input `TextBoxes` provided and click the **Calculate** `Button`. Verify that the output now accurately reflects the average of these values, which is 8.

h) ***Closing the application.*** Close your running application by clicking its close box.

i) ***Closing the IDE.*** Close the Visual Basic IDE by clicking its close box.

Programming Challenge

6.17 ***(Digit Extraction)*** Write an application that allows the user to enter a five-digit number into a `TextBox`. The application then separates the number into its individual digits and displays each digit in a `Label`. The application should look and behave similarly to Fig. 6.27. [*Hint:* You can use the `Mod` operator to extract the ones digit from a number. For instance, `12345 Mod 10` is `5`. You can use integer division (\) to "peel off" digits from a number. For instance, `12345 \ 100` is `123`. This allows you to treat the `3` in `12345` as a ones digit. Now you can isolate the `3` by using the `Mod` operator. Apply this technique to the rest of the digits.]

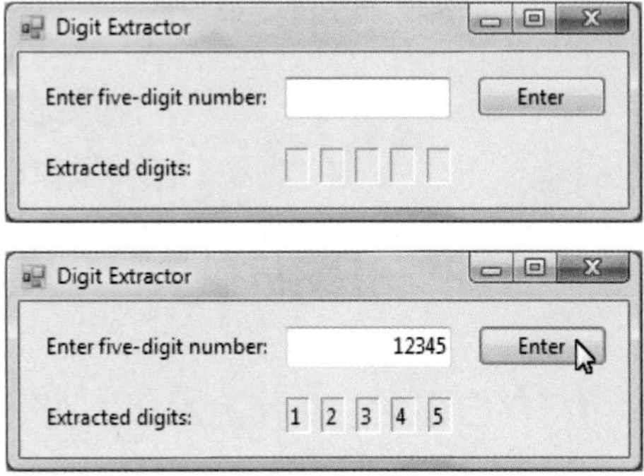

Figure 6.27 **Digit Extractor** application GUI.

a) ***Creating the application.*** Create a new project named `DigitExtractor`. Rename the `Form1.vb` file `DigitExtractor.vb`. Change the name of the `Form` to `DigitExtractorForm`. Add `Label`s, a `TextBox` and a `Button` to the application's `Form`. Name the `TextBox` `inputTextBox` and name the `Button` `enterButton`. Name the other controls logically based on the tips provided in earlier tutorials.

b) ***Adding an event handler for `enterButton`'s `Click` event.*** In **Design** view, double click `enterButton` to create the `enterButton_Click` event handler. In this event handler, create five variables of type `Integer`. Use integer division and the `Mod` operator to extract each digit. Store the digits in the five variables created.

c) ***Adding an event handler for `inputTextBox`'s `TextChanged` event.*** In **Design** view, double click `inputTextBox` to create the `inputTextBox_TextChanged` event handler. In this event handler, clear the five `Label`s used to display each digit. This event handler clears the output whenever new input is entered.

d) ***Running the application.*** Select **Debug > Start Debugging** to run your application. Enter a five-digit number and click the **Enter** `Button`. Enter a new five-digit number and verify that the previous output is cleared.

e) ***Closing the application.*** Close your running application by clicking its close box.

f) ***Closing the IDE.*** Close the Visual Basic IDE by clicking its close box.

7 TUTORIAL

Objectives

In this tutorial, you learn to:

- Understand basic problem-solving techniques.
- Understand control structures.
- Understand and create pseudocode.
- Use the `If...Then` and `If...Then...Else` selection statements to choose among alternative actions.
- Use the assignment operators.
- Use the debugger's **Watch** window.

Outline

Wage Calculator Application

Introducing Algorithms, Pseudocode and Program Control

Before writing an application, it is essential to have a thorough understanding of the problem you need to solve. This allows you to design a carefully planned approach to solving the problem. When writing an application, it is equally important to recognize the types of building blocks that are available and to use proven application-construction principles. In this tutorial, you'll learn the theory and principles of **structured programming**. Structured programming is a technique for organizing program control that helps you develop applications that are clear and easier to debug and modify. The techniques presented are applicable to most high-level languages, including Visual Basic.

7.1 Test-Driving the Wage Calculator Application

In this section, we preview this tutorial's **Wage Calculator** application. This application must meet the following requirements:

Application Requirements

A payroll company calculates the gross earnings per week of employees. Employees' weekly salaries are based on the number of hours they worked and their hourly wages. Create an application that accepts this information and calculates each employee's total (gross) earnings. The application assumes a standard work week of 40 hours. The wages for 40 or fewer hours are calculated by multiplying the employee's hourly wage by the number of hours worked. Any time worked over 40 hours in a week is considered "overtime" and earns time and a half. Salary for time and a half is calculated by multiplying the employee's hourly wage by 1.5 and multiplying the result of that calculation by the number of overtime hours worked. The total overtime earned is added to the user's gross earnings for the regular 40 hours of work to calculate the total earnings for that week.

This application calculates earnings from hourly wage and hours worked per week. Normally, an employee who has worked 40 or fewer hours is paid regular wages. The calculation differs if the employee has worked more than the standard 40-hour work week. In this tutorial, we introduce a programming construct known as a control structure that allows you to make this distinction and perform different calculations based on different user inputs. You begin by test-driving the completed application. Then you learn the additional Visual Basic capabilities needed to create your own version of this application.

Test-Driving the Wage Calculator Application

When using multiple TextBoxes vertically, align the TextBoxes on their right sides, and where possible make the TextBoxes the same size. Left align the descriptive Labels for such TextBoxes.

1. ***Opening the completed application.*** Open the directory `C:\Examples\Tutorial07\CompletedApplication\WageCalculator` to locate the **Wage Calculator** application. Double click `WageCalculator.sln` to open the application in the Visual Basic IDE.
2. ***Running the application.*** Select **Debug > Start Debugging** to run the application (Fig. 7.1). To organize the GUI, we vertically aligned the `TextBoxes` on their right sides and made the `TextBoxes` the same size. We also left aligned the `TextBoxes`' descriptive `Labels`.

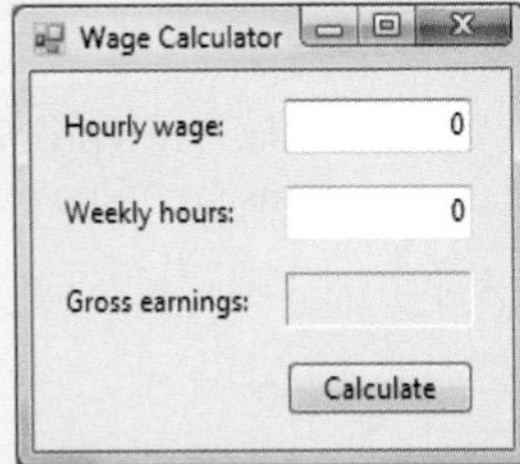

Figure 7.1 **Wage Calculator** application.

3. ***Entering the employee's hourly wage.*** Enter **10** in the **Hourly wage:** `TextBox`.
4. ***Entering the number of hours the employee worked.*** Enter **45** in the **Weekly hours:** `TextBox`.
5. ***Calculating the employee's gross earnings.*** Click the **Calculate** `Button`. The result (**$475.00**) is displayed in the **Gross earnings:** `TextBox` (Fig. 7.2). Note that the employee's earnings are the sum of the wages for the standard 40-hour work week (40 * 10) and the overtime pay (5 * 10 * 1.5).

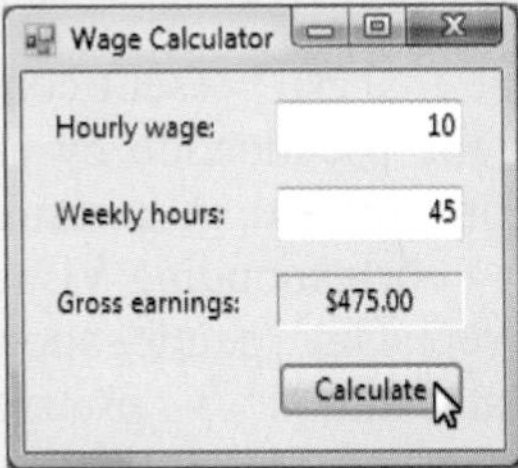

Figure 7.2 Calculating wages by clicking the **Calculate** `Button`.

6. ***Closing the application.*** Close your running application by clicking its close box.
7. ***Closing the IDE.*** Close the Visual Basic IDE by clicking its close box.

7.2 Algorithms

Computing problems can be solved by executing a series of actions in a specific order. A procedure for solving a problem, in terms of:

1. the actions to be executed and
2. the order in which these actions are to be executed

is called an **algorithm**. The following example demonstrates the importance of correctly specifying the order in which the actions are to be executed. Consider the "rise-and-shine algorithm" followed by one junior executive for getting out of bed and going to work: (1) get out of bed, (2) take off pajamas, (3) take a shower, (4) get dressed, (5) eat breakfast and (6) carpool to work. This routine prepares the executive for a productive day at the office.

However, suppose that the same steps are performed in a slightly different order: (1) get out of bed, (2) take off pajamas, (3) get dressed, (4) take a shower, (5) eat breakfast, (6) carpool to work. In this case, our junior executive shows up for work soaking wet.

Indicating the appropriate sequence in which to execute actions is equally crucial in computer programs. **Program control** refers to the task of ordering an application's statements correctly. In this tutorial, you'll begin to investigate the program-control capabilities of Visual Basic.

SELF-REVIEW

1. ________ refer(s) to the task of ordering an application's statements correctly.
   a) Actions
   b) Program control
   c) Control structures
   d) Visual programming

2. A(n) ________ is a plan for solving a problem in terms of the actions to be executed and the order in which these actions are to be executed.
   a) chart
   b) control structure
   c) algorithm
   d) ordered list

Answers: 1) b. 2) c.

7.3 Pseudocode

Pseudocode is an informal language that helps you formulate algorithms. The pseudocode we present is particularly useful in the development of algorithms that will be converted to structured portions of Visual Basic applications. Pseudocode resembles everyday English—it is convenient and user friendly, but it is not an actual computer-programming language.

Software Design Tip

Pseudocode helps you conceptualize an application during the application-design process. Pseudocode statements can be converted to Visual Basic at a later point.

Pseudocode statements are not executed on computers. Rather, pseudocode helps you think out an application before attempting to write it in a programming language, such as Visual Basic. In this tutorial, we provide several examples of pseudocode.

The pseudocode that we present consists solely of characters, so that you can create and modify the pseudocode by using editor programs, such as the Visual Basic code editor or Notepad. A carefully prepared pseudocode program can be converted easily to a corresponding Visual Basic application. Much of this conversion is as simple as replacing pseudocode statements with their Visual Basic equivalents. Let's look at an example of a pseudocode statement:

```
Assign 0 to the counter
```

This pseudocode statement provides an easy-to-understand task. You can put several such statements together to form an algorithm that can be used to meet application requirements. When you complete the pseudocode algorithm, you can then convert pseudocode statements to their equivalent Visual Basic statements. The pseudocode statement above, for instance, can be converted to the following Visual Basic statement:

```
counter = 0
```

Pseudocode normally describes only **executable statements**—the actions performed when the corresponding Visual Basic application is run. An example of a programming statement that is not executed is a declaration. The declaration

```
Dim number As Integer
```

informs the compiler of `number`'s type and instructs the compiler to reserve space in memory for this variable. The declaration does not cause any action, such as input, output or a calculation, to occur when the application executes, so we would not include this information in the pseudocode.

SELF-REVIEW

1. _________ is an informal language that helps you develop algorithms.
   a) Pseudocode b) VB-Speak
   c) Notation d) None of the above

2. Pseudocode _________.
   a) usually describes only declarations b) is executed on computers
   c) usually describes only executable lines of code
   d) usually describes declarations and executable lines of code

Answers: 1) a. 2) c.

7.4 Control Structures

Normally, statements in an application are executed one after another in the order in which they are written. This is called **sequential execution**. Visual Basic allows you to alter the order in which statements are executed. A **transfer of control** occurs when an executed statement does not directly follow the previously executed statement in the written application. This is common in computer programs.

All programs can be written in terms of only three control structures: the sequence structure, the selection structure and the repetition structure. The **sequence structure** is built into Visual Basic—unless directed to act otherwise, the computer executes Visual Basic statements sequentially—that is, one after the other in the order in which they appear in the application. The **activity diagram** in Fig. 7.3 illustrates a typical sequence structure, in which two calculations are performed in order. We discuss activity diagrams in detail following Fig. 7.3.

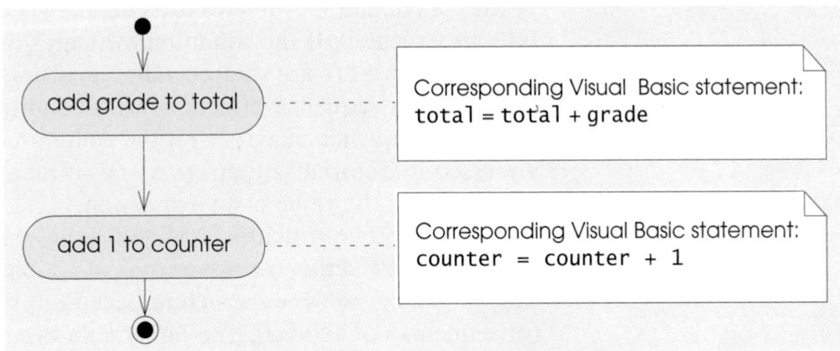

Figure 7.3 Sequence structure activity diagram.

Activity diagrams are part of the **Unified Modeling Language (UML)**—an industry standard for modeling software systems. An activity diagram models the activity (also called the **workflow**) of a portion of a software system. Such activities may include a portion of an algorithm, such as the sequence structure in Fig. 7.3. Activity diagrams are composed of special-purpose symbols, such as the **action-state symbol** (a rectangle with its left and right sides replaced with arcs curving outward), the **diamond symbol** and the **small circle symbol**; these symbols are connected by **transition arrows**, which represent the flow of the activity. Figure 7.3 does not include any diamond symbols—these are used in later activity diagrams.

Like pseudocode, activity diagrams help you develop and represent algorithms, although many programmers prefer pseudocode. Activity diagrams clearly show how control structures operate.

Consider the activity diagram for the sequence structure in Fig. 7.3. The activity diagram contains two **action states** that represent actions to perform. Each action state contains an **action expression**—for example, "add grade to total" or "add 1 to counter"—that specifies a particular action to perform. Other actions might include calculations or input/output operations. The arrows in the activity diagram are called transition arrows. These arrows represent **transitions**, indicating the order in which the actions represented by the action states occur—the application that implements the activities illustrated by the activity diagram in Fig. 7.3 first adds `grade` to `total`, then adds `1` to `counter`.

The **solid circle** located at the top of the activity diagram represents the activity's **initial state**—the beginning of the workflow before the application performs the modeled activities. The solid circle surrounded by a hollow circle that appears at the bottom of the activity diagram represents the **final state**—the end of the workflow after the application performs its activities.

Notice, in Fig. 7.3, the rectangles with the upper-right corners folded over. They look like sheets of paper and are called **notes** in the UML. Notes are like comments in Visual Basic applications—they are explanatory remarks that describe the purpose of symbols in the diagram. Figure 7.3 uses UML notes to show the Visual Basic code that you might associate with each action state in the activity diagram. A **dotted line** connects each note with the element that the note describes. Activity diagrams normally do not show the Visual Basic code that implements the activity, but we use notes here to show you how the diagram relates to Visual Basic code.

Selection Structures

Visual Basic provides three types of **selection structures**, which we discuss in this tutorial and in Tutorial 12. The **`If...Then`** selection structure performs (selects) an action (or sequence of actions) based on a condition. A **condition** is an expression with a **true** or **false** value that is used to make a decision. Conditions are **evaluated** (that is, tested) to determine whether their value is true or false. These values are of data type **`Boolean`** and are specified in Visual Basic code by using the keywords **`True`** and **`False`**. Sometimes we refer to a condition as a `Boolean` expression.

If the condition evaluates to `True`, the actions specified by the `If...Then` structure are executed. If the condition evaluates to `False`, the actions specified by the `If...Then` structure are skipped. The **`If...Then...Else`** selection structure performs an action (or sequence of actions) if a condition is true and performs a different action (or sequence of actions) if the condition is false. The `Select Case` structure, discussed in Tutorial 12, performs one of many actions (or sequences of actions), depending on the value of an expression.

The `If...Then` structure is called a **single-selection structure** because it selects or ignores a single action (or a sequence of actions). The `If...Then...Else` structure is called a **double-selection structure** because it selects between two different actions (or sequences of actions). The `Select Case` structure is called a **multiple-selection structure** because it selects among many different actions or sequences of actions.

Repetition Structures

Visual Basic provides seven types of **repetition structures** for performing a statement or group of statements repeatedly. These are listed below with the tutorials in which they are introduced:

- `While...End While`[1]
- `Do While...Loop` (Tutorial 9)
- `Do Until...Loop` (Tutorial 9)
- `Do...Loop While` (Tutorial 10)
- `Do...Loop Until` (Tutorial 10)
- `For...Next` (Tutorial 11)
- `For Each...Next` (Tutorial 20)

1. We do not discuss the `While...End While` loop in this book. This repetition structure behaves identically to the `Do While...Loop` and is provided for programmers familiar with previous versions of Visual Basic.

Keywords

The words `If`, `Then`, `Else`, `End`, `Select`, `Case`, `While`, `Do`, `Until`, `Loop`, `For`, `Next` and `Each` are all Visual Basic keywords—Appendix E includes a complete list of Visual Basic keywords. We discuss many of Visual Basic's keywords and their respective purposes throughout this book. Visual Basic has a much larger set of keywords than most other popular programming languages.

Control Structure Notes

Visual Basic has 11 control structures—the sequence structure, three types of selection structures and seven types of repetition structures. All Visual Basic applications are formed by combining as many of each type of control structure as is necessary. As with the sequence structure in Fig. 7.3, each control structure is drawn with two small circle symbols—a solid black one to represent the entry point to the control structure, and a solid black one surrounded by a hollow circle to represent the exit point.

All Visual Basic control structures are **single-entry/single-exit control structures**—each has exactly one entry point and one exit point. Such control structures make it easy to build applications—the control structures are attached to one another by connecting the exit point of one control structure to the entry point of the next. This is similar to stacking building blocks, so we call it **control-structure stacking**. The only other way to connect control structures is through **control-structure nesting**, whereby one control structure can be placed inside another. Thus, algorithms in Visual Basic applications are constructed from only 11 different types of control structures combined in only two ways—this is a model of simplicity. Control structures in Visual Basic are implemented as statements, so from this point forward (after the following exercises), we use the term "statement" in preference to the term "structure."

SELF-REVIEW

1. All Visual Basic applications can be written in terms of ________ types of control structures.

   a) one b) two
   c) three d) four

2. The process of application statements executing one after another in the order in which they are written is called ________.

   a) transfer of control b) sequential execution
   c) workflow d) None of the above

Answers: 1) c. 2) b.

7.5 `If...Then` Selection Statement

A selection statement chooses among alternative courses of action in an application. For example, suppose that the passing grade on a test is 60 (out of 100). The pseudocode statement

```
If student's grade is greater than or equal to 60
    Display "Passed"
```

determines whether the condition "student's grade is greater than or equal to 60" is true or false. If the condition is true, then "Passed" is displayed, and the next pseudocode statement in order is "performed." (Remember that pseudocode is not a real programming language.) If the condition is false, the display statement is ignored, and the next pseudocode statement in order is performed.

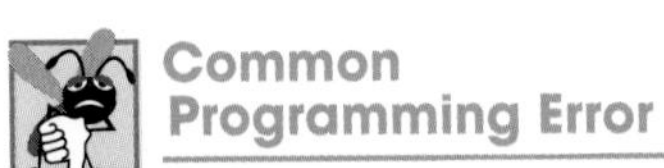

Omitting the **Then** keyword in an `If...Then` statement is a syntax error. The IDE helps prevent this error by inserting the **Then** keyword after you write the condition.

The preceding pseudocode *If* statement may be written in Visual Basic as

```
If studentGrade >= 60 Then
   displayLabel.Text = "Passed"
End If
```

The Visual Basic code corresponds closely to the pseudocode, demonstrating the usefulness of pseudocode as an application-development tool. The body (sometimes called a **block**) of the `If...Then` statement displays the string `"Passed"` in a `Label`. The keywords `End If` close an `If...Then` statement.

Good Programming Practice

Visual Basic indents the statements inside `If...Then` statements to improve readability.

Note the indentation in the `If...Then` statement. Such indentation enhances application readability. The Visual Basic compiler ignores whitespace characters, such as spaces, tabs and newlines used for indentation and vertical spacing, unless the whitespace characters are contained in strings.

The condition between keywords `If` and `Then` determines whether the statement(s) within the `If...Then` statement will execute. If the condition is true, the body of the `If...Then` statement executes. If the condition is false, the body is not executed. Conditions in `If...Then` statements can be formed by using the **equality operators** and **relational operators** (also called **comparison operators**), which are summarized in Fig. 7.4. The relational and equality operators all have the same level of precedence.

Common Programming Error

Adding spaces between the symbols in the operators <>, >= and <= (as in < >, > =, < =) is a syntax error that Visual Basic fixes automatically.

Common Programming Error

Reversal of the operators <>, >= and <= (as in ><, =>, =<) is a syntax error that Visual Basic fixes automatically.

Algebraic equality or relational operator	Visual Basic equality or relational operator	Example of Visual Basic condition	Meaning of Visual Basic condition
Relational operators			
>	>	`x > y`	x is greater than y
<	<	`x < y`	x is less than y
≥	>=	`x >= y`	x is greater than or equal to y
≤	<=	`x <= y`	x is less than or equal to y
Equality operators			
=	=	`x = y`	x is equal to y
≠	<>	`x <> y`	x is not equal to y

Figure 7.4 Equality and relational operators.

Figure 7.5 shows the syntax of the `If...Then` statement. A statement's **syntax** specifies how the statement must be formed to compile without syntax errors. Let's look closely at the syntax of an `If...Then` statement. The first line of Fig. 7.5 specifies that the statement must begin with the keyword `If` and be followed by a condition and the keyword `Then`. Note that we've italicized *condition*. This indicates that, when creating your own `If...Then` statement, you should replace the text *condition* with the actual condition that you would like evaluated. The second line indicates that you should replace *statements* with the actual statements that you want to be included in the body of the `If...Then` statement. Note that the text *statements* is placed within square brackets. These brackets do not appear in the actual `If...Then` statement. Instead, the square brackets indicate that certain portions of the statement are optional. In this example, the square brackets indicate that all statements in the `If...Then` statement's body are optional. Of course, if there are no statements in the body of the `If...Then` statement, then no actions will occur as part of that statement, regardless of the condition's value. The final line indicates that the statement ends with the `End If` keywords.

Syntax

```
If condition Then
    [ statements ]
End If
```

Figure 7.5 `If...Then` statement syntax.

Figure 7.6 illustrates the single-selection `If...Then` statement. This activity diagram contains what is perhaps the most important symbol in an activity diagram—the diamond, or **decision symbol**, which indicates that a decision is to be made. Note the two sets of square brackets above or next to the arrows leading from the decision symbol; these are called **guard conditions.** A decision symbol indicates that the workflow continues along a path determined by the symbol's associated guard conditions, which can be true or false. Each transition arrow emerging from a decision symbol has a guard condition (specified in square brackets above or next to the transition arrow). If a particular guard condition is true, the workflow enters the action state to which that transition arrow points. For example, in Fig. 7.6, if the grade is greater than or equal to 60, the application displays "Passed," then transitions to the final state of this activity. If the grade is less than 60, the application immediately transitions to the final state without displaying a message. Only one guard condition associated with a particular decision symbol can be true at once.

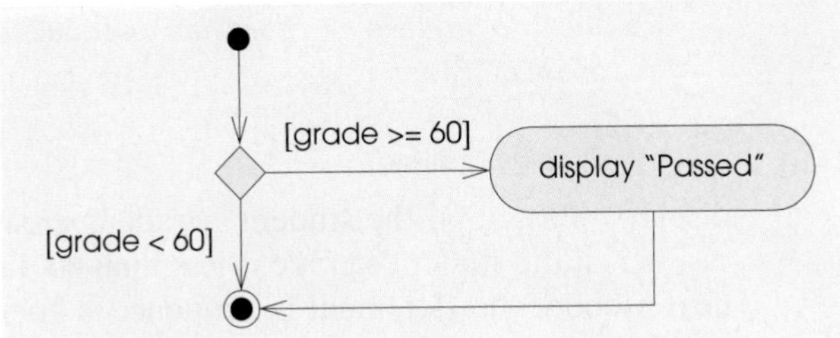

Figure 7.6 `If...Then` single-selection statement activity diagram.

Note that the `If...Then` statement (Fig. 7.6), is a single-entry/single-exit statement. The activity diagrams for the remaining control structures contain (aside from small circle symbols and transition arrows) only action-state symbols, indicating actions to be performed, and diamond symbols, indicating decisions to be made. Representing control structures in this way emphasizes the **action/decision model of programming**. To understand the process of structured programming better, we can envision 11 bins, each containing a different type of the 11 possible control structures. The control structures in each bin are empty, meaning that nothing is written in the action-state symbols and no guard conditions are written next to the decision symbols. Your task is to assemble an application, using as many control structures as the algorithm demands, combining those control statements in only two possible ways—stacking or nesting—and filling in the actions and the decisions' guard conditions in a manner appropriate to the algorithm. Again, each of these control structures is implemented in Visual Basic as a statement.

SELF-REVIEW

1. Which of the following `If...Then` statements correctly displays that a student received an A on an exam if the score was 90 or above?

a)
```
If studentGrade <> 90 Then
   displayLabel.Text = "Student received an A"
End If
```
b)
```
If studentGrade > 90 Then
   displayLabel.Text = "Student received an A"
End If
```
c)
```
If studentGrade = 90 Then
   displayLabel.Text = "Student received an A"
End If
```
d)
```
If studentGrade >= 90 Then
   displayLabel.Text = "Student received an A"
End If
```

2. The symbol ________ is not a Visual Basic operator.
   a) * b) ^
   c) % d) <>

Answers: 1) d. 2) c.

7.6 If...Then...Else Selection Statement and Conditional If Expressions

As you've learned, the `If...Then` selection statement performs an indicated action (or sequence of actions) only when the condition evaluates to `True`; otherwise, the action (or sequence of actions) is skipped. The `If...Then...Else` selection statement allows you to specify that a different action (or sequence of actions) is to be performed when the condition is true than when the condition is false. For example, the pseudocode statement

```
If student's grade is greater than or equal to 60
    Display "Passed"
Else
    Display "Failed"
```

displays "Passed" if the student's grade is greater than or equal to 60, but displays "Failed" if the student's grade is less than 60. In either case, after output occurs, the next pseudocode statement in sequence is "performed." The preceding pseudocod may be written in Visual Basic as

```
If studentGrade >= 60 Then
   displayLabel.Text = "Passed"
Else
   displayLabel.Text = "Failed"
End If
```

Good Programming Practice

Indent both body statements of an `If...Then...Else` statement to improve readability. (*Note:* The Visual Basic IDE does this automatically.)

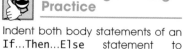

Note that the body of the `Else` clause is indented so that it lines up with the indented body of the `If` clause. A standard indentation convention should be applied consistently throughout your applications. It's difficult to read programs that do not use uniform spacing conventions. The IDE helps you maintain consistent indentation with its "smart indenting" feature, which is enabled by default for Visual Basic. The `If...Then...Else` selection statement follows the same general syntax as the `If...Then` statement. The `Else` keyword and any related statements are placed between the `If...Then` and closing `End If` keywords, as in Fig. 7.7.

Good Programming Practice

Apply a standard indentation convention consistently throughout your applications to enhance readability. Visual Basic's "smart indenting" feature helps you do this.

Syntax

```
If condition Then
   [ statements ]
Else
   [ statements ]
End If
```

Figure 7.7 `If...Then...Else` statement syntax.

The preceding `If...Then...Else` statement can also be written using a **conditional `If` expression**, as in

```
displayLabel.Text = If(studentGrade >= 60, "Passed", "Failed")
```

A conditional `If` expression starts with the keyword `If` and is followed by three expressions in parentheses—a condition, the value of the conditional expression if the condition is true and the value if the condition is false.

Figure 7.8 illustrates the flow of control in the `If...Then...Else` double-selection statement. Once again, aside from the initial state, transition arrows and final state, the only symbols in the activity diagram represent action states and decisions. In this example, the grade is either less than 60 or greater than or equal to 60. If the grade is less than 60, the application displays "Failed". If the grade is greater than or equal to 60, the application displays "Passed". We continue to emphasize this action/decision model of computing. Imagine again a deep bin containing as many empty double-selection statements as might be needed to build any Visual Basic application. Your job as a programmer is to assemble these selection statements (by stacking and nesting) with any other control statements required by the algorithm. You fill in the action states and decision symbols with action expressions and guard conditions appropriate to the algorithm.

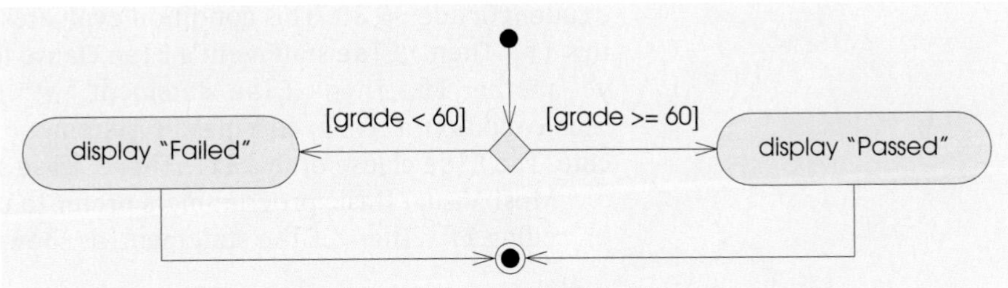

Figure 7.8 `If...Then...Else` double-selection statement activity diagram.

Nested `If...Then...Else` statements test for multiple conditions by placing `If...Then...Else` statements inside other `If...Then...Else` statements. For example, the following pseudocode displays "A" for exam grades greater than or equal to 90, "B" for grades in the range 80–89, "C" for grades in the range 70–79, "D" for grades in the range 60–69 and "F" for all other grades:

```
If student's grade is greater than or equal to 90
    Display "A"
Else
    If student's grade is greater than or equal to 80
        Display "B"
    Else
        If student's grade is greater than or equal to 70
            Display "C"
        Else
            If student's grade is greater than or equal to 60
                Display "D"
            Else
                Display "F"
```

The preceding pseudocode may be written in Visual Basic as shown in Fig. 7.9.

Good Programming Practice

If there are several levels of indentation, each level should be indented farther to the right by the same amount of space.

```
If studentGrade >= 90 Then
   displayLabel.Text = "A"
Else
   If studentGrade >= 80 Then
      displayLabel.Text = "B"
   Else
      If studentGrade >= 70 Then
         displayLabel.Text = "C"
      Else
         If studentGrade >= 60 Then
            displayLabel.Text = "D"
         Else
            displayLabel.Text = "F"
         End If
      End If
   End If
End If
```

Figure 7.9 Visual Basic code converted from pseudocode.

If `studentGrade` is greater than or equal to 90, the first condition evaluates to `True` and the statement `displayLabel.Text = "A"` is executed. With a value for `studentGrade` greater than or equal to 90, the remaining three conditions will evaluate to `True`. These conditions, however, are never evaluated, because they are placed within the `Else` portion of the outer `If...Then...Else` statement. The first condition is `True`, so all statements within the `Else` clause are skipped. Let's now assume that `studentGrade` contains the value `75`. The first condition is `False`, so the application executes the statements within the `Else` clause of this statement. This `Else` clause also contains an `If...Then...Else` statement, with the condition `studentGrade >= 80`. This condition evaluates to `False`, causing the statements in this `If...Then...Else` statement's `Else` clause to execute. This `Else` clause contains yet another `If...Then...Else` statement, with the condition `studentGrade >= 70`. This condition is `True`, causing the statement `displayLabel.Text = "C"` to execute. The `Else` clause of this `If...Then...Else` statement is then skipped.

Most Visual Basic programmers prefer to use the **`ElseIf` keyword** to write the preceding `If...Then...Else` statement, as shown in Fig. 7.10.

```
If studentGrade >= 90 Then
   displayLabel.Text = "A"
ElseIf studentGrade >= 80 Then
   displayLabel.Text = "B"
ElseIf studentGrade >= 70 Then
   displayLabel.Text = "C"
ElseIf studentGrade >= 60 Then
   displayLabel.Text = "D"
Else
   displayLabel.Text = "F"
End If
```

Figure 7.10 `If...Then...Else` statement using the `ElseIf` keyword.

Common Programming Error

The `Else` clause must always be last in an `If...Then...Else` statement—following an `Else` clause with another `Else` or `ElseIf` clause is a syntax error.

The two statements are equivalent, but you should use the latter statement—it avoids deep indentation of the code. Such deep indentation often leaves little room on a line, forcing lines to be split and decreasing code readability. Note that the final portion of the `If...Then...Else` statement uses the `Else` keyword to handle all the remaining possibilities. The `Else` clause must always be last in an `If...Then...Else` statement—following an `Else` clause with another `Else` or `ElseIf` clause is a syntax error. You should also note that the latter statement requires only one `End If`.

SELF-REVIEW

1. `If...Then...Else` is a _________-selection statement.

   a) single
   b) double
   c) triple
   d) nested

2. Placing an `If...Then...Else` statement inside another `If...Then...Else` statement is an example of _________.

   a) nesting `If...Then...Else` statements
   b) stacking `If...Then...Else` statements
   c) creating sequential `If...Then...Else` statements
   d) None of the above

Answers: 1) b. 2) a.

7.7 Constructing the Wage Calculator Application

This section builds the **Wage Calculator** by using the `If...Then...Else` statement. The `If...Then...Else` statement allows you to select between calculating regular wages and including overtime pay based on the number of hours worked. The following pseudocode describes the basic operation of the **Wage Calculator** application.

```
When the user clicks the Calculate Button
    Retrieve the number of hours worked and hourly wage from the TextBoxes

    If the number of hours worked is less than or equal to 40 hours
        Gross earnings equals hours worked times hourly wage
    Else
        Gross earnings equals 40 times hourly wage plus
        hours above 40 times wage and a half

    Display gross earnings
```

Visual Studio provides many programming tools to help you create powerful and effective applications. With so many tools available, it is often helpful to create a table to organize and choose the best GUI elements. Like pseudocode, these tables simplify the task of creating the application by outlining the application's actions. In addition to listing the application's actions, the table assigns controls and events to the actions described in the pseudocode.

Now that you've test-driven the **Wage Calculator** application and studied its pseudocode representation, you'll use an Action/Control/Event (ACE) table to help you convert the pseudocode to Visual Basic. Figure 7.11 lists the actions, controls and events that help you complete your own version of this application.

The `Labels` in the first row display information about the application to the user. These `Labels` guide the user through the application. The `Button` control, `calculateButton`, is used to calculate the employee's wages. Note that the third column of the table specifies that we'll be using this control's `Click` event to perform the calculations. The `TextBoxes` contain input from the user. The final control, `earningsResultLabel`, is a `Label` that displays the application's output.

Action/Control/Event (ACE) Table for the Wage Calculator Application

Action	Control	Event
Label the application's controls	wageLabel, hoursLabel, earningsLabel	Application is run
	calculateButton	Click
Retrieve the number of hours worked and hourly wage from the TextBoxes	wageTextBox, hoursTextBox	
If the number of hours worked is less than or equal to 40 hours Gross earnings equals hours worked times hourly wage		
Else Gross earnings equals 40 times hourly wage plus hours above 40 times wage and a half		
Display gross earnings	earningsResult-Label	

Figure 7.11 Action/Control/Event table for the **Wage Calculator** application.

We now apply our pseudocode and the ACE table to complete the **Wage Calculator** application. The following box guides you through the process of adding a `Click` event to the **Calculate** `Button` and declaring the variables you need to calculate the employee's wages. If you forget to add code to this `Click` event, the application won't respond when the user clicks the **Calculate** `Button`.

Declaring Variables in the Calculate `Button`'s `Click` Event Handler

1. ***Copying the template to your working directory.*** Copy the `C:\Examples\Tutorial07\TemplateApplication\WageCalculator` directory to your `C:\SimplyVB2008` directory.

2. ***Opening the Wage Calculator application's template file.*** Double click `WageCalculator.sln` in the `WageCalculator` directory to open the application in the Visual Basic IDE. If the application does not open in **Design** view, double click the **WageCalculator.vb** file in the **Solution Explorer**. If the **Solution Explorer** is not open, select **View > Solution Explorer**.

3. ***Adding the Calculate `Button` `Click` event handler.*** In this example, the event handler calculates the gross earnings when the **Calculate** `Button`'s `Click` event occurs. Double click the **Calculate** `Button`. An event handler is generated, and the IDE switches to **Code** view. Lines 3–6 of Fig. 7.12 display the generated event handler. Be sure to add the comments and line-continuation characters as shown in Fig. 7.12 so that the line numbers in your code match those presented in this tutorial.

Empty event handler

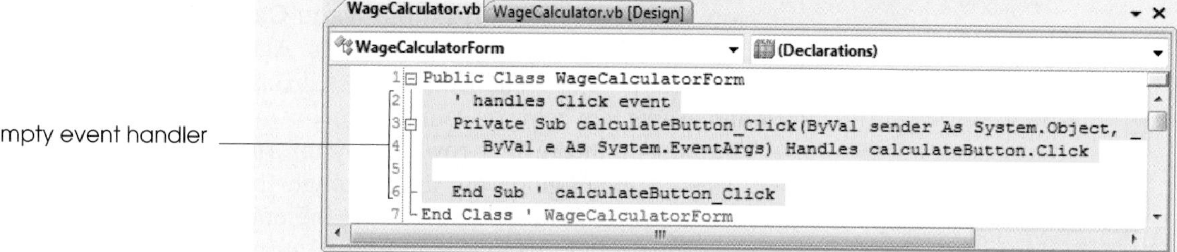
WageCalculator.vb
WageCalculator.vb [Design]
WageCalculatorForm
(Declarations)
1 Public Class WageCalculatorForm
2 ' handles Click event
3 Private Sub calculateButton_Click(ByVal sender As System.Object, _
4 ByVal e As System.EventArgs) Handles calculateButton.Click
5
6 End Sub ' calculateButton_Click
7 End Class ' WageCalculatorForm

Figure 7.12 Calculate `Button` event handler.

The `End Sub` keywords (line 6) indicate the end of event handler `calculateButton_Click`. The `End Class` keywords (line 7) indicate the end of class `WageCalculatorForm`. We often add comments so that the reader can easily determine which event handler or class is being closed without having to search for the beginning of that event handler or class in the file.

4. ***Declaring variables.*** This application uses the primitive data types `Double` and `Decimal`. A `Double` holds numbers with decimal points. Because hours and wages are often fractional numbers, `Integers` are not appropriate for this application. Add lines 6–9 of Fig. 7.13 into the body of event handler `calculateButton_Click`. Line 7 contains a variable declaration for `Double` `hours`, which holds the number of hours input by the user.

Variable declarations

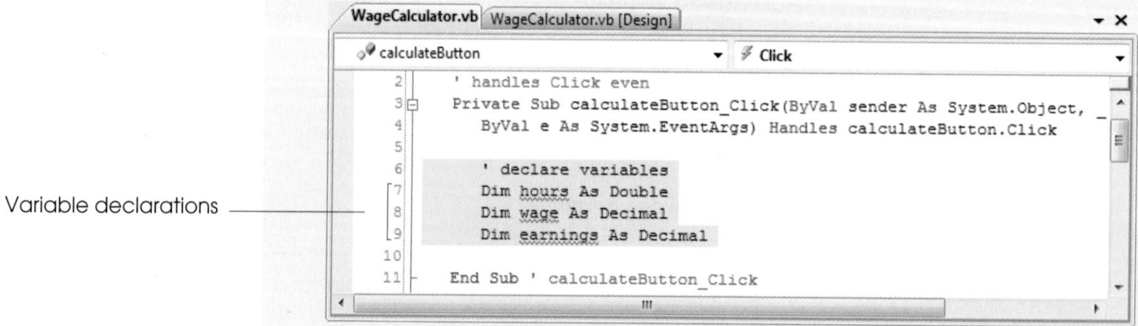
WageCalculator.vb
WageCalculator.vb [Design]
calculateButton
Click
2 ' handles Click even
3 Private Sub calculateButton_Click(ByVal sender As System.Object, _
4 ByVal e As System.EventArgs) Handles calculateButton.Click
5
6 ' declare variables
7 Dim hours As Double
8 Dim wage As Decimal
9 Dim earnings As Decimal
10
11 End Sub ' calculateButton_Click

Figure 7.13 Declaring variables of type `Double` and `Decimal`.

Type `Decimal` is used to store monetary amounts because this data type minimizes rounding errors in arithmetic calculations involving monetary amounts. Lines 8–9 declare `wage`, which stores the hourly wage input by the user, and `earnings`, which stores the total amount of earnings for the week.

(cont.)

Good Programming Practice

Constants (also called named constants) help make programs more readable by providing names for constant values.

5. ***Declaring a constant.*** Add line 11 of Fig. 7.14 to the end of event handler `calculateButton_Click`. Line 11 contains a **constant**, an identifier whose value cannot be changed after its initial declaration. Constants are declared with keyword **`Const`**. In this case, we assign to the constant `HOUR_LIMIT` the maximum number of hours worked before mandatory overtime pay (40). Note that we capitalize the constant's name to emphasize that it's a constant.

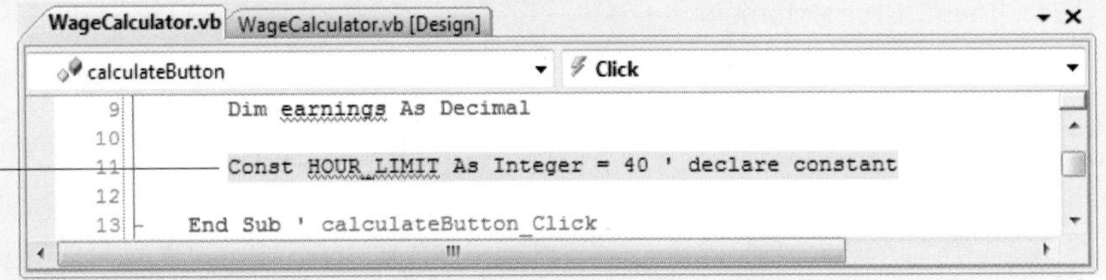
WageCalculator.vb
WageCalculator.vb [Design]
calculateButton
Click
9 Dim earnings As Decimal
10
11 Const HOUR_LIMIT As Integer = 40 ' declare constant
12
13 End Sub ' calculateButton_Click
Constant declaration

Figure 7.14 Creating a constant.

Good Programming Practice

Capitalize each letter in the name of a constant; separate each word in the name with an underscore.

6. ***Saving the project.*** Select **File > Save All** to save your modified code.

Now that you've declared variables, you can use them to retrieve input from the user, then use that input to compute and display the user's earnings. The following box walks you through using an `If...Then...Else` statement to determine the user's earnings.

Determining the User's Wages

1. ***Obtaining inputs from the TextBoxes.*** Add lines 13–15 of Fig. 7.15 to the end of event handler `calculateButton_Click`. Lines 14–15 assign values to `hours` and `wage` from the `TextBox`es into which the user enters data. The `Val` function returns the user input as `Double`s (lines 14–15). Visual Basic implicitly converts the `Double` result of `Val` to data type `Decimal` to assign the result to `wage` (line 15).

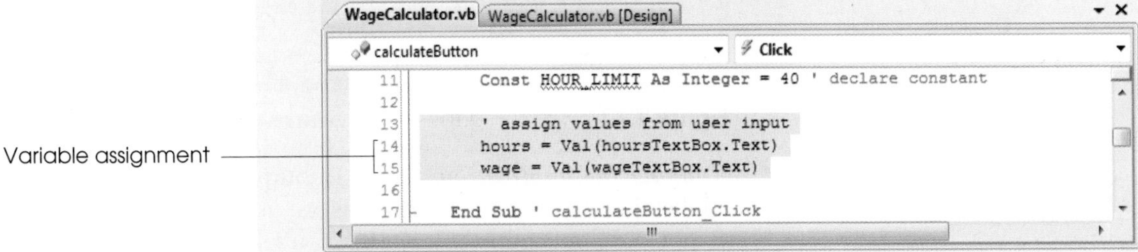
Variable assignment
WageCalculator.vb
WageCalculator.vb [Design]
calculateButton
Click
11 Const HOUR_LIMIT As Integer = 40 ' declare constant
12
13 ' assign values from user input
14 hours = Val(hoursTextBox.Text)
15 wage = Val(wageTextBox.Text)
16
17 End Sub ' calculateButton_Click

Figure 7.15 Assigning data to variables.

2. ***Determining wages based on hours worked.*** Begin to add the `If...Then...Else` statement shown in lines 17–28 of Fig. 7.16 to the end of event handler `calculateButton_Click`. First type lines 17–18, then press *Enter*. Note that the keywords `End If` are added for you by the IDE. Continue by adding lines 19–27 to the `If...Then...Else` statement. You might need to indent as you go. This `If...Then...Else` statement determines whether employees earn overtime in addition to their usual wages. Line 18 determines whether the value stored in `hours` is less than or equal to `HOUR_LIMIT`. If it is, then line 20 assigns the product of `hours` and `wage` to `earnings`. When you multiply a variable of data type `Double` by a variable of data type `Decimal`, Visual Basic implicitly converts the `Decimal` variable to a `Double`. The `Double` result is then implicitly converted to a `Decimal` when it is assigned to `Decimal` variable `earnings`.

Error-Prevention Tip

To reduce errors, the IDE sometimes adds keywords for you. One example is the adding of the keywords `End If` when an `If...Then` or an `If...Then...Else` statement is created. This eliminates the possibility that such keywords will be forgotten or misspelled.

(cont.)

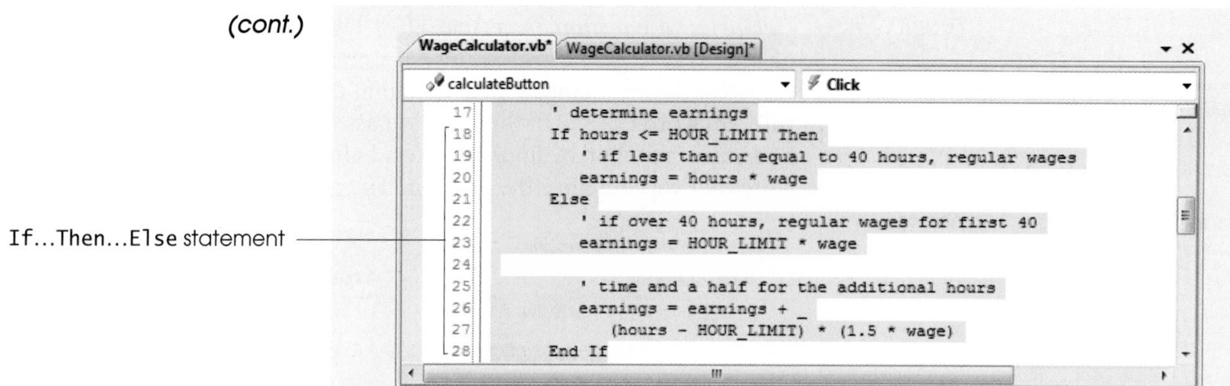

Figure 7.16 `If...Then...Else` statement to determine wages.

If, on the other hand, `hours` is not less than or equal to `HOUR_LIMIT`, then the application proceeds to the `Else` keyword in line 21. Line 23 computes the earnings for the hours worked up to the limit set by `HOUR_LIMIT` and assigns it to `earnings`. Lines 26–27 determine how many hours over `HOUR_LIMIT` there are (by using the expression `hours - HOUR_LIMIT`), then multiplies that by `1.5` times the user's hourly wage. This calculation results in the user's time-and-a-half pay for overtime hours, which is then added to `earnings`, and the result is assigned to `earnings`.

3. ***Displaying the result.*** Add lines 30–31 of Fig. 7.17 to the end of event handler `calculateButton_Click`. Line 31 assigns the value in `earnings` to the `Text` property of the `Label` `earningsResultLabel`, implicitly converting `earnings` from a `Decimal` to a string.

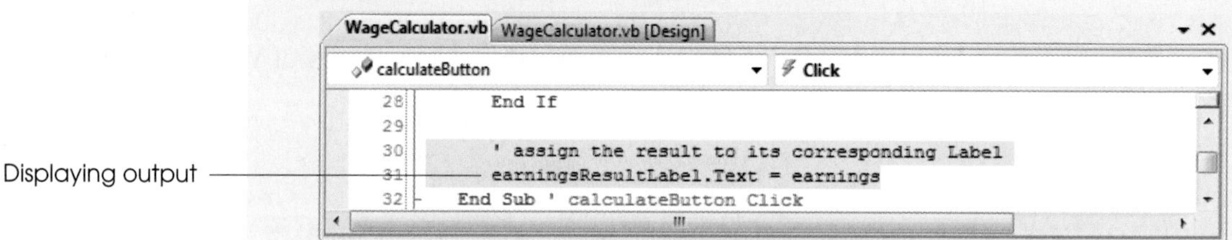

Figure 7.17 Assigning the result to `earningsResultLabel`.

4. ***Running the application.*** Select **Debug > Start Debugging** to run your application. Note that the output is not yet formatted as it should be in the completed application (Fig. 7.18). You learn how to add this functionality in Section 7.9.

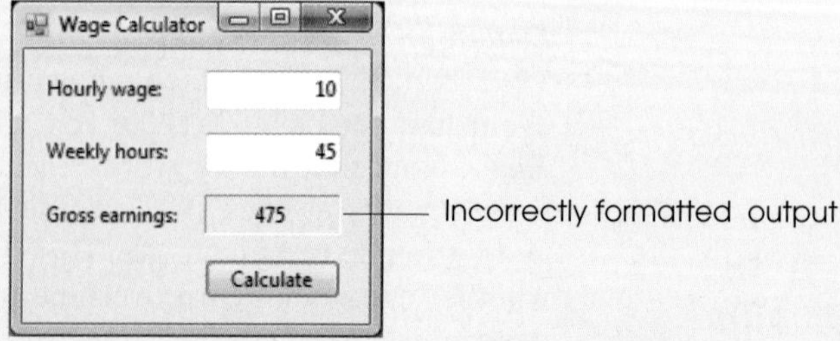

Figure 7.18 **Wage Calculator** with incorrectly formatted output.

5. ***Closing the application.*** Close your running application by clicking its close box.

SELF-REVIEW

1. The `Decimal` data type is used to store ________.
   a) letters and digits
   b) integers
   c) strings
   d) monetary amounts

2. Constants are declared with keyword ________.
   a) `Fixed`
   b) `Constant`
   c) `Final`
   d) `Const`

Answers: 1) d. 2) d.

7.8 Assignment Operators

Visual Basic provides several assignment operators for abbreviating assignment statements. For example, the statement

```
value = value + 3
```

which adds `3` to the value in `value`, can be abbreviated with the addition assignment operator += as

```
value += 3
```

The += operator adds the value of the right operand to the value of the left operand and stores the result in the left operand. Visual Basic provides assignment operators for several binary operators, including +, -, *, ^, / and \. When an assignment statement is evaluated, the expression to the right of the operator is always evaluated first, then assigned to the variable on the left. Figure 7.19 includes the assignment operators, sample expressions using these operators and explanations.

Assignment operators	Sample expression	Explanation	Assigns
Assume: `c = 4`			
+=	`c += 7`	`c = c + 7`	`11` to `c`
-=	`c -= 3`	`c = c - 3`	`1` to `c`
*=	`c *= 4`	`c = c * 4`	`16` to `c`
/=	`c /= 2`	`c = c / 2`	`2` to `c`
\=	`c \= 3`	`c = c \ 3`	`1` to `c`
^=	`c ^= 2`	`c = c ^ 2`	`16` to `c`

Figure 7.19 Assignment operators.

The following box demonstrates abbreviating our time-and-a-half calculation with the += operator. When you run the application again, notice that it runs the same as before—all that has changed is that one of the longer statements was made shorter.

Using the Addition Assignment Operator

1. ***Adding the addition assignment operator.*** Replace lines 26–27 of Fig. 7.16 with line 26 of Fig. 7.20.

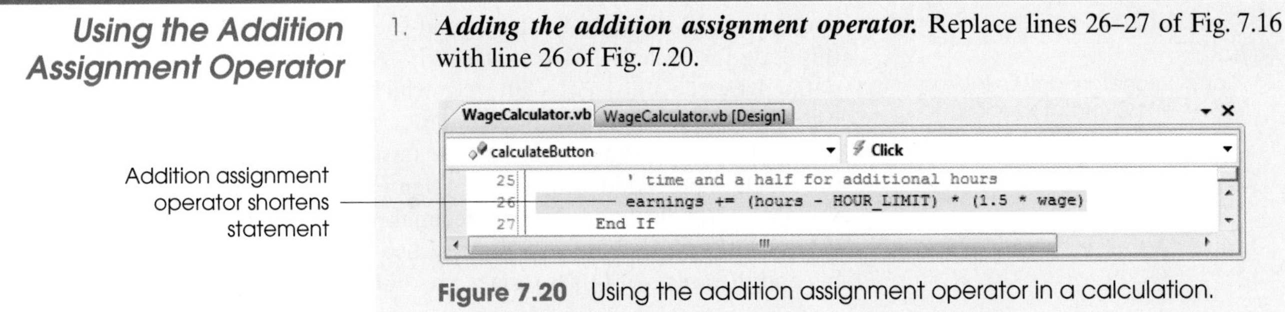

Figure 7.20 Using the addition assignment operator in a calculation.

(cont.)

In this step, we've used the addition assignment operator to make our statement shorter. Note that the statement still performs the same action—the time-and-a-half pay for the user is calculated and added to the regular wages earned.

2. ***Running the application.*** Select **Debug > Start Debugging** to run your application. Note that the application still does not format the output properly. The functionality of the application is the same as it was in the last box—we are now simply using the += operator to abbreviate a statement.

3. ***Closing the application.*** Close your running application by clicking its close box.

SELF-REVIEW

1. The *= operator ________.
   a) squares the value of the right operand and stores the result in the left operand
   b) adds the value of the right operand to the value of the left operand and stores the result in the left operand
   c) creates a new variable and assigns the value of the right operand to that variable
   d) multiplies the value of the left operand by the value of the right operand and stores the result in the left operand

2. If `number` is initialized with the value 5, what value will `number` contain after the expression `number -= 3` is executed?
   a) 3 b) 5
   c) 7 d) 2

Answers: 1) d. 2) d.

7.9 Formatting Text

There are several ways to format output in Visual Basic. In this section, we introduce method **`String.Format`** to control how text displays. Modifying the appearance of text for display purposes is known as **text formatting**. This method takes as an argument a **format control string**, followed by arguments that indicate the values to be formatted. The format control string argument specifies how the remaining arguments are to be formatted.

Recall that your **Wage Calculator** does not display the result of its calculation with the appropriate decimal and dollar sign that you saw when test-driving the application. Next, you learn how to apply currency formatting to the value in the **Gross earnings:** `TextBox`.

Formatting the Gross Earnings

GUI Design Tip

Format all monetary amounts using the C (currency) format specifier.

1. ***Modifying the Calculate `Button`'s `Click` event.*** If the IDE is not already in **Code** view, select **View > Code**. Replace line 31 of Fig. 7.17 with line 30 of Fig. 7.21. Line 30 sends the format control string, `"{0:C}"`, and the value to be formatted, `earnings`, to the `String.Format` method. The number zero indicates that argument `0` (`earnings`—the first argument after the format control string) should take the format specified by the letter after the colon; this letter is called the **format specifier**. In this case, we use the format defined by the uppercase letter `C`, which represents the **currency format**, used to display values as monetary amounts. The effect of the `C` format specifier varies, depending on the locale setting of your computer. In our case, the result is preceded with a dollar sign (`$`), uses a comma as the thousands separator and displays with two decimal places (representing cents) because we are in the United States. You may also specify the locale to use, but that is beyond the scope of this tutorial.

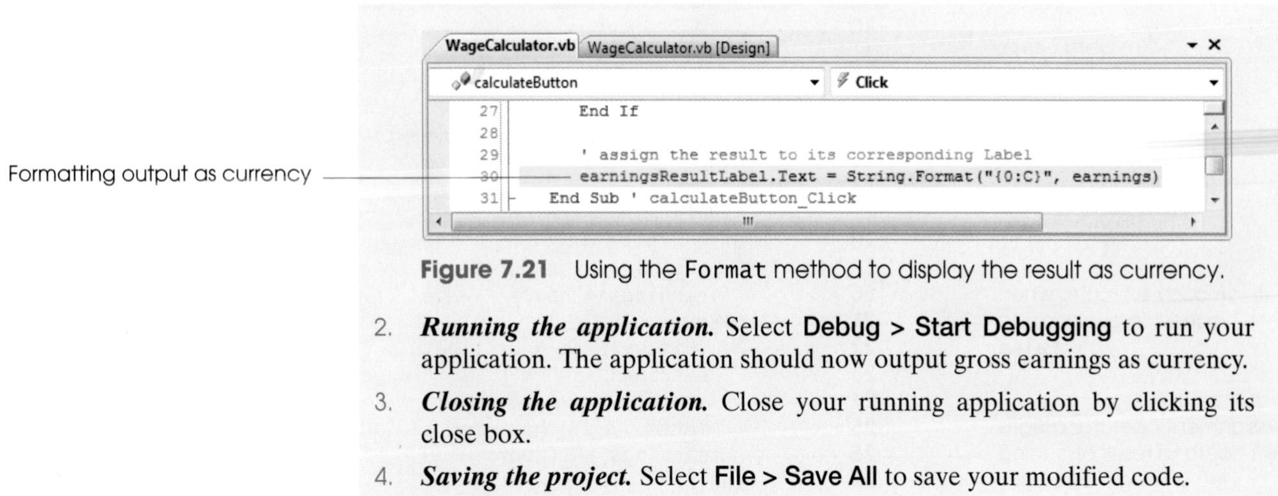

Figure 7.21 Using the `Format` method to display the result as currency.

2. ***Running the application.*** Select **Debug > Start Debugging** to run your application. The application should now output gross earnings as currency.
3. ***Closing the application.*** Close your running application by clicking its close box.
4. ***Saving the project.*** Select **File > Save All** to save your modified code.

Figure 7.22 shows several format specifiers. These format specifiers are case insensitive, so the uppercase letters may be used interchangeably with their lowercase equivalents. Note that format code `D` must be used only with integer types (such as `Integer`, `Byte`, `Short` and `Long`).

Format Specifier	**Description**
`C`	Currency. Formats the currency based on the computer's locale setting. For U.S. currency, precedes the number with `$`, separates every three digits with commas and sets the number of decimal places to two.
`E`	Scientific notation. Displays one digit to the left of the decimal point and six digits to the right of the decimal point, followed by the character `E` and a three-digit integer representing the exponent of a power of 10. For example, `956.2` is formatted as `9.562000E+002`.
`F`	Fixed point. Sets the number of decimal places to two.
`G`	General. Visual Basic chooses either `E` or `F` for you, depending on which representation generates a shorter string.
`D`	Decimal integer. Displays an integer as a whole number in standard base 10 format.
`N`	Number. Separates every three digits with a comma and sets the number of decimal places to two. (Varies by locale.)

Figure 7.22 Format specifiers for strings.

Figure 7.23 presents the source code for the **Wage Calculator** application. The lines of code that contain new programming concepts you learned in this tutorial are highlighted.

```
Public Class WageCalculatorForm
  ' handles Click event
  Private Sub calculateButton_Click(ByVal sender As System.Object, _
     ByVal e As System.EventArgs) Handles calculateButton.Click

     ' declare variables
     Dim hours As Double
     Dim wage As Decimal
     Dim earnings As Decimal
```

Figure 7.23 **Wage Calculator** application code. (Part 1 of 2.)

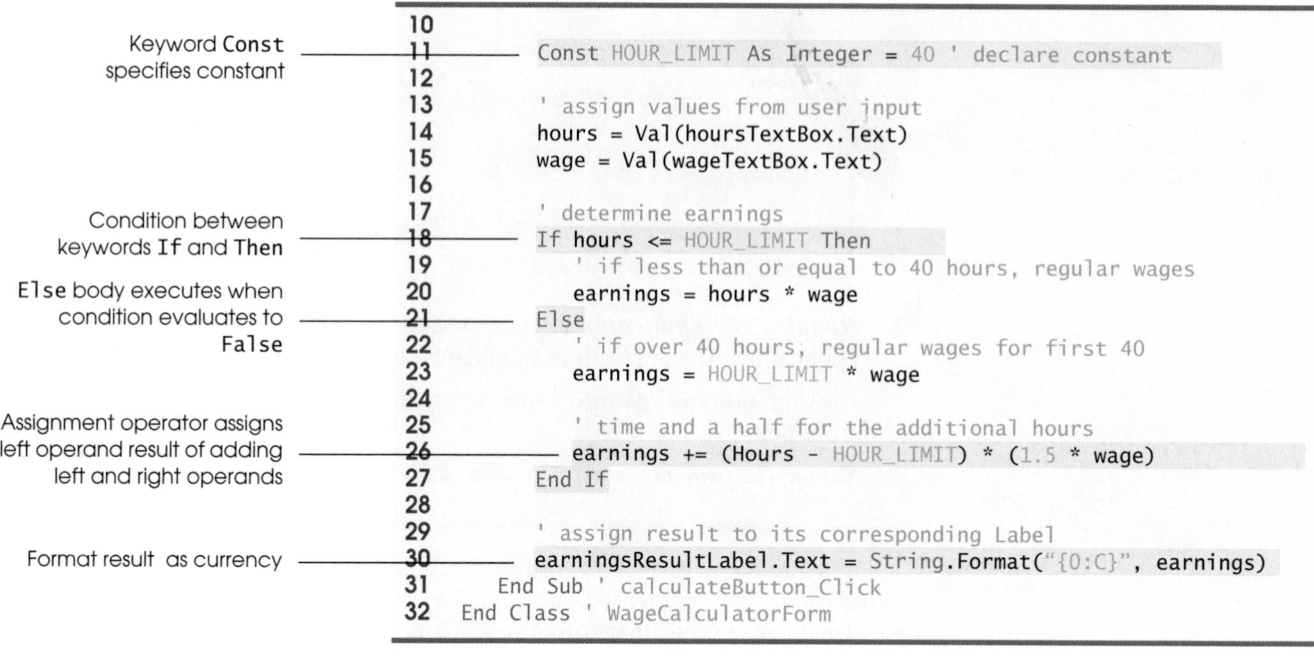
Keyword Const specifies constant
Condition between keywords If and Then
Else body executes when condition evaluates to False
Assignment operator assigns left operand result of adding left and right operands
Format result as currency

```
10
11        Const HOUR_LIMIT As Integer = 40 ' declare constant
12
13        ' assign values from user input
14        hours = Val(hoursTextBox.Text)
15        wage = Val(wageTextBox.Text)
16
17        ' determine earnings
18        If hours <= HOUR_LIMIT Then
19           ' if less than or equal to 40 hours, regular wages
20           earnings = hours * wage
21        Else
22           ' if over 40 hours, regular wages for first 40
23           earnings = HOUR_LIMIT * wage
24
25           ' time and a half for the additional hours
26           earnings += (Hours - HOUR_LIMIT) * (1.5 * wage)
27        End If
28
29        ' assign result to its corresponding Label
30        earningsResultLabel.Text = String.Format("{0:C}", earnings)
31     End Sub ' calculateButton_Click
32  End Class ' WageCalculatorForm
```

Figure 7.23 **Wage Calculator** application code. (Part 2 of 2.)

SELF-REVIEW

1. Method `String.Format` is used to _________.

   a) create constants
   b) control how text is formatted
   c) format Visual Basic statements
   d) All of the above

2. The _________ format displays values as monetary amounts.

   a) monetary
   b) cash
   c) currency
   d) dollar

Answers: 1) b. 2) c.

7.10 Using the Debugger: The Watch Window

Visual Studio includes several debugging windows that are accessible from the **Debug > Windows** submenu. The **Watch window**, which is available only in break mode, allows you to examine the value of a variable or expression. You can use the **Watch** window to view changes in a variable's value as the application executes, or you can change a variable's value yourself by entering the new value directly into the **Watch** window. Each expression or variable that is added to the **Watch** window is called a watch. In the following box, we demonstrate how to add, remove and manipulate watches by using the **Watch** window.

Using the Debugger: The Watch Window

1. ***Starting debugging.*** If the IDE is not in **Code** view, switch to **Code** view now. Set breakpoints in lines 15 and 20 (Fig. 7.24). Select **Debug > Start Debugging** to run the application. The **Wage Calculator** `Form` appears. Enter 12 into the **Hourly wage:** `TextBox` and 40 into the **Weekly hours:** `TextBox` (Fig. 7.25). Click the **Calculate** `Button`.

(cont.)

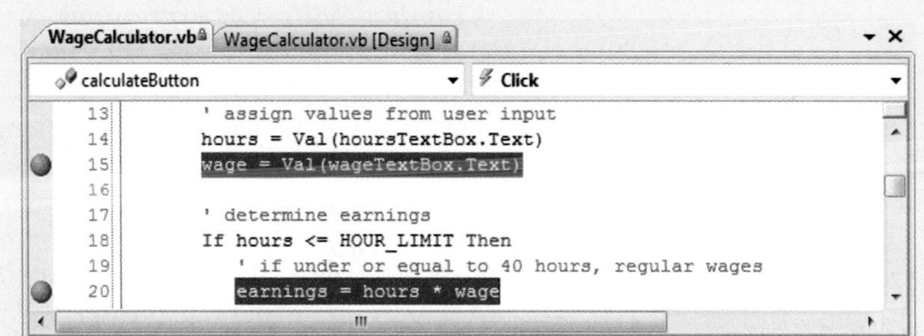

Figure 7.24 Breakpoints added to **Wage Calculator** application.

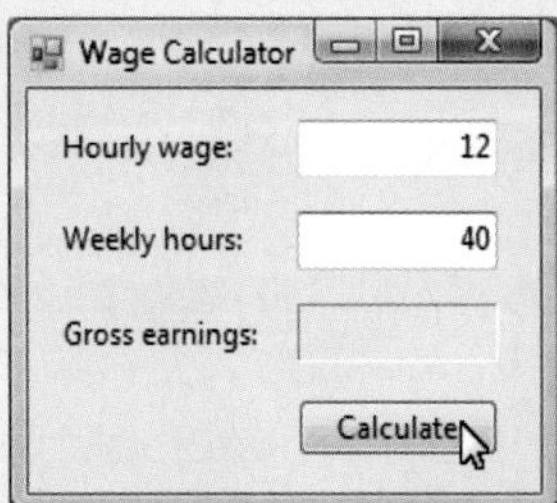

Figure 7.25 **Wage Calculator** application.

2. ***Suspending application execution.*** Clicking the **Calculate** `Button` causes event handler `calculateButton_Click` to execute until the breakpoint is reached. When the breakpoint is reached, application execution is paused, and the IDE switches into break mode. Note that the active window has been changed from the running application to the IDE. The **active window** is the window that is currently being used and is sometimes referred to as the window that has the **focus**. The **Wage Calculator** application is still running, but it may be hidden behind the IDE.

3. ***Examining data.*** Once the application has entered break mode, you are free to explore the values of various variables, using the debugger's **Watch** window. To display the **Watch** window, select **Debug > Windows > Watch**. The **Watch** window is initially empty. To add a watch, you can type an expression into the **Name** column. Single click in the first field of the **Name** column. Type `hours`, then press *Enter*. The value and type are added by the IDE (Fig. 7.26). Note that this value is `40.0`—the value assigned to `hours` in line 14. Type `wage` in the next row, then press *Enter*. The value displayed for `wage` is `0D`. The `D` indicates that the number stored in wage is of type `Decimal`. You can also highlight a variable name in the code and drag-and-drop that variable into the **Watch** window or right click the variable in the code and select **Add Watch**.

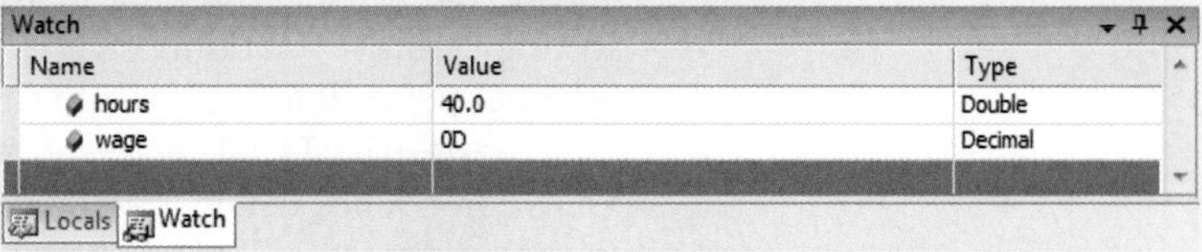

Figure 7.26 **Watch** window.

(cont.)

4. ***Examining different expressions.*** Add the expression `(wage + 3) * 5` into the **Watch** window. Note that the **Watch** window can evaluate arithmetic expressions, returning the value `15D`. Add the expression `wage = 3` into the **Watch** window—expressions containing the **=** symbol are treated as `Boolean` expressions instead of assignment statements. The value returned is `False`, because `wage` does not currently contain the value `3`. Add the expression `variableThatDoesNotExist` into the **Watch** window. This identifier does not exist in the current application, and therefore cannot be evaluated. An appropriate message is displayed in the **Value** field. Your **Watch** window should look similar to Fig. 7.27.

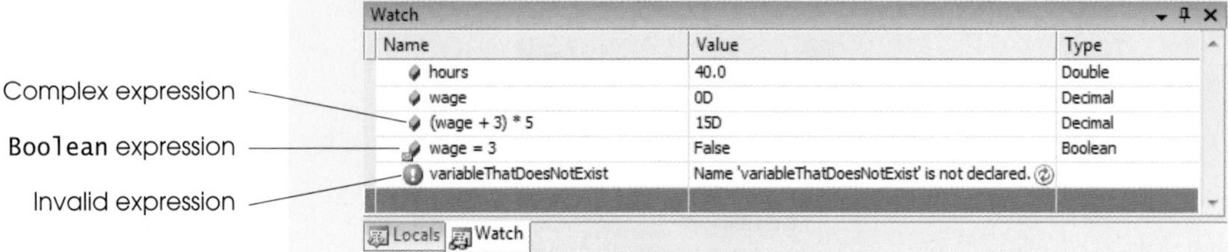

Figure 7.27 Examining expressions.

5. ***Removing an expression from the* Watch *window.*** At this point, we would like to clear the final expressions from the **Watch** window. To remove an expression, simply right click the expression in the **Watch** window and select **Delete Watch** (Fig. 7.28). Alternatively, you can click a variable in the **Watch** window and press the *Delete* key to remove the expression. Remove all the expressions that you added in *Step 4*.

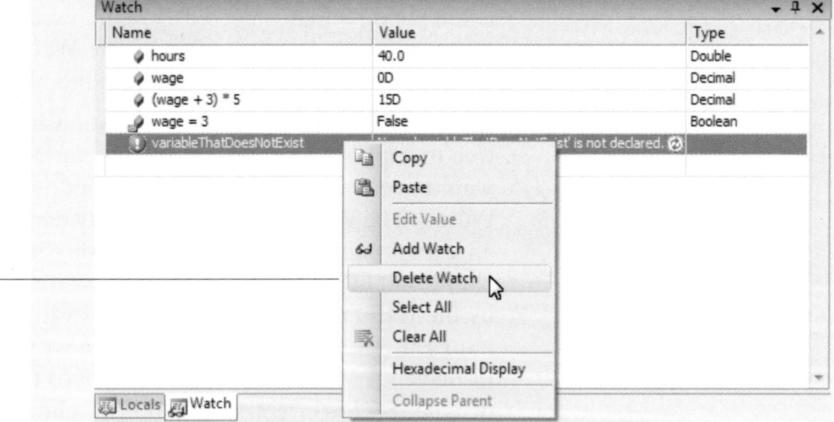

Figure 7.28 Deleting a watch.

6. ***Viewing modified values in a* Watch *window.*** Continue debugging by selecting **Debug > Continue**. The application continues to execute until the next breakpoint (line 20). Line 15 executes, assigning the wage value entered (`12`) to `wage`. The `If...Then` condition evaluates to `True` in line 18, and the application is once again suspended in line 20. Note that the value of `wage` has changed not only in the application, but also in the **Watch** window. Because the value has changed since the last time the application was suspended, the modified value is displayed in red (Fig. 7.29).

(cont.)

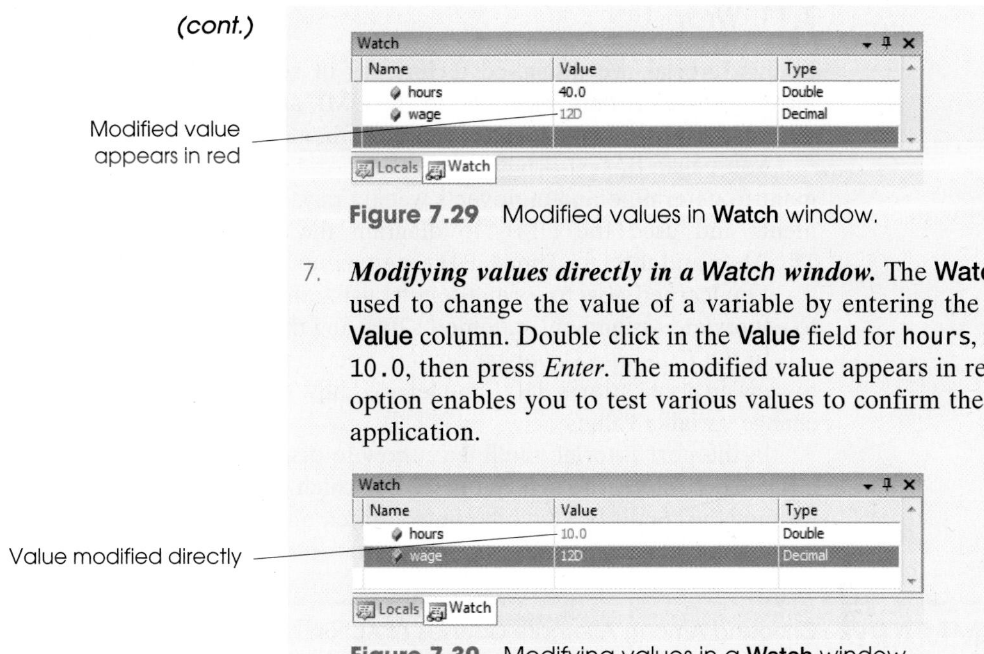

Figure 7.29 Modified values in **Watch** window.

7. ***Modifying values directly in a Watch window.*** The **Watch** window can be used to change the value of a variable by entering the new value in the **Value** column. Double click in the **Value** field for `hours`, replace `40.0` with `10.0`, then press *Enter*. The modified value appears in red (Fig. 7.30). This option enables you to test various values to confirm the behavior of your application.

Figure 7.30 Modifying values in a **Watch** window.

8. ***Viewing the application result.*** Select **Debug > Continue** to continue application execution. Once the event handler `calculateButton_Click` finishes execution, the focus is returned to the **Wage Calculator** window and the final result is displayed (Fig. 7.31). The result is `$120.00`, because we changed `hours` to `10.0` in the last step. The `TextBox` to the right of **Weekly hours:** still displays the value **40**, because we changed the value of `hours`, but not the `Text` property of either `TextBox`.

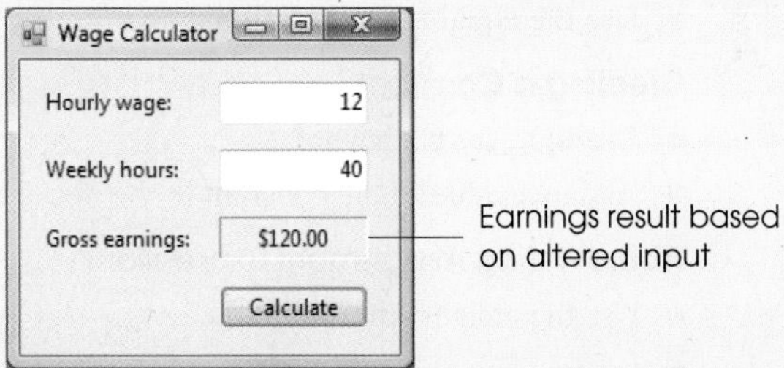

Figure 7.31 Output displayed after the debugging process.

9. ***Closing the application.*** To close your application, either click the running application's close box or select **Debug > Stop Debugging**.

10. ***Saving the project.*** Select **File > Save All** to save your modified code. [*Note:* Breakpoints will also be saved.]

11. ***Closing the IDE.*** Close the Visual Basic IDE by clicking its close box.

SELF-REVIEW

1. An application enters break mode when ________.
   a) **Debug > Start** is selected
   b) a breakpoint is reached
   c) the **Watch** window is used
   d) there is a syntax error

2. The **Watch** window allows you to ________.
   a) change variable values
   b) view variable type information
   c) evaluate expressions
   d) All of the above

Answers: 1) b. 2) d.

7.11 Wrap-Up

In this tutorial, we discussed techniques of solving programming problems. We introduced algorithms, pseudocode, the UML and control statements. We discussed different types of control statements and when each might be used.

You began by test-driving an application that used the `If...Then...Else` statement to determine an employee's weekly pay. You studied different control statements and used the UML to diagram the decision-making processes of the `If...Then` and the `If...Then...Else` statements.

You learned how to format text by using the method `String.Format` and how to abbreviate assignment statements by using the assignment operators.

In the *Using the Debugger* section, you learned how to use the **Watch** window to view an application's data. You learned how to add watches, remove watches and change variable values.

In the next tutorial you'll learn how to display message dialogs based on user input. You'll study the logical operators, which give you more expressive power for forming the conditions in your control statements, and you'll use the `CheckBox` control to allow the user to select from various options in an application.

SKILLS SUMMARY

Choosing Among Alternate Courses of Action

- Use the `If...Then` or `If...Then...Else` control statements.

Conceptualizing the Application Before Using Visual Studio 2008

- Use pseudocode.
- Create an Action/Control/Event (ACE) table.

Understanding Control Statements

- View the control statement's corresponding UML diagram.

Performing Comparisons

- Use the equality and relational operators.

Creating a Constant

- Use the `Const` keyword.
- Assign a value to the constant in the declaration.

Abbreviating Assignment Expressions

- Use the assignment operators.

Formatting a Value as a Monetary Amount

- Use the format code `C` in method `String.Format`.

Examining Data During Application Execution

- Use the debugger to set a breakpoint, and examine the **Watch** window.

KEY TERMS

action/decision model of programming—Representing control statements as UML activity diagrams with rounded rectangles indicating *actions* to be performed and diamond symbols indicating *decisions* to be made.

action expression (in the UML)—Used in an action state within a UML activity diagram to specify a particular action to perform.

action state—An action to perform in a UML activity diagram that is represented by an action-state symbol.

action-state symbol—A rectangle with its left and right sides replaced with arcs curving outward that represents an action to perform in a UML activity diagram.

active window—The window that is currently being used—sometimes referred to as the window that has the focus.

activity diagram—A UML diagram that models the activity (also called the workflow) of a portion of a software system.

algorithm—A procedure for solving a problem, specifying the actions to be executed and the order in which they are to be executed.

block—A group of code statements.

Boolean data type—A data type whose variable can have the value True or False.

condition—An expression with a True or False value that is used to make a decision.

conditional If expression—A shorthand representation of an If...Then...Else statement.

Const keyword—Used to declare a named constant.

control structure (control statement)—An application component that specifies the order in which statements execute (also known as the flow of control).

control structure (statement) nesting—Placing one control statement in the body of another control statement.

control structure (statement) stacking—A set of control statements in sequence. The exit point of one control statement is connected to the entry point of the next control statement in sequence.

constant—An identifier whose value cannot be changed after its initial declaration.

currency format—Used to display values as monetary amounts.

Decimal data type—Used to store monetary amounts.

decision symbol—The diamond-shaped symbol in a UML activity diagram that indicates that a decision is to be made.

diamond symbol—A symbol (also known as the decision symbol) in a UML activity diagram; this symbol indicates that a decision is to be made.

dotted line—A UML activity diagram symbol that connects each UML-style note with the element that the note describes.

double-selection statement—A statement, such as If...Then...Else, that selects between two different actions or sequences of actions.

Else keyword—Indicates the statements to be executed if the condition of the If...Then...Else statement is false.

ElseIf keyword—Keyword used for the nested conditions in nested If...Then...Else statements.

equality operators—Operators = (is equal to) and <> (is not equal to) that compare two values.

executable statements—Actions that are performed when the corresponding Visual Basic application is run.

final state—Represented by a solid circle surrounded by a hollow circle in a UML activity diagram; the end of the workflow after an application performs its activities.

focus—Designates the window currently in use.

format control string—A string that specifies how data should be formatted.

format specifier—Code that specifies the type of format that should be applied to a string for output.

formatting text—Modifying the appearance of text for display purposes.

guard condition—An expression contained in square brackets above or next to the arrows leading from a decision symbol in a UML activity diagram that determines whether workflow continues along a path.

If...Then statement—Selection statement that performs an action (or sequence of actions) based on a condition. This is also called the single-selection statement.

If...Then...Else statement—Selection statement that performs an action (or sequence of actions) if a condition is true and performs a different action (or sequence of actions) if the condition is false. This is also called the double-selection statement.

initial state—Represented by a solid circle in a UML activity diagram; the beginning of the workflow before the application performs the modeled activities.

multiple-selection statement—A statement that selects among many different actions or sequences of actions.

nested statement—A statement that is placed inside another control statement.

note—An explanatory remark (represented by a rectangle with a folded upper-right corner) describing the purpose of a symbol in a UML activity diagram.

program control—The task of ordering an application's statements in the correct order.

pseudocode—An informal language that helps you develop algorithms.

relational operators—Operators < (less than), > (greater than), <= (less than or equal to) and >= (greater than or equal to) that compare two values (also known as comparison operators).

repetition structure (or repetition statement)—Allows the programmer to specify that an action or sequence of actions should be repeated, depending on the value of a condition.

selection structure (or selection statement)—Selects among alternative courses of action.

sequence structure (or sequence statement)—Built into Visual Basic—unless directed to act otherwise, the computer executes Visual Basic statements sequentially.

sequential execution—Statements in an application are executed one after another in the order in which they are written.

single-entry/single-exit control structure (or statement)—A control statement that has one entry point and one exit point. All Visual Basic control statements are single-entry/single-exit control statements.

single-selection statement—The `If...Then` statement, which selects or ignores a single action or sequence of actions.

small circles (in the UML)—The solid circle in an activity diagram represents the activity's initial state, and the solid circle surrounded by a hollow circle represents the activity's final state.

solid circle (in the UML)—A UML activity diagram symbol that represents the activity's initial state.

`String.Format` method—Formats a string.

structured programming—A technique for organizing program control using sequence, selection and repetition structures to help you develop applications that are easy to understand, debug and modify.

syntax—Specifies how a statement must be formed to compile without syntax errors.

transfer of control—Occurs when an executed statement does not directly follow the previously executed statement in a running application.

transition—A change from one action state to another that is represented by transition arrows in a UML activity diagram.

UML (Unified Modeling Language)—An industry standard for modeling software systems graphically.

Watch window—A Visual Basic IDE window that allows you to view and modify variable values while an application is being debugged.

workflow—The activity of a portion of a software system.

GUI DESIGN GUIDELINES

Overall Design

- Format all monetary amounts using the `C` (currency) format specifier.

`TextBox`

- When using multiple `TextBoxes` vertically, align the `TextBoxes` on their right sides, and where possible make the `TextBoxes` the same size. Left-align the descriptive `Labels` for such `TextBoxes`.

CONTROLS, EVENTS, PROPERTIES & METHODS

`String` This class represents a series of characters treated as a single unit.

- ***Method***

  `Format`—Arranges the `String` in a specified format.

MULTIPLE-CHOICE QUESTIONS

7.1 In a condition, the ________ operator returns `False` if the left operand is larger than the right operand.

a) `=` b) `<`
c) `<=` d) All of the above

7.2 A _________ occurs when an executed statement does not directly follow the previously executed statement in the written application.

a) transition b) flow
c) logical error d) transfer of control

7.3 You can interact with the **Watch** window in _________.

a) run mode b) debug mode
c) break mode d) All of the above

7.4 The `If...Then` statement is called a _________ statement because it selects or ignores one action.

a) single-selection b) multiple-selection
c) double-selection d) repetition

7.5 The three types of control statements are the sequence statement, the selection statement and the _________ statement.

a) repeat b) looping
c) redo d) repetition

7.6 In an activity diagram, a rectangle with curved sides represents _________.

a) a complete algorithm b) a comment
c) an action d) the termination of the application

7.7 The `If...Then...Else` selection statement ends with the keywords _________.

a) `End If Then Else` b) `End If Else`
c) `End Else` d) `End If`

7.8 A variable of data type `Boolean` can be assigned keyword _________ or keyword _________.

a) `True, False` b) `Off, On`
c) `True, NotTrue` d) `Yes, No`

7.9 An identifier whose value cannot be changed after its initial declaration is called a _________.

a) `Double` b) constant
c) standard d) `Boolean`

7.10 The _________ operator assigns the result of adding the left and right operands to the left operand.

a) `+` b) `=+`
c) `+=` d) None of the above

EXERCISES

7.11 *(Currency Converter Application)* Develop an application that functions as a currency converter, as shown in Fig. 7.32. Users must provide a number in the **Dollars to convert:** `TextBox` and a currency name (as text) in the **Convert from dollars to:** `TextBox`. Clicking the **Convert** `Button` converts the specified amount into the indicated currency and displays it in a `Label`. Limit yourself to the following currencies as user input: Euros, Yen and Pesos. Use the following exchange rates: 1 Dollar = .69 Euros, 106.5 Yen and 11 Pesos.

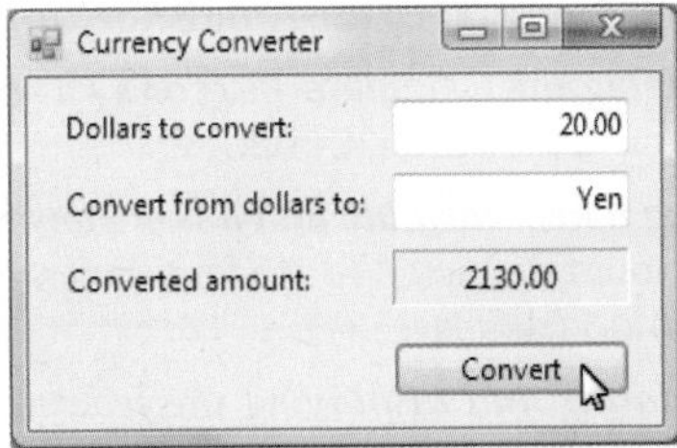

Figure 7.32 **Currency Converter** GUI.

a) ***Copying the template to your working directory.*** Copy the directory `C:\Examples\Tutorial07\Exercises\CurrencyConverter` to your `C:\SimplyVB2008` directory.

b) ***Opening the application's template file.*** Double click `CurrencyConverter.sln` in the `CurrencyConverter` directory to open the application.

c) ***Adding an event handler for the Convert `Button`'s `Click` event.*** Double click the **Convert** `Button` to generate an empty event handler for the `Button`'s `Click` event. The code for *Steps d–f* belongs in this event handler.

d) ***Obtaining the user input.*** Define a `Decimal` variable named `amount`. Use the `Val` function to convert the user input from the **Dollars to convert:** `TextBox` to a `Double`. Assign the result to variable `amount`. Visual Basic implicitly performs this conversion from `Double` to `Decimal`.

e) ***Performing the conversion.*** Use nested `If...Then...Else` statements to determine which currency the user entered. Assign the result of the conversion to `amount`. Display the result using method `String.Format` with format specifier `F`.

f) ***Running the application.*** Select **Debug > Start Debugging** to run your application. Enter a value in dollars to be converted and the name of the currency you wish to convert to. Click the **Convert** `Button` and, using the exchange rates above, verify that the correct output displays.

g) ***Closing the application.*** Close your running application by clicking its close box.

h) ***Closing the IDE.*** Close the Visual Basic IDE by clicking its close box.

7.12 ***(Wage Calculator That Performs Tax Calculations)*** Develop an application that calculates an employee's earnings, as shown in Fig. 7.33. The user should provide the hourly wage and number of hours worked per week. When the **Calculate** `Button` is clicked, the employee's gross earnings should display in the **Gross earnings:** `TextBox`. The **Less FWT:** `TextBox` should display the amount deducted for federal taxes and the **Net earnings:** `TextBox` should display the difference between the gross earnings and the federal tax amount. Assume that overtime wages are `1.5` times the hourly wage and federal taxes are 15% of gross earnings. The **Clear** `Button` should clear all fields.

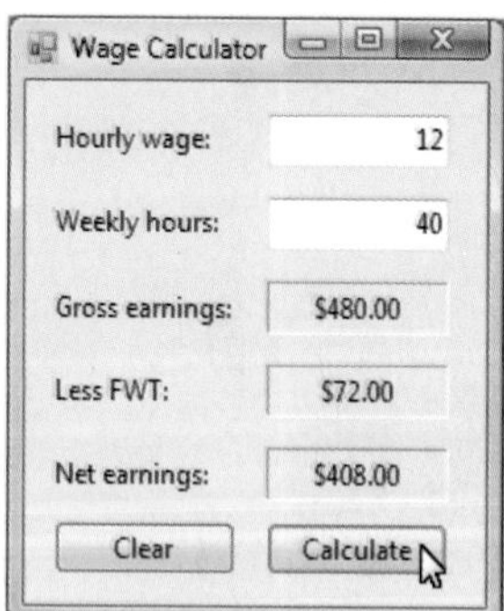

Figure 7.33 Wage Calculator GUI.

a) ***Copying the template to your working directory.*** Copy the directory `C:\Examples\Tutorial07\Exercises\ExpandedWageCalculator` to your `C:\SimplyVB2008` directory.

b) ***Opening the application's template file.*** Double click `WageCalculator.sln` in the `ExpandedWageCalculator` directory to open the application.

c) ***Modifying the Calculate `Button`'s `Click` event handler.*** Add the code for *Steps d–f* to `calculateButton_Click`.

d) ***Adding a new variable and a new constant.*** Declare variable `federalTaxes` to store the amount deducted for federal taxes. Declare constant `TAX_RATE` and assign it the value `0.15` (that is, 15%).

e) ***Calculating and displaying the federal taxes deducted.*** Multiply the total earnings (`earnings`) by the federal tax rate (`TAX_RATE`) to determine the amount to be removed for taxes. Assign the result to `federalTaxes`. Display this value using method `String.Format` with format specifier `C`.

f) ***Calculating and displaying the employee's net pay.*** Subtract `federalTaxes` from `earnings` to calculate the employee's net earnings. Display this value using method `String.Format` with format specifier C.

g) ***Creating an event handler for the* Clear *Button*.** Double click the **Clear** `Button` to generate an empty event handler for the `Click` event. This event handler should clear user input from the two `TextBoxes` and the results from the three `Labels`.

h) ***Running the application.*** Select **Debug > Start Debugging** to run your application. Enter an hourly wage and the number of hours worked. Click the **Calculate** `Button` and verify that the appropriate output is displayed for gross earnings, amount taken out for federal taxes and net earnings. Click the **Clear** `Button` and check that all fields are cleared.

i) ***Closing the application.*** Close your running application by clicking its close box.

j) ***Closing the IDE.*** Close the Visual Basic IDE by clicking its close box.

7.13 ***(Customer Charge Account Analyzer Application)*** Develop an application (as shown in Fig. 7.34) that determines whether a department-store customer has exceeded the credit limit on a charge account. Each customer enters an account number (an `Integer`), a balance at the beginning of the month (a `Decimal`), the total of all items charged this month (a `Decimal`), the total of all credits applied to the customer's account this month (a `Decimal`), and the customer's allowed credit limit (a `Decimal`). The application should input each of these facts, calculate the new balance (= *beginning balance – credits + charges*), display the new balance and determine whether the new balance exceeds the customer's credit limit. If the customer's credit limit is exceeded, the application should display a message (in a `Label` at the bottom of the `Form`) informing the customer of this fact. If the user changes the account number, the application should clear the other `TextBoxes`, the error message `Label` and the result `Label`.

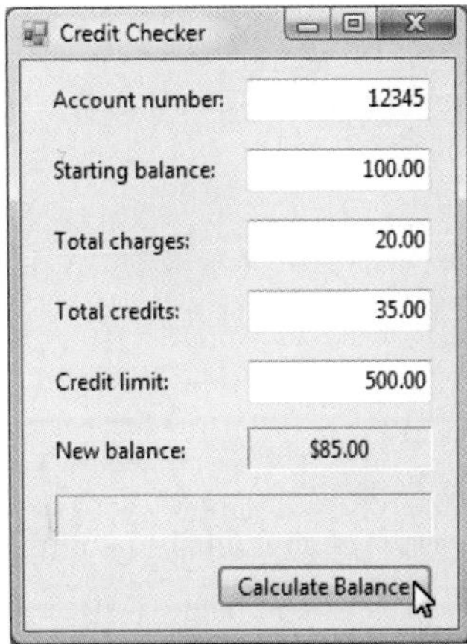

Figure 7.34 Credit Checker GUI.

a) ***Copying the template application to your working directory.*** Copy the directory `C:\Examples\Tutorial07\Exercises\CreditChecker` to `C:\SimplyVB2008`.

b) ***Opening the application's template file.*** Double click `CreditChecker.sln` in the `CreditChecker` directory to open the application.

c) ***Adding the* Calculate Balance *Button's* `Click` *event handler.*** Double click the **Calculate Balance** `Button` to generate the empty event handler for the `Click` event. The code for *Steps d–g* is added to this event handler.

d) ***Declaring variables.*** Declare four `Decimal` variables to store the starting balance, charges, credits and credit limit. Declare a fifth `Decimal` variable to store the new balance in the account after the credits and charges have been applied.

e) ***Obtaining user input.*** Obtain the user input from the `TextBoxes`' `Text` properties.

f) ***Calculating and displaying the new balance.*** Calculate the new balance by subtracting the total credits from the starting balance and adding the charges. Assign the result to a variable. Display the result formatted as currency.

g) ***Determining if the credit limit has been exceeded.*** If the new balance exceeds the specified credit limit, a message should be displayed in `errorLabel`.

h) ***Handling the Account number: TextBox's TextChanged event.*** Double click the **Account number:** `TextBox` to generate its `TextChanged` event handler. This event handler should clear the other `TextBoxes`, the error message `Label` and the result `Label`.

i) ***Running the application.*** Select **Debug > Start Debugging** to run your application. Enter an account number, your starting balance, the amount charged to your account, the amount credited to your account and your credit limit. Click the **Calculate Balance** `Button` and verify that the new balance displayed is correct. Enter an amount charged that exceeds your credit limit. Click the **Calculate Balance** `Button` and ensure that a message is displayed in the lower `Label`. Change the account number and check that all fields are cleared.

j) ***Closing the application.*** Close your running application by clicking its close box.

k) ***Closing the IDE.*** Close the Visual Basic IDE by clicking its close box.

What does this code do?

7.14 Assume that `ageTextBox` is a `TextBox` control and that the user has entered the value 27 into this `TextBox`. Determine the action performed by the following code:

```
Dim age As Integer

age = Val(ageTextBox.Text)

If age < 0 Then
   ageLabel.Text = "Enter a value greater than or equal to zero."
ElseIf age < 13 Then
   ageLabel.Text = "Child"
ElseIf age < 20 Then
   ageLabel.Text = "Teenager"
ElseIf age < 30 Then
   ageLabel.Text = "Young Adult"
ElseIf age < 65 Then
   ageLabel.Text = "Adult"
Else
   ageLabel.Text = "Senior Citizen"
End If
```

What's wrong with this code?

7.15 Assume that `ampmLabel` is a `Label` control. Find the error(s) in the following code:

```
Dim hour As Integer

hour = 14

If hour < 11 Then
   If hour > 0 Then
      ampmLabel.Text = "AM"
   End If
Else
   ampmLabel.Text = "PM"
ElseIf hour > 23 Then
   ampmLabel.Text = "Time Error."
End If
```

Using the Debugger

7.16 ***(Grade Calculator Application)*** Copy the `C:\Examples\Tutorial07\Debugger` directory to your working directory. This directory contains the `Grades` application, which takes a number from the user and displays the corresponding letter grade. For values 90–100 it should display **A**; for 80–89, **B**, for 70–79, **C**, for 60–69, **D** and for anything lower, an **F**. Run the application. Enter the value `85` in the `TextBox` and click **Calculate.** Note that the application displays **D** when it ought to display **B**. Select **View > Code** to enter the code editor and set as many breakpoints as you feel are necessary. Select **Debug > Start Debugging** to use the debugger to help you find the error(s). Figure 7.35 shows the incorrect output when the value 85 is input.

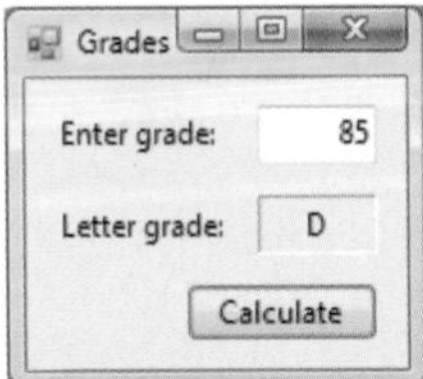

Figure 7.35 Incorrect output for **Grade** application.

Programming Challenge

7.17 *(**Encryption Application**)* A company transmits data over the telephone, but it's concerned that its phones could be tapped. All its data is transmitted as four-digit `Integer`s. The company has asked you to write an application that encrypts its data so that it may be transmitted more securely. Encryption is the process of transforming data for security reasons. Create a `Form` similar to Fig. 7.36. Your application should read four digits entered by the user and encrypt the information. Assume that the user inputs a single digit in each `TextBox`. Use the following technique to encrypt the number:

a) Replace each digit by (*the sum of that digit and* 7) `Mod` 10.

b) Swap the first digit with the third, and swap the second digit with the fourth.

Figure 7.36 **Encryption** application.

TUTORIAL

Objectives

In this tutorial, you learn to:

- Use CheckBoxes to allow users to select options.
- Use dialogs to display messages.
- Use logical operators to form more powerful conditions.

Outline

Dental Payment Application

Introducing CheckBoxes and Message Dialogs

Many Visual Basic applications use **message dialogs** that display messages to users. You encounter many dialogs while using a computer, from those that instruct you to select files or enter passwords to others that notify you of problems while using an application. In this tutorial, you'll use message dialogs to inform users of input problems.

You may have noticed that TextBoxes allow users to enter nearly any value as input. In some cases, you may want to use controls that provide users with predefined options. One way to do this is by providing CheckBoxes in your application. You'll also learn about logical operators, which you can use in your applications to make more involved decisions based on user input.

8.1 Test-Driving the Dental Payment Application

There are many procedures that dentists can perform. The office assistant may present you with a bill generated by a computer. In this tutorial, you'll program an application that prepares a bill for some basic dental procedures. This application must meet the following requirements:

> ***Application Requirements***
>
> *A dentist's office administrator wishes to create an application that employees can use to bill patients. The application must allow users to enter the patient's name and specify which services were performed during the visit. The application will then calculate the total charges. If a user attempts to calculate a bill before any services are specified, or before the patient's name is entered, an error message informing the user that necessary input is missing will be displayed.*

In the **Dental Payment** application, you'll use CheckBox controls and a message dialog to assist the user in entering data. You begin by test-driving the completed application. Then you learn the additional Visual Basic capabilities needed to create your own version of this application.

Test-Driving the Dental Payment Application

1. ***Opening the completed application.*** Open the directory `C:\Examples\Tutorial08\CompletedApplication\DentalPayment` to locate the **Dental Payment** application. Double click `DentalPayment.sln` to open the application in the Visual Basic IDE.

2. ***Running the Dental Payment application.*** Select **Debug > Start Debugging** to run the application (Fig. 8.1).

   Note that there are three square-shaped controls in the left column of the `Form`. These are known as **`CheckBox`** controls. A `CheckBox` is a small square that either is blank or contains a check mark. When a `CheckBox` is selected, a check mark appears in the box (☑). A `CheckBox` can be selected by simply clicking within the `CheckBox`'s small square or by clicking on the text of the `CheckBox`. A selected `CheckBox` can be unchecked in the same way. You will learn how to add `CheckBox` controls to a `Form` shortly.

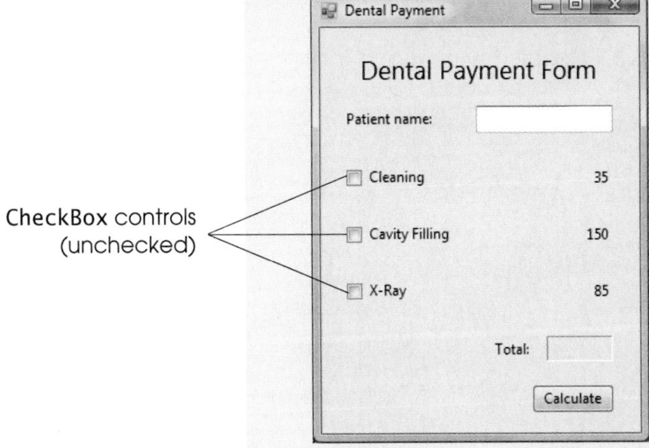

Figure 8.1 Running the completed **Dental Payment** application.

3. ***Attempting to calculate a total without entering input.*** Leave the **Patient name:** field blank, and deselect any `CheckBox`es that you've selected. Click the **Calculate** `Button`. Note that a message dialog appears indicating that you must enter data (Fig. 8.2). Close this dialog by clicking its **OK** `Button`.

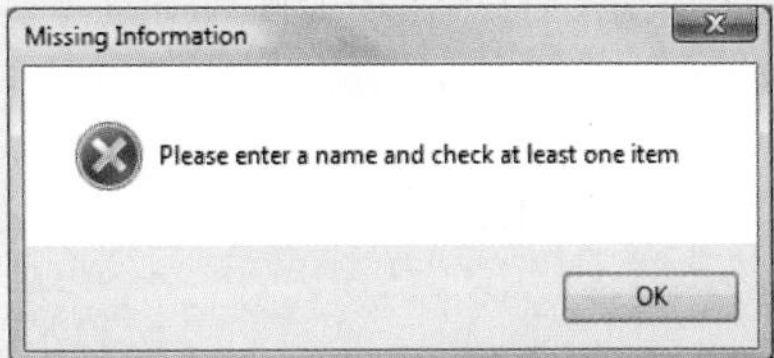

Figure 8.2 Message dialog appears when no name is entered and/or no `CheckBox`es are selected.

4. ***Entering quantities in the application.*** Type `Bob Jones` in the **Patient name:** field. Check all three `CheckBox`es by clicking each one. A check mark appears in each `CheckBox` (Fig. 8.3).

5. ***Unchecking the Cavity Filling CheckBox.*** Click the **Cavity Filling** `CheckBox` to remove its check mark. Only the **Cleaning** and **X-Ray** `CheckBox`es should now be selected (Fig. 8.4).

6. ***Determining the bill.*** Click the **Calculate** `Button`. This causes the application to total the price of the services performed during the dentist visit. The result is displayed in the **Total:** field (Fig. 8.5).

(cont.)

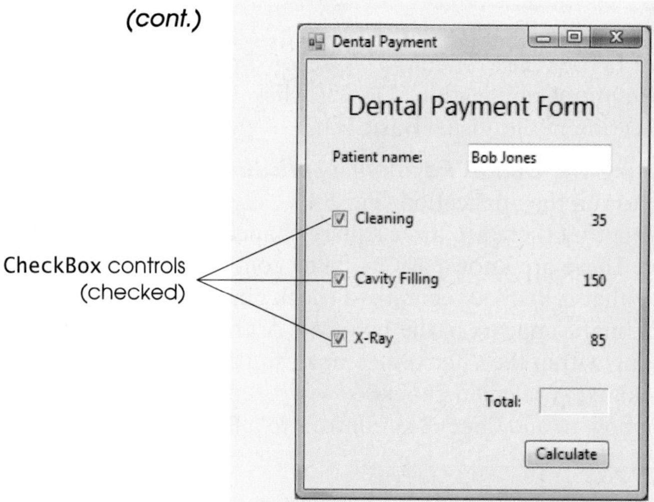

Figure 8.3 **Dental Payment** application with input entered.

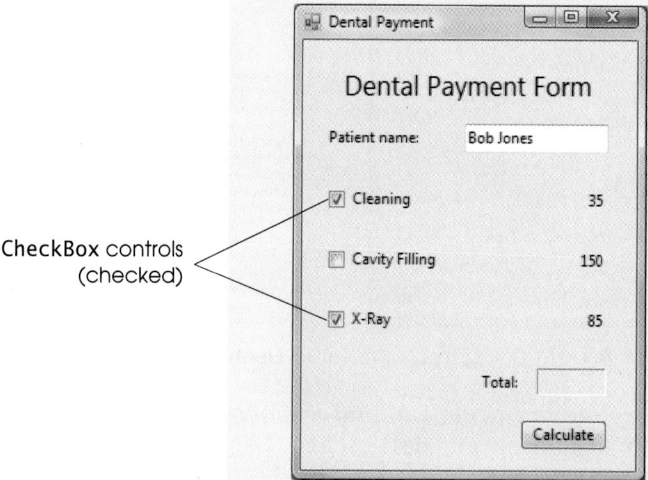

Figure 8.4 **Dental Payment** application with input changed.

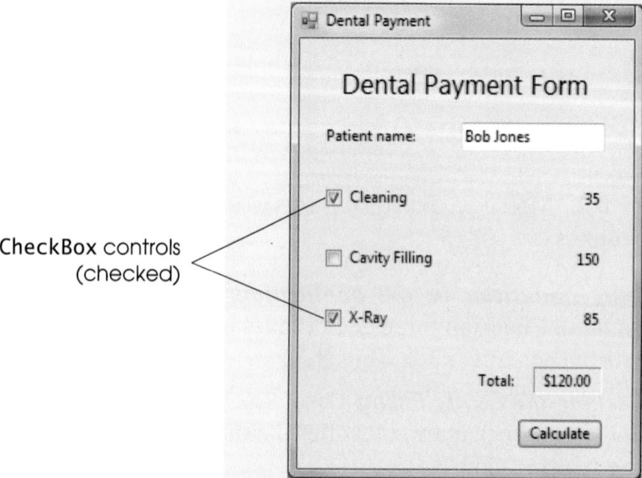

Figure 8.5 **Dental Payment** application with total calculated.

7. ***Closing the application.*** Close your running application by clicking its close box.
8. ***Closing the project.*** Close the project by selecting **File > Close Project**.

8.2 Designing the Dental Payment Application

Recall that pseudocode is an informal language that helps programmers develop algorithms. The following pseudocode describes the basic operation of the **Dental Payment** application, which runs when the user clicks **Calculate**:

```
When the user clicks the Calculate Button
    Clear previous output
    If user has not entered a patient name or has not selected any CheckBoxes
        Display message in dialog
    Else
        Initialize the total to zero
        If "Cleaning" CheckBox is selected
            Add cost of a cleaning to the total
        If "Cavity Filling" CheckBox is selected
            Add cost of receiving a cavity filling to the total
        If "X-Ray" CheckBox is selected
            Add cost of receiving an x-ray to the total
        Format total to be displayed as currency
        Display total
```

Now that you've test-driven the **Dental Payment** application and studied its pseudocode representation, you'll use an ACE table to help you convert the pseudocode to Visual Basic. Figure 8.6 lists the actions, controls and events that will help you complete your own version of this application. Data is input using a `TextBox` (`nameTextBox`) and `CheckBoxes` (`cleanCheckBox`, `cavityCheckBox` and `xrayCheckBox`). Output is displayed in `Label totalResultLabel` when a `Button` (`calculateButton`) is clicked.

Action/Control/Event (ACE) Table for the Dental Payment Application

Action	Control/Class/Object	Event
Label all the application's controls	`titleLabel`, `nameLabel`, `totalLabel`, `cleanCostLabel`, `fillingCostLabel`, `xrayCostLabel`	Application is run
	`calculateButton`	`Click`
Clear previous output	`totalResultLabel`	
If user has not entered a patient name or has not selected any CheckBoxes	`nameTextBox`, `cleanCheckBox`, `cavityCheckBox`, `xrayCheckBox`	
Display message in dialog	`MessageBox`	
Else Initialize the total to zero		
If "Cleaning" CheckBox is selected Add cost of a cleaning to the total	`cleanCheckBox`	
If "Cavity Filling" CheckBox is selected Add cost of receiving a cavity filling to the total	`cavityCheckBox`	

Figure 8.6 ACE table for **Dental Payment** application. (Part 1 of 2.)

Action	Control/Class/Object	Event
If "X-Ray" CheckBox is selected Add cost of receiving an x-ray to the total	xrayCheckBox	
Format total to be displayed as currency	String	
Display total	totalResultLabel	

Figure 8.6 ACE table for **Dental Payment** application. (Part 2 of 2.)

8.3 Using CheckBoxes

GUI Design Tip

A CheckBox's label should be descriptive and as short as possible. When a CheckBox's label contains more than one word, use book-title capitalization.

As mentioned earlier, a CheckBox is a small square that either is blank or contains a check mark. A CheckBox is known as a **state button** because it can be in the on/off [true/false] state. When a CheckBox is selected, a check mark appears in the box. Any number of CheckBoxes can be selected at a time, including none at all. The text that appears alongside a CheckBox is called the **CheckBox label**.

You can determine whether a CheckBox is on (that is, checked) by using the **Checked property**. If the CheckBox is checked, the Checked property contains the Boolean value True; otherwise, it contains False. [*Note:* A CheckBox can also have an indeterminate state if its ThreeState property is set to True. We do not discuss such CheckBoxes in this book.]

You'll now create the **Dental Payment** application from the template provided. The following box demonstrates how to add the CheckBoxes to your application. The application you build in the next two boxes does not display a dialog if the TextBox is empty and/or all the CheckBoxes are unchecked when the **Calculate** Button is clicked. You'll learn how to display that dialog in Section 8.4.

Adding CheckBoxes to the Form

1. ***Copying the template application to your working directory.*** Copy the C:\Examples\Tutorial08\TemplateApplication\DentalPayment directory to your C:\SimplyVB2008 directory.
2. ***Opening the Dental Payment application's template file.*** Double click DentalPayment.sln in the DentalPayment directory to open the application in the Visual Basic IDE. Double click DentalPayment.vb in the **Solution Explorer** if the form does not appear.
3. ***Adding CheckBox controls to the Form.*** Add a CheckBox to the Form by double clicking the

   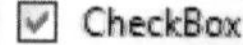

   icon in the **Toolbox**. Repeat this process until three CheckBoxes have been added to the Form.
4. ***Customizing the CheckBoxes.*** For this application, you'll modify the AutoSize, Location, Text, Size and Name properties of each CheckBox. First, set the AutoSize property of all three CheckBoxes to False. Next, change the Size property of all three CheckBoxes to 122, 24. Change the Name property of the first CheckBox to cleanCheckBox and set its Location property to 22, 113 and its Text property to Cleaning. Change the Name property of the second CheckBox to cavityCheckBox, its Location property to 22, 160 and its Text property to Cavity Filling. Change the Name property of the final CheckBox to xrayCheckBox, its Location property to 22, 207 and its Text property to X-Ray.
5. ***Saving the project.*** Select **File > Save All** to save your changes.

GUI Design Tip

Align groups of CheckBoxes either horizontally or vertically.

After placing the CheckBoxes on the Form and setting their properties, you need to code an event handler to enhance the application's functionality when users select CheckBoxes and click **Calculate**.

Adding the Calculate Button's Event Handler

1. ***Adding an event handler for `calculateButton`'s `Click` event.*** Double click the **Calculate** Button on the Form to create an event handler for that control's `Click` event.

2. ***Adding `If...Then` statements to calculate the patient's bill.*** Add lines 6–28 of Fig. 8.7 to your application. Be sure to include all blank lines and line-continuation characters shown in Fig. 8.7 to improve code readability and to ensure that your line numbers correspond to the figure's.

   Line 7 clears any text in the output `Label` that may be present from a previous calculation. Line 10 declares `Decimal` variable `total`, which stores the total charges for the patient. This variable is initialized to `0`. Lines 12–25 define three `If...Then` statements that determine whether the user has checked any of the Form's CheckBoxes. Each `If...Then` statement's condition compares a CheckBox's `Checked` property to `True`. For each `If...Then` statement, the dollar value of the service is added to `total` if the current CheckBox is checked. For example, if CheckBox `cleanCheckBox` is selected (line 13), line 14 uses the `Val` function to obtain the value from the `cleanCostLabel` and adds it to `total`. Line 28 displays the total (formatted as a currency amount) in `totalResultLabel`.

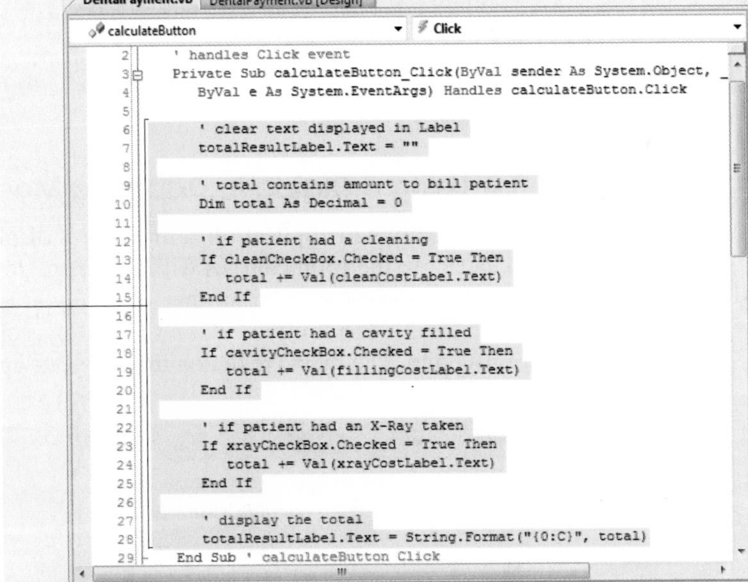

DentalPayment.vb*
DentalPayment.vb [Design]*
calculateButton
Click
2 ' handles Click event
3 Private Sub calculateButton_Click(ByVal sender As System.Object, _
4 ByVal e As System.EventArgs) Handles calculateButton.Click
5
6 ' clear text displayed in Label
7 totalResultLabel.Text = ""
8
9 ' total contains amount to bill patient
10 Dim total As Decimal = 0
11
12 ' if patient had a cleaning
13 If cleanCheckBox.Checked = True Then
14 total += Val(cleanCostLabel.Text)
15 End If
16
17 ' if patient had a cavity filled
18 If cavityCheckBox.Checked = True Then
19 total += Val(fillingCostLabel.Text)
20 End If
21
22 ' if patient had an X-Ray taken
23 If xrayCheckBox.Checked = True Then
24 total += Val(xrayCostLabel.Text)
25 End If
26
27 ' display the total
28 totalResultLabel.Text = String.Format("{0:C}", total)
29 End Sub ' calculateButton_Click
Add this highlighted code

Figure 8.7 Using the `Checked` property.

3. ***Running the application.*** Select **Debug > Start Debugging** to run your application. Note that the user is not required to enter a name or select any CheckBoxes before clicking the **Calculate** Button. If no CheckBoxes are selected, the bill displays the value **$0.00** (Fig. 8.8).

4. ***Selecting a CheckBox.*** Select the **Cleaning** CheckBox, and click the **Calculate** Button. The **Total:** field now displays **$35.00**.

5. ***Closing the application.*** Close your running application by clicking its close box.

(cont.)

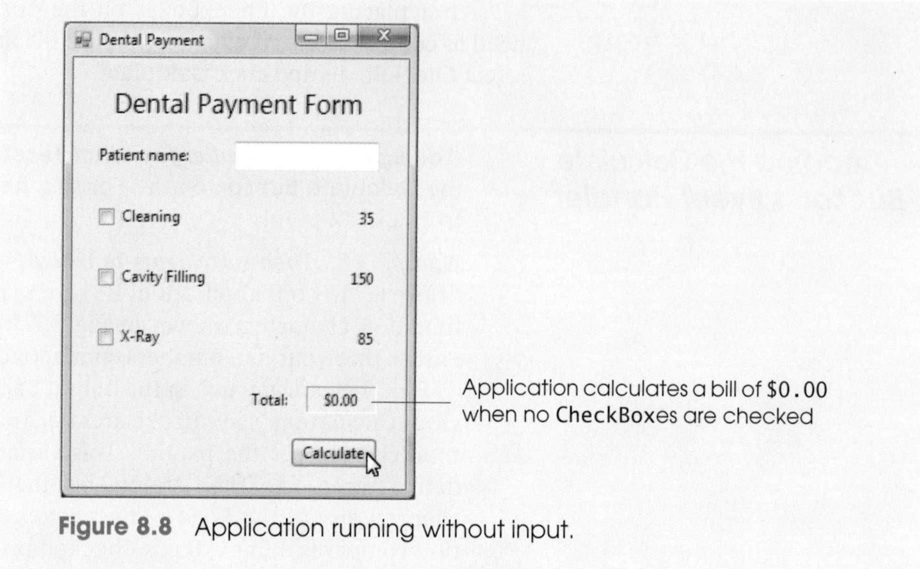

Figure 8.8 Application running without input.

SELF-REVIEW

1. The ________ property sets a CheckBox's label.
   a) Text b) Value
   c) Label d) Checked

2. Which property specifies whether a CheckBox is selected?
   a) Selected b) Checked
   c) Clicked d) Check

Answers: 1.) a. 2.) b.

8.4 Using a Dialog to Display a Message

In the completed application, a message is displayed in a dialog if the user attempts to calculate the total charges without specifying which services were performed or without entering a name. In this section, you learn how to display a dialog when a patient name is not input. When the dialog is closed, control returns to the application's Form. The message dialog used in your application is displayed in Fig. 8.9.

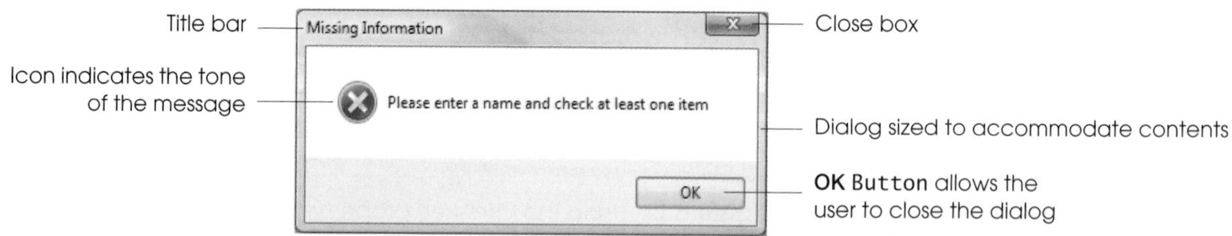

Figure 8.9 Dialog displayed by the application.

The message dialog contains a title bar and a close box. This dialog also contains a message (Please enter a name and check at least one item), an **OK** Button that allows the user to **dismiss** (close) the dialog (which the user must do to proceed) and an icon that indicates the tone of the message. (In this case, ⊗ indicates that a problem has occurred.)

Message dialogs are defined by class **MessageBox** and can be displayed by using method **MessageBox.Show**. The message dialog is customized by the arguments passed to MessageBox.Show. The following box demonstrates displaying a message dialog based on a condition.

GUI Design Tip

Text displayed in a dialog should be descriptive and as short as possible.

Displaying a Message Dialog Using `MessageBox.Show`

1. ***Adding an `If...Then` statement to the event handler for `calculateButton`'s `Click` event.*** The message should display only if the user does not enter the patient's name. Later, you'll add the code to determine if no `CheckBox` has been marked. Place the cursor in line 8 and press *Enter*. Then insert lines 9–12 of Fig. 8.10 into your event handler. Be sure to include a blank line after the `End If` keywords.

   Line 10 tests whether data was entered in the **Patient name:** `TextBox`. If no data has been entered, the expression `nameTextBox.Text = ""` evaluates to `True`. You'll add the body of this `If...Then` statement in *Step 2*.

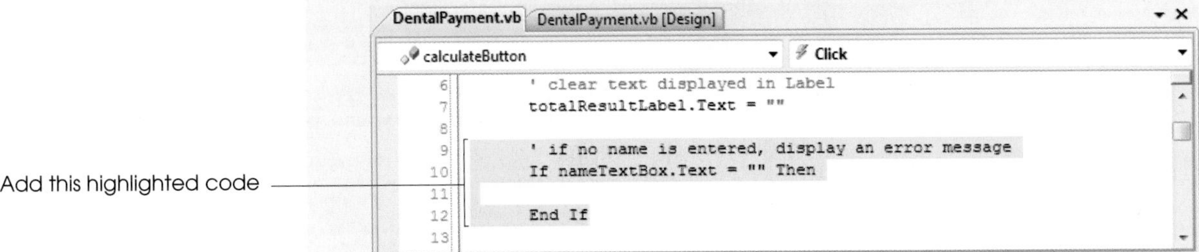

DentalPayment.vb
DentalPayment.vb [Design]
calculateButton
Click
6 ' clear text displayed in Label
7 totalResultLabel.Text = ""
8
9 ' if no name is entered, display an error message
10 If nameTextBox.Text = "" Then
11
12 End If
13
Add this highlighted code

Figure 8.10 Adding an `If...Then` statement to the `calculateButton` `Click` event handler to display a message dialog.

2. ***Adding code to display a message dialog.*** Insert lines 12–16 from Fig. 8.11 into the body of the `If...Then` statement you created in the preceding step. Change the `End If` (line 12 of Fig. 8.10) to `Else` (line 17 of Fig. 8.11). Note that the code you added to the `Click` event earlier (Fig. 8.7) now composes the body of the `Else` portion of your `If...Then...Else` statement. The `Else` is marked as a syntax error because the `If...Then...Else` statement is now missing the `End If` keywords. You add these keywords in *Step 3*.

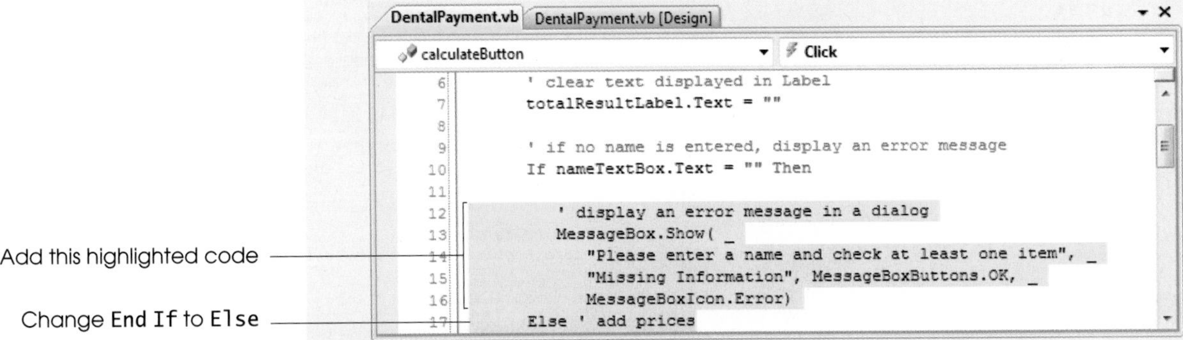

DentalPayment.vb
DentalPayment.vb [Design]
calculateButton
Click
6 ' clear text displayed in Label
7 totalResultLabel.Text = ""
8
9 ' if no name is entered, display an error message
10 If nameTextBox.Text = "" Then
11
12 ' display an error message in a dialog
13 MessageBox.Show(_
14 "Please enter a name and check at least one item", _
15 "Missing Information", MessageBoxButtons.OK, _
16 MessageBoxIcon.Error)
17 Else ' add prices
Add this highlighted code
Change End If to Else

Figure 8.11 Message dialog code that displays a message to users.

   Lines 13–16 call method `MessageBox.Show` using four arguments separated by commas. The first argument specifies the text that displays in the dialog, the second argument specifies the text that appears in its title bar, the third argument indicates which `Button`(s) to display at the bottom of the dialog and the fourth argument indicates which icon appears to the left of the dialog's text. We discuss the final two arguments in more detail shortly.

3. ***Closing the `If...Then...Else` statement.*** Scroll to the end of your event handler code. Insert the keywords `End If` (line 39 of Fig. 8.12) to terminate the `If...Then...Else` statement. Figure 8.13 displays the entire method `calculateButton_Click` after the new code has been added. Compare this code to your own to ensure that you've added the new code correctly.

(cont.)

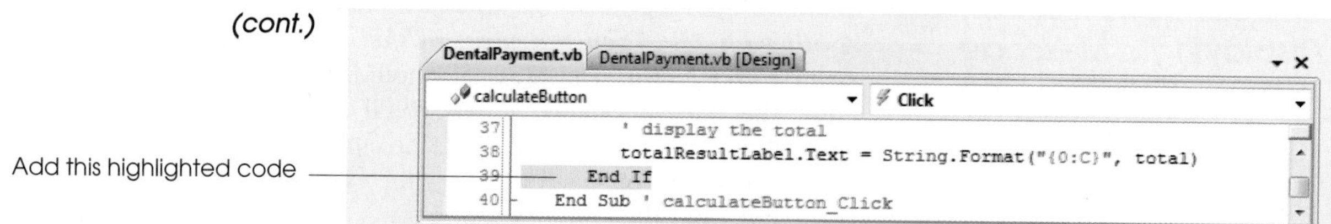

Figure 8.12 Ending the If...Then...Else statement.

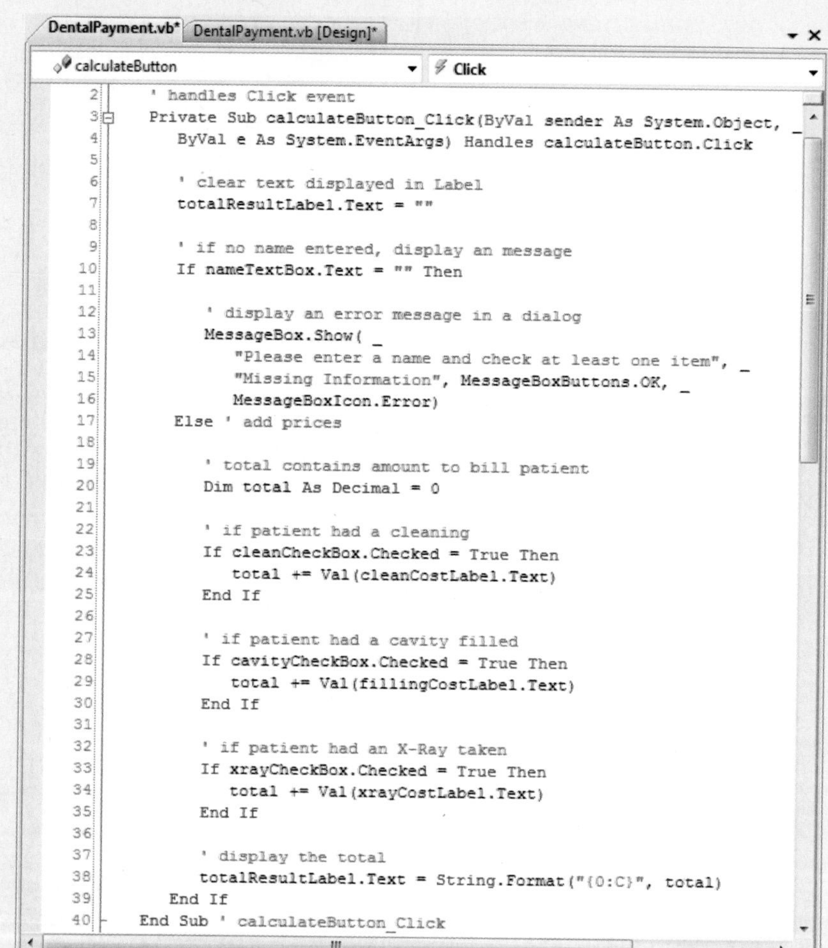

DentalPayment.vb*
DentalPayment.vb [Design]*
calculateButton
Click
' handles Click event
Private Sub calculateButton_Click(ByVal sender As System.Object, _
ByVal e As System.EventArgs) Handles calculateButton.Click
' clear text displayed in Label
totalResultLabel.Text = ""
' if no name entered, display an message
If nameTextBox.Text = "" Then
' display an error message in a dialog
MessageBox.Show(_
"Please enter a name and check at least one item", _
"Missing Information", MessageBoxButtons.OK, _
MessageBoxIcon.Error)
Else ' add prices
' total contains amount to bill patient
Dim total As Decimal = 0
' if patient had a cleaning
If cleanCheckBox.Checked = True Then
total += Val(cleanCostLabel.Text)
End If
' if patient had a cavity filled
If cavityCheckBox.Checked = True Then
total += Val(fillingCostLabel.Text)
End If
' if patient had an X-Ray taken
If xrayCheckBox.Checked = True Then
total += Val(xrayCostLabel.Text)
End If
' display the total
totalResultLabel.Text = String.Format("{0:C}", total)
End If
End Sub ' calculateButton_Click

Figure 8.13 Completed calculateButton_Click event handler.

4. ***Running the application.*** Select **Debug > Start Debugging** to run your application. Note that the user does not have to select any CheckBoxes before clicking the **Calculate** Button but must enter a name in the **Patient name:** TextBox. If none of the CheckBoxes is selected, the bill contains the value **$0.00** (Fig. 8.14). In the next section, you modify the code to test whether the user has selected any CheckBoxes. [*Note:* You cannot interact with the application's Form until you close the message dialog.]

5. ***Closing the application.*** Close your running application by clicking its close box.

(cont.)

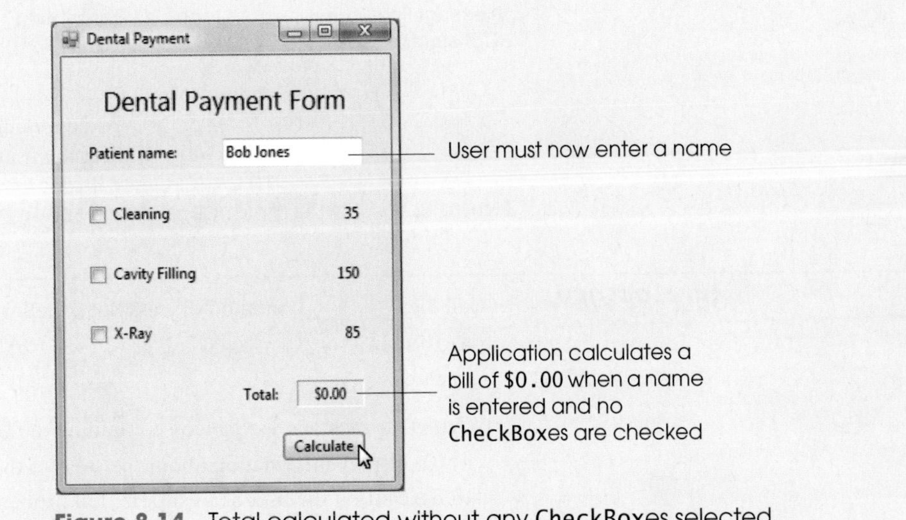

Figure 8.14 Total calculated without any `CheckBox`es selected.

In this example, you passed four arguments to method `MessageBox.Show`. As we discussed, the third argument specified the `Button`(s) to display in the dialog. You passed one of the **`MessageBoxButtons`** constants to method `MessageBox.Show`. You use only the `MessageBoxButtons.OK` constant in this book. Figure 8.15 lists the available `MessageBoxButtons` constants. Note that several `Button`s can be displayed at once. The fourth argument specified the icon to display in the dialog. To set the icon to display, you passed one of the **`MessageBoxIcon`** constants to method `MessageBox.Show`. Some of the available icon constants are shown in Fig. 8.16.

MessageBoxButtons Constants	**Description**
`MessageBoxButtons.OK`	**OK** `Button`. Allows the user to acknowledge a message.
`MessageBoxButtons.OKCancel`	**OK** and **Cancel** `Button`s. Allow the user to either continue or cancel an operation.
`MessageBoxButtons.YesNo`	**Yes** and **No** `Button`s. Allow the user to respond to a question.
`MessageBoxButtons.YesNoCancel`	**Yes**, **No** and **Cancel** `Button`s. Allow the user to respond to a question or cancel an operation.
`MessageBoxButtons.RetryCancel`	**Retry** and **Cancel** `Button`s. Allow the user either to retry or to cancel an operation that has failed.
`MessageBoxButtons.AbortRetryIgnore`	**Abort**, **Retry** and **Ignore** `Button`s. When one of a series of operations has failed, these `Button`s allow the user to abort the entire sequence, retry the failed operation or ignore the failed operation and continue.

Figure 8.15 Message dialog `MessageBoxButtons` constants.

MessageBoxIcon Constants	**Icon**	**Description**
`MessageBoxIcon.Exclamation`	⚠	Icon containing an exclamation point. Typically used to caution the user against potential problems.
`MessageBoxIcon.Information`	ℹ	Icon containing the letter "i." Typically used to display information about the state of the application.

Figure 8.16 Some message dialog `MessageBoxIcon` constants. (Part 1 of 2.)

MessageBoxIcon Constants	Icon	Description
MessageBoxIcon.None		No icon is displayed.
MessageBox-Icon.Error	⊗	Icon containing an × in a red circle. Typically used to alert the user to errors or critical situations.

Figure 8.16 Some message dialog MessageBoxIcon constants. (Part 2 of 2.)

SELF-REVIEW

1. Call the ________ method of class MessageBox to display a message dialog.
   a) Display b) Message
   c) Open d) Show

2. What is the message dialog icon containing the letter "i" typically used for?
   a) To display information about the state of the application
   b) To caution the user against potential problems
   c) To ask the user a question d) To alert the user to critical situations

Answers: 1.) d. 2.) a.

8.5 Logical Operators

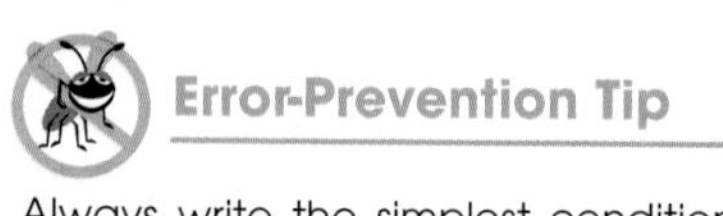

Error-Prevention Tip

Always write the simplest condition possible by limiting the number of logical operators used. Conditions with many logical operators can be hard to read and can introduce subtle bugs into your applications.

So far, you've studied only **simple conditions**, such as count <= 10, total > 1000, and number <> value. Each selection statement that you've used evaluated only one condition with one of the operators >, <, >=, <=, = or <>.

To handle multiple conditions more efficiently, Visual Basic provides **logical operators** that can be used to form complex conditions by combining simple ones. The logical operators are **And**, **AndAlso**, **Or**, **OrElse**, **Xor** and **Not**. We'll consider examples that use several of these operators. After you learn about logical operators, you'll use them to create a complex condition in your **Dental Payment** application to confirm that the user selected at least one CheckBox. See Appendix A for the complete list of operator precedence.

Using AndAlso

Suppose that you wish to ensure that two conditions are *both* true in an application before choosing a certain path of execution. In that case, you can use the logical AndAlso operator as follows:

```
If genderTextBox.Text = "Female" AndAlso age >= 65 Then
   seniorFemales += 1
End If
```

This If...Then statement contains two simple conditions. The condition genderTextBox.Text = "Female" determines whether a person is female, and the condition age >= 65 determines whether a person is a senior citizen. The = and >= operators have a higher precedence than operator AndAlso. The If...Then statement considers the combined condition

```
genderTextBox.Text = "Female" AndAlso age >= 65
```

This condition evaluates to True *if and only if* both of the simple conditions are true—i.e., genderTextBox.Text contains the value "Female" and age contains a value greater than or equal to 65. When this combined condition is true, variable seniorFemales is incremented by 1. However, if either or both of the simple conditions are false, the application skips the increment and proceeds to the statement following the If...Then statement. The readability of the preceding combined condition can be improved by adding redundant (that is, unnecessary) parentheses:

```
(genderTextBox.Text = "Female") AndAlso (age >= 65)
```

Figure 8.17 illustrates the outcome of using the `AndAlso` operator with two expressions. The table lists all four possible combinations of `True` and `False` values for *expression1* and *expression2*, which represent the left operand and the right operand, respectively. Such tables are called **truth tables**. Expressions that include relational operators, equality operators and logical operators evaluate to `True` or `False`.

expression1	expression2	expression1 AndAlso expression2
False	False	False
False	True	False
True	False	False
True	True	True

Figure 8.17 Truth table for the `AndAlso` operator.

Using `OrElse`

Now let's consider the `OrElse` operator. Suppose that you wish to ensure that either *or* both of two conditions are true before you choose a certain path of execution. You would use the `OrElse` operator, as in the following application segment:

```
If (semesterAverage >= 90) OrElse (finalExam >= 90) Then
   MessageBox.Show("Student grade is A", "Student Grade", _
      MessageBoxButtons.OK, MessageBoxIcon.Information)
End If
```

This statement also contains two simple conditions. The condition `semesterAverage >= 90` is evaluated to determine whether the student deserves an "A" in the course because of an outstanding performance throughout the semester. The condition `finalExam >= 90` is evaluated to determine whether the student deserves an "A" in the course because of an outstanding performance on the final exam. The `If...Then` statement then considers the combined condition

```
(semesterAverage >= 90) OrElse (finalExam >= 90)
```

When writing conditions that contain combinations of `AndAlso` and `OrElse` operators, use parentheses to ensure that the conditions evaluate properly. Otherwise, logic errors could occur because `AndAlso` has higher precedence than `OrElse`.

and awards the student an "A" if either or both of the conditions are true, meaning that the student performed well during the semester, performed well on the final exam or both. Note that the text `"Student grade is A"` is displayed unless both of the conditions are false. Figure 8.18 provides a truth table for the `OrElse` operator. Note that the `AndAlso` operator has a higher precedence than the `OrElse` operator. See Appendix A for a complete listing of operator precedence in Visual Basic.

expression1	expression2	expression1 OrElse expression2
False	False	False
False	True	True
True	False	True
True	True	True

Figure 8.18 Truth table for the `OrElse` operator.

Short-Circuit Evaluation

An expression containing operator `AndAlso` is evaluated only until truth or falsity is known. For example, evaluation of the expression

```
(genderTextBox.Text = "Female") AndAlso (age >= 65)
```

stops immediately if `genderTextBox.Text` is not equal to `"Female"` (which would mean that the entire expression is false). In this case, the evaluation of the second expression is irrelevant; once the first expression is known to be false, the whole expression must be false. Evaluation of the second expression occurs if and only if genderTextBox.Text is equal to "Female" (which would mean that the entire expression could still be true if the condition age >= 65 is true).

Similarly, an expression containing OrElse is evaluated only until its truth or falsity is known. For example, evaluation of the expression

```
If (semesterAverage >= 90) OrElse (finalExam >= 90) Then
```

stops immediately if semesterAverage is greater than or equal to 90 (which would mean that the entire expression is true). In this case, the evaluation of the second expression is irrelevant; once the first expression is known to be true, the whole expression must be true.

This way of evaluating logical expressions requires fewer operations, and therefore takes less time. This performance feature for the evaluation of AndAlso and OrElse expressions is called **short-circuit evaluation**. Visual Basic also provides the And and Or operators, which do not short-circuit. (They always evaluate their right operand regardless of whether or not the condition's truth or falsity is already known.) In Visual Basic applications, the performance benefit of using AndAlso and OrElse is negligible. One potential problem of using AndAlso/OrElse instead of And/Or is when the right operand contains a side effect, such as a function call that modifies a variable. Because such side effects might not occur when using short-circuit evaluation, subtle logic errors could occur. As a good programming practice, most Visual Basic programmers try to avoid writing conditions that contain side effects.

Using Xor

A condition containing the **logical exclusive OR** (Xor) operator is True *if and only if one of its operands results in a True value and the other results in a False value.* If both operands are True or both are False, the entire condition is false. Figure 8.19 presents a truth table for the logical exclusive OR operator (Xor). This operator always evaluates both of its operands (that is, there is no short-circuit evaluation).

expression1	expression2	expression1 Xor expression2
False	False	False
False	True	True
True	False	True
True	True	False

Figure 8.19 Truth table for the logical exclusive OR (Xor) operator.

Using Not

Visual Basic's Not (logical negation) operator enables you to "reverse" the meaning of a condition. Unlike the logical operators AndAlso, OrElse and Xor, each of which combines *two* expressions (that is, these are all *binary* operators), the Not operator is a *unary* operator, requiring only *one* operand. The Not operator is placed before a condition to choose a path of execution if the original condition (without the Not operator) is False. The Not operator is demonstrated by the following application segment:

```
If Not (grade = value) Then
   displayLabel.Text = "They are not equal!"
End If
```

The parentheses around the condition grade = value improve the readability of the condition. Most programmers prefer to write

```
Not (grade = value)
```

as

```
(grade <> value)
```

Figure 8.20 provides a truth table for the `Not` operator. In the following box you modify your **Dental Payment** application to use a complex expression.

expression	Not expression
`False`	`True`
`True`	`False`

Figure 8.20 Truth table for the `Not` operator (logical negation).

Using Logical Operators in Complex Expressions

1. ***Inserting a complex expression into the `Click` event handler.*** Replace lines 9–10 in `DentalPayment.vb` with lines 9–13 of Fig. 8.21.

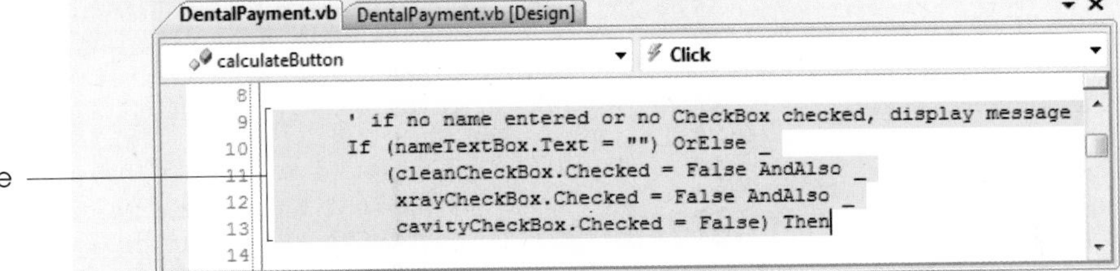

Add the highlighted code
DentalPayment.vb
DentalPayment.vb [Design]
calculateButton
Click
' if no name entered or no CheckBox checked, display message
If (nameTextBox.Text = "") OrElse _
(cleanCheckBox.Checked = False AndAlso _
xrayCheckBox.Checked = False AndAlso _
cavityCheckBox.Checked = False) Then

Figure 8.21 Using the `AndAlso` and `OrElse` logical operators.

Lines 10–13 define a more sophisticated logical expression than others we've used in this book. Note the use of `OrElse` and `AndAlso`. If the name is blank or if no `CheckBox` is checked, a dialog should appear. After the original expression (`nameTextBox.Text = ""`), you use `OrElse` to indicate that either the expression on the left (`nameTextBox.Text = ""`) or the expression "on the right" (which ensures that no `CheckBox`es have been checked) needs to be true for the entire expression to evaluate to `True` and execute the body of the `If...Then` statement. The complex expression "on the right" uses `AndAlso` twice to determine whether all three of the `CheckBox`es are unchecked. Note that because `AndAlso` has a higher precedence than `OrElse`, the parentheses in lines 10, 11 and 13 are redundant (unnecessary).

2. ***Running the application.*** Select **Debug > Start Debugging** to run your application. Note that users must enter a name and select at least one `CheckBox` before they click the **Calculate** `Button`. The application appears the same as in Figs. 8.1 and 8.4. You've now corrected the weakness from your earlier implementation of the **Dental Payment** application.

3. ***Closing the application.*** Close your running application by clicking its close box.

Figure 8.22 presents the source code for the **Dental Payment** application. The lines of code that contain new programming concepts that you learned in this tutorial are highlighted.

```
Public Class DentalPaymentForm
   ' handles Click event
   Private Sub calculateButton_Click(ByVal sender As System.Object, _
      ByVal e As System.EventArgs) Handles calculateButton.Click

      ' clear text displayed in Label
      totalResultLabel.Text = ""

```

Figure 8.22 Code for the **Dental Payment** application. (Part 1 of 2.)

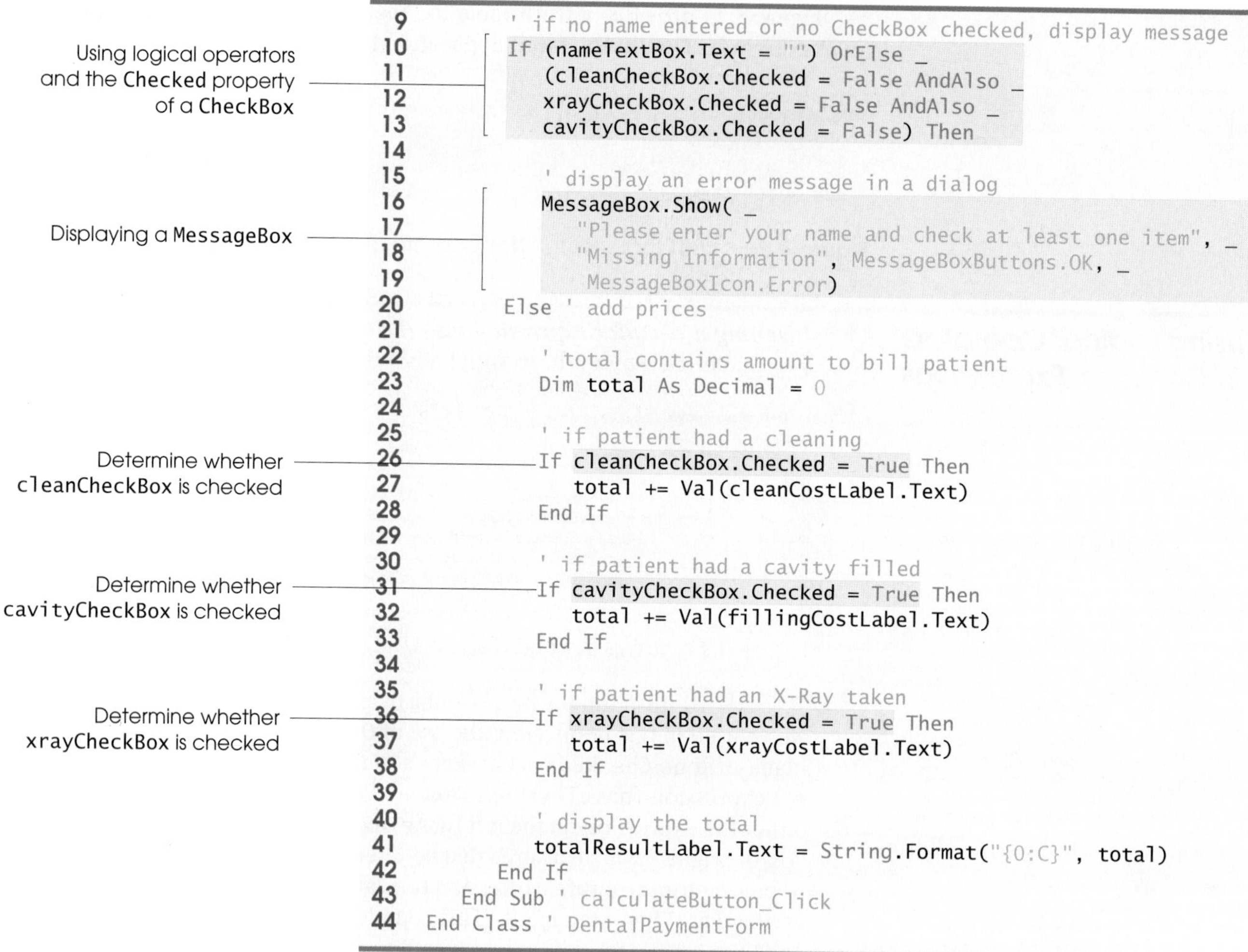
Using logical operators and the Checked property of a CheckBox
Displaying a MessageBox
Determine whether cleanCheckBox is checked
Determine whether cavityCheckBox is checked
Determine whether xrayCheckBox is checked

```
         ' if no name entered or no CheckBox checked, display message
         If (nameTextBox.Text = "") OrElse _
            (cleanCheckBox.Checked = False AndAlso _
            xrayCheckBox.Checked = False AndAlso _
            cavityCheckBox.Checked = False) Then

            ' display an error message in a dialog
            MessageBox.Show( _
               "Please enter your name and check at least one item", _
               "Missing Information", MessageBoxButtons.OK, _
               MessageBoxIcon.Error)
         Else ' add prices

            ' total contains amount to bill patient
            Dim total As Decimal = 0

            ' if patient had a cleaning
            If cleanCheckBox.Checked = True Then
               total += Val(cleanCostLabel.Text)
            End If

            ' if patient had a cavity filled
            If cavityCheckBox.Checked = True Then
               total += Val(fillingCostLabel.Text)
            End If

            ' if patient had an X-Ray taken
            If xrayCheckBox.Checked = True Then
               total += Val(xrayCostLabel.Text)
            End If

            ' display the total
            totalResultLabel.Text = String.Format("{0:C}", total)
         End If
      End Sub ' calculateButton_Click
   End Class ' DentalPaymentForm
```

Figure 8.22 Code for the **Dental Payment** application. (Part 2 of 2.)

SELF-REVIEW

1. A unary operator __________.

   a) requires exactly one operand
   b) requires two operands
   c) must use the AndAlso keyword
   d) can have no operands

2. The __________ operator is used to ensure that two conditions are both true.

   a) Xor
   b) AndAlso
   c) Also
   d) OrElse

Answers: 1.) a. 2.) b.

8.6 Designer-Generated Code

In Tutorial 6, you learned that every variable must be declared with a name and a type before you can use it in an application. Like the variables you've declared, GUI controls also must be declared before they are used. You might be wondering where these declarations are, since you have not seen them in any of the examples so far. A nice aspect of Visual Basic is that when you work in **Design** view to build and configure your application's GUI, Visual Basic automatically declares the controls for you. It also generates code that creates each control and configures its properties—including any changes that you make to the properties through the **Properties** window or by dragging and resizing controls on the Form.

To improve the readability of your application code, Visual Basic "hides" the GUI declarations and other GUI code it generates in a separate file that starts with the same name as the Form's .vb file, but ends with `Designer.vb`—in this tutorial, the file is named `DentalPaymentForm.Designer.vb`. By placing this code in a separate file, Visual Basic allows you to focus on your application's logic rather than the tedious details of building the GUI.

You can view these separate files and even edit them—though editing them is not recommended. To view the `Designer.vb` file for the **Dental Payment** application, click the **Show All Files** button (discussed in Section 2.5) in the **Solution Explorer**, then click the plus (+) sign next to `DentalPayment.vb` to expand its node. Double click `DentalPaymentForm.Designer.vb` to view the code.

Figure 8.23 shows the declarations that the IDE generated for all of the controls used in the **Dental Payment** application (lines 170–181). Note that the IDE declares each control's type with its fully qualified type name—that is, the namespace `System.Windows.Forms` followed by the type of the control. The controls declared in Fig. 8.23 are created by lines 25–36 in the completed application's `DentalPaymentForm.Designer.vb` file.

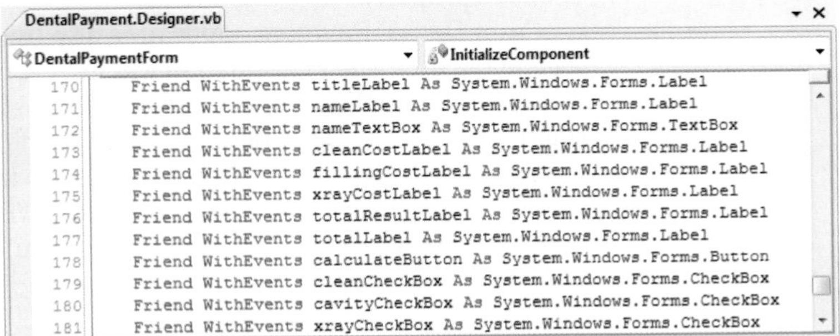

DentalPayment.Designer.vb

DentalPaymentForm | InitializeComponent

```
170 Friend WithEvents titleLabel As System.Windows.Forms.Label
171 Friend WithEvents nameLabel As System.Windows.Forms.Label
172 Friend WithEvents nameTextBox As System.Windows.Forms.TextBox
173 Friend WithEvents cleanCostLabel As System.Windows.Forms.Label
174 Friend WithEvents fillingCostLabel As System.Windows.Forms.Label
175 Friend WithEvents xrayCostLabel As System.Windows.Forms.Label
176 Friend WithEvents totalResultLabel As System.Windows.Forms.Label
177 Friend WithEvents totalLabel As System.Windows.Forms.Label
178 Friend WithEvents calculateButton As System.Windows.Forms.Button
179 Friend WithEvents cleanCheckBox As System.Windows.Forms.CheckBox
180 Friend WithEvents cavityCheckBox As System.Windows.Forms.CheckBox
181 Friend WithEvents xrayCheckBox As System.Windows.Forms.CheckBox
```

Figure 8.23 GUI declarations for the controls in the **Dental Payment** application.

In *Steps 3* and *4* of the box *Adding CheckBoxes to the Form* earlier in this tutorial, you placed three CheckBoxes on the Form and configured several of their properties. Figure 8.24 shows some of the statements that the IDE created based on your actions. For example, you set the Size property of each CheckBox to 122,24. Lines 123, 132 and 141 are the generated statements that change the size of the CheckBoxes. Similarly, you changed the locations of the CheckBoxes. The statements that change their locations appear in lines 121, 130 and 139.

DentalPayment.Designer.vb

DentalPaymentForm | InitializeComponent

```
118 '
119 'cleanCheckBox
120 '
121 Me.cleanCheckBox.Location = New System.Drawing.Point(22, 113)
122 Me.cleanCheckBox.Name = "cleanCheckBox"
123 Me.cleanCheckBox.Size = New System.Drawing.Size(122, 24)
124 Me.cleanCheckBox.TabIndex = 9
125 Me.cleanCheckBox.Text = "Cleaning"
126 Me.cleanCheckBox.UseVisualStyleBackColor = True
127 '
128 'cavityCheckBox
129 '
130 Me.cavityCheckBox.Location = New System.Drawing.Point(22, 160)
131 Me.cavityCheckBox.Name = "cavityCheckBox"
132 Me.cavityCheckBox.Size = New System.Drawing.Size(122, 24)
133 Me.cavityCheckBox.TabIndex = 10
134 Me.cavityCheckBox.Text = "Cavity Filling"
135 Me.cavityCheckBox.UseVisualStyleBackColor = True
136 '
137 'xrayCheckBox
138 '
139 Me.xrayCheckBox.Location = New System.Drawing.Point(22, 207)
140 Me.xrayCheckBox.Name = "xrayCheckBox"
141 Me.xrayCheckBox.Size = New System.Drawing.Size(122, 24)
142 Me.xrayCheckBox.TabIndex = 11
143 Me.xrayCheckBox.Text = "X-Ray"
144 Me.xrayCheckBox.UseVisualStyleBackColor = True
```

Figure 8.24 Statements that configure the CheckBox properties.

Everything you do with visual programming in **Design** view has consequences in the Designer.vb file, but the IDE handles the GUI code for you. This greatly simplifies the programming process and makes you more productive. This also eliminates many common programming errors and typos.

GUIs are tremendous tools for interfacing with computers. However, they require lots of code. Visual programming in **Design** view enables the IDE to generate most of this code for you, and the hidden Designer.vb file gets the GUI "out of the way" so you can concentrate on the logic of your application.

8.7 Wrap-Up

In this tutorial, you used CheckBox controls to provide a series of choices to users in the **Dental Payment** application. CheckBoxes provide options that can be selected by clicking them. When a CheckBox is selected, its square contains a check mark. You can determine whether a CheckBox is selected in your code by accessing its Checked property.

Your **Dental Payment** application also used a message dialog to display a message to the user when information was not entered appropriately. To implement the dialog in your application, you used the Show method of class MessageBox and constants provided by class MessageBoxButtons and MessageBoxIcon to display a message dialog containing Buttons and an icon. You used an If...Then...Else statement to calculate the cost of the dental visit or display a message dialog if the user was missing input. Later in this book you'll learn to avoid checking for invalid user input by disabling a control (such as a Button) when its events should not cause any action to occur.

You learned to use the logical AndAlso operator when both conditions must be true for the overall condition to be true—if either condition is false, the overall condition is false. You also learned that the logical OrElse operator requires at least one of its conditions to be true for the overall condition to be true—if both conditions are false, the overall condition is false. The logical Xor operator requires that exactly one of its conditions be true for the overall condition to be true—if both conditions are false or if both conditions are true, the overall condition is false. The logical Not operator reverses the Boolean result of a condition—True becomes False, and False becomes True. You then used the AndAlso and OrElse operators to form a complex expression.

Finally, you learned about the Designer.vb file that the IDE generates to store the code that builds the controls in your GUI. This file also contains the statements that configure the controls based on your actions in **Design** mode.

In the next tutorial, you'll learn more about Visual Basic's control structures. Specifically, you'll use repetition statements, which allow the programmer to specify that an action or a group of actions should be performed many times.

SKILLS SUMMARY

Adding a CheckBox to a Form

- Double click the CheckBox in the **Toolbox**.

Selecting a CheckBox

- Click the CheckBox when the application is running, and a check mark appears in the box.

Deselecting a CheckBox

- Click a checked CheckBox when the application is running to remove its check mark.

Determining Whether a CheckBox Is Selected

- Access the CheckBox's Checked property.

Displaying a Dialog

- Use method MessageBox.Show.

Combining Multiple Conditions

- Use the logical operators to form complex conditions by combining simple ones.

KEY TERMS

And operator—A logical operator used to ensure that two conditions are *both* true before choosing a certain path of execution. Does not perform short-circuit evaluation.

AndAlso operator—A logical operator used to ensure that two conditions are *both* true before choosing a certain path of execution. Performs short-circuit evaluation.

CheckBox control—A small square GUI element that either is empty or contains a check mark.

CheckBox label—The text that appears next to a CheckBox.

Checked property of the CheckBox control—Specifies whether the CheckBox is checked (True) or unchecked (False).

Designer.vb file—The file containing the declarations and statements that build an application's GUI.

dismiss a dialog—Synonym for closing a dialog.

logical exclusive OR (Xor) operator—A logical operator that is True if and only if one of its operands is True and the other is False.

logical operators—The operators (for example, AndAlso, OrElse, Xor and Not) that can be used to form complex conditions by combining simple ones.

message dialog—A window that displays messages to users or gathers input from users.

MessageBox class—Provides a method for displaying message dialogs.

MessageBoxButtons constants—The identifiers that specify the Buttons that can be displayed in a MessageBox dialog.

MessageBoxIcon constants—Identifiers that specify the icons that can be displayed in a MessageBox dialog.

MessageBox.Show method—Displays a message dialog.

Not (logical negation) operator—A logical operator that enables you to reverse the meaning of a condition: A True condition, when logically negated, becomes False, and a False condition, when logically negated, becomes True.

Or operator—A logical operator used to ensure that either *or* both of two conditions are true in an application before a certain path of execution is chosen.

OrElse operator—A logical operator used to ensure that either *or* both of two conditions are true in an application before a certain path of execution is chosen. Performs short-circuit evaluation.

repetition statements—Statements that allow the programmer to specify that an action or a group of actions should be performed many times.

short-circuit evaluation—The evaluation of the right operand in AndAlso and OrElse expressions occurs only if the first condition meets the criteria for the condition.

simple condition—Contains one expression that evaluates to True or False.

state button—A button that can be in the on/off (true/false) state.

truth table—A table that displays the Boolean result of a logical operator for all possible combinations of True and False values for its operands.

Xor (logical exclusive OR) operator—A logical operator that is True if and only if one of its operands is True and the other is False.

GUI DESIGN GUIDELINES

CheckBoxes

- A CheckBox's label should be descriptive and as short as possible. When a CheckBox label contains more than one word, use book-title capitalization.
- Align groups of CheckBoxes either horizontally or vertically.

Message Dialogs

- Text displayed in a dialog should be descriptive and as short as possible.

CONTROLS, EVENTS, PROPERTIES & METHODS

CheckBox ☑ CheckBox This control allows the user to select an option.

- ***In action***

- ***Properties***

  AutoSize—Allows for automatic resizing of the CheckBox.

  Checked—Specifies whether the CheckBox is checked (True) or unchecked (False).

  Location—Specifies the location of the CheckBox on the Form.

  Name—Specifies the name used to access the CheckBox control programmatically. The name should end with the suffix CheckBox.

  Size—Specifies the width and height (in pixels) of the CheckBox.

  Text—Specifies the text displayed next to the CheckBox.

MessageBox This class allows the user to display a message dialog.

- ***In action***

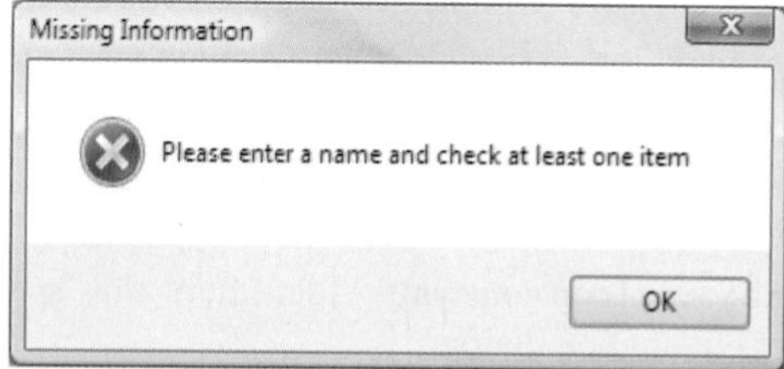

- ***Method***

  Show—Displays a message dialog. The user cannot interact with the application's Form until the message dialog is closed.

MessageBoxButtons This class provides constants used to specify the Buttons displayed in a message dialog.

- ***In action***

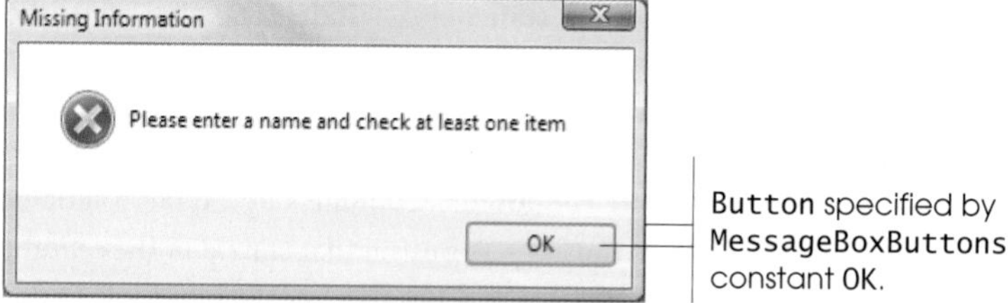

- ***Constants***

  OK—**OK** Button. Allows the user to acknowledge a message.

  OKCancel—**OK** and **Cancel** Buttons. Allow the user to either continue or cancel an operation.

  YesNo—**Yes** and **No** Buttons. Allow the user to respond to a question.

  YesNoCancel—**Yes**, **No** and **Cancel** Buttons. Allow the user to respond to a question or cancel an operation.

  RetryCancel—**Retry** and **Cancel** Buttons. Allow the user either to retry or to cancel an operation that has failed.

  AbortRetryCancel—**Abort**, **Retry** and **Ignore** Buttons. When one of a series of operations has failed, these Buttons allow the user to abort the entire sequence, retry the failed operation or ignore the failed operation and continue.

MessageBoxIcon This class provides constants used to specify the icon displayed in a message dialog.

- ***In action***

- ***Constants***

  `Exclamation`—Icon containing an exclamation point. Typically used to caution the user against potential problems.

  `Information`—Icon containing the letter "i." Typically used to display information about the state of the application.

  `None`—No icon is displayed in the message dialog.

  `Error`—Icon containing a white **×** in a red circle. Typically used to alert the user to errors or critical situations.

MULTIPLE-CHOICE QUESTIONS

8.1 How many `CheckBoxes` in a GUI can be selected at once?

a) `0`
b) `1`
c) `4`
d) any number

8.2 The first argument passed to method `MessageBox.Show` is ________.

a) the text displayed in the dialog's title bar
b) a constant representing the `Buttons` displayed in the dialog
c) the text displayed inside the dialog
d) a constant representing the icon that appears in the dialog

8.3 You can specify the `Button`(s) and icon to be displayed in a message dialog by using the `MessageBoxButtons` and ________ constants.

a) `MessageIcon`
b) `MessageBoxImages`
c) `MessageBoxPicture`
d) `MessageBoxIcon`

8.4 ________ are used to create complex conditions.

a) Assignment operators
b) Activity diagrams
c) Logical operators
d) Formatting codes

8.5 Operator `AndAlso` ________.

a) performs short-circuit evaluation
b) is not a keyword
c) is a comparison operator
d) evaluates to `False` if both operands are `True`

8.6 A `CheckBox` is selected when its `Checked` property is set to ________.

a) `On`
b) `True`
c) `Selected`
d) `Checked`

8.7 The condition *expression1* `AndAlso` *expression2* evaluates to `True` if ________.

a) *expression1* is `True` and *expression2* is `False`
b) *expression1* is `False` and *expression2* is `True`
c) both *expression1* and *expression2* are `True`
d) both *expression1* and *expression2* are `False`

8.8 The condition *expression1* `OrElse` *expression2* evaluates to `False` if ________.

a) *expression1* is `True` and *expression2* is `False`
b) *expression1* is `False` and *expression2* is `True`
c) both *expression1* and *expression2* are `True`
d) both *expression1* and *expression2* are `False`

8.9 The condition *expression1* `Xor` *expression2* evaluates to `True` if ________.

a) *expression1* is `True` and *expression2* is `False`
b) *expression1* is `False` and *expression2* is `True`
c) both *expression1* and *expression2* are `True`
d) Both a and b

8.10 The condition `Not(`*expression1* `AndAlso` *expression2*`)` evaluates to `True` if ________.

a) *expression1* is `True` and *expression2* is `False`
b) *expression1* is `False` and *expression2* is `True`
c) both *expression1* and *expression2* are `True`
d) both *expression1* and *expression2* are `False`

EXERCISES

8.11 ***(Enhanced Dental Payment Application)*** Modify the **Dental Payment** application from this tutorial to include additional services, as shown in Fig. 8.25. Add the proper functionality (using `If...Then` statements) to determine whether any of the new `CheckBoxes` are selected, and, if so, add the price of the service to the total bill. Display an error message in a dialog if the user selects the **Other** `CheckBox` but does not specify a price for the service.

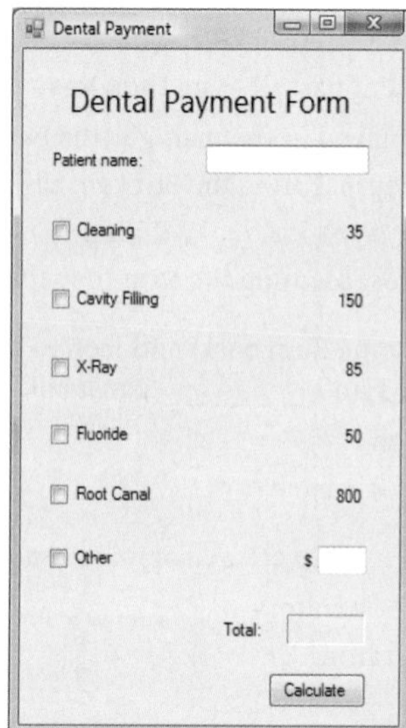

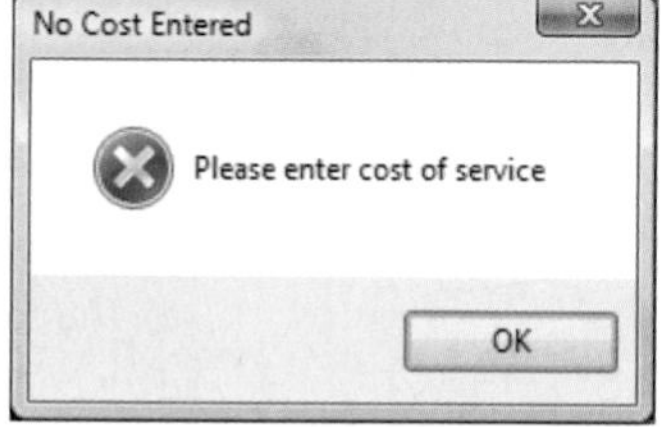

Figure 8.25 Enhanced **Dental Payment** application.

a) ***Copying the template to your working directory.*** Copy the directory `C:\Examples\Tutorial08\Exercises\DentalPaymentEnhanced` to your `C:\SimplyVB2008` directory.

b) ***Opening the application's template file.*** Double click `DentalPaymentEnhanced.sln` in the `DentalPaymentEnhanced` directory to open the application.

c) ***Adding CheckBoxes, Labels and a TextBox.*** Add two `CheckBoxes` and two `Labels` to the `Form`. The new `CheckBoxes` should be labeled **Fluoride** and **Root Canal**, respectively. Add these `CheckBoxes` and `Labels` beneath the `X-Ray CheckBox` and its price `Label`. The price for a fluoride treatment is $50; the price for a root canal is $800. Add a `CheckBox` labeled **Other** and a `Label` containing a dollar sign (**$**) to the `Form`, as shown in Fig. 8.25. Then add a `TextBox` to the right of the **$** `Label` in which the user can enter the cost of the service performed.

d) ***Modifying the Click event handler code.*** Add code to the `calculateButton_Click` event handler to determine whether the new `CheckBoxes` have been selected. This can be done by modifying the compound condition in the first `If...Then` statement in the event handler. Add an `ElseIf` clause to determine if the user selected the **Other** `CheckBox` but did not specify a price—if so, display an error message in a dialog. Also, use `If...Then` statements to update the bill amount.

e) ***Running the application.*** Select **Debug > Start Debugging** to run your application. Test your application by checking one or more of the new services. Click the **Calculate** `Button` and verify that the proper total is displayed. Test the application again by checking some of the services, then checking the **Other** `CheckBox` and entering a dollar value for this service. Click the **Calculate** `Button` and verify that the proper total is displayed, and that it includes the price for the "other" service.

f) ***Closing the application.*** Close your running application by clicking its close box.

g) ***Closing the IDE.*** Close the Visual Basic IDE by clicking its close box.

8.12 *(Fuzzy Dice Order Form Application)* Write an application that allows users to process orders for fuzzy dice, as shown in Fig. 8.26. The application should calculate the total price of the order, including tax and shipping. `TextBox`es for inputting the order number, the customer name and the shipping address are provided. Provide `CheckBox`es for selecting the fuzzy-dice color. The application should also contain a `Button` that, when clicked, calculates the subtotals for each type of fuzzy dice ordered and the total of the entire order (including tax and shipping). Use 5% for the tax rate. Shipping charges are $1.50 for up to 20 pairs of dice. If more than 20 pairs of dice are ordered, shipping is free.

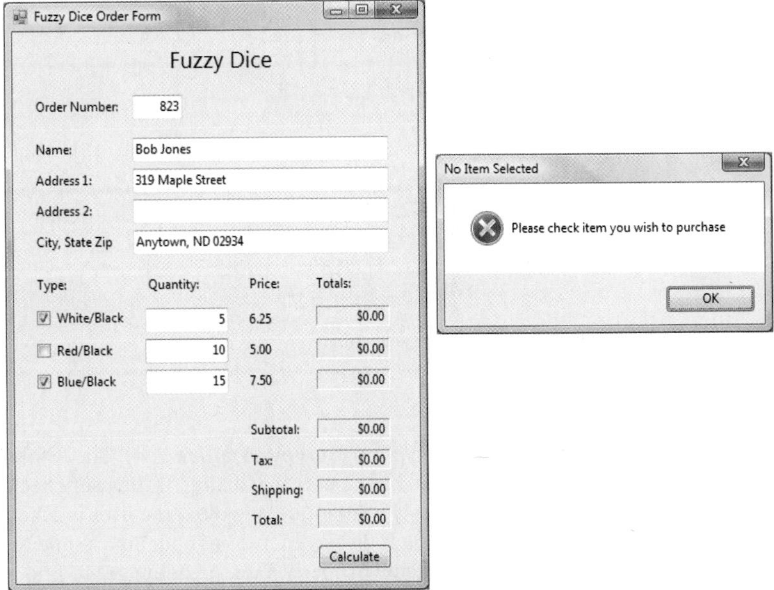

Figure 8.26 **Fuzzy Dice Order Form** application.

a) ***Copying the template to your working directory.*** Copy the directory `C:\Examples\Tutorial08\Exercises\FuzzyDiceOrderForm` to your `C:\SimplyVB2008` directory.

b) ***Opening the application's template file.*** Double click `FuzzyDiceOrderForm.sln` in the `FuzzyDiceOrderForm` directory to open the application.

c) ***Adding CheckBoxes to the Form.*** Add three `CheckBox`es to the `Form`. Label the first `CheckBox` **White/Black**, the second one **Red/Black** and the third **Blue/Black**.

d) ***Adding a `Click` event handler and its code.*** Create the `Click` event handler for the **Calculate** `Button`. The application should warn users if they specify an item's quantity without checking the item's corresponding `CheckBox`. For the total to be calculated, the user must enter an order number, a name and a shipping address. Use logical operators to ensure that these terms are met. If they aren't, display a message in a dialog.

e) ***Calculating the total cost.*** Calculate the subtotal, tax, shipping and total, and display the results in their corresponding `Label`s.

f) ***Running the application.*** Select **Debug > Start Debugging** to run your application. Test the application by providing quantities for checked items. Ensure that your application is calculating 5% sales tax. Verify that shipping is free if more than 20 pairs of dice are ordered. Also, determine whether your code containing the logical operators works correctly by specifying a quantity for an item that is not checked. For instance, in Fig. 8.26, a quantity is specified for **Red/Black** dice, but the corresponding `CheckBox` is not selected. This should cause the message dialog in Fig. 8.26 to appear.

g) ***Closing the application.*** Close your running application by clicking its close box.

h) ***Closing the IDE.*** Close the Visual Basic IDE by clicking its close box.

What does this code do? ▶

8.13 Assume that `nameTextBox` is a `TextBox` and that `otherCheckBox` is a `CheckBox` next to which is another `TextBox` called `otherTextBox`, in which the user should specify a value. What does this code segment do?

```
If (nameTextBox.Text = "" OrElse _
   (otherCheckBox.Checked = True AndAlso _
   otherTextBox.Text = "")) Then

   MessageBox.Show("Please enter a name or value", _
      "Input Error", MessageBoxButtons.OK, _
      MessageBoxIcon.Error)

End If
```

What's wrong with this code? ▶

8.14 Assume that `nameTextBox` is a `TextBox`. Find the error(s) in the following code:

```
If nameTextBox.Text = "John Doe" Then

   MessageBox.Show("Welcome, John!", _
      MessageBoxIcon.Exclamation)

End If
```

Using the Debugger ▶

8.15 ***(Sibling Survey Application)*** The **Sibling Survey** application displays the siblings selected by the user in a dialog. If the user checks either the **Brother(s)** or **Sister(s)** `CheckBox` and the **No Siblings** `CheckBox`, the user is asked to verify the selection. Otherwise, the user's selection is displayed in a `MessageBox`. While testing this application, you noticed that it does not execute properly. Use the debugger to find and correct the logic error(s) in the code. This exercise is located in the `C:\Examples\Tutorial08\Exercises\Debugger\SiblingSurvey` directory. Figure 8.27 shows the correct output for the application.

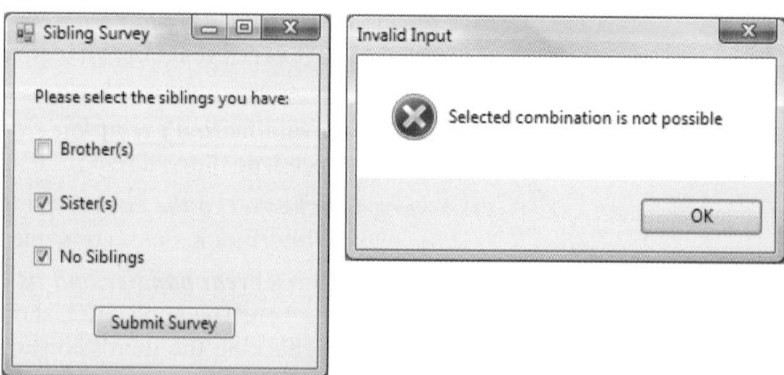

Figure 8.27 Correct output for the **Sibling Survey** application.

Programming Challenge ▶

8.16 ***(Modified Fuzzy Dice Order Form Application)*** Modify the **Fuzzy Dice Order Form** application from Exercise 8.12 to determine whether customers should receive a 7% discount on their purchase (Fig. 8.28). Customers ordering more than $500 (before tax and shipping) in fuzzy dice are eligible for this discount.

Figure 8.28 Modified **Fuzzy Dice Order Form** application.

a) ***Opening the application***. Open the application you created in Exercise 8.12.

b) ***Adding the discount `Label`***. Add two `Label`s to the `Form` to display the discount. Place the `Label`s below the **Subtotal** `Label` as shown in Fig. 8.28.

c) ***Determining whether the total cost is over $500***. Use an `If...Then` statement to determine whether the subtotal is greater than $500.

d) ***Displaying the discount and subtracting the discount from the total***. If a customer orders more than $500, display a message dialog, as shown in Fig. 8.28, that informs the user that the customer is entitled to a 7% discount. The message dialog should contain an `Information` icon and an **OK** `Button`. Calculate 7% of the total amount before taxes and shipping, and display the discount amount in the **Discount:** field. Subtract this amount from the subtotal, and update the **Total:** fields.

e) ***Running the application.*** Select **Debug > Start Debugging** to run your application. Confirm that your application calculates and displays the discount properly.

f) ***Closing the application.*** Close your running application by clicking its close box.

g) ***Closing the IDE.*** Close the Visual Basic IDE by clicking its close box.

TUTORIAL

Objectives

In this tutorial, you learn to:

- Use the Do While...Loop and Do Until...Loop repetition statements to execute statements in an application repeatedly.
- Use counter-controlled repetition.
- Display information in ListBoxes.
- Concatenate strings.

Outline

Car Payment Calculator Application

Introducing the Do While...Loop and Do Until...Loop Repetition Statements

This tutorial continues the discussion of structured programming that we began in Tutorial 7. We introduce **repetition statements**, which are control statements that can repeat actions based on a condition's value. You perform many repetitive tasks based on conditions. For example, each time you turn a page in this book (while there are more pages to read), you are repeating a simple task, namely turning a page, based on a condition, namely that there are more pages to read.

Performing tasks repeatedly is an important part of structured programming. Repetition statements are used in many types of applications. In this tutorial, you learn to use the Do While...Loop and the Do Until...Loop repetition statements. You use a repetition statement in the **Car Payment Calculator** application that you build. Later tutorials introduce additional repetition statements.

9.1 Test-Driving the Car Payment Calculator Application

The following problem statement requires an application that repeats a calculation four times—you'll use a repetition statement to solve this problem. The application must meet the following requirements:

Application Requirements

Typically, banks offer car loans for periods ranging from two to five years (24 to 60 months). Borrowers repay the loans in monthly installments. The amount of each monthly payment is based on the length of the loan, the amount borrowed and the interest rate. Create an application that allows the customer to enter the price of a car, the down-payment amount and the annual interest rate of the loan. The application should display the loan's duration in months and the monthly payments for two-, three-, four- and five-year loans. The variety of options allows the user to easily compare repayment plans and choose the most appropriate.

You begin by test-driving the completed application. Then you learn the additional Visual Basic capabilities needed to create your own version of this application.

Test-Driving the Car Payment Calculator Application

1. ***Opening the completed application.*** Open the directory `C:\Examples\Tutorial09\CompletedApplication\CarPaymentCalculator` to locate the **Car Payment Calculator** application. Double click `CarPayment-Calculator.sln` to open the application in the Visual Basic IDE.
2. ***Running the application.*** Select **Debug > Start Debugging** to run the application (Fig. 9.1). Note the new GUI control—the `ListBox` control, which allows users to view and/or select from multiple items in a list. Users cannot add items to, or remove items from, a `ListBox` by interacting directly with it. The `ListBox` does not accept keyboard input—users cannot add or delete selected items. You must write code that adds items to, or removes items from, a `ListBox`.

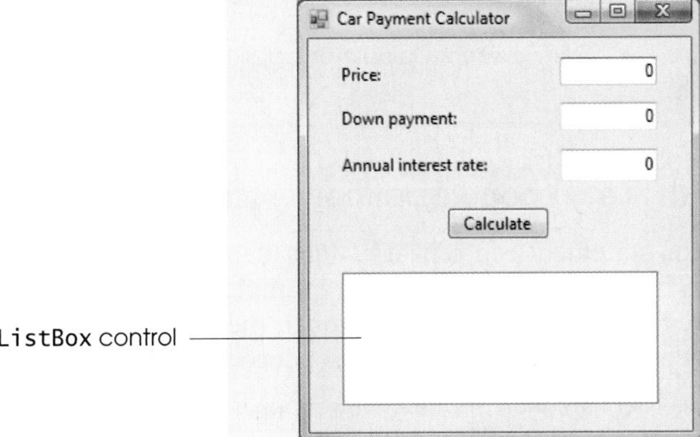

Figure 9.1 **Car Payment Calculator** application before data has been entered.

3. ***Entering quantities in the application.*** Enter 16900 in the **Price:** `TextBox`. Enter 6000 in the **Down payment:** `TextBox`. Enter `7.5` in the **Annual interest rate:** `TextBox`. The `Form` appears as in Fig. 9.2.

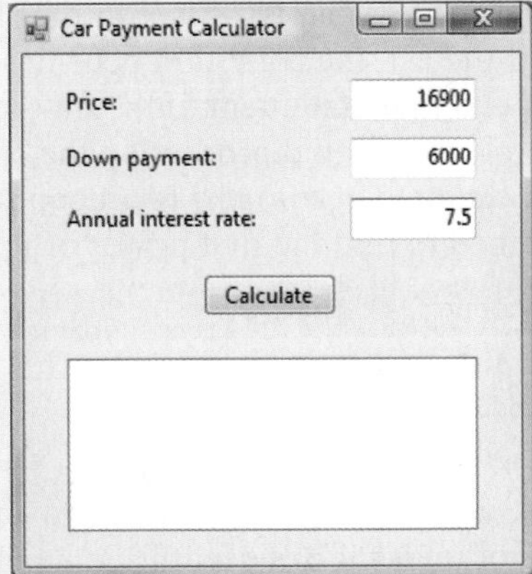

Figure 9.2 **Car Payment Calculator** application after data has been entered.

4. ***Calculating the monthly payment amounts.*** Click the **Calculate** `Button`. The application displays the monthly payment amounts in the `ListBox` (Fig. 9.3). The information is organized in tabular format.
5. ***Closing the application.*** Close your running application by clicking its close box.
6. ***Closing the IDE.*** Close the Visual Basic IDE by clicking its close box.

(cont.)

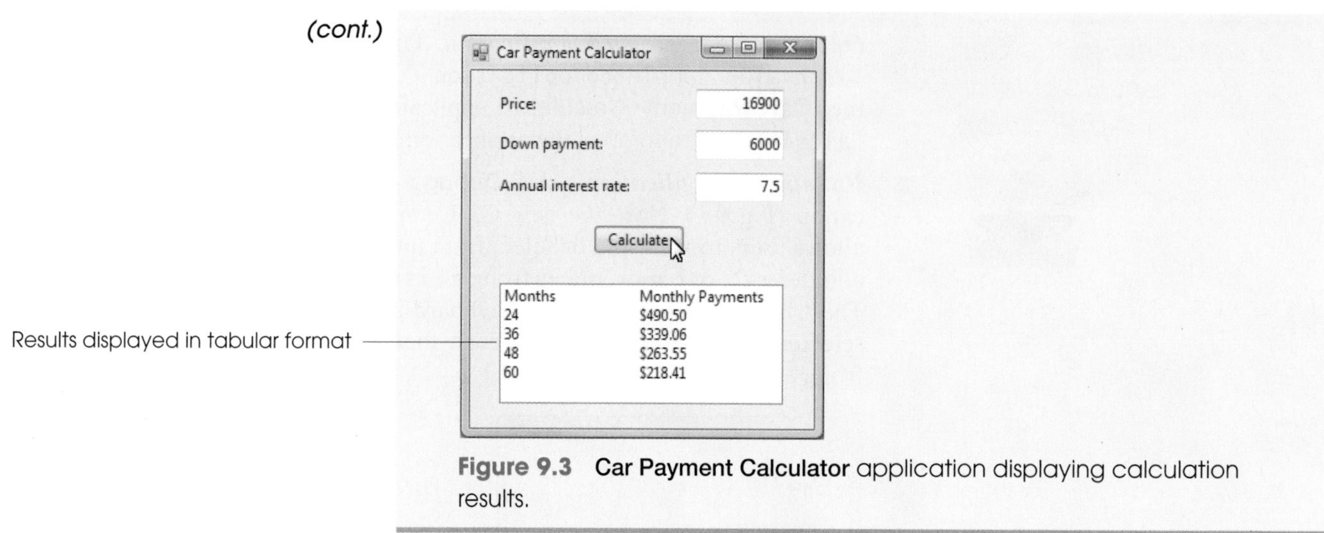

Figure 9.3 **Car Payment Calculator** application displaying calculation results.

9.2 Do While...Loop Repetition Statement

A repetition statement can repeat actions, depending on the value of a condition (which can be either true or false). For example, if you go to the grocery store with a list of items to purchase, you go through the list until you have each item. This process is described by the following pseudocode statements:

```
Do while there are more items on my shopping list
    Put next item in cart
    Cross it off my list
```

These statements describe the repetitive actions that occur during a shopping trip. The condition "there are more items on my shopping list" can be true or false. If it is true, then the actions "Put next item in cart" and "Cross it off my list" are performed in sequence. In an application, these actions execute repeatedly while the condition remains true. The statements indented in this repetition statement constitute its **body**. When the last item on the shopping list has been put in the cart and crossed off the list, the condition becomes false. At this point, the repetition terminates, and the first statement after the repetition statement executes. In the shopping example, you would proceed to the checkout station.

Common Programming Error

Provide in the body of every Do While...Loop statement an action that eventually causes the condition to become false. If you do not, the repetition statement never terminates, causing an error called an **infinite loop**. Such an error causes the application to "hang up." When an infinite loop occurs in your application, return to the IDE and select **Debug > Stop Debugging**.

As an example of a Do While...Loop statement, let's look at an application segment designed to find the first power of 3 greater than 50.

```
Dim product As Integer = 3

Do While product <= 50
   product *= 3
Loop
```

The application segment declares and initializes variable product to 3, taking advantage of a Visual Basic feature that allows variable initialization to be incorporated into a declaration. The condition in the Do While...Loop statement, product <= 50, is referred to as the **loop-continuation condition**. While the loop-continuation condition remains true, the Do While...Loop statement executes its body repeatedly. When the loop-continuation condition becomes false, the Do While...Loop statement finishes executing, and product contains the first power of 3 larger than 50.

Let's examine the execution of the preceding code in detail. When the Do While...Loop statement is entered, the value of product is 3 and the loop-continuation condition (3 <= 50) is true. Each time the loop executes, the variable product is multiplied by 3, taking on the values 3, 9, 27 and 81, successively. When product becomes 81, the condition in the Do While...Loop statement, product <= 50, evaluates to `False`. When the repetition ends, the final value of `product` is `81`, which is, indeed, the first power of 3 greater than `50`. Application execution continues with the next statement after the `Do While...Loop` statement. If a `Do While...Loop` statement's condition is initially false, the body does not execute and your application simply continues executing with the next statement after the keyword `Loop`. The following box describes each step as the above repetition statement executes.

Executing the Do While...Loop Repetition Statement

1. The application declares variable `product` and sets its value to `3`.
2. The application enters the `Do While...Loop` repetition statement.
3. The loop-continuation condition is checked. The condition evaluates to `True` (`product` is less than or equal to `50`), so the application continues executing at the next statement in the loop's body.
4. The number (currently `3`) stored in `product` is multiplied by `3` and the result is assigned to `product`; `product` now contains the number `9`.
5. The loop-continuation condition is checked. The condition evaluates to `True` (`product` is less than or equal to `50`), so the application continues executing at the next statement in the loop's body.
6. The number (currently `9`) stored in `product` is multiplied by `3` and the result is assigned to `product`; `product` now contains the number `27`.
7. The loop-continuation condition is checked. The condition evaluates to `True` (`product` is less than or equal to `50`), so the application continues executing at the next statement in the loop's body.
8. The number (currently `27`) stored in `product` is multiplied by `3` and the result is assigned to `product`; `product` now contains the number `81`.
9. The loop-continuation condition is checked. The condition evaluates to `False` (`product` is not less than or equal to `50`), so the application exits the `Do While...Loop` repetition statement and continues executing at the first statement after keyword `Loop`.

Let's use a UML activity diagram to illustrate the flow of control in the preceding `Do While...Loop` repetition statement. The UML activity diagram in Fig. 9.4 contains an initial state, transition arrows, a merge, a decision, two guard conditions, an action state, three notes and a final state. The action state represents the statement in which the value of `product` is multiplied by 3.

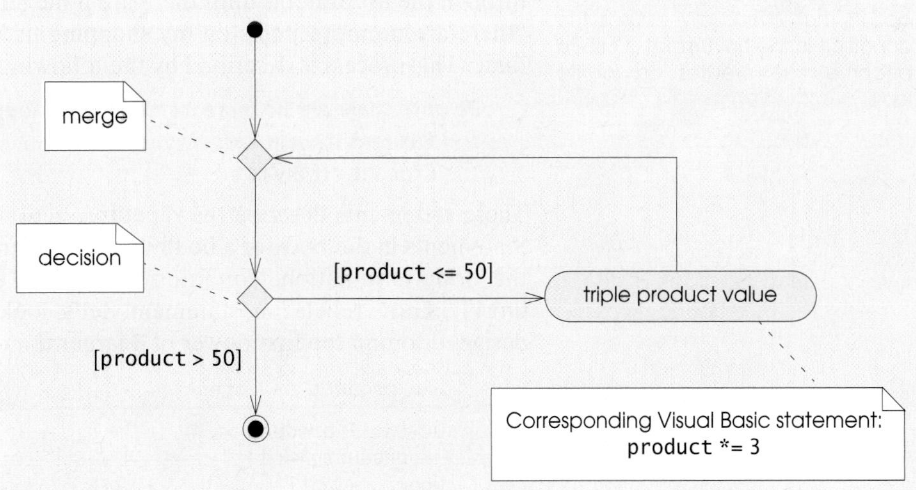

Figure 9.4 `Do While...Loop` repetition statement UML activity diagram.

The activity diagram clearly shows the repetition. The transition arrow emerging from the action state points back to the merge, creating a **loop**. The guard conditions are tested each time the loop iterates while the guard condition `product <= 50` remains true. Eventually, the guard condition `product > 50` becomes true. At this point, the `Do While...Loop` statement terminates, and control passes to the next statement in the application following the loop.

Figure 9.4 introduces the UML's **merge symbol**. The UML represents both the merge symbol and the decision symbol as diamonds. The merge symbol joins two flows of activity into one. In this diagram, the merge symbol joins the transitions from the initial state and from the action state, so they both flow into the loop-continuation guard decision, which determines whether the loop body statement should begin (or continue) executing. In this case, the UML activity diagram enters its action state when the loop-continuation guard condition `product <= 50` is true.

Although the UML represents both the decision and the merge symbols with the diamond shape, the symbols can be distinguished by the number of "incoming" and "outgoing" transition arrows. A decision symbol has one transition arrow pointing to the diamond and two (or more) transition arrows pointing out from the diamond to indicate possible transitions from that point. In addition, each transition arrow pointing out of a decision symbol has a guard condition next to it. A merge symbol has two (or more) transition arrows pointing to the diamond and only one transition arrow pointing from the diamond, to indicate multiple activity flows merging.

SELF-REVIEW

1. The body of a `Do While...Loop` statement executes ________.
   a) at least once
   b) never
   c) while its condition is true
   d) while its condition is false

2. The UML represents both the merge symbol and the decision symbol as ________.
   a) rectangles with rounded sides
   b) diamonds
   c) small black circles
   d) ovals

Answers: 1) c. 2) b.

9.3 Do Until...Loop Repetition Statement

Common Programming Error

Failure to provide the body of a `Do Until...Loop` statement with an action that eventually causes the condition in the `Do Until...Loop` to become true creates an infinite loop.

Unlike the `Do While...Loop` repetition statement, the **`Do Until...Loop`** repetition statement determines whether its condition is false before repetition can continue, and the loop terminates when its condition becomes true. This is known as a **loop-termination condition**. For example, you can think of grocery shopping as looping through the list of items until there are none left on the list. Note that the condition "there are no more items on my shopping list" must be false for the loop to continue. This process is described by the following pseudocode statements:

```
Do until there are no more items on my shopping list
    Put next item in cart
    Cross it off my list
```

These statements describe the repetitive actions that occur during a shopping trip. Statements in the body of a `Do Until...Loop` are executed repeatedly for as long as the loop-termination condition remains `False`. As an example of a `Do Until...Loop` repetition statement, let's look again at an application segment designed to find the first power of 3 larger than 50:

```
Dim product As Integer = 3

Do Until product > 50
   product *= 3
Loop
```

The following box describes each step as the repetition statement executes.

Executing the Do Until...Loop Repetition Statement

1. The application declares variable `product` and sets its value to 3.
2. The application enters the `Do Until...Loop` repetition statement.
3. The loop-termination condition is checked. The condition evaluates to `False` (`product` is not greater than 50), so the application continues executing at the next statement in the loop's body.
4. The number (currently 3) stored in `product` is multiplied by 3 and the result is assigned to `product`; `product` now contains the number 9.
5. The loop-termination condition is checked. The condition evaluates to `False` (`product` is not greater than 50), so the application continues executing at the next statement in the loop's body.
6. The number (currently 9) stored in `product` is multiplied by 3 and the result is assigned to `product`; `product` now contains the number 27.
7. The loop-termination condition is checked. The condition evaluates to `False` (`product` is not greater than 50), so the application continues executing at the next statement in the loop's body.
8. The number (currently 27) stored in `product` is multiplied by 3 and the result is assigned to `product`; `product` now contains the number 81.
9. The loop-termination condition is checked. The condition now evaluates to `True` (`product` is greater than 50), so the application exits the `Do Until...Loop` repetition statement and continues executing at the first statement after keyword `Loop`.

The UML activity diagram in Fig. 9.5 illustrates the flow of control for the `Do Until...Loop` repetition statement. This activity diagram is the same as the `Do While...Loop` repetition statement's activity diagram. Once again, note that (besides the initial state, transition arrows, a final state and three notes) the only symbols in the diagram represent an action state, a decision and a merge.

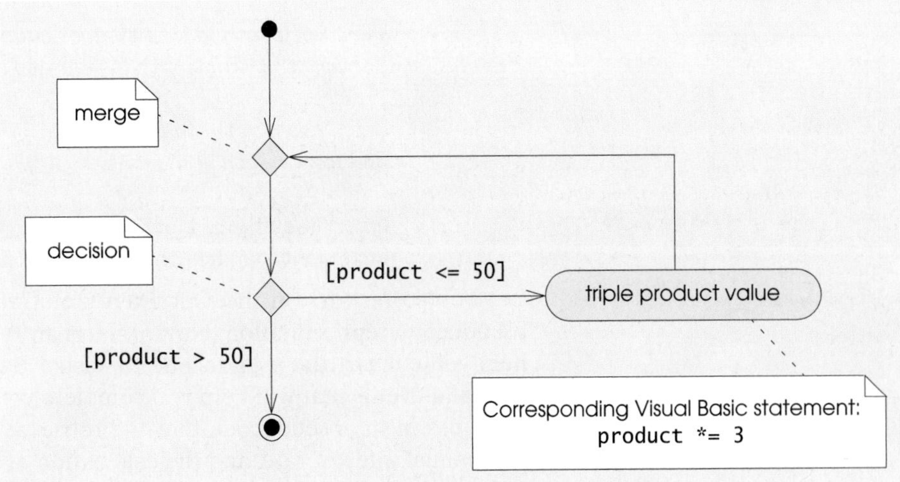

Figure 9.5 `Do Until...Loop` repetition statement UML activity diagram.

SELF-REVIEW

1. A `Do Until...Loop` repetition statement differs from a `Do While...Loop` repetition statement in _________.
   a) that a `Do While...Loop` repetition statement loops as long as the loop-continuation condition remains `False`, whereas a `Do Until...Loop` repetition statement loops as long as the loop-continuation condition remains `True`

b) that a Do Until...Loop repetition statement loops as long as the loop-termination condition remains False, whereas a Do While...Loop repetition statement loops as long as the loop-continuation condition remains True

c) that a Do Until...Loop repetition statement always executes at least once

d) no way. There is no difference between the Do Until...Loop and Do While...Loop repetition statements

2. Statements in the body of a Do Until...Loop execute repeatedly for as long as the _________ remains False.

a) loop-continuation condition
b) do-loop condition
c) loop-termination condition
d) until-loop condition

Answer: 1) b. 2) c.

9.4 Constructing the Car Payment Calculator Application

Now that you've learned the Do While...Loop and Do Until...Loop repetition statements, you're ready to construct the **Car Payment Calculator** application.

The following pseudocode describes the basic operation of the **Car Payment Calculator** application that occurs when a user enters information and clicks the **Calculate** Button:

```
When the user clicks the Calculate Button
    Initialize loan length to two years
    Clear the ListBox of any previous calculation results
    Add a header to the ListBox

    Get down payment from a TextBox
    Get sticker price from a TextBox
    Get annual interest rate from a TextBox

    Calculate loan amount (sticker price – down payment)
    Calculate monthly interest rate (annual interest rate / 12)

    Do while loan length is less than or equal to five years
        Convert the loan length in years to number of months

        Calculate monthly payment based on loan amount, monthly interest rate
        and loan length in months

        Insert result into ListBox
        Increment loan length in years by one year
```

You've test-driven the **Car Payment Calculator** application and studied its pseudocode representation. Now you use an Action/Control/Event (ACE) table to help you convert the pseudocode to Visual Basic. Figure 9.6 lists the actions, controls and events that will help you complete your own version of this application.

Note in the pseudocode that the retrieval of the down payment, sticker price and annual interest rate, and the calculation of the loan amount and monthly interest rate occur before the repetition statement because they need to be performed only once. Statements that have different results in each iteration are included in the repetition statement. The repetition statement's body includes: converting loan length in years to loan length in months, calculating the monthly payment amount, displaying the calculation's result and incrementing the loan length in years.

Action/Control/Event (ACE) Table for the Car Payment Calculator

Action	Control	Event
Label all the application's controls	`priceLabel`, `downPaymentLabel`, `interestLabel`	Application is run
	`calculateButton`	`Click`
Initialize loan length to two years		
Clear the ListBox of any previous calculation results	`paymentsListBox`	
Add a header to the ListBox	`paymentsListBox`	
Get down payment from a TextBox	`downPaymentTextBox`	
Get sticker price from a TextBox	`priceTextBox`	
Get annual interest rate from a TextBox	`interestTextBox`	
Calculate loan amount		
Calculate monthly interest rate		
Do while loan length is less than or equal to five years Convert the loan length in years to number of months		
Calculate monthly payment based on loan amount, monthly interest rate and loan length in months		
Insert result into ListBox	`paymentsListBox`	
Increment loan length in years by one year		

Figure 9.6 **Car Payment Calculator** application ACE table.

The application displays the calculation results in a `ListBox`. Next, you add and customize the `ListBox` that displays the results.

Adding a `ListBox` to the Car Payment Calculator Application

1. ***Copying the template to your working directory.*** Copy the `C:\Examples\Tutorial09\TemplateApplication\CarPaymentCalculator` directory to your `C:\SimplyVB2008` directory.
2. ***Opening the Car Payment Calculator application's template file.*** Double click `CarPaymentCalculator.sln` in the `CarPaymentCalculator` directory to open the application in the Visual Basic IDE. The `TextBox`es for user input and the **Calculate** `Button` are provided for you.
3. ***Adding a `ListBox` control to the Form.*** Double click the `ListBox` control,

   ListBox

   in the **Toolbox**. Change the `ListBox`'s `Name` property to `paymentsListBox`. Set the `Location` property to `24, 166` and the `Size` property to `230, 94`. Figure 9.7 shows the `Form` with the `ListBox` control. Note that the `ListBox` displays its `Name` property in **Design** view—the name is not displayed when the application is running.
4. ***Saving the project.*** Select **File > Save All** to save your changes.

Append the `ListBox` suffix to all `ListBox` control names.

A `ListBox` should be large enough to display all of its contents or large enough that scrollbars can be used easily.

(cont.)

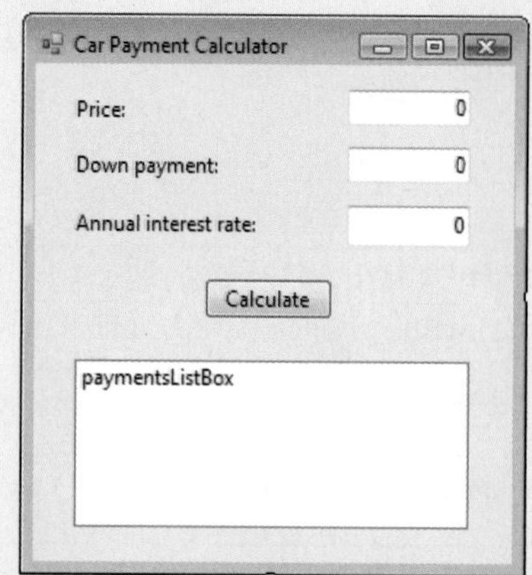
Car Payment Calculator
Price:
0
Down payment:
0
Annual interest rate:
0
Calculate
paymentsListBox

Figure 9.7 `ListBox` added to **Car Payment Calculator** application's `Form`.

After adding the `ListBox`, you must add an event handler to the application to respond when the user clicks the **Calculate** `Button`. Event handler `calculateButton_Click` updates the `ListBox`'s contents. The following box describes how to add items to a `ListBox` and how to clear a `ListBox`.

Using Code to Change a `ListBox`'s Contents

1. ***Adding the Calculate `Button`'s event handler.*** Double click the **Calculate** `Button` to generate the empty event handler `calculateButton_Click`.
2. ***Clearing the `ListBox` control.*** Add lines 6–7 of Fig. 9.8 to `calculateButton_Click`. Each time the user clicks the **Calculate** `Button`, any content previously displayed in the `ListBox` is removed. To remove all content from the `ListBox`, call method **`Clear`** on property **`Items`** (line 7). Content can be added and deleted from the `ListBox` by using its `Items` property. The `Items` property returns an object that contains a list of items displayed in the `ListBox`. Note that we've added comments in lines 2 and 8, and broken the first line of `calculateButton_Click` into two lines for readability.

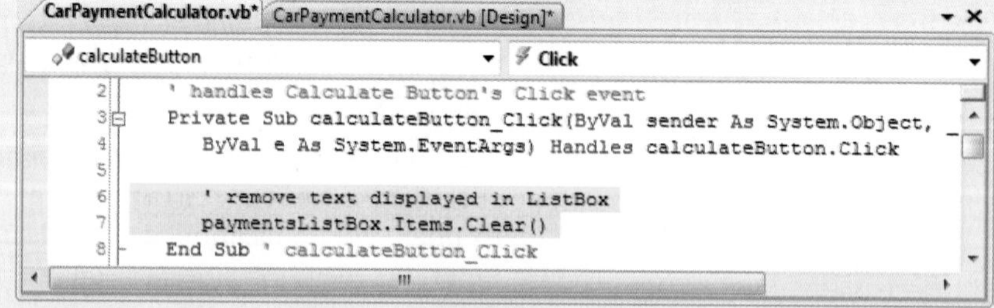
CarPaymentCalculator.vb*
CarPaymentCalculator.vb [Design]*
calculateButton
Click
2 ' handles Calculate Button's Click event
3 Private Sub calculateButton_Click(ByVal sender As System.Object, _
4 ByVal e As System.EventArgs) Handles calculateButton.Click
5
6 ' remove text displayed in ListBox
7 paymentsListBox.Items.Clear()
8 End Sub ' calculateButton_Click

Figure 9.8 Clearing the contents of a `ListBox`.

File
New
Open...
Close

GUI Design Tip

Use headers in a `ListBox` when you are displaying tabular data. Adding headers improves readability by describing the information that is displayed in the `ListBox`.

3. ***Adding content to the `ListBox` control.*** Add lines 9–11 of Fig. 9.9 to `calculateButton_Click`. The `ListBox` displays the number of monthly payments and the amount per payment. To clarify what information is being displayed, a line of text—called a **header**—needs to be added to the `ListBox`. Method **`Add`** (lines 10–11 of Fig. 9.9) adds the header—the column headings `"Months"` and `"Monthly Payment"` separated by two tab characters—to the `ListBox`'s `Items` property.

(cont.)

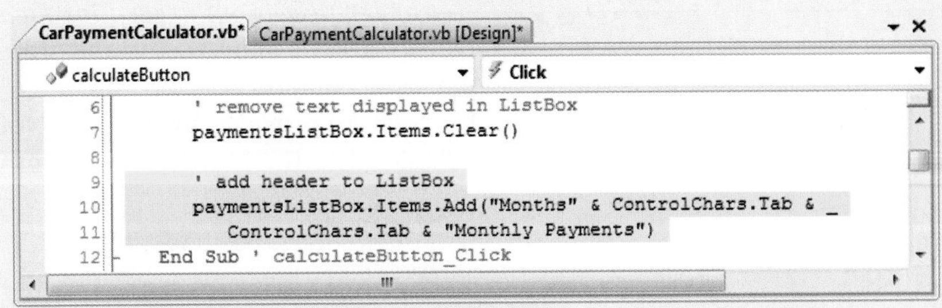
CarPaymentCalculator.vb* CarPaymentCalculator.vb [Design]*
calculateButton
Click
6 ' remove text displayed in ListBox
7 paymentsListBox.Items.Clear()
8
9 ' add header to ListBox
10 paymentsListBox.Items.Add("Months" & ControlChars.Tab & _
11 ControlChars.Tab & "Monthly Payments")
12 End Sub ' calculateButton_Click

Figure 9.9 Adding a header to a `ListBox`.

The ampersand symbol (&) is called the **string-concatenation operator.** This operator combines (or concatenates) its two operands into one string value by appending the text in the right operand to the end of the text in the left operand. In lines 10–11, the header is created by joining the values `"Months"` and `"Monthly Payments"` with two `ControlChars.Tab` constants. The constant `ControlChars.Tab` inserts a tab character into the string. The application uses two tab characters of separation between the columns (Fig. 9.3). [*Note:* The .NET Framework Class Library type `ControlChars` provides constants for several special characters, including `Tab`, `CrLf` and `NewLine`. Many of these constants have corresponding Visual Basic constants, such as `vbTab`, `vbCrLf` and `vbNewline`.]

4. ***Saving the project.*** Select **File > Save All** to save your modified code.

Now that you've learned how to change a `ListBox`'s contents, you need to declare variables and obtain user input for the calculation. The following box shows you how to initialize the **Car Payment Calculator** application's variables. The box also guides you through converting the annual interest rate to the monthly interest rate and shows you how to calculate the amount of the loan.

Declaring Variables and Retrieving User Input

1. ***Declaring variables.*** Add lines 6–13 of Fig. 9.10 to the application above the code you added in the preceding box. Variables `years` and `months` store the length of the loan in years and months. The calculation requires the length in months, but the loop-continuation condition uses the number of years. Variables `price`, `downPayment` and `interest` store the user input from the `TextBox`es. Variable `monthlyPayment` stores the result of the monthly payment calculation. Variables `loanAmount` and `monthlyInterest` store calculation results.

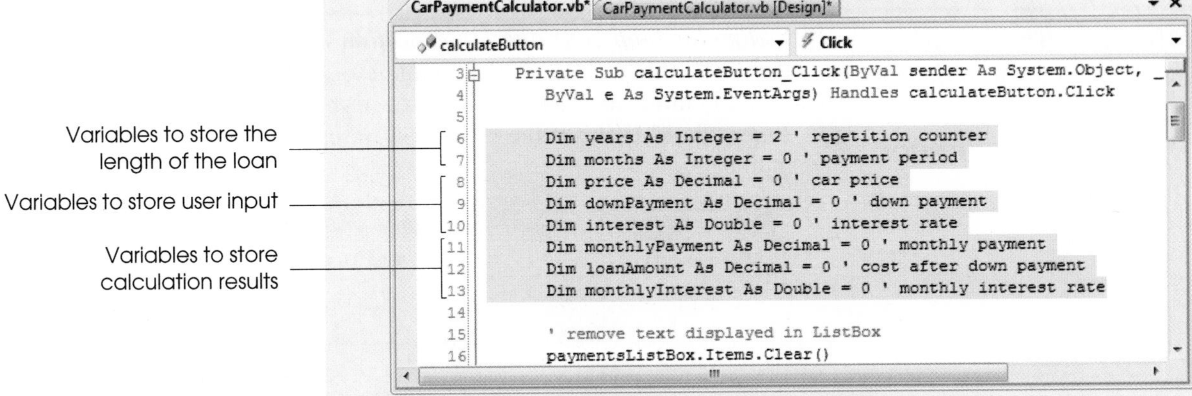
Variables to store the length of the loan
Variables to store user input
Variables to store calculation results
CarPaymentCalculator.vb* CarPaymentCalculator.vb [Design]*
calculateButton
Click
3 Private Sub calculateButton_Click(ByVal sender As System.Object, _
4 ByVal e As System.EventArgs) Handles calculateButton.Click
5
6 Dim years As Integer = 2 ' repetition counter
7 Dim months As Integer = 0 ' payment period
8 Dim price As Decimal = 0 ' car price
9 Dim downPayment As Decimal = 0 ' down payment
10 Dim interest As Double = 0 ' interest rate
11 Dim monthlyPayment As Decimal = 0 ' monthly payment
12 Dim loanAmount As Decimal = 0 ' cost after down payment
13 Dim monthlyInterest As Double = 0 ' monthly interest rate
14
15 ' remove text displayed in ListBox
16 paymentsListBox.Items.Clear()

Figure 9.10 Variables for the **Car Payment Calculator** application.

(cont.)

2. ***Retrieving user input needed for the calculation.*** Add lines 22–26 of Fig. 9.11 below the code you added in the preceding box. Lines 24–26 retrieve the down payment (`downPayment`), the price (`price`) and the annual interest rate (`interest`) provided by the user. Note that line 26 divides the interest rate by 100 to obtain the decimal equivalent (for example, 5% becomes .05).

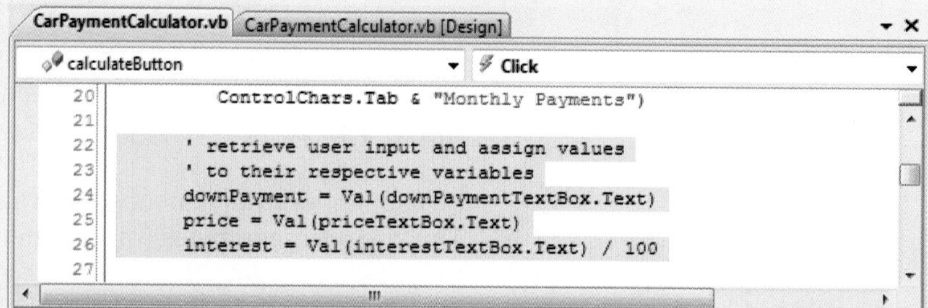

Figure 9.11 Retrieving input in the **Car Payment Calculator** application.

3. ***Calculating values used in the calculation.*** The application computes the amount of the loan by subtracting the down payment from the price. Add lines 28–30 of Fig. 9.12 to calculate the amount borrowed (line 29) and the monthly interest rate (line 30). These calculations need to occur only once, so they are placed before the `Do While...Loop` statement. Variables `loanAmount` and `monthlyInterest` are used in the calculation of monthly payments, which you'll add to your application shortly.

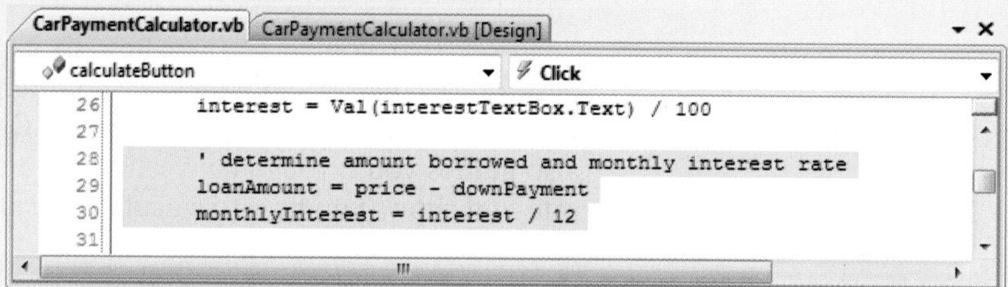

Figure 9.12 Determining amount borrowed and monthly interest rate.

4. ***Saving the project.*** Select **File > Save All** to save your modified code.

Next, you add a repetition statement to the application to calculate the monthly payment for four loans. The repetition statement performs this calculation for loans that last two, three, four and five years.

Calculating the Monthly Payment Amounts with a Do While...Loop Repetition Statement

1. ***Setting the loop-continuation condition.*** Add lines 32–33 of Fig. 9.13 below the lines that calculate the amount of the loan (`loanAmount`) and the monthly interest rate (`monthlyInterest`). After you type line 33 and press *Enter*, the IDE closes the repetition statement by adding the keyword `Loop` in line 35.

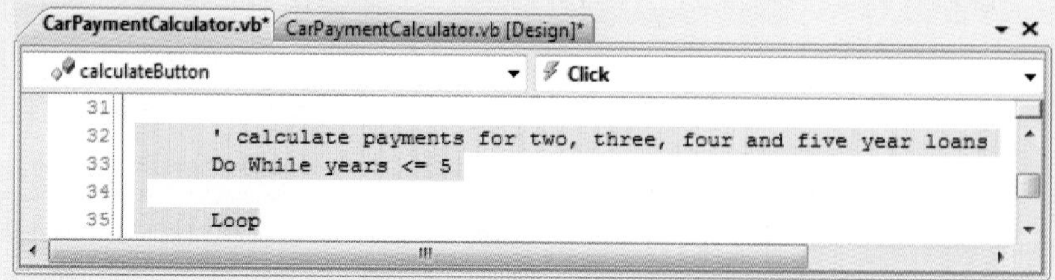

Figure 9.13 Loop-continuation condition.

(cont.)

Recall that the shortest loan in this application lasts two years, so you initialized `years` to `2` in line 6 (Fig. 9.10). The loop-continuation condition (`years <= 5`) in Fig. 9.13 specifies that the `Do While...Loop` statement executes while `years` remains less than or equal to `5`. This loop is an example of **counter-controlled repetition**. This technique uses a variable called a **counter** (`years`) to control the number of times that a set of statements executes. Counter-controlled repetition also is called **definite repetition**, because the number of repetitions is known before the repetition statement begins executing. In this example, repetition terminates when the counter (`years`) exceeds `5`.

2. ***Calculating the payment period.*** Add lines 34–35 of Fig. 9.14 to the `Do While...Loop` repetition statement to calculate the number of payments (that is, the length of the loan in months). The number of months changes with each iteration of the loop, and the calculation result changes based on the length of the payment period. Variable `months` takes on the values `24`, `36`, `48` and `60`, on successive iterations.

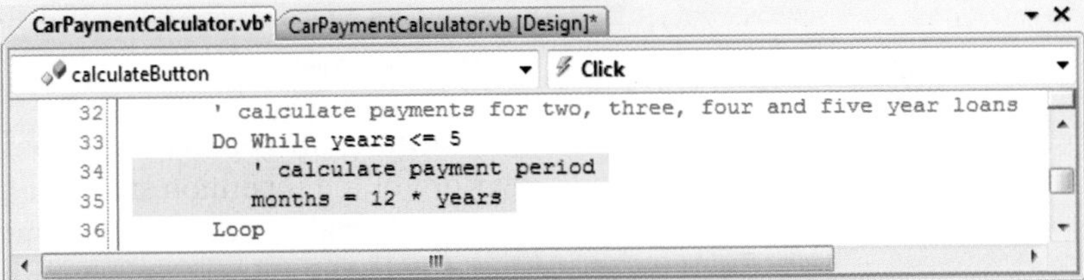
CarPaymentCalculator.vb*
CarPaymentCalculator.vb [Design]*
calculateButton
Click
32 ' calculate payments for two, three, four and five year loans
33 Do While years <= 5
34 ' calculate payment period
35 months = 12 * years
36 Loop

Figure 9.14 Converting the loan duration from years to months.

3. ***Computing the monthly payment.*** Add lines 37–39 of Fig. 9.15 to the `Do While...Loop` repetition statement. Lines 38–39 (Fig. 9.15) use the `Pmt` function to calculate the user's monthly payment. The **`Pmt`** function (which is built into Visual Basic) returns a `Double` value that specifies the monthly payment amount on a loan for a constant interest rate (`monthlyInterest`) and a given time period (`months`). Line 39 passes to `Pmt` the interest rate, the total number of payments (equal to the number of months in the payment period) and the amount borrowed. Note that the amount borrowed is passed as a negative value. Borrowed amounts are represented by negative values, because they represent a removal of cash from the person or organization that is lending money. The `Double` return value of `Pmt` is converted to type `Decimal` when you assign it to `Decimal` variable `monthlyPayment`.

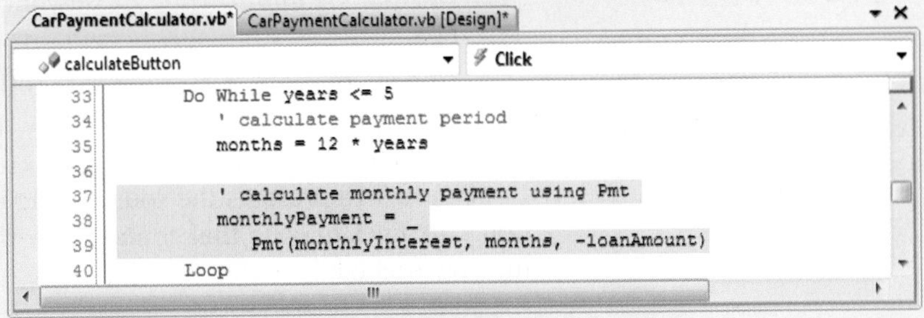
CarPaymentCalculator.vb*
CarPaymentCalculator.vb [Design]*
calculateButton
Click
33 Do While years <= 5
34 ' calculate payment period
35 months = 12 * years
36
37 ' calculate monthly payment using Pmt
38 monthlyPayment = _
39 Pmt(monthlyInterest, months, -loanAmount)
40 Loop

Figure 9.15 `Pmt` function returns monthly payment.

(cont.)

4. ***Displaying the monthly payment amount.*** Add lines 41–44 of Fig. 9.16 to the application. The number of monthly payments and the monthly payment amounts are displayed beneath the header in the `ListBox`. To add this content to the `ListBox`, call method `Add` (lines 42–44 of Fig. 9.16). Lines 43–44 use method `String.Format` to display `monthlyPayment` in currency format. Note that the two tab characters ensure that the monthly payment amount is placed in the second column. The space provided by the extra tab character makes the application's output more readable.

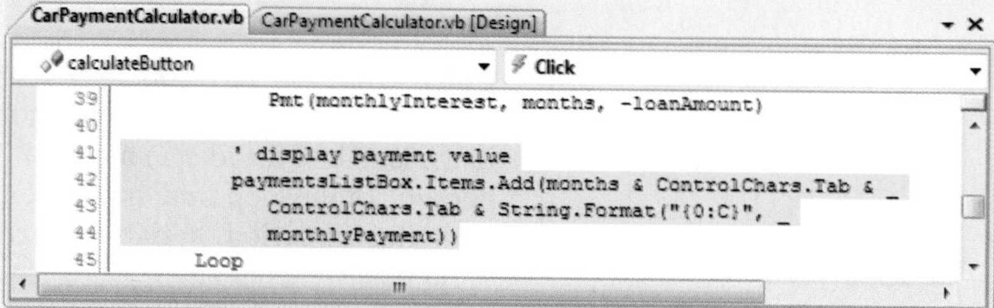

Figure 9.16 Displaying the number of months and the amount of each monthly payment.

5. ***Incrementing the counter variable.*** Add line 46 of Fig. 9.17 before the closing keyword of the repetition statement. Line 46 increments the counter variable (`years`). Variable `years` is incremented in each iteration until it equals 6. Then the loop-continuation condition (`years` <= 5) evaluates to `False` and the repetition ends.

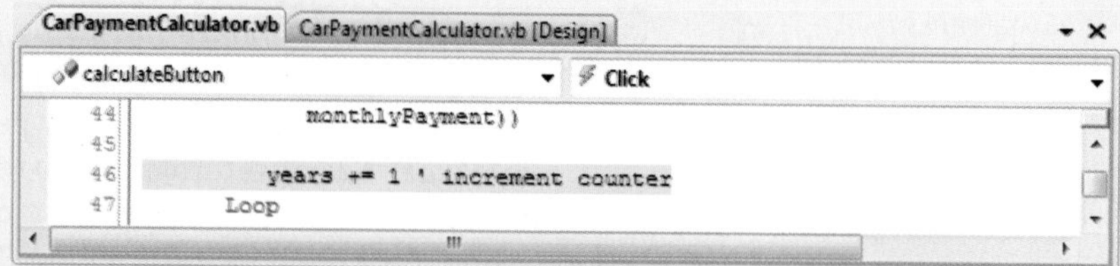

Figure 9.17 Incrementing the counter.

6. ***Running the application.*** Select **Debug > Start Debugging** to run your application. The application should calculate and display monthly payments. Enter values for a car's price, down payment and annual interest rate and click the **Calculate** `Button` to verify that the application is working correctly.

7. ***Closing the application.*** Close your running application by clicking its close box.

8. ***Closing the IDE.*** Close the Visual Basic IDE by clicking its close box.

Figure 9.18 presents the source code for the **Car Payment Calculator** application. The lines of code that contain new programming concepts you learned in this tutorial are highlighted.

```
Public Class CarPaymentCalculatorForm
   ' handles Calculate Button's Click event
   Private Sub calculateButton_Click(ByVal sender As System.Object, _
      ByVal e As System.EventArgs) Handles calculateButton.Click

      Dim years As Integer = 2 ' repetition counter
```

Figure 9.18 **Car Payment Calculator** application code. (Part 1 of 2.)

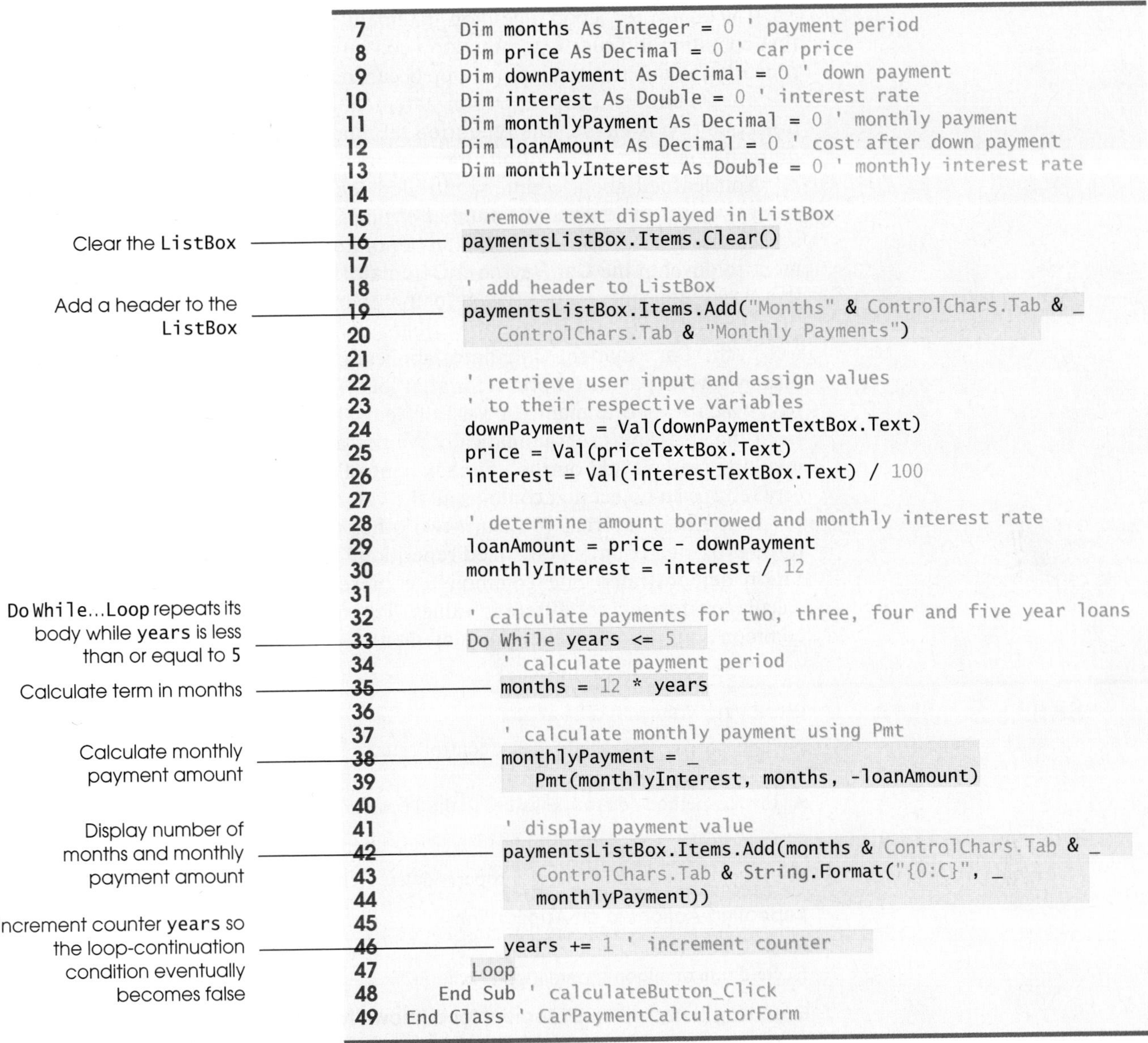

```
        Dim months As Integer = 0 ' payment period
        Dim price As Decimal = 0 ' car price
        Dim downPayment As Decimal = 0 ' down payment
        Dim interest As Double = 0 ' interest rate
        Dim monthlyPayment As Decimal = 0 ' monthly payment
        Dim loanAmount As Decimal = 0 ' cost after down payment
        Dim monthlyInterest As Double = 0 ' monthly interest rate

        ' remove text displayed in ListBox
        paymentsListBox.Items.Clear()

        ' add header to ListBox
        paymentsListBox.Items.Add("Months" & ControlChars.Tab & _
           ControlChars.Tab & "Monthly Payments")

        ' retrieve user input and assign values
        ' to their respective variables
        downPayment = Val(downPaymentTextBox.Text)
        price = Val(priceTextBox.Text)
        interest = Val(interestTextBox.Text) / 100

        ' determine amount borrowed and monthly interest rate
        loanAmount = price - downPayment
        monthlyInterest = interest / 12

        ' calculate payments for two, three, four and five year loans
        Do While years <= 5
           ' calculate payment period
           months = 12 * years

           ' calculate monthly payment using Pmt
           monthlyPayment = _
              Pmt(monthlyInterest, months, -loanAmount)

           ' display payment value
           paymentsListBox.Items.Add(months & ControlChars.Tab & _
              ControlChars.Tab & String.Format("{0:C}", _
              monthlyPayment))

           years += 1 ' increment counter
        Loop
     End Sub ' calculateButton_Click
  End Class ' CarPaymentCalculatorForm
```

Clear the ListBox
Add a header to the ListBox
Do While...Loop repeats its body while years is less than or equal to 5
Calculate term in months
Calculate monthly payment amount
Display number of months and monthly payment amount
Increment counter years so the loop-continuation condition eventually becomes false

Figure 9.18 **Car Payment Calculator** application code. (Part 2 of 2.)

SELF-REVIEW

1. Counter-controlled repetition is also called _________ because the number of repetitions is known before the loop begins executing.
   a) definite repetition b) known repetition
   c) sequential repetition d) counter repetition

2. The line of text added to a `ListBox` to describe the information that will be displayed is called a _________.
   a) title b) starter
   c) header d) clarifier

Answers: 1) a. 2) c.

9.5 Wrap-Up

In this tutorial, you began using repetition statements. You used the `Do While...Loop` and the `Do Until...Loop` statements to repeat actions in an application, depending on a loop-continuation condition or a loop-termination condition, respectively.

The Do While...Loop repetition statement executes as long as its loop-continuation condition is True. When the loop-continuation condition becomes False, the repetition terminates. An infinite loop occurs if this condition never becomes False.

The Do Until...Loop repetition statement executes as long as its loop-termination condition is False. The repetition terminates when the loop-termination condition becomes True. An infinite loop occurs if this condition never becomes True.

You learned about counter-controlled repetition, in which a repetition statement "knows" in advance the number of times it will iterate, and a variable known as a counter precisely counts that number of iterations. You used a repetition statement to develop the **Car Payment Calculator** application in which you calculated the monthly payments for a given loan amount and a given interest rate for loan durations of two, three, four and five years.

In the **Car Payment Calculator** application, you used the ListBox control to display several payment options for a car loan. You learned about the ListBox control, which is used to maintain a list of items. Items can be added to and removed from the ListBox programmatically. Values are added to a ListBox control by invoking method Add on the ListBox control's Items property. The Items property returns an object that contains all the values displayed in the ListBox.

In the next tutorial, you learn two other repetition statements, and you continue exploring counter-controlled repetition. The **Car Payment Calculator** application demonstrated one common use of repetition statements—performing a calculation for several different values. The next application introduces another common application of repetition statements—summing a series of numbers.

SKILLS SUMMARY

Displaying Values in a ListBox

- Property Items of the ListBox control returns an object that contains the values to be displayed in a ListBox.
- Invoke method Add to add values to the Items property.

Clearing a ListBox's Contents

- Method Clear of the Items's property deletes (clears) all the values in the ListBox.

Repeating Actions in an Application

- Use a repetition statement that depends on the true or false value of a loop-continuation condition or a loop-termination condition.

Executing a Repetition Statement for a Known Number of Repetitions

- Use counter-controlled repetition with a counter variable to determine the number of times that a set of statements will execute.

Using the Do While...Loop Repetition Statement

- This repetition statement executes while the loop-continuation condition is True.
- An infinite loop occurs if the condition never becomes False.

Using the Do Until...Loop Repetition Statement

- This repetition statement executes until the loop-termination condition is True.
- An infinite loop occurs if the condition never becomes True.

Concatenating Strings

- Use the & operator to build a new string from two existing strings. The contents of the right operand are appended to the contents of the left operand to create the new string.

KEY TERMS

Add method of Items—Adds an item to a ListBox control.

body of a control statement—The set of statements that are enclosed in a control statement.

Clear method of Items—Deletes all the values in a ListBox control.

ControlChars.Tab constant—Represents a tab character.

counter—A variable used to determine the number of times the body of a repetition statement executes.

counter-controlled repetition—A technique that uses a counter variable to determine the number of times that the body of a repetition statement executes. Also called definite repetition.

definite repetition—See counter-controlled repetition.

`Do Until...Loop` repetition statement—A control statement that executes a set of body statements *until* its loop-termination condition becomes `True`.

`Do While...Loop` repetition statement—A control statement that executes a set of body statements *while* its loop-continuation condition is `True`.

header—A line of text at the top of a `ListBox` that clarifies the information being displayed.

infinite loop—An error in which a repetition statement never terminates.

`Items` property of the `ListBox` control—Returns an object containing all the values in the `ListBox`.

`ListBox` control—Allows the user to view items in a list. Items can be added to or removed from the list programmatically.

loop—Another name for a repetition statement.

loop-continuation condition—The condition used in a repetition statement (such as a `Do While...Loop`) that enables repetition to continue while the condition is `True` and that causes repetition to terminate when the condition becomes `False`.

loop-termination condition—The condition used in a repetition statement (such as a `Do Until...Loop`) that enables repetition to continue while the condition is `False` and that causes repetition to terminate when the condition becomes `True`.

merge symbol (in the UML)—A diamond symbol in the UML that joins two flows of activity into one flow of activity.

`Pmt` function—A built-in Visual Basic function that, given an interest rate, the total number of payments and a monetary loan amount, returns a `Double` value specifying the amount per payment.

repetition statement—Allows you to specify that an action or actions should be repeated, depending on the value of a condition.

string-concatenation operator (&)—This operator combines its two operands into one string value.

GUI DESIGN GUIDELINES

`ListBox`

- A `ListBox` should be large enough to display all of its content or large enough that scrollbars may be used easily.
- Use headers in a `ListBox` when you are displaying tabular data. Adding headers improves readability by describing the information that is displayed in the `ListBox`.

CONTROLS, EVENTS, PROPERTIES & METHODS

`ListBox` ListBox This control allows the user to view and select from items in a list.

- ***In action***

Months	Monthly Payments
24	$490.50
36	$339.06
48	$263.55
60	$218.41

- ***Properties***

`Items`—Returns an object that contains the items displayed in the `ListBox`.

`Location`—Specifies the location of the `ListBox` on the `Form`.

`Name`—Specifies the name used to access the properties of the `ListBox` programatically. The name should be appended with the `ListBox` suffix.

`Size`—Specifies the width and height (in pixels) of the `ListBox`.

- ***Methods***

  Items.Add—Adds an item to the Items property.

  Items.Clear—Deletes all the values in the ListBox's Items property.

MULTIPLE-CHOICE QUESTIONS

9.1 The ________ statement executes until its loop-termination condition becomes True.

a) Do While...Loop b) Do Until...Loop
c) Do d) Loop

9.2 The ________ statement executes until its loop-continuation condition becomes False.

a) Do While...Loop b) Do Until...Loop
c) Do d) Do While

9.3 A(n) ________ loop occurs when a condition in a Do While...Loop never becomes False.

a) infinite b) undefined
c) nested d) indefinite

9.4 A ________ is a variable that helps control the number of times that a set of statements executes.

a) repeater b) counter
c) loop d) repetition control statement

9.5 The ________ control allows users to add and view items in a list.

a) ListItems b) SelectBox
c) ListBox d) ViewBox

9.6 In a UML activity diagram, a(n) ________ symbol joins two flows of activity into one flow of activity.

a) merge b) combine
c) action state d) decision

9.7 Property ________ returns an object containing all the values in a ListBox.

a) All b) List
c) ListItemValues d) Items

9.8 Items's method ________ deletes all the values in a ListBox.

a) Remove b) Delete
c) Clear d) Del

9.9 Items's method ________ adds an item to a ListBox.

a) Include b) Append
c) Add d) None of the above

9.10 Function ________ calculates monthly payments on a loan based on a fixed interest rate.

a) MonPmt b) Payment
c) MonthlyPayment d) Pmt

EXERCISES

9.11 ***(Table of Powers Application)*** Write an application that displays a table of numbers from 1 to an upper limit, along with each number's squared value (for example, the number n to the power 2, or n ^ 2) and cubed value (the number n to the power 3, or n ^ 3). The user specifies the upper limit, and the results are displayed in a ListBox, as in Fig. 9.19.

a) ***Copying the template to your working directory.*** Copy the directory C:\Examples\Tutorial09\Exercises\TableOfPowers to your C:\SimplyVB2008 directory.

b) ***Opening the application's template file.*** Double click TableOfPowers.sln in the TableOfPowers directory to open the application.

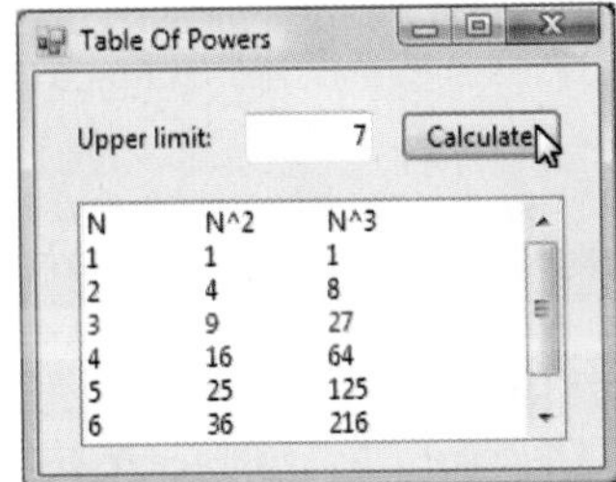

Figure 9.19 **Table of Powers** application's `Form`.

c) ***Adding a `ListBox`.*** Add a `ListBox` to the application, as shown in Fig. 9.19. Name the `ListBox` `resultsListBox`.

d) ***Adding the Upper limit: `TextBox` event handler.*** Double click the **Upper limit:** `TextBox` to generate an event handler for this `TextBox`'s `TextChanged` event. In this event handler, clear the `ListBox`.

e) ***Adding the Calculate `Button` event handler.*** Double click the **Calculate** `Button` to generate the empty event handler `calculateButton_Click`. Add the code specified by the remaining steps to this event handler.

f) ***Clearing the `ListBox`.*** Use method `Clear` on the `Items` property to clear the `ListBox` of any previous data.

g) ***Obtaining the upper limit supplied by the user.*** Assign the value entered by the user in the **Upper limit:** `TextBox` to a variable. Note that the `TextBox`'s `Name` property is set to `inputTextBox`.

h) ***Adding a header.*** Use method `Add` on the `Items` property to insert a header in the `ListBox`. The header should label three columns—`N`, `N^2` and `N^3`. Column headings should be separated by tab characters.

i) ***Calculating the powers from 1 to the specified upper limit.*** Use a `Do Until...Loop` to calculate the squared value and the cubed value of each number from `1` to the upper limit, inclusive. Add an item to the `ListBox` containing the current number being analyzed, its squared value and its cubed value.

j) ***Incrementing the counter.*** Remember to increment the counter appropriately each time through the loop.

k) ***Running the application.*** Select **Debug > Start Debugging** to run your application. Enter an upper limit and click the **Calculate** `Button`. Verify that the table of powers displayed contains the correct values.

l) ***Closing the application.*** Close your running application by clicking its close box.

m) ***Closing the IDE.*** Close the Visual Basic IDE by clicking its close box.

9.12 ***(Mortgage Calculator Application)*** A bank offers mortgages that can be repaid in 5, 10, 15, 20, 25 or 30 years. Write an application that allows the user to enter the price of a house (the amount of the mortgage) and the annual interest rate. When the user clicks the **Calculate** `Button`, the application displays a table of the mortgage length in years together with the monthly payment, as shown in Fig. 9.20.

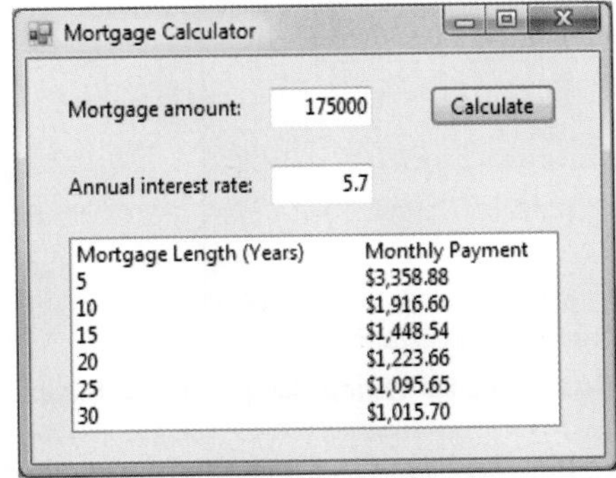

Figure 9.20 **Mortgage Calculator** application's `Form`.

a) ***Copying the template to your working directory.*** Copy the directory `C:\Examples\Tutorial09\Exercises\MortgageCalculator` to your `C:\SimplyVB2008` directory.

b) ***Opening the application's template file.*** Double click `MortgageCalculator.sln` in the `MortgageCalculator` directory to open the application.

c) ***Adding a `ListBox`.*** Add a `ListBox` as shown in Fig. 9.20. Name the `ListBox` `resultsListBox`.

d) ***Adding a Calculate `Button` event handler.*** Double click the **Calculate** `Button` to generate the empty event handler `calculateButton_Click`. Add the code specified in the remaining steps to your event handler.

e) ***Converting the annual interest rate to the monthly interest rate.*** To convert the annual interest rate from a percent value into its `Double` equivalent, divide the annual rate by `100`. Then divide the `Double` annual rate by `12` to obtain the monthly rate.

f) ***Clearing the `ListBox`.*** Use method `Clear` on the `Items` property to clear the `ListBox` of any previous data.

g) ***Displaying a header.*** Use method `Add` to display a header in the `ListBox`. The header should be the column headers `"Mortgage Length (Years)"` and `"Monthly Payment"`, separated by a tab character.

h) ***Using a repetition statement.*** Add a `Do While...Loop` repetition statement to calculate six monthly payment options for the user's mortgage. Each option has a different number of years that the mortgage can last. For this exercise, use the following numbers of years: `5`, `10`, `15`, `20`, `25` and `30`.

i) ***Converting the length of the mortgage from years to months.*** Convert the number of years to months.

j) ***Calculating the monthly payments for six different mortgages.*** Use the `Pmt` function to compute the monthly payments. Pass to the function the monthly interest rate, the number of months in the mortgage and the mortgage amount. Remember that the mortgage amount must be negative, because it represents an amount of money being paid out by the lender.

k) ***Displaying the results.*** Use method `Add` on the `Items` property to display the length of the mortgage in years and the monthly payment in the `ListBox`. Use three tab characters to ensure that the monthly payment appears in the second column.

l) ***Running the application.*** Select **Debug > Start Debugging** to run your application. Enter a mortgage amount and annual interest rate, then click the **Calculate** `Button`. Verify that the monthly payments displayed contain the correct values.

m) ***Closing the application.*** Close your running application by clicking its close box.

n) ***Closing the IDE.*** Close the Visual Basic IDE by clicking its close box.

9.13 ***(Office Supplies Application)*** Create an application that allows the user to make a list of office supplies to buy, as shown in Fig. 9.21. The user should enter the supply item in a `TextBox` and click the **Buy** `Button` to add it to the `ListBox`. The **Clear** `Button` removes all the items from the `ListBox`.

Figure 9.21 **Office Supplies** application's `Form`.

a) ***Copying the template to your working directory.*** Copy the `C:\Examples\Tutorial09\Exercises\OfficeSupplies` directory to your `C:\SimplyVB2008` directory.

b) ***Opening the application's template file.*** Double click `OfficeSupplies.sln` in `OfficeSupplies` directory to open the application.

c) ***Adding a `ListBox`.*** Add a `ListBox` to the `Form`. Name the `ListBox` `suppliesListBox`. Place and size it as shown in Fig. 9.21.

d) ***Adding an event handler for the Buy `Button`.*** Double click the **Buy** `Button` to generate the event handler `buyButton_Click`. The event handler should obtain the user input from the `TextBox`. The user input is then added as an item into the `ListBox`. After the input is added to the `ListBox`, clear the **Supply:** `TextBox`.

e) ***Adding an event handler for the Clear `Button`.*** Double click the **Clear** `Button` to generate the event handler `clearButton_Click`. The event handler should use the `Clear` method on the `Items` property to clear the `ListBox`.

f) ***Running the application.*** Select **Debug > Start Debugging** to run your application. Enter several items into the **Supply:** `TextBox` and click the **Buy** `Button` after entering each item. Verify that each item is added to the `ListBox`. Click the **Clear** `Button` and verify that all items are removed from the `ListBox`.

g) ***Closing the application.*** Close your running application by clicking its close box.

h) ***Closing the IDE.*** Close the Visual Basic IDE by clicking its close box.

What does this code do?

9.14 What is the result of the following code?

```
Dim x As Integer = 1
Dim mysteryValue As Integer = 1

Do While x < 6
   mysteryValue *= x
   x += 1
Loop

displayLabel.Text = mysteryValue
```

What's wrong with this code?

9.15 Find the error(s) in the following code:

a) Assume that the variable `x` is declared and initialized to `1`. The loop should total the numbers from `1` to `10`.

```
Dim total As Integer = 0

Do Until x <= 10
   total += x
   x += 1
Loop
```

b) Assume that the variable `counter` is declared and initialized to `1`. The loop should sum the numbers from `1` to `100`.

```
Do While counter <= 100
   total += counter
Loop

counter += 1
```

c) Assume that the variable `counter` is declared and initialized to `1000`. The loop should iterate from `1000` to `1`.

```
Do While counter > 0
   numbersListBox.Items.Add(counter)
   counter += 1
Loop
```

d) Assume that the variable `counter` is declared and initialized to `1`. The loop should execute five times, adding the numbers `1–5` to a `ListBox`.

```
Do While counter < 5
   numbersListBox.Items.Add(counter)
   counter += 1
Loop
```

Using the Debugger ▶

9.16 *(Odd Numbers Application)* The **Odd Numbers** application should display all of the odd integers between one and the number input by the user. Copy the **Odd Numbers** application from `C:/Examples/Tutorial09/Exercises/Debugger` to your working directory. Run the application. Note that an infinite loop occurs after you enter a value into the **Upper limit:** `TextBox` and click the **View** `Button`. Select **Debug > Stop Debugging** to close the running application.Use the debugger to find and fix the error(s) in the application. Figure 9.22 displays the correct output for the application.

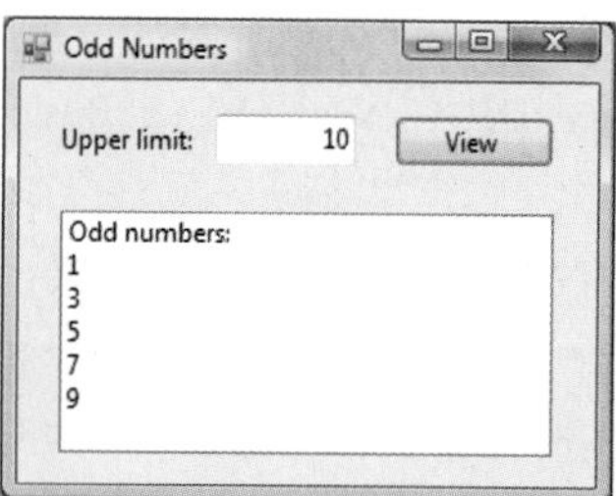

Figure 9.22 Correct output for the **Odd Numbers** application.

Programming Challenge ▶

9.17 *(To-Do List Application)* Use a `ListBox` as a to-do list. Enter each item in a `TextBox`, and add it to the `ListBox` by clicking a `Button`. The item should be displayed in a numbered list, as in Fig. 9.23. To do this, we introduce property `Count`, which returns the number of items in a `ListBox`'s `Items` property. The following is a sample call to assign the number of items displayed in `sampleListBox` to an `Integer` variable:

```
count = sampleListBox.Items.Count
```

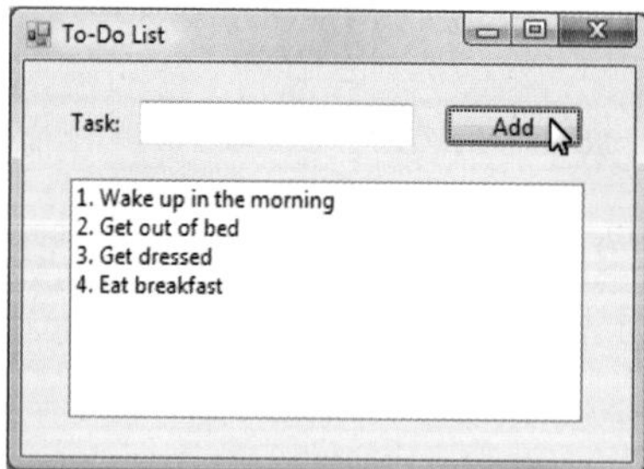

Figure 9.23 **To-Do List** application's `Form`.

TUTORIAL 10

Class Average Application

Introducing the Do...Loop While and Do...Loop Until Repetition Statements

Objectives

In this tutorial, you learn to:

- Use the Do...Loop While statement.
- Use the Do...Loop Until statement.
- Further understand counter-controlled repetition.
- Transfer the focus to a control.
- Enable and disable Buttons.

Outline

This tutorial continues the discussion of repetition statements that we began in Tutorial 9. In the preceding tutorial, we examined Do While...Loop and Do Until...Loop repetition statements, which test their loop-continuation and loop-termination conditions before an iteration. This tutorial introduces two additional repetition statements, Do...Loop While and Do...Loop Until, which test their conditions *after* each iteration. As a result, the body statements contained in these repetition statements are performed at least once.

You'll also learn how to disable and enable controls on a Form. When a control, such as a Button, is disabled, it no longer responds to the user. You'll use this feature to prevent the user from causing errors in your applications. This tutorial also introduces the concept of transferring the focus of the application to a control. Proper use of the focus makes an application easier to use.

10.1 Test-Driving the Class Average Application

This application must meet the following requirements:

Application Requirements

A teacher regularly gives quizzes to a class of 10 students. The grades on these quizzes are integers in the range from 0 to 100 (0 and 100 are both valid grades). The teacher would like you to develop an application that computes the class average for one quiz.

The class average is equal to the sum of the grades divided by the number of students who took the quiz. The algorithm for solving this problem must input each of the grades, total the grades, perform the averaging calculation and display the result. You begin by test-driving the completed application. Then you learn the additional Visual Basic capabilities needed to create your own version of this application.

Test-Driving the Class Average Application

1. ***Opening the completed application.*** Open the directory `C:\Examples\Tutorial10\CompletedApplication\ClassAverage` to locate the **Class Average** application. Double click `ClassAverage.sln` to open the application in the Visual Basic IDE.

2. ***Running the Class Average application.*** Select **Debug > Start Debugging** to run the application (Fig. 10.1).

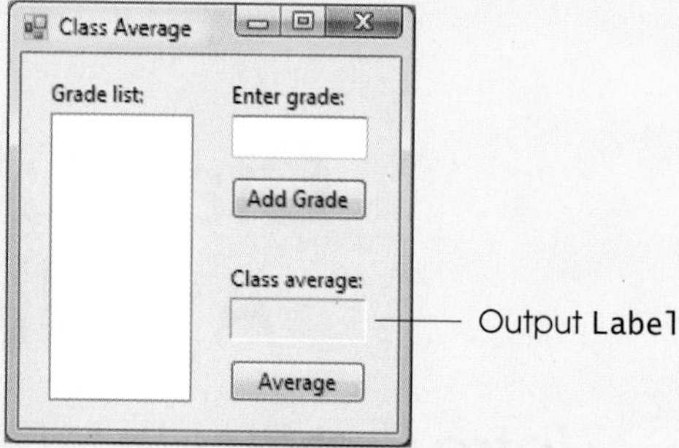

Figure 10.1 **Class Average** application's `Form` in run mode.

3. ***Entering quiz grades.*** Enter `85` as the first quiz grade in the **Enter grade:** `TextBox`, and click the **Add Grade** `Button`. The grade displays in the `ListBox`, as in Fig. 10.2. After you click the **Add Grade** `Button`, the cursor appears in the **Enter grade:** `TextBox`. When a control is selected (for example, the **Enter grade:** `TextBox`), it is said to have the **focus** of the application. You learn to set the focus to a control as you build this tutorial's application. As a result of the application's focus being transferred to the **Enter grade:** `TextBox`, you can type another grade without navigating to the `TextBox` with the mouse or the *Tab* key. Transferring the focus to a particular control tells the user what information the application expects next. [*Note:* If you click the **Average** `Button` before 10 grades have been input, a runtime error occurs. Select **Debug > Stop Debugging** to close the running application. Repeat *Step 2*. You'll fix this problem in the exercises.]

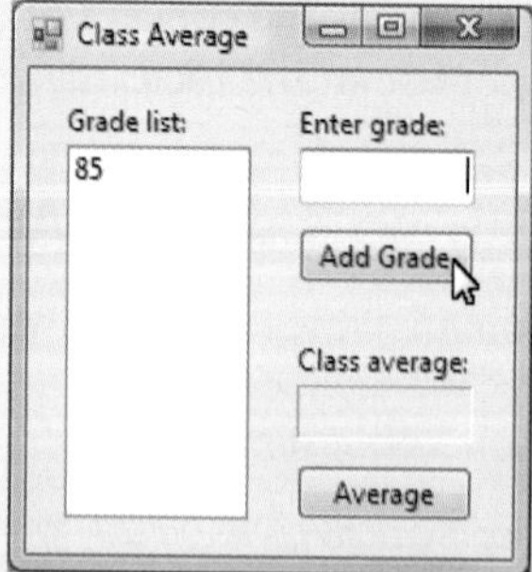

Figure 10.2 Entering grades in the **Class Average** application.

4. ***Repeating* Step 3 *nine times.*** Enter nine other grades between 0 and 100, and click the **Add Grade** `Button` after each entry. After 10 grades are displayed in the **Grade list:** `ListBox`, the `Form` will look similar to Fig. 10.3. Note that the **Add Grade** `Button` is disabled once you have entered 10 grades. That is, its color is gray, and clicking the `Button` does not invoke its event handler.

5. ***Calculating the class average.*** Click the **Average** `Button` to calculate the average of the 10 quizzes. The class average is displayed in an output `Label` above the **Average** `Button` (Fig. 10.4). Note that the **Add Grade** `Button` is now enabled.

(cont.)

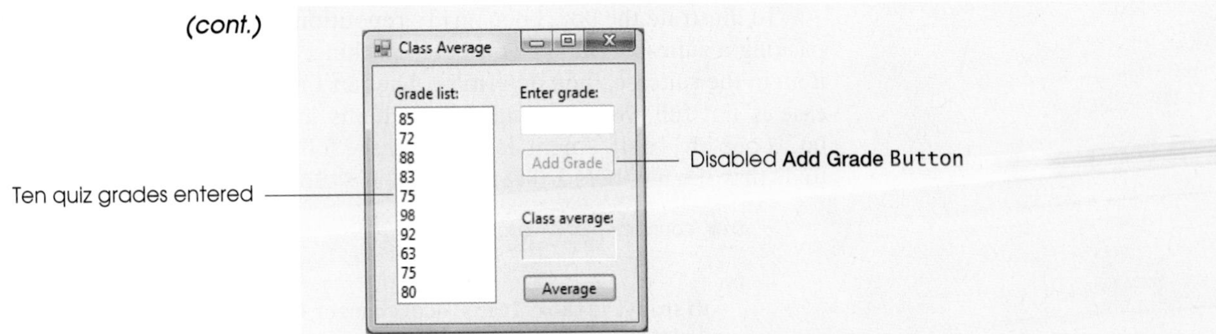

Figure 10.3 **Class Average** application after 10 grades have been input.

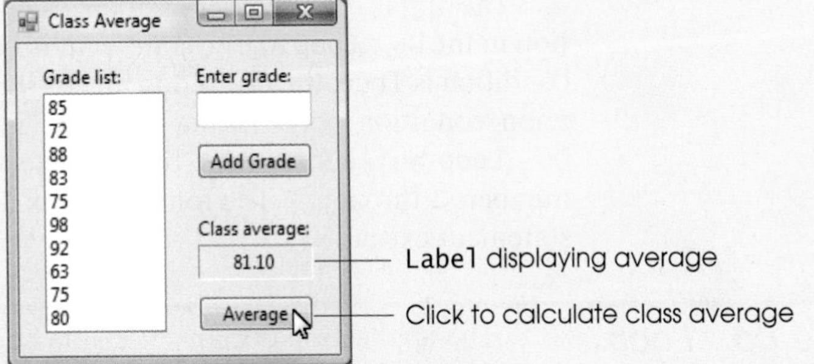

Figure 10.4 Displaying the class average.

6. ***Entering another set of grades.*** You can calculate the class average for another set of 10 grades without restarting the application. Enter a grade in the `TextBox`, and click the **Add Grade** `Button`. Note that the **Grade list:** `ListBox` and the **Class average:** field are cleared when you start entering another set of grades (Fig. 10.5).

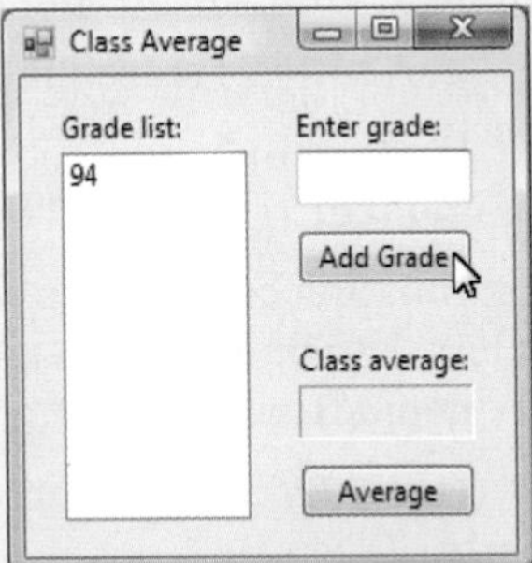

Figure 10.5 Entering a new set of grades.

7. ***Closing the application.*** Close your running application by clicking its close box.
8. ***Closing the IDE.*** Close the Visual Basic IDE by clicking its close box.

10.2 Do...Loop While Repetition Statement

An infinite loop occurs when the loop-continuation condition in a `Do...Loop While` statement never becomes `False`.

The `Do...Loop While` repetition statement is similar to the `Do While...Loop` statement; both statements iterate while their loop-continuation conditions are `True`. In the `Do While...Loop` statement, the loop-continuation condition is tested at the beginning of the loop, before the body of the loop is performed. The `Do...Loop While` statement tests the loop-continuation condition *after* the loop body is performed. Therefore, in a `Do...Loop While` statement, the loop body always executes at least once. When a `Do...Loop While` statement terminates, execution continues with the statement after the `Loop While` keywords.

To illustrate the Do...Loop While repetition statement, consider the example of packing a suitcase: Before you begin packing, the suitcase is empty. You place an item in the suitcase, then determine whether the suitcase is full. As long as the suitcase is not full, you continue to put items in the suitcase. As an example of a Do...Loop While statement, let's look at the following application segment designed to display the numbers 1 through 3 in a ListBox:

```
Dim counter As Integer = 1

Do
   displayListBox.Items.Add(counter)
   counter += 1
Loop While counter <= 3
```

The application segment initializes counter to 1. The loop-continuation condition in the Do...Loop While statement is counter <= 3. While the loop-continuation condition is True, the Do...Loop While statement executes. When the loop-continuation condition becomes False (that is, when counter is greater than 3), the Do...Loop While statement finishes executing and displayListBox contains the numbers 1 through 3. The following box describes each step as the above repetition statement executes.

Executing the Do...Loop While Repetition Statement

1. The application declares variable counter and sets its value to 1.
2. The application enters the Do...Loop While repetition statement.
3. The number (currently 1) stored in counter is added to displayListBox's Items property.
4. The value of counter is increased by 1; counter now contains 2.
5. The loop-continuation condition is checked. The condition evaluates to True (counter is less than or equal to 3), so the application continues executing at the first statement after the Do statement.
6. The number (currently 2) stored in counter is added to displayListBox's Items property.
7. The value of counter is increased by 1; counter now contains 3.
8. The loop-continuation condition is checked. The condition evaluates to True (counter is less than or equal to 3), so the application continues executing at the first statement after the Do statement.
9. The number (currently 3) stored in counter is added to displayListBox's Items property.
10. The value of counter is increased by 1; counter now contains 4.
11. The loop-continuation condition is checked. The condition evaluates to False (counter is not less than or equal to 3), so the application exits the Do...Loop While repetition statement.

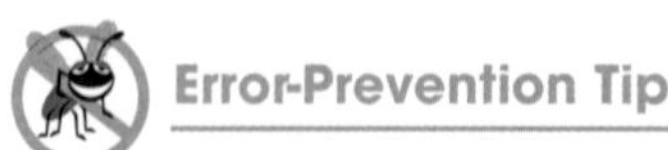

Including a final value in the condition of a repetition statement (and choosing the appropriate relational operator) can reduce the occurrence of off-by-one errors. For example, in a Do While...Loop statement used to print the values 1–10, the loop-continuation condition should be counter <= 10, rather than counter < 10 (which is an off-by-one error) or counter < 11 (which is correct, but less clear).

If you mistyped the loop-continuation condition as counter < 3 or counter <= 2, the ListBox would display only 1 and 2. Including an incorrect relational operator (such as the less-than sign in counter < 3) or an incorrect final value for a loop counter (such as the 2 in counter <= 2) in the condition of any repetition statement, or using an incorrect initial value (such as counter = 0) can cause **off-by-one errors**, which occur when a loop executes for one more or one less iteration than is necessary.

Figure 10.6 illustrates the UML activity diagram for the general Do...Loop While statement. This diagram makes it clear that the loop-continuation guard condition ([counter <= 3]) does not evaluate until after the loop performs the action state at least once. Recall that action states can include one or more Visual Basic statements executed one after the other (sequentially) as in the preceding example. When you use a Do...Loop While repetition statement in building an application, you would provide the appropriate action state and the guard conditions for your application.

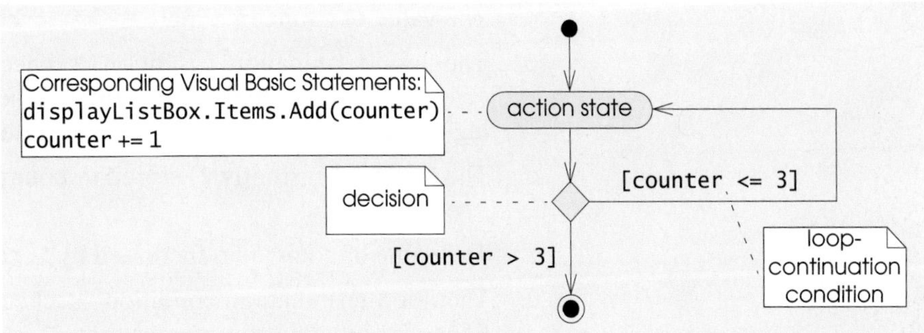

Figure 10.6 Do...Loop While repetition statement UML activity diagram.

SELF-REVIEW

1. The Do...Loop While statement repeats when the loop-continuation condition _________.
   a) is False after the loop body executes
   b) is False before the loop body executes
   c) is True after the loop body executes
   d) is True before the loop body executes

2. An infinite loop occurs when the loop-continuation condition in a Do While...Loop or Do...Loop While statement _________.
   a) never becomes True
   b) never becomes False
   c) is False
   d) is tested repeatedly

Answers: 1) c. 2) b.

10.3 Do...Loop Until Repetition Statement

The **Do...Loop Until** statement is similar to the Do Until...Loop statement, except that in the Do...Loop Until statement the loop-termination condition is tested *after* the loop body is performed. Therefore, the loop body executes at least once. When a Do...Loop Until terminates, execution continues with the statement after the Loop Until keywords.

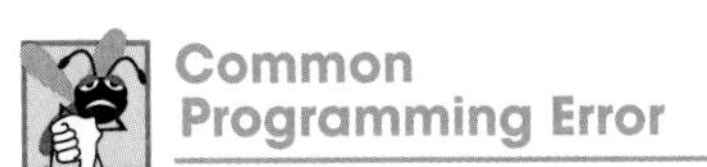

Common Programming Error

An infinite loop occurs when the loop-termination condition in a Do...Loop Until statement never becomes True.

Again, consider the suitcase-packing example. Before you begin packing, the suitcase is empty. You place an item in the suitcase, then determine whether the suitcase is full. As long as the condition "the suitcase is full" is False, you continue to put items into the suitcase.

As an example of a Do...Loop Until statement, let's look at another application segment designed to display the numbers 1 through 3 in a ListBox:

```
Dim counter As Integer = 1

Do
   displayListBox.Items.Add(counter)
   counter += 1
Loop Until counter > 3
```

The application segment initializes counter to 1, and the loop-termination condition in the Do...Loop Until statement is counter > 3. While the loop-termination condition is False, the Do...Loop Until statement executes. When the loop-termination condition becomes True, the Do...Loop Until statement finishes executing and displayListBox contains the numbers 1 through 3. The following box describes each step as the repetition statement executes.

Executing the Do...Loop Until Repetition Statement

1. The application declares variable counter and sets its value to 1.
2. The application enters the Do...Loop Until repetition statement.
3. The number (currently 1) stored in counter is added to displayListBox's Items property.
4. The value of counter is increased by 1; counter now contains 2.
5. The loop-termination condition is checked. The condition evaluates to False (counter is not greater than 3), so the application continues executing at the first statement after the Do statement.
6. The number (currently 2) stored in counter is added to displayListBox's Items property.
7. The value of counter is increased by 1; counter now contains 3.
8. The loop-termination condition is checked. The condition evaluates to False (counter is not greater than 3), so the application continues executing at the first statement after the Do statement.
9. The number (currently 3) stored in counter is added to displayListBox's Items property.
10. The value of counter is increased by 1; counter now contains 4.
11. The loop-termination condition is checked. The condition now evaluates to True (counter is greater than 3), so the application exits the Do...Loop Until repetition statement.

The Do...Loop Until UML activity diagram (Fig. 10.7) makes it clear that the loop-termination guard condition is not evaluated until after the body is executed at least once. This UML diagram indicates the exact same guard conditions as detailed in Fig. 10.6. The only difference for a Do...Loop Until repetition statement is that it continues to execute when the loop-termination guard condition is False. When the guard condition evaluates to True, the repetition ends and program control moves to the next statement following the Loop Until keywords.

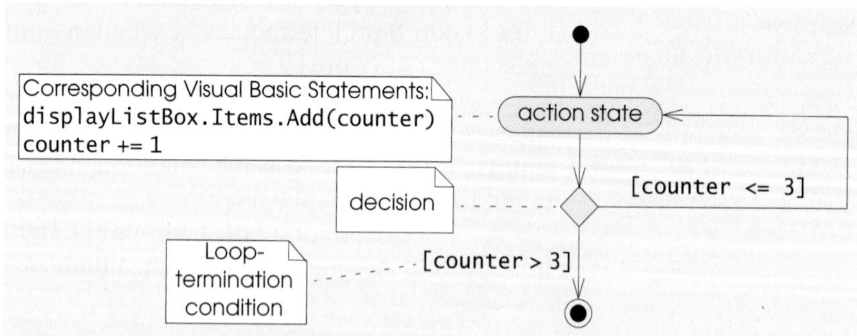

Figure 10.7 Do...Loop Until repetition statement UML activity diagram.

SELF-REVIEW

1. The Do...Loop Until statement checks the loop-termination condition ________.
   a) for False after the loop body executes
   b) for False before the loop body executes
   c) for True after the loop body executes
   d) for True before the loop body executes

2. When a Do...Loop Until terminates, execution continues with the ________.
   a) Loop Until clause
   b) statement after keywords Loop Until
   c) statements inside Do and Loop Until
   d) Do clause

Answers: 1) c. 2) b.

10.4 Creating the Class Average Application

Now that you've learned the `Do...Loop While` and `Do...Loop Until` repetition statements, you can begin to develop the **Class Average** application. First, you use pseudocode to list the actions to execute and to specify the order of execution. You use counter-controlled repetition to input the grades one at a time. Recall that this technique uses a variable called a counter to determine the number of times that a set of statements executes. In this example, repetition terminates when the counter exceeds 10 because we are assuming, for simplicity, that the user enters only 10 grades. The following pseudocode describes the operation of the **Class Average** application when the **Add Grade** `Button` is clicked and when the **Average** `Button` is clicked:

```
When the user clicks the Add Grade Button
    If an average has already been calculated for a set of grades
        Clear the output Label and the ListBox

    Retrieve grade entered by user in the Enter grade: TextBox
    Display the grade in the ListBox
    Clear the Enter grade: TextBox
    Transfer focus to the Enter grade: TextBox

    If the user has entered 10 grades
        Disable the Add Grade Button
        Transfer focus to the Average Button
When the user clicks the Average Button
    Set total to zero
    Set grade counter to zero

    Do
        Read the next grade in the ListBox
        Add the grade to the total
        Add one to the grade counter
    Loop While the grade counter is less than 10

    Calculate the class average by dividing the total by 10
    Display the class average
    Enable the Add Grade Button
    Transfer focus to the Enter grade: TextBox
```

Now that you've test-driven the **Class Average** application and studied its pseudocode representation, you use an ACE table to help you convert the pseudocode to Visual Basic. Figure 10.8 lists the actions, controls and events that will help you complete your own version of this application.

We label the application's GUI, using `Label`s `gradeLabel`, `averageLabel` and `gradeListLabel`. The user enters grades in `gradeTextBox` and clicks the `addButton`. The `Click` event then Adds the value that the user entered in `gradeTextBox` to the `ListBox`, using method `gradesListBox.Items.Add`. When the user has entered 10 grades and clicked `averageButton`, the application retrieves each value from the `ListBox`, adds it to the total and computes the class average by dividing by 10. The class average is then displayed in `averageResultLabel`.

Action/Control/Event Table for the Class Average Application

Action	Control	Event
Label all the application's controls	`gradeLabel`, `gradeListLabel`, `averageLabel`	

Figure 10.8 ACE table for the **Class Average** application. (Part 1 of 2.)

Action	Control	Event
	addButton	Click
If an average has already been calculated for a set of grades	averageResult-Label	
Clear the output Label and the ListBox	averageResult-Label, gradesListBox	
Retrieve grade entered by user in the Enter grade: TextBox	gradeTextBox	
Display the grade in the ListBox	gradesListBox	
Clear the Enter grade: TextBox	gradeTextBox	
Transfer focus to the Enter grade: TextBox	gradeTextBox	
If the user has entered 10 grades	gradesListBox	
Disable the Add Grade Button	addButton	
Transfer focus to the Average Button	averageButton	
	averageButton	Click
Set total to zero		
Set grade counter to zero		
Do		
Read the next grade in the ListBox	gradesListBox	
Add the grade to the total		
Add one to the grade counter		
Loop While the grade counter is less than 10		
Calculate the class average by dividing the total by 10		
Display the class average	averageResult-Label	
Enable the Add Grade Button	addButton	
Transfer focus to the Enter grade: TextBox	gradeTextBox	

Figure 10.8 ACE table for the **Class Average** application. (Part 2 of 2.)

Now that we've formulated an algorithm for solving the **Class Average** problem, we can begin adding functionality to the template application. To display in the **Grade list:** ListBox a grade entered in the **Enter grade:** TextBox, the user clicks the **Add Grade** Button. If the application is already displaying grades in the **Grade list:** ListBox and the class average in the **Class average:** Label, the values are first cleared. The following box guides you through adding this functionality to the **Add Grade** Button's event handler.

Entering Grades in the Class Average Application

1. ***Copying the template to your working directory.*** Copy the C:\Examples\Tutorial10\TemplateApplication\ClassAverage directory to your C:\SimplyVB2008 directory.
2. ***Opening the Class Average application's template file.*** Double click ClassAverage.sln in the ClassAverage directory to open the application in the Visual Basic IDE. Double click ClassAverage.vb in the **Solution Explorer** to display the Form (Fig. 10.9).

(cont.)

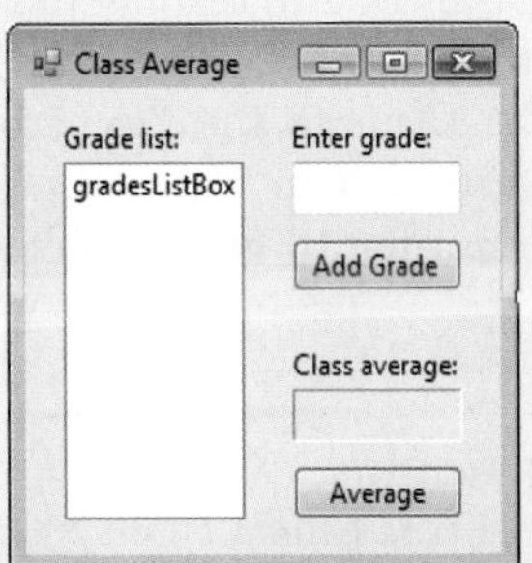

Figure 10.9 Class Average application's `Form` in **Design** view.

3. ***Adding an event handler for the* Add Grade *Button.*** Each time the user enters a grade in the **Class Average** application, they must click the **Add Grade** `Button`. Double click the `Button` labeled **Add Grade** to create event handler `addButton_Click`.

4. ***Clearing the `ListBox` and the* Class average: *`Label` of any output from a previous calculation.*** Add lines 6–10 (Fig. 10.10) to event handler `addButton_Click`. Remember to place a comment before each event handler (line 2), and recall that we use the line-continuation character to split long lines (lines 3–4). To determine whether there was a previous calculation, test whether `averageResultLabel` displays any text by comparing the `Text` property's value to the empty string (line 7). If `averageResultLabel` displays the result of a previous calculation, set its `Text` property to the empty string (line 8). Line 9 clears the grades from the `ListBox`.

Clearing the grade list and class average

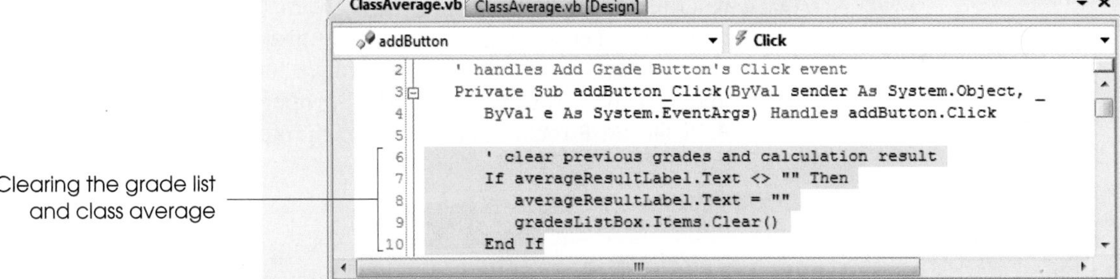

ClassAverage.vb
ClassAverage.vb [Design]
addButton
Click
2 ' handles Add Grade Button's Click event
3 Private Sub addButton_Click(ByVal sender As System.Object, _
4 ByVal e As System.EventArgs) Handles addButton.Click
5
6 ' clear previous grades and calculation result
7 If averageResultLabel.Text <> "" Then
8 averageResultLabel.Text = ""
9 gradesListBox.Items.Clear()
10 End If

Figure 10.10 Clearing the output `Label` and `ListBox` after a calculation.

5. ***Displaying each grade in the `ListBox` control.*** Add lines 12–14 of Fig. 10.11 to event handler `addButton_Click` below the `If...Then` statement. Line 13 Adds the grade entered in `gradeTextBox` to `gradesListBox`'s `Items` property. The grade is displayed in the `ListBox`.

Adding a numeric grade to the `ListBox` and clearing the user input from the `TextBox`

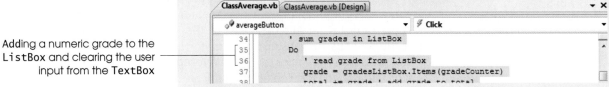

ClassAverage.vb | ClassAverage.vb [Design]

averageButton | Click

```
34      ' sum grades in ListBox
35      Do
36         ' read grade from ListBox
37         grade = gradesListBox.Items(gradeCounter)
```

Figure 10.11 Adding the grade input to the `ListBox` and clearing the **Enter grade:** `TextBox`.

6. ***Preparing for the next grade to be entered.*** Method `Clear` (line 14 of Fig. 10.11) deletes the grade from the `TextBox` to prepare the application for the next grade to be entered. Using this method functions the same as assigning `""` or `String.Empty` to the `TextBox`'s `Text` property.

7. ***Saving the project.*** Select **File > Save All** to save your modified code.

You've added the code to display the grade entered in the **Enter grade:** TextBox in the ListBox when the user clicks the **Add Grade** Button. Next, you learn how to transfer the focus to the TextBox for the next grade entry after the user clicks the **Add Grade** Button. The following box also shows you how to disable the **Add Grade** Button after 10 grades have been entered and its functionality is no longer needed.

Transferring the Focus to a Control and Disabling a Button

1. ***Transferring the focus to a control.*** Add line 15 (Fig. 10.12) to event handler addButton_Click. Line 15 calls gradeTextBox's **Focus** method to place the cursor in the TextBox for the next grade input. This process is called **transferring the focus**. Here the focus is transferred from the Button the user just clicked to the TextBox in which the user will input the next value.

Transferring the focus of the application to the TextBox

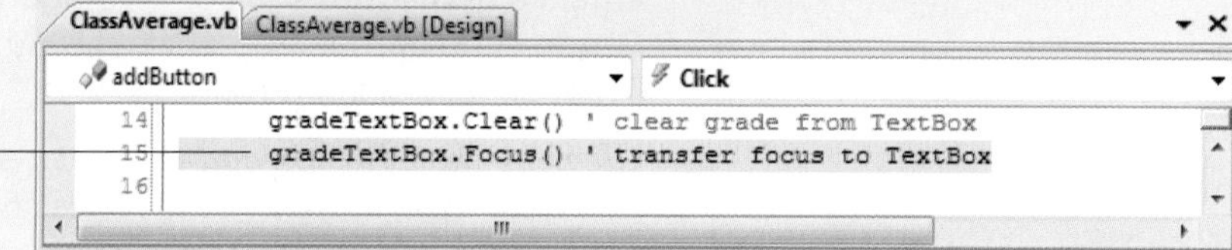

Figure 10.12 Transferring the focus to the TextBox control.

GUI Design Tip

Transfer the focus to the control that should be used next.

GUI Design Tip

Disable Buttons when their function should not be available to users.

2. ***Disabling the Add Grade Button to prohibit users from entering more than 10 grades.*** Your application should accept exactly 10 grades. If the number of grades already entered by the user is equal to 10, then the application should prevent the user from entering more grades. Add lines 17–21 of Fig. 10.13 to event handler addButton_Click. Line 18 determines whether 10 or more grades have been entered, using the >= comparison operator. Items's **Count** property returns the number of items displayed in the **Grade list:** ListBox. If 10 grades have been entered, line 19 disables addButton by setting its **Enabled** property to False. Clicking the disabled **Add Grade** Button will not cause the addButton_Click event handler to execute.

Disabling the **Add grade** Button and transferring the focus to the **Average** Button

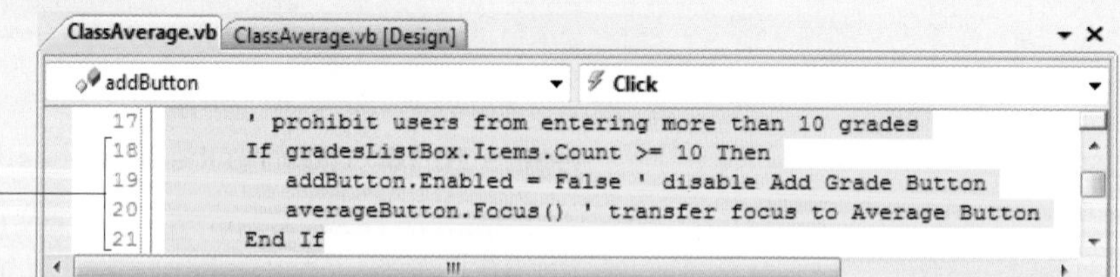

Figure 10.13 Application accepts only 10 grades.

Common Programming Error

A control must be enabled in order to receive focus.

3. ***Transferring the focus to the Average Button after 10 grades have been entered.*** After 10 grades have been entered, it does not make sense for the application to transfer the focus to the TextBox. Instead, line 20 invokes method Focus to transfer the focus to the **Average** Button. This way, you can press *Enter* or *Space* to invoke **Average** Button's event handler, without navigating to the Button or using the mouse pointer.
4. ***Saving the project.*** Select **File > Save All** to save your modified code.

After 10 grades have been entered and displayed in the ListBox, the **Add Grade** Button's event handler transfers the focus to the **Average** Button. When the user clicks the **Average** Button, the application calculates and displays the average of the 10 grades. The following box shows you how to sum the grades with a Do...Loop Until repetition statement before the average calculation. The box also covers displaying the result in the **Class average:** Label.

Calculating the Class Average

1. ***Adding an event handler for the Average* `Button`.** Double click the **Average** `Button` to generate event handler `averageButton_Click`.
2. ***Initializing variables used in the class-average calculation.*** Add lines 28–32 of Fig. 10.14 to event handler `averageButton_Click`. Line 29 declares `Integer` `total`. You use `total` to calculate the sum of the 10 grades (you need this sum later when you calculate the average grade). Line 30 declares the counter (`gradeCounter`). It's important that variables used as totals and counters have appropriate initial values before they are used. If a numerical variable is not initialized before its first use, Visual Basic initializes it to a default value of `0`. However, notice in Fig. 10.14 that all of the variables are manually initialized to `0`. This makes the program clearer. Variable `grade` (line 31) temporarily stores each grade read from the `ListBox`. Although the grades entered are `Integer`s, the result of the averaging calculation can be a floating-point value (such as the `81.10` result in Fig. 10.4); therefore, you declare `Double` variable `average` (line 32) to store the class average.

Initializing variables

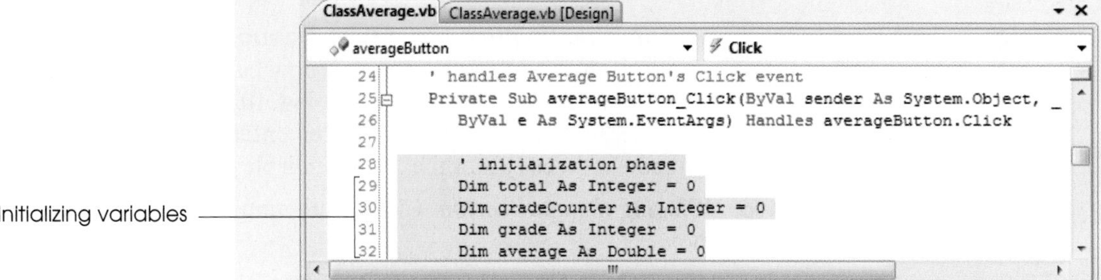

Figure 10.14 Initialization phase of class-average calculation.

3. ***Summing the grades displayed in the* `ListBox`.** Add lines 34–40 of Fig. 10.15 to event handler `averageButton_Click`. The `Do...Loop Until` statement (lines 35–40) sums the grades that it reads from the `ListBox`. Line 40 indicates that the statement should iterate until the value of `gradeCounter` is greater than or equal to `10`. [*Note:* In Exercise 10.12 you modify the application to handle any number of grades.] Line 37 reads the current value from the `ListBox`, using the `ListBox`'s `Items` collection, and stores that value in `grade`. The items in a `ListBox` are accessed by their position number, starting from position number `0`. Line 38 adds `grade` to the previous value of `total` and assigns the result to `total`, using the `+=` assignment operator. Variable `gradeCounter` is incremented (line 39) to indicate that another grade has been processed. (Incrementing the counter ensures that the condition at line 40 eventually becomes `True`, terminating the loop.)

Using the `Do...Loop Until` repetition statement to sum grades in the `ListBox`

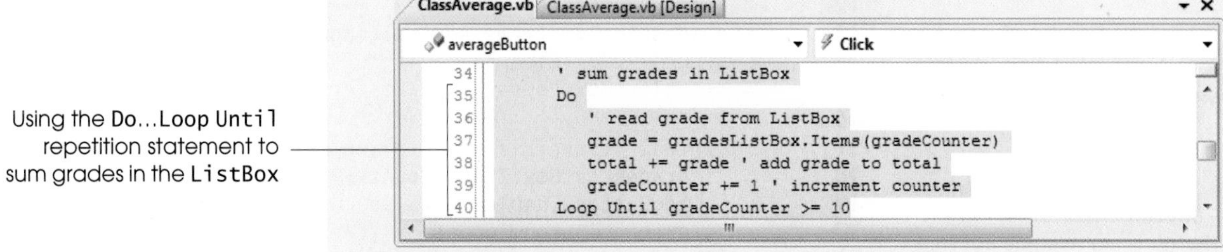

Figure 10.15 `Do...Loop Until` summing grades.

(cont.)

GUI Design Tip

Enable a disabled Button when its function should be available to the user once again.

4. ***Calculating and displaying the average.*** Add lines 42–45 of Fig. 10.16 to event handler averageButton_Click. Line 42 assigns the result of the average calculation to variable average. Line 43 displays the value of variable average. Note the use of the F format specifier to display average in floating-point format. After the average is displayed, another set of 10 grades can be entered. To allow this, you need to enable the **Add Grade** Button by setting property Enabled to True (line 44). Line 45 transfers the focus to the **Enter grade:** TextBox.

Calculating the class average, enabling the **Add Grade** Button and transferring the focus to the **Enter Grade:** TextBox

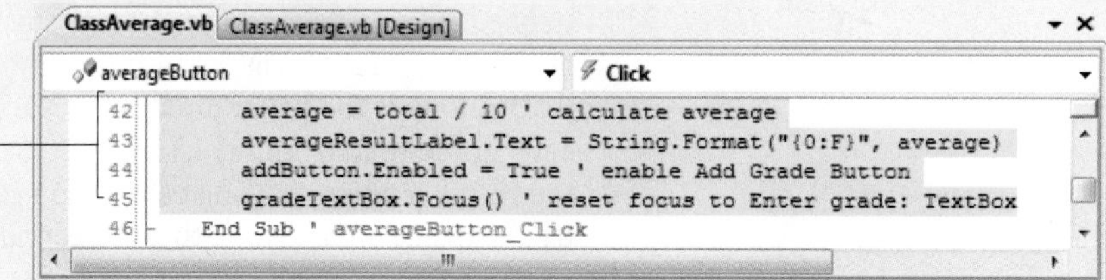

Figure 10.16 Displaying the result of the average calculation.

5. ***Running the application.*** Select **Debug > Start Debugging** to run your application. Your application can now calculate and display the class average. Enter the 10 grades shown in Fig. 10.3 using the **Enter grade:** TextBox and the **Add Grade** Button. After entering 10 grades, click the **Average** Button and verify that the average displayed is correct.

6. ***Closing the application.*** Close your running application by clicking its close box.

7. ***Closing the IDE.*** Close the Visual Basic IDE by clicking its close box.

Figure 10.17 presents the source code for the **Class Average** application. The lines of code that contain new programming concepts you learned in this tutorial are highlighted.

Clearing gradeTextBox

Transferring focus to gradeTextBox

Disabling the **Add Grade** Button and transferring the focus to the **Average** Button

```
Public Class ClassAverageForm
   ' handles Add Grade Button's Click event
   Private Sub addButton_Click(ByVal sender As System.Object, _
      ByVal e As System.EventArgs) Handles addButton.Click

      ' clear previous grades and calculation result
      If averageResultLabel.Text <> "" Then
         averageResultLabel.Text = ""
         gradesListBox.Items.Clear()
      End If

      ' display grade in ListBox
      gradesListBox.Items.Add(Val(inputTextBox.Text))
      gradeTextBox.Clear() ' clear grade from TextBox
      gradeTextBox.Focus() ' transfer focus to TextBox

      ' prohibit users from entering more than 10 grades
      If gradesListBox.Items.Count >= 10 Then
         addButton.Enabled = False ' disable Add Grade Button
         averageButton.Focus() ' transfer focus to Average Button
      End If
   End Sub ' addButton_Click

   ' handles Average Button's Click event
   Private Sub averageButton_Click(ByVal sender As System.Object, _
      ByVal e As System.EventArgs) Handles averageButton.Click
```

Figure 10.17 **Class Average** application code. (Part 1 of 2.)

Accessing a grade in the ListBox via the Items property

Using a Do...Loop Until statement to total all the grades

Enabling the **Add Grade** Button and transferring the focus to the **Enter grade:** TextBox

```
      ' initialization phase
      Dim total As Integer = 0
      Dim gradeCounter As Integer = 0
      Dim grade As Integer = 0
      Dim average As Double = 0

      ' sum grades in ListBox
      Do
         ' read grade from ListBox
         grade = gradesListBox.Items(gradeCounter)
         total += grade ' add grade to total
         gradeCounter += 1 ' increment counter
      Loop Until gradeCounter >= 10

      average = total / 10 ' calculate average
      averageResultLabel.Text = String.Format("{0:F}", average)
      addButton.Enabled = True ' enable Add Grade Button
      gradeTextBox.Focus() ' reset focus to Enter grade: TextBox
   End Sub ' averageButton_Click
End Class ' ClassAverageForm
```

Figure 10.17 **Class Average** application code. (Part 2 of 2.)

1. If you do not want a Button to call its event handler method when the Button is clicked, set property _________ to _________

   a) Enabled, False b) Enabled, True

   c) Disabled, True d) Disabled, False

2. _________ a TextBox selects that TextBox to receive user input.

   a) Enabling b) Clearing

   c) Transferring the focus to d) Disabling

Answers: 1) a. 2) c.

10.5 Wrap-Up

In this tutorial, you learned how to use the Do...Loop While and the Do...Loop Until repetition statements. We provided the syntax and included UML activity diagrams that explained how each statement executes. You used the Do...Loop Until statement in the **Class Average** application that you developed.

The Do...Loop While repetition statement executes as long as its loop-continuation condition is True. This repetition statement always executes at least once. When the loop-continuation condition becomes False, the repetition terminates. This repetition statement enters an infinite loop if the loop-continuation condition never becomes False.

The Do...Loop Until repetition statement also executes at least once. It executes as long as its loop-termination condition is False. When the loop-termination condition becomes True, the repetition terminates. The Do...Loop Until statement enters an infinite loop if the loop-termination condition never becomes True.

You also learned more sophisticated techniques for creating polished graphical user interfaces for your applications. You now know how to invoke method Focus to transfer the focus in an application, indicating that the next action the user takes should involve this control. You also learned how to disable Buttons that should not be available to a user at certain times during an application's execution, and you learned how to enable those Buttons again.

In the next tutorial, you continue studying repetition statements. You learn how to use the For...Next repetition statement, which is particularly useful for counter-controlled repetition.

SKILLS SUMMARY

Do...Loop While Repetition Statement

- Iterates while its loop-continuation condition is True.
- Tests the loop-continuation condition after the loop body is performed.
- Always executes the loop body at least once.
- Becomes an infinite loop if the loop-continuation condition never becomes False.

Do...Loop Until Repetition Statement

- Iterates until its loop-termination condition becomes True.
- Tests the loop-termination condition after the loop body is performed.
- Always executes the loop body at least once.
- Becomes an infinite loop if the loop-termination condition never becomes True.

Disabling a Button

- Set Button property Enabled to False.

Determining the Number of Items in a ListBox

- Use the Count property of the ListBox's Items property.

Enabling a Button

- Set Button property Enabled to True.

Transferring the Focus to a Control

- Call method Focus.

KEY TERMS

Count property of Items—Returns the number of ListBox items.

Do...Loop Until repetition statement—A control statement that executes a set of statements at least once until the loop-termination condition becomes True after the loop executes.

Do...Loop While repetition statement—A control statement that executes a set of statements at least once while the loop-continuation condition is True after the loop executes.

Enabled property—Specifies whether a control such as a Button appears enabled (True) or disabled (False).

Focus method—Transfers the focus of the application to the control on which the method is called.

off-by-one error—The kind of logic error that occurs, for example, when a loop executes for one more or one less iteration than is intended.

transferring the focus—Selecting a control in an application.

GUI DESIGN GUIDELINES

Overall Design

- Transfer the focus to the control that should be used next.

Button

- Disable a Button when its function should not be available to users.
- Enable a disabled Button when its function should once again be available to users.

CONTROLS, EVENTS, PROPERTIES & METHODS

Button Button When clicked, commands the application to perform an action.

- ***In action***

Calculate Total

- ***Event***

Click—Raised when the user clicks the Button.

- ***Properties***

Enabled—Determines whether the Button's event handler executes when the Button is clicked.

`Location`—Specifies the location of the `Button` on the `Form` relative to the `Form`'s top-left corner.

`Name`—Specifies the name used to access the `Button` programmatically. The name should be appended with the `Button` suffix.

`Size`—Specifies the width and height (in pixels) of the `Button`.

`Text`—Specifies the text displayed on the `Button`.

- ***Method***

`Focus`—Transfers the focus of the application to the `Button` that calls it.

`ListBox` ListBox This control allows the user to view and select from items in a list.

- ***In action***

Months	Monthly Payments
24	$490.50
36	$339.06
48	$263.55
60	$218.41

- ***Properties***

`Items`—Returns an object that contains the items displayed in the `ListBox`.

`Items.Count`—Returns the number of items in the `ListBox`.

`Location`—Specifies the location of the `ListBox` on the `Form` relative to the `Form`'s top-left corner.

`Name`—Specifies the name used to access the `ListBox` programmatically. The name should be appended with the `ListBox` suffix.

`Size`—Specifies the width and height (in pixels) of the `ListBox`.

- ***Methods***

`Items.Add`—Adds an item to the `Items` property.

`Items.Clear`—Deletes all the values in the `ListBox`'s `Items` property.

`TextBox` TextBox This control allows the user to input data from the keyboard.

- ***In action***

0

- ***Event***

`TextChanged`—Raised when the text in the `TextBox` is changed.

- ***Properties***

`Location`—Specifies the location of the `TextBox` on the `Form` relative to the `Form`'s top-left corner.

`Name`—Specifies the name used to access the `TextBox` programmatically. The name should be appended with the `TextBox` suffix.

`Size`—Specifies the width and height (in pixels) of the `TextBox`.

`Text`—Specifies the initial text displayed in the `TextBox`.

`TextAlign`—Specifies how the text is aligned within the `TextBox`.

`Width`—Specifies the width (in pixels) of the `TextBox`.

- ***Methods***

`Clear`—Removes the text from the `TextBox` that calls it.

`Focus`—Transfers the focus of the application to the `TextBox` that calls it.

MULTIPLE-CHOICE QUESTIONS

10.1 A(n) ________ occurs when a loop-continuation condition in a `Do...Loop While` never becomes `False`.

a) infinite loop
b) counter-controlled loop
c) control statement
d) nested control statement

10.2 Set property _________ to `True` to enable a `Button`.

a) `Disabled` b) `Focus`
c) `Enabled` d) `ButtonEnabled`

10.3 The _________ statement executes at least once and continues executing until its loop-termination condition becomes `True`.

a) `Do While...Loop` b) `Do...Loop Until`
c) `Do...Loop While` d) `Do Until...Loop`

10.4 The _________ statement executes at least once and continues executing until its loop-continuation condition becomes `False`.

a) `Do...Loop Until` b) `Do Until...Loop`
c) `Do While...Loop` d) `Do...Loop While`

10.5 Method _________ transfers the focus to a control.

a) `GetFocus` b) `Focus`
c) `Transfer` d) `Activate`

10.6 A _________ contains the sum of a series of values.

a) total b) counter
c) condition d) loop

10.7 Property _________ of _________ contains the number of items in a `ListBox`.

a) `Count`, `ListBox` b) `ListCount`, `Items`
c) `ListCount`, `ListBox` d) `Count`, `Items`

10.8 A(n) _________ occurs when a loop executes for one more or one less iteration than is necessary.

a) infinite loop b) counter-controlled loop
c) off-by-one error d) nested control statement

10.9 A `Do...Loop Until` repetition statement's loop-termination condition is evaluated _________.

a) only the first time the body executes b) before the body executes
c) after the body executes d) None of the above

10.10 If its continuation condition is initially `False`, a `Do...Loop While` repetition statement _________.

a) never executes b) executes while the condition is `False`
c) executes until the condition becomes `True` d) executes only once

EXERCISES

10.11 ***(Modified* Class Average *Application)*** Modify the **Class Average** application, as in Fig. 10.18, so that **Average** `Button` is disabled until 10 grades have been entered.

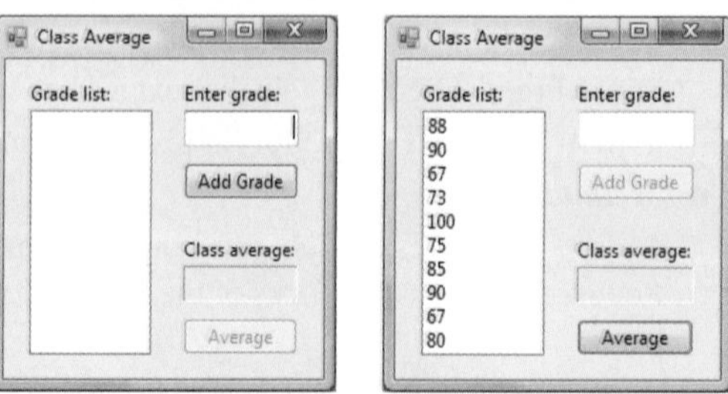

Figure 10.18 Modified **Class Average** application.

a) ***Copying the template to your working directory.*** Copy the directory `C:\Examples\Tutorial10\Exercises\ModifiedClassAverage` to your `C:\SimplyVB2008` directory.

b) ***Opening the application's template file.*** Double click `ClassAverage.sln` in the `ModifiedClassAverage` directory to open the application.

c) ***Initially disabling the Average `Button`.*** Use the **Properties** window to modify the **Average** `Button` in the `Form` so that it is disabled when the application first executes by setting its `Enabled` property to `False`.

d) ***Enabling the Average `Button` after 10 grades have been entered.*** Add code to the `addButton_Click` event handler so that the **Average** `Button` becomes enabled when 10 grades have been entered.

e) ***Disabling the Average `Button` after the calculation has been performed.*** Add code to the `averageButton_Click` event handler so that the **Average** `Button` is disabled once the calculation result has been displayed.

f) ***Running the application.*** Select **Debug > Start Debugging** to run your application. Enter 10 grades and ensure that the **Average** `Button` is disabled until all 10 grades are entered. Verify that the **Add Grade** `Button` is disabled after 10 grades are entered. Once the **Average** `Button` is enabled, click it and verify that the average displayed is correct. The **Average** `Button` should then become disabled again, and the **Add Grade** `Button` should be enabled.

g) ***Closing the application.*** Close your running application by clicking its close box.

h) ***Closing the IDE.*** Close the Visual Basic IDE by clicking its close box.

10.12 *(Class Average Application That Handles Any Number of Grades)* Rewrite the **Class Average** application to handle any number of grades, as in Fig. 10.19. Note that the application does not know how many grades the user will enter, so the `Buttons` must be enabled at all times.

a) ***Copying the template to your working directory.*** Copy the directory `C:\Examples\Tutorial10\Exercises\UndeterminedClassAverage` to your `C:\SimplyVB2008` directory.

b) ***Opening the application's template file.*** Double click `ClassAverage.sln` in the `UndeterminedClassAverage` directory to open the application.

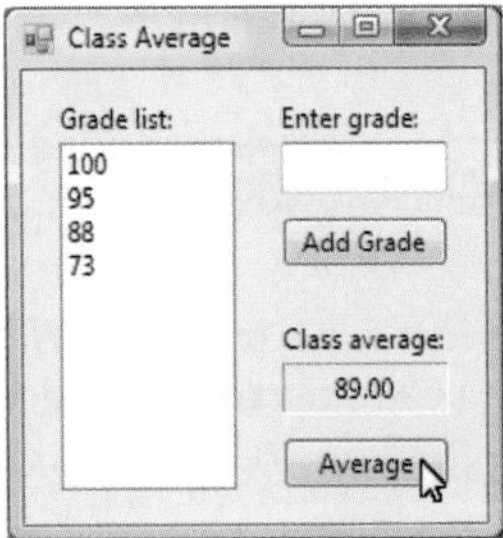

Figure 10.19 Modified **Class Average** application handling an unspecified number of grades.

c) ***Never disabling the Add Grade `Button`.*** Remove code from the `addButton_Click` event handler so that the **Add Grade** `Button` is not disabled after entering 10 grades.

d) ***Summing the grades in the `ListBox`.*** Modify code in the `averageButton_Click` event handler so that `gradeCounter` increments until it's equal to the number of grades entered. Use `gradesListBox.Items.Count` to determine the number of items in the `ListBox`. The number returned by the `Count` property will be zero if there are no grades entered. Use an `If...Then` selection statement to avoid division by zero and display a message dialog to the user if there are no grades entered when the user clicks the **Average** `Button`.

e) ***Calculating the class average.*** Modify the code in the `averageButton_Click` event handler so that `average` is computed by using the actual number of grades rather than the value `10`.

f) ***Running the application.*** Select **Debug > Start Debugging** to run your application. Enter 10 grades and click the **Average** Button. Verify that the average displayed is correct. Follow the same actions but this time for 15 grades, then for 5 grades. Each time, verify that the appropriate average is displayed.

g) ***Closing the application.*** Close your running application by clicking its close box.

h) ***Closing the IDE.*** Close the Visual Basic IDE by clicking its close box.

10.13 ***(Arithmetic Calculator Application)*** Write an application that allows the user to enter a series of numbers and manipulate them. The application should provide users with the option of adding or multiplying the numbers. Users should enter each number in a TextBox. After entering each number, the user clicks a Button, and the number is inserted in a ListBox. The GUI should behave as in Fig. 10.20.

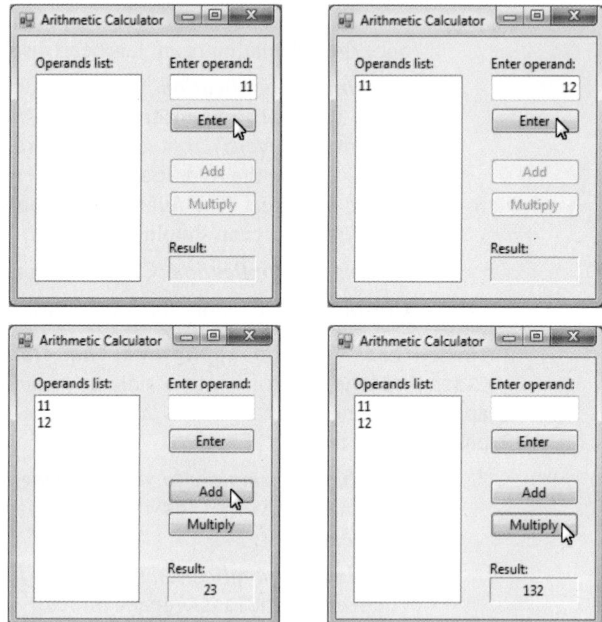

Figure 10.20 **Arithmetic Calculator** application.

a) ***Copying the template to your working directory.*** Copy the directory C:\Examples\Tutorial10\Exercises\ArithmeticCalculator to your C:\SimplyVB2008 directory.

b) ***Opening the application's template file.*** Double click ArithmeticCalculator.sln in the ArithmeticCalculator directory to open the application.

c) ***Adding a ListBox to display the entered numbers.*** Add a ListBox. Place and size it as in Fig. 10.20.

d) ***Creating an event handler for the Enter Button.*** Create the Click event handler for the **Enter** Button. If the result of a previous calculation is displayed, this event handler should clear the result, clear the ListBox and disable the addition and multiplication Buttons. It should then insert the current number in the **Operands list:** ListBox. When the ListBox contains at least two numbers, the event handler should then enable the addition and multiplication Buttons.

e) ***Summing the values in the ListBox.*** Define the Click event handler for the **Add** Button. This event handler should compute the sum of all the values in the **Operands list:** ListBox and display the result in resultLabel.

f) ***Multiplying the values in the ListBox.*** Define the Click event handler for the **Multiply** Button. This event handler should compute the product of all the values in the **Operands list:** ListBox and display the result in resultLabel.

g) ***Running the application.*** Select **Debug > Start Debugging** to run your application. Enter two values, then click the **Add** and **Multiply** Buttons. Verify that the results displayed are correct. Also, make sure that the **Add** and **Multiply** Buttons are not enabled until two values have been entered. Enter a new value and verify that the previous result and the ListBox is cleared. Enter two more values, then click the **Add** and **Multiply** Buttons. Verify that the results displayed are correct.

h) ***Closing the application.*** Close your running application by clicking its close box.

i) ***Closing the IDE.*** Close the Visual Basic IDE by clicking its close box.

What does this code do?

10.14 What is the result of the following code?

```
Dim y As Integer
Dim x As Integer
Dim mysteryValue As Integer

x = 1
mysteryValue = 0

Do
   y = x ^ 2
   displayListBox.Items.Add(y)
   mysteryValue += 1
   x += 1
Loop While x <= 10

resultLabel.Text = mysteryValue
```

What's wrong with this code?

10.15 Find the error(s) in the following code. This code should add 10 to the value in y and store it in z. It then should reduce the value of y by one and repeat until y is less than 10. Last, resultLabel should display the final value of z.

```
Dim y As Integer = 10
Dim z As Integer = 2

Do
   z = y + 10
Loop Until y < 10

y -= 1

resultLabel.Text = z
```

Using the Debugger

10.16 ***(Factorial Application)*** The **Factorial** application calculates the factorial of an integer input by the user. The factorial of an integer is the product of the integers from one to that number. For example, the factorial of 3 is 6 (1 × 2 × 3). Copy the **Factorial** application from C:\Examples\Tutorial10\Exercises\Factorial to your working directory. While testing the application, you noticed that it did not execute correctly. Use the debugger to find and correct the logic error(s) in the application. Figure 10.21 displays the correct output for the **Factorial** application.

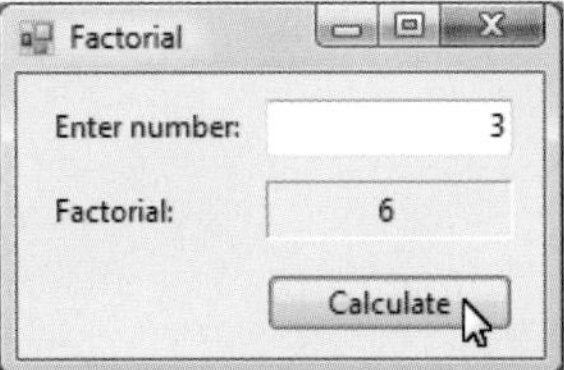

Figure 10.21 Correct output for the **Factorial** application.

Programming Challenge

10.17 ***(Restaurant Bill Application)*** Develop an application that calculates a restaurant bill. The user should be able to enter the item ordered, the quantity of the item ordered and the price per item. When the user clicks the **Add Item** Button, your application should display the number ordered, the item ordered and the price per unit in three ListBoxes, as shown in Fig. 10.22. When the user clicks the **Total Bill** Button, the application should calculate the total cost. For each entry in the ListBox, multiply the cost of each item by the number of items ordered.

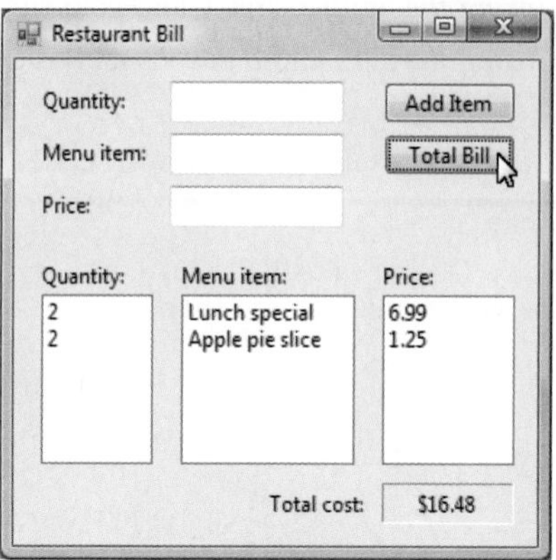

Figure 10.22 **Restaurant Bill** application's Form.

T U T O R I A L 11

Interest Calculator Application

Introducing the For...Next Repetition Statement and NumericUpDown Control

Objectives

In this tutorial, you learn to:

- Execute statements repeatedly with the `For...Next` repetition statement.
- Obtain user input with the `NumericUpDown` control.
- Display information, using a multiline `TextBox`.
- Use type `String`.

Outline

As you learned in Tutorials 9 and 10, applications are often required to repeat actions. Using a `Do` repetition statement allowed you to specify a condition and test it either before entering the loop or after executing the body of the loop. In the **Car Payment Calculator** application and the **Class Average** application, a counter was used to determine the number of times the loop should iterate. In fact, the use of counters in repetition statements is so common in applications that Visual Basic provides an additional control statement specially designed for such cases—the `For...Next` repetition statement. In this tutorial, you use the `For...Next` repetition statement to create an **Interest Calculator** application.

11.1 Test-Driving the Interest Calculator Application

The **Interest Calculator** application calculates the amount of money in your savings account. You begin with a certain amount of money and are paid interest for a period of time. Users specify the principal amount (the initial amount of money in the account), the interest rate and the number of years for which interest will be calculated. The application then displays the results. This application must meet the following requirements:

Application Requirements

You are considering investing $1,000.00 in a savings account that yields 5% interest compounded annually, and you want to forecast how your investment will grow. Assuming that you leave all interest on deposit, calculate and display the amount of money in the account at the end of each year over a period of n *years. To compute these amounts, use the following formula:*

$$a = p(1 + r)^n$$

where

p is the original amount of money invested (the principal)
r is the annual interest rate (for example, .05 is equivalent to 5%)
n is the number of years
a is the amount on deposit at the end of the *n*th year.

You begin by test-driving the completed application. Then you learn the additional Visual Basic capabilities needed to create your own version of this application.

Test-Driving the Interest Calculator Application

1. ***Opening the completed application.*** Open the directory `C:\Examples\Tutorial11\CompletedApplication\InterestCalculator` to locate the **Interest Calculator** application. Double click `InterestCalculator.sln` to open the application in the Visual Basic IDE.

2. ***Running the Interest Calculator application.*** Select **Debug > Start Debugging** to run the application (Fig. 11.1).

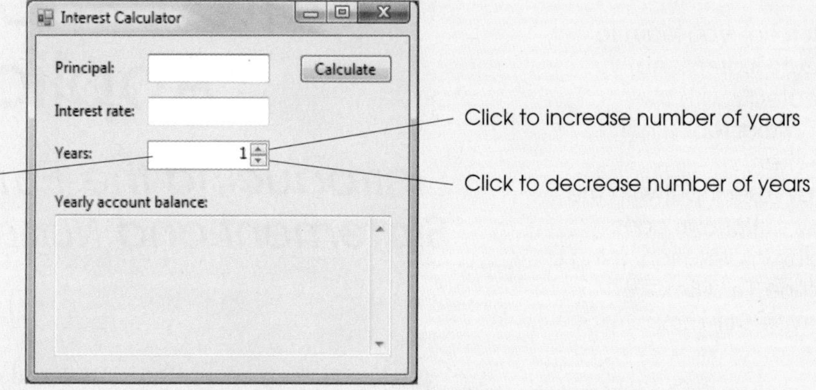

Figure 11.1 Completed **Interest Calculator** application.

3. ***Providing a principal value.*** Once the application is running, provide a value in the **Principal:** `TextBox`. Input `1000`, as specified in the problem statement.

4. ***Providing an interest-rate value.*** Next, type a value in the **Interest Rate:** `TextBox`. We specified the interest rate 5% in the problem statement, so enter 5 in the **Interest Rate:** `TextBox`.

5. ***Providing the duration of the investment.*** Now, choose the number of years for which you want to calculate the amount in the savings account. In this case, select `10` by entering it using the keyboard or by clicking the up arrow in the **Years:** `NumericUpDown` control repeatedly until the value reads `10`.

6. ***Calculating the amount.*** After you input the necessary information, click the **Calculate** `Button`. The amount of money in your account at the end of each year during a period of `10` years displays in the multiline `TextBox`. The application should look similar to Fig. 11.2.

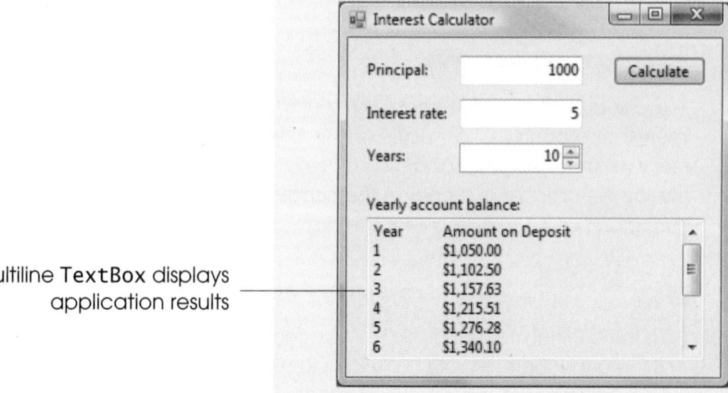

Figure 11.2 Output of completed **Interest Calculator** application.

(cont.)

7. ***Closing the application.*** Close your running application by clicking its close box.
8. ***Closing the IDE.*** Close the Visual Basic IDE by clicking its close box.

11.2 Essentials of Counter-Controlled Repetition

In Tutorials 9 and 10, you learned how to use counter-controlled repetition. The four essential elements of counter-controlled repetition are:

1. the *name* of a *control variable* (or loop counter) that is used to determine whether the loop continues to iterate
2. the *initial value* of the control variable
3. the *increment* (or *decrement*) by which the control variable is modified during each iteration of the loop (that is, each time the loop is performed)
4. the *condition* that tests for the *final value* of the control variable (to determine whether looping should continue).

The example in Fig. 11.3 uses the four elements of counter-controlled repetition. This `Do While...Loop` statement is similar to the **Car Payment Calculator** application's loop in Tutorial 9.

```
1  Dim years As Integer = 2 ' control variable
2
3  Do While years <= 5
4     months = 12 * years ' calculate payment period
5
6     ' calculate payment value
7     monthlyPayment = _
8        (monthlyInterest, months, -loanAmount)
9
10    ' display payment value
11    paymentsListBox.Items.Add(months & ControlChars.Tab & _
12       ControlChars.Tab & String.Format("{0:C}", monthlyPayment))
13
14    years += 1 ' increment counter
15 Loop
```

Figure 11.3 Counter-controlled repetition example.

Recall that the **Car Payment Calculator** application calculates and displays monthly car payments over periods of two to five years. The declaration in line 1 *names* the control variable (`years`), indicating that it is of data type `Integer`. This declaration includes an initialization, which sets the variable to an *initial value* of `2`.

Consider the `Do While...Loop` statement (lines 3–15). Line 4 uses the `years` variable to calculate the number of months over which car payments are to be made. Lines 7–8 use the `Pmt` function to determine the monthly payment for the car. This value depends on the interest rate, the duration of the loan in months, the car's price, and the down-payment amount. Lines 11–12 display the amount in a `ListBox`. Line 14 increments the control variable `years` by `1` for each iteration of the loop. The condition in the `Do While...Loop` statement (line 3) tests whether the value of the control variable is less than or equal to `5`, meaning that `5` is the *final value* for which the condition is true. The body of this `Do While...Loop` is performed even when the control variable is `5`. The loop terminates when the control variable exceeds `5` (that is, when `years` has a value of `6`).

SELF-REVIEW

1. Counter-controlled repetition ________ the control variable after each iteration.
   a) increments b) initializes
   c) decrements d) Either a or c

2. What aspect of the control variable determines whether looping should continue?
   a) name b) initial value
   c) type d) final value

Answers: 1) d. 2) d.

11.3 Introducing the For...Next Repetition Statement

The **For...Next** repetition statement makes it easier for you to write code to perform counter-controlled repetition. This statement specifies all four elements essential to counter-controlled repetition. The For...Next statement takes less time to code and is easier to read than an equivalent Do repetition statement.

Let's examine the first line of the For...Next repetition statement (Fig. 11.4), which we call the **For...Next header**. The For...Next header specifies all four essential elements for counter-controlled repetition. The line should be read *"for the values of* counter *starting at 2 and ending at 10, do the following statements, then add (step) two to* counter*."*

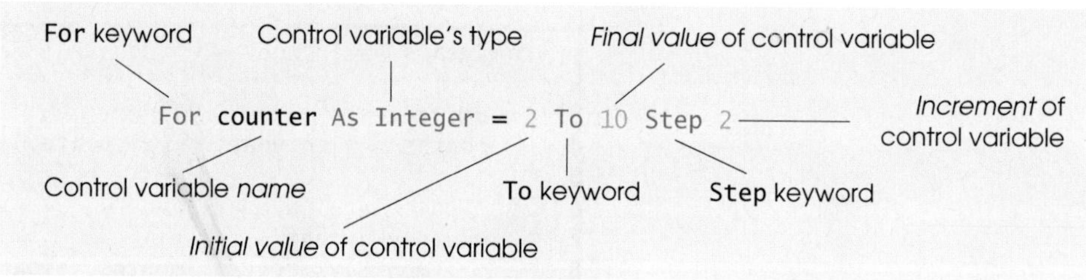

Figure 11.4 For...Next header components.

A For...Next statement such as

```
For counter As Integer = 2 To 10 Step 2
   body statement(s)
Next
```

begins with the keyword **For**. Then the statement declares and initializes a control variable (in this case, Integer control variable counter is declared and set to 2). Note that you do not use the Dim keyword to declare the control variable in a For...Next header. Following the initial value of the control variable is the keyword **To**, followed by the final value of the control variable. You can then use the **Step** keyword to specify the amount by which to increase (or decrease) the control variable each time the loop body completes execution. If you wish to decrease the value of the control variable each time through the loop, simply use a negative number after the Step keyword. When using a negative Step value, the final value must be less than the starting value—otherwise the loop body does not execute. The Step keyword is optional. If you omit the Step keyword, the control variable increments by one after each repetition, by default.

The body of a For...Next statement is placed after the For...Next header. The keyword **Next** marks the end of the For...Next repetition statement, much as the keyword Loop marks the end of a Do While...Loop statement. Optionally, you can include the name of the control variable to the right of the Next keyword (e.g., Next counter). Some programmers like to do this to help make the program clearer, especially in nested For...Next statements. When you declare the control variable in the For...Next statement's header (as we did above), the control vari-

Common Programming Error

Attempting to access the control variable in code after the loop results in a compilation error, because the variable no longer exists.

able exists only until the loop terminates execution. The following box describes each step as the above repetition statement executes.

Executing the For...Next Repetition Statement

1. The application declares variable `counter` and sets its value to 2.
2. The loop-continuation condition is checked. The condition evaluates to `True` (`counter` is 2, which is less than or equal to 10), so the application executes the body of the `For...Next` repetition statement.
3. The value of `counter` is increased by 2; `counter` now contains 4.
4. The loop-continuation condition is checked. The condition evaluates to `True` (`counter` is 4, which is less than or equal to 10), so the application executes the body of the `For...Next` repetition statement.
5. The value of `counter` is increased by 2; `counter` now contains 6.
6. The loop-continuation condition is checked. The condition evaluates to `True` (`counter` is 6, which is less than or equal to 10), so the application executes the body of the `For...Next` repetition statement.
7. The value of `counter` is increased by 2; `counter` now contains 8.
8. The loop-continuation condition is checked. The condition evaluates to `True` (`counter` is 8, which is less than or equal to 10), so the application executes the body of the `For...Next` repetition statement.
9. The value of `counter` is increased by 2; `counter` now contains 10.
10. The loop-continuation condition is checked. The condition evaluates to `True` (`counter` is 10, which is less than or equal to 10), so the application executes the body of the `For...Next` repetition statement.
11. The value of `counter` is increased by 2; `counter` now contains 12.
12. The loop-continuation condition is checked. The condition evaluates to `False` (`counter` is 12, which is not less than or equal to 10), so the application exits the `For...Next` repetition statement.

The `For...Next` statement can be represented by other repetition statements. For example, an equivalent `Do While...Loop` statement for Fig. 11.4 is

```
counter = 2

Do While counter <= 10
   body statement(s)
   counter += 2
Loop
```

Note that the `For...Next` statement's header (Fig. 11.4) implies the loop-continuation condition (`counter <= 10`), which is shown explicitly in the preceding `Do While...Loop` statement. The starting value, ending value and increment portions of a `For...Next` header can contain arithmetic expressions. The expressions are evaluated once (when the `For...Next` statement begins executing) and then used as the starting value, ending value and increment of the `For...Next` header. For example, assume that `a = 2` and `b = 10`. The header

```
For i As Integer = a To (4 * a * b) Step (b \ a)
```

is equivalent to the header

```
For i As Integer = 2 To 80 Step 5
```

If the implied loop-continuation condition is initially `False` (for example, if the starting value is greater than the ending value and the increment value is positive), the For...Next statement's body is not performed. Instead, execution proceeds with the statement after the For...Next statement.

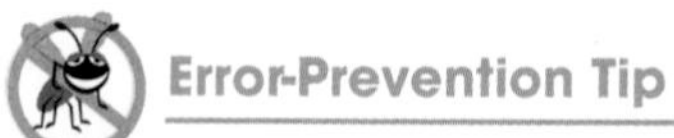

Error-Prevention Tip

Although the value of the control variable can be changed in the body of a For...Next loop, avoid doing so, because this practice can lead to subtle errors.

The control variable frequently is displayed or used in calculations in the For...Next body, but it does not have to be. It is common to use the control variable only to control repetition and not use it in the For...Next body.

The UML activity diagram for the For...Next statement is similar to that of the Do While...Loop statement. For example, the UML activity diagram of the For...Next statement

```
For counter As Integer = 1 To 10
   displayListBox.Items.Add(counter * 10)
Next
```

is shown in Fig. 11.5. This activity diagram shows that the initialization occurs only once and that incrementing occurs *after* each execution of the body statement. Note that, besides small circles and transition arrows, the activity diagram contains only action states, merge symbols and decision symbols.

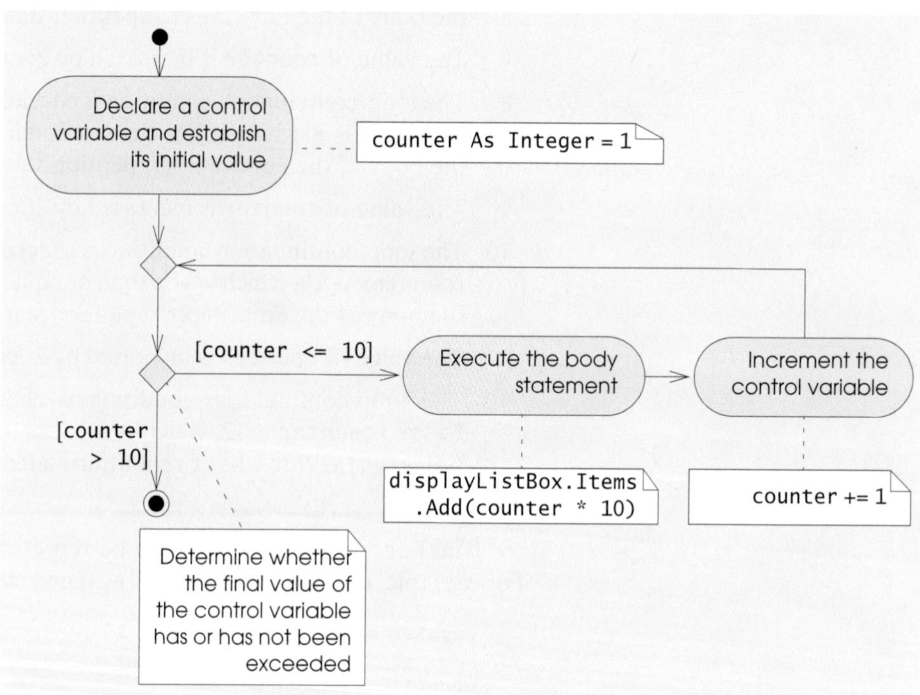

Figure 11.5 For...Next repetition statement UML activity diagram.

Good Programming Practice

Vertical spacing above and below control statements, as well as indentation of the bodies of control statements, enhances readability.

The For...Next header indicates each item needed to conduct counter-controlled repetition with a control variable. To help solidify your understanding of this new repetition statement, let's consider how the Do While...Loop statement of Fig. 11.3 can be replaced by a For...Next statement.

The converted code is shown in Fig. 11.6. When the For...Next statement begins execution, line 1 of Fig. 11.6 declares Integer control variable years and initializes it to 2.

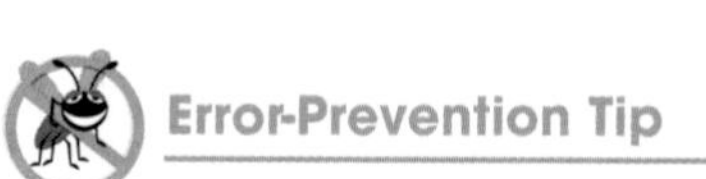

Error-Prevention Tip

If you use a For...Next loop for counter-controlled repetition, off-by-one errors (which occur when a loop executes for one more or one less iteration than is necessary) are normally avoided, because the terminating value is clear.

The implied loop-continuation condition years <= 5 (which depends on the control variable's final value) is tested in line 1. Keyword To is required in the For...Next statement. The value before this keyword specifies the initial value of years; the value that follows it specifies the value tested for loop continuation (in this case, 5). Keyword Step is optional and is not used here. Step specifies the increment (the amount that is added to years each time the For...Next body is executed). If Step is not included, then the increment is 1, by default.

Common Programming Error

Counter-controlled loops should not be controlled with floating-point variables. These are represented only approximately in the computer's memory, possibly resulting in imprecise counter values and inaccurate tests for termination that could lead to logic errors.

```
1  For years As Integer = 2 To 5
2     months = 12 * years ' calculate payment period
3
4     ' calculate payment value
5     value = Pmt(monthlyRate, months, -loanAmount)
6
7     ' display payment value
8     paymentsListBox.Items.Add(months & ControlChars.Tab & _
9        ControlChars.Tab & String.Format("{0:C}", value))
10 Next
```

Figure 11.6 Code segment for the **Car Payment Calculator** application that demonstrates the `For...Next` statement.

The initial value of `years` is 2, so the implied loop-continuation condition is satisfied and the payment calculations within the `For...Next` body are executed.

After execution of the `For...Next` body, the `Next` keyword is reached (line 10). This keyword marks the end of the `For...Next` repetition statement. When `Next` is reached, `years` is incremented by `1` (the default increment amount), and the loop begins again with the implied loop-continuation condition test.

This process repeats until the implied loop-continuation condition becomes `False` as `years` becomes greater than `5`, then repetition terminates.

Local Type Inference

In each `For...Next` statement presented so far, we declared and initialized the control variable in the `For...Next` statement's header. The Visual Basic 2008 compiler provides a new feature—called **local type inference**—that enables it to infer a local variable's type based on the context in which the variable is initialized. A local variable is any variable declared in the body of a method (such as an event handler). For example, in the declaration

```
Dim x = 7
```

the compiler infers that the variable x should be of type `Integer`, because the compiler assumes that whole-number values, like 7, are of type `Integer`. Similarly, in the declaration

```
Dim y = -123.45
```

the compiler infers that the variable y should be of type `Double`, because the compiler assumes that floating-point number values, like `-123.45`, are of type `Double`.

You can also use local type inference with control variables in the header of a `For...Next` statement. For example, in Fig. 11.6, line 1 could be written as

```
For years = 2 To 5
```

In this case, `years` is of type `Integer` because it is initialized with a whole-number value (2). We prefer to explicitly declare the type of a variable in our examples.

The local type inference feature is one of several new Visual Basic 2008 features that support Language Integrated Query (LINQ). We'll use local type inference when we present LINQ examples in Tutorials 20, 21, 23, 24, 30 and 32.

SELF-REVIEW

1. If the `Step` clause is omitted, the increment of a `For...Next` statement defaults to ______.

   a) `2`   b) `1`
   c) `0`   d) `-1`

2. The value before the `To` keyword in a `For...Next` statement specifies the _________.

   a) initial value of the counter variable   b) final value of the counter variable
   c) increment   d) number of times the statement iterates

Answers: 1) b. 2) a.

11.4 Examples Using the For...Next Statement

The following examples demonstrate different ways of varying the control variable in a For...Next statement. In each case, we write the appropriate For...Next header:

a) Vary the control variable from 1 to 100 in increments of 1.

```
For i As Integer = 1 To 100
```
or
```
For i As Integer = 1 To 100 Step 1
```

b) Vary the control variable from 100 to 1 in increments of -1 (decrements of 1).

```
For i As Integer = 100 To 1 Step -1
```

c) Vary the control variable from 7 to 77 in increments of 7.

```
For i As Integer = 7 To 77 Step 7
```

d) Vary the control variable from 20 to -20 in increments of -2 (decrements of 2).

```
For i As Integer = 20 To -20 Step -2
```

e) Vary the control variable over the sequence of the following values: 2, 5, 8, 11, 14, 17, 20.

```
For i As Integer = 2 To 20 Step 3
```

f) Vary the control variable over the sequence of the following values: 99, 88, 77, 66, 55, 44, 33, 22, 11, 0.

```
For i As Integer = 99 To 0 Step -11
```

SELF-REVIEW

1. Which of the following is the appropriate For...Next header for varying the control variable over the following sequence of values: 25, 20, 15, 10, 5?

   a) For i As Integer = 5 To 25 Step 5
   b) For i As Integer = 25 To 5 Step -5
   c) For i As Integer = 5 To 25 Step -5
   d) For i As Integer = 25 To 5 Step 5

2. Which of the following statements describes the For...Next header

   ```
   For i As Integer = 81 To 102
   ```

   a) Vary the control variable from 81 to 102 in increments of 1.
   b) Vary the control variable from 81 to 102 in increments of 0.
   c) Vary the control variable from 102 to 81 in increments of -1.
   d) Vary the control variable from 81 to 102 in increments of 2.

Answers: 1) b. 2) a.

11.5 Constructing the Interest Calculator Application

Our solution to this tutorial's problem statement computes interest over a given number of years by using the For...Next statement. This repetition statement performs the calculation for every year that the money remains on deposit.

The following pseudocode describes the basic operation of the **Interest Calculator** application when the **Calculate** Button is clicked:

```
When the user clicks the Calculate Button
    Get the values for the principal, interest rate and years entered by the user
    Store a header String to be added to the output TextBox

    For each year (starting at 1 and ending with the number of years entered)
        Calculate the current value of the investment
        Append the year and the current value of the investment to the String
            that will be displayed in the output TextBox
Display the final output in the output TextBox
```

The template application we provide for this tutorial contains the **Calculate** `Button` plus two `Label`s and their corresponding `TextBox`es: for **Principal:** and for **Interest Rate:**. The `Form` has a **Years:** `Label`, but you insert the `NumericUpDown` control for this input. The **`NumericUpDown`** control limits a user's choices for the number of years to a specific range. You then create a multiline `TextBox` with a scrollbar and add it to the application's GUI. Finally, you add functionality with a `For...Next` statement. Now that you've test-driven the **Interest Calculator** application and studied its pseudocode representation, you use an ACE table to help you convert the pseudocode to Visual Basic. Figure 11.7 lists the actions, controls and events that help you complete your own version of this application.

Action/Control/Event (ACE) Table for the Interest Calculator Application

Action	Control	Event
Label the application's controls	`principalLabel`, `rateLabel`, `yearsLabel`, `yearlyAccount-Label`	Application is run
	`calculateButton`	`Click`
Get the values for the principal, interest rate and years entered by user	`principalText-Box`, `rateTextBox`, `yearUpDown`	
Store a header to be added to the output TextBox		
For each year (starting at 1 and ending with the number of years entered) Calculate the current value of the investment		
Append the year and the current value of the investment to the String that will be displayed in the output TextBox		
Display the final output in the output TextBox	`resultTextBox`	

Figure 11.7 ACE table for **Interest Calculator** application.

In the following box, you begin building the **Interest Calculator** application. First, you add a `NumericUpDown` control to allow the user to specify the number of years. This control provides up and down arrows that allow the user to scroll through the control's range of values. The box shows you how to set the limits of the range (maximum and minimum values). We use `10` as the maximum value and `1` as the minimum value for this control. The **`Increment`** property specifies by how much the current number in the `NumericUpDown` control changes when the user clicks the control's up (for incrementing) or down (for decrementing) arrow. This application uses the `Increment` property's default value, 1.

Adding and Customizing a `NumericUpDown` Control

1. ***Copying the template to your working directory.*** Copy the `C:\Examples\Tutorial11\TemplateApplication\InterestCalculator` directory to your `C:\SimplyVB2008` directory.
2. ***Opening the* Interest Calculator *application's template file.*** Double click `InterestCalculator.sln` in the `InterestCalculator` directory to open the application in the Visual Basic IDE (Fig. 11.8). Double click the `InterestCalculator.vb` file in the **Solution Explorer** if the `Form` is not already visible.

(cont.)

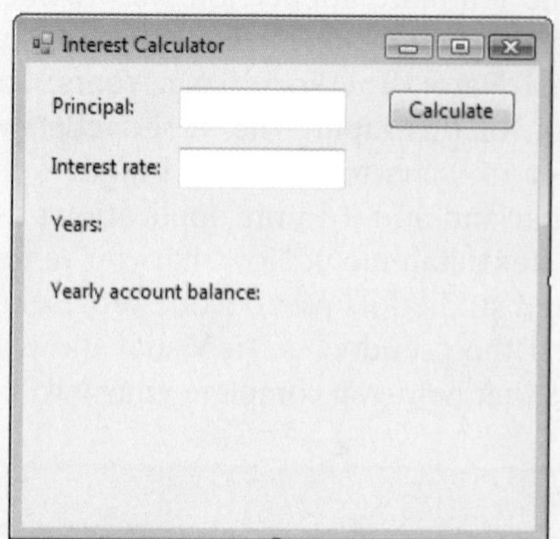

Figure 11.8 The **Interest Calculator** application in **Design** view.

3. ***Adding a NumericUpDown control.*** Double click NumericUpDown

   NumericUpDown

   in the **Toolbox** to add it to the Form. Change the control's Name property to yearUpDown. To improve code readability, append the UpDown suffix to NumericUpDown control names.

4. ***Setting the NumericUpDown control's location and size.*** Set yearUpDown's Location property to 91, 82 and its Width property to 100 so that it aligns horizontally and vertically with the TextBoxes above it.

5. ***Setting property TextAlign.*** Set property TextAlign to Right. The number now appears right aligned in the control.

Append the UpDown suffix to NumericUpDown control names.

Use a NumericUpDown control to limit the range of user input.

A NumericUpDown control should follow the same GUI Design Guidelines as a TextBox. (See Appendix C.)

6. ***Setting range limits for the NumericUpDown control.*** By default, this control sets 0 as the minimum and 100 as the maximum. To change these values, set the **Maximum** property of the **Years:** NumericUpDown control to 10. Then set its **Minimum** property to 1. This limits users to selecting values between 1 and 10 for the number of years. If the user inputs a value less than Minimum or greater than Maximum, the value is automatically set to the minimum or maximum value, respectively, when the control loses focus. Note that the NumericUpDown control displays 1, the value of its Minimum property. Your Form should now look like Fig. 11.9.

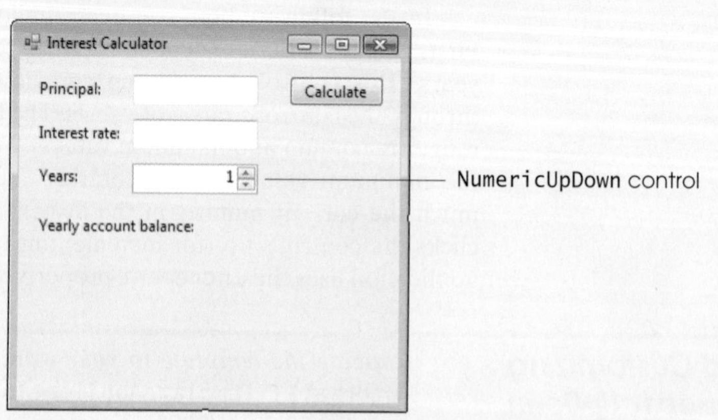

Figure 11.9 NumericUpDown control added to **Interest Calculator** application.

7. ***Saving the project.*** Select **File > Save All** to save your modified code.

The **Interest Calculator** application displays the results of its calculations in a multiline TextBox, which is simply a TextBox that can display more than one line of text. You can configure the TextBox to have a scrollbar, so that, if the TextBox is too small to display its contents, the user can scroll up and down to view the entire contents of the box. Next, you'll create this TextBox.

Adding and Customizing a Multiline TextBox with a Scrollbar

1. ***Adding a TextBox to the Form.*** Double click the TextBox control in the **Toolbox** to add a TextBox to the Form. Name the TextBox resultTextBox.
2. ***Creating a multiline TextBox.*** Select the TextBox's **Multiline** property, and change its value from False to True. Doing so allows the TextBox to contain multiple lines.
3. ***Setting the size and location of the TextBox.*** Set the TextBox's Location property to 16, 140 and the Size property to 274, 111, so that it aligns horizontally with the controls above it.
4. ***Setting property ReadOnly.*** To ensure that the user cannot change the output in the **Yearly account balance:** TextBox, set the **ReadOnly** property to True.
5. ***Inserting a vertical scrollbar.*** Using scrollbars allows you to keep the size of a TextBox small while still allowing the user to view all the information in that TextBox. The length of the text could exceed the height of the TextBox, so enable the vertical scrollbar by setting resultTextBox's **ScrollBars** property to **Vertical**. A vertical scrollbar appears on the right side of the TextBox. By default, property ScrollBars is set to **None**. You can also set property ScrollBars to **Horizontal** or **Both**. A horizontal scrollbar appears at the bottom of the TextBox. The value Both indicates that horizontal and vertical scrollbars should be displayed—the horizontal scroll bar is only displayed if the text exceeds the width of the TextBox. Note that, even without scrollbars, the user can scroll through the text by using the arrow keys. The scrollbar is initially disabled on your Form. A scrollbar is enabled only when it is needed (that is, when there is too much text in the TextBox). Your Form should look like Fig. 11.10.

GUI Design Tip

If a TextBox will display multiple lines of output, set the Multiline property to True and left align the output by setting the TextAlign property to Left.

GUI Design Tip

If a TextBox is used to display output, set the ReadOnly property to True to ensure that the user cannot change the output.

GUI Design Tip

If a multiline TextBox will display many lines of output, limit the TextBox height and use a vertical scrollbar to allow users to view additional lines of output.

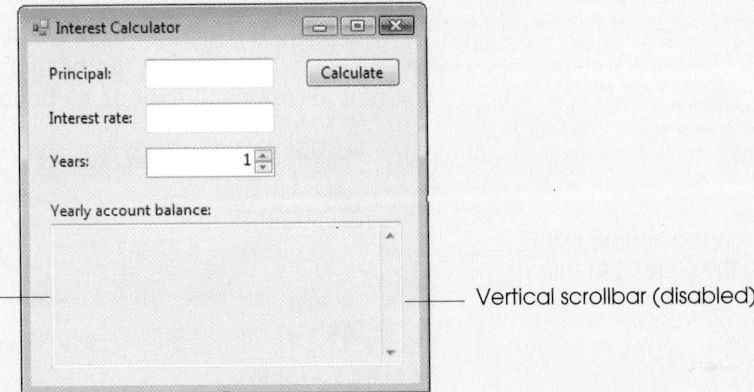

Figure 11.10 Multiline TextBox with vertical scrollbar added to the Form.

6. ***Saving the project.*** Select **File > Save All** to save your modified code.

Now that you've finished designing the GUI, you'll add functionality to your application. When the user clicks the **Calculate** Button, you want the application to retrieve the input, then output a table containing the amount on deposit at the end of each year. You do this by adding code to the Button's Click event handler.

Adding a Click Event Handler

1. ***Creating the event handler.*** Double click the **Calculate** Button. The **Calculate** Button Click event handler appears in the application's code.

2. ***Adding code to event handler calculateButton_Click.*** Add lines 6–14 of Fig. 11.11 to the calculateButton_Click event handler. Lines 7–10 declare the variables needed to store user inputs, calculation results and the output. Variable principal stores the amount of the principal as entered by the user and rate stores the interest rate. Variable amount stores the result of the interest calculation.

   Line 10 declares a String variable output. String variables store a series of characters. The most commonly used characters are letters and numbers, although there are also many special characters, such as $, *, ^, tabs and newlines. A list of characters you are likely to use is found in Appendix B. You actually have been using Strings all along—Labels and TextBoxes both store values in the Text property as values of type String. In fact, when you assign a numeric data type, such as an Integer, to the Text property of a Label, the Integer value is implicitly converted to a String. Lines 13–14 retrieve the principal and the interest rate from TextBoxes.

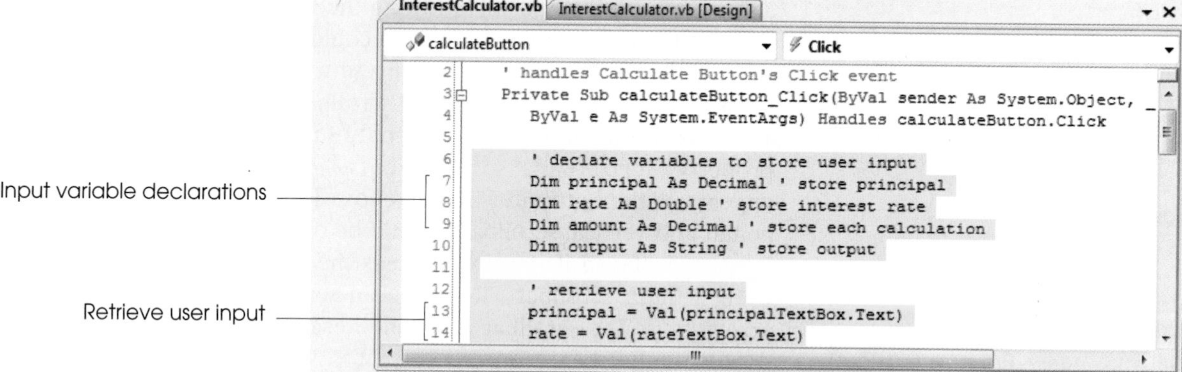

Figure 11.11 Application code for retrieving and storing user input.

The multiline TextBox displays the results in two columns. Add lines 16–18 of Fig. 11.12 to assign the header to output. The header labels the two columns as Year and Amount on Deposit, respectively.

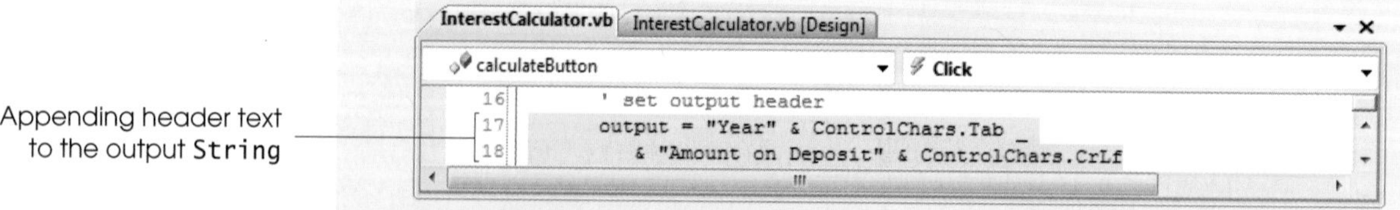

Figure 11.12 Application code for appending the header text to the String variable.

Recall that you cleared values in a Label in Tutorial 6 by setting the Text property to the empty string (""), which represents a String value with no characters. When assigning new text to a String variable, you must begin and end the text with a double quotation mark ("). The opening and closing double quotation marks must appear on the same line; otherwise, a syntax error occurs. For example, if you wanted to store the word Year in the String variable year, you would use the following statement:

```
year = "Year"
```

(cont.)

You can append a `String` or a character to the end of another `String` by using the concatenation operator (&). In lines 17–18 of Fig. 11.12, you use the `ControlChars.Tab` constant to insert a tab character between the word `Year` and the text `Amount on Deposit`. You then insert a newline character (`ControlChars.CrLf`), so that the next series of text will appear in the next line of output.

3. ***Saving the project.*** Select **File > Save All** to save your modified code.

The `For...Next` statement in lines 21–26 of Fig. 11.13 performs the interest calculations for the specified number of years. You create the `For...Next` statement in the next box.

Calculating Cumulative Interest with a For...Next Statement

Good Programming Practice

Place a blank line before and after each control statement to make it stand out in the code.

1. ***Declaring and initializing the control variable and establishing the loop-continuation test.*** Add lines 20–26 of Fig. 11.13 to the `calculateButton_Click` event handler. Note that the keyword `Next` appears once you press *Enter* at the end of line 21.

   Line 21 is the `For...Next` header which declares the control variable `yearCounter` and initializes it to `1`. The value after the keyword `To` sets the implied loop-continuation condition. This loop continues while the control variable is less than or equal to the number of years specified by the user.

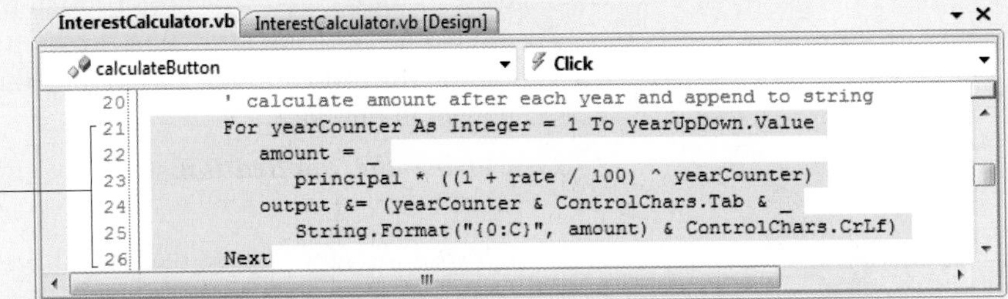
InterestCalculator.vb
InterestCalculator.vb [Design]
calculateButton
Click
20 ' calculate amount after each year and append to string
21 For yearCounter As Integer = 1 To yearUpDown.Value
22 amount = _
23 principal * ((1 + rate / 100) ^ yearCounter)
24 output &= (yearCounter & ControlChars.Tab & _
25 String.Format("{0:C}", amount) & ControlChars.CrLf)
26 Next
Using the For...Next statement to format and append text to the output String

Figure 11.13 Application code for the `For...Next` statement.

2. ***Performing the interest calculation.*** The `For...Next` statement executes its body once for each year up to the value of `yearUpDown`'s **`Value`** property, which contains the number of years selected by the user. The control variable `yearCounter` increases from `1` to `yearUpDown.Value` in increments of 1. Add lines 22–23 of Fig. 11.13 to perform the calculation from the formula

   $$a = p(1 + r)^n$$

   where *a* is `amount`, *p* is `principal`, *r* is `rate` and *n* is `yearCounter`. Note that the calculation in line 23 also divides `rate` by `100`. This implies that the user must enter an interest-rate value in percentage format (for example, the user should enter the number `5.5` to represent 5.5%).

3. ***Appending the calculation to the output string.*** Add lines 24–25 of Fig. 11.13. These lines append additional text to the end of `output`, using the **&= operator**. The &= operator (which behaves much like the += operator) appends the right operand to the text in the left operand. This new value is then assigned to the variable in the left operand. The text includes the current `yearCounter` value, a tab character (`ControlChars.Tab`) to position to the second column, the result of the call `String.Format("{0:C}", amount)` and, finally, a newline character (`ControlChars.CrLf`) to start the next output on the next line. Recall that the `C` (for "currency") formatting code indicates that its corresponding argument (`amount`) should be displayed in monetary format.

(cont.)

4. ***Reaching the Next keyword.*** After the body of the loop is performed, application execution reaches keyword Next, which is now in line 26. The counter (yearCounter) is incremented by 1, and the loop begins again with the implied loop-continuation test.

5. ***Terminating the For...Next statement.*** The For...Next statement executes until the control variable exceeds the number of years specified by the user.

6. ***Displaying the result of the calculations.*** After exiting the For...Next statement, output is ready to be displayed to the user in resultTextBox. Add line 28 of Fig. 11.14 to display the header and the results in the multiline TextBox.

Displaying in the multiline TextBox the result of the calculations performed in the For...Next statement

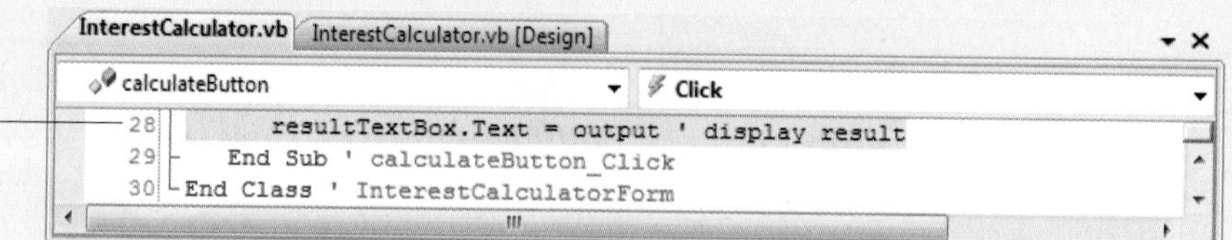
InterestCalculator.vb
InterestCalculator.vb [Design]
calculateButton
Click
28 resultTextBox.Text = output ' display result
29 End Sub ' calculateButton_Click
30 End Class ' InterestCalculatorForm

Figure 11.14 Application code for displaying calculation results.

7. ***Running the application.*** Select **Debug > Start Debugging** to run your application. Your application can now calculate and display the amount on deposit for each year. Enter 1000 in the **Principal:** TextBox, 5 in the **Interest Rate:** TextBox and 10 in the **Years:** NumericUpDown control. Click the **Calculate** Button and verify that the results are the same as those displayed in Fig. 11.2.

8. ***Closing the application.*** Close your running application by clicking its close box.

9. ***Closing the IDE.*** Close the Visual Basic IDE by clicking its close box.

Figure 11.15 presents the source code for the **Interest Calculator** application. The lines of code that contain new programming concepts you learned in this tutorial are highlighted.

Use the Value property of yearUpDown

Declare a variable of type String

Construct a header for the TextBox as a String

```
Public Class InterestCalculatorForm
  ' handles Calculate Button's Click event
  Private Sub calculateButton_Click(ByVal sender As System.Object, _
     ByVal e As System.EventArgs) Handles calculateButton.Click

     ' declare variables to store user input
     Dim principal As Decimal ' store principal
     Dim rate As Double ' store interest rate
     Dim amount As Decimal ' store each calculation
     Dim output As String ' store output

     ' retrieve user input
     principal = Val(principalTextBox.Text)
     rate = Val(rateTextBox.Text)

     ' set output header
     output = "Year" & ControlChars.Tab _
        & "Amount on Deposit" & ControlChars.CrLf

```

Figure 11.15 **Interest Calculator** application. (Part 1 of 2.)

Loop from 1 to the value specified by the user in the `yearUpDown` control

Append result of calculation to the `String` named `output`

Display results in `resultTextBox`

```
      ' calculate amount after each year and append to string
      For yearCounter = 1 To yearUpDown.Value
         amount = _
            principal * ((1 + rate / 100) ^ yearCounter)
         output &= (yearCounter & ControlChars.Tab & _
            String.Format("{0:C}", amount) & ControlChars.CrLf)
      Next

      resultTextBox.Text = output ' display result
   End Sub ' calculateButton_Click
End Class ' InterestCalculatorForm
```

Figure 11.15 **Interest Calculator** application. (Part 2 of 2.)

SELF-REVIEW

1. The __________ property determines by how much the current number in a `NumericUpDown` control changes when the user clicks the up arrow or the down arrow.

   a) `Amount` b) `Step`
   c) `Increment` d) `Next`

2. Which `For...Next` header alters the control variable from `1` to `50` in increments of 5?

   a) `For i = 1 To 50 Step 50` b) `For 1 To 50 Step 5`
   c) `For i = 1 To 50 Step = 5` d) `For i = 1 To 50 Step 5`

Answers: 1) c. 2) d.

11.6 Wrap-Up

In this tutorial, you learned that the essential elements of counter-controlled repetition are the name of a control variable, the initial value of the control variable, the increment (or decrement) by which the control variable is modified each time through the loop and the condition that tests the value of the control variable. We then explored the `For...Next` repetition statement, which combines these essentials of counter-controlled repetition in its header.

After becoming familiar with the `For...Next` repetition statement, you changed the **Car Payment Calculator** application's `Do While...Loop` statement into a `For...Next` statement. You then built an **Interest Calculator** after analyzing the pseudocode and the ACE table for this application. In the **Interest Calculator**'s GUI, you added new design elements, including a `NumericUpDown` control, useful for handling numeric input, and a multiline `TextBox` that contained a scrollbar.

In the next tutorial, you learn to use the `Select Case` multiple-selection statement. You've learned that the `If...Then...Else` selection statement can be used in code to select between multiple courses of action on the value of a condition. The `Select Case` multiple-selection statement can save development time and improve code readability if the number of conditions is large. You'll use a `Select Case` multiple-selection statement to build a **Security Panel** application.

SKILLS SUMMARY

Using the For...Next Repetition Statement

- Declare a control variable and specify its initial value before keyword `To`.
- Specify the value tested for loop continuation after keyword `To`.
- Use optional keyword `Step` to specify the increment (or decrement).
- Use keyword `Next` to mark the end of the repetition statement.
- Use the `For...Next` statement to help eliminate off-by-one errors.

Creating a Multiline TextBox with a Vertical Scrollbar

- Insert a `TextBox` onto the `Form`.
- Set `TextBox` property `Multiline` to `True`.
- Set `TextBox` property `ScrollBar` to `Vertical`.

Specifying a NumericUpDown Control's Maximum Value

- Use NumericUpDown property Maximum.

Specifying a NumericUpDown Control's Minimum Value

- Use NumericUpDown property Minimum.

Changing the Current Number in a NumericUpDown Control

- Click the NumericUpDown control's up or down arrow or type a new value.

Specifying by How Much the Current Number in a NumericUpDown Control Changes When the User Clicks an Arrow

- Use NumericUpDown property Increment.

Obtaining the Value of a NumericUpDown Control

- Use NumericUpDown property Value.

KEY TERMS

&= operator—Modifies the String on its left side by appending the value on its right side to the end of the String.

For...Next header—The first line of a For...Next repetition statement. The For...Next header specifies all four essential elements for counter-controlled repetition.

For...Next repetition statement—Repetition statement that handles the details of counter-controlled repetition. The For...Next statement uses all four elements essential to counter-controlled repetition in one line of code (the name of a control variable, the initial value, the increment or decrement value and the final value).

For keyword—Begins the For...Next statement.

Horizontal value of ScrollBars property—Used to display a horizontal scrollbar on the bottom of a TextBox.

Increment property of a NumericUpDown control—Specifies by how much the current number in the NumericUpDown control changes when the user clicks the control's up (for incrementing) or down (for decrementing) arrow.

local type inference—Visual Basic 2008 compiler feature that enables it to infer a local variable's type based on the context in which the variable is initialized.

Maximum property of a NumericUpDown control—Determines the maximum input value in a particular NumericUpDown control.

Minimum property of a NumericUpDown control—Determines the minimum input value in a particular NumericUpDown control.

Multiline property of a TextBox control—Specifies whether the TextBox is capable of displaying multiple lines of text. If the property value is True, the TextBox may contain multiple lines of text; if the value of the property is False, the TextBox can contain only one line of text.

None value of ScrollBars property—Used to display no scrollbars on a TextBox.

NumericUpDown control—Allows you to specify maximum and minimum numeric input values. Also allows you to specify an increment (or decrement) when the user clicks the up (or down) arrow.

ReadOnly property of a TextBox control—Determines whether the user can change the value of a TextBox.

ScrollBars property of a TextBox control—Specifies whether a TextBox has a scrollbar and, if so, of what type. By default, property ScrollBars is set to None.

Step keyword—Optional component of the For...Next header that specifies the increment or decrement (that is, the amount added to or subtracted from the control variable each time the loop is executed).

String data type—Stores a series of characters.

To keyword—Used to specify a range of values. Commonly used in For...Next headers to specify the initial and final values of the statement's control variable.

Vertical value of ScrollBars property—Used to display a vertical scrollbar on the right side of a TextBox.

GUI DESIGN GUIDELINES

TextBox

- If a TextBox will display multiple lines of output, set the Multiline property to True and left align the output by setting the TextAlign property to Left.
- If a TextBox is used to display output, set the ReadOnly property to True to ensure that the user cannot change the output.
- If a multiline TextBox will display many lines of output, limit the TextBox height and use a vertical scrollbar to allow users to view additional lines of output.

NumericUpDown

- A NumericUpDown control should follow the same GUI Design Guidelines as a TextBox.
- Use a NumericUpDown control to limit the range of numeric user input.

CONTROLS, EVENTS, PROPERTIES & METHODS

NumericUpDown NumericUpDown This control allows you to specify maximum and minimum numeric input values.

- ***In action***

- ***Properties***

Increment—Specifies by how much the current number in the NumericUpDown control changes when the user clicks the control's up (for incrementing) or down (for decrementing) arrow.

Location—Specifies the location of the NumericUpDown control on the Form relative to the Form's top-left corner.

Maximum—Determines the maximum input value in a particular NumericUpDown control.

Minimum—Determines the minimum input value in a particular NumericUpDown control.

Name—Specifies the name used to access the NumericUpDown control programmatically. The name should be appended with the UpDown suffix.

Size—Specifies the width and height (in pixels) of the NumericUpDown control.

TextAlign—Specifies how the text is aligned within the NumericUpDown control.

Value—Specifies the value in the NumericUpDown control.

Width—Specifies the width (in pixels) of the NumericUpDown.

TextBox abl TextBox This control allows the user to input data from the keyboard.

- ***In action***

- ***Event***

TextChanged—Raised when the text in the TextBox is changed.

- ***Properties***

Location—Specifies the location of the TextBox on the Form relative to the Form's top-left corner.

Multiline—Specifies whether the TextBox is capable of displaying multiple lines of text.

Name—Specifies the name used to access the TextBox programmatically. The name should be appended with the TextBox suffix.

ReadOnly—Determines whether the value of a TextBox can be changed by the user.

ScrollBars—Specifies whether the multiline TextBox contains a vertical and/or horizontal scrollbar.

Size—Specifies the width and height (in pixels) of the TextBox.

Text—Specifies the text displayed in the TextBox.

TextAlign—Specifies how the text is aligned within the TextBox.

Width—Specifies the width (in pixels) of the TextBox.

- ***Methods***

  Clear—Removes the text from the TextBox that calls it.

  Focus—Transfers the focus of the application to the TextBox that calls it.

MULTIPLE-CHOICE QUESTIONS

11.1 "Hello" has data type ________.

a) String
b) StringLiteral
c) Character
d) StringText

11.2 A ________ provides the ability to enter or display multiple lines of text in the same control.

a) TextBox
b) NumericUpDown
c) MultilineTextBox
d) multiline NumericUpDown

11.3 The For...Next header specifies ________.

a) the control variable and its initial value
b) the increment or decrement
c) the loop-continuation condition
d) all four essentials of counter controlled repetition

11.4 ________ is optional in a For...Next header when the control variable's increment is 1.

a) Keyword To
b) The initial value of the control variable
c) Keyword Step
d) The final value of the control variable

11.5 Setting TextBox property ScrollBars to ________ creates only a vertical scrollbar.

a) True
b) Vertical
c) Up
d) Both

11.6 ________ is used to determine whether a For...Next loop continues to iterate.

a) The initial value of the control variable
b) Keyword For
c) Keyword Step
d) The final value of the control variable

11.7 In a For...Next loop, the control variable is incremented (or decremented) ________.

a) after the body of the loop executes
b) when keyword To is reached
c) while the loop-continuation condition is False
d) while the body of the loop executes

11.8 Setting a NumericUpDown control's ________ properties ensures that the user cannot enter invalid values in the control.

a) Increment and Locked
b) ScrollBars and ReadOnly
c) Minimum and Maximum
d) ReadOnly and InValid

11.9 The ________ and ________ properties limit the values users can select in the NumericUpDown control.

a) Maximum, Minimum
b) Top, Bottom
c) High, Low
d) Max, Min

11.10 The For...Next header ________ can be used to vary the control variable over the odd numbers in the range 1–9.

a) For i As Integer = 1 To 10 Step 1
b) For i As Integer = 1 To 10 Step 2
c) For i As Integer = 1 To 10 Step -1
d) For i As Integer = 1 To 10 Step -2

EXERCISES

11.11 ***(Present Value Calculator Application)*** A bank wants to show its customers how much they would need to invest now (i.e., the "present value") to achieve a specified financial goal (i.e., the "future value") in 5, 10, 15, 20, 25 or 30 years. Users must provide their financial goal (the amount of money desired after the specified number of years have elapsed), an interest rate and the length of the investment in years. Create an application that calculates and displays the principal (initial amount to invest) needed to achieve the user's financial goal. Your application should allow the user to invest money for 5, 10, 15, 20, 25 or 30 years. For example, a customer who wants to reach the financial goal of $15,000 over a period of 5 years when the interest rate is 6.6% will need to invest $10,896.96, as shown in Fig. 11.16. Use the &= operator and a `For...Next` loop to accomplish this.

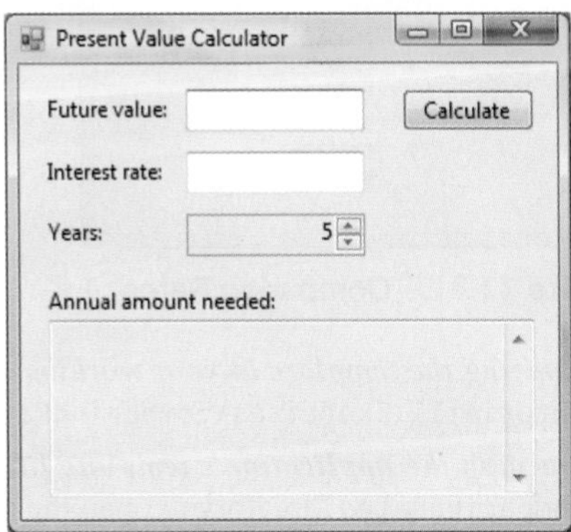

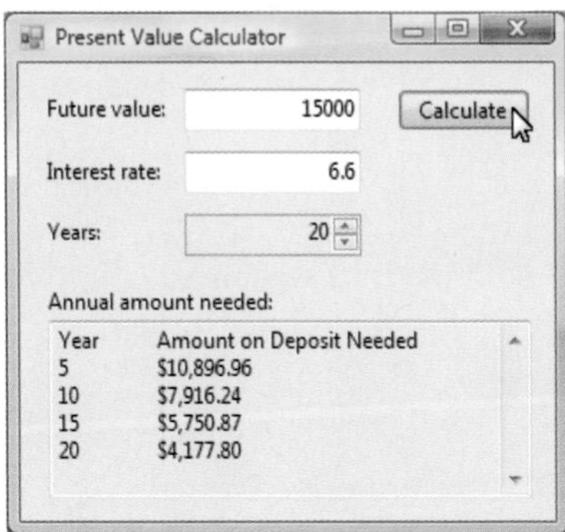

Figure 11.16 **Present Value Calculator** GUI.

a) ***Copying the template to your working directory.*** Copy the directory `C:\Examples\Tutorial11\Exercises\PresentValue` to your `C:\SimplyVB2008` directory.

b) ***Opening the application's template file.*** Double click `PresentValue.sln` in the `PresentValue` directory to open the application.

c) ***Adding the `NumericUpDown` control.*** Place and size the `NumericUpDown` control so that it follows the GUI Design Guidelines. Set the `NumericUpDown` control's `Name` property to `yearUpDown`. Set the `NumericUpDown` control to increment the number of years by 5. To allow the user to select only a duration that is in the specified range of values, set the `yearUpDown` control's `ReadOnly` property to `True`. This forces the user to select a value using the `yearUpDown` control's up and down arrows, which select values in intervals of 5.

d) ***Adding a multiline `TextBox`.*** Add a `TextBox` to the `Form` below the `NumericUpDown` control and set its `Name` property to `resultTextBox`. Set the `TextBox` to display multiple lines and a vertical scrollbar. Resize and position the `TextBox` on the `Form` so that it follows the GUI Design Guidelines. Ensure that the user cannot modify the text in the `TextBox`.

e) ***Adding a `Click` event handler and adding code.*** Add a `Click` event handler for the **Calculate** `Button`. Once in **Code** view, add code to the application such that, when the **Calculate** `Button` is clicked, the multiline `TextBox` displays the necessary principal for each five-year interval. Use the following version of the present-value calculation formula:

$$p = a / (1 + r)^n$$

where

p is the amount needed to achieve the future value
a is the future-value amount
r is the annual interest rate (for example, .05 is equivalent to 5%)
n is the number of years.

f) ***Running the application.*** Select **Debug > Start Debugging** to run your application. Enter amounts for the future value, interest rate and number of years. Click the **Calculate** `Button` and verify that the year intervals and the amount on deposit needed for each are correct. Test the application again, this time entering `30` for the number of years. Verify that the vertical scrollbar appears to display all of the output.

g) ***Closing the application.*** Close your running application by clicking its close box.

h) ***Closing the IDE.*** Close the Visual Basic IDE by clicking its close box.

11.12 *(**Compound Interest: Comparing Rates** Application)* Write an application that calculates the amount of money in an account after 10 years for interest-rate amounts of 5–10%. For this application, users must provide the initial principal.

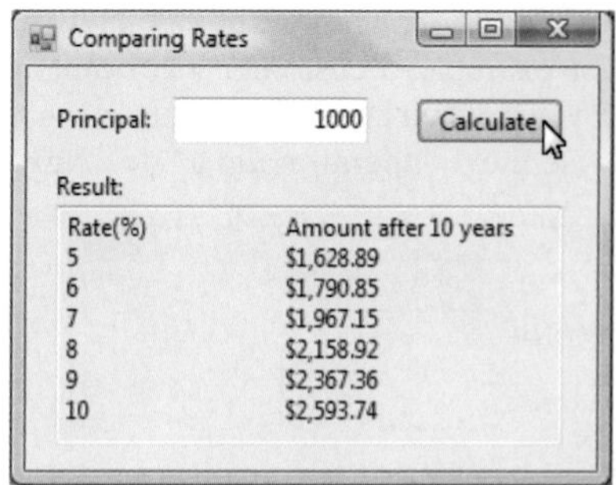

Figure 11.17 **Comparing Rates** GUI.

a) ***Copying the template to your working directory.*** Copy the directory `C:\Examples\Tutorial11\Exercises\ComparingRates` to your `C:\SimplyVB2008` directory.

b) ***Opening the application's template file.*** Double click `ComparingRates.sln` in the `ComparingRates` directory to open the application.

c) ***Adding a multiline `TextBox`.*** Add a `TextBox` to the `Form` below the **Result:** `Label`. Set the `TextBox` to display multiple lines. Resize and position the `TextBox` on the `Form` so that it follows the GUI Design Guidelines (Fig. 11.17). Ensure that the user cannot modify the text in the `TextBox`.

d) ***Adding a `Click` event handler and adding code.*** Add a `Click` event handler for the **Calculate** `Button`. Once in **Code** view, add code to the application such that, when the **Calculate** `Button` is clicked, the multiline `TextBox` displays the amount in the account after 10 years for interest rates of 5, 6, 7, 8, 9 and 10%. Use the following version of the interest-calculation formula:

$$a = p\,(1 + r)^{n}$$

where

a is the investment's value at the end of the nth year
p is the original amount invested (the principal)
r is the annual interest rate (for example, .05 is equivalent to 5%)
n is the number of years.

e) ***Running the application.*** Select **Debug > Start Debugging** to run your application. Enter the principal amount for an account and click the **Calculate** `Button`. Verify that the correct amounts after 10 years are displayed, based on interest-rate amounts of 5–10%.

f) ***Closing the application.*** Close your running application by clicking its close box.

g) ***Closing the IDE.*** Close the Visual Basic IDE by clicking its close box.

11.13 *(Validating Input to the **Interest Calculator** Application)* Enhance the **Interest Calculator** application with error checking. Test whether the user has entered valid values for the principal and interest rate. If the user enters an invalid value, display a message in the multiline `TextBox`. Figure 11.18 demonstrates the application handling an invalid input.

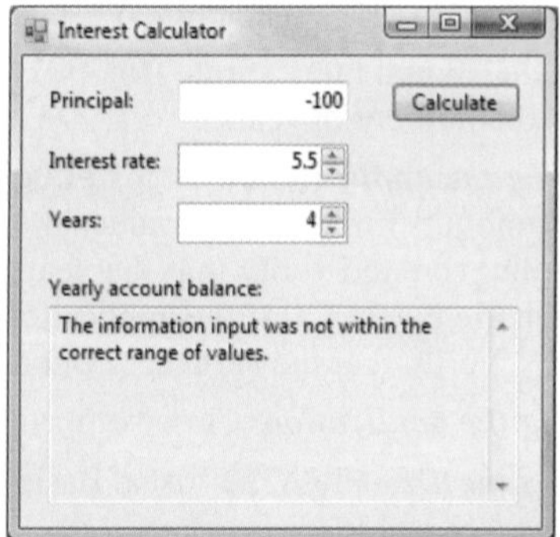

Figure 11.18 **Interest Calculator** application with error checking.

a) ***Copying the template to your working directory.*** Copy the directory `C:\Examples\Tutorial11\Exercises\InterestCalculatorEnhancement` to your `C:\SimplyVB2008` directory.

b) ***Opening the application's template file.*** Double click `InterestCalculator.sln` in the `InterestCalculatorEnhancement` directory to open the application.

c) ***Adding a `NumericUpDown` control.*** Replace the **Interest rate:** `TextBox` with a `NumericUpDown` control. Allow the user to enter values in the range of `0` to `100` only. Set the `DecimalPlaces` property to `1`. This allows users to specify a value with up to one decimal place. Set the `Interval` to `0.1`.

d) ***Modifying the `Click` event handler.*** Modify the code in the **Calculate** `Button`'s `Click` event handler to validate the input. The principal must be a positive amount. Also, retrieve the interest rate from the **Interest rate:** `NumericUpDown`.

e) ***Displaying the error message.*** Display the text `"The information input was not within the correct range of values."` in `resultTextBox` if the principal value is not valid.

f) ***Running the application.*** Select **Debug > Start Debugging** to run your application. Enter invalid data for the principal and interest rate. The invalid data for the interest rate is automatically adjusted to be within the minimum and maximum values allowed by the `NumericUpDown` control. The invalid data for the principal can include negative numbers or values that start with letters. Verify that entering invalid data for the principal and clicking the **Calculate** `Button` results in the error message displayed in Fig. 11.18.

g) ***Closing the application.*** Close your running application by clicking its close box.

h) ***Closing the IDE.*** Close the Visual Basic IDE by clicking its close box.

What does this code do? ▶

11.14 What is the value of `result` after the following code executes? Assume that `power`, `result` and `number` are all declared as `Integers`.

```
power = 5
number = 10
result = number

For i As Integer = 1 To (power - 1)
   result *= number
Next
```

What's wrong with this code? ▶

11.15 Identify and correct the error(s) in each of the following:

a) This statement should display in a `ListBox` all numbers from 100 to 1 in descending order.

```
For counter As Integer = 100 To 1
   displayListBox.Items.Add(counter)
Next
```

b) The following code should display in a `ListBox` the odd `Integers` from `19` to `1` in descending order.

```
For counter As Integer = 19 To 1 By -1
   displayListBox.Add(counter)
Next
```

Using the Debugger ▶

11.16 *(**Savings Calculator** Application)* The **Savings Calculator** application calculates the amount that the user will have on deposit after one year. The application gets the initial amount on deposit from the user, and assumes that the user will add $100 to the account every month for the entire year. No interest is added to the account. While testing the application, you noticed that the amount calculated by the application was incorrect. Use the debugger to locate and correct any logic error(s). Figure 11.19 displays the correct output for this application.

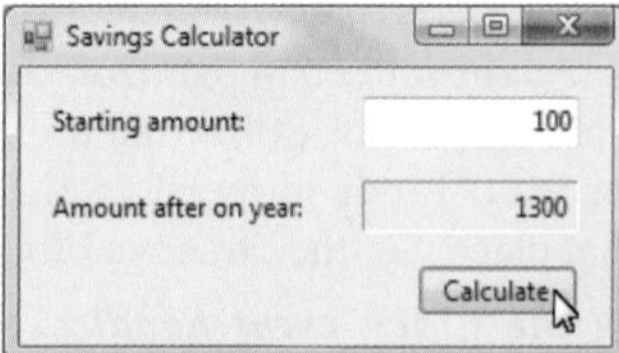

Figure 11.19 Correct output for the **Savings Calculator** application.

Programming Challenge

11.17 ***(Pay Raise Calculator Application)*** Develop an application that computes the amount of money an employee makes each year over a user-specified number of years. The employee receives an hourly wage and a pay raise once every year. For simplicity, assume that employees work 40 hours a week, 52 weeks a year. The user specifies the hourly wage and the amount of the raise (in percent per year).

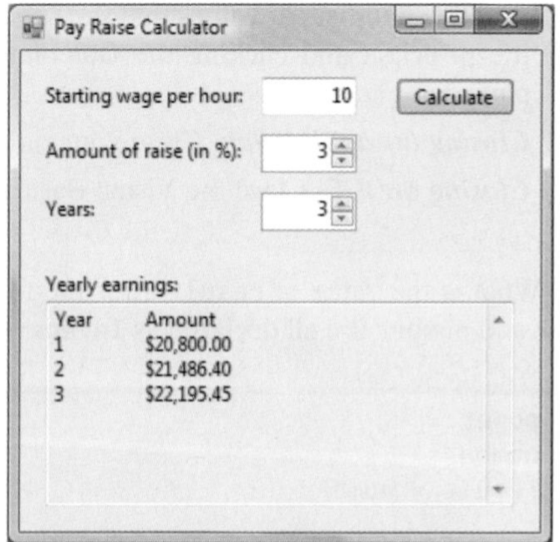

Figure 11.20 **Pay Raise** GUI.

a) ***Copying the template to your working directory.*** Copy the directory `C:\Examples\Tutorial11\Exercises\PayRaise` to your `C:\SimplyVB2008` directory.

b) ***Opening the application's template file.*** Double click `PayRaise.sln` in the `PayRaise` directory to open the application.

c) ***Adding controls to the Form.*** Add two `NumericUpDown` controls to the `Form`. The first `NumericUpDown` control should allow the user to specify the pay-raise percentage. The user should be able to specify percentages only in the range of 3–8%. Create the second `NumericUpDown` control for users to select the number of years in the range 1–50. Then add a multiline `TextBox` control to the application. Set its `ScrollBar` property to display a vertical scrollbar. Ensure that the user cannot modify the text in the `NumericUpDown` and `TextBox` controls. Resize and move the controls you created so that they follow the GUI Design Guidelines as in Fig. 11.20.

d) ***Adding a `Click` event handler and adding code.*** Add a `Click` event handler for the **Calculate** `Button`. Once in **Code** view, add code to use the `For...Next` statement to compute the yearly salary amounts, based on the yearly pay raise.

e) ***Running the application.*** Select **Debug > Start Debugging** to run your application. Enter a starting wage per hour, the size of the yearly raise and the number of years worked. Click the **Calculate** `Button` and verify that the correct amount after each year is displayed in the **Yearly earnings:** `TextBox`.

f) ***Closing the application.*** Close your running application by clicking its close box.

g) ***Closing the IDE.*** Close the Visual Basic IDE by clicking its close box.

TUTORIAL 12

Objectives

In this tutorial, you learn to:

- Use the `Select Case` multiple-selection statement.
- Use `Case` statements.
- Use the `Is` keyword.
- Obtain the current date and time.
- Display the date and time.
- Use `TextBox` property `PasswordChar`.

Outline

Security Panel Application

Introducing the `Select Case` Multiple-Selection Statement

In the last tutorial, you learned to use the `For...Next` statement, which is the most concise statement for performing counter-controlled repetition. In this tutorial, you learn about the `Select Case` multiple-selection statement. The `Select Case` statement is used to simplify code that uses several `ElseIf` statements sequentially when an application must choose among many possible actions to perform.

12.1 Test-Driving the Security Panel Application

In this tutorial, you use the `Select Case` multiple-selection statement to construct a **Security Panel** application. This application must meet the following requirements:

Application Requirements

A lab wants to install a security panel outside a laboratory room. Only authorized personnel may enter the lab, using their security codes. The following are valid security codes (also called access codes) and the groups of employees they represent:

Values	*Group*
1645–1689	*Technicians*
8345	*Custodians*
9998, 1006–1008	*Scientists*

Once a security code is entered, access is either granted or denied. All access attempts are written to a window below the keypad. If access is granted, the date, time and group (scientists, custodians, etc.) are written to the window. If access is denied, the date, the time and the message "Access Denied" are written to the window. Furthermore, the user can enter any one-digit access code to summon a security guard for assistance. The date, the time and the message "Assistance Requested" are then written to the window to indicate that the request has been received.

You begin by test-driving the completed application. Then you learn the additional Visual Basic capabilities needed to create your own version of this application.

Test-Driving the Security Panel Application

1. ***Opening the completed application.*** Open the directory `C:\Examples\Tutorial12\CompletedApplication\SecurityPanel` to locate the **Security Panel** application. Double click `SecurityPanel.sln` to open the application in the Visual Basic IDE.

2. ***Running the Security Panel application.*** Select **Debug > Start Debugging** to run the application (Fig. 12.1). At the top of the `Form`, you are provided with a `TextBox` that displays an asterisk for each digit in the security code entered using the GUI keypad. Note that the GUI keypad looks much like a real-world keypad. The **C** `Button` clears your current input, and the **#** `Button` causes the application to process the security code entered. Results are displayed in the `ListBox` at the bottom of the `Form`.

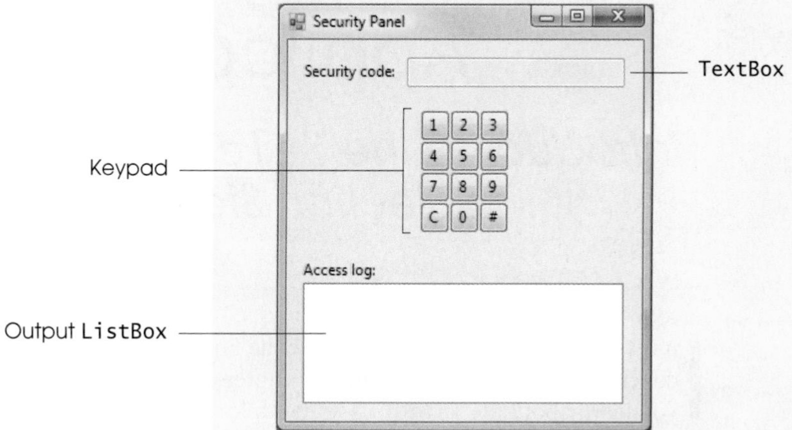

Figure 12.1 **Security Panel** application executing.

3. ***Entering an invalid security code.*** Use the keypad to enter the invalid security code `1212`. Note that an asterisk (*) is displayed in the `TextBox` (Fig. 12.2) for each numeric key you click on the `Form`. These characters prevent other people from seeing the code entered. Next, click the **#** `Button`. A message indicating that access is denied appears in the `ListBox`, as in Fig. 12.3. Note that the `TextBox` is cleared when the **#** `Button` is pressed.

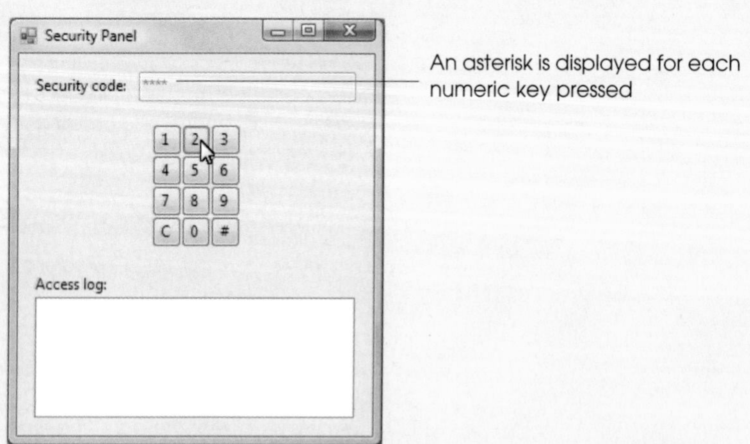

Figure 12.2 Asterisks displayed in **Security code:** field.

GUI Design Tip

If your GUI is modeling a real-world object, its design should mimic the physical appearance of the object.

(cont.)

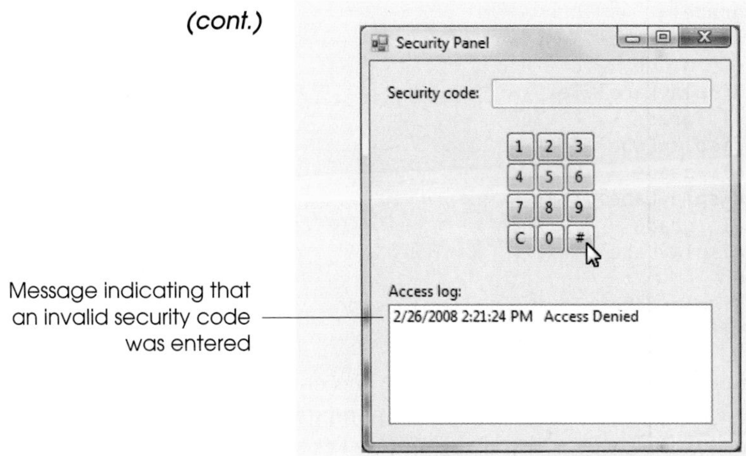

Figure 12.3 **Security Panel** displaying **Access Denied** message.

4. ***Using the* C Button.** Press a few numeric keys, then click the **C** `Button`. Note that all the asterisks displayed in the `TextBox` disappear. Users often make mistakes when keystroking or when clicking `Buttons`, so the **C** `Button` allows users to make a "fresh start."

5. ***Entering a valid security code.*** Use the keypad to enter `1006`, then click the **#** `Button`. Note that a second message appears in the `ListBox`, as in Fig. 12.4.

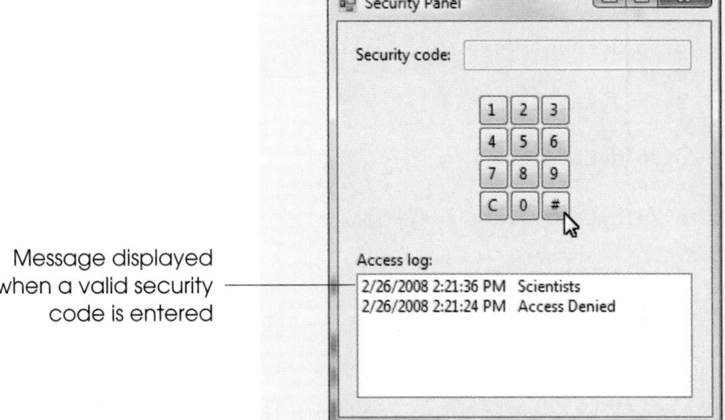

Figure 12.4 **Security Panel** application confirming a valid security-code entry.

6. ***Closing the application.*** Close your running application by clicking its close box.

7. ***Closing the IDE.*** Close the Visual Basic IDE by clicking its close box.

12.2 Introducing the `Select Case` Multiple-Selection Statement

In this section, you learn how to use the **`Select Case` multiple-selection statement**. For comparison purposes, we provide an `If...Then...Else` multiple-selection statement that displays a text message based on a student's grade:

```
If grade = "A" Then
   displayLabel.Text = "Excellent!"
ElseIf grade = "B" Then
   displayLabel.Text = "Very good!"
ElseIf grade = "C" Then
   displayLabel.Text = "Good."
ElseIf grade = "D" Then
   displayLabel.Text = "Poor."
ElseIf grade = "F" Then
   displayLabel.Text = "Failure."
Else
   displayLabel.Text = "Invalid grade."
End If
```

This statement can be used to produce the correct output when selecting among multiple values of grade. [*Note:* String comparisons are case sensitive—"A" is not equal to "a".] However, by using the Select Case statement, you can simplify every instance like

```
If grade = "A" Then
```

to one like

```
Case "A"
```

and eliminate the If and ElseIf keywords.

The following Select Case multiple-selection statement performs the same functionality as the preceding If...Then...Else statement:

Good Programming Practice

Visual Basic automatically indents the statements in the body of each Case to improve readability.

```
Select Case grade
   Case "A"
      displayLabel.Text = "Excellent!"
   Case "B"
      displayLabel.Text = "Very good!"
   Case "C"
      displayLabel.Text = "Good."
   Case "D"
      displayLabel.Text = "Poor."
   Case "F"
      displayLabel.Text = "Failure."
   Case Else
      displayLabel.Text = "Invalid grade."
End Select
```

Common Programming Error

When using the optional Case Else statement in a Select Case statement, failing to place the Case Else as the last Case is a syntax error.

Common Programming Error

Case statements that have the same value in their expression lists result in logic errors. At runtime, only the body of the first matching Case executes.

The Select Case statement begins with the keywords Select Case followed by a **test expression** (also called a **controlling expression**) and terminates with keywords **End Select**. The test expression is specified once, in the first line of the Select Case statement, and is used in each Case statement. The preceding Select Case statement contains five **Case statements** and the optional **Case Else statement**. Each Case statement contains the keyword Case followed by an **expression list**. The expression list can contain any built-in data type, such as strings ("A") or numeric values (707 and 9.9). Each Case statement's expression list is compared to grade—the Select Case statement's controlling expression. Although a Select Case statement can have any number of Cases, only one Case Else is allowed.

Figure 12.5 shows the UML activity diagram for this Select Case multiple-selection statement. The first condition to be evaluated is grade = "A". If this condition is True, the text "Excellent!" is displayed, and control proceeds to the first statement after the Select Case statement. If the condition evaluates to False (that is, grade <> "A"), the statement continues by testing the next condition, grade = "B". If this condition is True, the text "Very good!" is displayed, and control proceeds to the first statement after the Select Case statement. If the condition is False (that is, grade <> "B"), the statement continues to test the next condition. This process continues until a matching Case is found or until the final condition evaluates to `False` (`grade <> "F"`). If the latter occurs, the `Case Else`'s body is executed, and the text `"Invalid grade."` is displayed. The application then continues with the first statement after the `Select Case` statement.

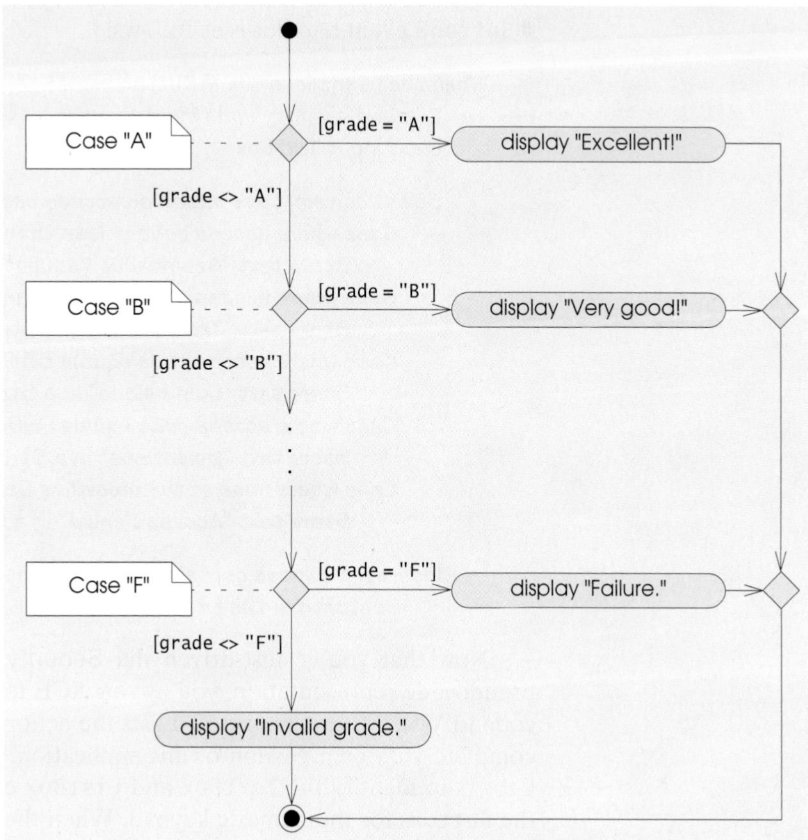

Figure 12.5 `Select Case` multiple-selection statement UML activity diagram.

SELF-REVIEW

1. `Select Case` is a ________-selection statement.
   a) multiple
   b) double
   c) single
   d) None of the above

2. When does the `Case Else` body execute?
   a) Every time a `Select Case` statement executes
   b) When more than one `Case` is matched
   c) When all `Case`s are matching `Case` statements in a `Select Case` statement
   d) None of the above

Answers: 1) a. 2) d.

12.3 Constructing the Security Panel Application

The **Security Panel** application contains 10 `Buttons` that display digits. (We call these numeric `Buttons`.) You'll create an event handler for each `Button`'s `Click` event. These `Buttons` make up the GUI keypad. The following pseudocode describes the `Click` event handler for each of these numeric `Buttons`:

```
If a numeric Button is clicked
    Concatenate Button's digit to the TextBox's Text property value
```

Later in this tutorial, you convert this pseudocode into Visual Basic code and create the `Click` event handlers for each numeric `Button`. The user then can use the numeric Buttons to enter digits and have them concatenated to the text in a TextBox.

In addition to the numeric Buttons, this application also contains a **C** Button and a **#** Button. The **C** Button clears the Form's TextBox. The pseudocode for the **#** Button's event handler is as follows:

```
When the user clicks the # Button
    Retrieve security code input by user
    Clear input TextBox

    Select correct Case based on access code
        Case where access code is less than 10
            Store text "Assistance Requested" in a String variable
        Case where access code is in the range 1645 to 1689
            Store text "Technicians" in a String variable
        Case where access code equals 8345
            Store text "Custodians" in a String variable
        Case where access code equals 9998 or is in the range 1006 to 1008
            Store text "Scientists" in a String variable
        Case where none of the preceding Cases match
            Store text "Access Denied" in a String variable

    Insert a message containing the current time and the String variable's
        contents in the ListBox
```

Now that you've test-driven the **Security Panel** application and studied its pseudocode representation, you use an ACE table to help you convert the pseudocode to Visual Basic. Figure 12.6 lists the actions, controls and events that help you complete your own version of this application. The first row specifies that you use Labels to identify the TextBox and ListBox controls. The second row introduces the Buttons for the numeric keypad. When these Buttons are clicked, their values are concatenated to the text in the TextBox's Text property. The next row indicates that securityCodeTextBox stores the security code that is input by the user. The next two rows specify that the user can click the **Clear** Button to clear the TextBox. The rest of the table indicates the functionality of the enterButton.

Action/Control/Event (ACE) Table for the Security Panel Application

Action	Control	Event
Label the application's fields	securityCodeLabel, accessLogLabel	
	oneButton, twoButton, threeButton, fourButton, fiveButton, sixButton, sevenButton, eightButton, nineButton, zeroButton	Click
Concatenate Button's digit to the TextBox's Text property value	securityCodeTextBox	
	clearButton	Click
Clear input TextBox	securityCodeTextBox	

Figure 12.6 ACE table for **Security Panel** application. (Part 1 of 2.)

Action	Control	Event
	enterButton	Click
Retrieve security code input by user	securityCodeText-Box	
Clear input TextBox	securityCodeText-Box	
Select correct Case based on access code		
Case where access code is less than 10 Store text "Assistance Requested"		
Case where access code is in the range 1645 to 1689 Store text "Technicians"		
Case where access code equals 8345 Store text "Custodians"		
Case where access code equals 9998 or is in the range 1006 to 1008 Store text "Scientists"		
Case where none of preceding Cases match Store text "Access Denied"		
Insert a message containing the current time and the String variable's contents in the ListBox	logEntryListBox	

Figure 12.6 ACE table for **Security Panel** application. (Part 2 of 2.)

Now that you are familiar with the `Select Case` multiple-selection statement, you use it to build the **Security Panel** application.

Using the PasswordChar Property

1. ***Copying the template to your working directory.*** Copy the `C:\Examples\Tutorial12\TemplateApplication\SecurityPanel` directory to your `C:\SimplyVB2008` directory.
2. ***Opening the Security Panel application's template file.*** Double click `SecurityPanel.sln` in the `SecurityPanel` directory.
3. ***Displaying the * character in the TextBox.*** Select the **Security code:** `TextBox` at the top of the `Form`, and set this `TextBox`'s `PasswordChar` property to * in the **Properties** window. Text displayed in a `TextBox` can be hidden or **masked** with the character specified in property **PasswordChar**. **Masking characters** are displayed rather than the actual text that the user types. However, the `TextBox`'s `Text` property does contain the text the user typed. For example, if a user enters `5469`, the `TextBox` displays ****, yet stores `"5469"` in its `Text` property. Now any character displayed in this `TextBox` displays as the * character.
4. ***Disabling the TextBox.*** The primary reason for using a `TextBox` instead of a `Label` to display the access code is to use the `PasswordChar` property. To prevent users from modifying the text in the `TextBox`, set its **Enabled** property to `False`. You can also accomplish this using the `ReadOnly` property.
5. ***Creating the enterButton_Click event handler.*** Double click the `#` `Button` to create the `enterButton_Click` event handler.

GUI Design Tip

Mask passwords or other sensitive pieces of information in `TextBoxes`.

(cont.)

6. ***Declaring and initializing variables.*** Add lines 6–10 of Fig. 12.7 to the enterButton_Click event handler. Lines 6–7 declare variables accessCode and message to store the user's security code (access code) and the message displayed to the user (based on the access code entered), respectively. Line 9 sets the accessCode variable to the security code input by the user. The securityCodeTextBox initially contains the empty string. If the user clicks the # Button without entering a security code, the Val function returns 0. Line 10 clears the **Security code:** TextBox.

Declaring event handler's variables

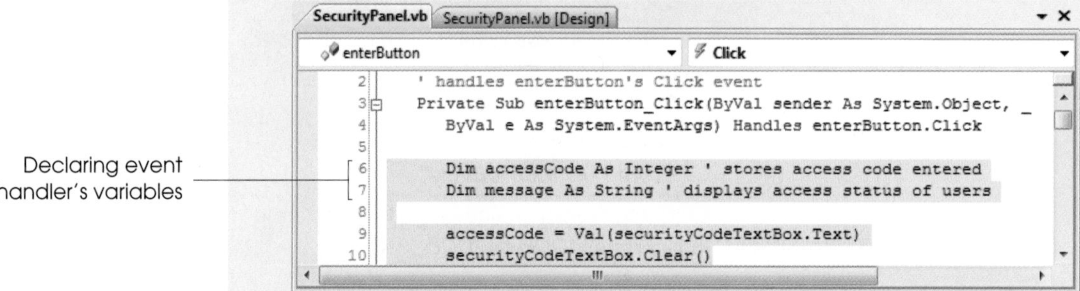

Figure 12.7 Variable declarations for enterButton_Click.

7. ***Saving the project.*** Select **File > Save All** to save your modified code.

Now that you've designed the GUI for your application, declared the variables for your event handler and obtained a value for variable accessCode, let's continue by creating your Select Case statement, as shown in the following box. This statement determines the user's access level based on the code input.

Adding a Select Case Statement to the Application

1. ***Adding a Select Case statement to enterButton_Click.*** Add line 12 from Fig. 12.8 to the enterButton_Click event handler and press *Enter*. Keywords End Select (line 14) are added below the Select Case line that you just added. Line 12 begins the Select Case statement, which contains the controlling expression accessCode—the access code entered by the user. Recall that this expression (the value accessCode) is compared sequentially with each Case until either a match occurs or the End Select statement is reached. If a matching Case is found, the body of the Case executes and program control proceeds to the first statement after the End Select statement.

Creating a Select Case statement

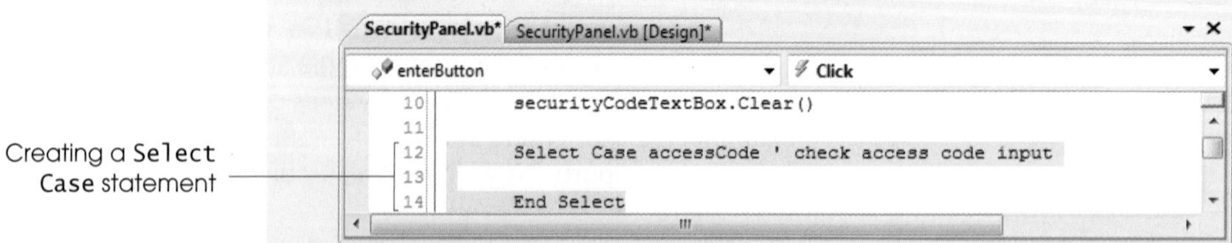

Figure 12.8 Select Case statement.

2. ***Adding a Case to the Select Case statement.*** Add lines 13–14 from Fig. 12.9 to the Select Case statement. The first Case statement tests whether accessCode is less than 10. Keyword Is followed by a relational or equality operator can be used to compare the controlling expression and the value to the right of the operator. In this case, if the value in accessCode is less than 10, the code in the body of the Case statement executes and message is assigned the text "Assistance Requested", which is displayed after the body of the Select Case statement completes.

(cont.)

Is keyword can be used for relational and equality comparisons

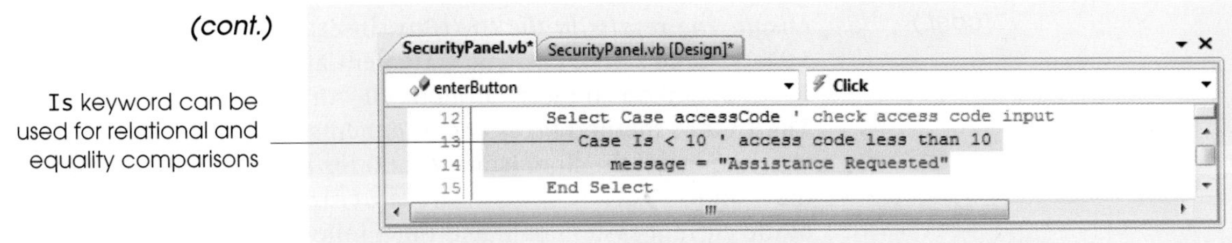

Figure 12.9 First Case added to Select Case statement.

3. ***Specifying Cases for the remaining access codes.*** Add lines 15–20 from Fig. 12.10 to the Select Case statement.

To keyword can be used to specify a range of values to test

Comma used to separate multiple expressions in a Case

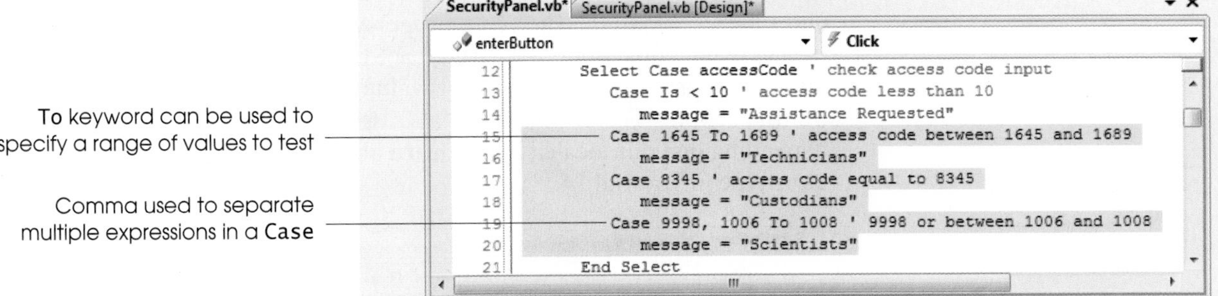

Figure 12.10 Cases specified for remaining access codes.

Common Programming Error

If the value on the left side of the To keyword in a Case statement is larger than the value on the right side, the Case is ignored during application execution, potentially causing a logic error. The compiler issues a warning in this case.

The Case statement in lines 15–16 determines whether the value of accessCode is in the range 1645 to 1689, inclusive. Keyword To is used to specify the range. If the user enters an access code in this range, the body of the Case statement sets message to "Technicians".

The next Case statement (lines 17–18) checks for a specific number. If accessCode matches the value 8345, then the statement in that Case is executed. Specifying a single value in a Case statement is common.

The next Case statement (lines 19–20) determines whether accessCode is 9998 or a number in the range 1006 to 1008, inclusive. Note that when multiple values or value ranges are provided in a Case statement, they are separated by commas.

4. ***Adding a Case Else to the Select Case statement.*** Add lines 21–22 from Fig. 12.11 to the Select Case statement. These lines contain the optional Case Else, which is executed when the controlling expression does not match any of the previous Cases. If used, the Case Else must follow all other Case statements. In your application, the body of the Case Else statement sets variable message to "Access Denied". The required keywords End Select (line 23 of Fig. 12.11) terminate the Select Case statement.

Case Else statement executes when no other Case matches

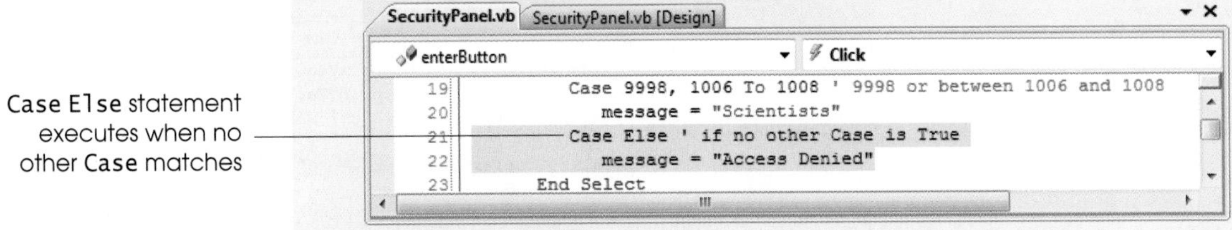

Figure 12.11 Case Else of the Select Case statement.

(cont.)

5. ***Displaying results in the* `ListBox`.** Insert lines 25–26 of Fig. 12.12 after the `Select Case` statement. The statement at line 26 uses the `Items` property's **`Insert`** method to insert an item into the `ListBox` at a specified position. The `Insert` method takes two arguments—the first specifies the position at which to insert the item (starting at `0` for the first item), the second specifies the item to insert. Line 26 inserts a `String` in `logEntryListBox` consisting of the current system date and time, followed by three spaces and the value assigned to `message`. This item, the `String`, is inserted as the first item (as specified by the first argument, `0`) in the `ListBox`, so the messages are displayed in reverse chronological order. The first part of method `Insert`'s second argument contains the expression `Date.Now`. The .NET Framework Class Library provides a **`Date`** type that can be used to store and display date and time information. The `Date` property **`Now`** returns the system time and date. Passing this value as part of a `String` in the second argument to method `Insert` (line 26) causes this value to be converted and displayed as a `String`. [*Note:* The format used to display the `Date` as a `String` varies depending on your locale.] You'll learn about how a date is stored using the `Date` type in Tutorial 14.

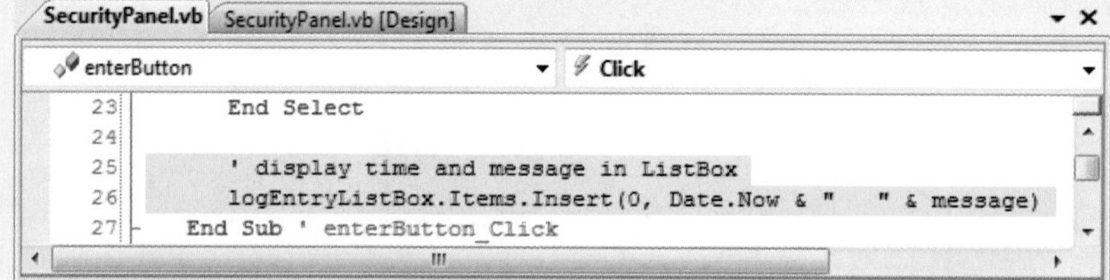

Figure 12.12 Updating the **Security Panel** application's `ListBox`.

6. ***Saving the project.*** Select **File > Save All** to save your modified code.

Now that you've defined the `enterButton_Click` event handler, you focus on the numeric `Buttons`. You create event handlers for each numbered `Button` and for the **C** `Button`.

Programming the Remaining Event Handlers

1. ***Creating the* `zeroButton_Click` *event handler.*** In **Design** view, double click the **0** `Button` (`zeroButton`) to create the `zeroButton_Click` event handler.

2. ***Coding the* `zeroButton_Click` *event handler.*** Add line 33 of Fig. 12.13 to the event handler. Line 33 appends the `String` `"0"` to the end of `securityCodeTextBox`'s `Text` property value. You do this to append the numeric `Button`'s value to the access code in the `TextBox`.

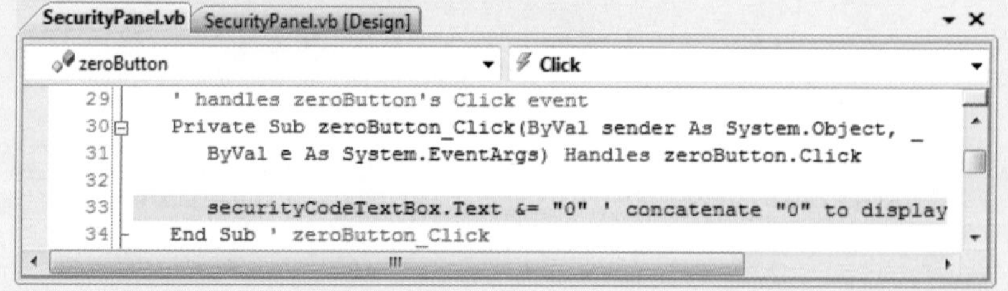

Figure 12.13 Event handler `zeroButton_Click`.

(cont.)

3. ***Defining the other numeric `Buttons`' event handlers.*** Repeat *Steps 1–2* for the remaining numeric `Buttons` (**1** through **9**). Be sure to substitute the `Button`'s number for the quoted value (for example, `oneButton_Click` sets `securityCodeTextBox`'s number as `&= "1"`). Figure 12.14 shows the event handlers for `Buttons` `oneButton` and `twoButton`.

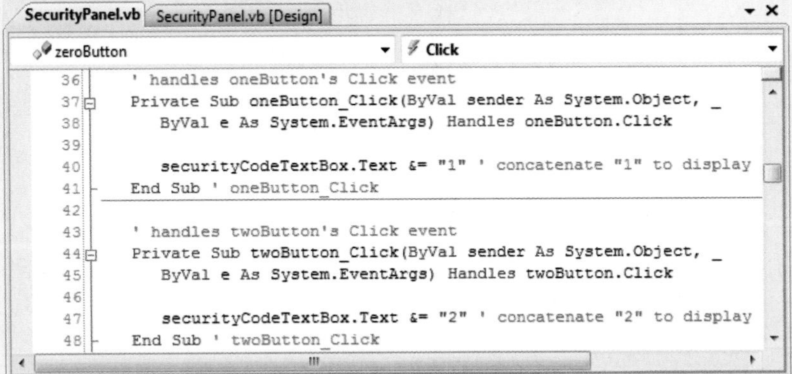

Figure 12.14 Event handlers `oneButton_Click` and `twoButton_Click`.

4. ***Defining the `clearButton_Click` event handler.*** Double click the **C** `Button`, and add line 103 as shown in Fig. 12.15 to clear the **Security code:** `TextBox`.

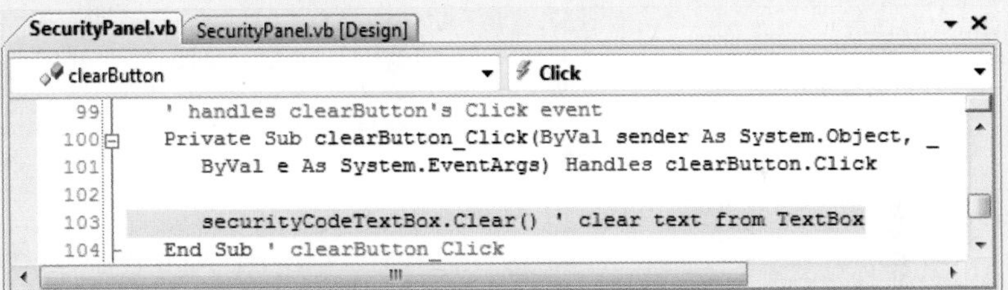

Figure 12.15 Event handler `clearButton_Click` defined.

5. ***Running the application.*** Select **Debug > Start Debugging** to run your application. Enter several security codes and verify that the correct output is displayed in the `ListBox`.

6. ***Closing the application.*** Close your running application by clicking its close box.

7. ***Closing the IDE.*** Close the Visual Basic IDE by clicking its close box.

Figure 12.16 presents the source code for the **Security Panel** application. The lines of code that contain new programming concepts you learned in this tutorial are highlighted. Look over the code carefully to make sure that you've added all of the event handlers correctly.

```
Public Class SecurityPanelForm
   ' handles enterButton's Click event
   Private Sub enterButton_Click(ByVal sender As System.Object, _
      ByVal e As System.EventArgs) Handles enterButton.Click

      Dim accessCode As Integer ' stores access code entered
      Dim message As String ' displays access status of users

```

Figure 12.16 **Security Panel** application. (Part 1 of 3.)

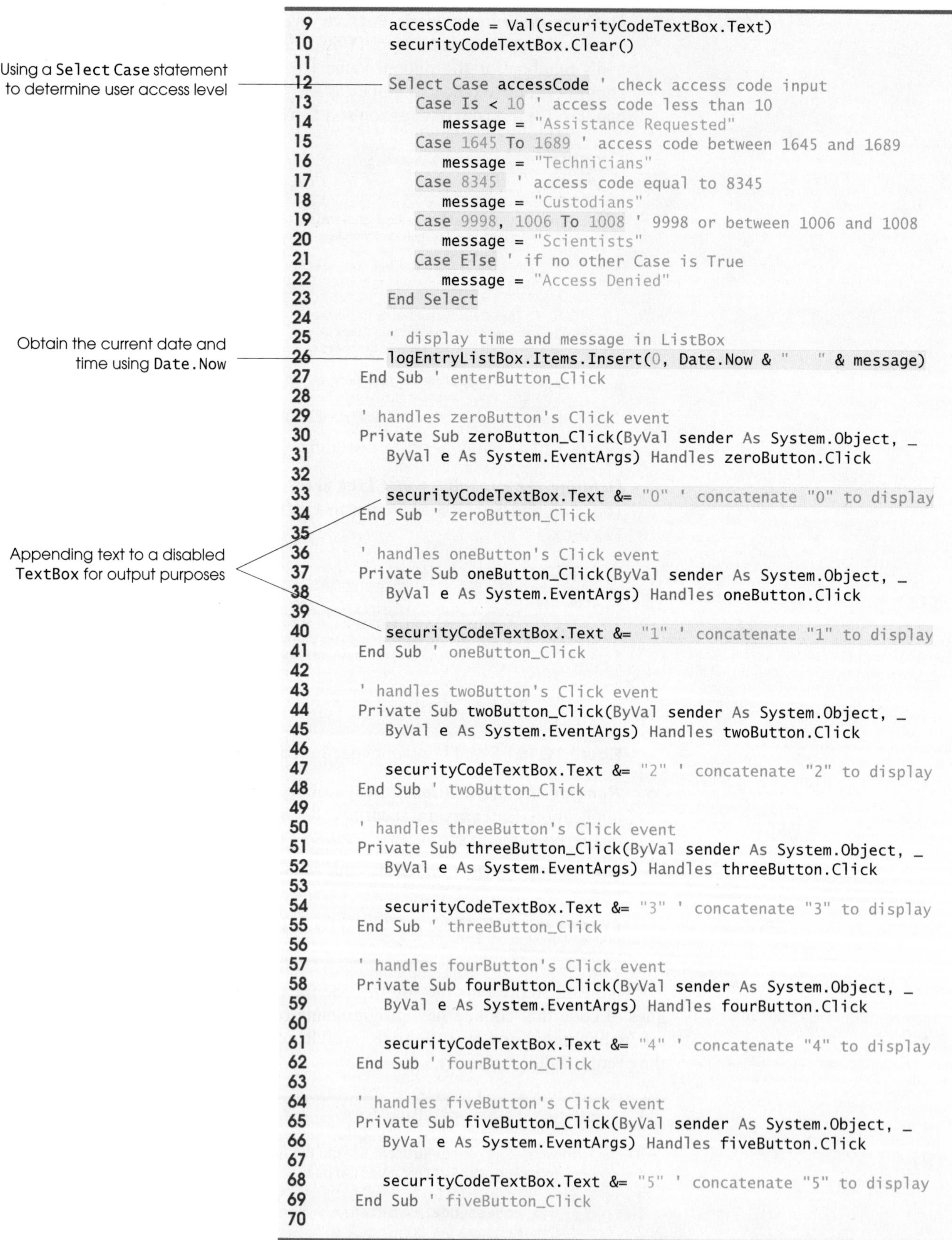
Using a Select Case statement to determine user access level
Obtain the current date and time using Date.Now
Appending text to a disabled TextBox for output purposes

```
      accessCode = Val(securityCodeTextBox.Text)
      securityCodeTextBox.Clear()

      Select Case accessCode ' check access code input
         Case Is < 10 ' access code less than 10
            message = "Assistance Requested"
         Case 1645 To 1689 ' access code between 1645 and 1689
            message = "Technicians"
         Case 8345  ' access code equal to 8345
            message = "Custodians"
         Case 9998, 1006 To 1008 ' 9998 or between 1006 and 1008
            message = "Scientists"
         Case Else ' if no other Case is True
            message = "Access Denied"
      End Select

      ' display time and message in ListBox
      logEntryListBox.Items.Insert(0, Date.Now & "   " & message)
   End Sub ' enterButton_Click

   ' handles zeroButton's Click event
   Private Sub zeroButton_Click(ByVal sender As System.Object, _
      ByVal e As System.EventArgs) Handles zeroButton.Click

      securityCodeTextBox.Text &= "0" ' concatenate "0" to display
   End Sub ' zeroButton_Click

   ' handles oneButton's Click event
   Private Sub oneButton_Click(ByVal sender As System.Object, _
      ByVal e As System.EventArgs) Handles oneButton.Click

      securityCodeTextBox.Text &= "1" ' concatenate "1" to display
   End Sub ' oneButton_Click

   ' handles twoButton's Click event
   Private Sub twoButton_Click(ByVal sender As System.Object, _
      ByVal e As System.EventArgs) Handles twoButton.Click

      securityCodeTextBox.Text &= "2" ' concatenate "2" to display
   End Sub ' twoButton_Click

   ' handles threeButton's Click event
   Private Sub threeButton_Click(ByVal sender As System.Object, _
      ByVal e As System.EventArgs) Handles threeButton.Click

      securityCodeTextBox.Text &= "3" ' concatenate "3" to display
   End Sub ' threeButton_Click

   ' handles fourButton's Click event
   Private Sub fourButton_Click(ByVal sender As System.Object, _
      ByVal e As System.EventArgs) Handles fourButton.Click

      securityCodeTextBox.Text &= "4" ' concatenate "4" to display
   End Sub ' fourButton_Click

   ' handles fiveButton's Click event
   Private Sub fiveButton_Click(ByVal sender As System.Object, _
      ByVal e As System.EventArgs) Handles fiveButton.Click

      securityCodeTextBox.Text &= "5" ' concatenate "5" to display
   End Sub ' fiveButton_Click

```

Figure 12.16 **Security Panel** application. (Part 2 of 3.)

```
      ' handles sixButton's Click event
      Private Sub sixButton_Click(ByVal sender As System.Object, _
         ByVal e As System.EventArgs) Handles sixButton.Click

         securityCodeTextBox.Text &= "6" ' concatenate "6" to display
      End Sub ' sixButton_Click

      ' handles sevenButton's Click event
      Private Sub sevenButton_Click(ByVal sender As System.Object, _
         ByVal e As System.EventArgs) Handles sevenButton.Click

         securityCodeTextBox.Text &= "7" ' concatenate "7" to display
      End Sub ' sevenButton_Click

      ' handles eightButton's Click event
      Private Sub eightButton_Click(ByVal sender As System.Object, _
         ByVal e As System.EventArgs) Handles eightButton.Click

         securityCodeTextBox.Text &= "8" ' concatenate "8" to display
      End Sub ' eightButton_Click

      ' handles nineButton's Click event
      Private Sub nineButton_Click(ByVal sender As System.Object, _
         ByVal e As System.EventArgs) Handles nineButton.Click

         securityCodeTextBox.Text &= "9" ' concatenate "9" to display
      End Sub ' nineButton_Click

      ' handles clearButton's Click event
      Private Sub clearButton_Click(ByVal sender As System.Object, _
         ByVal e As System.EventArgs) Handles clearButton.Click

         securityCodeTextBox.Clear() ' clear text from TextBox
      End Sub ' clearButton_Click
   End Class ' SecurityPanelForm
```

Figure 12.16 **Security Panel** application. (Part 3 of 3.)

SELF-REVIEW

1. A `Case` that handles all values larger than a specified value must precede the > operator with keyword ________.

   a) `Select` b) `Is`
   c) `Case` d) `All`

2. Use a(n) ________ to separate multiple conditions in a `Case` statement.

   a) period b) asterisk
   c) comma d) colon

Answers: 1) b. 2) c.

12.4 Wrap-Up

In this tutorial, you learned how to use the `Select Case` multiple-selection statement and discovered its similarities to the `If...Then...Else` statement. You studied a UML activity diagram that illustrates the flow of control in `Select Case` statements.

You then applied what you learned to create your **Security Panel** application. You set a `TextBox`'s `PasswordChar` property to `*` in the **Properties** window to mask the text in the `TextBox`. You used a `Select Case` statement to determine whether the user entered a correct security code. You also defined a `Case Else` statement, which executes if a valid security code is not provided. You used `Date.Now` to obtain the system time and date. Finally, you learned how to insert an item at a specified position in a `ListBox` using the `Items.Insert` method.

In the next tutorial, you'll learn how to construct applications from small, manageable pieces of reusable code called procedures. You'll use this capability to enhance an example you created earlier in the book.

SKILLS SUMMARY

Creating a Select Case Statement

- Use the keywords Select Case followed by a controlling expression.
- Use the keyword Case followed by an expression to compare with the controlling expression.
- Define the statements that execute if the Case's expression matches the controlling expression.
- Use the keywords Case Else followed by statements to execute if the controlling expression does not match any of the provided Cases. Case Else, if used, must be the last Case statement.
- Use the keywords End Select to end the Select Case statement.

Masking User Input in a TextBox

- Set the TextBox's PasswordChar property to the desired character, typically the asterisk (*), to mask the user input.
- Retrieve the value typed by the user in the Text property.

Retrieving the Current Date and Time

- Use property Now of type Date, which, when converted to a String, displays the current date in the format 12/31/2002 11:59:59 P.M. (depending on locale).

Inserting an Item at the Beginning of a ListBox

- Use the Items property's Insert method with the first argument 0.

KEY TERMS

Case Else statement—Optional statement whose body executes if the Select Case's test expression does not match an expression of any Case.

Case statement—Statement whose body executes if the Select Case's test expression matches the Case's expression.

controlling expression—Value compared sequentially with each Case until either a match occurs or the End Select statement is reached. Also known as a test expression.

Date type—A type whose properties can be used to store and display date and time information.

Enabled property of a TextBox—Determines whether the TextBox responds to user input.

End Select keywords—Terminates the Select Case statement.

expression list—Multiple expressions separated by commas. Used for Cases in Select Case statements, when certain statements should execute based on more than one condition.

Insert method of a ListBox's Items property—Inserts an item in a ListBox at the location specified by its first argument.

Is keyword—A keyword that, when followed by a comparison operator, can be used to compare the controlling expression of a Select Case statement and a value.

masking—Hiding text such as passwords or other sensitive pieces of information that should not be observed by other people as they are typed. Masking is achieved by using the PasswordChar property of the TextBox for which you would like to hide data. The actual data entered is retained in the TextBox's Text property.

masking character—Used to replace each character displayed in a TextBox when the TextBox's data is masked for privacy.

multiple-selection statement—Performs one of many actions (or sequences of actions) depending on the value of the controlling expression.

Now property of Date type—Returns the current system time and date.

PasswordChar property of a TextBox—Specifies the masking character for a TextBox.

Select Case statement—The multiple-selection statement used to make a decision by comparing an expression to a series of conditions. The algorithm then takes different actions based on those values.

GUI DESIGN GUIDELINES

Overall Design

- If your GUI is modeling a real-world object, its design should mimic the physical appearance of the object.

TextBox

- Mask passwords or other sensitive pieces of information in TextBoxes.

CONTROLS, EVENTS, PROPERTIES & METHODS

TextBox TextBox This control allows the user to input data from the keyboard.

- ***In action***

0

- ***Event***

  TextChanged—Raised when the text in the TextBox is changed.

- ***Properties***

  Enabled—Determines whether the user can enter data (True) in the TextBox or not (False).

  Location—Specifies the location of the TextBox on the Form relative to the Form's top-left corner.

  Multiline—Specifies whether the TextBox is capable of displaying multiple lines of text.

  Name—Specifies the name used to access the TextBox programmatically. The name should be appended with the TextBox suffix.

  PasswordChar—Specifies the masking character to be used when displaying data in the TextBox.

  ReadOnly—Determines whether the value of a TextBox can be changed by the user.

  ScrollBars—Specifies whether the TextBox contains scrollbars.

  Size—Specifies the width and height (in pixels) of the TextBox.

  Text—Specifies the text displayed in the TextBox.

  TextAlign—Specifies how the text is aligned within the TextBox.

  Width—Specifies the width (in pixels) of the TextBox.

- ***Methods***

  Clear—Removes text from the TextBox that calls it.

  Focus—Transfers the focus of the application to the TextBox that calls it.

ListBox ListBox This control allows the user to view and select from items in a list.

- ***In action***

Months	Monthly Payments
24	$490.50
36	$339.06
48	$263.55
60	$218.41

- ***Properties***

  Items—Returns an object that contains the items displayed in the ListBox.

  Items.Count—Returns the number of items in the ListBox.

  Items.Item—Returns the value at the specified index in the ListBox.

  Location—Specifies the location of the ListBox on the Form relative to the Form's top-left corner.

  Name—Specifies the name used to access the ListBox programmatically. The name should be appended with the ListBox suffix.

  Size—Specifies the width and height (in pixels) of the ListBox.

- ***Methods***

  Items.Add—Adds an item to the end Items property.

`Items.Clear`—Deletes all the values in the `ListBox`'s `Items` property.

`Items.Insert`—Inserts the item specified by its second argument into the `Items` property at the location (starting at `0` for the first item) specified by its first argument.

MULTIPLE-CHOICE QUESTIONS

12.1 The ________ keywords signify the end of a `Select Case` statement.

a) `End Case` b) `End Select`
c) `End Select Case` d) `Case End`

12.2 The expression ________ returns the current system time and date.

a) `Date.DateTime` b) `Date.SystemDateTime`
c) `Date.Now` d) `Date.SystemTimeDate`

12.3 You can hide information entered into a `TextBox` by setting the `TextBox`'s ________ property to a character that will be displayed for every character the user enters.

a) `PrivateChar` b) `Mask`
c) `MaskingChar` d) `PasswordChar`

12.4 Which of the following is a syntax error?

a) Having duplicate `Case` statements in the same `Select Case` statement
b) Having a `Case` statement in which the value to the left of a `To` keyword is larger than the value to the right
c) Preceding a `Case` statement with the `Case Else` statement in a `Select Case` statement
d) Using keyword `Is` in a `Select Case` statement

12.5 Keyword ________ is used to specify a range in a `Case` statement.

a) `Also` b) `Between`
c) `To` d) `From`

12.6 ________ separates multiple values tested in a `Case` statement.

a) A comma b) An underscore
c) Keyword `Also` d) A semicolon

12.7 The ________ method inserts a value at a specified location in a `ListBox`.

a) `Append` b) `Items.Insert`
c) `InsertAt` d) `Items.Add`

12.8 If the value on the left of the `To` keyword in a `Case` statement is larger than the value on the right, ________.

a) a syntax error occurs
b) the body of the `Case` statement executes
c) the body of the `Case` statement never executes
d) the statement causes a runtime error

12.9 The expression following the keywords `Select Case` is called a ________.

a) guard condition b) controlling expression
c) selection expression d) case expression

12.10 To prevent a user from modifying text in a `TextBox`, set its ________ property to `False`.

a) `Enabled` b) `Text`
c) `TextChange` d) `Editable`

EXERCISES

12.11 ***(Sales Commission Calculator Application)*** Develop an application that calculates a salesperson's commission from the number of items sold (Fig. 12.17). Assume that all items have a fixed price of $10 per unit. Use a `Select Case` statement to implement the following sales commission schedule:

Fewer than 10 items sold = 1% commission
Between 10 and 40 items sold = 2% commission
Between 41 and 100 items sold = 4% commission
More than 100 items sold = 8% commission

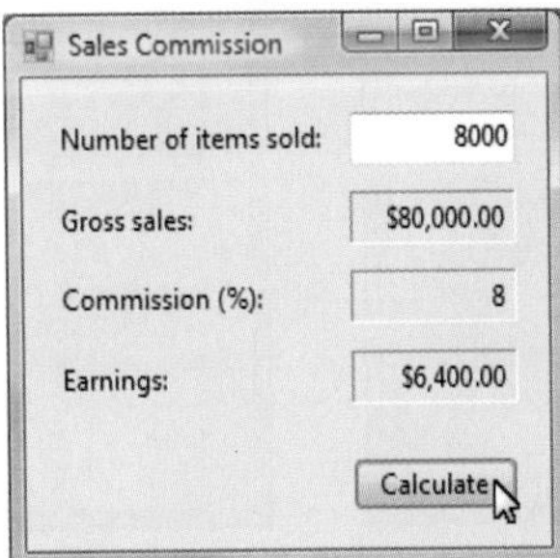

Figure 12.17 Sales Commission Calculator GUI.

a) ***Copying the template to your working directory.*** Copy the directory `C:\Examples\Tutorial12\Exercises\SalesCommissionCalculator` to your `C:\SimplyVB2008` directory.

b) ***Opening the application's template file.*** Double click `SalesCommissionCalculator.sln` in the `SalesCommissionCalculator` directory to open the application.

c) ***Defining an event handler for the `Button`'s `Click` event.*** Create an event handler for the **Calculate** `Button`'s `Click` event.

d) ***Displaying the salesperson's gross sales.*** In your new event handler, multiply the number of items that the salesperson has sold by `10`, and display the resulting gross sales as a monetary amount.

e) ***Calculating the salesperson's commission percentage.*** Use a `Select Case` statement to compute the salesperson's commission percentage from the number of items sold. The rate that is selected is applied to all the items the salesperson sold.

f) ***Displaying the salesperson's earnings.*** Multiply the salesperson's gross sales by the commission percentage determined in the preceding step to calculate the salesperson's earnings. Remember to divide by `100` to obtain the percentage.

g) ***Running the application.*** Select **Debug > Start Debugging** to run your application. Enter a value for the number of items sold and click the **Calculate** `Button`. Verify that the gross sales displayed is correct, that the percentage of commission is correct and that the earnings displayed is correct based on the commission assigned.

h) ***Closing the application.*** Close your running application by clicking its close box.

i) ***Closing the IDE.*** Close the Visual Basic IDE by clicking its close box.

12.12 *(Cash Register Application)* Use the numeric keypad from the **Security Panel** application to build a **Cash Register** application (Fig. 12.18). In addition to numbers, the cash register should include a decimal-point `Button`. Apart from this numeric operation, there should be **Enter**, **Delete**, **Clear** and **Total** `Buttons`. For simplicity, sales tax should be calculated based on the total amount purchased. Use a `Select Case` statement to compute sales tax. Add the tax amount to the subtotal to calculate the total. Display the subtotal, tax and total for the user. Use the following sales-tax percentages, which are based on the amount of money spent:

Amounts under $100 = 10% (.10) sales tax
Amounts between $100 and $500 = 7.5% (.075) sales tax
Amounts above $500 = 5% (.05) sales tax

a) ***Copying the template to your working directory.*** Copy the directory `C:\Examples\Tutorial12\Exercises\CashRegister` to your `C:\SimplyVB2008` directory.

b) ***Opening the application's template file.*** Double click `CashRegister.sln` in the `CashRegister` directory to open the application.

c) ***Defining event handlers for the numeric `Buttons` and decimal point in the keypad.*** Create event handlers for each of these `Button`'s `Click` events. Have each event handler concatenate the proper value to the `TextBox` at the top of the `Form`.

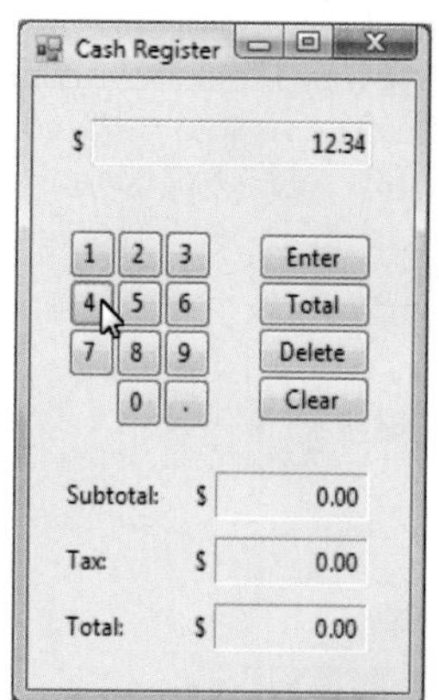

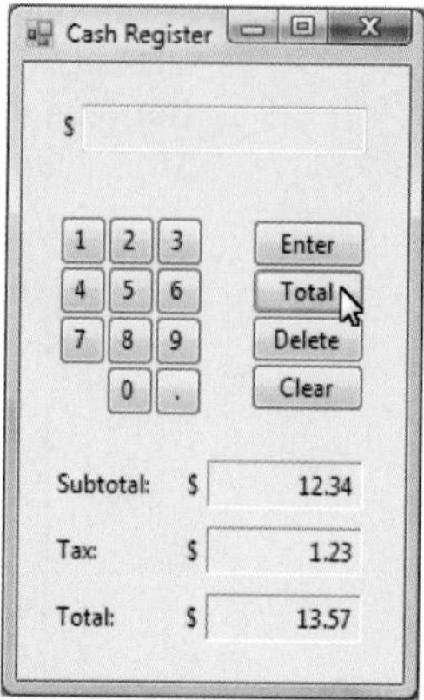

Figure 12.18 **Cash Register** GUI.

d) ***Defining an event handler for the Enter `Button`'s `Click` event.*** Create an event handler for the `enterButton`'s `Click` event. Have this event handler add the current amount to the subtotal, display the new subtotal and clear the current price entered.

e) ***Defining an event handler for the Total `Button`'s `Click` event.*** Create an event handler for the `totalButton`'s `Click` event. Have this event handler use the subtotal to compute the tax amount and then the total. Display this information in the appropriate `Label`s.

f) ***Defining an event handler for the Clear `Button`'s Click event.*** Create an event handler for the `clearButton`'s `Click` event. Have this event handler clear the user input and display the value `0.00` for the subtotal, sales tax and total.

g) ***Defining an event handler for the Delete `Button`'s `Click` event.*** Create an event handler for the `deleteButton`'s `Click` event. Have this event handler clear only the data in the `TextBox`.

h) ***Running the application.*** Select **Debug > Start Debugging** to run your application. Use the keypad to enter various dollar amounts, clicking the **Enter** `Button` after each. Verify that the **Subtotal:** field updates after each new entry. After several amounts have been entered, click the **Total** `Button` and verify that the appropriate sales tax and total are displayed. Enter several values again and click the **Delete** `Button` to clear the current input. Click the **Clear** `Button` to clear all the output values.

i) ***Closing the application.*** Close your running application by clicking its close box.

j) ***Closing the IDE.*** Close the Visual Basic IDE by clicking its close box.

12.13 *(Income Tax Calculator Application)* Create an application that computes the amount of income tax that a person must pay, depending upon salary. Income tax should be calculated for each portion of income in each range. For example, if the user earns $25,000, they pay 10% on the first $7,825 and 15% on the remaining $17,175. Your application should perform as shown in Fig. 12.19. Use the following income ranges and corresponding tax rates:

Not over $7,825 = 10% income tax
$7,826 – 31,850 = 15% income tax
$31,851 – 77,100 = 25% income tax
$77,101 – 160,850 = 28% income tax
$160,850 – 349,700 = 33% income tax
Over $349,700 = 35% income tax

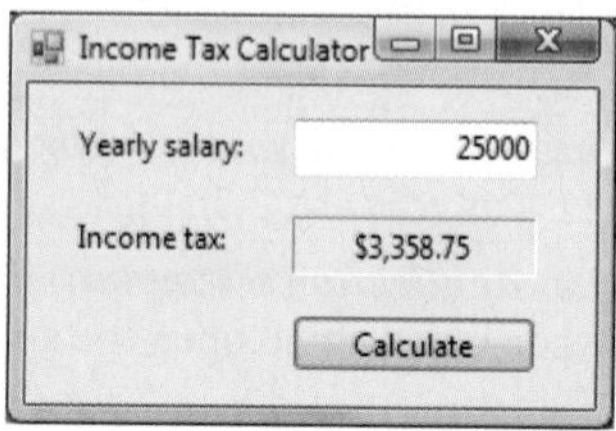

Figure 12.19 **Income Tax Calculator** GUI.

a) ***Copying the template to your working directory.*** Copy the directory `C:\Examples\Tutorial12\Exercises\IncomeTaxCalculator` to your `C:\SimplyVB2008` directory.

b) ***Opening the application's template file.*** Double click `IncomeTaxCalculator.sln` in the `IncomeTaxCalculator` directory to open the application.

c) ***Defining an event handler for the* Calculate *Button's* Click *event.*** Use the designer to create an event handler for the `calculateButton`'s `Click` event. Have this event handler use a `Select Case` statement to determine the user's income-tax percentage. Display the result in the output `Label`.

d) ***Using the TextChanged even to clear the output.*** Double click the **Yearly salary:** `TextBox` to create its `TextChanged` event. Clear the output `Label` when the user changes the value in the `TextBox`.

e) ***Running the application.*** Select **Debug > Start Debugging** to run your application. Enter a yearly salary and click the **Calculate** `Button`. Verify that the appropriate income tax is displayed, based on the ranges listed in the exercise description.

f) ***Closing the application.*** Close your running application by clicking its close box.

g) ***Closing the IDE.*** Close the Visual Basic IDE by clicking its close box.

What does this code do?

12.14 What is output by the following code? Assume that `donationButton` is a `Button`, `donationTextBox` is a `TextBox` and `messageLabel` is an output `Label`.

```
Private Sub donationButton_Click(ByVal sender As _
   System.Object, ByVal e As System.EventArgs) _
   Handles donationButton.Click

   Select Case Val(donationTextBox.Text)
      Case 0
         messageLabel.Text = "Please consider donating to our cause."
      Case 1 To 100
         messageLabel.Text = "Thank you for your donation."
      Case Is > 100
         messageLabel.Text = "Thank you very much for your donation!"
      Case Else
         messageLabel.Text = "Please enter a valid amount."
   End Select
End Sub
```

What's wrong with this code?

12.15 This `Select Case` statement should determine whether an `Integer` is even or odd. Find the error(s) in the following code:

```
Select Case value Mod 2
   Case 0
      outputLabel.Text = "Odd Integer"
   Case 1
      outputLabel.Text = "Even Integer"
End Select
```

Using the Debugger

12.16 *(**Discount Calculator** Application)* Copy the `C:\Examples\Tutorial07\DiscountCalculator` directory to your `C:\SimplyVB2008` directory. The **Discount Calculator** application determines the discount the user receives, based on how much money the user spends. A 15% discount is received for purchases over $200, a 10% discount is received for purchases between $150 and $200, a 5% discount is received for purchases between $100 and $149 and a 2% discount is received for purchases between $50 and $99. While testing your application, you notice that the application is not calculating the discount properly for some values. Use the debugger to find and fix the logic error(s) in the application. Figure 12.20 displays the correct output for the application.

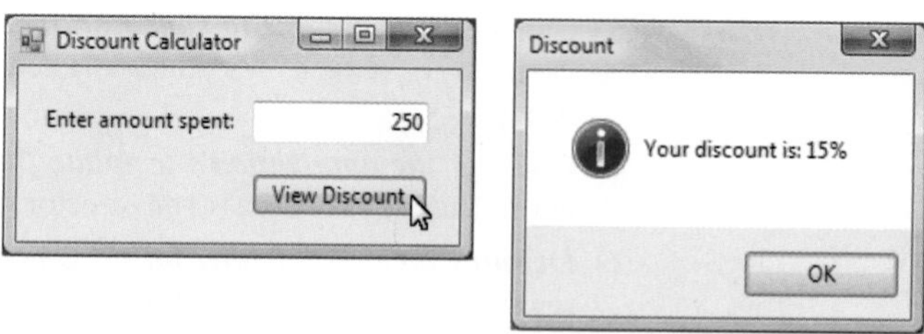

Figure 12.20 Correct output for the **Discount Calculator** application.

Programming Challenge

12.17 ***(Enhanced Cash Register Application)*** A store is holding a sale. Modify the **Cash Register** application (Exercise 12.12) to calculate the discount received based on the total amount spent after taxes. The discount should be displayed in a dialog box as well as in the **Discount:** `Label`. Figure 12.21 displays the enhanced **Cash Register** application GUI. The store offers the following discounts based on the total amount spent:

Under $200 = 10% discount
$200 – 500 = 20% discount
Over $500 = 30% discount

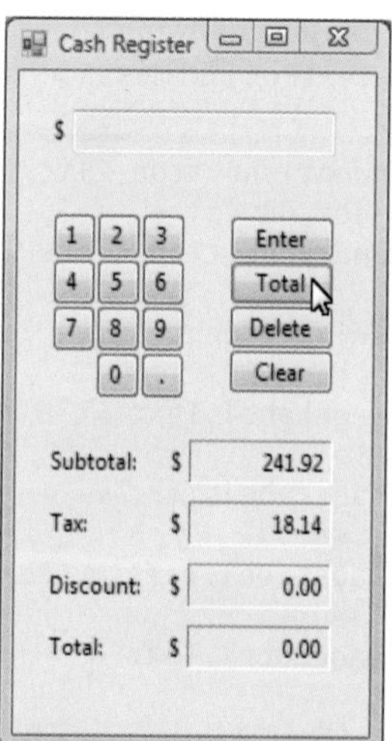

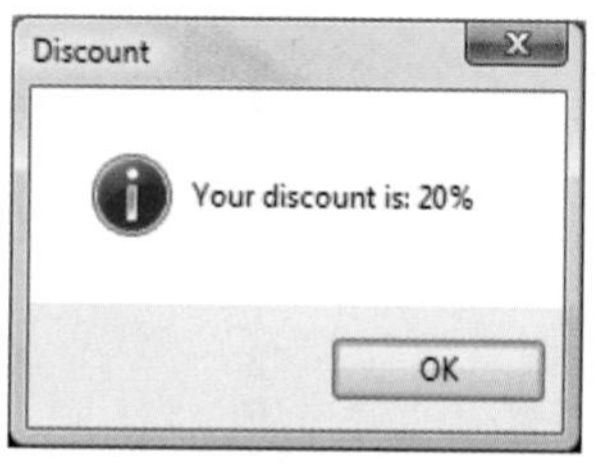

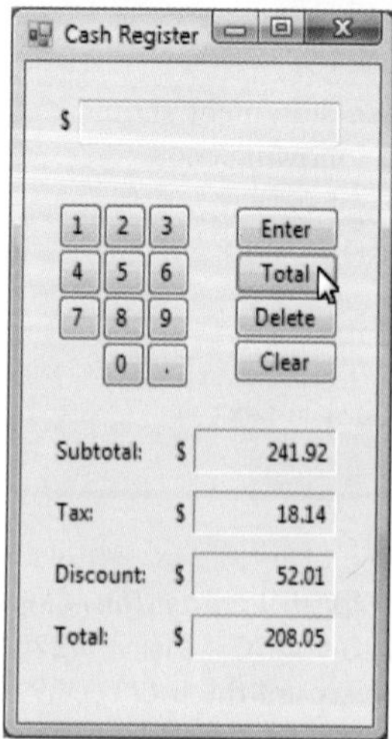

Figure 12.21 **Enhanced Cash Register** GUI.

TUTORIAL 13

Enhancing the Wage Calculator Application

Introducing Function Procedures and Sub Procedures

Objectives

In this tutorial, you learn to:

- Construct applications modularly from pieces called procedures.
- Work with "built-in" procedures.
- Distinguish between `Function` procedures and `Sub` procedures, and determine when each should be used.
- Create your own `Function` procedures and `Sub` procedures.
- Use the Debugging controls on the **Standard** Toolbar.

Outline

Most software applications that solve real-world problems are much larger than the applications presented in the first few tutorials of this text. Experience has shown that the best way to develop and maintain a large application is to construct it from smaller, more manageable pieces. This technique is known as **divide and conquer** (also called **componentization**). These manageable pieces include program components—known as **procedures**—that simplify the design, implementation and maintenance of large applications. In this tutorial, you learn how to create two kinds of procedures—namely, `Function` procedures and `Sub` procedures.

13.1 Test-Driving the Enhanced Wage Calculator Application

Use procedures to enhance the **Wage Calculator** application that you created in Tutorial 7. This application must meet the following requirements:

Application Requirements

Recall the problem statement from Tutorial 7: A payroll company calculates the gross earnings per week of employees. Employees' weekly salaries are based on the number of hours they worked and their hourly wages. Create an application that accepts this information and calculates each employee's total (gross) earnings. The application assumes a standard work week of 40 hours. The wages for 40 or fewer hours are calculated by multiplying the employee's hourly wage by the number of hours worked. Any time worked over 40 hours in a week is considered "overtime" and earns time and a half. Salary for time and a half is calculated by multiplying the employee's hourly wage by 1.5 and multiplying the result of that calculation by the number of overtime hours worked. The total overtime earned is added to the user's gross earnings for the regular 40 hours of work to calculate the total earnings for that week.

The completed application has the same functionality as the application in Tutorial 7, but uses procedures to better organize the code. This application calculates earnings based on an employee's hourly wage and the number of hours worked per week. An employee who works 40 or fewer hours earns the hourly wage multiplied by the number of hours worked. The calculation differs if the employee has worked more than the standard 40-hour work week. In this tutorial, you learn about procedures that perform calculations based on input values that may differ with each execution of the application. You begin by test-driving the completed application. Then you learn the additional Visual Basic technologies needed to create your own version of this application.

Test-Driving the Enhanced Wage Calculator Application

1. ***Opening the completed application.*** Open the directory `C:\Examples\Tutorial13\CompletedApplication\WageCalculator2` to locate the **Wage Calculator** application. Double click `WageCalculator2.sln` to open the application in the Visual Basic IDE.
2. ***Running the Wage Calculator application.*** Select **Debug > Start Debugging** to run the application.
3. ***Entering the employee's hourly wage.*** Enter `10` in the **Hourly wage:** `TextBox` (Fig. 13.1).

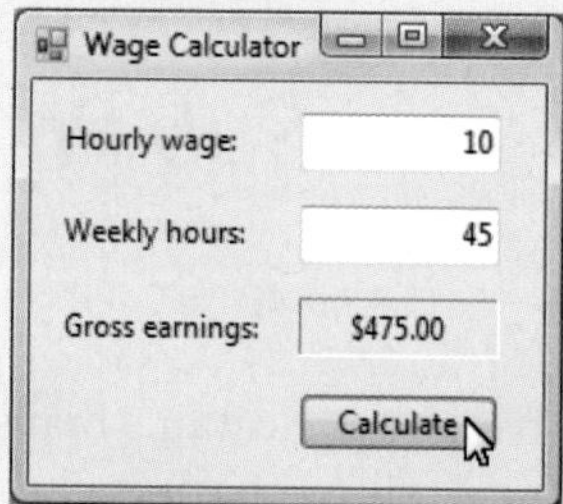

Figure 13.1 **Wage Calculator** running.

4. ***Entering the number of hours the employee worked.*** Enter `45` in the **Weekly hours:** `TextBox`.
5. ***Calculating wages earned.*** Click the **Calculate** `Button`. The result (`$475.00`) is displayed in the **Gross earnings:** `Label`.
6. ***Closing the application.*** Close the running application by clicking its close box.
7. ***Closing the IDE.*** Close the Visual Basic IDE by clicking its close box.

13.2 Classes and Procedures

The key to creating large applications is to break them into smaller pieces. In object-oriented programming, these pieces consist primarily of classes, which can be further broken down into **methods**. In Visual Basic programming, methods are implemented by writing procedures. We frequently refer to procedures as methods.

Programmers typically combine **programmer-defined** classes and methods with preexisting (also called predefined) code available in the .NET Framework Class Library. Using preexisting code saves time, effort and money. The concept of **reusing code** increases efficiency for application developers. Figure 13.2 explains several preexisting Visual Basic methods.

You've already used several preexisting classes and methods in the .NET Framework Class Library. For example, all of the GUI controls you've used in your applications are defined in the .NET Framework Class Library as classes. You have also used .NET Framework Class Library class methods, such as method `Format` of class `String`, to display output properly in your applications. Without method `String.Format`, you would have needed to code this functionality yourself—a task that would have included many lines of code and programming techniques that have not been introduced yet. You'll learn many more .NET Framework Class Library classes and methods in this book.

Procedure	Description	Example
`Math.Max(x, y)`	Returns the larger value of x and y	`Math.Max(2.3, 12.7)` is `12.7` `Math.Max(-2.3, -12.7)` is `-2.3`
`Math.Min(x, y)`	Returns the smaller value of x and y	`Math.Min(2.3, 12.7)` is `2.3` `Math.Min(-2.3, -12.7)` is `-12.7`
`Math.Sqrt(x)`	Returns the square root of x	`Math.Sqrt(9)` is `3.0` `Math.Sqrt(2)` is `1.4142135623731`
`Pmt(x, y, z)`	Calculates loan payments where x specifies the interest rate, y specifies the number of payment periods and z specifies the principal value of the loan	`Pmt(0.05, 12, -4000)` is `451.301640083261`

`Val(x)`	Returns the numeric value of x	`Val("5")` is `5`
		`Val("5a8")` is `5`
		`Val("a5")` is `0`

`String.Format(` *formatString*, *listOfArguments*`)`	Returns a formatted `String`. The first parameter, *formatString*, specifies the formatting and *listOfArguments* specifies the values to format	`String.Format("{0:C}", 1.23)` is `"$1.23"`

Figure 13.2 Some predefined Visual Basic methods.

However, the .NET Framework Class Library cannot provide every conceivable feature that you might want, so Visual Basic allows you to create your own programmer-defined procedures to meet the unique requirements of your applications. Two types of procedures exist: **`Function` procedures** and **`Sub` procedures**. In the next section, you learn about `Function` procedures; in Section 13.4, you learn about `Sub` procedures. Throughout this tutorial, the term "procedure" refers to both `Function` procedures and `Sub` procedures, unless otherwise noted.

SELF-REVIEW

1. ________ provides the programmer with preexisting classes that perform common tasks.
   a) The Framework Class Library
   b) The `PreExisting` keyword
   c) The Framework Code Library
   d) The `Library` keyword

2. Programmers normally use ________.
   a) programmer-defined procedures
   b) preexisting procedures
   c) both programmer-defined and preexisting procedures
   d) neither programmer-defined nor preexisting procedures

Answers: 1) a. 2) c.

13.3 `Function` Procedures

Software Design Tip

Use procedures to increase the clarity and organization of your applications. This not only helps others understand your applications, but it also helps you develop, test and debug your applications.

The applications presented earlier in this book call .NET Framework Class Library methods (such as `String.Format`) to help accomplish the applications' tasks. You now learn how to write your own programmer-defined procedures. You first learn how to create procedures in the context of two small applications, before you create the enhanced **Wage Calculator** application. The first application uses the Pythagorean theorem to calculate the length of the hypotenuse of a right triangle, and the second application determines the maximum of three numbers. Let us begin by reviewing the Pythagorean theorem. A right triangle (a triangle with a 90-degree angle) always satisfies the following relationship—the sum of the squares of the two smaller sides of the triangle equals the square of the largest side of the triangle, which is known as the hypotenuse. In this application, the two smaller sides are called sides A and B, and their lengths are used to calculate the length of the hypotenuse. Follow the steps in the next box to create the application.

Creating the Hypotenuse Calculator *Application*

1. ***Copying the template to your working directory.*** Copy the `C:\Examples\Tutorial13\TemplateApplication\HypotenuseCalculator` directory to your `C:\SimplyVB2008` directory.

2. ***Opening the* Hypotenuse Calculator *application's template file.*** Double click `HypotenuseCalculator.sln` in the `HypotenuseCalculator` directory to open the application in the Visual Basic IDE. When you open the `Form` in **Design** view, you'll see the GUI shown in Fig. 13.3. When this application is running, the user enters the lengths of a triangle's two shorter sides into the **Length of side A:** and **Length of side B:** `TextBoxes`, then clicks the **Calculate Hypotenuse** `Button`. The completed application calculates the length of the hypotenuse and displays the result in the **Length of hypotenuse:** output `Label`.

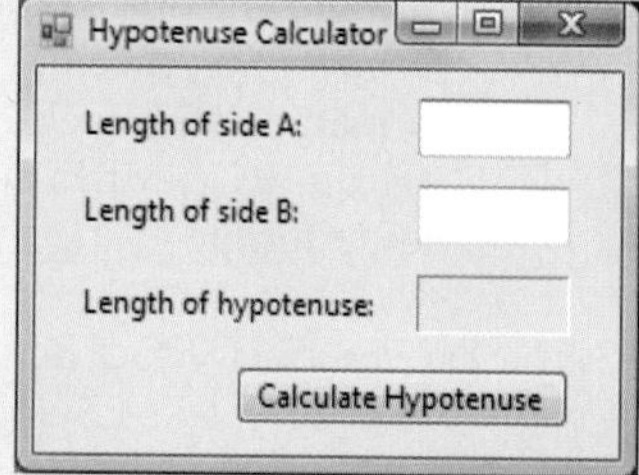

Figure 13.3 **Hypotenuse Calculator** GUI.

3. ***Viewing the template application code.*** Switch to **Code** view, and examine the code provided in the template, shown in Fig. 13.4.

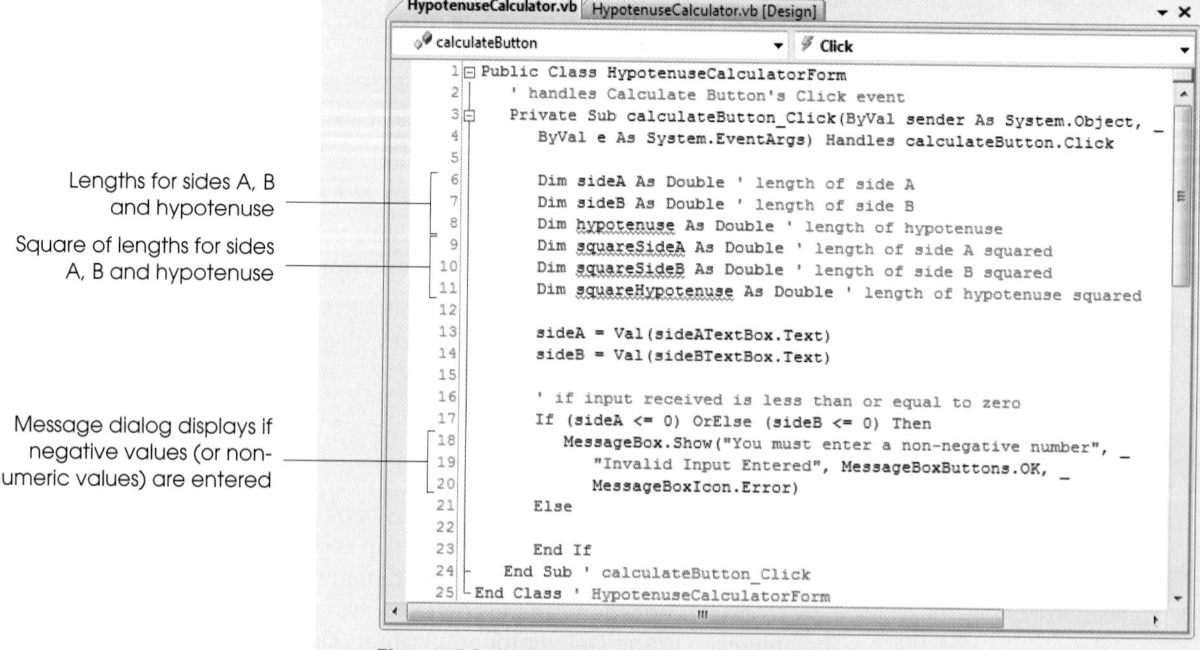

HypotenuseCalculator.vb
HypotenuseCalculator.vb [Design]
calculateButton
Click
Lengths for sides A, B and hypotenuse
Square of lengths for sides A, B and hypotenuse
Message dialog displays if negative values (or non-numeric values) are entered
Public Class HypotenuseCalculatorForm
' handles Calculate Button's Click event
Private Sub calculateButton_Click(ByVal sender As System.Object, _
ByVal e As System.EventArgs) Handles calculateButton.Click
Dim sideA As Double ' length of side A
Dim sideB As Double ' length of side B
Dim hypotenuse As Double ' length of hypotenuse
Dim squareSideA As Double ' length of side A squared
Dim squareSideB As Double ' length of side B squared
Dim squareHypotenuse As Double ' length of hypotenuse squared
sideA = Val(sideATextBox.Text)
sideB = Val(sideBTextBox.Text)
' if input received is less than or equal to zero
If (sideA <= 0) OrElse (sideB <= 0) Then
MessageBox.Show("You must enter a non-negative number", _
"Invalid Input Entered", MessageBoxButtons.OK, _
MessageBoxIcon.Error)
Else
End If
End Sub ' calculateButton_Click
End Class ' HypotenuseCalculatorForm

Figure 13.4 **Hypotenuse Calculator** template code.

(cont.)

Good Programming Practice

Add comments at the beginning of a procedure to indicate its purpose.

Good Programming Practice

Add comments at the end of your procedures, indicating which procedure is being terminated.

We've provided an incomplete event handler for the **Calculate Hypotenuse** `Button`. This event handler contains six declarations (lines 6–11). Variables `sideA` and `sideB` contain the lengths of sides A and B, entered by the user. Variable `hypotenuse` contains the length of the hypotenuse, which is calculated shortly. Variable `squareSideA` stores the length of side A, squared. Similarly, variables `squareSideB` and `squareHypotenuse` store the squares of the lengths of side B and the hypotenuse, respectively. Lines 13–14 store the user input for the lengths of sides A and B. Lines 17–23 contain an `If...Then...Else` statement. The `If` statement's body displays a message dialog if a negative value (or zero) is input as the length of side A or side B, or both. The `Else`'s body, which executes only if you enter values greater than zero, should calculate the length of the hypotenuse.

4. ***Creating an empty `Function` procedure.*** Add lines 26–28 of Fig. 13.5 after event handler `calculateButton_Click`, then press *Enter*. The keywords `End Function` are added by the IDE (line 30). You learn about these keywords shortly. Note that we added a comment in line 30 to identify the procedure being terminated.

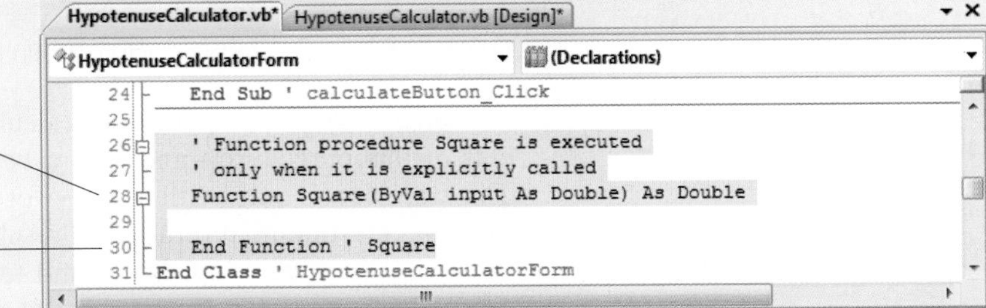

Figure 13.5 `Function` procedure `Square`.

Good Programming Practice

Choosing meaningful procedure names and parameter names makes applications more readable and reduces the need for excessive comments.

5. ***Understanding the `Function` procedure.*** The procedure begins in line 28 (Fig. 13.5) with keyword `Function`, followed by a **procedure name** (in this case, `Square`). The procedure name can be any valid identifier. The procedure name is followed by a set of parentheses containing a parameter declaration.

   The declaration in the parentheses is known as the **parameter list**, where variables (called **parameters**) are declared. Parameters enable a procedure to receive data that helps the procedure perform its task. Although this parameter list contains only one declaration, the parameter list can contain zero or more declarations separated by commas. The parameter list declares each parameter's name and type. Note that the declarations of parameters here use the keyword `ByVal` instead of keyword `Dim`. We discuss keyword `ByVal` shortly. Parameters are used only in the `Function` procedure body.

   A `Function` procedure returns one value after it performs its task. To specify the type of the returned value, the parameter list is followed by the keyword `As`, which is in turn followed by a data type (`Double` in this example). The type that follows `As`, known as the **return type**, indicates the type of the result returned from the `Function` (in this case, `Double`). The first line of a procedure (including the keyword `Function`, the procedure name, the parameter list and the return type) is often called the **procedure header**. The procedure header for `Square` declares one parameter, `input`, to be of type `Double` and sets the return type of `Square` to be `Double`.

Software Design Tip

To promote reusability, each procedure should perform a single well-defined task, and the procedure name should express that task effectively and concisely.

(cont.)

Good Programming Practice

Procedure names should be verbs and should begin with an uppercase first letter. Each subsequent word in the name should begin with an uppercase first letter. This naming convention is known as Pascal case.

The `Function` procedure of Fig. 13.5 ends on line 30 with the keywords **`End Function`**. The declarations and statements that appear after the procedure header but before the keywords `End Function` form the **procedure body**. The procedure body contains code that performs actions, generally by manipulating the parameters from the parameter list, and returns a result. In the next step, you add statements to the body of procedure `Square`. The procedure header, the body and the keywords `End Function` collectively make up the **procedure definition**.

6. ***Adding code to the body of a `Function` procedure.*** You want your `Function` procedure to perform the squaring functionality needed in this application. Add lines 30–31 of Fig. 13.6 to `Square`'s body.

Calculate the square using the ^ operator

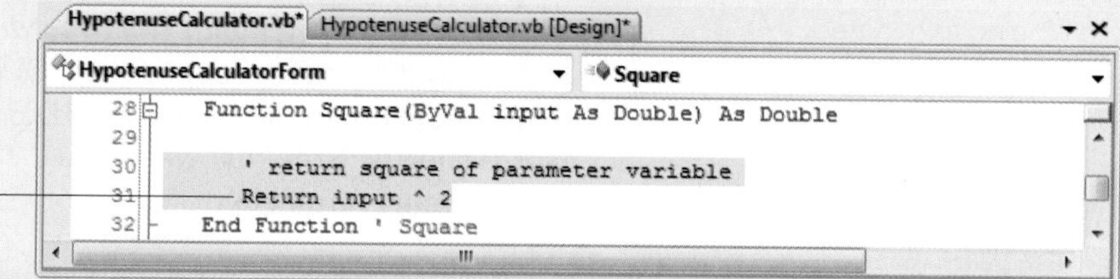

Figure 13.6 `Square` procedure definition.

Good Programming Practice

Placing a blank line between procedure definitions enhances application readability.

Line 31 uses the ^ operator to calculate the square of `input`—the parameter of this procedure—and uses a **`Return` statement** to return this value. This statement begins with the keyword **`Return`**, followed by an expression. The `Return` statement returns the result of the expression following keyword `Return`, in this case `input ^ 2`, and terminates execution of the procedure. This value is returned to the point at which the procedure was called. You write the code to call the procedure in the next step.

7. ***Invoking procedure `Square`.*** Now that you've created your procedure, you can call it from your event handler. Add lines 22–24 of Fig. 13.7 to your application, in the `Else` block of the `If...Then...Else` statement. These lines call `Square` by using the procedure name followed by a set of parentheses that contain the procedure's argument. In this case, the arguments are the variables `sideA` and `sideB`, which contain the user input. In each call, the argument's value is passed to procedure `Square` and stored in its parameter `input`.

Calling procedure `Square`

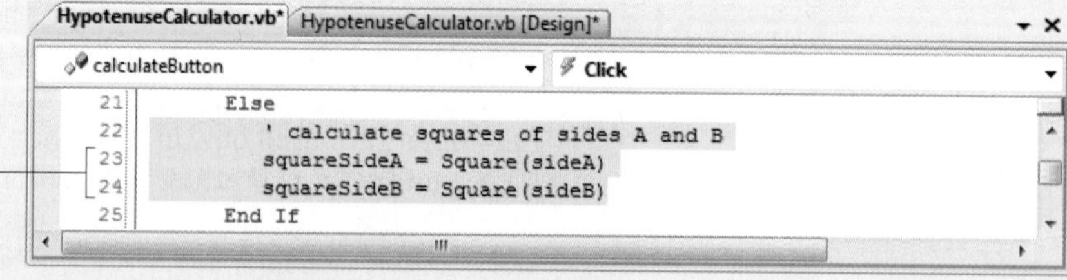

Figure 13.7 Invoking procedure `Square`.

Good Programming Practice

Selecting descriptive parameter names makes the information provided by the *Parameter Info* feature more meaningful.

Note that typing the opening parenthesis after a procedure name causes the Visual Basic IDE to display a window containing the procedure's argument names and types (Fig. 13.8). This is the ***Parameter Info*** feature of the IDE, which provides you with information about procedures and their arguments. The *Parameter Info* feature displays information for programmer-defined procedures as well as for .NET Framework Class Library methods.

(cont.)

Parameter Info window

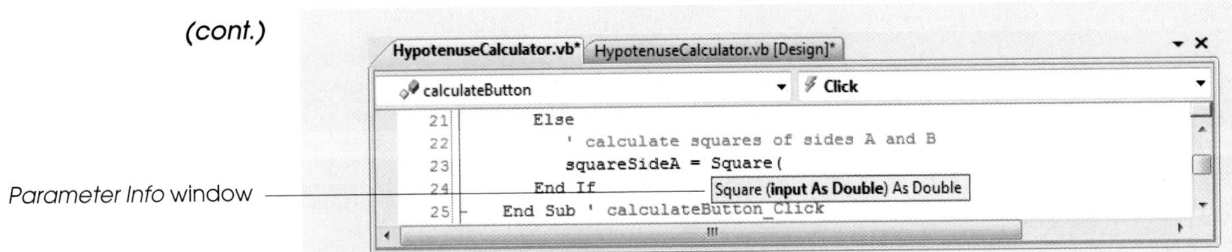

Figure 13.8 *Parameter Info* window.

A procedure is **invoked** (that is, made to perform its designated task) by a **procedure call**. The procedure call specifies the procedure name and provides information (**arguments**) that the **callee** (the procedure being called) requires to do its job. Each argument is assigned to one of the procedure's parameters when the procedure is called. The number of arguments in the call must match the number of parameters in the definition. After completing its task, the called procedure returns control to the **caller** (the **calling procedure**). For example, we have typically called function `Val` as follows:

```
result = Val(inputTextBox.Text)
```

where `Val` is the name of the function, and `inputTextBox.Text`'s value is the argument passed to this function. `Val` uses its argument to perform its defined task (returning the value of `inputTextBox.Text` as a number).

When program control reaches line 23 of Fig. 13.7, the application calls `Function` procedure `Square`. At this point, the application makes a copy of the value stored in variable `sideA` (the user input), and program control transfers to the first line of `Square`.

Keyword **`ByVal`**, specified in procedure `Square`'s parameter declaration, indicates that a copy of the argument's value (the length of side A) should be passed to `Square`. `Square` receives the copy of the value input by the user and stores it in the parameter `input`. When the `Return` statement in `Square` is reached, the value to the right of keyword `Return` is returned to the point in line 23 where `Square` was called, and the procedure's execution completes (any remaining statements of the procedure's body are not executed), and the parameter that was holding the copy of the value is discarded.

Program control also transfers to this point, and the application continues by assigning the return value of `Square` to variable `squareSideA`. These same actions occur again when program control reaches the second call to `Square` in line 24. With this call, the value passed to `Square` is the value stored in variable `sideB`, and the value returned is assigned to variable `squareSideB`. We now need to determine the hypotenuse using the values of `squareSideA` and `squareSideB`.

8. ***Calling a preexisting method of the .NET Framework Class Library.*** Add lines 26–34 of Fig. 13.9 to the `Else`'s body of the `If...Then...Else` statement in your application. Line 28 adds the square of side A and the square of side B, resulting in the square of the hypotenuse, which is assigned to variable `squareHypotenuse`. Line 32 then calls .NET Framework Class Library method **`Sqrt`** of class `Math` (by using the dot operator). This method calculates the square root of the square of the hypotenuse to find the length of the hypotenuse, then formats the result and displays it in the `outputLabel`.

Error-Prevention Tip

Small procedures are easier to test, debug and understand than large ones.

9. ***Running the application.*** Select **Debug > Start Debugging** to run your application. Enter 3 into the **Length of side A:** `TextBox` and 4 into the **Length of side B:** `TextBox`. Click the **Calculate Hypotenuse** `Button`. The output is shown in Fig. 13.10.

(cont.)

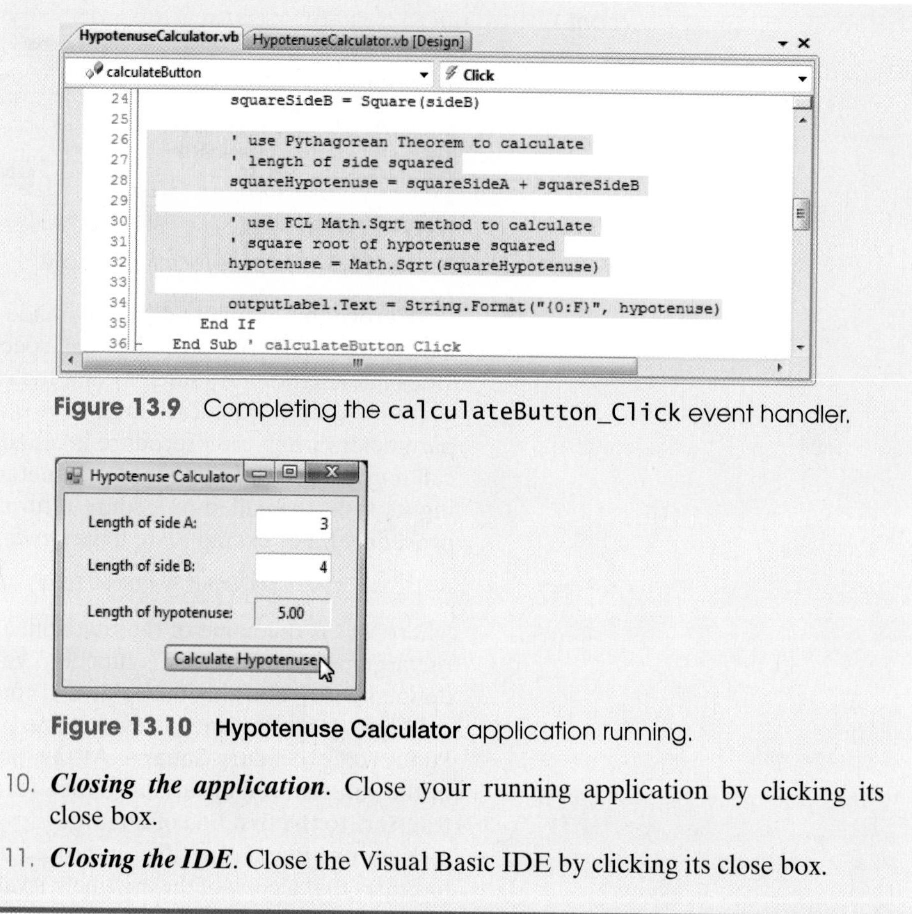

Figure 13.9 Completing the `calculateButton_Click` event handler.

Figure 13.10 **Hypotenuse Calculator** application running.

10. ***Closing the application.*** Close your running application by clicking its close box.
11. ***Closing the IDE.*** Close the Visual Basic IDE by clicking its close box.

You've now successfully created a `Function` procedure and tested it by running the application to confirm that it works correctly. This `Function` procedure can now be used in any Visual Basic application where you wish to calculate the square of a `Double`. All you need to do is include the procedure definition in your application. This is an example of code reuse, which helps you create applications faster.

As demonstrated in the **Hypotenuse Calculator** application, the procedure call used to call a `Function` procedure follows the format

name(*argument list*)

The procedure header and procedure calls all must agree with regard to the number, types and order of parameters.

There must be one argument in the argument list of the procedure call for each parameter in the parameter list of the procedure header. The arguments also must be compatible with the parameters' types (that is, Visual Basic must be able to assign the value of the argument to its corresponding parameter). For example, a parameter of type `Double` could receive the value of `53547.350009`, `22` or `-.03546`, but not `"hello"`, because a `Double` variable cannot contain a `String`. If a procedure does not receive any values, the parameter list is empty (that is, the procedure name is followed by an empty set of parentheses). You study procedure parameters in more detail in Tutorial 15.

As you saw in the preceding example, the statement

`Return` *expression*

can occur anywhere in a `Function` procedure body and returns the value of *expression* to the caller. If necessary, Visual Basic attempts to convert the value of *expression* to the `Function` procedure's return type. `Functions` `Return` exactly one value. When a `Return` statement executes, control returns immediately to the point at which that `Function` procedure was called.

You now create another `Function` procedure. This procedure, which is part of the **Maximum** application, returns the largest of three numbers input by the user. In the following box, you create the **Maximum** application.

Creating a `Function` Procedure That Returns the Largest of Three Numbers

1. ***Copying the template to your working directory.*** Copy the `C:\Examples\Tutorial13\TemplateApplication\Maximum` directory to your directory `C:\SimplyVB2008`.

2. ***Opening the Maximum application's template file.*** Double click `Maximum.sln` in the `Maximum` directory to open the application in the Visual Basic IDE. Switch to **Design** view (Fig. 13.11).

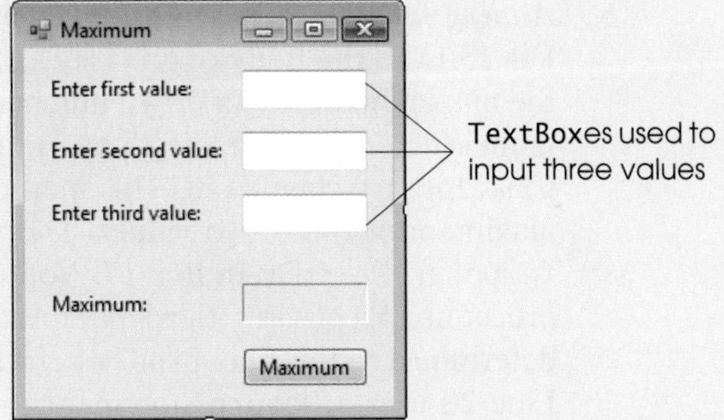

Figure 13.11 **Maximum** application in **Design** view.

3. ***Creating an event handler for the Maximum `Button`.*** Double click the **Maximum** `Button` to create an event handler for this `Button`'s `Click` event. Add a comment in line 2 of Fig. 13.12 and split the header over two lines, as shown in lines 3–4. Add lines 6–7 to the event handler. Lines 6–7 call `Function` procedure `Maximum` and pass it the three values the user has input into the application's `TextBoxes`. Note that `Maximum` has been underlined in blue, indicating a compilation error. This occurs because `Function` procedure `Maximum` has not yet been defined. You define `Maximum` in the next step. This compilation error occurs whenever you call a procedure that is not recognized by the Visual Basic IDE. Misspelling the name of a procedure in a procedure call also causes a compilation error. Finally, add the comment after keywords `End Sub` in line 8.

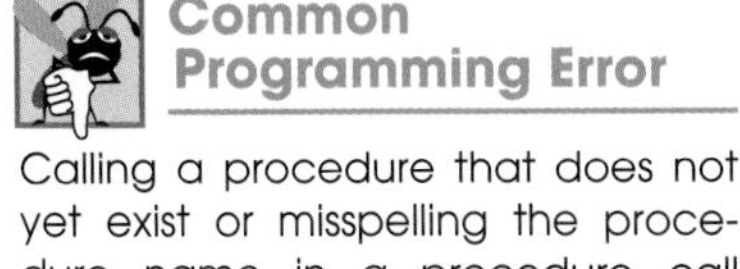

Calling a procedure that does not yet exist or misspelling the procedure name in a procedure call results in a compilation error.

Calling a procedure that has not yet been defined is an error

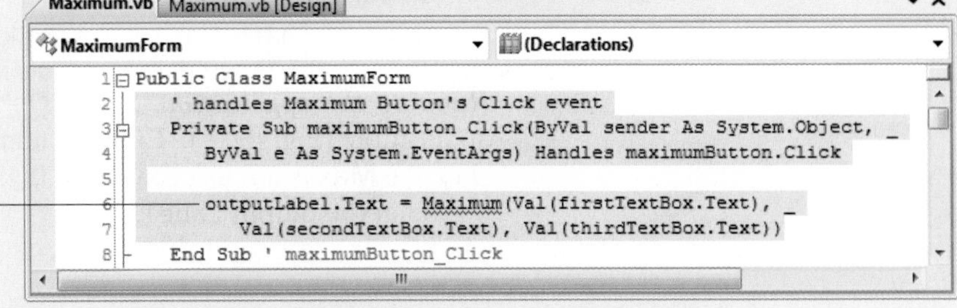

Figure 13.12 Invoking `Function` procedure `Maximum`.

4. ***Creating `Function` procedure `Maximum`.*** Add lines 10–12 of Fig. 13.13 after event handler `maximumButton_Click`, then press *Enter*. Note that the keywords `End Function` are added for you by the IDE. The parameter list specifies that the values of the three arguments passed to `Maximum` are stored in parameters `one`, `two` and `three`. The parameter list is followed by the keyword `As` and the return type `Double`.

(cont.)

Empty Function procedure Maximum

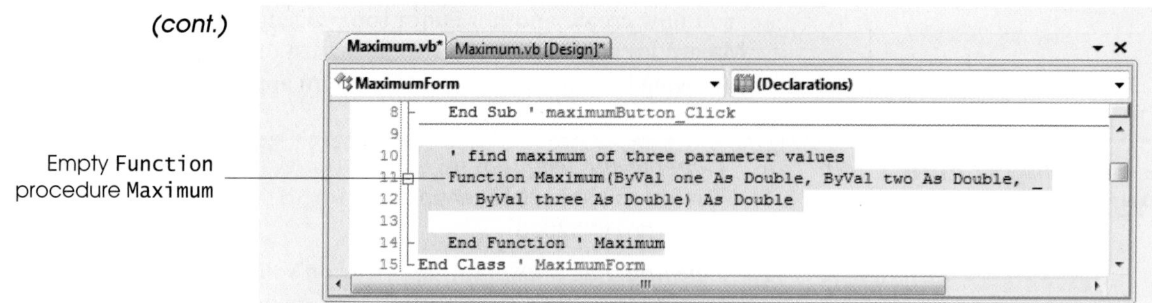

Figure 13.13 Maximum Function procedure.

5. ***Adding functionality to Function procedure Maximum.*** Add lines 14–20 of Fig. 13.14 to the body of Maximum. Line 14 creates a variable that contains the maximum of the first two numbers passed to this procedure. This maximum is determined in line 17 by using the Max method of .NET Framework Class Library class Math. This method takes two Doubles and returns the maximum of these two values. The value returned is assigned to variable temporaryMaximum in line 17. You then compare that value to Function procedure Maximum's third parameter, three, in line 18. The maximum determined in this line, finalMaximum, is the maximum of the three values. Line 20 uses a Return statement to return this value. The Return statement terminates execution of the procedure and returns the result of finalMaximum to the calling procedure. The result is returned to the point (line 6 of Fig. 13.12) where Maximum was called and is assigned to outputLabel's Text property.

Calling Math.Max to determine the maximum of two values

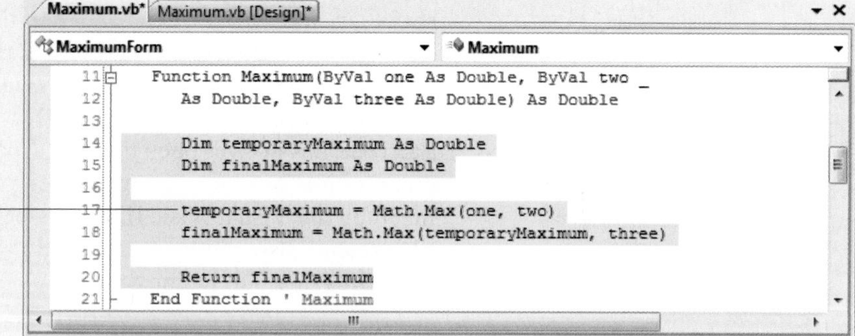

Figure 13.14 Math.Max returns the larger of its two arguments.

6. ***Running the application.*** Select **Debug > Start Debugging** to run your application (Fig. 13.15). Enter a numeric value into each TextBox, and click the **Maximum** Button. Note that the largest of the three values is displayed in the output Label.

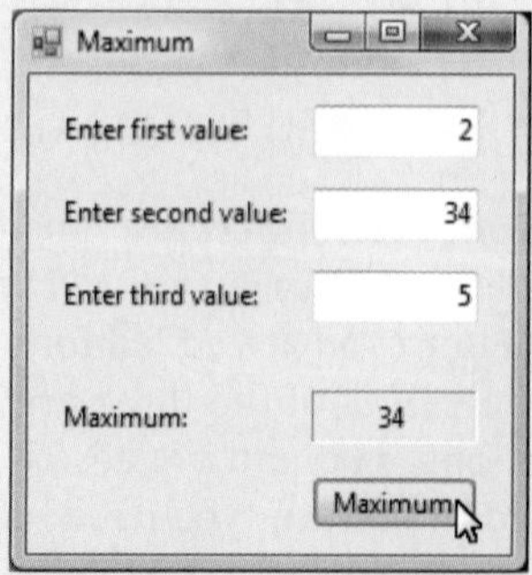

Figure 13.15 **Maximum** application running.

(cont.)

7. ***Closing the application***. Close your running application by clicking its close box.
8. ***Closing the IDE***. Close the Visual Basic IDE by clicking its close box.

SELF-REVIEW

1. A procedure is invoked by a(n) ________.
   a) callee b) caller
   c) argument d) parameter
2. The ________ statement in a `Function` procedure sends a value back to the calling procedure.
   a) `Return` b) `Back`
   c) `End` d) None of the above

Answers: 1) b. 2) a.

13.4 Using Sub Procedures in the Wage Calculator Application

The **Calculate** `Button`'s `Click` event handler in the original version of the **Wage Calculator** application (Tutorial 7) calculated wages and displayed the result in a `Label`. In the following box, you'll write `Sub` procedure `DisplayPay` to perform these tasks. **`Sub` procedures** are similar to `Function` procedures, with one important difference: `Sub` procedures do not return a value to the caller. When the user clicks the **Calculate** `Button`, event handler `calculateButton_Click` calls `Sub` procedure `DisplayPay`.

Creating a Sub Procedure within the Wage Calculator Application

1. ***Copying the template to your working directory.*** Copy the `C:\Examples\Tutorial13\TemplateApplication\WageCalculator2` directory to your `C:\SimplyVB2008` directory.
2. ***Opening the Wage Calculator application's template file.*** Double click `WageCalculator2.sln` in the `WageCalculator2` directory to open the application in the Visual Basic IDE.
3. ***Creating the `calculateButton_Click` event handler.*** View the application's `Form` in **Design** view. Double click the **Calculate** `Button` to generate the `Click` event handler.
4. ***Entering functionality to `calculateButton_Click`.*** Add lines 6–15 of Fig. 13.16 to the empty event handler. This code calls procedure `DisplayPay` to calculate and display the wages. Lines 11–12 retrieve the user input from the `TextBoxes` and assign the values to variables declared in lines 7–8. Line 15 calls procedure `DisplayPay`, which you define shortly. This procedure call takes two arguments: the hours worked (`userHours`) and the hourly wage (`wage`). Note that the call to `DisplayPay` is underlined in blue because the procedure has not yet been defined; for the moment, this is a compilation error.
5. ***Creating a `Sub` procedure.*** After event handler `calculateButton_Click`, add `Sub` procedure `DisplayPay` to your application (lines 18–39 of Fig. 13.17).

   Procedure `DisplayPay` receives the argument values and stores them in the parameters `hours` and `rate`. Note that the syntax of a `Sub` procedure is the same as the syntax of a `Function` procedure, with a few small changes. In particular, the `Function` and `End Function` keywords are replaced with the **`Sub`** and **`End Sub`** keywords (lines 19 and 39 of Fig. 13.17), respectively. Another difference is that there is no return type, because `Sub` procedures do not return values.

(cont.)

Call to DisplayPay

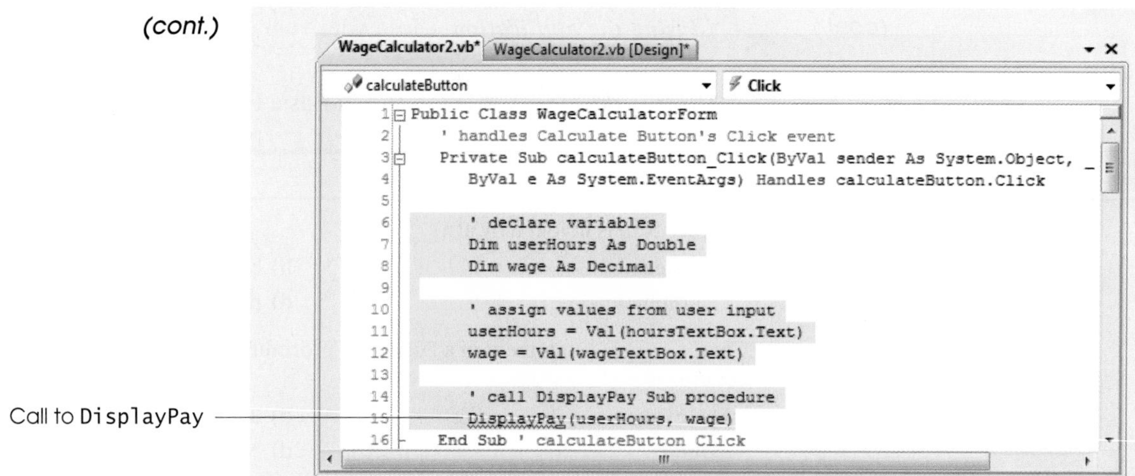

```
1  Public Class WageCalculatorForm
2     ' handles Calculate Button's Click event
3     Private Sub calculateButton_Click(ByVal sender As System.Object, _
4        ByVal e As System.EventArgs) Handles calculateButton.Click
5
6        ' declare variables
7        Dim userHours As Double
8        Dim wage As Decimal
9
10       ' assign values from user input
11       userHours = Val(hoursTextBox.Text)
12       wage = Val(wageTextBox.Text)
13
14       ' call DisplayPay Sub procedure
15       DisplayPay(userHours, wage)
16    End Sub ' calculateButton_Click
```

Figure 13.16 calculateButton_Click calls DisplayPay.

DisplayPay calculates and displays the user's gross earnings

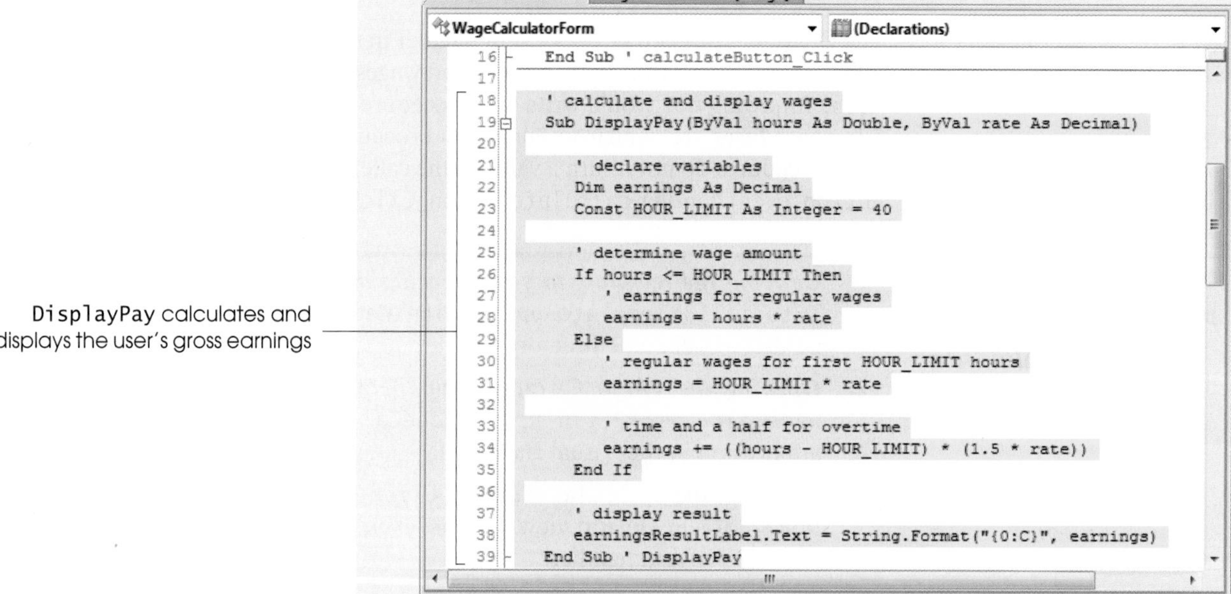

```
16    End Sub ' calculateButton_Click
17
18    ' calculate and display wages
19    Sub DisplayPay(ByVal hours As Double, ByVal rate As Decimal)
20
21       ' declare variables
22       Dim earnings As Decimal
23       Const HOUR_LIMIT As Integer = 40
24
25       ' determine wage amount
26       If hours <= HOUR_LIMIT Then
27          ' earnings for regular wages
28          earnings = hours * rate
29       Else
30          ' regular wages for first HOUR_LIMIT hours
31          earnings = HOUR_LIMIT * rate
32
33          ' time and a half for overtime
34          earnings += ((hours - HOUR_LIMIT) * (1.5 * rate))
35       End If
36
37       ' display result
38       earningsResultLabel.Text = String.Format("{0:C}", earnings)
39    End Sub ' DisplayPay
```

Figure 13.17 Sub procedure DisplayPay definition.

Common Programming Error

Declaring a variable in a procedure's body with the same name as a parameter in the procedure header is a compilation error.

Note that the variable earnings and the constant HOUR_LIMIT have been moved to the DisplayPay procedure. (In Fig. 7.14 of Tutorial 7, they were located within the calculateButton_Click event handler.) They are no longer needed in calculateButton_Click, so they have been removed from that event handler.

Lines 26–35 define the If...Then...Else statement that determines whether overtime must be calculated. The condition for this statement determines whether hours is less than or equal to constant HOUR_LIMIT. If it is, then the employee's earnings without overtime are calculated. Otherwise, the employee's earnings including overtime are calculated. Line 38 displays the result (formatted as currency) in a Label.

When control reaches the End Sub statement, control returns to the calling procedure, calculateButton_Click (line 15 of Fig. 13.16).

6. ***Saving the project.*** Select **File > Save All** to save your modified code.

The following box shows you how to add `Function` procedure `CheckOvertime` to the **Wage Calculator** application. `CheckOvertime` determines whether an employee has worked overtime.

Creating a `Function` Procedure within the Wage Calculator Application

1. ***Creating a `Function` procedure header.*** Add `Function` procedure `CheckOvertime` (lines 41–50 of Fig. 13.18) to your application, after the `DisplayPay` procedure definition. Note that the return type of the procedure is `Boolean`—the value returned by the procedure must be a `Boolean` (that is, a constant, variable or expression that evaluates to `True` or `False`).

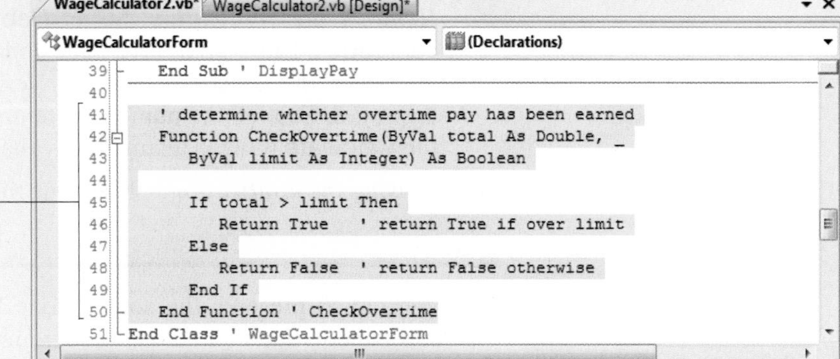

WageCalculator2.vb*
WageCalculator2.vb [Design]*
WageCalculatorForm
(Declarations)
39 End Sub ' DisplayPay
40
41 ' determine whether overtime pay has been earned
42 Function CheckOvertime(ByVal total As Double, _
43 ByVal limit As Integer) As Boolean
44
45 If total > limit Then
46 Return True ' return True if over limit
47 Else
48 Return False ' return False otherwise
49 End If
50 End Function ' CheckOvertime
51 End Class ' WageCalculatorForm

`CheckOvertime` determines if the user has worked overtime

Common Programming Error

Failure to return a value from a `Function` procedure causes the procedure to return the default value for the *return-type* (0 for numeric types, `False` for `Boolean`s, `Nothing` for so-called reference types), often resulting in logic errors.

Figure 13.18 `Function` procedure `CheckOverTime` definition.

When the program calls `CheckOvertime`, program control transfers to the beginning of this procedure (line 42). The arguments passed to this procedure (passed in the procedure call, which you write in the next step) are stored in the parameters `total` (the total hours worked) and `limit` (the maximum hours before overtime is paid). Line 46 returns the `Boolean` value `True`, to indicate that the employee has worked overtime; line 48 returns the `Boolean` value `False`, to indicate that the employee has not worked overtime. Program control and the value (either `True` or `False`) are returned to the line where `CheckOvertime` was initially called.

2. ***Modifying `Sub` procedure `DisplayPay`.*** In `Sub` procedure `DisplayPay`, replace the statement (line 26 of Fig. 13.17)

```
If hours <= HOUR_LIMIT Then
```

with line 26 of Fig. 13.19. We modify `DisplayPay` so that it now calls `Function` procedure `CheckOvertime` to determine whether the employee qualifies for overtime pay.

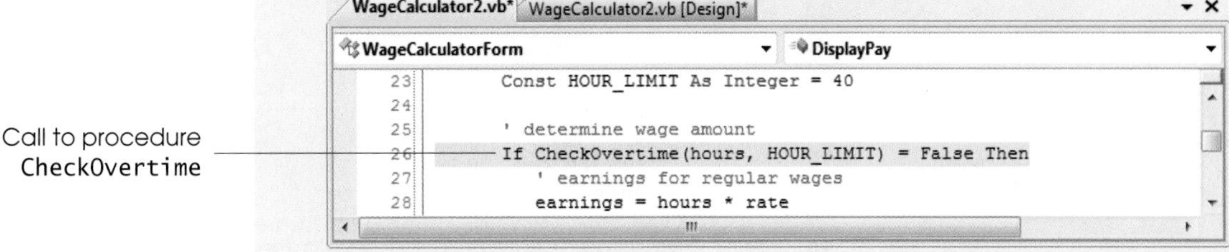

Figure 13.19 `DisplayPay` calls `Function` procedure `CheckOvertime`.

Line 26 calls `Function` procedure `CheckOvertime` in the `If` statement's condition. At this point, the application copies the values of `hours` and `HOUR_LIMIT` (the arguments in the procedure call), and control transfers to the header of `Function` procedure `CheckOvertime`.

(cont.)

The parameters in CheckOvertime's header are initialized to copies of hours's value and HOUR_LIMIT's value. The value returned from CheckOvertime is compared to the value False in line 26. Note that this line can also be written as

```
If Not CheckOvertime(hours, HOUR_LIMIT) Then
```

Now when the **Calculate** Button is clicked, DisplayPay is called and executed. Recall that Function procedure CheckOvertime is called by the DisplayPay Sub procedure. This sequence of calls is repeated every time the user clicks the **Calculate** Button.

3. ***Running the application***. Select **Debug > Start Debugging** to run your application. Enter an hourly wage and number of hours worked (under 40), then click the **Calculate** Button. Verify that the appropriate earnings are displayed. Change the number of hours worked to a value over 40 and click the **Calculate** Button again. Verify that the appropriate output is displayed.

4. ***Closing the application***. Close your running application by clicking its close box.

Figure 13.20 presents the source code for the **Wage Calculator** application. The lines of code that contain new programming concepts you learned in this tutorial are highlighted.

Call to Sub procedure that calculates and displays wages (line 15)

Sub procedure header specifies parameter names and types (line 19)

Call to Function procedure that determines if user has worked overtime (line 26)

```
1  Public Class WageCalculatorForm
2     ' handles Calculate Button's Click event
3     Private Sub calculateButton_Click(ByVal sender As System.Object, _
4        ByVal e As System.EventArgs) Handles calculateButton.Click
5
6        ' declare variables
7        Dim userHours As Double
8        Dim wage As Decimal
9
10       ' assign values from user input
11       userHours = Val(hoursTextBox.Text)
12       wage = Val(wageTextBox.Text)
13
14       ' call DisplayPay Sub procedure
15       DisplayPay(userHours, wage)
16    End Sub ' calculateButton_Click
17
18    ' calculate and display wages
19    Sub DisplayPay(ByVal hours As Double, ByVal rate As Decimal)
20
21       ' declare variables
22       Dim earnings As Decimal
23       Const HOUR_LIMIT As Integer = 40
24
25       ' determine wage amount
26       If CheckOvertime(hours, HOUR_LIMIT) = False Then
27          ' earnings for regular wages
28          earnings = hours * rate
29       Else
30          ' regular wages for first HOUR_LIMIT hours
31          earnings = HOUR_LIMIT * rate
32
33          ' time and a half for overtime
34          earnings += ((hours - HOUR_LIMIT) * (1.5 * rate))
35       End If
36
```

Figure 13.20 Code for **Wage Calculator** application. (Part 1 of 2.)

End Sub keywords indicate the end of Sub procedure definition

Function procedure header specifies parameter names and types as well as a return type

End Function keywords indicate the end of Function procedure definition

```
      ' display result
      earningsResultLabel.Text = String.Format("{0:C}", earnings)
   End Sub ' DisplayPay

   ' determine whether overtime pay has been earned
   Function CheckOvertime(ByVal total As Double, _
      ByVal limit As Integer) As Boolean

      If total > limit Then
         Return True ' return True if over limit
      Else
         Return False ' return False otherwise
      End If
   End Function ' CheckOvertime
End Class ' WageCalculatorForm
```

Figure 13.20 Code for **Wage Calculator** application. (Part 2 of 2.)

SELF-REVIEW

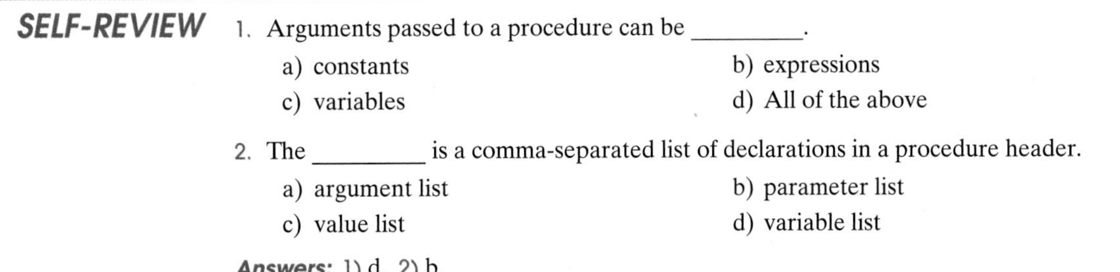

1. Arguments passed to a procedure can be ________.
   a) constants b) expressions
   c) variables d) All of the above

2. The ________ is a comma-separated list of declarations in a procedure header.
   a) argument list b) parameter list
   c) value list d) variable list

Answers: 1) d. 2) b.

13.5 Using the Debugger: Debugging Controls

Now you continue your study of the debugger by learning about the debugging controls on the **Standard** toolbar (Fig. 13.21). These `ToolStripButtons` provide convenient access to commands in the **Debug** menu. If the **Standard** toolbar isn't visible in the IDE, select **View > Toolbars > Standard**. In this section, you learn how to use the debug `ToolStripButtons` to verify that a procedure's code is executing correctly. In the following box, we use the debug `ToolStripButtons` to examine the **Wage Calculator** application.

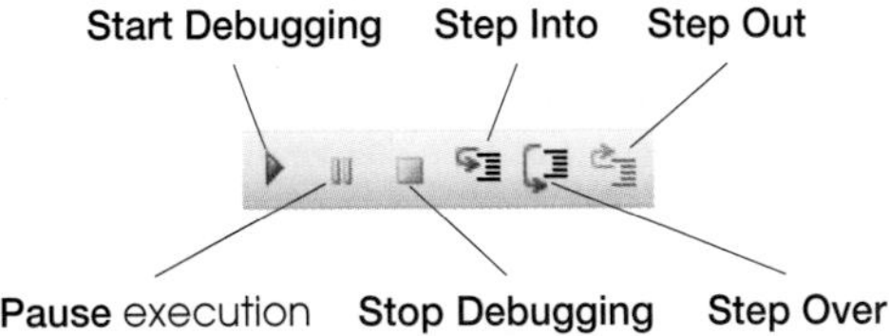

Figure 13.21 Debugging controls on the **Standard** toolbar.

Using the Debugger: Debugging Controls

1. ***Opening the completed application.*** If your completed **Wage Calculator** application is not open, double click the `WageCalculator2.sln` file in the directory `C:\SimplyVB2008\WageCalculator2` to open it.

2. ***Setting a breakpoint.*** Set a breakpoint in line 15 by clicking in the margin indicator bar (Fig. 13.22).

3. ***Starting the debugger.*** To start the debugger, select **Debug > Start Debugging**, or click the **Start Debugging** `ToolStripButton` (▶) on the **Standard** toolbar. The **Wage Calculator** application executes. Enter the value `7.50` in the **Hourly wage:** `TextBox`, and enter `35` in the **Weekly hours:** `TextBox`. Click the **Calculate** `Button`.

(cont.)

Breakpoint set at a line containing a procedure call

```
WageCalculator2.vb   WageCalculator2.vb [Design]
calculateButton      Click
12        wage = Val(wageTextBox.Text)
13
14        ' call DisplayPay Sub procedure
15        DisplayPay(userHours, wage)
16     End Sub ' calculateButton_Click
```

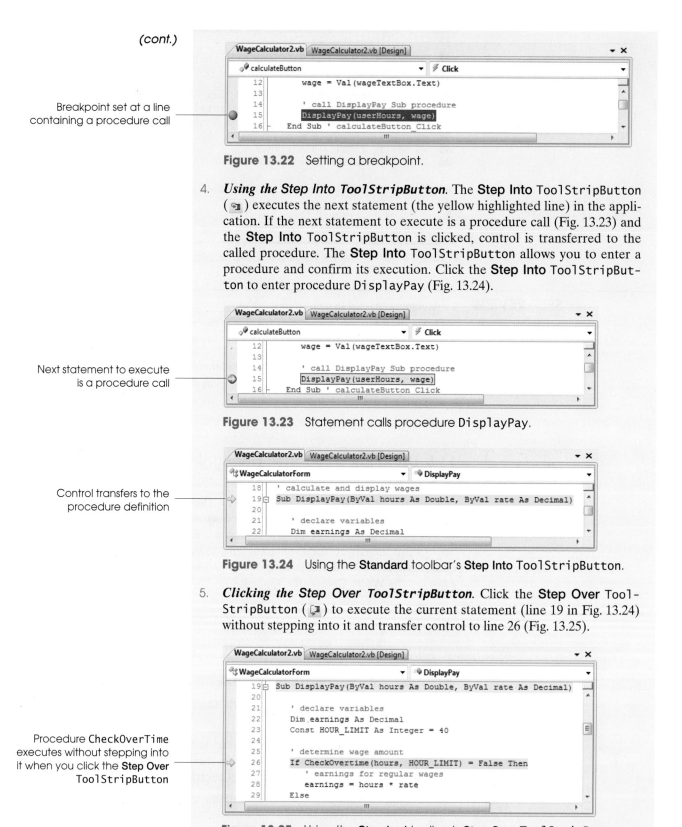

Figure 13.22 Setting a breakpoint.

4. ***Using the Step Into ToolStripButton.*** The **Step Into** ToolStripButton ( ) executes the next statement (the yellow highlighted line) in the application. If the next statement to execute is a procedure call (Fig. 13.23) and the **Step Into** ToolStripButton is clicked, control is transferred to the called procedure. The **Step Into** ToolStripButton allows you to enter a procedure and confirm its execution. Click the **Step Into** ToolStripButton to enter procedure DisplayPay (Fig. 13.24).

Next statement to execute is a procedure call

```
WageCalculator2.vb   WageCalculator2.vb [Design]
calculateButton      Click
12        wage = Val(wageTextBox.Text)
13
14        ' call DisplayPay Sub procedure
15        DisplayPay(userHours, wage)
16     End Sub ' calculateButton Click
```

Figure 13.23 Statement calls procedure DisplayPay.

Control transfers to the procedure definition

```
WageCalculator2.vb   WageCalculator2.vb [Design]
WageCalculatorForm   DisplayPay
18     ' calculate and display wages
19     Sub DisplayPay(ByVal hours As Double, ByVal rate As Decimal)
20
21        ' declare variables
22        Dim earnings As Decimal
```

Figure 13.24 Using the **Standard** toolbar's **Step Into** ToolStripButton.

5. ***Clicking the Step Over ToolStripButton.*** Click the **Step Over** ToolStripButton ( ) to execute the current statement (line 19 in Fig. 13.24) without stepping into it and transfer control to line 26 (Fig. 13.25).

Procedure CheckOverTime executes without stepping into it when you click the **Step Over** ToolStripButton

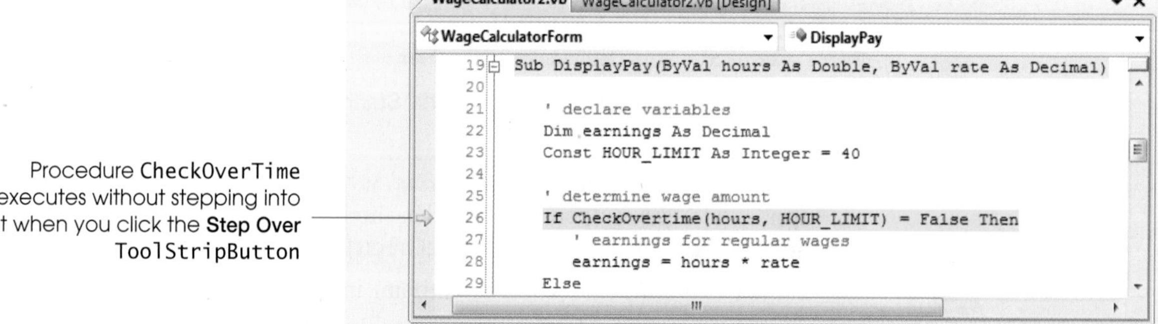

Figure 13.25 Using the **Standard** toolbar's **Step Over** ToolStripButton.

(cont.)

6. ***Clicking the* Step Over ToolStripButton *again*.** Click the **Step Over** `ToolStripButton`. **Step Over** behaves like the **Step Into** when the next statement to execute does not contain a procedure call. If the next statement to execute contains a procedure call, the called procedure executes in its entirety (without transferring control and entering the procedure), and the yellow arrow advances to the next executable line in the current procedure (Fig. 13.26).

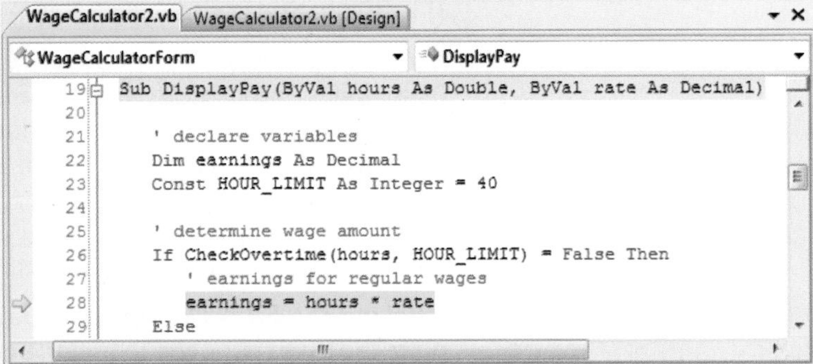

Figure 13.26 Using the **Standard** toolbar's **Step Over** `ToolStripButton` again.

7. ***Setting a breakpoint*.** Set a breakpoint at the end of procedure `DisplayPay` in line 39 (`End Sub`) of Fig. 13.27. You will make use of this breakpoint in the next step.

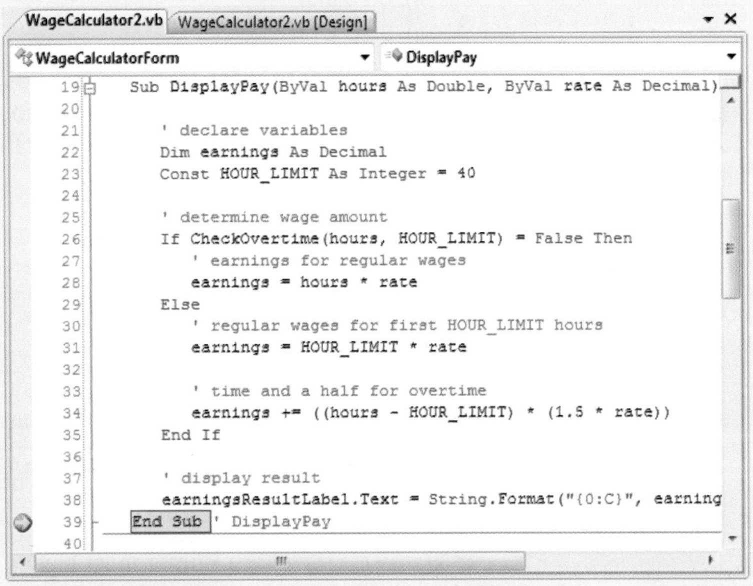

Figure 13.27 Using the **Standard** toolbar's **Continue** `ToolStripButton`.

8. ***Using the* Continue ToolStripButton.** Clicking the **Continue** `ToolStripButton` (▶) executes any statements between the next executable statement and the next breakpoint or the end of the current event handler, whichever comes first. Note that there is one executable statement (line 38) before the breakpoint that was set in *Step 7*. Click the **Continue** `ToolStripButton`. The next executable statement is now line 39 (Fig. 13.27). This feature is particularly useful when you have many lines of code before the next breakpoint that you do not want to step through line by line.

(cont.)

9. ***Using the Stop Debugging ToolStripButton.*** Click the **Stop Debugging** ToolStripButton ( ) to end the debugging session and return the IDE to design mode.
10. ***Starting the debugger.*** We have one last feature to present that requires you to start the debugger again. Start the debugger, as you did in *Step 3*, entering the same values as input.
11. ***Using the Step Into ToolStripButton.*** Keep the breakpoint in line 15 (Fig. 13.22) and remove the breakpoint from line 39. Repeat *Step 4*.
12. ***Clicking the Step Out ToolStripButton.*** After you've stepped into the DisplayPay procedure, click the **Step Out** ToolStripButton ( ) to execute the statements in the procedure and return control to line 15, which contains the procedure call. Often, in lengthy procedures, you want to look at a few key lines of code and then continue debugging the caller's code. This feature is useful for such situations, where you do not want to continue stepping through the entire procedure line by line.
13. ***Clicking the Stop Debugging ToolStripButton.*** Click the **Stop Debugging** ToolStripButton to end the debugging session.
14. ***Closing the IDE.*** Close the Visual Basic IDE by clicking its close box.

SELF-REVIEW

1. During debugging, the ________ ToolStripButton executes the remaining statements in the current procedure call and returns program control to the place where the procedure was called.

    a) **Step Into** b) **Step Out**
    c) **Step Over** d) **Steps**

2. The ________ ToolStripButton behaves like the **Step Into** ToolStripButton when the next statement to execute does not contain a procedure call.

    a) **Step Into** b) **Step Out**
    c) **Step Over** d) **Steps**

Answers: 1) b. 2) c.

13.6 Optional Parameters

It is not uncommon for a program to invoke a procedure repeatedly with the same argument value for a particular parameter. In such cases, you can specify that such a parameter is an **Optional parameter** that has a default value. In a procedure call, when the argument for an Optional parameter is omitted, the compiler rewrites the procedure call and inserts the Optional parameter's default value. There are three rules for using Optional parameters:

- Each Optional parameter must have a default value.
- The default value must be a constant expression (typically a literal value, such as a numeric value or a string literal).
- All parameters that appear after an Optional parameter in the parameter list, must also be Optional parameters.

Consider the Function BoxVolume that calculates the volume of a box (i.e., length times width times height):

```
Function BoxVolume( Optional ByVal length As Integer = 1, _
   Optional ByVal width As Integer = 1, _
   Optional ByVal height As Integer = 1 ) As Integer

   Return length * width * height
End Function ' BoxVolume
```

In this case, all three parameters are optional, as specified by the Optional keyword before each parameter's declaration. Notice that each parameter has a default value specified with an = and a literal value (1). If BoxVolume is invoked with fewer than three Integer arguments, the value 1 will be specified for each omitted argument. You can now invoke Function BoxVolume several different ways:

```
BoxVolume() ' returns 1; default values used for length, width, height
BoxVolume(10) ' returns 10; default values used for width, height
BoxVolume(10, 20) ' returns 200; default value used for height
BoxVolume(10, 20, 30) ' returns 6000; no default values used
BoxVolume(, 20, 30) ' returns 600; default value used for length
BoxVolume(10, , 30) ' returns 300; default value used for width
```

Arguments can be omitted for any of the parameters. For example, the last two method calls omitted the length and width parameters, respectively. Notice that comma placeholders are used when an omitted argument is not the last argument in the call.

13.7 Wrap-Up

In this tutorial, you learned about the difference between Function and Sub procedures, and you learned how procedures can be used to better organize an application. From this point forward, we frequently refer to Function and Sub procedures simply as methods. This tutorial introduced you to the concept called code reuse, showing how time and effort can be saved by using preexisting code. You used preexisting code provided by the .NET Framework Class Library and learned to create your own code that can be used in other applications.

You learned the syntax for creating and invoking the two types of procedures. You learned the components of a procedure, including the procedure header, parameter list, and (in the case of Function procedures) the return type and Return statement. After learning how to develop and write procedures, you learned about the order of execution that occurs from the line where a procedure is called (invoked) to the procedure definition, and returning control back to the point of invocation. In this tutorial's applications, you created three Function procedures—Square, Maximum and CheckOvertime—and a Sub procedure (DisplayPay).

After creating the procedures in this tutorial, you learned how to debug the procedures in the application by using the ToolStripButtons in the **Standard** toolbar. These ToolStripButtons (including **Step Into**, **Step Out** and **Step Over**) can be used to determine whether a procedure is executing correctly. Finally, you learned how to declare and use Optional parameters.

In the next tutorial, you'll learn about such controls as GroupBoxes and DateTimePickers and use them to build a **Shipping Time** application. This application controls information about a package being shipped from one location to another.

SKILLS SUMMARY

Creating a Function Procedure

- Use keyword Function to begin the procedure.
- Specify a parameter list declaring each parameter's name and type. In the parameter list, use keyword ByVal in place of keyword Dim.
- Place the keyword As and the return type after the parenthesis that terminates the parameter list.
- Press *Enter* to generate the terminating End Function statement.
- Add code to the procedure's body to perform a specific task.
- Return a value with the Return statement.

Using a Function Procedure

- Use a Function procedure when a value needs to be returned to the caller.

Returning a Value from a Function Procedure

- Use the Return keyword followed by the value to be returned.

Creating a Sub Procedure

- Start the procedure header with keyword Sub.
- Specify a parameter list declaring each parameter's name and type. In the parameter list, use keyword ByVal in place of keyword Dim.
- Press *Enter* to generate the terminating End Sub statement.
- Add code to the procedure's body to perform a specific task.

Invoking a Procedure

- Specify the procedure name and any arguments in parentheses.
- Ensure that the arguments passed match the procedure definition's parameters in number, type and order.

Using the Debugging Controls in the Standard Toolbar

- To execute a procedure while stepping through your code in the debugger, click the **Step Into** ToolStripButton if you'd like to view the execution of that procedure's body statements.
- To step out of a procedure in the debugger, click the **Step Out** ToolStripButton to return to the caller.
- When you wish to execute a procedure in your code without stepping through it in the debugger, click the **Step Over** ToolStripButton.

Specifying Optional Parameters in a Procedure Definition

- Place the keword Optional before the declaration each parameter that should have a default value.
- Follow the parameter's type with an = and its default value.

KEY TERMS

argument—Information provided to a procedure call.

ByVal keyword—The keyword specifying that the calling procedure should pass a copy of its argument's value in the procedure call to the called procedure.

callee—The procedure being called.

caller—The procedure that calls another procedure. Also known as the calling procedure.

componentization—*See* divide-and-conquer technique.

divide-and-conquer technique—Constructing large applications from small, manageable pieces to make development and maintenance of large applications easier.

End Function keywords—Indicates the end of a Function procedure.

End Sub keywords—Indicates the end of a Sub procedure.

Function keyword—Begins the definition of a Function procedure.

Function procedure—A procedure similar to a Sub procedure, with one important difference: Function procedures return a value to the caller, whereas Sub procedures do not.

invoking a procedure—Causing a procedure to perform its designated task.

Max method of class Math—A method of class Math which returns the greater of its two arguments.

method—A procedure contained in a class.

Min method of class Math—A method of class Math which returns the lesser of its two arguments.

Optional parameter—A parameter that is specified with a default value. If the corresponding argument is omitted in the procedure call, the default value is supplied by the compiler.

***Parameter Info* feature of the IDE**—Provides information about procedures and their arguments.

parameter—A variable declared in a procedure's parameter list that can be used in the body of the procedure.

parameter list—A comma-separated list in which the procedure declares each parameter's name and type.

procedure—A set of instructions for performing a particular task.

procedure body—The declarations and statements that appear after the procedure header but before the keywords `End Sub` or `End Function`. The procedure body contains Visual Basic code that performs actions, generally by manipulating or interacting with the parameters from the parameter list.

procedure call—Invokes a procedure, specifies the procedure name and provides arguments that the callee (the procedure being called) requires to perform its task.

procedure definition—The procedure header, body and ending statement.

procedure header—The first line of a procedure (including the keyword `Sub` or `Function`, the procedure name, the parameter list and the `Function` procedure return type).

procedure name—Follows the keyword `Sub` or `Function` and distinguishes one procedure from another. A procedure name can be any valid identifier.

programmer-defined procedure—A procedure created by a programmer to meet the unique needs of a particular application.

`Return` keyword—Signifies the return statement that sends a value back to the procedure's caller.

`Return` statement—Used to return a value from a procedure.

return type—Data type of the result returned from a `Function` procedure.

reusing code—The practice of using existing code to build new code. Reusing code saves time, effort and money.

`Sqrt` method of class `Math`—A method of class `Math` which returns the square root of its argument.

`Sub` keyword—Begins the definition of a `Sub` procedure.

`Sub` procedure—A procedure similar to a `Function` procedure, with one important difference: `Sub` procedures do not return a value to the caller, whereas `Function` procedures do.

CONTROLS, EVENTS, PROPERTIES & METHODS

`Math` This class provides methods used to perform common arithmetic calculations.

- ***Methods***

  `Min`—Returns the lesser of two numeric values.

  `Max`—Returns the greater of two numeric values.

  `Sqrt`—Returns the square root of a numeric value.

MULTIPLE-CHOICE QUESTIONS

13.1 A procedure defined with keyword `Sub` _________.

a) must specify a return type
b) does not accept arguments
c) returns a value
d) does not return a value

13.2 The technique of developing large applications from small, manageable pieces is known as _________.

a) divide and conquer
b) returning a value
c) click and mortar
d) a building-block algorithm

13.3 What is the difference between `Sub` and `Function` procedures?

a) `Sub` procedures return values, `Function` procedures do not.
b) `Function` procedures return values, `Sub` procedures do not.
c) `Sub` procedures accept parameters, `Function` procedures do not.
d) `Function` procedures accept parameters, `Sub` procedures do not.

13.4 What occurs after a procedure call is made?

a) Control is given to the called procedure. After the procedure is run, the application continues execution at the point where the procedure call was made.

b) Control is given to the called procedure. After the procedure is run, the application continues execution with the statement after the called procedure's definition.

c) The statement before the procedure call is executed.

d) The application terminates.

13.5 `Function`s can return ________ value(s).

a) zero
b) exactly one
c) one or more
d) any number of

13.6 Which of the following must be true when making a procedure call?

a) The number of arguments in the procedure call must match the number of parameters in the procedure header.

b) The argument types must be compatible with their corresponding parameter types.

c) Both a and b
d) None of the above

13.7 Which of the following statements correctly returns the variable `value` from a `Function` procedure?

a) `Return Dim value`
b) `Return value As Integer`
c) `value Return`
d) `Return value`

13.8 The ________ `ToolStripButton` executes the next statement in the application. If the next statement to execute contains a procedure call, the called procedure executes in its entirety.

a) **Step Into**
b) **Step Out**
c) **Step Over**
d) **Steps**

13.9 The first line of a procedure (including the keyword `Sub` or `Function`, the procedure name, the parameter list and the `Function` procedure return type) is known as the procedure ________.

a) body
b) title
c) caller
d) header

13.10 Method ________ of class `Math` calculates the square root of the value passed as an argument.

a) `SquareRoot`
b) `Root`
c) `Sqrt`
d) `Square`

EXERCISES

13.11 ***(Temperature Converter Application)*** Write an application that performs temperature conversions (Fig. 13.28). The application should perform two types of conversions: degrees Fahrenheit to degrees Celsius, and degrees Celsius to degrees Fahrenheit.

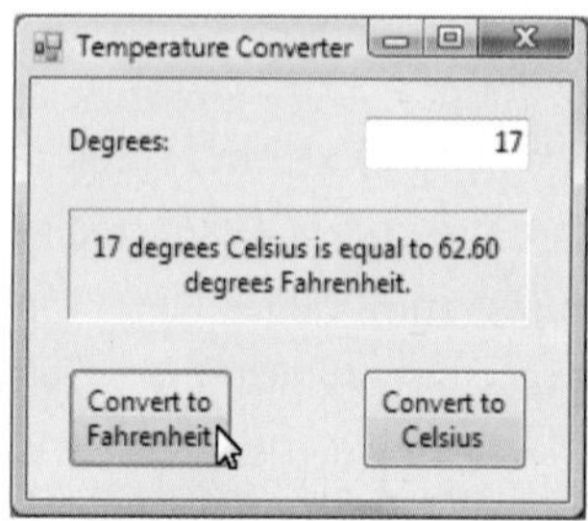

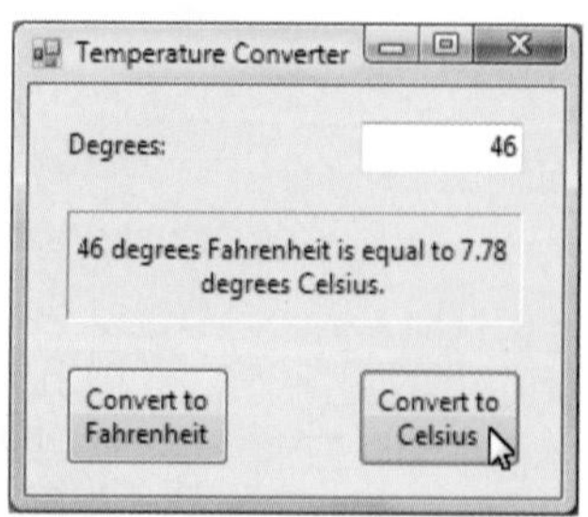

Figure 13.28 **Temperature Converter** GUI.

a) ***Copying the template to your working directory.*** Copy the directory `C:\Examples\Tutorial13\Exercises\TemperatureConversion` to your `C:\SimplyVB2008` directory.

b) ***Opening the application's template file.*** Double click `TemperatureConversion.sln` in the `TemperatureConversion` directory to open the application.

c) ***Converting Fahrenheit to Celsius.*** To convert degrees Fahrenheit to degrees Celsius, use this formula:

```
celsius = (5 / 9) * (fahrenheit - 32)
```

d) ***Converting Celsius to Fahrenheit.*** To convert degrees Celsius to degrees Fahrenheit, use this formula:

```
fahrenheit = (9 / 5) * celsius + 32
```

e) ***Adding event handlers to your application.*** Double click each `Button` to add the proper event handlers to your application. These event handlers call procedures (that you define in the next step) to convert the degrees entered to either Fahrenheit or Celsius. Each event handler displays the result in the application's output `Label`.

f) ***Adding `Function` procedures to your application.*** Create `Function` procedures to perform each conversion, using the formulas above. The user should provide the temperature to convert.

g) ***Formatting the temperature output.*** To format the temperature information, use the `String.Format` method. Use `F` as the formatting code to limit the temperature to two decimal places.

h) ***Running the application.*** Select **Debug > Start Debugging** to run your application. Enter a temperature value. Click the **Convert to Fahrenheit** `Button` and verify that the correct output is displayed based on the formula given. Click the **Convert to Celsius** `Button` and again verify that the output is correct.

i) ***Closing the application.*** Close your running application by clicking its close box.

j) ***Closing the IDE.*** Close the Visual Basic IDE by clicking its close box.

13.12 *(Display Square Application)* Write an application that displays a solid square composed of a character input by the user (Fig. 13.29). The user also should input the size.

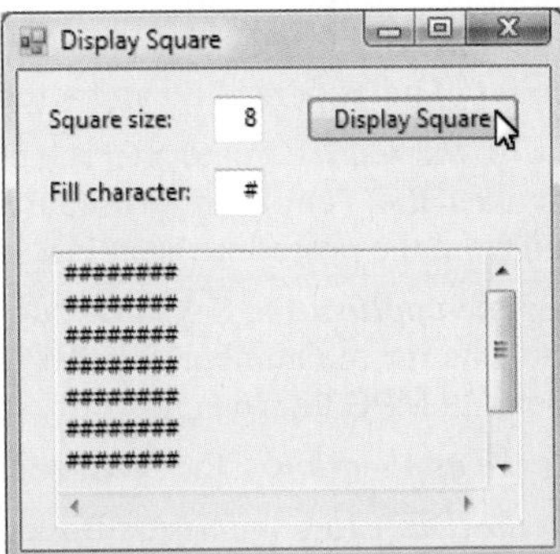

Figure 13.29 **Display Square** application.

a) ***Copying the template to your working directory.*** Copy the directory `C:\Examples\Tutorial13\Exercises\DisplaySquare` to your `C:\SimplyVB2008` directory.

b) ***Opening the application's template file.*** Double click `DisplaySquare.sln` in the `DisplaySquare` directory to open the application.

c) ***Adding a Sub procedure.*** Write a `Sub` procedure `DisplaySquare` to display the solid square. The size (the length of each side) should be specified by the `Integer` parameter `size`. The character that fills the square should be specified by the `String` parameter `fillCharacter`. Use a `For...Next` statement nested within another `For...Next` statement to create the square. The outer `For...Next` specifies what row is currently being displayed. The inner `For...Next` appends all the characters that form the row to a display `String`. Use the multiline `TextBox` provided to display the square. For example, if `size` is 8 and `fillCharacter` is #, the application should look similar to Fig. 13.29.

d) ***Adding an event handler for your Button's Click event.*** Double click the **Display Square** `Button` to create the event handler. Program the event handler to call procedure `DisplaySquare`.

e) ***Running the application.*** Select **Debug > Start Debugging** to run your application. Enter a size for the square (that is, the length of each side) and a fill character. Click the **Display Square** `Button`. A square should be displayed of the size you specified, using the character you specified.

f) ***Closing the application.*** Close your running application by clicking its close box.

g) ***Closing the IDE.*** Close the Visual Basic IDE by clicking its close box.

13.13 ***(Miles Per Gallon Application)*** Drivers often want to know the miles per gallon their cars get so they can estimate gasoline costs. Develop an application that allows the user to input the number of miles driven and the number of gallons used for a tank of gas, and displays the corresponding miles per gallon.

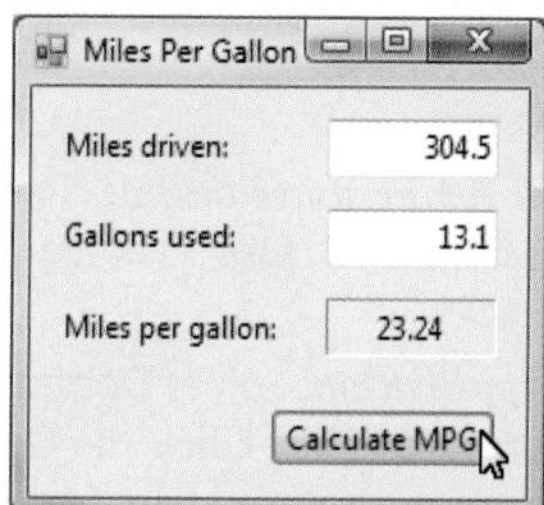

Figure 13.30 **Miles Per Gallon** application.

a) ***Copying the template to your working directory.*** Copy the directory `C:\Examples\Tutorial13\Exercises\MilesPerGallon` to your `C:\SimplyVB2008` directory.

b) ***Opening the application's template file.*** Double click `MilesPerGallon.sln` in the `MilesPerGallon` directory to open the application.

c) ***Calculating the miles per gallon.*** Write a `Function` procedure `MilesPerGallon` that takes the number of miles driven and gallons used (entered by the user), calculates the amount of miles per gallon and returns the miles per gallon for a tankful of gas.

d) ***Displaying the result.*** Create a `Click` event handler for the **Calculate MPG** `Button` that invokes the `Function` procedure `MilesPerGallon` and displays the result returned from the procedure as in Fig. 13.30.

e) ***Running the application.*** Select **Debug > Start Debugging** to run your application. Enter a value for the number of miles driven and the number of gallons used. Click the **Calculate MPG** `Button` and verify that the correct output is displayed.

f) ***Closing the application.*** Close your running application by clicking its close box.

g) ***Closing the IDE.*** Close the Visual Basic IDE by clicking its close box.

What does this code do?

13.14 What does the following code do? Assume that this procedure is invoked by using `Mystery(70, 80)`.

```
Sub Mystery(ByVal number1 As Integer, ByVal number2 As Integer)
   Dim x As Integer
   Dim y As Double

   x = number1 + number2
   y = x / 2

   If y <= 60 Then
      resultLabel.Text = "<= 60"
   Else
      resultLabel.Text = "Result is " & y
   End If
End Sub ' Mystery
```

What's wrong with this code?

13.15 Find the error(s) in the following code, which should take an `Integer` value as a parameter and return the value of the parameter multiplied by two.

```
Function TimesTwo(ByVal number As Integer) As Integer
   Dim result As Integer

   result = number * 2
End Function ' TimesTwo
```

Using the Debugger

13.16 *(Gas Pump Application)* The **Gas Pump** application (Fig. 13.31) calculates the cost of gas at a local gas station. This gas station charges `$3.13` per gallon for **Regular** grade gas, `$3.33` per gallon for **Special** grade gas and `$3.45` per gallon for **Super +** grade gas. The user enters the number of gallons to purchase and clicks the desired grade. The application calls a `Sub` procedure to compute the total cost from the number of gallons entered and the selected grade, then displays the result. While testing the application, you noticed that one of your totals was incorrect, given the input.

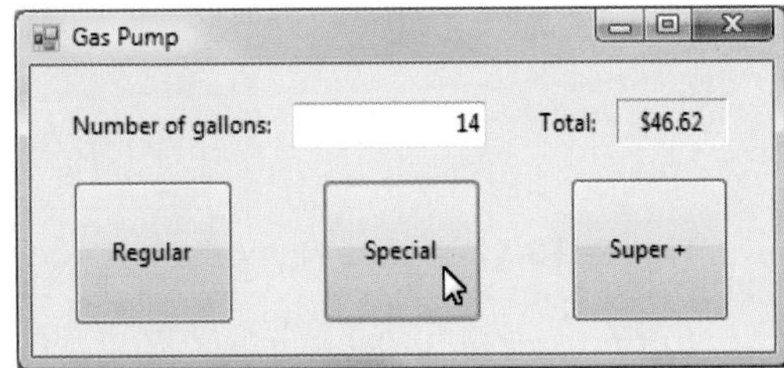

Figure 13.31 **Gas Pump** application executing correctly.

a) ***Copying the template to your working directory.*** Copy the directory `C:\Examples\Tutorial13\GasPump` to your `C:\SimplyVB2008` directory.

b) ***Opening the application's template file.*** Double click `GasPump.sln` in the `GasPump` directory to open the application.

c) ***Running the application.*** Select **Debug > Start Debugging** to run your application. Determine which total is incorrect.

d) ***Setting a breakpoint.*** Set a breakpoint at the beginning of the event handler that is providing incorrect output. For instance, if the **Regular** `Button` is providing incorrect output when clicked, add a breakpoint at the beginning of that `Button`'s `Click` event handler. Use the debugger to help find any logic error(s) in the application.

e) ***Modifying the application.*** Once you've located the error(s), modify the application so that it behaves correctly.

f) ***Running the application.*** Select **Debug > Start Debugging** to run your application. Enter a number of gallons and click the **Regular**, **Special** and **Super +** `Buttons`. After each `Button` is clicked, verify that the total displayed is correct based on the prices given in this exercise's description.

g) ***Closing the application.*** Close your running application by clicking its close box.

h) ***Closing the IDE.*** Close the Visual Basic IDE by clicking its close box.

Programming Challenge

13.17 *(Prime Numbers Application)* An `Integer` greater than 1 is said to be prime if it is divisible by only 1 and itself. For example, 2, 3, 5 and 7 are prime numbers, but 4, 6, 8 and 9 are not. Write an application that takes two numbers (representing a lower bound and an upper bound) and determines all of the prime numbers within the specified bounds, inclusive.

a) ***Creating the application.*** Create an application named `PrimeNumbers` and have its GUI appear as shown in Fig. 13.32. Add an event handler for the **Calculate Primes** `Button`'s `Click` event.

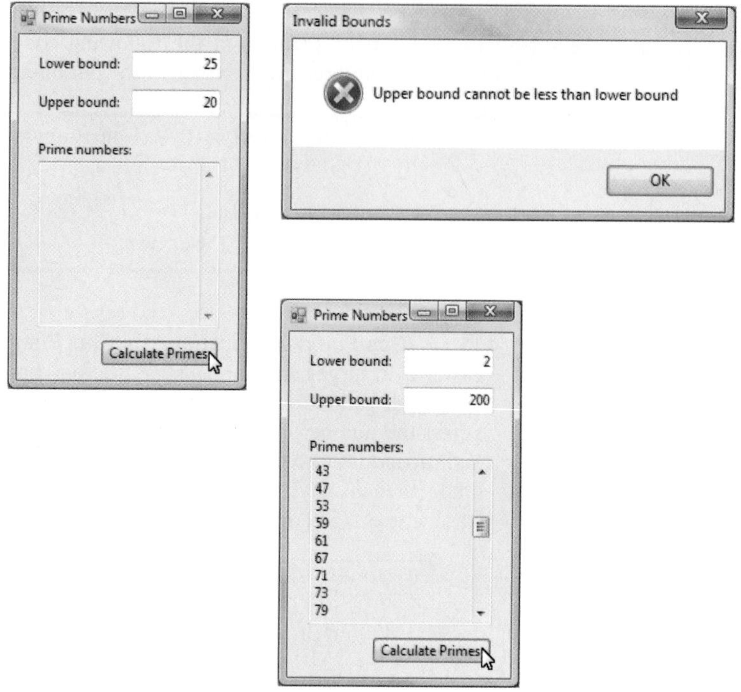

Figure 13.32 Prime Numbers application.

b) ***Checking for prime numbers.*** Write a `Function` procedure `Prime` that returns `True` if a number is prime, `False` otherwise. To determine if a number is prime, write a `For...Next` statement that counts from 2 to the square root of the number. In the body of the loop, use the `Mod` operator (Tutorial 6) to determine whether the number is divisible by the counter variable's value (that is, the remainder is 0). If so, the number is not prime.

c) ***Limiting user input.*** Allow users to enter a lower bound (`lower`) and an upper bound (`upper`). Prevent the user from entering bounds less than or equal to 1, or an upper bound that is smaller than the lower bound.

d) ***Displaying the prime numbers.*** Call `Function` procedure `Prime` from your event handler to determine which numbers between the lower and upper bounds are prime. Then have the event handler display the prime numbers in a multiline, scrollable `TextBox`, as in Fig. 13.32.

e) ***Running the application.*** Select **Debug > Start Debugging** to run your application. Enter a lower bound and an upper bound that is smaller than the lower bound. Click the **Calculate Primes** `Button`. You should receive an error message. Enter negative bounds and click the **Calculate Primes** `Button`. Again, you should receive an error message. Enter valid bounds and click the **Calculate Primes** `Button`. This time, the primes within that range should be displayed.

f) ***Closing the application.*** Close your running application by clicking its close box.

g) ***Closing the IDE.*** Close the Visual Basic IDE by clicking its close box.

T U T O R I A L

Objectives

In this tutorial, you learn to:

- Create and manipulate `Date` variables.
- Execute code at regular intervals using a `Timer` control.
- Retrieve `Date` input with a `DateTimePicker` control.
- Group controls using a `GroupBox` control.

Outline

Shipping Time Application

Using `Dates` and `Timers`

Many companies, from airlines to shipping companies, rely on date and time information in their daily operations. These companies often require applications that reliably perform date and time calculations. In this tutorial, you create an application that performs calculations using the `Date` primitive type, which allows you to store and manipulate date and time information. You also learn how to use a `DateTimePicker` control to retrieve date and time information from the user. Finally, you learn how to use a `Timer`—a Windows `Forms` control that executes code at specified time intervals.

14.1 Test-Driving the Shipping Time Application

In this tutorial, you build the **Shipping Time** application. This application must meet the following requirements:

Application Requirements

A seafood distributor has asked you to create an application that calculates the delivery time for fresh seafood shipped from Portland, Maine, to its distribution center in Las Vegas, Nevada, where only the freshest seafood is accepted. The distributor has arrangements with local airlines to guarantee that seafood ships on flights that leave either at noon or at midnight. However, for security reasons, the airport requires the distributor to drop off the seafood at the airport at least one hour before each flight. When the distributor specifies the drop-off time, the application should display the delivery time in Las Vegas. This application should take into account the three-hour time difference (it's three hours earlier in Las Vegas) and the six-hour flight time between the two cities. The application should allow the user to select drop-off times within the current day (seafood must be shipped within a day to guarantee freshness). The application should also include a running clock that displays the current time.

This application calculates the shipment's delivery time from the user's drop-off time, taking into account such factors as transit time and time zones. You use the `DateTimePicker` control to enable the user to enter the drop-off time. You use the `Date` properties and methods to calculate the delivery time. You begin by test-driving the completed application. Then you learn the additional Visual Basic capabilities needed to create your own version of this application.

Test-Driving the Shipping Time Application

1. ***Opening the completed application.*** Open the directory `C:\Examples\Tutorial14\CompletedApplication\ShippingTime` to locate the **Shipping Time** application. Double click `ShippingTime.sln` to open the application in the Visual Basic IDE.
2. ***Running the Shipping Time application.*** Select **Debug > Start Debugging** to run the application (Fig. 14.1).

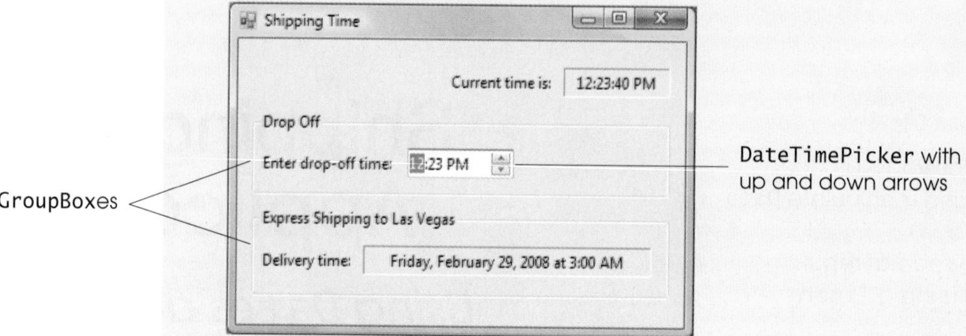

Figure 14.1 **Shipping Time** application.

3. ***Entering a drop-off time.*** The default drop-off time is set to your computer's current time when you execute the application. When you change the drop-off time, the **Delivery time:** `Label` displays the delivery time based on the new time. Note that if you select a time before 11:00 A.M., the shipment arrives in Las Vegas at 3:00 P.M. If you specify a time between 11:00 A.M. and 11:00 P.M., the shipment arrives in Las Vegas at 3:00 A.M. the following day. Finally, if you specify a time after 11:00 P.M., the shipment arrives at 3:00 P.M. on the following day.

   The time displayed in the **Current time is:** `Label` updates to the current time once each second. However, the drop-off time displayed in the `DateTimePicker` changes only if you select different values by using the up and down arrows or by typing in a new value.
4. ***Closing the application.*** Click your running application's close box.
5. ***Closing the IDE.*** Close the Visual Basic IDE by clicking its close box.

14.2 Date Variables

Error-Prevention Tip

Always store dates in a `Date` variable. Storing dates in variables of other types can lead to conversion errors and loss of data.

Choosing the correct data type in which to store information can decrease development time by simplifying code. For example, if you are using whole numbers, variables of type `Integer` are your best choice; if you need to store monetary values, you should use variables of type `Decimal`. If you want to store date information (such as the day, month, year and time), you could use separate variables to keep track of the month, day of the week, year and other date-related information. This would be a complicated task and could slow the development of applications that require date and time information.

Declaring a Date Variable

The primitive type `Date` simplifies manipulation, storage and display of date (and time) information. `Date` is the Visual Basic keyword that corresponds to the **`DateTime`** type in the .NET Framework Class Library—they can be used interchangeably. A **`Date`** variable stores information about a point in time (for example, 12:00:00 A.M. on January 1, 2008). Using code, you can access a `Date`'s properties, including the day, the hour and the minute. Your **Shipping Time** application requires calculations involving time, so you use `Date` variables to store and manipulate this information.

You use the New keyword when creating a Date value. In the code, the statement

Date constructor

```
Dim delivery As Date = New Date(2003, 1, 1, 0, 0, 0)
```

Date variable

declares a new Date variable named delivery. The New keyword calls the Date's constructor. A **constructor** is a procedure that initializes an object when it's created. You learn how to write your own constructors in Tutorial 19. Note that this particular constructor takes six arguments—year, month, day, hour, minute and second. These values are described in Fig. 14.2.

Argument	Range	Description
Initializing a Date *variable using* New Date(*year*, *month*, *day*, *hour*, *minute*, *second*)		
year	Integer values 1–9999	Specifies the year.
month	Integer values 1–12	Specifies the month of the year.
day	Integer values 1–*number of days in month*	Specifies the day of the month. Each month has 28 to 31 days depending on the month and year.
hour	Integer values 0–23	Specifies the hour of the day on a 24 hour clock. The value 0 represents 12:00 A.M.
minute	Integer values 0–59	Specifies the minute of the hour.
second	Integer values 0–59	Specifies the number of elapsed seconds in the current minute.

Figure 14.2 Date constructor arguments.

Type Date actually has many so-called overloaded constructors. **Method overloading** allows you to create multiple methods with the same name but different **signatures**—that is, with different numbers and types of parameters, or with parameters ordered differently (by type). When an overloaded method is called, the compiler selects the proper method by examining the number, types and order (by type) of the arguments. Often, method overloading is used to create several methods with the same name that perform similar tasks on different sets of parameters (e.g., multiple constructors that enable you to initialize objects in different ways). If a type provides overloaded constructors or methods, *IntelliSense* shows a tooltip containing one of the available overloads. You can cycle through the others by clicking anywhere inside the tooltip. This tooltip appears after you type the opening parenthesis after the constructor or method name. Figure 14.3 shows an overloaded Date constructor that takes only three arguments—year, month and day. As you can see in the tooltip, this is one of Date's 11 overloaded constructors.

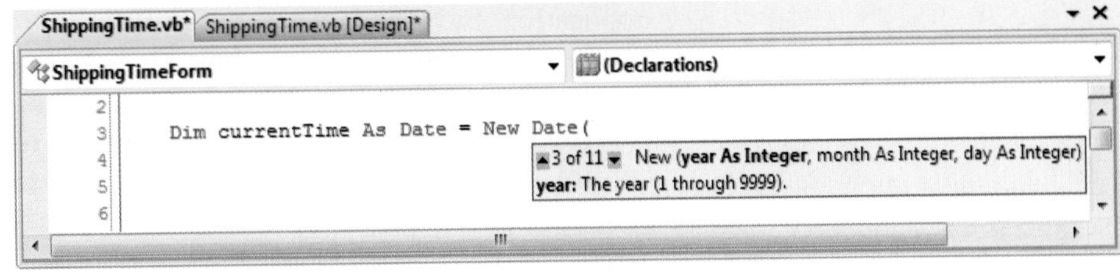

Figure 14.3 *IntelliSense* showing overloaded Date constructors.

Using Date Members

After assigning a value to a Date variable, you can access its properties using the member-access (dot) operator, as follows:

```
Dim year = delivery.Year ' retrieves Date delivery's year
Dim month = delivery.Month ' retrieves Date delivery's month
```

```
Dim day = delivery.Day ' retrieves Date delivery's day
Dim hour = delivery.Hour ' retrieves Date delivery's hour
Dim minute = delivery.Minute ' retrieves Date delivery's minute
Dim second = delivery.Second ' retrieves Date delivery's second
```

In this tutorial, you use several Date properties and methods that can be accessed through the member-access operator.

Values in Date variables cannot be added like numeric-primitive data types such as Integers and Decimals—though you can compare Dates with relational operators as you would numeric data. Instead of using arithmetic operators to add or subtract values in Date variables, you must call the correct method, using the member-access operator. Figure 14.4 demonstrates how to perform various calculations with Date variables.

Common Programming Error

Date methods do not modify the Date value on which they are called. You must assign the result of the method to a variable of type Date.

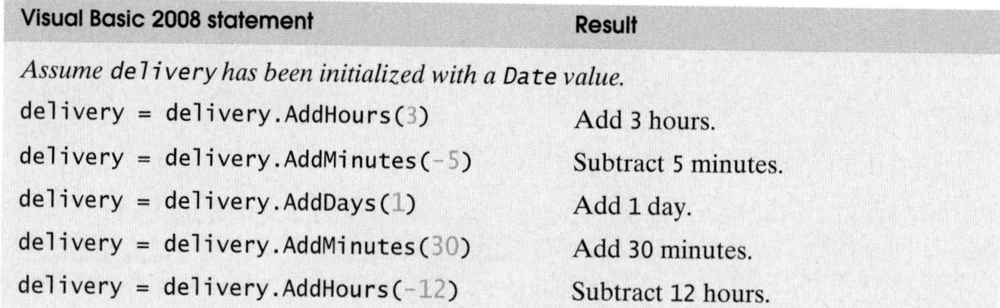

Visual Basic 2008 statement	Result
Assume delivery *has been initialized with a* Date *value.*	
delivery = delivery.AddHours(3)	Add 3 hours.
delivery = delivery.AddMinutes(-5)	Subtract 5 minutes.
delivery = delivery.AddDays(1)	Add 1 day.
delivery = delivery.AddMinutes(30)	Add 30 minutes.
delivery = delivery.AddHours(-12)	Subtract 12 hours.

Figure 14.4 Date methods that perform various calculations.

Note that an "add" method does not actually change the value of the Date variable on which it is called. Instead, each "add" method returns a Date value containing the result of the calculation. To change the value of Date variable delivery, you must assign to delivery the value returned by the "add" method.

Visual Basic provides a simple way to assign the current date and time to a Date variable. You can use the Now property to assign your computer's current date and time to a Date variable:

```
Dim currentTime As Date = Date.Now
```

Note that this assignment does not require keyword New. This is because the Date.Now property returns a Date value. Much like methods MessageBox.Show and String.Format, you can access the Now property of the Date type by following the name of the type with the member-access operator and the property name. Methods and properties accessible through the type's name, rather than a variable of that type, are known as Shared members. The MSDN online documentation uses the S symbol to indicate a Shared member.

Now that you're familiar with Date variables, you design the **Shipping Time** application by using two new controls—the GroupBox control and the DateTimePicker control. A GroupBox control groups related controls visually by drawing a labeled box around them. GroupBoxes are especially useful for grouping controls, such as CheckBoxes, that represent related choices. The DateTimePicker control allows users to enter date and time information.

SELF-REVIEW

1. You can use the ________ method to subtract 2 days from a Date value.
   a) SubtractDays b) AddDays
   c) SubDays d) SubtractTime

2. The Date methods that perform calculations using Date values ________.
   a) return a new Date value b) modify the Date value(s)
   c) do not return values d) Either a or b

Answers: 1) b. 2) c.

14.3 Creating the Shipping Time Application: Design Elements

You're now ready to begin analyzing the problem statement and developing pseudocode. The following pseudocode describes the basic operation of the **Shipping Time** application:

```
When the Form loads:
    Set range of possible drop-off times to any time in the current day
    Call sub procedure DisplayDeliveryTime to determine and display the
        shipment's delivery time

When the user changes the drop-off time:
    Call sub procedure DisplayDeliveryTime to determine and display the
        shipment's delivery time

After one second has elapsed:
    Update and display the current time

When the DisplayDeliveryTime procedure gets called:
    Call function DepartureTime to determine the time the shipment's flight
        departs
    Add three hours to determine the delivery time (takes into account 6 hours
        for time of flight minus 3 hours for the time difference)
    Display the delivery time

When the DepartureTime procedure gets called:
    Select correct Case based on the hour the shipment was dropped off
        Case where the drop-off hour is between the values 0 and 10
            Delivery set to depart on noon flight of current day
        Case where the drop off hour is 23
            Delivery set to depart on noon flight of next day
        Case where none of the preceding Cases match
            Delivery set to depart on midnight flight of current day
```

Now that you've test-driven the **Shipping Time** application and studied its pseudocode representation, you use an ACE table to help you convert the pseudocode to Visual Basic. Figure 14.5 lists the actions, controls and events that help you complete your own version of this application.

Action/Control/Event (ACE) Table for the Shipping Time Application

Action	Control	Event/Method
Label the application's controls	`currentTimeIsLabel`, `dropOffLabel`, `deliveryTimeLabel`	Application is run
	`ShippingTimeForm`	`Load`
Set range of possible drop-off times to any time in the current day	`dropOffDateTimePicker`	
Call sub procedure DisplayDevliveryTime to determine and display the shipment's delivery time	`dropOffDateTimePicker`, `lasVegasTimeLabel`	

Figure 14.5 ACE table for the **Shipping Time** application. (Part 1 of 2.)

Action	Control	Event/Method
	dropOff-DateTimePicker	ValueChanged
Call sub procedure DisplayDevliveryTime to determine and display the shipment's delivery time	dropOff-DateTimePicker, lasVegasTime-Label	
	clockTimer	Tick
Update and display the current time	currentTime-Label	
		Display-DeliveryTime
Call function DepartureTime to determine the time the shipment's flight departs	dropOff-DateTimePicker	
Add three hours to determine the delivery time		
Display the delivery time	lasVegasTime-Label	
		DepartureTime
Select correct Case based on the hour the shipment was dropped off	dropOff-DateTimePicker	
Case where drop-off hour is 0–10		
Delivery set to depart on noon flight		
Case where drop-off hour is 23		
Delivery set to depart on noon flight of next day		
Case where none of the preceding Cases match		
Delivery set to depart on midnight flight of current day		

Figure 14.5 ACE table for the **Shipping Time** application. (Part 2 of 2.)

The following box demonstrates how to insert a GroupBox control into your application.

Placing Controls in a GroupBox

1. ***Copying the template to your working directory.*** Copy the C:\Examples\Tutorial14\TemplateApplication\ShippingTime to your C:\SimplyVB2008 directory.

2. ***Opening the Shipping Time application's template file.*** Double click ShippingTime.sln in the ShippingTime directory to open the application in the Visual Basic IDE.

3. ***Displaying the template Form.*** Double click ShippingTime.vb in the **Solution Explorer** window to display the Form in the IDE.

4. ***Inserting a GroupBox control in the Form.*** The template includes a GroupBox that displays the seafood-shipment delivery time. Add a second GroupBox to contain the drop-off time by double clicking the GroupBox control,

GroupBox

GUI Design Tip

GroupBox titles should be concise and should use book-title capitalization.

(cont.)

Good Programming Practice

Append the `GroupBox` suffix to `GroupBox` control names.

in the **Containers** tab of the **Toolbox**. Change the `Text` property to `Drop Off` and the `Name` property to `dropOffGroupBox`. Place the `GroupBox` above the provided `GroupBox` and make them the same size. After these modifications, your `Form` should look like Fig. 14.6.

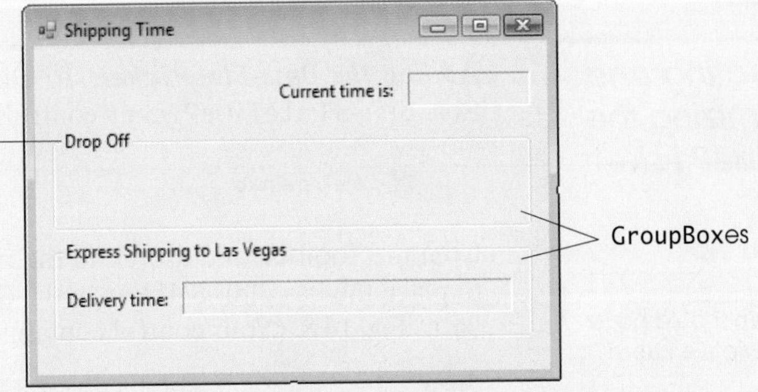

Figure 14.6 `GroupBox` controls on the **Shipping Time** `Form`.

5. ***Creating `Label`s inside the GroupBox.*** To place a `Label` inside the `GroupBox`, click the `Label` control in the **Toolbox**, then click inside the `GroupBox` (Fig. 14.7). Change the `Label`'s `Text` property to `Enter drop-off time:` and its `Name` property to `dropOffLabel`. Then change the position of the `Label` by setting its `Location` property to `6, 33`—this value aligns it with the **Delivery time:** `Label`.

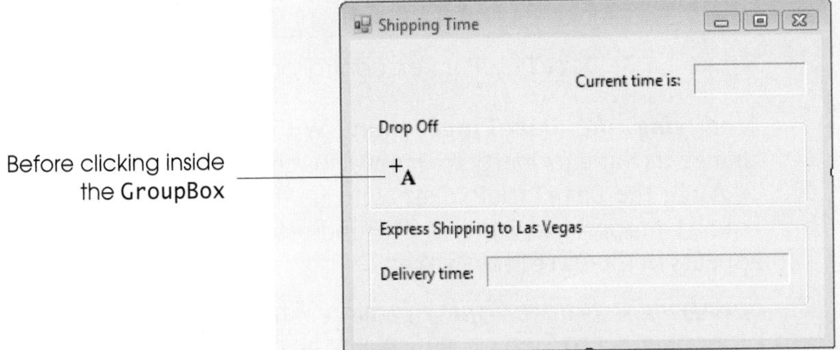

Figure 14.7 Adding a `Label` to a `GroupBox`.

GUI Design Tip

Use `GroupBox`es to group related controls in a box with a title.

Note that the `Location` values you entered are measured from the top-left corner of the `GroupBox`, not from the top-left corner of the `Form`. Objects that contain controls, such as `Form`s, `GroupBox`es and `Panel`s (which you will use in Tutorial 19) are called **containers**. The `Location` of a control is measured from the top-left corner of its container object.

If a `GroupBox` is placed over a control that is already on the `Form`, the control will be behind the `GroupBox` (that is, the `GroupBox` hides the control by covering it). To avoid this problem, remove all controls from the area in which you wish to place the `GroupBox` control before inserting it. You can then either drag and drop existing controls into the `GroupBox` or add new controls as needed as described earlier.

6. ***Saving the project.*** Select **File > Save All** to save your changes.

You've now added a `GroupBox` and a `Label` to the **Shipping Time** application to display the drop-off time. In the following box, you add a `DateTimePicker` control to retrieve the drop-off time from the user.

Recall that the `DateTimePicker` retrieves date and time information from the user. The `DateTimePicker` allows you to select from several predefined date and time formats (for example, date formats like 12/31/2008 and Friday, December 31, 2008; and time formats like 2:00:00 PM), or you can create your own format. The date and time information is then stored in a variable of type Date, which you can manipulate using Date methods. Note that the format limits the date and/or time information the user can see, but does not alter the Date value stored in the DateTimePicker.

Creating and Customizing the DateTimePicker

GUI Design Tip

Each DateTimePicker should have a corresponding descriptive Label.

Good Programming Practice

Append the DateTimePicker suffix to DateTimePicker control names.

GUI Design Tip

Use a DateTimePicker to retrieve date and time information from the user.

Error-Prevention Tip

Be cautious when using the CustomFormat property to specify a DateTimePicker's display. The format may be interpreted differently based on your locale.

Error-Prevention Tip

If the user is to specify a date and/or time, use a DateTimePicker control to prevent the user from entering invalid date or time values.

1. ***Adding the DateTimePicker.*** To add a DateTimePicker to your application, drag a DateTimePicker control

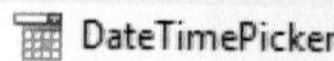

from the **Toolbox** and drop it to the right of the **Enter drop-off time:** Label to place the DateTimePicker in the GroupBox. Your Form should look similar to Fig. 14.8. (Your control contains your computer's current date.)

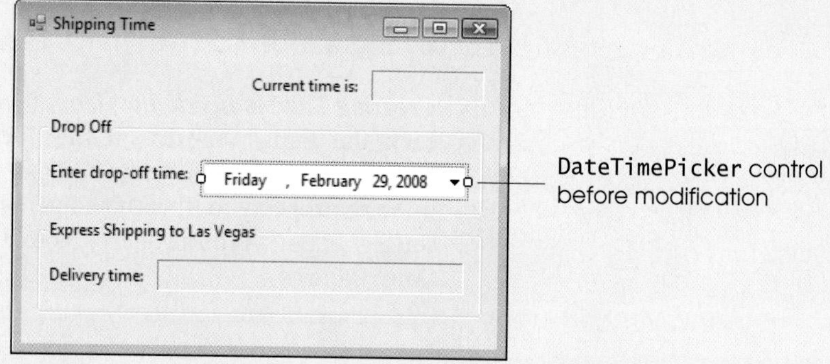

Figure 14.8 DateTimePicker control on the Form.

2. ***Modifying the DateTimePicker.*** With the DateTimePicker selected, change its Name property to dropOffDateTimePicker.

   Align the DateTimePicker with its descriptive Label. Next, change its Format property to Custom. This indicates that you'll specify how the date appears in the DateTimePicker.

3. ***Specifying a custom display format.*** When the DateTimePicker's Format property is set to Custom, it displays the date and time using the custom format that you specify in the CustomFormat property. Note that the DateTimePicker now displays the date in the format 1/1/2008, the default format when the Format property is set to Custom and you have not set CustomFormat property.

   Set the value of the CustomFormat property to hh:mm tt. Note that the CustomFormat property is case sensitive. The "hh" displays the hour as a number from 01 to 12, the ":" inserts a colon and the "mm" indicates that the number of minutes from 00 to 59 should follow the colon. The "tt" indicates that AM or PM should appear, depending on the time of day. You can find an extensive list of date and time formats at http://msdn2.microsoft.com/en-us/library/8kb3ddd4.aspx. Note that the Format property eliminates the problem of a user's entering a letter or symbol when the application expects a number—the DateTimePicker does not allow values in any format other than what you specify in the Format or CustomFormat properties. The DateTimePicker also prevents the user from specifying an invalid time, such as 32:15. Resize the DateTimePicker to a size appropriate for this time-only format.

(cont.)

GUI Design Tip

If the user is to specify a time of day or a date and time, set the DateTimePicker's ShowUpDown property to True. If the user is to specify only a date, set the DateTimePicker's ShowUpDown property to False to allow the user to select a day from the month calendar.

4. ***Using up and down arrows in the DateTimePicker.*** Set the DateTimePicker's **ShowUpDown** property to True. This setting allows the user to select the date or time by clicking the up or down arrows that appear on the right side of the control, much like a NumericUpDown control. When the property is set to False (which is the default), a down arrow appears on the right side of the control (Fig. 14.8). Clicking the down arrow causes a month calendar to appear, allowing the user to select a date (but not a time). A demonstration of the month calendar is shown in the Controls, Events, Properties & Methods section at the end of this tutorial. The user needs to enter only the time of day, so you use up and down arrows to allow the user to select the time (Fig. 14.9).

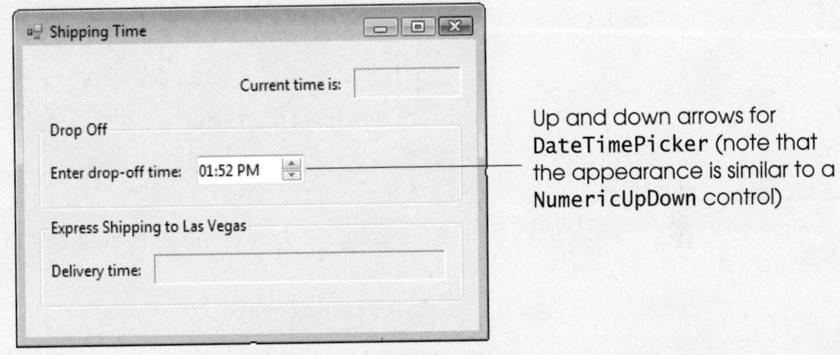

Figure 14.9 Customized DateTimePicker control on the Form.

5. ***Saving the project.*** Select **File > Save All** to save your modified code.

The final control you add to the Form is a Timer. You use the Timer control to generate events that help you display the current time of day on the Form.

Creating a Timer Control

1. ***Adding a Timer control.*** A **Timer** control is an object that can run code every millisecond (1/1000 of a second) by generating a **Tick** event. By default, the Timer runs code every 100 milliseconds (1/10 of a second). Each time the Tick event occurs, its event handler executes. You can customize the "wake period" (the amount of time between Timer Tick events) and the code it executes (the event handler for the Tick event) so that a certain task is performed once every "wake up" period.

   Add a Timer to the Form by clicking the Timer control,

   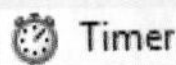

   in the **Components** tab of the **Toolbox** and dragging and dropping it anywhere on the Form. Note that the Timer does not actually appear on the Form—it appears below the Form designer in an area called the **component tray** (Fig. 14.10). The Timer control is placed in the component tray because it's not part of the graphical user interface—users never see the Timer control.

2. ***Customizing the Timer control.*** Rename the Timer by setting its Name property to clockTimer. To allow the Timer to generate Tick events, set the Timer's Enabled property to True. Then set its **Interval** property to 1000, which specifies the number of milliseconds between Tick events (1,000 milliseconds = 1 second).

Good Programming Practice

Append the Timer suffix to Timer control names.

3. ***Saving the project.*** Select **File > Save All** to save your modified code.

(cont.)

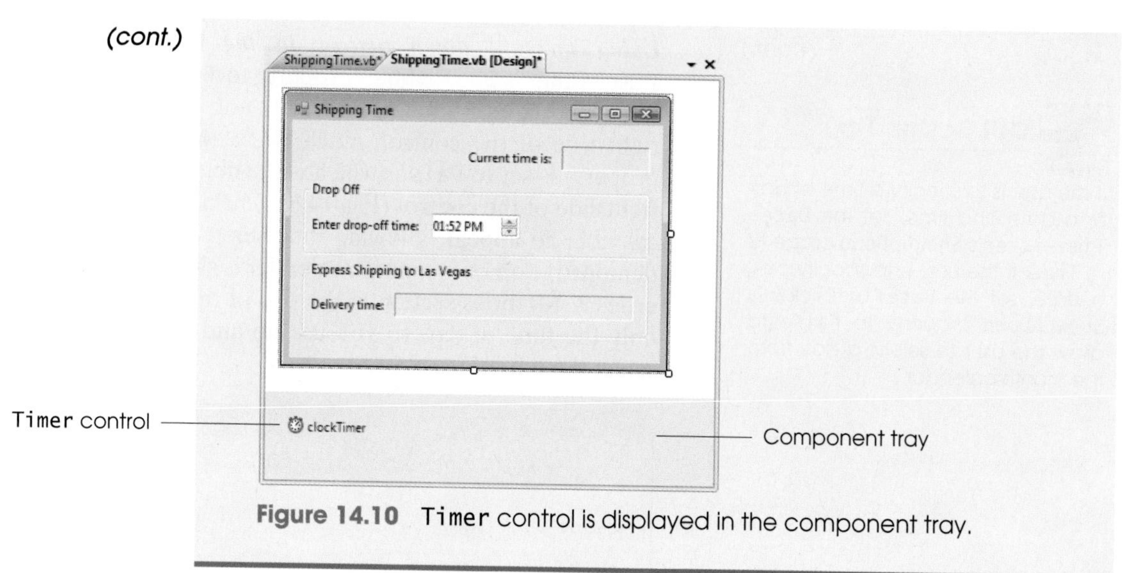

Figure 14.10 `Timer` control is displayed in the component tray.

SELF-REVIEW

1. By default, the `Timer` control generates a `Tick` event every ________.
   a) second
   b) 100 seconds
   c) 100 milliseconds
   d) half a second

2. Setting the `Format` property of the `DateTimePicker` control to ________ allows you to specify how the date appears in the `DateTimePicker`.
   a) `Custom`
   b) `Unique`
   c) `User`
   d) `Other`

Answers: 1) c. 2) a.

14.4 Creating the Shipping Time Application: Inserting Code

Now that you've completed the visual design of the **Shipping Time** application, you complete the application by inserting code. You begin coding the application's functionality by creating a clock in the application that updates the current time every second. You then write code that displays the delivery time from Portland to Las Vegas. You implement this feature by inserting code that runs when the `Form` loads or whenever the user specifies a new drop-off time. In the following box, you write the code to create the clock.

Coding the Shipping Time Application's Clock

1. ***Inserting code to handle the Timer's `Tick` event.*** Double click the `Timer` control in the component tray to generate the empty event handler for the `Tick` event. Add lines 6–8 of Fig. 14.11 to the body of the event handler. Be sure to format the event handler as shown in Fig. 14.11 to ensure that your line numbers match those in the text.

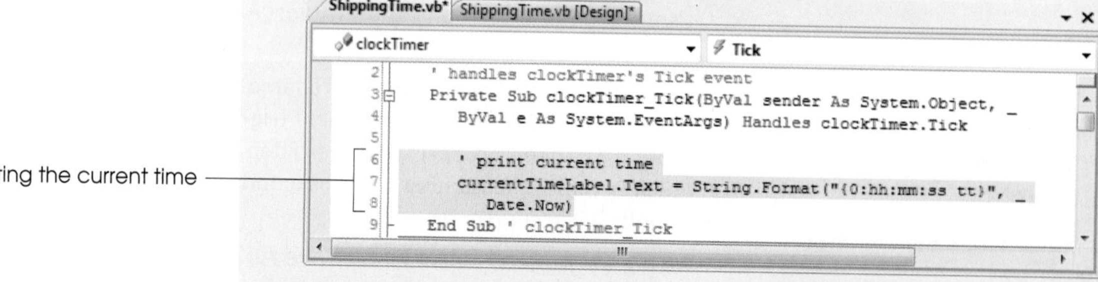

Figure 14.11 Inserting code for a `Tick` event.

(cont.)

Lines 3–9 define the `Tick` event handler, which executes every second. `Date` property `Now` retrieves your computer's current time. The event handler takes this information and formats it to match the format you specify, `"{hh:mm:ss tt}"`. The `Text` property of `currentTimeLabel` is then set to the formatted `String` for display to the user. Recall that in the method `String.Format` the `0` corresponds to the argument that will be formatted (that is, `Date.Now`) and the text following the colon contains the format information for that argument's value. You're already familiar with the purpose of `hh:mm` and `tt`. The `:ss` following `mm` indicates that a colon followed by the number of seconds (00–59) should be displayed.

2. ***Saving the project.*** Select **File > Save All** to save your modified code.

Now that you've coded your application's clock, using the `Timer`'s `Tick` event handler, you insert code to display a delivery time when the application opens. You begin by creating a `Load` event handler for your application.

Using Code to Display a Delivery Time

1. ***Adding the `ShippingTimeForm_Load` event handler.*** When an application runs, the `Form` is displayed. However, sometimes you also want a specific action to occur when the application opens but before the `Form` displays. To run code when the application first opens, create an event handler for the `Form`'s **`Load`** event. To create a `Load` event handler, return to the Windows `Form` Designer by clicking the **ShippingTime.vb [Design]** tab. Double click an empty area in the `Form` to generate the `Load` event handler and enter **Code** view. Be careful not to double click a control on the `Form`; this generates the control's event handler instead. You can double click the `Form`'s title bar to ensure that you don't accidentally create an event handler for another control.

2. ***Storing the current date.*** Add line 16 from Fig. 14.12 into the `Load` event handler to store the current date in variable `currentTime`. (You store the date as a variable so that you can preserve information about the current date for later use in the event handler.) Be sure to add the comments and line-continuation characters as shown in Fig. 14.12 so that the line numbers in your code match those presented in this tutorial.

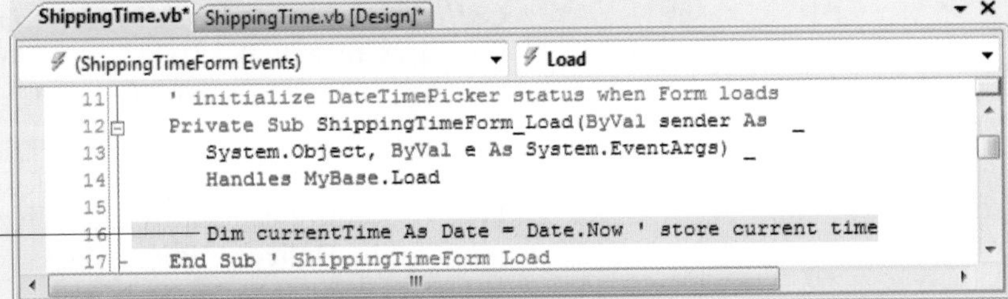

Storing the current time in currentTime
ShippingTime.vb*
ShippingTime.vb [Design]*
(ShippingTimeForm Events)
Load
11 ' initialize DateTimePicker status when Form loads
12 Private Sub ShippingTimeForm_Load(ByVal sender As _
13 System.Object, ByVal e As System.EventArgs) _
14 Handles MyBase.Load
15
16 Dim currentTime As Date = Date.Now ' store current time
17 End Sub ' ShippingTimeForm Load

Figure 14.12 Storing the current time.

3. ***Setting the drop-off hours.*** Add lines 18–23 of Fig. 14.13 to the `ShippingTimeForm_Load` event handler. These lines set the `MinDate` and `MaxDate` properties for `dropOffDateTimePicker`. The **`MinDate`** property specifies the earliest value that the `DateTimePicker` allows the user to enter. The **`MaxDate`** property specifies the latest value that the `DateTimePicker` allows the user to enter. Together, these two properties set the range of drop-off times from which the user can select.

(cont.)

Setting the range of drop-off times

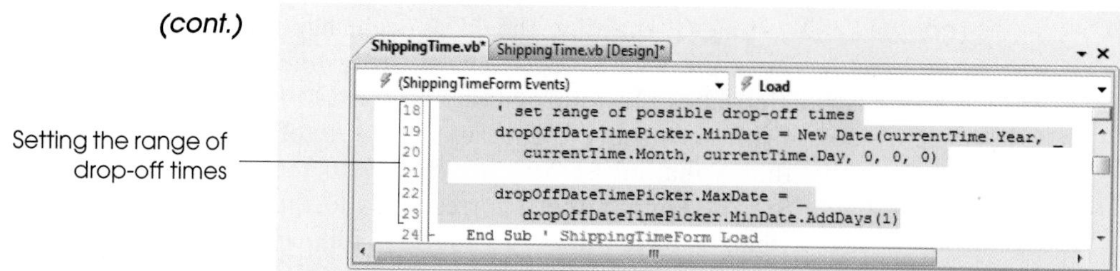

Figure 14.13 Setting the `MinDate` and `MaxDate` properties.

To guarantee freshness, the seafood shipment should be dropped off at the airline within the current day; therefore, the earliest drop-off time (`MinDate`) is set to 12:00 A.M. of the current day (lines 19–20), and the latest drop-off time (`MaxDate`) is set to 12:00 A.M. the following day (lines 22–23). Note that the `MaxDate` value is calculated by adding one day to the `MinDate` value using the `AddDays` method. Recall that the `AddDays` method does not change the `Date` value on which it operates—it returns a new `Date` value. This value is assigned to the `MaxDate` property in line 22.

The `Date` constructor (called in line 19) creates a value that stores a date and a time of midnight. Recall that the first parameter is the year, the second is the month and the third is the day. The last three parameters specify the hour, minute and number of seconds. A `Date` variable's `Year` property returns the value of its year as an `Integer` (for example, `2008`). Its `Month` property returns the value of the `Date` variable's month as an `Integer` (for example, `6` for June). Finally, the `Date` variable's `Day` property returns the day of the month (an `Integer` between `1` and `31`, depending on the month and year).

The `Date` type also provides property **Today**, which returns the current date with the time set to `00:00:00` (midnight). You can use this property to return the current date when you do not need any information about the time. You could have used property `Today` instead of property `Now` in the `Form`'s `Load` event handler. The `DateTimePicker`'s `MinDate` property would be set to the value returned by `Date.Today` (midnight of the current day). The `MaxDate` property would be set by adding one day to the `MinDate` property. We used the `Now` property to give you more practice using the `Date` constructor and to demonstrate the `Year`, `Month` and `Day` properties.

4. ***Calling the `DisplayDeliveryTime` procedure.*** Add lines 25–26 of Fig. 14.14 to call the `DisplayDeliveryTime` procedure. Note that `DisplayDeliveryTime` is underlined in blue. This is due to the compilation error you introduce when you call a procedure that has not yet been written. You write this procedure later in this tutorial. The `DisplayDeliveryTime` procedure calculates the delivery time in Las Vegas and displays the result in the **Delivery time:** `Label`.

Displaying the delivery time

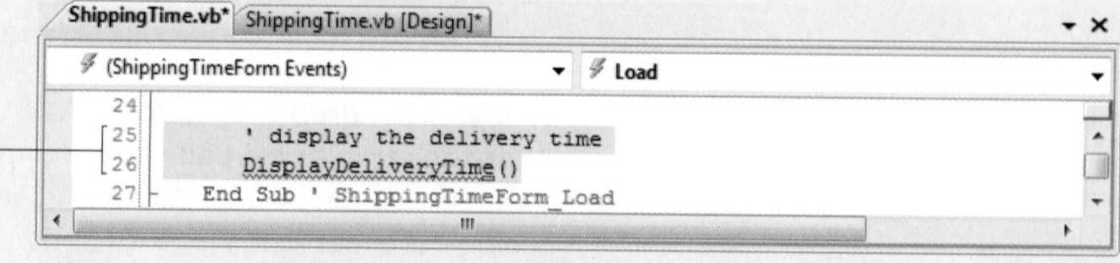

Figure 14.14 Calling the `DisplayDeliveryTime` procedure.

5. ***Saving the project.*** Select **File > Save All** to save your modified code.

So far, you've added functionality that calls `DisplayDeliveryTime` to display the delivery time when the application runs initially. However, you should allow a user to select any drop-off time and instantly see when the seafood shipment will be delivered. In the following box, you learn how to handle the `DateTimePicker`'s `ValueChanged` event, which occurs when the user changes the `DateTimePicker`'s value.

Coding the `ValueChanged` Event Handler

1. ***Creating the `ValueChanged` event handler.*** Click the **ShippingTime.vb [Design]** tab. Double click the `DateTimePicker` control `dropOffDateTimePicker` to generate its `ValueChanged` event handler.

2. ***Inserting code in the event handler.*** Insert lines 34–35 of Fig. 14.15 into the event handler. This code runs when the user changes the time in the `DateTimePicker`. Be sure to add the comments and line-continuation characters as shown in Fig. 14.15 so that the line numbers in your code match those presented in this tutorial.

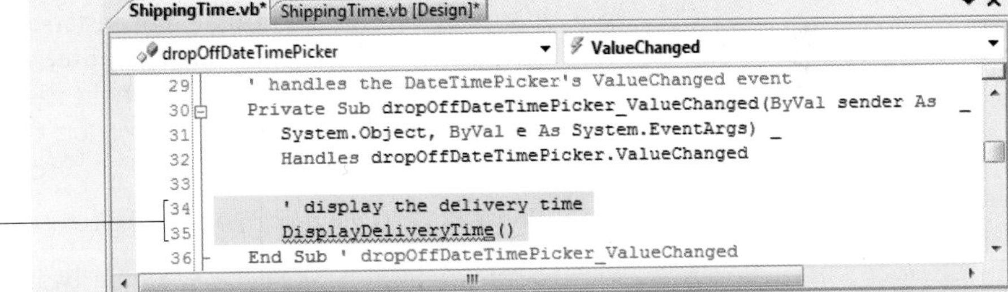
Calculating and displaying the delivery time
ShippingTime.vb*
ShippingTime.vb [Design]*
dropOffDateTimePicker
ValueChanged
29 ' handles the DateTimePicker's ValueChanged event
30 Private Sub dropOffDateTimePicker_ValueChanged(ByVal sender As _
31 System.Object, ByVal e As System.EventArgs) _
32 Handles dropOffDateTimePicker.ValueChanged
33
34 ' display the delivery time
35 DisplayDeliveryTime()
36 End Sub ' dropOffDateTimePicker_ValueChanged

Figure 14.15 Inserting code in the `ValueChanged` event handler.

The `ValueChanged` event handler also uses the `DisplayDeliveryTime` procedure to calculate and display the delivery time in Las Vegas. In the next box, you write the `DisplayDeliveryTime` procedure, after which the compilation error no longer appears.

3. ***Saving the project.*** Select **File > Save All** to save your modified code.

Though you've called the `DisplayDeliveryTime` procedure in two event handlers, you still need to write the procedure. Next, you use `Date` methods to calculate and display the delivery time in an output `Label`.

Coding the `DisplayDeliveryTime` Procedure

1. ***Creating the `DisplayDeliveryTime` procedure.*** Add lines 38–47 of Fig. 14.16 below the `ValueChanged` event handler. Line 41 calls the procedure `DepartureTime`. Note that `DepartureTime` is underlined in blue. This is due to the compilation error you introduce when you call a procedure that has not yet been written. You write this procedure in the following box. The `DepartureTime` procedure determines which flight (midnight or noon) the seafood shipment will use. It returns a `Date` value representing the flight's departure time. Line 41 stores this value in the `Date` variable `delivery`.

2. ***Calculating and displaying the delivery time.*** Line 44 calculates the delivery time by adding three hours to the departure time (see the discussion following this box). Lines 45–46 display the Las Vegas delivery time by calling the `Date` types's `ToLongDateString` and `ToShortTimeString` methods. A `Date` variable's `ToLongDateString` method returns the date as a `String` in the format "Wednesday, October 30, 2008." A `Date` variable's `ToShortTimeString` returns the time as a `String` in the format "4:00 PM."

(cont.)

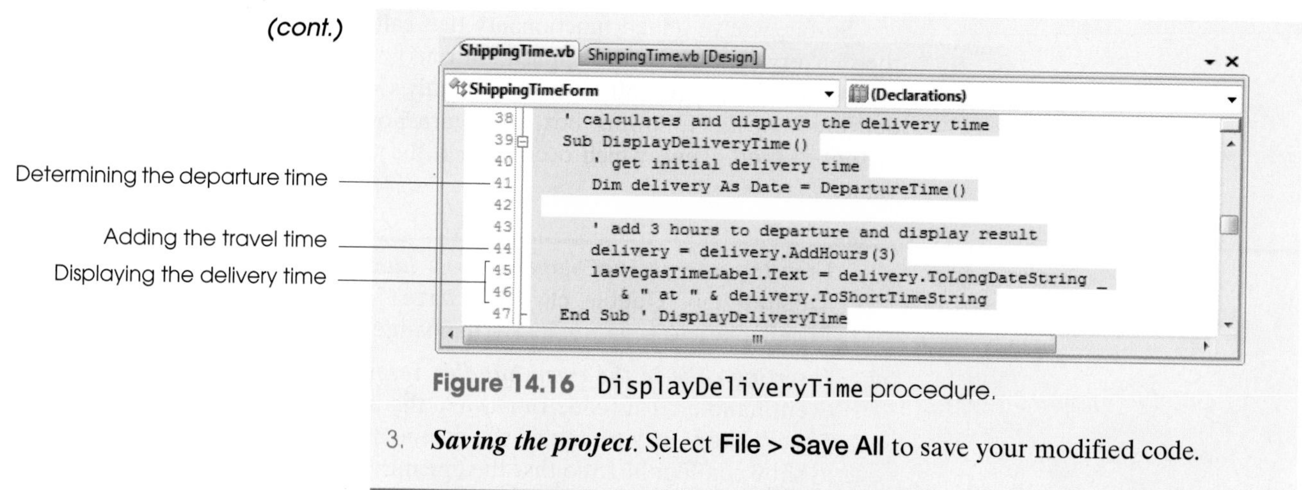
Determining the departure time
Adding the travel time
Displaying the delivery time
ShippingTime.vb
ShippingTime.vb [Design]
ShippingTimeForm
(Declarations)
38 ' calculates and displays the delivery time
39 Sub DisplayDeliveryTime()
40 ' get initial delivery time
41 Dim delivery As Date = DepartureTime()
42
43 ' add 3 hours to departure and display result
44 delivery = delivery.AddHours(3)
45 lasVegasTimeLabel.Text = delivery.ToLongDateString _
46 & " at " & delivery.ToShortTimeString
47 End Sub ' DisplayDeliveryTime

Figure 14.16 `DisplayDeliveryTime` procedure.

3. ***Saving the project.*** Select **File > Save All** to save your modified code.

When calculating the shipment's delivery time, you must account for the time-zone difference and the flight time. For instance, if you send a shipment from Portland, Maine to Las Vegas, it travels west three time zones (the time in Las Vegas is three hours earlier) and spends six hours in transit. If you drop off the shipment at 5:00 P.M. in Portland, the shipment leaves on the midnight flight and arrives in Las Vegas at

`12:00 A.M.` + (*time zone change* + *flight time*) = `12:00 A.M. + (-3 + 6)` *hours*

which is 3:00 A.M. Las Vegas time. Similarly, if the shipment takes the noon flight to Las Vegas, it arrives at 3:00 P.M. in Las Vegas.

To complete the application, you need to code the `DepartureTime Function` procedure. You use a `Select Case` statement and `Date` methods to return a `Date` containing the departure time (noon or midnight) for the seafood shipment's flight.

Coding the `DepartureTime` Procedure

1. ***Writing the `DepartureTime` procedure.*** Insert lines 49–53 of Fig. 14.17 into your code below the `DisplayDeliveryTime` procedure. Line 51 stores the current date in the `Date` variable `currentDate`. Line 52 declares the `Date` variable `departTime`, the variable you use to store the `DepartureTime Function` procedure's return value.

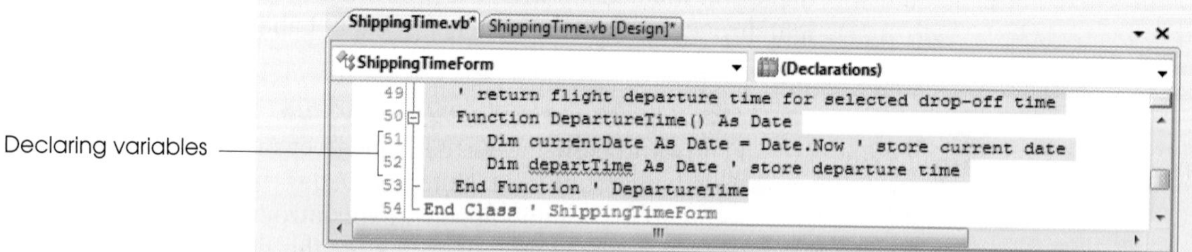
Declaring variables
ShippingTime.vb*
ShippingTime.vb [Design]*
ShippingTimeForm
(Declarations)
49 ' return flight departure time for selected drop-off time
50 Function DepartureTime() As Date
51 Dim currentDate As Date = Date.Now ' store current date
52 Dim departTime As Date ' store departure time
53 End Function ' DepartureTime
54 End Class ' ShippingTimeForm

Figure 14.17 Inserting procedure `DepartureTime` into the application.

2. ***Determining which flight the shipment uses.*** Insert lines 54–67 of Fig. 14.18 after the variable declarations and before the `End Function` statement. The `Select Case` statement that begins at line 55 uses the hour specified by the user in the `DateTimePicker` as the controlling expression. The `DateTimePicker`'s `Value` property (which is of type `Date`) contains the value selected by the user. The `Date`'s `Hour` property returns the hour of the `Date` stored in the `DateTimePicker`'s `Value` property. Recall that the `Hour` property stores the hour value as an `Integer` in the range of `0` to `23`.

(cont.)

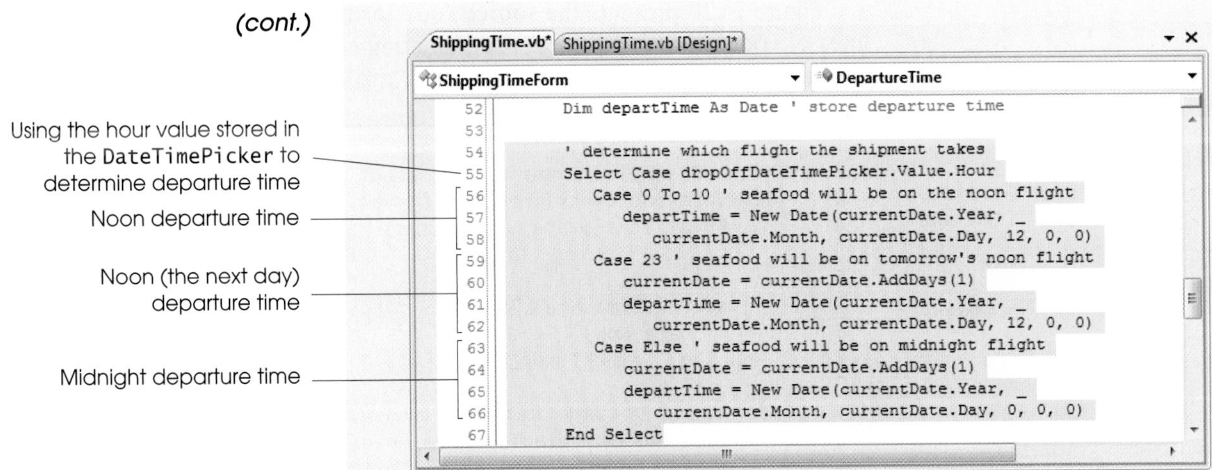
Using the hour value stored in the DateTimePicker to determine departure time
Noon departure time
Noon (the next day) departure time
Midnight departure time
ShippingTime.vb* ShippingTime.vb [Design]*
ShippingTimeForm
DepartureTime
52 Dim departTime As Date ' store departure time
53
54 ' determine which flight the shipment takes
55 Select Case dropOffDateTimePicker.Value.Hour
56 Case 0 To 10 ' seafood will be on the noon flight
57 departTime = New Date(currentDate.Year, _
58 currentDate.Month, currentDate.Day, 12, 0, 0)
59 Case 23 ' seafood will be on tomorrow's noon flight
60 currentDate = currentDate.AddDays(1)
61 departTime = New Date(currentDate.Year, _
62 currentDate.Month, currentDate.Day, 12, 0, 0)
63 Case Else ' seafood will be on midnight flight
64 currentDate = currentDate.AddDays(1)
65 departTime = New Date(currentDate.Year, _
66 currentDate.Month, currentDate.Day, 0, 0, 0)
67 End Select

Figure 14.18 Determining the seafood shipment's flight departure time.

The first `Case` statement's expression list (line 56) determines whether the `DateTimePicker`'s value is between midnight (`Hour` = `0`) and 10:59 A.M. (`Hour` = `10`). If so, the seafood shipment takes the noon flight to Las Vegas. (Recall that the shipment must arrive at the airport at least one hour before the flight leaves.) The first `Case` statement's body (lines 57–58) stores the departure time of noon on the current day in the variable `departTime`.

The next `Case` statement's expression list (line 59) determines whether the value in the `DateTimePicker` is between 11:00 P.M. and 11:59 P.M. (`Hour` = `23`). If the drop-off time occurs between 11:00 P.M. and 11:59 P.M, the seafood shipment takes the noon flight to Las Vegas the next day. The body of this `Case` (lines 60–62) stores the departure time of noon on the next day in the variable `departTime`.

The `Case Else`'s body executes if the controlling expression matches neither of the other two `Case`s (the value in the `DateTimePicker` is between 11:00 A.M. and 10:59 P.M.). In this case, the seafood shipment takes the midnight flight to Las Vegas. The `Case Else` (lines 64–66) stores the departure time of midnight in the variable `departTime`. Note that because midnight occurs on the following day, the `Date` variable representing midnight should contain a `Day` property value corresponding to the next day (line 64).

3. ***Returning the delivery time.*** Insert line 69 of Fig. 14.19 into the `DepartureTime` procedure following the `End Select` statement. Line 69 returns the `Date` value containing the flight departure time.

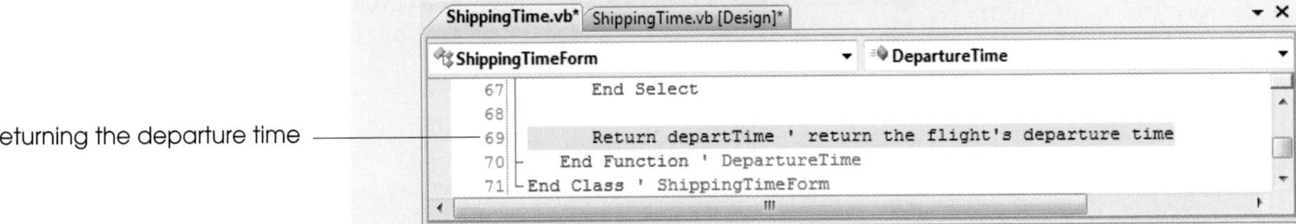
Returning the departure time
ShippingTime.vb* ShippingTime.vb [Design]*
ShippingTimeForm
DepartureTime
67 End Select
68
69 Return departTime ' return the flight's departure time
70 End Function ' DepartureTime
71 End Class ' ShippingTimeForm

Figure 14.19 Returning the flight departure time.

4. ***Running the application.*** Select **Debug > Start Debugging** to run your application.
5. ***Closing the application.*** Close your running application by clicking its close box.
6. ***Closing the IDE.*** Close the Visual Basic IDE by clicking its close box.

Figure 14.20 presents the source code for the **Shipping Time** application. The lines of code that contain new programming concepts you learned in this tutorial are highlighted.

```
Public Class ShippingTimeForm
   ' handles clockTimer's Tick event
   Private Sub clockTimer_Tick(ByVal sender As System.Object, _
      ByVal e As System.EventArgs) Handles clockTimer.Tick

      ' print current time
      currentTimeLabel.Text = String.Format("{0:hh:mm:ss tt}", _
         Date.Now)
   End Sub ' clockTimer_Tick

   ' initialize DateTimePicker status when Form loads
   Private Sub ShippingTimeForm_Load(ByVal sender As _
      System.Object, ByVal e As System.EventArgs) _
      Handles MyBase.Load

      Dim currentTime As Date = Date.Now ' store current time

      ' set range of possible drop-off times
      dropOffDateTimePicker.MinDate = New Date(currentTime.Year, _
         currentTime.Month, currentTime.Day, 0, 0, 0)

      dropOffDateTimePicker.MaxDate = _
         dropOffDateTimePicker.MinDate.AddDays(1)

      ' display the delivery time
      DisplayDeliveryTime()
   End Sub ' ShippingTimeForm_Load

   ' handles the DateTimePicker's ValueChanged event
   Private Sub dropOffDateTimePicker_ValueChanged(ByVal sender As _
      System.Object, ByVal e As System.EventArgs) _
      Handles dropOffDateTimePicker.ValueChanged

      ' display the delivery time
      DisplayDeliveryTime()
   End Sub ' dropOffDateTimePicker_ValueChanged

   ' calculates and displays the delivery time
   Sub DisplayDeliveryTime()
      ' get initial delivery time
      Dim delivery As Date = DepartureTime()

      ' add 3 hours to departure and display result
      delivery = delivery.AddHours(3)
      lasVegasTimeLabel.Text = delivery.ToLongDateString _
         & " at " & delivery.ToShortTimeString
   End Sub ' DisplayDeliveryTime

   ' return flight departure time for selected drop-off time
   Function DepartureTime() As Date
      Dim currentDate As Date = Date.Now ' store current date
      Dim departTime As Date ' store departure time

      ' determine which flight the shipment takes
      Select Case dropOffDateTimePicker.Value.Hour
         Case 0 To 10 ' seafood will be on the noon flight
            departTime = New Date(currentDate.Year, _
               currentDate.Month, currentDate.Day, 12, 0, 0)
```

Figure 14.20 **Shipping Time** application code. (Part 1 of 2.)

```
            Case 23 ' seafood will be on tomorrow's noon flight
                currentDate = currentDate.AddDays(1)
                departTime = New Date(currentDate.Year, _
                    currentDate.Month, currentDate.Day, 12, 0, 0)
            Case Else ' seafood will be on midnight flight
                currentDate = currentDate.AddDays(1)
                departTime = New Date(currentDate.Year, _
                    currentDate.Month, currentDate.Day, 0, 0, 0)
        End Select

        Return departTime ' return the flight's departure time
    End Function ' DepartureTime
End Class ' ShippingTimeForm
```

Figure 14.20 **Shipping Time** application code. (Part 2 of 2.)

SELF-REVIEW

1. The `ToShortTimeString` method is called on a `Date` variable to return its value in the format ________.

   a) `11 o'clock` b) `23:00`
   c) `11:00` d) `11:00 PM`

2. `DateTimePicker` properties ________ and ________ specify the earliest and latest dates that can be selected, respectively.

   a) `MinDate`, `MaxDate` b) `Now`, `Later`
   c) `Minimum`, `Maximum` d) `Early`, `Late`

Answers: 1) d. 2) a.

14.5 Wrap-Up

In this tutorial, you learned how to use the `Date` type to manipulate date and time information. You used variables of this type to calculate and display delivery times in your **Shipping Time** application. To help users enter date and time information, you used a `DateTimePicker` control. You observed how a `DateTimePicker` control can display custom date and time formats and limit user input. To help you group controls on the `Form` visually, you used the `GroupBox` control. You also learned how to use the `Timer` control to execute code at fixed intervals specified in milliseconds.

You then used three new event handlers to help you complete the **Shipping Time** application. You learned that the `Form`'s `Load` event handler executes code when the application is opened initially. You used this event to set initial values in your application. You then learned how to use the `DateTimePicker` control's `ValueChanged` event handler to execute code when the control's value changes. You used this event handler to update the delivery time each time the user entered a new time. Finally, you learned about the `Timer`'s `Tick` event handler, which you used to update and display the current time in a `Label` that serves as a clock.

In the next tutorial, you'll use the **Fund Raiser** application to introduce two key concepts—arguments and scope rules. Learning these concepts will help you understand how Visual Basic keeps track of variables throughout your application.

SKILLS SUMMARY

Executing Code When the Application Opens

- Use the `Form`'s `Load` event handler to execute code when the application first opens.

Storing and Manipulating Date and Time Information

- Use a `Date` variable (which corresponds to the `DateTime` built-in type) to store and manipulate date and time information. A `Date` variable stores information about a point in time (e.g., 12:00:00 A.M. on January 1, 2003). This information can be formatted for display in predefined long or short formats or in custom (programmer-defined) formats.

Using Date Variables

- Use keyword New to create a new Date value.
- Use property Date.Now to obtain your computer's current date and time for the local time zone.
- Use the member-access operator (.) to access properties of a Date variable, such as Years, Hours, etc.
- Use Date methods, such as AddHours and AddDays, to add or subtract time from values in Date variables. Then assign the value returned by the method to a Date variable.

Using a GroupBox Control

- Use a GroupBox control to group related controls visually. To add a GroupBox to the Form, double click the GroupBox control in the **Toolbox** or drag a GroupBox control from the **Toolbox** onto a Form.
- Use property Text to configure the title of a GroupBox.

Placing Controls Inside a GroupBox

- Place a control inside the GroupBox by clicking the control's name in the **Toolbox**, then clicking inside the GroupBox. You also can drag the control from the **Toolbox** or the Form and drop it inside the GroupBox.

Using the DateTimePicker Control

- Use a DateTimePicker control to get date and time information from the user.
- Set property Format to Custom to indicate that you will specify how the date appears in the DateTimePicker. Specify the format in property CustomFormat.
- Set property ShowUpDown to True to allow the user to select the date or time by clicking an up or down arrow. If this property's value is False, a monthly calendar drops down, allowing the user to pick a date.
- Use the DateTimePicker's ValueChanged event handler to execute code when the value in the DateTimePicker changes.

Using the Timer Control

- Use a Timer control to execute code (the Tick event handler) at specified intervals.
- To add a Timer control to the Form, click the Timer in the **Toolbox**, then click anywhere on the Form. You also can double click the Timer in the **Toolbox**. The Timer control appears in the component tray.
- Specify the number of milliseconds between Tick events using the Interval property.
- Set the Enabled property to True so that the Tick event is raised once per Interval.

KEY TERMS

component tray—The area below the Windows Form Designer that contains controls, such as Timers, that are not part of the graphical user interface.

constructor—A procedure that initializes an object when it is created.

container—An object, such as a GroupBox or Form, that contains other controls.

CustomFormat property of a DateTimePicker control—The DateTimePicker property that contains your format string with which to display the date and/or time when DateTimePicker Format property is set to Custom.

DateTime primitive type—The .NET Framework Class Library type that corresponds to the Date keyword.

Date variable—A variable of type Date, capable of storing date and time data.

DateTimePicker control—Retrieves date and time information from the user.

Format property of a DateTimePicker control—The DateTimePicker property that allows you to specify a predefined or custom format with which to display the date and/or time.

GroupBox control—Groups related controls visually.

Interval property of a Timer control—The Timer property that specifies the number of milliseconds between Tick events.

Load event of a Form—Raised when an application initially executes.

MaxDate property of a DateTimePicker control—The DateTimePicker property that specifies the latest value that the DateTimePicker allows the user to enter.

method overloading—Allows you to create multiple methods with the same name but different signatures.

MinDate property of a DateTimePicker control—Specifies the earliest value that the control allows the user to enter.

New keyword—Used to call a constructor when creating an object.

Now property of type Date—The Date property that retrieves your computer's current time.

signature—Specifies a procedure's parameters and their types.

ShowUpDown property of a DateTimePicker control—The DateTimePicker property that, when True, allows the user to specify the time using up and down arrows, and, when False, allows the user to specify the date using a calendar.

Tick event of a Timer control—Raised after the number of milliseconds specified in the Timer control's Interval property has elapsed (if Enabled is True).

Timer control—Generates Tick events to run code at specified intervals.

Today property of type Date—Returns the current date with the time set to midnight.

ToLongDateString method of type Date—Returns a String containing the date in the format "Wednesday, October 30, 2002."

ToShortTimeString method of type Date—Returns a String containing the time in the format "4:00 PM."

Value property of a DateTimePicker control—Stores the value (such as a time) in a DateTimePicker control.

ValueChanged event of a DateTimePicker control—Raised when a user selects a new day or time in the DateTimePicker control.

GUI DESIGN GUIDELINES

DateTimePicker

- Use a DateTimePicker to retrieve date and time information from the user.
- Each DateTimePicker should have a corresponding descriptive Label.
- If the user is to specify a time of day or a date and time, set the DateTimePicker's ShowUpDown property to True. If the user is to specify only a date, set the DateTimePicker's ShowUpDown property to False to allow the user to select a day from the month calendar.

GroupBox

- GroupBox titles should be concise and should use book-title capitalization.
- Use GroupBoxes to group related controls in a box with a title.

CONTROLS, EVENTS, PROPERTIES & METHODS

Date This type provides properties and methods to store and manipulate date and time information.

- ***Properties***

  Day—Returns the day stored in a Date variable.

  Hour—Returns the hour stored in a Date variable.

  Minute—Returns the minute stored in a Date variable.

  Month—Returns the month stored in a Date variable.

  Now—Returns the system's current date and time.

  Second—Returns the second stored in the Date variable.

  Today—Returns the system's current date with the time set to 00:00:00 (midnight).

  Year—Returns the year stored in a Date variable.

- ***Methods***

  AddDays—Creates a new Date value that is the specified number of days later (or earlier) in time.

  AddHours—Creates a new Date value that is the specified number of hours later (or earlier) in time.

AddMinutes—Creates a new Date value that is the specified number of minutes later (or earlier) in time.

ToLongDateString—Returns a String containing the date in the format "Wednesday, October 30, 2002."

ToShortTimeString—Returns a String containing the time in the format "4:00 PM."

DateTimePicker DateTimePicker This control is used to retrieve date and time information from the user.

- ***In action***

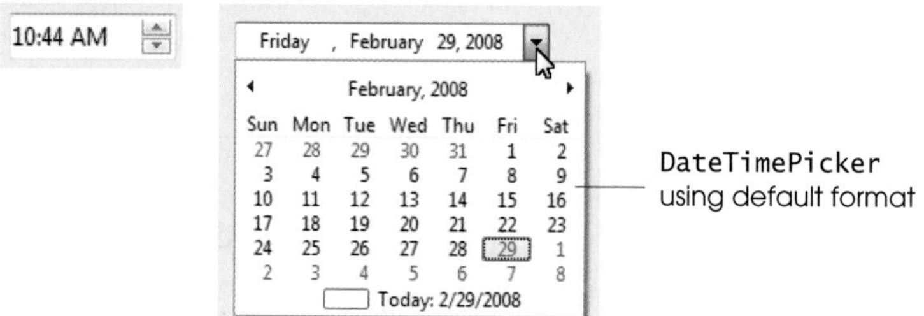

DateTimePicker using default format

- ***Event***

  ValueChanged—Raised when the Value property is changed.

- ***Properties***

  CustomFormat—Sets a custom format string to use when displaying the date and/or time.

  Format—Specifies the format in which the date and time are displayed on the control. Long specifies that the date is to be displayed in the format "Monday, December 09, 2002." Short specifies that the date is to be displayed in the format "12/9/2002." Time specifies that the time is to be displayed in the format "8:39:53 PM." Custom allows you to specify a custom format in which to display the date and/or time.

  Location—Specifies the location of the DateTimePicker control relative to the top-left corner of the container (e.g., a Form or a GroupBox).

  MinDate—Specifies the minimum date and/or time that can be selected.

  MaxDate—Specifies the maximum date and/or time that can be selected.

  Name—Specifies the name used to access the DateTimePicker control programmatically. The name should be appended with the DateTimePicker suffix.

  ShowUpDown—Specifies whether the up and down arrows (True) are displayed on the control for time values. If False, a down arrow is displayed for accessing a drop-down calendar.

  Size—Specifies the width and height (in pixels) of the DateTimePicker control.

  Value—Stores the date and/or time in the DateTimePicker control.

GroupBox GroupBox This control groups related controls visually in a box with a title.

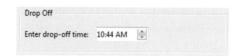

- ***In action***

  Drop Off

  Enter drop-off time: 10:44 AM

- ***Properties***

  Location—Specifies the location of the GroupBox control relative to the top-left corner of the container (e.g., a Form or a GroupBox).

  Name—Specifies the name used to access the GroupBox control programmatically. The name should be appended with the GroupBox suffix.

  Size—Specifies the width and height (in pixels) of the GroupBox control.

  Text—Specifies the text displayed on the GroupBox.

Timer Timer This control wakes up at specified intervals of time to execute code in its Tick event handler.

- *Event*

  Tick—Raised after the number of milliseconds specified in the Interval property has elapsed.

- *Properties*

  Enabled—Determines whether the Timer is running (True). The default is False.

  Interval—Specifies the time interval (in milliseconds) between Tick events.

  Name—Specifies the name used to access the Timer control programmatically. The name should be appended with the Timer suffix.

MULTIPLE-CHOICE QUESTIONS

14.1 The _________ allows you to store and manipulate date information easily.

a) Date type b) DatePicker control
c) GroupBox control d) Now property

14.2 You can _________ a Date variable.

a) add hours to b) add days to
c) subtract hours from d) All of the above

14.3 To subtract one day from Date variable day's value, assign the value returned by _________ to day.

a) day.AddHours(-24) b) day.SubtractDays(1)
c) day.AddDays(-1) d) Both a and c

14.4 The time 3:45 and 35 seconds in the afternoon would be formatted as 03:45:35 PM according to the format string _________.

a) "hh:mm:ss" b) "hh:mm:ss tt"
c) "hh:mm:ss am:pm" d) "h:m:s tt"

14.5 A(n) _________ event occurs before the Form is displayed.

a) LoadForm b) InitializeForm
c) Load d) FormLoad

14.6 Timer property Interval sets the rate at which Tick events occur in _________.

a) nanoseconds b) microseconds
c) milliseconds d) seconds

14.7 To set Date variable time five hours earlier, use _________.

a) time = time.SubtractHours(5) b) time = time.AddHours(-5)
c) time = time.AddHours(5) d) time.AddHours(-5)

14.8 A _________ is a container.

a) GroupBox b) Form
c) Timer d) Both a and b

14.9 A Date variable stores hour values in the range _________.

a) 1 to 12 b) 0 to 12
c) 0 to 24 d) 0 to 23

14.10 A DateTimePicker's _________ property specifies the format string with which to display the date.

a) CustomFormat b) FormatString
c) Format d) Text

EXERCISES

14.11 *(World Clock Application)* Create an application that displays the current time in Los Angeles, Atlanta, London and Tokyo. Use a `Timer` to update the clock every second. Assume that your local time is the time in Atlanta. Atlanta is three hours later than Los Angeles. London is five hours later than Atlanta. Tokyo is nine hours later than London. The application should look similar to Fig. 14.21.

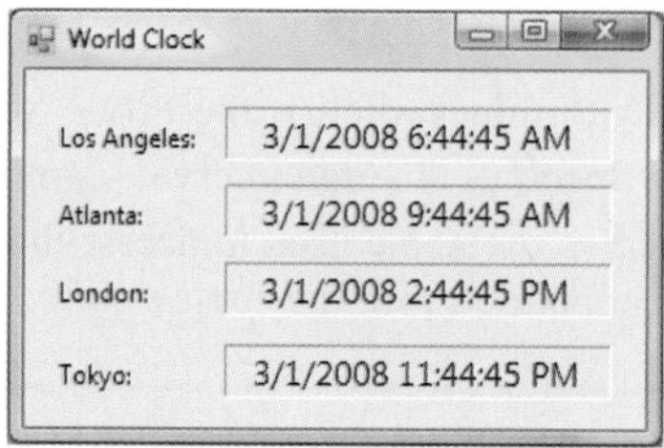

Figure 14.21 World Clock GUI.

a) ***Copying the template to your working directory.*** Copy the directory `C:\Examples\Tutorial14\Exercises\WorldClock` to your `C:\SimplyVB2008` directory.

b) ***Opening the application's template file.*** Double click `WorldClock.sln` in the `WorldClock` directory to open the application.

c) ***Adding a `Timer` to the `Form`.*** Add a `Timer` control to the **World Clock** application. Set the `Timer` control's `Name` property to `clockTimer`. The Timer should generate a Tick event every 1,000 milliseconds (one second).

d) ***Adding a `Tick` event handler for `clockTimer`.*** Add a `Tick` event handler for `clockTimer`. The event handler should calculate and display the current times for Los Angeles, Atlanta, London and Tokyo.

e) ***Running the application.*** Select **Debug > Start Debugging** to run your application. Look at the clock on your machine to verify that the time for Los Angeles is three hours earlier, the time in Atlanta is the same as what your clock says, the time in London is five hours later, and the time in Tokyo is 14 hours later (nine hours later than London).

f) ***Closing the application.*** Close your running application by clicking its close box.

g) ***Closing the IDE.*** Close the Visual Basic IDE by clicking its close box.

14.12 *(Shipping Time Application Enhancement)* During the winter, a distribution center in Denver, Colorado, needs to receive seafood shipments to supply the local ski resorts. Enhance the **Shipping Time** application by adding Denver, Colorado, as another shipping destination. Denver is two time zones west of Portland, Maine, meaning that the time is two hours earlier than Portland. Because there are no direct flights to Denver, shipments from Portland take eight hours.

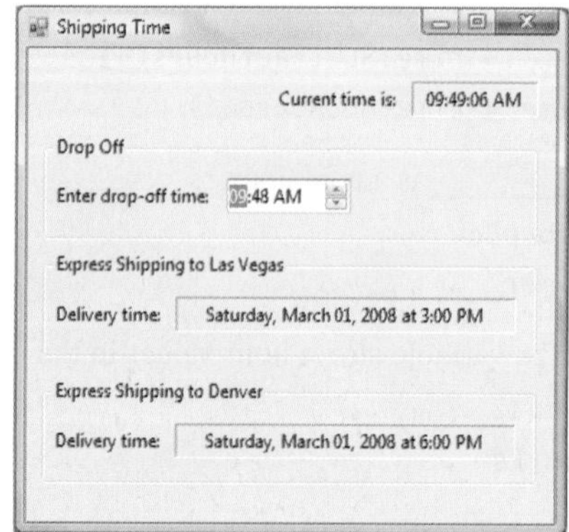

Figure 14.22 Enhanced Shipping Time GUI.

a) ***Copying the template to your working directory.*** Copy the directory `C:\Examples\Tutorial14\Exercises\ShippingTimeEnhanced` to your `C:\SimplyVB2008` directory.

b) ***Opening the application's template file.*** Double click `ShippingTime.sln` in the `ShippingTimeEnhanced` directory to open the application.

c) ***Inserting a GroupBox.*** Resize the `Form` to fit the **Express Shipping to Denver** `GroupBox` as shown in Fig. 14.22. Add a `GroupBox` to the `Form`. Change the `Text` property of the `GroupBox` to indicate that it contains the delivery time in Denver. Resize and position the `GroupBox` so that it resembles the GUI shown in Fig. 14.22.

d) ***Inserting `Labels`.*** In the `GroupBox` you just created, add an output `Label` to display the delivery time for a seafood shipment to Denver and a corresponding descriptive `Label`.

e) ***Inserting code to the `DisplayDeliveryTime` procedure.*** Add code to `DisplayDeliveryTime` procedure to compute and display the delivery time in Denver.

f) ***Running the application.*** Select **Debug > Start Debugging** to run your application. Select various drop-off times, and ensure that the delivery times are correct for both Las Vegas and Denver.

g) ***Closing the application.*** Close your running application by clicking its close box.

h) ***Closing the IDE.*** Close the Visual Basic IDE by clicking its close box.

14.13 *(Alarm Application)* Create an application that allows the user to set an alarm clock. The application should allow the user to set the time of the alarm by using a `DateTimePicker`. While the alarm is set, the user should not be able to modify the `DateTimePicker`. If the alarm is set and the current time matches or exceeds the time in the `DateTimePicker`, play the computer's "beep" sound. (Your computer must have the necessary hardware for sound enabled.) The user should be able to cancel an alarm by using a **Reset** `Button`. This `Button` is disabled when the application starts.

Figure 14.23 Alarm GUI.

a) ***Copying the template to your working directory.*** Copy the directory `C:\Examples\Tutorial14\Exercises\AlarmClock` to your `C:\SimplyVB2008` directory.

b) ***Opening the application's template file.*** Double click `AlarmClock.sln` in the `AlarmClock` directory to open the application.

c) ***Inserting a `DateTimePicker`.*** Add a `DateTimePicker` control to the `Form`. Set the `DateTimePicker` to display only the time, as shown in Fig. 14.23. Resize and position the `DateTimePicker` control so that it appears as it does in Fig. 14.23.

d) ***Coding the Set `Button`'s `Click` event handler.*** Add a `Click` event handler for the **Set** `Button`. This event handler should disable the **Set** `Button` and the `DateTimePicker` and enable the **Reset** `Button`.

e) ***Coding the `Timer`'s `Tick` event handler.*** Define the `Tick` event handler for the `Timer`. A `Tick` event should occur every 1,000 milliseconds (one second). Update the current time once a second. If the alarm is set and the current time matches or exceeds the time in the `DateTimePicker`, play the computer's "beep" sound by calling the `Beep` function. To call the `Beep` function, type `Beep()` on its own line in your code. Recall that you can use relational operators with `Date` values.

f) ***Coding the Reset `Button`'s `Click` event handler.*** Define the `Click` event handler for the **Reset** `Button`. When the **Reset** `Button` is clicked, the GUI should be set back to its original state.

g) ***Running the application.*** Select **Debug > Start Debugging** to run your application. Use the `DateTimePicker` and the **Set** `Button` to set a time for the alarm to go off.

Wait for that time to verify that the alarm makes beeping sounds. Click the **Reset** Button to set a new time for the alarm to go off.

h) ***Closing the application.*** Close your running application by clicking its close box.

i) ***Closing the IDE.*** Close the Visual Basic IDE by clicking its close box.

What does this code do? ▶ **14.14** This code creates a Date variable. What date does this variable contain?

```
Dim day As Date = New Date(2003, 1, 2, 3, 4, 5)
```

What's wrong with this code? ▶ **14.15** The following lines of code are supposed to create a Date variable and increment its hour value by two. Find the error(s) in the code.

```
Dim currentDay As Date = Date.Now
currentDay.AddHours(2)
```

Programming Challenge ▶ **14.16** *(Fee Calculator)* Create an application that computes the fee for parking a car in a parking garage (Fig. 14.24). The user should provide the **Time In:** and **Time Out:** values by using DateTimePickers. The application should calculate the cost of parking in the garage for the specified amount of time. Assume that parking costs $3 an hour. When calculating the total time spent in the garage, you can ignore the seconds value, but treat the minutes value as a fraction of an hour (1 minute is 1/60 of an hour). For simplicity, assume that no overnight parking is allowed, so each car leaves the garage on the same day in which it arrives.

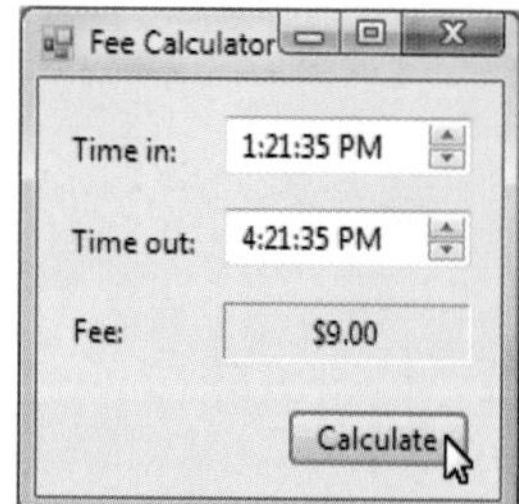

Figure 14.24 Fee Calculator GUI.

a) ***Copying the template to your working directory.*** Copy the directory C:\Examples\Tutorial14\Exercises\FeeCalculator to your C:\SimplyVB2008 directory.

b) ***Opening the application's template file.*** Double click FeeCalculator.sln in the FeeCalculator directory to open the application.

c) ***Inserting the DateTimePicker controls.*** Add two DateTimePicker controls to the Form. Set the DateTimePickers so that they show the time only. Set the Size and Location properties of each DateTimePicker control so that they appear as in Fig. 14.24.

d) ***Writing the Function procedure Fee.*** Define a Function procedure Fee that accepts two Dates as parameters—the value of the **Time In:** DateTimePicker and the value of the **Time Out:** DateTimePicker. Using this information, procedure Fee should calculate the fee for parking in the garage. The Function procedure should then return this value as a Decimal.

e) ***Coding the Calculate Button's Click event handler.*** Add the Click event handler for the **Calculate** Button. This event handler should call Fee to obtain the amount due. It should then display the amount (formatted as currency) in a Label.

f) ***Running the application.*** Select **Debug > Start Debugging** to run your application. Use the DateTimePickers' up and down arrows to select the time the car was placed in the garage and the time the car was taken out of the garage. Click the **Calculate** Button and verify that the correct fee is displayed.

g) ***Closing the application.*** Close your running application by clicking its close box.

h) ***Closing the IDE.*** Close the Visual Basic IDE by clicking its close box.

TUTORIAL 15

Objectives

In this tutorial, you learn to:

- Create variables that can be used in all the `Form`'s procedures.
- Pass arguments by reference, using `ByRef`, so that the called procedure can modify the caller's variables.
- Eliminate subtle data-type errors by enabling `Option Strict` in your projects.
- Change a value from one data type to another, using methods of class `Convert`.

Outline

Fund Raiser Application

Introducing Scope, Pass-by-Reference and `Option Strict`

In this tutorial, you learn several important Visual Basic concepts. First, you learn how to declare variables outside of a class's procedure definitions. These variables can be referenced from any procedure within your `Form`'s code. Next, you learn another technique for passing arguments to procedures. In the procedures that you've created so far, the application has made a copy of the argument's value, and any changes the called procedure made to the copy did not affect the original variable's value. You learn how to pass an argument to a procedure—using a technique called pass-by-reference—so that changes made to the parameter's value in the procedure are also made to the original variable in the caller. You learn how the Visual Basic compiler handles conversions between different data types and how to enable a feature called `Option Strict` to avoid subtle errors that can occur when a value of one type is assigned to a variable of an incompatible type. In addition, you become familiar with methods from class `Convert` that allow you to explicitly convert data from one type to another.

15.1 Test-Driving the Fund Raiser Application

In this tutorial, you create a fund raiser application that determines how much donated money is available after operating costs. This application must meet the following requirements:

Application Requirements

An organization is hosting a fund raiser to collect donations. A portion of each donation is used to cover the operating expenses of the organization—the rest of the donation goes to the charity. Create an application that allows the organization to keep track of the total amount of money raised. The application should deduct 17% of each donation for operating costs—the remaining 83% is given to the charity. The application should display the amount of each donation after the 17% for operating expenses is deducted—it also should display the total amount raised for the charity (that is, the total amount donated less operating costs) for all donations up to that point.

The user inputs the amount of a donation into a `TextBox` and clicks a `Button` to calculate the net amount of the donation that the charity receives after operating expenses have been deducted. In addition, the total amount of money raised for the charity is updated and displayed. You begin by test-driving the completed application. Then you learn the additional Visual Basic technologies needed to create your own version of this application.

Test-Driving the Fund Raiser Application

1. ***Opening the completed application.*** Open the directory `C:\Examples\Tutorial15\CompletedApplication\FundRaiser` to locate the **Fund Raiser** application. Double click `FundRaiser.sln` to open the application in the Visual Basic IDE.

2. ***Running the* Fund Raiser *application.*** Select **Debug > Start Debugging** to run the application (Fig. 15.1).

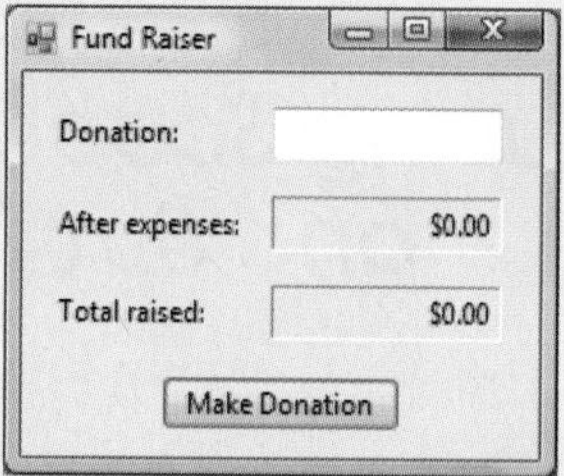

Figure 15.1 **Fund Raiser** application's `Form`.

3. ***Entering a donation in the application.*** Enter `1500` in the **Donation:** `TextBox`. Click the **Make Donation** `Button`. The application calculates the amount of the donation after the operating expenses have been deducted and displays the result ($1245.00) in the **After expenses:** field. Because this is the first donation entered, this amount is repeated in the **Total raised:** field (Fig. 15.2).

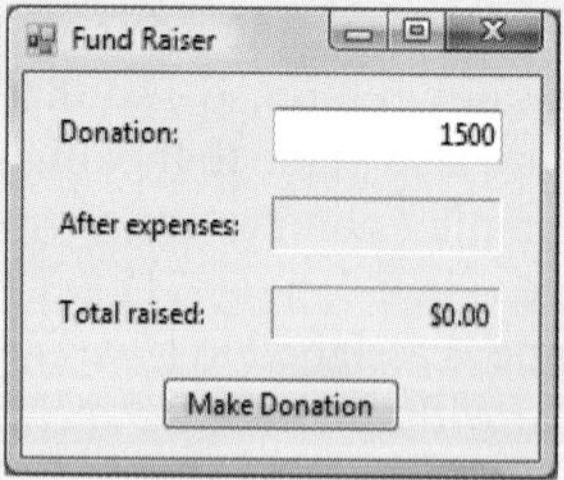

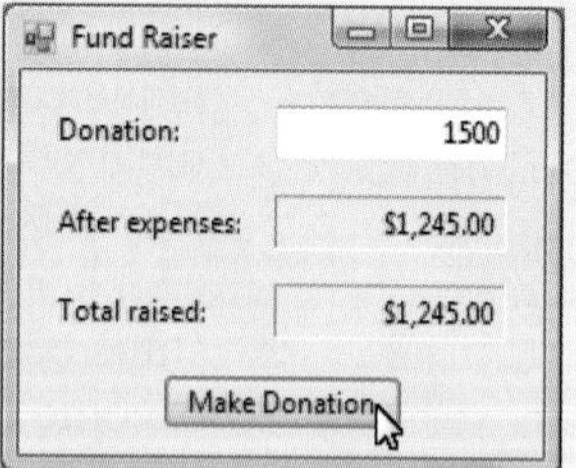

Figure 15.2 **Fund Raiser** application's `Form` with first donation entered.

4. ***Entering additional donations.*** Enter more donations, and click the **Make Donation** `Button`. Note that the total raised increases with each additional donation (Fig. 15.3).

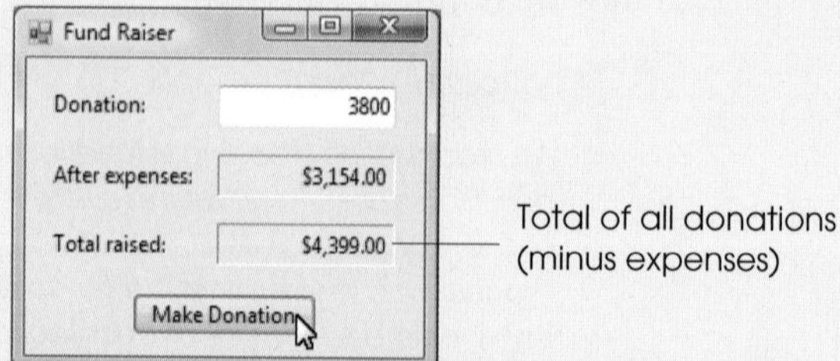

Figure 15.3 Making further donations.

5. ***Closing the application.*** Close your running application by clicking its close box.

6. ***Closing the IDE.*** Close the Visual Basic IDE by clicking its close box.

15.2 Constructing the Fund Raiser Application

The following pseudocode statements describe the basic operation of the **Fund Raiser** application:

```
When the user changes the current donation amount in the TextBox:
    Clear Label that displays amount of current donation that goes toward
        charity

When the user clicks the Make Donation Button:
    Obtain amount of current donation from TextBox
    Call function CalculateDonation to calculate amount of current donation that
        goes toward charity (amount after operating costs)
    Display amount of current donation that goes toward charity
    Update total amount raised for charity (from all donations received)
    Display total amount raised for charity

When the CalculateDonation procedure gets called:
    Calculate operating costs (multiply the donated amount by the operating-
        cost percentage)
    Calculate amount of donation that goes toward charity (subtract operating
        costs from donated amount)
```

Now that you've test-driven the **Fund Raiser** application and studied its pseudocode representation, you use an ACE table to help you convert the pseudocode to Visual Basic. Figure 15.4 lists the actions, controls and events that help you complete your own version of this application.

Action/Control/Event Table for the Fund Raiser Application

Action	Control	Event/Method
Label all the application's controls	donationLabel, donatedLabel, totalLabel	Application is run
	donationTextBox	TextChanged
Clear Label that displays amount of current donation that goes toward charity	donatedValueLabel	
	donateButton	Click
Obtain amount of current donation from TextBox	donationTextBox	
Call function CalculateDonation to calculate amount of current donation that goes toward charity		
Display amount of current donation that goes toward charity	donatedValueLabel	
Update total amount raised for charity		
Display total amount raised for charity	totalValueLabel	
		Calculate-Donation
Calculate operating costs		
Calculate amount of donation that goes toward charity		

Figure 15.4 **Fund Raiser** application's ACE table.

You're now ready to begin programming the **Fund Raiser** application. First, you declare the variables needed in the application. In this discussion, you learn a new concept—scope. The **scope** of a variable's identifier is the portion of an application in which the identifier can be referenced. Some identifiers can be referenced throughout an application—others can be referenced only from limited portions of an application (such as within a single procedure). You now add code to your application to illustrate these various scopes.

Examining Scope with the Fund Raiser Application

1. ***Copying the template.*** Copy the `C:\Examples\Tutorial15\TemplateApplication\FundRaiser` directory to your `C:\SimplyVB2008` directory.

2. ***Opening the Fund Raiser application's template file.*** Double click `FundRaiser.sln` in the `FundRaiser` directory to open the application in the Visual Basic IDE (Fig. 15.5).

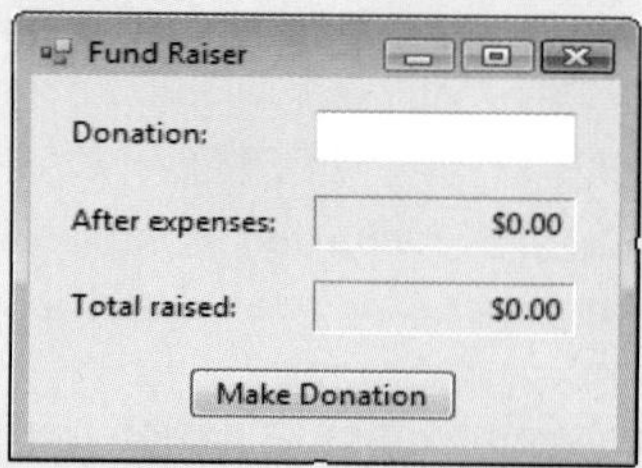

Figure 15.5 **Fund Raiser** template application's `Form`.

3. ***Placing declarations in the code file.*** Select **View > Code**, and add lines 2–3 of Fig. 15.6 to `FundRaiser.vb`. In this application, you need a variable that stores the total amount of money raised for charity.

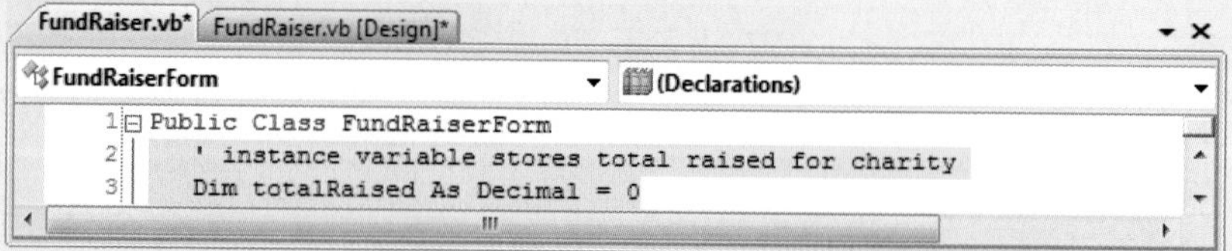

Figure 15.6 Declaring an instance variable in class `FundRaiserForm`.

This variable is initialized when the `Form` first loads and must retain its value while the application executes (that is, it cannot be created each time a procedure is invoked). Variable `totalRaised` stores the total amount of money raised. This variable is an **instance variable**—a variable declared inside a class, but outside any of the class's procedure definitions. All procedures in class `FundRaiserForm` have access to this variable and can modify its value.

Instance variables have **module scope**. Module scope begins at the identifier after keyword `Class` and terminates at the `End Class` statement. This scope enables any procedure in a class to access all instance variables defined in the same class. A `Form`'s module-scope instance variables are created when the `Form` is created (normally, when the application begins executing).

4. ***Creating the `Click` event handler for the Make Donation `Button`.*** Select **View > Designer** to return to **Design** view. Double click the **Make Donation** `Button` to generate its `Click` event handler `donateButton_Click`. Split the procedure header over two lines, as in lines 27–28 of Fig. 15.7, and place the comments in lines 26 and 30 around the event handler.

(cont.)

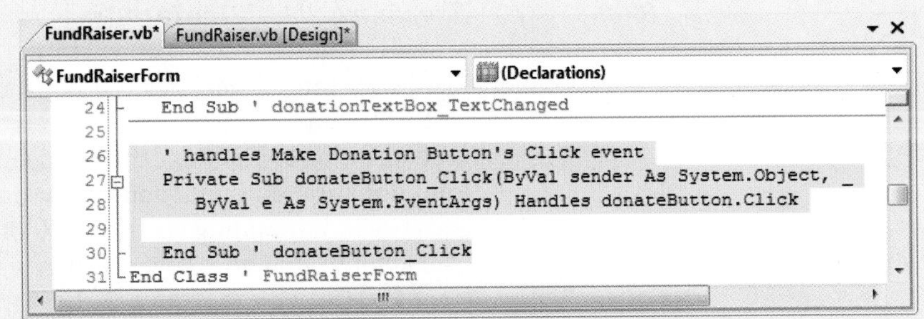

Figure 15.7 Adding a `Click` event handler to the application.

5. ***Declaring local variables in event handler `donateButton_Click`.*** Add lines 30–31 of Fig. 15.8 to event handler `donateButton_Click`. Variable `donation` (line 30) stores the donation amount. Variable `afterCosts` (line 31) stores the donation amount after the operating expenses have been deducted.

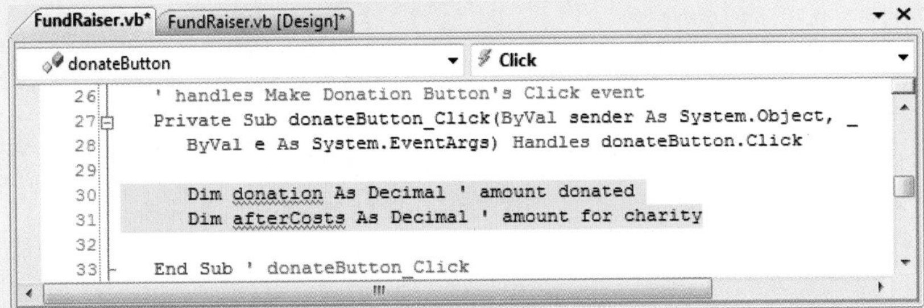

Figure 15.8 Declaring local variables in the `donateButton_click` event handler.

In Visual Basic, identifiers, such as `donation` and `afterCosts`, that are declared inside a procedure (but outside a control statement, such as a `Do While...Loop`) have **procedure scope**. Procedure scope begins at the identifier's declaration and ends at the last statement of the procedure. Identifiers with procedure scope cannot be referenced outside of the procedure in which they are declared. A procedure's parameters also have procedure scope.

Identifiers declared inside control statements (such as inside an `If...Then` statement) have **block scope**, which begins at the identifier's declaration and ends at the enclosing block's final statement (for example, `Else` or `End If`).

Variables with either procedure scope or block scope are called **local variables**, because they cannot be referenced outside the procedure or block in which they are declared. If a local variable (that is, a variable with either block scope or procedure scope) has the same name as an instance variable (that is, a variable with module scope), the instance variable is hidden in the block or procedure by the local variable. Any expression containing the variable name uses the local variable's value and not the instance variable's value. The instance variable's value is not destroyed, though—you can still access the instance variable by preceding its name with the keyword `Me` and a dot (`.`). Tutorial 19 discusses the `Me` keyword in more detail.

Error-Prevention Tip

Hidden variable names can sometimes lead to subtle logic errors. Use unique names for all variables, regardless of scope, to prevent an instance variable from becoming hidden.

(cont.)

6. ***Examining the `CalculateDonation` procedure.*** The template application provides the `CalculateDonation Function` procedure (lines 5–16 of Fig. 15.9). Line 9 declares the constant `COSTS`, which stores the operating-cost percentage. This constant also is "local" to the procedure and cannot be used elsewhere. The `Function` procedure accepts one parameter value—the total donation amount (`donatedAmount`). The amount of the donation that goes toward operating costs is 17% of the initial donation. The net donation (the amount that goes toward charity) is calculated by multiplying local constant `COSTS` (with the value `0.17`), by the donation amount and subtracting this result from the donation amount.

Parameter `donatedAmount` has procedure scope because it is declared in the procedure header

Local variable `netDonation` has procedure scope because it is declared in the procedure body

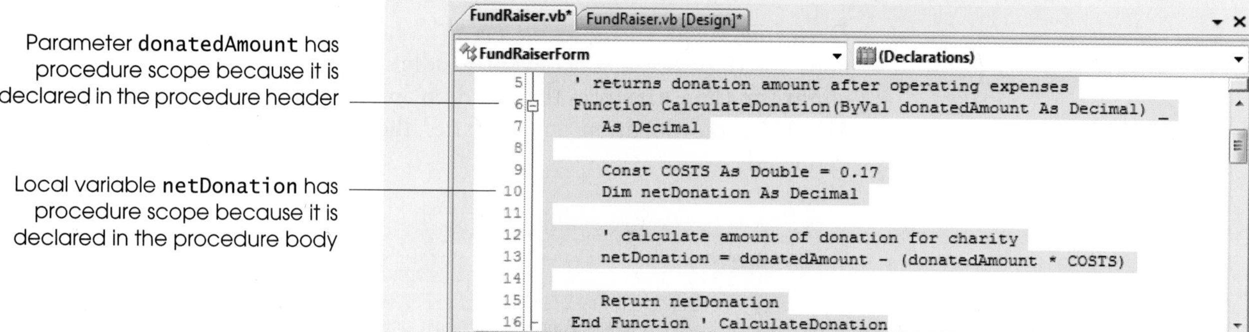
FundRaiser.vb*
FundRaiser.vb [Design]*
FundRaiserForm
(Declarations)
5 ' returns donation amount after operating expenses
6 Function CalculateDonation(ByVal donatedAmount As Decimal) _
7 As Decimal
8
9 Const COSTS As Double = 0.17
10 Dim netDonation As Decimal
11
12 ' calculate amount of donation for charity
13 netDonation = donatedAmount - (donatedAmount * COSTS)
14
15 Return netDonation
16 End Function ' CalculateDonation

Figure 15.9 `Function` procedure `CalculateDonation` provided in the template application.

Procedure `CalculateDonation` subtracts the operating cost from the donation amount (`donatedAmount`) and assigns the result to `netDonation` (line 13). The `Function` procedure then returns the `Decimal` result (line 15).

7. ***Demonstrating the difference between module scope and procedure scope.*** Now we demonstrate the limits of procedure scope. In line 13 of Fig. 15.10, temporarily replace the constant `COSTS` with the variable `donation`, which is declared as a local variable in `donateButton_Click` (line 30 in Fig. 15.8). Note the jagged line under `donation` to indicate an error. Variables with procedure scope can be accessed and modified only in the procedure in which they are defined. The error message displayed when the mouse pointer rests on `donation` indicates that `donation` is not declared. This variable is "local" to `donateButton_Click`, so `Function CalculateDonation` cannot "see" the declaration of `donation`. Replace `donation` with `COSTS` in line 13.

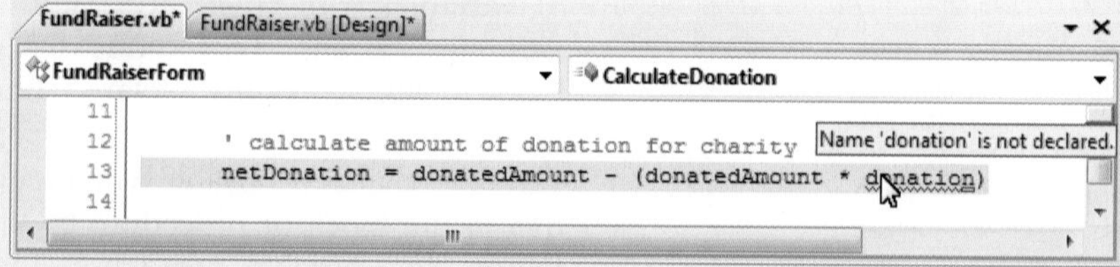
FundRaiser.vb*
FundRaiser.vb [Design]*
FundRaiserForm
CalculateDonation
11
12 ' calculate amount of donation for charity
13 netDonation = donatedAmount - (donatedAmount * donation)
14
Name 'donation' is not declared.

Figure 15.10 Demonstrating procedure scope.

8. ***Obtaining the donation amount.*** Add lines 33–34 of Fig. 15.11 to event handler `donateButton_Click`. You obtain the donation amount from the `donationTextBox` (line 34).

(cont.)

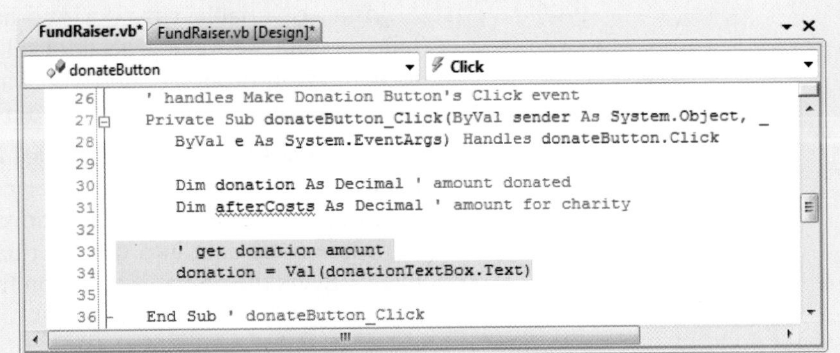

Figure 15.11 Obtaining the donation amount.

9. ***Calculating and displaying the donation amount after the operating expenses.*** Add lines 36–40 of Fig. 15.12 to the event handler. Line 37 invokes procedure `CalculateDonation` with the amount of the donation (`donation`). The result of this procedure—the net amount that goes to charity after the deduction for operating costs—is assigned to variable `afterCosts`. The donation amount after operating costs is formatted as a currency string and displayed in the **After expenses:** `Label` (line 40).

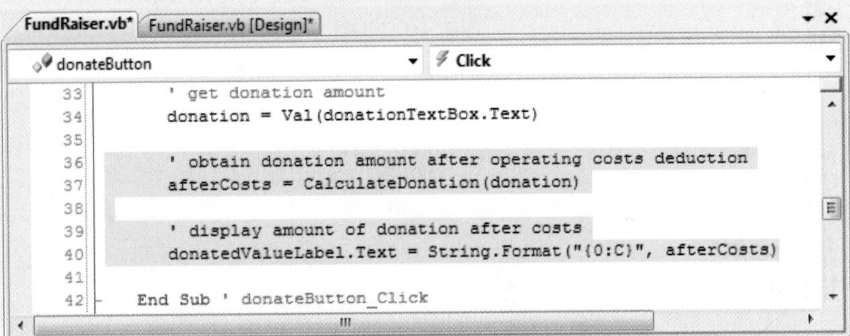

Figure 15.12 Calculating and displaying the donation amount after operating expenses.

10. ***Updating and displaying the fund raiser total.*** Add lines 42–46 of Fig. 15.13 to the event handler. Line 43 updates instance variable `totalRaised`, which stores the total amount given to the charity after the operating costs have been deducted. Line 46 displays the total amount raised for charity.

    Note that `totalRaised` is not declared as a local variable in this event handler and does not have a jagged line beneath it. Recall that `totalRaised` is an instance variable, declared in line 3 of Fig. 15.6. Instance variables may be used in any of the class's procedures.

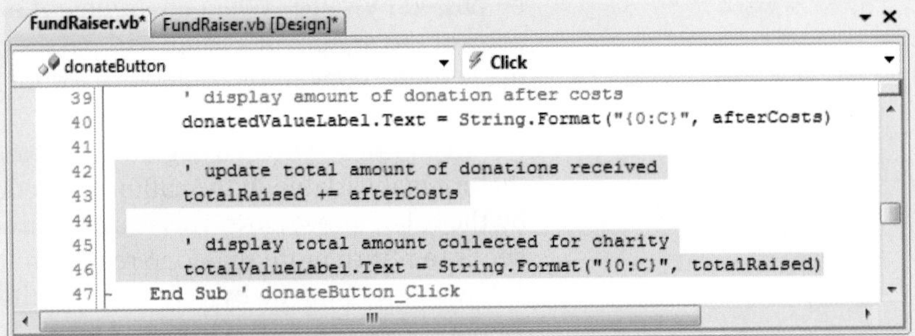

Figure 15.13 Updating and displaying the total amount raised for charity.

(cont.)

Instance variable `totalRaised` has module scope, and therefore maintains its value between procedure calls. Variables with procedure scope, such as `donation`, do not retain their values between procedure calls and are reinitialized each time their procedure is invoked.

11. ***Clearing the After expenses: `Label` to display the next result.*** The template application includes event handler `donationTextBox_TextChanged` (lines 18–24 of Fig. 15.14) for the **Donation:** `TextBox`'s `TextChanged` event. When the user enters data into the `TextBox`, the `TextChanged` event occurs and line 23 clears the previous donation from the **After expenses:** `Label`.

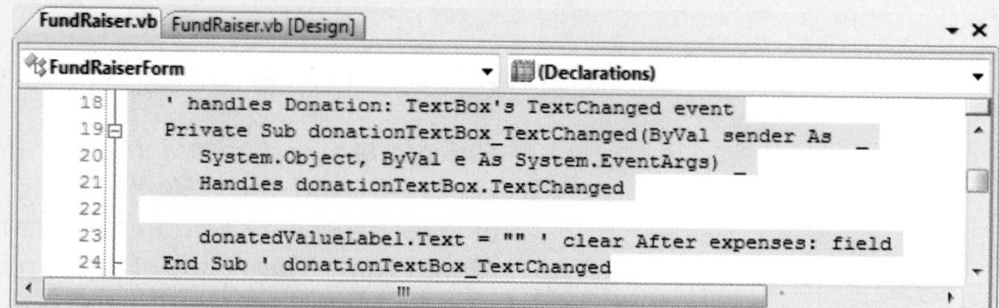

Figure 15.14 Clearing the **Donation:** `TextBox`.

12. ***Running the application.*** Select **Debug > Start Debugging** to run your application. Enter several donation values to see that they are added to the total donation amount each time the **Make Donation** `Button` is clicked. The application now runs and displays the correct output.

13. ***Closing the application.*** Close your running application by clicking its close box.

SELF-REVIEW

1. Instance variables have ________ scope.

   a) block b) procedure
   c) module d) None of the above

2. Variables with either procedure scope or block scope are called ________.

   a) instance variables b) local variables
   c) class variables d) hidden variables

Answers: 1) c. 2) b.

15.3 Passing Arguments: Pass-by-Value vs. Pass-by-Reference

Arguments are passed to procedures in one of two ways—**pass-by-value** or **pass-by-reference**. The keyword `ByVal` (which we have used in all our procedures until now, including event handlers generated by Visual Basic) indicates that an argument will be passed by value. When an argument is passed by value, the application makes a copy of the argument's value and passes the copy to the called procedure. Changes made to the copy in the called procedure do not affect the original variable's value in the calling procedure.

In contrast, when an argument is passed by reference (using keyword `ByRef`), the original variable in the calling procedure can be accessed and modified directly by the called procedure. This is useful in some situations, such as when a procedure needs to return more than one result. In the following box, you use keyword `ByRef` to pass an argument by reference to the procedure that calculates the donation amount after operating costs.

Passing Arguments with `ByRef` *in the Fund Raiser Application*

1. ***Passing variable*** `afterCosts` ***by reference.*** Replace line 37 in the event handler `donateButton_Click` with line 37 of Fig. 15.15. We now pass two variables to procedure `CalculateDonation`. Note that because procedure `CalculateDonation` currently accepts only one argument, the second argument (`afterCosts`) is flagged as a compilation error. In the following steps, we resolve this error by rewriting procedure `CalculateDonation` so that it accepts two arguments. The first argument (in this case, `donation`) is passed by value. The second argument (in this case, `afterCosts`) is passed by reference. When the `CalculateDonation` procedure returns, variable `afterCosts` contains the portion of the donation that the charity receives. Therefore, no assignment statement is necessary.

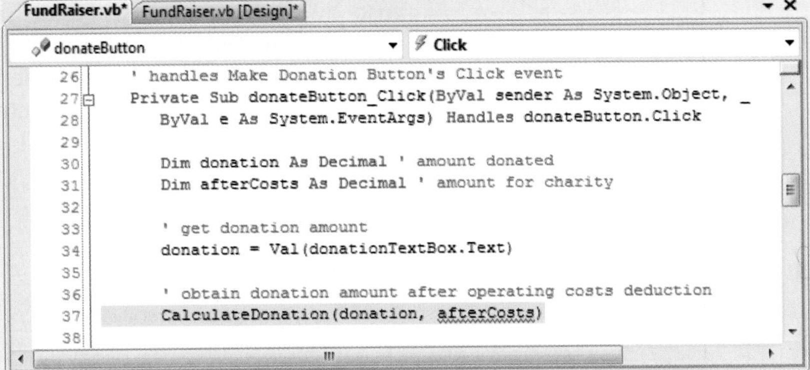
FundRaiser.vb*
FundRaiser.vb [Design]*
donateButton
Click
26 ' handles Make Donation Button's Click event
27 Private Sub donateButton_Click(ByVal sender As System.Object, _
28 ByVal e As System.EventArgs) Handles donateButton.Click
29
30 Dim donation As Decimal ' amount donated
31 Dim afterCosts As Decimal ' amount for charity
32
33 ' get donation amount
34 donation = Val(donationTextBox.Text)
35
36 ' obtain donation amount after operating costs deduction
37 CalculateDonation(donation, afterCosts)
38

Figure 15.15 Passing variable `afterCosts` by reference.

2. ***Removing the old*** `CalculateDonation Function` ***procedure.*** Delete the `CalculateDonation Function` procedure (lines 5–16 of Fig. 15.16) from `FundRaiser.vb`.

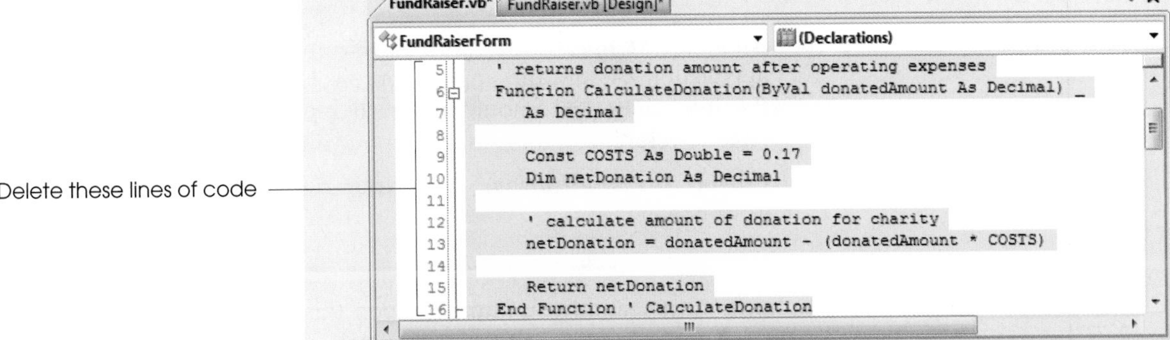
Delete these lines of code
FundRaiser.vb*
FundRaiser.vb [Design]*
FundRaiserForm
(Declarations)
5 ' returns donation amount after operating expenses
6 Function CalculateDonation(ByVal donatedAmount As Decimal) _
7 As Decimal
8
9 Const COSTS As Double = 0.17
10 Dim netDonation As Decimal
11
12 ' calculate amount of donation for charity
13 netDonation = donatedAmount - (donatedAmount * COSTS)
14
15 Return netDonation
16 End Function ' CalculateDonation

Figure 15.16 `Function` procedure `CalculateDonation` to be removed.

3. ***Coding the new*** `CalculateDonation Sub` ***procedure.*** Add lines 5–9 of Fig. 15.17 in your code. Lines 6–7 specify procedure `CalculateDonation`'s header. Keyword `ByRef` (line 7) indicates that variable `netDonation` is passed by reference. This means that any changes made to variable `netDonation` in `CalculateDonation` affect `donateButton_Click`'s local variable `afterCosts`. Since it's no longer necessary for `CalculateDonation` to return a value, `CalculateDonation` is now created as a `Sub` procedure rather than a `Function` procedure.

(cont.)

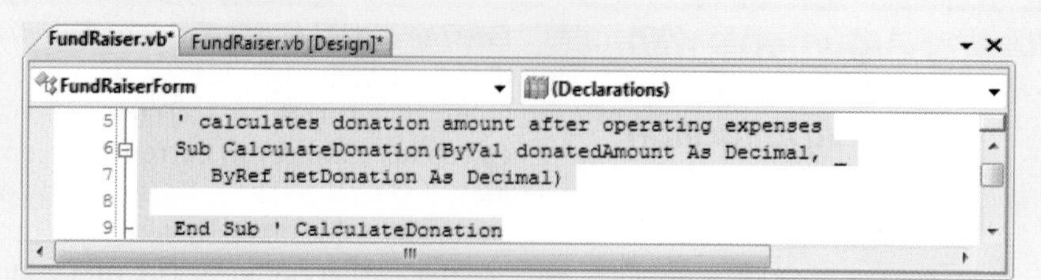
FundRaiser.vb* FundRaiser.vb [Design]*
FundRaiserForm
(Declarations)
' calculates donation amount after operating expenses
Sub CalculateDonation(ByVal donatedAmount As Decimal, _
ByRef netDonation As Decimal)
End Sub ' CalculateDonation

Figure 15.17 `CalculateDonation` Sub procedure.

4. ***Calculating the donation amount for charity after operating costs.*** Add lines 9–12 of Fig. 15.18 to Sub procedure `CalculateDonation`. Line 12 calculates the amount of the donation that goes toward charity after operating costs have been deducted. Note that this is the same calculation that was performed in line 13 of the original `Function` procedure `CalculateDonation` in Fig. 15.16. The only difference is that assigning the calculation result to variable `netDonation` actually assigns the value to local variable `afterCosts` in `donateButton_Click`. You do not need to return the calculation result.

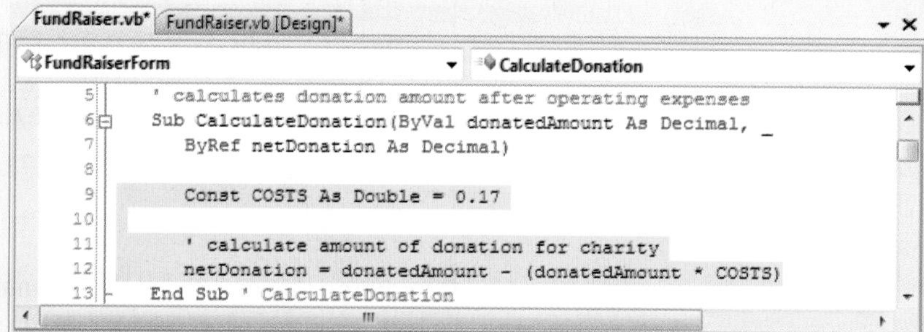
FundRaiser.vb* FundRaiser.vb [Design]*
FundRaiserForm
CalculateDonation
' calculates donation amount after operating expenses
Sub CalculateDonation(ByVal donatedAmount As Decimal, _
ByRef netDonation As Decimal)
Const COSTS As Double = 0.17
' calculate amount of donation for charity
netDonation = donatedAmount - (donatedAmount * COSTS)
End Sub ' CalculateDonation

Figure 15.18 Calculating the donation that goes toward charity after operating costs have been deducted.

5. ***Running the application.*** Select **Debug > Start Debugging** to run your application. Again, the application displays the correct results, adding to the total donation amount for each input. This solution, however, uses pass-by-reference rather than pass-by-value.

6. ***Closing the application.*** Close your running application by clicking its close box.

In the next section you improve upon this application again by using `Option Strict`, which helps you write cleaner code.

Value Types and Reference Types

Data types in Visual Basic are divided into two categories—**value types** and **reference types**. A variable of a value type (such as `Integer`) simply contains a value of that type. For example, the declaration

```
Dim count As Integer = 7
```

places the value 7 into the `Integer` variable `count`.

By contrast, a variable of a reference type contains the location where an object is stored in memory. Such a variable is said to refer to an object. For example, the variables you use to interact with the controls in a GUI are all reference-type variables that refer to objects of the various control types (e.g., `Button`, `TextBox`, etc.). Reference type instance variables are initialized by default to the value `Nothing`—

indicating that the variable does not yet refer to an object. Except for type String, Visual Basic's primitive types are value types—String is a reference type. Value types are defined in Visual Basic using the keyword Structure. All other types are reference types.

To interact with an object, you must use a variable that references the object to invoke (i.e., call) the object's methods and access the object's properties. For example, the statement

```
currentTimeLabel.Text = String.Format("{0:hh:mm:ss tt}", Date.Now)
```

uses the variable currentTimeLabel (of reference-type Label) to access the Label's Text property and assign it a formatted String.

The distinction between value types and reference types is important when passing arguments to methods. By default, arguments are passed by value. When a reference-type variable is passed to a procedure by value, a copy of the variable's value—the location of the object to which the variable refers—is passed. Because the procedure receives an object's location, the procedure can modify the object. In effect, the variable is passed by value (you cannot make it refer to a different object), but the object to which the variable refers is passed by reference. If you want to change which object a reference-type variable refers to, you could pass that variable to a procedure by reference.

SELF-REVIEW

1. Keyword ________ indicates pass-by-reference.
   a) Reference b) ByRef
   c) ByReference d) PassByRef
2. When an argument is passed by reference, the called procedure can access and modify ________.
   a) the caller's original data directly b) a copy of the caller's data
   c) other procedures' local variables d) None of the above

Answers: 1) b. 2) a.

15.4 Option Strict

When a computer accesses data, it needs to know its type in order for the data to make sense. Imagine you are purchasing a book from an online store that ships internationally. You notice that the price for the book is 20, but no currency is associated with the price—it could be dollars, euros, pesos, yen or some other currency. Therefore, it's important to know what type of currency is being used. If the currency is different from the one that you normally use, you need to perform a conversion to get the price.

Similar conversions occur many times in an application. The Visual Basic compiler determines a data type, and, with that knowledge, it can add two Integers or combine two Strings of text. Visual Basic can convert one data type to another, as long as the conversion "makes sense." For example, you are allowed to assign an Integer value to a Decimal variable without writing code that tells the application how to do the conversion. These types of assignments perform so-called **implicit conversions**. When an attempted conversion does not make sense, such as assigning "hello" to an Integer variable, an error occurs. Figure 15.19 lists some of Visual Basic's data types and their allowed implicit conversions. [*Note*: We do not discuss every data type in this book. Consult the Visual Basic documentation to learn more about Visual Basic data types.]

The types listed in the right column are "larger" types in that they can store more data than the types in the left column. For example, Integer types (left column) can be converted to Long types (right column, which includes four other data

Data Type	Can be implicitly converted to these (larger) types
Boolean	Object
Byte	Short, Integer, Long, Decimal, Single, Double or Object
Char	String or Object
Date	Object
Decimal	Single, Double or Object
Double	Object
Integer	Long, Decimal, Single, Double or Object
Long	Decimal, Single, Double or Object
Object	none
Short	Integer, Long, Decimal, Single, Double or Object
Single	Double or Object
String	Object

Figure 15.19 Some data types and their allowed implicit conversions.

types). An Integer variable can store values in the approximate range ±2.1 billion—a Long variable can store numbers in the approximate range $\pm 9 \times 10^{18}$ (9 followed by 18 zeros). This means that any Integer value can be assigned to a Long variable without losing any data. These kinds of conversions are called implicit **widening conversions**, because the value of a "smaller" type (Integer) is being assigned to a variable of a "larger" type (Long) that can represent a wider range of values.

When a "larger" type, such as Double, is assigned to a "smaller" type, such as Integer, either a runtime error occurs because the value being assigned is too large to be stored in the smaller type or the assignment is permitted. Consider the following code:

```
Dim value1 As Double = 4.6
Dim value2 As Integer = value1
```

Common Programming Error

Narrowing conversions can result in loss of data, which can cause subtle logic errors.

Variable value2 will be assigned 5—the result of implicitly converting the Double value 4.6 to an Integer. Such conversions are called implicit **narrowing conversions**. They can introduce subtle errors in applications, because the actual value being assigned could have been altered without your being aware of it—a dangerous practice. For example, if you were expecting variable value2 to be assigned a value other than 5 (such as 4.6 or 4), a logic error would occur.

Visual Basic provides a project setting called **Option Strict** that, when set to On, disallows implicit narrowing conversions. If you attempt an implicit narrowing conversion, the compiler issues a compilation error. Later, we show how you can override this by performing narrowing conversions explicitly. First, however, you learn how to enable Option Strict, which is set to Off by default. The following box demonstrates how to set Option Strict to On through the Visual Basic IDE.

Enabling Option Strict

1. ***Opening the project's property pages.*** In the **Solution Explorer**, right click the project name (FundRaiser) to display a context menu. Select **Properties** to open the **FundRaiser** property pages tab (Fig. 15.20). You also can double click the project's My Project folder in the **Solution Explorer**.

(cont.)

FundRaiser | FundRaiser.vb | FundRaiser.vb [Design]

Application
Compile
Debug
References
Resources
Settings
Signing
My Extensions
Security
Publish

Assembly name: FundRaiser
Root namespace: FundRaiser
Application type: Windows Forms Application
Icon: (Default Icon)
Startup form: FundRaiserForm
Assembly Information... | View UAC Settings
Enable application framework
Windows application framework properties
Enable XP visual styles
Make single instance application
Save My.Settings on Shutdown
Authentication mode: Windows
Shutdown mode: When startup form closes
Splash screen: (None) | View Application Events

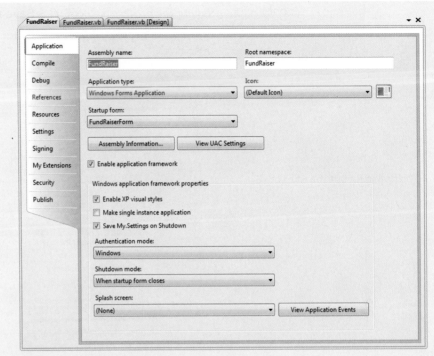

Figure 15.20 **FundRaiser**'s property page tab.

2. ***Selecting the*** **`Compile`** ***category.*** On the left side of the **FundRaiser** property pages tab, select the **Compile** category (Fig. 15.21). Toward the top of the **Compile** category's page is a `ComboBox` labeled **Option Strict:**. By default, the option is set to `Off`.

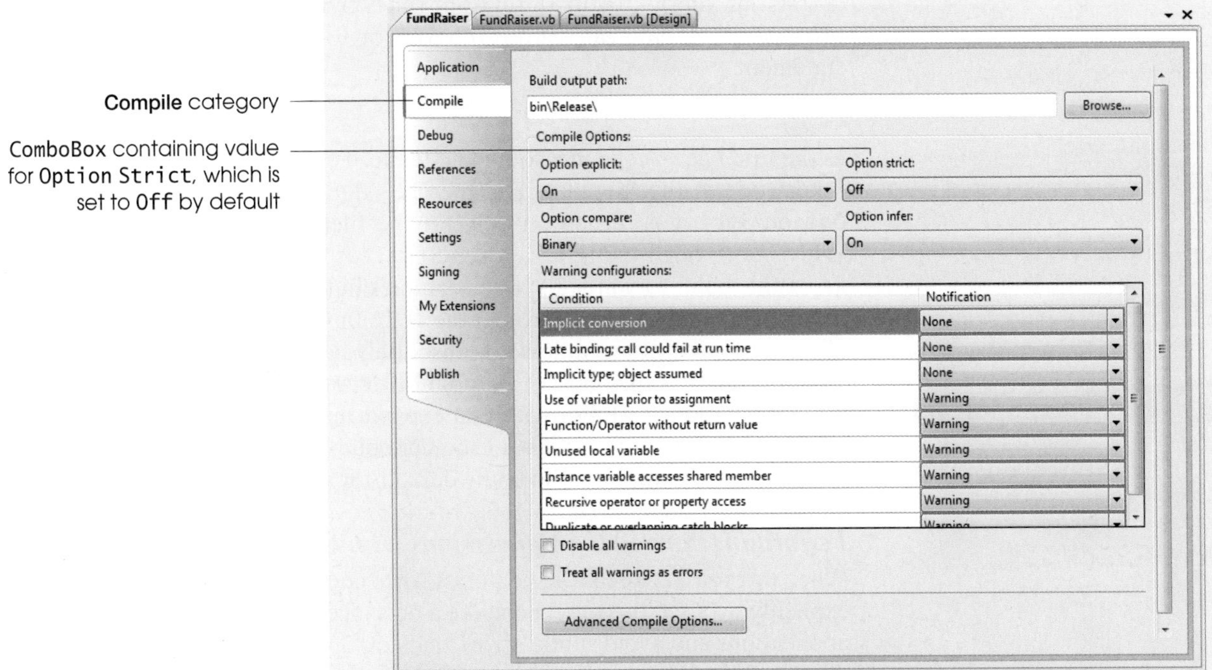

Figure 15.21 Selecting **Compile** in the **FundRaiser**'s property pages.

3. ***Setting*** **`Option Strict`** ***to*** **`On`**. Select **On** in the `ComboBox` labeled **Option Strict:** (Fig. 15.22). `Option Strict` is now set to `On` for this application.

(cont.)

4. ***Saving the project.*** Select **File > Save All** to save your modified code.
5. ***Closing the property pages tab.*** Close the property pages tab by clicking its close box.

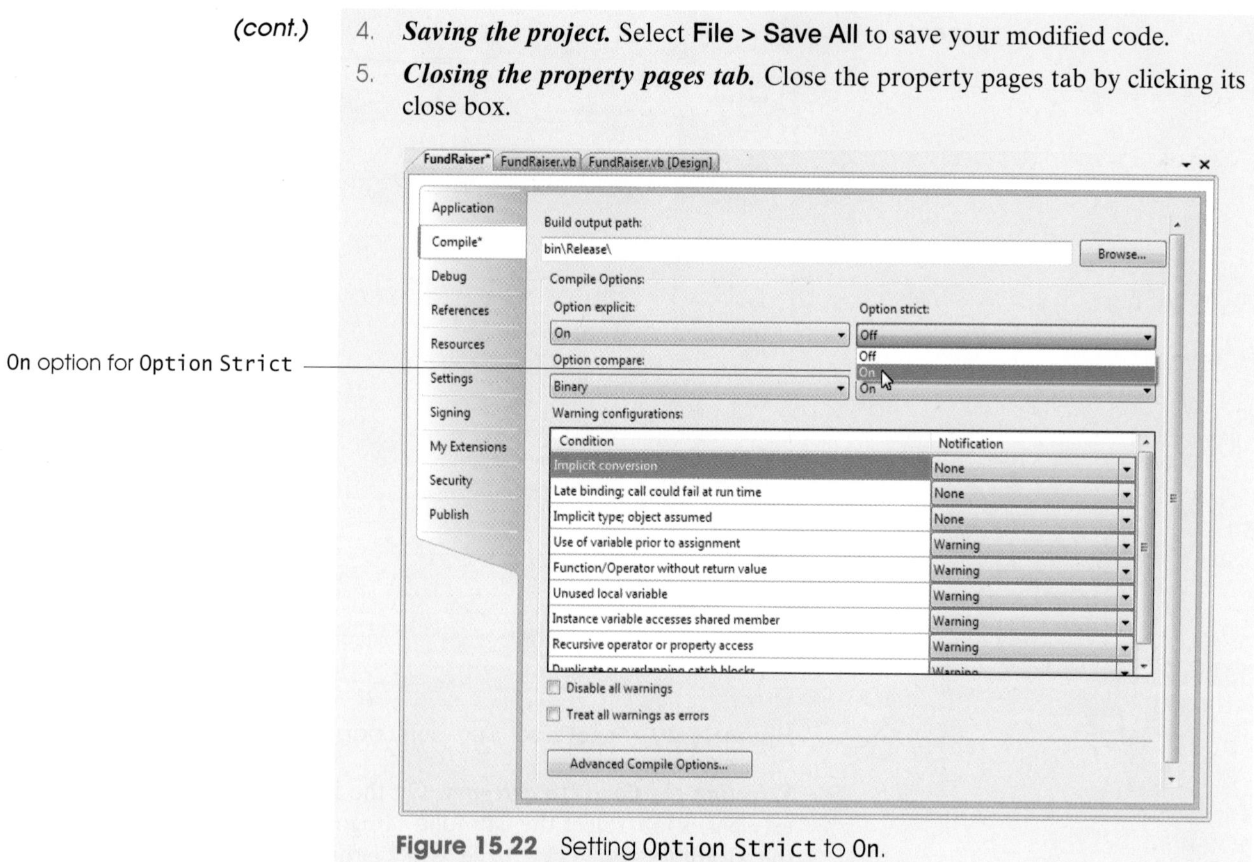

Figure 15.22 Setting `Option Strict` to `On`.

As an alternative to setting `Option Strict` to `On` through the application's property pages, you can set `Option Strict` to `On` programmatically by adding the statement

```
Option Strict On
```

as the first line of code in a source-code file. This statement must appear before any other code in the file, including the class definition. When set programmatically, `Option Strict` is turned on only for the file(s) in which the statement appears. When set through the IDE, `Option Strict` is turned on for all files in the project. From this point forward, all code examples in the remainder of this book have had `Option Strict` set to `On` through the IDE. `Option Strict` should be set to `On` for all of your applications unless it is absolutely necessary to turn it off.

Set `Option Strict` to `On` in *every* application to avoid subtle errors that can be introduced by implicit narrowing conversions.

You can set `Option Strict` to `On` by default for each new application you create. Select **Tools > Options...**, then expand the **Projects and Solutions** node and select **VB Defaults**. Select **On** in the `ComboBox` labeled **Option Strict:** (Fig. 15.23). `Option Strict` will be set to `On` by default for all new applications you create.

Performing Narrowing Conversions with `Option Strict` Set to `On`

When `Option Strict` is `On`, you must write code to perform narrowing conversions explicitly. At first, this may seem like a nuisance, but it helps you create more robust applications and avoid subtle errors that could result from implicit conversions. The .NET framework provides methods in class **`Convert`** (Fig. 15.24) that help you perform conversions when `Option Strict` is `On`. Visual Basic also provides keywords that perform similar conversions. For example, the conversions performed by `Convert` methods `ToInt32`, `ToDecimal` and `ToDouble` also can be done using the Visual Basic conversion functions `CInt`, `CDec` and `CDbl` respectively. We use the methods of class `Convert` in this book. In addition to these methods, every object in Visual Basic defines a `ToString` method, which converts the object to a `String`.

(cont.)

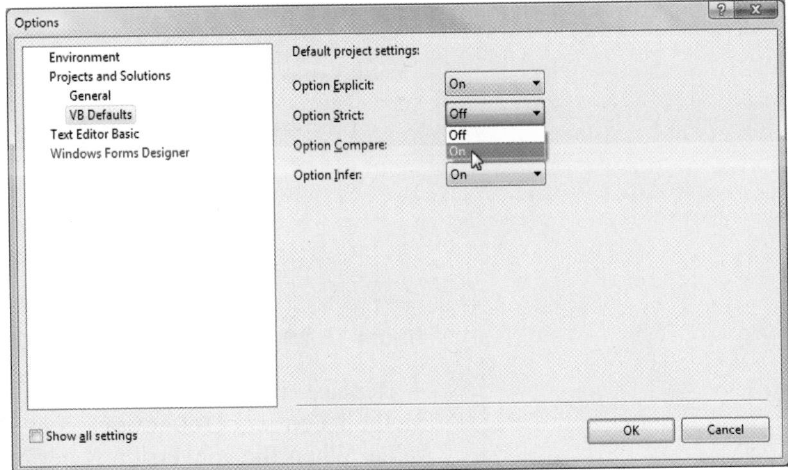

Figure 15.23 Setting default for `Option Strict` to `On`.

Convert To	Use Convert Method	Sample Statement
`Integer`	`ToInt32`	`value = Convert.ToInt32( _ inputTextBox.Text)`
`Decimal`	`ToDecimal`	`value = Convert.ToDecimal( _ Pmt(monthlyInterest, _ months,-loanAmount))`
`Double`	`ToDouble`	`rate = Convert.ToDouble( _ rateTextBox.Text) / 100`

Figure 15.24 Three of class `Convert`'s methods.

The name of each conversion method in class `Convert` begins with the word `To`, followed by the name of the data type to which the method converts its argument. For example, to convert a `String` input by the user in `inputTextBox` to an `Integer`, use the statement

```
number = Convert.ToInt32(inputTextBox.Text)
```

`Int32` is the .NET type that Visual Basic's `Integer` keyword represents. Conversions in statements that call `Convert` methods or Visual Basic's conversion functions are called **explicit conversions**. In the following box, you learn to use explicit conversions.

Using Class `Convert` in the Fund Raiser Application

1. ***Converting a `Double` amount to a `Decimal` value.*** Note that line 12 in Fig. 15.25 is underlined. Place the mouse pointer over the jagged line. An error message displays, indicating that `Option Strict` prohibits an implicit conversion from `Double` to `Decimal`. Multiplying a `Decimal` (`donatedAmount`) and a `Double` (`COSTS`) results in a `Double` value. The result is then assigned to the `Decimal` parameter `netDonation`, causing an implicit conversion from `Double` to `Decimal`. This conversion is not allowed by `Option Strict` because converting from `Double` to `Decimal` could result in data loss. You can also view this error by selecting **View > Error List** to open the **Error List** window.

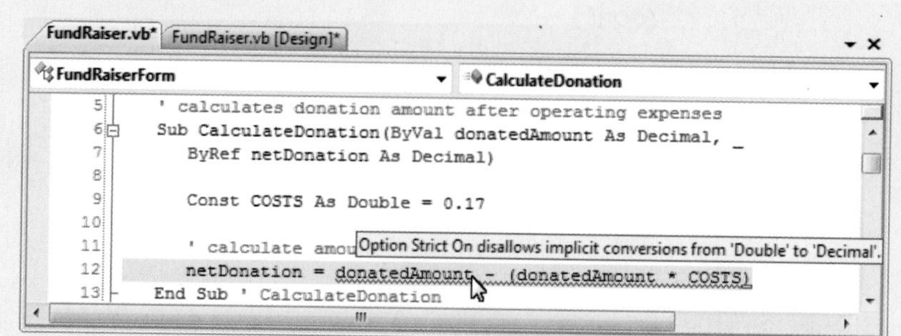

Figure 15.25 `Option Strict` prohibits implicit narrowing conversions.

Replace the underlined expression with lines 12–13 of Fig. 15.26. Method `Convert.ToDecimal` converts the `Double` value to a `Decimal` value. When the conversion is performed explicitly with a call to method `Convert.ToDecimal`, the jagged lines disappear. This error also could be corrected by declaring the `COSTS` constant as a `Decimal`. We declared it as a `Double` to demonstrate converting a `Double` value to a `Decimal` using method `Convert.ToDecimal`.

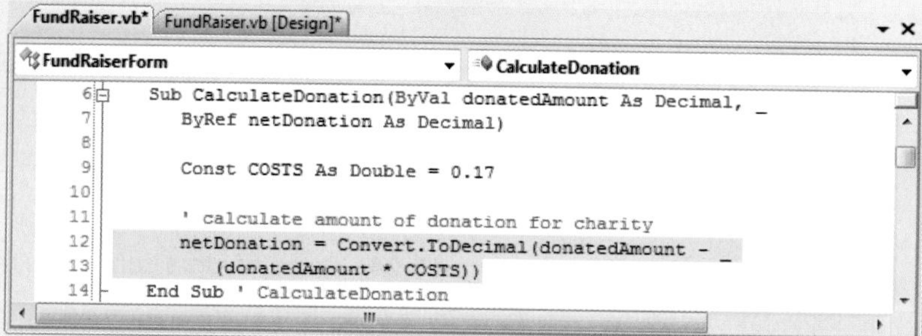

Figure 15.26 Explicitly performing a narrowing conversion with `Convert.ToDecimal`.

2. ***Converting the user input from a `String` to a `Decimal`.*** Line 32 of Fig. 15.27 is underlined. The error message that appears when the mouse pointer rests on this line indicates that `Option Strict` prohibits an implicit conversion from `Double` to `Decimal`.

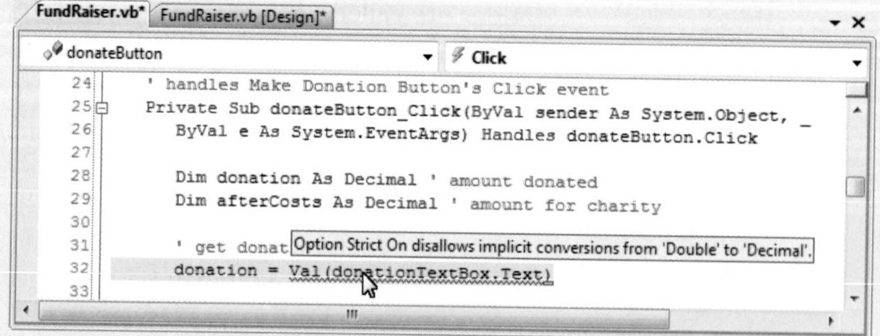

Figure 15.27 `Option Strict` prohibits a narrowing conversion from type `Double` to type `Decimal`.

Replace the underlined expression with line 32 of Fig. 15.28. Method `Convert.ToDecimal` explicitly converts `donationTextBox.Text` to a `Decimal`. After this change is made, the jagged line disappears. Recall that the `Val` function returns `0` if its argument cannot be converted to a `Double`. The methods of class `Convert` generate exceptions if their argument cannot be converted. Tutorial 25 discusses exceptions in detail.

(cont.)

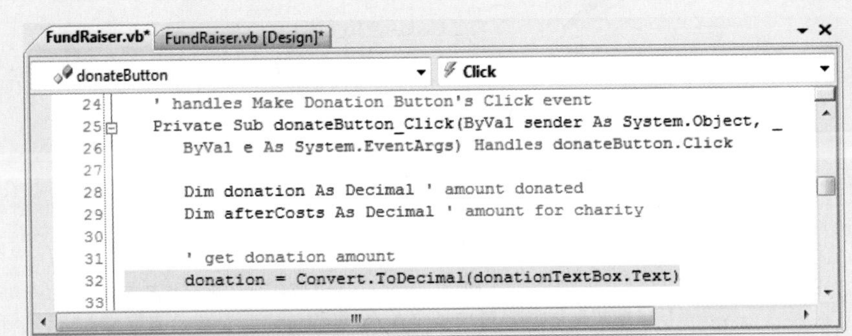

Figure 15.28 Explicitly converting a `Double` to type `Decimal` with `Convert.ToDecimal`.

Note that each method in class `Convert` has multiple versions for converting various types to the type specified in the method name. For example, there are versions of `Convert.ToDecimal` to convert values of every primitive type to type `Decimal`.

3. ***Running the application.*** Select **Debug > Start Debugging** to run your application. Enter a donation amount and click the **Make Donation Button**. Verify that the total raised and the amount after expenses are correct. Enter more donations, each time verifying the output.
4. ***Closing the application.*** Close your running application by clicking its close box.
5. ***Closing the IDE.*** Close the Visual Basic IDE by clicking its close box.

Figure 15.29 presents the source code for the **Fund Raiser** application. The lines of code that contain new programming concepts you learned in this tutorial are highlighted.

Instance variable declaration

Procedure `CalculateDonation` determines the amount of donation after operating costs—parameter `netDonation` is modified directly (using `ByRef`)

Converting the calculation result to type `Decimal`

```
Public Class FundRaiserForm
   ' instance variable stores total raised for charity
   Dim totalRaised As Decimal = 0

   ' returns donation amount after operating expenses
   Sub CalculateDonation(ByVal donatedAmount As Decimal, _
      ByRef netDonation As Decimal)

      Const COSTS As Double = 0.17

      ' calculate amount of donation for charity
      netDonation = Convert.ToDecimal(donatedAmount - _
         (donatedAmount * COSTS))
   End Sub ' CalculateDonation

   ' handles Donation: TextBox's TextChanged event
   Private Sub donationTextBox_TextChanged(ByVal sender As _
      System.Object, ByVal e As System.EventArgs) _
      Handles donationTextBox.TextChanged

      donatedValueLabel.Text = "" ' clear After expenses: field
   End Sub ' donationTextBox_TextChanged

   ' handles Make Donation Button's Click event
   Private Sub donateButton_Click(ByVal sender As System.Object, _
      ByVal e As System.EventArgs) Handles donateButton.Click
```

Figure 15.29 **Fund Raiser** application's code. (Part 1 of 2.)

Convert donation amount from a Double to a Decimal value

afterCosts is passed by reference

```

      Dim donation As Decimal ' amount donated
      Dim afterCosts As Decimal ' amount for charity

      ' get donation amount
      donation = Convert.ToDecimal(donationTextBox.Text)

      ' obtain donation amount after operating costs deduction
      CalculateDonation(donation, afterCosts)

      ' display amount of donation after costs
      donatedValueLabel.Text = String.Format("{0:C}", afterCosts)

      ' update total amount of donations received
      totalRaised += afterCosts

      ' display total amount collected for charity
      totalValueLabel.Text = String.Format("{0:C}", totalRaised)
   End Sub ' donateButton_Click
End Class ' FundRaiserForm
```

Figure 15.29 **Fund Raiser** application's code. (Part 2 of 2.)

SELF-REVIEW

1. When Option Strict is set to On, you must explicitly perform ________.
   a) narrowing conversions
   b) widening conversions
   c) all type conversions
   d) no conversions

2. The methods in ________ are used to change data types explicitly.
   a) class Strict
   b) class Change
   c) class Convert
   d) class Conversion

Answers: 1) a. 2) c.

15.5 Wrap-Up

In this tutorial, you learned concepts about data types and variables, and you built the **Fund Raiser** application to demonstrate these concepts.

You learned how to create instance variables, which are declared inside a class but outside any of the class's procedure definitions. Instance variables have module scope—they are accessible to all procedures in the class in which they are declared. In this tutorial, you declared your instance variable in the FundRaiserForm class. In Tutorial 19, you learn how to create your own classes and how to declare instance variables in them. Before this tutorial, all the variables you declared were local variables—that is, variables with either procedure scope or block scope. Variables with procedure scope are accessible only within the procedure in which they are declared. Variables with block scope are accessible only within the block (such as the body of an If...Then statement) in which they are declared.

You learned the difference between passing arguments by value and by reference. When passing by value, the calling procedure makes a copy of the argument's value and passes the copy to the called procedure. Changes to the called procedure's copy do not affect the original variable value in the calling procedure. When passing by reference, the original data can be accessed and modified directly by the called procedure. You now know how to use keyword ByVal to pass arguments by value and keyword ByRef to pass arguments by reference. You also learned to distinguish between value types and reference types.

You also learned about data-type conversions. You learned that narrowing conversions (such as converting a Double to a Decimal) can result in data loss and that widening conversions (such as a conversion from Integer to Double) don't have this problem. You learned that setting Option Strict to On causes the Visual Basic compiler to flag implicit narrowing conversions as compilation errors and forces you to perform such conversions explicitly.

In the next tutorial, you learn about random-number generation, and you create an application that simulates the dice game called craps.

SKILLS SUMMARY

Setting `Option Strict` to On in the Current Project

- Right click the project name in the **Solution Explorer** and select **Properties**.
- Select **Compile** from the categories in the property pages.
- Set the **Option strict:** `ComboBox` to **On**.

Setting `Option Strict` to On by Default for All New Applications

- Select **Tools > Options...**.
- Expand the **Projects and Solutions** node and select **VB Defaults**.
- Set the **Option Strict:** `ComboBox` to **On**.

Passing Arguments

- Arguments can be passed by value (`ByVal`) or by reference (`ByRef`).

Passing Arguments by Value

- In the procedure header, place keyword `ByVal` before the name of each parameter that is to be passed by value.
- The application makes a copy of the argument's value and passes the copy to the called procedure.
- Changes to the called procedure's copy do not affect the original argument value.

Passing Arguments by Reference

- In the procedure header, place keyword `ByRef` before the name of each parameter that is to be passed by reference.
- Called procedures can access and modify original arguments directly.

Understanding Scope

- Instance variables have module scope and can be accessed by all procedures in the same class.
- Local variables have either procedure scope or block scope.
- Variables with procedure scope cannot be referenced outside the procedure in which they are declared.
- Variables with block scope cannot be referenced outside the block (such as the body of an `If...Then` statement) in which they are declared.

Converting Between Data Types

- Use the appropriate method of class Convert to perform an explicit conversion from one data type to another.

KEY TERMS

block scope—Variables declared inside control statements, such as an `If...Then` statement, have block scope. Block scope begins at the identifier's declaration and ends at the block's final statement (for example, `Else` or `End If`).

`ByRef` keyword—Used to pass an argument by reference.

`ByVal` keyword—Used to pass an argument by value.

`Convert` class—Provides methods for converting data types.

explicit conversion—An operation that converts a value of one type to another type using code to (explicitly) tell the application to do the conversion. An example of an explicit conversion is to convert a value of type `Double` to type `Decimal` using a `Convert` method.

implicit conversion—An operation that converts a value of one type to another type without writing code to (explicitly) tell the application to do the conversion.

instance variable—Declared inside a class but outside any procedure of that class. Instance variables have module scope.

local variable—Declared inside a procedure or block, such as the body of an `If...Then` statement. Local variables have either procedure scope or block scope.

module scope—Variable declared inside a class definition but outside any of the classes procedures have module scope. Module scope begins at the identifier after keyword `Class` and terminates at the `End Class` statement, enables all procedures in the same class to access all instance variables defined in that class.

narrowing conversion—A conversion where the value of a "larger" type is being assigned to a variable of a "smaller" type, where the larger type can store more data than the smaller type. Narrowing conversions can result in loss of data, which can cause subtle logic errors.

`Option Strict`—When set to `On`, disallows implicit narrowing conversions (for example, conversion from `Double` to `Decimal`). If you attempt an implicit narrowing conversion, the compiler issues a compilation error.

pass-by-reference—When an argument is passed by reference, the called procedure can access and modify the caller's argument value directly. Keyword `ByRef` indicates pass-by-reference (also called call-by-reference).

pass-by-value—When an argument is passed by value, the application makes a copy of the argument's value and passes the copy to the called procedure. With pass-by-value, changes to the called procedure's copy do not affect the caller's argument value. Keyword `ByVal` indicates pass-by-value (also called call-by-value).

procedure scope—Variables declared inside a procedure but outside a control statement have procedure scope. Variables with procedure scope cannot be referenced outside the procedure in which they are declared.

reference type—A type that stores the location of an object. Any type that is not a value type is a reference type. Primitive type `String` is a reference type.

scope—The portion of an application in which an identifier (such as a variable name) can be referenced. Some identifiers can be referenced throughout an application—others can be referenced only from limited portions of an application (such as within a single procedure or block).

widening conversion—A conversion in which the value of a "smaller" type is assigned to a variable of a "larger" type—that is, a type that can store more data than the smaller type.

value type—A type that is defined as a `Structure` in Visual Basic. A variable of a value type contains a value of that type. The primitive types (other than `String`) are value types.

MULTIPLE-CHOICE QUESTIONS

15.1 In the property pages tab, _________ must be selected to access `Option Strict`.

a) Compile
b) Designer Defaults
c) General
d) Imports

15.2 When `Option Strict` is set to `On`, variables _________.

a) are passed by value
b) are passed by reference
c) might need to be converted explicitly to a different type to avoid errors
d) are used only within the block in which they are declared

15.3 A variable declared inside a class, but outside a procedure, is called a(n) _________.

a) local variable
b) hidden variable
c) instance variable
d) constant variable

15.4 Visual Basic provides methods in class _________ to convert from one data type to another.

a) `ChangeTo`
b) `Convert`
c) `ConvertTo`
d) `ChangeType`

15.5 When `Option Strict` is _________, the implicit conversion from a `Decimal` to an `Integer` results in an error.

a) `On`
b) `True`
c) `Off`
d) `False`

15.6 Keyword _________ indicates pass-by-reference.

a) `ByReference`
b) `ByRef`
c) `Ref`
d) `Reference`

15.7 With _________, changes made to a parameter variable's value do not affect the value of the variable in the calling procedure.

a) `Option Strict`
b) pass-by-value
c) pass-by-reference
d) None of the above

15.8 Instance variables _________.

a) can be accessed by a procedure in the same class
b) have module scope
c) Neither of the above
d) Both of the above

15.9 Assigning a "smaller" type to a "larger" type is a _________ conversion.

a) narrowing
b) shortening
c) widening
d) lengthening

15.10 A value of type `Single` can be implicitly converted to _________ when `Option Strict` is `On`.

a) `Integer`
b) `Double`
c) Neither of the above
d) Both of the above

EXERCISES

15.11 *(Task List Application)* Create an application that allows the user to add items to a daily task list. The application should also display the number of tasks to be performed. Use method `ToString` to display the number of tasks in a `Label`. The application should look like the GUI in Fig. 15.30.

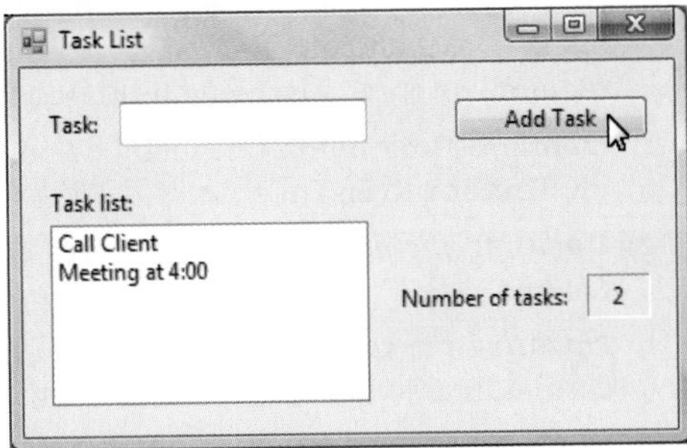

Figure 15.30 **Task List** application's GUI.

a) ***Copying the template to your working directory.*** Copy the directory `C:\Examples\Tutorial15\Exercises\TaskList` to your `C:\SimplyVB2008` directory.

b) ***Opening the application's template file.*** Double click `TaskList.sln` in the `TaskList` directory to open the application.

c) ***Setting `Option Strict` to `On`.*** Use the directions provided in the box, *Enabling `Option Strict`*, to set `Option Strict` to `On`.

d) ***Creating an instance variable.*** Declare `numberOfTasks` as an instance variable of class `TaskListForm`. This variable is used to keep track of how many tasks have been entered.

e) ***Adding the Add Task `Button`'s `Click` event handler.*** Double click the **Add Task** `Button` to generate the empty event handler `addButton_Click`. This event handler should display the user input in the `ListBox` and clear the user input from the `TextBox`. The event handler should also update the `Label` that displays the number of tasks. Use method `ToString` to display the number of tasks in the `Label`. Finally, the event handler should transfer the focus to the `TextBox`.

f) ***Running the application.*** Select **Debug > Start Debugging** to run your application. Enter several tasks, and click the **Add Task** `Button` after each. Verify that each task is added to the **Task list:** ListBox, and that the number of tasks is incremented with each new task.

g) ***Closing the application.*** Close your running application by clicking its close box.

h) ***Closing the IDE.*** Close the Visual Basic IDE by clicking its close box.

15.12 *(Quiz Average Application)* Develop an application that computes a student's average quiz score for all of the quiz scores entered. The application should look like the GUI in Fig. 15.31. Use method Convert.ToInt32 to convert the user input to an Integer. Use instance variables with module scope to keep track of the sum of all the quiz scores entered and the number of quiz scores entered.

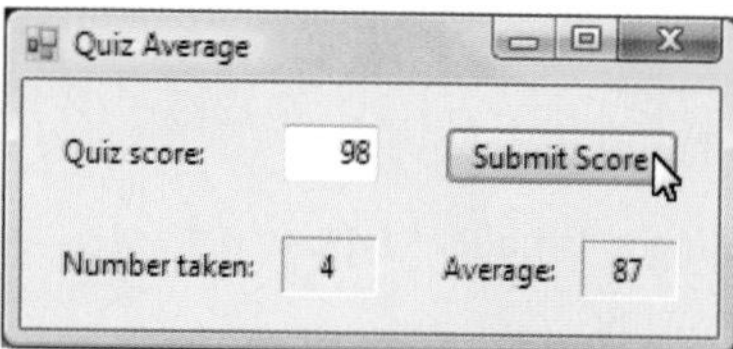

Figure 15.31 **Quiz Average** application's GUI.

a) ***Copying the template to your working directory.*** Copy the directory C:\Examples\Tutorial15\Exercises\QuizAverage to your C:\SimplyVB2008 directory.

b) ***Opening the application's template file.*** Double click QuizAverage.sln in the QuizAverage directory to open the application.

c) ***Setting Option Strict to On.*** Use the directions provided in the box, *Enabling Option Strict*, to set Option Strict to On.

d) ***Adding instance variables.*** Add two instance variables—totalScore, which keeps track of the sum of all the quiz scores entered, and taken, which keeps track of the number of quiz scores entered.

e) ***Adding the Submit Score Button's event handler.*** Double click the **Submit Score** Button to generate the empty event handler submitButton_Click. The code required by *Steps f–k* should be placed in this event handler.

f) ***Obtaining user input.*** Use method Convert.ToInt32 to convert the user input from the TextBox to an Integer.

g) ***Updating the number of quiz scores entered.*** Increment the number of quiz scores entered.

h) ***Updating the sum of all the quiz scores entered.*** Add the current quiz score to the current total to update the sum of all the quiz scores entered.

i) ***Calculating the average score.*** Divide the sum of all the quiz scores entered by the number of quiz scores entered to calculate the average score.

j) ***Displaying the average score.*** Use method ToString to display the average quiz grade in the **Average:** field.

k) ***Displaying the number of quizzes taken.*** Use method ToString to display the number of quiz scores entered in the **Number taken:** field.

l) ***Running the application.*** Select **Debug > Start Debugging** to run your application. Enter several quiz scores, clicking the **Submit Score** Button after each. With each new score, verify that the **Number taken:** field is incremented and that the average is updated correctly.

m) ***Closing the application.*** Close your running application by clicking its close box.

n) ***Closing the IDE.*** Close the Visual Basic IDE by clicking its close box.

15.13 *(Modified Maximum Application)* Modify the **Maximum** application from Tutorial 13 (Fig. 15.32) to use keyword ByRef to pass a fourth argument to procedure Maximum by reference. Use methods from class Convert to perform any necessary type conversions.

a) ***Copying the template to your working directory.*** Copy the directory C:\Examples\Tutorial15\Exercises\Maximum to your C:\SimplyVB2008 directory.

b) ***Opening the application's template file.*** Double click Maximum.sln in the Maximum directory to open the application.

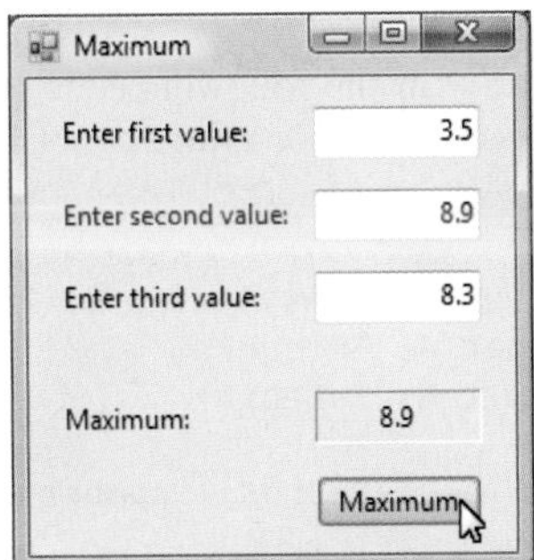

Figure 15.32 Modified **Maximum** application's GUI.

c) ***Setting `Option Strict` to `On`.*** Use the directions provided in the box, *Enabling `Option Strict`*, to set `Option Strict` to `On`.

d) ***Adding a local variable.*** Add local variable `max` of type `Double` to event handler `maximumButton_Click`. The code required in *Steps d–f* should be placed in this event handler. Variable `max` stores the result of procedure `Maximum`.

e) ***Passing four arguments to procedure `Maximum`.*** Use method `Convert.ToDouble` to convert the user input from the `TextBox`es to `Double`s. Pass these three values as the first three arguments to procedure `Maximum`. Pass local variable `max` as the fourth argument to procedure `Maximum`.

f) ***Displaying the maximum value.*** Use method `ToString` to display local variable `max` in the **Maximum:** field.

g) ***Changing procedure `Maximum` to a `Sub` procedure.*** Change procedure `Maximum` to a `Sub` procedure. Make sure that `Sub` procedure `Maximum` no longer returns a value and does not specify a return type. The modifications required in *Steps g–h* should be performed on this `Sub` procedure.

h) ***Adding a fourth parameter to procedure `Maximum`.*** Add a fourth parameter `finalMaximum` of type `Double` to `Maximum`'s procedure header. Use keyword `ByRef` to specify that this argument is passed by reference. Remove the declaration of variable `finalMaximum` from the body of procedure `Maximum`.

i) ***Running the application.*** Select **Debug > Start Debugging** to run your application. Enter three different values into the input fields and click the **Maximum** `Button`. Verify that the largest value is displayed in the **Maximum:** field.

j) ***Closing the application.*** Close your running application by clicking its close box.

k) ***Closing the IDE.*** Close the Visual Basic IDE by clicking its close box.

What does this code do? ▶ **15.14** What is displayed in `displayLabel` when the user clicks the `enterButton`?

```
Public Class ScopeTestForm
   Dim value2 As Integer = 5

   Private Sub enterButton_Click(ByVal sender As System.Object, _
      ByVal e As System.EventArgs) Handles enterButton.Click

      Dim value1 As Integer = 10
      Dim value2 As Integer = 3

      Test(value1)
      displayLabel.Text = value1.ToString()
   End Sub ' enterButton_Click

   Sub Test(ByRef value1 As Integer)
      value1 *= value2
   End Sub ' Test
End Class ' ScopeTestForm
```

What's wrong with this code?

15.15 Find the error(s) in the following code (the procedure should assign the value 14 to variable `result`). Assume that `Option Strict` is set to `On`.

```
Sub Sum()
   Dim numberWords As String = "4"
   Dim number As Integer = 10
   Dim result As Integer

   result = numberWords + number
End Sub ' Sum
```

Programming Challenge

15.16 ***(Schedule Book Application)*** Develop an application that allows the user to enter a schedule of appointments and their respective times. Create the `Form` in Fig. 15.33 and name the application **Schedule Book**. Add a `Function` procedure called `TimeTaken` that returns a `Boolean` value. Each time a user enters a new appointment, `Function` procedure `TimeTaken` determines whether the user has scheduled more than one appointment at the same time. If `TimeTaken` returns `True`, the user is notified via a message dialog. Otherwise, the appointment is added to the `ListBoxes`. Set `Option Strict` to `On`, and use methods from class `Convert` as necessary.

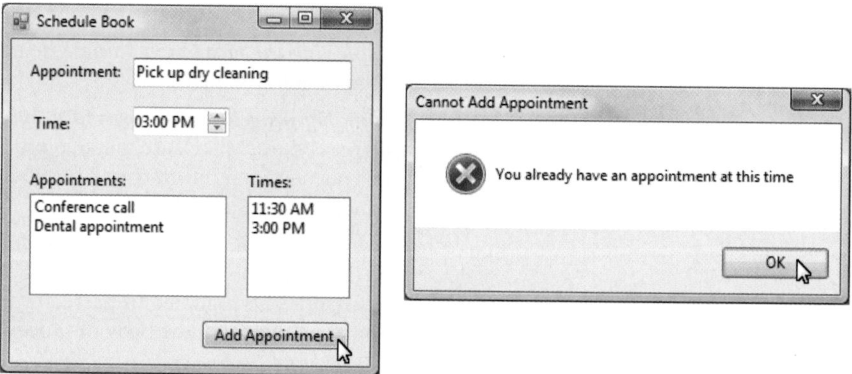

Figure 15.33 **Schedule Book** application's GUI.

TUTORIAL 16

Objectives

In this tutorial, you learn to:

- Code simulation techniques that employ random-number generation.
- Use class `Random` methods to generate random numbers.
- Use enumerations to enhance code readability.
- Read images from files.

Outline

Craps Game Application

Introducing Random-Number Generation and Enum

You now learn a popular type of application—simulation and game playing. In this tutorial, you develop a **Craps Game** application. There is something in the air of a casino that invigorates many people—from the high rollers at the plush mahogany-and-felt craps tables to the quarter-poppers at the one-armed bandits. Many of these individuals are drawn by the element of chance—the possibility that luck will convert a pocketful of money into a mountain of wealth.

You can introduce the element of chance into computer applications using random numbers. This tutorial's **Craps Game** application introduces several new concepts, including random-number generation and enumerations. It also uses important concepts that you learned previously, including instance variables, procedures and the `Select Case` multiple-selection control statement.

16.1 Test-Driving the Craps Game Application

One popular game of chance is a dice game known as "craps," played in casinos worldwide. This application must meet the following requirements:

Application Requirements

Create an application that simulates playing the game of craps. In this game, a player rolls two dice. Each die has six faces. Each face contains one, two, three, four, five or six spots. After the dice have come to rest, the sum of the spots on the two top faces is calculated. If the sum is 7 or 11 on the first throw, the player wins. If the sum is 2, 3 or 12 on the first throw (called "craps"), the player loses (the "house" wins). If the sum is 4, 5, 6, 8, 9 or 10 on the first throw, that sum becomes the player's "point." To win, a player must continue rolling the dice until the point value is rolled. The player loses by rolling a 7 before rolling the point.

Creating this application teaches you two important concepts—random-number generation and enumerations. You begin by test-driving the completed application. Then you learn the additional Visual Basic capabilities needed to create your own version of this application.

Test-Driving the Craps Game Application

1. ***Opening the completed application.*** Open the directory `C:\Examples\Tutorial16\CompletedApplication\CrapsGame` to locate the **Craps Game** application. Double click `CrapsGame.sln` to open the application in the Visual Basic IDE.

2. ***Running the Craps Game application.*** Select **Debug > Start Debugging** to run the application (Fig. 16.1).

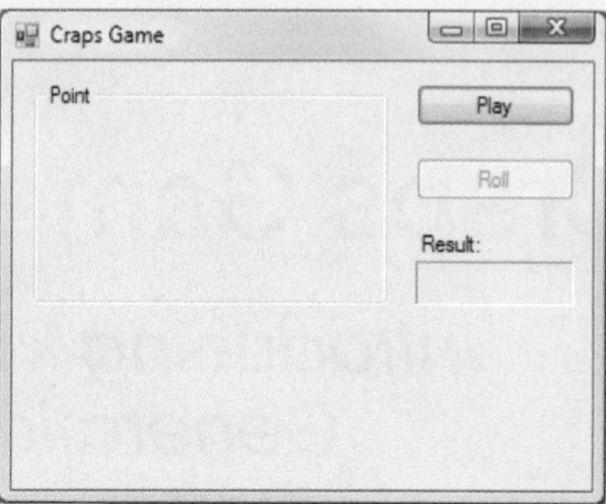

Figure 16.1 **Craps Game** application's initial appearance.

3. ***Starting the game.*** Click the **Play** `Button`. There are three possible outcomes at this point.

■ The player wins by rolling 7 or 11 (Fig. 16.2).

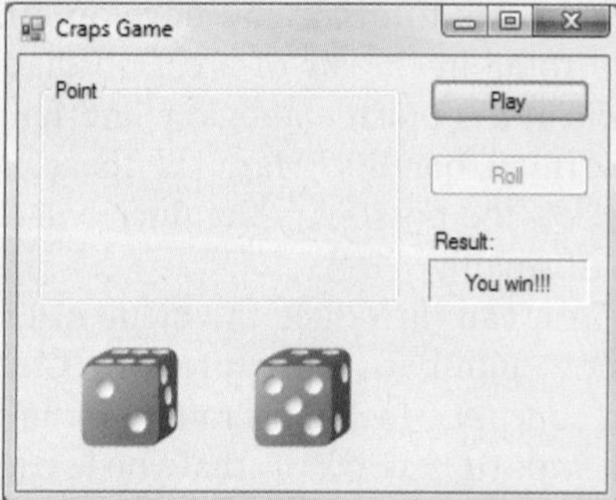

Figure 16.2 Player wins on first roll by rolling 7 or 11.

■ The player loses by rolling 2, 3 or 12 (Fig. 16.3).

Figure 16.3 Player loses on first roll by rolling 2, 3 or 12.

■ Otherwise, the roll becomes the player's point (4, 5, 6, 8, 9 or 10), which is then displayed for the remainder of the game (Fig. 16.4).

Note that in this application unlike the real game of craps, the value of the roll is computed using the forward-facing die faces instead of the top faces. This makes reading the die faces easier.

(cont.)

Figure 16.4 First roll sets the point that the player must match to win.

4. ***Continuing the game.*** If the application displays **Roll again!**, as in Fig. 16.4, click the **Roll** `Button` repeatedly until either you win by matching your point value (Fig. 16.5) or you lose by rolling a 7 (Fig. 16.6). When the game ends, you can click **Play** to start over.

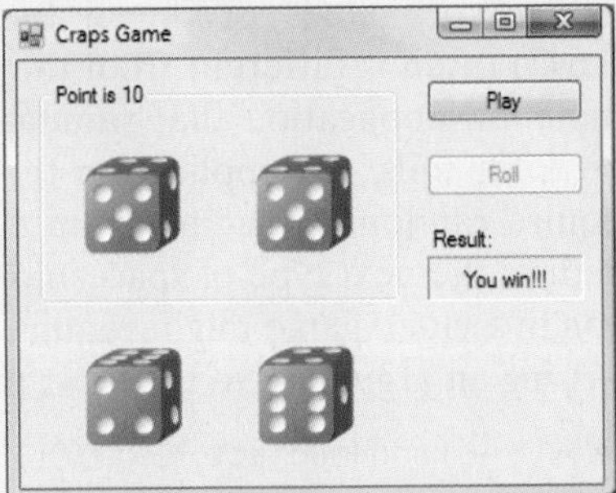

Figure 16.5 Winning the game by matching your point before rolling a 7.

Figure 16.6 Losing by rolling a 7 before matching your point.

5. ***Closing the application.*** Close your running application by clicking its close box.
6. ***Closing the IDE.*** Close the Visual Basic IDE by clicking its close box.

16.2 Random-Number Generation

Now you learn how to use an object of class **`Random`** to introduce the element of chance into your applications. You learn more about working with objects of existing classes over the next few tutorials; then you'll learn to create your own classes and objects of those classes in Tutorial 19. Consider the following statements:

```
Dim randomObject As New Random()
Dim randomNumber As Integer = randomObject.Next()
```

The first statement declares `randomObject` as a reference of type `Random` and assigns it a `New Random` object. A reference-type variable contains a **reference** to an object. Recall that keyword New creates a new object in memory. When you create an object, New returns a reference to that object, which you typically store in a reference-type variable so you can interact with the object. Notice that the assignment operator (=) is not required in this statement.

The second statement declares Integer variable randomNumber and assigns it the value returned by calling Random's Next method on randomObject. The **Next** method generates a positive Integer value between zero and the largest possible Integer, which is the constant **Int32.MaxValue** (the value 2,147,483,647). You can use the Next method to generate random values of type Integer or use **NextDouble** method to generate random values of type Double. The NextDouble method returns a positive Double value from 0.0 up to, but not including, 1.0. Class Random does not contain a Next method for any other data type.

If the Next method were to produce truly random values, then every value in this range would have an equal chance (or probability) of being chosen when Next is called. The values returned by Next are actually **pseudorandom numbers**—a sequence of values produced by a complex mathematical calculation. This mathematical calculation comes close, but is not exactly random in choosing numbers.

The range of values produced by Next (that is, values between 0 and 2,147,483,647) often is different from the range needed in a particular application. For example, an application that simulates coin tossing might require only 0 for heads and 1 for tails. An application that simulates the rolling of a six-sided die would require random Integers from 1 to 6. Similarly, an application that randomly predicts the next type of spaceship (out of four possibilities) that flies across the horizon in a video game might require random Integers from 1 to 4.

By passing an argument to the Next method as follows

```
value = 1 + randomObject.Next(6)
```

you can produce integers in the range from 1 to 6. When a single argument is passed to Next, the values returned by Next are in the range from 0 up to, but not including, the value of that argument. In the preceding statement, Next produces values in the range 0–5. You can change the range of numbers produced by adding 1 to the previous result, so that the return values are in the range 1–6. This new range corresponds nicely with the roll of a six-sided die, for example.

You may also pass two arguments to Next to produce a range of numbers. For example, the preceding statement also could be written as

```
value = randomObject.Next(1, 7) ' from 1 up to, but not including, 7
```

Note that you must use 7 as the second argument to the Next method to produce integers in the range 1–6. The first argument indicates the minimum value in the desired range. The second is equal to *one more than the maximum value desired.*

As with method Next, the range of values produced by method NextDouble (that is, values greater than or equal to 0.0 and less than 1.0) is also usually different from the range needed in a particular application. By multiplying the value returned from method NextDouble as follows

```
value = 6 * randomObject.NextDouble()
```

you can produce Double values in the range from 0.0 to 6.0 (not including 6.0). Figure 16.7 shows examples of the ranges returned by calls to methods Next and NextDouble.

Method call	Resulting range
randomObject.Next()	0 to one less than Int32.MaxValue
randomObject.Next(30)	0 to 29

Figure 16.7 Next and NextDouble method calls with corresponding ranges. (Part 1 of 2.)

Method call	Resulting range
`10 + randomObject.Next(10)`	10 to 19
`randomObject.Next(10, 20)`	10 to 19
`randomObject.Next(5, 100)`	5 to 99
`randomObject.NextDouble()`	0.0 to less than 1.0
`8 * randomObject.NextDouble()`	0.0 to less than 8.0

Figure 16.7 `Next` and `NextDouble` method calls with corresponding ranges. (Part 2 of 2.)

SELF-REVIEW

1. The statement ________ returns a number in the range from 8 to 300.
   a) `randomObject.Next(8, 300)`
   b) `randomObject.Next(8, 301)`
   c) `1 + randomObject.Next(8, 300)`
   d) None of the above

2. The statement ________ returns a number in the range 15 to 35.
   a) `randomObject.Next(15, 36)`
   b) `randomObject.Next(15, 35)`
   c) `10 + randomObject.Next(5, 26)`
   d) Both a and c

Answers: 1) b. 2) d.

16.3 Constructing the Craps Game Application

The following pseudocode describes the operation of the **Craps Game** application:

```
When the player clicks the Play Button:
    Roll the dice using random numbers
    Display images corresponding to the numbers on the rolled dice
    Calculate the sum of both dice

    Select correct case based on the sum of the two dice:

        Case where first roll is 7 or 11
            Display the winning message

        Case where first roll is 2, 3 or 12
            Display the losing message

        Case where none of the preceding Cases are true
            Set the value of the point to the sum of the dice
            Display point value
            Display message to roll again
            Display images for user's point
            Disable the Play Button
            Enable the Roll Button

When the player clicks the Roll Button:
    Roll the dice using random numbers
    Display images corresponding to the numbers on the rolled dice
    Calculate the sum of both dice

    If the player rolls the same value as the point
        Display the winning message
        Disable the Roll Button
        Enable the Play Button

    Else If the player rolls a 7
        Display the losing message
        Disable the Roll Button
        Enable the Play Button
```

Now that you've test-driven the **Craps Game** application and studied its pseudocode representation, you use an ACE table to help you convert the pseudocode to Visual Basic. Figure 16.8 lists the actions, controls and events that will help you complete your own version of this application.

Action/Control/Event (ACE) Table for the Craps Game Application

Action	Control/Object	Event
Label the application's controls	resultLabel, pointDiceGroupBox	
	playButton	Click
Roll the dice using random numbers	randomObject	
Display images corresponding to the numbers on the rolled dice	die1Picture, die2Picture	
Calculate the sum of both dice		
Select correct case based on sum:		
Case where first roll is 7 or 11 Disable the Roll Button	rollButton	
Display the winning message	statusLabel	
Case where first roll is 2, 3 or 12 Disable the Roll Button	rollButton	
Display the losing message	statusLabel	
Case where none of the preceding Cases are true Set the value of the point to the sum of the dice		
Display the point value	pointDiceGroupBox	
Display message to roll again	statusLabel	
Display images for user's point	pointDie1Picture, pointDie2Picture	
Disable the Play Button	playButton	
Enable the Roll Button	rollButton	
	rollButton	Click
Roll the dice using random numbers	randomObject	
Display images corresponding to the numbers on the rolled dice	die1Picture, die2Picture	
Calculate the sum of both dice		
If the player rolls the same value as the point Display the winning message	statusLabel	
Disable the Roll Button	rollButton	
Enable the Play Button	playButton	
Else if the player rolls a 7 Display the losing message	statusLabel	
Disable the Roll Button	rollButton	
Enable the Play Button	playButton	

Figure 16.8 ACE table for the **Craps Game** application.

In the following boxes, you create an application to simulate playing the game of craps. Note that the numbers 2, 3, 7, 11 and 12 have special meanings during a game of craps. Throughout the game, you use these numbers (as constants) quite often. In this case, it would be helpful to create a group of related constants and assign them meaningful names for use in your application. You can do this by using an **enumeration**. With enumerations, you can create constant identifiers that describe various significant dice combinations in craps, such as SNAKE_EYES (2), TREY (3), CRAPS (7), LUCKY_SEVEN (7), YO_LEVEN (11) and BOX_CARS (12). By providing descriptive identifiers for a group of related constants, enumerations enhance program readability and ensure that numbers are consistent throughout the application. In the following box you learn how to use enumerations.

Introducing Enumerations and Declaring Instance Variables

1. ***Copying the template to your working directory.*** Copy the `C:\Examples\Tutorial16\TemplateApplication\CrapsGame` directory to your `C:\SimplyVB2008` directory.

2. ***Opening the application's template file.*** Double click `CrapsGame.sln` in the `CrapsGame` directory to open the application in the Visual Basic IDE. Figure 16.9 displays the `Form` in **Design** view. Remember to follow the steps in Tutorial 15 to turn `Option Strict On` before going any further.

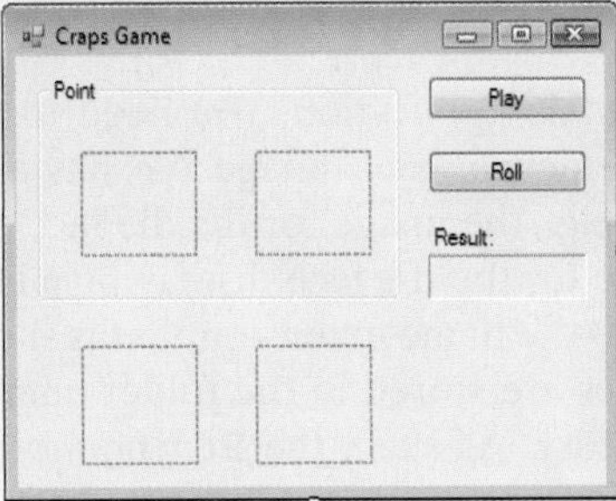
Craps Game
Point
Play
Roll
Result:

Figure 16.9 Template **Craps Game** `Form` in **Design** view.

3. ***Declaring an enumeration.*** Add lines 2–3 of Fig. 16.10 to your application, then press *Enter*. Note that keywords `End Enum` appear. Enumerations begin with the keyword **`Enum`** (line 3), and end with the keywords **`End Enum`** (line 10). The name of the enumeration (`DiceNames`) follows the keyword `Enum` (line 3). Now add lines 4–9 of Fig. 16.10 into your application between the lines containing keywords `Enum` and `End Enum`.

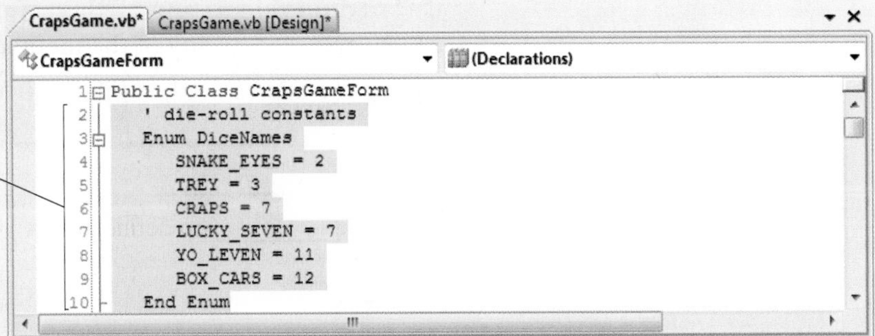
Defining an enumeration
CrapsGame.vb*
CrapsGame.vb [Design]*
CrapsGameForm
(Declarations)
1 Public Class CrapsGameForm
2 ' die-roll constants
3 Enum DiceNames
4 SNAKE_EYES = 2
5 TREY = 3
6 CRAPS = 7
7 LUCKY_SEVEN = 7
8 YO_LEVEN = 11
9 BOX_CARS = 12
10 End Enum

Figure 16.10 Enumeration `DiceNames` in the **Craps Game** application.

Good Programming Practice

Use enumerations to group related constants and enhance code readability.

Common Programming Error

You can specify an enumeration's type after its name by using the keyword `As` followed by `Byte`, `SByte`, `Short`, `UShort`, `Integer`, `UInteger`, `Long`, or `ULong`. If no type is specified, enumeration constants are of type `Integer` by default. Attempting to create enumerations of other types results in compilation errors.

We use enumerations here to make the code easier to read, especially for someone who is unfamiliar with the application. You can refer to the numbers using the enumeration name and the member-access operator. For instance, use `DiceNames.SNAKE_EYES` for the number `2`, `DiceNames.TREY` for the number `3`, `DiceNames.CRAPS` and `DiceNames.LUCKY_SEVEN` for the number `7`, `DiceNames.YO_LEVEN` for the number `11` and `DiceNames.BOX_CARS` for the number `12`. Note that you can assign the same value to multiple enumeration constants, as you did in lines 6 and 7. You are not required to provide values for the constants in an enumeration. If no values are specified, the constants are automatically assigned consecutive values starting from `0`.

(cont.)

4. ***Declaring constants and instance variables.*** Several methods require the use of the same variables and constants throughout the lifetime of the application. As you learned in Tutorial 15, you declare instance variables for this purpose. Add lines 12–19 of Fig. 16.11 below the enumeration definition.

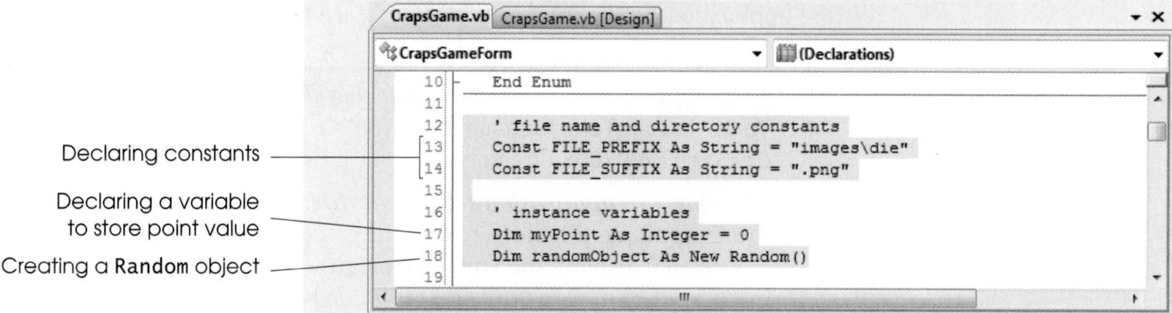
CrapsGame.vb
CrapsGame.vb [Design]
CrapsGameForm
(Declarations)
10 End Enum
11
12 ' file name and directory constants
13 Const FILE_PREFIX As String = "images\die"
14 Const FILE_SUFFIX As String = ".png"
15
16 ' instance variables
17 Dim myPoint As Integer = 0
18 Dim randomObject As New Random()
19
Declaring constants
Declaring a variable to store point value
Creating a Random object

Figure 16.11 Instance variables added to the **Craps Game** application.

In this application, you need to access images for the six die faces. For convenience, each image file has a name that differs only by one character—e.g., the image for the die face displaying 1 is named `die1.png`, and the image for the die face displaying 6 is named `die6.png`. Recall that `png` is an image-file name extension that is short for Portable Network Graphic. These images are stored in the folder named `images` in your project's `bin\Debug` directory. As such, the `String images\die1.png` would correctly indicate the location of the die face displaying 1 relative to the `bin\Debug` directory. To help create a `String` representing the path to the image, `Strings FILE_PREFIX (images\die)` and `FILE_SUFFIX (.png)` are used (as constants) to store the prefix and suffix of the file name (lines 13–14).

The game of craps requires that you store the user's point, once established on the first roll, for the game's duration. Therefore, variable `myPoint` (line 17 of Fig. 16.11) is declared as an `Integer` to store the value of the dice on the first roll. You use the `Random` object referenced by `randomObject` (line 18) to "roll" the dice and generate those values. These variables are declared outside of any methods (giving them module scope) so that they can be accessed by any of the methods in the class.

5. ***Saving the project.*** Select **File > Save All** to save your modified code.

SELF-REVIEW

1. Use keyword ________ to define groups of related constants.

   a) `ReadOnly` b) `Enum`
   c) `Constants` d) `Enumeration`

2. The constants defined in an `Enum` ________.

   a) may use repeated values
   b) can be accessed using the `Enum`'s name followed by the member access operator
   c) are not required to declare a value
   d) All of the above

Answers: 1) b. 2) b.

16.4 Using Random Numbers in the Craps Game Application

Now that you've declared an enumeration and instance variables, you'll add code to execute when the user clicks the **Craps Game** application's `Buttons`. The following box explains how to add the code that executes when the user clicks **Play**.

Coding the Play Button's Click Event Handler

1. ***Creating the Play Button's Click event handler.*** Return to the **Design** view to display the Form. Double click the **Play** Button to generate the **Play** Button's Click event handler and view the code file. (The **Play** Button is used to begin a new game of craps.)

2. ***Removing Images from a PictureBox and rolling dice.*** Begin coding the Click event handler by adding lines 24–33 from Fig. 16.12 into the playButton_Click event handler. Be sure to add the comments and line-continuation characters, as shown in Fig. 16.12, so that the line numbers in your code match those presented in this tutorial. [*Note:* RollDice is underlined in blue because the procedure is not yet defined.]

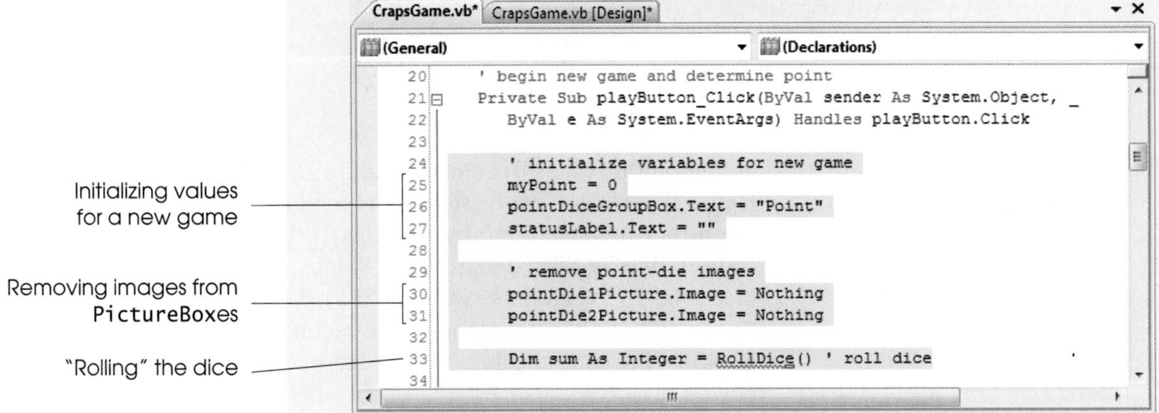
CrapsGame.vb*
CrapsGame.vb [Design]*
(General)
(Declarations)
20 ' begin new game and determine point
21 Private Sub playButton_Click(ByVal sender As System.Object, _
22 ByVal e As System.EventArgs) Handles playButton.Click
23
24 ' initialize variables for new game
25 myPoint = 0
26 pointDiceGroupBox.Text = "Point"
27 statusLabel.Text = ""
28
29 ' remove point-die images
30 pointDie1Picture.Image = Nothing
31 pointDie2Picture.Image = Nothing
32
33 Dim sum As Integer = RollDice() ' roll dice
34
Initializing values for a new game
Removing images from PictureBoxes
"Rolling" the dice

Figure 16.12 playButton_Click event handler definition.

Lines 25–27 initialize variables for a new game. Line 25 sets variable myPoint, the craps game point value, to 0. Line 26 changes the text displayed on the GroupBox to Point, using the GroupBox's Text property. As you saw in the test-drive, the GroupBox's Text property is used to display the point value. Finally, line 27 clears the value of the output Label because the user is starting a new game.

Lines 30–31 remove any images from the PictureBoxes used to display the point die. Though there are no images when the application is first run, if the user chooses to continue playing after completing a game, the images from the previous game must be cleared. Setting the Image property to keyword Nothing indicates that there is no image to display. Keyword **Nothing** is used to indicate that a variable does not refer to an object.

Line 33 declares the variable sum and assigns it the value returned by rolling the dice. This is accomplished by calling the RollDice procedure, which you define later in this tutorial. [*Note:* Again, RollDice is underlined in blue because the procedure is not yet defined.] The RollDice Function procedure not only rolls dice and returns the sum of their values, but also displays the die images in the lower two PictureBoxes.

3. ***Using a Select Case statement to determine the result of rolling the dice.*** Recall that if the player rolls 7 or 11 on the first roll, the player wins, but if the player rolls 2, 3 or 12 on the first roll, the player loses. Add lines 35–36 of Fig. 16.13 to the playButton_Click event handler beneath the code you added in the previous step, then press *Enter*. Note that the keywords End Select are autogenerated. Now add lines 37–46 of Fig. 16.13 into the playButton_Click event handler between the Select and End Select keywords.

(cont.)

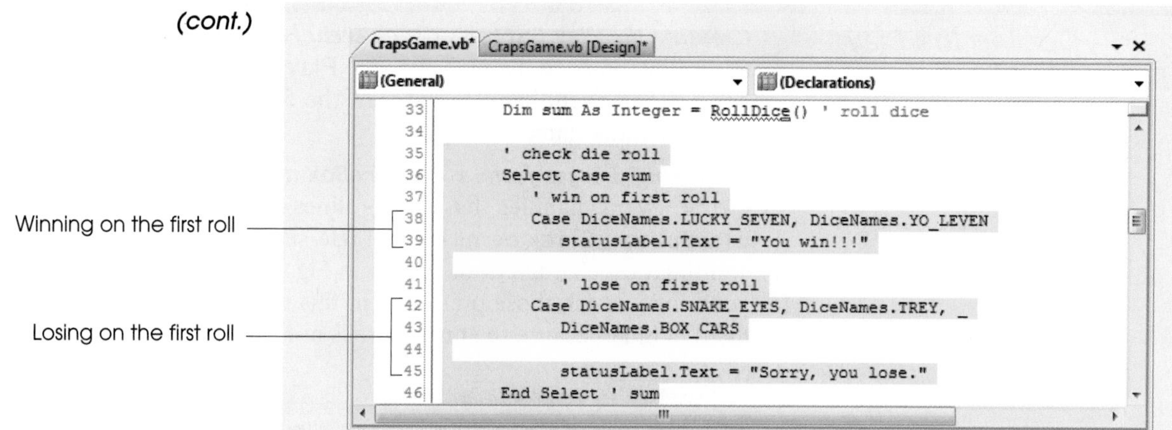
Winning on the first roll
Losing on the first roll
CrapsGame.vb*
CrapsGame.vb [Design]*
(General)
(Declarations)
33 Dim sum As Integer = RollDice() ' roll dice
35 ' check die roll
36 Select Case sum
37 ' win on first roll
38 Case DiceNames.LUCKY_SEVEN, DiceNames.YO_LEVEN
39 statusLabel.Text = "You win!!!"
41 ' lose on first roll
42 Case DiceNames.SNAKE_EYES, DiceNames.TREY, _
43 DiceNames.BOX_CARS
45 statusLabel.Text = "Sorry, you lose."
46 End Select ' sum

Figure 16.13 `Select Case` statement in `playButton_Click`.

The first `Case` statement (lines 38–39) selects values `7` and `11`, using the enumeration values `DiceNames.LUCKY_SEVEN` and `DiceNames.YO_LEVEN`. Recall that several expressions can be specified in the same `Case` statement when they are separated by commas. If the sum of the dice is `7` or `11`, the code in line 39 displays `"You win!!!"` in the output `statusLabel`. If the dice total 2 (`DiceNames.SNAKE_EYES`), 3 (`DiceNames.TREY`) or 12 (`DiceNames.BOX_CARS`), the code in the second `Case` statement executes (lines 42–45). This code displays a message in `statusLabel` indicating that the player has lost.

4. ***Using the Case `Else` statement to continue the game.*** If the player did not roll a 2, 3, 7, `11` or 12, then the value of the dice becomes the point and the player must roll again. Add lines 46-53 of Fig. 16.14 within the `Select Case` statement to implement this rule.

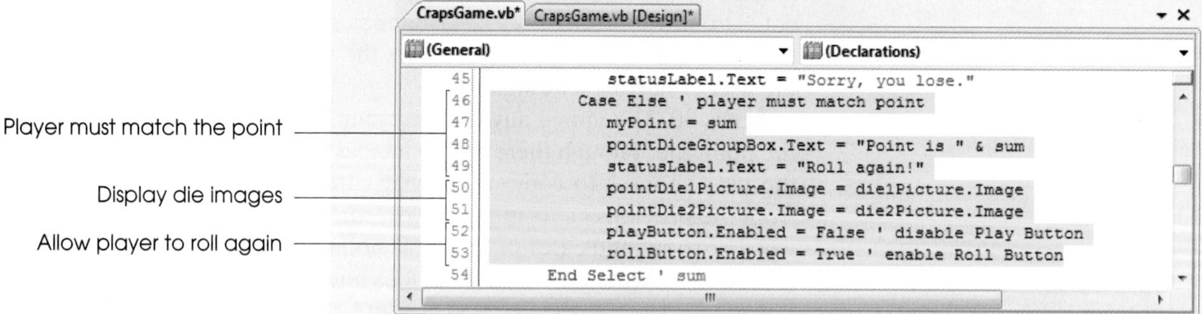
Player must match the point
Display die images
Allow player to roll again
CrapsGame.vb*
CrapsGame.vb [Design]*
(General)
(Declarations)
45 statusLabel.Text = "Sorry, you lose."
46 Case Else ' player must match point
47 myPoint = sum
48 pointDiceGroupBox.Text = "Point is " & sum
49 statusLabel.Text = "Roll again!"
50 pointDie1Picture.Image = die1Picture.Image
51 pointDie2Picture.Image = die2Picture.Image
52 playButton.Enabled = False ' disable Play Button
53 rollButton.Enabled = True ' enable Roll Button
54 End Select ' sum

Figure 16.14 `Case Else` statement in `playButton_Click`.

The first line of the `Case Else` statement's body (line 47) sets the instance variable `myPoint` to the sum of the die values. Next, line 48 changes the text in the `GroupBox`, using its `Text` property to display the value of the current point. Line 49, changes the `statusLabel` to notify the user to roll again.

If the user must match the point, you display the die images corresponding to the result of the dice roll. In Tutorial 3, you learned how to insert an image into a `PictureBox` in the Windows `Form` Designer. To set the image for a `PictureBox`, you used its `Image` property. You can also use code to set this property. To display the die faces for the point in the `GroupBox`, set the `Image` property of each `PictureBox` in the `GroupBox` to the same `Image` property value as its corresponding `PictureBox` below the `GroupBox` (lines 50–51).

(cont.)

Recall that the `RollDice` method (which you define shortly) sets the `Image` properties of the lower `PictureBoxes`. Finally, the **Play** `Button` is disabled (line 52) and the **Roll** `Button` is enabled (line 53), limiting users to clicking the **Roll** `Button` for the rest of the game. Line 54 ends the `Select Case` statement.

5. ***Saving the project.*** Select **File > Save All** to save your modified code.

The **Roll** `Button` is enabled after the user clicks **Play** and does not win or lose on the first roll, so you must code an event handler for it. You define the event handler in the following box.

Coding the Roll `Button`'s `Click` Event Handler

1. ***Generating the Roll `Button`'s `Click` event handler.*** Return to **Design** view, and double click the **Roll** `Button` to generate the **Roll** `Button`'s `Click` event handler and open the code window.

2. ***Rolling the dice.*** The user clicks the **Roll** `Button` to try to match the point, which requires rolling dice. Add line 61 of Fig. 16.15, which rolls the dice, displays the die images and stores the sum of the dice in variable `sum`. [*Note:* `RollDice` is underlined in blue because the procedure is not yet defined. You define it to roll the dice and display the die images shortly.]

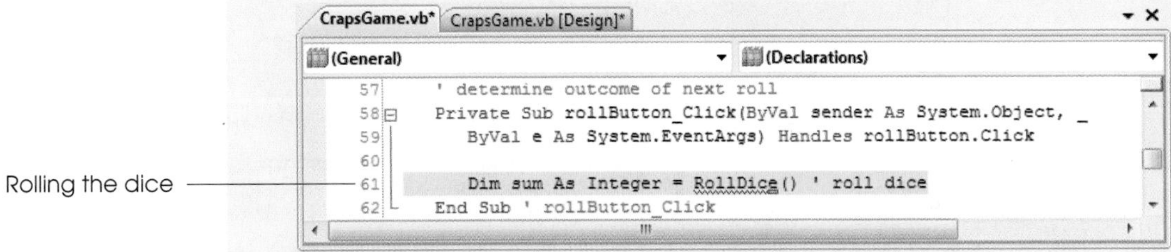

CrapsGame.vb* CrapsGame.vb [Design]*
(General)
(Declarations)
57 ' determine outcome of next roll
58 Private Sub rollButton_Click(ByVal sender As System.Object, _
59 ByVal e As System.EventArgs) Handles rollButton.Click
60
61 Dim sum As Integer = RollDice() ' roll dice
62 End Sub ' rollButton_Click
Rolling the dice

Figure 16.15 Rolling the dice in `rollButton_Click`.

3. ***Determining the output of the roll.*** If the roll matches the point, the user wins and the game ends. However, if the user rolls a 7 (`DiceNames.CRAPS`), the user loses and the game ends. Add lines 63–72 of Fig. 16.16 into the `rollButton_Click` event handler to incorporate this processing into your **Craps Game** application.

   The `If...Then` statement (lines 64–67) determines whether the sum of the dice in the current roll matches the point. If so, the program displays a winning message in `statusLabel`. It then allows the user to start a new game, by disabling the **Roll** `Button` and enabling the **Play** `Button`.

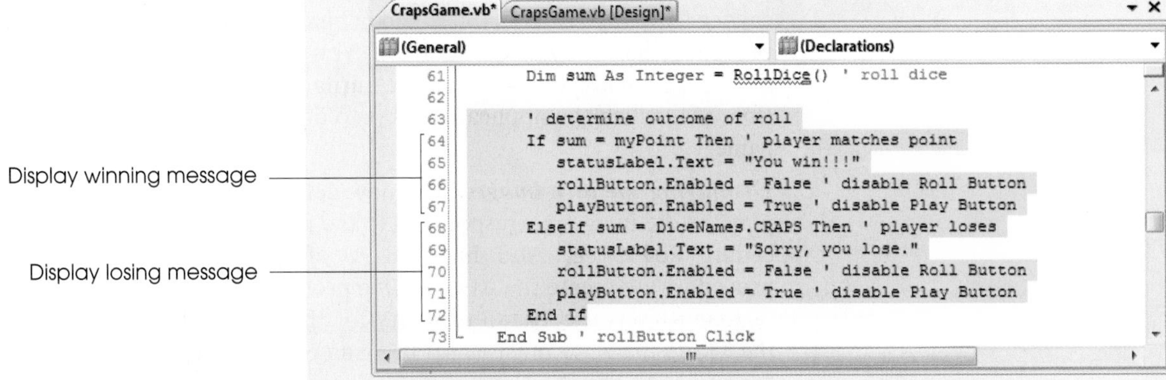

CrapsGame.vb* CrapsGame.vb [Design]*
(General)
(Declarations)
61 Dim sum As Integer = RollDice() ' roll dice
62
63 ' determine outcome of roll
64 If sum = myPoint Then ' player matches point
65 statusLabel.Text = "You win!!!"
66 rollButton.Enabled = False ' disable Roll Button
67 playButton.Enabled = True ' disable Play Button
68 ElseIf sum = DiceNames.CRAPS Then ' player loses
69 statusLabel.Text = "Sorry, you lose."
70 rollButton.Enabled = False ' disable Roll Button
71 playButton.Enabled = True ' disable Play Button
72 End If
73 End Sub ' rollButton_Click
Display winning message
Display losing message

Figure 16.16 Determining the outcome of a roll.

(cont.)

The `ElseIf` statement (lines 68–71) determines whether the sum of the dice in the current roll is `7` (`DiceNames.CRAPS`). If so, the application displays a message that the user has lost (in `statusLabel`) and ends the game by disabling the **Roll** `Button` and enabling the **Play** `Button`. If the player neither matches the point nor rolls a 7, then the player is allowed to roll again by clicking the **Roll** `Button`.

4. ***Saving the project.*** Select **File > Save All** to save your modified code.

In the following box, you add code to the application to simulate rolling dice and to display the dice in the appropriate `PictureBoxes`.

Using Random Numbers to Simulate Rolling Dice

1. ***Creating a Random object and simulating die rolling.*** This application will roll and display dice many times as it executes. Therefore, it is a good idea to create two procedures: one to roll the dice (`RollDice`) and one to display a die (`DisplayDie`). Define `Function` procedure `RollDice` first, by adding lines 75–86 of Fig. 16.17.

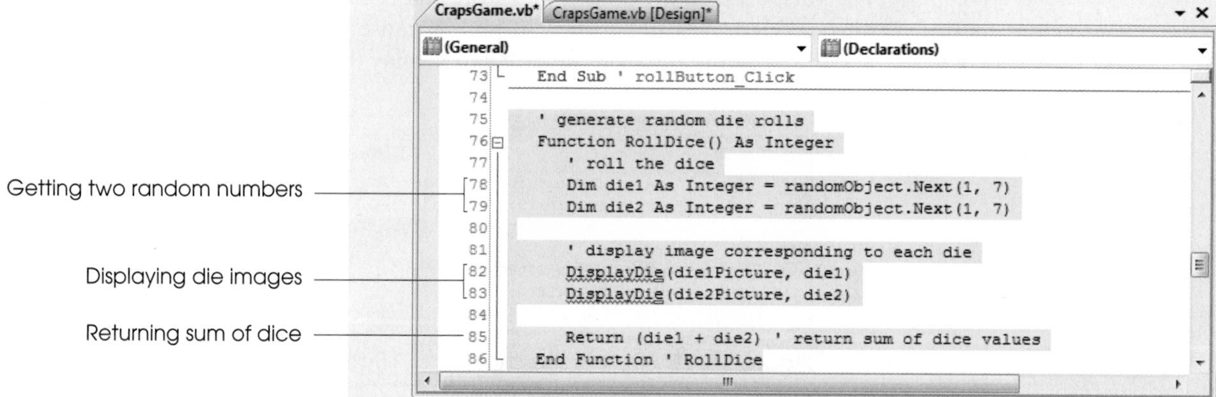

Figure 16.17 `RollDice` procedure definition.

This code sets the values of `die1` and `die2` to the values returned by `randomObject.Next(1, 7)`, which is an `Integer` random number between `1` and `6` (lines 78 and 79). Remember that the number returned is always less than the second argument.

The procedure then calls `DisplayDie` (lines 82 and 83), a procedure that displays the image of the die face corresponding to each number. The first parameter in `DisplayDie` is the `PictureBox` that displays the image, and the second parameter is the number that appears on the face of the die. The calls to `DisplayDie` are underlined in blue as compilation errors because the procedure has not yet been defined. You define the `DisplayDie` procedure in *Step 2*. Finally, the procedure returns the sum of the values of the dice (line 85), which the application uses to determine the outcome of the craps game.

2. ***Displaying the dice images.*** You now define procedure `DisplayDie` to display the die images corresponding to the random numbers generated in procedure `RollDice`. Add lines 88–92 of Fig. 16.18 (after the `RollDice` procedure) to create the `DisplayDie` procedure.

Line 91 sets the `Image` property for the specified `PictureBox`. Because the `Image` property must be set using an object of type `Image`, you must create an `Image` object.

(cont.)

Displaying a die image

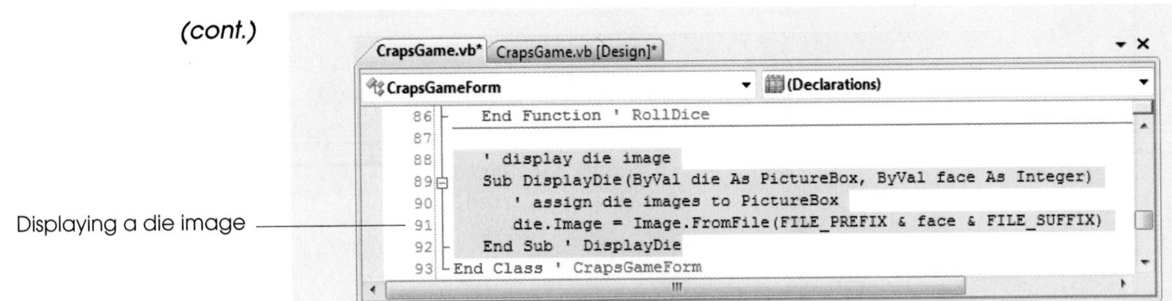

Figure 16.18 `DisplayDie` procedure definition.

The `Image` class's `FromFile` method helps create `Image` objects. `Image.FromFile` returns an `Image` object containing the image located at the path you specify. To specify the location, pass a `String` representing the path to the `FromFile` method. In this case, you concatenate `FILE_PREFIX & face & FILE_SUFFIX` to create the file's path. If the value of `face` is `1`, the expression would represent the string `images\die1.png`—the image in the `images` folder of a die face showing 1. The application searches for the specified file in the directory in which its executable file (.exe) is located, in this case `C:\SimplyVB2008\CrapsGame\bin\Debug\`. This starting location combined with the file path created using the String constants indicates that the image is located at `C:\SimplyVB2008\CrapsGame\bin\Debug\images\die1.png`. If the image cannot be found at the location you specify, an exception is raised. You learn how to handle exceptions in Tutorial 25. You can use Windows Explorer to verify that this is the correct location. This image is then displayed in the `PictureBox` by using its `Image` property.

3. ***Running the application.*** Select **Debug > Start Debugging** to run your completed application and enjoy the game!
4. ***Closing the application.*** Close your running application by clicking its close box.
5. ***Closing the IDE.*** Close the Visual Basic IDE by clicking its close box.

Figure 16.19 presents the source code for the **Craps Game** application. The lines of code that contain new programming concepts you learned in this tutorial are highlighted. As part of the project settings, `Option Strict` is set to `On` (to prevent implicit narrowing conversions).

Defining an enumeration

```
Public Class CrapsGameForm
   ' die-roll constants
   Enum DiceNames
      SNAKE_EYES = 2
      TREY = 3
      CRAPS = 7
      LUCKY_SEVEN = 7
      YO_LEVEN = 11
      BOX_CARS = 12
   End Enum

   ' file name and directory constants
   Const FILE_PREFIX As String = "images\die"
   Const FILE_SUFFIX As String = ".png"

```

Figure 16.19 **Craps Game** application's code. (Part 1 of 3.)

Creating a **Random** object

Removing the images from both point **PictureBoxes**

Using **Enum** constants

Using **Enum** constants

Generating random numbers

```
   ' instance variables
   Dim myPoint As Integer = 0
   Dim randomObject As New Random()

   ' begin new game and determine point
   Private Sub playButton_Click(ByVal sender As System.Object, _
      ByVal e As System.EventArgs) Handles playButton.Click

      ' initialize variables for new game
      myPoint = 0
      pointDiceGroupBox.Text = "Point"
      statusLabel.Text = ""

      ' remove point-die images
      pointDie1Picture.Image = Nothing
      pointDie2Picture.Image = Nothing

      Dim sum As Integer = RollDice() ' roll dice

      ' check die roll
      Select Case sum
         ' win on first roll
         Case DiceNames.LUCKY_SEVEN, DiceNames.YO_LEVEN _
            statusLabel.Text = "You win!!!"

         ' lose on first roll
         Case DiceNames.SNAKE_EYES, DiceNames.TREY, _
            DiceNames.BOX_CARS

            statusLabel.Text = "Sorry, you lose."
         Case Else ' player must match point
            myPoint = sum
            pointDiceGroupBox.Text = "Point is " & sum
            statusLabel.Text = "Roll again!"
            pointDie1Picture.Image = die1Picture.Image
            pointDie2Picture.Image = die2Picture.Image
            playButton.Enabled = False ' disable Play Button
            rollButton.Enabled = True ' enable Roll Button
      End Select ' sum
   End Sub ' playButton_Click

   ' determine outcome of next roll
   Private Sub rollButton_Click(ByVal sender As System.Object, _
      ByVal e As System.EventArgs) Handles rollButton.Click

      Dim sum As Integer = RollDice() ' roll dice

      ' determine outcome of roll
      If sum = myPoint Then ' player matches point
         statusLabel.Text = "You win!!!"
         rollButton.Enabled = False ' disable Roll Button
         playButton.Enabled = True ' enable Play Button
      ElseIf sum = DiceNames.CRAPS Then ' player loses
         statusLabel.Text = "Sorry, you lose."
         rollButton.Enabled = False ' disable Roll Button
         playButton.Enabled = True ' enable Play Button
      End If
   End Sub ' rollButton_Click

   ' generate random die rolls
   Function RollDice() As Integer
      ' roll the dice
      Dim die1 As Integer = randomObject.Next(1, 7)
      Dim die2 As Integer = randomObject.Next(1, 7)
```

Figure 16.19 **Craps Game** application's code. (Part 2 of 3.)

Using code to display an image

```

        ' display image corresponding to each die
        DisplayDie(die1Picture, die1)
        DisplayDie(die2Picture, die2)

        Return (die1 + die2) ' return sum of dice values
    End Function ' RollDice

    ' display die image
    Sub DisplayDie(ByVal die As PictureBox, ByVal face As Integer)
        ' assign die images to PictureBox
        die.Image = Image.FromFile(FILE_PREFIX & face & FILE_SUFFIX)
    End Sub ' DisplayDie
End Class ' CrapsGameForm
```

Figure 16.19 **Craps Game** application's code. (Part 3 of 3.)

SELF-REVIEW

1. Use the ________ method of class Image to create an Image object from a file.
   a) `Image`
   b) `ImageFile`
   c) `Image.ImageFile`
   d) `Image.FromFile`

2. To clear the image in a `PictureBox`, set its `Image` property to ________.
   a) "" (double quotes)
   b) `Nothing`
   c) `None`
   d) `Empty`

Answers: 1) c. 2) b.

16.5 Wrap-Up

In this tutorial, you created the **Craps Game** application to simulate playing the popular dice game called craps. You learned about the `Random` class and how it can be used to generate random numbers by creating a `Random` object and calling method `Next` on it. You then learned how to specify the range of values within which random numbers should be generated by passing various arguments to method `Next`. You also learned about enumerations, which enhance program readability by using descriptive identifiers to represent constants in an application.

Using your knowledge of random-number generation and event handlers, you wrote code that added functionality to your **Craps Game** application. You used random-number generation to simulate the element of chance. In addition to "rolling dice" in code, you learned how to use a `PictureBox` to display an image by using code. In the next tutorial, you learn how to use arrays, which allow you to use one name to store many values. You apply your knowledge of random numbers and arrays to create a **Flag Quiz** application that tests your knowledge of various nations' flags.

SKILLS SUMMARY

Generating Random Numbers

- Create an object of class `Random`, and call this object's `Next` or `NextDouble` methods.

Generating Random Numbers within a Specified Range

- Call the `Random` class's `Next` method with one argument to produce values from 0 up to, but not including the argument value.
- Call the `Random` class's `Next` method with two arguments to produce values from the first argument's value up to, but not including, the second argument's value.

Using Enumerations

- Begin the declaration of an enumeration with keyword `Enum`. Then, use a list of descriptive names and set each one to the value it represents. End the enumeration with keywords `End Enum`.

- You can refer to the enumeration values using the enumeration name and the member-access operator followed by the name of the constant.

Creating an Image Object

- Pass a String representing the image's location to the Image.FromFile method.

Clearing a Reference's Values

- Assign the Nothing keyword to the variable storing the reference you wish to clear.

KEY TERMS

End Enum keywords—Ends an enumeration.

Enum keyword—Begins an enumeration.

enumeration—A group of related, named constants.

Image.FromFile—A method of class Image that returns an Image object containing the image located at the path you specify.

Int32.MaxValue constant—The largest possible 32-bit Integer (2,147,483,647).

Next method of class Random—A method of class Random that, when called with no arguments, generates a positive Integer value between zero and the constant Int32.MaxValue. When called with arguments, the method generates an Integer value in a range constrained by those arguments.

NextDouble method of class Random—A method of class Random that generates a positive Double value that is greater than or equal to 0.0 and less than 1.0.

Nothing keyword—Used to clear a reference's value.

pseudorandom numbers—A sequence of values produced by a complex mathematical calculation that simulates random-number generation.

Random class—Contains methods to generate pseudorandom numbers.

reference—Keyword New creates a new object in memory and returns a reference to that object. You typically store an object's reference in a reference-type variable so you can interact with the object.

CONTROLS, EVENTS, PROPERTIES & METHODS

Image This class provides functionality to manipulate images.

- ***Method***

  FromFile—Used to specify the image to load and where it is located.

Random This class is used to generate random numbers.

- ***Methods***

  Next—When called with no arguments, generates a positive Integer value between zero and the largest possible Integer, which is the constant Int32.MaxValue (2,147,483,647). When called with one argument, generates a positive Integer value from zero up to, but not including, the argument passed to it. When called with two arguments, generates a positive Integer value in the range from the first argument's value up to, but not including, the second argument's value.

  NextDouble—Generates a positive Double value that is greater than or equal to 0.0 and less than 1.0.

MULTIPLE-CHOICE QUESTIONS

16.1 A Random object can generate pseudorandom numbers of type ________.

a) Integer b) Single
c) Double d) Both a and c

16.2 Constant identifiers within enumerations (e.g. SNAKE_EYES, TREY, CRAPS, etc.) ________ be assigned the same numeric value.

a) cannot b) can
c) must d) should

16.3 The `Next` method of class `Random` can be called using ________.

a) one argument
b) no arguments
c) two arguments
d) All of the above

16.4 The statement ________ assigns `value` a random number in the range 5–20.

a) `value = randomObject.Next(5, 21)`
b) `value = randomObject.Next(4, 20)`
c) `value = randomObject.Next(5, 20)`
d) `value = randomObject.Next(4, 21)`

16.5 The ________ method takes a paramenter that specifies the file from which an image is loaded.

a) `Next` in class `Random`
b) `FromFile` in class `Image`
c) `File` in class `Image`
d) None of the above

16.6 The values returned by the methods of class `Random` are ________ numbers.

a) pseudorandom
b) completely random
c) ordered
d) None of the above

16.7 When creating random numbers, the second argument passed to the `Next` method is ________.

a) equal to the maximum value you wish to be generated
b) equal to one more than the maximum value you wish to be generated
c) equal to one less than the maximum value you wish to be generated
d) equal to the minimum value you wish to be generated

EXERCISES

16.8 ***(Guess the Number Application)*** Develop an application that generates a random number and prompts the user to guess the number (Fig. 16.20). When the user clicks the **New Game** `Button`, the application chooses a number in the range `1` to `100` at random. The user enters guesses into the **Guess:** `TextBox` and clicks the **Enter** `Button`. If the guess is correct, the game ends, and the user can start a new game. If the guess is not correct, the application should indicate whether the guess is higher or lower than the correct number.

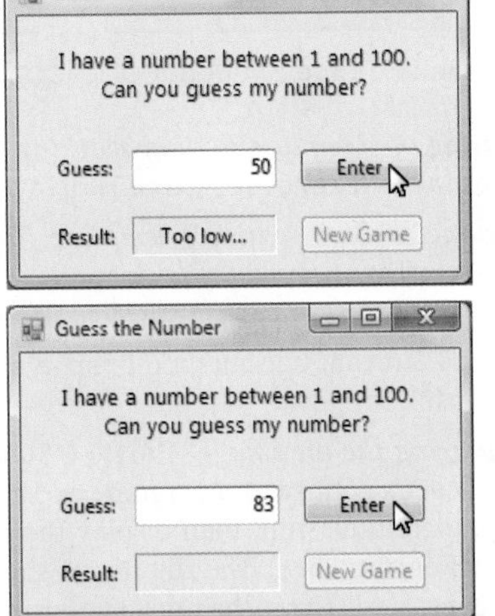

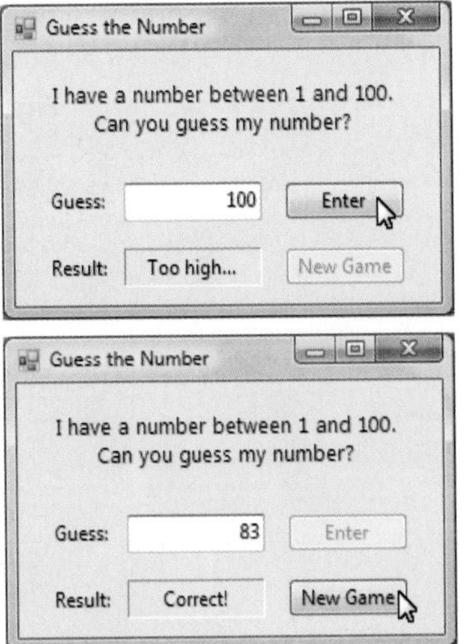

Figure 16.20 **Guess the Number** application.

a) ***Copying the template to your working directory.*** Copy the directory `C:\Examples\Tutorial16\Exercises\GuessNumber` to your `C:\SimplyVB2008` directory.

b) ***Opening the application's template file.*** Double click `GuessNumber.sln` in the `GuessNumber` directory to open the application.

c) ***Creating a `Random` object.*** Create two instance variables. The first variable should reference a `Random` object, and the second variable should store a randomly generated number in the range of `1` to `100`.

d) ***Adding a Click event handler for the Enter Button.*** Add a Click event handler for the **Enter** Button that retrieves the value entered by the user and compares it to the random number. If the guess is correct, display **Correct!** in the output Label. Then disable the **Enter** Button and enable the **New Game** Button. If the user's guess is higher than the correct answer, display **Too high...** in the output Label. If the user's guess is lower than the correct answer, display **Too low...** in the output Label. Place the focus on the **Guess:** TextBox.

e) ***Adding a Click event handler for the New Game Button.*** Add a Click event handler for the **New Game** Button that generates a new random number for the instance variable. The event handler should then disable the **New Game** Button, enable the **Enter** Button and clear the **Result:** Label and the **Guess:** TextBox.

f) ***Adding a TextChanged event handler for the Guess: TextBox.*** Add a TextChanged event handler for the **Guess:** TextBox that clears the **Result:** Label.

g) ***Running the application.*** Select **Debug > Start Debugging** to run your application. Enter guesses (clicking the **Enter** Button after each) until you have successfully determined the answer. Click the **New Game** Button and test the application again.

h) ***Closing the application.*** Close your running application by clicking its close box.

i) ***Closing the IDE.*** Close the Visual Basic IDE by clicking its close box.

16.9 *(Dice Simulator Application)* Develop an application that simulates rolling two six-sided dice. Your application should have a **Roll** Button that, when clicked, displays two dice images corresponding to random numbers. It should also display the number of times each face has appeared. Your application should look like Fig. 16.21.

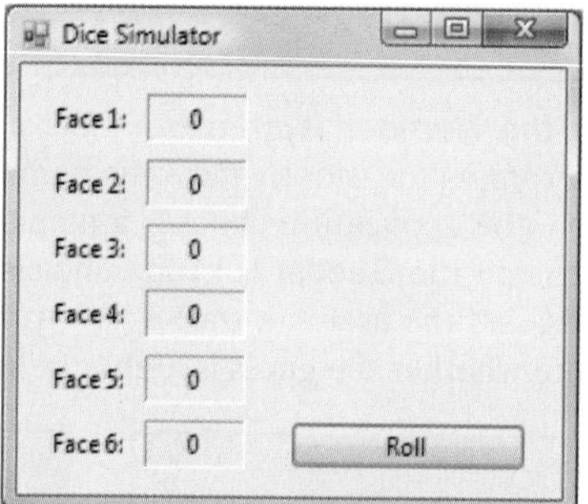

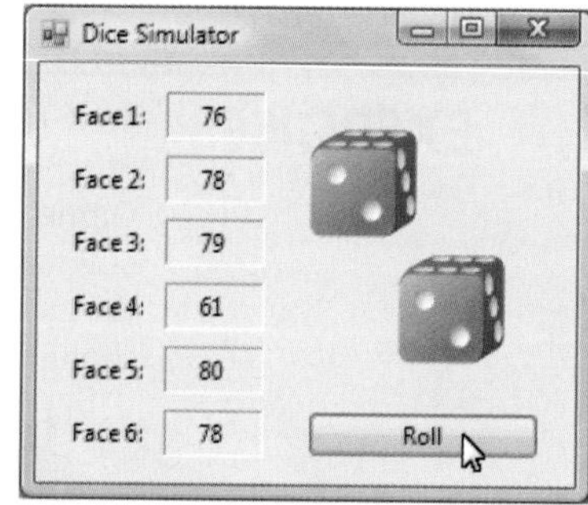

Figure 16.21 **Dice Simulator** application.

a) ***Copying the template to your working directory.*** Copy the directory C:\Examples\Tutorial16\Exercises\DiceSimulator to your C:\SimplyVB2008 directory.

b) ***Opening the application's template file.*** Double click DiceSimulator.sln in the DiceSimulator directory to open the application.

c) ***Adding a Click event handler for the Roll Button.*** Add a Click event handler for the **Roll** Button. Call method DisplayDie twice in this event handler to display the images for both dice

d) ***Displaying the die image.*** Create a Sub procedure named DisplayDie that takes a PictureBox control as an argument. This method should generate a random number to simulate a die roll, then display the die image in the corresponding PictureBox control on the Form. The die image should correspond to the random number that was generated. To set the image, refer to the code presented in Fig. 16.19.

e) ***Displaying the frequency.*** Add a Sub procedure called DisplayFrequency to be called from DisplayDie that uses a Select Case statement to update the number of times each face has appeared. Create an enumeration for the dice faces which will be used in the Select Case statement.

f) ***Running the application.*** Select **Debug > Start Debugging** to run your application. Click the **Roll** Button several times. Each time, two die faces are displayed. Verify after each roll that the appropriate face values on the left are incremented. You can perform several hundred rolls quickly by placing the focus on the Roll Button (by clicking it) and holding down the Enter key. The frequency of each face should be similar.

g) ***Closing the application.*** Close your running application by clicking its close box.

h) ***Closing the IDE.*** Close the Visual Basic IDE by clicking its close box.

16.10 ***(Lottery Picker Application)*** A lottery commission offers four different lottery games to play: Three-number, Four-number, Five-number and Five-number + one lotteries. Each game has independent numbers. Develop an application that randomly picks numbers for all four games and displays the generated numbers in a GUI (Fig. 16.22). You should use two digits to display all numbers by using the `D2` format specifier in a call to `String.Format`. The games are played as follows:

- Three-number lotteries require players to choose three numbers in the range 0–9.
- Four-number lotteries require players to choose four numbers in the range 0–9.
- Five-number lotteries require players to choose five numbers in the range 1–39.
- Five-number + 1 lotteries require players to choose five numbers in the range 1–49 and an additional number in the range of 1–42.

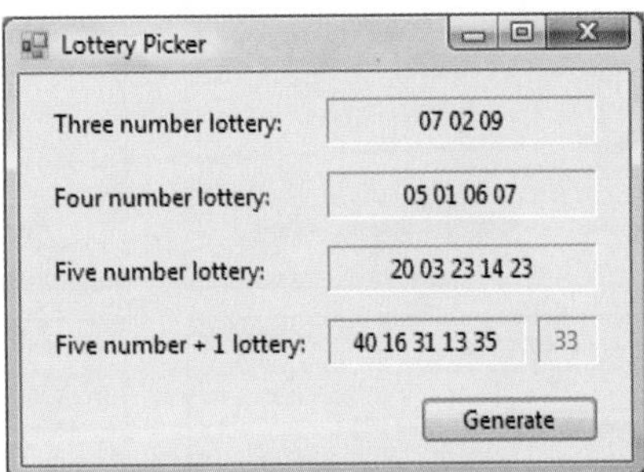

Figure 16.22 **Lottery Picker** application.

a) ***Copying the template to your working directory.*** Copy the directory `C:\Examples\Tutorial16\Exercises\LotteryPicker` to your `C:\SimplyVB2008` directory.

b) ***Opening the application's template file.*** Double click `LotteryPicker.sln` in the `LotteryPicker` directory to open the application.

c) ***Generating random numbers.*** Create a `Function` procedure that generates a random number within a given range and returns it as a `String`. Create another `Function` procedure which generates a specified number of digits within a given range and returns the digits as a `String`. Use the previous `Function` to help implement this `Function`.

d) ***Drawing numbers for the games.*** Add code into your application to call the previously created procedure in order to generate numbers for all four games. To make the application simple, allow repetition of numbers.

e) ***Running the application.*** Select **Debug > Start Debugging** to run your application. Click the **Generate** `Button` multiple times. Make sure the values displayed are within the ranges described in the exercise description.

f) ***Closing the application.*** Close your running application by clicking its close box.

g) ***Closing the IDE.*** Close the Visual Basic IDE by clicking its close box.

What does this code do? ▶

16.11 What does the following code do?

```
Sub PickRandomNumbers()

   Dim number1 As Integer
   Dim number As Double
   Dim number2 As Integer
   Dim randomObject As New Random()

```

```
        number1 = randomObject.Next()
        number = 5 * randomObject.NextDouble()
        number2 = randomObject.Next(1, 10)
        integer1Label.Text = Convert.ToString(number1)
        double1Label.Text = Convert.ToString(number)
        integer2Label.Text = Convert.ToString(number2)
    End Sub ' PickRandomNumbers
```

Programming Challenge

16.12 ***(Multiplication Teacher Application)*** Develop an application that helps children learn multiplication. Use random-number generation to produce two positive one-digit integers that display in a question, such as "How much is 6 times 7?" The student should type the answer into a `TextBox`. If the answer is correct, then the application randomly displays one of three messages in a `Label`, **Very Good!**, **Excellent!** or **Great Job!**. If the student is wrong, the `Label` displays the message **No. Please try again**. The GUI and sample user interactions are shown in Fig. 16.23.

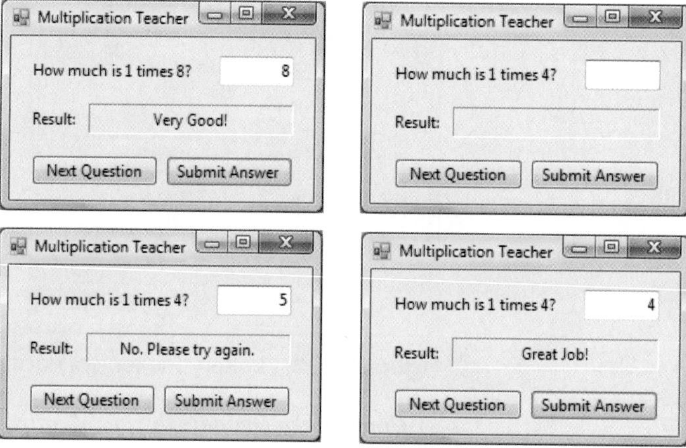

Figure 16.23 **Multiplication Teacher** application.

a) ***Copying the template to your working directory.*** Copy the directory `C:\Examples\Tutorial16\Exercises\MultiplicationTeacher` to your `C:\SimplyVB2008` directory.

b) ***Opening the application's template file.*** Double click `MultiplicationTeacher.sln` in the `MultiplicationTeacher` directory to open the application.

c) ***Generating the questions.*** Add a procedure into your application to generate each new question.

d) ***Displaying a new question.*** Add code into your application to call the procedure created in the preceding step when the user clicks the **Next Question** `Button`, as well as when the `Form` loads.

e) ***Determining whether the right answer was entered.*** When the user clicks the **Submit Answer** `Button`, determine whether the student answered the question correctly, and display the appropriate message.

f) ***Displaying a random message.*** Add a procedure `GenerateOutput` that displays a random message congratulating the student for answering correctly. This method should be called if the student answered the question correctly.

g) ***Running the application.*** Select **Debug > Start Debugging** to run your application. Enter several correct answers and at least one incorrect answer. Verify that **No. Please try again.** is displayed when you are incorrect, and one of the other responses is displayed at random when you are correct.

h) ***Closing the application.*** Close your running application by clicking its close box.

i) ***Closing the IDE.*** Close the Visual Basic IDE by clicking its close box.

TUTORIAL 17

Flag Quiz Application

Introducing One-Dimensional Arrays and ComboBoxes

Objectives

In this tutorial, you learn to:

- Create and initialize arrays.
- Store information in an array.
- Refer to individual elements of an array.
- Sort arrays.
- Use ComboBoxes to display options in a drop-down list.
- Replace characters in a String.

Outline

This tutorial introduces basic concepts and features of **data structures**. Data structures group and organize related data. **Arrays** are data structures that consist of data items of the same type. You'll learn how to create arrays and how to access the information they contain. You'll also learn how to sort a String array's information alphabetically.

This tutorial's **Flag Quiz** application includes a ComboBox control. A ComboBox presents user options in a drop-down list that opens when you click the down arrow at the right side of the control. You may also type into the ComboBox control to locate an item. This is the first time that you add a ComboBox to an application, but you've used them many times before in the Visual Studio environment. For example, when you activated Option Strict in Tutorial 15, you selected **On** from a ComboBox.

17.1 Test-Driving the Flag Quiz Application

You now create an application that tests a student's knowledge of the flags of various countries. The application uses arrays to store information, such as the country names and Boolean values that determine whether a country name has been previously selected by the application as a correct answer. This application must meet the following requirements:

Application Requirements

A geography teacher would like to quiz students on their knowledge of the flags of various countries. The teacher has asked you to write an application that displays a flag and allows the student to select the corresponding country from a list. The application should inform the user of whether the answer is correct and display the next flag. The application should display five flags randomly chosen from the flags of Australia, Brazil, China, Italy, Russia, South Africa, Spain and the United States. When the application is run, a given flag should be displayed only once.

You begin by test-driving the completed application. Then you learn the additional Visual Basic capabilities needed to create your own version of this application.

Test-Driving the Flag Quiz Application

1. ***Opening the completed application.*** Open the directory `C:\Examples\Tutorial17\CompletedApplication\FlagQuiz` to locate the **Flag Quiz** application. Double click `FlagQuiz.sln` to open the application in the Visual Basic IDE.

2. ***Running the Flag Quiz application.*** Select **Debug > Start Debugging** to run the application (Fig. 17.1). Note that you might see a different flag when you run the application, because the application randomly selects which flag to display.

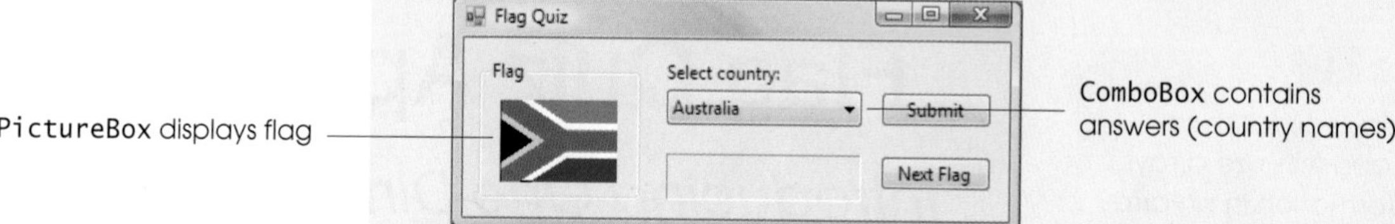

Figure 17.1 **Flag Quiz** application running.

3. ***Selecting an answer.*** The `ComboBox` contains eight country names. One country name corresponds to the displayed flag and is the correct answer. The scrollbar allows you to browse through the `ComboBox`'s drop-down list. Select an answer from the `ComboBox`, as shown in Fig. 17.2.

Figure 17.2 Selecting an answer from the `ComboBox`.

4. ***Submitting a correct answer.*** Click the **Submit** `Button` to check your answer. If it's correct, the message `"Correct!"` is displayed in an output `Label` (Fig. 17.3). Note that the **Submit** `Button` is now disabled and the **Next Flag** `Button` is enabled.

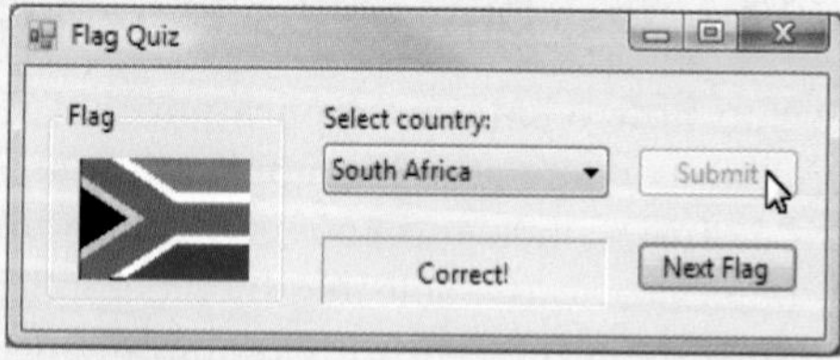

Figure 17.3 Submitting the correct answer.

5. ***Displaying the next flag.*** Click the **Next Flag** `Button` to display a different flag (Fig. 17.4). Note that the **Submit** `Button` is now enabled, the **Next Flag** `Button` is disabled, the `ComboBox` displays **Australia** (the first country listed in the `ComboBox`) and the output `Label` is cleared.

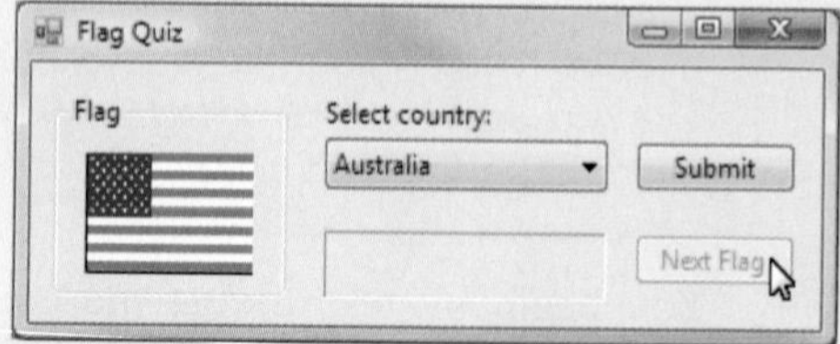

Figure 17.4 Displaying the next flag.

(cont.)

6. ***Submitting an incorrect answer.*** To demonstrate the application's response, select an incorrect answer and click **Submit**, as in Fig. 17.5. The application displays `"Sorry, incorrect."` in the output `Label`.

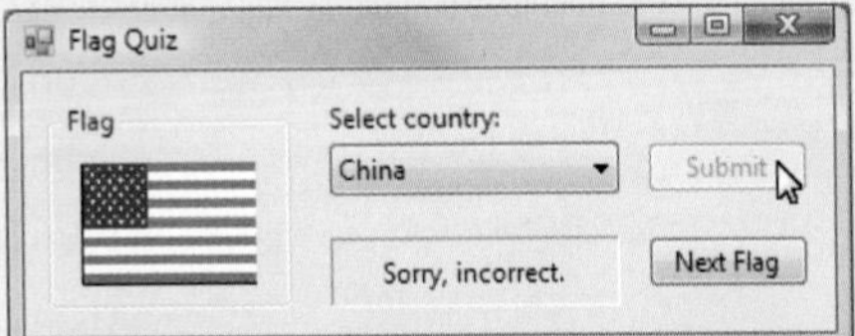

Figure 17.5 Submitting an incorrect answer.

7. ***Finishing the quiz.*** After the application displays five flags and the user has submitted five answers, the quiz ends (Fig. 17.6). Note that the two `Buttons` and the `ComboBox` are disabled.

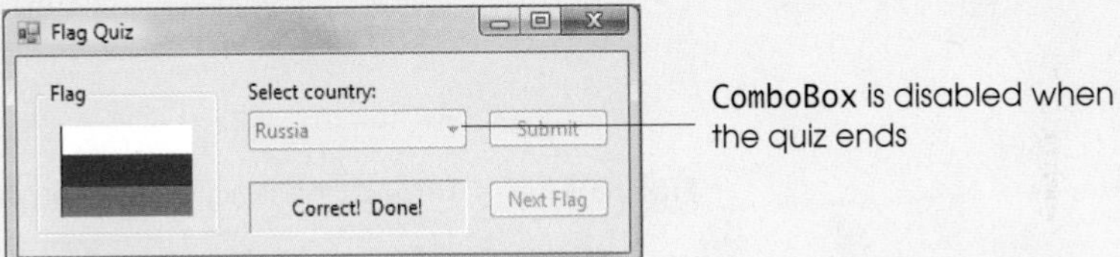

Figure 17.6 Finishing the quiz.

8. ***Closing the application.*** Click your running application's close box.
9. ***Closing the IDE.*** Close the Visual Basic IDE by clicking its close box.

17.2 Introducing Arrays

An array is a group of variables that all contain data items of the same name and type. Array names follow the same conventions that apply to other identifiers. To refer to a particular location in an array, you specify the name of the array and the **position number** of the location, which is a value that indicates a specific location within an array. Position numbers begin at `0` (zero).

Figure 17.7 depicts an `Integer` array named `netUnitsSold`. This array contains 13 items, also called **elements**. Each array element represents the net number of "units sold" of a particular book in one month at a bookstore. For example, `netUnitsSold(1)` is the net sales of that book for January (month 1), `netUnitsSold(2)` is the net sales for February, and so on. In this example, you simply ignore the first element of the array, because there is no month zero.

Each array element is referred to by providing the name of the array followed by the position number of the element in parentheses `()`. The position numbers for the elements in an array begin with `0`. Thus, the element `0` of array `netUnitsSold` is referred to as `netUnitsSold(0)`, element 1 of array `netUnitsSold` is referred to as `netUnitsSold(1)`, element 6 of array `netUnitsSold` is referred to as `netUnitsSold(6)` and so on. Element *i* of array `netUnitsSold` is referred to as `netUnitsSold(i)`. The position number in parentheses is called an **index** or a **subscript**. An index must be either zero, a positive integer or an integer expression that yields a non-negative result. If an application uses an expression as an index, the expression is evaluated first to determine the index. For example, if variable `value1` is equal to `5`, and variable `value2` is equal to `6`, then the statement

```
netUnitsSold(value1 + value2) += 2
```

adds `2` to array element `netUnitsSold(11)`. Note that an **indexed array name** (the array name followed by an index enclosed in parentheses)—like any other variable name—can be used on the left side of an assignment to place a new value into an array element.

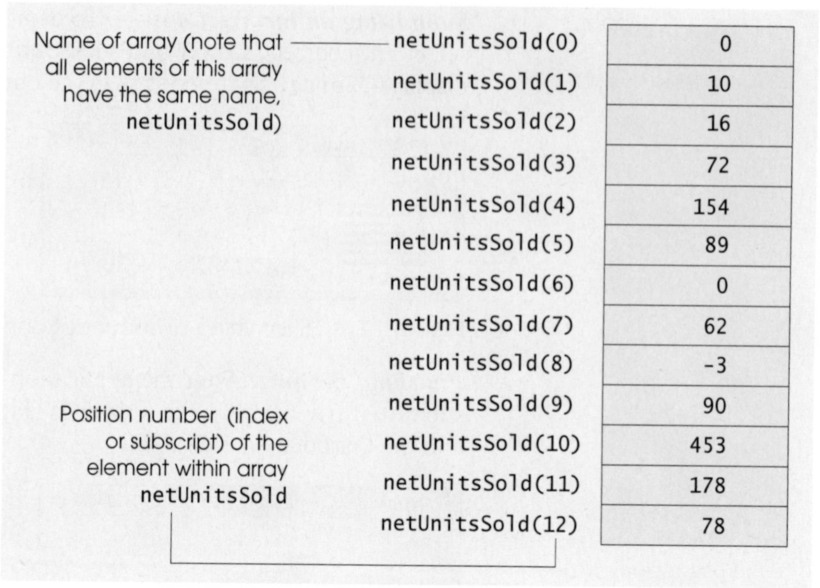

Figure 17.7 Array consisting of 13 elements.

Let's examine array netUnitsSold in Fig. 17.7 more closely. The name of the array is netUnitsSold. The 13 elements of the array are referred to as netUnitsSold(0) through netUnitsSold(12). The value of netUnitsSold(1) is 10, the value of netUnitsSold(2) is 16, the value of netUnitsSold(3) is 72, the value of netUnitsSold(7) is 62 and the value of netUnitsSold(11) is 178. A positive value for an element in this array indicates that more books were sold than were returned. A negative value for an element in this array indicates that more books were returned than were sold. A value of zero indicates that the number of books sold was equal to the number of books returned.

Values stored in arrays can be used in various calculations and applications. For example, to determine the net units sold in the first three months of the year, then store the result in variable firstQuarterUnits, we would write

```
firstQuarterUnits = _
   netUnitsSold(1) + netUnitsSold(2) + netUnitsSold(3)
```

You use only **one-dimensional** arrays, such as netUnitsSold, in this tutorial. The indexed array names of one-dimensional arrays use only one index. In the next tutorial, you study two-dimensional arrays—their indexed array names use two indices.

SELF-REVIEW

1. The number that refers to a particular element of an array is called its ________.
   a) value
   b) size
   c) indexed array name
   d) index (or subscript)

2. The indexed array name of one-dimensional array units's element 2 is ________.
   a) units{2}
   b) units(2)
   c) units[0,2]
   d) units[2]

Answers: 1) d. 2) b.

17.3 Declaring and Allocating Arrays

To declare an array, you provide the array's name and data type. The following statement declares the array in Fig. 17.7:

```
Dim netUnitsSold As Integer()
```

The parentheses that follow the data type indicate that `netUnitsSold` is an array. Arrays can be declared to contain any data type. In an array of a primitive data type, every element contains one value of the declared type. For example, every element of an `Integer` array contains an `Integer` value.

Before you can use an array, you must specify its size and allocate memory for it. Arrays are represented as objects in Visual Basic, and all objects are typically allocated by using keyword `New`. The value stored in the array variable is actually a reference to the array object. To allocate memory for the array `netUnitsSold` after it has been declared, use the statement

```
netUnitsSold = New Integer(0 To 12) {}
```

Attempting to access elements in the array by using an index outside the array bounds results in an `IndexOutOfRangeException`. We discuss exceptions in Tutorial 25.

Array bounds determine what indices can be used to access an element in the array. Here, the array bounds are `0` and `12` (one less than the number of elements in the array). Note that because of array element `0`, the actual number of array elements (13) is one larger than the upper bound specified in the allocation (`12`).

If you know the number of elements at the time you declare the array, you can write the array declaration as

```
Dim netUnitsSold(0 To 12) As Integer
```

which creates a 13-element array. In this case, the compiler implicitly uses the `New` keyword for you.

The required braces (`{` and `}`) are called an **initializer list** and specify the initial element values. When the initializer list is empty, as it is here, the array elements are initialized to the default value for the array's data type. Again, these default values are `0` for numeric primitive-data-type variables (such as `Integer`), `False` for `Boolean` variables and `Nothing` for references. Recall that keyword `Nothing` denotes an empty reference (that is, a value indicating that a reference variable has not been assigned an object). The initializer list also can contain a comma-separated list specifying the initial values of the elements in the array. For example,

```
Dim salesPerDay As Integer()
salesPerDay = New Integer() {0, 2, 3, 6, 1, 4, 5, 6}
```

declares and allocates an array containing eight `Integer` values. The compiler determines the array bounds from the number of elements in the initializer list. Thus, it is not necessary to specify the size of the array when you use a nonempty initializer list.

If you specify an upper bound when initializing an array, it is a compilation error if you provide too many or too few values in the initializer list.

You can specify both the array bounds and an initializer list, as in:

```
Dim temperatures As Double() = _
   New Double(0 To 3) {23.45, 34.98, 78.98, 53.23}
```

Note that the upper bound is one less than the number of items in the array. The preceding statement can also be written as

```
Dim temperatures As Double() = {23.45, 34.98, 78.98, 53.23}
```

In this case, the compiler determines the array bounds from the number of elements in the initializer list and implicitly uses the `New` keyword for you.

Arrays can also be initialized using implicit lower bounds. For example, the preceding statement could have been written as follows:

```
Dim temperatures As Double() = _
   New Double(3) {23.45, 34.98, 78.98, 53.23}
```

Note that the value `0` and the keyword `To` are not included in the parentheses.

Often, the elements of an array are used in a calculation. The following box demonstrates declaring and initializing an array and accessing its elements.

Computing the Sum of an Array's Elements

1. ***Copying the template to your working directory.*** Copy the `C:\Examples\Tutorial17\TemplateApplication\SumArray` directory to your `C:\SimplyVB2008` directory.

2. ***Opening the Sum Array application's template file.*** Double click `SumArray.sln` in the `SumArray` directory to open the application in the Visual Basic IDE.

3. ***Adding the Button's `Click` event handler.*** Double click the **Sum Array** `Button` in **Design** view (Fig. 17.8) to generate the empty event handler `sumButton_Click`.

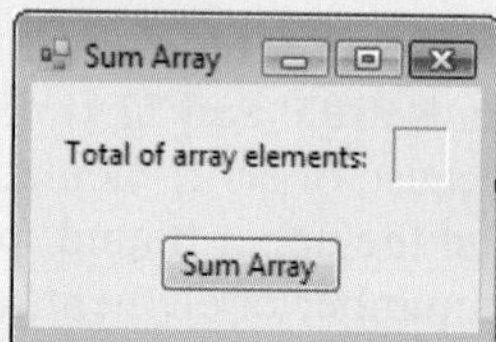

Figure 17.8 **Sum Array** application's `Form` in **Design** view.

4. ***Combining the declaration and allocation of an array.*** Add lines 6–8 of Fig. 17.9 to the event handler. Line 7 combines the declaration and allocation of an array into one statement. Variable `array` is a reference to an array of `Integer`s containing 10 elements that are initialized with the values from 1 to 10. Line 8 declares and initializes variable `total`, which will be used to sum the values in the array.

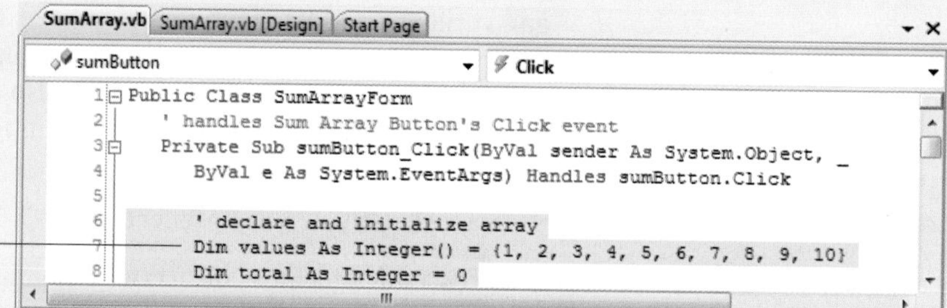

Creating an array of `Integers`

Figure 17.9 Declaring an array in the event handler.

Error-Prevention Tip

Use method `GetUpperBound` when you need to find an array's highest index. Using an actual numerical value for the upper bound instead could lead to errors if you change the number of array elements.

Error-Prevention Tip

It is important to note the difference between the "seventh element of the array" and "array element seven." Array indices begin at 0, which means that the former has the index 6, whereas the latter has the index 7. This confusion is a common source of "off-by-one" errors.

5. ***Calculating the sum.*** Add lines 10–16 (Fig. 17.10) to the event handler. The `For...Next` loop (lines 11–14) retrieves each element's value (one at a time), which is added to `total` (line 13). Method **`GetUpperBound`** (line 11) returns the index of the last element in the array. Method `GetUpperBound` takes one argument, indicating a dimension of the array. For one-dimensional arrays, such as `array`, `GetUpperBound`'s argument is always `0`, to indicate the first (and only) dimension (or row) of the array. In this case, `array.GetUpperBound(0)` returns `9`. We discuss arrays with two dimensions in Tutorial 18.

   Every array in Visual Basic "knows" its own length. The **length** (or the number of elements) of the array (`10` in this case) is returned by the expression `array.Length`.

   We could have set the upper bound in the `For...Next` loop as

   ```
   array.Length - 1
   ```

   which returns `9`. The value returned by method `GetUpperBound` is the last index in the array—one less than the value of the array's **`Length`** property.

(cont.)

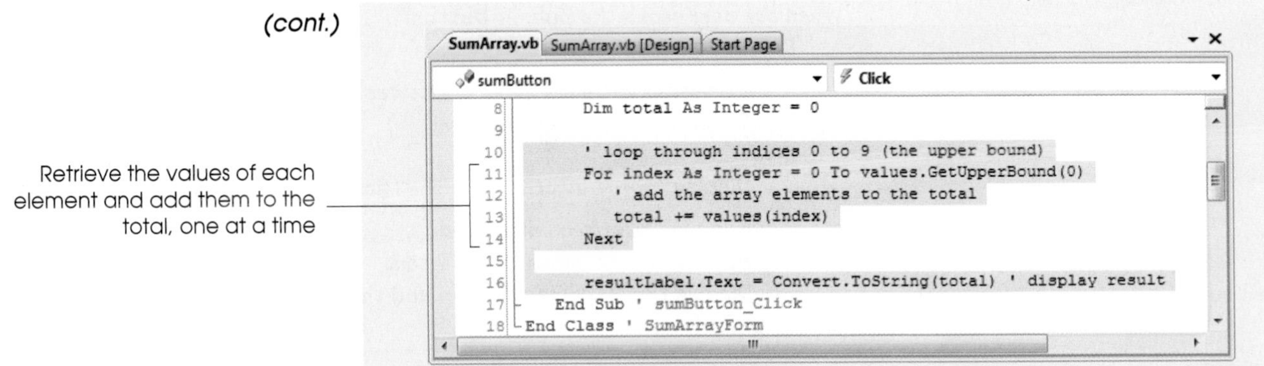

Figure 17.10 Calculating the sum of the values of an array's elements.

6. ***Displaying the result.*** Line 16 displays the sum of the array element values.
7. ***Running the application.*** Select **Debug > Start Debugging** to run your application. The result of adding the integers from 1 to 10, inclusive, is displayed when you click the **Sum Array** `Button` (Fig. 17.11).

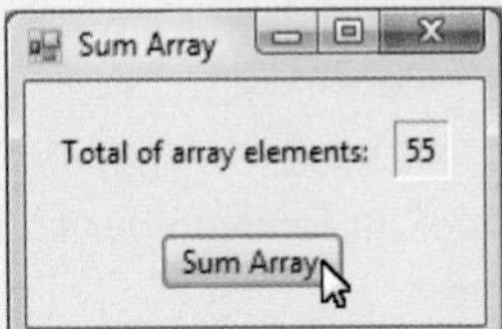

Figure 17.11 Displaying the sum of the values of an array's elements.

8. ***Closing the application.*** Close your running application by clicking its close box.
9. ***Closing the IDE.*** Close the Visual Basic IDE by clicking its close box.

SELF-REVIEW

1. Arrays can be allocated using keyword ________.

   a) `Declare` b) `Create`
   c) `New` d) `Allocate`

2. An array's length is ________.

   a) one more than the array's last index b) one less than the array's last index
   c) the same as the array's last index d) returned by method `GetUpperBound`

Answers: 1) c. 2) a.

17.4 Constructing the Flag Quiz Application

Before you begin building the **Flag Quiz** application, you need to develop the application using pseudocode and an ACE table. The following pseudocode describes the basic operation of the **Flag Quiz** application:

```
When the Form loads:
    Sort the country names alphabetically
    Place country names in the ComboBox
    Call DisplayFlag to randomly select a flag and display it
```

When the user clicks the Submit Button:
    Retrieve the selected country name

    If the selected value matches the correct answer
        Display "Correct!" in the Label
    Else
        Display "Sorry, incorrect." in the Label

    If five images have been displayed
        Append "Done!" to the Label's text
        Disable the Next Flag Button and the ComboBox
    Else
        Enable Next Flag Button

    Disable Submit Button

When the user clicks the Next Flag Button:
    Call DisplayFlag to randomly select a flag and display it
    Clear the Label's text
    Set ComboBox to display its first item
    Update the number of flags shown
    Enable Submit Button
    Disable Next Flag Button

When DisplayFlag is called:
    Call GetUniqueRandomNumber to obtain the index of a flag that has not yet
        been used
    Obtain the name of the country from the countries array
    Call BuildPathName to get the image's path and file name
    Display the flag in a PictureBox

When GetUniqueRandomNumber is called:
    Create a Random object
    Select the index of a flag that has not been used
    Set the corresponding element of the used array to true
    Return the index

When BuildPathName is called:
    Use String method Replace to remove spaces from the country String
    Return a String containing the corresponding image's path and file name

Now that you've test-driven the **Flag Quiz** application and studied its pseudocode representation, you use an ACE table to help you convert the pseudocode to Visual Basic. Figure 17.12 lists the actions, controls and events that help you complete your own version of this application.

Action/Control/Event (ACE) Table for the Flag Quiz Application

Action	Control/Class/Object	Event
Label the application's controls	`flagGroupBox`, `selectLabel`	
	`FlagQuizForm`	`Load`
Sort the countries alphabetically	`Array`	
Place country names in the ComboBox	`countriesCombo-Box`	
Call DisplayFlag to randomly select a flag and display it		

Figure 17.12 **Flag Quiz** application's ACE table. (Part 1 of 3.)

Action	Control/Class/ Object	Event
	submitButton	Click
Retrieve the selected country name	countriesComboBox	
If the selected value matches the correct answer Display "Correct!" in the Label	feedbackLabel	
Else Display "Sorry, incorrect." in Label	feedbackLabel	
If five images have been displayed Append "Done!" to Label's text	feedbackLabel	
Disable the Next Flag Button and the ComboBox	nextButton, countriesComboBox	
Else Enable Next Flag Button	nextButton	
Disable Submit Button	submitButton	
	nextButton	Click
Call DisplayFlag to randomly select a flag and display it		
Clear the Label's text	feedbackLabel	
Set ComboBox to display its first item	countriesComboBox	
Update the number of flags shown		
Enable Submit Button	submitButton	
Disable Next Flag Button	nextButton	
		DisplayFlag
Call GetUniqueRandomNumber to obtain the index of a flag that has not yet been used		
Obtain the name of the country from the countries array	countries	
Call BuildPathName to get the image's path and file name		
Enable Submit Button	submitButton	
Display the flag in a PictureBox	flagPicture	
		GetUniqueRandomNumber
Create a Random object	randomObject	
Select the index of a flag that has not been used	randomObject, used (array)	
Set the corresponding element of the used array to true	used (array)	
Return the index		

Figure 17.12 **Flag Quiz** application's ACE table. (Part 2 of 3.)

Action	Control/Class/Object	Event
		BuildPathName
Use String method Replace to remove spaces from the country String	country	
Return a String containing the corresponding image's path and file name	country	

Figure 17.12 **Flag Quiz** application's ACE table. (Part 3 of 3.)

The following box shows you how to initialize the variables used in the application. In particular, the application requires two one-dimensional arrays.

Initializing Important Variables

1. ***Copying the template to your working directory.*** Copy the `C:\Examples\Tutorial17\TemplateApplication\FlagQuiz` directory to your `C:\SimplyVB2008` directory.

2. ***Opening the* Flag Quiz *application's template file.*** Double click `FlagQuiz.sln` in the `FlagQuiz` directory to open the application in the Visual Basic IDE.

3. ***Declaring the array of country names.*** Add lines 2–4 of Fig. 17.13 to the application. Lines 3–4 declare and initialize array `countries` as an instance variable of class `FlagQuizForm`. Each element is a `String` containing the name of a country. These lines assign the initializer list to the array, combining the declaration and initialization into one statement. The compiler determines the size of the array (in this case, eight elements) based on the number of items in the initializer list.

Creating an array of `Strings` to store country names

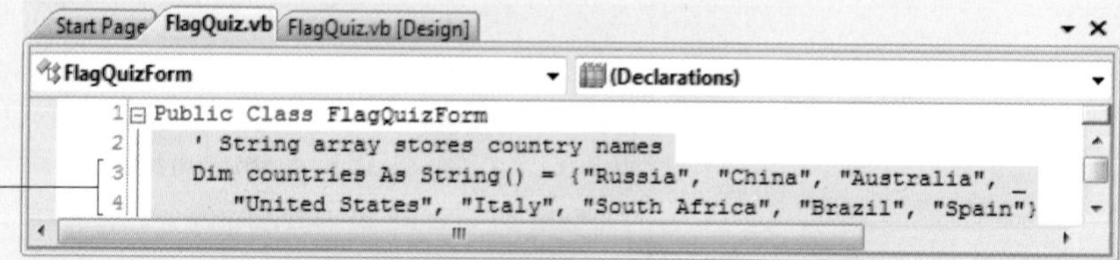

Figure 17.13 `String` array that stores country names.

4. ***Creating a `Boolean` array.*** The application should not display any flag more than once. Since the application uses random-number generation to pick a flag, the same flag could be selected more than once—just as, when you roll a six-sided die many times, a die face could be repeated. You'll use a `Boolean` array to keep track of which flags have been displayed. Add lines 6–8 of Fig. 17.14 to `FlagQuiz.vb`. Lines 7–8 declare and create `Boolean` array named `used`.

Creating an array of `Boolean` values with the same number of elements as the array of country names

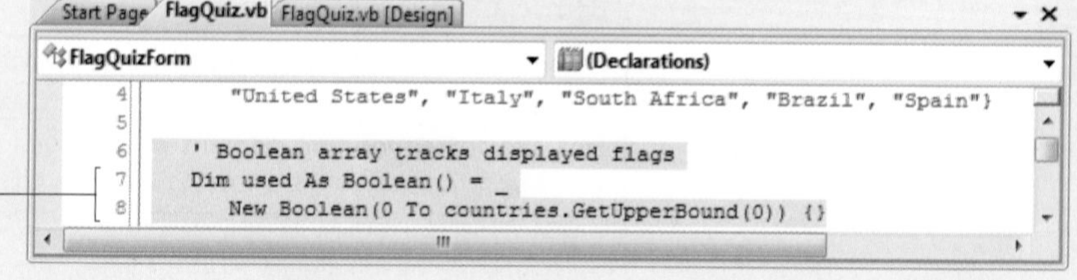

Figure 17.14 `Boolean` array that keeps track of displayed flags.

(cont.)

Method GetUpperBound returns array countries's highest index, which is used as the upper bound of used. Therefore, array used has the same size as array countries. The elements of used correspond to the elements of countries—used(0) specifies whether the flag corresponding to the country name in countries(0) (Russia) has been displayed. By default, each uninitialized element in a Boolean array is False. The application will set an element of used to True if its corresponding flag has been displayed.

5. ***Initializing a counter and a variable to store the answer.*** Add lines 10–11 of Fig. 17.15 to FlagQuiz.vb. The application ensures that only five flags are displayed by incrementing variable count, which is initialized to 1 (line 10). The correct answer (the name of the country whose flag is displayed) is stored in country (line 11).

Creating instance variables

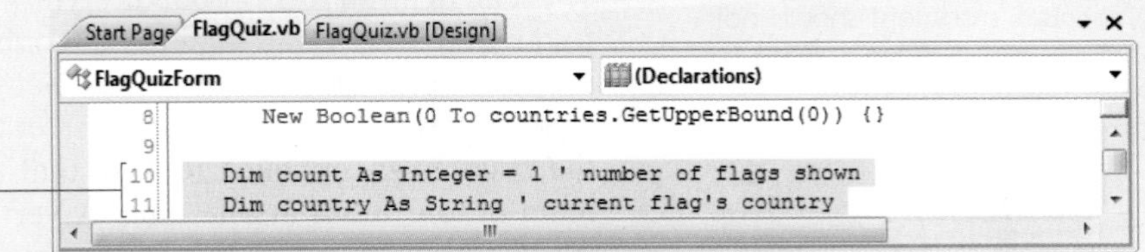

Figure 17.15 Instance variables used throughout the application.

6. ***Saving the project.*** Select **File > Save All** to save your modified code.

GUI Design Tip

Each ComboBox should be accompanied by a descriptive Label describing the ComboBox's contents.

Now you add another control to the **Flag Quiz** application template. The **Flag Quiz** application allows students to select answers from a ComboBox. The **ComboBox** control combines features of a TextBox and a ListBox. A ComboBox usually appears as a TextBox with a down arrow to its right. The user can click the down arrow to display a list of predefined items. If a user chooses an item from this list, that item is displayed in the ComboBox. If the list contains more items than the drop-down list can display at one time, a vertical scrollbar appears. The following box shows you how to assign an array's elements to a ComboBox before the Form is displayed to the user.

Adding and Customizing a ComboBox

1. ***Adding a ComboBox to the Form.*** Double click FlagQuiz.vb in the **Solution Explorer** to display the application's Form (Fig. 17.16). Add a ComboBox to the Form by double clicking the

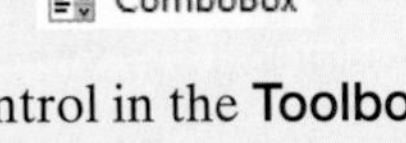

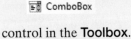

control in the **Toolbox**.

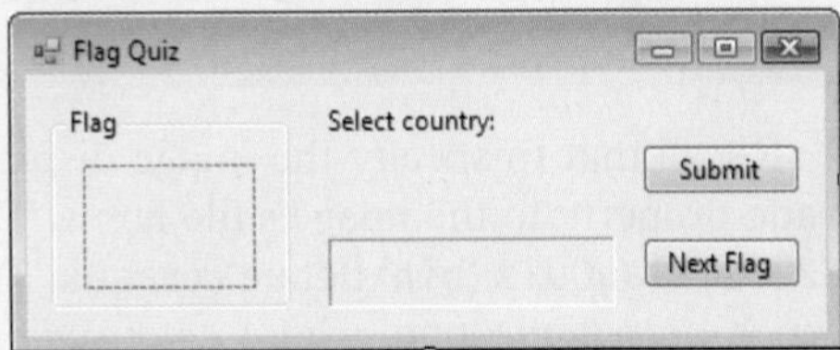

Figure 17.16 **Flag Quiz** template application's Form.

2. ***Customizing the ComboBox.*** Change the Name property of the ComboBox to countriesComboBox. Position the ComboBox just below the **Select country:** Label and match its width with that of the output Label below it. The Form should look like Fig. 17.17.

(cont.)

Good Programming Practice

Append the ComboBox suffix to ComboBox control names.

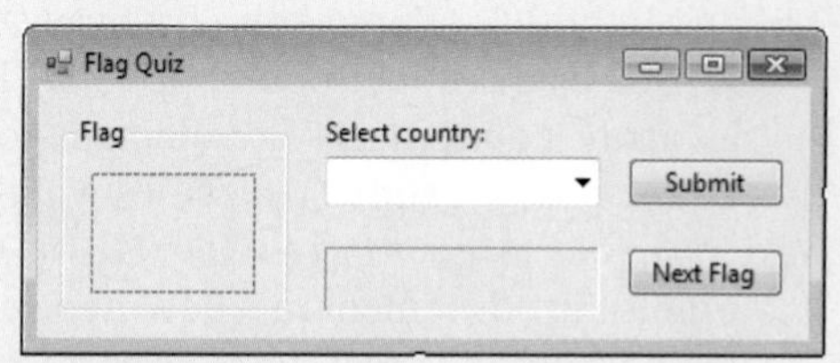

Figure 17.17 ComboBox added to **Flag Quiz** application's Form.

GUI Design Tip

If a ComboBox's content should not be editable, set its DropDownStyle property to DropDownList.

3. ***Setting the appearance of ComboBox.*** Property **DropDownStyle** determines the ComboBox's appearance. Value **DropDownList** specifies that the ComboBox is not editable (the user cannot type text in its TextBox). You can click the arrow button to display a drop-down list from which you can select an item. In this ComboBox style, if you press the key that corresponds to the first letter of an item in the ComboBox, that item is selected and displayed in the ComboBox's TextBox. Set the DropDownStyle property of the ComboBox to DropDownList. Then, set the **MaxDropDownItems** property of the countriesComboBox to 4, so that the drop-down list displays a maximum of four items at one time. A vertical scrollbar is added to the drop-down list to allow users to scroll through the remaining items.

4. ***Generating an event handler to add items to the ComboBox during the Load event.*** The ComboBox should contain a list of country names when the Form is displayed. The Form's Load event occurs before the Form is displayed—as a result, you should add the items to the ComboBox in the Form's Load event handler. Double click the Form to generate the empty event handler FlagQuizForm_Load.

5. ***Displaying items in the ComboBox.*** Format the FlagQuizForm_Load event handler as shown in Fig. 17.18 and add lines 17–18. ComboBox property **DataSource** (line 18) specifies the source of the items displayed in the ComboBox. In this case, the source is array countries.

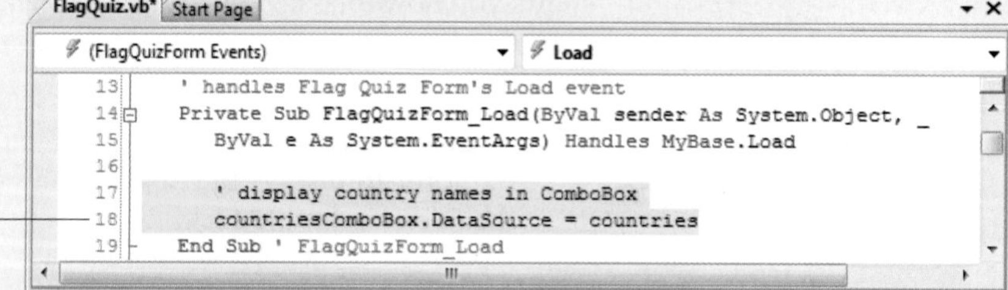

Figure 17.18 Assigning the String elements of an array to a ComboBox.

6. ***Saving the project.*** Select **File > Save All** to save your modified code.

Recall that to specify the image displayed in a PictureBox, you need to set its Image property to the image's file name. The flag images are located at C:\SimplyVB2008\FlagQuiz\bin\Debug\images. The name of each flag-image file is of the form *countryname*.png, where *countryname* has no whitespace. The following box shows how the application constructs the full path name needed to locate and display each flag.

Building a Flag-Image File's Path Name

1. ***Creating a procedure to build the flag-image file's path name.*** Add lines 21–25 of Fig. 17.19 to the **Flag Quiz** application after event handler `FlagQuizForm_Load`. Function `BuildPathName` constructs and returns a relative path that includes the name of a flag-image's file. The country name is retrieved from instance variable `country` (the correct answer). Line 23 uses the `String.Format` method to create a `String` that begins with `images\` followed by the country name and the `.png` image file-name extension.

Removing whitespace from a country name

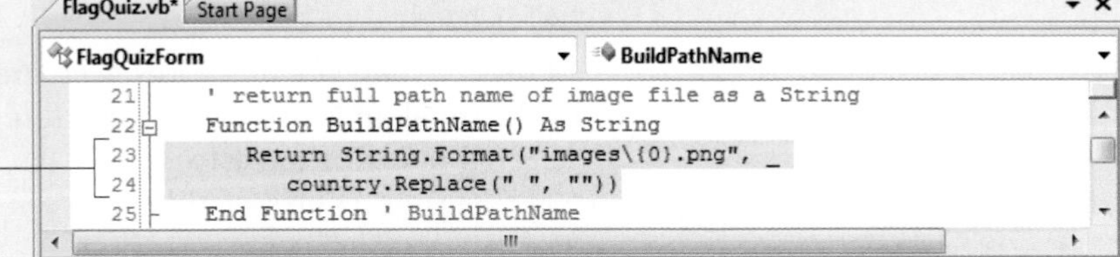

Figure 17.19 Removing whitespace from the country name.

Some countries—for example, South Africa and the United States—have space characters in their names, but the flag-image file names do not contain spaces. Line 24 uses `String` method **`Replace`** to replace occurrences of the space character with an empty `String`. The `Replace` method takes two arguments—a `String` to replace in the original `String` and a `String` with which to replace all occurrences of the first argument. Method `Replace` returns a new `String` with the specified replacements. If there are no occurrences of the first argument in the `String`, the method returns a copy of the original `String`. [*Note:* `String` methods, such as `Remove`, do not modify the `String` object for which they are called. The `String` object returned by these methods contains a copy of the modified `String`.]

2. ***Saving the project.*** Select **File > Save All** to save your modified code.

To ensure that the user is not asked the same question twice, a flag must be displayed no more than once when running the application. The application uses the `Boolean` array `used` to track which flags have been displayed. The following box shows you how to ensure that the application displays a flag no more than once.

Selecting a Unique Flag to Display

1. ***Creating the `GetUniqueRandomNumber` procedure.*** Add lines 27–28 of Fig. 17.20 to the **Flag Quiz** application after procedure `BuildPathName`. Line 28 is the header for the `GetUniqueRandomNumber` procedure. `GetUniqueRandomNumber` returns the index of a country name whose flag has not been displayed.

Determining whether a country's flag has been displayed previously

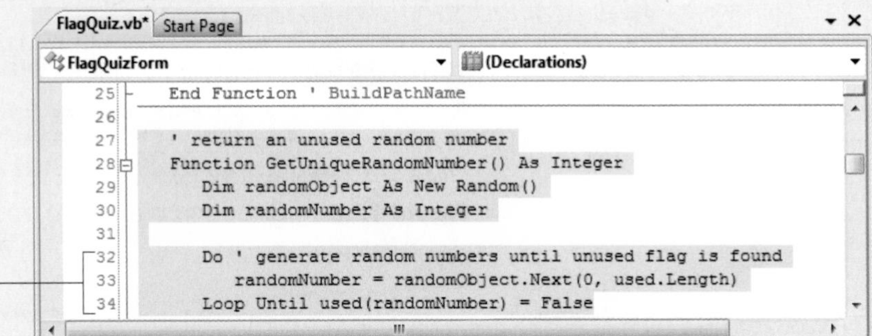

Figure 17.20 Generating a unique index.

(cont.)

2. ***Generating a random index.*** Add line 29 of Fig. 17.20 to the procedure GetUniqueRandomNumber. To select the next flag to display, you create a Random object that you'll use to select random flags.

3. ***Ensuring that each flag displays only once.*** Add lines 30–34 of Fig. 17.20 to GetUniqueRandomNumber. Method Next (line 33) of class Random generates a random index between 0 and used.Length (the number of country names). If the index has been selected previously, the element of used at the generated index is True. The Do...Loop Until statement (lines 32–34) iterates until it finds an unused flag (that is, until used(randomNumber) is False).

4. ***Indicating that the index has been used.*** Add lines 36–37 of Fig. 17.21 to the GetUniqueRandomNumber procedure. Line 37 sets the element at the selected index of used to True. This indicates that the flag has been used. Checking the values in this array ensures that the index will not be used again in the application.

Indicate that the unused flag will be displayed and return the flag's index for use

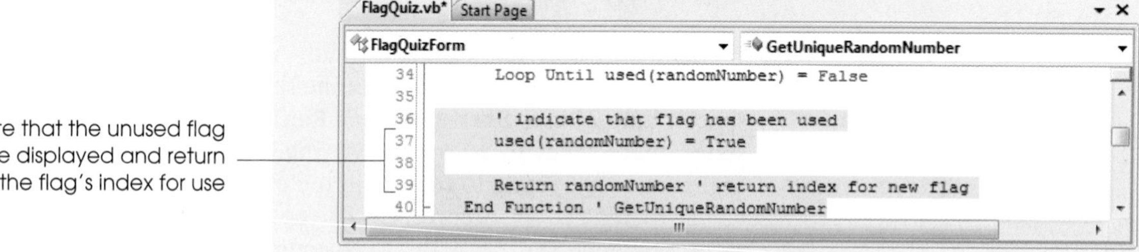

Figure 17.21 Returning the unique index.

5. ***Returning the unique random number.*** Add line 39 of Fig. 17.21 to the GetUniqueRandomNumber procedure to return the unique random index.

6. ***Saving the project.*** Select **File > Save All** to save your modified code.

With the full path name and a unique flag selected, the application can display that flag. The following box shows how to display the selected flag.

Displaying a Flag

1. ***Creating the DisplayFlag procedure.*** Add lines 42–43 of Fig. 17.22 to the **Flag Quiz** application after procedure GetUniqueRandomNumber. Procedure DisplayFlag selects a random country name and displays that country's flag.

Getting the index of an unused flag

Retrieving the flag's corresponding country name

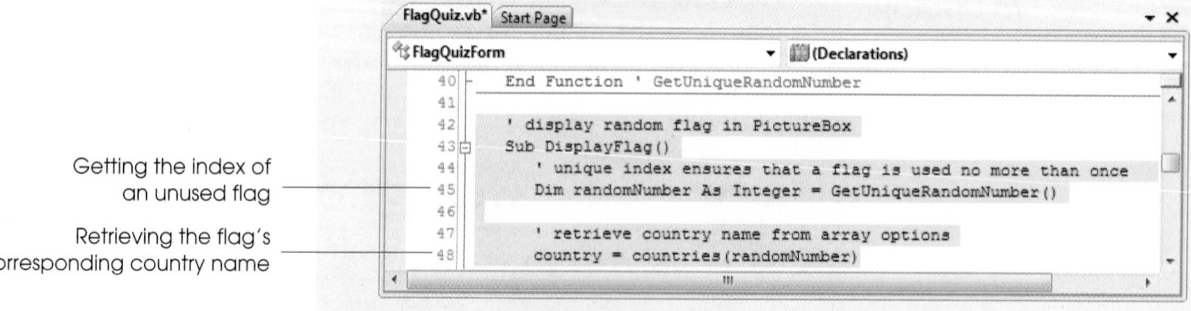

Figure 17.22 Choosing a random country name.

(cont.)

2. ***Obtaining a unique index.*** Add lines 44–45 of Fig. 17.22 to the `DisplayFlag` procedure. Line 45 invokes `GetUniqueRandomNumber` to find an index of a flag that has not been displayed during the application's execution and assigns the index to `randomNumber`.
3. ***Retrieving a country name.*** Add lines 47–48 of Fig. 17.22 to the `DisplayFlag` procedure. Line 48 obtains the flag's corresponding country name from index `randomNumber` of `String` array `countries` and assigns it to instance variable `country`, which represents the correct answer.
4. ***Building the flag image's path name.*** Add lines 50–51 of Fig. 17.23 to the `DisplayFlag` procedure. Line 51 invokes procedure `BuildPathName`. The procedure returns the flag image's path name, which is assigned to `path`.

Getting the path name of the flag and displaying the flag image

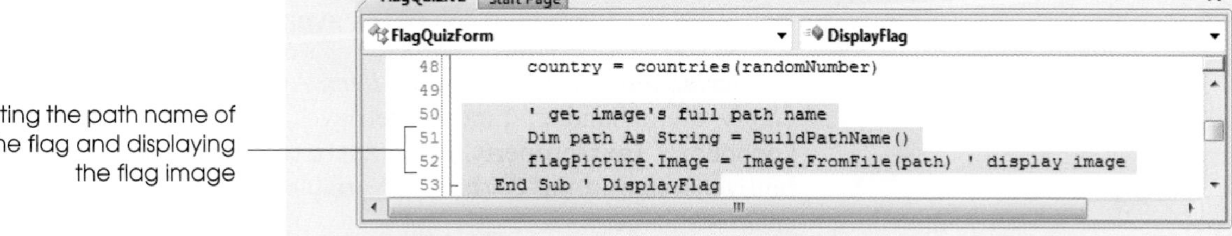

Figure 17.23 Displaying a flag image.

5. ***Displaying the flag image.*** Add line 52 of Fig. 17.23 to the `DisplayFlag` procedure. Line 52 sets `flagPicture`'s `Image` property to the `Image` object returned by method `Image.FromFile`. Recall that method `Image.FromFile` returns an `Image` object from the specified file.
6. ***Displaying a flag when the application is run.*** When the `Form` loads, the first flag image in the quiz is displayed. The `Form`'s `Load` event handler should invoke procedure `DisplayFlag`. Add line 20 of Fig. 17.24 to event handler `FlagQuizForm_Load`.
7. ***Saving the project.*** Select **File > Save All** to save your modified code.

Displaying a flag when application is first run

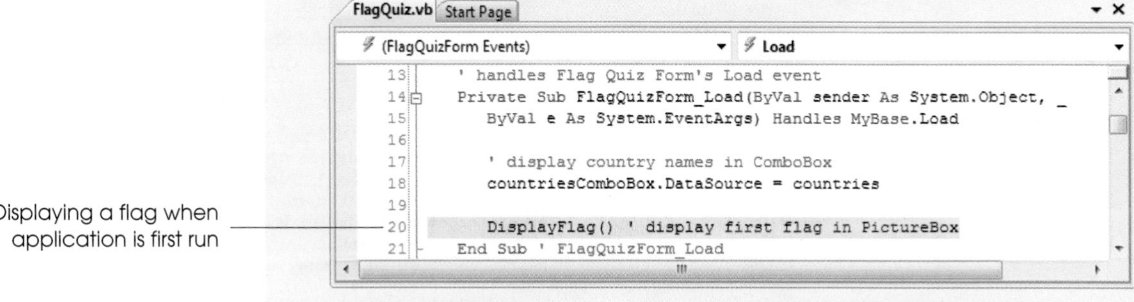

Figure 17.24 Displaying a flag when the `Form` is loaded.

The user submits an answer by selecting a country name from the `ComboBox` and clicking the **Submit** `Button`. The application displays whether the user's answer is correct. If the application is finished (that is, five flags have been displayed), the application informs the user that the quiz is done—otherwise, the application enables the user to view the next flag. The following box implements this functionality.

Processing a User's Answer

1. ***Adding the Submit `Button`'s `Click` event handler.*** Double click the **Submit** `Button` to generate the `Click` event handler `submitButton_Click`. Format it as shown in lines 57–59 of Fig. 17.25.

(cont.)

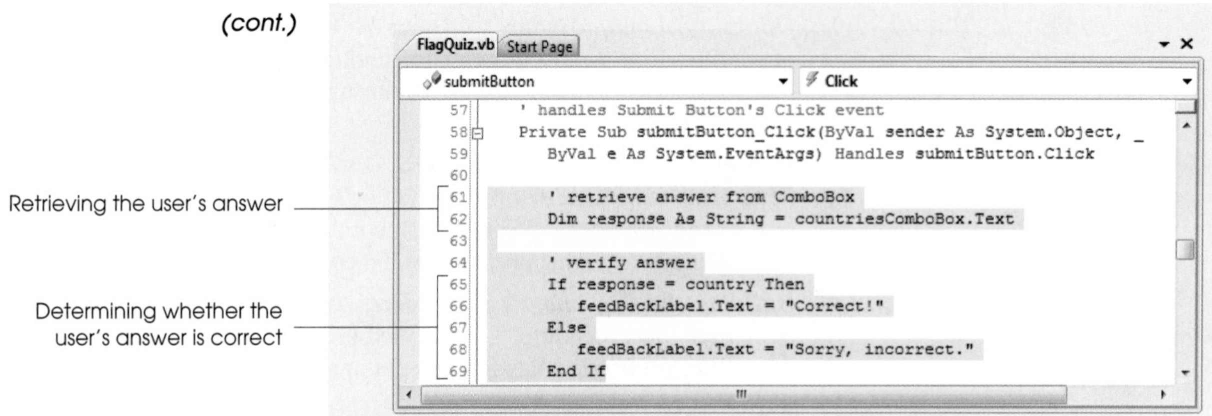

Figure 17.25 Submit `Button` `Click` event handler.

2. ***Retrieving the selected ComboBox item.*** Add lines 61–62 of Fig. 17.25 to the empty event handler. Line 62 retrieves the user's answer by using the `ComboBox`'s `Text` property. Property `Text` returns the `String` that is currently selected in the `ComboBox`. Variable `response` contains the selected country's name.

3. ***Verifying the user's answer.*** Add lines 64–69 of Fig. 17.25 to `submitButton_Click`. The `If...Then...Else` statement (lines 65–69) determines whether the user's response matches the correct answer and displays `"Correct!"` in the `Label` if the user's response matches the correct answer (line 66); otherwise, it displays `"Sorry, incorrect."` (line 68).

4. ***Informing the user that the quiz is over when five flags have been displayed.*** Add lines 71–80 of Fig. 17.26 to the `submitButton_Click` event handler. If five flags have been displayed, the `Label` displays text informing the user that the quiz is over (line 73), the `nextButton` is disabled (line 74) and the `countriesComboBox` is disabled (line 75)—by setting its `Enabled` property to `False`.

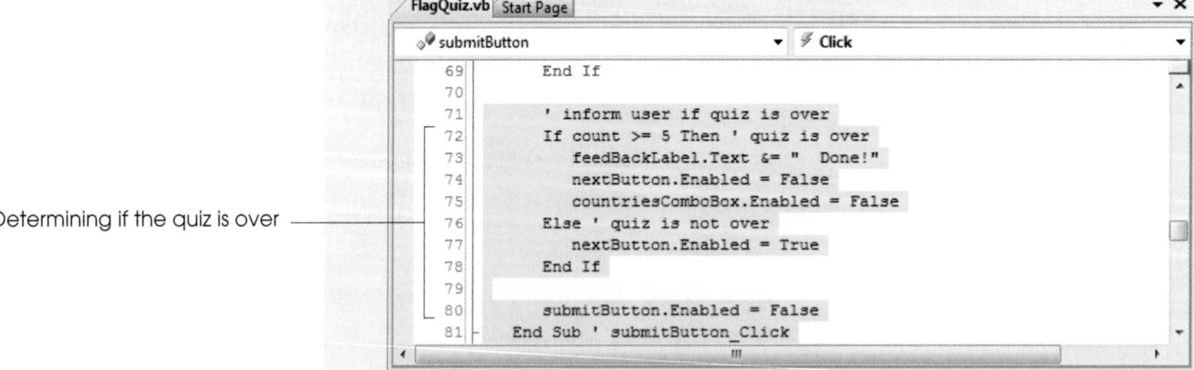

Figure 17.26 Testing whether the quiz is finished.

5. ***Continuing the quiz when fewer than five flags have been shown.*** If the quiz is not finished (that is, `count` is less than `5`), the application enables the **Next Flag** `Button` (line 77). The functionality of the **Next Flag** `Button` will be discussed in the next box. Line 80 disables the `submitButton`.

6. ***Saving the project.*** Select **File > Save All** to save your modified code.

The user requests the next flag in the quiz by clicking the **Next Flag** `Button`. The application then displays the next flag and increments the number of flags shown. In the following box, you implement this functionality.

Displaying the Next Flag

1. ***Adding the Next Flag `Button`'s `Click` event handler to the application.*** Return to **Design** view (**View > Designer**). Double click the **Next Flag** `Button` to generate the `Click` event handler `nextButton_Click`. Format it as shown in lines 83–85 of Fig. 17.27.

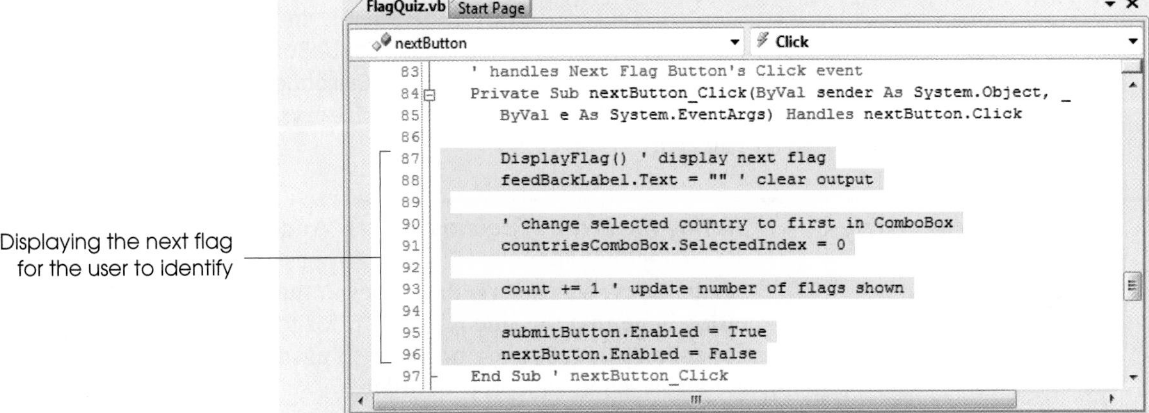

FlagQuiz.vb
Start Page
nextButton
Click
83 ' handles Next Flag Button's Click event
84 Private Sub nextButton_Click(ByVal sender As System.Object, _
85 ByVal e As System.EventArgs) Handles nextButton.Click
86
87 DisplayFlag() ' display next flag
88 feedBackLabel.Text = "" ' clear output
89
90 ' change selected country to first in ComboBox
91 countriesComboBox.SelectedIndex = 0
92
93 count += 1 ' update number of flags shown
94
95 submitButton.Enabled = True
96 nextButton.Enabled = False
97 End Sub ' nextButton_Click
Displaying the next flag for the user to identify

Figure 17.27 **Next Flag** `Button` `Click` event handler.

2. ***Displaying the next flag.*** Add line 87 of Fig. 17.27 to the empty event handler. This line calls procedure `DisplayFlag` to place the next flag in the `PictureBox`.
3. ***Clearing the previous results.*** Add line 88 of Fig. 17.27 to the event handler to clear the output `Label`, deleting the results of the previous question.
4. ***Resetting the ComboBox.*** Add lines 90–91 of Fig. 17.27 to the event handler. Line 91 sets property `SelectedIndex` of `countriesComboBox` to `0`, which selects and displays the first item in the `ComboBox`'s drop-down list.
5. ***Updating the number of flags shown.*** Add line 93 of Fig. 17.27 to the event handler to update instance variable `count` to indicate that one more flag has been shown.
6. ***Enabling the Submit `Button` and disabling the Next Flag `Button`.*** Add lines 95–96 of Fig. 17.27 to the event handler. Line 95 enables the **Submit** `Button` and line 96 disables the **Next Flag** `Button`. This is a visual reminder to the user that an answer must be submitted before another flag can be displayed.
7. ***Saving the project.*** Select **File > Save All** to save your modified code.

SELF-REVIEW

1. Property ________ specifies the source of the data displayed in the `ComboBox`.
   a) `ComboData` b) `Source`
   c) `DataList` d) `DataSource`

2. `ComboBox` property ________ is 0 when the first `ComboBox` item is selected.
   a) `SelectedIndex` b) `SelectedValue`
   c) `Index` d) `SelectedNumber`

Answers: 1) d. 2) a.

17.5 Sorting Arrays

Sorting data refers to arranging the data into some particular order, such as ascending or descending order. Sorting is one of the most popular computing capabilities. For example, a bank sorts checks by account number so that it can prepare individual bank statements at the end of each month. Telephone companies sort account information by last name and, within last-name listings, by first name, to make it easy to find phone numbers. Virtually every organization must sort some data, and often, massive amounts of it. In this section, you learn how to sort the values in an array so that you can alphabetize the list of countries in the **Flag Quiz** application.

Users are able to find a country name in the `ComboBox` faster if the country names are alphabetized. [*Note:* Class `ComboBox` contains property `Sorted`, which, when set to `True`, sorts the items in the `ComboBox` alphabetically. We do not use this property because this tutorial focuses on arrays.] The following box shows you how to sort an array.

Sorting an Array

1. ***Sorting the array of country names.*** Add line 17 of Fig. 17.28 to event handler `FlagQuizForm_Load`. Line 17 passes array `countries` to method `Array.Sort`, which sorts the values in the array into ascending alphabetical order. Note that this line is placed prior to assigning array `countries` to the `ComboBox`'s `DataSource` property to ensure that the items in the `ComboBox` are displayed in alphabetical order.

Alphabetizing country names in the array

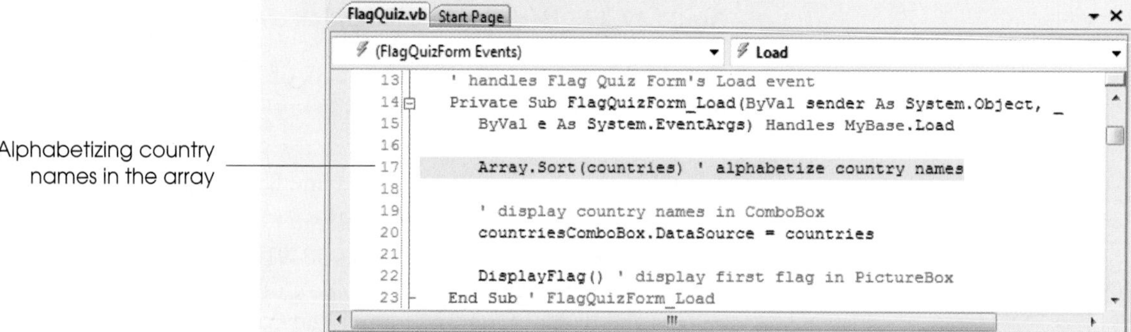

Figure 17.28 Sorting the array of country names.

2. ***Running the application.*** Select **Debug > Start Debugging** to run your application. The country names should now be alphabetized. Enter different answers and make sure that the proper message is displayed based on whether the answer is correct. Make sure that after five answers have been entered, the text **Done!** is appended to the current message displayed.

3. ***Closing the application.*** Close your running application by clicking its close box.

4. ***Closing the IDE.*** Close the Visual Basic IDE by clicking its close box.

Figure 17.29 presents the source code for the **Flag Quiz** application. The lines of code that contain new programming concepts you learned in this tutorial are highlighted.

Declaring and initializing an array in one statement

```
Public Class FlagQuizForm
   ' String array stores country names
   Dim countries As String() = {"Russia", "China", "Australia", _
      "United States", "Italy", "South Africa", "Brazil", "Spain"}
```

Figure 17.29 **Flag Quiz** application's code. (Part 1 of 3.)

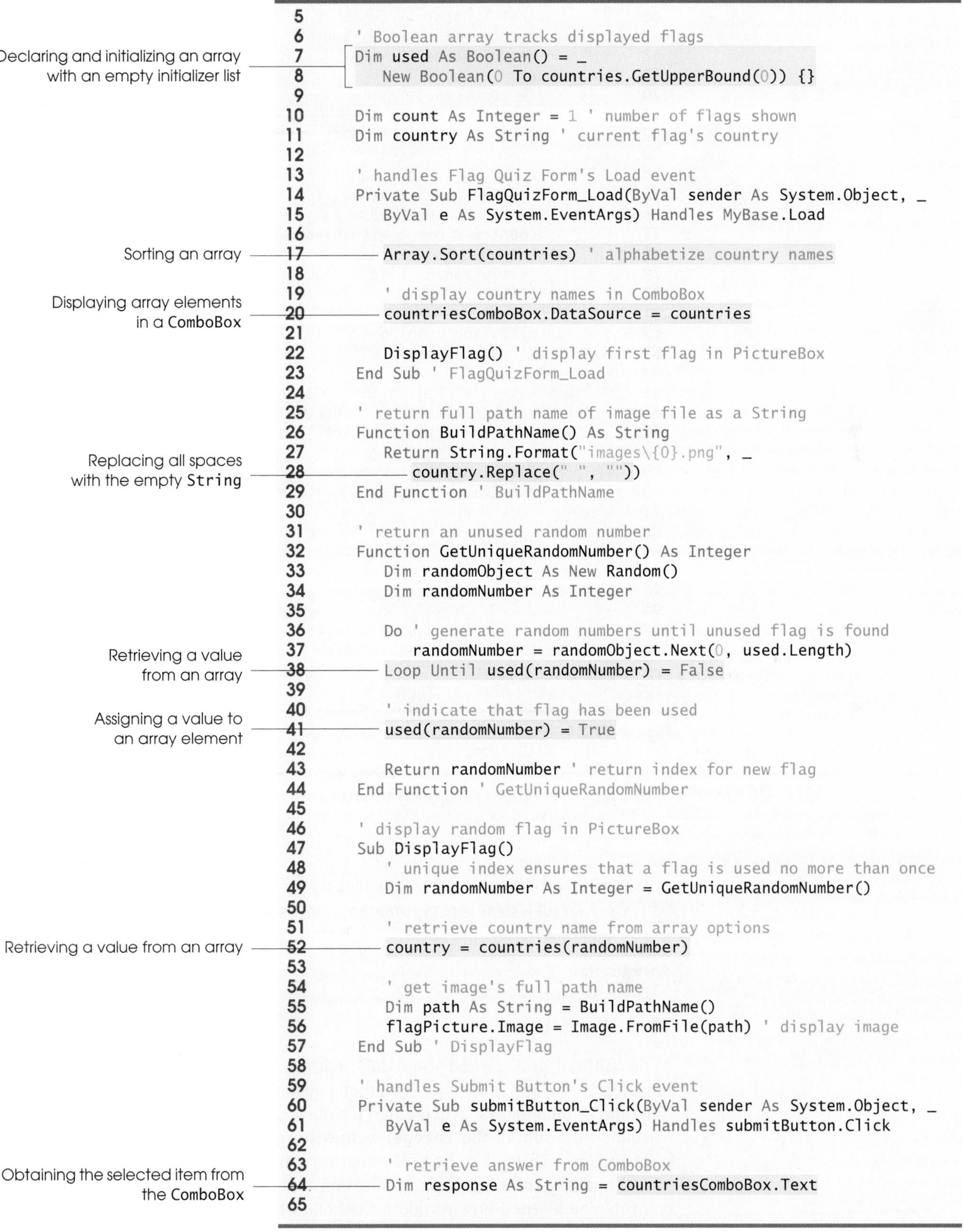


```

   ' Boolean array tracks displayed flags
   Dim used As Boolean() = _
      New Boolean(0 To countries.GetUpperBound(0)) {}

   Dim count As Integer = 1 ' number of flags shown
   Dim country As String ' current flag's country

   ' handles Flag Quiz Form's Load event
   Private Sub FlagQuizForm_Load(ByVal sender As System.Object, _
      ByVal e As System.EventArgs) Handles MyBase.Load

      Array.Sort(countries) ' alphabetize country names

      ' display country names in ComboBox
      countriesComboBox.DataSource = countries

      DisplayFlag() ' display first flag in PictureBox
   End Sub ' FlagQuizForm_Load

   ' return full path name of image file as a String
   Function BuildPathName() As String
      Return String.Format("images\{0}.png", _
         country.Replace(" ", ""))
   End Function ' BuildPathName

   ' return an unused random number
   Function GetUniqueRandomNumber() As Integer
      Dim randomObject As New Random()
      Dim randomNumber As Integer

      Do ' generate random numbers until unused flag is found
         randomNumber = randomObject.Next(0, used.Length)
      Loop Until used(randomNumber) = False

      ' indicate that flag has been used
      used(randomNumber) = True

      Return randomNumber ' return index for new flag
   End Function ' GetUniqueRandomNumber

   ' display random flag in PictureBox
   Sub DisplayFlag()
      ' unique index ensures that a flag is used no more than once
      Dim randomNumber As Integer = GetUniqueRandomNumber()

      ' retrieve country name from array options
      country = countries(randomNumber)

      ' get image's full path name
      Dim path As String = BuildPathName()
      flagPicture.Image = Image.FromFile(path) ' display image
   End Sub ' DisplayFlag

   ' handles Submit Button's Click event
   Private Sub submitButton_Click(ByVal sender As System.Object, _
      ByVal e As System.EventArgs) Handles submitButton.Click

      ' retrieve answer from ComboBox
      Dim response As String = countriesComboBox.Text

```

Figure 17.29 **Flag Quiz** application's code. (Part 2 of 3.)

```
        ' verify answer
        If response = country Then
           feedBackLabel.Text = "Correct!"
        Else
           feedBackLabel.Text = "Sorry, incorrect."
        End If

        ' inform user if quiz is over
        If count >= 5 Then ' quiz is over
           feedBackLabel.Text &= " Done!"
           nextButton.Enabled = False
           countriesComboBox.Enabled = False
        Else ' quiz is not over
           nextButton.Enabled = True
        End If

        submitButton.Enabled = False
     End Sub ' submitButton_Click

     ' handles Next Flag Button's Click event
     Private Sub nextButton_Click(ByVal sender As System.Object, _
        ByVal e As System.EventArgs) Handles nextButton.Click

        DisplayFlag() ' display next flag
        feedBackLabel.Text = "" ' clear output

        ' change selected country to first in ComboBox
        countriesComboBox.SelectedIndex = 0

        count += 1 ' update number of flags shown

        submitButton.Enabled = True
        nextButton.Enabled = False
     End Sub ' nextButton_Click
  End Class ' FlagQuizForm
```

Setting the selected **ComboBox** item

Figure 17.29 **Flag Quiz** application's code. (Part 3 of 3.)

SELF-REVIEW

1. The process of ordering the elements of an array is called ________ the array.
   a) allocating
   b) sorting
   c) declaring
   d) initializing

2. Which of the following sorts array `averageRainfall`?
   a) `Array(averageRainfall).Sort()`
   b) `Sort.Array(averageRainfall)`
   c) `Sort(averageRainfall)`
   d) `Array.Sort(averageRainfall)`

Answers: 1) b. 2) d.

17.6 Wrap-Up

In this tutorial, you learned about data structures called arrays, which normally contain elements of the same type. You then learned how to create, initialize and access one-dimensional arrays. You created a simple application called **Sum Array**, which calculated the sum of the `Integer` values stored in an array. You studied pseudocode and an ACE table to help you begin creating the **Flag Quiz** application.

In building the **Flag Quiz** application, you were introduced to the `ComboBox` control. You learned how to add a `ComboBox` to the `Form` and modify the `ComboBox`'s appearance. You then populated the `ComboBox` with data from an array. You reviewed how to display images in a `PictureBox` and how to generate random numbers by using an object of class `Random`.

You were introduced to `String` method `Replace` (for replacing characters in a `String`). You learned how to sort an array by using method `Array.Sort`.

In the next tutorial, you learn how to create more sophisticated arrays with two dimensions, and use them to implement a student grades application. Two-dimensional arrays are like tables organized in rows and columns.

SKILLS SUMMARY

Creating an Array

- Declare the array using the format:

  `Dim` *arrayName* `As` *arrayType*`()`

  where *arrayName* is the reference name of the array, and *arrayType* is the type of data that will be stored in the array.
- If you know the number of elements in advance you can use

  `Dim` *arrayName*`(0 To` *maxIndex*`) As` *arrayType*

  or

  `Dim` *arrayName* `As` *arrayType*`() = New` *arrayType*`(0 To` *maxIndex*`) {}`

  to specify an array with a high index of *maxIndex*.

Assigning an Array Object to an Array Variable

- Use keyword `New` as in the statement:

  arrayName `= New` *arrayType*`()` {*arrayInitializerList*}

  where *arrayInitializerList* is a comma-separated list of the items that initialize the elements of the array.

Declaring and Initializing an Array with an Initializer List

- Use keyword `New` as in the statement:

  `Dim` *arrayName* `As` *arrayType*`() = New` *arrayType*`()` {*arrayInitializerList*}

  or use the shorthand notation

  `Dim` *arrayName* `As` *arrayType*`() =` {*arrayInitializerList*}

  in which the compiler implicitly uses the keyword `New`.

Referring to Element *n* of an Array

- Enclose the index *n* in parentheses after the array name.

Obtaining the Number of Elements in an Array

- Use property `Length`.

Obtaining the Index of the Last Element in a One-Dimensional Array

- Invoke method `GetUpperBound` with `0` as its argument, or use *arrayName*`.Length - 1`.

Combining `TextBox` Features With `ListBox` Features

- Use a `ComboBox` control.

Setting the Maximum Number of Drop-Down Items a ComboBox's List Displays

- Use property `MaxDropDownItems`.

Specifying the Source of Data Displayed in a ComboBox

- Use property `DataSource`.

Obtaining the Selected Text in a ComboBox

- Use `ComboBox` property `Text`.

Changing the Style of a ComboBox

- Use property `DropDownStyle`.

Sorting an Array into Ascending Order

- Pass the array to be sorted as the argument to method `Array.Sort`.

Replacing Characters in a String

- Use method Replace with two String arguments—the substring to locate and replace, and the replacement String.
- The method returns a copy of the original String with appropriate replacements (if any).

KEY TERMS

array—A data structure containing data items of the same type.

array bounds—Integers that determine what indices can be used to access an element in an array. The lower bound is 0; the upper bound is the length of the array minus one.

Array.Sort method—Sorts the values of an array into ascending order.

ComboBox control—Combines a TextBox with a ListBox.

DataSource property of class ComboBox—Specifies the source of items listed in a ComboBox.

data structure—Groups and organizes related data.

DropDownList value of DropDownStyle property —Specifies that a ComboBox is not editable.

DropDownStyle property of class ComboBox—Property of the ComboBox control that specifies the appearance of the ComboBox.

element—An item in an array.

Enabled property of class ComboBox—Specifies whether a user can select an item from a ComboBox.

GetUpperBound method of class Array—Returns an array's highest index.

index—An array element's position number, also called a subscript. An index must be zero, a positive integer or an integer expression that yields a non-negative result. If an application uses an expression as an index, the expression is evaluated first, to determine the index.

indexed array name—The array name followed by an index enclosed in parentheses. The indexed array name can be used on the left side of an assignment statement to place a new value into an array element. The indexed array name can be used in the right side of an assignment to retrieve the value of that array element.

initializer list—The required braces ({ and }) surrounding the initial values of the elements in an array. When the initializer list is empty, the elements in the array are initialized to the default value for the array's data type.

length of an array—The number of elements in an array.

Length property of class Array—Contains the length of (or number of elements in) an array.

MaxDropDownItems property of class ComboBox—Property of the ComboBox control that specifies how many items can be displayed in the drop-down list. If the ComboBox has more elements than this, it provides a scrollbar to access all of them.

one-dimensional array—An array that uses only one index.

position number—A value that indicates a specific location within an array. Position numbers begin at 0 (zero).

Replace method of class String—Returns a copy of the String for which it is called. Replaces all occurrences of the characters in its first String argument with the characters in its second String argument.

SelectedIndex property of class ComboBox—Specifies the index of the selected item. Returns -1 if no item is selected.

Sorted property of class ComboBox—When set to True, sorts the items in a ComboBox alphabetically.

subscript—*See* index.

Text property of class ComboBox—Returns the currently selected String in the ComboBox.

GUI DESIGN GUIDELINES

ComboBoxes

- Each ComboBox should have a descriptive Label that describes the ComboBox's contents.
- If a ComboBox's content should not be editable, set its DropDownStyle property to DropDownList.

CONTROLS, EVENTS, PROPERTIES & METHODS

ComboBox ComboBox This control allows the user to select from a drop-down list of options.

- ***In action***

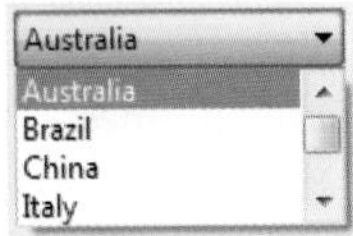

- ***Properties***

`DataSource`—Specifies the source of the items listed in a `ComboBox`.

`DropDownStyle`—Specifies a `ComboBox`'s appearance.

`Enabled`—Specifies whether a user can select an item from the `ComboBox`.

`Location`—Specifies the location of the `ComboBox` control relative to the top-left corner of the container (e.g., a `Form` or a `GroupBox`).

`MaxDropDownItems`—Specifies the maximum number of items the `ComboBox` can display in its drop-down list. If the `ComboBox` has more elements than this, it provides a scrollbar to access all of them.

`Name`—Specifies the name used to access the `ComboBox` control programmatically. The name should be appended with the `ComboBox` suffix.

`SelectedIndex`—Specifies the index of the selected item. Returns `-1` if no item is selected.

`Size`—Specifies the width and height (in pixels) of the `ComboBox` control.

`Sorted`—When set to `True`, displays the `ComboBox` options in alphabetical order or ascending order.

`Text`—The currently selected `String` in the `ComboBox`.

`Array` This data structure stores a fixed number of elements of the same type.

- ***Property***

`Length`—Specifies the number of elements in the array.

- ***Methods***

`GetUpperBound`—Returns the array's highest index.

`Sort`—Orders an array's elements. An array of numerical values would be organized in ascending order, and an array of `String`s would be organized in alphabetical order.

`String` The `String` class represents a series of characters treated as a single unit.

- ***Methods***

`Format`—Arranges a `String` in a specified format.

`Replace`—Returns a copy of the `String` for which it is called. Replaces all occurrences of the characters in its first `String` argument with the characters in its second `String` argument.

MULTIPLE-CHOICE QUESTIONS

17.1 Arrays can be declared to hold values of ________.

a) type `Double` b) type `Integer`
c) type `String` d) any data type

17.2 An array's elements are related by the fact that they have the same name and ________.

a) constant value b) subscript
c) type d) value

17.3 Method ________ returns an array's highest index.

a) `GetUpperBound` b) `GetUpperLimit`
c) `GetHighestIndex` d) `GetUpperSubscript`

17.4 The first element in every array is the ________.

a) subscript
b) zeroth element
c) length of the array
d) smallest value in the array

17.5 Arrays ________.

a) are controls
b) always have one dimension
c) keep data in sorted order at all times
d) are objects

17.6 The initializer list can ________.

a) be used to determine the size of the array
b) contain a comma-separated list of initial values for the array elements
c) be empty
d) All of the above

17.7 Which method call sorts array `words` in ascending order?

a) `Array.Sort(words)`
b) `words.SortArray()`
c) `Array.Sort(words, 1)`
d) `Sort(words)`

17.8 The `ComboBox` control combines a `TextBox` control with a ________ control.

a) `DateTimePicker`
b) `ListBox`
c) `NumericUpDown`
d) `Label`

17.9 To search for a period (`.`) in a `String` called `test`, use the expression ________.

a) `String.Search(test, ".")`
b) `String.IndexOf(test, ".")`
c) `test.IndexOf(".")`
d) `test.Search(".")`

17.10 Property ________ contains the size of an array.

a) `Elements`
b) `ArraySize`
c) `Length`
d) `Size`

EXERCISES

17.11 ***(Enhanced Flag Quiz Application)*** Enhance the **Flag Quiz** application by counting the number of questions that were answered correctly (Fig. 17.30). After all the questions have been answered, display a message in a `Label` that describes how well the user performed. The following table shows which messages to display:

Number of correct answers	Message
5	`Excellent!`
4	`Very good`
3	`Good`
2	`Poor`
1 or 0	`Fail`

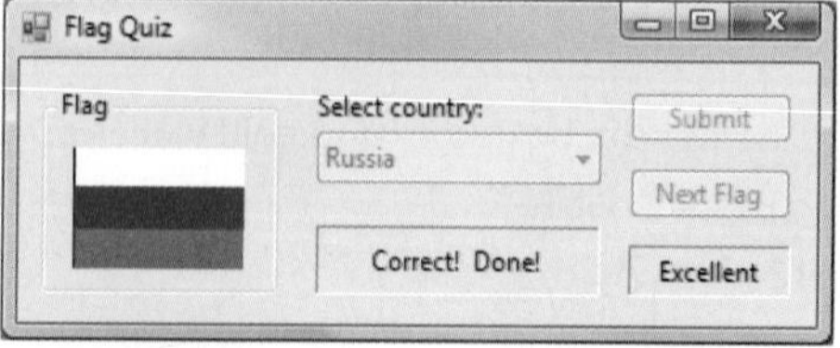

Figure 17.30 Enhanced **Flag Quiz** application's GUI.

a) ***Copying the template to your working directory.*** Copy the directory `C:\Examples\Tutorial17\Exercises\FlagQuiz2` to your `C:\SimplyVB2008` directory.

b) ***Opening the application's template file.*** Double click `FlagQuiz2.sln` in the `FlagQuiz2` directory to open the application.

c) ***Adding a variable to count the number of correct answers.*** Add an instance variable `numberCorrect`, and initialize it to `0`. You use this variable to count the number of correct answers submitted by the user.

d) ***Counting the correct answers.*** Increment `numberCorrect` in the **Submit** `Button`'s event handler whenever the submitted answer is correct.

e) ***Displaying the message.*** Write a procedure `DisplayMessage` that displays a message in `scoreLabel` depending on the value of `numberCorrect`. Call this procedure from the **Submit** `Button`'s event handler when the quiz is completed.

f) ***Running the application.*** Select **Debug > Start Debugging** to run your application. The finished application should behave as in Fig. 17.30. Run the application a few times and enter a different number of correct answers each time to verify that the correct feedback is displayed.

g) ***Closing the application.*** Close your running application by clicking its close box.

h) ***Closing the IDE.*** Close the Visual Basic IDE by clicking its close box.

17.12 *(Salary Survey Application)* Use a one-dimensional array to solve the following problem: A company pays its salespeople on a commission basis. The salespeople receive $200 per week, plus 9% of their gross sales for that week. For example, a salesperson who grosses $5,000 in sales in a week receives $200 plus 9% of $5,000, a total of $650. Write an application (using an array of counters) that determines how many of the salespeople earned salaries in each of the following ranges (assuming that each salesperson's salary is truncated to an integer amount): $200–299, $300–399, $400–499, $500–599, $600–699, $700–799, $800–899, $900–999 and over $999.

Allow the user to enter the sales for each employee in a `TextBox`. The user clicks the **Calculate** `Button` to calculate the salesperson's salary. When the user is done entering this information, clicking the **Show Totals** `Button` displays how many of the salespeople earned salaries in each of the above ranges. The finished application should behave like Fig. 17.31.

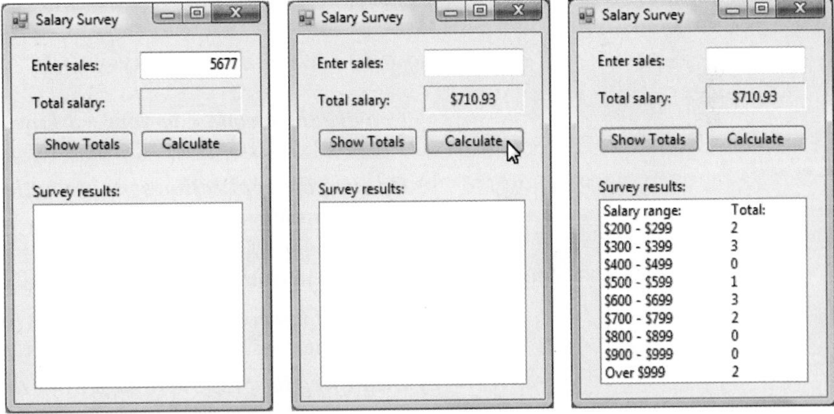

Figure 17.31 **Salary Survey** application's GUI.

a) ***Copying the template to your working directory.*** Copy the directory `C:\Examples\Tutorial17\Exercises\SalarySurvey` to your `C:\SimplyVB2008` directory.

b) ***Opening the application's template file.*** Double click `SalarySurvey.sln` in the `SalarySurvey` directory to open the application.

c) ***Creating an array of salary ranges.*** Create a `String` array, and initialize it to contain the salary ranges (the `Strings` displayed in the `ListBox`'s first column).

d) ***Creating an array that represents the number of salaries in each range.*** Create an empty `Integer` array to store the number of employees who earn salaries in each range.

e) ***Creating an event handler for the Calculate `Button`.*** Write event handler `calculateButton_Click`. Obtain the user input from the **Enter sales:** `TextBox`. Calculate the commission due to the employee and add that amount to the base salary. Increment the element in array `salaries` that corresponds to the employee's salary range. This event handler should also display the employee's salary in the **Total salary:** `Label`.

f) ***Writing an event handler for the Show Totals Button.*** Create event handler `totalsButton_Click` to display the salary distribution in the `ListBox`. Use a `For...Next` statement to display the range (an element in array `salaryRanges`) and the number of employees whose salary falls in that range (an element in array `salaries`).

g) ***Running the application.*** Select **Debug > Start Debugging** to run your application. Enter several sales amounts using the **Calculate** `Button`. Click the **Show Totals** `Button` and verify that the proper amounts are displayed for each salary range, based on the salaries calculated from your input.

h) ***Closing the application.*** Close your running application by clicking its close box.

i) ***Closing the IDE.*** Close the Visual Basic IDE by clicking its close box.

17.13 ***(Cafeteria Survey Application)*** Twenty students were asked to rate, on a scale from 1 to 10, the quality of the food in the student cafeteria, with 1 being "awful" and 10 being "excellent." Allow the user input to be entered using a `ComboBox`. Use an `Integer` array to store the frequency of each rating. Display the frequencies as a histogram in a multiline, scrollable `TextBox`. Figure 17.32 demonstrates the completed application.

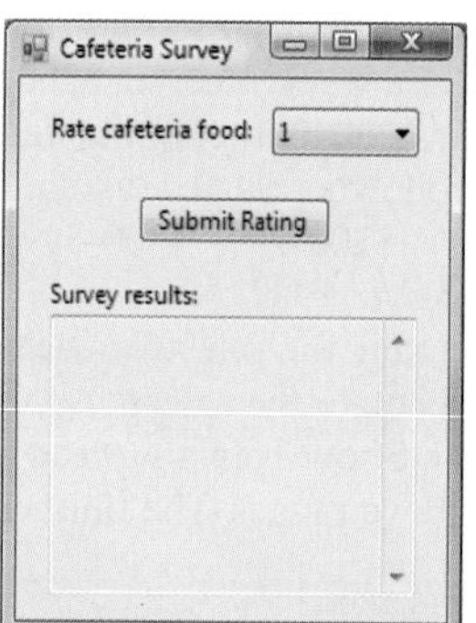

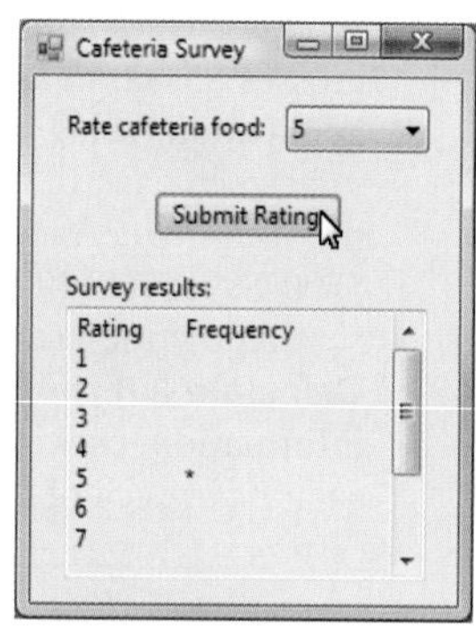

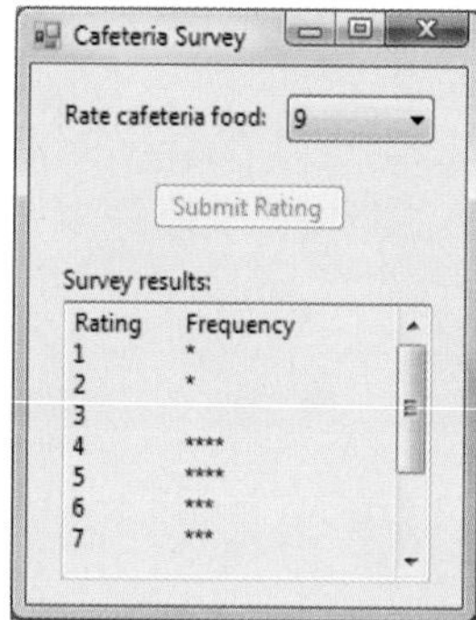

Figure 17.32 Cafeteria Survey GUI.

a) ***Copying the template to your working directory.*** Copy the directory `C:\Examples\Tutorial17\Exercises\CafeteriaSurvey` to your `C:\SimplyVB2008` directory.

b) ***Opening the application's template file.*** Double click `CafeteriaSurvey.sln` in the `CafeteriaSurvey` directory.

c) ***Creating an array of the possible ratings.*** Create an array of 10 integers, called `choices`, to contain the integers in the range 1–10, inclusive.

d) ***Adding a ComboBox.*** Add a `ComboBox` to the GUI as in Fig. 17.32. The `ComboBox` will display the possible ratings. Set property `DropDownStyle` to `DropDownList`.

e) ***Displaying the possible ratings when the application starts.*** Write the event handler for the `Load` event so that the `DataSource` of the `ComboBox` is set to `choices` when the application starts.

f) ***Creating an array to store the responses.*** Create an `Integer` array of length `11` named `responses`. This will be used to store the number of responses in each of the 10 categories (element 0 will not be used).

g) ***Counting the number of responses.*** Create an `Integer` variable named `responseCounter` to keep track of how many responses have been input.

h) ***Storing the responses.*** Write the event handler `submitButton_Click` to increment `responseCounter`. Store the response in array `responses`. Call procedure `DisplayHistogram` to display the results.

i) ***Creating procedure `DisplayHistogram`.*** The procedure template is already provided for you in the application template. Add a header to the `TextBox`. Use nested `For...Next` loops to display the ratings in the first column. The second column uses asterisks to indicate how many students surveyed submitted the corresponding rating.

j) ***Running the application.*** Select **Debug > Start Debugging** to run your application. Enter 20 responses using the **Submit Rating** `Button`. Verify that the resulting histogram displays the responses entered.

k) ***Closing the application.*** Close your running application by clicking its close box.

l) ***Closing the IDE.*** Close the Visual Basic IDE by clicking its close box.

What does this code do?

17.14 This function declares `numbers` as its parameter. What does it return?

```
Function Mystery(ByVal numbers As Integer()) As Integer()
   Dim length As Integer = numbers.Length - 1
   Dim tempArray As Integer() = New Integer(0 To length) {}

   For i As Integer = length To 0 Step -1
      tempArray(length - i) = numbers(i)
   Next

   Return tempArray
End Function ' Mystery
```

What's wrong with this code?

17.15 The code that follows uses a `For...Next` loop to sum the elements in an array. Find the error(s) in the following code:

```
Sub SumArray()
   Dim sum As Integer
   Dim numbers As Integer() = {1, 2, 3, 4, 5, 6, 7, 8}

   For counter As Integer = 0 To numbers.Length
      sum += numbers(counter)
   Next
End Sub ' SumArray
```

Programming Challenge

17.16 ***(Road Sign Test Application)*** Write an application that tests the user's knowledge of road signs. Your application should display a random sign image and ask the user to select the sign name from a `ComboBox`. This application should look like Fig. 17.33. [*Hint:* The application is similar to the **Flag Quiz** application.] You can find the images in `C:\Examples\Tutorial17\Exercises\images`. Remember to set `Option Strict` to `On`.

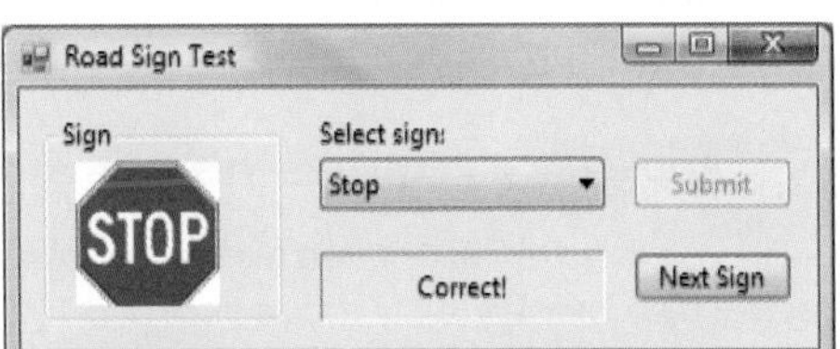

Figure 17.33 **Road Sign Test** GUI.

TUTORIAL

Student Grades Application

Introducing Two-Dimensional Arrays and RadioButtons

Objectives

In this tutorial, you learn to:

- Understand the similarities and differences between one-dimensional and two-dimensional arrays.
- Declare and manipulate two-dimensional arrays.
- Understand how to use two-dimensional arrays.
- Use nested `For...Next` loops.
- Use `RadioButton`s to enable users to select exactly one option out of several.

Outline

In this tutorial, you learn about two-dimensional arrays, which allow you to store multiple values of the same type organized into rows and columns. Two-dimensional arrays are useful for representing tabular data. For example, an instructor could use a two-dimensional array whose rows represent the students in a class and whose columns represent the grades the students received on each of the class's exams. You also learn about the `RadioButton` control, which enables users to choose only one of several options.

18.1 Test-Driving the Student Grades Application

You implement the **Student Grades** application by using a two-dimensional array. This application must meet the following requirements:

Application Requirements

A teacher issues three tests to a class of 10 students. The grades on these tests are integers in the range from 0 to 100. The teacher has asked you to develop an application to keep track of each student's average and the class average. The teacher has also asked that there be a choice to view the grades as either numbers or letters. Letter grades should be calculated according to the grading system:

90–100	A
80–89	B
70–79	C
60–69	D
Below 60	F

The application should allow a user to input the student's three test grades, then compute each student's average and the class average. The application should display number grades by default.

The student's average is equal to the sum of the student's three grades divided by three. The class average is equal to the sum of all of the students' grades divided by the number of tests taken. You begin by test-driving the completed application. Then you learn the additional Visual Basic capabilities needed to create your own version of this application.

Test-Driving the Student Grades Application

1. ***Opening the completed application.*** Open the directory `C:\Examples\Tutorial18\CompletedApplication\StudentGrades` to locate the **Student Grades** application. Double click `StudentGrades.sln` to open the application in the Visual Basic IDE.

2. ***Running the Student Grades application.*** Select **Debug > Start Debugging** to run the application (Fig. 18.1).

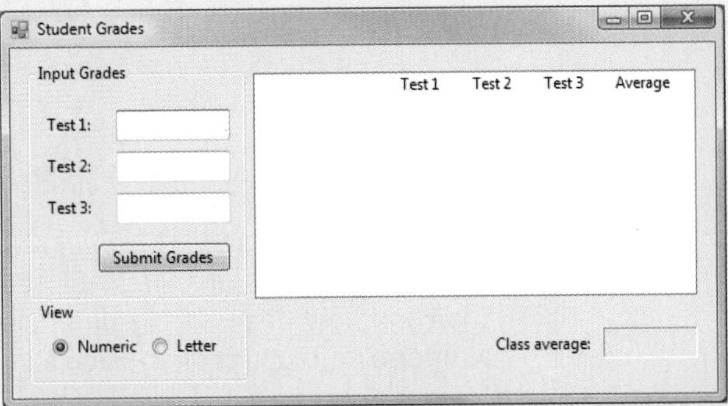

Figure 18.1 Running the completed **Student Grades** application.

3. ***Entering data.*** Type `87`, `94` and `93` in the **Test 1:**, **Test 2:** and **Test 3:** `TextBox`es, respectively (Fig. 18.2). Click the **Submit Grades** `Button` to calculate the student's average and display the student's test scores and average in the `ListBox` (Fig. 18.3). Enter grades for nine more students. Once 10 students have been entered, all the controls in the **Input Grades** `GroupBox` are disabled (Fig. 18.4).

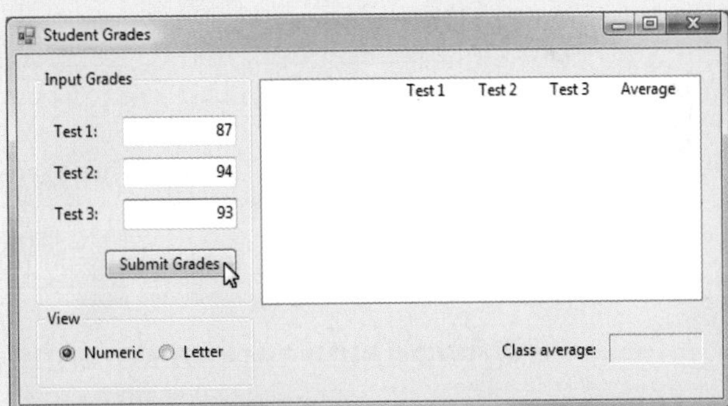

Figure 18.2 Inputting data to the **Student Grades** application.

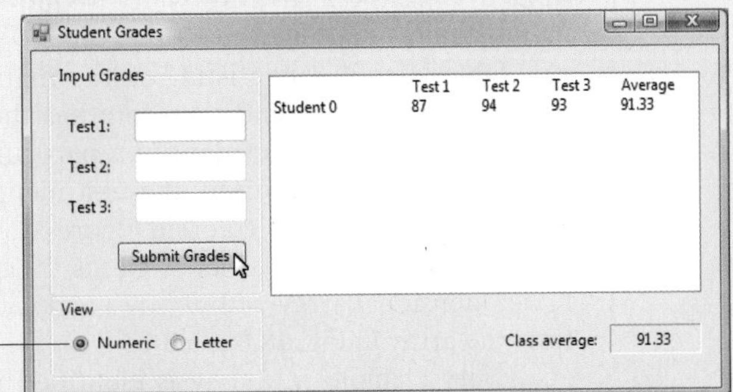

Figure 18.3 Displaying the student's numerical grade.

(cont.)

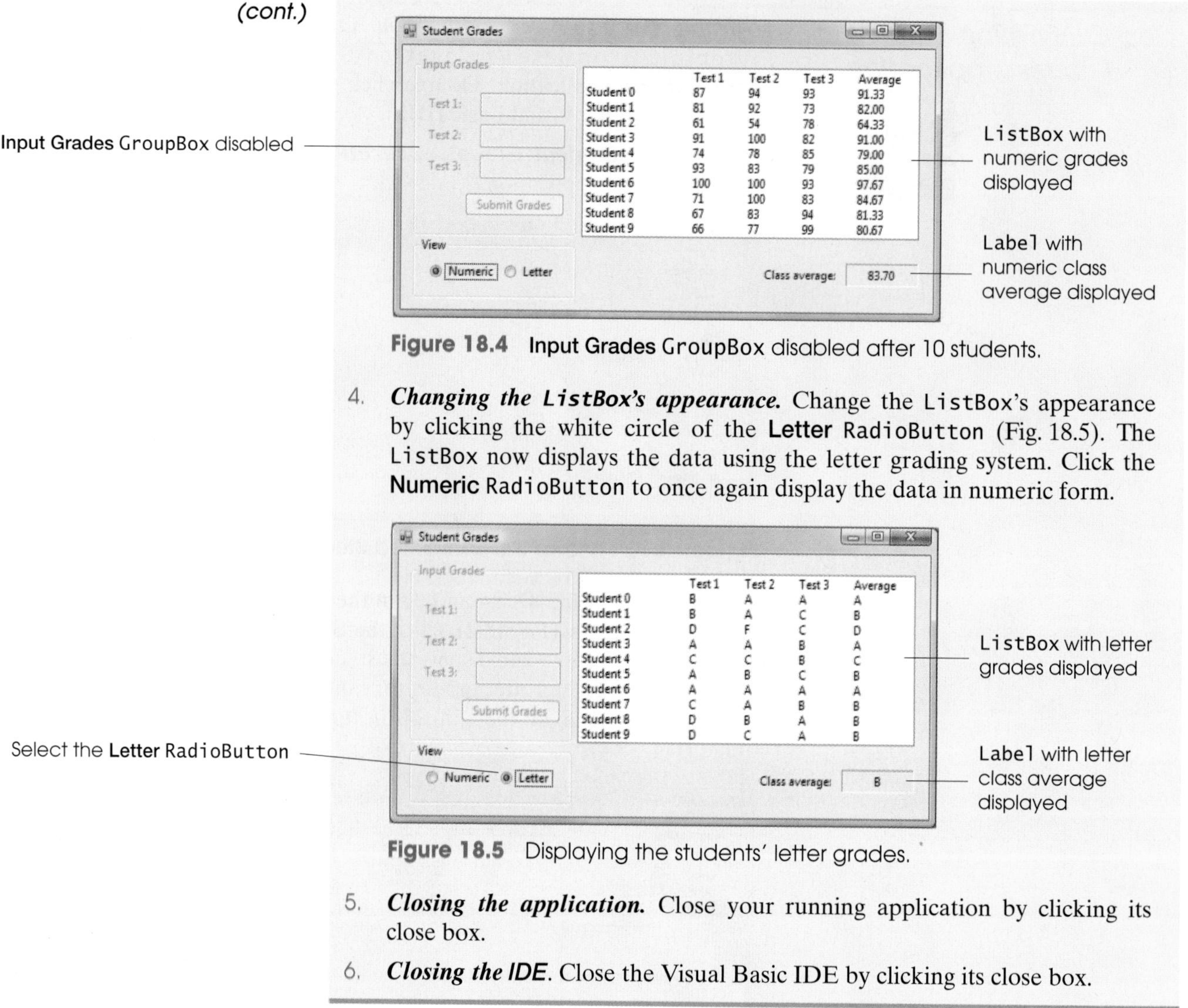

	Test 1	Test 2	Test 3	Average
Student 0	87	94	93	91.33
Student 1	81	92	73	82.00
Student 2	61	54	78	64.33
Student 3	91	100	82	91.00
Student 4	74	78	85	79.00
Student 5	93	83	79	85.00
Student 6	100	100	93	97.67
Student 7	71	100	83	84.67
Student 8	67	83	94	81.33
Student 9	66	77	99	80.67

Figure 18.4 Input Grades GroupBox disabled after 10 students.

4. ***Changing the ListBox's appearance.*** Change the `ListBox`'s appearance by clicking the white circle of the **Letter** `RadioButton` (Fig. 18.5). The `ListBox` now displays the data using the letter grading system. Click the **Numeric** `RadioButton` to once again display the data in numeric form.

	Test 1	Test 2	Test 3	Average
Student 0	B	A	A	A
Student 1	B	A	C	B
Student 2	D	F	C	D
Student 3	A	A	B	A
Student 4	C	C	B	C
Student 5	A	B	C	B
Student 6	A	A	A	A
Student 7	C	A	B	B
Student 8	D	B	A	B
Student 9	D	C	A	B

Figure 18.5 Displaying the students' letter grades.

5. ***Closing the application.*** Close your running application by clicking its close box.

6. ***Closing the IDE.*** Close the Visual Basic IDE by clicking its close box.

18.2 Two-Dimensional Rectangular Arrays

So far, you've studied one-dimensional arrays, which contain one sequence (or row) of values. In this section, we introduce **two-dimensional arrays** (sometimes called **double-subscripted arrays**), which require two indices to identify particular elements. **Rectangular arrays** are two-dimensional arrays that are often used to represent **tables** of values consisting of information arranged in **rows** and **columns**. Each row is the same size and therefore has the same number of columns (hence, the term "rectangular"). To identify a particular table element, you must specify the two indices—by convention, the first identifies the element's row, and the second identifies the element's column. Figure 18.6 illustrates a two-dimensional rectangular array, named `array`, that contains three rows and four columns. A rectangular two-dimensional array with *m* rows and *n* columns is called an ***m*-by-*n* array**; therefore, the array in Fig. 18.6 is a 3-by-4 array.

Every element in `array` is identified in Fig. 18.6 by an element name of the form `array(i, j)`, where `array` is the name of the array and `i` and `j` are the indices that uniquely identify the row and column of each element in `array`. All row numbers and column numbers in two-dimensional arrays begin with zero, so the elements in the first row each have a first index of `0`; the elements in the last column each have a second index of `3` (Fig. 18.6).

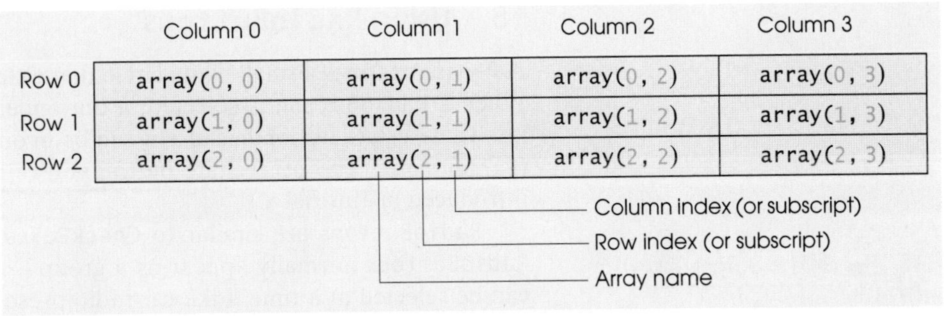

	Column 0	Column 1	Column 2	Column 3
Row 0	array(0, 0)	array(0, 1)	array(0, 2)	array(0, 3)
Row 1	array(1, 0)	array(1, 1)	array(1, 2)	array(1, 3)
Row 2	array(2, 0)	array(2, 1)	array(2, 2)	array(2, 3)

Column index (or subscript)
Row index (or subscript)
Array name

Figure 18.6 Two-dimensional rectangular array with three rows and four columns.

Two-dimensional arrays are initialized much like one-dimensional arrays. For example, a two-dimensional rectangular array, numbers, with two rows and two columns, could be declared and initialized with

```
Dim numbers As Integer(,) = New Integer(0 To 1, 0 To 1) {}
numbers(0, 0) = 1
numbers(0, 1) = 2
numbers(1, 0) = 3
numbers(1, 1) = 4
```

Note that a comma (,) is required inside the parentheses following the data type to indicate that the array is two-dimensional. Similar to one-dimensional arrays, if you know the number of rows and columns at the time you declare the two-dimensional array, you can write the declaration as

```
Dim numbers(0 To 1, 0 To 1) As Integer
```

which creates a two-dimensional array with two rows and two columns. In this case, the compiler implicitly uses the New keyword and initializes all the elements to 0.

Two-dimensional arrays also may be initialized using an initializer list. The preceding initialization could be written on one line as:

```
Dim numbers As Integer(,) = New Integer(,) {{1, 2}, {3, 4}}
```

The values in the initializer list are grouped by row using nested braces, with 1 and 2 initializing numbers(0, 0) and numbers(0, 1), respectively, and 3 and 4 initializing numbers(1, 0) and numbers(1, 1), respectively. The preceding declaration can also be written as

```
Dim numbers As Integer(,) = {{1, 2}, {3, 4}}
```

In this case, the compiler implicitly uses the New keyword to create the array object.

Recall from Tutorial 17 that you can specify the lower bounds of an array implicitly or explicitly. The same is true for each dimension of a two-dimensional array. Accordingly, the array numbers also can be allocated as follows:

```
Dim numbers As Integer(,) = New Integer(1, 1) {}
```

or

```
Dim numbers(1, 1) As Integer
```

SELF-REVIEW

1. Arrays that use two indices are referred to as ________ arrays.
   a) single-subscripted
   b) two-dimensional
   c) double
   d) one-dimensional

2. The expression ________ creates an Integer array of two rows and five columns.
   a) New Integer(0 To 2, 0 To 5) {}
   b) New Integer(0 To 1, 0 To 5) {}
   c) New Integer(0 To 1, 0 To 4) {}
   d) New Integer(0 To 2, 0 To 4) {}

Answers: 1) b. 2) c.

18.3 Using RadioButtons

A **RadioButton** is a small white circle that either is blank or contains a smaller dot. When a RadioButton is selected, a dot appears in the circle. A RadioButton is known as a state button because it can be in only the "on" (True) state or the "off" (False) state. (The other state button you've studied is the CheckBox, which was introduced in Tutorial 8.)

RadioButtons are similar to CheckBoxes in that they are state buttons, but RadioButtons normally appear as a group—only one RadioButton in the group can be selected at a time. Like car-radio preset buttons, which can select only one station at a time, RadioButtons represent a set of **mutually exclusive options**—a set of options of which only one can be selected at a time. By default, all RadioButtons added directly to the Form become part of the same group. To separate RadioButtons into several groups, each RadioButton group must be in a different container (such as a GroupBox).

GUI Design Tip

Use RadioButtons when the user must choose only one option from a group.

GUI Design Tip

Always place each group of RadioButtons in a separate container (such as a GroupBox).

The RadioButton control's **Checked** property indicates whether the RadioButton is checked (contains a small dot) or unchecked (blank). If the RadioButton is checked, the Checked property returns the Boolean value True. If the RadioButton is not checked, the Checked property returns False.

A RadioButton also generates an event when its checked state changes. Event **CheckedChanged** occurs when a RadioButton is either selected or deselected.

The following pseudocode describes the basic operation of the **Student Grades** application:

```
When the user clicks the Submit Grades Button:
    Retrieve the student's grades from the TextBoxes
    Add the student's test scores to the array
    Display the student's test scores and average in the ListBox
    Display the class's average in the Class average: Label
    Clear the student's test scores from the TextBoxes

    If 10 students have been entered
        Disable the input controls

When the user selects the Numeric RadioButton:
    Display each student's numeric test scores and average in the ListBox
    Display the class's numeric average in the Class average: Label

When the user selects the Letter RadioButton:
    Display each student's letter test scores and average in the ListBox
    Display the class's letter average in the Class average: Label
```

Your **Student Grades** application uses the RadioButton control's CheckedChanged event handler to update the ListBox and **Class average:** Label when the user selects either letter or numeric grades for display.

Now that you've test-driven the **Student Grades** application and studied its pseudocode representation, you use an ACE table to help you convert the pseudocode to Visual Basic. Figure 18.7 lists the actions, controls and events that help you complete your own version of this application.

Action/Control/Event (ACE) Table for the Student Grades Application

Action	Control	Event
Label the application's components	inputGroupBox, viewGroupBox, test1Label, test2Label, test3Label, classAverageLabel	Application is run

Figure 18.7 ACE table for the **Student Grades** application. (Part 1 of 2.)

Action	Control	Event
	submitButton	Click
Retrieve the student's grades from the TextBoxes	test1TextBox, test2TextBox, test3TextBox	
Add the student's test scores to the array		
Display the student's test scores and average in the ListBox	gradesListBox	
Display the class's average in the Class average: Label	averageLabel	
Clear the student's test scores from the TextBoxes	test1TextBox, test2TextBox, test3TextBox	
If 10 students have been entered		
Disable the input controls	inputGroupBox	
	numericRadio-Button	Check-Changed
Display each student's numeric test scores and average in the ListBox	gradesListBox	
Display the class's numeric average in the Class average: Label	averageLabel	
	letterRadioButton	Check-Changed
Display each student's letter test scores average in the ListBox	gradesListBox	
Display the class's letter average in the Class average: Label	averageLabel	

Figure 18.7 ACE table for the **Student Grades** application. (Part 2 of 2.)

Now you build your **Student Grades** application, using a two-dimensional array and `RadioButton`s. The `RadioButton`s allow the user to view the students' grades as letters or numbers.

Adding RadioButtons to the View GroupBox

1. ***Copying the template to your working directory.*** Copy the `C:\Examples\Tutorial18\TemplateApplication\StudentGrades` directory to your `C:\SimplyVB2008` directory.
2. ***Opening the Student Grades application's template file.*** Double click `StudentGrades.sln` in the `StudentGrades` directory to open the application in the Visual Basic IDE.
3. ***Adding RadioButtons to the View GroupBox.*** Select the **View** `GroupBox` on the `Form`. Add a `RadioButton` to the `GroupBox` by double clicking the **RadioButton** control,

   RadioButton

   in the **Toolbox**. Repeat this process so that two `RadioButton`s are added to the `GroupBox`. Note that, as with `CheckBoxes`, each `RadioButton` control contains a `Text` property.

(cont.)

4. ***Customizing the RadioButtons.*** Align the RadioButtons horizontally. Rename the left RadioButton by changing its Name property to numericRadioButton, and set its Text property to Numeric. Then set the right RadioButton control's Name property to letterRadioButton, and set its Text property to Letter. Set the Checked property of numericRadioButton to True. Your Form should look similar to Fig. 18.8.

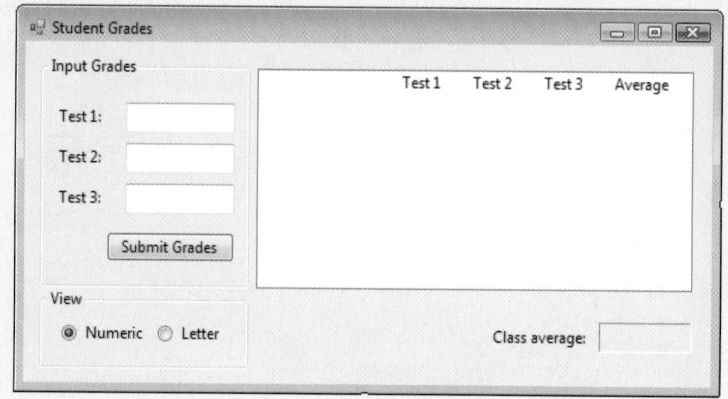

Figure 18.8 RadioButtons placed in the GroupBox.

5. ***Saving the project.*** Select **File > Save All** to save your modified code.

GUI Design Tip

Align groups of RadioButtons either horizontally or vertically.

Good Programming Practice

Append the RadioButton suffix to RadioButton control names.

Error-Prevention Tip

To avoid subtle logic errors, one RadioButton in a group is often selected by default, by setting its Checked property to True. This can be done using code or by setting the value using the **Properties** window.

SELF-REVIEW

1. The ________ property determines whether a RadioButton is selected.
   a) Selected
   b) Clicked
   c) Checked
   d) Enabled
2. The ________ event is raised when a RadioButton is either selected or deselected.
   a) CheckedChanged
   b) Changed
   c) SelectedChanged
   d) None of the above

Answers: 1) c. 2) a.

18.4 Inserting Code into the Student Grades Application

Now that you've placed the controls on the Form, you are ready to write code to interact with the data given by the user. First you declare a two-dimensional array to contain the student test scores.

Declaring a Two-Dimensional Array

1. ***Declaring a two-dimensional array.*** Add lines 2–3 of Fig. 18.9 to your code. Line 2 declares a 10-by-3 array of Integers to contain the test scores. Each row in the array represents a student. Each column represents a test. Note the studentCount instance variable (line 3), which contains the number of students entered by the user so far.

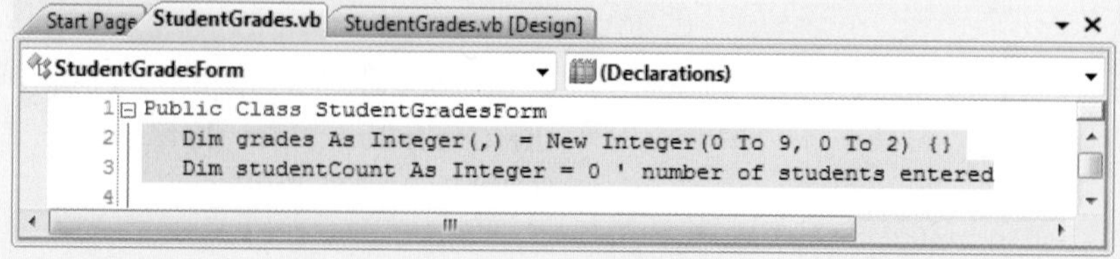

Figure 18.9 Declaring a two-dimensional array.

2. ***Saving the project.*** Select **File > Save All** to save your modified code.

The template code provides an incomplete version of the **Submit Grades** `Button`'s `Click` event handler. You now use the two-dimensional array that you declared in the previous box to finish this event handler.

Finishing the Submit Grades `Button`'s `Click` Event Handler

1. ***Retrieving the student's test scores.*** Double click the **Submit Grades** `Button` to display its `Click` event handler in **Code** view. Add lines 9–12 of Fig. 18.10 to your code. Lines 10–12 add the student's test scores to the `grades` array using the `studentCount` instance variable to add the scores to the appropriate row. You store each test score in a separate column of the array.

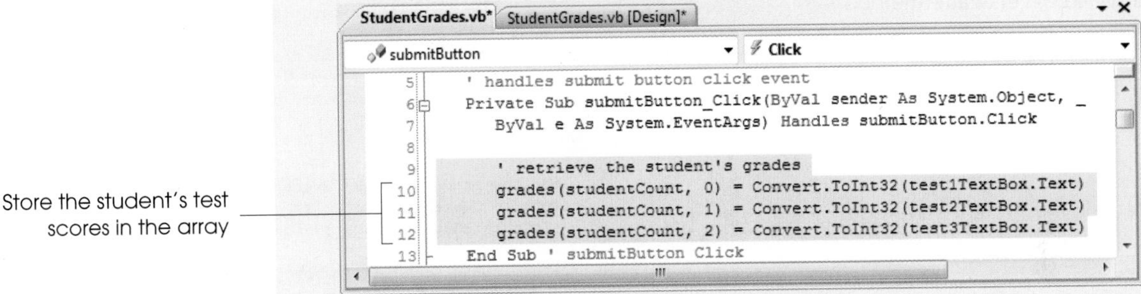
StudentGrades.vb*
StudentGrades.vb [Design]*
submitButton
Click
5 ' handles submit button click event
6 Private Sub submitButton_Click(ByVal sender As System.Object, _
7 ByVal e As System.EventArgs) Handles submitButton.Click
8
9 ' retrieve the student's grades
10 grades(studentCount, 0) = Convert.ToInt32(test1TextBox.Text)
11 grades(studentCount, 1) = Convert.ToInt32(test2TextBox.Text)
12 grades(studentCount, 2) = Convert.ToInt32(test3TextBox.Text)
13 End Sub ' submitButton Click
Store the student's test scores in the array

Figure 18.10 Storing the student's test scores.

2. ***Displaying the output.*** Insert lines 14–41 of Fig. 18.11 into your code. Line 15–16 declare and initialize a `String` variable used to create the output that is added to the `ListBox`. Lines 19–30 use a `For...Next` statement to iterate over each of the student's test scores. Line 19 calls array method `GetUpperBound` to set the final value of the control variable. Recall from Tutorial 17 that method `GetUpperBound` returns the highest index of the dimension specified by the argument passed to the method. In this case, you retrieve the highest index of the array's second dimension, indicated by passing `1` as the argument to `GetUpperBound`. This returns the index of the last column in the `grades` array. Line 21 uses the `Checked` property of `letterRadioButton` to determine how the user wants to view the students' grades. Line 24 calls the `LetterGrade` method to determine the letter grade corresponding to a given numeric grade retrieved from the array—this method has been provided for you in the template. Line 23 adds the letter grade to the `output String`. The `Else` branch of the decision (lines 25–29) adds the information to the `output String` in numeric form.

   Lines 33–34 add the student's test average to the `output String`, adding a `Tab` character for proper formatting. Line 34 passes the row containing the current student's grades to method `CalculateStudentAverage`, which returns the student's test average as a `String`. Note that the `CalculateStudentAverage` method is underlined in blue, indicating a compilation error. This occurs because the method has not been defined yet—you create this method in later steps. Line 38 increments the number of students for which grades have been entered. Line 41 displays the class's test average in the **Class average:** `Label`. Note that method `CalculateClassAverage` is underlined in blue, again indicating a compilation error. You create this method in later steps.

(cont.)

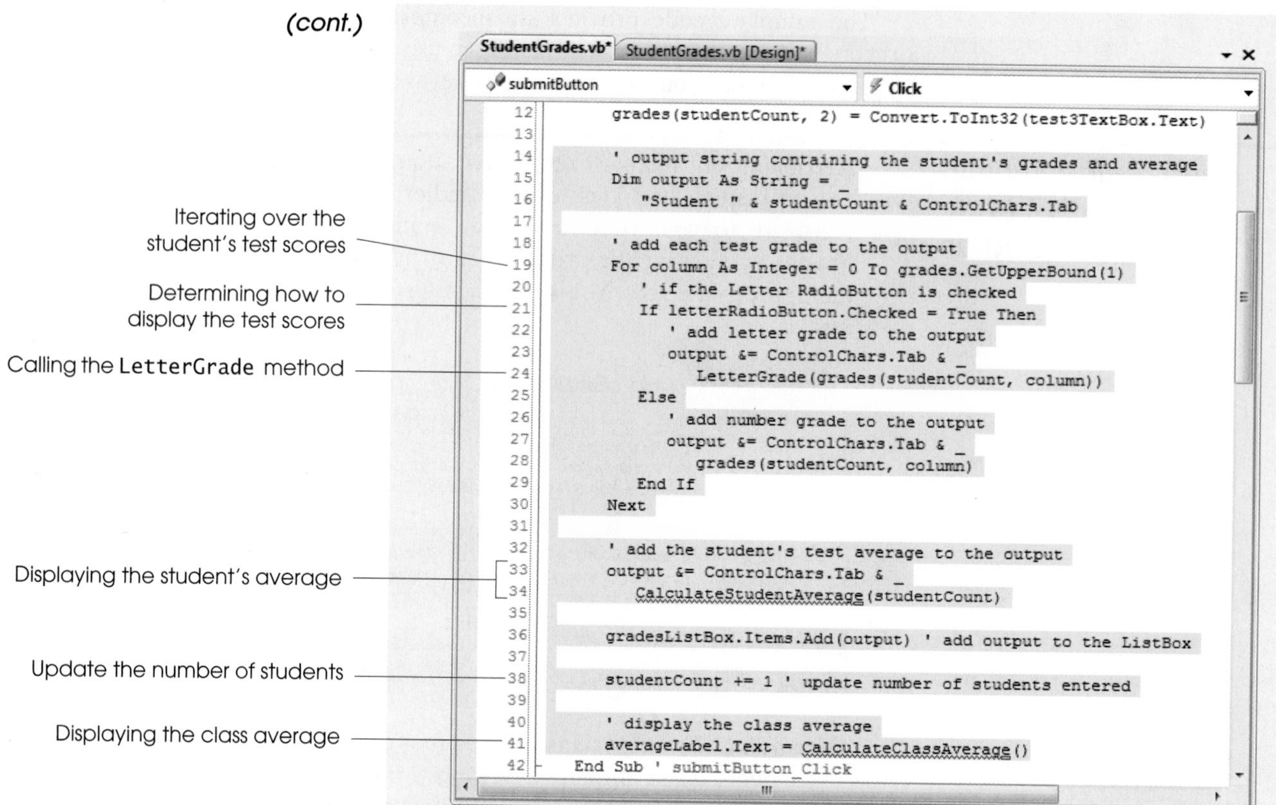
StudentGrades.vb* StudentGrades.vb [Design]*
submitButton
Click
grades(studentCount, 2) = Convert.ToInt32(test3TextBox.Text)
' output string containing the student's grades and average
Dim output As String = _
"Student " & studentCount & ControlChars.Tab
' add each test grade to the output
For column As Integer = 0 To grades.GetUpperBound(1)
' if the Letter RadioButton is checked
If letterRadioButton.Checked = True Then
' add letter grade to the output
output &= ControlChars.Tab & _
LetterGrade(grades(studentCount, column))
Else
' add number grade to the output
output &= ControlChars.Tab & _
grades(studentCount, column)
End If
Next
' add the student's test average to the output
output &= ControlChars.Tab & _
CalculateStudentAverage(studentCount)
gradesListBox.Items.Add(output) ' add output to the ListBox
studentCount += 1 ' update number of students entered
' display the class average
averageLabel.Text = CalculateClassAverage()
End Sub ' submitButton_Click
Iterating over the student's test scores
Determining how to display the test scores
Calling the LetterGrade method
Displaying the student's average
Update the number of students
Displaying the class average

Figure 18.11 Displaying the output.

3. ***Clearing the input and disabling the input controls.*** Insert lines 43–52 of Fig. 18.12 into your code. Lines 44–46 remove the user's input from each `TextBox`. Line 47 places the focus on the **Test 1:** `TextBox`. If `grades` array is full (line 50), line 51 disables the **Input Grades** `GroupBox` so that no more grades can be entered—disabling a `GroupBox` disables all the controls it contains. Note that in line 50 you add one to the result of `grades.GetUpperBound(0)` to obtain the number of rows in the array. Recall from Tutorial 17 that arrays provide a `Length` property which returns the number of elements in an array. You cannot use the `Length` property in this situation because `grades` is a two-dimensional array. The `Length` property of a rectangular two-dimensional array returns the total number of elements in the array, in this case 30 (10 rows times 3 columns).

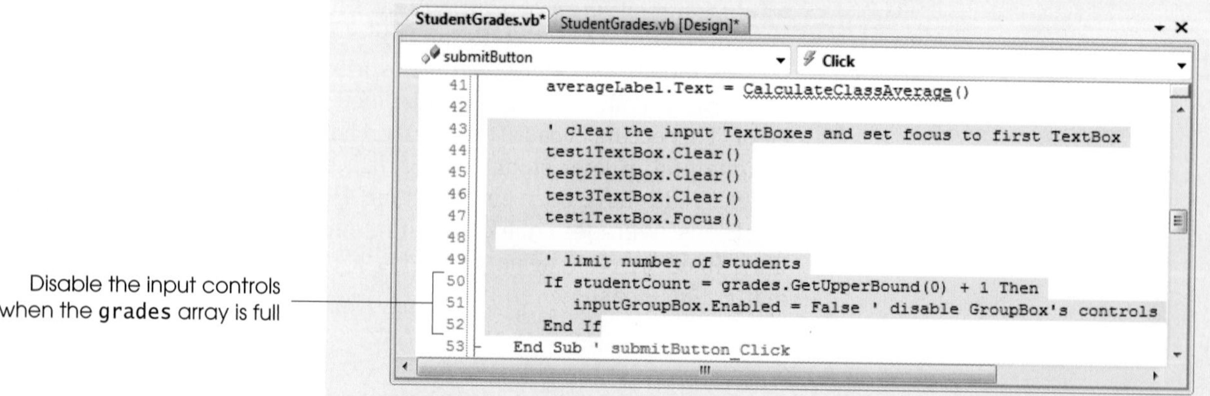
StudentGrades.vb* StudentGrades.vb [Design]*
submitButton
Click
41 averageLabel.Text = CalculateClassAverage()
42
43 ' clear the input TextBoxes and set focus to first TextBox
44 test1TextBox.Clear()
45 test2TextBox.Clear()
46 test3TextBox.Clear()
47 test1TextBox.Focus()
48
49 ' limit number of students
50 If studentCount = grades.GetUpperBound(0) + 1 Then
51 inputGroupBox.Enabled = False ' disable GroupBox's controls
52 End If
53 End Sub ' submitButton_Click
Disable the input controls when the grades array is full

Figure 18.12 Application does not allow more than 10 data entries.

4. ***Saving the project.*** Select **File > Save All** to save your modified code.

In the previous box, you called methods `CalculateStudentAverage` and `CalculateClassAverage`, which are not yet defined, to display the appropriate data. You create these methods in the next box.

Coding Methods to Average Test Grades

1. ***Coding the `CalculateStudentAverage` method.*** Add lines 55–76 of Fig. 18.13 above the `LetterGrade` method. Lines 60–62 use a `For...Next` statement to sum the grades contained in the row of the `grades` array specified by the argument passed to the method. Line 67 uses the `letterRadioButton`'s `Checked` property to determine how the user wants to view the average. Lines 69 and 72 calculate the student's average test score by dividing the sum of the test scores by the number of tests taken. Line 69 also calles method `LetterGrade`. Recall that the first column in a two-dimensional array has index `0`. You must add one to the last column's index (`GetUpperBound(1)`) to determine the number of columns in each row. Line 71 calls `String.Format` with the format control string `"{0:F}"` to format the test average with exactly two digits following the decimal point. You can follow the `F` format specifier with a number to set a different **precision**—the number of digits following the decimal point. The default precision is two. Line 75 returns the `String` containing the student's test average.

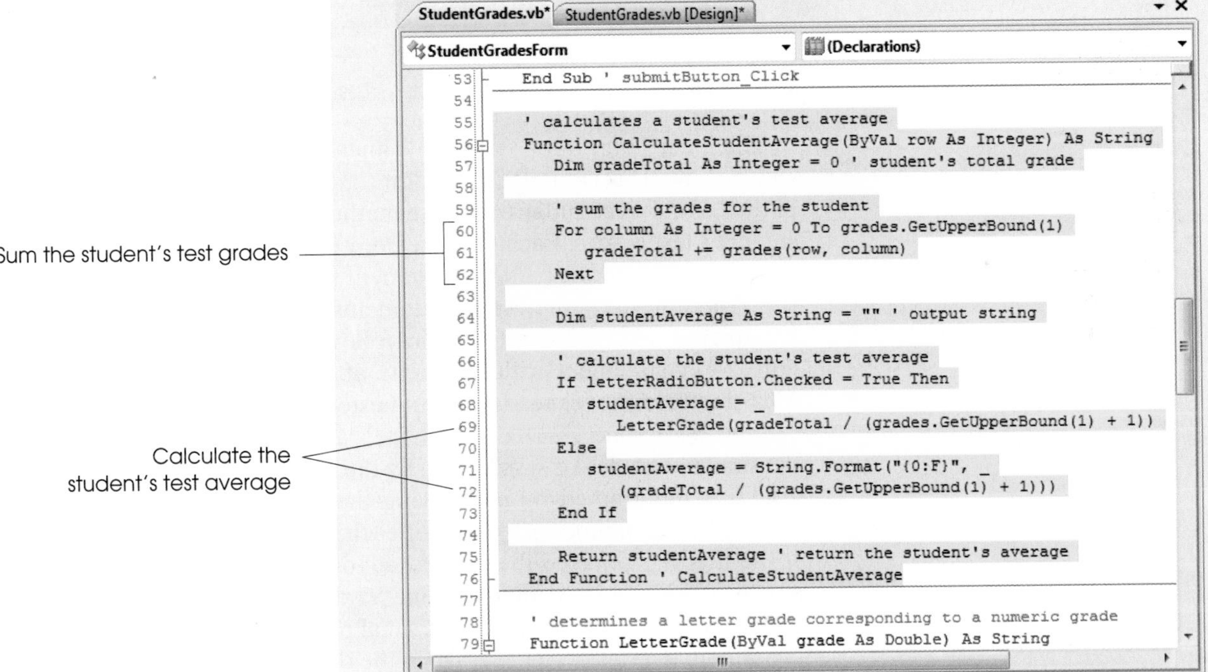

StudentGrades.vb*
StudentGrades.vb [Design]*
StudentGradesForm
(Declarations)
53 End Sub ' submitButton_Click
54
55 ' calculates a student's test average
56 Function CalculateStudentAverage(ByVal row As Integer) As String
57 Dim gradeTotal As Integer = 0 ' student's total grade
58
59 ' sum the grades for the student
60 For column As Integer = 0 To grades.GetUpperBound(1)
61 gradeTotal += grades(row, column)
62 Next
63
64 Dim studentAverage As String = "" ' output string
65
66 ' calculate the student's test average
67 If letterRadioButton.Checked = True Then
68 studentAverage = _
69 LetterGrade(gradeTotal / (grades.GetUpperBound(1) + 1))
70 Else
71 studentAverage = String.Format("{0:F}", _
72 (gradeTotal / (grades.GetUpperBound(1) + 1)))
73 End If
74
75 Return studentAverage ' return the student's average
76 End Function ' CalculateStudentAverage
77
78 ' determines a letter grade corresponding to a numeric grade
79 Function LetterGrade(ByVal grade As Double) As String
Sum the student's test grades
Calculate the student's test average

Figure 18.13 Calculating a student's test average.

2. ***Coding the `CalculateClassAverage` method.*** Add lines 78–102 of Fig. 18.14 below the `CalculateStudentAverage` method. Method `CalculateClassAverage` calculates the class's test average and returns it as a `String`. Lines 83–88 use **nested `For...Next` statements** to iterate over the columns in each row. The outer `For...Next` statement's header (line 83) declares the `row` control variable and sets the initial value to `0` (the first row) and the final value to `studentCount - 1` (the last row in which grades have been entered). Notice that you must subtract `1` from `studentCount` because the first row's index is `0`. This `For...Next` statement iterates over each row containing student grades.

(cont.)

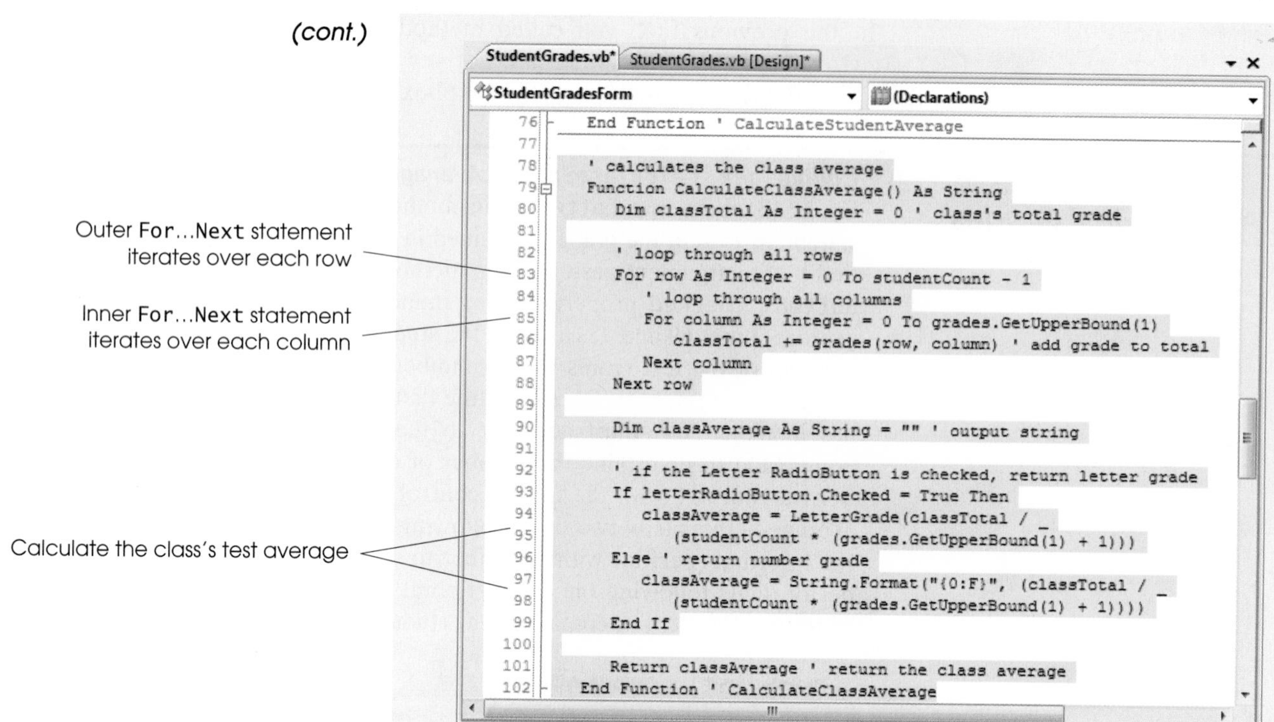

StudentGrades.vb*
StudentGrades.vb [Design]*
StudentGradesForm
(Declarations)
Outer For...Next statement iterates over each row
Inner For...Next statement iterates over each column
Calculate the class's test average
76 End Function ' CalculateStudentAverage
78 ' calculates the class average
79 Function CalculateClassAverage() As String
80 Dim classTotal As Integer = 0 ' class's total grade
82 ' loop through all rows
83 For row As Integer = 0 To studentCount - 1
84 ' loop through all columns
85 For column As Integer = 0 To grades.GetUpperBound(1)
86 classTotal += grades(row, column) ' add grade to total
87 Next column
88 Next row
90 Dim classAverage As String = "" ' output string
92 ' if the Letter RadioButton is checked, return letter grade
93 If letterRadioButton.Checked = True Then
94 classAverage = LetterGrade(classTotal / _
95 (studentCount * (grades.GetUpperBound(1) + 1)))
96 Else ' return number grade
97 classAverage = String.Format("{0:F}", (classTotal / _
98 (studentCount * (grades.GetUpperBound(1) + 1))))
99 End If
101 Return classAverage ' return the class average
102 End Function ' CalculateClassAverage

Figure 18.14 Calculating the class's test average.

The inner `For...Next` statement (lines 85–87) sums all the grades in the current row. This is similar to the `For...Next` statement used in lines 60–62 of the `CalculateStudentAverage` method (Fig. 18.13) which sums a single student's test grades. Each time the body of the outer `For...Next` statement executes, the inner `For...Next` statement sums all the grades for the current row. These nested `For...Next` statements sum all the grades contained in the `grades` array. Note that you followed the `Next` keyword of each `For...Next` statement with the name of the statement's control variable. This greatly improves readability of nested `For...Next` statements.

Lines 94–95 and 97–98 calculate the class's average test score by dividing the summed grades (`classTotal`) by the number of grades. The number of grades is determined by multiplying the number of students (`studentCount`) by the number of grades for each student (the number of columns). If the user has selected the **Letter** `RadioButton`, line 94 formats the average as a letter grade; otherwise line 97 displays the average as a number with exactly two digits after the decimal point. Line 101 returns the `String` containing the class's test average in the desired format (letter or numeric).

3. ***Saving the project.*** Select **File > Save All** to save your modified code.

You now code event handlers to enhance the application's functionality by allowing the user to select whether the results are presented as letter grades or numeric grades.

Coding Event Handlers for the RadioButtons

1. ***Creating the numericRadioButton_CheckedChanged event handler.*** In **Design** view, double click the **Numeric** `RadioButton` to generate its `CheckedChanged` event handler. Add lines 130–135 of Fig. 18.15 to the event handler. Recall that a `RadioButton`'s `CheckedChanged` event occurs both when it is selected and when it is deselected. Line 131 tests whether the `numericRadioButton` is selected. If so, and the number of students entered is greater than `0` (line 132), the event handler calls method `DisplayClassGrades` to display the grades in the proper form. Note that `DisplayClassGrades` is underlined in blue, indicating a compilation error, because you have not yet defined it. You define this method later in this box.

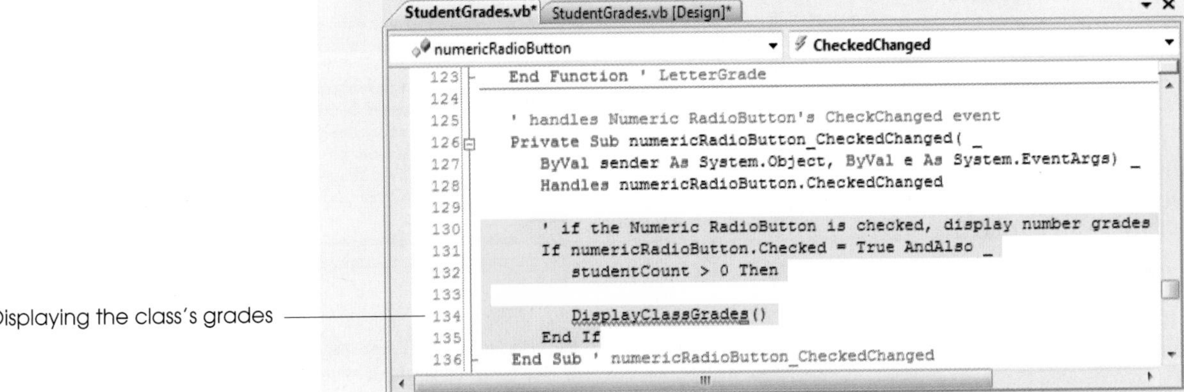
StudentGrades.vb* StudentGrades.vb [Design]*
numericRadioButton
CheckedChanged
123 End Function ' LetterGrade
124
125 ' handles Numeric RadioButton's CheckChanged event
126 Private Sub numericRadioButton_CheckedChanged(_
127 ByVal sender As System.Object, ByVal e As System.EventArgs) _
128 Handles numericRadioButton.CheckedChanged
129
130 ' if the Numeric RadioButton is checked, display number grades
131 If numericRadioButton.Checked = True AndAlso _
132 studentCount > 0 Then
133
134 DisplayClassGrades()
135 End If
136 End Sub ' numericRadioButton_CheckedChanged
Displaying the class's grades

Figure 18.15 Method `numericRadioButton_CheckedChanged`.

2. ***Creating the letterRadioButton_CheckedChanged event handler.*** In **Design** view, double click the **Letter** `RadioButton` to generate its `CheckedChanged` event handler. Add lines 143–148 of Fig. 18.16 to the event handler. This event handler performs the similar checks and actions as the `numericRadioButton`'s `CheckChanged` event handler.

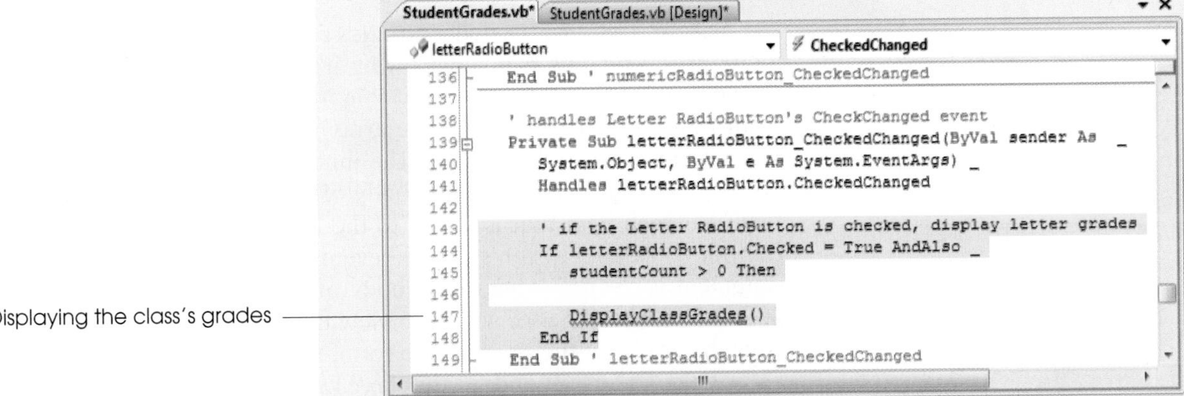
StudentGrades.vb* StudentGrades.vb [Design]*
letterRadioButton
CheckedChanged
136 End Sub ' numericRadioButton_CheckedChanged
137
138 ' handles Letter RadioButton's CheckChanged event
139 Private Sub letterRadioButton_CheckedChanged(ByVal sender As _
140 System.Object, ByVal e As System.EventArgs) _
141 Handles letterRadioButton.CheckedChanged
142
143 ' if the Letter RadioButton is checked, display letter grades
144 If letterRadioButton.Checked = True AndAlso _
145 studentCount > 0 Then
146
147 DisplayClassGrades()
148 End If
149 End Sub ' letterRadioButton_CheckedChanged
Displaying the class's grades

Figure 18.16 Method `letterRadioButton_CheckedChanged`.

3. ***Creating the DisplayClassGrades method.*** Add lines 151–186 of Fig. 18.17 below the **Letter** `RadioButton`'s `CheckedChanged` event handler. Method `DisplayClassGrades` displays each student's grades and test average, as well as the class average, in the format selected by the user (numeric or letter). Line 153 clears the `ListBox` using its `Clear` method. Lines 156–159 replace the header displayed at the top of the `ListBox`.

(cont.)

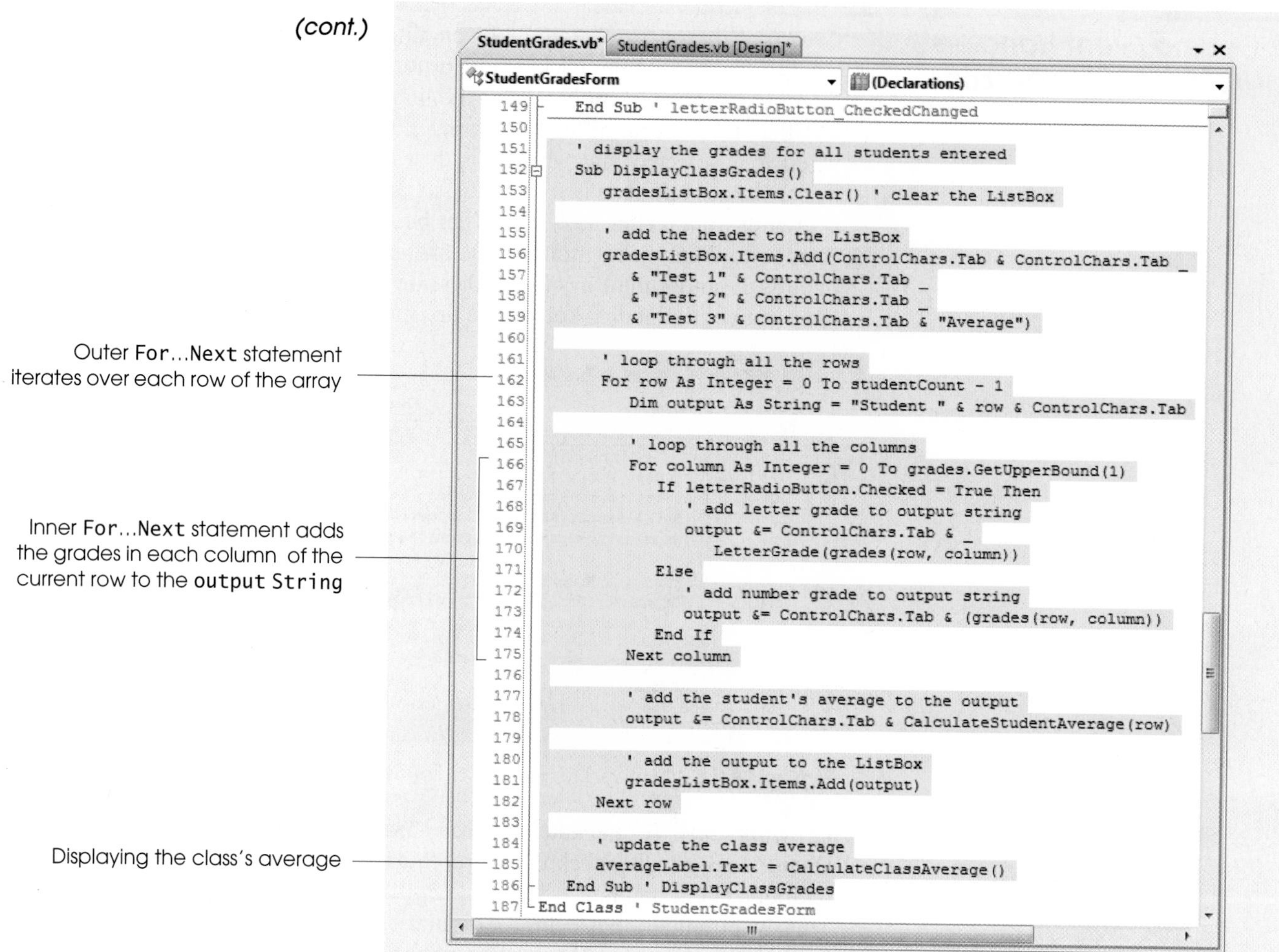
StudentGrades.vb*
StudentGrades.vb [Design]*
StudentGradesForm
(Declarations)
Outer For...Next statement iterates over each row of the array
Inner For...Next statement adds the grades in each column of the current row to the output String
Displaying the class's average

```
149   End Sub ' letterRadioButton_CheckedChanged
150
151   ' display the grades for all students entered
152   Sub DisplayClassGrades()
153      gradesListBox.Items.Clear() ' clear the ListBox
154
155      ' add the header to the ListBox
156      gradesListBox.Items.Add(ControlChars.Tab & ControlChars.Tab _
157         & "Test 1" & ControlChars.Tab _
158         & "Test 2" & ControlChars.Tab _
159         & "Test 3" & ControlChars.Tab & "Average")
160
161      ' loop through all the rows
162      For row As Integer = 0 To studentCount - 1
163         Dim output As String = "Student " & row & ControlChars.Tab
164
165         ' loop through all the columns
166         For column As Integer = 0 To grades.GetUpperBound(1)
167            If letterRadioButton.Checked = True Then
168               ' add letter grade to output string
169               output &= ControlChars.Tab & _
170                  LetterGrade(grades(row, column))
171            Else
172               ' add number grade to output string
173               output &= ControlChars.Tab & (grades(row, column))
174            End If
175         Next column
176
177         ' add the student's average to the output
178         output &= ControlChars.Tab & CalculateStudentAverage(row)
179
180         ' add the output to the ListBox
181         gradesListBox.Items.Add(output)
182      Next row
183
184      ' update the class average
185      averageLabel.Text = CalculateClassAverage()
186   End Sub ' DisplayClassGrades
187 End Class ' StudentGradesForm
```

Figure 18.17 Method `DisplayClassGrades`.

Lines 162–182 use nested `For...Next` statements to iterate over each grade in the `grades` array, displaying it in the chosen format. As in the `CalculateClassAverage` method (Fig. 18.14), the outer `For...Next` statement iterates over the rows of the array while the inner `For...Next` statement iterates over the columns. The inner `For...Next` statement uses the `output String` (declared in the body of the outer `For...Next` statement) to create each item that is added to the `ListBox`, much as you did in the **Submit Grades** `Button`'s `Click` event handler. The `If...Then...Else` statement (lines 167–174) in the body of the inner `For...Next` statement determines how the user wishes to view the grades (numeric or letter) and adds the grade, in the appropriate form, to the `output String`. The inner `For...Next` statement ends at the `Next` keyword in line 175. Note that you place the name of the statement's control variable after the `Next` keyword to improve readability. The body of the outer `For...Next` statement then adds the current student's average to the `output String` (line 178) and adds the `String` to the `gradesListBox`. Line 182 marks the end of the outer `For...Next` statement with keyword `Next`, followed by the name of the statement's control variable to increase readability. Line 185 displays the class's average in the `averageLabel`.

4. ***Running the application.*** Select **Debug > Start Debugging** to run your application. Test your application to ensure that it functions as the completed application does.

(cont.)

5. ***Closing the application***. Close your running application by clicking its close box.

6. ***Closing the IDE***. Close the Visual Basic IDE by clicking its close box.

Figure 18.18 presents the source code for the **Student Grades** application. The lines of code that contain new programming concepts you learned in this tutorial are highlighted.

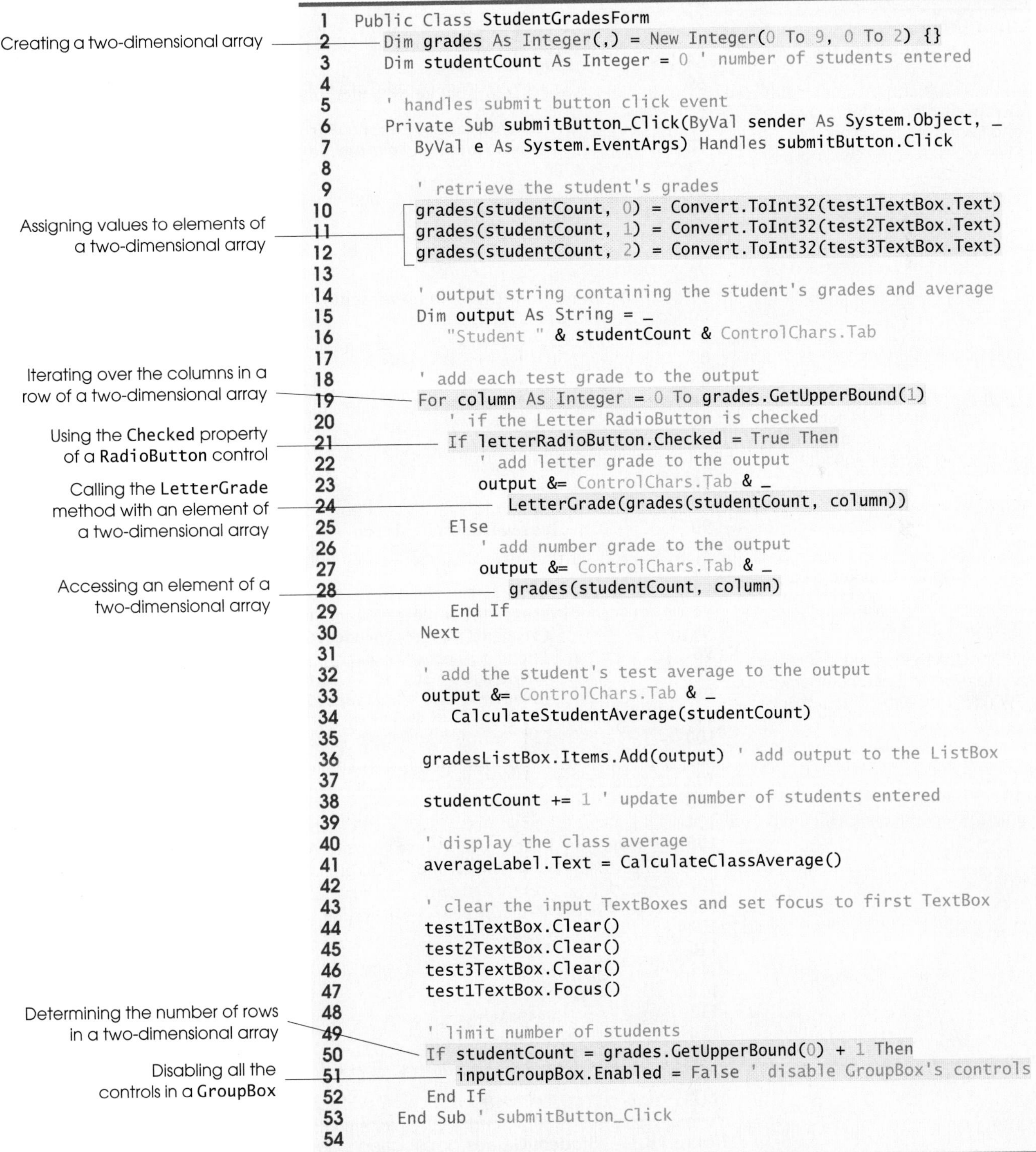


```
Public Class StudentGradesForm
   Dim grades As Integer(,) = New Integer(0 To 9, 0 To 2) {}
   Dim studentCount As Integer = 0 ' number of students entered

   ' handles submit button click event
   Private Sub submitButton_Click(ByVal sender As System.Object, _
      ByVal e As System.EventArgs) Handles submitButton.Click

      ' retrieve the student's grades
      grades(studentCount, 0) = Convert.ToInt32(test1TextBox.Text)
      grades(studentCount, 1) = Convert.ToInt32(test2TextBox.Text)
      grades(studentCount, 2) = Convert.ToInt32(test3TextBox.Text)

      ' output string containing the student's grades and average
      Dim output As String = _
         "Student " & studentCount & ControlChars.Tab

      ' add each test grade to the output
      For column As Integer = 0 To grades.GetUpperBound(1)
         ' if the Letter RadioButton is checked
         If letterRadioButton.Checked = True Then
            ' add letter grade to the output
            output &= ControlChars.Tab & _
               LetterGrade(grades(studentCount, column))
         Else
            ' add number grade to the output
            output &= ControlChars.Tab & _
               grades(studentCount, column)
         End If
      Next

      ' add the student's test average to the output
      output &= ControlChars.Tab & _
         CalculateStudentAverage(studentCount)

      gradesListBox.Items.Add(output) ' add output to the ListBox

      studentCount += 1 ' update number of students entered

      ' display the class average
      averageLabel.Text = CalculateClassAverage()

      ' clear the input TextBoxes and set focus to first TextBox
      test1TextBox.Clear()
      test2TextBox.Clear()
      test3TextBox.Clear()
      test1TextBox.Focus()

      ' limit number of students
      If studentCount = grades.GetUpperBound(0) + 1 Then
         inputGroupBox.Enabled = False ' disable GroupBox's controls
      End If
   End Sub ' submitButton_Click

```

Figure 18.18 **Student Grades** application's code. (Part 1 of 4.)

Iterating over the columns in a row of a two-dimensional array

Using the **Checked** property of a **RadioButton** control

Calculating the student's average and formatting it as a number with two digits after the decimal point

Using nested **For...Next** statements to iterate over the columns in each row of a two-dimensional array

Using the **Checked** property of a **RadioButton** control

Calculating the class's average and formatting it as a number with two digits after the decimal point

```
   ' calculates a student's test average
   Function CalculateStudentAverage(ByVal row As Integer) As String
      Dim gradeTotal As Integer = 0 ' student's total grade

      ' sum the grades for the student
      For column As Integer = 0 To grades.GetUpperBound(1)
         gradeTotal += grades(row, column)
      Next

      Dim studentAverage As String = "" ' output string

      ' calculate the student's test average
      If letterRadioButton.Checked = True Then
         studentAverage = _
            LetterGrade(gradeTotal / (grades.GetUpperBound(1) + 1))
      Else
         studentAverage = String.Format("{0:F}", _
            (gradeTotal / (grades.GetUpperBound(1) + 1)))
      End If

      Return studentAverage ' return the student's average
   End Function ' CalculateStudentAverage

   ' calculates the class average
   Function CalculateClassAverage() As String
      Dim classTotal As Integer = 0 ' class's total grade

      ' loop through all rows
      For row As Integer = 0 To studentCount - 1
         ' loop through all columns
         For column As Integer = 0 To grades.GetUpperBound(1)
            classTotal += grades(row, column) ' add grade to total
         Next column
      Next row

      Dim classAverage As String = "" ' output string

      ' if the Letter RadioButton is checked, return letter grade
      If letterRadioButton.Checked = True Then
         classAverage = LetterGrade(classTotal / _
            (studentCount * (grades.GetUpperBound(1) + 1)))
      Else ' return number grade
         classAverage = String.Format("{0:F}", (classTotal / _
            (studentCount * (grades.GetUpperBound(1) + 1))))
      End If

      Return classAverage ' return the class average
   End Function ' CalculateClassAverage

   ' determines a letter grade corresponding to a numeric grade
   Function LetterGrade(ByVal grade As Double) As String
      Dim output As String ' the letter grade to return

      ' determine the correct letter grade
      Select Case grade
         Case Is >= 90
            output = "A"
         Case Is >= 80
            output = "B"
         Case Is >= 70
            output = "C"
         Case Is >= 60
            output = "D"
```

Figure 18.18 **Student Grades** application's code. (Part 2 of 4.)

Handling the CheckedChanged event of a RadioButton control

Handling the CheckedChanged event of a RadioButton control

Outer For...Next statement iterates over the rows of a two-dimensional array

Inner For...Next statement iterates over the columns of a row in a two-dimensional array

Using the control variable's name to improve readability of nested For...Next statements

Using the control variable's name to improve readability of nested For...Next statements

```
         Case Else
            output = "F"
      End Select

      Return output ' return the letter grade
   End Function ' LetterGrade

   ' handles Numeric RadioButton's CheckChanged event
   Private Sub numericRadioButton_CheckedChanged(ByVal sender As _
      System.Object, ByVal e As System.EventArgs) _
      Handles numericRadioButton.CheckedChanged

      ' if the Numeric RadioButton is checked, display number grades
      If numericRadioButton.Checked = True AndAlso _
         studentCount > 0 Then

         DisplayClassGrades()
      End If
   End Sub ' numericRadioButton_CheckedChanged

   ' handles Letter RadioButton's CheckChanged event
   Private Sub letterRadioButton_CheckedChanged(ByVal sender As _
      System.Object, ByVal e As System.EventArgs) _
      Handles letterRadioButton.CheckedChanged

      ' if the Letter RadioButton is checked, display letter grades
      If letterRadioButton.Checked = True AndAlso _
         studentCount > 0 Then

         DisplayClassGrades()
      End If
   End Sub ' letterRadioButton_CheckedChanged

   ' display the grades for all students entered
   Sub DisplayClassGrades()
      gradesListBox.Items.Clear() ' clear the ListBox

      ' add the header to the ListBox
      gradesListBox.Items.Add(ControlChars.Tab & ControlChars.Tab _
         & "Test 1" & ControlChars.Tab _
         & "Test 2" & ControlChars.Tab _
         & "Test 3" & ControlChars.Tab & "Average")

      ' loop through all the rows
      For row As Integer = 0 To studentCount - 1
         Dim output As String = "Student " & row & ControlChars.Tab

         ' loop through all the columns
         For column As Integer = 0 To grades.GetUpperBound(1)
            If letterRadioButton.Checked = True Then
               ' add letter grade to output string
               output &= ControlChars.Tab & _
                  LetterGrade(grades(row, column))
            Else
               ' add number grade to output string
               output &= ControlChars.Tab & (grades(row, column))
            End If
         Next column

         ' add the student's average to the output
         output &= ControlChars.Tab & CalculateStudentAverage(row)

         ' add the output to the ListBox
         gradesListBox.Items.Add(output)
      Next row
```

Figure 18.18 **Student Grades** application's code. (Part 3 of 4.)

```

         ' update the class average
         averageLabel.Text = CalculateClassAverage()
      End Sub ' DisplayClassGrades
End Class ' StudentGradesForm
```

Figure 18.18 **Student Grades** application's code. (Part 4 of 4.)

SELF-REVIEW

1. A container can contain ________ RadioButton(s).

   a) exactly two
   b) no more than one
   c) no more than three
   d) any number of

2. When one RadioButton in a container is selected, ________.

   a) others can be selected at the same time
   b) a logic error will occur
   c) all others will be deselected
   d) Both a and c

3. Typically, ________ statements are used to iterate over each element in a two-dimensional array.

   a) Do While...Loop
   b) nested For...Next
   c) Do...Loop Until
   d) nested Do...Loop While

Answers: 1.) d. 2.) c. 3.) b.

18.5 Wrap-Up

In this tutorial, you learned how to declare and assign values to a two-dimensional array. You used code to store user input in a two-dimensional array. You also learned how to use For...Next statements to iterate over the rows or columns in a two-dimensional array. You used nested For...Next statements to iterate over every element in the two-dimensional array.

To help you complete the **Student Grades** application, you used RadioButtons. You learned that you must group related RadioButtons in separate containers. Initially, zero or one RadioButton in a container is selected and only one can be selected at a time. You learned how to determine a RadioButton's state by examining its Checked property. You also learned that selecting or deselecting a RadioButton calls its CheckedChanged event handler.

In the next tutorial, you learn about classes. (Recall that you've been using classes all along, from the Form class that represents the application's GUI to the Random class that you use to generate random numbers.) You create your own classes for use in your applications.

SKILLS SUMMARY

Creating a Two-Dimensional Array

- Declare the array using the format:

  Dim *arrayName* As *arrayType*(,)

  where *arrayName* is the reference name of the array, and *arrayType* is the type of data that will be stored in the array. The comma (,) in the parentheses indicates that the array is two-dimensional.

Assigning an Object to an Array Variable

- Use keyword New as in the statement:

  arrayName = New *arrayType*(,) {{*arrayInitializerList*}, {*arrayInitializerList*},...}

  where *arrayInitializerList* is a comma-separated list of the items that initialize the elements of one row in the array. You can also use

  arrayName = New *arrayType*(,) {}

  to create the array and initialize its elements to the default value for *arrayType*.

Referring to Element *m, n* of a Two-Dimensional Array

- Follow the array name by (*m*, *n*), where *m* is the row index and *n* is the column index.

Obtaining the Number of Rows and Columns in a Two-Dimensional Array

- Pass `0` (the first dimension of the array) to method `GetUpperBound` to retrieve the index of the last row.
- Pass `1` (the second dimension of the array) to method `GetUpperBound` to retrieve the index of the last column.

Using Two-Dimensional Arrays

- Declare a rectangular array to create a table of values (each row contains the same number of columns).
- Use a `For...Next` statement to iterate over the rows or columns of the two-dimensional array.
- Use nested `For...Next` statements to iterate over every element in the two-dimensional array.

Using a `RadioButton`

- Use a `RadioButton` in an application to present the user with mutually exclusive options.

Selecting a `RadioButton` at Runtime

- Click the white circle of the `RadioButton`. A small dot appears inside the white circle.

Determining Whether a `RadioButton` Is Selected

- Access the `RadioButton`'s `Checked` property.

Executing Code When a `RadioButton`'s State Has Changed

- Use the `CheckedChanged` event handler, which executes when a `RadioButton` is selected or deselected.
- Inspect the `RadioButton`'s `Checked` property to determine whether it was selected or deselected.

KEY TERMS

`Checked` property of `RadioButton` control—When `True`, displays a small dot in the control. When `False`, the control displays an empty white circle.

`CheckedChanged` event—Raised when a `RadioButton`'s state changes.

column—The second dimension of a two-dimensional array.

double-subscripted array—*See* two-dimensional array.

`Enabled` property of `GroupBox` control—When `False`, disables all controls contained in the `GroupBox`.

***m*-by-*n* array**—A two-dimensional array with *m* rows and *n* columns.

mutually exclusive options—A set of options of which only one can be selected at a time.

nested `For...Next` statements—A `For...Next` statement defined in the body of another `For...Next` statement. Commonly used to iterate over the elements of a two-dimensional array.

precision—Specifies the number of digits to the right of the decimal point in a formatted floating-point value.

`RadioButton` control—Appears as a small circle that is either blank (unchecked) or contains a smaller dot (checked). Usually these controls appear in groups of two or more. Exactly one `RadioButton` in a group is selected at one time.

rectangular array—A type of two-dimensional array that can represent tables of values consisting of information arranged in rows and columns. Each row contains the same number of columns.

row—The first dimension of a two-dimensional array.

table—A two-dimensional array used to contain information arranged in rows and columns.

two-dimensional array—An array that contains multiple rows of values.

GUI DESIGN GUIDELINES

RadioButton

- Use RadioButtons when the user must choose only one option from a group.
- Always place each group of RadioButtons in a separate container (such as a GroupBox).
- Align groups of RadioButtons either horizontally or vertically.

CONTROLS, EVENTS, PROPERTIES & METHODS

RadioButton RadioButton This control allows the user to select only one of several options.

- ***In action***

Numeric

- ***Event***

CheckedChanged—Raised when the control is either selected or deselected.

- ***Properties***

Checked—Set to True if the control is selected and False if it is not selected.

Location—Specifies the location of the RadioButton control relative to the top-left corner of the container (e.g., a Form or a GroupBox).

Name—Specifies the name used to access the RadioButton control programmatically. The name should be appended with the RadioButton suffix.

Size—Specifies the width and height (in pixels) of the RadioButton control.

Text—Specifies the text displayed in the label to the right of the RadioButton.

GroupBox GroupBox This control groups related controls visually in a box with a title.

- ***In action***

- ***Properties***

Location—Specifies the location of the GroupBox control relative to the top-left corner of the container (e.g., a Form or a GroupBox).

Enabled—When set to False, disables all controls contained in the GroupBox.

Name—Specifies the name used to access the GroupBox control programmatically. The name should be appended with the GroupBox suffix.

Size—Specifies the width and height (in pixels) of the GroupBox control.

Text—Specifies the text displayed on the GroupBox.

MULTIPLE-CHOICE QUESTIONS

18.1 When declaring an array, a(n) _________ is required inside parentheses in order to indicate that the array is two-dimensional.

a) comma
b) asterisk
c) period
d) apostrophe

18.2 A two-dimensional array in which each row contains the same number of columns is called a _________ array.

a) data
b) rectangular
c) tabular
d) All of the above

18.3 In an *m*-by-*n* array, the *m* stands for _________.

a) the number of columns in the array
b) the total number of array elements
c) the number of rows in the array
d) the number of elements in each row

18.4 Which of the following statements assigns an array of five rows and three columns to a two-dimensional `Integer` array named `array`?

a)
```
array = _
   New Integer(0 To 5, 0 To 3) {}
```
b)
```
array = _
   New Integer(0 To 4, 0 To 2){}
```
c)
```
array = _
   New Integer(0 To 4, 0 To 3) {}
```
d)
```
array = _
   New Integer(0 To 5, 0 To 2) {}
```

18.5 A `RadioButton` is a type of _________ control.

a) check
b) change
c) state
d) action

18.6 Use a _________ to group `RadioButton`s on the `Form`.

a) `GroupBox` control
b) `ComboBox` control
c) `ListBox` control
d) None of the above

18.7 The _________ event handler is invoked when the user selects a `RadioButton`.

a) `Selected`
b) `CheckedChanged`
c) `ButtonChanged`
d) `CheckSelected`

18.8 The _________ property is set to `True` when a `RadioButton` is selected.

a) `Selected`
b) `Chosen`
c) `On`
d) `Checked`

18.9 Two-dimensional arrays are often used to represent _________.

a) a pie chart
b) distances
c) lines
d) tables

18.10 Which of the following statements assigns an array of three rows and three columns to a two-dimensional array of integers `array`?

a)
```
Dim array As Integer()() = _
   New Integer()() {{1, 2, 3}, {4, 5, 6}, {7, 8, 9}}
```
b)
```
Dim array As Integer() = _
   {{1, 2, 3}, {4, 5, 6}, {7, 8, 9}}
```
c)
```
Dim array As Integer(,) = _
   New Integer(,) {{1, 2, 3}, {4, 5, 6}, {7, 8, 9}}
```
d) All of the above

EXERCISES

18.11 ***(Food Survey Application)*** A school cafeteria is giving an electronic survey to its students to improve their lunch menu. Create an application that uses a two-dimensional array to store votes for the survey. Provide `RadioButton`s to allow students to indicate whether they like or dislike a particular food (Fig. 18.19).

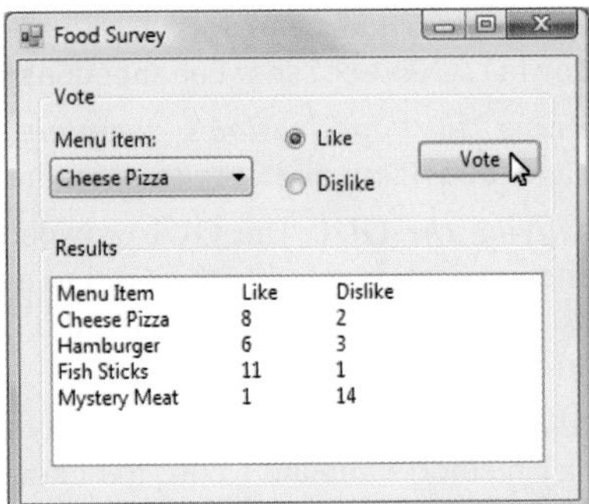

Figure 18.19 Food Survey application.

a) ***Copying the template to your working directory.*** Copy the directory `C:\Examples\Tutorial18\Exercises\FoodSurvey` to your `C:\SimplyVB2008` directory.

b) ***Opening the application's template file.*** Double click FoodSurvey.sln in the FoodSurvey directory to open the application.

c) ***Adding RadioButtons to the Vote GroupBox.*** Add two RadioButtons to the **Vote** GroupBox. Name one likeRadioButton and the other dislikeRadioButton. Change their Text properties to Like and Dislike, respectively. Set the Checked property of likeRadioButton to True.

d) ***Declaring a two-dimensional Integer array.*** Declare a two-dimensional Integer array named votes, with four rows and two columns. Each row corresponds to a menu item in the ComboBox. The columns store the number of "like" and "dislike" votes, respectively. The items in ComboBox provided in the template application were added through the IDE using the ComboBox's Items property.

e) ***Creating event handler voteButton_Click.*** Generate the Click event handler for the **Vote** Button. Create a local Integer variable index. This variable should contain the index of the selected item in the **Menu item:** ComboBox. Use the Checked property to determine whether the student likes or dislikes the selected menu item and update the votes array accordingly.

f) ***Displaying the data.*** Create a Sub procedure named DisplayVotes. Add a header to the resultsListBox as in Fig. 18.19. Use a For...Next statement to iterate through each row in the votes array. Add the menu item, the number of "like" votes and the number of "dislike" votes to the ListBox. Call this procedure from the **Vote** Button's Click event handler.

g) ***Running the application.*** Select **Debug > Start Debugging** to run your application. Choose either the **Like** or **Dislike** RadioButton. Click the **Vote** Button and verify that the displayed information is updated correctly. Make several more votes and make sure that the numbers are correct.

h) ***Closing the application.*** Close your running application by clicking its close box.

i) ***Closing the IDE.*** Close the Visual Basic IDE by clicking its close box.

18.12 ***(Enhanced Gas Pump Application)*** Enhance the **Gas Pump** application from Exercise 13.16 by allowing the user to choose the grade of gasoline using RadioButtons (Fig. 18.20). The total should be updated when the user selects a different grade of gasoline. It should be cleared when the user changes the number of gallons.

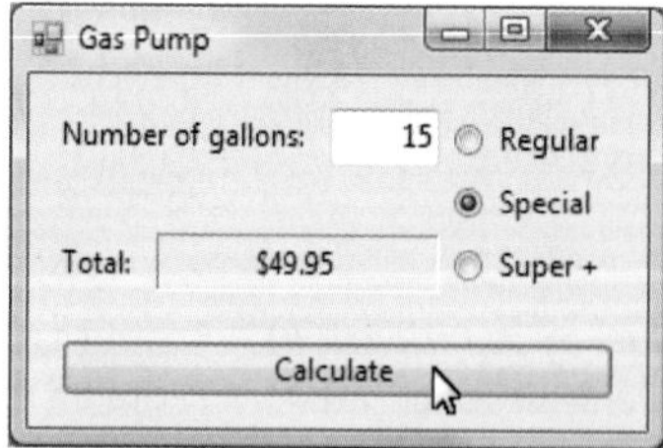

Figure 18.20 Enhanced **Gas Pump** application.

a) ***Copying the template to your working directory.*** Copy the directory C:\Examples\Tutorial18\Exercises\EnhancedGasPump to your C:\SimplyVB2008 directory.

b) ***Opening the application's template file.*** Double click GasPump.sln in the EnhancedGasPump directory to open the application.

c) ***Modifying the GUI.*** The GUI provided in the template is that of the original **Gas Pump** application. Modify this GUI to appear as in Fig. 18.20. Replace the three Buttons with three RadioButtons. Add a **Calculate** Button. Reposition and resize the controls.

d) ***Modifying the Total method.*** Modify the Select Case statement provided in the Total method template to use the Checked property of each RadioButton to determine the price per gallon. Also, use a Double instance variable to store the number of gallons instead of an Integer.

e) ***Adding a ResetPump method.*** Create the ResetPump method to reset the **Gas Pump** application. Clear the TextBox and output Label and set the gallons instance variable to 0.

f) ***Coding the Calculate `Button`'s `Click` event handler.*** Double click the **Calculate** `Button` to generate its `Click` event handler. Use an `If...Then` statement to determine if the user entered a number of gallons to purchase. If so, retrieve the number of gallons from the `TextBox` and store it in the `gallons` instance variable. Call `Sub` procedure `Total` to display the total cost of the purchase.

g) ***Coding the `CheckedChanged` event handlers.*** Double click each of the `RadioButtons` to generate their `CheckedChanged` event handlers. These event handlers should reset the application.

h) ***Coding the `TextChanged` event handler.*** Double click the **Number of gallons:** `TextBox` to generate its `TextChanged` event handler. To ensure that the price displayed is always relative to the number of gallons in the `TextBox`, the `TextChanged` event handler should reset the **Total:** `Label` and the `gallons` instance variable.

i) ***Running the application.*** Select **Debug > Start Debugging** to run your application. Test your application to ensure that it displays the correct total according to the grade selected.

j) ***Closing the application.*** Close your running application by clicking its close box.

k) ***Closing the IDE.*** Close the Visual Basic IDE by clicking its close box.

What does this code do?

18.13 What is returned by the following code? Assume that `GetStockPrices` is a `Function` procedure that returns a 2-by-31 array, with the first row containing the stock price at the beginning of the day and the last row containing the stock price at the end of the day, for each day of the month.

```
Function Mystery() As Integer()
   Dim prices As Integer(,) = New Integer(0 To 1, 0 To 30) {}

   prices = GetStockPrices()

   Dim result As Integer() = New Integer(30) {}

   For i As Integer = 0 To 30
      result(i) = prices(1, i) - prices(0, i)
   Next

   Return result
End Function ' Mystery
```

What's wrong with this code?

18.14 Find the error(s) in the following code. The `TwoDArrays` procedure should create a two-dimensional array and initialize all its values to one.

```
Sub TwoDArrays()
   Dim array As Integer(,)

   array = New Integer(0 To 3, 0 To 3) {}

   ' assign 1 to all cell values
   For i As Integer = 0 To 3
      array(i, i) = 1
   Next
End Sub ' TwoDArrays
```

Programming Challenge

18.15 ***(Sales Report Application)*** A clothing manufacturer has asked you to create an application that calculates its total sales for a week. Sales values should be input separately for each clothing item, but the amount of sales for each of the five weekdays should be input all at once. The application should calculate the total amount of sales for each item in the week and also the total sales for the manufacturer for all the items in the week. Because the manufacturer is a small company, it produces at most 10 items in any week. The application is shown in Fig. 18.21.

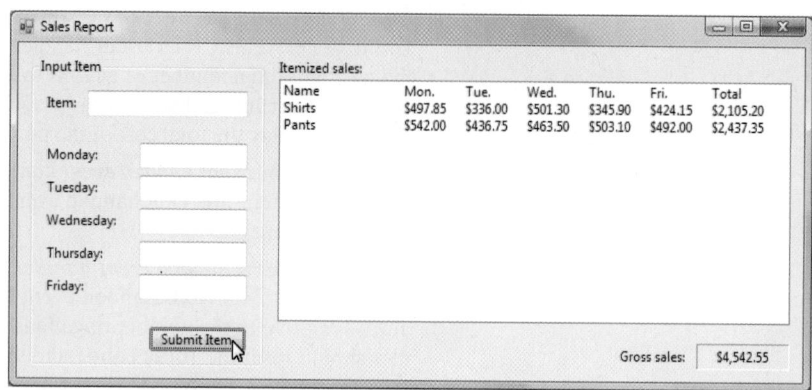

Figure 18.21 **Sales Report** application.

a) ***Copying the template to your working directory.*** Copy the directory `C:\Examples\Tutorial18\Exercises\SalesReport` to your `C:\SimplyVB2008` directory.

b) ***Opening the application's template file.*** Double click `SalesReport.sln` in the `SalesReport` directory to open the application.

c) ***Declaring a two-dimensional `Decimal` array.*** Declare a two-dimensional `Decimal` array named `itemSales`, with 10 rows and five columns.

d) ***Inputting data from the user.*** Add code to the beginning of the **Submit Item** `Button`'s `Click` event handler to retrieve the data input by the user. Assign the item name to the one-dimensional `itemNames` array, indexed with `itemCount` (which stores the number of items added). Assign the daily sales data to the two-dimensional `itemSales` array. The first index in this array is `itemCount`, and the second ranges from `0` to `4` depending on the day of the week (Monday–Friday). Finally, increment variable `itemCount` to record that another item's sales data has been added.

e) ***Iterating over all the items added.*** Add a `For...Next` statement after the `output` variable's declaration in the `DisplaySales` procedure. Iterate over each item added by the user. For each item, assign its name to `String ouput`. Append two tab characters to format the output properly.

f) ***Iterating over the days in the week.*** Add a nested `For...Next` statement to the body of the `For...Next` statement from the previous step. This `For...Next` statement iterates over the daily sales (the columns in the `itemSales` array). Append the daily sales (formatted as currency) followed by a tab character to the `output String`. Add the daily sales amount to the weekly total.

g) ***Calculating the total sales and outputting an item's sales.*** After iterating over the daily sales, add the weekly sales to the gross sales. Format the gross sales as currency and display it in the **Gross sales:** `Label`. Add code to append the weekly sales to `output`. Then add `output` to the `ListBox` using the `Add` method of `ListBox` property `Items`.

h) ***Running the application.*** Select **Debug > Start Debugging** to run your application. Test your application to ensure that it runs correctly, as in Fig. 18.21.

i) ***Closing the application.*** Close your running application by clicking its close box.

j) ***Closing the IDE.*** Close the Visual Basic IDE by clicking its close box.

TUTORIAL 19

Microwave Oven Application

Building Your Own Classes and Objects

Objectives

In this tutorial, you learn to:

- Create your own classes.
- Create and use objects of your own classes.
- Control access to object instance variables.
- Use keyword `Private`.
- Create your own properties.
- Use the `Panel` control.
- Use `String` methods `PadLeft` and `Substring`.

Outline

In earlier tutorials, you used the following application-development methodology: You analyzed many typical problems that required an application to be built and determined what classes from the .NET Framework Class Library were needed to implement each application. You then selected appropriate methods from these classes and created any necessary procedures to complete each application.

You have now seen several .NET classes. Each GUI control is defined as a class. When you add a control to your application from the **Toolbox**, an object (also known as an instance) of that class is created and added to your application. You have also seen .NET classes that are not GUI controls. Classes `String` and `Random`, for example, have been used to create `String` objects (for textual data) and `Random` objects (for generating random numbers), respectively. When you create and use an object of a class in an application, your application is known as a **client** of that class.

In this tutorial, you'll learn to create and use your own classes (sometimes known as **programmer-defined classes** or **programmer-defined types**). Creating your own classes is a key part of object-oriented programming (OOP). As with procedures, classes can be reused. Visual Basic applications typically are created by using a combination of .NET classes and methods and programmer-defined classes and methods. You have already created several procedures in this book. Note that all of these procedures were created within classes, because all of your applications have been defined as classes (each `Form` you've created is a class). In this tutorial (and for the remainder of the book), you'll refer to a class's procedures as methods, which is the industry-preferred term for procedures located within a class.

You'll create a microwave oven simulator where the user will enter an amount of time for the microwave to cook food. To handle the time data, you'll create a class called `Time`. This class stores a number of minutes and seconds (which your **Microwave Oven** application will use to keep track of the remaining cook time) and provides properties whereby clients of this class can change the number of minutes and seconds.

19.1 Test-Driving the Microwave Oven Application

In this tutorial you'll build your own class as you construct your **Microwave Oven** application. This application must meet the following requirements:

Application Requirements

*An electronics company is considering building microwave ovens. The company has asked you to develop an application that simulates a microwave oven. The oven contains a keypad that allows the user to specify the microwave cook time, which is displayed for the user. Once a time is entered, the user clicks the **Start** `Button` to begin the cooking process. The microwave's glass window changes color (from gray to yellow) to simulate the oven's light that remains on while the food is cooking, and a timer counts down one second at a time. Once the time expires, the color of the microwave's glass window returns to gray (indicating that the microwave's light is now off) and the microwave displays the text "Done!" The user can click the **Clear** `Button` at any time to stop the microwave and enter a new time. The user should be able to enter a number of minutes no larger than 59 and a number of seconds no larger than 59; otherwise, the invalid portion of the cook time is set to zero. A beep is sounded whenever a `Button` is clicked and when the microwave oven has finished a countdown.*

You begin by test-driving the completed application. Then you learn the additional Visual Basic technologies that you need to create your own version of this application.

Test-Driving the Microwave Oven Application

1. ***Opening the completed application.*** Open the directory `C:\Examples\Tutorial19\CompletedApplication\MicrowaveOven` to locate the **Microwave Oven** application. Double click `MicrowaveOven.sln` to open the application in the Visual Basic IDE.

2. ***Running the Microwave Oven application.*** Select **Debug > Start Debugging** to run the application (Fig. 19.1). The application contains a large rectangle on the left (representing the microwave oven's glass window) and a keypad on the right, including a `Label` with the text **Microwave Oven**. The numeric `Buttons` are used to enter the cook time, which is displayed in the `Label` on the top right. Note that the keypad `Buttons` appear flat, to give the application a more "real-world" appearance. To create this appearance, the `Buttons`' **`FlatStyle`** property has been set to **`Flat`**. Similarly, the `Label`'s `BorderStyle` property has been set to **`FixedSingle`**.

Microwave Oven

Microwave's glass window

Microwave Oven

Label

1 2 3
4 5 6
7 8 9
0

Numeric keypad (Buttons appear flat)

Start Clear

Figure 19.1 **Microwave Oven** application's `Form`.

(cont.)

3. ***Entering a time.*** Click the following numeric `Buttons` in order: **1**, **2**, **3**, **4** and **5**. Each time you click a keypad `Button`, you'll hear a beeping sound. (If you don't hear a beeping sound, please check your computer's settings to ensure that the volume of your machine's speaker has not been lowered or muted.)

   Note that you can enter no more than four digits (the first two for the minutes and the second two for the seconds)—any extra digits will not appear (Fig. 19.2). The number of minutes and the number of seconds must each be 59 or less. If the user enters an invalid number of minutes or seconds (such as 89), the invalid amount is set to zero.

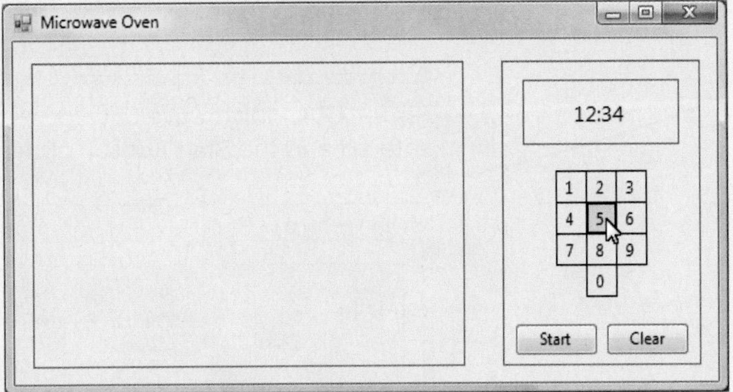

Figure 19.2 **Microwave Oven** application accepts only four digits.

4. ***Entering invalid data.*** Click the **Clear** `Button` to clear your input. Click the following numeric `Buttons` in order: **7**, **2**, **3** and **5** (Fig. 19.3). This input is invalid because the number of minutes, 72, is larger than the maximum allowed value, 59, so the number of minutes is reset to zero when the **Start** `Button` is clicked. Click the **Start** `Button` now. Note that the number of minutes has been reset to **00** (Fig. 19.4). Also note that the microwave oven's window has changed to yellow, to simulate the light that goes on inside the oven so that the user can watch the food cooking.

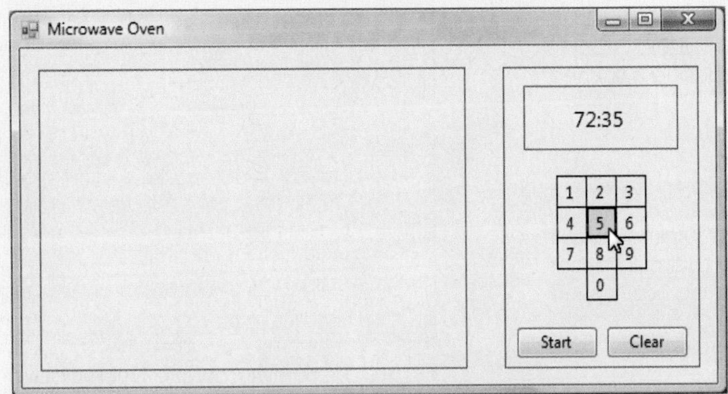

Figure 19.3 **Microwave Oven** application with invalid input.

5. ***Entering valid data.*** Click the **Clear** `Button` to enter a new cook time. Click `Button` **5** (to indicate five seconds); then, click **Start** (Fig. 19.5).

6. ***Viewing the application after the cooking time has expired.*** Wait five seconds. Note that the display `Label` shows the time counting down by 1 each second. When the time has reached zero, the oven beeps, the display `Label` changes to contain the text **Done!** and the microwave oven's window changes back to the same color as the `Form` (Fig. 19.6).

(cont.)

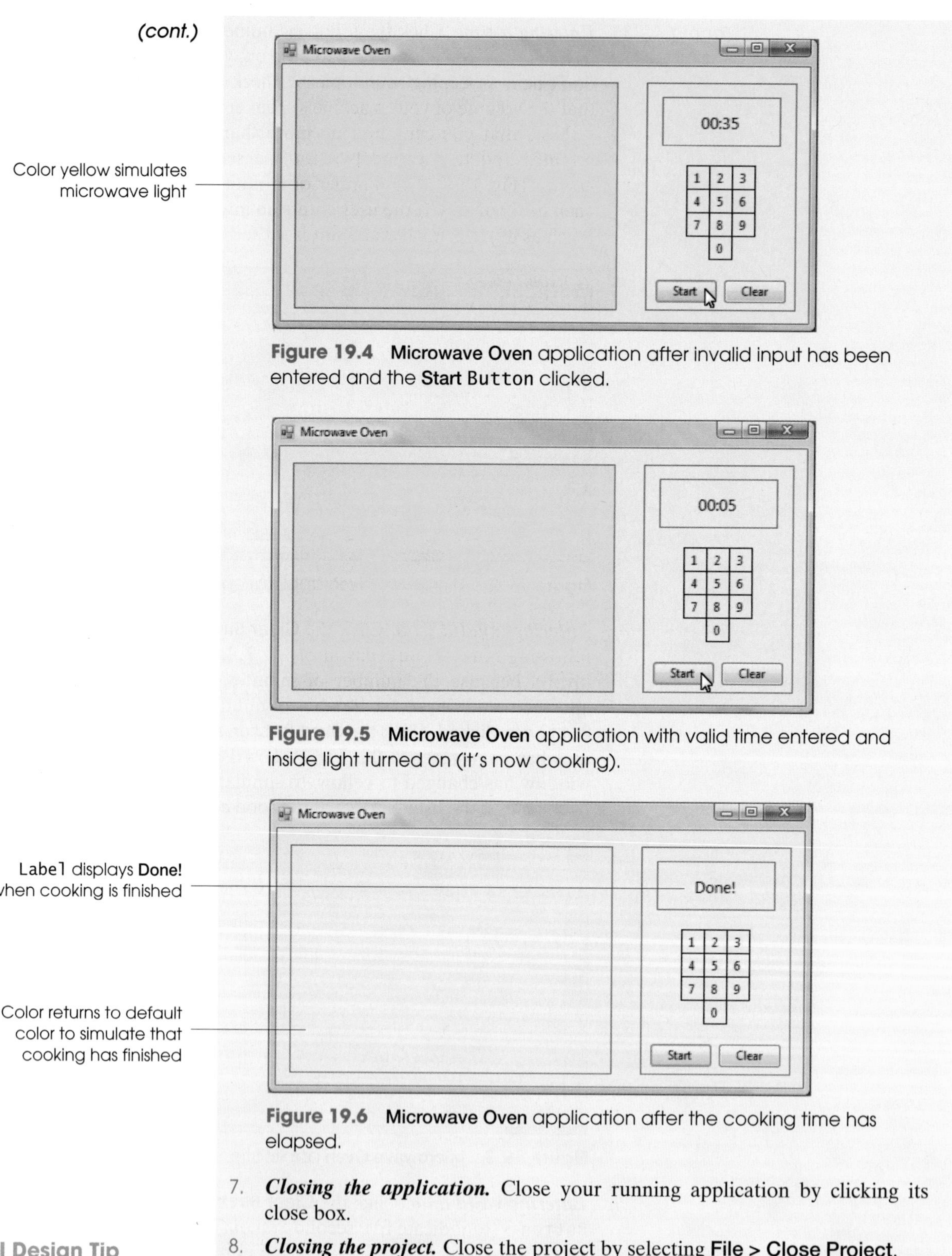

Figure 19.4 **Microwave Oven** application after invalid input has been entered and the **Start** `Button` clicked.

Figure 19.5 **Microwave Oven** application with valid time entered and inside light turned on (it's now cooking).

Figure 19.6 **Microwave Oven** application after the cooking time has elapsed.

7. ***Closing the application.*** Close your running application by clicking its close box.
8. ***Closing the project.*** Close the project by selecting **File > Close Project.**

GUI Design Tip

Use `Panels` to organize groups of related controls where the purpose of the controls is obvious. If the purpose of the controls is not obvious, use a `GroupBox` rather than a `Panel`, because `GroupBoxes` can contain captions.

19.2 Designing the Microwave Oven Application

In Tutorial 14, you learned to use `GroupBoxes` to group various controls. The **Microwave Oven** application groups controls using a **`Panel` control**. The main difference between `Panels` and `GroupBoxes` is that `GroupBoxes` can display a caption. The **Microwave Oven** application requires two `Panels`—one to contain the controls of the application, and the other to represent the microwave oven's glass window. The template application provided for you contains one of these `Panel`s.

The **Microwave Oven** application contains a class (called `Time`) whose objects store the cook time in minutes and seconds. All the controls you have used (including the `Form` itself) are defined as classes. You'll begin by creating the `Time` class. The following pseudocode describes the basic operation of class `Time`:

```
When the time object is created:
    Assign input to variables for number of minutes and number of seconds

When setting the number of minutes:

    If the number of minutes is less than 60
        Set the number of minutes to specified value
    Else
        Set the number of minutes to 0

When setting the number of seconds:

    If the number of seconds is less than 60
        Set the number of seconds to specified value
    Else
        Set the number of seconds to 0
```

When an object of class `Time` is created, the number of minutes and number of seconds are initialized. Any invalid number (minutes or seconds) is set to 0. The following pseudocode describes the basic operation of your **Microwave Oven** class:

```
When the user clicks a numeric Button:
    Sound beep
    Display the formatted time

When the user clicks the Start Button:
    Store the minutes and seconds
    Display the formatted time
    Begin countdown—Start timer
    Turn the microwave light on

When the timer ticks (once per second):
    Decrease time by one second
    Display new time

    If new time is zero
        Stop the countdown
        Sound beep
        Display text "Done!"
        Turn the microwave light off

When the user clicks the Clear Button:
    Display the text "Microwave Oven"
    Clear input and time data
    Stop the countdown
    Turn the microwave light off
```

The user enters input by clicking the numeric `Button`s. Each time a numeric `Button` is clicked, the number on that `Button` is appended to the end of the cook time displayed in the GUI's `Label`. At most, four digits can be displayed. After entering the cook time, the user can click the **Start** `Button` to begin the cooking process or click the **Clear** `Button` and enter a new time. Each `Button` makes a beeping sound when clicked. If the **Start** `Button` is clicked, a countdown using a `Timer` control begins, and the microwave oven's window changes to yellow, indicating that the oven's light is on (so that the user can watch the food cook). Each second, the display is updated to show the remaining cooking time. When the countdown finishes, another beep is sounded, the display `Label` displays the text

Done! and the microwave oven's light is turned off by changing the window's color back to its default gray.

Now that you've test-driven the **Microwave Oven** application and studied its pseudocode representation, you'll use an ACE table to help you convert the pseudocode to Visual Basic. Figure 19.7 lists the actions, controls and events that will help you complete your own version of this application.

Action/Control/Event (ACE) Table for the Microwave Oven Application

Action	Control/Object	Event
	`oneButton, twoButton, threeButton, fourButton, fiveButton, sixButton, sevenButton, eightButton, nineButton, zeroButton`	`Click`
Sound beep		
Display the formatted time	`displayLabel`	
	`startButton`	`Click`
Store the minutes and seconds	`timeObject`	
Display the formatted time	`displayLabel`	
Begin countdown—Start timer	`clockTimer`	
Turn microwave light on	`windowPanel`	
	`clockTimer`	`Tick`
Decrease time by one second	`timeObject`	
Display new time	`displayLabel`	
If new time is zero	`timeObject`	
Stop the countdown	`clockTimer`	
Sound beep		
Display text "Done!"	`displayLabel`	
Turn the microwave light off	`windowPanel`	
	`clearButton`	`Click`
Display the text "Microwave Oven"	`displayLabel`	
Clear input and time data	`timeIs, timeObject`	
Stop the countdown	`clockTimer`	
Turn microwave light off	`windowPanel`	

Figure 19.7 ACE table for the **Microwave Oven** application.

Input is sent to the application when the user clicks one of the numeric `Buttons`. Values are displayed in `displayLabel` as they are entered. Once all input has been entered, the user clicks the **Start** `Button` to begin the countdown. The `Form`'s `windowPanel` background color is set to yellow to simulate the microwave oven's light being turned on, and `clockTimer` updates `displayLabel` each second during the countdown. To clear the input and start over, the user can click the **Clear** `Button`. In the following box, you begin creating your **Microwave Oven** application by adding the second `Panel` to the `Form` and viewing the template code.

Adding a `Panel` Control to the Microwave Oven Application

1. ***Copying the template to your working directory.*** Copy the `C:\Examples\Tutorial19\TemplateApplication\MicrowaveOven` directory to your `C:\SimplyVB2008` directory.

(cont.)

GUI Design Tip

Although it is possible to have a `Panel` without a border (by setting the `BorderStyle` property to `None`), use borders on your `Panels` to improve user interface readability and organization.

Good Programming Practice

Use the `Panel` suffix when naming panels.

2. ***Opening the* Microwave Oven *application's template file.*** Double click `MicrowaveOven.sln` in the `MicrowaveOven` directory to open the application in the Visual Basic IDE.

3. ***Adding a* `Panel` *to the* Form.** Add a `Panel` control to the `Form` by double clicking the `Panel` control (Panel) in the **Containers** tab of the **Toolbox**. Name the control `windowPanel` because this `Panel` represents your microwave oven's window. Set the `Panel`'s `Size` property to `328, 224` and its `Location` property to `14, 16`. Set the `BorderStyle` property to `FixedSingle`, to display a thin black rectangle surrounding your `Panel`.

4. ***Viewing the template code.*** Before you add code to this application, switch to code view, and examine the code provided. Line 4 of Fig. 19.8 declares instance variable `timeIs`, a `String` that will store user input.

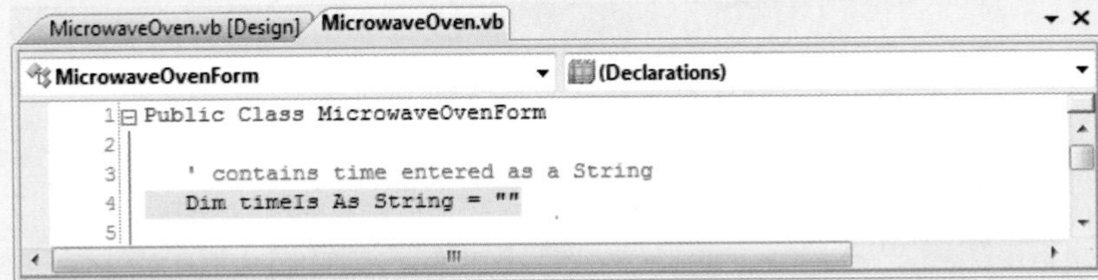

Figure 19.8 Variable `timeIs` contains the user's input.

The template code also contains event handlers for the numeric `Buttons`' `Click` events. Each `Button` is clicked when the user wants to append the current `Button`'s digit to the amount of cooking time. Let's look at one of these event handlers closely (Fig. 19.9). Line 10 calls function **Beep**, which causes your computer to make a beeping sound. Each event handler for the numeric keypad `Buttons` begins with a call to `Beep`, appends the current `Button`'s number to `timeIs` (line 11) and calls method `DisplayTime` (line 12), which displays the current cooking time in the application's `Label`. There are 10 of these event handlers—one for each digit from 0 to 9.

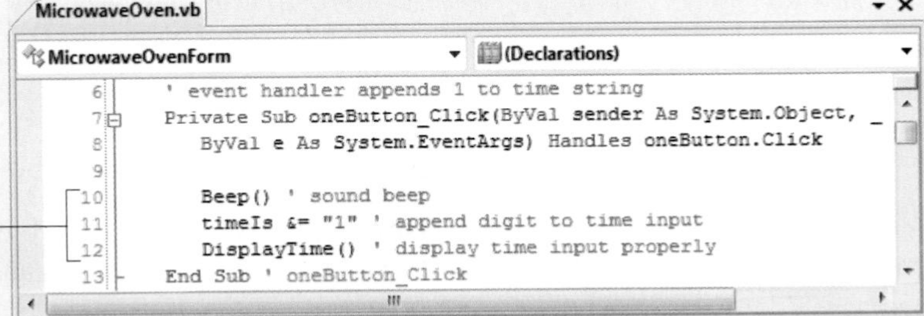

Figure 19.9 Typical numeric event handler.

GUI Design Tip

A `Panel` can display scrollbars when it is not large enough to display all of its controls. To increase usability, we suggest avoiding the use of scrollbars on `Panels`. If a `Panel` is not large enough to display all of its contents, increase the size of the `Panel` or place the content in multiple `Panels`.

`MicrowaveOven.vb` contains four more methods that you define in this tutorial. The first is the `startButton_Click` event handler in lines 96–100 of Fig. 19.10. This event handler starts the microwave oven's cooking process, which in this simulation consists of a time countdown and changing the window's color to yellow, simulating the oven's light being on.

Event handler `clearButton_Click` (lines 102–106) clears the time entered. The **Clear** `Button` is used to change the time entered or terminate cooking early. The event handler resets the time to all zeros and displays the text **Microwave Oven**. Method `DisplayTime` (lines 108–111) displays the cooking time as it's being entered. Event handler `clockTimer_Tick` (lines 113–117) changes the application's `Label` during the countdown.

5. ***Saving the project.*** Select **File > Save All** to save your modified code.

(cont.)

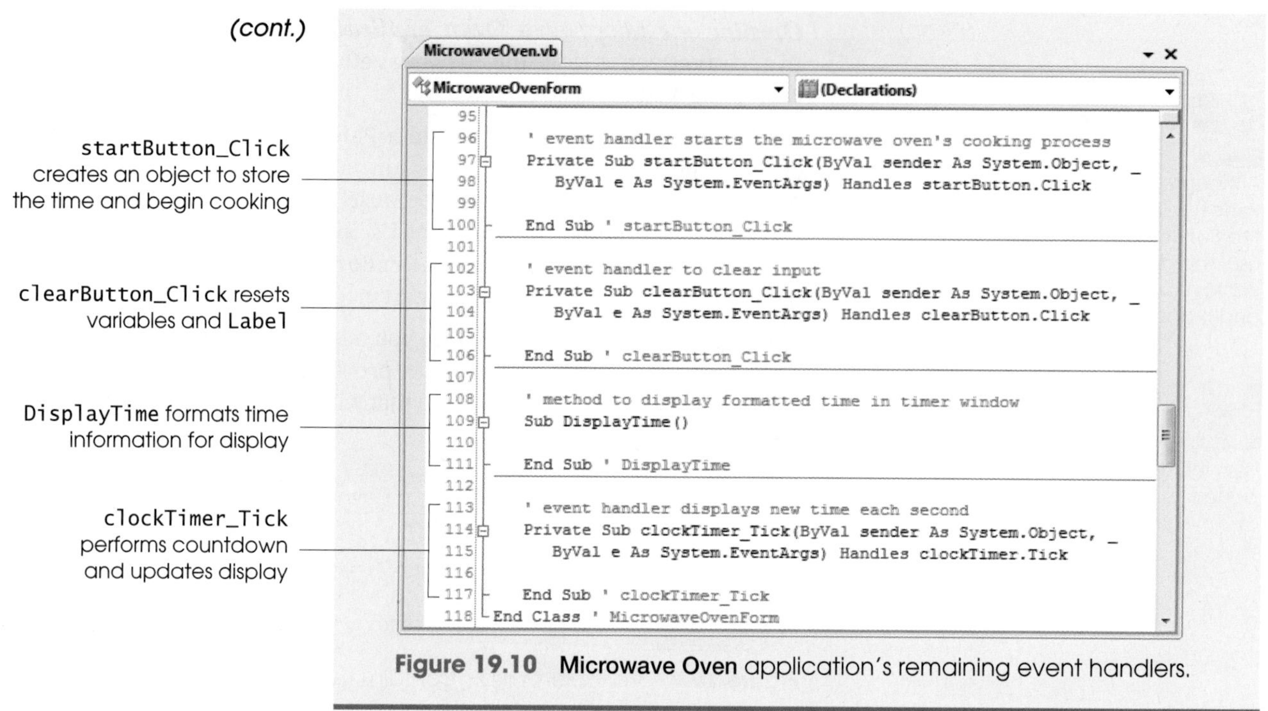
MicrowaveOven.vb
MicrowaveOvenForm
(Declarations)
' event handler starts the microwave oven's cooking process
Private Sub startButton_Click(ByVal sender As System.Object, _
ByVal e As System.EventArgs) Handles startButton.Click
End Sub ' startButton_Click
' event handler to clear input
Private Sub clearButton_Click(ByVal sender As System.Object, _
ByVal e As System.EventArgs) Handles clearButton.Click
End Sub ' clearButton_Click
' method to display formatted time in timer window
Sub DisplayTime()
End Sub ' DisplayTime
' event handler displays new time each second
Private Sub clockTimer_Tick(ByVal sender As System.Object, _
ByVal e As System.EventArgs) Handles clockTimer.Tick
End Sub ' clockTimer_Tick
End Class ' MicrowaveOvenForm
startButton_Click creates an object to store the time and begin cooking
clearButton_Click resets variables and Label
DisplayTime formats time information for display
clockTimer_Tick performs countdown and updates display

Figure 19.10 **Microwave Oven** application's remaining event handlers.

SELF-REVIEW

1. A Panel is different from a GroupBox in that a _________.
   a) GroupBox can be used to organize controls, whereas a Panel cannot
   b) Panel contains a caption, whereas a GroupBox does not
   c) GroupBox contains a caption, whereas a Panel does not
   d) Panel can be used to organize controls, whereas a GroupBox cannot

2. Function Beep causes the computer to _________.
   a) make three beeping sounds in sequence
   b) make a beeping sound
   c) display a message dialog and make a beeping sound
   d) set off the system alarm and pause the application

Answers: 1) c. 2) b.

19.3 Adding a New Class to the Project

Next, you learn how to add a class to your application. This class is used to create objects that contain the time in minutes and seconds.

Adding a Class to the Microwave Oven Application

1. ***Adding a new class to the project.*** Select **Project > Add Class**. In the dialog that appears (Fig. 19.11), enter the class name (Time) in the **Name:** field and click **Add**. Note that the class name (ending with the .vb file extension) appears in the **Solution Explorer** below the project name (Fig. 19.12).

2. ***Viewing the code that has been added to this class.*** If Time.vb does not open for you when it is created, double click the file in the **Solution Explorer**. Note that a few lines of code have been added for you (Fig. 19.13). Line 1, which begins the Time class definition, contains the keywords Public and Class, followed by the name of the class (in this case, Time). Keyword **Class** indicates that what follows is a class definition. You'll learn about keyword Public in Section 19.7. The keywords **End Class** (line 3) indicate the end of the class definition. Any code placed between these two lines forms the class definition's body. Any methods or variables defined in the body of a class are considered to be **members** of that class.

(cont.)

Select **Class** as new item

Name of new class

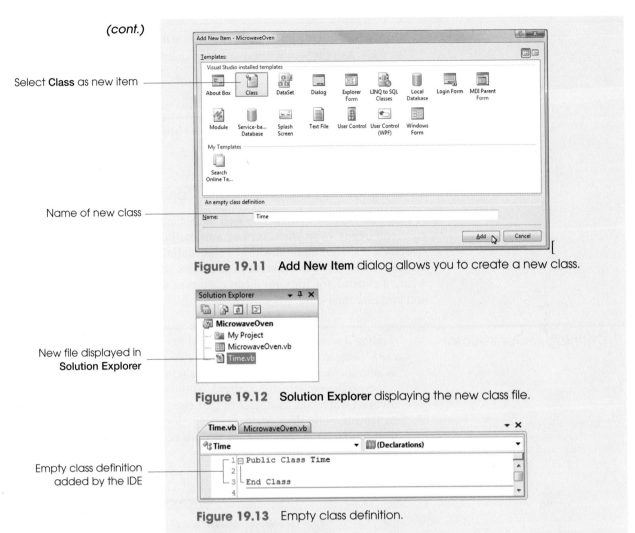

Figure 19.11 **Add New Item** dialog allows you to create a new class.

New file displayed in **Solution Explorer**

Figure 19.12 **Solution Explorer** displaying the new class file.

Empty class definition added by the IDE

```
1 Public Class Time
2
3 End Class
4
```

Figure 19.13 Empty class definition.

3. ***Adding instance variables to your application.*** Add lines 1–2 of Fig. 19.14 to `Time.vb`, above the class definition. Always add comments indicating the name and purpose of your class files. Add lines 6–8 to the `Time` class definition.

   Lines 7–8 declare each of the two `Integer` instance variables—`minuteValue` and `secondValue`. The `Time` class stores a time value containing minutes and seconds—the value for minutes is stored in `minuteValue`, and the value for seconds is stored in `secondValue`. Finally, be sure to add a comment in line 10 where the class definition is terminated.

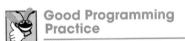

Good Programming Practice

Add comments at the beginning of your classes to increase readability. The comments should indicate the name of the file that contains the class and the purpose of the class being defined.

Instance variables store minute and second information

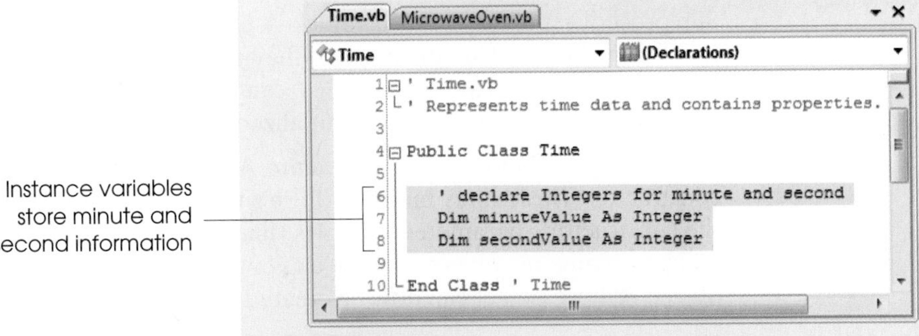

Figure 19.14 `Time`'s instance variables.

4. ***Saving the project.*** Select **File > Save All** to save your modified code.

SELF-REVIEW

1. To add a class to a project in the Visual Basic IDE, select _________.
   a) **File > Add Class**
   b) **File > Add File > Add Class**
   c) **Project > Add Class**
   d) **Project > Add File > Add Class**

2. A class definition ends with the keyword(s) _________.
   a) `Class End`
   b) `End Class`
   c) `EndClass`
   d) `End`

Answers: 1) c. 2) b.

19.4 Initializing Class Objects: Constructors

A class can contain methods as well as instance variables. You have already used method `Format` from class `String` and method `Next` from class `Random`. A **constructor** is a special method within a class definition that is used to initialize a class's instance variables. The constructor is always named `New`. In the following box, you create a constructor for your `Time` class that allows clients to create `Time` objects and initialize their data.

Defining a Constructor

1. ***Adding a constructor to a class.*** Add lines 10–11 of Fig. 19.15 to the body of class `Time`, then press *Enter*. The keywords `End Sub` are added for you, just as with the other `Sub` procedures you've created in this text.

   `New` is the constructor method. You write code for the constructor that is invoked whenever an object of that class is **instantiated** (created). This constructor method then performs the actions in its body, which you add in the next few steps. A constructor's actions consist mainly of statements that initialize the class's instance variables.

New is the constructor method

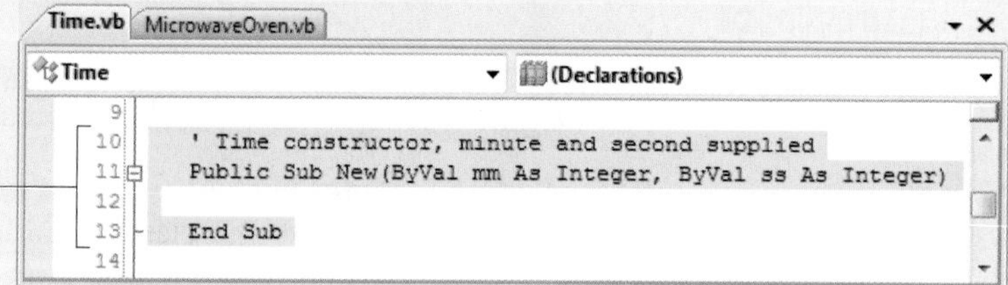

Figure 19.15 Empty constructor.

   Constructors can take arguments (you'll see how to provide arguments to constructors momentarily) but cannot return values. An important difference between constructors and other methods is that constructors cannot specify a return data type—for this reason, Visual Basic constructors are implemented as `Sub` procedures rather than `Function` procedures, because `Sub` procedures cannot return values. A class's instance variables can be initialized in the constructor or when they are defined in the class definition. Variable `secondValue`, for instance, can be initialized where it is declared (line 8 of Fig. 19.14) or it can be initialized in `Time`'s constructor.

Common Programming Error

Attempting to declare a constructor as a `Function` procedure instead of as a `Sub` procedure and attempting to `Return` a value from a constructor are both syntax errors.

2. ***Initializing variables in a constructor.*** Add lines 13–14 of Fig. 19.16 to the constructor. These lines initialize `Time`'s instance variables to the values of the constructor's parameter variables (line 11 of Fig. 19.15). When a client of a class creates an object of that class, values are often specified for that object. A `Time` object can now be created with the statement

```
timeObject = New Time(5, 3)
```

Error-Prevention Tip

Providing a constructor to ensure that every object is initialized with meaningful values can help eliminate logic errors.

(cont.)

which appears in the client. The `Time` object is created and the constructor executes. The constructor's parameters, the values `5` and `3`, are used to initialize `secondValue` and `minuteValue`.

Initialize instance variables

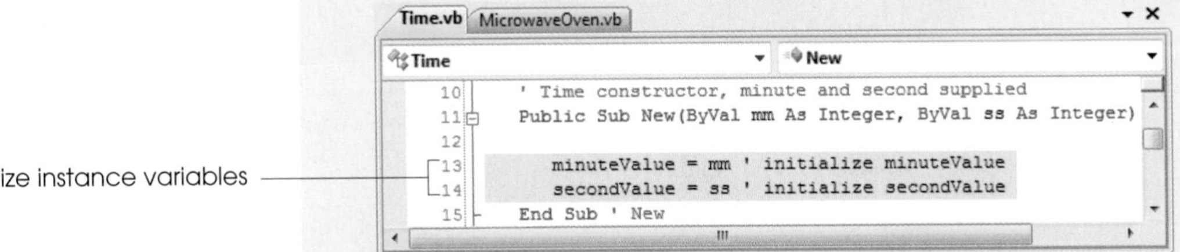

Figure 19.16 Constructor initializing instance variables.

3. ***Creating a `Time` object.*** After defining the class, you can use it as a type (just as you would use `Integer` or `Double`) in declarations. View `MicrowaveOven.vb` by selecting the **MicrowaveOven.vb** tab above the code editor. Add lines 6–7 of Fig. 19.17 to your application. Note the use of the class name, `Time`, as a type. Just as you can create many variables from a data type, such as `Integer`, you can create many objects from class types. You can create your own class types as needed; this is one reason why Visual Basic is known as an **extensible language**—the language can be "extended" with new data types. Note that, after you type `As` in line 7, *IntelliSense* displays a window of available types. Your `Time` class is displayed in the *IntelliSense* window (Fig. 19.18).

Declare `timeObject` of programmer-defined type `Time`

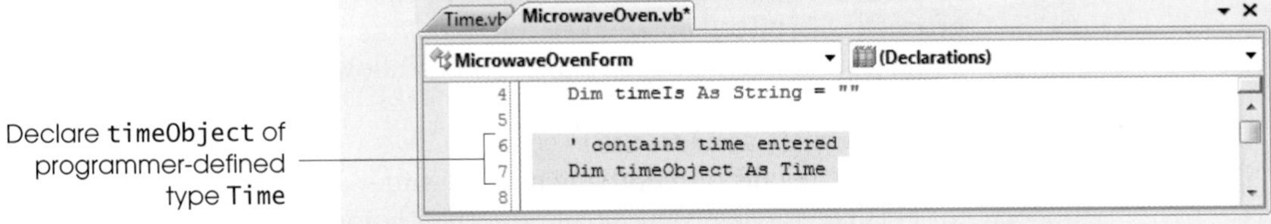

Figure 19.17 Declaring an object of type `Time`.

`Time` appears as a type in the IDE

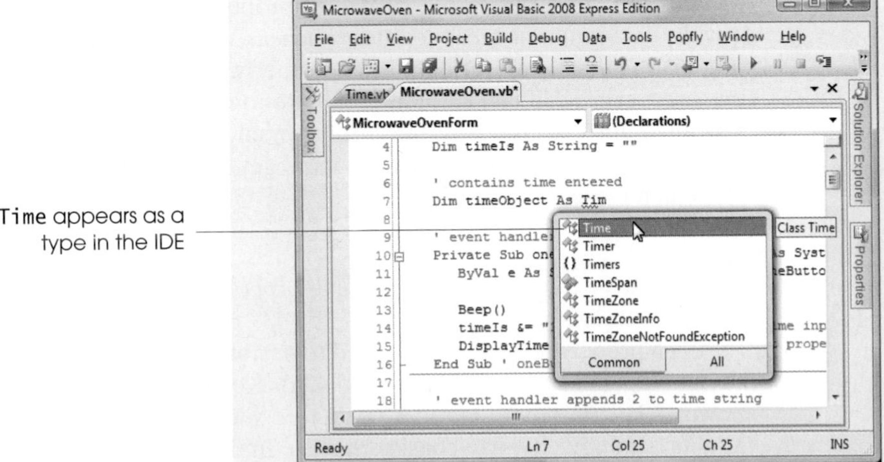

Figure 19.18 `Time` appearing as a type in an *IntelliSense* window.

4. ***Saving the project.*** Select **File > Save All** to save your modified code.

SELF-REVIEW

1. A(n) ________ language is one that can be "extended" with new data types.
   a) data
   b) extensible
   c) typeable
   d) extended

2. Variables can be initialized ________.
   a) when they are declared
   b) to their default values
   c) in a constructor
   d) All of the above

Answers: 1) b. 2) d.

19.5 Properties

Clients of a class usually want to manipulate that class's instance variables. For example, assume a class (`Person`) that stores information about a person, including age information (stored in `Integer` instance variable `age`). Clients who create an object of class `Person` might want to modify `age`—perhaps incorrectly, by assigning a negative value to `age`, for example. Classes often provide **properties** to allow clients to access and modify instance variables safely. The syntax used to access properties is the same as the syntax used to access instance variables. You've already seen and used several properties in previous tutorials. For instance, many GUI controls contain a `Text` property, used to get or set the text displayed by a control. When a value is assigned to a property, the code in the property definition is executed. The code in the property typically checks the value to be assigned and rejects invalid data. In this tutorial, you learn how to create your own properties to help clients of a class read and modify the class's instance variables. You create two properties, `Minute` and `Second`, for your `Time` class. `Minute` allows clients to access variable `minuteValue` safely, and `Second` allows clients to access variable `secondValue` safely.

Good Programming Practice

Capitalize the first letter of a property's name.

A **property definition** may consist of two **accessors**—methodlike code units that handle the details of modifying and returning data. The **Set accessor** allows clients to set (that is, assign values to) properties. For example, when the code

```
timeObject.Minute = 35
```

executes, the `Set` accessor of the `Minute` property executes. `Set` accessors typically provide data-validation capabilities (such as range checking) to ensure that the value of each instance variable is set properly. In your **Microwave Oven** application, users can specify an amount of minutes only in the range 0 to 59. Values not in this range are discarded by the `Set` accessor, and `minuteValue` is assigned the value 0. The **Get accessor** allows clients to get (that is, obtain the value of) a property. When the code

```
minuteValue = timeObject.Minute
```

executes, the `Get` accessor of the `Minute` property executes and returns the value of the `minuteValue` instance variable.

Each property is typically defined to perform validity checking—to ensure that the data assigned to the property is valid. Keeping an object's data valid is also known as keeping that data in a **consistent state**. Property `Minute` keeps instance variable `minuteValue` in a consistent state. In the following box, you'll create properties `Minute` and `Second` for class `Time`, defining `Get` and `Set` accessors for each.

Defining Properties

1. ***Adding property `Minute` to class `Time`.*** View `Time.vb` by selecting the **Time.vb** tab above the code editor. Add lines 17–18 of Fig. 19.19 below the constructor, then press *Enter* to add property `Minute` to class `Time`. Lines 19–25 are added for you automatically by the IDE.

(cont.)

Good Programming Practice

Name each property with a capital first letter.

Note the syntax used in a property definition. You begin in line 18 with the keyword `Public` (which is discussed in Section 19.7), followed by the keyword **`Property`**, which indicates that you are defining a property. The keyword `Property` is followed by the name of the property (in this case, `Minute`) and a set of parentheses, which is similar to the way you define methods. The first line of the property concludes with the keyword `As` followed by a data type (in this case, `Integer`), indicating the data type of any value assigned to, or read from, this property.

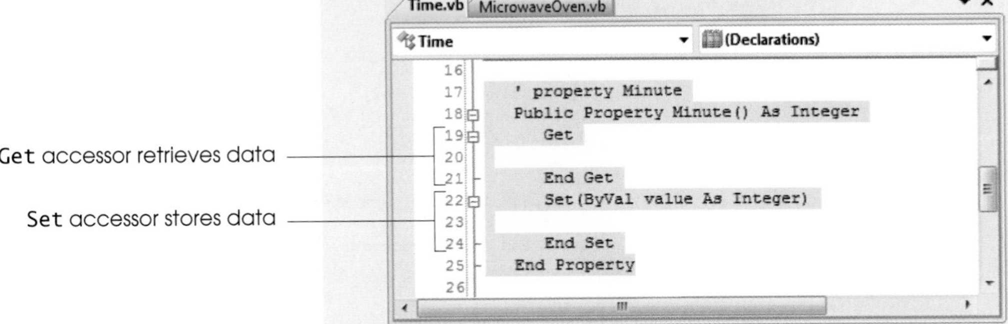
Time.vb
MicrowaveOven.vb
Time
(Declarations)
Get accessor retrieves data
Set accessor stores data
16
17 ' property Minute
18 Public Property Minute() As Integer
19 Get
20
21 End Get
22 Set(ByVal value As Integer)
23
24 End Set
25 End Property
26

Figure 19.19 Empty `Minute` property.

The keyword **`Get`** in line 19 indicates the beginning of this property's `Get` accessor. The keywords **`End Get`** in line 21 indicate the end of the `Get` accessor. Any code that you insert between these two lines makes up the `Get` accessor's body and is executed when a client of this class attempts to read a value from the `Minute` property, as with the code

```
minutes = timeObject.Minute
```

Typically, the `Get` property simply returns the value.

The keyword **`Set`** in line 22 indicates the beginning of this property's `Set` accessor. The keywords **`End Set`** in line 24 indicate the end of the `Set` accessor. Any code that you insert between these two lines makes up the `Set` accessor's body and is executed automatically (that's the beauty of properties) when a client of this class attempts to assign a value to the `Minute` property, as with the code `timeObject.Minute = 35`. The value assigned is stored in the parameter specified in line 22, which by default uses the identifier `value`. This identifier is used to access the value assigned to property `Minute`. The property ends in line 25 with the keywords **`End Property`**.

2. ***Defining the `Get` accessor.*** Add line 21 of Fig. 19.20 to your `Get` accessor. Also add a comment (line 19) above the `Get` accessor, to increase readability. When property `Minute` is referenced, you want your `Get` accessor to return the value of `minuteValue` just as a method (function) would return a value, so you use the keyword `Return` in line 21, followed by the identifier `minuteValue`. Finally, add a comment in line 22 to indicate the end of the `Get` accessor.

Returning data from a property

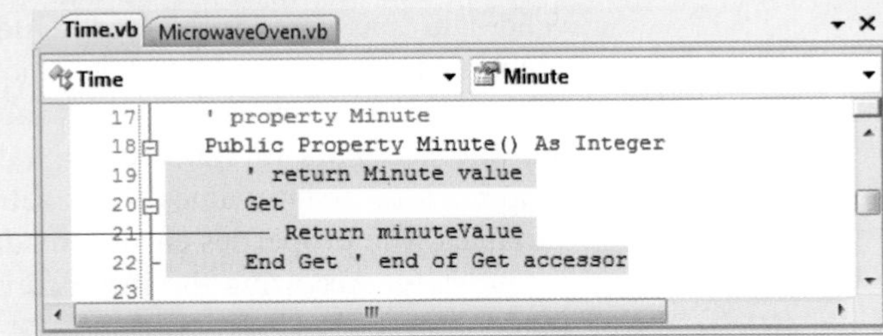
Time.vb
MicrowaveOven.vb
Time
Minute
17 ' property Minute
18 Public Property Minute() As Integer
19 ' return Minute value
20 Get
21 Return minuteValue
22 End Get ' end of Get accessor
23

Figure 19.20 `Get` accessor definition.

(cont.)

3. ***Defining the* Set *accessor.*** Add lines 26–31 of Fig. 19.21 to your `Set` accessor. Also add a comment (line 24) above the `Set` accessor, to increase readability. When property `Minute` is assigned a value, you want to test whether the value to be assigned is valid. You do not want to accept a minutes value greater than 59, a condition that is tested in line 27. If the number of minutes is valid, it is assigned to `minuteValue` in line 28. Otherwise, the value `0` is assigned to `minuteValue` in line 30. Finally, add a comment at line 32 to indicate the end of the `Set` accessor.

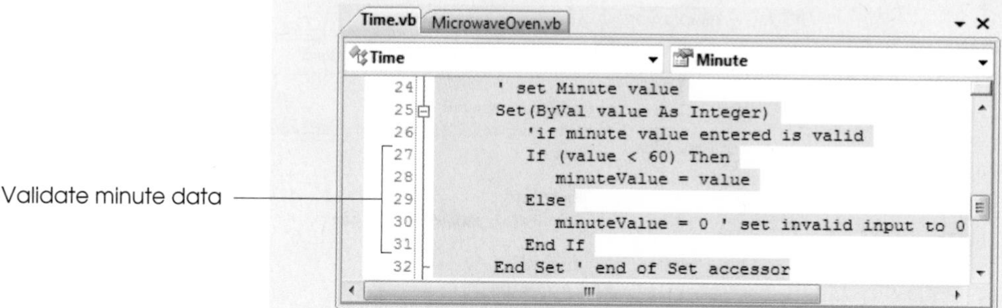

Time.vb
MicrowaveOven.vb
Time
Minute
24 ' set Minute value
25 Set(ByVal value As Integer)
26 'if minute value entered is valid
27 If (value < 60) Then
28 minuteValue = value
29 Else
30 minuteValue = 0 ' set invalid input to 0
31 End If
32 End Set ' end of Set accessor
Validate minute data

Figure 19.21 `Set` accessor definition.

4. ***Adding property* Second *to class* Time.** Add lines 35–36 of Fig. 19.22 to your application, then press *Enter*. Lines 37–43 are added for you automatically by the IDE.

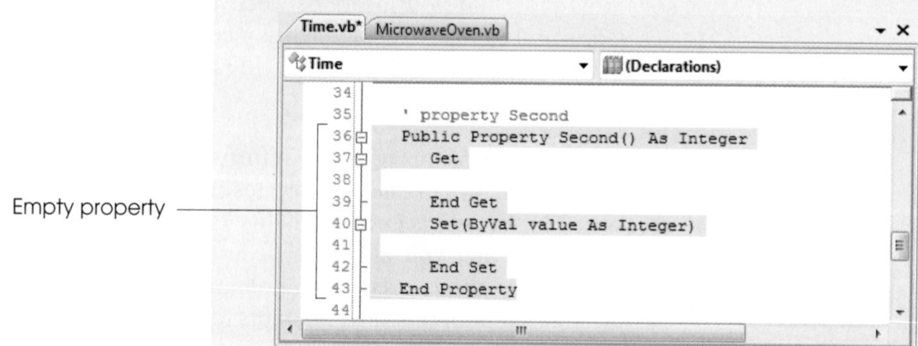

39 End Get

42 End Set

Empty property

Figure 19.22 `Second` property.

5. ***Defining the* Second *property's accessors.*** Add comments above each accessor (lines 37 and 42 of Fig. 19.23). Add line 39 to property `Second`'s `Get` accessor and lines 44–49 to property `Second`'s `Set` accessor. Note that this property is similar to `Minute`, except that variable `secondValue` is being modified and read, as opposed to variable `minuteValue`. Finally, you should add comments at the end of each accessor (lines 40 and 50) to increase readability.

6. ***Assigning values to properties.*** Change lines 13–14 of Fig. 19.16 to lines 13–14 of Fig. 19.24. Now that you have defined properties to ensure that only valid data is assigned to `minuteValue` and `secondValue`, you can use these properties to safely initialize instance variables in the class's constructor. When a client calls `New` and passes values for `mm` and `ss`, the constructor calls the `Set` accessors to validate the values. You should not bypass a class's properties to assign values to or retrieve values from the class's instance variables. The properties ensure the data is valid, keeping the data in a consistent state. Accessing the instance variables directly bypasses this validation.

(cont.)

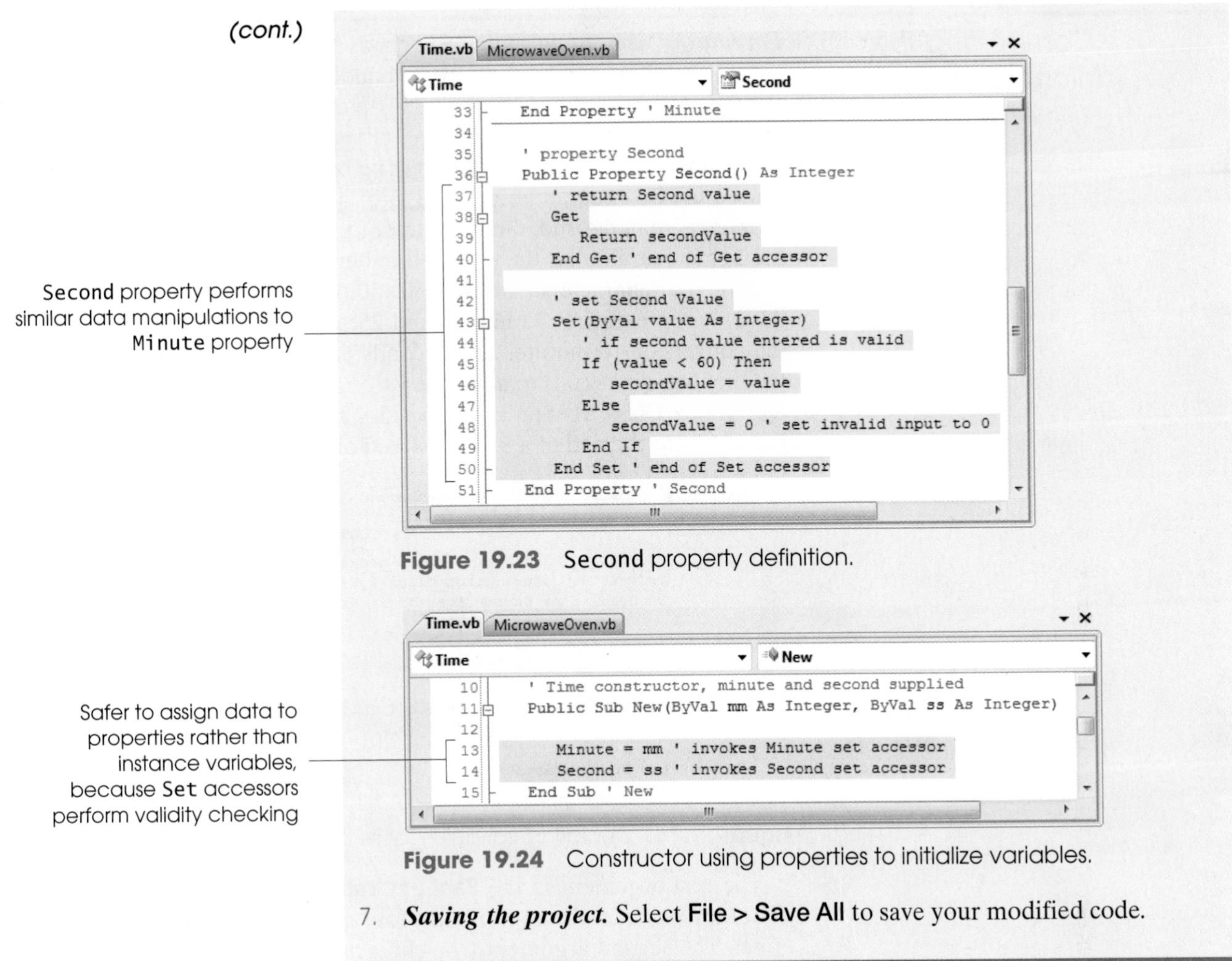

`Second` property performs similar data manipulations to `Minute` property

Figure 19.23 `Second` property definition.

Safer to assign data to properties rather than instance variables, because `Set` accessors perform validity checking

Figure 19.24 Constructor using properties to initialize variables.

7. ***Saving the project.*** Select **File > Save All** to save your modified code.

SELF-REVIEW

1. A(n) _________ can ensure that a value is appropriate for a data member before the data member is assigned that value.
   a) `Get` accessor
   b) `Access` accessor
   c) `Modify` accessor
   d) `Set` accessor

2. Properties can contain both _________ accessors.
   a) `Return` and `Value`
   b) `Get` and `Value`
   c) `Get` and `Set`
   d) `Return` and `Set`

Answers: 1) d. 2) c.

19.6 Completing the Microwave Oven Application

Now that you've completed your `Time` class, you'll use an object of this class to maintain the cooking time in your application. Follow the steps in the next box to add this functionality to your application.

Completing the Microwave Oven Application

1. ***Formatting user input.*** View `MicrowaveOven.vb` in the code editor. Add lines 103–107 of Fig. 19.25 to event handler `startButton_Click`. Variables `second` and `minute` (lines 103–104) store the second and minute values entered by the user. Line 107 uses `String` method **`PadLeft`**, which appends characters to the beginning of a `String` based on the its length. This method can be used to guarantee the length of a `String`—if the `String` has fewer characters than desired, method `PadLeft` adds characters to the beginning of the `String` until it has the proper number of characters. You want `timeIs` to contain four characters (for example, `"0325"` rather than `"325"` for a time of `"3:25"`, representing 3 minutes and 25 seconds). Having four digits makes the conversion to minutes and seconds easier. You can now simply convert the first two digits (`03`) to a minute value and the last two digits (`25`) to a second value. Class `String` also provides method **`PadRight`**, which appends characters to the end of a `String` based on its length.

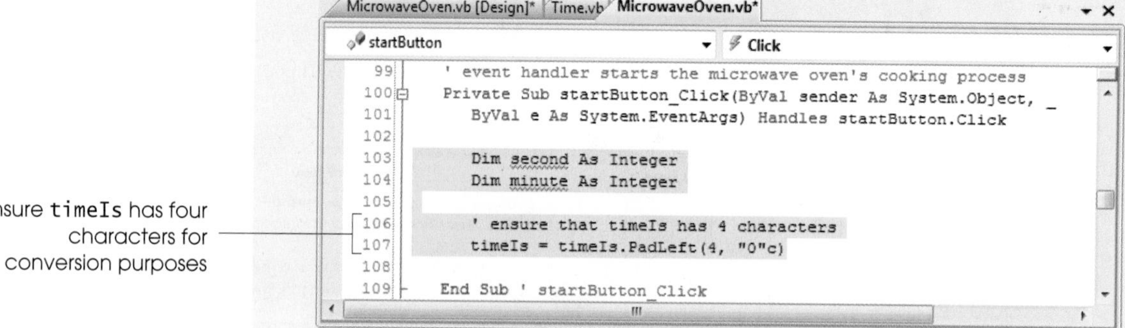
MicrowaveOven.vb [Design]*
Time.vb
MicrowaveOven.vb*
startButton
Click
99 ' event handler starts the microwave oven's cooking process
100 Private Sub startButton_Click(ByVal sender As System.Object, _
101 ByVal e As System.EventArgs) Handles startButton.Click
102
103 Dim second As Integer
104 Dim minute As Integer
105
106 ' ensure that timeIs has 4 characters
107 timeIs = timeIs.PadLeft(4, "0"c)
108
109 End Sub ' startButton_Click
Ensure timeIs has four characters for conversion purposes

Figure 19.25 Declaring variables for second and minute values.

The first argument in the `PadLeft` call, `4`, specifies the desired length of `timeIs`. If `timeIs` already contains four or more characters, `PadLeft` has no effect. The second argument (the character `0`) specifies the character that is appended to the beginning of the `String`. Note that specifying only `"0"` as the second argument causes an error, because `"0"` is of type `String`. Method `PadLeft` expects the second argument to be a single character of data type **`Char`**. You obtain the character `0` by using the literal value `"0"c` to indicate that `0` is a `Char`, not a `String`. The letter `c` following the closing double quote is Visual Basic's syntax for a **character literal**. If you do not specify the second argument, `PadLeft` uses spaces by default.

2. ***Converting user input to `Integers`.*** Add lines 109–111 of Fig. 19.26 to event handler `startButton_Click`. Line 110 calls method `Convert.ToInt32` to convert the last two characters of `timeIs` to an `Integer` and assign this value to `second`. The last two characters are selected from `timeIs` by using method **`Substring`**, which returns part of a `String`. The argument passed to `Substring`, `2`, indicates that the subset of characters returned from this method should begin with the character at position 2, and continue to the end of the `String`. Remember that the character at position 2 is actually the third character in the `String`, because the position values of a `String` begin at 0. In the example `"0325"`, calling `Substring` with the argument `2` returns `"25"`. Line 111 selects the first two characters of `timeIs`, converts the value to an `Integer`, and assigns this value to `minute`. The call to `Substring` in line 111 takes two arguments. The first argument, `0`, indicates that the characters returned from this method start with the first character (at position 0) of `timeIs`. The second argument, `2`, indicates that only two characters from the starting position are to be returned. In the example `"0325"`, calling `Substring` with the arguments `0` and `2` returns `"03"`.

(cont.)

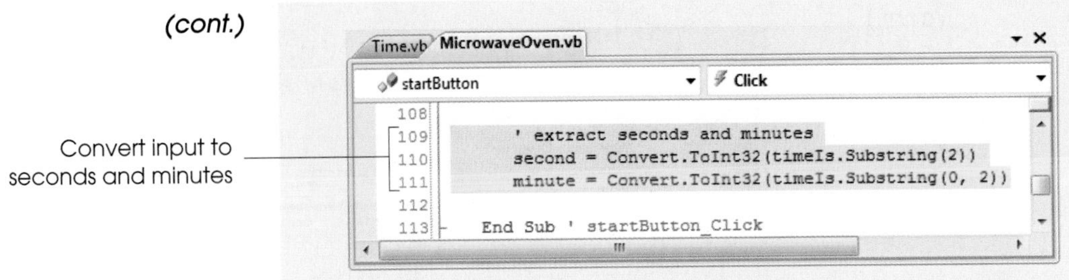
Convert input to seconds and minutes
Time.vb
MicrowaveOven.vb
startButton
Click
108
109 ' extract seconds and minutes
110 second = Convert.ToInt32(timeIs.Substring(2))
111 minute = Convert.ToInt32(timeIs.Substring(0, 2))
112
113 End Sub ' startButton_Click

Figure 19.26 Form minute and second values from input.

3. ***Creating a `Time` object.*** Add lines 113–114 of Fig. 19.27 to `startButton_Click`. Line 114 creates an object of type `Time`. When the object is instantiated, operator `New` allocates the memory in which the `Time` object will be stored; then the `Time` constructor (which must be named `New`) is called with the values of `minute` and `second` to initialize the `Time` object's instance variables. The `New` operator then returns a reference to the newly created object; this reference is assigned to `timeObject`.

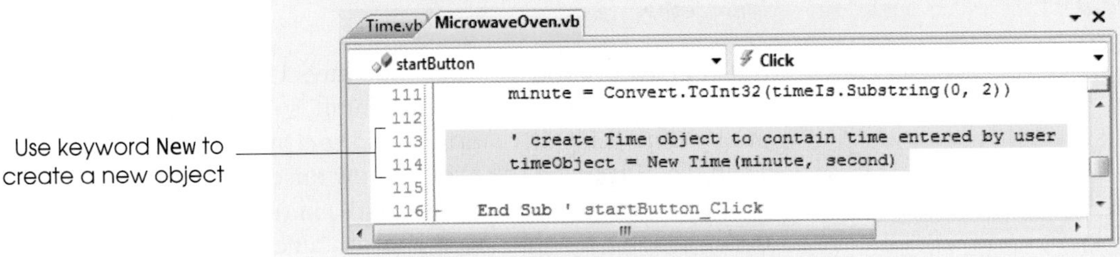
Use keyword New to create a new object
Time.vb
MicrowaveOven.vb
startButton
Click
111 minute = Convert.ToInt32(timeIs.Substring(0, 2))
112
113 ' create Time object to contain time entered by user
114 timeObject = New Time(minute, second)
115
116 End Sub ' startButton_Click

Figure 19.27 Creating a `Time` object.

4. ***Accessing a `Time` object's properties.*** Add lines 116–117 of Fig. 19.28 to `startButton_Click`. These lines use the newly created `Time` object and method `String.Format` to display the cooking time properly. You want the resulting `String` to contain two digits (for the minute), a colon (`:`) and finally another two digits (for the second). For example, if the time entered was 3 minutes and 20 seconds, the `String` that will display for the user is `"03:20"`. To achieve this result, you pass to the method the format control string `"{0:D2}:{1:D2}"`, which indicates that arguments `0` and `1` (the first and second arguments after the format `String` argument) take the format `D2` (base 10 decimal number format using two digits) for display purposes—thus, `8` would be converted to `08`. The colon between the curly braces `}` and `{` is included in the output, separating the minutes from the seconds. The arguments after the format-control string access `timeObject`'s minute and second values, using the `Minute` and `Second` properties. Note that `Time`'s properties appear in the *IntelliSense* window (Fig. 19.29) when you try to access the object's members (using the dot operator).

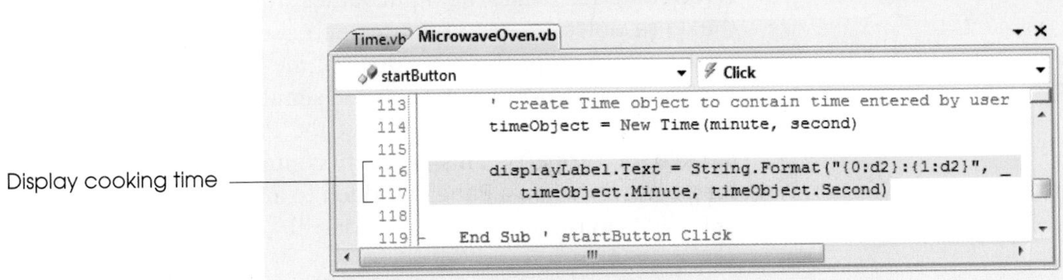
Display cooking time
Time.vb
MicrowaveOven.vb
startButton
Click
113 ' create Time object to contain time entered by user
114 timeObject = New Time(minute, second)
115
116 displayLabel.Text = String.Format("{0:d2}:{1:d2}", _
117 timeObject.Minute, timeObject.Second)
118
119 End Sub ' startButton Click

Figure 19.28 Displaying time information with separating colon.

(cont.)

Time's properties appear in *IntelliSense*

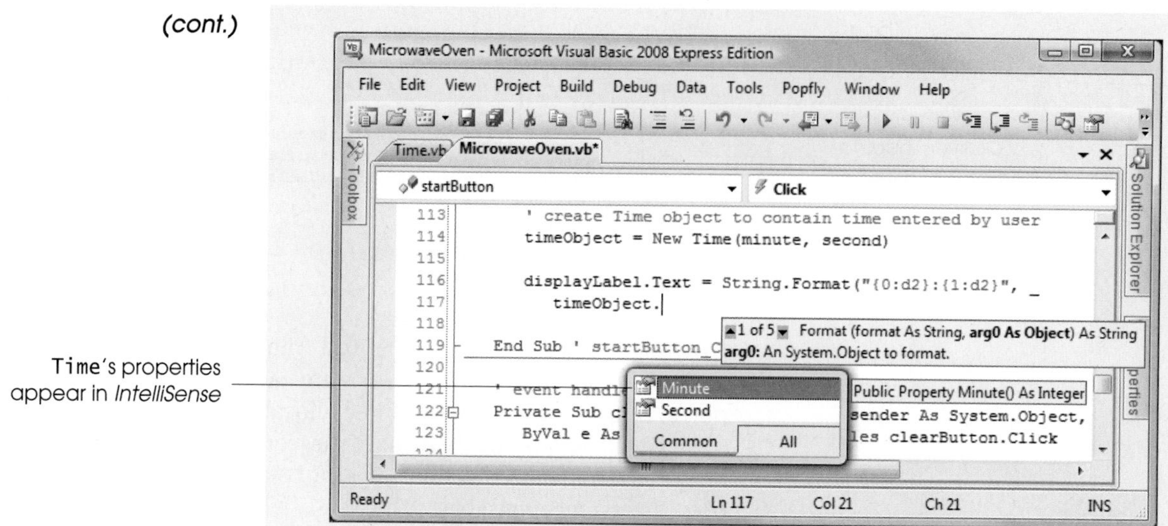

Figure 19.29 Properties of a programmer-defined type also appear in *IntelliSense*.

5. ***Starting the cooking process.*** Add lines 119–123 of Fig. 19.30 to your application. Line 119 clears the user's input, so that the user can enter new input at any time. Line 121 starts the `Timer` by setting its `Enabled` property to `True`. The `Timer`'s `Tick` event is now raised once per second—its `Interval` property is set to 1000 (milliseconds) in the template. You'll implement the event handler for this event shortly. Line 123 sets the `Panel`'s `BackColor` property to yellow to simulate the light inside the microwave oven. The color yellow is assigned to property `BackColor` using property `Yellow` of structure `Color`. The **`Color`** structure contains several predefined colors as properties.

Start timer and turn light on to indicate microwave oven is cooking

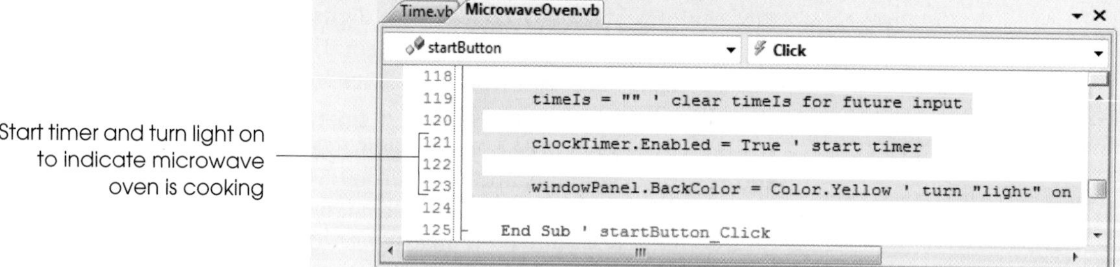

Figure 19.30 Starting the microwave oven countdown.

6. ***Clearing the cook time.*** Add lines 131–136 of Fig. 19.31 to event handler `clearButton_Click`. Line 132 sets the application's `Label` to **Microwave Oven**. Line 133 clears the input values stored in `timeIs`, and line 134 resets the `Time` object to zero minutes and zero seconds. Line 135 disables the `Timer`, which stops the countdown. Line 136 sets the `Panel`'s background back to the `Panel`'s original color to simulate turning off the light inside the microwave oven. Note that we set the `Panel`'s color using the **`DefaultBackColor`** property. This property contains the default background color for a control. When a `Panel` is added to a `Form`, its background takes on the default background color of the control.

(cont.)

Resetting **Microwave Oven** application

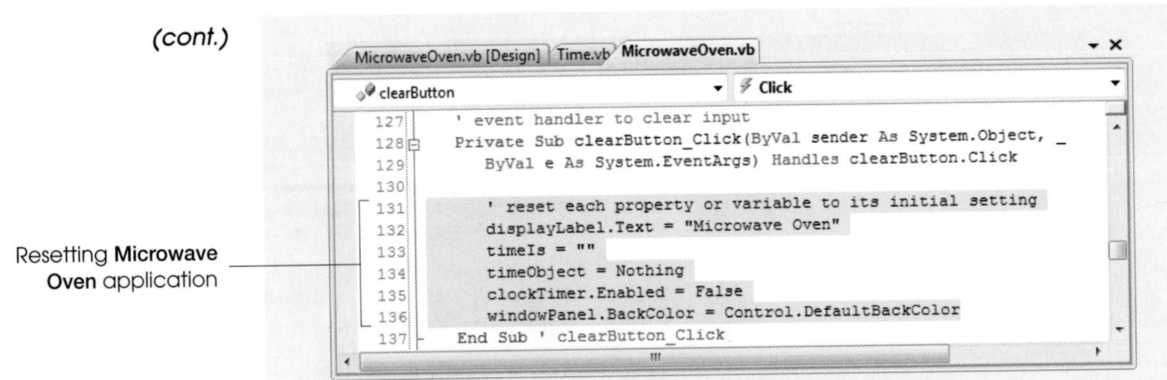

MicrowaveOven.vb [Design]
Time.vb
MicrowaveOven.vb
clearButton
Click
127 ' event handler to clear input
128 Private Sub clearButton_Click(ByVal sender As System.Object, _
129 ByVal e As System.EventArgs) Handles clearButton.Click
130
131 ' reset each property or variable to its initial setting
132 displayLabel.Text = "Microwave Oven"
133 timeIs = ""
134 timeObject = Nothing
135 clockTimer.Enabled = False
136 windowPanel.BackColor = Control.DefaultBackColor
137 End Sub ' clearButton_Click

Figure 19.31 Clearing the **Microwave Oven** input.

7. ***Displaying data as it is being input.*** Add lines 142–150 of Fig. 19.32 to method `DisplayTime`. This method is called each time the user enters another digit for the cooking time. Lines 142–143 declare variables `second` and `minute`, which store the current number of seconds and minutes. Line 145 declares `display`, which stores the user's current input in the proper display format. Lines 148–150 remove any extra digits entered by the user. (Recall that the user may enter a maximum of four digits.) Line 148 uses `String` property **`Length`**, which returns the number of characters in a `String`, to determine whether `timeIs` has more than four digits.

   If it does, line 149 uses `String` method `Substring` to remove the extra digits. The arguments (`0` followed by `4`) indicate that the substring returned should begin with the first character in `timeIs` and continue for four characters. The result is assigned back to `timeIs`, ensuring that any characters appended past the first four are removed.

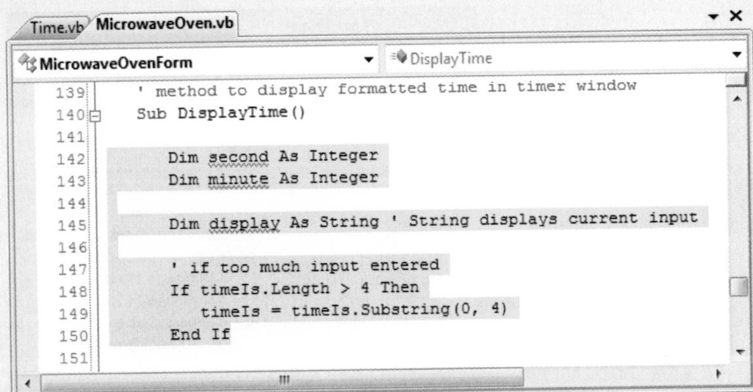

Time.vb
MicrowaveOven.vb
MicrowaveOvenForm
DisplayTime
139 ' method to display formatted time in timer window
140 Sub DisplayTime()
141
142 Dim second As Integer
143 Dim minute As Integer
144
145 Dim display As String ' String displays current input
146
147 ' if too much input entered
148 If timeIs.Length > 4 Then
149 timeIs = timeIs.Substring(0, 4)
150 End If
151

Figure 19.32 Modifying invalid user input.

8. ***Completing the `DisplayTime` method.*** Add lines 152–160 of Fig. 19.33 to method `DisplayTime`. These lines are similar to those of event handler `startButton_Click`. Line 152 appends zeros to the front of `timeIs` if fewer than four digits were entered. Lines 155–156 use method `Substring` to isolate the number of seconds and minutes currently entered. Lines 159–160 then use method `Format` to display the input correctly.

(cont.)

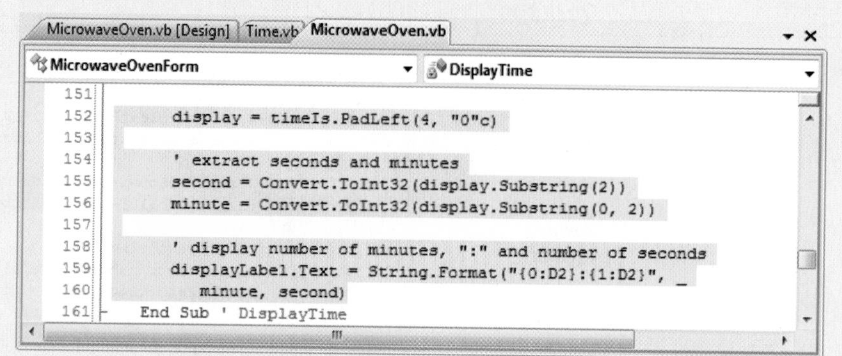

```
            display = timeIs.PadLeft(4, "0"c)

            ' extract seconds and minutes
            second = Convert.ToInt32(display.Substring(2))
            minute = Convert.ToInt32(display.Substring(0, 2))

            ' display number of minutes, ":" and number of seconds
            displayLabel.Text = String.Format("{0:D2}:{1:D2}", _
               minute, second)
         End Sub ' DisplayTime
```

Figure 19.33 Display current input.

9. ***Performing the countdown.*** Add lines 167–182 of Fig. 19.34 to event handler `clockTimer_Tick`. Remember that this event handler executes every second for as long as the `Timer` is enabled. Lines 168–182 modify the display `Label` once per second so that the time remaining is shown to the user.

   If the value of seconds is greater than zero (line 168), the number of seconds is decremented by one (line 169). If the value of seconds is zero but the value of minutes is greater than zero (line 172), the number of minutes is decremented by one (line 173) and the number of seconds is reset to 59 for the new minute (line 174). If the number of seconds is zero and the number of minutes is zero, the cooking process is stopped—the `Timer` is disabled (line 178), a beep is sounded (line 179), the display `Label` is set to **Done!** (line 180) and the window `Panel`'s background color is set back to its default background color (line 181).

Modify time appropriately during countdown

```
163      ' event handler displays new time each second
164      Private Sub clockTimer_Tick(ByVal sender As System.Object, _
165         ByVal e As System.EventArgs) Handles clockTimer.Tick
166
167         ' perform countdown, subtract one second
168         If timeObject.Second > 0 Then
169            timeObject.Second -= 1
170            displayLabel.Text = String.Format("{0:D2}:{1:D2}", _
171               timeObject.Minute, timeObject.Second)
172         ElseIf timeObject.Minute > 0 Then
173            timeObject.Minute -= 1
174            timeObject.Second = 59
175            displayLabel.Text = String.Format("{0:D2}:{1:D2}", _
176               timeObject.Minute, timeObject.Second)
177         Else ' countdown finished
178            clockTimer.Enabled = False ' stop timer
179            Beep()
180            displayLabel.Text = "Done!" ' inform user time is finished
181            windowPanel.BackColor = Control.DefaultBackColor
182         End If
183      End Sub ' clockTimer_Tick
```

Figure 19.34 Modifying the display during countdown.

10. ***Running the application.*** Select **Debug > Start Debugging** to run your application. Enter a cook time and click the **Start** `Button`. The application should now count down correctly, as you have defined the `Tick` event handler for `clockTimer`. Click the **Clear** `Button` and verify that the input is cleared and the countdown is stopped.

11. ***Closing the application.*** Close your running application by clicking its close box.

SELF-REVIEW

1. The ________ property returns the number of characters in a `String`.
   a) `Length` b) `Size`
   c) `Char` d) `Width`

2. The expression `example.Substring(0, 7)` returns the character(s) ________.
   a) that begin at position seven and run backward to position zero
   b) that begin at position zero and continue for seven characters
   c) at position zero and position seven d) at position zero, repeated seven times

Answers: 1) a. 2) b.

Common Programming Error

Attempting to access a `Private` class member from outside its class is a compilation error.

Software Design Tip

Declare all instance variables of a class as `Private`. When necessary, provide `Public` properties to set and get the values of `Private` instance variables.

19.7 Controlling Access to Members

Keywords `Public` and `Private` are called **access modifiers**. You defined properties with access modifier `Public` earlier in this tutorial. Class members that are declared with access modifier `Public` are available to any client of the class. Declaring instance variables, properties or methods with access modifier `Private` makes them available only to methods and properties of the class. Attempting to access a class's `Private` data from outside the class definition is a compilation error. Normally, instance variables are declared `Private`, whereas methods and properties are declared `Public`. There are advanced access modifiers (`Protected` and `Friend`) that are beyond the scope of this book. In the following box, you declare this application's instance variables as `Private`.

Controlling Access to Members

Good Programming Practice

Group all `Private` class members in a class definition, followed by all `Public` class members to enhance clarity and readability.

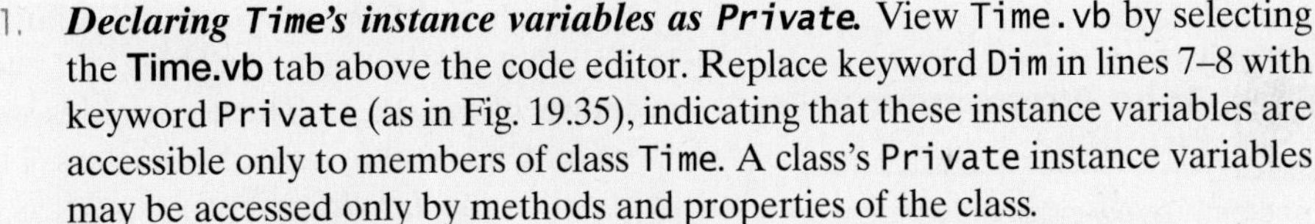

1. ***Declaring `Time`'s instance variables as `Private`.*** View `Time.vb` by selecting the **Time.vb** tab above the code editor. Replace keyword `Dim` in lines 7–8 with keyword `Private` (as in Fig. 19.35), indicating that these instance variables are accessible only to members of class `Time`. A class's `Private` instance variables may be accessed only by methods and properties of the class.

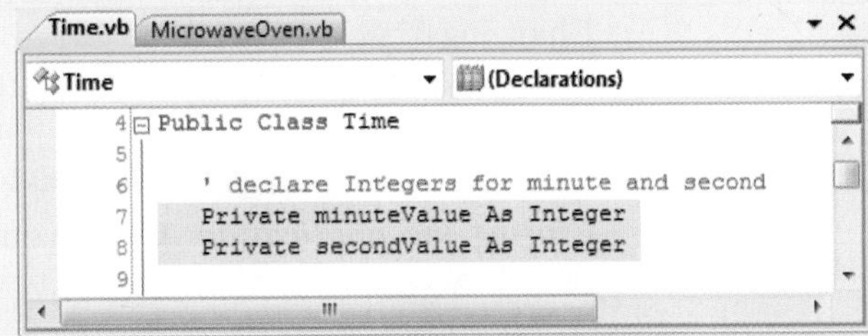
Time.vb
MicrowaveOven.vb
Time
(Declarations)
4 Public Class Time
5
6 ' declare Integers for minute and second
7 Private minuteValue As Integer
8 Private secondValue As Integer
9

Figure 19.35 `Time`'s instance variables are `Private`.

2. ***Declaring `MicrowaveOvenForm`'s instance variables as `Private`.*** View `MicrowaveOven.vb` by selecting the **MicrowaveOven.vb** tab above the code editor. Replace keyword `Dim` in lines 4 and 7 with keyword `Private` (as in Fig. 19.36), indicating that these instance variables are accessible only to members of class `MicrowaveOvenForm`.

Software Design Tip

It is possible to declare the `Get` and `Set` accessors with different access modifiers. One of the accessors must have the same access as the property, and the other must be more restrictive than the property. For example, in a `Public` property, the `Get` accessor could be `Public` and the `Set` accessor could be `Private` to create a property that is "read-only" to the class's clients.

3. ***Setting method `DisplayTime` as `Private`.*** Add keyword `Private` to the beginning of method `DisplayTime` (line 140 of Fig. 19.37). As with variables, methods are declared `Private` to make them accessible only to other members of the current class. In this example only the class that defines your **Microwave Oven** uses method `DisplayTime`, so you should make this method `Private`.

   Note that the event handlers you have created throughout this book have the keyword `Private` automatically added to their headers. You now know that this occurs because event handlers are specific to the `Form`'s class, and not the entire application, which includes class `Time`.

(cont.)

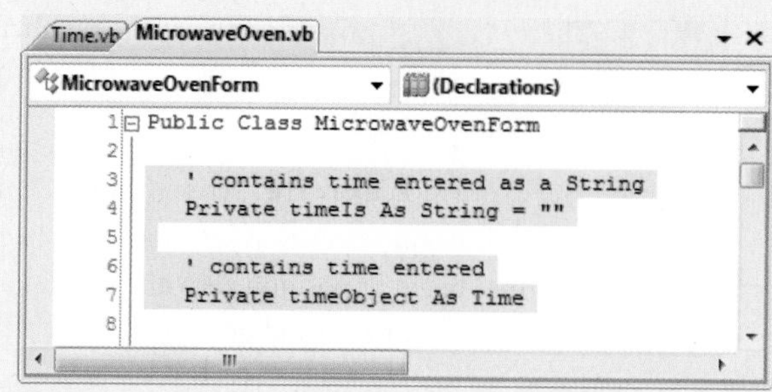

Figure 19.36 **Microwave Oven**'s instance variables are `Private`.

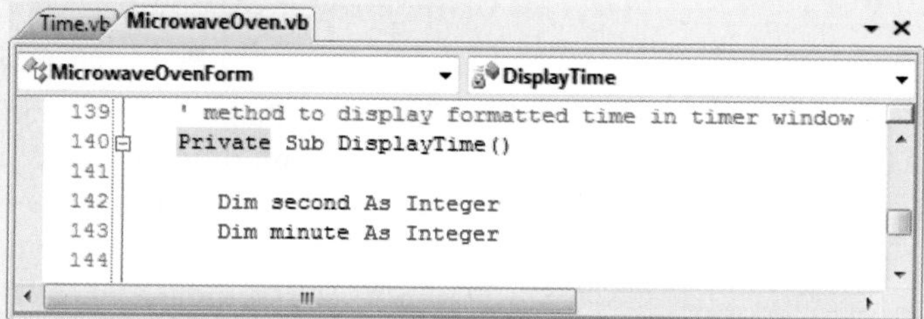

Figure 19.37 **Microwave Oven**'s methods are `Private`.

4. ***Running the application.*** Select **Debug > Start Debugging** to run your application. Note that the application performs exactly as it did at the end of the last box. This occurs because when instance variables are declared by using keyword `Dim`, they are by default `Private` variables. For example, recall that the instance variables of `Time` did not appear in the *IntelliSense* window of Fig. 19.29. These variables were `Private` by default, and therefore not accessible outside of class `Time`. Inaccessible variables do not appear in the *IntelliSense* window. It is a good practice always to precede instance variables with a member-access modifier (usually `Private`). Changing `DisplayTime` to be `Private` did not affect the application either, because your code does not attempt to access this method from outside the class in which it is defined. Note that you cannot use the `Private` access modifier to declare local variables in a method, you must use `Dim`.

5. ***Closing the application.*** Close your running application by clicking its close box.

Good Programming Practice

For clarity, every instance variable or property definition should be preceded by a member-access modifier.

Figures 19.38 and 19.39 present the source code for the **Microwave Oven** application. The lines of code that contain new programming concepts that you learned in this tutorial are highlighted.

```
Public Class MicrowaveOvenForm

   ' contains time entered as a String
   Private timeIs As String = ""

   ' contains time entered
   Private timeObject As Time

   ' event handler appends 1 to time string
   Private Sub oneButton_Click(ByVal sender As System.Object, _
      ByVal e As System.EventArgs) Handles oneButton.Click

      Beep() ' sound beep
```

Make a "beep" sound by calling method `Beep`

Figure 19.38 **Microwave Oven** application code. (Part 1 of 4.)

```
      timeIs &= "1" ' append digit to time input
      DisplayTime() ' display time input properly
   End Sub ' oneButton_Click

   ' event handler appends 2 to time string
   Private Sub twoButton_Click(ByVal sender As System.Object, _
      ByVal e As System.EventArgs) Handles twoButton.Click

      Beep() ' sound beep
      timeIs &= "2" ' append digit to time input
      DisplayTime() ' display time input properly
   End Sub ' twoButton_Click

   ' event handler appends 3 to time string
   Private Sub threeButton_Click(ByVal sender As System.Object, _
      ByVal e As System.EventArgs) Handles threeButton.Click

      Beep() ' sound beep
      timeIs &= "3" ' append digit to time input
      DisplayTime() ' display time input properly
   End Sub ' threeButton_Click

   ' event handler appends 4 to time string
   Private Sub fourButton_Click(ByVal sender As System.Object, _
      ByVal e As System.EventArgs) Handles fourButton.Click

      Beep() ' sound beep
      timeIs &= "4" ' append digit to time input
      DisplayTime() ' display time input properly
   End Sub ' fourButton_Click

   ' event handler appends 5 to time string
   Private Sub fiveButton_Click(ByVal sender As System.Object, _
      ByVal e As System.EventArgs) Handles fiveButton.Click

      Beep() ' sound beep
      timeIs &= "5" ' append digit to time input
      DisplayTime() ' display time input properly
   End Sub ' fiveButton_Click

   ' event handler appends 6 to time string
   Private Sub sixButton_Click(ByVal sender As System.Object, _
      ByVal e As System.EventArgs) Handles sixButton.Click

      Beep() ' sound beep
      timeIs &= "6" ' append digit to time input
      DisplayTime() ' display time input properly
   End Sub ' sixButton_Click

   ' event handler appends 7 to time string
   Private Sub sevenButton_Click(ByVal sender As System.Object, _
      ByVal e As System.EventArgs) Handles sevenButton.Click

      Beep() ' sound beep
      timeIs &= "7" ' append digit to time input
      DisplayTime() ' display time input properly
   End Sub ' sevenButton_Click

   ' event handler appends 8 to time string
   Private Sub eightButton_Click(ByVal sender As System.Object, _
      ByVal e As System.EventArgs) Handles eightButton.Click

      Beep() ' sound beep
      timeIs &= "8" ' append digit to time input
```

Figure 19.38 **Microwave Oven** application code. (Part 2 of 4.)

```
      DisplayTime() ' display time input properly
   End Sub ' eightButton_Click

   ' event handler appends 9 to time string
   Private Sub nineButton_Click(ByVal sender As System.Object, _
      ByVal e As System.EventArgs) Handles nineButton.Click

      Beep() ' sound beep
      timeIs &= "9" ' append digit to time input
      DisplayTime() ' display time input properly
   End Sub ' nineButton_Click

   ' event handler appends 0 to time string
   Private Sub zeroButton_Click(ByVal sender As System.Object, _
      ByVal e As System.EventArgs) Handles zeroButton.Click

      Beep() ' sound beep
      timeIs &= "0" ' append digit to time input
      DisplayTime() ' display time input properly
   End Sub ' zeroButton_Click

   ' event handler starts the microwave oven's cooking process
   Private Sub startButton_Click(ByVal sender As System.Object, _
      ByVal e As System.EventArgs) Handles startButton.Click

      Dim second As Integer
      Dim minute As Integer

      ' ensure that timeIs has 4 characters
      timeIs = timeIs.PadLeft(4, "0"c)

      ' extract seconds and minutes
      second = Convert.ToInt32(timeIs.Substring(2))
      minute = Convert.ToInt32(timeIs.Substring(0, 2))

      ' create Time object to contain time entered by user
      timeObject = New Time(minute, second)

      displayLabel.Text = String.Format("{0:D2}:{1:D2}", _
         timeObject.Minute, timeObject.Second)

      timeIs = "" ' clear timeIs for future input

      clockTimer.Enabled = True ' start timer

      windowPanel.BackColor = Color.Yellow ' turn "light" on

   End Sub ' startButton_Click

   ' event handler to clear input
   Private Sub clearButton_Click(ByVal sender As System.Object, _
      ByVal e As System.EventArgs) Handles clearButton.Click

      ' reset each property or variable to its initial setting
      displayLabel.Text = "Microwave Oven"
      timeIs = ""
      timeObject = Nothing
      clockTimer.Enabled = False
      windowPanel.BackColor = Control.DefaultBackColor
   End Sub ' clearButton_Click

   ' method to display formatted time in timer window
   Private Sub DisplayTime()
```

Creating a new object of a programmer-defined type

Accessing variables of a programmer-defined type

Use property `BackColor` to change the `Panel`'s color

Figure 19.38 **Microwave Oven** application code. (Part 3 of 4.)

Method Substring returns a subset of characters in a String

Method PadLeft called to ensure that String timeIs contains four characters

```
      Dim second As Integer
      Dim minute As Integer

      Dim display As String ' String displays current input

      ' if too much input entered
      If timeIs.Length > 4 Then
         timeIs = timeIs.Substring(0, 4)
      End If

      display = timeIs.PadLeft(4, "0"c)

      ' extract seconds and minutes
      second = Convert.ToInt32(display.Substring(2))
      minute = Convert.ToInt32(display.Substring(0, 2))

      ' display number of minutes, ":" and number of seconds
      displayLabel.Text = String.Format("{0:D2}:{1:D2}", _
         minute, second)
   End Sub ' DisplayTime

   ' event handler displays new time each second
   Private Sub clockTimer_Tick(ByVal sender As System.Object, _
      ByVal e As System.EventArgs) Handles clockTimer.Tick

      ' perform countdown, subtract one second
      If timeObject.Second > 0 Then
         timeObject.Second -= 1
         displayLabel.Text = String.Format("{0:D2}:{1:D2}", _
            timeObject.Minute, timeObject.Second)
      ElseIf timeObject.Minute > 0 Then
         timeObject.Minute -= 1
         timeObject.Second = 59
         displayLabel.Text = String.Format("{0:D2}:{1:D2}", _
            timeObject.Minute, timeObject.Second)
      Else ' no more seconds
         clockTimer.Enabled = False ' stop timer
         Beep()
         displayLabel.Text = "Done!" ' inform user time is finished
         windowPanel.BackColor = Control.DefaultBackColor
      End If
   End Sub ' clockTimer_Tick
End Class ' MicrowaveOvenForm
```

Figure 19.38 **Microwave Oven** application code. (Part 4 of 4.)

Keyword Class used to define a class

New is the constructor

Assign data to properties, rather than directly to instance variables

End Sub keywords end the constructor definition

```
' Time.vb
' Represents time data and contains properties.

Public Class Time

   ' declare Integers for minute and second
   Private minuteValue As Integer
   Private secondValue As Integer

   ' Time constructor, minute and second supplied
   Public Sub New(ByVal mm As Integer, ByVal ss As Integer)

      Minute = mm ' invokes Minute Set accessor
      Second = ss ' invokes Second Set accessor
   End Sub ' New

```

Figure 19.39 Class Time. (Part 1 of 2.)

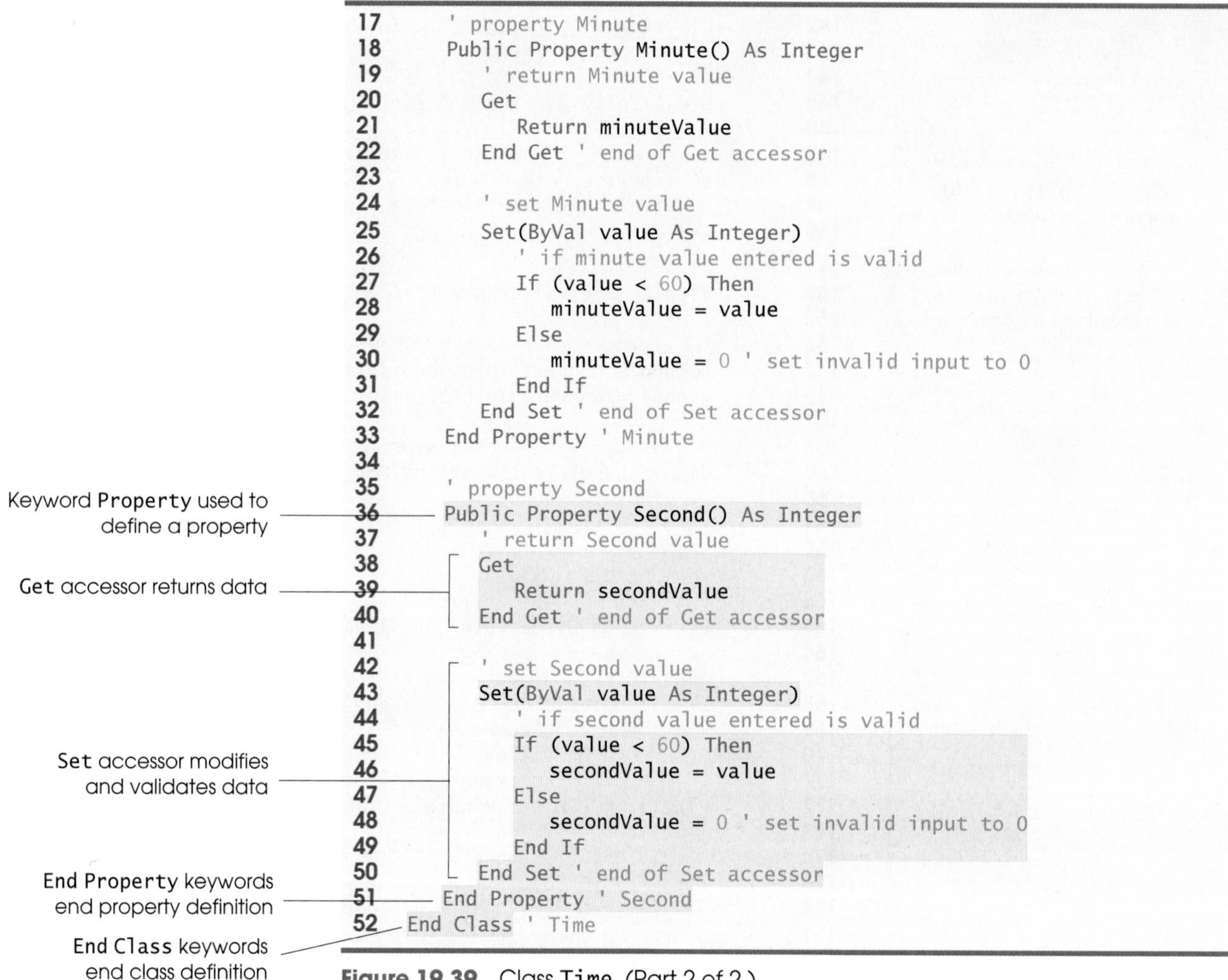

```
      ' property Minute
      Public Property Minute() As Integer
         ' return Minute value
         Get
            Return minuteValue
         End Get ' end of Get accessor

         ' set Minute value
         Set(ByVal value As Integer)
            ' if minute value entered is valid
            If (value < 60) Then
               minuteValue = value
            Else
               minuteValue = 0 ' set invalid input to 0
            End If
         End Set ' end of Set accessor
      End Property ' Minute

      ' property Second
      Public Property Second() As Integer
         ' return Second value
         Get
            Return secondValue
         End Get ' end of Get accessor

         ' set Second value
         Set(ByVal value As Integer)
            ' if second value entered is valid
            If (value < 60) Then
               secondValue = value
            Else
               secondValue = 0 ' set invalid input to 0
            End If
         End Set ' end of Set accessor
      End Property ' Second
   End Class ' Time
```


Figure 19.39 Class Time. (Part 2 of 2.)

SELF-REVIEW

1. Instance variable declarations should be preceded by which of the following keywords.

   a) `Dim` b) `Private`
   c) `Public` d) Any of the above

2. Instance variables are considered _________ by default.

   a) `Private` b) `Public`
   c) `Dimensional` d) None of the above

Answers: 1) b. 2) a.

19.8 Using the Debugger: The Locals Window

Now you'll enhance your knowledge of the debugger by studying the capabilities of the **Locals** window. This window allows you to view the values stored in an object's instance variables. In this section, you learn how to view the contents of `timeObject`'s instance variables to verify that your application is executing correctly. In the following box, you use this window to examine the state of the `Time` object in the **Microwave Oven** application.

Using the Debugger: Using the Locals Window

1. ***Viewing the application code.*** View `MicrowaveOven.vb` by selecting the **MicrowaveOven.vb** tab above the code editor.

2. ***Setting breakpoints.*** Set breakpoints in lines 168 and 181 by clicking in the margin indicator bar (Fig. 19.40). You can set breakpoints in your application to examine an object's instance variables at certain places during execution. In the **Microwave Oven** application, `clockTimer`'s `Tick` event handler modifies the properties of `timeObject`. Setting breakpoints in lines 168 and 181 allows you to suspend execution before and after certain properties have been modified, ensuring that data is being modified properly.

```
163     ' event handler displays new time each second
164     Private Sub clockTimer_Tick(ByVal sender As System.Object, _
165        ByVal e As System.EventArgs) Handles clockTimer.Tick
166
167        ' perform countdown, subtract one second
168        If timeObject.Second > 0 Then
169           timeObject.Second -= 1
170           displayLabel.Text = String.Format("{0:D2}:{1:D2}", _
171              timeObject.Minute, timeObject.Second)
172        ElseIf timeObject.Minute > 0 Then
173           timeObject.Minute -= 1
174           timeObject.Second = 59
175           displayLabel.Text = String.Format("{0:D2}:{1:D2}", _
176              timeObject.Minute, timeObject.Second)
177        Else ' countdown finished
178           clockTimer.Enabled = False ' stop timer
179           Beep()
180           displayLabel.Text = "Done!" ' inform user time is finished
181           windowPanel.BackColor = Control.DefaultBackColor
182        End If
183     End Sub ' clockTimer_Tick
```

Figure 19.40 **Microwave Oven** application with breakpoints added.

3. ***Starting the debugger.*** Start the debugger by selecting **Debug > Start Debugging.**

4. ***Opening the Locals window.*** Open the **Locals** window (Fig. 19.41) by selecting **Debug > Windows > Locals** while the debugger is running. The **Locals** window allows you to view the state of the variables in the current scope. Recall that the scope of a variable's identifier is the portion of an application in which the identifier can be referenced. The `Timer`'s `Tick` event is a method of the `Form` class, so all the instance variables and controls of the `Form` are viewable in the **Locals** window. This means that you can view the values of the properties of `timeObject`, because `timeObject` is an instance variable of the `Form` class.

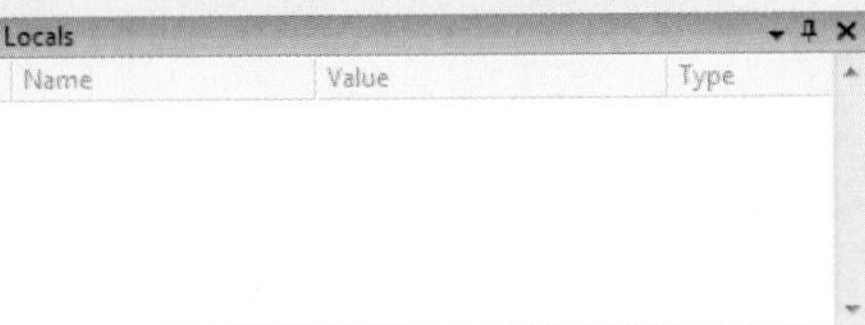

Figure 19.41 Empty **Locals** window.

5. ***Setting the time.*** Set the microwave oven's time to `1:01`, and click the **Start** `Button`.

(cont.)

6. ***Using the Locals window.*** While execution is still halted, look at the **Locals** window. If the **Locals** window is now hidden, reselect **Debug > Windows > Locals.** The **Locals** window lists all the variables that are in the scope of `clockTimer`'s `Tick` event handler. To view the contents of `timeObject`, click the plus box next to the word **Me.** Scroll down until you reach `timeObject`, and click the plus box next to it. This shows all the members of `timeObject`, their current values and their types (Fig. 19.42). Note that it displays different icons for the objects instance variables and properties.

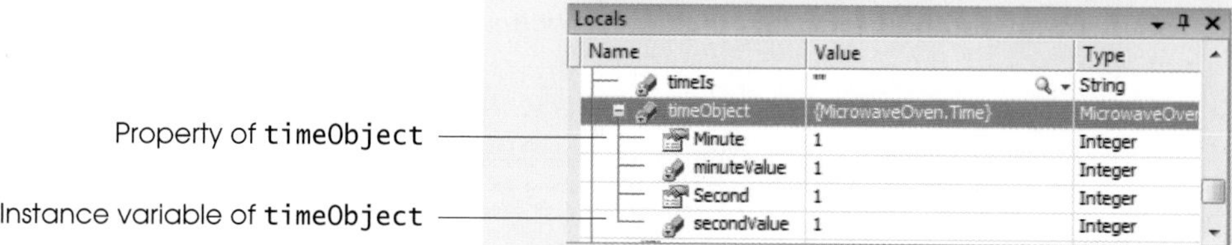

Figure 19.42 **Locals** window displaying the state of `timeObject`.

7. ***Continuing program execution.*** Click the debug toolbar's **Continue** `Button`, and view the values of the `timeObject`'s members. Note that the value for the amount of seconds (as represented by variable `secondValue` and property `Second`) appears in red (Fig. 19.43) to indicate it has changed. Click the **Continue** `Button` again.

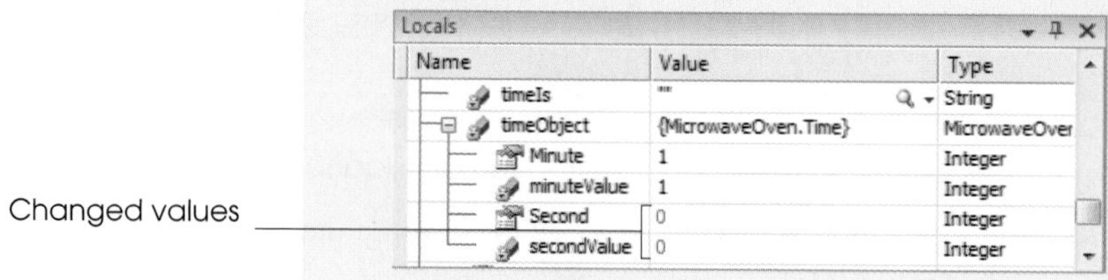

Figure 19.43 **Locals** window displaying changed variables.

8. ***Changing the value of a variable.*** In the **Locals** window, double click the value for property `Second`. Type `0` and press *Enter* to set the microwave oven's time to zero (Fig. 19.44). The **Locals** window allows you to change the values of variables to verify that program execution is correct at certain points without having to run the program again for each value. Now set the value of the `Second` property to `100`. Note that the `Second` property validates the data and sets the value to `0`.

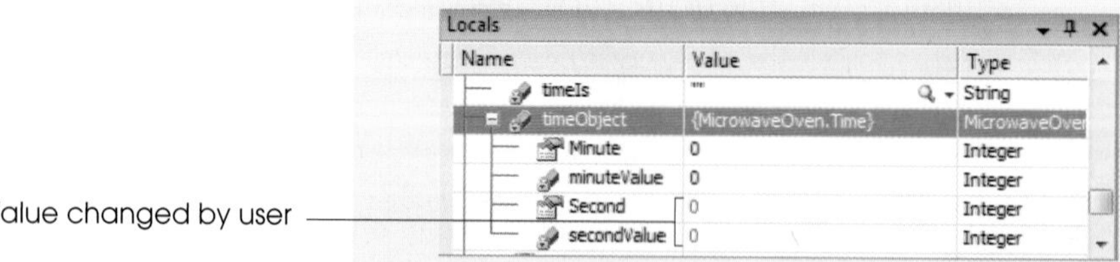

Figure 19.44 Changing the value of a variable in the **Locals** window.

9. ***Continuing execution.*** Click the **Continue** `Button`. Execution continues until the breakpoint in line 181 is reached.
10. ***Stopping the debugger.*** Click the **Stop Debugging** `Button` to end the debugging session.
11. ***Closing the application.*** Close your running application by clicking its close box.
12. ***Clearing the breakpoints.*** Clear the breakpoints you set in the application.
13. ***Closing the IDE.*** Close the Visual Basic IDE by clicking its close box.

In this section, you learned how to use the **Locals** window to view the state of an object and verify that your application is executing correctly.

SELF-REVIEW

1. The **Locals** window allows you to ________.
   a) change the value stored in an instance variable of an object
   b) view all of the variables in the current scope
   c) view the values stored in all of the variables in the current scope
   d) All of the above

2. When a variable's value changes, it becomes ________ in the **Locals** window.
   a) red b) italic
   c) blue d) bold

Answers: 1) d. 2) a.

19.9 Wrap-Up

In previous tutorials, you used .NET classes and methods to add functionality to your applications. In this tutorial, you learned how to create your own classes, also known as programmer-defined classes, to provide functionality not available in the .NET Framework Class Library. Visual Basic applications typically are created by using a combination of .NET classes and methods, and programmer-defined classes and methods.

You created a microwave-oven simulator using a programmer-defined class called `Time`. You added a class definition file to your application to create the `Time` class; then you added instance variables, a constructor, and properties to that class. You defined your constructor to initialize the class's instance variables. For each property, you defined `Get` and `Set` accessors that allow the class's instance variables to be safely accessed and modified. You then applied what you learned about classes and properties to create a `Time` object. You used the properties of class `Time` to access and display the number of minutes and number of seconds that the user specified as the microwave oven's cook time. You also learned how to control access to the members of class `Time` through the use of `Public` and `Private` member-access modifiers. You learned how `Panel`s can organize controls (much like `GroupBox`es), and used a `Panel` to simulate the microwave oven's door. You learned how to create a beeping sound. You even learned some new ways to manipulate strings using the `Substring` and `PadLeft` methods. You concluded the tutorial by learning how to view an application's values using the debugger's **Locals** window.

In the next tutorial, you learn about collections. The .NET Framework Class Library provides several collection classes that enable you to store collections of data in an organized way. A collection can be thought of as a group of items. You'll use collections to create a **Shipping Hub** application that stores information about several packages that are being shipped to various states. Each package is defined by using a `Package` programmer-defined class. Several `Package` objects are maintained by using collections.

SKILLS SUMMARY

Defining a `Public` Property

- Use keywords `Public Property` followed by the property name and a set of parentheses.
- After the parentheses, specify the property's type with the `As` keyword.
- Press *Enter*. Empty `Get` and `Set` accessors are added for you by the IDE, followed by the keywords `End Property`. The `Get` accessor begins with keyword `Get` and ends with keywords `End Get`. The `Set` accessor begins with keyword `Set` and ends with keywords `End Set`.
- In the `Get` accessor, provide code to return the requested data.
- In the `Set` accessor, provide code to modify the relevant data. Be sure to validate the data.

Adding a Class File to Your Project

- Select **Project > Add Class**.
- Enter a name for the class.

Creating a Constructor

- Use keywords `Public Sub New`, followed by a set of parentheses enclosing any constructor parameters.
- Press *Enter*. The keywords `End Sub` are added by the IDE.
- Add code to initialize the object's data.

Adding a `Panel` to Your Application

- Double click the `Panel` control in the **Containers** tab of the **Toolbox**, or drag the `Panel` control from the **Toolbox** to the `Form`. We recommend appending `Panel` to `Panel` control names.

KEY TERMS

access modifier—Keywords used to specify what members of a class a client may access. Includes keywords `Public` and `Private`.

accessors—Methodlike code units that handle the details of modifying and returning data.

`Beep`—Causes your computer to make a beep sound.

`Char` data type—Primitive type that represents a character.

`Class` Keyword—Reserved word required to begin a class definition.

character literal—A single character represented as a value of type `Char`. Create a character literal by placing a single character in double quotes followed by the letter `c` (e.g., `"0"c`).

client—When an application creates and uses an object of a class, the application is known as a client of the class.

`Color` structure—Contains several predefined colors as properties.

consistent state—A way to maintain the values of an object's instance variables such that the values are always valid.

constructor—A special class method that initializes a class's variables.

`DefaultBackColor` property—Contains the default background color for a control.

`End Class` Keywords—Reserved words required to end a class definition.

extensible language—A language that can be "extended" with new data types. Visual Basic is an extensible language.

`FixedSingle` value of the `BorderStyle` property of a `Label`—Specifies that the `Label` will display a thin, black border.

`Flat` value of the `FlatStyle` property of a `Button`—Specifies that a `Button` will appear flat.

`FlatStyle` property of a `Button`—Determines whether the `Button` will appear flat or three-dimensional.

`Get` accessor—Used to retrieve a value of a property.

`Get`/`End Get` keywords—Reserved words that define a property's `Get` accessor.

instantiate an object—Create an object (or instance) of a class.

`Length` property of class `String`—Returns the number of characters in a `String`.

Locals window—Allows you to view the state of the variables and properties in the current scope during debugging.

members of a class—Methods, variables and properties declared within the body of a class.

`PadLeft` method of class `String`—Adds characters to the beginning of a string until the length of the string equals the specified length.

`PadRight` method of class `String`—Adds characters to the end of a string until the length of the string equals the specified length.

`Panel` control—Used to group controls. Unlike `GroupBoxes`, `Panels` do not have captions.

`Private` keyword—Member-access modifier that makes members accessible only to the class that defines the members.

programmer-defined class (programmer-defined type)—A class defined by a programmer, as opposed to classes predefined in the Framework Class Library.

property—Contains accessors—portions of code that handle the details of modifying and returning data.

property definition—Defines the accessors for a property.

Property/End Property keywords—Reserved words indicating the definition of a class property.

Public keyword—Member-access modifier that makes instance variables or methods accessible wherever the application has a reference to that object.

Set accessor—Provides data-validation capabilities to ensure that the value is set properly.

Set/End Set keywords—Reserved words that define a property's Set accessor.

Substring method of class String—Returns characters from a string, corresponding to the arguments passed by the user, that indicate the start position within a String and the number of characters to return.

GUI DESIGN GUIDELINES

Panel

- Use Panels to organize groups of related controls where the purpose of the controls is obvious. If the purpose of the controls is not obvious, use a GroupBox rather than a Panel, because GroupBoxes can contain captions.
- Although it is possible to have a Panel without a border (by setting the BorderStyle property to None), use borders on your Panels to improve user interface readability and organization.
- A Panel can display scrollbars when it is not large enough to display all of its controls. To increase usability, we suggest avoiding the use of scrollbars on Panels. If a Panel is not large enough to display all of its contents, increase the size of the Panel.

CONTROLS, EVENTS, PROPERTIES & METHODS

Button [ab] Button This control allows the user to raise an action or event.

- ***In action***

- ***Event***

  Click—Raised when the user clicks the Button.

- ***Properties***

  Enabled—Determines whether the Button's event handler is executed when the Button is clicked.

  FlatStyle—Determines whether the Button appears flat or three-dimensional.

  Location—Specifies the location of the Button on the Form relative to the top-left corner.

  Name—Specifies the name used to access the Button programmatically. The name should be appended with the Button suffix.

  Size—Specifies the height and width (in pixels) of the Button.

  Text—Specifies the text displayed on the Button.

- ***Method***

  Focus—Transfers the focus of the application to the Button that calls it.

Label A Label This control displays text on the Form that the user cannot modify.

- ***In action***

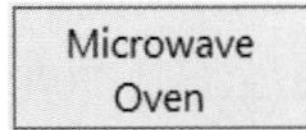

- ***Properties***

  BorderStyle—Specifies the appearance of the Label's border.

  Font—Specifies the font name, style and size of the text displayed in the Label.

  Location—Specifies the location of the Label on the Form relative to the top-left corner.

Name—Specifies the name used to access the Label programmatically. The name should be appended with the Label suffix.

Size—Specifies the width and height (in pixels) of the Label.

Text—Specifies the text displayed on the Label.

TextAlign—Specifies how the text is aligned within the Label.

Panel Panel This control is used to organize various controls. Unlike a GroupBox control, the Panel control does not display a caption.

- ***In action***

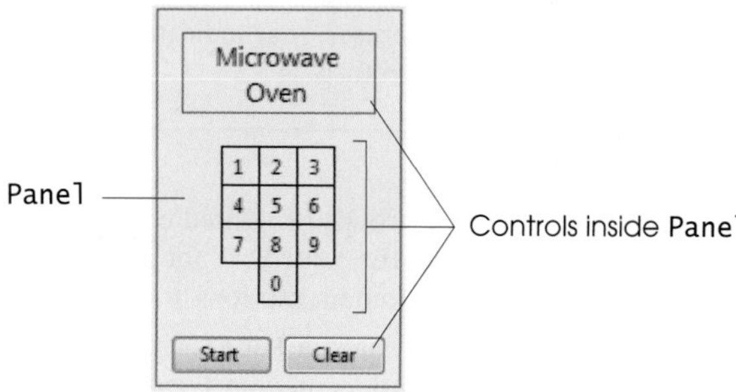

- ***Properties***

DefaultBackColor—Returns the default background color of a Panel control.

Name—Specifies the name of the Panel.

Size—Specifies the size of the Panel.

Location—Specifies the Panel's location on the Form relative to the top-left corner.

BorderStyle—Specifies the Panel's border style. Options include None (displaying no border), FixedSingle (a single-line border) and Fixed3D (a three-dimensional border).

None—Specifies that the Panel will not display a border.

FixedSingle—Specifies that the Panel will display a thin, black border.

Fixed3D—Specifies that the Panel will display a three-dimensional border.

BackColor—Specifies the background color of the Panel.

String The String class represents a series of characters treated as a single unit.

- ***Property***

Length—Returns the number of characters in the String.

- ***Methods***

Format—Arranges the string in a specified format.

IndexOf—Returns the index of the specified character(s) in a String.

Insert—Returns a copy of the String for which it is called with the specified character(s) inserted.

PadLeft—Returns a copy of a String with padding characters inserted at the beginning.

Remove—Returns a copy of the String for which it is called with the specified character(s) removed.

Substring—Returns a substring from a String.

ToLower—Returns a copy of the String for which it is called with any uppercase letters converted to lowercase letters.

MULTIPLE-CHOICE QUESTIONS

19.1 A Button appears flat if its _________ property is set to Flat.

a) BorderStyle b) FlatStyle
c) Style d) BackStyle

19.2 Keyword _________ introduces a class definition.

a) NewClass b) ClassDef
c) VBClass d) Class

19.3 Keyword _________ is used to create an object.

a) `CreateObject` b) `Instantiate`
c) `Create` d) `New`

19.4 `String` characters are of data type _________.

a) `Char` b) `StringCharacter`
c) `Character` d) `strCharacter`

19.5 The _________ is used to retrieve the value of an instance variable.

a) `Get` accessor of a property b) `Retrieve` method of a class
c) `Client` method of a class d) `Set` accessor of a property

19.6 When you enter the header for a constructor in the Visual Basic IDE, then press *Enter*, the keywords _________ are created for you.

a) `End Public Class` b) `End Procedure`
c) `End Sub` d) `End`

19.7 An important difference between constructors and other methods is that _________.

a) constructors cannot specify a return data type
b) constructors cannot specify any parameters
c) other methods are implemented as `Sub` procedures
d) constructors can assign values to instance variables

19.8 A class can yield many _________, just as a primitive data type can yield many values.

a) names b) objects (instances)
c) values d) types

19.9 The `Set` accessor enables you to _________.

a) provide range checking b) modify data
c) provide data validation d) All of the above

19.10 Instance variables declared `Private` are not accessible _________.

a) outside the class b) by other methods of the same class
c) by members of another class d) inside the same class

EXERCISES

19.11 ***(Triangle Creator Application)*** Create an application that allows the user to enter the lengths for the three sides of a triangle as `Integers`. The application should then determine whether the triangle is a right triangle (two sides of the triangle form a 90-degree angle), an equilateral triangle (all sides of equal length) or neither. The application's GUI is completed for you (Fig. 19.45). You must create a class to represent a triangle object and define the event handler for the **Create** `Button`.

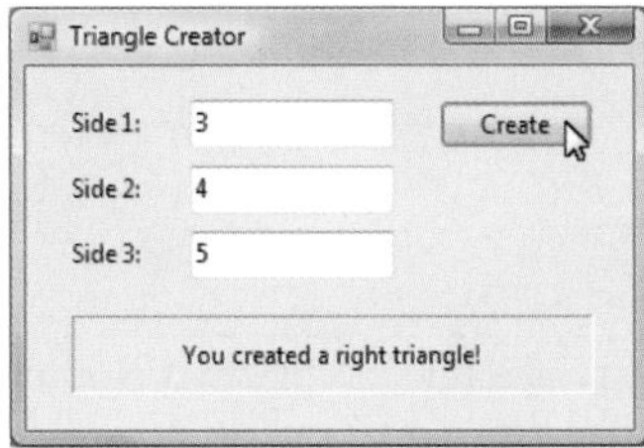

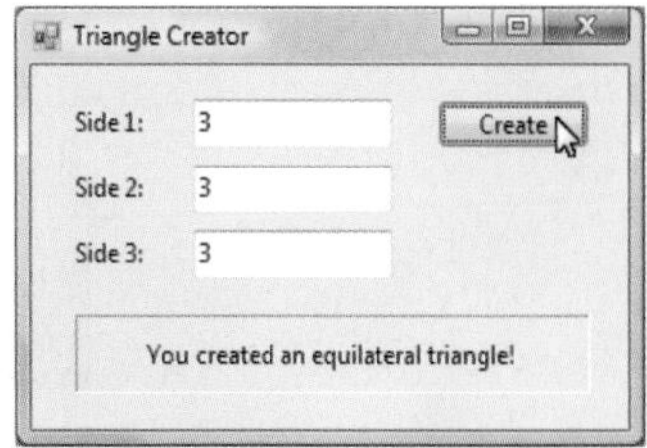

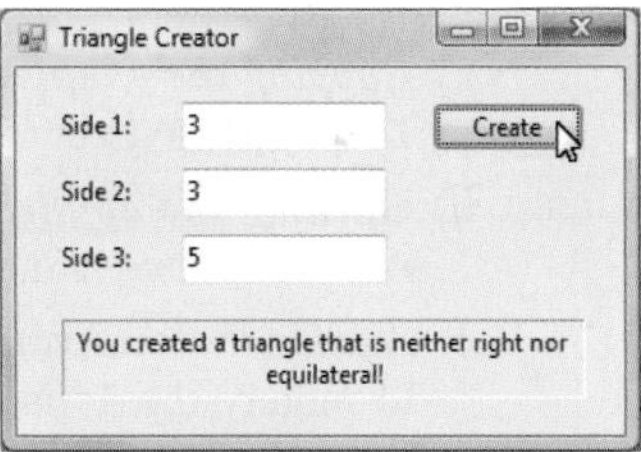

Figure 19.45 **Triangle Creator** application with all possible outputs.

a) ***Copying the template to your working directory.*** Copy the directory `C:\Examples\Tutorial19\Exercises\Triangle` to your `C:\SimplyVB2008` directory.

b) ***Opening the application's template file.*** Double click `Triangle.sln` in the `Triangle` directory to open the application.

c) ***Creating the `Triangle` class.*** Add a class to the project, and name it `Triangle`. This is where you define the properties of the `Triangle` class.

d) ***Defining the necessary constructor and properties.*** Define a constructor that takes the lengths of the three sides of the triangle as arguments. Create three properties that enable clients to access and modify the lengths of the three sides. If the user enters a negative value, that side should be assigned the value zero and the dispaly updated.

e) ***Adding additional features.*** Create two more properties in the `Triangle` class—one determines whether the sides form a right triangle, the other an equilateral triangle. Use the Pythagorean theorem ($a^2 + b^2 = c^2$) to test for a right triangle. These properties are considered **read-only**, because you would naturally define only the `Get` accessor. There is no simple `Set` accessor that can make a triangle a right triangle or an equilateral triangle without first modifying the lengths of the triangle's sides. To create a read-only property (where the `Set` accessor is omitted), precede keyword `Property` with the keyword **`ReadOnly`**.

f) ***Adding code to event handler.*** Now that you have created your `Triangle` class, you can use it to create objects in your application. Double click the **Create** `Button` in **Design** view to generate the event handler. Create new variables to store the three lengths from the `TextBoxes`; then use those values to create a new `Triangle` object.

g) ***Displaying the result.*** Use an `If...ElseIf` statement to determine whether the triangle is a right triangle, an equilateral triangle or neither. Display the result in a `Label`.

h) ***Running the application.*** Select **Debug > Start Debugging** to run your application. Add various inputs until you have created an equilateral triangle, a right triangle and a triangle that is neither right nor equilateral. Verify that the proper output is displayed for each.

i) ***Closing the application.*** Close your running application by clicking its close box.

j) ***Closing the IDE.*** Close the Visual Basic IDE by clicking its close box.

19.12 *(Modified **Microwave Oven** Application)* Modify the tutorial's **Microwave Oven** application to include an additional digit to represent the hour. Allow the user to enter up to 9 hours, 59 minutes and 59 seconds (Fig. 19.46).

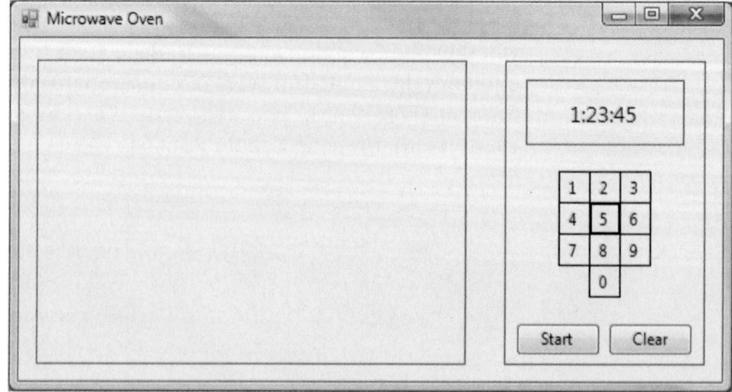

Figure 19.46 Modified **Microwave Oven** application's GUI.

a) ***Copying the template to your working directory.*** Copy the directory `C:\Examples\Tutorial19\Exercises\MicrowaveOven2` to your `C:\SimplyVB2008` directory.

b) ***Opening the application's template file.*** Double click `MicrowaveOven2.sln` in the `MicrowaveOven2` directory to open the application.

c) ***Adding the hour variable.*** To allow cooking time that includes the hour digit, you need to modify the `Time` class. Define a new `Private` instance variable to represent the hour. Change `Time`'s constructor to receive the hour as its first argument (now the constructor should have three arguments). You also have to modify the **Start** `Button` event handler, **Clear** `Button` event handler and the `DisplayTime` method to include an hour variable.

d) ***Adding the `Hour` property.*** Use the `Minute` and `Second` properties as your template to create the property for the hour. Remember, the hour must be less than 10.

e) ***Changing the padding amount.*** Change the calls to the `PadLeft` method to be consistent with the new time format.

f) ***Extracting the hour.*** Add a call to the `Substring` method so that hour gets the first digit in the `timeIs String`. Also, change the calls to the `Substring` method for minute and second so that they extract the proper digits from the `timeIs String`.

g) ***Accessing the first five digits.*** Change the `If...Then` statement from the `DisplayTime` method to take and display the first five digits entered by the user.

h) ***Edit the `Timer` object.*** Edit the `clockTimer_Tick` event handler to provide changes to hours and its corresponding minutes and seconds.

i) ***Displaying the time.*** Edit the `Format String` so that the display `Label` includes the hour.

j) ***Running the application.*** Select **Debug > Start Debugging** to run your application. Enter various times and verify that the application counts down properly.

k) ***Closing the application.*** Close your running application by clicking its close box.

l) ***Closing the IDE.*** Close the Visual Basic IDE by clicking its close box.

19.13 *(**Account Information Application**)* The local bank wants you to create an application that allows it to view clients' information. The interface is created for you (Fig. 19.47); you need to implement the `Client` class. Once the application is completed, the bank manager should be able to click the **Next** or **Previous** `Button` to run through each client's information. The information is stored in four arrays containing first names, last names, account numbers and account balances, respectively.

Figure 19.47 **Account Information** application GUI.

a) ***Copying the template to your working directory.*** Copy the directory `C:\Examples\Tutorial19\Exercises\AccountInformation` to your `C:\SimplyVB2008` directory.

b) ***Opening the application's template file.*** Double click `AccountInformation.sln` in the `AccountInformation` directory to open the application.

c) ***Determining variables for the class.*** Examine the code from `AccountInformation.vb`, including all the properties that the `Client` object uses to retrieve the information.

d) ***Creating the `Client` class.*** Create a new class, and call it `Client`. Add this class to the project. Define four `Private` instance variables to represent each value the Client class should contain. Create properties that allow clients to get and set these values. Use the properties in a constructor to initialize the instance variables.

e) ***Defining each property.*** Each `Private` variable should have a corresponding property allowing the user to set or get the `Private` variable's value. Note that the account number should not be negative.

f) ***Adding more information.*** In the `AccountInformationForm_Load` event handler, add one more value to each array to create another account.

g) ***Running the application.*** Select **Debug > Start Debugging** to run your application. Click the **Previous** and **Next** `Button`s to ensure that each account's information is displayed properly.

h) ***Closing the application.*** Close your running application by clicking its close box.

i) ***Closing the IDE.*** Close the Visual Basic IDE by clicking its close box.

What does this code do?

19.14 What does the following code do? The first code listing contains the definition of class `Shape`. Each `Shape` object represents a closed shape with a number of sides. The second code listing contains a method (`Mystery`) created by a client of class `Shape`. What does this method do?

```
Public Class Shape

   Private sides As Integer

   ' constructor with number of sides
   Public Sub New(ByVal value As Integer)
      Side = value
   End Sub ' New

   ' set and get side value
   Public Property Side() As Integer
      ' return sides
      Get
         Return sides
      End Get ' end of Get accessor

      ' set sides
      Set(ByVal value As Integer)
         If value > 0 Then
            sides = value
         Else
            sides = 0
         End If
      End Set ' end of Set accessor
   End Property ' Side
End Class ' Shape
```

```
Public Function Mystery(ByVal shapeObject As Shape) As String
   Dim shape As String

   ' determine case with shapeObject.Side
   Select Case shapeObject.Side
      Case Is < 3
         shape = "Not a Shape"
      Case 3
         shape = "Triangle"
      Case 4
         shape = "Square"
      Case Else
         shape = "Polygon"
   End Select

   Return shape
End Function ' Mystery
```

What's wrong with this code?

19.15 Find the error(s) in the following code. The following method should create a new `Shape` object with `numberSides` sides. Assume the `Shape` class from Exercise 19.14.

```
Private Sub ManipulateShape(ByVal numberSides As Integer)
   Dim shapeObject As Shape = New Shape(3)

   shape.sides = numberSides
End Sub ' ManipulateShape
```

Using the Debugger ▶

19.16 ***(View Name Application)*** The **View Name** application allows the user to enter the user's first and last names. When the user clicks the **View Name** `Button`, a `MessageBox` that displays the user's first and last names appears. The application creates an instance of `Class Name`. This class uses its property definitions to set the first-name and last-name instance variables. Copy the `ViewNames` folder from `C:\Examples\Tutorial19\Exercises\Debugger` to your `C:\SimplyVB2008` folder. Open and run the application. While testing your application, you noticed that the `MessageBox` did not display the correct output. Use the debugger to find the logic error(s) in the application. The correct output is displayed in Fig. 19.48.

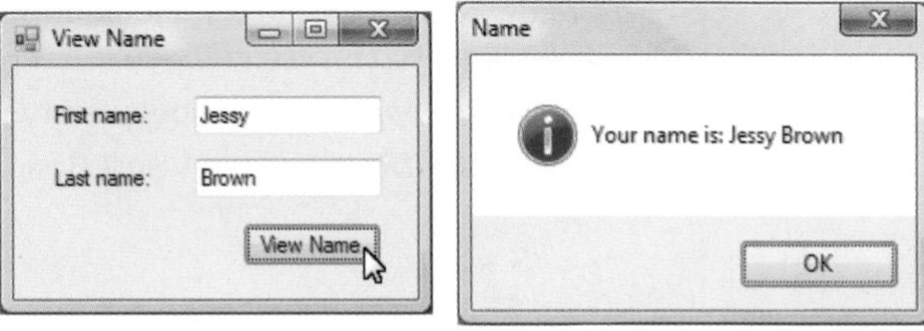

Figure 19.48 **View Name** application with correct output.

Programming Challenge ▶

19.17 ***(DVD Burner Application)*** Create an application that simulates a DVD burner. Users create a DVD with their choice of title and bonus materials. The GUI is provided for you (Fig. 19.49). You create a class (`DVD`) to represent the DVD object and another class (`Bonus`) to represent bonus materials for a DVD object.

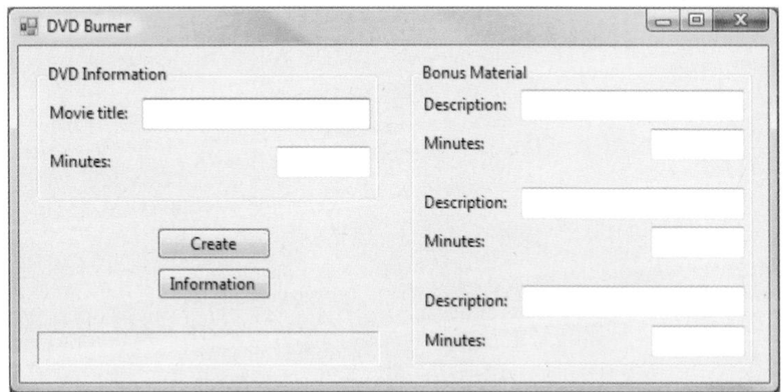

Figure 19.49 **DVD Burner** application's GUI.

a) ***Copying the template to your working directory.*** Copy the directory `C:\Examples\Tutorial19\Exercises\DVDBurner` to your `C:\SimplyVB2008` directory.

b) ***Opening the application's template file.*** Double click `DVDBurner.sln` in the `DVDBurner` directory to open the application.

c) ***Creating the bonus material object.*** Create a class, and name it `Bonus`. The class's objects each represent one bonus-material item on the DVD. Each `Bonus` object should have a name (description) and a length (in minutes).

d) ***Creating the DVD class.*** Create a class, and name it `DVD`. This class contains the movie title and the length of the movie. The class should also include an array of three `Bonus` items. Create properties that allow clients to get and set the movie's title and length. Create a `ReadOnly` property to get the movie's bonus material as a `String` containing each bonus item's name and length.

e) ***Creating the necessary variables.*** Before you define the **Create** `Button`'s event handler, create a `DVD` class instance variable. Inside the **Create** `Button`'s event handler, create the necessary variables to store the information from the `TextBoxes` on the GUI. This is also where you need to create the array of `Bonus` objects to store the bonus materials.

f) ***Adding bonus-material information.*** Add the description and length of each specified bonus item to the `Bonus` array you created in the preceding step.

g) ***Creating a DVD object.*** Use information about the movie, its title, length and the array of bonus materials to make your DVD object.

h) ***Displaying the output.*** The **Information** `Button`'s `Click` event handler is already defined for you. Locate the event handler, add a `String` containing the complete information on the DVD object that you created earlier and display this `String` to a `MessageBox`.

i) ***Running the application.*** Select **Debug > Start Debugging** to run your application. Enter information for several DVDs. After information is entered for each, click the **Create** `Button`. Then click the **Information** `Button` and verify that the information being displayed is correct for your newly created DVD.

j) ***Closing the application.*** Close your running application by clicking its close box.

k) ***Closing the IDE.*** Close the Visual Basic IDE by clicking its close box.

T U T O R I A L **20**

Objectives

In this tutorial, you learn to:

- Use generic collections.
- Create and manipulate a `List(Of T)` object.
- Use Language Integrated Query (LINQ) to select elements from a collection.
- Set the `MaxLength` property of a `TextBox`.
- Specify the tab order in a GUI using the `TabStop` and `TabIndex` properties of the controls.
- Create an access key for a control.
- Use a `For Each...Next` loop to iterate through a collection.
- Obtain a `String` representation of an object.

Outline

Shipping Hub Application

Introducing Generic Collections, LINQ, `For Each...Next` and Access Keys

Though most business can be conducted over phone lines and using e-mail messages, often it is necessary to send packages by a shipping company. As the pace of business increases, shipping companies seek an efficient means to transfer packages from one location to another. One approach is to send packages to a central location (a hub) before they reach their final destination. In this tutorial, you develop a **Shipping Hub** application to simulate package processing at a shipping warehouse. You use collections, which provide a quick and easy way to organize and manipulate the data used by your application. The tutorial focuses on the `List` collection, which provides data-storage capabilities similar to an array, but with much greater flexibility. You learn to use the `For Each...Next` repetition statement to iterate through the objects in a collection. You also learn to use part of Visual Basic's new Language-Integrated Query (LINQ) capabilities to select elements from a collection based on a condition—known as filtering the collection.

20.1 Test-Driving the Shipping Hub Application

In this section, you test-drive the **Shipping Hub** application, which must meet the following requirements:

Application Requirements

*A shipping company receives packages at its headquarters, which functions as its shipping hub. After receiving the packages, the company ships them to a distribution center in one of the following states: Alabama, Florida, Georgia, Kentucky, Mississippi, North Carolina, South Carolina, Tennessee, West Virginia or Virginia. The company needs an application to track the packages that pass through its shipping hub. For each package that arrives at the hub, the user clicks the application's **Scan New** `Button`, to generate a package ID number. Once a package has been scanned, the user should be able to enter the shipping address for it. The user should be able to navigate through the list of scanned packages by using **< BACK** or **NEXT >** `Buttons` and by viewing a list of all packages destined for a particular state.*

This application stores a list of packages in a `List(Of Packages)` object. You use the `For Each...Next` repetition statement to access the objects stored in the `List`. You begin by test-driving the completed application. Then you learn the additional Visual Basic technologies needed to create your own version of the application.

Test-Driving the Shipping Hub Application

1. ***Opening the completed application.*** Open the directory `C:\Examples\Tutorial20\CompletedApplication\ShippingHub` to locate the **Shipping Hub** application. Double click `ShippingHub.sln` to open the application in the Visual Basic IDE.

2. ***Running the Shipping Hub application.*** Select **Debug > Start Debugging** to run the application (Fig. 20.1).

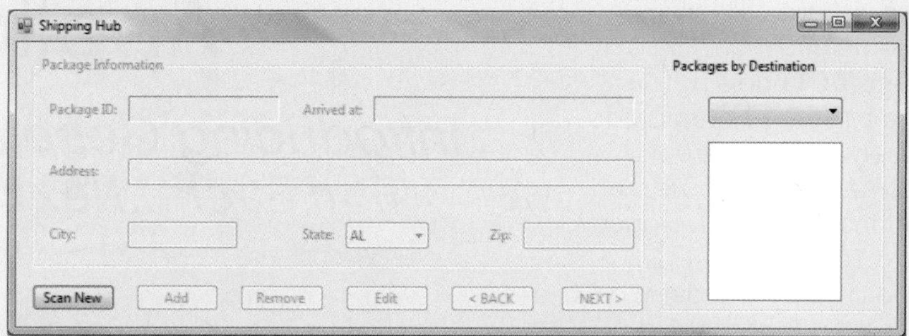

Figure 20.1 **Shipping Hub** application when first run.

3. ***Scanning a new package.*** Click the **Scan New** `Button`. The application displays a package ID number and the arrival time, enables the `TextBoxes` and allows the user to enter the package information (Fig. 20.2). The package ID number for your first package will most likely be different than the one shown here because it's randomly generated each time the application executes.

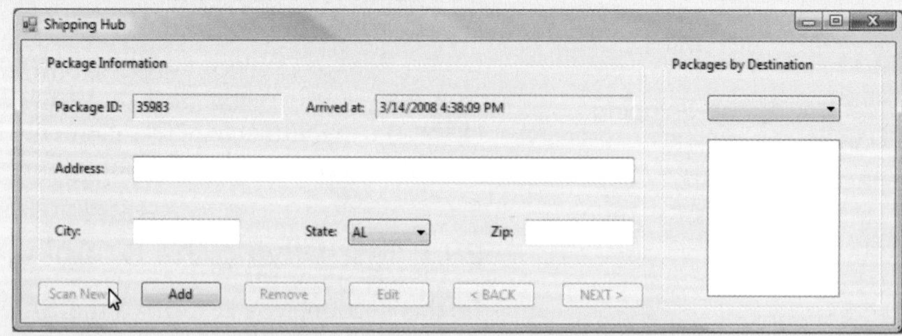

Figure 20.2 Scanning a new package.

4. ***Using the Tab key.*** Type `318 Some Street` in the **Address:** `TextBox`, then press the *Tab* key. Note that the cursor moves to the **City:** `TextBox` (Fig. 20.3).

5. ***Adding a package to the list of packages.*** Type `Point Pleasant` in the **City:** field, then press the *Tab* key. Select **WV** from the **State:** `ComboBox`, then press the *Tab* key. Type `25550` in the **Zip:** field, and click the **Add** `Button` to add the package to the application's `List`.

GUI Design Tip

Using the Tab key is an efficient way for users to navigate through the controls in a GUI.

(cont.)

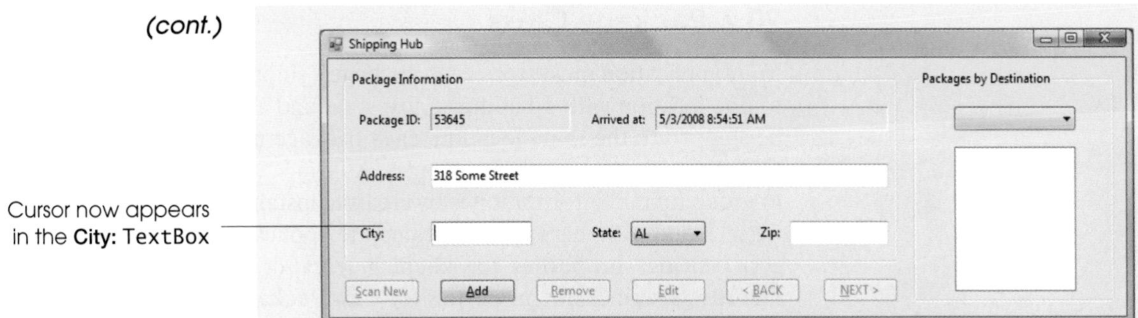

Figure 20.3 Pressing the *Tab* key moves the cursor to the next `TextBox`.

Note that you cannot enter more than five numbers in the **Zip:** field because the **Zip:** `TextBox`'s `MaxLength` property is set to 5. The **`MaxLength`** property determines the maximum number of characters that the user can enter into a `TextBox`. The values in the **State:** `ComboBox` were added using its **`Items`** property in the Windows `Form` Designer. When the program is not running, you can switch to **Design** view and select the **State:** `ComboBox`. Then, click the **Edit Items** link at the bottom of the **Properties** window. The dialog that opens allows you to edit the items in the `ComboBox`'s drop down.

6. ***Removing, editing and browsing packages.*** The application's **NEXT >** and **< BACK** `Buttons` allow the user to navigate the list of packages. The user can click on the **Remove** `Button` to delete packages and on the **Edit** `Button` to update a particular package's information. Experiment with the various `Buttons` by adding, removing and editing packages. Use the following sample data:

   - 9 Some Road, Goose Creek, SC, 29445
   - 234 Some Place, Tamassee, SC, 29686
   - 46 Some Avenue, Mammoth Cave, KY, 42259
   - 3 Some Street, Yazoo City, MS, 39194

7. ***Viewing all packages going to a state.*** The `ComboBox` on the right side of the application allows the user to select a state. When a state is selected, all of the package ID numbers of packages destined for that state are displayed in the `ListBox` (Fig. 20.4). If the `ListBox` contains more package numbers than it can display, a vertical scrollbar appears automatically.

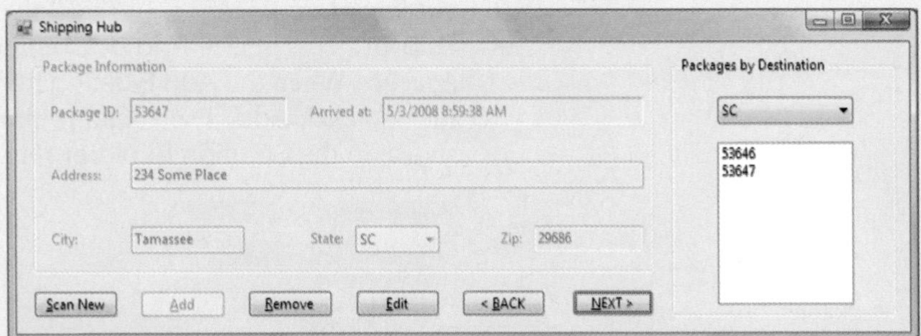

Figure 20.4 Viewing all packages going to South Carolina.

8. ***Closing the application.*** Close your running application by clicking its close box.

9. ***Closing the IDE.*** Close the Visual Basic IDE by clicking its close box.

20.2 Package Class

Your application must store each package's shipping information. Each package ships to one location with an address, city, state and zip code. Since multiple packages can be shipped to the same location, each package needs a unique identification number to distinguish it from other packages. As you learned in Tutorial 19, a convenient way to group related information is by creating instances of a class. The Package class that we included with this example's template application (but not did not add to the project) provides properties for keeping track of package information. The table in Fig. 20.5 describes the properties for class Package. You must add the Package class to the **Shipping Hub** application before you can use it to create objects of this class. You learn how to add the Package class to the **Shipping Hub** application in the next box.

Property	Description
Address	Provides access to instance variable addressValue, which represents the package's address as a String.
City	Provides access to instance variable cityValue, which represents the package's city as a String.
State	Provides access to instance variable stateValue, which stores the package's state as a String. It uses the standard two-letter state abbreviations. For example, NC is used for North Carolina.
Zip	Provides access to instance variable zipValue. Represents the zip code as a String.
PackageNumber	Provides access to instance variable packageNumberValue, which stores the package's identification number as an Integer.
ArrivalTime	Provides access to instance variable timeValue, which stores the package's arrival time as a Date.

Figure 20.5 Properties of class Package.

Adding a Class to an Application

1. ***Copying the template to your working directory.*** Copy the C:\Examples\Tutorial20\TemplateApplication\ShippingHub directory to your C:\SimplyVB2008 directory.
2. ***Opening the Shipping Hub application's template file.*** Double click ShippingHub.sln in the ShippingHub directory to open the application in the Visual Basic IDE.
3. ***Adding class Package.*** In the **Solution Explorer**, right click the **ShippingHub** project. Select **Add > Existing Item...** from the context menu that appears. When the **Add Existing Item** dialog appears, select the Package.vb file and click **Add**. The Package class is now included in the application and shown in the **Solution Explorer** (Fig. 20.6).

Package class added to the ShippingHub project

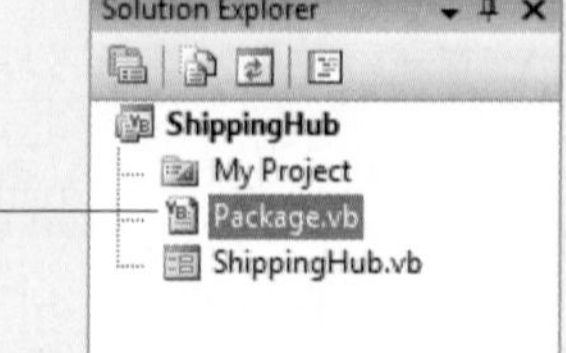

Figure 20.6 **Solution Explorer** with Package.vb added.

20.3 Using Properties TabIndex and TabStop

Many applications require users to enter information into multiple TextBoxes. It is awkward for users to have to select each TextBox using the mouse. Most applications allow the user to press the *Tab* key to navigate between the controls on the Form. To ensure ease of use, the focus must be transferred to the proper control when the *Tab* key is pressed. The **TabIndex** property allows you to specify the order in which focus transfers between controls when *Tab* is pressed. However, some controls, such as a read-only TextBox, should not be selected using the *Tab* key. The **TabStop** property specifies whether the user can select the control using the *Tab* key. Setting this property to False prevents the control from being selected by using the *Tab* key. You set both of these properties in the following box.

Setting Properties TabIndex and TabStop

GUI Design Tip

Set a control's TabStop property to True only if the control is used to receive user input.

GUI Design Tip

Use the TabIndex property to define the logical order in which the user should enter data. Usually the order transfers the focus of the application from top to bottom and left to right.

1. ***Opening ShippingHub.vb.*** Double click ShippingHub.vb in the **Solution Explorer** to open the file in **Design** view. The **Shipping Hub** application requires that the user enter the package information into its TextBoxes. To make it easy for the user to enter the data, you'll allow the user to press the *Tab* key to access the proper control.

2. ***Setting property TabStop.*** The TabStop property defaults to True for controls that receive user input. Make sure that the TabStop property is set to True for the **Address:**, **City:**, and **Zip:** TextBoxes, the **State:** and **Packages by Destination** ComboBoxes and the six Buttons.

3. ***Using the Tab Order view in the Windows Form Designer.*** The IDE provides a view called **Tab Order** to help visualize the tab order. To use the **Tab Order** view, select the Form by clicking it, then select **View > Tab Order**. White numbers indicating the TabIndex appear in blue boxes in the upper-left corner of the control (Fig. 20.7). The first time you click a control in this view, its TabIndex value is set to zero, as displayed in the TabIndex box (Fig. 20.7). Subsequent clicks will increment the value by one.

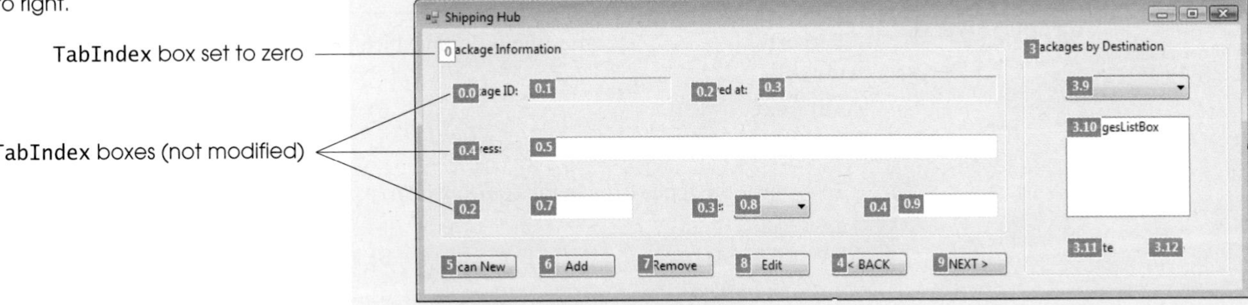

Figure 20.7 Setting the TabIndex properties using the **Tab Order** view of the **Shipping Hub** application.

Begin by clicking the **Package Information** GroupBox. Note that its value becomes 0 and the background of the surrounding box changes to white (Fig. 20.7). Then click the **Address:** TextBox. Now the value changes to 0.0. The first zero refers to the TabIndex of the container (in this case, the GroupBox), and the second zero refers to the TabIndex for that control within the container.

Continue setting the tab indices by clicking the **City:** TextBox, then the **State:** ComboBox and finally the **Zip:** TextBox. Finish setting the tab indices for the GroupBox by clicking each control that has not been changed. Controls that have not been changed display a box with a blue background.

(cont.)

4. ***Setting the TabIndex properties for the rest of the application.*** Continue setting the TabIndex properties by clicking the **Scan New** Button. Then click the remaining unchanged controls in the order indicated in Fig. 20.8. When all the application's controls have been ordered, the TabIndex boxes will once again display a blue background. Exit the **Tab Order** view by selecting **View > Tab Order** or by pressing the *Esc* key.

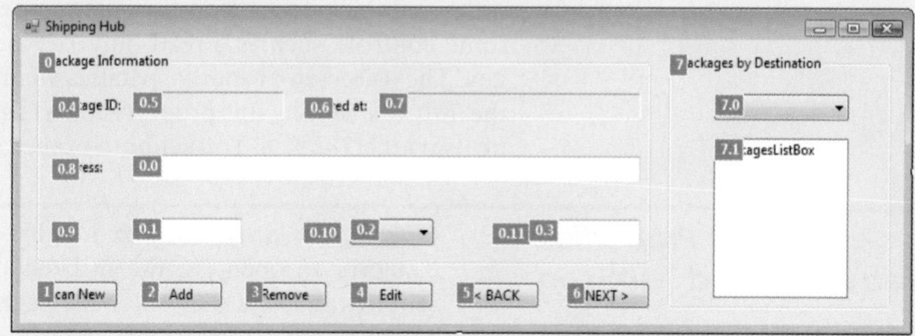

Figure 20.8 **Tab Order** view of the **Shipping Hub** application.

5. ***Saving the project.*** Select **File > Save All** to save your modified code.

Designing your GUI with the tab order in mind helps you add the controls in the order they should receive the focus. If this is not possible, proper use of the TabIndex and TabStop properties enables users to enter data into an application more efficiently. Most controls have TabIndex and TabStop properties. TabIndex values on a Form or within a GroupBox should be unique—two controls cannot receive the focus at the same time. For its TabIndex property, by default, the first control added to the Form has a value of 0, the second control a value of 1, the third control a value of 2 (one more than the last control's value), and so on.

SELF-REVIEW

1. Property ________ specifies the order in which controls receive the focus when *Tab* is pressed.

   a) Text   b) TabStop
   c) Index   d) TabIndex

2. To prevent the focus from being transferred to a control using the *Tab* key, set property ________ to ________.

   a) TabIndex, 0   b) TabStop, False
   c) TabControl, True   d) TabIndex, Nothing

Answers: 1) d. 2) b.

20.4 Using Access Keys

Many applications allow users to interact with controls such as Buttons and menus via the keyboard. **Access keys** (or keyboard shortcuts) allow the user to perform an action on a control using the keyboard.

To specify an access key for a control, insert an & (ampersand) symbol in the control's Text property before the letter you wish to use as an access key. If you wish to use "s" as the access key on the **Scan New** Button, set its Text property to &Scan New. You can specify many access keys in an application, but each letter used as an access key in a container should be unique. To use the access key, you must press and hold the *Alt* key, then press the access key character on the keyboard (release both keys after pressing the access key character). In this case of the **Scan New** Button, you would press and hold the *Alt* key, then press the *S* key (also written as *Alt+S*). You would then release both keys. The effect of using the access key is the same as clicking the button.

Access keys are often used on `Button` controls and on the `MainMenu` control, which will be introduced in Tutorial 21. To display an ampersand character on a control, type && in its `Text` property. Follow the steps in the next box to use access keys in your **Shipping Hub** application.

Creating Access Keys

1. ***Creating an access key for the* Scan New `Button`.** Insert an & symbol before the letter `S` in the `Text` property of the **Scan New** `Button` (Fig. 20.9). Press *Enter* or click outside the field to update the property. Note that the letter `S` is now underlined on the `Button` (Fig. 20.9). If the user presses *Alt*, then *S*, during execution, this has the same effect as "clicking" the **Scan New** `Button`—the `Click` event is raised. Depending on your system configuration, you may need to press the *Alt* key to display the underline under the access key character at execution time.

GUI Design Tip

Use access keys to allow users to "click" a control using the keyboard.

Using the & symbol to create an access key (there is no space between & and S)

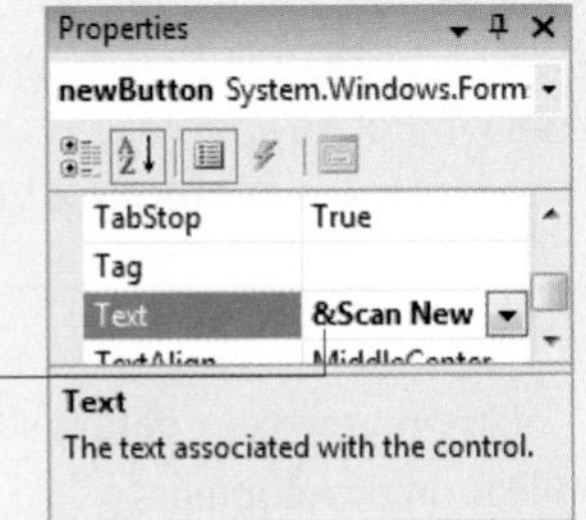

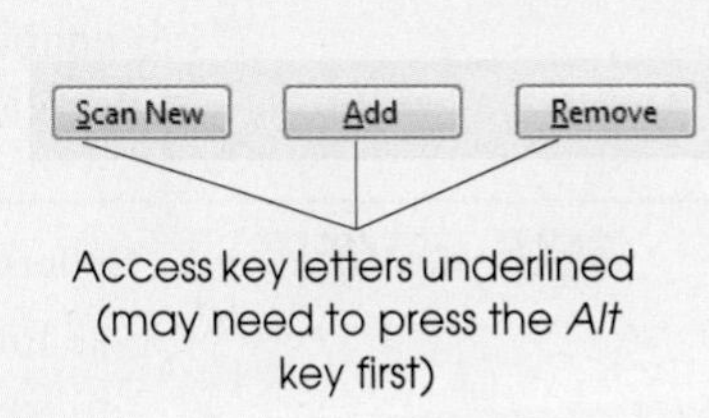

Access key letters underlined (may need to press the *Alt* key first)

Figure 20.9 Creating an access key.

2. ***Inserting access keys for the remaining* `Buttons`.** Use the `Text` properties of the remaining `Buttons` to create access keys. Precede the `B` on the **< BACK** `Button` with an ampersand. Repeat this process for the `A` on the **Add** `Button`, the `R` on the **Remove** `Button`, the `E` on the **Edit** `Button` and the `N` on the **NEXT >** `Button`. Note that the access key does not have to be the first letter in the control's text.

3. ***Saving the project.*** Select **File > Save All** to save your modified code.

SELF-REVIEW

1. When creating an access key, the ________ the ampersand is/are underlined.

   a) character preceding b) character following
   c) characters following d) characters preceding

2. Press the ________ key, then the underlined character on a `Button`, to use the access key.

   a) *Control* b) *Shift*
   c) *Alt* d) *Tab*

Answers: 1) b. 2) c.

20.5 Collections

The .NET Framework Class Library provides several classes, called **collections**, which you can use to store groups of related objects. These classes provide methods that facilitate the storage and organization of your data without requiring any knowledge of the details of how the objects are being stored. This capability improves your application-development time because you do not have to write code to organize your data efficiently—the methods in the collection classes are proven to be reliable and efficient.

Software Design Tip

Use a `List` to store a group of values when the number of elements in the group varies during the running of an application.

In Tutorials 17 and 18, you learned how to declare and use arrays in your applications. You may have noticed a limitation to arrays—once an array is declared, its size does not change automatically to match its data set. This poses a problem if the number of items in the array needs to change repeatedly over time.

Class `List(Of T)` (from namespace `System.Collections.Generic`) provides a convenient solution to this problem. **`List(Of T)`** is a generic collection. Generic classes specify a set of related classes with a single class declaration. The generic class `List(Of T)` specifies a set of classes which provide the functionality for a `List` of any data type. The identifier `T` is a placeholder (known as a type parameter) which you replace with an actual type (known as the type argument) when you declare an instance of the generic `List(Of T)` collection. For example,

```
Dim list As List(Of Integer)
```

declares a `List` collection that can store only `Integer` values, and

```
Dim list2 As List(Of Package)
```

declares `list2` as a `List` of `Package`s. The generic `List` collection provides all of the capabilities of an array, as well as dynamic resizing capabilities. **Dynamic resizing** enables the `List` object to increase its size to accommodate new elements and to decrease its size to conserve memory when elements are removed.

SELF-REVIEW

1. Collections _________.
   a) force you to focus on how your data is stored
   b) speed up application development
   c) allow you to focus on the details of your application
   d) Both b and c

2. One limitation of arrays is that _________.
   a) their size cannot change automatically
   b) they can store only primitive data types
   c) `String`s cannot be placed in them
   d) All of the above

Answers: 1) d. 2) a.

20.6 Shipping Hub Application: Using Class `List(Of T)`

By now, you are familiar with designing GUIs and writing methods and event handlers. This tutorial's template file provides much of the application's functionality so that you can concentrate on using a `List`. You are encouraged to study the full source code at the end of the tutorial to understand how the application is implemented. The following pseudocode statements describe the basic operation of your **Shipping Hub** application:

When the Form loads:
Generate a random initial package ID number and arrival time
Set the SelectedIndex of the State ComboBox to 0
Create an empty List of Packages

When the user clicks the Scan New Button:
Generate the next package ID number
Create a new Package object
Display the new Package's package number and arrival time
Enable the TextBoxes, the ComboBox and the Add Button

When the user clicks the Add Button:
Retrieve address, city, state and zip code values; and disable input controls
Add the package to the List
Enable the Package Information GroupBox and the approptiate Buttons
Disable the Add Button
Add the package number to the ListBox

```
    Change the Packages by Destination ComboBox value to the package's
        destination state
    Enable the New Button

When the user clicks the < BACK Button:
    Display the previous package in the List

When the user clicks the NEXT > Button:
    Display the next package in the List

When the user clicks the Remove Button:
    Remove the package from the Packages by Destination ListBox
    Remove the package from the List

When the user clicks the Edit Button:
    Change the Button to read Update
    Allow the user to modify package address information

When the user clicks the Update Button:
    Update the package's information in the List
    Disable controls that allow user input, and change the
        Update Button to read Edit

When the user chooses a different state in the Packages by Destination
ComboBox:
    Display the package number for each package destined for that
        state in the ListBox
```

The **Shipping Hub** application must store a list of packages through which the user can navigate using the **NEXT >** and **< BACK** `Buttons`. Each time the application runs, it must allow for any number of packages to be added. Since arrays don't resize automatically, you'd be limited by the number of values that you could store in the array. [*Note:* You can manually resize an array with the Visual Basic keywords `ReDim` and `Preserve`, which we do not cover in this book.] The `List` collection solves this problem by combining the functionality of an array with dynamic resizing capabilities.

Now that you've test-driven the **Shipping Hub** application and studied its pseudocode representation, you use an ACE table to help you convert the pseudocode to Visual Basic. Figure 20.10 lists the actions, controls and events that help you complete your own version of this application.

Action/Control/Event (ACE) Table for the Shipping Hub Application

Action	Control/Object	Event
Label the application's controls	`informationGroupBox`, `listByGroupBox`, `arrivedLabel`, `packageIDLabel`, `addressLabel`, `cityLabel`, `stateLabel`, `zipLabel`	Application is run
	`ShippingHubForm`	`Load`
Generate a random initial package ID number and arrival time	`randomObject`	
Set the SelectedIndex of the State ComboBox to 0	`stateComboBox`	
Create an empty List of Packages	`list`	

Figure 20.10 ACE table for the **Shipping Hub** application. (Part 1 of 3.)

Action	Control/Object	Event
	newButton	Click
Generate the next package ID number		
Create a new Package object	packageObject	
Display the new Package's package number and arrival time	packageNumber-Label, arrivalTimeLabel	
Enable the TextBoxes, the CboBox and the Add Button	addButton, addressTextBox, cityTextBox, stateComboBox, zipTextBox	
	addButton	Click
Enable the Package Information GroupBox and the approptiate Buttons	informationGroup-Box, (call SetBut-tons with True as an argument for the Buttons)	
Disable the Add Button	addButton	
Add the package to the List	list	
Add the package number to the ListBox	packagesListBox	
Change the Packages by Destination ComboBox value to the package's destination state	stateComboBox	
Enable the New Button	newButton	
	backButton	Click
Display the previous package in the List	list, packageNumber-Label, arrivalTimeLabel addressTextBox, cityTextBox, stateComboBox, zipTextBox	
	nextButton	Click
Display the next package in the List	list, packageNumber-Label, arrivalTimeLabel addressTextBox, cityTextBox, stateComboBox, zipTextBox	
	removeButton	Click
Remove the package from the Packages by Destination ListBox	packagesListBox	
Remove the package from the List	list	
	editUpdateButton	Click
Change the Button to read Update	editUpdateButton	
Allow the user to modify package address information	addressTextBox, cityTextBox, stateComboBox, zipTextBox	

Figure 20.10 ACE table for the **Shipping Hub** application. (Part 2 of 3.)

Action	Control/Object	Event
	`editUpdateButton`	`Click`
Update the package's information in the List	`list`	
Disable controls that allow user input, and change the Update Button to read Edit	`addressTextBox`, `cityTextBox`, `stateComboBox`, `zipTextBox`, `editUpdateButton`	
	`viewPackages-ComboBox`	`Selected-Index-Changed`
Display the package number for each package destined for that state in the ListBox	`packagesListBox`	

Figure 20.10 ACE table for the **Shipping Hub** application. (Part 3 of 3.)

In this tutorial, you focus on using a `List` in the **Shipping Hub** application. You begin by creating a `List(Of Package)` object.

Creating a List of Packages

1. ***Declaring a `List(Of Package)`.*** Insert line 3 of Fig. 20.11 in the `ShippingHub` class to declare `List(Of Package) list`. Note the use of the member-access operator (`.`) to gain access to the `List` class, which is located in namespace `System.Collections.Generic`.

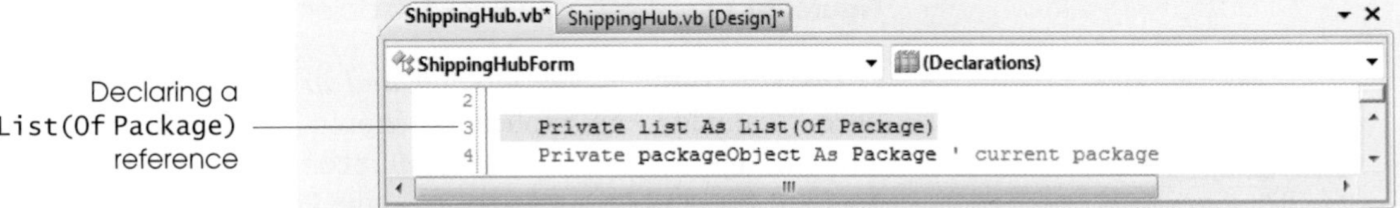

Figure 20.11 Declaring the `List(Of Package)` reference.

2. ***Initializing the `List(Of Package)`.*** To use the `List` instance variable declared in *Step 1*, you must create a new `List(Of Package)` object. You then assign a reference to the `List(Of Package)` object to the instance variable. Insert line 21 (Fig. 20.12) to the `Form`'s `Load` event handler. This line uses the `New` keyword to create an empty `List(Of Package)` object when the application loads. Note that line 19 uses `stateComboBox`'s `SelectedIndex` property to show the first state in the list.

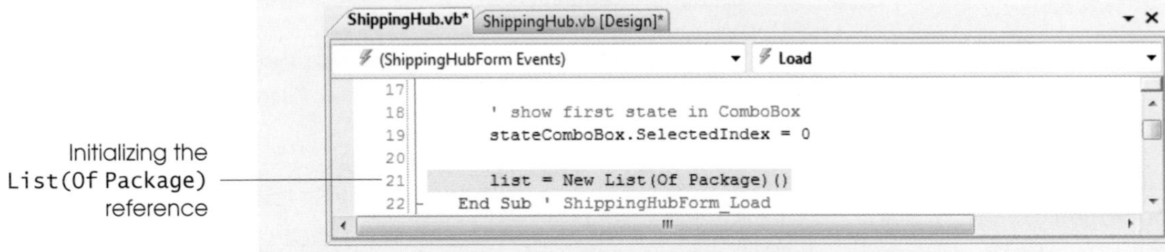

Figure 20.12 Creating a `List(Of Package)` object.

3. ***Saving the project.*** Select **File > Save All** to save your modified code.

Now that you've created a `List` object, you insert code that allows the user to add `Package`s to the `List`. To accomplish this, you create a reference to an object of class `Package` and use `List`'s `Add` method to store the reference in the `List`. Recall that you've already added the Package class to your application. You now create Packages and add them to your List.

Adding and Removing Packages

1. ***Creating a package.*** The user clicks the **Scan New** Button when a new package arrives at the shipping hub. When this occurs, the application creates a package number and allows the user to enter the shipping address. Insert lines 28–29 from Fig. 20.13 into the **Scan New** Button's Click event handler. Line 28 increments packageID (declared at line 7) to ensure that all packages have a unique identification number. Line 29 passes the package number as an argument to the constructor for class Package. The value that you pass to the Package constructor can then be accessed using its PackageNumber property. Every time line 29 executes, it uses the same reference, packageObject, to refer to a new Package object. However, the previous Package object is not lost each time a new Package is created. This is because each Package reference will be stored in the List.

Create a new Package object with a unique ID

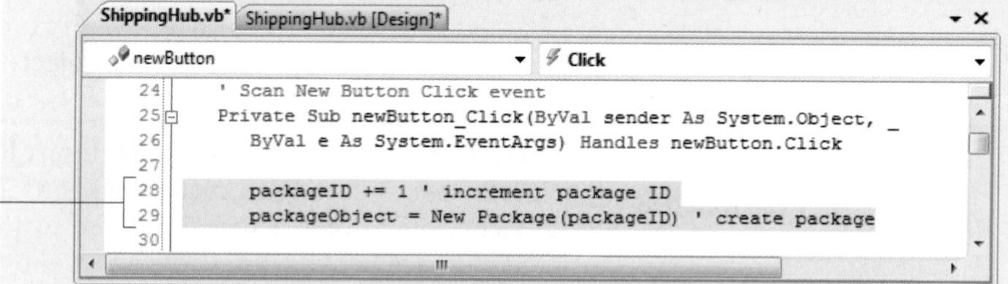

ShippingHub.vb*
ShippingHub.vb [Design]*
newButton
Click
24 ' Scan New Button Click event
25 Private Sub newButton_Click(ByVal sender As System.Object, _
26 ByVal e As System.EventArgs) Handles newButton.Click
27
28 packageID += 1 ' increment package ID
29 packageObject = New Package(packageID) ' create package
30

Figure 20.13 Creating a Package object.

2. ***Displaying the package number and arrival time.*** After the package has been "scanned," the application should display the package's arrival time and package number. In the newButton_Click event handler, insert lines 32–35 of Fig. 20.14. Lines 32–33 use the Package's PackageNumber property to display the package identification number in a Label. The ToString method returns a String representation of an object, and is available for all types. For instance, a Date structure's ToString method returns the date as a String, in the format 11/29/2008 9:34:00 AM (recall that this depends on the user's locale). However, be aware that for some .NET classes, ToString merely returns the class name. Lines 34–35 use the Package's ArrivalTime property to display the arrival time (the current time) in a Label. The Package's ArrivalTime property is set to the current time in the Package class's constructor. Recall that the ArrivalTime property is already defined for you in the Package class.

Displaying arrival time and package ID number in Labels

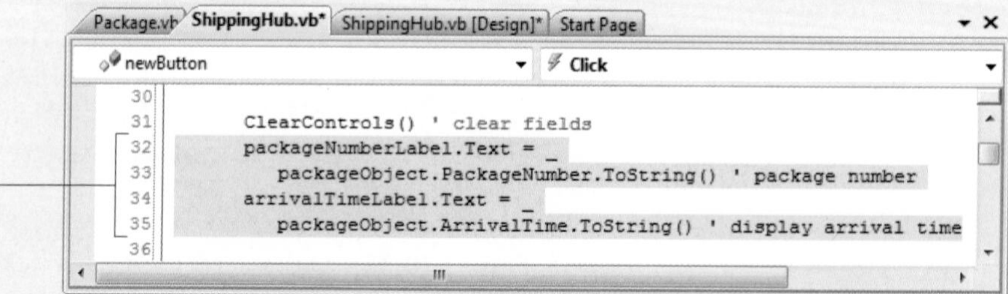

Figure 20.14 Displaying the package's number and arrival time.

(cont.)

3. ***Adding a package to the `List`.*** The user clicks the **Add** `Button` to add the package to the `List` after entering the package's information. Add line 50 of Fig. 20.15 to the **Add** `Button`'s `Click` event handler. This line stores the package information by adding the `Package` object to `list` using the `List`'s `Add` method.

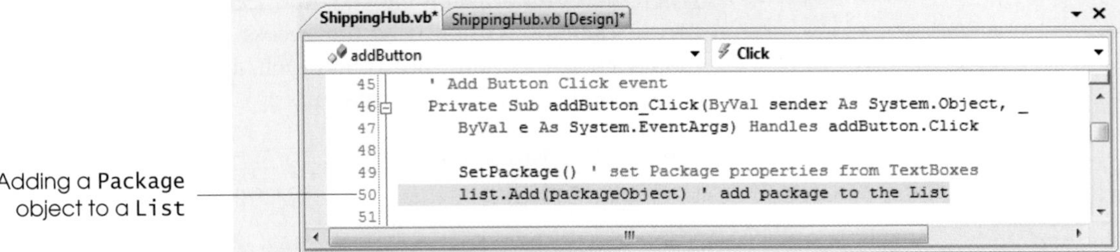

Figure 20.15 Adding a package to the `List`.

Each time you add a `Package` to the `List` by calling the `Add` method, the `Package` is placed at the end of the `List`. With arrays, you refer to a value's location by its index. Similarly, in a `List`, you can refer to an element's location in the `List` as the element's **index**. Like an array, the index of an element at the beginning of the `List` is zero, and the index of an element at the end of the `List` is one less than the number of elements in the `List`.

4. ***Removing a package from the `List`.*** When the user selects a package and clicks the **Remove** `Button`, the application should remove the `Package` from the `List`. The `List` class provides a simple way to remove elements from the `List`. Insert line 105 (Fig. 20.16) into the **Remove** `Button`'s `Click` event handler. This line uses the **`RemoveAt`** method to remove a package from the `List`. The argument passed to the method `RemoveAt` is the index (stored in variable `position`) of the `Package` in the `List`. Variable `position` keeps track of the index and is incremented or decremented each time the user clicks the **NEXT >** or **< BACK** `Buttons`.

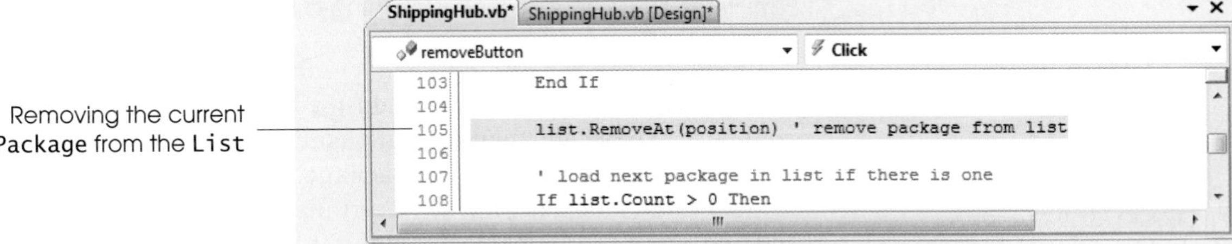

Figure 20.16 Removing a `Package` from the `List`.

If a `Package` at index 3 is removed from the `List`, the `Package` that was previously at index 4 will then be located at index 3. Whenever an object is removed from a `List`, the indices update accordingly. Note that line 108 of Fig. 20.16 uses the `Count` property of class `List`. Like the `Length` property of an array, the **`Count`** property returns the number of elements currently stored in the `List`.

5. ***Saving the project.*** Select **File > Save All** to save your modified code.

Once a `Package` has been added to the `List`, the **Shipping Hub** application disables the `TextBoxes` so that the user does not accidentally modify the package information. An **Edit** `Button` is provided to allow users to modify any of the package information except for the arrival time and the package identification number. When the user clicks the **Edit** `Button`, its event handler should enable the controls that allow the user to modify the package data. You add functionality to accomplish this in the following box.

Updating Package Information

1. ***Changing the Edit Button's Text property.*** Add lines 134–135 of Fig. 20.17 before the Else clause in the editUpdateButton_Click event handler. When the **Edit** Button is clicked, line 135 changes the text on the **Edit** Button to &Update (using U as the access key). This indicates that the user should click the same Button, which now is labeled **Update**, to submit changes to the package information.

Using code to change the text displayed on a Button

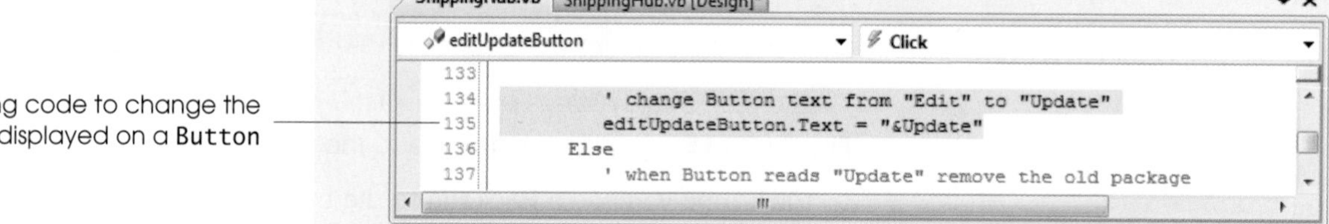

Figure 20.17 Changing the **Edit** Button to display **Update**.

2. ***Updating the package data.*** Insert lines 140–141 of Fig. 20.18 into the editUpdateButton_Click event handler. When the user chooses to alter the package information, the Package is removed from the List and a new one with the updated address information is added.

Updating the List with new package information

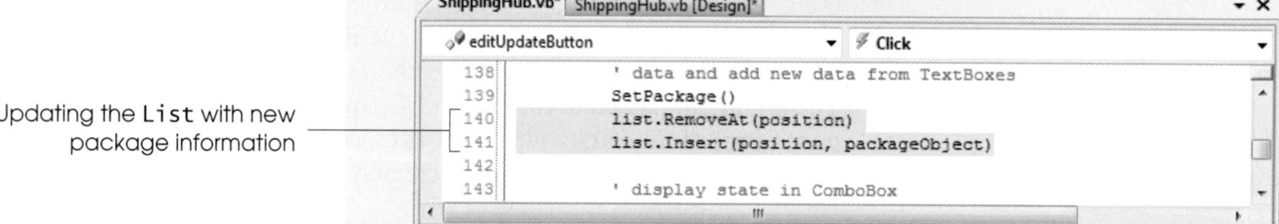

Figure 20.18 Removing and inserting a Package to update data.

Line 140 removes the old Package object from the List. Line 141 uses class List's Insert method to add the package to the List. The Insert method is like the Add method, but Insert allows you to specify the index in the List at which to insert the Package. The first argument to the Insert method is the index at which to insert the Package (in this case, position), and the second argument contains the Package to insert into the List (package). Using the Insert method allows you to place the updated Package object at the same index in the List as the Package object you just removed, thus maintaining the package IDs in sequential order. [*Note:* We could have modified the existing Package object, but we chose to introduce other methods of the List collection here.]

3. ***Changing the Button's Text property to Edit.*** After the user clicks the **Update** Button, the TextBoxes are once again disabled. Since the user's changes have been applied, you should reset the text on the **Update** Button to read **Edit**. Insert line 151 of Fig. 20.19 into the event handler to reset the text on the Button to **Edit**. Note once again the use of the & to enable the Button's access key.

4. ***Saving the project.*** Select **File > Save All** to save your modified code.

(cont.)

Using code to display the text on the Button

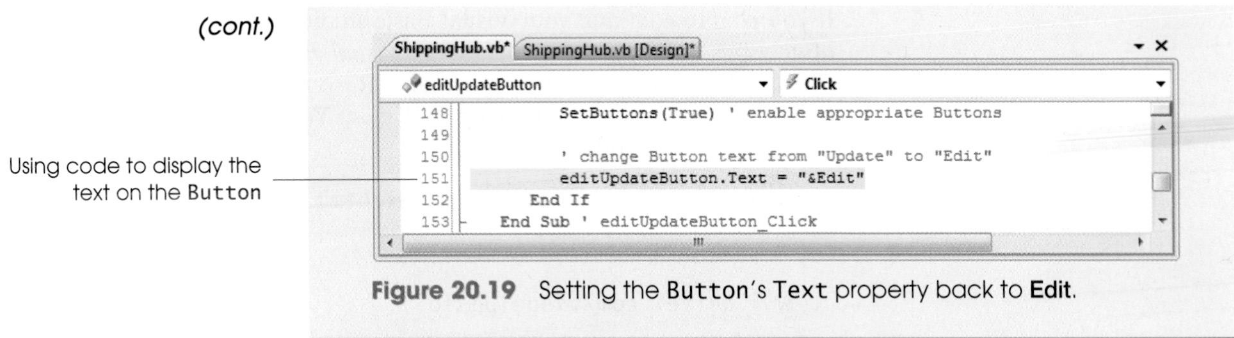

Figure 20.19 Setting the Button's Text property back to **Edit**.

The user navigates the List by clicking the **NEXT >** and **< BACK** Buttons. Each time the user chooses to view a different package in the List, the package information displayed in the Form's controls must be updated. To display a package's information, you must retrieve the information from the List that contains the Package objects. You learn how to do this in the following box.

Displaying a Package

1. ***Retrieving package data.*** Insert lines 167–168 from Fig. 20.20 into your application's LoadPackage method. To display the information, you must retrieve the data from the List using the elements index enclosed in parentheses, as you did with arrays. Line 168 assigns to packageObject the Package stored at index position.

Retrieving a Package object from a List

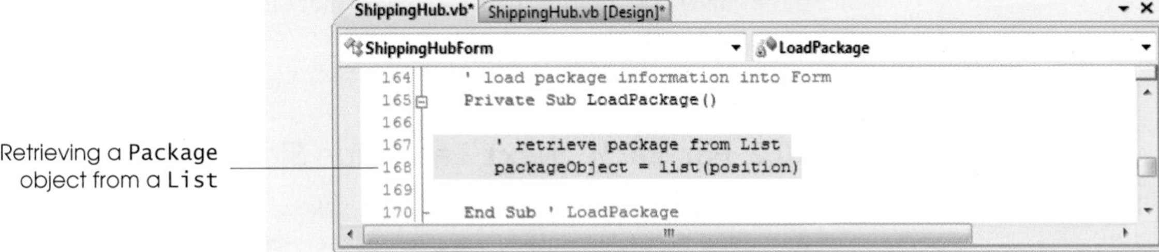

Figure 20.20 Retrieving a Package from the List.

2. ***Displaying the package information.*** Insert lines 170–178 of Fig. 20.21 into your application. These lines retrieve the package information from packageObject and display the data in the corresponding controls on the Form. Lines 176 and 178 use the ToString method to convert the arrival time and package number to their String representations.

Displaying data stored in the Package object

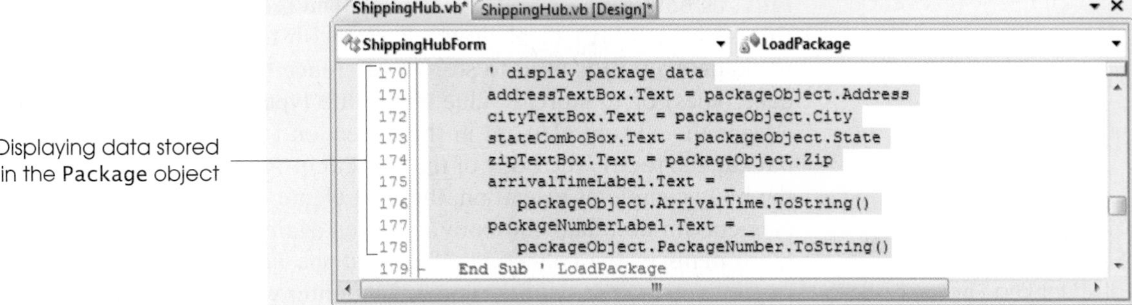

Figure 20.21 Displaying the package data in the Form's controls.

3. ***Saving the project.*** Select **File > Save All** to save your modified code.

In this section, you learned that a generic List collection stores references to any single type. The complete details of generics are beyond the scope of this book.

If you plan to continue your Visual Basic studies, we provide a thorough treatment of generics and generic collections in *Visual Basic 2008 How to Program, Fourth Edition*. We also provide tutorials and Resource Centers with additional Visual Basic 2008 information at `www.deitel.com`. You can find tutorials on Visual Basic generics and many other topics at

```
www.deitel.com/articles/index.html
```

Our Visual Basic Resource Center

```
www.deitel.com/visualbasic
```

includes articles on many Visual Basic 2008 features, including generics. Go to our Resource Centers for lots of additional information on the subjects in this book and new developments in VB.

SELF-REVIEW

1. Method ________ of class `List` can be used to add an object at a specific location in the `List`.
   a) `AddAt` b) `Insert`
   c) `AddObjectAt` d) `Add`

2. The **Shipping Hub** application uses a `List` because class `List` ________.
   a) can store a variable number of objects
   b) allows the addition and removal of packages
   c) allows the insertion of items into any index in the `List`
   d) All of the above

Answers: 1) b. 2) d.

20.7 For Each...Next Repetition Statement

Visual Basic provides the **For Each...Next** repetition statement for iterating through all the elements in an array or a collection. Instead of setting initial, final and increment values for a counter variable, the `For Each...Next` statement uses a control variable that can be assigned each element in the collection. Assuming that you have created a `List` called `list` that contains `Package` objects, the code

Good Programming Practice

Use a `For Each...Next` repetition statement to iterate through values in an array or collection without using a counter variable.

```
For Each packageObject As Package In list
   packagesListBox.Items.Add(packageObject.PackageNumber)
Next
```

adds each package's ID number to a `ListBox`. The `For Each...Next` statement requires both a group and an element. The **group** specifies the array or collection (in this case, `list`) through which you wish to iterate. The **element** (in this case, `packageObject`) is used to store a reference to an object in the group (for reference types) or to store a value (for value types). The `For Each...Next` statement assigns the current element in the collection to the element variable (in this case, `packageObject`). The body of the `For Each...Next` statement then executes. When the body completes execution, the next element in the collection is assigned to the element variable and the body executes again. This continues until there are no more items in the collection. Note that the `For Each...Next` statement does not require you to specify initial and final counter values, and thus it simplifies access to groups of values. Note that body statement in the preceding `For Each...Next` statement uses `paclageListBox`'s `Items` property (a collection). The **`Items`** property stores the items displayed in a `ListBox` or `ComboBox`.

Common Programming Error

If the element in a `For Each...Next` statement cannot be converted to the same type as the groups's objects, a compilation error occurs. For example, if a `List` contained `Date` values, declaring a reference to a `Package` object as the element would cause a compilation error.

Figure 20.22 shows the UML activity diagram for the preceding `For Each...Next` statement. It is similar to the UML diagram for the `For...Next` statement in Tutorial 11. The only difference is that the `For Each...Next` continues to execute the body until all elements in the array or collection have been accessed.

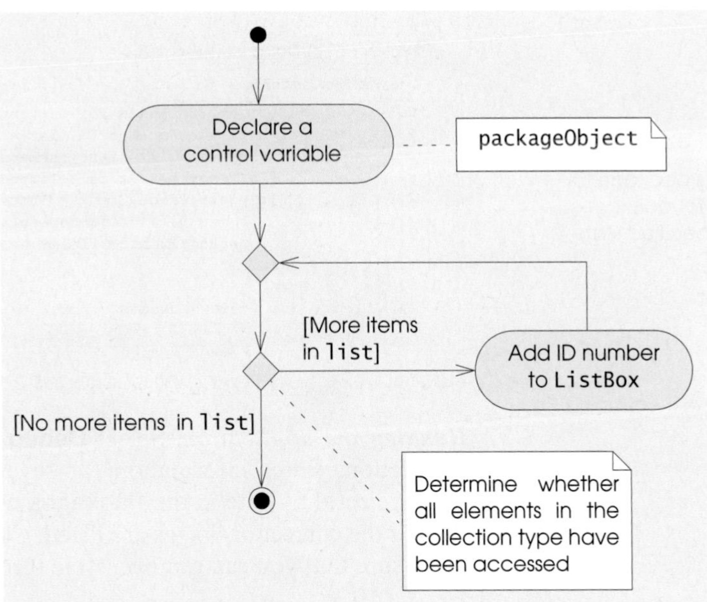

Figure 20.22 UML activity diagram for `For Each...Next` repetition statement.

When the user selects a state from the `ComboBox`, the application displays the package number for each package destined for that state. You now use the `For Each...Next` statement in the **Shipping Hub** application to add this functionality.

Inserting a For Each...Next Statement

1. ***Inserting a For Each...Next statement.*** Add lines 221–222 of Fig. 20.23 to your application, then press *Enter*. Note that the `Next` keyword is added for you by the IDE. Line 222 is the header of the repetition statement. This line declares control variable `viewPackage` of type `Package`. The loop iterates through `list`, assigning the next element in the `List` (beginning with the first `Package` object) to control variable `viewPackage` before executing the body of the loop during each iteration. Note that you've added this code to a `ComboBox`'s `SelectedIndexChanged` event handler. The **`SelectedIndexChanged`** event occurs when the value selected in the `ComboBox` changes.

For Each...Next header

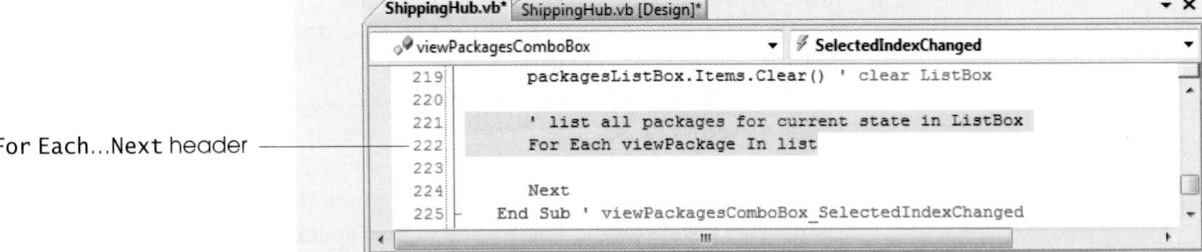

Figure 20.23 Writing a `For Each...Next` statement.

2. ***Determining a package's destination state.*** Insert lines 223–228 of Fig. 20.24 into your application. These lines contain an `If...Then` statement that tests each package's destination state against the state name displayed in the **Packages by Destination** `ComboBox`. If these state names match, line 227 displays the package number in the `ListBox`.

(cont.)

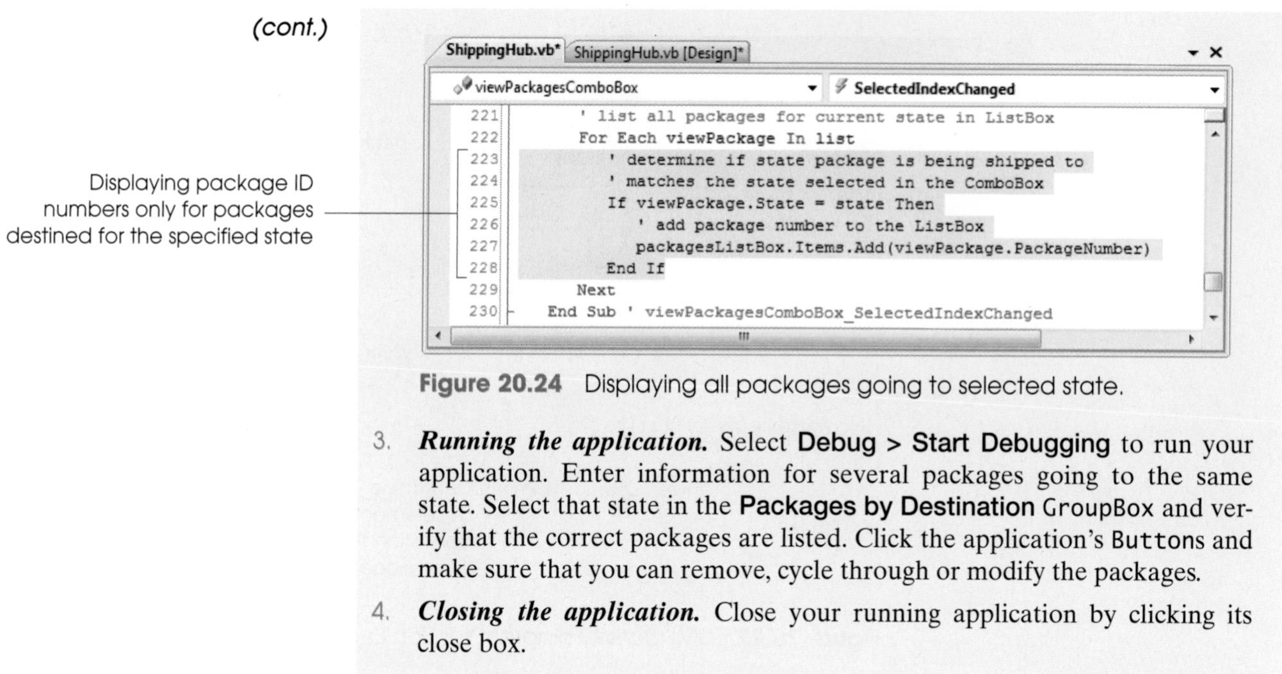

Figure 20.24 Displaying all packages going to selected state.

3. ***Running the application.*** Select **Debug > Start Debugging** to run your application. Enter information for several packages going to the same state. Select that state in the **Packages by Destination** `GroupBox` and verify that the correct packages are listed. Click the application's `Buttons` and make sure that you can remove, cycle through or modify the packages.
4. ***Closing the application.*** Close your running application by clicking its close box.

20.8 Language-Integrated Query (LINQ)

In the previous section, you used a `For Each...Next` repetition statement to iterate through a `List` of `Packages` to find those destined for a selected state. This technique is sometimes known as filtering a collection based on certain criteria (i.e., conditions). This is typical of how many older applications perform search operations. Visual Basic 2008 and the .NET 3.5 framework introduce **Language-Integrated Query (LINQ)** capabilities, which can be used to the task of filtering collections.

A **query** retrieves specific information from a data source, such as a collection. LINQ enables you to write queries directly in your Visual Basic code. With LINQ, you can query arrays, collections and other data sources such as XML documents and SQL databases. In this tutorial, we use LINQ to Objects to query collections. We discuss LINQ to SQL in Tutorial 24, **Address Book** Application, and LINQ to XML in Tutorial 32, Weather Viewer.

A typical LINQ query contains three clauses—a `From` clause, a `Where` clause and a `Select` clause. The **`From`** clause, which must appear first in a LINQ query, specifies a **range variable** and the data source to query. The range variable represents each item in the data source, much like the control variable in a `For Each...Next` statement. The **`Where`** clause specifies the conditions that must be met for the item to be included in the results. The expression in the `Where` clause must evaluate to a `Boolean`. If the expression evaluates to `True`, the item is included in the results. The **`Select`** clause specifies the value(s) placed in the results. For example, assuming that you've created a `List` of `Package` objects called `list`, the LINQ to Objects query

```
Dim cityQuery = From p In list _
                Where p.City = "Boston" _
                Select p
```

selects all the `Packages` in `list` that are destined for Boston. The query iterates through each `Package` in `list` and checks whether the `Package`'s `City` property equals `"Boston"`. If the expression in the `Where` clause evaluates to `True`, the `Select` clause includes the corresponding `Package` in the result, which is a collection of 0 or more `Packages` (because we are querying a `List(Of Package)`). LINQ uses **deferred execution**—the query does not execute until you attempt to iterate through the query results.

Notice that there are no type declarations in this sample query. To implement some of the advanced features of LINQ, Visual Basic 2008 can use local type inference to infer the type of a variable based on the context in which it is initialized. The compiler knows that `list` contains `Package` objects. So it infers that `p` is of the type `Package`. We discuss the type of `cityQuery` in the following box.

This example query is similar to the `For Each...Next` statement you wrote in the previous box. In the following box you learn to use LINQ to select from the `List` all the `Packages` destined for a specified state.

Using LINQ to Select Packages from a `List`

1. ***Declaring a LINQ query.*** Add lines 222–225 of Fig. 20.25 to your application. These lines declare a LINQ query that selects from `list` all the `Packages` destined for the specified state (local variable `state`). Recall that the compiler infers the type of the range variable (`p`). In this case, the type is `Package` because the compiler knows that `list` contains `Package` objects. The `Where` clause determines whether the `Package`'s `State` property is equal to the state selected in the `viewPackagesComboBox`.

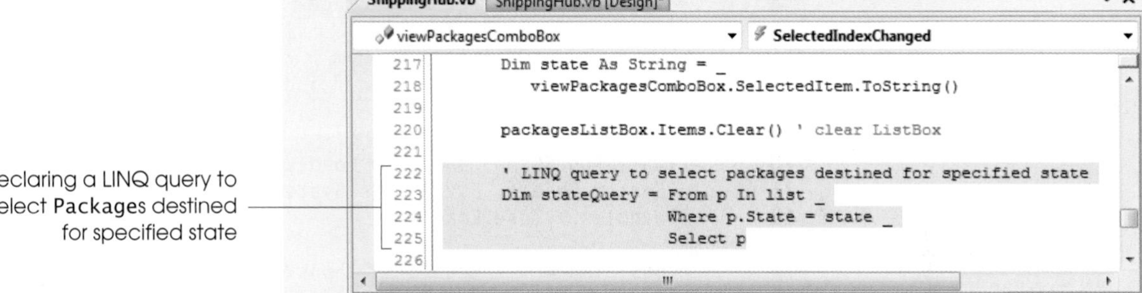
Declaring a LINQ query to select Packages destined for specified state
ShippingHub.vb*
ShippingHub.vb [Design]*
viewPackagesComboBox
SelectedIndexChanged
217 Dim state As String = _
218 viewPackagesComboBox.SelectedItem.ToString()
219
220 packagesListBox.Items.Clear() ' clear ListBox
221
222 ' LINQ query to select packages destined for specified state
223 Dim stateQuery = From p In list _
224 Where p.State = state _
225 Select p
226

Figure 20.25 Declaring a LINQ query.

2. ***Using a `For Each...Next` statement to iterate through the query results.*** Replace the `For Each...Next` statement from Fig. 20.24 with lines 227–231 of Fig. 20.26. This `For Each...Next` statement iterates over the results from the `stateQuery`. The query results are contained in an `IEnumerable(Of Package)` object. **`IEnumerable`** is an **interface**—a set of methods that can be called on an object to tell the object to perform some task or return some piece of information. The `IEnumerable` interface provides methods to iterate through a set of objects, such as an array or a collection. Arrays and collections implement the `IEnumerable` interface—you can call any `IEnumerable` method on an array or collection object to iterate through its elements. The `For Each...Next` statement implicitly calls these `IEnumerable` methods. As such, a `For Each...Next` statement can iterate over any object that implements the `IEnumerable` interface. This means you can use a `For Each...Next` statement to iterate over the results of any LINQ query. The `For Each...Next` statement in lines 228–231 adds the `PackageNumber` of each `Package` returned by `stateQuery` to the `packagesListBox`. Note that execution of the `stateQuery` is deferred until program control reaches line 228, where we begin iterating through the results.

3. ***Closing the application.*** Close your running application by clicking its close box.

4. ***Closing the IDE.*** Close Visual Basic IDE by clicking its close box.

(cont.)

Use a For Each...Next statement to display the results of the query

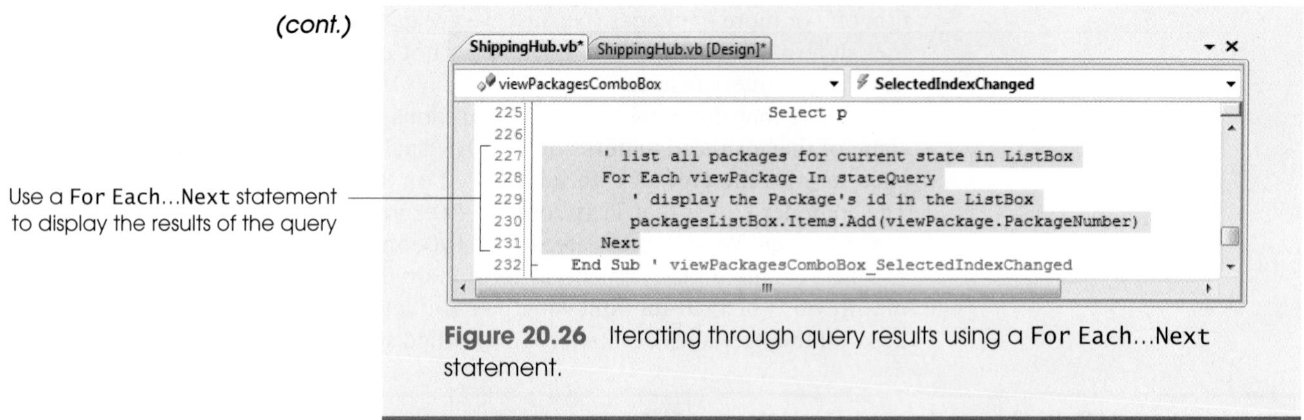

Figure 20.26 Iterating through query results using a For Each...Next statement.

Figure 20.27 presents the source code for the **Shipping Hub** application. The lines of code that contain new programming concepts that you learned in this tutorial are highlighted.

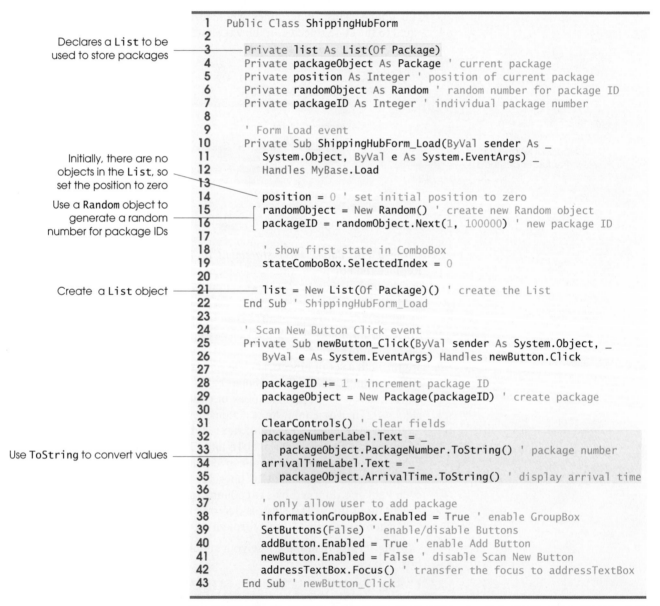

Declares a List to be used to store packages

Initially, there are no objects in the List, so set the position to zero

Use a Random object to generate a random number for package IDs

Create a List object

Use ToString to convert values

```
Public Class ShippingHubForm

   Private list As List(Of Package)
   Private packageObject As Package ' current package
   Private position As Integer ' position of current package
   Private randomObject As Random ' random number for package ID
   Private packageID As Integer ' individual package number

   ' Form Load event
   Private Sub ShippingHubForm_Load(ByVal sender As _
      System.Object, ByVal e As System.EventArgs) _
      Handles MyBase.Load

      position = 0 ' set initial position to zero
      randomObject = New Random() ' create new Random object
      packageID = randomObject.Next(1, 100000) ' new package ID

      ' show first state in ComboBox
      stateComboBox.SelectedIndex = 0

      list = New List(Of Package)() ' create the List
   End Sub ' ShippingHubForm_Load

   ' Scan New Button Click event
   Private Sub newButton_Click(ByVal sender As System.Object, _
      ByVal e As System.EventArgs) Handles newButton.Click

      packageID += 1 ' increment package ID
      packageObject = New Package(packageID) ' create package

      ClearControls() ' clear fields
      packageNumberLabel.Text = _
         packageObject.PackageNumber.ToString() ' package number
      arrivalTimeLabel.Text = _
         packageObject.ArrivalTime.ToString() ' display arrival time

      ' only allow user to add package
      informationGroupBox.Enabled = True ' enable GroupBox
      SetButtons(False) ' enable/disable Buttons
      addButton.Enabled = True ' enable Add Button
      newButton.Enabled = False ' disable Scan New Button
      addressTextBox.Focus() ' transfer the focus to addressTextBox
   End Sub ' newButton_Click
```

Figure 20.27 Complete code listing for the **Shipping Hub** application. (Part 1 of 4.)

```
   ' Add Button Click event
   Private Sub addButton_Click(ByVal sender As System.Object, _
      ByVal e As System.EventArgs) Handles addButton.Click

      SetPackage() ' set Package properties from TextBoxes
      list.Add(packageObject) ' add package to the List

      informationGroupBox.Enabled = False ' disable GroupBox
      SetButtons(True) ' enable appropriate Buttons

      ' package cannot be added until Scan New is clicked
      addButton.Enabled = False ' disable Add Button

      ' if package's state displayed, add ID to ListBox
      If stateComboBox.Text = viewPackagesComboBox.Text Then
         packagesListBox.Items.Add(packageObject.PackageNumber)
      End If

      viewPackagesComboBox.Text = packageObject.State ' list package
      newButton.Enabled = True ' enable Scan New Button
   End Sub ' addButton_Click

   ' Back Button Click event
   Private Sub backButton_Click(ByVal sender As System.Object, _
      ByVal e As System.EventArgs) Handles backButton.Click

      ' move backward one package in the list
      If position > 0 Then
         position -= 1
      Else ' wrap to end of list
         position = list.Count - 1
      End If

      LoadPackage() ' load package data from item in list
   End Sub ' backButton_Click

   ' Next Button Click event
   Private Sub nextButton_Click(ByVal sender As System.Object, _
      ByVal e As System.EventArgs) Handles nextButton.Click

      ' move forward one package in the list
      If position < list.Count - 1 Then
         position += 1
      Else
         position = 0 ' wrap to beginning of list
      End If

      LoadPackage() ' load package data from item in list
   End Sub ' nextButton_Click

   ' Remove Button click event
   Private Sub removeButton_Click(ByVal sender As _
      System.Object, ByVal e As System.EventArgs) _
      Handles removeButton.Click

      ' remove ID from ListBox if state displayed
      If stateComboBox.Text = viewPackagesComboBox.Text Then
         packagesListBox.Items.Remove(packageObject.PackageNumber)
      End If

      list.RemoveAt(position) ' remove package from list

```

When the user clicks the **< BACK** `Button`, decrement the position. If the position was zero, set the position to the last object in the `List`

When the user clicks the **NEXT >** `Button`, increment the position. If the position was the last object in the array, set the position to zero

Figure 20.27 Complete code listing for the **Shipping Hub** application. (Part 2 of 4.)

Set the position to the next package in the `List`

```
      ' load next package in list if there is one
      If list.Count > 0 Then
         ' if not at first position, go to previous one
         If position > 0 Then
            position -= 1
         End If

         LoadPackage() ' load package data from item in list
      Else
         ClearControls() ' clear fields
      End If

      SetButtons(True) ' enable appropriate Buttons
   End Sub ' removeButton_Click

   ' Edit/Update Button Click event
   Private Sub editUpdateButton_Click(ByVal sender As _
      System.Object, ByVal e As System.EventArgs) _
      Handles editUpdateButton.Click

      ' when Button reads "Edit", allow user to
      ' edit package information only
      If editUpdateButton.Text = "&Edit" Then
         informationGroupBox.Enabled = True ' enable GroupBox
         SetButtons(False)
         editUpdateButton.Enabled = True

         ' change Button text from "Edit" to "Update"
         editUpdateButton.Text = "&Update"
      Else
         ' when Button reads "Update" remove the old package
         ' data and add new data from TextBoxes
         SetPackage()
         list.RemoveAt(position)
         list.Insert(position, packageObject)

         ' display state in ComboBox
         viewPackagesComboBox.Text = packageObject.State

         ' when done, return to normal operating state
         informationGroupBox.Enabled = False ' disable GroupBox
         SetButtons(True) ' enable appropriate Buttons

         ' change Button text from "Update" to "Edit"
         editUpdateButton.Text = "&Edit"
      End If
   End Sub ' editUpdateButton_Click

   ' set package properties
   Private Sub SetPackage()
      packageObject.Address = addressTextBox.Text
      packageObject.City = cityTextBox.Text
      packageObject.State = _
         stateComboBox.SelectedItem.ToString()
      packageObject.Zip = zipTextBox.Text
   End Sub ' SetPackage

   ' load package information into Form
   Private Sub LoadPackage()

      ' retrieve package from list
      packageObject = list(position)

```

Using & in the `Text` property of a `Button` to create an access key

Removing and inserting items from/into a `List`

Using & in the `Text` property of a `Button` to create an access key

Retrieve data from user, and store it in the `Package` object

Figure 20.27 Complete code listing for the **Shipping Hub** application. (Part 3 of 4.)

```
        ' display package data
        addressTextBox.Text = packageObject.Address
        cityTextBox.Text = packageObject.City
        stateComboBox.Text = packageObject.State
        zipTextBox.Text = packageObject.Zip
        arrivalTimeLabel.Text = _
           packageObject.ArrivalTime.ToString()
        packageNumberLabel.Text = _
           packageObject.PackageNumber.ToString()
    End Sub ' LoadPackage

    ' clear all the input controls on the Form
    Private Sub ClearControls()
        addressTextBox.Clear()
        cityTextBox.Clear()
        zipTextBox.Clear()
        stateComboBox.SelectedText = ""
        arrivalTimeLabel.Text = ""
        packageNumberLabel.Text = ""
    End Sub ' ClearControls

    ' enable/disable Buttons
    Private Sub SetButtons(ByVal state As Boolean)
        removeButton.Enabled = state
        editUpdateButton.Enabled = state
        nextButton.Enabled = state
        backButton.Enabled = state

        ' disable navigation if not multiple packages
        If list.Count < 2 Then
           nextButton.Enabled = False
           backButton.Enabled = False
        End If

        ' if no items, disable Remove and Edit/Update Buttons
        If list.Count = 0 Then
           editUpdateButton.Enabled = False
           removeButton.Enabled = False
        End If
    End Sub ' SetButtons

    ' event raised when user selects a new state in ComboBox
    Private Sub viewPackagesComboBox_SelectedIndexChanged( _
        ByVal sender As System.Object, ByVal e As System.EventArgs) _
        Handles viewPackagesComboBox.SelectedIndexChanged

        Dim state As String = _
           viewPackagesComboBox.SelectedItem.ToString()

        packagesListBox.Items.Clear() ' clear ListBox

        ' LINQ query to select packages destined for specified state
        Dim stateQuery = From p In list _
                         Where p.State = state _
                         Select p

        ' list all packages for current state in ListBox
        For Each viewPackage As Package In stateQuery
           ' display the Package's id in the ListBox
           packagesListBox.Items.Add(viewPackage.PackageNumber)
        Next
    End Sub ' viewPackagesComboBox_SelectedIndexChanged
End Class ' ShippingHubForm
```

Using `ToString` to convert values

Enable or disable `Buttons` depending on value of `state`

Declare a LINQ query to select `Packages` destined for specified state

Figure 20.27 Complete code listing for the **Shipping Hub** application. (Part 4 of 4.)

SELF-REVIEW

1. The group in a For Each...Next repetition statement represents _________.
   a) the counter used for iteration
   b) the reference used for iteration
   c) an array or collection
   d) the guard condition

2. The _________ statement provides a convenient way to iterate through values in an array or collection.
   a) Do While...Loop
   b) For...Next
   c) For Each...Next
   d) None of the above

Answers: 1) c. 2) c.

20.9 Wrap-Up

In this tutorial, you learned how to use the TabStop and TabIndex properties to enhance the **Shipping Hub** application's usability. You learned how to determine which controls receive the application's focus when the *Tab* key is pressed using the TabStop property. You then used **View > Tab Order** to help you specify the order in which controls receive the focus when the *Tab* key is pressed. To further enhance the user interface, you created access keys to allow the user to "click" Buttons in the **Shipping Hub** application by pressing the *Alt* key and then the access key for the particular Button.

You learned about using the List collection. You used List methods to add a Package object to a List and delete the Package from a specific index in a List. You then wrote code to insert a Package object into the List at a specific index. These methods helped you store, edit and navigate a List of Packages in the **Shipping Hub** application.

You learned about the For Each...Next repetition statement. You declared a control variable for use in the repetition statement and used that reference in the For Each...Next statement to iterate through each element in a group (which can be an array or a collection). Then you used the For Each...Next statement to iterate through Package objects in the List in your **Shipping Hub** application.

Finally, you learned to use LINQ to Objects to create queries that selected objects from a collection based on specified conditions. You also learned how to use a For Each...Next statement to iterate through the results of the query.

In the next tutorial, you learn about keyboard events, which are events raised when the user presses and releases keys on the keyboard. You also learn the Dictionary collection and use LINQ to Objects to filter the collection of controls on a Form.

SKILLS SUMMARY

Using the TabIndex and TabStop Properties

- Set the TabIndex properties of controls on your Form using numbers to specify the order in which to transfer the focus of the application when the user presses the *Tab* key. Using **View > Tab Order** helps in configuring the order of this process.
- Set the TabStop property of a control to False if a control is not used by the user to input data. Set the TabStop property of a control to True if focus should be transferred to the control using the *Tab* key.

Creating Access Keys

- Insert the & symbol in a control's Text property before the character you wish you use as an access key (keyboard shortcut).

Creating a List

- Assign a reference to a List to an object of type System.Collections.Generic.List using keyword New.

```
Dim list As New List(Of Integer)()
```

Limiting the Number of Characters that Can Be Typed in a `TextBox`

- Set the `TextBox`'s `MaxLength` property.

Using a `List`

- Call `List` method `Add` on a `List` object to add the method's argument to the end of the `List`.
- Call `List` method `RemoveAt` on a `List` object to remove the object from the `List` at the index specified by the method's argument.
- Call `List` method `Insert` on a `List` object to add the object specified by the second argument to the `List` at the index specified by the first argument.
- Use `List` property `Count` on a `List` object to obtain the number of its elements.

Using a `For Each...Next` Repetition Statement

- Declare a variable of the same type as the elements you wish to access in a group (that is, an array or a collection).
- Specify the variable as the control variable in the `For Each...Next` repetition statement and the array or collection through which you wish to iterate. The loop repeats and the body of the `For Each...Next` repetition statement executes for each element in the group. The value accessed at the beginning of each iteration is stored in the control variable for the body of the loop.

Using Language-Integrated Query (LINQ) to Select Objects

- Declare a variable and assign a LINQ query to it. A basic LINQ query consists of a `From` clause, a `Where` clause and a `Select` clause.
- Specify in the `From` clause an element variable name and the array or collection from which to select elements.
- Specify in the `Where` clause the conditions that must be met to include an element in the results.
- Specify in the `Select` clause the information to select from the element.
- To execute the LINQ query, iterate over its results.

KEY TERMS

access key—Keyboard shortcut that allows the user to perform an action on a control using the keyboard.

`Add` method of class `List`—Adds a specified object to the end of a `List`.

collection—A class used to store groups of related objects.

`Count` property of `List`—Returns the number of objects contained in the `List`.

deferred execution—A LINQ query is not executed until you begin to iterate over its results.

dynamic resizing—A capability that allows certain objects (such as `List`s) to increase or decrease in size based on the addition or removal of elements from that object. Enables the `List` object to increase its size to accommodate new elements and to decrease its size when elements are removed.

element of a `For Each...Next` statement—Used to store a reference to the current value of the collection being iterated.

`For Each...Next` repetition statement—Iterates through elements in an array or collection.

`From` clause (of a LINQ query)—Specifies a range variable and the data source to query.

group (of a `For Each...Next` statement)—Specifies the array or collection through which you wish to iterate.

index of a `List`—The value with which you can refer to a specific element in an `List`, based on the element's location in the `List`.

`IEnumerable` interface—Provides methods to iterate through a set of objects, such as an array or a collection.

`Insert` method of class `List`—Inserts a specified object into the specified location of a `List`.

interface—Specifies a set of methods that can be called on an object which implements the interface to perform certain tasks.

`Items` property of `ComboBox`—Collection containing the values displayed in a `ComboBox`.

Language-Integrated Query (LINQ)—Provides support for writing queries in Visual Basic.

List(Of T) class—Has the same capabilities as an array, as well as dynamic resizing.

MaxLength property of TextBox—Specifies the maximum number of characters that can be input into a TextBox.

query (LINQ)—Retrieves specific information from a data source, such as a collection.

range variable (LINQ)—The control variable for a LINQ query.

RemoveAt method of class List—Removes the object located at a specified location of a List.

Select clause (of a LINQ query)—Specifies the value(s) placed in the results of the query.

SelectedIndexChanged event of ComboBox—Raised when a new value is selected in a ComboBox.

System.Collections.Generic namespace—Contains collection classes such as List.

TabIndex property—A control property that specifies the order in which focus is transferred to controls on the Form when the *Tab* key is pressed.

TabStop property—A control property that specifies whether a control can receive the focus when the *Tab* key is pressed.

ToString method—Returns a String representation of the object or data type on which the method is called.

Where clause (of a LINQ query)—Specifies the conditions that must be met for an item to be included in the results.

GUI DESIGN GUIDELINES

Overall Design

- Set a control's TabStop property to True only if the control is used to receive user input.
- Use the TabIndex property to define the logical order in which the user should enter data. Usually the order transfers the focus of the application from top to bottom and left to right.
- Use access keys to allow users to "click" a control using the keyboard.

CONTROLS, EVENTS, PROPERTIES & METHODS

List This class is used to store a variable number of objects of any specified type.

- ***Property***

  Count—Returns the number of objects contained in the List.

- ***Methods***

  Add—Adds an object to the the end of a List.

  Insert—Adds an object to the List object at a specific index.

  RemoveAt—Removes an object from the List object at the specified index.

ComboBox ComboBox This control allows users to select options from a drop-down list.

- ***In action***

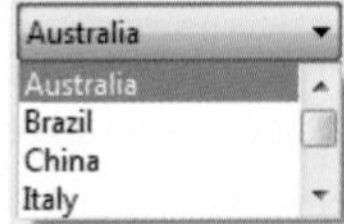

- ***Event***

  SelectedIndexChanged—Raised when a new value is selected in the ComboBox.

- ***Properties***

  DataSource—Specifies the source of the items displayed in a ComboBox.

  DropDownStyle—Determines the ComboBox's style.

  Enabled—Determines whether the user can enter data (True) in the ComboBox or not (False).

  Items—Collection containing the values displayed in a ComboBox.

`Location`—Specifies the location of the `ComboBox` control relative to the top-left corner of the container (e.g., a `Form` or a `GroupBox`).

`MaxDropDownItems`—Determines the maximum number of items to be displayed when the user clicks the drop-down arrow.

`Name`—Specifies the name used to access the `ComboBox` control programmatically. The name should be appended with the `ComboBox` suffix.

`SelectedItem`—Contains the item selected by the user.

`TabIndex`—Specifies the order in which focus is transferred to controls when *Tab* is pressed.

`TabStop`—Specifies whether the user can select the control using the *Tab* key.

`Text`—Specifies the text displayed in the `ComboBox`.

TextBox [abl] TextBox This control allows the user to input data from the keyboard.

- ***In action***

- ***Event***

`TextChanged`—Raised when the text in the `TextBox` is changed.

- ***Properties***

`Enabled`—Determines whether the user can enter data in the `TextBox` or not.

`Location`—Specifies the location of the `TextBox` control relative to the top-left corner of the container (e.g., a `Form` or a `GroupBox`).

`MaxLength`—Specifies the maximum number of characters that can be input into the `TextBox`.

`Multiline`—Specifies whether the `TextBox` is capable of displaying multiple lines of text.

`Name`—Specifies the name used to access the `TextBox` programmatically. The name should be appended with the `TextBox` suffix.

`PasswordChar`—Specifies the masking character to be used when displaying data in the `TextBox`.

`ReadOnly`—Determines whether the value of a `TextBox` can be changed.

`ScrollBars`—Specifies whether a multiline `TextBox` contains a scrollbar.

`Size`—Specifies the width and height (in pixels) of the `TextBox`.

`TabIndex`—Specifies the order in which focus is transferred to controls when *Tab* is pressed.

`TabStop`—Specifies whether the user can select the control using the *Tab* key.

`Text`—Specifies the text displayed in the `TextBox`.

`TextAlign`—Specifies how the text is aligned within the `TextBox`.

- ***Method***

`Focus`—Transfers the focus of the application to the `TextBox` that calls it.

MULTIPLE-CHOICE QUESTIONS

20.1 ________ are specifically designed to store groups of values.

a) Collections b) Properties
c) Accessors d) None of the above

20.2 The ________ key provides a quick and convenient way to navigate through controls on a `Form`.

a) *Tab* b) *Enter*
c) *Caps Lock* d) *Alt*

20.3 A `List` differs from an array in that a `List` can ________.

a) store objects of any type b) resize itself dynamically
c) be accessed programmatically d) Both b and c

20.4 The element in a `For Each...Next` statement ________.

a) must be of type `Integer`
b) must be of (or convertible to) the same type as the group elements
c) must be of type `List`
d) None of the above

20.5 The control that receives the focus the first time *Tab* is pressed has a `TabIndex` property set to ________.

a) `First` b) `0`
c) `Next` d) `1`

20.6 Users should be able to use the *Tab* key to transfer the focus to ________.

a) only `Buttons`
b) only `TextBoxes`
c) only controls that have an `AcceptTab` property
d) only the controls that receive user input

20.7 To ensure that the proper controls obtain the focus when the *Tab* key is pressed, use the ________.

a) `TabIndex` property b) `TabStop` and `TabIndex` properties
c) `TabStop` property d) `Focus` property

20.8 To add a value to the end of a `List`, call the ________ method.

a) `Add` b) `AddToEnd`
c) `AddAt` d) `InsertAt`

20.9 To remove a value from a specific index in the `List`, use method ________.

a) `Remove` b) `RemoveAt`
c) `Delete` d) `DeleteAt`

20.10 A LINQ query can be used ________ .

a) to select elements from a collection b) in a `For Each...Next` statement
c) to select elements from an array d) All of the above

EXERCISES

20.11 ***(Modified** Shipping Hub **Application)*** Modify the **Shipping Hub** application created in this tutorial, so that the user can double click a package in the `packagesListBox`. When a package number is double clicked, the package's information should be displayed in a `MessageBox` (Fig. 20.28).

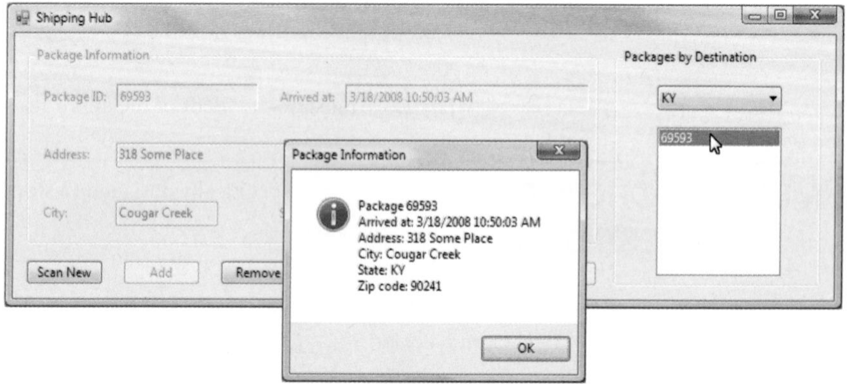

Figure 20.28 Modified **Shipping Hub** application GUI.

a) ***Copying the template to your working directory.*** Copy the directory `C:\Examples\Tutorial20\Exercises\ShippingHubModified` to your `C:\SimplyVB2008` directory.

b) ***Opening the application's template file.*** Double click `ShippingHubModified.sln` in the `ShippingHubModified` directory to open the application.

c) ***Viewing the event handler.*** Click **ShippingHub.vb** in the **Solution Explorer** and select **View > Code**. Scroll to the end of the code listing to locate the `ListBox`'s `DoubleClick` event handler. A `ListBox`'s `DoubleClick` event is raised when the control is double clicked.

d) ***Initializing necessary variables.*** Create a reference of type `Package` to hold the `Package` selected from the `List`. Create a `String` variable to store the information about the given package. Write code in the `DoubleClick` event handler to declare the `Package tempPackage` and the `String packageInfo`.

e) ***Writing a LINQ query.*** Create a LINQ query that selects from `list` the `Package` with the `PackageNumber` that is selected in the `ListBox`. Create an `Integer` variable to store the number selected in the `ListBox` and use that variable in your LINQ query. Do not initialize the `Integer` variable yet.

f) ***Checking whether the user has selected a valid item.*** To determine whether the user has selected a valid item (and not an empty element in the `ListBox`), write an `If...Then` statement to make sure that an item is selected in the `ListBox`. [*Hint:* A `SelectedIndex` value of `-1` means that no item is currently selected.]

g) ***Retrieving the correct `Package`.*** If a valid item is selected from the `ListBox`, assign the selected package ID number to the `Integer` variable you created in *Step e*. Assign to `tempPackage` the first element in the query results. You can use the query's `First` property to access this element. Note that each `Package` has a unique `PackageNumber`—only one `Package` is returned by the query. However, the query returns an `IEnumerable` from which you must explicitly select the first item to assign it to a reference of type `Package`. Place all the package information in the `String` you declared in *Step d*.

h) ***Inserting the `Else` statement.*** Create an `Else` statement to notify the user if an invalid item has been selected from the `ListBox`. If this occurs, add a message to the `packageInfo String` displayed in the `MessageBox`.

i) ***Displaying the `MessageBox`.*** Call the `MessageBox`'s `Show` method to display the text you've added to the `packageInfo String`. This displays either the information for the package selected or a message stating that an invalid package has been selected.

j) ***Running the application.*** Select **Debug > Start Debugging** to run your application. Add several packages. In the **Packages by Destination** `GroupBox`, select a state for which there are packages being sent. Double click one of the packages listed in the **Packages by Destination** `ListBox`, and verify that the correct information is displayed in a `MessageBox`.

k) ***Closing the application.*** Close your running application by clicking its close box.

l) ***Closing the IDE.*** Close the Visual Basic IDE by clicking its close box.

20.12 *(`Controls` Collection Application)* Visual Basic provides many different types of collections. One such collection is the `Controls` collection, which provides access to all of the controls on a `Form`. Create an application that uses the `Controls` collection and a `For Each...Next` loop to iterate through each control on the `Form`. As each control is encountered, add its name to a `ListBox`, and change the control's background color (in Fig. 20.29, `Color.Wheat`, is used).

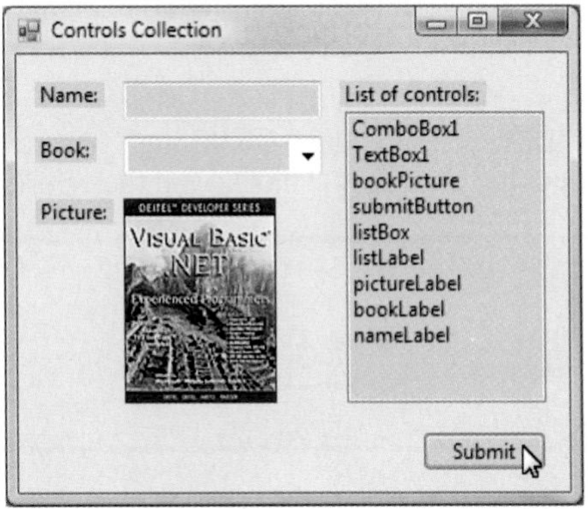

Figure 20.29 `Controls` Collection GUI.

a) ***Copying the template to your working directory.*** Copy the directory `C:\Examples\Tutorial20\Exercises\ControlsCollection` to your `C:\SimplyVB2008` directory.

b) ***Opening the application's template file.*** Double click `ControlsCollection.sln` in the `ControlsCollection` directory to open the application.

c) ***Generating an event handler.*** Switch to **Design** view. Double click the **Submit** `Button` to create an event handler for the `Click` event.

d) ***Declaring a control variable.*** Declare a reference of type `Control`. This reference represents each element in the `For Each...Next` statement as it iterates through each `Control` on the `Form`.

e) ***Clearing the*** **`ListBox`**. To ensure that the information in the `ListBox` is updated each time the **Submit** `Button` is clicked, clear the `ListBox` of all items.

f) ***Writing a*** **`For Each...Next`** ***statement.*** To create the `For Each...Next` statement, use the control variable that you created to iterate through the `Form`'s `Controls` collection.

g) ***Adding each control's name to the*** **`ListBox`**. Use the `ListBox`'s `Items.Add` method to insert the name of each control on the `Form`. Recall that a control's `Name` property contains the name of the control.

h) ***Changing the control's background color.*** Use the `Control`'s `BackColor` property to change its background color. Set the property to a new color using a member of the `Color` structure. [*Hint:* Type the word `Color` followed by the member-access operator to display a list of predefined colors using the *IntelliSense* feature.] Note that the color of the `PictureBox` does not appear to change, because its image displays in the control's foreground.

i) ***Running the application.*** Select **Debug > Start Debugging** to run your application. Click the **Submit** `Button`. Verify that the controls' background colors change, and that all the controls are listed in the **List of controls:** `ListBox`.

j) ***Closing the application.*** Close your running application by clicking its close box.

k) ***Closing the IDE.*** Close the Visual Basic IDE by clicking its close box.

What does this code do?

20.13 What is the result of executing the following code?

```
Dim listItem As Integer
Dim output As String = ""

Dim list As New System.Collections.Generic.List(Of Integer)()
list.Add(1)
list.Add(3)
list.Add(5)

For Each listItem In list
   output &= (" " & listItem)
Next

MessageBox.Show(output, "Mystery", _
   MessageBoxButtons.OK, MessageBoxIcon.Information)
```

What's wrong with this code?

20.14 This code should iterate through an array of `Packages` in `list` and display each package's number in `displayLabel`. Find the error(s) in the following code.

```
Dim value As System.Collections.Generic.List(Of Package)

For Each value In list
  displayLabel.Text &= (" " & value.PackageNumber)
Next
```

Programming Challenge

20.15 ***(Enhanced Shipping Hub Application)*** Enhance the **Shipping Hub** application created in Exercise 20.11 to allow the user to move a maximum of five packages from the warehouse to a truck for shipping (Fig. 20.30). If you have not completed Exercise 20.11, follow the steps in Exercise 20.11 before proceeding with this exercise. If you have completed Exercise 20.11, copy the code you added to the `packagesListBox` `DoubleClick` event handler to the same event handler in this application before beginning this exercise.

a) ***Copying the template to your working directory.*** Copy the directory `C:\Examples\Tutorial20\Exercises\ShippingHubEnhanced` to your `C:\SimplyVB2008` directory.

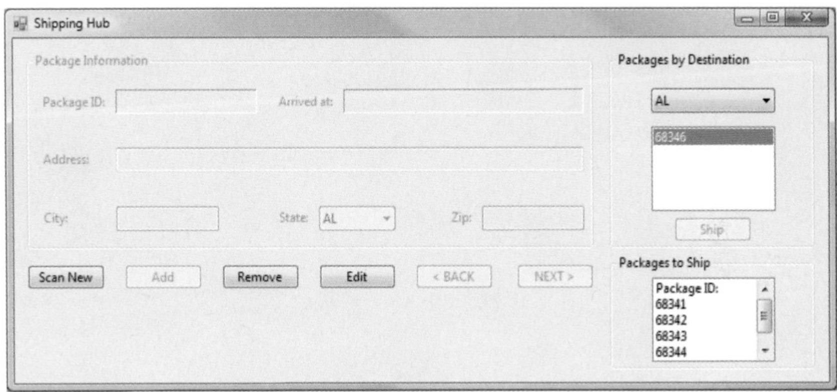

Figure 20.30 Enhanced **Shipping Hub** GUI.

b) ***Opening the application's template file.*** Double click `ShippingHubEnhanced.sln` in the `ShippingHubEnhanced` directory to open the application.

c) ***Enabling the Ship `Button`.*** The **Ship** `Button` should not be enabled until a package is selected in `packageListBox`. Double click `packageListBox` in **Design** view to define its `SelectedIndexChanged` event handler. Use the `Button`'s `Enabled` property to enable the `Button` if the `SelectedIndex` of the `ListBox` is not `-1`. This means that when the user selects a package from the `ListBox`, the user can send it to the truck by clicking the **Ship** `Button`. Also, insert a line of code after the `For Each...Next` statement in the `viewPackagesComboBox_SelectedIndexChanged` event handler to disable the **Ship** `Button` when a user chooses a different state.

d) ***Defining the Ship `Button`'s `Click` Event.*** Double click the **Ship** `Button` in **Design** view to define the `Click` event handler.

e) ***Creating temporary variables.*** Create two temporary `Package` references to store the correct package's information. Use `tempPackage` as the reference to the element in the collection of a `For Each...Next` statement, and the `truckPackage` as a reference to the package added to the truck.

f) ***Using the `If...Then...Else` statement.*** Use an `If...Then...Else` statement to allow packages to be placed onto the truck if the number of packages on the truck is less than five.

g) ***Using a LINQ query.*** Use a LINQ query to select from `list` the `Package` whose `PackageNumber` is selected in the `ListBox`. Assign the selected `Package` to the `truckPackage` reference.

h) ***Adding the package to the truck.*** Add the selected `Package` to the truck by adding the reference to `truckPackage` to the truck's `List`, `truckList`.

i) ***Removing the package.*** Use `List`'s `Remove` method to delete the `Package` meant for the truck from `list`. Also remove the `Package`'s `PackageNumber` from `packagesListBox`.

j) ***Displaying the Packages in the `ListBox`.*** Clear the `truckListBox`, then add `"Package ID:"` as a header. Use a `For Each...Next` statement that iterates through each `Package` in `truckList` and displays each `Package`'s `PackageNumber` in `truckListBox`.

k) ***Refreshing the GUI.*** Call the ClearControls and SetButtons methods to clear the TextBoxes and enable the appropriate Buttons. Set the **Ship** Button's Enabled property to False.

l) ***Coding the Else statement.*** Display a MessageBox that notifies the user if the number of packages on the truck is already five. Then disable the **Ship** Button.

m) ***Running the application.*** Select **Debug > Start Debugging** to run your application. Add several packages. Add several Packages to the **Packages to Ship** ListBox. Verify that you can add only five Packages to this ListBox.

n) ***Closing the application.*** Close your running application by clicking its close box.

o) ***Closing the IDE.*** Close the Visual Basic IDE by clicking its close box.

T U T O R I A L

Typing Application

Introducing Keyboard Events, Menus, Dialogs and the `Dictionary` Collection

Objectives

In this tutorial, you learn to:

- Handle keyboard events.
- Create menus for your Windows applications.
- Use dialogs to display messages.
- Use the `ShowDialog` method of the **Font** and **Color** dialogs.
- Display the **Font** dialog to enable users to choose fonts.
- Display the **Color** dialog to enable users to choose colors.
- Use operator `IsNot` to compare references.
- Use a `Dictionary` to store pairs of keys and values.
- Use LINQ to Objects to search a `Form`'s `Controls` collection.

Outline

Text-editor applications enable you to perform many tasks, from writing e-mails to creating business proposals. These applications often use menus and dialogs to help you customize the appearance of your document. They also respond to keys pressed on the keyboard either by displaying characters or by performing actions (such as accessing menus or dialogs). In this tutorial, you learn how to handle **keyboard events**, which occur when keys on the keyboard are pressed and released. Handling keyboard events allows you to specify the action that the application is to take when a particular key is pressed. When you handle the key events in this application, you use LINQ to Objects, the `Form`'s `Controls` collection and a `Dictionary` collection to locate the correct `Button` to highlight on the GUI. You then learn how to add menus to your application. By now, you are familiar with using various menus and dialogs provided by Windows applications. You learn to create menus that group related commands and allow the user to select various actions to perform in the application. Finally, you learn about the **Font** and **Color** dialogs, which allow the user to change the appearance of text in the application.

21.1 Test-Driving the Typing Application

In this tutorial, you create a **Typing** Application to help students learn how to type. This application must meet the following requirements:

> ***Application Requirements***
>
> *A high-school course teaches students how to type. The instructor would like to use a Windows application that allows students to watch what they are typing on the screen without looking at the keyboard. You have been asked to create an application that displays what the student types. The application has to display a virtual keyboard that highlights any key the student presses on the real keyboard. This application must also contain menu commands for selecting the font style and color of the text displayed, clearing the text displayed and inverting the background and foreground colors of the display.*

This application allows the user to type text. As the user presses each key, the application highlights the corresponding key on the GUI and adds the character to a TextBox. The user can select the color and style of the characters typed, invert the background and foreground colors and clear the TextBox. You begin by test-driving the completed application. Then you learn the additional Visual Basic capabilities that you need to create your own version of this application.

Test-Driving the Typing Application

1. ***Opening the completed application.*** Open the directory C:\Examples\Tutorial21\CompletedApplication\Typing to locate the **Typing** application. Double click Typing.sln to open the application in the Visual Basic IDE.
2. ***Running the Typing Application.*** Select **Debug > Start Debugging** to run the application. Once the application has loaded, type the sentence "Programming in Visual Basic is simple." As you type, the corresponding keys light up on the Form's virtual keyboard and the text is displayed in the TextBox (Fig. 21.1). [*Note:* This application assumes that only one key is pressed at a time; however, capital letters do work.]

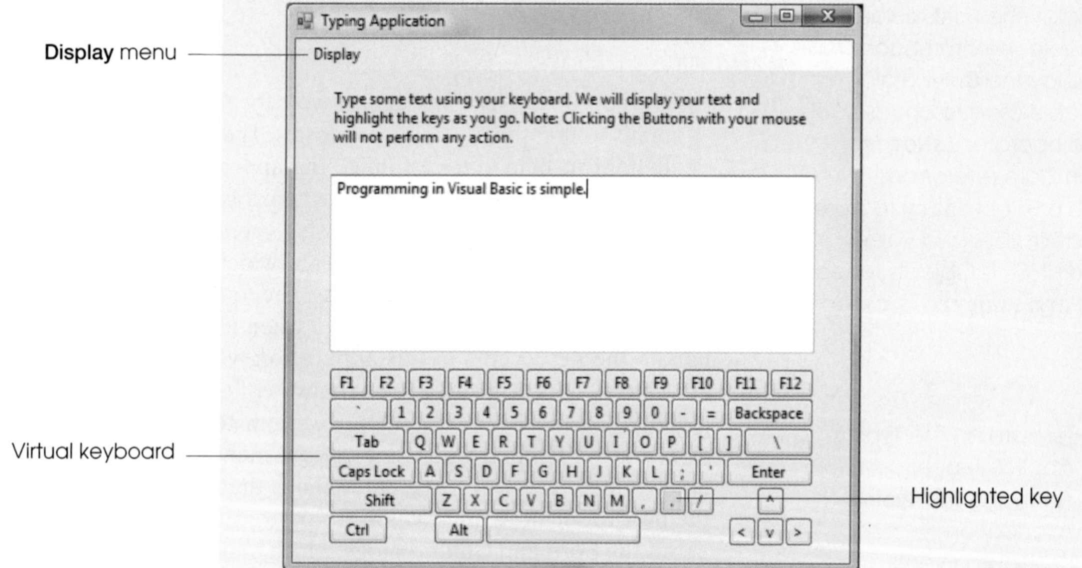

Figure 21.1 **Typing** application with key pressed.

3. ***Changing the font.*** Select **Display > Text > Font...** (Fig. 21.2) to open the **Font** dialog shown in Fig. 21.3. The **Font** dialog allows you to choose the font style for the application's output. Select Segoe UI from the **Font:** ComboBox, select Bold from the **Font style:** ComboBox and select 11 from the **Size:** ComboBox. Click the **OK** Button. Note that the text you typed in *Step 2* is now bold and bigger.
4. ***Changing the color of the font.*** Select **Display > Text > Color...** to display the **Color** dialog (Fig. 21.4). This dialog allows you to choose the color of the text displayed. Select a color, and click **OK**.

(cont.)

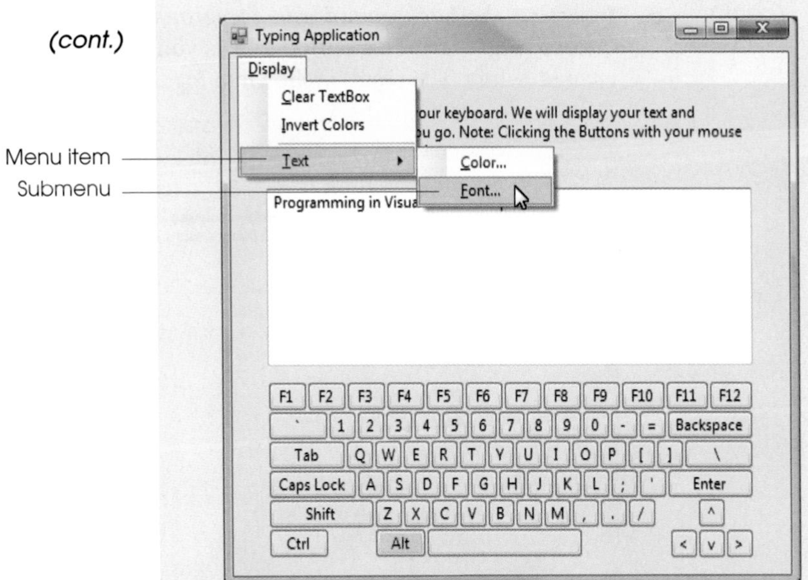

Figure 21.2 Selecting the **Font...** menu item.

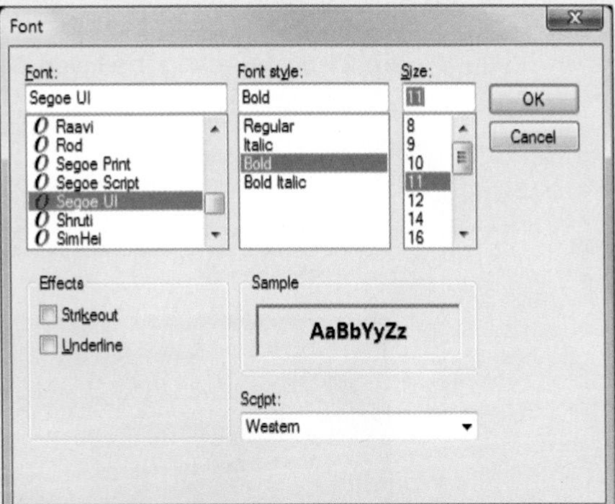

Figure 21.3 **Font** dialog displayed when **Display > Text > Font...** is selected.

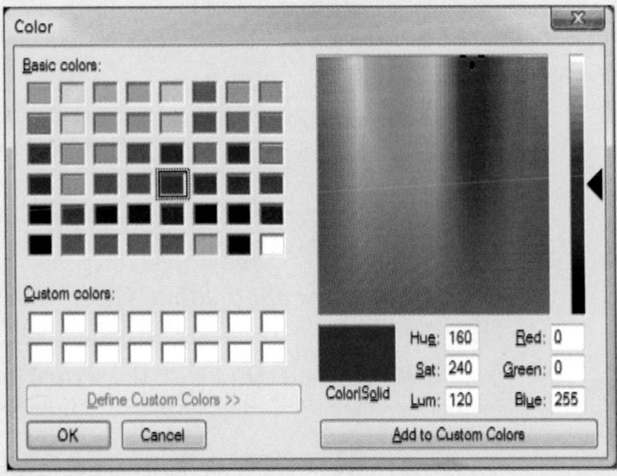

Figure 21.4 **Color** dialog displayed when **Display > Text > Color...** is selected.

(cont.)

5. ***Inverting the background and foreground colors.*** Select **Display > Invert Colors** (Fig. 21.5). This option allows you to swap the background and foreground colors. The result is shown in Fig. 21.6.

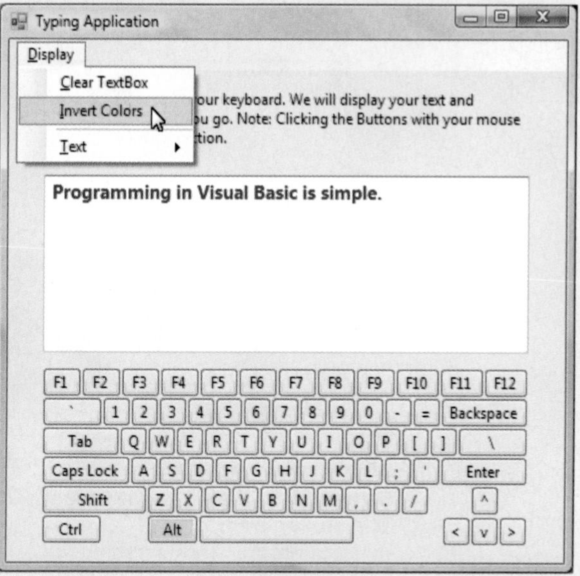

Figure 21.5 Selecting the **Invert Colors** menu item.

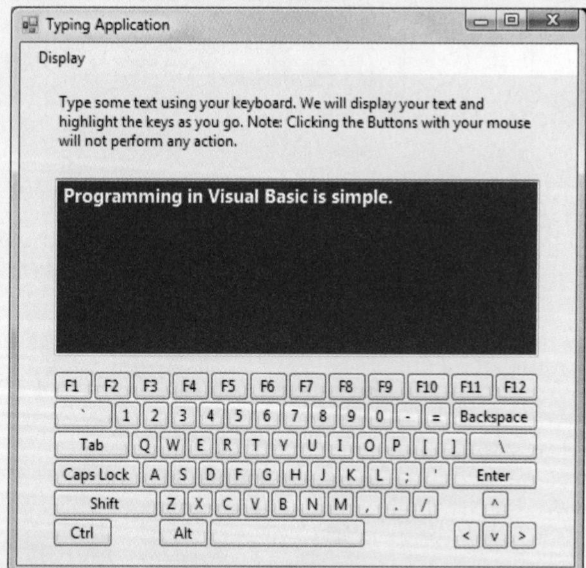

Figure 21.6 Output with colors inverted.

6. ***Clearing the TextBox.*** Select **Display > Clear TextBox** to remove all the text from the `TextBox`.

7. ***Closing the application.*** Close your running application by clicking its close box.

8. ***Closing the IDE.*** Close the Visual Basic IDE by clicking its close box.

21.2 Analyzing the Typing Application

Before you begin building the **Typing** application, you should analyze the application's components. The following pseudocode describes the basic operation of the **Typing** application:

When the user presses a key:
    Highlight the corresponding Button on the GUI

When the user releases a key:
    Reset the corresponding Button's background color to the Button's default background color

When the user selects the Color... menu item:
    Display the Color dialog
    Update the TextBox text's color

When the user selects the Font... menu item:
    Display the Font dialog
    Update the TextBox text's font

When the user selects the Clear TextBox menu item:
    Clear the TextBox

When the user selects the Invert Colors menu item:
    Swap the TextBox's background and foreground colors

Now that you've test-driven the **Typing** application and studied its pseudocode representation, you use an ACE table to help you convert the pseudocode to Visual Basic. Figure 21.7 lists the actions, controls and events that help you complete your own version of this application. [*Note:* The number of `Buttons` is large and no `Button` events are used; therefore, the `Buttons` in the virtual keyboard are not included in the ACE table.]

*Action/Control/Event (ACE) Table for the **Typing** Application*

Action	Control	Event
Label the application's controls	`promptLabel`	Application is run
	`outputTextBox`	`KeyPress`, `KeyDown`
Highlight the corresponding Button on the GUI	keyboard `Buttons`	
	`outputTextBox`	`KeyUp`
Reset the corresponding Button's background color to the Button's default background color	keyboard `Buttons`	
	`colorMenuItem`	`Click`
Display the Color dialog	`dialog`	
Update the TextBox text's color	`outputTextBox`	
	`fontMenuItem`	`Click`
Display the Font dialog	`dialog`	
Update the TextBox text's font	`outputTextBox`	
	`clearMenuItem`	`Click`
Clear the TextBox	`outputTextBox`	
	`invertMenuItem`	`Click`
Swap the TextBox's background and foreground colors	`outputTextBox`	

Figure 21.7 ACE table for the **Typing** Application.

21.3 Keyboard Events

You now learn to handle keyboard events, which occur when keys on the keyboard are pressed and released. All keyboard events are raised by the control that currently has the focus. In the **Typing** application, these events are raised by the `Text-`

Box control. You first learn about the outputTextBox's **KeyDown** event, which occurs when a key is pressed while the outputTextBox has the focus. In the following box, you insert the code to handle the event when the user presses a key. This event handler processes control keys (e.g., *Shift*, *Enter*, *Tab*), function keys (e.g., *F1*, *F2*, etc.) and the arrow keys only. You learn to process the letter, digit and symbol keys in a subsequent box.

Coding the KeyDown Event Handler

1. ***Copying the template to your working directory.*** Copy the C:\Examples\Tutorial21\TemplateApplication\Typing directory to your working directory C:\SimplyVB2008.

2. ***Opening the Typing application's template file.*** Double click Typing.sln in the Typing directory to open the application in the Visual Basic IDE.

3. ***Determining whether the pressed key is a control key, function key or arrow key.*** Add lines 10–11 of Fig. 21.8 to your code, then press *Enter* to add the End If keywords.

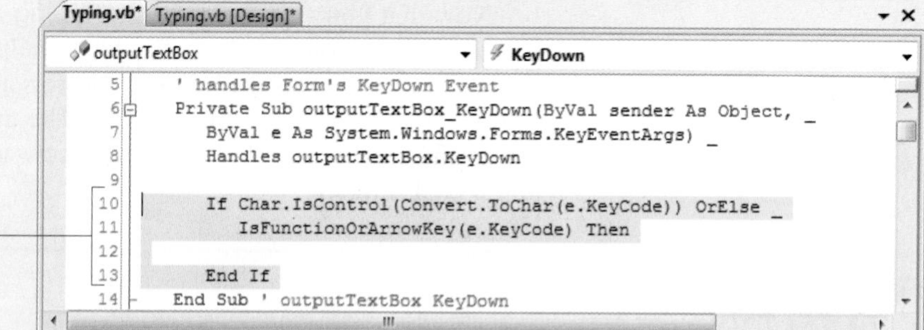

Determine whether the pressed key is a control key, function key or arrow key

Figure 21.8 Determining whether the pressed key is a control key, function key or arrow key.

When a key is pressed, the KeyDown event is raised for the control that has the focus. As you've seen in previous tutorials, event handlers specify two parameters—sender and e. The **sender** Object is the GUI component that raised the event (this is also known as the source of the event), and e contains data for the event. In this case, e (which is of type **KeyEventArgs**) contains a **KeyCode** property (used in lines 10–11) that specifies which key was pressed as a value from the Keys enumeration.

The **Keys enumeration** represents keyboard keys using meaningful names. Recall that enumerations are used to assign meaningful names to constant values. In this case, each value in the Keys enumeration is an Integer that represents a key. In the method IsFunctionOrArrowKey (lines 69–82 of Fig. 21.9), Keys.F1 and Keys.F12 (line 73) represent the *F1* and *F12* keys, respectively. Similarly, Keys.Up, Keys.Down, Keys.Left and Keys.Right (line 75) represent the four arrow keys. You can find a listing of the constants in the Keys enumeration at http://msdn.microsoft.com/en-us/library/system.windows.forms.keys.aspx.

Line 10 uses the Char class's **IsControl** method to determine whether the pressed key is a control character. This method receives a Char as an argument, so you convert e.KeyCode to a Char with Convert method ToChar. Line 11 calls method IsFunctionOrArrowKey in the template code to determine whether the key pressed is a function or arrow key.

(cont.)

```
' determine whether pressed key is a function or arrow key
Function IsFunctionOrArrowKey(ByVal code As Keys) As Boolean
   Dim result As Boolean

   Select Case code
      Case Keys.F1 To Keys.F12
         result = True
      Case Keys.Up, Keys.Down, Keys.Left, Keys.Right
         result = True
      Case Else
         result = False ' not a match
   End Select

   Return result
End Function ' isFunctionOrArrowKey
```

Figure 21.9 Method `IsFunctionOrArrowKey` provided in the template.

4. ***Determining which* `Button` *to highlight using LINQ to Objects.*** Add lines 13–21 of Fig. 21.10 to your code. Line 14 declares variable `pressed`. Visual Basic infers the type of this variable from the result of the LINQ expression (lines 15–21).

Using LINQ to Objects to query the `Form`'s `Controls` collection and locate the `Button` that matches the pressed key

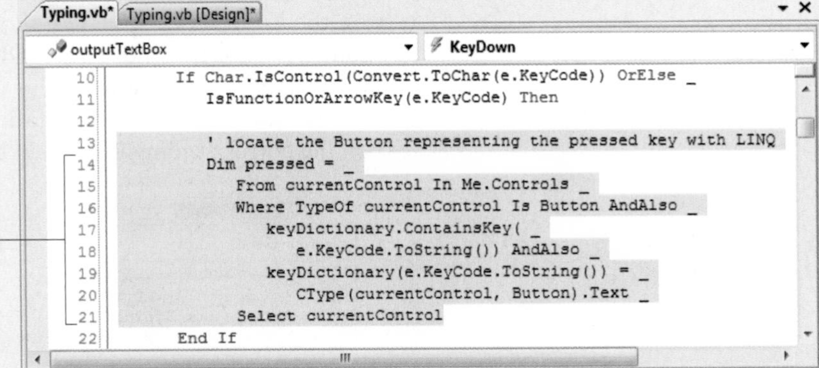

```
10       If Char.IsControl(Convert.ToChar(e.KeyCode)) OrElse _
11          IsFunctionOrArrowKey(e.KeyCode) Then
12
13          ' locate the Button representing the pressed key with LINQ
14          Dim pressed = _
15             From currentControl In Me.Controls _
16             Where TypeOf currentControl Is Button AndAlso _
17                keyDictionary.ContainsKey( _
18                   e.KeyCode.ToString()) AndAlso _
19                keyDictionary(e.KeyCode.ToString()) = _
20                   CType(currentControl, Button).Text _
21             Select currentControl
22       End If
```

Figure 21.10 Using LINQ to locate the `Button` that matches the pressed key.

Line 15 iterates through the controls in the `Form`'s `Controls` collection. Recall that Visual Basic infers the type of the LINQ query's range variable (`currentControl`). Lines 16–20 specify the criteria for selecting a control from the collection. The expression

```
TypeOf currentControl Is Button
```

uses a **`TypeOf...Is`** expression (line 16)—which determines whether `currentControl` is of the type `Button`. The `Controls` collection contains the controls placed directly on the `Form`, but the application changes the background color of only `Button` controls. The preceding expression ensures that only `Button`s are selected. [*Note:* A control is part of the `Controls` collection of the container in which the control is placed. The LINQ query assumes that all of the controls are placed directly on the `Form`, not in nested containers (e.g., `GroupBox`es or `Panel`s).]

(cont.)

The rest of the condition (lines 17–20) uses a `Dictionary` collection to help map the `KeyCode` of the pressed key to the `Text` of a `Button` in the GUI. A **`Dictionary`** is a collection of key/value pairs. The key in the pair is used to determine the storage location for the corresponding value and to locate that value when it is required later for use in the application. In the template code for this application, we provided you with a predefined `Dictionary` named `keyDictionary` that maps the `String` representations of various control-key, function-key and arrow-key `KeyCode`s to the `String`s that appear on the `Button`s representing those keys in the GUI.

Line 3 in the code

```
Private keyDictionary As New Dictionary(Of String, String)
```

defines instance variable `keyDictionary` and assigns it a new `Dictionary` that stores pairs of `String`s. When you define a `Dictionary`, you must specify the types of its keys and its values, similar to how you declared the type of elements stored in a `List` in Tutorial 20. The keys and values are not required to be the same type.

The `Form`'s `Load` event handler (Fig. 21.11) uses `Dictionary` method **`Add`** to insert key/value pairs in `keyDictionary`. Lines 59–61 add pairs of `String`s representing the function keys. The `String` representation of a function key's `KeyCode` is the same as the text on the function key and the text on the GUI's corresponding `Button`. So, the key/value pair for the *F1* key consists of the `String`s `"F1"` and `"F1"`. Lines 64–74 add key/value pairs for the control keys and arrow keys in the GUI. The first argument to each call to `Add` is the `String` representation of the `KeyCode` and the second is the text on the corresponding `Button` in the GUI.

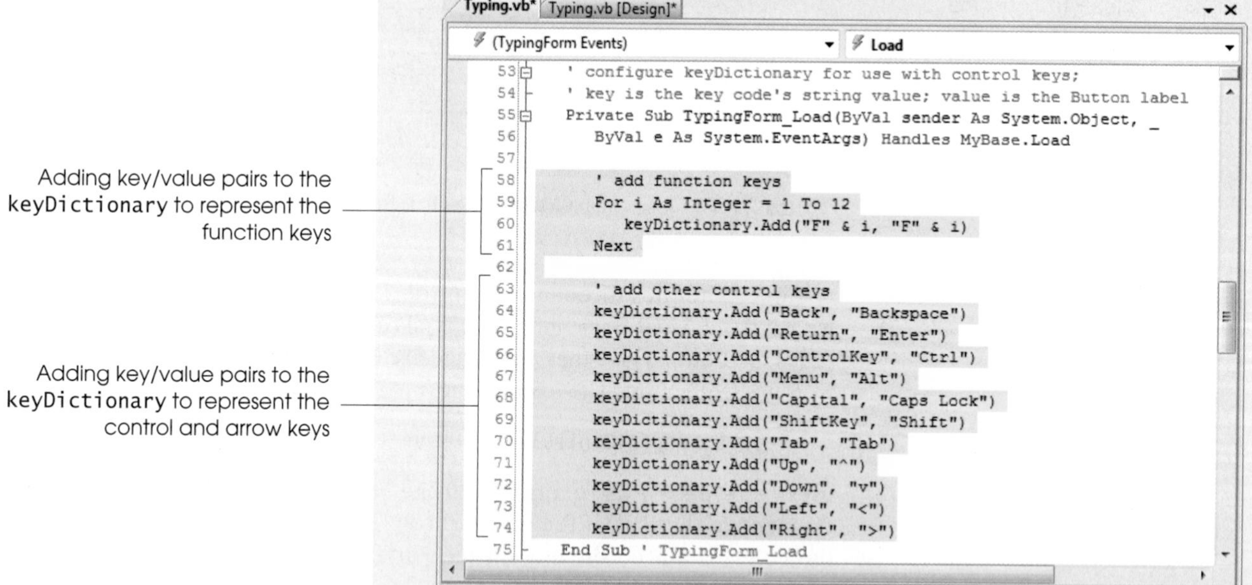

Typing.vb*
Typing.vb [Design]*
(TypingForm Events)
Load
53 ' configure keyDictionary for use with control keys;
54 ' key is the key code's string value; value is the Button label
55 Private Sub TypingForm_Load(ByVal sender As System.Object, _
56 ByVal e As System.EventArgs) Handles MyBase.Load
57
58 ' add function keys
59 For i As Integer = 1 To 12
60 keyDictionary.Add("F" & i, "F" & i)
61 Next
62
63 ' add other control keys
64 keyDictionary.Add("Back", "Backspace")
65 keyDictionary.Add("Return", "Enter")
66 keyDictionary.Add("ControlKey", "Ctrl")
67 keyDictionary.Add("Menu", "Alt")
68 keyDictionary.Add("Capital", "Caps Lock")
69 keyDictionary.Add("ShiftKey", "Shift")
70 keyDictionary.Add("Tab", "Tab")
71 keyDictionary.Add("Up", "^")
72 keyDictionary.Add("Down", "v")
73 keyDictionary.Add("Left", "<")
74 keyDictionary.Add("Right", ">")
75 End Sub ' TypingForm_Load
Adding key/value pairs to the keyDictionary to represent the function keys
Adding key/value pairs to the keyDictionary to represent the control and arrow keys

Figure 21.11 Adding key/value pairs to the `keyDictionary`.

Lines 17–18 in the LINQ expression's `Where` clause (Fig. 21.10) use the `Dictionary`'s **`ContainsKey`** method to determine whether the `KeyCode`'s `String` representation appears as a key in the `Dictionary`, in which case the method returns `True`. Lines 19–20

```
keyDictionary(e.KeyCode.ToString()) = _
   CType(currentControl, Button).Text
```

(cont.)

get the `String` representation of the `KeyCode` and use it as a key in the `Dictionary` to obtain the corresponding value. Next, the value is compared with the `currentControl`'s `Text` property. If they match, the LINQ expression selects the control (line 19). For example, if the user presses *F5* and the `String "F5"` matches the text on one of the `Buttons` in the GUI, the LINQ query selects the control. The **CType** operator (line 18) converts a variable to another type. The `Controls` collection represents each control as a reference of type `Control`, so variable `currentControl`'s type is `Control`. The expression `CType(currentControl, Button)` converts the variable's type to `Button`, so the `Button`'s `Text` property can be used in the code. An exception is raised if `CType` cannot convert the specified object to the specified type (we discuss exceptions in detail in Tutorial 25). However, you know this conversion will succeed because the `Where` clause has already checked that `currentControl` is of type `Button`.

5. ***Changing the color of a* `Button`.** Add lines 23–25 of Fig. 21.12 to your code. Line 21 determines whether the collection returned by the LINQ expression (`pressed`) contains any elements. If it does, line 22 calls method `ChangeColor` (provided in the template code) to change the `Button`'s background color to yellow. The expression `pressed.First` represents the first item in the LINQ result. Recall from Tutorial 20 that a LINQ query returns a collection of items that match the criteria in the `Where` clause. Again, the type of this item is `Control`, so `CType` is used to convert it to a `Button`.

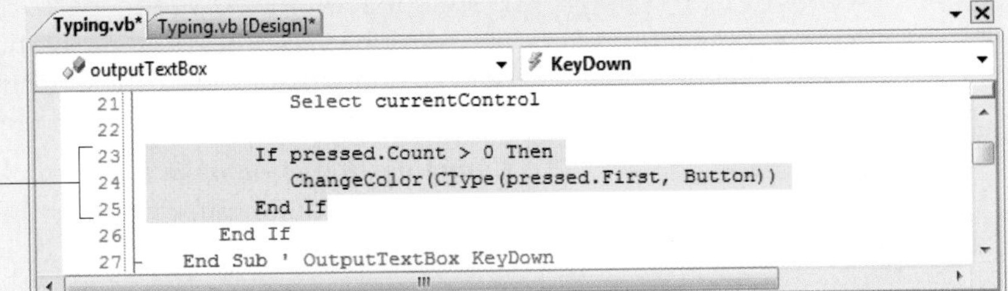
If there is a Button that matches the pressed key, change the Button's background color
Typing.vb* Typing.vb [Design]*
outputTextBox
KeyDown
21 Select currentControl
22
23 If pressed.Count > 0 Then
24 ChangeColor(CType(pressed.First, Button))
25 End If
26 End If
27 End Sub ' OutputTextBox KeyDown

Figure 21.12 Changing the color of the `Button` that corresponds to the pressed key.

6. ***Saving the project.*** Select **File > Save All** to save your modified code.

The `KeyDown` event handler in this application does not test whether any of the letter, digit or symbol keys were pressed. It is often inconvenient to use the `KeyDown` event handler to detect keyboard events because the `KeyEventArgs` object's `KeyCode` property is case insensitive. If you try to handle letters in the `KeyDown` event handler, the event's `KeyCode` property does not indicate whether the letter is lowercase or uppercase. This is not appropriate for the **Typing** application, because the user should be able to type uppercase and lowercase letters. Visual Basic provides the **KeyPress** event handler, which can recognize both uppercase and lowercase letters. You learn how to use the `KeyPress` event handler in the following box.

Coding to the KeyPress Event Handler

1. ***Determining which* `Button` *to highlight using LINQ to Objects.*** Add lines 34–40 of Fig. 21.13 to the `KeyPress` event handler. Line 35 declares variable `pressed`. Once again, Visual Basic infers the type of this variable from the result of the LINQ expression (lines 36–40).

(cont.)

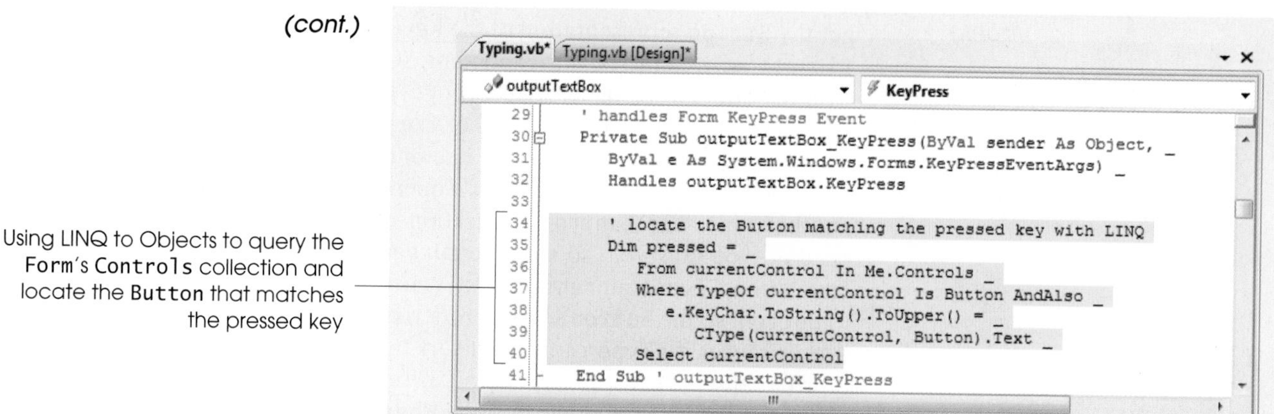

Figure 21.13 Determining the Button that matches the pressed key.

Line 36 iterates through the Form's Controls collection. Lines 37–39 specify the criteria for selecting a control from the collection. The first part of the condition (line 37) determines whether currentControl's type is Button. The second part determines whether the uppercase version of the pressed key matches the Text property of the currentControl. Variable e refers to the **KeyPressEventArgs** object that is passed as an argument to the event handler. Property **KeyChar** is a Char that represents the character on the key that was pressed. Method **ToUpper** converts the String representation of the KeyChar property to uppercase. This conversion is necessary because the Text properties of the Buttons are uppercase and String comparisons are case sensitive in Visual Basic by default. If both parts of the condition are true, the currentControl is selected (line 40).

2. ***Changing the color of a Button.*** Add lines 42–48 of Fig. 21.14 to your code. Line 42 determines whether the KeyChar contains a space. If so, the space bar was pressed and line 43 calls ChangeColor with spaceButton as an argument. Line 45 determines whether the collection returned by the LINQ expression contains any elements. If so, line 46 calls method ChangeColor to change the corresponding Button's background color to yellow. Recall that a LINQ query does not execute until you access its results (line 45).

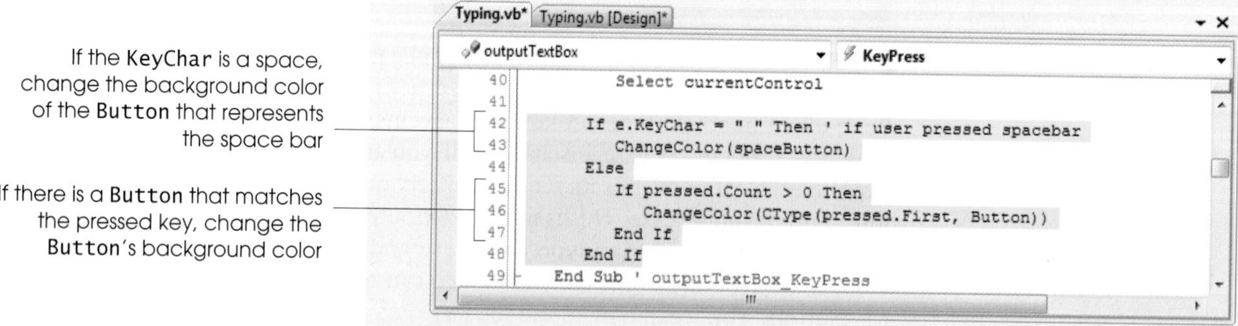

Figure 21.14 Changing the color of the Button that corresponds to the pressed key.

3. ***Running the application.*** Select **Debug > Start Debugging** to run your application. As you type, the Button corresponding to the key you press on the keyboard is highlighted and the text is added to the TextBox. The characters typed are added to the TextBox as part of its built-in key processing. Notice that the Button remains highlighted until another key is pressed.

4. ***Saving the project.*** Select **File > Save All** to save your modified code.

Software Design Tip

Use the `KeyPress` event handler for letter and number key events. Use the `KeyDown` event handler for modifier and control key events.

You may be wondering why you could not just use the `KeyPress` event handler to test for all of the keys on the keyboard. Control keys, such as *F1*, do not raise the `KeyPress` event. The `KeyPress` event cannot test for the modifier keys (*Ctrl*, *Shift* and *Alt*). **Modifier keys** do not display characters on the keyboard but can be used to modify the way that applications respond to a keyboard event. For instance, pressing the *Shift* key while pressing a letter in a text editor displays the uppercase form of the letter. You use the `KeyDown` event handler to handle the event raised when a modifier key is pressed.

The **`KeyUp`** event is raised when a key is released by the user. It is raised regardless of whether the key press is handled by the `KeyPress` or the `KeyDown` event handler. The **Typing** application uses the `KeyUp` event handler to remove the highlight color from `Buttons` on the GUI when the user releases the corresponding key. You learn how to add the `KeyUp` event handler to your application in the following box.

Creating the KeyUp Event Handler

1. ***Creating the KeyUp event handler.*** An empty `KeyUp` event handler is provided, to maintain clarity in the template application. However, if you want to generate `KeyUp`, `KeyDown` or `KeyPress` event handlers for other controls, begin by selecting the control for which you wish to add the event handler. In the **Typing** application select `outputTextbox` from the **Class Name** `ComboBox` in the top left corner of the code editor. Then select the appropriate event handler from the **Method Name** `ComboBox` in the top right corner of the code editor, as shown in Fig. 21.15. When you select an event name from the **Method Name** `ComboBox`, that event handler is generated in your code.

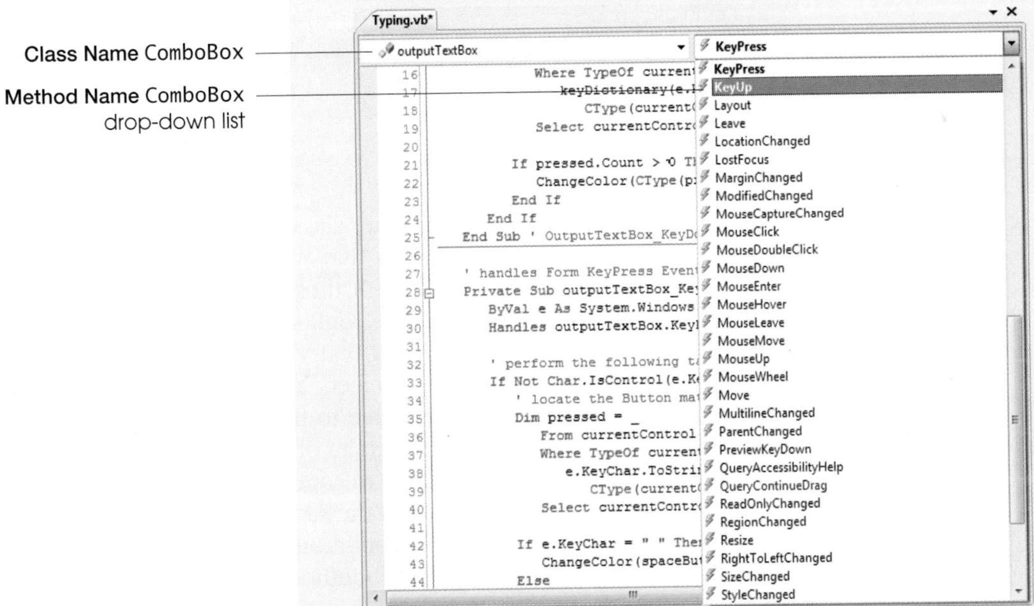

Figure 21.15 Generating the `KeyUp` event handler.

2. ***Writing code in the KeyUp event handler.*** Insert line 56 of Fig. 21.16 in your application. The `KeyUp` event handler executes whenever a key is released—therefore, you need to change the color of the released `Button` back to that `Button`'s default color. Line 56 calls `ResetColor`, provided for you in the template, to perform this action.

3. ***Running the application.*** Select **Debug > Start Debugging** to run your application. Notice that the highlighting is removed when the key is released.

(cont.)

Resetting a **Button**'s color after a key is released

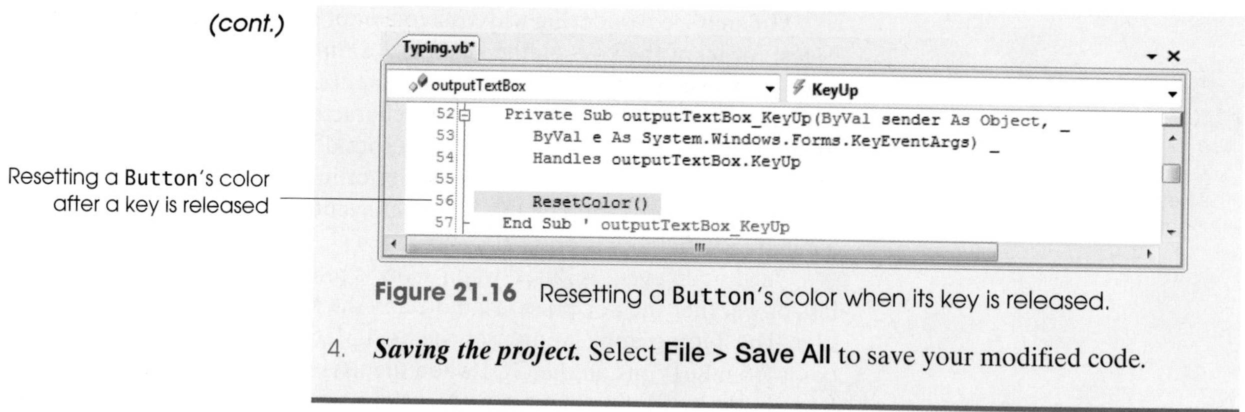

Figure 21.16 Resetting a **Button**'s color when its key is released.

4. ***Saving the project.*** Select **File > Save All** to save your modified code.

Next, you examine the `ResetColor` method that we provided for you in the template. This method uses the `IsNot` operator—a helpful tool for determining whether a reference type variable refers to an object or contains the `Nothing` reference.

SELF-REVIEW

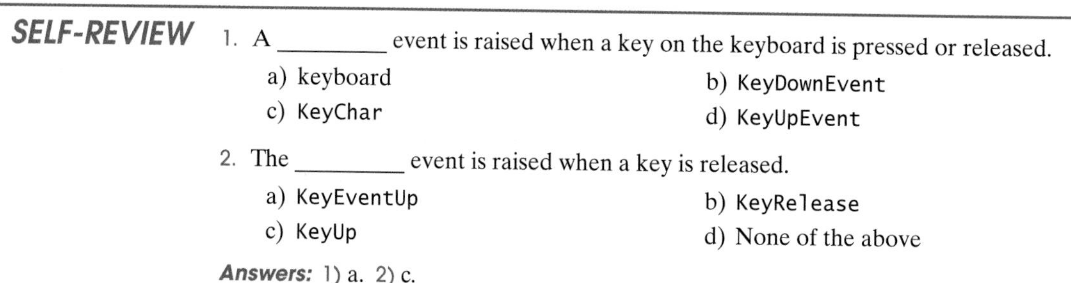

1. A _________ event is raised when a key on the keyboard is pressed or released.
   a) keyboard
   b) `KeyDownEvent`
   c) `KeyChar`
   d) `KeyUpEvent`

2. The _________ event is raised when a key is released.
   a) `KeyEventUp`
   b) `KeyRelease`
   c) `KeyUp`
   d) None of the above

Answers: 1) a. 2) c.

21.4 IsNot Operator

In Tutorial 19, you learned how to create classes and objects of those classes. You also learned that you can use variables that store references to objects, known as reference type variables, to interact with those objects. Sometimes it is useful to know whether a reference type variable contains a reference to an object or it currently contains a `Nothing` reference, so that you can determine whether the variable can be used to manipulate an object. You can use the **`IsNot`** operator to compare a reference type variable's value to the value `Nothing`. Such a condition evaluates to `True` if the variable refers to an object—otherwise, the condition evaluates to `False`. You can also use `IsNot` to compare two reference type variables to determine whether or not they refer to the same object. If they do not, the condition evaluates to `True`; otherwise, the condition evaluates to `False`.

Figure 21.17 shows the `ResetColor` method that you called to restore the color of a `Button` when the corresponding key is released. Line 68 uses the `IsNot` operator to ensure that `lastButton`—an instance variable used to store the previously pressed `Button`—actually refers to a `Button`. If `lastButton` does not refer to a `Button` object, line 69 will not execute.

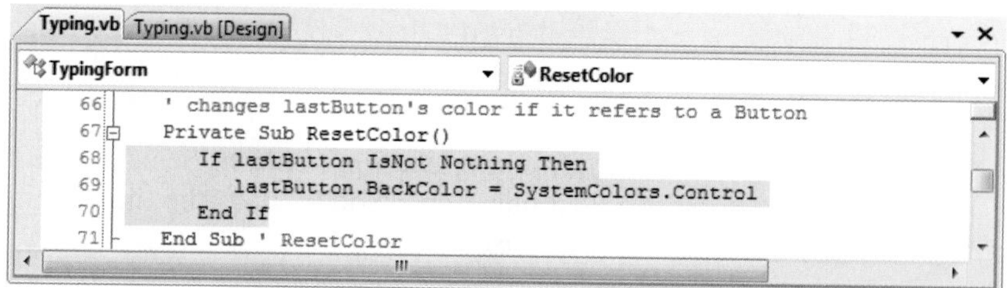

Figure 21.17 `IsNot` operator inside the `ResetColor` method

Your application highlights the corresponding `Buttons`, displays the output in a `TextBox`, and changes the `Buttons` back to their normal color, so that the user can see what is being typed. Now you allow the user to alter the appearance of the text in the `TextBox`. To do this, you use the `MenuStrip` control, which creates a menu that allows the user to select various options to format the `TextBox`.

21.5 Menus

Menus allow you to group related commands for Windows applications. Although most menus and commands vary among applications, some—such as **Open** and **Save**—are common to many applications. Menus are an important part of GUIs because they organize commands without cluttering the GUI. In this section, you learn how to enhance the **Typing** application by adding menus that allow the user to control how to display text in the `TextBox`.

Creating a Menu

5. ***Creating a `MenuStrip` control.*** Switch to **Design** view. Double click `MenuStrip` in the **Menus & Toolbars** tab of the **Toolbox** to add a `MenuStrip` to your application (Fig. 21.18). When you do this, a `MenuStrip` control appears in the component tray. Also, a box that reads **Type Here** appears on the top of your `Form`. This represents a **menu item**—an item that the user can select in a menu. When you type text in the **Type Here** field, Visual Studio creates a **`ToolStripMenuItem`** to represent the menu item. To edit menu items, click the **MenuStrip** icon in the component tray, the menu on the `Form`, or a menu item. This puts the IDE in **Menu Designer mode**, which allows you to create and edit menus and menu items. Change the `Name` property of the `MenuStrip` control to `menuBar`.

`ToolStripMenuItem` field

`MenuStrip` control in the component tray

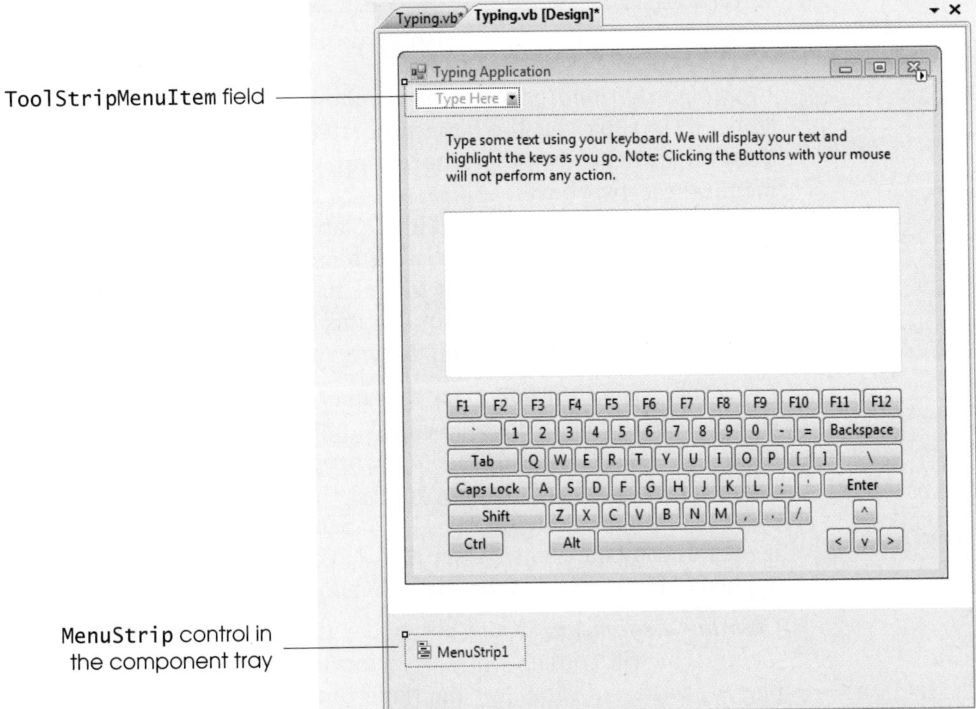

Figure 21.18 `MenuStrip` control added to the **Typing** application.

(cont.)

Good Programming Practice

We suggest appending the `MenuItem` suffix to `ToolStripMenuItem` controls.

6. ***Creating the first menu item.*** Click in the **Type Here** box, type `&Display` and press *Enter*. This sets the text to be displayed in that menu item and indicates that the letter `D` is the access key. Then change the `Name` property of the `ToolstripMenuItem` to `displayMenuItem`. Note that when you clicked the **Type Here** field, two more fields appeared (Fig. 21.19). The one on the right represents a new menu item that can be created to the right of the **Display** menu item. The field below the **Display** menu item represents a menu item that appears when the **Display** menu item is selected. You use the **Display** menu item to display all of the options that allow the user to customize the output displayed in the `TextBox`.

Menu item

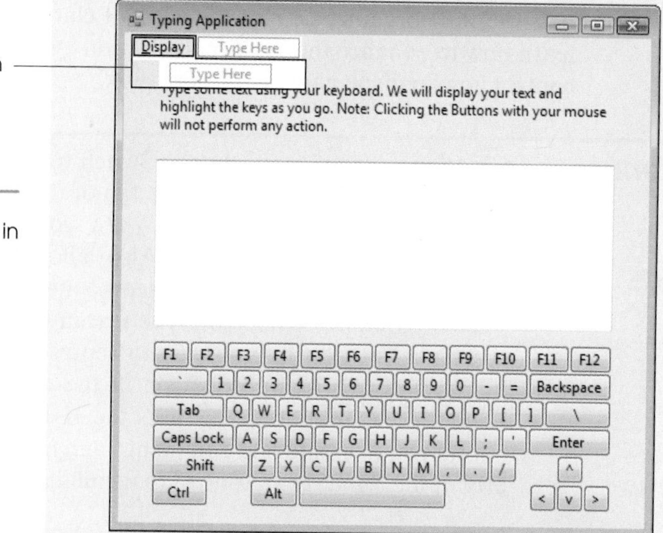

Figure 21.19 Creating the **Display** menu.

GUI Design Tip

Use book-title capitalization in menu-item text.

7. ***Creating additional menu items.*** In the box below the **Display** menu, type `&Clear TextBox`. Set the `Name` property of this menu item to `clearMenuItem`. Once again, two more boxes appear. Every time you add an item to a menu, these two boxes appear (Fig. 21.20). Entering text in the right box turns the menu item on the left into a submenu. The right box is now a menu item in that submenu. A **submenu** is a menu within another menu. The box that appears on the bottom of the menu allows you to add another item to that menu. Type `&Invert Colors` in this box to add another menu item. Set the `Name` property of this menu item to `invertMenuItem`.

8. ***Inserting a separator bar.*** Click the small arrow on the right side of the **Type Here** box to display a drop-down list containing items that may be added to the menu. Select **Separator** from the drop-down list (Fig. 21.21). Note that a **separator bar**, which is a gray, recessed horizontal rule, appears below the **Invert Colors** menu item (Fig. 21.22). Separator bars are used to group submenus and menu items. A separator bar also can be created by typing a hyphen (`-`) in the `Text` property of a menu item.

GUI Design Tip

Use separator bars in a menu to group related menu items.

9. ***Creating a submenu.*** In the box under the separator bar, type `&Text`. This menu item will contain options to format the appearance of the text displayed in the `TextBox`. Set the `Name` property of this menu item to `textMenuItem`. All menu items can contain both menu items and submenus. Insert `&Color...` and `&Font...` as menu items in the **Text** submenu, naming them `colorMenuItem` and `fontMenuItem`, respectively (Fig. 21.22).

GUI Design Tip

If clicking a menu item opens a dialog, an ellipsis (...) should follow the menu item's text.

(cont.)

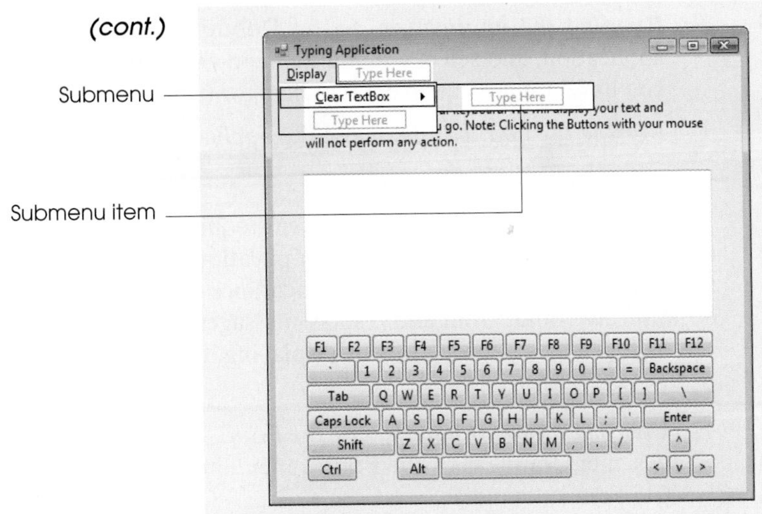

Figure 21.20 Adding items to the menu.

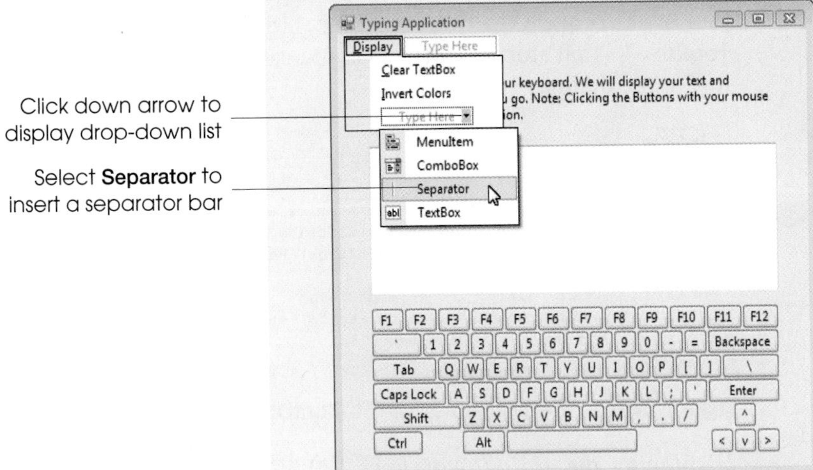

Figure 21.21 Adding a separator bar to group menu items.

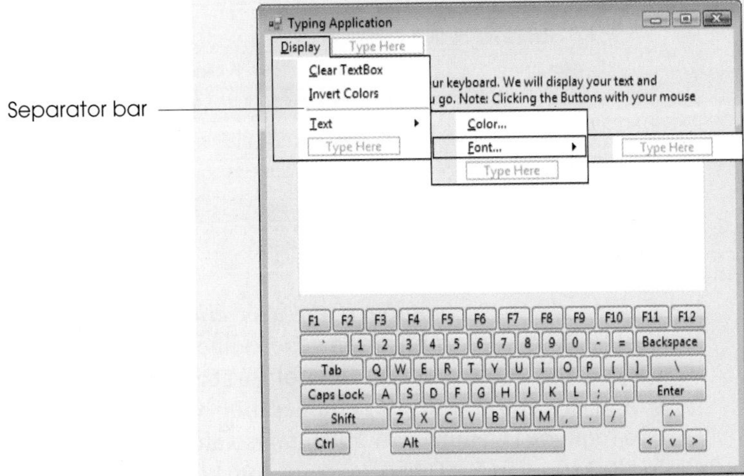

Figure 21.22 Adding a submenu to a menu item.

(cont.)

10. ***Running the application***. Select **Debug > Start Debugging** to run your application, and select a menu item. At this point, nothing happens, because you have not created event handlers for the menu items.
11. ***Closing the application.*** Close the application by clicking its close box.

Like any other control, a menu item requires an event handler to perform an action when it is clicked. The **Typing** application introduces the **Font** and **Color** dialogs to allow users to customize the appearance of what is being typed. Dialogs allow you to receive input from and display messages to users. You learn how to use the Font dialog in the following box by displaying it from a menu item's event handler.

Coding the Font... Menu Item's Click Event Handler

1. ***Creating an event handler for the Font... menu item***. In the Windows Form designer, double click the **Font...** menu item that you created to generate its Click event handler.
2. ***Declaring the dialog variables***. Add lines 117–118 of Fig. 21.23 to your code. Line 117 creates a new FontDialog object that allows the user to select the font style to apply to the text. Line 118 declares a variable of type DialogResult that stores information indicating which Button the user clicked to exit the dialog.

Declaration for the FontDialog and its result

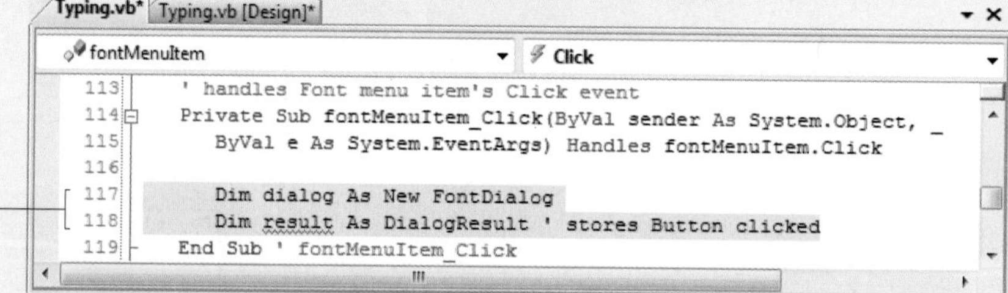

Figure 21.23 Declarations for the **FontDialog** and its DialogResult.

3. ***Displaying the dialog***. Add lines 120–121 of Fig. 21.24 to your event handler. These lines call the ShowDialog method to display the **Font** dialog to the user and assign the return value of ShowDialog to variable result.

Showing the dialog and assigning the result

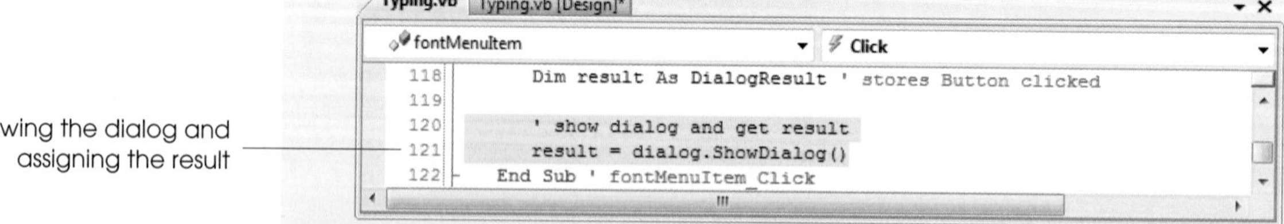

Figure 21.24 Opening the **Font** dialog.

4. ***Exiting the event handler if the user clicks Cancel.*** Add lines 123–126 of Fig. 21.25 to your application. These lines determine whether the user has clicked the **Font** dialog's **Cancel** Button. Line 124 compares the value stored in result with the enumeration value DialogResult.Cancel. The DialogResult enumeration contains values corresponding to standard dialog Button names. This provides a convenient way to determine which Button the user has clicked. If the user clicks the **Cancel** Button, no action takes place and the method exits using the Return statement (line 125). Since this method is a Sub procedure, you can use Exit Sub in place of Return to exit the method.

(cont.)

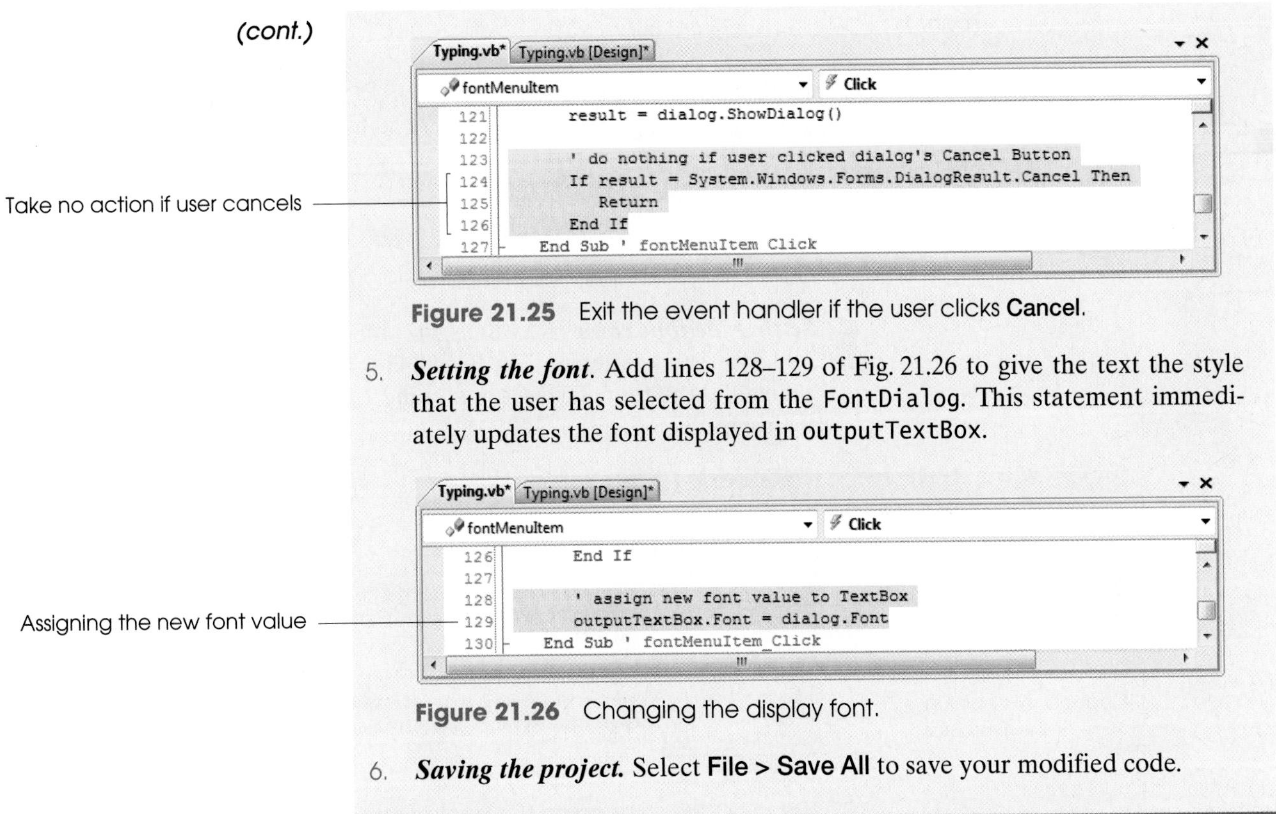

Figure 21.25 Exit the event handler if the user clicks **Cancel**.

5. ***Setting the font.*** Add lines 128–129 of Fig. 21.26 to give the text the style that the user has selected from the `FontDialog`. This statement immediately updates the font displayed in `outputTextBox`.

Figure 21.26 Changing the display font.

6. ***Saving the project.*** Select **File > Save All** to save your modified code.

The user of the **Typing** application should also be able to select the color of the font displayed in the `TextBox`. You learn how to display the **Color** dialog from an event handler in the following box.

Coding the Color... Menu Item's `Click` Event Handler

1. ***Creating an event handler for the Color... menu item.*** Double click the **Color...** menu item to generate its `Click` event handler.

2. ***Declaring the dialog variables.*** Add lines 136–137 of Fig. 21.27 to your application. Line 136 creates a new `ColorDialog` object that allows the user to select the color of the text. Line 137 declares a `DialogResult` variable to store the value of the `Button` clicked by the user.

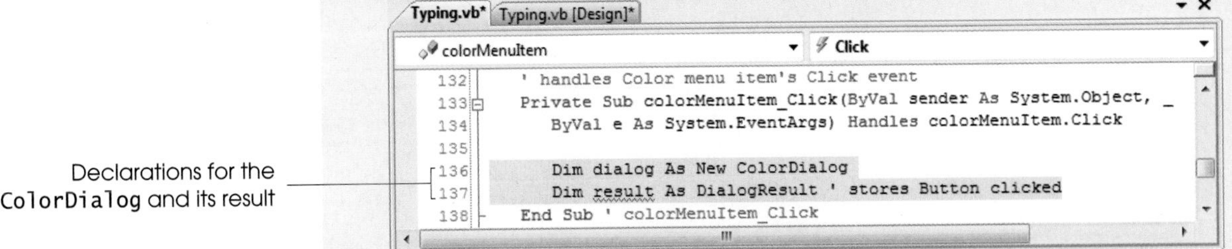

Figure 21.27 Declarations for the **Color** dialog and its `DialogResult`.

3. ***Setting the `ColorDialog`'s open mode.*** Add lines 139–140 of Fig. 21.28 to your application. The `ColorDialog` object allows you to specify which color options the dialog presents to the user of your application. To display the **Color** dialog as shown in Fig. 21.4, the `FullOpen` option must be set to `True` (line 139). If this option is set to `False`, only the left half of the dialog is displayed. Line 140 opens the **Color** dialog using the `ShowDialog` method.

(cont.)

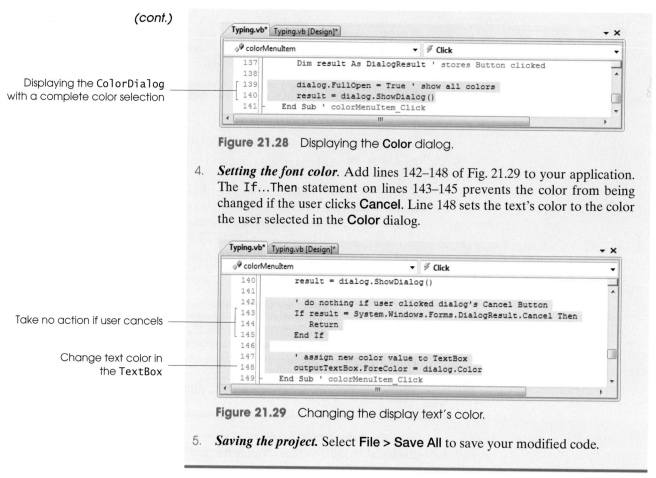

Displaying the `ColorDialog` with a complete color selection

```
Typing.vb*  Typing.vb [Design]*
colorMenuItem                     Click
137        Dim result As DialogResult ' stores Button clicked
138
139        dialog.FullOpen = True ' show all colors
140        result = dialog.ShowDialog()
141     End Sub ' colorMenuItem_Click
```

Figure 21.28 Displaying the **Color** dialog.

4. ***Setting the font color.*** Add lines 142–148 of Fig. 21.29 to your application. The `If...Then` statement on lines 143–145 prevents the color from being changed if the user clicks **Cancel**. Line 148 sets the text's color to the color the user selected in the **Color** dialog.

Take no action if user cancels

Change text color in the `TextBox`

```
Typing.vb*  Typing.vb [Design]*
colorMenuItem                     Click
140        result = dialog.ShowDialog()
141
142        ' do nothing if user clicked dialog's Cancel Button
143        If result = System.Windows.Forms.DialogResult.Cancel Then
144           Return
145        End If
146
147        ' assign new color value to TextBox
148        outputTextBox.ForeColor = dialog.Color
149     End Sub ' colorMenuItem_Click
```

Figure 21.29 Changing the display text's color.

5. ***Saving the project.*** Select **File > Save All** to save your modified code.

The user should be able to clear all of the text in the `TextBox` using the **Clear TextBox** menu item. You learn how to do this in the following box.

Clearing the `TextBox`

1. ***Generating an event handler for the Clear TextBox menu item.*** Double click the **Clear TextBox** menu item to generate its `Click` event.
2. ***Clearing the text.*** Add line 155 of Fig. 21.30 to your application. This line calls the `Clear` method to erase the text in the `TextBox`. Calling the `Clear` method on a `TextBox` has the same effect as setting its `Text` property to the empty string.

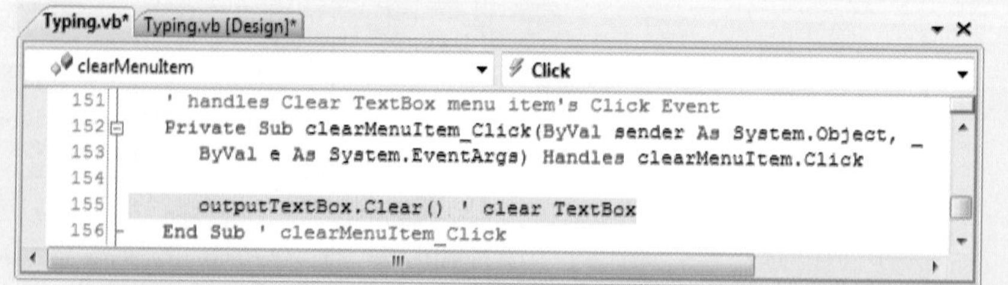

Figure 21.30 Calling the `Clear` method of class `TextBox` to erase the text.

3. ***Saving the project.*** Select **File > Save All** to save your modified code.

The user should be able to swap the foreground and background colors of the `TextBox`. You learn how to accomplish this in the following box.

Inverting Colors

1. ***Creating an event handler for the* Invert Colors *menu item.*** Double click the **Invert Colors** menu item in **Design** view to create its `Click` event handler (Fig. 21.31).

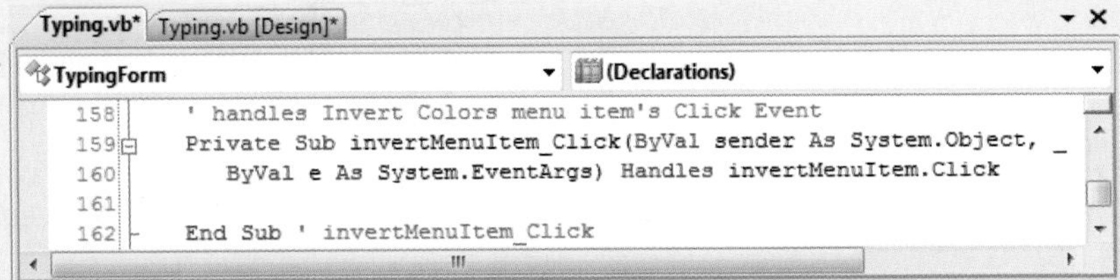
Typing.vb* Typing.vb [Design]*
TypingForm
(Declarations)
158 ' handles Invert Colors menu item's Click Event
159 Private Sub invertMenuItem_Click(ByVal sender As System.Object, _
160 ByVal e As System.EventArgs) Handles invertMenuItem.Click
161
162 End Sub ' invertMenuItem_Click

Figure 21.31 Empty event handler for **Invert Color** menu item.

2. ***Inverting the colors.*** Insert lines 162–166 of Fig. 21.32 to your application. Line 162 declares a `Color` variable to store a color value. To swap colors, you must use a temporary variable to hold one of the colors that you want to swap. A **temporary variable** is used to store data when swapping values. Such a variable is no longer needed after the swap occurs. Without a temporary variable, you would lose the value of one color property (by reassigning its value) before you could assign its color to the other property.

   Line 164 assigns the temporary `Color` variable the background color of the `TextBox`. Line 165 then sets the background color to the foreground color. Finally, line 166 assigns the text color the value stored in the temporary `Color` variable, which contains the `TextBox`'s background color from before the swap.

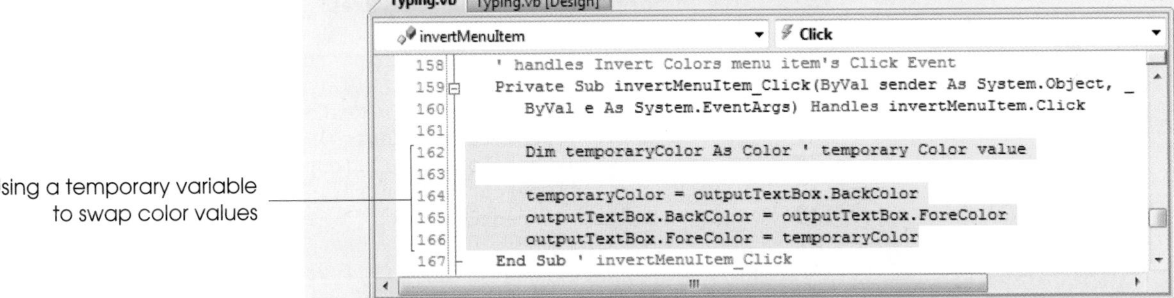
Using a temporary variable to swap color values
Typing.vb* Typing.vb [Design]*
invertMenuItem
Click
158 ' handles Invert Colors menu item's Click Event
159 Private Sub invertMenuItem_Click(ByVal sender As System.Object, _
160 ByVal e As System.EventArgs) Handles invertMenuItem.Click
161
162 Dim temporaryColor As Color ' temporary Color value
163
164 temporaryColor = outputTextBox.BackColor
165 outputTextBox.BackColor = outputTextBox.ForeColor
166 outputTextBox.ForeColor = temporaryColor
167 End Sub ' invertMenuItem_Click

Figure 21.32 Swapping the background and foreground colors.

3. ***Running the application.*** Select **Debug > Start Debugging** to run your application. Enter text using your keyboard. The keys you press should be highlighted in the virtual keyboard on the `Form`. Use the menu to change the color of the text, then invert the colors of the text and the `TextBox`. Finally, use the menus to change the text's font, then clear the `TextBox`.

4. ***Closing the application.*** Close your running application by clicking its close box.

5. ***Closing the IDE.*** Close the Visual Basic IDE by clicking its close box.

Figure 21.33 presents the source code for the **Typing** application. The lines of code that contain new programming concepts you learned in this tutorial are highlighted.

Instance variable to store which **Button** the user pressed

Converting a KeyCode to a **Char** using **Convert.ToChar**

Determining a **Control**'s type using **TypeOf**

Determining if the **Dictionary** contains a key matching the **KeyCode**'s **String** representation

Converting a Control to a **Button** using **CType**

Determining if the key pressed is a control character

```
Public Class TypingForm
   Private lastButton As Button ' reference to last Button pressed
   Private keyDictionary As New Dictionary(Of String, String)

   ' handles Form's KeyDown Event
   Private Sub outputTextBox_KeyDown(ByVal sender As Object, _
      ByVal e As System.Windows.Forms.KeyEventArgs) _
      Handles outputTextBox.KeyDown

      If Char.IsControl(Convert.ToChar(e.KeyCode)) OrElse _
         IsFunctionOrArrowKey(e.KeyCode) Then

         ' locate the Button representing the pressed key with LINQ
         Dim pressed = _
            From currentControl In Me.Controls _
            Where TypeOf currentControl Is Button AndAlso _
               keyDictionary.ContainsKey( _
                  e.KeyCode.ToString()) AndAlso _
               keyDictionary(e.KeyCode.ToString()) = _
                  CType(currentControl, Button).Text _
            Select currentControl

         If pressed.Count > 0 Then
            ChangeColor(CType(pressed.First, Button))
         End If
      End If
   End Sub ' OutputTextBox_KeyDown

   ' handles Form KeyPress Event
   Private Sub outputTextBox_KeyPress(ByVal sender As Object, _
      ByVal e As System.Windows.Forms.KeyPressEventArgs) _
      Handles outputTextBox.KeyPress

      ' locate the Button matching the pressed key with LINQ
      Dim pressed = _
         From currentControl In Me.Controls _
         Where TypeOf currentControl Is Button AndAlso _
            e.KeyChar.ToString().ToUpper() = _
               CType(currentControl, Button).Text _
         Select currentControl

      If e.KeyChar = " " Then ' if user pressed spacebar
         ChangeColor(spaceButton)
      Else
         If pressed.Count > 0 Then
            ChangeColor(CType(pressed.First, Button))
         End If
      End If
   End Sub ' outputTextBox_KeyPress

   ' handles the TextBox's KeyUp event
   Private Sub outputTextBox_KeyUp(ByVal sender As Object, _
      ByVal e As System.Windows.Forms.KeyEventArgs) _
      Handles outputTextBox.KeyUp

      ResetColor()
   End Sub ' outputTextBox_KeyUp

   ' highlight Button passed as argument
   Private Sub ChangeColor(ByVal buttonPassed As Button)
      ResetColor()
      buttonPassed.BackColor = Color.Yellow
      lastButton = buttonPassed ' save Button to reset color later
   End Sub ' ChangeColor
```

Figure 21.33 **Typing** application code listing. (Part 1 of 3.)

Using the **IsNot** operator to determine whether **lastButton** refers to **Nothing**

Adding items to a Dictionary

Create **FontDialog** and **DialogResult** variables

Display dialog and get **Button** clicked to exit the dialog

```
' changes lastButton's color if it refers to a Button
Private Sub ResetColor()
   If lastButton IsNot Nothing Then
      lastButton.BackColor = SystemColors.Control
   End If
End Sub ' ResetColor

' configure keyDictionary for use with control keys;
' key is the key code's string value; value is the Button label
Private Sub TypingForm_Load(ByVal sender As System.Object, _
   ByVal e As System.EventArgs) Handles MyBase.Load

   ' add function keys
   For i As Integer = 1 To 12
      keyDictionary.Add("F" & i, "F" & i)
   Next

   ' add other control keys
   keyDictionary.Add("Back", "Backspace")
   keyDictionary.Add("Return", "Enter")
   keyDictionary.Add("ControlKey", "Ctrl")
   keyDictionary.Add("Menu", "Alt")
   keyDictionary.Add("Capital", "Caps Lock")
   keyDictionary.Add("ShiftKey", "Shift")
   keyDictionary.Add("Tab", "Tab")
   keyDictionary.Add("Up", "^")
   keyDictionary.Add("Down", "v")
   keyDictionary.Add("Left", "<")
   keyDictionary.Add("Right", ">")
End Sub ' TypingForm_Load

' determine whether pressed key is a function or arrow key
Function IsFunctionOrArrowKey(ByVal code As Keys) As Boolean
   Dim result As Boolean

   Select Case code
      Case Keys.F1 To Keys.F12
         result = True
      Case Keys.Up, Keys.Down, Keys.Left, Keys.Right
         result = True
      Case Else
         result = False ' not a match
   End Select

   Return result
End Function ' isFunctionOrArrowKey

' handles Font menu item's Click event
Private Sub fontMenuItem_Click(ByVal sender As System.Object, _
   ByVal e As System.EventArgs) Handles fontMenuItem.Click

   Dim dialog As FontDialog = New FontDialog()
   Dim result As DialogResult ' stores Button clicked

   ' show dialog and get result
   result = dialog.ShowDialog()

   ' do nothing if user clicked dialog's Cancel Button
   If result = System.Windows.Forms.DialogResult.Cancel Then
      Return
   End If

```

Figure 21.33 **Typing** application code listing. (Part 2 of 3.)

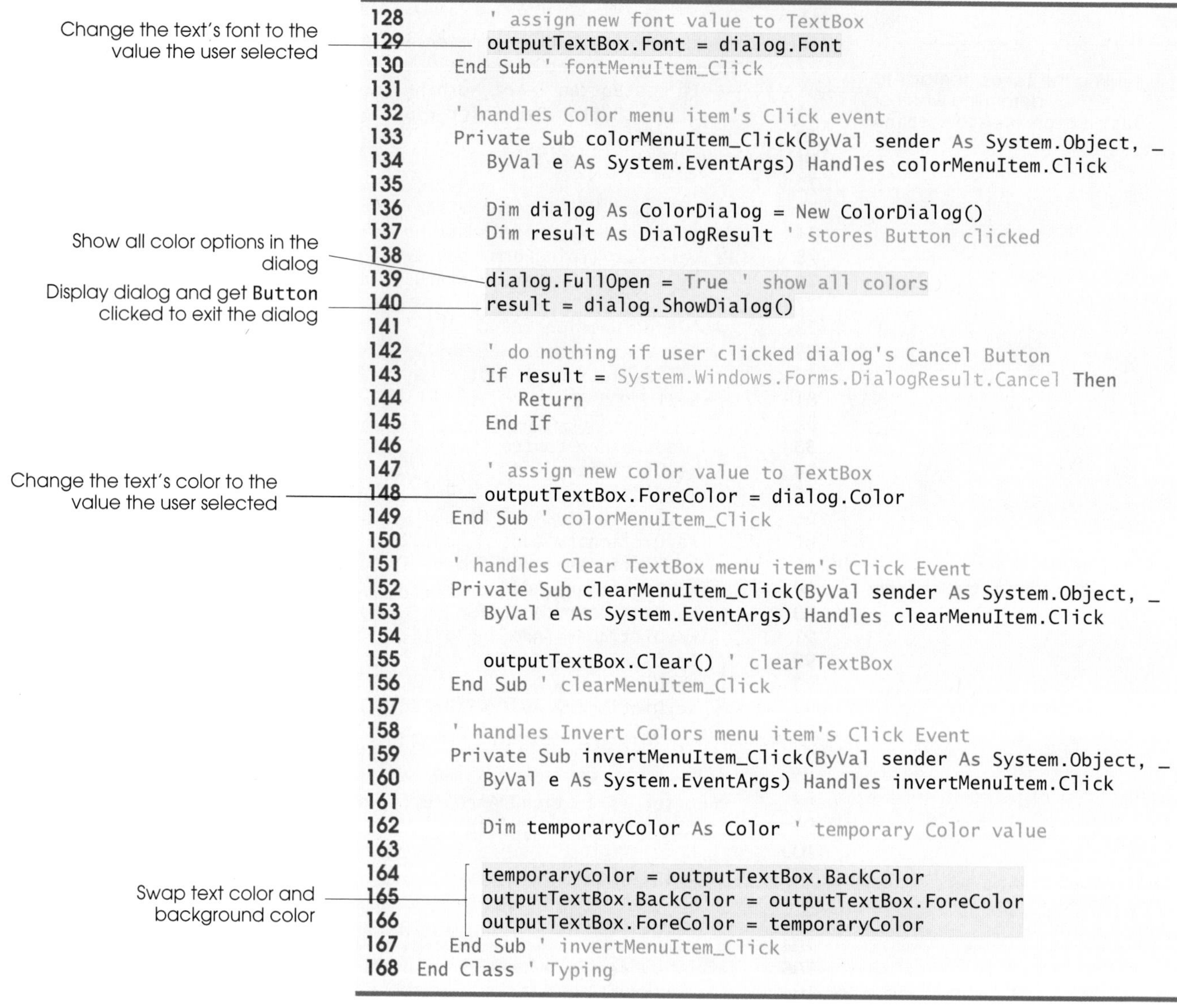
Change the text's font to the value the user selected
Show all color options in the dialog
Display dialog and get Button clicked to exit the dialog
Change the text's color to the value the user selected
Swap text color and background color

```
         ' assign new font value to TextBox
         outputTextBox.Font = dialog.Font
      End Sub ' fontMenuItem_Click

      ' handles Color menu item's Click event
      Private Sub colorMenuItem_Click(ByVal sender As System.Object, _
         ByVal e As System.EventArgs) Handles colorMenuItem.Click

         Dim dialog As ColorDialog = New ColorDialog()
         Dim result As DialogResult ' stores Button clicked

         dialog.FullOpen = True ' show all colors
         result = dialog.ShowDialog()

         ' do nothing if user clicked dialog's Cancel Button
         If result = System.Windows.Forms.DialogResult.Cancel Then
            Return
         End If

         ' assign new color value to TextBox
         outputTextBox.ForeColor = dialog.Color
      End Sub ' colorMenuItem_Click

      ' handles Clear TextBox menu item's Click Event
      Private Sub clearMenuItem_Click(ByVal sender As System.Object, _
         ByVal e As System.EventArgs) Handles clearMenuItem.Click

         outputTextBox.Clear() ' clear TextBox
      End Sub ' clearMenuItem_Click

      ' handles Invert Colors menu item's Click Event
      Private Sub invertMenuItem_Click(ByVal sender As System.Object, _
         ByVal e As System.EventArgs) Handles invertMenuItem.Click

         Dim temporaryColor As Color ' temporary Color value

         temporaryColor = outputTextBox.BackColor
         outputTextBox.BackColor = outputTextBox.ForeColor
         outputTextBox.ForeColor = temporaryColor
      End Sub ' invertMenuItem_Click
   End Class ' Typing
```

Figure 21.33 **Typing** application code listing. (Part 3 of 3.)

SELF-REVIEW

1. Menus can contain ________.

   a) commands that the user can select
   b) submenus
   c) separator bars
   d) All of the above

2. ________ allow you to receive input from and display messages to users.

   a) Dialogs
   b) Enumerations
   c) Separator bars
   d) All of the above

Answers: 1) d. 2) a.

21.6 Wrap-Up

In this tutorial, you learned how to process keyboard events by using the KeyDown and KeyPress event handlers that are invoked when the user presses various keys on the keyboard. You used LINQ to Objects and a Dictionary collection to help map the key that was pressed to a specific Button in the GUI. You learned how to use the TypeOf...Is expression to determine if a control is a Button. You then learned how to use the KeyUp event handler to handle the event raised when the user releases a key. You also learned how to use the IsNot operator to determine if a reference variable contains a reference to an object or Nothing.

You added menus to the **Typing** application. You learned that menus allow you to add controls to your application without cluttering the GUI. You also learned how to code a menu item's Click event handler to alter the displayed text in the **Typing** application. You learned how to display the **Color** and **Font** dialogs so that the user could specify the font style and color of the text in the TextBox. You also learned how to use the DialogResult enumeration to determine which Button the user pressed to exit a dialog.

In the next tutorial, you learn about the methods in the String class that allow you to manipulate Strings. These methods help you build a screen-scraper application that can search text for a particular value.

SKILLS SUMMARY

Adding Keyboard Event Handlers to Your Application

- Select the control for which you want to add the event handler from the **Class Name** ComboBox.
- Select the desired event handler from the **Method Name** ComboBox.

Executing Code When the User Presses a Letter Key on the Keyboard

- Use the KeyPress event handler.
- Use property KeyChar to determine which key was pressed.

Executing Code When the User Presses a Key That Is Not a Letter

- Use the KeyDown event handler.
- Use property KeyCode to determine which key was pressed.

Executing Code When the User Releases a Key

- Use the KeyUp event handler.

Using the Dictionary Collection

- Call Dictionary method Add on a Dictionary object to add the key/value pair to the Dictionary.
- Use the Dictionary's name followed by an items key in parentheses to retrieve the key's value from the Dictionary, much like an array.

Converting an Object to a Different Type

- Use the CType method to convert the object to the desired type. An exception is raised if the conversion fails.

Adding Menus to Your Application

- Double click the MenuStrip control in the **Toolbox**.
- Add menu items to the menu by typing the item's name in the **Type Here** boxes that appear in Menu Designer mode.
- Add submenus by typing a menu item's name in the **Type Here** box that appears to the right of the submenu's name.
- Use a menu item's Click event handler to perform an action when that menu item is selected by the user.

Adding a Font Dialog to Your Application

- Use keyword New to create a new FontDialog object.
- Use a DialogResult variable to store the Button the user clicked to exit the dialog.
- Use method ShowDialog to display the dialog and obtain the Button user selected to exit the dialog.

Adding a Color Dialog to Your Application

- Use keyword New to create a new ColorDialog object.
- Use a DialogResult variable to store the Button the user clicked to exit the dialog.

- Set the FullOpen option to True to provide the user with the full range of colors.
- Use method ShowDialog to display the dialog and obtain the Button user selected to exit the dialog.

KEY TERMS

Add method of class Dictionary—Adds a key/value pair to a Dictionary collection.

Cancel value of DialogResult enumeration—Used to determine whether the user clicked the **Cancel** Button of a dialog.

Char structure—Stores characters (such as letters and symbols).

ColorDialog class—Used to display a dialog from which the user can select colors.

ContainsKey method of class Dictionary—Determines whether the Dictionary contains the key specified as an argument.

CType operator—Converts the object passed as the first argument to the type passed as the second argument.

DialogResult enumeration—An enumeration that contains values corresponding to standard dialog Button names.

Dictionary collection—A collection of key/value pairs.

FontDialog class—Used to display a dialog from which the user can choose a font and its style.

FullOpen property of class ColorDialog—Property that, when True, enables the ColorDialog to provide a full range of color options when displayed.

IsControl method of structure Char—Determines whether the Char passed as an argument represents a control key.

IsNot operator—Determines whether two reference variables contain references to different objects or whether a single reference variable refers to an object.

keyboard event—Raised when a key on the keyboard is pressed or released.

KeyChar property of class KeyPressEventArgs—Contains data about the key that raised the KeyPress event.

KeyCode property of class KeyEventArgs—Contains data about the key that raised the KeyDown event.

KeyDown event—Generated when a key is initially pressed. Used to handle the event raised when a key that is not a letter or number key is pressed.

KeyEventArgs class—Stores information about special modifier keys.

KeyPress event—Generated when a key is pressed. Used to handle the event raised when a letter or number key is pressed.

KeyPressEventArgs class—Stores information about character keys.

Keys enumeration—Contains values representing keyboard keys.

KeyUp event—Generated when a key is released.

menu—Design element that groups related commands for Windows applications. Although these commands depend on the application, some—such as **Open** and **Save**—are common to many applications. Menus are an integral part of GUIs, because they organize commands without cluttering the GUI.

Menu Designer mode in the Visual Basic IDE—Design mode in the IDE that allows you to create and edit menus and menu items.

menu item—Command located in a menu that, when selected, causes the application to perform an action.

MenuStrip control—Allows you to add menus to your application.

modifier key—Key such as *Shift*, *Alt* or *Control* that modifies the way that an application responds to a keyboard event.

sender event argument—Event argument that contains a reference to the object that raised the event (also called the source of the event).

separator bar—Bar placed in a menu to separate related menu items.

ShowDialog method of class FontDialog or ColorDialog—The method that displays the dialog on which it is called.

submenu—Menu within another menu.

temporary variable—Used to store data when swapping values.

`ToUpper` method of class `String`—Returns the uppercase representation of a `String`. Similarly, `ToLower` returns the lowercase representation of a `String`.

`ToolStripMenuItem` class—Class which represents an individual menu item in a `MenuStrip`.

`TypeOf...Is` expression—Returns True if the object referenced by the variable is of the specified type.

GUI DESIGN GUIDELINES

`MenuStrip`

- Use book-title capitalization in menu-item text.
- Use separator bars in a menu to group related menu items.
- If clicking a menu item opens a dialog, an ellipsis (...) should follow the menu item's text.

CONTROLS, EVENTS, PROPERTIES & METHODS

`Char` This structure represents a character.

- *Method*

  `IsControl`—Determines if the Char represents a control character.

`ColorDialog` ColorDialog This control allows the user to select a color.

- *Properties*

  `Color`—Contains the color selected by the user. The default color is black.

  `FullOpen`—When `True`, displays an extended color palette. If this property is set to `False`, a dialog with fewer options is displayed.

- *Method*

  `ShowDialog`—Displays the **Color** dialog to the user.

`FontDialog` FontDialog This control allows the user to select a font and customize its size and style.

- *Property*

  `Font`—Contains the font specified by the user.

- *Method*

  `ShowDialog`—Displays the **Font** dialog to the user.

`KeyEventArgs` This class represents arguments passed to the `KeyDown` event handler.

- *Property*

  `KeyCode`—Contains data about the key that raised the `KeyDown` event.

`KeyPressEventArgs` This class represents arguments passed to the `KeyPress` event handler.

- *Property*

  `KeyChar`—Contains data about the key that raised the `KeyPress` event.

`MenuStrip` MenuStrip This control allows you to group related commands for a Windows application.

- *In action*

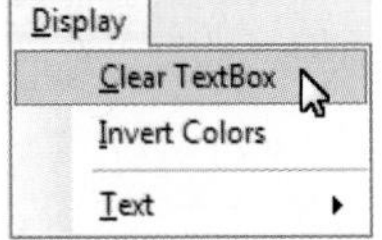

- *Event*

`Click`—Raised when the user clicks a menu item or presses an access key that represents an item.

`Dictionary` This class is used to store a variable number of key/value pairs.

- ***Methods***

  `Add`—Adds a key/value pair to the `Dictionary` object.

  `ContainsKey`—Returns `True` if the `Dictionary` contains the specified key.

`TextBox` TextBox This control allows the user to input data from the keyboard.

- ***In action***

  0

- ***Events***

  `KeyDown`—Raised when a key is pressed. `KeyDown` is case insensitive. It cannot recognize lowercase letters.

  `KeyPress`—Raised when a key is pressed. `KeyPress` cannot handle modifier keys.

  `KeyUp`—Raised when a key is released by the user.

  `TextChanged`—Raised when the text in the `TextBox` is changed.

- ***Properties***

  `Enabled`—Determines whether the user can enter data in the `TextBox` or not.

  `Font`—Specifies the font used to display text in the `TextBox`.

  `ForeColor`—Specifies color of the text in the `TextBox`.

  `Location`—Specifies the location of the `TextBox` control relative to the top-left corner of the container (e.g., a `Form` or a `GroupBox`).

  `MaxLength`—Specifies the maximum number of characters that can be input into the `TextBox`.

  `Multiline`—Specifies whether the `TextBox` is capable of displaying multiple lines of text.

  `Name`—Specifies the name used to access the `TextBox` programmatically. The name should be appended with the `TextBox` suffix.

  `PasswordChar`—Specifies the masking character to be used when displaying data in the `TextBox`.

  `ReadOnly`—Determines whether the value of a `TextBox` can be changed.

  `ScrollBars`—Specifies whether a multiline `TextBox` contains a scrollbar.

  `Size`—Specifies the width and height (in pixels) of the `TextBox`.

  `TabIndex`—Specifies the order in which focus is transferred to controls when *Tab* is pressed.

  `TabStop`—Specifies whether the user can select the control using the *Tab* key.

  `Text`—Specifies the text displayed in the `TextBox`.

  `TextAlign`—Specifies how the text is aligned within the `TextBox`.

- ***Methods***

  `Clear`—Removes the text from the `TextBox` that calls it.

  `Focus`—Transfers the focus of the application to the `TextBox` that calls it.

MULTIPLE-CHOICE QUESTIONS

21.1 When creating a menu, typing a(n) _________ in front of a menu-item name creates an access key for that item.

a) & b) !
c) $ d) #

21.2 *Alt*, *Shift* and *Control* are _________ keys.

a) modifier b) special
c) function d) None of the above

21.3 `KeyChar` is a property of _________.

a) `KeyEventArgs`
b) `Key`
c) `KeyArgs`
d) `KeyPressEventArgs`

21.4 Typing a hyphen (`-`) as a menu item's `Text` property will create a(n) _________.

a) separator bar
b) access shortcut
c) new submenu
d) keyboard shortcut

21.5 A _________ provides a group of related commands for Windows applications.

a) separator bar
b) hot key
c) menu
d) margin indicator bar

21.6 The _________ enumeration specifies key codes and modifiers.

a) `Keyboard`
b) `Key`
c) `KeyboardTypes`
d) `Keys`

21.7 The _________ event is raised when a key is pressed by the user.

a) `KeyPress`
b) `KeyHeld`
c) `KeyDown`
d) Both a and c

21.8 Which of the following is not a keyboard event?

a) `KeyPress`
b) `KeyDown`
c) `KeyUp`
d) `KeyClicked`

21.9 Which of the following is not a structure?

a) `Char`
b) `Color`
c) `String`
d) `Date`

21.10 The _________ type allows you to determine which `Button` the user clicked to exit a dialog.

a) `DialogButtons`
b) `DialogResult`
c) `Buttons`
d) `ButtonResult`

EXERCISES

21.11 ***(Inventory Application with Keyboard Events)*** Enhance the **Inventory** application that you developed in Tutorial 4 to prevent the user from entering input that is not a number. Use keyboard events to allow the user to press the number keys, the left and right arrows and the *Backspace* keys. If any other key is pressed, display a `MessageBox` instructing the user to enter a number (Fig. 21.34).

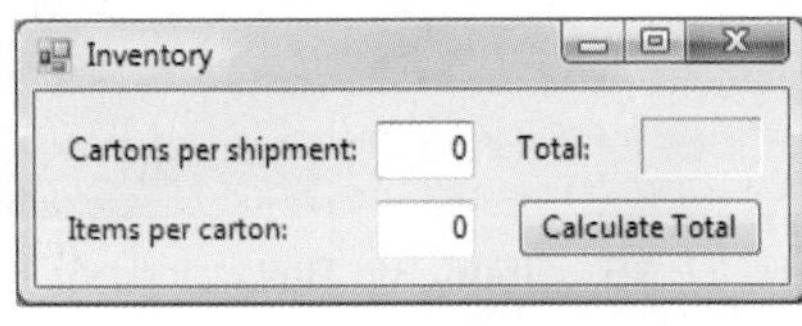

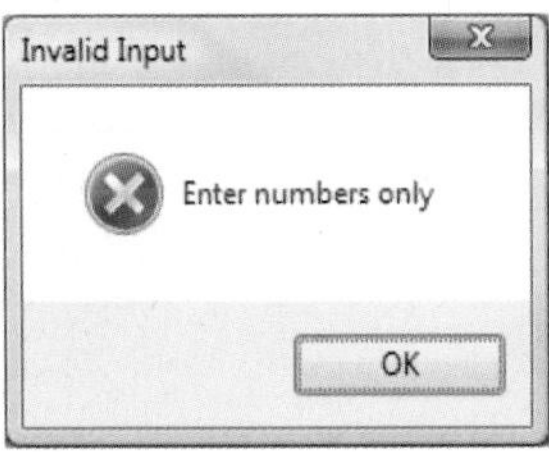

Figure 21.34 **Inventory** application with ley events.

a) ***Copying the template to your working directory.*** Copy the directory `C:\Examples\Tutorial21\Exercises\KeyEventInventory` to your `C:\SimplyVB2008` directory.

b) ***Opening the application's template file.*** Double click `KeyEventInventory.sln` in the `KeyEventInventory` directory to open the application.

c) ***Adding the KeyDown event handler for the first TextBox.*** Use the **Class Name** and **Method Name** `ComboBox`es to add an empty `KeyDown` event handler for the **Cartons per shipment:** `TextBox`.

d) ***Adding a `Select Case` statement.*** Add a `Select Case` statement to the `KeyDown` event handler that uses the `Keys` enumeration to determine whether a number key, a left or right arrow, *Enter* or the *Backspace* key was pressed.

e) ***Adding the Case Else statement.*** Add a Case Else statement that executes when a key other than a valid one for this application was pressed. If an invalid key was pressed, clear the TextBox and display a MessageBox that instructs the user to enter a number.

f) ***Adding the KeyDown event handler for the second TextBox.*** Repeat *Steps c–e*, but this time create a KeyDown event handler for the **Items per carton:** TextBox. This event handler should have the same functionality as the one for the **Cartons per shipment:** TextBox.

g) ***Running the application.*** Select **Debug > Start Debugging** to run your application. Try entering letters or pressing the up- and down-arrow keys in the TextBoxes. A MessageBox should be displayed. Enter valid input and click the **Calculate Total** Button. Verify that the correct output is displayed.

h) ***Closing the application.*** Close your running application by clicking its close box.

i) ***Closing the IDE.*** Close the Visual Basic IDE by clicking its close box.

21.12 *(Bouncing Ball Game)* Write an application that allows the user to play a game, in which the goal is to prevent a bouncing ball from falling off the bottom of the Form. When the user presses the *S* key, a blue ball bounces off the top, left and right sides (the "walls") of the Form. A horizontal bar on the bottom of the Form serves as a paddle to prevent the ball from hitting the bottom of the Form. (The ball can bounce off the paddle, but not the bottom of the Form.) The user can move the paddle using the left and right arrow keys. If the ball hits the paddle, it bounces up, and the game continues. If the ball hits the bottom of the Form, the game ends. The paddle's width decreases every 20 seconds to make the game more challenging. The GUI and the bouncing ball are provided for you (Fig. 21.35).

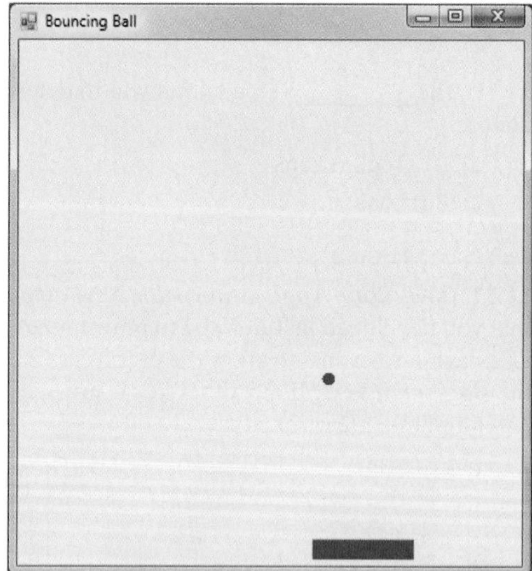

Figure 21.35 **Bouncing Ball** application.

a) ***Copying the template to your working directory.*** Copy the directory C:\Examples\Tutorial21\Exercises\BouncingBall to your C:\SimplyVB2008 directory.

b) ***Opening the application's template file.*** Double click BouncingBall.sln in the BouncingBall directory to open the application.

c) ***Creating the KeyDown event handler.*** Insert a KeyDown event handler for the Form.

d) ***Writing code to start the game.*** Write an If...Then statement in the KeyDown event handler that tests whether the user presses the *S* key. You can use the KeyDown event handler for the *S* key in this case because you do not care whether the user presses an uppercase *S* or a lowercase *S*. If the user presses the *S* key, start the two Timers provided in the template (set their Enabled properties to True).

e) ***Inserting code to move the paddle left.*** Add an ElseIf statement that tests whether the user pressed the left-arrow key and whether the paddle's horizontal position (rectangleX) is greater than zero. If the paddle's horizontal position equals zero, the left edge of the paddle is touching the left wall and the paddle should not be allowed to move farther to the left. If both the conditions in the `If...Then` are true, decrease the paddle's *x*-position by `10`.

f) ***Inserting code to move the paddle right.*** Add an `ElseIf` statement that tests whether the user pressed the right-arrow key and whether the paddle's *x*-coordinate is less than the width of the `Form` minus the width of the paddle (`rectangleWidth`). If the paddle's *x*-coordinate equals the `Form`'s width minus the width of the paddle, the paddle's right edge is touching the right wall and the paddle should not be allowed to move farther to the right. If both the conditions in the `If...Then` statement are true, increase the paddle's *x*-coordinate by `10`.

g) ***Running the application.*** Select **Debug > Start Debugging** to run your application. Press the *S* key to begin the game and use the paddle to keep the bouncing ball from dropping off the `Form`. Continue doing this until 20 seconds have passed, and verify that the paddle is decreased in size at that time.

h) ***Closing the application.*** Close your running application by clicking its close box.

i) ***Closing the IDE.*** Close the Visual Basic IDE by clicking its close box.

21.13 *(Form Painter Application)* Create a menu for the **Form Painter** application that allows the user to select the size and color of the paint and the color of the `Form` (Fig. 21.36). The **Form Painter** application is provided for you.

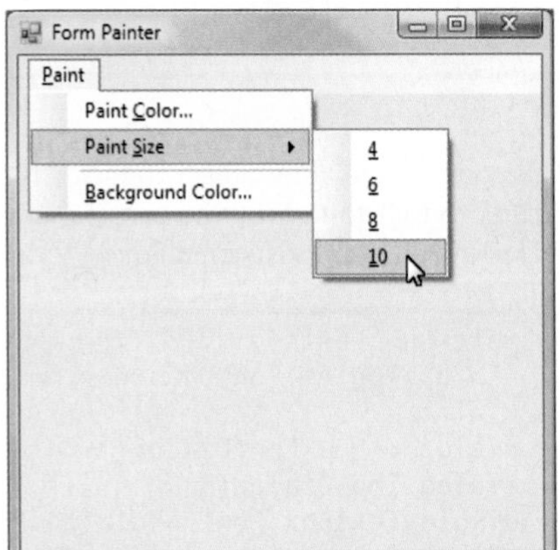

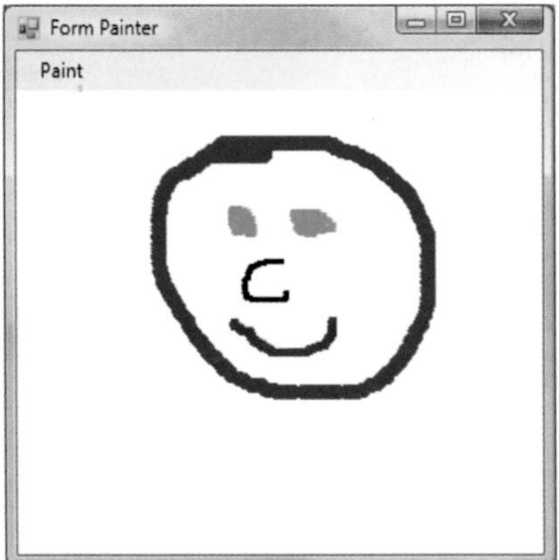

Figure 21.36 Modified **Painter** GUI.

a) ***Copying the template to your working directory.*** Copy the directory `C:\Examples\Tutorial21\Exercises\FormPainter` to your `C:\SimplyVB2008` directory.

b) ***Opening the application's template file.*** Double click `FormPainter.sln` in the `FormPainter` directory to open the application.

c) ***Creating the menus.*** Create a menu titled **Paint** that contains a **Paint Color...** menu item, a **Paint Size** submenu that contains menu items **4**, **6**, **8** and **10**, a separator bar and a **Background Color...** menu item.

d) ***Changing the paint color.*** Add an event handler for the **Paint Color...** menu item. This event handler should display a **Color** dialog that allows the user to change the value stored in `paintColor`.

e) ***Changing the paint size.*** Add an event handler for each of the **Paint Size** submenu's menu items. Each event handler should change the value stored in `diameter` to the value displayed on the menu (that is, clicking the **4** menu item changes the value of `diameter` to `4`).

f) ***Changing the background color.*** Add an event handler for the **Background Color...** menu item. This event handler should display a **Color** dialog that allows the user to change the value stored in `backgroundColor` and also change the `BackColor` property of the `Form`. To change the background color of the `Form`, assign the value specifying the background color to `BackColor`. For instance, the statement `BackColor = Color.White` changes the background color of the `Form` to white.

g) ***Running the application.*** Select **Debug > Start Debugging** to run your application. Use the menus to draw shapes of various colors and brush sizes. Use the other menu option to change the color of the `Form`.

h) ***Closing the application.*** Close your running application by clicking its close box.

i) ***Closing the IDE.*** Close the Visual Basic IDE by clicking its close box.

What does this code do?

21.14 What is the result of the following code?

```
Private Sub colorMenuItem_Click(ByVal sender As _
   System.Object, ByVal e As System.EventArgs) _
   Handles colorMenuItem.Click

   Dim dialog As ColorDialog = New ColorDialog()
   Dim result As DialogResult

   dialog.FullOpen = True

   result = dialog.ShowDialog()

   If result = System.Windows.Forms.DialogResult.Cancel Then
     Return
   End If

   BackColor = dialog.Color
End Sub ' colorMenuItem_Click
```

What's wrong with this code?

21.15 This code should allow a user to pick a font from a **Font** dialog and set the text in `displayTextBox` to that font. Find the error(s) in the following code, assuming that a `TextBox` named `displayTextBox` exists on a `Form`.

```
Private Sub Fonts()
   Dim dialog As FontDialog

   dialog = New FontDialog()
   dialog.ShowDialog()
   displayTextBox.Font = dialog.Font
End Sub
```

Programming Challenge

21.16 ***(Dvorak Keyboard Application)*** Create an application that simulates the letters on the Dvorak keyboard. A Dvorak keyboard allows faster typing by placing the most commonly used keys in the most accessible locations. Use keyboard events to create an application similar to the **Typing** application that simulates the Dvorak keyboard instead of the standard keyboard. The correct Dvorak key should be highlighted on the virtual keyboard, and the correct character should be displayed in the `TextBox`. The keys and characters map as follows:

- On the top row, the *P* key of the Dvorak keyboard maps to the *R* key on a standard keyboard, and the *L* key of the Dvorak keyboard maps to the *P* key on a standard keyboard.
- On the middle row, the *A* key remains in the same position, and the *S* key on the Dvorak keyboard maps to the semicolon key on the standard keyboard.
- On the bottom row, the *Q* key on the Dvorak keyboard maps to the *X* key on the standard keyboard, and the *Z* key maps to the question-mark key.
- All of the other keys on the Dvorak keyboard map to the locations shown in Fig. 21.37.

a) ***Copying the template to your working directory.*** Copy the directory `C:\Examples\Tutorial21\Exercises\DvorakKeyboard` to your `C:\SimplyVB2008` directory.

b) ***Opening the application's template file.*** Double click `DvorakKeyboard.sln` in the `DvorakKeyboard` directory to open the application.

c) ***Creating the Dvorak key mapping***. Use a `Dictionary` to map the text of the key pressed to the text of its corresponding Dvorak key. Initialize this `Dictionary` in the `Form`'s `Load` event.

d) ***Creating the KeyPress event handler***. Use the **Class Name** and **Method Name** `ComboBoxes` to add a `KeyPress` event handler for the `TextBox`.

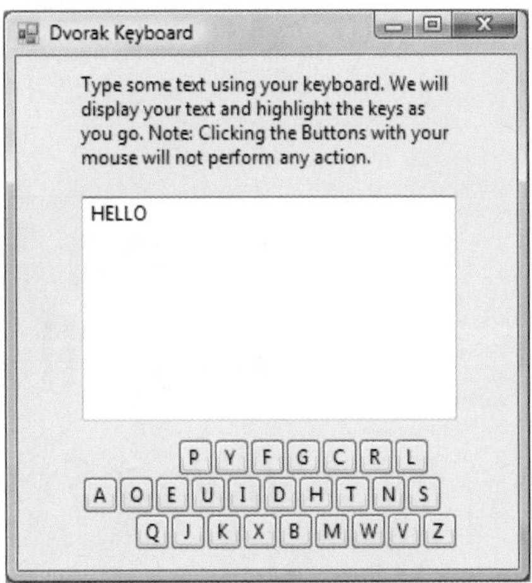

Figure 21.37 **Dvorak Keyboard** GUI.

e) ***Creating a LINQ statement***. Add a LINQ query statement to the `KeyPress` event handler. The LINQ query statement should select the `Button` in the Dvorak keyboard which corresponds to the key pressed on the user's keyboard. If a Dvorak key was pressed, highlight it on the GUI and display the character in the `TextBox` by appending the `Button`'s text to the `TextBox`'s `Text` property. Note that the `TextBox` does not display the actual key pressed on the keyboard. The `ReadOnly` property has been set to `True` to prevent user input from displaying in the `TextBox`. The `BackColor` property has been set to `White` to maintain a familiar appearance.

f) ***Running the application.*** Select **Debug > Start Debugging** to run your application. Use your keyboard to enter text. Verify that the text entered is correct based on the rules in the exercise description. Make sure that the correct `Buttons` on the `Form` are highlighted as you enter text.

g) ***Closing the application.*** Close your running application by clicking its close box.

h) ***Closing the IDE.*** Close the Visual Basic IDE by clicking its close box.

22 TUTORIAL

Screen Scraping Application

Introducing `String` Processing

Objectives

In this tutorial, you learn to:

- Manipulate `String` objects.
- Use properties and methods of class `String`.
- Search for substrings within `String`s.
- Extract substrings within `String`s.
- Replace substrings within `String`s.

Outline

This tutorial introduces Visual Basic's `String`-processing capabilities. The techniques presented in this tutorial can be used to create applications that manipulate text. Earlier tutorials introduced class `String` from the `System` namespace and several of its methods. In this tutorial, you learn how to search `String`s, retrieve characters from `String` objects and replace characters in a `String`. You create an application that uses these `String`-processing capabilities to manipulate a `String` containing **HTML** (**HyperText Markup Language**). HTML is a technology for describing web pages. Extracting desired information from the HTML that composes a web page is called **screen scraping**. Applications that perform screen scraping can be used to extract specific information, such as weather conditions or stock prices, from web pages so that the information can be formatted and manipulated more easily by computer applications. In this tutorial, you create a simple **Screen Scraping** application.

22.1 Test-Driving the Screen Scraping Application

This application must meet the following requirements:

Application Requirements

An online European auction house wants to expand its business to include bidders from the United States. However, all of the auction house's web pages currently display their prices in euros, not dollars. The auction house wants to generate separate web pages for American bidders that display the prices of auction items in dollars. These new web pages will be generated by using screen-scraping techniques on the already existing web pages. You have been asked to build a prototype application that tests the screen-scraping functionality. The application must search a sample string of HTML and extract information about the price of a specified auction item. For testing purposes, a `ComboBox` should be provided that contains auction items listed in the HTML. The selected item's amount must then be converted to dollars. Assume the exchange rate is one euro to 1.58 dollars (that is, one euro is equivalent to $1.58). The price (in dollars) and sample HTML are displayed in `Label`s.

The **Screen Scraping** application searches for the name of a specified auction item in a string of HTML. Users select the item for which to search from a `ComboBox`. The application then extracts and displays the price in dollars of this item. You begin by test-driving the completed application. Then, you learn the additional Visual Basic capabilities needed to create your own version of the application.

Test-Driving the Screen Scraping Application

1. ***Opening the completed application.*** Open the directory `C:\Examples\Tutorial22\CompletedApplication\ScreenScraping` to locate the **Screen Scraping** application. Double click `ScreenScraping.sln` to open the application in the Visual Basic IDE.

2. ***Running the application***. Select **Debug > Start Debugging** to run the application (Fig. 22.1). Note that the HTML string is displayed in a `Label` at the bottom of the `Form`.

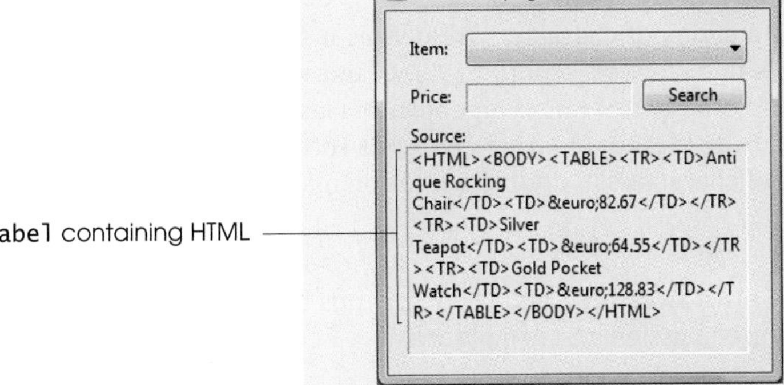

Figure 22.1 **Screen Scraping** application's `Form`.

3. ***Selecting an item name.*** The `ComboBox` contains three item names. Select an item name from the `ComboBox`, as shown in Fig. 22.2.

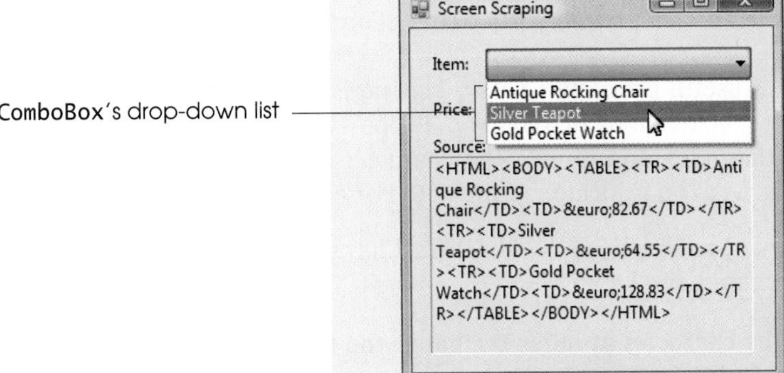

Figure 22.2 Selecting an item name from the `ComboBox`.

4. ***Searching for an item's price.*** Click the **Search** `Button` to display the price for the selected item. The extracted price is displayed in a `Label` (Fig. 22.3).

5. ***Closing the application.*** Close your running application by clicking its close box.

6. ***Closing the IDE.*** Close the Visual Basic IDE by clicking its close box.

(cont.)

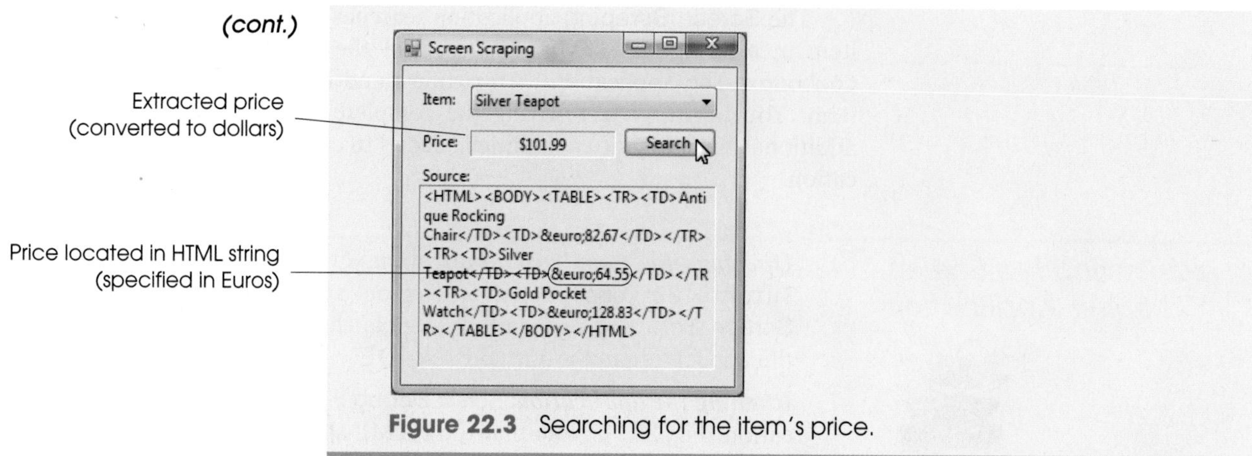

Figure 22.3 Searching for the item's price.

22.2 Fundamentals of Strings

A string is a series of characters treated as a single unit. These characters can be uppercase letters, lowercase letters, digits and various **special characters**, such as +, -, *, /, $ and others. A string is an object of class `String` in the `System` namespace. You write **string literals**, or **string constants** (often called **literal `String` objects**), as sequences of characters in double quotation marks, as follows:

```
"This is a string!"
```

You've already created and used `String`s in previous tutorials. You know that a declaration can assign a `String` literal to a `String` variable. For example, the declaration

```
Dim myColor As String = "blue"
```

initializes `myColor` to refer to the literal `String` object `"blue"`.

Like arrays, `String`s always know their own size. `String` property **`Length`** returns the length of the `String` (that is, the number of characters in the `String`). For example, the expression `myColor.Length` evaluates to `4` for the `String` `"blue"`.

Another useful property of class `String` is **`Chars`**, which returns the character located at a specific index in a `String`. Property `Chars` takes an `Integer` argument specifying the index and returns the character at that index. As in arrays, the first element of a `String` is located at index `0`. For example, the following code

```
If string1.Chars(0) = string2.Chars(0) Then _
   messageLabel.Text = "The first characters are the same."
```

compares the character at index `0` (that is, the first character) of `string1` with the character at index `0` of `string2`.

In earlier tutorials, you used several methods of class `String` to manipulate `String` objects. Figure 22.4 lists some of these methods. Note that the example expression `" My String"` intentionally begins with a blank space. You learn new `String` methods later in this tutorial.

Any `String` method or operator that appears to modify a `String` actually returns a new `String` that contains the results. For example, `String` method `ToUpper` does not actually modify the original `String`, but instead returns a new `String` in which each lowercase letter has been converted to uppercase. This occurs because `String`s are **immutable** objects—that is, characters in `String`s cannot be changed after the `String`s are created.

Method	Description	Sample Expression (assume text = " My String")
PadLeft(*length*, *char*)	Returns a copy of a String with character *char* inserted at the beginning until the String is *length* characters long.	text.PadLeft(12, "!"c) Returns: "!! My String"
PadRight(*length*, *char*)	Returns a copy of a String with character *char* inserted at the end until the String is *length* characters long.	text.PadRight(12, "!"c) Returns: " My String!!"
ToLower()	Returns a copy of the String with all uppercase letters converted to lowercase.	text.ToLower() Returns: " my string"
ToUpper()	Returns a copy of the String with all lowercase letters converted to uppercase.	text.ToUpper() Returns: " MY STRING"

Figure 22.4 String methods introduced in earlier tutorials.

SELF-REVIEW

1. The _________ property of the class String returns the number of characters in the String.
   a) MaxChars b) Length
   c) CharacterCount d) TotalLength

2. A String can be composed of _________.
   a) digits b) lowercase letters
   c) special characters d) All of the above

Answers: 1) b. 2) d.

22.3 Analyzing the Screen Scraping Application

Before building the **Screen Scraping** application, you must analyze its components. The following pseudocode describes the basic operation of the **Screen Scraping** application.

```
When the Form loads:
    Display the HTML that contains the items' prices in a Label

When the user clicks the Search Button:
    Search the HTML for the item the user selected from the ComboBox
    Extract the item's price
    Convert the item's price from euros to dollars
    Display the item's price in a Label
```

Now that you have test-driven the **Screen Scraping** application and studied its pseudocode representation, you use an ACE table to help you convert the pseudocode to Visual Basic. Figure 22.5 lists the actions, controls and events that help you complete your own version of this application.

Action/Control/Event (ACE) Table for the Screen Scraping Application

Action	Control/Object	Event
Label the application's controls	itemLabel priceLabel sourceLabel	Application is run
	ScreenScraping-Form	Load
Display the HTML that contains the items' prices in a Label	htmlLabel	
	searchButton	Click
Search the HTML for the item the user selected from the ComboBox	itemsComboBox	
Extract the item's price		
Convert the item's price from euros to dollars		
Display the item's price in a Label	resultLabel	

Figure 22.5 ACE table for **Screen Scraping** application.

Now that you've analyzed the **Screen Scraping** application's components, you learn about the String methods that you need to construct the application.

22.4 Locating Substrings in Strings

Many applications search for a character or set of characters in a String. For example, a word-processing application allows users to search their documents. Class String provides methods that make it possible to search for **substrings** (or sequences of characters) in a String. In the following box, you begin building the **Screen Scraping** application.

Locating the Selected Item's Price

1. ***Copying the template to your working directory.*** Copy the C:\Examples\Tutorial22\TemplateApplication\ScreenScraping directory to your C:\SimplyVB2008 directory.
2. ***Opening the Screen Scraping application's template file.*** Double click ScreenScraping.sln in the ScreenScraping directory to open the application in the Visual Basic IDE. Double click ScreenScraping.vb in the **Solution Explorer** to display the application's Form in **Design** view.
3. ***Creating a Click event handler for the Search Button.*** Double click the **Search** Button on the application's Form to generate the event handler searchButton_Click. Add the comments in lines 13 and 17 of Fig. 22.6.

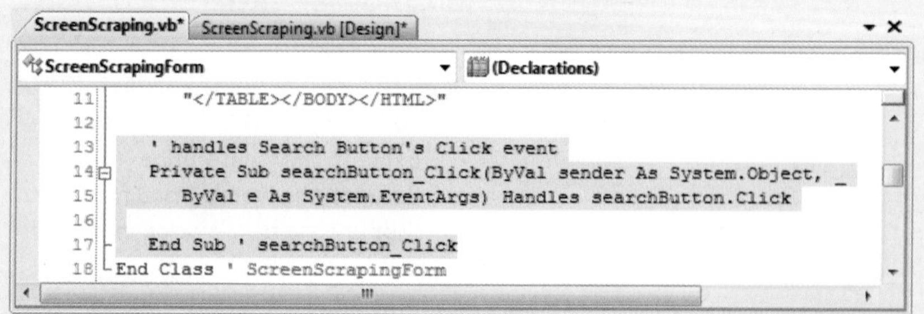
ScreenScraping.vb*
ScreenScraping.vb [Design]*
ScreenScrapingForm
(Declarations)
11 "</TABLE></BODY></HTML>"
12
13 ' handles Search Button's Click event
14 Private Sub searchButton_Click(ByVal sender As System.Object, _
15 ByVal e As System.EventArgs) Handles searchButton.Click
16
17 End Sub ' searchButton_Click
18 End Class ' ScreenScrapingForm

Figure 22.6 searchButton_Click event handler.

(cont.)

4. ***Declaring three Integer variables, a String reference and a Decimal variable.*** Add lines 17–21 of Fig. 22.7 to the `searchButton_Click` event handler. These lines declare `Integer` variables `itemLocation`, `priceBegin` and `priceEnd`, `String` variable `price` and `Decimal` variable `dollars`.

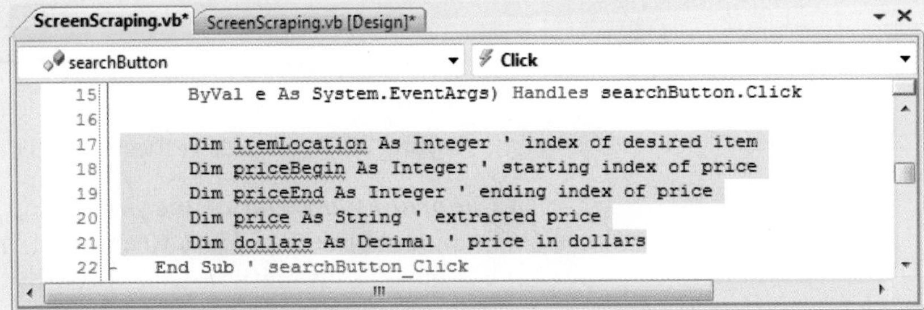
ScreenScraping.vb* ScreenScraping.vb [Design]*
searchButton
Click
15 ByVal e As System.EventArgs) Handles searchButton.Click
17 Dim itemLocation As Integer ' index of desired item
18 Dim priceBegin As Integer ' starting index of price
19 Dim priceEnd As Integer ' ending index of price
20 Dim price As String ' extracted price
21 Dim dollars As Decimal ' price in dollars
22 End Sub ' searchButton_Click

Figure 22.7 `searchButton_Click` event-handler declarations.

5. ***Locating the specified item name.*** Add lines 23–25 of Fig. 22.8 to event handler `searchButton_Click`. Lines 24–25 call `String` method **`IndexOf`** to locate the first occurrence of the specified item name in the HTML string stored in the `html` instance variable. There are three overloaded versions of `IndexOf` that search for substrings in a `String`. Lines 24–25 use the version of `IndexOf` that takes a single argument—the substring for which to search. (The specified item name is the `String` representation of the `SelectedItem` in `itemsComboBox`.)

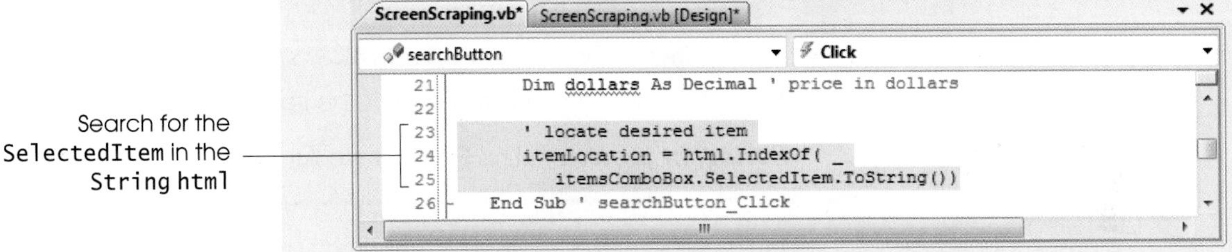
Search for the SelectedItem in the String html
ScreenScraping.vb* ScreenScraping.vb [Design]*
searchButton
Click
21 Dim dollars As Decimal ' price in dollars
23 ' locate desired item
24 itemLocation = html.IndexOf(_
25 itemsComboBox.SelectedItem.ToString())
26 End Sub ' searchButton_Click

Figure 22.8 Locating the desired item name.

`Option Strict` is set to `On`, so you must convert `SelectedItem` (which is of type `Object`) to a `String`, by using method `ToString`, before passing the selected item to method `IndexOf`. If `IndexOf` finds the specified substring (in this case, the item name), `IndexOf` returns the index at which the substring begins in the `String`. For example, the return value `0` means that the substring begins at the first element of the `String`. If `IndexOf` does not find the substring, it returns `-1`. The result is stored in variable `itemLocation`.

6. ***Locating the start of the price.*** Add lines 27–29 of Fig. 22.9 to event handler `searchButton_Click`. Lines 28–29 locate the index at which the item's price begins. Lines 28–29 use a version of method `IndexOf` that takes two arguments—the substring to find and the starting index in the `String` at which the search begins. The method does not examine any characters prior to the starting index (specified by `itemLocation`). The third version of method `IndexOf` takes three arguments—the substring to find, the index at which to start searching and the number of characters to search. You do not use this version of `IndexOf` in the **Screen Scraping** application.

The first price that follows the specified item name in the HTML is the desired price; therefore, you can begin the search at `itemLocation`. The substring to find is `"€"`. This is the HTML representation of the euro symbol, which appears before every price value in the HTML. The index returned from method `IndexOf` is stored in variable `priceBegin`.

(cont.)

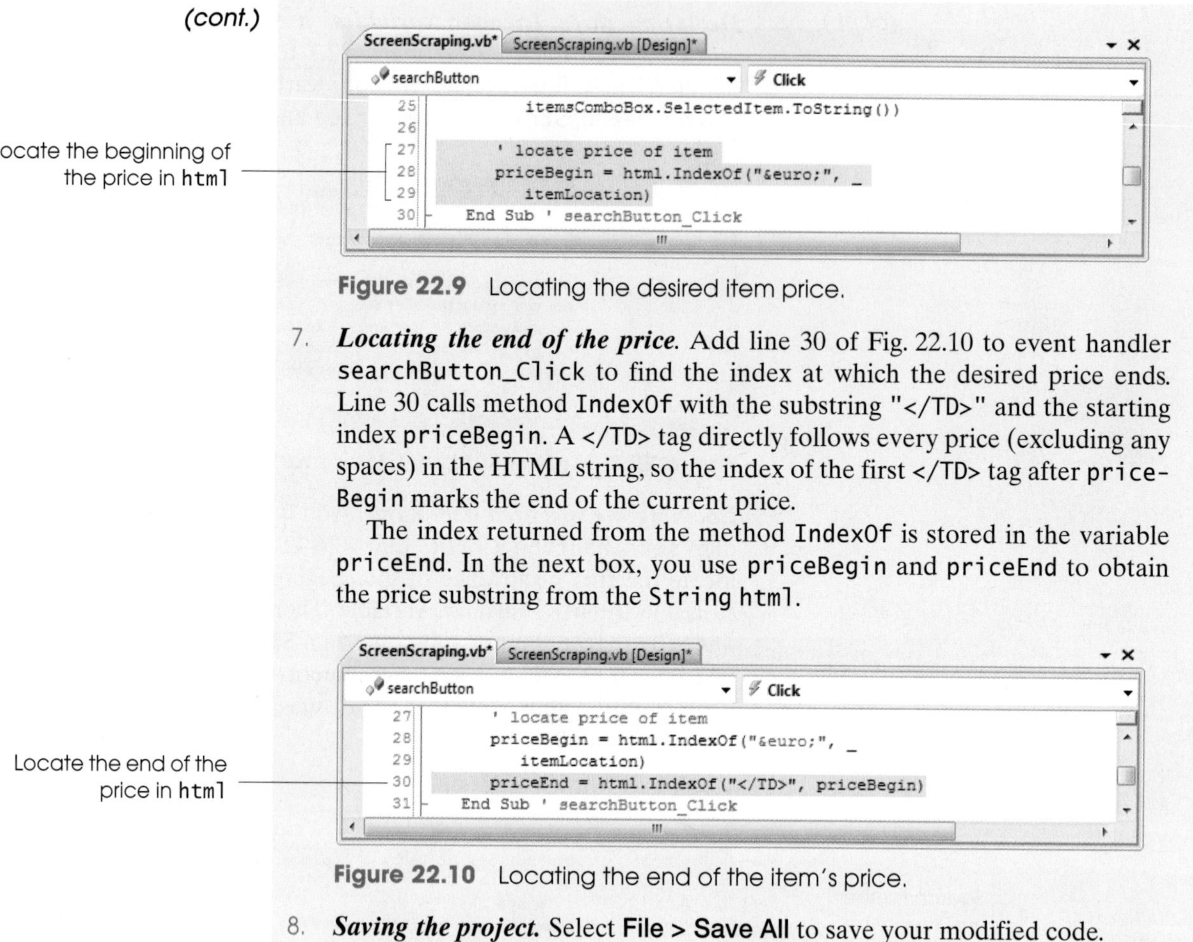
Locate the beginning of the price in html
ScreenScraping.vb* ScreenScraping.vb [Design]*
searchButton
Click
25 itemsComboBox.SelectedItem.ToString())
26
27 ' locate price of item
28 priceBegin = html.IndexOf("€", _
29 itemLocation)
30 End Sub ' searchButton_Click

Figure 22.9 Locating the desired item price.

7. ***Locating the end of the price.*** Add line 30 of Fig. 22.10 to event handler `searchButton_Click` to find the index at which the desired price ends. Line 30 calls method `IndexOf` with the substring "</TD>" and the starting index `priceBegin`. A </TD> tag directly follows every price (excluding any spaces) in the HTML string, so the index of the first </TD> tag after `priceBegin` marks the end of the current price.

   The index returned from the method `IndexOf` is stored in the variable `priceEnd`. In the next box, you use `priceBegin` and `priceEnd` to obtain the price substring from the `String html`.

Locate the end of the price in html
ScreenScraping.vb* ScreenScraping.vb [Design]*
searchButton
Click
27 ' locate price of item
28 priceBegin = html.IndexOf("€", _
29 itemLocation)
30 priceEnd = html.IndexOf("</TD>", priceBegin)
31 End Sub ' searchButton_Click

Figure 22.10 Locating the end of the item's price.

8. ***Saving the project.*** Select **File > Save All** to save your modified code.

The **`LastIndexOf`** method is similar to method `IndexOf`. Method `LastIndexOf` locates the *last* occurrence of a substring in a `String`—it performs the search starting from the end of the `String` and searches toward the beginning. If method `LastIndexOf` finds the substring, it returns the starting index of the specified substring in the `String`; otherwise, `LastIndexOf` returns -1.

There are three overloaded versions of `LastIndexOf` that search for substrings in a `String`. The first version takes a single argument—the substring for which to search. The second version takes two arguments—the substring for which to search and the highest index from which to begin searching backward for the substring. The third version of method `LastIndexOf` takes three arguments—the substring for which to search, the starting index from which to start searching backward and the number of characters to search. Figure 22.11 shows examples of the three versions of `LastIndexOf`. Note that the example expression " My String" intentionally begins with a blank space.

Method	Example Expression (assume text = " My String")	Returns
LastIndexOf(*string*)	text.LastIndexOf("n")	8
LastIndexOf(*string, integer*)	text.LastIndexOf("n", 6)	-1
	text.LastIndexOf("y", 6)	2
LastIndexOf(*string, integer, integer*)	text.LastIndexOf("m", 7, 3)	-1
	text.LastIndexOf("r", 7, 3)	6

Figure 22.11 `LastIndexOf` examples.

SELF-REVIEW

1. Method ________ locates the first occurrence of a substring.

   a) `IndexOf` b) `FirstIndexOf`
   c) `FindFirst` d) `Locate`

2. The third argument passed to the `LastIndexOf` method is ________.

   a) the starting index from which to start searching backward
   b) the starting index from which to start searching forward
   c) the length of the substring to locate
   d) the number of characters to search

Answers: 1) a. 2) d.

22.5 Extracting Substrings from `String`s

Once you've located a substring in a `String`, you might want to retrieve the substring from the `String`. The following box uses the `Substring` method to retrieve the price of the selected item from the HTML string.

Retrieving the Desired Item's Price

1. ***Extracting the price.*** Add lines 32–34 of Fig. 22.12 to the `searchButton_Click` event handler. Recall from Tutorial 19 that class `String` provides two versions of the `Substring` method, each of which returns a new `String` object that contains a copy of a part of an existing `String` object.

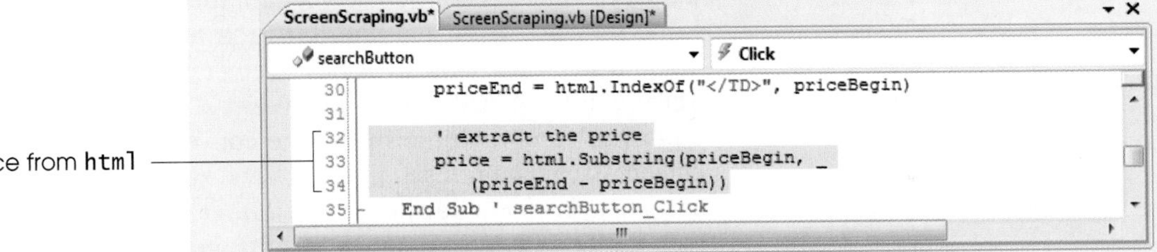
Extract price from html
ScreenScraping.vb*
ScreenScraping.vb [Design]*
searchButton
Click
30 priceEnd = html.IndexOf("</TD>", priceBegin)
31
32 ' extract the price
33 price = html.Substring(priceBegin, _
34 (priceEnd - priceBegin))
35 End Sub ' searchButton_Click

Figure 22.12 Retrieving the desired price.

Lines 33–34 extract the price, using the version of the `Substring` method that takes two `Integer` arguments. The first argument (`priceBegin`) specifies the starting index from which the method copies characters from the original `String`.

The second argument (`priceEnd - priceBegin`) specifies the length of the substring to be copied. The substring returned (`price`) contains a copy of the specified characters from the original `String`. In this case, the substring returned is the item's price (in euros).

The other version of method `Substring` takes one `Integer` argument. The argument specifies the starting index from which the method copies characters in the original `String`. The substring returned contains a copy of the characters from the starting index to the end of the `String`.

2. ***Saving the project.*** Select **File > Save All** to save your modified code.

SELF-REVIEW

1. The `Substring` method ________.

   a) accepts either one or two arguments
   b) returns a new `String` object
   c) creates a `String` object by copying part of an existing `String` object
   d) All of the above

2. The second argument passed to method Substring specifies ________.
   a) the last index of the String to copy
   b) the length of the substring to copy
   c) the index from which to begin copying backward
   d) a character which, when reached, signifies that copying is to stop

Answers: 1) d. 2) b.

22.6 Replacing Substrings in Strings

Perhaps you want to replace certain characters in Strings. Class String provides the **Replace** method to replace occurrences of one substring with a different substring. The Replace method takes as arguments a String to replace in the original String and a String with which to replace all occurrences of the first argument. Method Replace returns a new String with the specified replacements. The original String remains unchanged. If there are no occurrences of the first argument in the String, the method returns a copy of the original String. The following box uses method Replace to convert the extracted price from euros to dollars.

Converting the Price to Dollars

1. ***Converting the price.*** Add lines 36–39 of Fig. 22.13 to searchButton_Click. Line 37 uses String method Replace to return a new String object in which every occurrence in price of substring "€" (the euro currency symbol) is replaced with substring "" (the empty String)—there is one replacement in this example. Note that you assign the value returned from method Replace to price. This is required because method Replace returns a new String—it does not modify the original String. Line 38 calls method Convert.ToDecimal to retrieve the price as a Decimal and multiplies it by the conversion rate (1.58D). (You can find current exchange rates at http://www.xe.com/ucc/.) The D in line 38 indicates that 1.58 is a Decimal value rather than a Double. Recall that a Decimal multiplied by a Double results in a Double. Specifying 1.58 as a Decimal removes the need to convert the result of the multiplication. The price in dollars is assigned to Decimal variable dollars. Line 39 calls String method Format to display the price in resultLabel as currency.

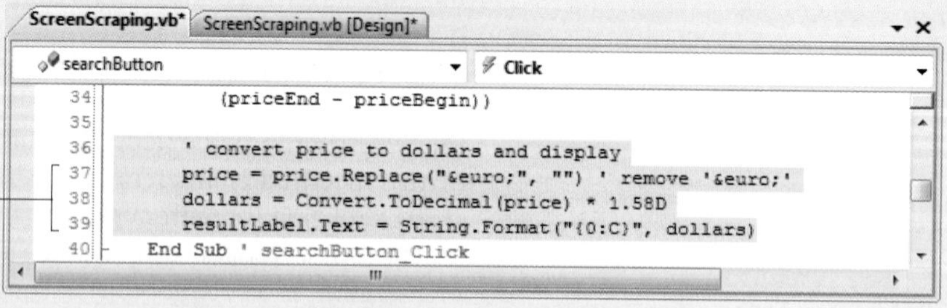

   Replace "€" with "" and convert the amount to dollars

   ```
   34            (priceEnd - priceBegin))
   35
   36         ' convert price to dollars and display
   37        price = price.Replace("&euro;", "") ' remove '&euro;'
   38        dollars = Convert.ToDecimal(price) * 1.58D
   39        resultLabel.Text = String.Format("{0:C}", dollars)
   40     End Sub ' searchButton_Click
   ```

   Figure 22.13 Converting the price to dollars.

2. ***Saving the project.*** Select **File > Save All** to save your modified code.

Method Replace also is used when the Form for the **Screen Scraping** application first loads. The following box uses method Replace to ensure that the HTML string displays correctly in a Label.

Displaying the HTML String

1. ***Creating a Load event handler for the Form.*** In **Design** view, double click the Form to generate an empty Load event handler. This event handler executes when the application runs.

(cont.)

2. ***Formatting the Load event handler.*** Add the comments in lines 42 and 47 of Fig. 22.14 around event handler `ScreenScrapingForm_Load`. Also, split the procedure header over three lines using line-continuation characters, as in lines 43–44 of Fig. 22.14, to improve its readability.

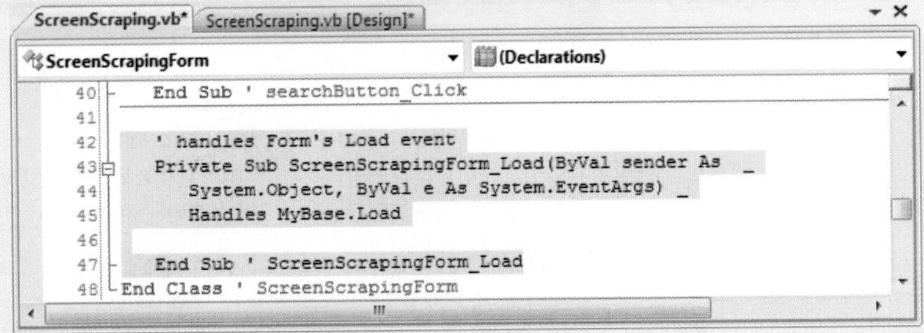

Figure 22.14 Load event for the `Form`.

3. ***Displaying the HTML string in a `Label`.*** Add lines 47–48 of Fig. 22.15 to `ScreenScrapingForm_Load`. Line 48 calls `String` method `Replace` to replace every occurrence of `"€"` in the HTML string with `"&€"`. As explained previously, the substring `"€"` is the HTML for the euro symbol. For this text to display in a `Label` correctly, you must prefix it with an additional ampersand (&) so that the `"e"` in `"euro"` is not confused with an access key. The value returned from `Replace` is displayed in `htmlLabel`.

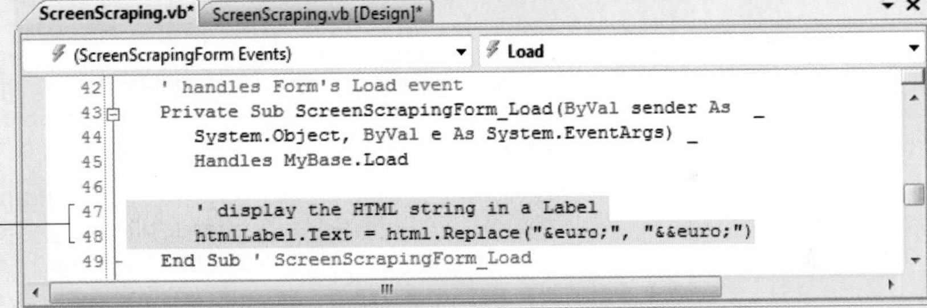

Figure 22.15 Displaying the HTML string in a `Label`.

4. ***Running the application.*** Select **Debug > Start Debugging** to run your application. Select the different items from the **Item** `ComboBox`, clicking the **Search** `Button` after each selection. Make sure that in each case, the proper price is extracted and converted to dollars.

5. ***Closing the application.*** Close your running application by clicking its close box.

6. ***Closing the IDE.*** Close the Visual Basic IDE by clicking its close box.

SELF-REVIEW

1. If there are no occurrences of the substring in the `String`, method `Replace` returns ________.

   a) `0` b) `-1`
   c) `nothing` d) a copy of the original `String`

2. `String` method `Replace` replaces ________ occurrence(s) of the substring in the `String`.

   a) the first b) the last
   c) all of the d) None of the above

Answer: 1) d. 2) c.

22.7 Other String Methods

Class `String` provides several additional methods that allow you to manipulate `Strings`. Figure 22.16 lists some of these methods and provides a description of what each method does.

Method	Description	Sample Expression (assume `text = " My String"`)
`EndsWith(`*string*`)`	Returns `True` if a `String` ends with argument *string*; otherwise, returns `False`.	`text.EndsWith("ing")` Returns: `True`
`Insert(`*index*, *string*`)`	Returns a copy of the `String` with the argument *string* inserted at *index*.	`text.Insert(0, "This is")` Returns: `"This is My String"`
`Join(`*separator*, *array*`)`	Concatenates the elements in a `String` array, separated by the first argument. A new `String` containing the concatenated elements is returned.	`Dim array As String() = _ New String() _ {"a", "b", "c"}` `String.Join(";", array)` Returns: `"a;b;c"`
`Split()`	Splits the words in a `String` whenever a space is reached.	`Dim array As String() = _ text.Split()` Returns: A `String` array containing `"My"` and `"String"`
`StartsWith(`*string*`)`	Returns `True` if a `String` starts with argument *string*; otherwise, returns `False`.	`text.StartsWith("Your")` Returns: `False`
`Trim()`	Removes any whitespace (that is, blank lines, spaces and tabs) from the beginning and end of a `String`. Methods `TrimStart` and `TrimEnd` are similar.	`text.Trim()` Returns: `"My String"`

Figure 22.16 Description of some other `String` methods.

Figure 22.17 presents the source code for the **Screen Scraping** application. The lines of code that contain new programming concepts you learned in this tutorial are highlighted.

```
Public Class ScreenScrapingForm

   ' String of HTML to extract prices from
   Dim html As String = "<HTML><BODY><TABLE>" & _
      "<TR><TD>Antique Rocking Chair</TD>" & _
      "<TD>&euro;82.67</TD></TR>" & _
      "<TR><TD>Silver Teapot</TD>" & _
      "<TD>&euro;64.55</TD></TR>" & _
      "<TR><TD>Gold Pocket Watch</TD>" & _
      "<TD>&euro;128.83</TD></TR>" & _
      "</TABLE></BODY></HTML>"

   ' handles Search Button's Click event
   Private Sub searchButton_Click(ByVal sender As System.Object, _
      ByVal e As System.EventArgs) Handles searchButton.Click
```

Figure 22.17 **Screen Scraping** application's code listing. (Part 1 of 2.)

```
        Dim itemLocation As Integer ' index of desired item
        Dim priceBegin As Integer ' starting index of price
        Dim priceEnd As Integer ' ending index of price
        Dim price As String ' extracted price
        Dim dollars As Decimal ' price in dollars

        ' locate desired item
        itemLocation = html.IndexOf( _
           itemsComboBox.SelectedItem.ToString())

        ' locate price of item
        priceBegin = html.IndexOf("&euro;", _
           itemLocation)
        priceEnd = html.IndexOf("</TD>", priceBegin)

        ' extract the price
        price = html.Substring(priceBegin, _
           (priceEnd - priceBegin))

        ' convert price to dollars and display
        price = price.Replace("&euro;", "") ' remove '&euro;'
        dollars = Convert.ToDecimal(price) * 1.58D
        resultLabel.Text = String.Format("{0:C}", dollars)
     End Sub ' searchButton_Click

     ' handles load event procedure for the Form
     Private Sub ScreenScrapingForm_Load( _
        ByVal sender As System.Object, ByVal e As System.EventArgs) _
        Handles MyBase.Load

        ' display the HTML string in a Label
        htmlLabel.Text = html.Replace("&euro;", "&&euro;")
     End Sub ' ScreenScrapingForm_Load
  End Class ' ScreenScrapingForm
```

Search for the `SelectedItem` in the `String html`

Locate the beginning of the price in `html`

Locate the end of the price in `html`

Extract the price from `html`

Replace "`€`" with the empty `String`

Replace "`€`" with "`&&euro`"

Figure 22.17 **Screen Scraping** application's code listing. (Part 2 of 2.)

SELF-REVIEW

1. The ________ method removes all whitespace characters that appear at the beginning and end of a `String`.

   a) `RemoveSpaces` b) `NoSpaces`
   c) `Trim` d) `Truncate`

2. The `StartsWith` method returns ________ if a `String` begins with the method's `String` argument.

   a) `True` b) `False`
   c) `1` d) the index of the substring

Answers: 1) c. 2) a.

22.8 Wrap-Up

In this tutorial, you studied class `String` from the `System` namespace. You learned how to create and manipulate `String` objects. You learned how to locate, retrieve and replace substrings in `Strings`. You reviewed several methods from class `String` that were used in earlier tutorials and learned several additional methods. You applied your knowledge of `Strings` in Visual Basic to create a simple **Screen Scraping** application that retrieves the price of an item in euros from an HTML `String` and converts it to dollars.

In the next tutorial, you learn how data is represented in a computer, you're introduced to the concepts of files and streams, and you learn how to store data in sequential files.

SKILLS SUMMARY

Determining the Size of a `String`

- Use `String` property `Length`.

Locating Substrings in `Strings`

- Use `String` method `IndexOf` to locate the first occurrence of a substring.
- Use `String` method `LastIndexOf` to locate the last occurrence of a substring.

Retrieving Substrings from `Strings`

- Use `String` method `Substring` with one argument to obtain a substring that begins at the specified starting index and contains the remainder of the original `String`.
- Use `String` method `Substring` with two arguments to specify the starting index and the length of the substring.

Replacing Substrings in `Strings`

- Use `String` method `Replace` to replace occurrences of one substring with another substring.

Comparing Substrings to the Beginning or End of a `String`

- Use `String` method `StartsWith` to determine whether a `String` starts with a particular substring.
- Use `String` method `EndsWith` to determine whether a `String` ends with a particular substring.

Removing Whitespace from a `String`

- Use `String` method `Trim` to remove all whitespace characters that appear at the beginning and end of a `String`.

KEY TERMS

`Chars` property of class `String`—Returns the character located at a specific index in a `String`.

`EndsWith` method of class `String`—Determines whether a `String` ends with a particular substring.

HTML (HyperText Markup Language)—A technology for describing web pages.

immutable—Describes an object that cannot be changed after it is created. In Visual Basic, `Strings` are immutable.

`IndexOf` method of class `String`—Returns the index of the first occurrence of a substring in a `String`. Returns `-1` if the substring is not found.

`Insert` method of class `String`—Returns a new `String` object with the specified substring inserted at the given index of the original `String`.

`Join` method of class `String`—Concatenates the elements in a `String` array, separated by the first argument. A new `String` containing the concatenated elements is returned.

`LastIndexOf` method of class `String`—Returns the index of the last occurrence of a substring in a `String`. Returns `-1` if the substring is not found.

`Length` property of class `String`—Returns the number of characters in the `String` for which it is called.

literal `String` object—A `String` constant written as a sequence of characters in double quotation marks (also called a string literal).

`Replace` method of class `String`—Returns a new `String` object in which every occurrence of a substring is replaced with a different substring.

screen scraping—The process of extracting desired information from the HTML that composes a web page.

special characters—Characters that are neither digits nor letters.

`Split` method of class `String`—Splits the words in a `String` whenever a space is reached.

`StartsWith` method of class `String`—Determines whether a `String` starts with a particular substring.

string constant—A `String` constant written as a sequence of characters in double quotation marks (also called a string literal).

string literal—A `String` constant written as a sequence of characters in double quotation marks (also called a literal `String` object).

substring—A sequence of characters in a `String`.

`Substring` method of class `String`—Creates a new `String` object by copying part of an existing `String` object.

`Trim` method of class `String`—Removes all whitespace characters from the beginning and end of a `String`.

CONTROLS, EVENTS, PROPERTIES & METHODS

`String` The `String` class represents a series of characters treated as a single unit.

- ***Properties***

  `Chars`—Returns the character located at a specific index in the `String`.

  `Length`—Returns the number of characters in the `String`.

- ***Methods***

  `EndsWith`—Determines whether a `String` ends with a particular substring.

  `Format`—Arranges the string in a specified format.

  `IndexOf`—Returns the index of the specified character(s) in a `String`. Returns `-1` if the substring is not found.

  `Insert`—Returns a copy of the `String` for which it is called with the specified character(s) inserted.

  `Join`—Concatenates the elements in a `String` array, separated by the first argument. A new `String` containing the concatenated elements is returned.

  `LastIndexOf`—Returns the index of the last occurrence of a substring in a `String`. Returns `-1` if the substring is not found.

  `PadLeft`—Inserts characters at the beginning of a `String`.

  `Remove`—Returns a copy of the `String` for which it is called with the specified character(s) removed.

  `Replace`—Returns a new `String` object in which every occurrence of a substring is replaced with a different substring.

  `StartsWith`—Determines whether a `String` starts with a particular substring.

  `Substring`—Returns a substring from a `String`.

  `ToLower`—Returns a copy of the `String` for which it is called with any uppercase letters converted to lowercase letters.

  `ToUpper`—Returns a copy of the `String` for which it is called with any lowercase letters converted to uppercase letters.

  `Trim`—Removes all whitespace characters from the beginning and end of a `String`.

MULTIPLE-CHOICE QUESTIONS

22.1 Extracting desired information from web pages is called _________.

a) web crawling b) screen scraping
c) querying d) redirection

22.2 If method `IndexOf` does not find the specified substring, it returns _________.

a) `False` b) `0`
c) `-1` d) None of the above

22.3 The `String` class allows you to _________ `Strings`.

a) search b) retrieve characters from
c) replace characters in d) All of the above

22.4 _________ is a technology for describing web content.

a) Class `String`
b) A `String` literal
c) HTML
d) A screen scraper

22.5 The `String` class is located in the _________ namespace.

a) `String`
b) `System.Strings`
c) `System.IO`
d) `System`

22.6 The _________ method creates a new `String` object by copying part of an existing `String` object.

a) `StringCopy`
b) `Substring`
c) `CopyString`
d) `CopySubString`

22.7 All `String` objects are _________.

a) the same size
b) always equal to each other
c) preceded by at least one whitespace character
d) immutable

22.8 The `IndexOf` method with two arguments does not examine any characters that occur prior to the _________.

a) starting index
b) first match
c) last character of the `String`
d) None of the above

22.9 The _________ method determines whether a `String` ends with a particular substring.

a) `CheckEnd`
b) `StringEnd`
c) `EndsWith`
d) `EndIs`

22.10 The _________ method returns an array of `String`s.

a) `Join`
b) `Split`
c) `Replace`
d) None of the above

EXERCISES

22.11 ***(Supply Cost Calculator Application)*** Write an application that calculates the cost of all the supplies added to the user's shopping list (Fig. 22.18). The application should contain two `ListBox`es. The first contains all the supplies offered and their respective prices. Users should be able to select the desired supplies from the first `ListBox` and add them to the second `ListBox`. Provide a **Calculate** `Button` that displays the total price for the user's shopping list (the contents of the second `ListBox`).

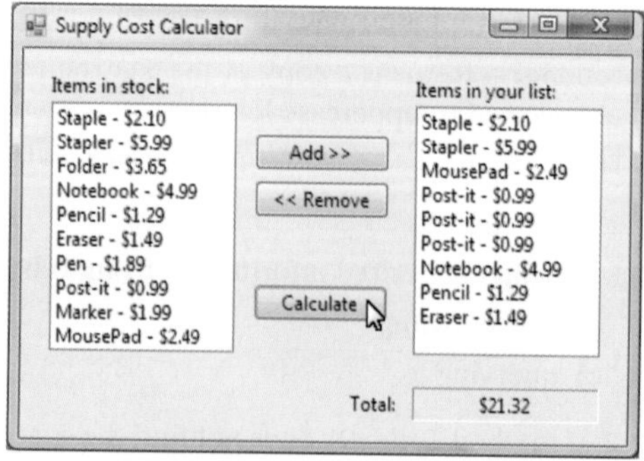

Figure 22.18 **Supply Cost Calculator** application's GUI.

a) ***Copying the template to your working directory.*** Copy the directory `C:\Examples\Tutorial22\Exercises\SupplyCalculator` to your `C:\SimplyVB2008` directory.

b) ***Opening the application's template file.*** Double click `SupplyCalculator.sln` in the `SupplyCalculator` directory to open the application.

c) ***Adding code to the Add >> `Button`.*** Double click the **Add >>** `Button` to create an empty event handler. Insert code in the event handler that adds the selected item from the first ListBox to shoppingListBox. Be sure to check that an item is selected in the first ListBox before attempting to add an item to shoppingListBox.

d) ***Enabling the Buttons.*** Once the user adds something to the shoppingListBox, set the Enabled properties of the **<< Remove** and **Calculate** Buttons to True.

e) ***Deselecting the items.*** Once the item is added to the shoppingListBox, make sure that it is deselected in the stockListBox. Also, clear the **Total:** Label to indicate to the user that a new total price must be calculated.

f) ***Adding code to the << Remove Button.*** Double click the **<< Remove** Button to create an empty event handler. The **Items in your list:** ListBox's SelectionMode property has been set to MultiExtended to allow the user to select multiple items. Use a Do While loop to remove any selected items in the shoppingListBox. Be sure to check that at least one item is selected before attempting to remove an item. [*Hint:* Method shoppingListBox.Items.RemoveAt(index) will remove the item located at index from the shoppingListBox. When an item is removed, the SelectedIndex property points to the next selected item, if there is one.] If there are no items remaining in the shoppingListBox, disable the **<< Remove** and **Calculate** Buttons. Also, clear the **Total:** Label to indicate to the user that a new total price must be calculated.

g) ***Adding code to the Calculate Button.*** Double click the **Calculate** Button to create an empty event handler. Use a For...Next statement to loop through all the items in the shoppingListBox. Convert each item from the ListBox into a String. Then use the String method Substring to extract the price of each item.

h) ***Displaying the total.*** Convert the String representing each item's price to a Decimal, and add this to the overall total (of type Decimal). Remember to output the value in currency format.

i) ***Running the application.*** Select **Debug > Start Debugging** to run your application. Use the **Add >>** and **<< Remove** Buttons to add and remove items from the **Items in your list:** ListBox. Click the **Calculate** Button and verify that the total price displayed is correct.

j) ***Closing the application.*** Close your running application by clicking its close box.

k) ***Closing the IDE.*** Close the Visual Basic IDE by clicking its close box.

22.12 *(Encryption Application)* Write an application that encrypts a message from the user (Fig. 22.19). The application should be able to encrypt the message in two different ways: substitution cipher and transposition cipher (both described below). The user should be able to enter the message in a TextBox and select the desired method of encryption. Display the encrypted message in a Label.

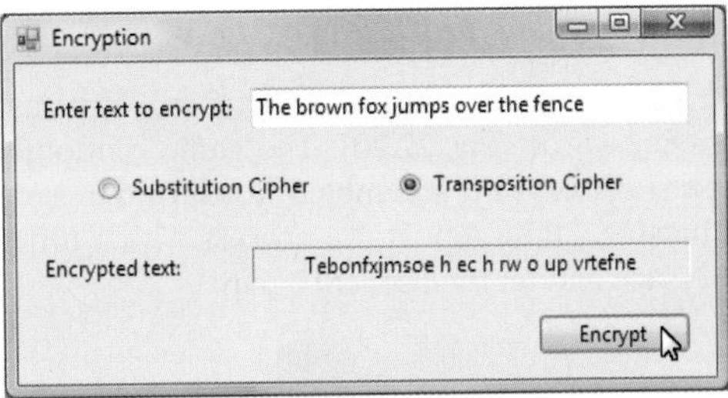

Figure 22.19 **Encryption** application's GUI.

In a substitution cipher, every character in the English alphabet is represented by a different character in the substitution alphabet. Every time a letter occurs in the English sentence, it is replaced by the letter at the corresponding index of the substitution alphabet. In a transposition cipher, two Strings are created. The first new String contains all characters at the even indices of the input String. The second new String contains all of the characters at the odd indices. The new Strings are concatenated, with a space between them, to form the encrypted text. For example, a transposition cipher for the word "code" would be "cd oe."

a) ***Copying the template to your working directory.*** Copy the directory C:\Examples\Tutorial22\Exercises\Encryption to your C:\SimplyVB2008 directory.

b) ***Opening the application's template file.*** Double click `Encryption.sln` in the `Encryption` directory to open the application.

c) ***Adding code to the Encrypt `Button`.*** Double click the **Encrypt** `Button` to create an empty event handler.

d) ***Determining the cipher method.*** Use `If...Then...Else` statements to determine which method of encryption the user has selected and call the appropriate procedure.

e) ***Locating the `SubstitutionCipher` method.*** Locate the `SubstitutionCipher` procedure. The English and substitution alphabet `Strings` are defined for you in this procedure.

f) ***Converting the text input to lowercase.*** Add code to the `SubstitutionCipher` method that uses the `ToLower` method of class `String` to make all the characters in the input `String` (`plainTextBox.Text`) lowercase.

g) ***Performing the substitution encryption.*** Use a `For...Next` statement to iterate through each character of the input `String`. Use `String` method `IndexOf` to find the index of the input character in the `String` holding the English alphabet. Attach the character from the `cipherAlphabet` at the corresponding index to the cipher text.

h) ***Displaying the `String`.*** Now that the `String` has been substituted with all the corresponding cipher characters, assign the cipher `String` to `cipherTextLabel`.

i) ***Locating the `TranspositionCipher` method.*** Locate the `TranspositionCipher` method. Define two `String` variables, each representing a word.

j) ***Extracting the first word.*** Use a `For...Next` statement to retrieve all the "even" indices (starting from 0) from the input `String`. Increment the control variable by 2 each time, and add the characters located at even indices to the first `String` created in *Step i*.

k) ***Extracting the second word.*** Use another `For...Next` statement to retrieve all the "odd" indices (starting from 1) from the same input `String`. Increment the control variable by 2, and add the characters at odd indices to the second `String` that you created in *Step i*.

l) ***Outputting the result.*** Add the two `Strings` together with a space in between, and output the result to `cipherTextLabel`.

m) ***Running the application.*** Select **Debug > Start Debugging** to run your application. Enter text into the **Enter text to encrypt:** `TextBox`. Select the **Substitution Cipher** `RadioButton` and click the **Encrypt** `Button`. Verify that the output is the properly encrypted text using the substitution cipher. Select the **Transposition Cipher** `RadioButton` and click the **Encrypt** `Button`. Verify that the output is the properly encrypted text using the transposition cipher.

n) ***Closing the application.*** Close your running application by clicking its close box.

o) ***Closing the IDE.*** Close the Visual Basic IDE by clicking its close box.

22.13 *(**Anagram Game** Application)* Write an **Anagram Game** that contains an array of 20 pre-set words (Fig. 22.20). The game randomly selects a word and scrambles its letters. A `Label` displays the scrambled word for the user to guess. If the user guesses correctly, display a message, then repeat the process with a different word. If the guess is incorrect, display a message and let the user try again.

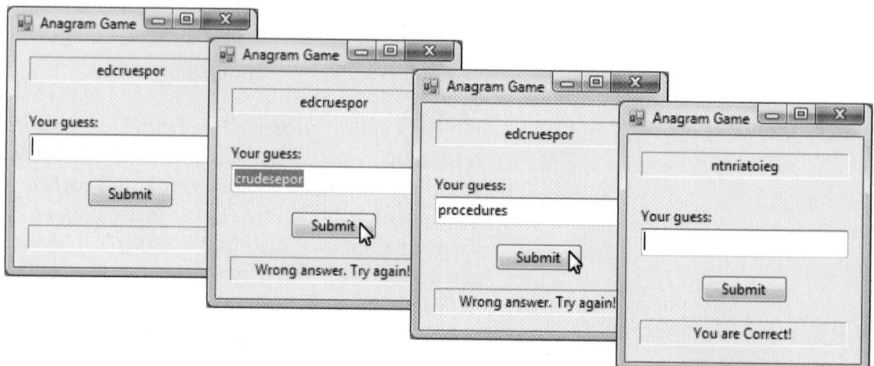

Figure 22.20 **Anagram Game** application's GUI.

a) ***Copying the template to your working directory.*** Copy the directory `C:\Examples\Tutorial22\Exercises\Anagram` to your `C:\SimplyVB2008` directory.

b) ***Opening the application's template file.*** Double click `Anagram.sln` in the `Anagram` directory to open the application.

c) ***Locating the `GenerateAnagram` method.*** Locate the `GenerateAnagram` method. It is the first method after the `AnagramForm_Load` event handler.

d) ***Picking a random word.*** Generate a random number to use as the index of the word in the `anagram` array. Retrieve a word from the `anagram` array, using the random number as an index. Store the word in another `String` variable.

e) ***Generate the scrambled word.*** Generate a second random number to store the index of a character to be moved. Use a `For...Next` statement to iterate through the word 20 times. In the body of the loop, pass the second random number to the `Chars` property of class `String`. Append the character returned by `Chars` to the end of the `String`, and remove it from its original position. Next, generate a new random number to move a different character during the next iteration of the loop. Remember to output the final word to `anagramLabel`.

f) ***Defining the Submit `Button`.*** Double click the **Submit** `Button` to generate an empty event handler.

g) ***Testing the user's input.*** Use an `If...Then...Else` statement to determine whether the user's input matches the actual word. If the user is correct, clear the `TextBox`, place the focus on the `TextBox` and generate a new word. Otherwise, select the user's text (using the `TextBox`'s `SelectAll` method) and place the focus on the `TextBox`.

h) ***Running the application.*** Select **Debug > Start Debugging** to run your application. Submit correct answers and incorrect answers, and verify that the appropriate message is displayed each time.

i) ***Closing the application.*** Close your running application by clicking its close box.

j) ***Closing the IDE.*** Close the Visual Basic IDE by clicking its close box.

What does this code do?

22.14 What is assigned to `result` when the following code executes?

```
Dim word1 As String = "CHORUS"
Dim word2 As String = "d i n o s a u r"
Dim word3 As String = "The theme is string."
Dim result As String

result = word1.ToLower()
result = result.Substring(4)
word2 = word2.Replace(" ", "")
word2 = word2.Substring(4, 4)
result = word2 & result

word3 = word3.Substring(word3.IndexOf(" ") + 1, 3)

result = word3.Insert(3, result)
```

What's wrong with this code?

22.15 This code should remove all commas from `test` and convert all lowercase letters to uppercase letters. Find the error(s) in the following code.

```
Dim test As String = "Bug,2,Bug"

test = test.ToUpper()
test = test.Replace("")
```

Programming Challenge

22.16 ***(Pig Latin Application)*** Write an application that encodes English-language phrases into pig Latin (Fig. 22.21). Pig Latin is a form of coded language often used for amusement. Many different methods are used to form pig Latin phrases. For simplicity, use the following method to form the pig Latin words:

> *To form a pig Latin word from an English-language phrase, the translation proceeds one word at a time. To translate an English word into a pig Latin word, place the first letter of the English word (if it is not a vowel) at the end of the English word and add the letters "ay." If the first letter of the English word is a vowel, place it at the end of the word and add "y." Using this method, the word "jump" becomes "umpjay," the word "the" becomes "hetay" and the word "ace" becomes "ceay." Blanks between words remain blanks.*

Assume the following: The English phrase consists of words separated by blanks, there are no punctuation marks and all words have two or more letters. Enable the user to input a sentence. The `TranslateToPigLatin` method translates the sentence into pig Latin, word by word. [*Hint:* You need to use the `Join` and `Split` methods of class `String` demonstrated in Fig. 22.16 to form the pig Latin phrases.]

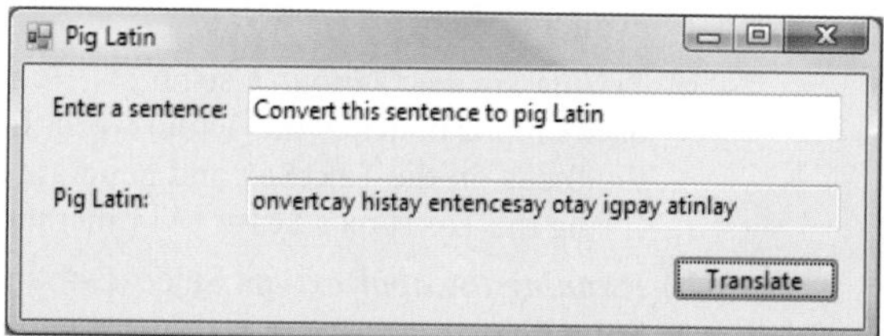

Figure 22.21 **Pig Latin** application.

a) ***Copying the template to your working directory.*** Copy the `C:\Examples\Tutorial22\Exercises\PigLatin` directory to your `C:\SimplyVB2008` directory.

b) ***Opening the application's template file.*** Double click `PigLatin.sln` in the `PigLatin` directory to open the application.

c) ***Splitting the sentence.*** Use method `Split` on the `String` passed to the `TranslateToPigLatin` method. Assign the result of this operation to `words`.

d) ***Retrieving the word's first letter.*** Declare a `For...Next` statement that iterates through your array of words. As you iterate through the array, store each word's first letter in `temporary`.

e) ***Determining the suffix.*** Use an `If...Then...Else` statement to determine whether the first letter is a vowel, then determine the suffix for each word. Store this suffix in `suffix`.

f) ***Generating new words.*** Generate the new words by arranging each word's pieces in the proper order.

g) ***Returning the new sentence.*** When the `For...Next` statement finishes, use method `Join` to combine all of the elements in `words`, and `Return` the new pig Latin sentence.

h) ***Running the application.*** Select **Debug > Start Debugging** to run your application. Enter a sentence and click the **Translate** `Button`. Verify that the sentence is correctly converted into pig Latin.

i) ***Closing the application.*** Close your running application by clicking its close box.

j) ***Closing the IDE.*** Close the Visual Basic IDE by clicking its close box.

Objectives

In this tutorial, you learn to:

- Create, read from, write to and update files.
- Understand a computer's data hierarchy.
- Become familiar with sequential-access file processing.
- Use `StreamReader` and `StreamWriter` classes to read from, and write to, sequential-access files.
- Use the `OpenFileDialog` component.
- Add and configure a `MonthCalendar` control.
- Use LINQ to query a sequential-access file.

Outline

Ticket Information Application

Introducing Sequential-Access Files

You've used variables and arrays to store data temporarily—the data is lost when a method or application terminates. When you want to store data for a longer period of time, you can use files. A **file** is a collection of data that is given a name, such as `data.txt` or `Welcome.sln`. Data in files exists even after the application that created the data terminates—such data is called **persistent data**. Computers store files on **secondary storage media**, including magnetic disks (for example, the hard drive of your computer), optical disks (for instance, CD-ROMs or DVDs), flash drives and magnetic tapes.

File processing—which includes creating, reading from, writing to and updating files—is an important capability of Visual Basic. It enables Visual Basic to support commercial applications that typically process massive amounts of persistent data. In this tutorial, you learn about **sequential-access files**, which contain information that is read from a file in the order in which it was originally written to the file. You learn how to create, open and write to a sequential-access file by building a **Write Event** application. This application allows the user to create or open a **text file** (a file containing human-readable characters) and to input the date, time, price and description of a community event (such as a concert or a sporting match).

You then learn how to read data from a file by building the **Ticket Information** application. This application displays data from a text file named `calendar.txt` created by the **Write Event** application.

23.1 Test-Driving the Ticket Information Application

Many communities and businesses use computer applications to allow their members and customers to view information about upcoming events, such as movies, concerts, sports and other activities. The **Write Event** application that you build in Section 23.4 writes the community-event information to a sequential-access file. The **Ticket Information** application that you build in this tutorial displays the data stored in the file generated by the **Write Event** application. This application must meet the following requirements:

Application Requirements

A local town has asked you to write an application that allows its residents to view community events for the current month. Events taking place in the town include concerts, sporting events, movies and other forms of entertainment. When the user selects a date, the application must indicate whether there are events scheduled for that day. The application must list the scheduled events and allow the user to select one. When the user selects an event, the application must display its time and price and a brief description of the event. The community-event information is stored in a sequential-access file named `calendar.txt`.

Your application allows a user to select a date from a `MonthCalendar` control. Then the application opens the `calendar.txt` file and reads its contents to display information about events scheduled for the selected date. You begin by test-driving the completed application. Then you learn the additional Visual Basic capabilities needed to create your own version of the application.

Test-Driving the Ticket Information Application

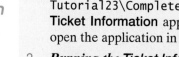

1. ***Opening the completed application.*** Open the directory `C:\Examples\Tutorial23\CompletedApplication\TicketInformation` to locate the **Ticket Information** application. Double click `TicketInformation.sln` to open the application in the Visual Basic IDE.
2. ***Running the Ticket Information application.*** Select **Debug > Start Debugging** to run the application (Fig. 23.1). The calendar reflects the day and month on which you actually run the application. [*Note:* On Windows XP, the `MonthCalendar` control looks somewhat different from the version on Windows Vista in Fig. 23.1.] The `MonthCalendar` control is similar to the `DateTimePicker` control (Tutorial 14), except that a `MonthCalendar` allows you to select a range of dates, whereas the `DateTimePicker` allows you to select the time, but no more than one date. For simplicity, you should select only one date. In addition, the application deals only with the current month, but the `MonthCalendar` control allows the user to view calendars of previous or future months by using the arrow buttons.

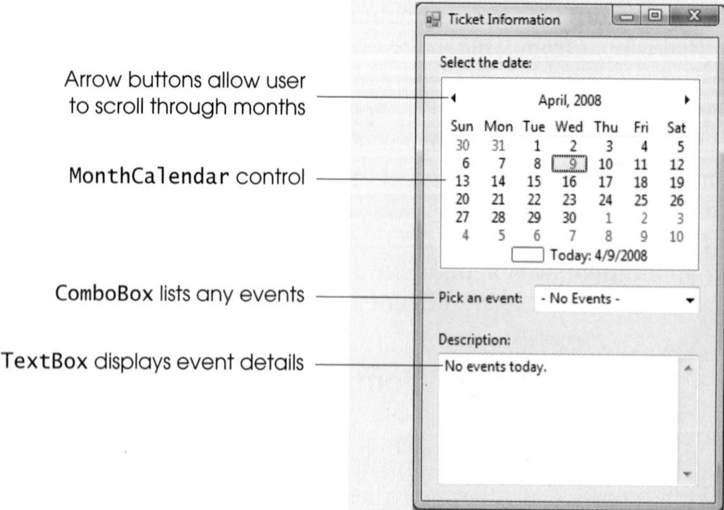

Figure 23.1 **Ticket Information** application's GUI.

(cont.)

3. ***Getting event information.*** Select the 13th day of the current month in the `MonthCalendar`. Note that the `ComboBox` displays `"- No Events -"` (Fig. 23.2). This is because there are no events scheduled for the 13th. Select the 19th day of the month. The `ComboBox` now displays `"- Events -"`. Click the `ComboBox` to view the scheduled events and select **Comedy club**. The time, the price and description of the event appear in the **Description:** `TextBox` (Fig. 23.2).

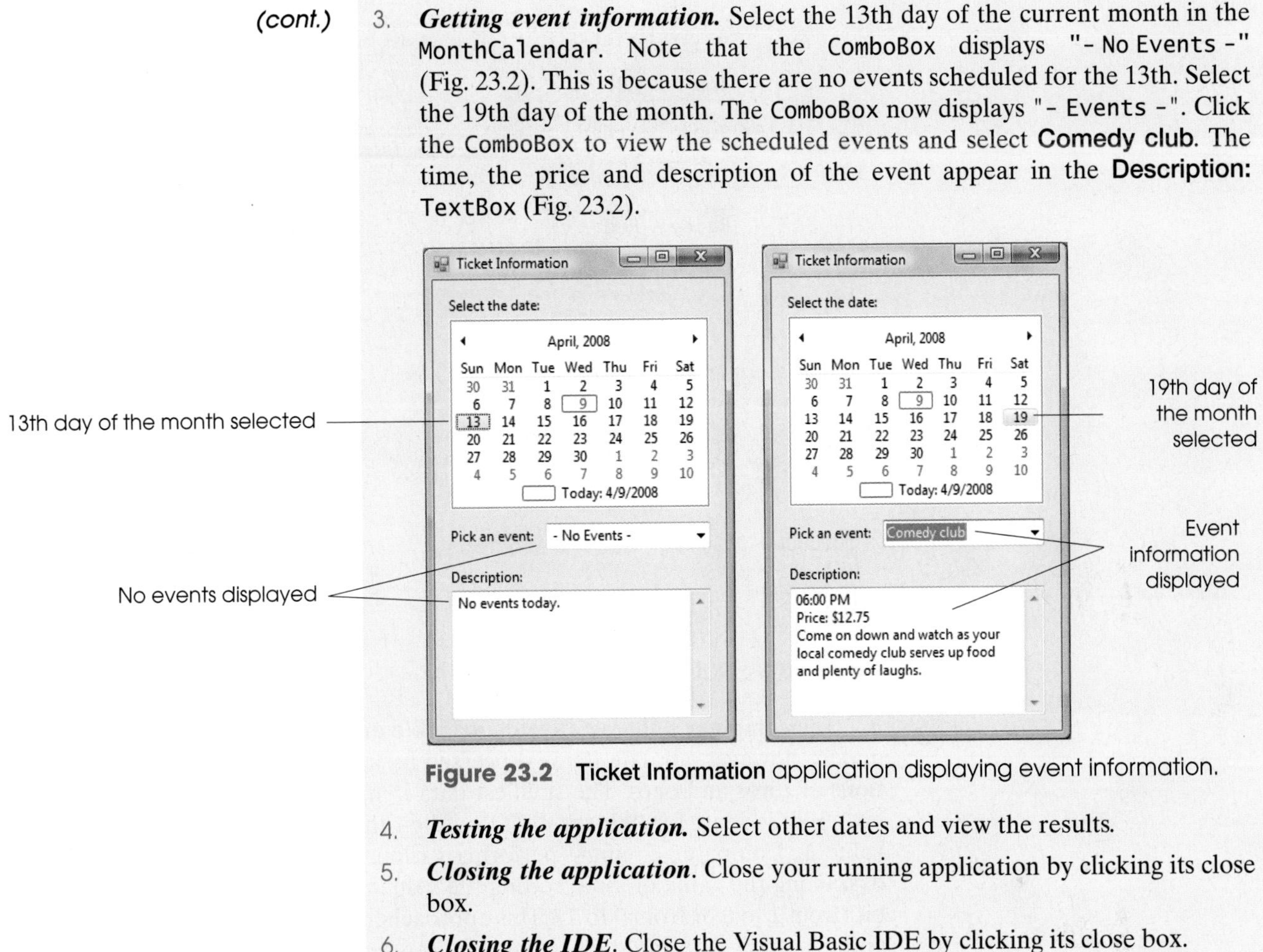

Figure 23.2 Ticket Information application displaying event information.

4. ***Testing the application.*** Select other dates and view the results.
5. ***Closing the application.*** Close your running application by clicking its close box.
6. ***Closing the IDE.*** Close the Visual Basic IDE by clicking its close box.

SELF-REVIEW

1. The _______ control allows a user to select a range of dates.
   a) `DateTimePicker` b) `MonthCalendar`
   c) `ComboBox` d) `TextBox`

2. The `MonthCalendar` control is similar to the _______ control.
   a) `DateTimePicker` b) `ComboBox`
   c) `TextBox` d) `Timer`

Answers: 1) b. 2) a.

23.2 Data Hierarchy

Data items processed by computers form a **data hierarchy** (Fig. 23.3) in which data items become larger and more complex in structure as they progress from bits, to characters, to fields and to larger data structures.

Throughout this book, you've been manipulating data in your applications. The data has been in several forms—**decimal digits** (0, 1, 2, 3, 4, 5, 6, 7, 8 and 9), letters (A–Z and a–z) and **special symbols** ($, @, %, &, *, (,), -, +, ", :, ?, / and many others). Digits, letters and special symbols are referred to as characters. The set of all characters used to write applications and represent data items on a particular computer is called that computer's **character set**.

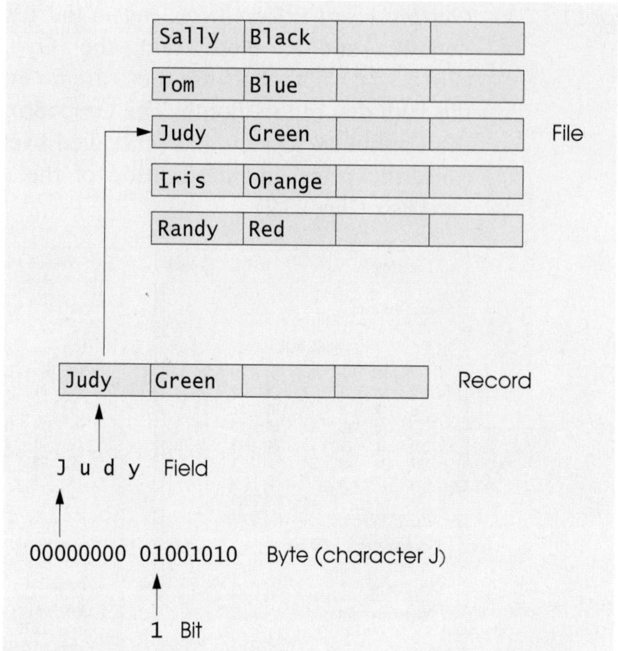

Figure 23.3 Data hierarchy.

The computer's character set is readable and understandable by humans. Ultimately, however, all data items processed by a computer are reduced to combinations of zeros and ones. The smallest data item that computers support is called a **bit**. "Bit" is short for "**binary digit**"—a digit that can hold only the value 0 or the value 1. Computer circuitry performs various simple bit manipulations, such as examining the value of a bit, setting the value of a bit and reversing the value of a bit (from 1 to 0 or from 0 to 1). This approach has been adopted because it is simple and economical to build electronic devices that can assume two stable states—0 representing one state and 1 representing the other. It is remarkable that the extensive functions performed by computers involve only the most fundamental manipulations of 0s and 1s.

Because computers can process only 0s and 1s, every character in a computer's character set is represented as a pattern of 0s and 1s. **Bytes** are composed of eight bits. Characters in Visual Basic are **Unicode** characters, which are composed of two bytes. Programming with data in the low-level form of bits is difficult, so programmers create applications and data items with characters, and computers manipulate and process these characters as patterns of bits.

Just as characters are composed of bits, **fields** are composed of characters. A field is a group of characters that conveys meaning. For example, a field consisting of uppercase and lowercase letters can represent a person's name.

Typically, a **record**, which is usually represented as a `Class` in Visual Basic, is a collection of several related fields (called instance variables in Visual Basic). In a payroll system, for example, a record for a particular employee might include the following fields:

1. Employee identification number
2. Name
3. Address
4. Hourly pay rate
5. Number of exemptions claimed
6. Year-to-date earnings
7. Amount of taxes withheld

Thus, a record is a group of related fields. In the preceding example, each field is associated with the same employee.

A group of related records is stored in a file. A company's payroll file normally contains one record for each employee. Hence, a payroll file for a small company might contain only 22 records, whereas one for a large company might contain 100,000 records. It is not unusual for a company to have many files, some containing millions, billions or even trillions of characters of information.

To facilitate the retrieval of specific records from a file, at least one field in each record is chosen as a record key. A **record key** uniquely identifies a record as belonging to a particular person or entity and distinguishes that record from all other records. Therefore, the record key must be unique. In the payroll record just described, the employee identification number normally would be chosen as the record key, because each employee's identification number is different.

There are many ways to organize records in a file. The most common type of organization is called a sequential-access file, in which records typically are stored in order by a record-key field. In a payroll file, records are sometimes placed in order by employee identification number. The first employee record in the file contains the lowest employee identification number, and subsequent records contain increasingly higher employee identification numbers.

Most businesses use many different files to store data. For example, a company might have payroll files, accounts receivable files (listing money due from clients), accounts payable files (listing money due to suppliers), inventory files (listing facts about all the items handled by the business) and many other types of files. Sometimes a group of related files is called a **database**. A collection of programs designed to create and manage databases is called a **database management system** (DBMS). You learn about databases in Tutorial 24.

SELF-REVIEW

1. The smallest data item a computer can process is called a ________.
   a) database b) byte
   c) file d) bit

2. A group of related records is stored in ________.
   a) file b) field
   c) bit d) byte

Answers: 1) d. 2) a.

23.3 Files and Streams

Common Programming Error

Attempting to open a file from multiple programs at once (or even the same program) is a logic error. A file can be opened by only one program at a time.

Files are viewed as sequential **streams** of bytes (Fig. 23.4). When a file is opened, Visual Basic creates an object and associates a stream with that object. To perform file processing in Visual Basic, you must import the `System.IO` namespace, which includes definitions of stream classes, such as `StreamReader` (for text input from a file) and `StreamWriter` (for text output to a file).

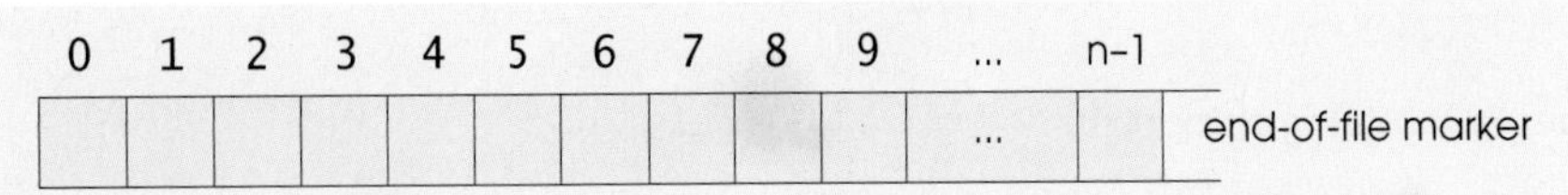

Figure 23.4 Visual Basic's conceptual view of an *n*-byte file.

23.4 Writing to a File—Creating the Write Event Application

An important aspect of the **Ticket Information** application is its ability to read data sequentially from a file. You need to create the file from which the **Ticket Information** application reads its data. Therefore, before you create the **Ticket Information** application, you must learn how to write to a sequential-access file.

The **Write Event** application enables the user to create a new file or open an existing file. The user might want to create a new file for events or update an existing file by adding more event information. You add this functionality in the following box.

Adding a Dialog to Open or Create a File

1. ***Copying the template to your working directory.*** Copy the `C:\Examples\Tutorial23\TemplateApplication\WriteEvent` directory to your `C:\SimplyVB2008` directory.
2. ***Opening the Write Event application's template file.*** Double click `WriteEvent.sln` in the `WriteEvent` directory to open the application in the Visual Basic IDE.
3. ***Adding a dialog to the Form.*** The application uses the `OpenFileDialog` component to customize the **Open** dialog. To add an `OpenFileDialog` to the application, double click the `OpenFileDialog` component

   OpenFileDialog

   in the **All Windows Forms** category of the **Toolbox**. The control's name appears in the component tray at the bottom of the **Design** view. Change the control's `Name` property to `openFileDialog`. Change its `FileName` property to `calendar.txt`, which is the default file name displayed in the **Open** dialog. [*Note:* This is the name of the file from which the **Ticket Information** application retrieves information.] The **Open** dialog normally allows the user to open only existing files, but you also want the user to be able to create a file. For this reason, set property `CheckFileExists` to `False` so that the **Open** dialog allows the user to specify a new file name. If the user specifies a file that does not exist, the file is created and opened. Figure 23.5 shows the application in **Design** view after the `OpenFileDialog` component has been added and renamed.

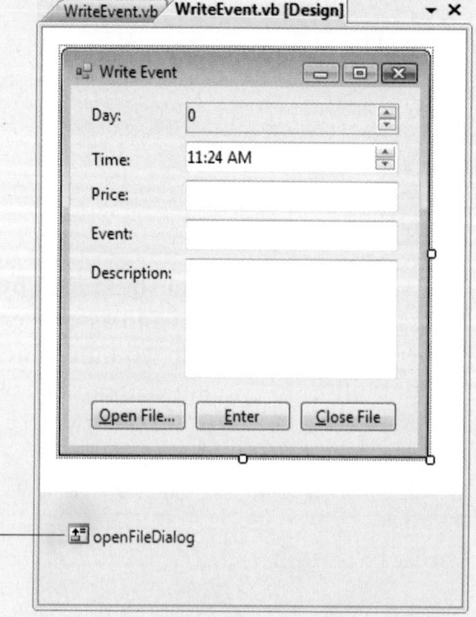

Figure 23.5 `openFileDialog` added and renamed.

4. ***Saving the project.*** Select **File > Save All** to save your modified code.

The **Write Event** application stores the user-input information in a text file. It expects the user to open or create a file with the extension `.txt`. If the user does not do so, the application displays an error message. The following box guides you through adding this functionality.

Determining Whether a File Name Is Valid

1. ***Adding method `CheckValidity`.*** Add lines 3–6 of Fig. 23.6 to the application. Method `CheckValidity` receives a file name as a `String` and returns a `Boolean` value. If the file name is valid, the `Function` returns `True`. Otherwise, the `Function` returns `False`.

`CheckValidity` `Function` procedure header

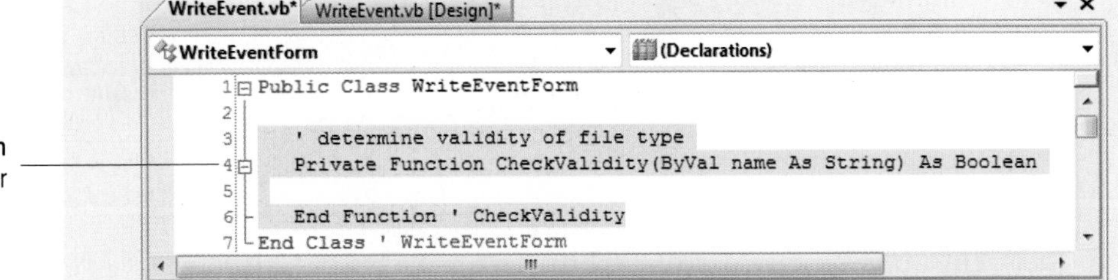

Figure 23.6 Method `CheckValidity` header.

2. ***Displaying a `MessageBox` to indicate an invalid file name.*** Add lines 5–11 of Fig. 23.7 to method `CheckValidity`. `String` method `EndsWith` (line 6) returns `False` if the value of variable `name` does not end with `.txt`, the extension that indicates a text file. In this case, lines 7–9 display a `MessageBox` informing the user that the application expects a text file.

Displaying error message if incorrect file type is provided

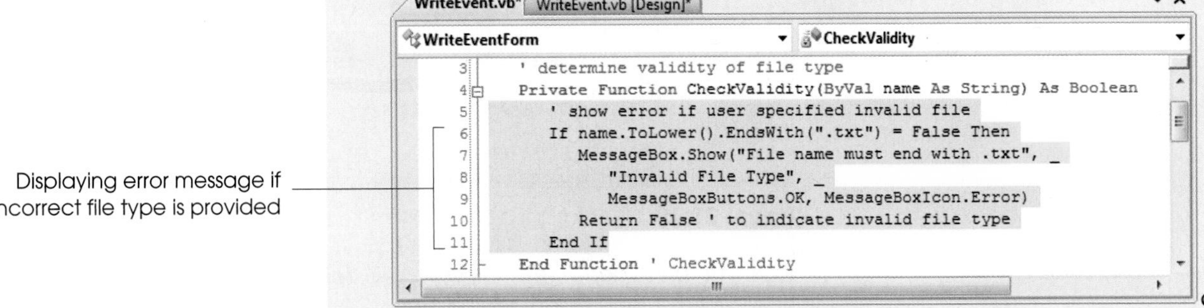

Figure 23.7 Displaying an error message indicating an invalid file name.

3. ***Receiving a valid file name.*** Add lines 11–16 of Fig. 23.8 to the `If...Then` statement. If a valid file name is entered, method `CheckValidity` should return `True`. The GUI should indicate that the user cannot create or open another file, but the user may enter data into the file or close the file. For this reason, line 13 disables the **Open File...** `Button`, while lines 14–15 enable the **Enter** and **Close File** `Buttons`, respectively. The method returns `True` (line 16) to indicate that the user entered a valid file name.

Enabling and disabling `Buttons`

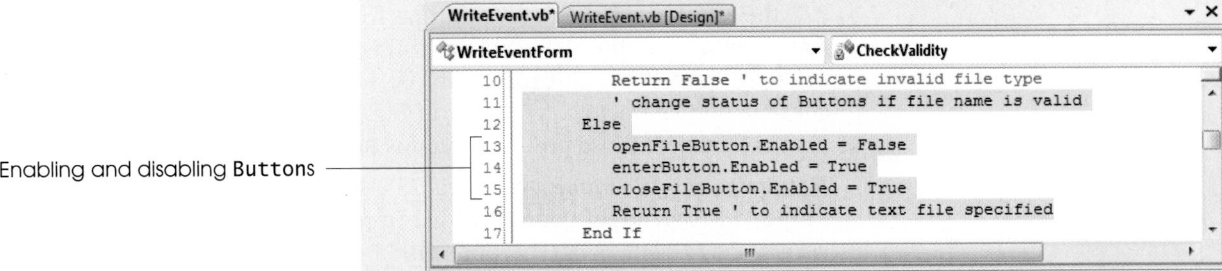

Figure 23.8 Changing the GUI if a valid file name is entered.

4. ***Saving the project.*** Select **File > Save All** to save your modified code.

You've added the `OpenFileDialog` component to allow users to open a file and a method that determines whether the user has entered a valid file name. Now you add code that associates the specified file with a stream.

Creating a `StreamWriter` Object

1. ***Importing namespace `System.IO` to enable file processing.*** To access the classes that enable you to perform file processing with sequential-access files without preceding each class name with "`System.`", add line 1 of Fig. 23.9 to import namespace `System.IO`.

Importing namespace `System.IO`

```
WriteEvent.vb | WriteEvent.vb [Design]
(General)                (Declarations)
1  Imports System.IO
2
3  Public Class WriteEventForm
```

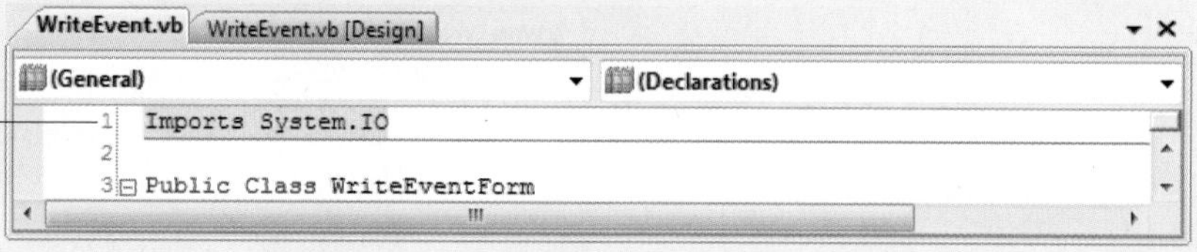

Figure 23.9 `System.IO` namespace imported into class `WriteEventForm`.

2. ***Declaring a `StreamWriter` variable.*** Namespace `System.IO` includes class `StreamWriter`, which is used to create objects for writing text to a file. You use a `StreamWriter` to write data into the file created or opened by the user. Add line 5 of Fig. 23.10 to the `WriteEventForm` class definition to declare the variable that holds a `StreamWriter` object.

Declaring `StreamWriter` variable

```
WriteEvent.vb* | WriteEvent.vb [Design]*
WriteEventForm           (Declarations)
1  Imports System.IO
2
3  Public Class WriteEventForm
4
5     Private output As StreamWriter
6
7     ' determine validity of file type
```

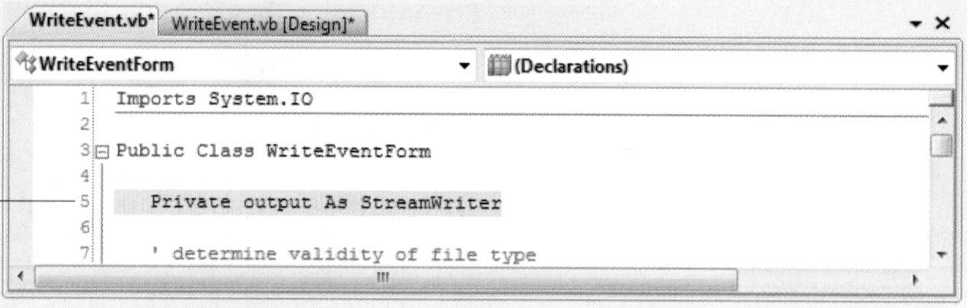

Figure 23.10 Declaring a `StreamWriter` variable.

3. ***Creating the Open File... `Button`'s `Click` event handler.*** Switch to **Design** view and double click the **Open File...** `Button` on the **Write Event** application's `Form` to create the empty `openFileButton_Click` event handler.

4. ***Displaying the Open dialog.*** Add lines 28–34 of Fig. 23.11 to the event handler. When the user clicks the **Open File...** `Button`, the **`ShowDialog`** method of the `OpenFileDialog` component displays the **Open** dialog to allow the user to open a file (line 29) and returns a value of type `DialogResult`. If the user specifies a file that does not exist, it is created. Line 29 assigns the return value of method `ShowDialog` to a `DialogResult` variable named `result`. The value of the `DialogResult` variable specifies what `Button` the user clicked in the **Open** dialog. If the user clicked the **Cancel** `Button` (line 32), the event handler exits without performing the actions in the `If...Then` statement. At this point, the user can still open or create a file by clicking the enabled **Open File...** `Button` again. Be sure to add the comments and line-continuation characters, as shown in Fig. 23.11, so that the line numbers in your code match those presented in this tutorial.

5. ***Retrieving the file name.*** Add lines 33–34 of Fig. 23.12 to the `If` statement. Property `FileName` of `OpenFileDialog` specifies the full path of the file the user selected (line 34). The application stores the path and file name in `fileName`.

(cont.)

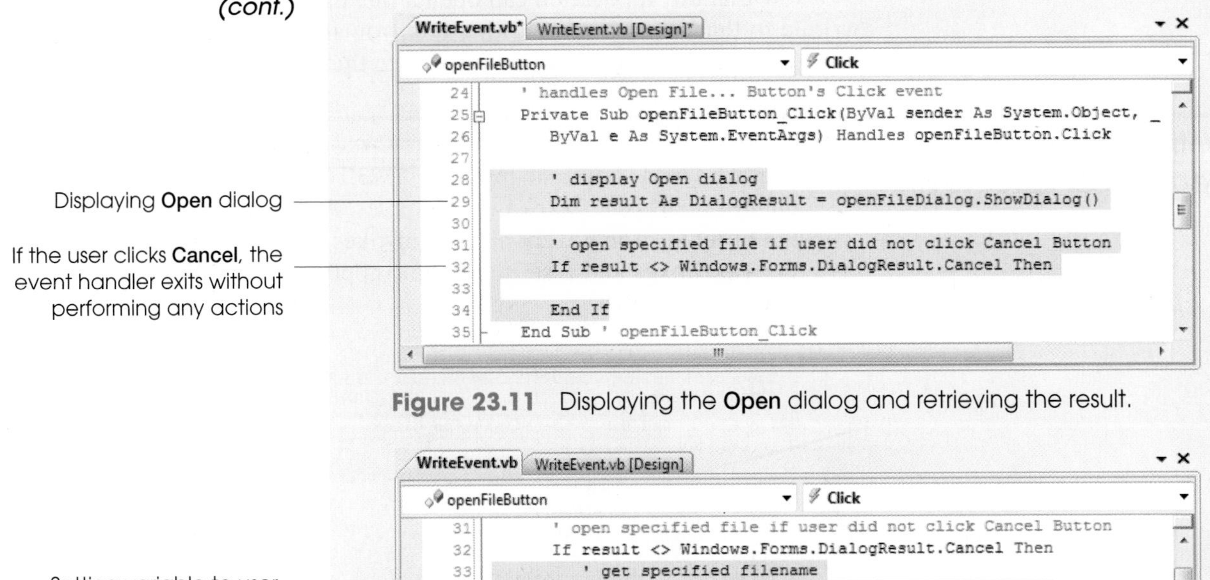

Figure 23.11 Displaying the **Open** dialog and retrieving the result.

Figure 23.12 Retrieving the name and path of selected file.

6. ***Checking for a valid file type.*** Add lines 36–40 of Fig. 23.13 to the event handler. Line 37 invokes method `CheckValidity` (which you defined earlier in this tutorial) to determine whether the specified file is a text file (that is, the file name ends with `".txt"`).

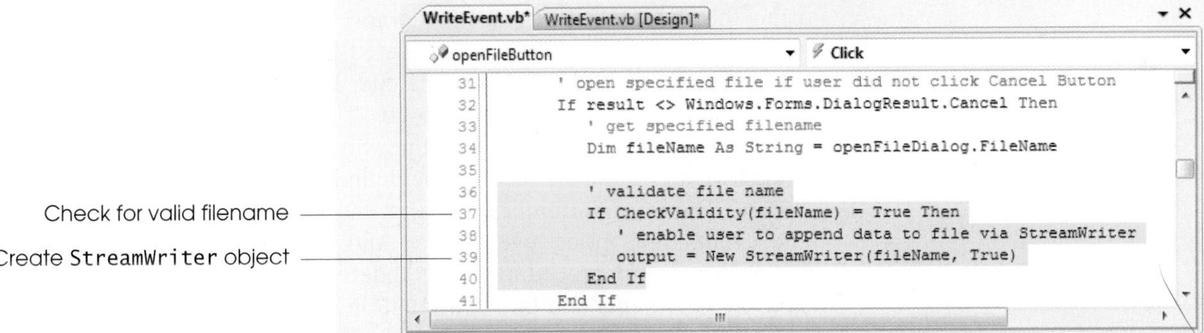

Figure 23.13 Validating the filename and initializing a `StreamWriter` object.

7. ***Initializing a `StreamWriter` object.*** Line 39 initializes `StreamWriter` object `output`, which is used to write to the file specified by the user. Note that the `StreamWriter` constructor takes two arguments. The first indicates the name of the file (specified by variable `fileName`) to which you write information. The second is a `Boolean` value that determines whether the `StreamWriter` appends information to the end of the file. You pass value `True`, so that any information written to the file is appended to the end of the file if the file already exists. If you pass value `False`, any existing content is deleted and replaced.

8. ***Saving the project.*** Select **File > Save All** to save your modified code.

Common Programming Error

When you open an existing file by invoking the `StreamWriter` constructor with a `False` second argument, data previously contained in the file is lost.

Now that the application can open a file, the user can input information that is written to that file. In the following box, you add code that makes the **Enter** Button's Click event handler write the data to the text file.

Writing Information to a Sequential-Access File

1. ***Clearing user input from the TextBoxes and resetting the NumericUpDown control.*** Add lines 44–50 of Fig. 23.14 to the application below the openFileButton_Click event handler. After the user's input is processed, the **Enter** Button's event handler invokes method ClearUserInput to clear the TextBoxes and reset the NumericUpDown control's value to 1 (the first day of the month).

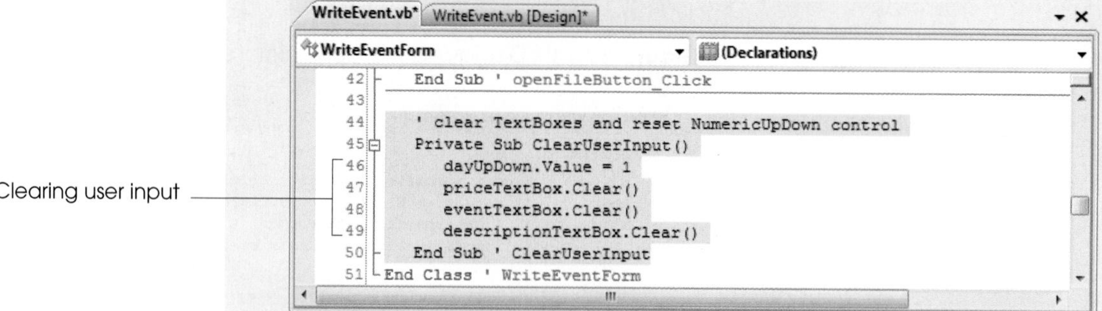
WriteEvent.vb*
WriteEvent.vb [Design]*
WriteEventForm
(Declarations)
42 End Sub ' openFileButton_Click
43
44 ' clear TextBoxes and reset NumericUpDown control
45 Private Sub ClearUserInput()
46 dayUpDown.Value = 1
47 priceTextBox.Clear()
48 eventTextBox.Clear()
49 descriptionTextBox.Clear()
50 End Sub ' ClearUserInput
51 End Class ' WriteEventForm
Clearing user input

Figure 23.14 Clearing user input.

2. ***Creating the enterButton_Click event handler.*** In **Design** view, double click the **Enter** Button to create the enterButton_Click event handler.

3. ***Defining the enterButton_Click event handler.*** Add lines 56–62 of Fig. 23.15 to the event handler. Lines 57–60 write the user input to the file by using the StreamWriter's **Write** method. The Write method writes its argument to the file. Each field is separated by a *Tab* character—this makes it easier to extract the data from the file. Line 61 writes the last field using StreamWriter's **WriteLine** method. The WriteLine method writes its argument to the file, followed by a newline character. Each record in the file ends with a newline character—the delimiter we chose to mark the end of a record. The information is written to the file in the following order: day of the event, time, price, event name and description. Line 62 invokes the ClearUserInput procedure that you defined in *Step 1* of this box. Be sure to add the comments and line-continuation characters, as shown in Fig. 23.15, so that the line numbers in your code match those presented in this tutorial.

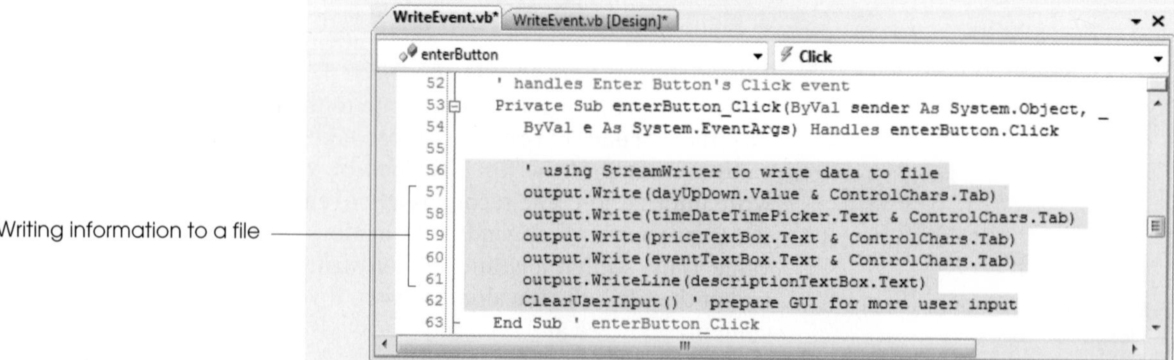
WriteEvent.vb*
WriteEvent.vb [Design]*
enterButton
Click
52 ' handles Enter Button's Click event
53 Private Sub enterButton_Click(ByVal sender As System.Object, _
54 ByVal e As System.EventArgs) Handles enterButton.Click
55
56 ' using StreamWriter to write data to file
57 output.Write(dayUpDown.Value & ControlChars.Tab)
58 output.Write(timeDateTimePicker.Text & ControlChars.Tab)
59 output.Write(priceTextBox.Text & ControlChars.Tab)
60 output.Write(eventTextBox.Text & ControlChars.Tab)
61 output.WriteLine(descriptionTextBox.Text)
62 ClearUserInput() ' prepare GUI for more user input
63 End Sub ' enterButton_Click
Writing information to a file

Figure 23.15 StreamWriter writing to a file.

4. ***Saving the project.*** Select **File > Save All** to save your modified code.

You should always close the file after you've finished processing it to ensure that you don't lose any data. You add this capability to the **Close File** `Button`'s `Click` event handler in the following box.

Closing the `StreamWriter`

1. ***Create the `closeFileButton_Click` event handler.*** In **Design** view, double click the **Close File** `Button` of the **Write Event** application's `Form`. The `closeFileButton_Click` event handler appears in the `WriteEvent.vb` file.

2. ***Defining the `closeFileButton_Click` event handler.*** Add lines 69–74 of Fig. 23.16 to the event handler. Line 69 uses the `StreamWriter`'s `Close` method to close the stream. Line 72 re-enables the **Open File...** `Button` in case the user would like to create or update another sequential-access file. Lines 73–74 disable the **Enter** and **Close File** `Buttons`, because users should not be able to click these `Buttons` when a file is not open.

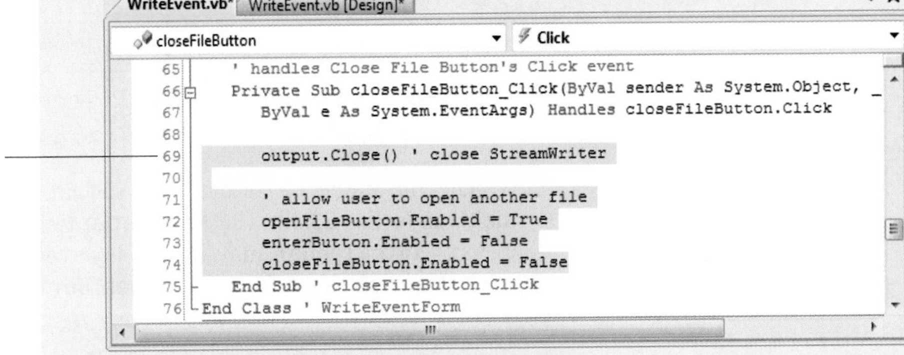

WriteEvent.vb*
WriteEvent.vb [Design]*
closeFileButton
Click
65 ' handles Close File Button's Click event
66 Private Sub closeFileButton_Click(ByVal sender As System.Object, _
67 ByVal e As System.EventArgs) Handles closeFileButton.Click
68
69 output.Close() ' close StreamWriter
70
71 ' allow user to open another file
72 openFileButton.Enabled = True
73 enterButton.Enabled = False
74 closeFileButton.Enabled = False
75 End Sub ' closeFileButton_Click
76 End Class ' WriteEventForm
Closing StreamWriter object

Figure 23.16 Closing the `StreamWriter`.

3. ***Saving the project.*** Select **File > Save All** to save your modified code.

You have now successfully created the **Write Event** application. You test this application to see how it works and view the file contents in the following box.

Writing Event Information to a File

1. ***Running the Write Event application.*** Select **Debug > Start Debugging** to run your application (Fig. 23.17).

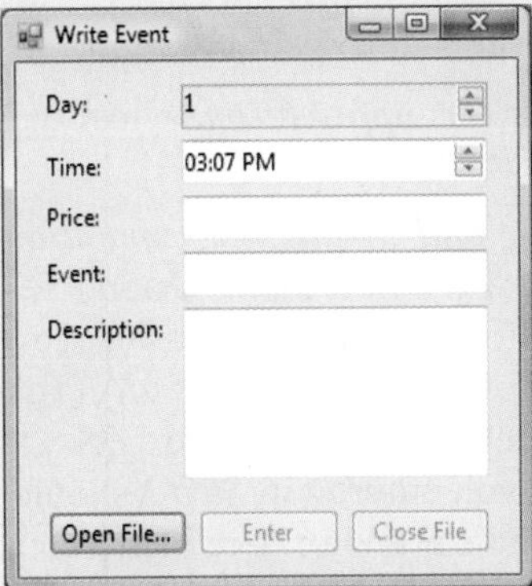

Figure 23.17 **Write Event** application running.

2. ***Creating a file.*** Click the **Open File...** `Button` to display the **Open** dialog. To open the existing `calendar.txt` file, brows to `C:\Examples\Tutorial-23_TicketInfo\TemplateApplication\TicketInformation\TicketInformation\bin\Debug` (Fig. 23.18).

(cont.)

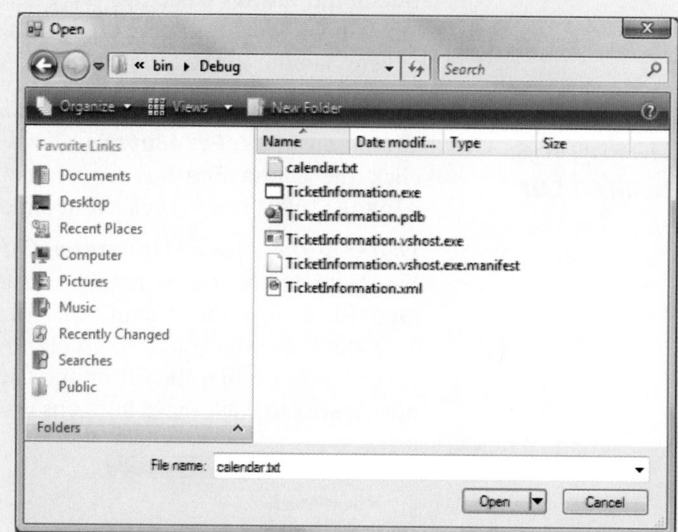

Figure 23.18 **Open** dialog displaying contents of the template **Ticket Information** application's `Debug` folder.

The file name `calendar.txt` should be displayed in the **File name:** field, as in Fig. 23.18. The **File name:** field may not display the extension (`.txt`), or `calendar` may be displayed with a capital "`C`" based on your computer's settings. Click the **Open** `Button` to open the existing `calendar.txt` file.

3. ***Inputting event information.*** In the **Day:** `NumericUpDown` control, select `4` to indicate that the event is scheduled on the fourth day of the month. Enter `2:30 PM` in the **Time:** `DateTimePicker`. Type `12.50` in the **Price:** `TextBox`. Enter `Arts and Crafts Fair` in the **Event:** `TextBox`. In the **Description:** `TextBox`, enter the information `Take part in creating various types of arts and crafts at this fair`. Click the **Enter** `Button` to add this event's information to the `calendar.txt` file.

4. ***Inputting more event information.*** Write more event information to the file by repeating *Step 3* with your own set of events.

5. ***Closing the file.*** When you have entered all the events you wish, click the **Close File** `Button`. This closes the `calendar.txt` file and prevents any more events from being written.

6. ***Closing the application.*** Close your running application by clicking its close box.

7. ***Opening and closing the sequential-access file.*** Use the IDE to open `calendar.txt`. Select **File > Open File...** to display the **Open** dialog. Navigate to the folder `C:\Examples\Tutorial23_TicketInfo\TemplateApplication\TicketInformation\TicketInformation\bin\Debug`, select the `calendar.txt` file and click **Open**. Scroll through the file. The information you entered in *Step* 3 should appear in the file, similar to Fig. 23.19. Close the `calendar.txt` file.

Day and time of event, ticket price, event name and description

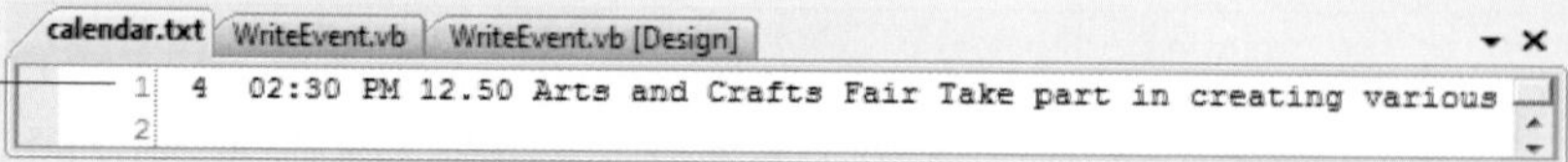

Figure 23.19 Sequential-access file generated by **Write Event** application.

8. ***Closing the IDE.*** Close the Visual Basic IDE by clicking its close box.

Figure 23.20 presents the source code for the **Write Event** application. The lines of code that contain new programming concepts you've learned so far in this tutorial are highlighted.

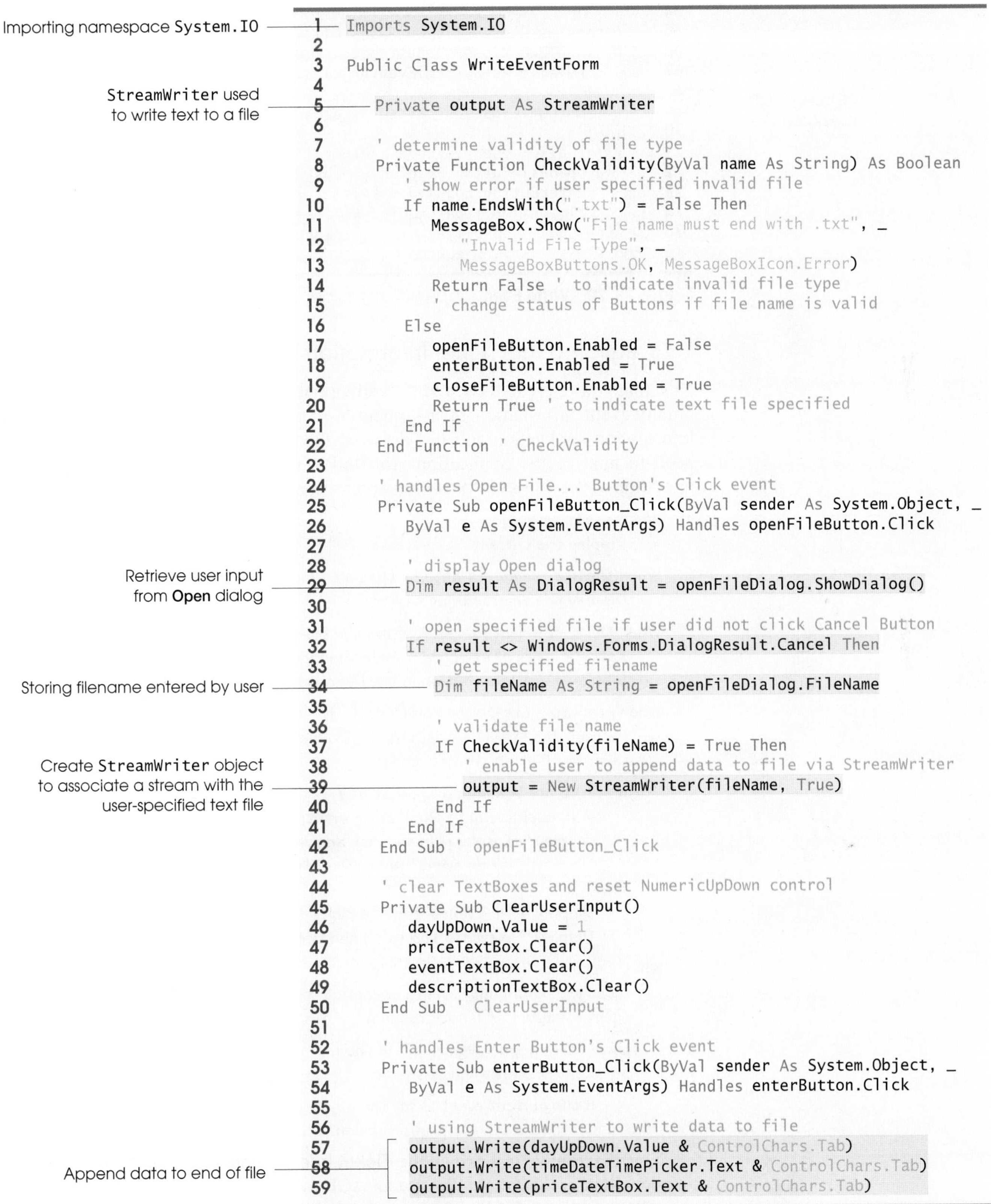
Importing namespace System.IO
StreamWriter used to write text to a file
Retrieve user input from Open dialog
Storing filename entered by user
Create StreamWriter object to associate a stream with the user-specified text file
Append data to end of file

```
Imports System.IO

Public Class WriteEventForm

   Private output As StreamWriter

   ' determine validity of file type
   Private Function CheckValidity(ByVal name As String) As Boolean
      ' show error if user specified invalid file
      If name.EndsWith(".txt") = False Then
         MessageBox.Show("File name must end with .txt", _
            "Invalid File Type", _
            MessageBoxButtons.OK, MessageBoxIcon.Error)
         Return False ' to indicate invalid file type
         ' change status of Buttons if file name is valid
      Else
         openFileButton.Enabled = False
         enterButton.Enabled = True
         closeFileButton.Enabled = True
         Return True ' to indicate text file specified
      End If
   End Function ' CheckValidity

   ' handles Open File... Button's Click event
   Private Sub openFileButton_Click(ByVal sender As System.Object, _
      ByVal e As System.EventArgs) Handles openFileButton.Click

      ' display Open dialog
      Dim result As DialogResult = openFileDialog.ShowDialog()

      ' open specified file if user did not click Cancel Button
      If result <> Windows.Forms.DialogResult.Cancel Then
         ' get specified filename
         Dim fileName As String = openFileDialog.FileName

         ' validate file name
         If CheckValidity(fileName) = True Then
            ' enable user to append data to file via StreamWriter
            output = New StreamWriter(fileName, True)
         End If
      End If
   End Sub ' openFileButton_Click

   ' clear TextBoxes and reset NumericUpDown control
   Private Sub ClearUserInput()
      dayUpDown.Value = 1
      priceTextBox.Clear()
      eventTextBox.Clear()
      descriptionTextBox.Clear()
   End Sub ' ClearUserInput

   ' handles Enter Button's Click event
   Private Sub enterButton_Click(ByVal sender As System.Object, _
      ByVal e As System.EventArgs) Handles enterButton.Click

      ' using StreamWriter to write data to file
      output.Write(dayUpDown.Value & ControlChars.Tab)
      output.Write(timeDateTimePicker.Text & ControlChars.Tab)
      output.Write(priceTextBox.Text & ControlChars.Tab)
```

Figure 23.20 **Write Event** application's code. (Part 1 of 2.)

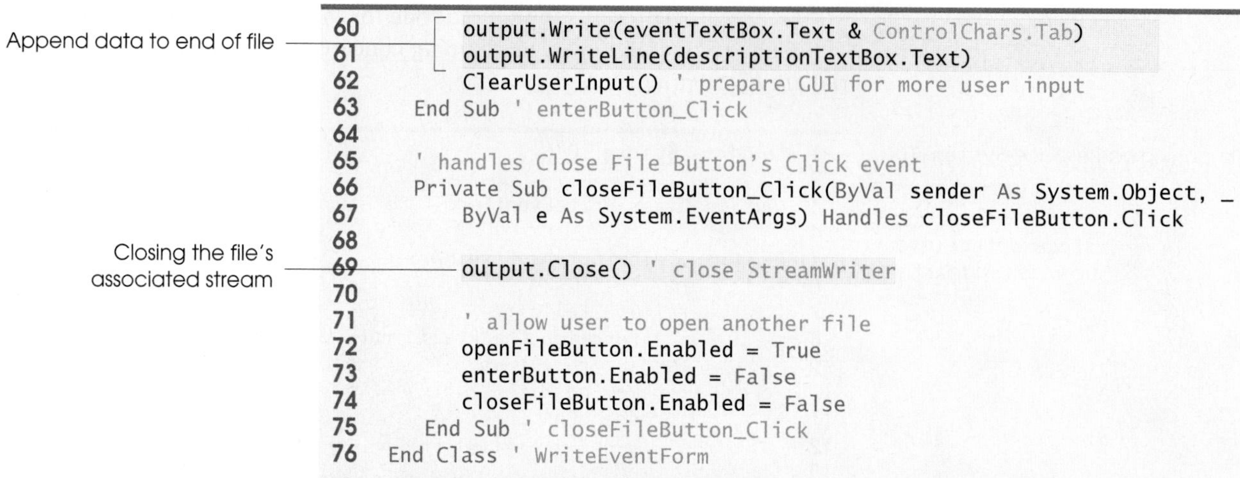
Append data to end of file
Closing the file's associated stream

```
         output.Write(eventTextBox.Text & ControlChars.Tab)
         output.WriteLine(descriptionTextBox.Text)
         ClearUserInput() ' prepare GUI for more user input
     End Sub ' enterButton_Click

     ' handles Close File Button's Click event
     Private Sub closeFileButton_Click(ByVal sender As System.Object, _
         ByVal e As System.EventArgs) Handles closeFileButton.Click

         output.Close() ' close StreamWriter

         ' allow user to open another file
         openFileButton.Enabled = True
         enterButton.Enabled = False
         closeFileButton.Enabled = False
     End Sub ' closeFileButton_Click
End Class ' WriteEventForm
```

Figure 23.20 **Write Event** application's code. (Part 2 of 2.)

23.5 Building the Ticket Information Application

Now that you've created the **Write Event** application to enable a user to write community-event information to a sequential-access text file, you create the **Ticket Information** application you test-drove at the beginning of the tutorial. First you need to analyze the application. The following pseudocode describes the basic operation of the **Ticket Information** application:

```
When the Form loads:
    Display the current day's events

When the user selects a date on the calendar:
    Display the selected day's events

When the user selects an event from the Pick an event: ComboBox:
    Retrieve index of selected item in the Pick an event: ComboBox
    Display event information in the Description: TextBox

When procedure CreateEventList is called:
    Extract data for the selected day from calendar.txt
    Clear the Pick an event: ComboBox

    If events are scheduled for that day
        Add each event to the Pick an event: ComboBox
        Display "- Events -" in the Pick an event: ComboBox
        Display "Pick an event." in the Description: TextBox
    Else
        Display "- No Events -" in the Pick an event: ComboBox
        Display "No events today." in the Description: TextBox

When procedure ExtractData is called:
    Clear the community events collection
    Open calendar.txt file for reading

    Until there are no events left in the file
        Read the next line of the file

        If the current event is for the day selected by the user
            Store the event information
```

Now that you've test-driven the **Ticket Information** application and studied its pseudocode representation, you use an ACE table to help you convert the pseudocode to Visual Basic. Figure 23.21 lists the actions, controls and events that help you complete your own version of this application.

Action/Control/Event (ACE) Table for the Ticket Information Application

Action	Control	Event/Method
Label the application's controls	dateLabel, eventLabel, description-Label	Application is run
	TicketInfor-mationForm	Load
Display the current day's events	eventComboBox	
	dateMonth-Calendar	DateChanged
Display the selected day's events	eventComboBox, description-TextBox	
	eventComboBox	Selected-IndexChanged
Retrieve index of selected item in the Pick an event: ComboBox	eventComboBox	
Display event information in the Description: TextBox	description-TextBox	
		Create-EventList
Extract data for the selected day from calendar.txt	dateMonth-Calendar	
Clear the Pick an event: ComboBox	eventComboBox	
If events are scheduled for that day Add each event to the Pick an event: ComboBox	eventComboBox, community-Events	
Display "- Events -" in the Pick an event: ComboBox	eventComboBox	
Display "Pick an event." in the Description: TextBox	description-TextBox	
Else Display "- No Events -" in the Pick an event: ComboBox	eventComboBox	
Display "No events today." in the Description: TextBox	description-TextBox	
		ExtractData
Clear the community events collection	community-Events	
Open calendar.txt file for reading	input	
Until there are no events left in the file	input	
Read the next line of the file	input	
If the current event is for the day selected by the user Store the event information	community-Events	

Figure 23.21 ACE table for the **Ticket Information** application.

The **Ticket Information** application allows the user to view the information for a specific date by selecting the date from a `MonthCalendar` control. The following box guides you through configuring the `MonthCalendar` control.

Adding a `MonthCalendar` Control

1. ***Copying the template to your working directory.*** Copy the `C:\Examples\Tutorial23\TemplateApplication\TicketInformation` directory to your `C:\SimplyVB2008` directory.
2. ***Opening the* Ticket Information *template application.*** Double click `TicketInformation.sln` in the `TicketInformation` directory to open the application in the Visual Basic IDE and view the template's `Form`. The template also provides the empty methods `CreateEventList` and `ExtractData`. You add code to these methods later.
3. ***Adding a `MonthCalendar` control to the `Form`.*** Double click the `MonthCalendar` control

   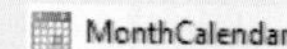

   in the **All Windows Forms** group of the **Toolbox**. The **Properties** window displays the control's properties. Change the `Name` property to `dateMonthCalendar`. Position the `MonthCalendar` control as in Fig. 23.22.

   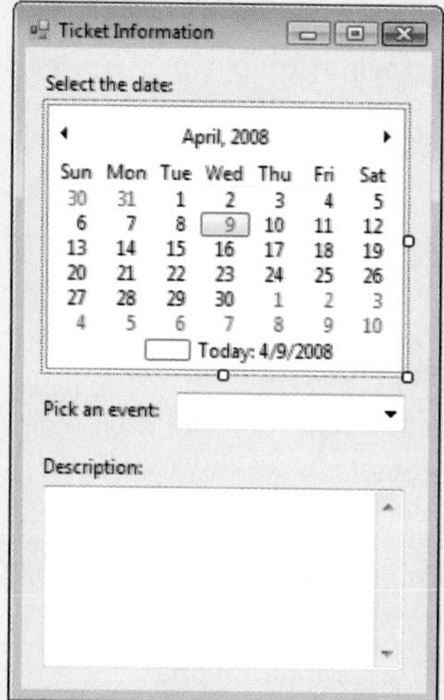

   Figure 23.22 `Ticket Information` template application's `Form`.

4. ***Saving the project.*** Select **File > Save All** to save your modified code.

Good Programming Practice

Append the `MonthCalendar` suffix to `MonthCalendar` control names.

Now that you've added the `MonthCalendar` control, you can begin writing code for the **Ticket Information** application. For this application, you define two `Sub` procedures named `CreateEventList` and `ExtractData`. Before adding any functionality to the application, you import `System.IO` and create an instance variable in the next box.

Beginning to Build the Ticket Information Application

1. ***Importing namespace `System.IO`.*** Switch to **Code** view. Add line 1 of Fig. 23.23 before the class definition to import namespace `System.IO`, which allows the application to use class `StreamReader` to read information from a sequential-access file.

   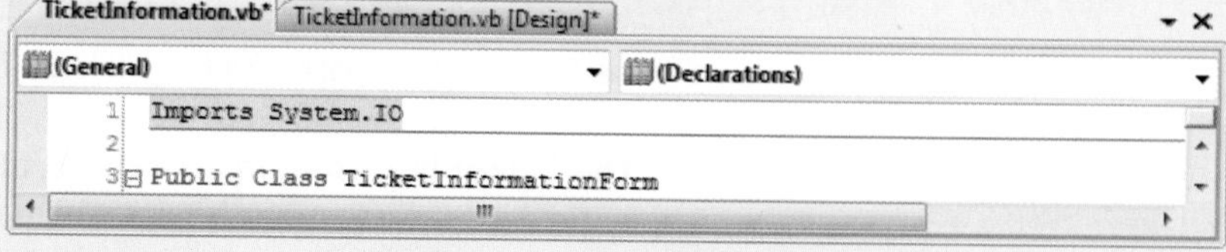

   Figure 23.23 Importing the `System.IO` namespace.

(cont.)

2. ***Adding a*** `List` ***of*** `CommunityEvents`***.*** Add lines 5–7 of Fig. 23.24 to the application. To keep track of information, you store the event information read from the file in `List(Of CommunityEvent) communityEvents` (lines 6–7). Note that the type `CommunityEvent` is underlined, indicating a compilation error—the type is undefined. We provided this class for you with the template application. In the **Solution Explorer**, right click the **TicketInformation** project. Select **Add > Existing Item...** from the context menu that appears. When the **Add Existing Item** dialog appears, select the `CommunityEvent.vb` file and click **Add**. The `CommunityEvent` class stores the information about an event. The class includes properties `Day`, `Time`, `Price`, `Name` and `Description`. You can view the code for the `CommunityEvent` class by double clicking the `CommunityEvent.vb` file in the **Solution Explorer**.

Creating a `List` of `CommunityEvents`

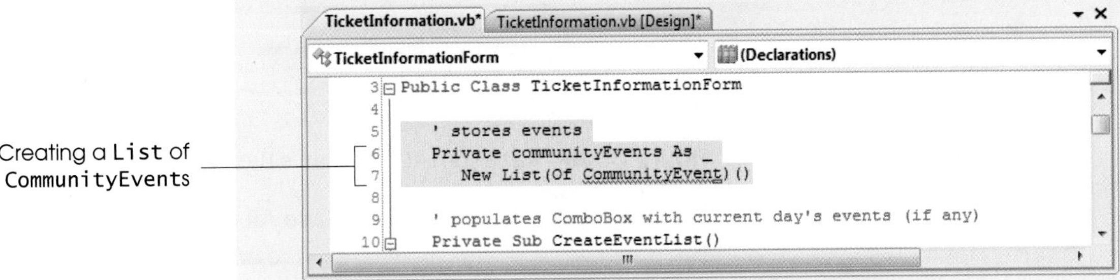

Figure 23.24 `List` declared to hold event information.

3. ***Saving the project.*** Select **File > Save All** to save your modified code.

When you run the **Ticket Information** application, by default, the current day is selected in the `MonthCalendar` control. The application shows the list of the day's events in the `ComboBox`. Recall that, if there are no events for the day, the `ComboBox` displays `"- No Events -"`. In the following box, you invoke a method from the `Form`'s `Load` event handler to set the display in the `ComboBox` appropriately.

Handling the Form's Load Event

1. ***Defining the Form's Load event.*** Double click the `Form` in **Design** view to generate event handler `TicketInformationForm_Load`. Add lines 24–25 of Fig. 23.25 to the event handler. Line 25 invokes the `CreateEventList` method. You'll soon add code to `CreateEventList` to populate the `ComboBox` with any events scheduled for the current day.

You add code to the `CreateEventList` procedure later

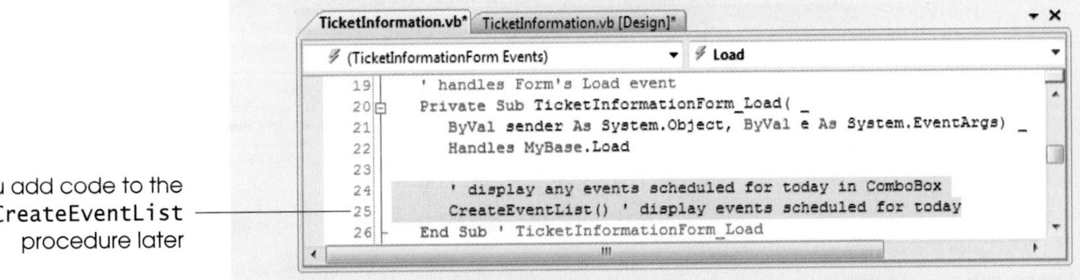

Figure 23.25 `Load` event handler calling method `CreateEventList`.

2. ***Saving the project.*** Select **File > Save All** to save your modified code.

When the user selects a date in the `MonthCalendar` control, the `DateChanged` event is raised. You add code to the event handler to invoke the `CreateEventList` method in the following box.

Handling the MonthCalendar's DateChanged Event

1. ***Creating the MonthCalendar's DateChanged event handler.*** In **Design** view, double click the MonthCalendar to generate the empty event handler dateMonthCalendar_DateChanged.
2. ***Invoking the CreateEventList method.*** Add lines 34–35 of Fig. 23.26 to the dateMonthCalendar_DateChanged event handler. Line 35 invokes method CreateEventList, which you define in the next box.

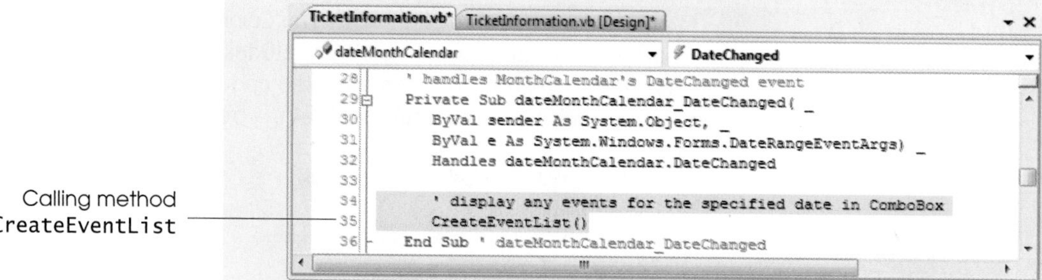

Figure 23.26 dateMonthCalendar's DateChanged event handler.

3. ***Saving the project.*** Select **File > Save All** to save your modified code.

The application invokes method CreateEventList from the Form's Load event and dateMonthCalendar's DateChanged event. The CreateEventList method populates the ComboBox with event names if there are any events for the day the user chooses—otherwise, it indicates that the event list is empty. You define this functionality in the following box.

Defining the CreateEventList Method

1. ***Setting variables and clearing the ComboBox in the CreateEventList method.*** Add lines 12–18 of Fig. 23.27 to the CreateEventList method. The CreateEventList method first declares a control variable, currentEvent (line 12), that is used to iterate through the events. Line 15 invokes the ExtractData method (which you define in the next box), passing the Date that is currently selected in the MonthCalendar. The ExtractData method stores event information in the List communityEvents that was created at lines 6–7. The date is specified by the MonthCalendar control's **SelectionStart** property. The MonthCalendar control allows you to select a range of dates. SelectionStart is the first date in the range selected. The Clear method of the ComboBox's Items property removes any events currently displayed in the ComboBox (line 18).

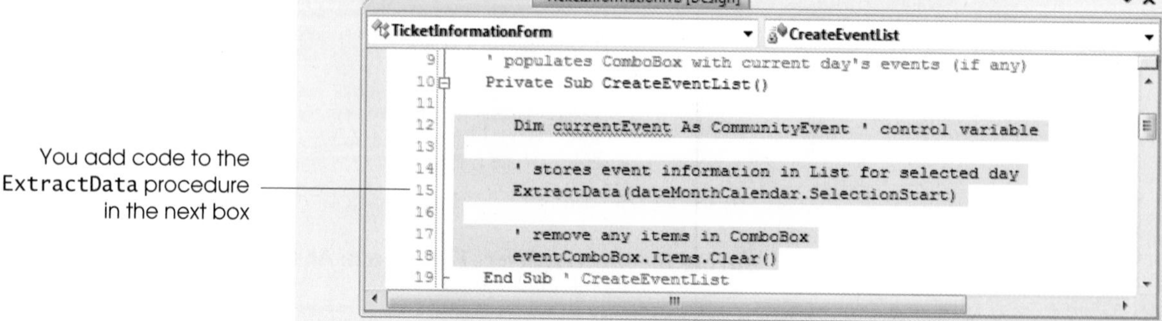

Figure 23.27 CreateEventList calls method ExtractData and clears the ComboBox.

(cont.)

2. ***Setting events displayed in the ComboBox.*** Add lines 20–34 of Fig. 23.28 to the `CreateEventList` method. If there are events scheduled for the chosen day (i.e., `Count` is greater than 0; line 21), then the `For Each...Next` statement (lines 22–25) iterates through `List communityEvents` and adds the name of each event to the `ComboBox`. The `CreateEventList` method informs the user that there are events scheduled for the specified day by using the `Text` properties of the `ComboBox` and `TextBox` (lines 28–29). If there are events for the chosen day, then the `ComboBox` displays `"- Events -"` and the `Textbox` displays `"Pick an event."`—otherwise, the `ComboBox` displays `"- No events -"` and the `Textbox` displays `"No events today."` (lines 32–33).

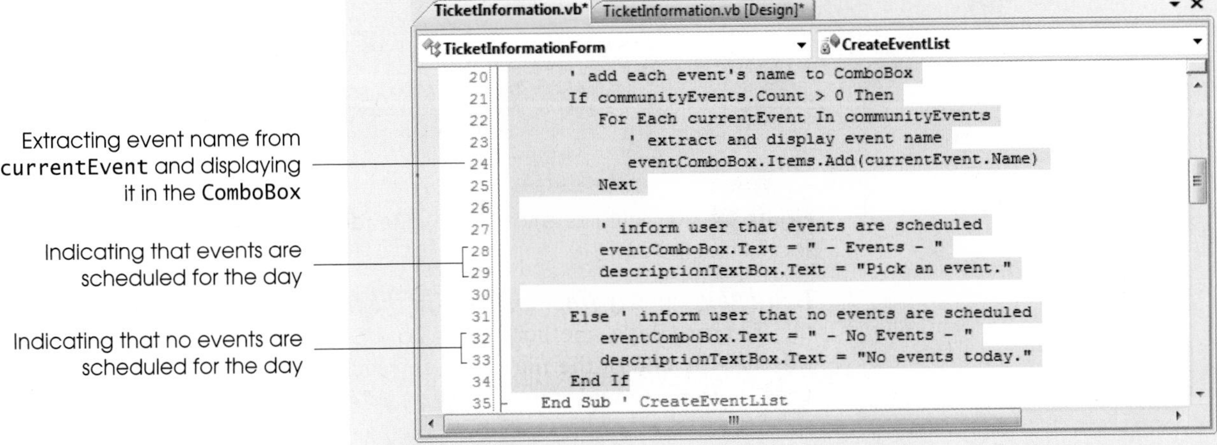

Figure 23.28 Displaying the events scheduled for the specified day.

3. ***Saving the project.*** Select **File > Save All** to save your modified code.

As described in *Step 1* of the previous box, the `ExtractData` method uses a variable of type `Date` (`currentDate`) as its only parameter. The `ExtractData` method creates `CommunityEvent` objects from the information in `calendar.txt` and adds the `CommunityEvents` to the `List`. You define the `ExtractData` method in the following box.

Reading a Sequential-Access File

1. ***Adding variables to the ExtractData method.*** Add lines 39–44 of Fig. 23.29 to the `ExtractData` method. The `Date` selected in the `MonthCalendar` control is passed to the `ExtractData` method as the parameter `currentDate`. Line 40 assigns to `chosenDay` the selected day returned by the `Day` property of the `currentDate` parameter. The `eventInfo` variable (line 41) is an array of `Strings` used to store the event information retrieved from the file. The `fileDay` variable (line 42) stores the day of the event read from the file. Line 44 calls `List` method `Clear` to clear the `List` of `CommunityEvents`.

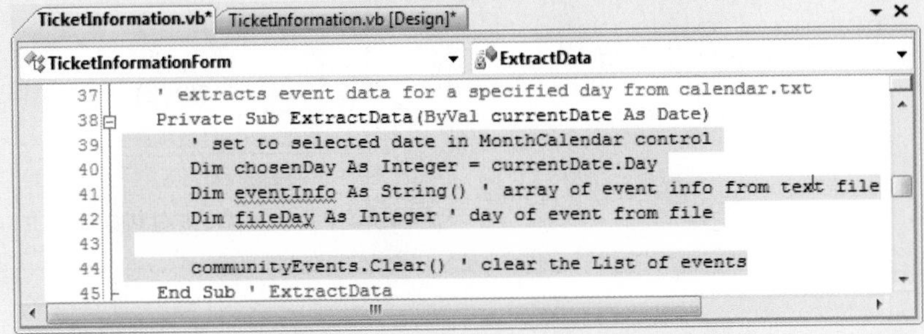

Figure 23.29 `ExtractData` method's variable declarations.

(cont.)

2. ***Creating a StreamReader to read from the file.*** Add lines 46–48 of Fig. 23.30 to the method. To read from the file, `ExtractData` creates a new `StreamReader` object (line 47), passing the name of the file to be read (`"calendar.txt"`). Recall that you wrote information to this file using the **Write Event** application earlier in this tutorial. [*Note:* The data file is in the same directory as the application's executable (`C:\SimplyVB2008\TicketInformation\TicketInformation\bin\Debug`), so you do not need to use the full path name.] `String` variable `line` (line 48) stores a line of text read from the file.

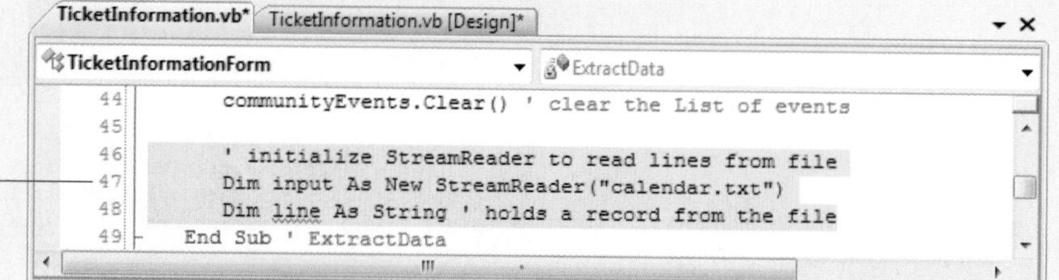

Figure 23.30 Initializing the `StreamReader` used to read data from a sequential-access file.

3. ***Extracting the day from an event in the file.*** Add lines 50–58 of Fig. 23.31 to the `ExtractData` method. The `Do Until...Loop` statement determines whether the end of the file has been reached. When this condition becomes `True`, looping should stop. The `StreamReader` object's **`EndOfStream`** property returns `True` if the end of the file has been reached (line 51). The **`ReadLine`** method (line 52) of the `StreamReader` reads one line of text from the specified stream (`input`) and returns the characters as a `String`, or `Nothing` if the end of file is reached. Line 52 assigns the line read from the file to `line`. Recall that each field in the record is separated by a *Tab* character. Line 55 calls `String` method `Split`, passing the *Tab* character constant as an argument, and assigns the resulting array of `Strings` to array `eventInfo`. In Tutorial 22 you used the `Split` method with no arguments to split a `String` wherever a space appeared. The argument passed to the `Split` method (in this case `ControlChars.Tab`) specifies the character (or characters) at which to split the `String`. This character (or characters) is called a **delimiter** and is used to mark the boundaries between fields in a record. Line 57 converts the first field in the record (that is, the day of the event) read from the file to an `Integer` and assigns that value to `fileDay`.

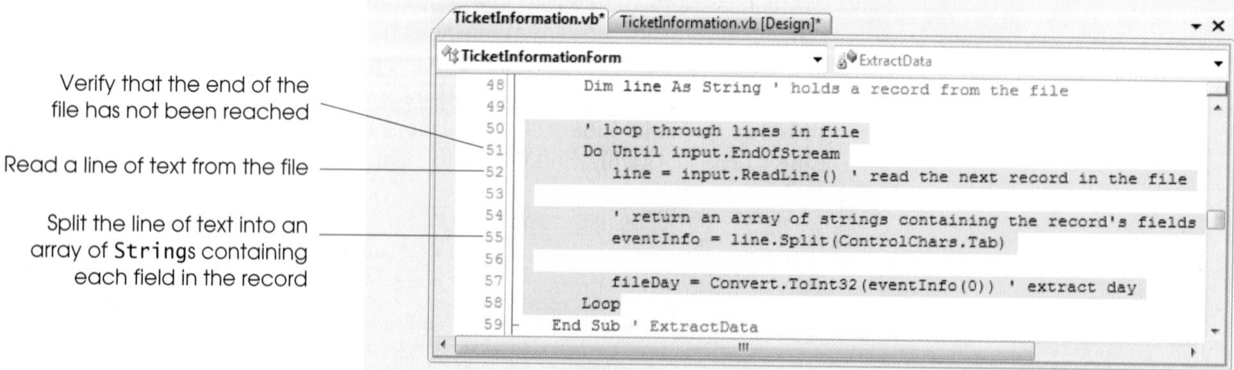

Figure 23.31 Extracting the day from an event entry in the file.

(cont.)

4. ***Storing event information read from the sequential-access file.*** Add lines 59–70 of Fig. 23.32 to the `ExtractData` method's `Do Until...Loop` statement. The loop reads each event sequentially from the file. If the day of the event read from the file (`fileDay`) and the specified day (`chosenDay`) are the same (line 60), then the event information (day, time, ticket price, name and description) is stored in a `CommunityEvent` object and added to the `List` (lines 62–69). Line 62 creates a new `CommunityEvent` object to store the event's information. Lines 63–67 assign each of the event's fields (stored in array `eventInfo`) to the corresponding property of class `CommunityEvent`. Line 69 adds the `CommunityEvent` object to the `List`.

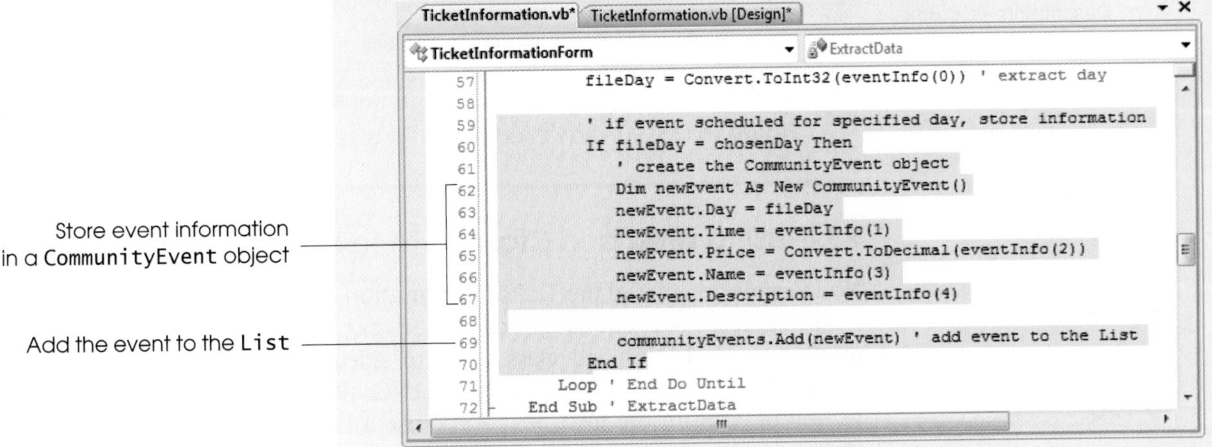

Figure 23.32 Storing event information in the `List` of `CommunityEvents`.

5. ***Saving the project.*** Select **File > Save All** to save your modified code.

The `ComboBox` displays the names of any events scheduled for the date specified in the `MonthCalendar` control. When the user selects the community event from the `ComboBox`, the `SelectedIndexChanged` event is raised and the description of the community event is displayed in the `TextBox`. The next box explains how to add this functionality.

Handling the SelectedIndexChanged Event

1. ***Creating the ComboBox's SelectedIndexChanged event handler.*** Double click the **Pick an event:** `ComboBox` in **Design** view to generate the empty event handler `eventComboBox_SelectedIndexChanged`.

2. ***Displaying event information.*** Add lines 98–106 of Fig. 23.33 to the event handler. When the user selects an event in the `ComboBox`, the `eventComboBox_SelectedIndexChanged` event handler displays information about the event in the `descriptionTextBox`. The `SelectedIndex` property of the `ComboBox` returns the index number of the selected event, which is equivalent to the index of the event in the `communityEvents List`. The event handler sets the `TextBox`'s `Text` property to the time that the event starts (line 104), the ticket price (lines 105) and the event's description (line 106).

3. ***Running the application.*** Select **Debug > Start Debugging** to run your application. Select various dates and view the event information. Select the fourth day of the current month. You should be able to view the arts and crafts fair event added earlier in the tutorial.

4. ***Closing the application.*** Close your running application by clicking its close box.

(cont.)

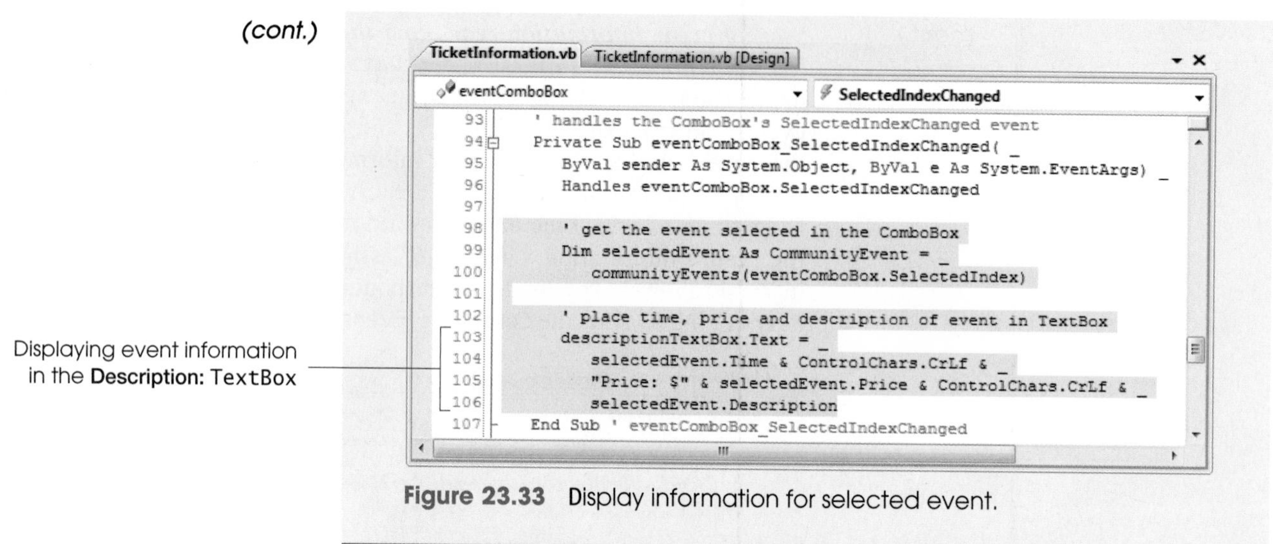

Figure 23.33 Display information for selected event.

23.6 Using LINQ and Class `File` to Extract Data from a Text File

You've now completed the **Ticket Information** application using the `StreamReader` class to access the event data in `calendar.txt`. Next, you modify the `ExtractData` method using LINQ and class `File` to select the desired events from `calendar.txt`. As you've already learned, LINQ allows you to search any array or collection of data. In the next box, you'll use a LINQ query to replace the entire `Do Until...Loop` statement and several of the method's local variables. The following box guides you through creating the LINQ query.

Using LINQ to Select Events From a Text File

1. ***Removing the `Do Until...Loop` and local variables.*** Delete the `Do Until...Loop` statement from the `ExtractData` method. Also delete the local variables `eventInfo`, `fileDay`, `input` and `line` (Fig. 23.34).

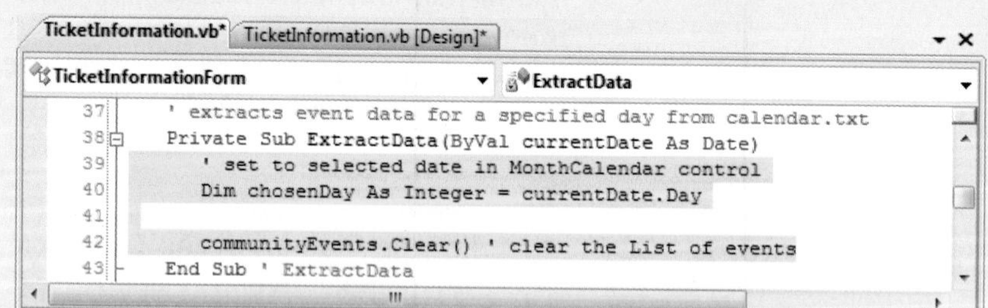

Figure 23.34 Removed `Do Until...Loop` and local variables.

2. ***Writing the `From` clause.*** Add lines 44–46 of Fig. 23.35. Line 45 declares local variable `eventQuery` to store the LINQ query used to search the data from `calendar.txt`. The `From` clause (line 46) specifies the range variable (`line`) and the data source. A LINQ data source can be any object that implements the `IEnumerable` interface, such as an array or collection. Class **`File`** provides methods for file manipulation including reading, creating, copying and deleting files. `File` method **`ReadAllLines`** returns an array of `String`s in which each element is a line from the text file passed as an argument. Because an array implements interface `IEnumerable`, you can use LINQ to search the array. The query's range variable (`line`) is of type `String`. The compiler uses local type inference to determine the type. In this case, it infers type `String`, because we are querying the array of `String`s returned by method `ReadAllLines`.

(cont.)

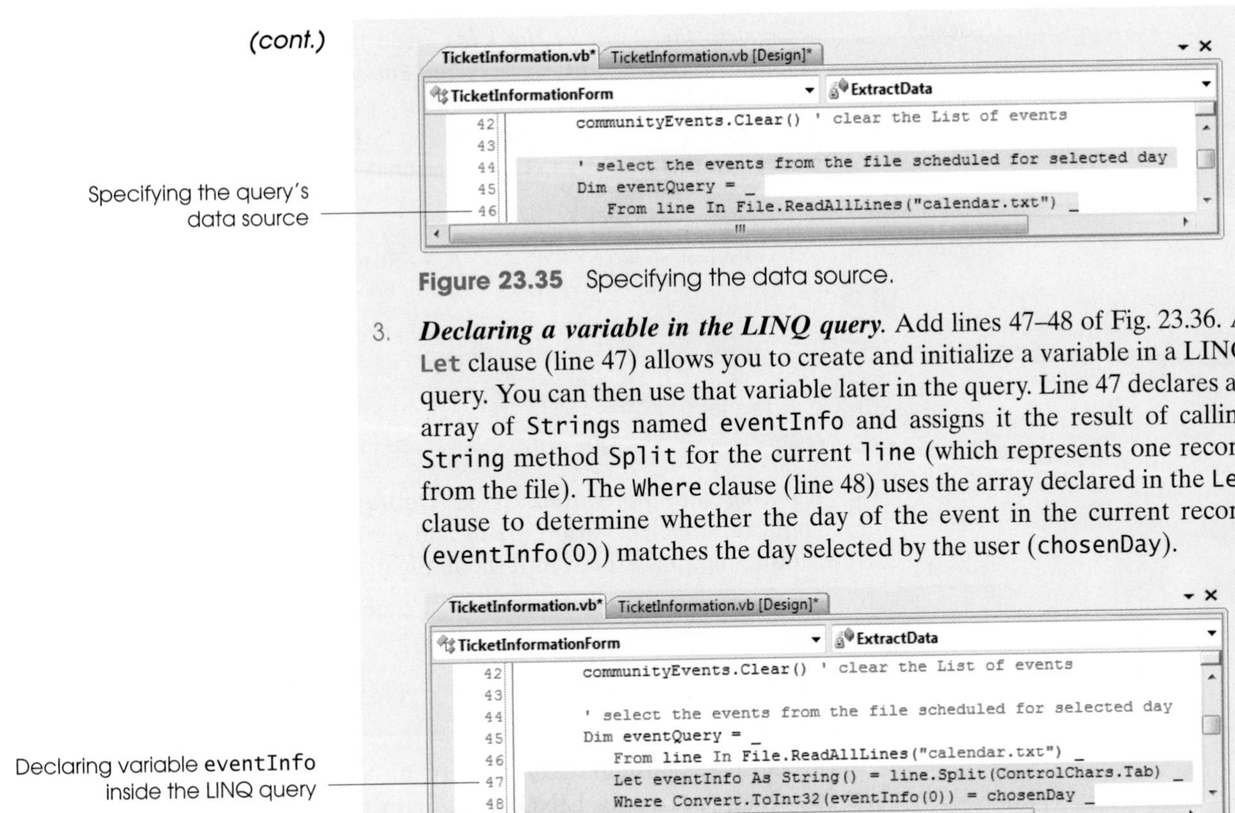

Figure 23.35 Specifying the data source.

3. ***Declaring a variable in the LINQ query.*** Add lines 47–48 of Fig. 23.36. A `Let` clause (line 47) allows you to create and initialize a variable in a LINQ query. You can then use that variable later in the query. Line 47 declares an array of `String`s named `eventInfo` and assigns it the result of calling `String` method `Split` for the current `line` (which represents one record from the file). The `Where` clause (line 48) uses the array declared in the `Let` clause to determine whether the day of the event in the current record (`eventInfo(0)`) matches the day selected by the user (`chosenDay`).

Figure 23.36 Declaring a variable in a LINQ query.

4. ***Selecting the events for the specified day.*** Add lines 49–56 of Fig. 23.37. As a LINQ query executes, it can create new objects which are returned as the query's result. Line 49 creates a new `CommunityEvent` object. The `With` keyword (line 49) specifies that the property names used in the expressions between the curly braces (lines 50–56) are from the new `CommunityEvent` object. Lines 51–55 assign values you read from the file (stored in `eventInfo`) to the `CommunityEvent` object's corresponding properties. This use of the `With` keyword is called an **object initializer**. Object initializers can be used anywhere you can create an object using the normal syntax. The use of object initializers in a `Select` clause allows you to return any type of object from a LINQ query—you do not have to return the same type of object contained in the data source you are querying.

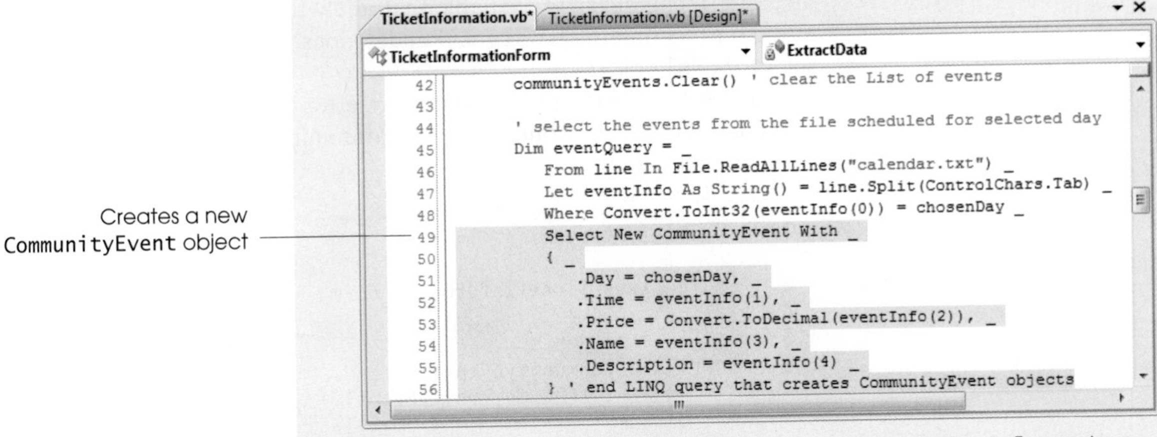

Figure 23.37 Creating `CommunityEvent` objects in the `Select` clause.

(cont.)

5. ***Assigning the result to the `List`.*** Add lines 58–59 below the LINQ query (Fig. 23.38). Line 59 uses interface `IEnumerable`'s `ToList` method to assign the events selected from `calendar.txt` to the `List` object `communityEvents`. Method `ToList` returns a `List` of the items selected by the LINQ query—in this case, a `List(Of CommunityEvent)`.

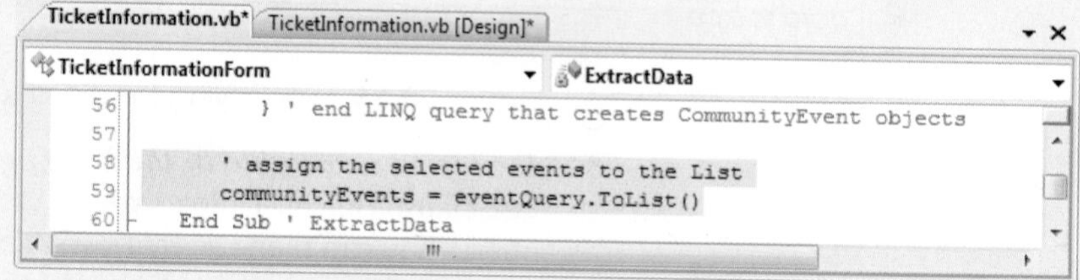

TicketInformation.vb*
TicketInformation.vb [Design]*
TicketInformationForm
ExtractData
56 } ' end LINQ query that creates CommunityEvent objects
57
58 ' assign the selected events to the List
59 communityEvents = eventQuery.ToList()
60 End Sub ' ExtractData

Figure 23.38 Assigning the query result to the `List`.

6. ***Running the application.*** Select **Debug > Start Debugging** to run your application. Select various dates and view the event information. The application functions exactly as it did in the previous box.
7. ***Closing the application.*** Close your running application by clicking its close box.
8. ***Closing the IDE.*** Close the Visual Basic IDE by clicking its close box.

This example of using LINQ to query the content from a text file illustrates several important features of LINQ, including variable declarations (the `Let` clause) and object initializers (the `With` keyword). The most important feature, as noted earlier, is that you can use the same syntax to query different types of data sources. However, using LINQ to query a text file in the manner shown here does have some disadvantages. In particular, the query must first read the entire text file before continuing execution. This could be problematic for large files. The `StreamReader` is able to read one line of the file, then execute the remaining portion of the loop before reading the next line. Reading the entire file doesn't noticeably affect the **Ticket Information** application because the file being queried is quite small.

Imagine an application that searches a file for a single specific record. The `StreamReader` is required to read the file only until the point at which the desired record is found. If the record is located in the first line of the file, then one line only of the file must be read. The LINQ query reads the entire file no matter where the record is located in the file. It is not uncommon for a company to store hundreds, even thousands of records in a single file. Such a large file would cause the LINQ implementation to perform noticeably slower, or the program could run out of memory. Techniques are available that allow the LINQ query to read a single line of the file at a time, as the `StreamReader` does, but these techniques are beyond the scope of this book.

Figure 23.39 presents the source code for the **Ticket Information** application. The lines of code that contain new programming concepts you learned in this tutorial are highlighted.

Importing namespace `System.IO`

```
Imports System.IO

Public Class TicketInformationForm

   ' stores events
   Private communityEvents As _
      New List(Of CommunityEvent)()

```

Figure 23.39 **Ticket Information** application's code. (Part 1 of 3.)

```
    ' populates ComboBox with current day's events (if any)
    Private Sub CreateEventList()

       Dim currentEvent As CommunityEvent ' control variable

       ' stores event information in List for selected day
       ExtractData(dateMonthCalendar.SelectionStart)

       ' remove any items in ComboBox
       eventComboBox.Items.Clear()

       ' add each new event name to ComboBox
       If communityEvents.Count > 0 Then
          For Each currentEvent In communityEvents
             ' extract and display event name
             eventComboBox.Items.Add(currentEvent.Name)
          Next

          ' inform user that events are scheduled
          eventComboBox.Text = " - Events - "
          descriptionTextBox.Text = "Pick an event."

       Else ' inform user that no events are scheduled
          eventComboBox.Text = " - No Events - "
          descriptionTextBox.Text = "No events today."
       End If
    End Sub ' CreateEventList

    ' extracts event data for a specified day from calendar.txt
    Private Sub ExtractData(ByVal currentDate As Date)
       ' set to selected date in MonthCalendar control
       Dim chosenDay As Integer = currentDate.Day

       communityEvents.Clear() ' clear the List of events

       ' select the events from the file scheduled for selected day
       Dim eventQuery = _
          From line In File.ReadAllLines("calendar.txt") _
          Let eventInfo As String() = line.Split(ControlChars.Tab) _
          Where Convert.ToInt32(eventInfo(0)) = chosenDay _
          Select New CommunityEvent With _
          { _
             .Day = chosenDay, _
             .Time = eventInfo(1), _
             .Price = Convert.ToDecimal(eventInfo(2)), _
             .Name = eventInfo(3), _
             .Description = eventInfo(4) _
          } ' end LINQ query that creates CommunityEvent objects

       ' assign the selected events to the List
       communityEvents = eventQuery.ToList()
    End Sub ' ExtractData

    ' handles Form's Load event
    Private Sub TicketInformationForm_Load( _
       ByVal sender As System.Object,ByVal e As System.EventArgs) _
       Handles MyBase.Load

       ' display any events scheduled for today in ComboBox
       CreateEventList()
    End Sub ' TicketInformationForm_Load

```

Retrieve an array containing each line of `calendar.txt`

Split `line` into array of `Strings`

Check whether the `chosenDay` the day from the line being processed

Creating a `CommunityEvent` object with an object initializer

Retrieve a `List` containing each `CommunityEvent` object in the query result

Figure 23.39 **Ticket Information** application's code. (Part 2 of 3.)

```
    ' handles MonthCalendar's DateChanged event
    Private Sub dateMonthCalendar_DateChanged( _
       ByVal sender As System.Object, _
       ByVal e As System.Windows.Forms.DateRangeEventArgs) _
       Handles dateMonthCalendar.DateChanged

       ' display any events for the specified date in ComboBox
       CreateEventList()
    End Sub ' dateMonthCalendar_DateChanged

    ' handles ComboBox's SelectedIndexChanged event
    Private Sub eventComboBox_SelectedIndexChanged(ByVal sender As _
       System.Object, ByVal e As System.EventArgs) _
       Handles eventComboBox.SelectedIndexChanged

       ' get the event selected in the ComboBox
       Dim selectedEvent As CommunityEvent = _
          communityEvents(eventComboBox.SelectedIndex)

       ' place time, price and description of event in TextBox
       descriptionTextBox.Text =
          selectedEvent.Time & ControlChars.CrLf & _
          "Price: $" & selectedEvent.Price & ControlChars.CrLf & _
          selectedEvent.Description
    End Sub ' eventComboBox_SelectedIndexChanged
End Class ' TicketInformationForm
```

Figure 23.39 **Ticket Information** application's code. (Part 3 of 3.)

23.7 Wrap-Up

In this tutorial, you learned how to store data in sequential-access files. Data in files is called persistent data because it is maintained after the application that generated it terminates. Computers store files on secondary storage devices.

Sequential-access files store data items in the order in which they are written to the file. They are part of the data hierarchy in which computers process data items. These files are composed of records, which are collections of related fields. Fields contain characters composed of bytes. Bytes are composed of the smallest data items that computers can support—bits.

You learned how Visual Basic views each file as a sequential stream of bytes with an end-of-file marker. You learned how to create a sequential-access file in the **Write Event** application by associating a `StreamWriter` object with a specified file name. You used the `StreamWriter` to add information to that file. After creating a file of community events with the **Write Event** application, you developed the **Ticket Information** application using a `StreamReader` object to read information from that file sequentially. The user selects a date in the **Ticket Information** application's `MonthCalendar` control and extracts event information from a sequential-access file about any events scheduled for the specified date.

Next, you modified the **Ticket Information** application to use a LINQ query to select events scheduled for the specified date from the sequential-access file. You learned how to create a variable in a LINQ query using a `Let` clause. You also learned how to create objects in a LINQ query using object initializers.

In the next tutorial, you study databases, which were briefly mentioned earlier in this tutorial. Databases provide another common mechanism for maintaining persistent data. You learn to use LINQ to retrieve information from a database.

SKILLS SUMMARY

Displaying the Open Dialog

- Add an `OpenFileDialog` component to your application by double clicking `OpenFileDialog` in the **Toolbox**.

- Invoke the OpenFileDialog's ShowDialog method.

Retrieving the Filename from the Open Dialog

- Use the FileName property of the OpenFileDialog object.

Writing Lines of Text to a Sequential-Access File

- Import namespace System.IO.
- Create a StreamWriter object by passing two arguments to the constructor—the name of the file to open for writing and a Boolean value that determines whether information is appended to the file or replaces the current contents of the file.
- Use the Write and WriteLine methods of class StreamWriter to write information to the file.
- Call the Close method of class StreamWriter to close the file.

Reading Lines of Text from a Sequential-Access File

- Import namespace System.IO.
- Create a StreamReader object by passing the name of the file to open for reading to the constructor.
- Use the ReadLine method of class StreamReader to read information from the file.
- Call the Close method of class StreamReader to close the file.

Adding a MonthCalendar Control

- Double click the MonthCalendar control in the **Toolbox** to add a MonthCalendar to the application.

Handling a MonthCalendar Control's DateChanged Event

- Double click the MonthCalendar control in **Design** view to generate the DateChanged event handler.
- Property SelectionStart returns the first (or only) date selected.

Retrieving Information from Text from a Sequential-Access File Using LINQ

- Import namespace System.IO.
- Specify the String array returned from method ReadAllLines of class File as the data source in the From clause.
- Declare a String array in a Let clause and assign it the String array returned from String method Split called on a String representing a record in the file.
- Use a Where clause to specify the constraints for selecting the record.
- Use a Select clause to specify the information returned by the query.

KEY TERMS

binary digit—A digit that can assume one of two values.

bit—Short for "binary digit"—a digit that can assume one of two values.

byte—Eight bits.

character set—The set of all characters used to write applications and represent data items on a particular computer. Visual Basic uses the Unicode character set.

CheckFileExists property of class OpenFileDialog—Enables the user to display a warning if a specified file does not exist.

Close method of class StreamWriter or StreamReader—Used to close the stream.

database—Can be a group of related files.

database management system (DBMS)—Collection of programs designed to create and manage databases.

data hierarchy—Collection of data items processed by computers that become larger and more complex in structure as you progress from bits, to characters, to fields and up to larger data structures.

DateChanged event of MonthCalendar control—Raised when a new date (or a range of dates) is selected.

decimal digits—The digits 0, 1, 2, 3, 4, 5, 6, 7, 8 and 9.

delimiter—Marks the boundaries between fields in a record of a text file.

EndOfStream property of class StreamReader—Returns a Boolean value indicating whether the end of the file has been reached.

field—Group of characters that conveys some meaning. For example, a field consisting of uppercase and lowercase letters can represent a person's name.

file—Collection of data that is assigned a name. Used for long-term persistence of large amounts of data, even after the application that created the data terminates.

File class—Provides methods for file manipulations including creating, copying and deleting files.

FileName property of class OpenFileDialog—Specifies the file name selected in the dialog.

MonthCalendar control—Displays a calendar from which a user can select a range of dates.

object initializer—Uses keyword With to assign property values to a newly created object.

OpenFileDialog component—Enables an application to use the **Open** dialog, which allows users to specify a file to be opened

persistent data—Data maintained in files which exists after the application that created the data terminates.

ReadAllLines method of class File—Returns an array of Strings containing each line of the file.

ReadLine method of class StreamReader—Reads a line from a file and returns it as a String.

record—A collection of related fields. Usually a Class in Visual Basic composed of several fields (called member variables in Visual Basic).

record key—Identifies a record and distinguishes it from all other records.

secondary storage media—Devices such as magnetic disks, optical disks and magnetic tapes on which computers store files.

SelectionStart property of MonthCalendar control—Returns the first (or only) date selected.

sequential-access file—File containing data that is read in the order in which it was written to the file.

ShowDialog method of class OpenFileDialog—Displays the **Open** dialog and returns the result of the user interaction with the dialog.

special symbols—$, @, %, &, *, (,), -, +, ", :, ?, / and the like.

stream—A sequence of characters.

StreamReader class—Provides methods for reading information from a file.

StreamWriter class—Provides methods for writing information to a file.

text file—A file containing human-readable characters.

ToList method of interface IEnumerable—Returns a List of the items contained in an IEnumerable object.

Unicode—A character set containing characters that are composed of two bytes. Characters are represented in Visual Basic using the Unicode character set.

With keyword—Specifies that the subsequent property assignment statements contained between curly braces refer to the newly created object in an object initializer.

Write method of class StreamWriter—Writes a String to a file.

WriteLine method of class StreamWriter—Writes a String and a line terminator to a file.

CONTROLS, EVENTS, PROPERTIES & METHODS

ComboBox ComboBox This control allows users to select options from a drop-down list.

- ***In action***

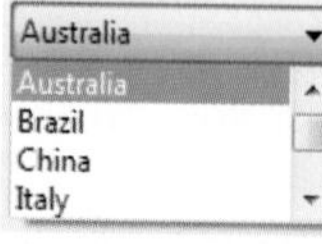

- ***Event***

SelectedIndexChanged—Raised when a new value is selected in the ComboBox.

- ***Properties***

  `DataSource`—Allows you to add items to the ComboBox.

  `DropDownStyle`—Determines the ComboBox's style.

  `Enabled`—Determines whether the user can select items from the ComboBox.

  `Items.Item`—Retrieves the value at the specified index.

  `Items`—Specifies the values the user can select from the ComboBox.

  `Location`—Specifies the location of the ComboBox control relative to the top-left corner of the container (e.g., a Form or a GroupBox).

  `MaxDropDownItems`—Determines the maximum number of items to be displayed when the user clicks the drop-down arrow.

  `Name`—Specifies the name used to access the ComboBox control programmatically. The name should be appended with the ComboBox suffix.

  `SelectedValue`—Contains the item selected by the user.

  `TabIndex`—Specifies the order in which focus is transferred to controls when *Tab* is pressed.

  `TabStop`—Specifies whether the user can select the control using the *Tab* key.

  `Text`—Specifies the text displayed in the ComboBox.

- ***Methods***

  `Items.Add`—Adds an item to the ComboBox.

  `Items.Clear`—Deletes all the values in the ComboBox.

`File` This class provides methods for file manipulations including creating, copying and deleting files.

- ***Method***

  `ReadAllLines`—Returns an array of Strings containing each line of the file.

`MonthCalendar` MonthCalendar This control displays a calendar from which the user can select a date or a range of dates.

- ***In action***

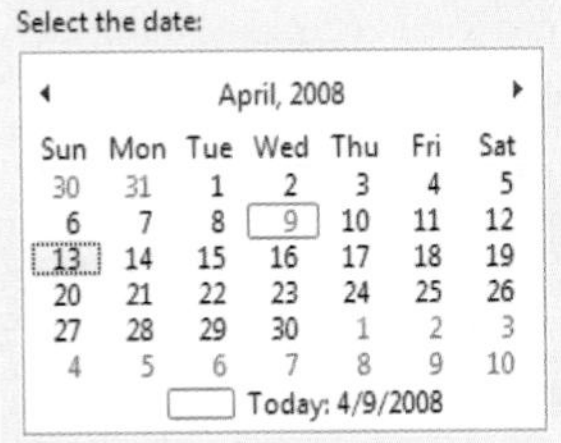

- ***Event***

  `DateChanged`—Raised when a new date (or a range of dates) is selected.

- ***Properties***

  `Name`—Specifies the name used to access the properties of the MonthCalendar control in the application code. The name should be appended with the MonthCalendar suffix.

  `SelectionStart`—Returns the first (or only) date selected.

`OpenFileDialog` OpenFileDialog This object enables an application to use the **Open** dialog.

- ***Properties***

  `CheckFileExists`—Enables the user to display a warning if a specified file does not exist.

  `FileName`—Sets the default file name displayed in the dialog. It can also be used to retrieve the name of the file selected by the user.

  `Name`—Specifies the name used to access the OpenFileDialog component programmatically.

- ***Method***

  `ShowDialog`—Displays the **Open** dialog and returns the result of the user interaction with the dialog.

`StreamWriter` This class is used to write data to a file.

- ***Methods***

  `Close`—Used to close the stream.

  `Write`—Writes the data specified in its argument.

  `WriteLine`—Writes the data specified in its argument, followed by a newline character.

`StreamReader` This class is used to read data from a file.

- ***Property***

  `EndOfStream`—Returns a `Boolean` value indicating whether the end of the file has been reached.

- ***Methods***

  `Close`—Closes the stream.

  `ReadLine`—Reads a line of data from a particular file and returns it as a `String`.

MULTIPLE-CHOICE QUESTIONS

23.1 Data maintained in a file is called _________.

a) persistent data b) bits
c) secondary data d) databases

23.2 Methods from the _________ class can be used to write data to a file.

a) `StreamReader` b) `FileWriter`
c) `StreamWriter` d) `WriteFile`

23.3 Namespace _________ provides the classes and methods you need to perform file processing.

a) `System.IO` b) `System.Files`
c) `System.Stream` d) `System.Windows.Forms`

23.4 Sometimes a group of related files is called a _________.

a) field b) database
c) collection d) byte

23.5 A(n) _________ allows the user to select a file to open.

a) `CreateFileDialog` b) `OpenFileDialog`
c) `MessageBox` d) None of the above

23.6 Digits, letters and special symbols are referred to as _________.

a) constants b) `Integers`
c) characters d) None of the above

23.7 The _________ method reads a line from a file.

a) `ReadLine` b) `Read`
c) `ReadAll` d) `ReadToNewline`

23.8 A _________ contains information that is read in the order it was written.

a) sequential-access file b) `StreamWriter`
c) `StreamReader` d) None of the above

23.9 The smallest data item that a computer can support is called a _________.

a) character set b) character
c) special symbol d) bit

23.10 Methods from the ________ class can be used to read data from a file.

a) `StreamWriter` b) `FileReader`
c) `StreamReader` d) `ReadFile`

EXERCISES

23.11 *(Birthday Saver Application)* Create an application that stores people's names and birthdays in a file (Fig. 23.40). The user creates a file and inputs each person's first name, last name and birthday on the `Form`. The information is then written to the file.

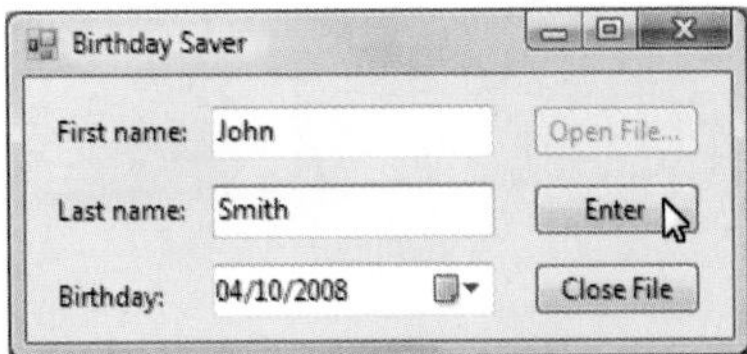

Figure 23.40 **Birthday Saver** application's GUI.

a) ***Copying the template to your working directory.*** Copy the directory `C:\Examples\Tutorial23\Exercises\BirthdaySaver` to your `C:\SimplyVB2008` directory.

b) ***Opening the application's template file.*** Double click `BirthdaySaver.sln` in the `BirthdaySaver` directory to open the application (Fig. 23.40).

c) ***Adding and customizing an `OpenFileDialog` component.*** Add an `OpenFileDialog` component to the `Form`. Change its `Name` property to `openFileDialog`. Set the `CheckFileExists` property to `False`.

d) ***Importing namespace `System.IO`.*** Import `System.IO` to allow file processing.

e) ***Declaring a `StreamWriter` object.*** Declare a `StreamWriter` object that can be used throughout the entire class.

f) ***Defining the Open File... `Button`'s `Click` event handler.*** Double click the **Open File...** `Button` to create the `openButton_Click` event handler. Write code to display the **Open** dialog. If the user clicks the **Cancel** `Button` in the dialog, the event handler performs no further actions. Otherwise, determine whether the user provided a file name that ends with the `.txt` extension. If not, display a `MessageBox` asking the user to select an appropriate file. If the user specified a valid file name, perform *Step g*.

g) ***Initializing the `StreamWriter`.*** Initialize the `StreamWriter` in the event handler `openButton_Click`, passing the user-input file name as an argument. Allow the user to append information to the file by passing the `Boolean` value `True` as the second argument to the `StreamWriter`. Enable the **Enter** and **Close File** `Buttons`. Disable the **Open File...** `Button`.

h) ***Defining the Enter `Button`'s `Click` event handler.*** Double click the **Enter** `Button` to create the event handler `enterButton_Click`. This event handler writes the name of the person and the person's birthday on a line in the file. Finally, the `TextBoxes` on the `Form` are cleared, and the `DateTimePicker`'s value is set back to the current date.

i) ***Defining the Close File `Button`'s `Click` event handler.*** Double click the **Close File** `Button` to create the `closeButton_Click` event handler. Close the `StreamWriter` connection and reset the `Buttons` to their initial state in this event handler.

j) ***Running the application.*** Select **Debug > Start Debugging** to run your application. Open a file by clicking the **Open File...** `Button`. After a file has been opened, use the input fields provided to enter birthday information. After each person's name and birthday are typed in, click the **Enter** `Button`. When you are finished, close the file by clicking the **Close File** `Button`. Browse to the file and ensure that its contents contain the birthday information that you entered.

k) ***Closing the application.*** Close your running application by clicking its close box.

l) ***Closing the IDE.*** Close the Visual Basic IDE by clicking its close box.

23.12 *(Photo Album Application)* Create an application that displays images for the user, as shown in Fig. 23.41. This application should display the current image in a large `PictureBox` and display the previous and next images in smaller `PictureBoxes`. A description of the book represented by the large image should be displayed in a multiline `TextBox`.

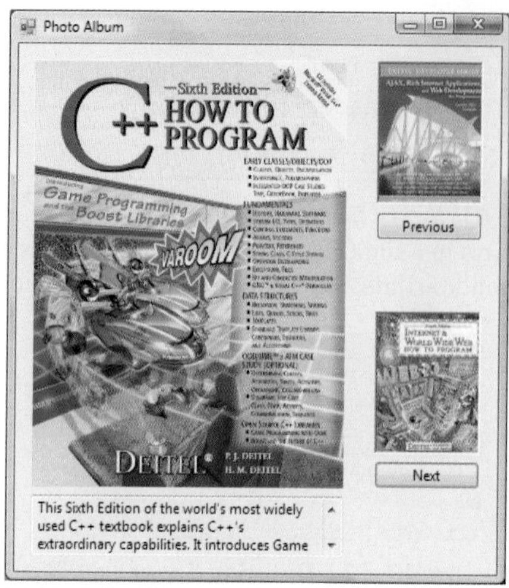

Figure 23.41 **Photo Album** application GUI.

a) ***Copying the template to your working directory.*** Copy the directory `C:\Examples\Tutorial23\Exercises\PhotoAlbum` to your `C:\SimplyVB2008` directory.

b) ***Opening the application's template file.*** Double click `PhotoAlbum.sln` in the `PhotoAlbum` directory to open the application.

c) ***Importing `System.IO` namespace.*** Import namespace `System.IO` to allow file processing.

d) ***Creating instance variables.*** Create instance variable `current` to represent the current image that is displayed, and set it to `0`. Create the `largeImage` array (to store the `String` path names of six large images), the `smallImage` array (to store the `String` path names of six small images) and the `descriptions` array (to store the descriptions of the six books represented by the images).

e) ***Defining the `RetrieveData` procedure.*** Create a `Sub` procedure named `RetrieveData` to store the path names of the larger images in `largeImage` and the path names of the smaller images in `smallImage`. (The images are placed in your application's `bin\Debug` folder in the subfolders `images\large` and `images\small`.) Sequential-access file `books.txt` (in the project's `bin\Debug` folder) stores the file name of each image. The file is organized such that the file name of the small and large images and the book's description are on a single line, separated by a *Tab* character. The files have similar names. The small image's file name ends with `_thumb.jpg` (that is, *filename*`_thumb.jpg`), while the large image's file name ends with `_large.jpg` (that is, *filename*`_large.jpg`). The description of the book, which should be stored in array `descriptions`, follows the file name. Write code to read this data from the file and place it into arrays. [*Note:* There are only two fields in each record—the file name used for *both* images and the book description.]

f) ***Defining the `DisplayPicture` procedure.*** Create a `Sub` procedure named `DisplayPicture` to display the current image in the large `PictureBox`, to display the previous and next images in the smaller `PictureBoxes`, and to place the description of the large image in the `TextBox`.

g) ***Using `If...Then...Else` in the `DisplayPicture` procedure.*** Use an `If...Then...Else` statement to display the images on the `Form`. If the `Integer` instance variable is `0`, display the image of the first book. Also, display the next book's image in the next image `PictureBox`. However, since there is no previous image, nothing should be displayed in the previous image `PictureBox`, and the **Previous** `Button` should be disabled. If the last image is displayed in the large `PictureBox`, then disable the **Next** `Button`, and do not display anything in the next image `PictureBox`. Otherwise, all three `PictureBoxes` should display their corresponding images, and the **Previous** and **Next** `Buttons` should be enabled.

h) ***Defining the `PhotoAlbumForm_Load` event handler.*** Double click the `Form` to create the `PhotoAlbumForm_Load` event handler. Invoke methods `RetrieveData` and `DisplayPicture` in this event handler.

i) ***Defining the `previousButton_Click` event handler.*** Double click the **Previous Image** `Button` to create the `previousButton_Click` event handler. In this event handler, decrease the `Integer` instance variable by `1` and invoke procedure `DisplayPicture`.

j) ***Defining the `nextButton_Click` event handler.*** Double click the **Next** `Button` to create the `nextButton_Click` event handler. In this event handler, increment the `Integer` instance variable by `1` and invoke the `DisplayPicture` procedure.

k) ***Running the application.*** Select **Debug > Start Debugging** to run your application. Click the **Previous** and **Next** `Buttons` to ensure that the proper images and descriptions are displayed.

l) ***Closing the application.*** Close your running application by clicking its close box.

m) ***Closing the IDE.*** Close the Visual Basic IDE by clicking its close box.

23.13 ***(Car Reservation Application)*** Create an application that allows a user to reserve a car for the specified day (Fig. 23.42). A small car-reservation company can rent out only four cars per day. Let the application allow the user to specify a certain day. If four cars have already been reserved for that day, then indicate to the user that no vehicles are available.

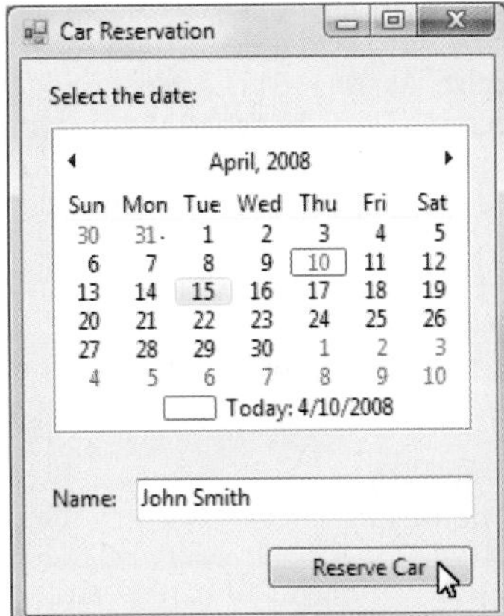

Figure 23.42 **Car Reservation** application GUI.

a) ***Copying the template to your working directory.*** Copy the directory `C:\Examples\Tutorial23\Exercises\CarReservation` to your `C:\SimplyVB2008` directory.

b) ***Opening the application's template file.*** Double click `CarReservation.sln` in the `CarReservation` directory to open the application.

c) ***Adding a `MonthCalendar` control to the `Form`.*** Drag and drop a `MonthCalendar` control on the `Form`. Set its `Name` property to `dateMonthCalendar`. Position the `MonthCalendar` control as shown in Fig. 23.42.

d) ***Importing `System.IO` namespace.*** Import namespace `System.IO` to allow file processing.

e) ***Determining the number of reservations.*** Create a method named `NumberOfReservations` that takes one argument of type `Date`. The procedure should use a LINQ that searches the `reservations.txt` file for reservations made for the selected date. The procedure should return the number of cars rented for the day selected. [*Hint:* Use the query result's `Count` method to determine the number of elements in the result.]

f) ***Defining a `Sub` procedure.*** Create a `Sub` procedure named `CheckReservations`. This procedure should invoke the `NumberOfReservations` method, passing in the user-selected day as an argument. The `CheckReservations` method should then retrieve the number returned by `NumberOfReservations` and determine whether four cars have been rented for that day. If four cars have been rented, then display a message dialog to the user stating that no cars are available that day for rental. If fewer than four cars have been rented for that day, create a `StreamWriter` object, passing `reservations.txt` as the first argument and `True` as the second argument to specify that data should be appended to any existing data. Write the day and the user's name to the reservations.txt file and display a message dialog to the user stating that a car has been reserved.

g) ***Defining the reserveButton_Click event handler.*** Double click the **Reserve Car** Button to create the reserveButton_Click event handler. In this event handler, invoke the CheckReservations procedure and clear the **Name:** TextBox.

h) ***Running the application.*** Select **Debug > Start Debugging** to run your application. Enter several reservations, including four reservations for the same day. Enter a reservation for a day that already has four reservations to ensure that a message dialog is displayed.

i) ***Closing the application.*** Close your running application by clicking its close box. Open reservations.txt to ensure that the proper data has been stored (based on the reservations entered in *Step h*).

j) ***Closing the IDE.*** Close the Visual Basic IDE by clicking its close box.

What does this code do?

23.14 What is the result of the following code?

```
Dim path1 As String = "oldfile.txt"
Dim path2 As String = "newfile.txt"
Dim output As New StreamWriter(path2)
Dim input As New StreamReader(path1)

Dim line As String = input.ReadLine()

Do While line <> Nothing
   output.WriteLine(line)
   line = input.ReadLine()
Loop

output.Close()
input.Close()
```

What's wrong with this code?

23.15 Find the error(s) in the following code, which is supposed to read a line from somefile.txt, convert the line to uppercase and then append it to somefile.txt.

```
Dim path As String = "somefile.txt"
Dim output As New StreamWriter(path, True)
Dim input As New StreamReader(path)

Dim contents As String = input.ReadLine()

contents = contents.ToUpper()
output.Write(contents)
output.Close()
input.Close()
```

Programming Challenge

23.16 *(**File Scrape Application**)* Create an application, similar to the screen-scraping application of Tutorial 22, that opens a user-specified file and searches the file for the price of a book, returning it to the user (Fig. 23.43). [*Hint:* Use the ReadToEnd method of class StreamReader to retrieve the entire contents of a file as a single String. The book price appears, for example, in the sample booklist.htm file as Our Price: <b>$59.99</b>.]

Figure 23.43 **File Scrape** application GUI.

a) ***Copying the template to your working directory.*** Copy the directory `C:\Examples\Tutorial23\Exercises\FileScrape` to your `C:\SimplyVB2008` directory. Note that two HTML files—`booklist.htm` and `bookpool.htm`—are provided for you in the project's `bin\Debug` folder.

b) ***Opening the application's template file.*** Double click `FileScrape.sln` in the `FileScrape` directory to open the application.

c) ***Creating an event handler.*** Create an event handler for the **Open...** `Button` that allows the user to select a file to search for prices. Once the file has been opened, enable the **Search** `Button`.

d) ***Creating a second event handler.*** Create an event handler for the **Search** `Button`. This event handler should search the specified HTML file for the book price. When the price is found, display it in the `resultLabel`.

e) ***Running the application.*** Select **Debug > Start Debugging** to run your application. Click the **Open...** `Button` and select one of the `.htm` files provided in the `FileScrape` directory. Click the **Search** `Button` and view the price of the book. For `booklist.htm`, the price should be $59.99, and for `bookpool.htm` the price should be $39.50.

f) ***Closing the application.*** Close your running application by clicking its close box.

g) ***Closing the IDE.*** Close the Visual Basic IDE by clicking its close box.

24 TUTORIAL

Objectives

In this tutorial, you learn to:

- Connect to databases.
- Create LINQ to SQL classes.
- View the contents of a SQL Server Express database.
- Add database controls to Windows `Forms`.
- Use the **Data Sources** window.
- Use LINQ to query a database.
- Read information from and update information in databases.

Outline

Address Book Application

Introducing Database Programming

In the last tutorial, you learned how to create sequential-access files and how to search through such files to locate information. Sequential-access files are inappropriate for so-called **instant-access applications**, in which information must be located immediately. An electronic address book can be constructed as an instant-access application for rapid access to specific contact information. A large company's address book may have hundreds of thousands of listings—however, when a specific person's contact information is requested, it is retrieved almost immediately. This type of instant access is made possible by databases. Individual database records can be accessed directly (and quickly) without sequentially searching through large numbers of other records, as is required with sequential-access files. In this tutorial, you study databases and LINQ to SQL as you create an **Address Book** application.

Databases have been used in business applications for decades. Each new version of Visual Basic has increased support for interacting with databases, making it easier with each release. The introduction of LINQ greatly simplifies the process of accessing and updating information contained in a database. Previous versions required the use of **Structured Query Language** (**SQL**) to manipulate data in the database. SQL—pronounced "sequel," or as its individual letters—is the international standard language used almost universally with databases to perform **queries** (i.e., to request information that satisfies given criteria) and to manipulate data.

LINQ, which is modeled after SQL, allows you to interact with the database directly in your code. In most cases, you no longer need to use SQL directly (though LINQ uses SQL behind the scenes and you can still create custom SQL statements as necessary). Visual Studio generates a set of LINQ to SQL classes based on the structure of a database. Visual Studio's *IntelliSense* displays these classes and their properties. The LINQ to SQL classes help you interact with your database and build powerful data-driven applications quickly and easily. You manipulate the database using the same LINQ syntax you used to manipulate data contained in objects in previous chapters. This uniform syntax is a key advantage of LINQ.

24.1 Test-Driving the Address Book Application

An electronic address book provides quick and easy access to stored contact information. It also allows new contact information to be added and existing contact information to be updated or deleted. This application must meet the following requirements:

Application Requirements

You have been asked to create an address book application that stores the first name, last name, e-mail address and phone number of multiple people in a database table. Each entry should be stored as a different row in the table. The user should be able to navigate through the data, add rows, delete rows and save changes to the data. Specific entries should be retrievable by searching the data by last name.

You begin by test-driving the completed application. Then you learn the additional Visual Basic capabilities needed to create your own version of this application.

Test-Driving the Address Book Application

1. ***Opening the completed application.*** Open the directory `C:\Examples\Tutorial24\CompletedApplication\AddressBook` to locate the **Address Book** application. Double click `AddressBook.sln` to open the application in the Visual Basic IDE.

2. ***Running the application.*** Select **Debug > Start Debugging** to run the application (Fig. 24.1). The database provided with this example initially contains six entries. The `BindingNavigator` at the top of the `Form` (discussed in Section 24.3) is the strip of `Buttons` below the window's title bar. It is an auto-generated set of controls that allows you to manipulate the data displayed in the `Form`'s other controls.

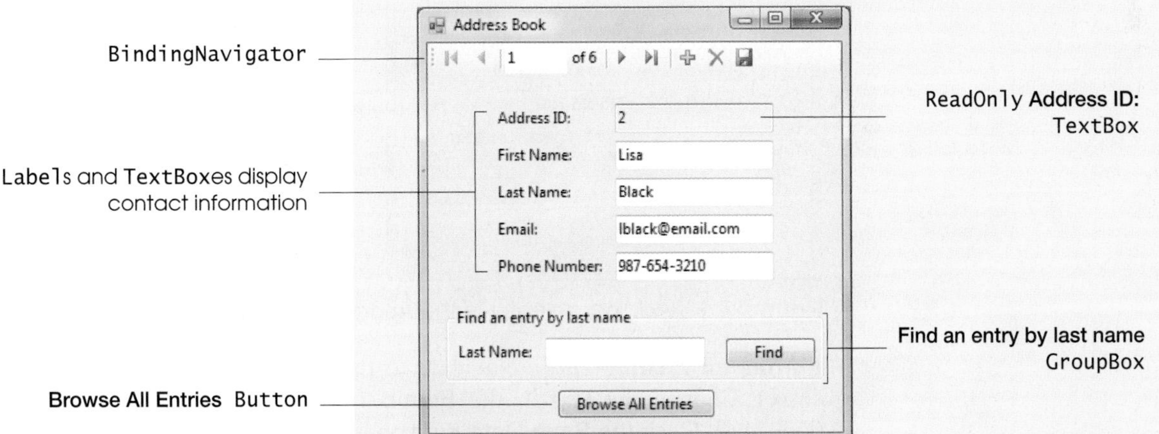

Figure 24.1 **Address Book** application.

3. ***Browsing the entries.*** The `BindingNavigator` allows you to browse through the entries. Click the **Move next**, **Move last**, **Move previous** and **Move first** `Buttons` (Fig. 24.2) to navigate through the **Address Book** entries. Notice that the entries are in alphabetical order by last name.

(cont.)

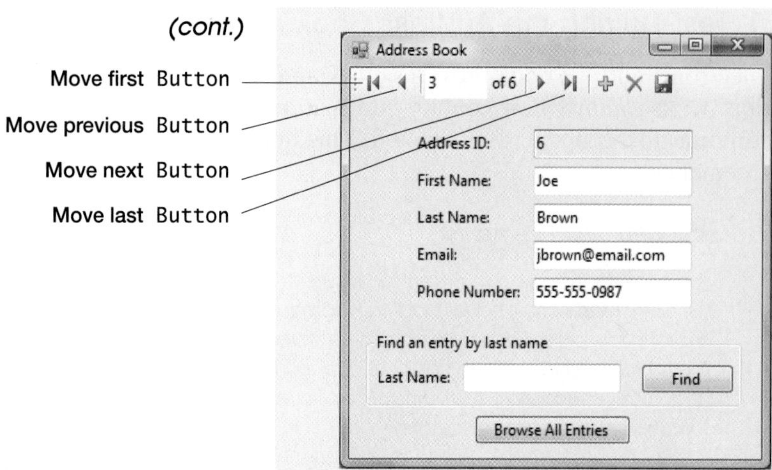

Figure 24.2 Navigating the entries in the **Address Book** application.

4. ***Adding a new entry.*** Click the **Add new** `Button` in the `BindingNavigator` at the top of the `Form`. The **Address ID:** `TextBox` is automatically filled in with the value `0`—this field's value is generated by the database when you save the new record. Fill in the **First Name:**, **Last Name:**, **Email:** and **Phone Number:** `TextBoxes` as shown in Fig. 24.3, then click the **Save Data** `Button` in the `BindingNavigator`. When you click the **Save Data** `Button`, the value in the **Address ID:** `TextBox` updates to the database-generated **Address ID** value (in this case, 7).

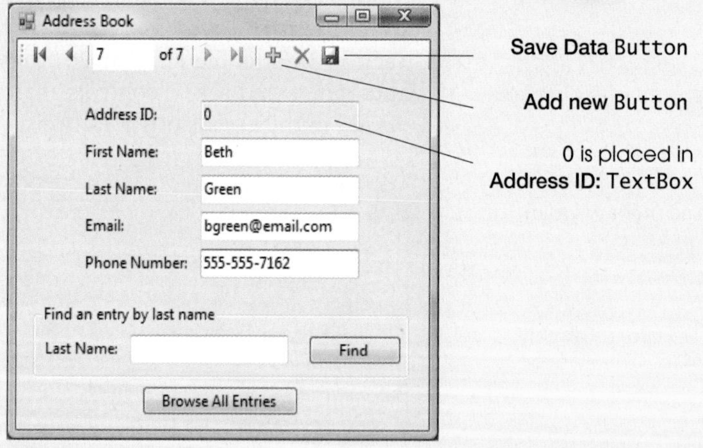

Figure 24.3 Adding an entry in the **Address Book** application.

5. ***Editing an existing entry.*** Navigate to the entry for Lisa Black (the first entry). Change the text in the **Email:** `TextBox` to `black.l@email.com` (Fig. 24.4). Click the **Save Data** `Button` in the `BindingNavigator` to save the changes to this entry. [*Note:* If you edit entries, remember to click the **Save Data** `Button` after updating an entry.]

6. ***Searching all entries by last name.*** To search the entries by last name, enter a last name in the **Last Name:** `TextBox` of the **Find an entry by last name** `GroupBox`, then click the **Find** `Button`. Using this method, search for the last name `Brown`. The `BindingNavigator` now allows you to navigate through only those entries containing the last name `Brown` (Fig. 24.5). Note that the `BindingNavigator` now shows `1 of 2`, because there are only two entries with the last name `Brown`. If you search for a last name that is not in the database table, then nothing is returned by the application and the `Form`'s `TextBoxes` are cleared.

(cont.)

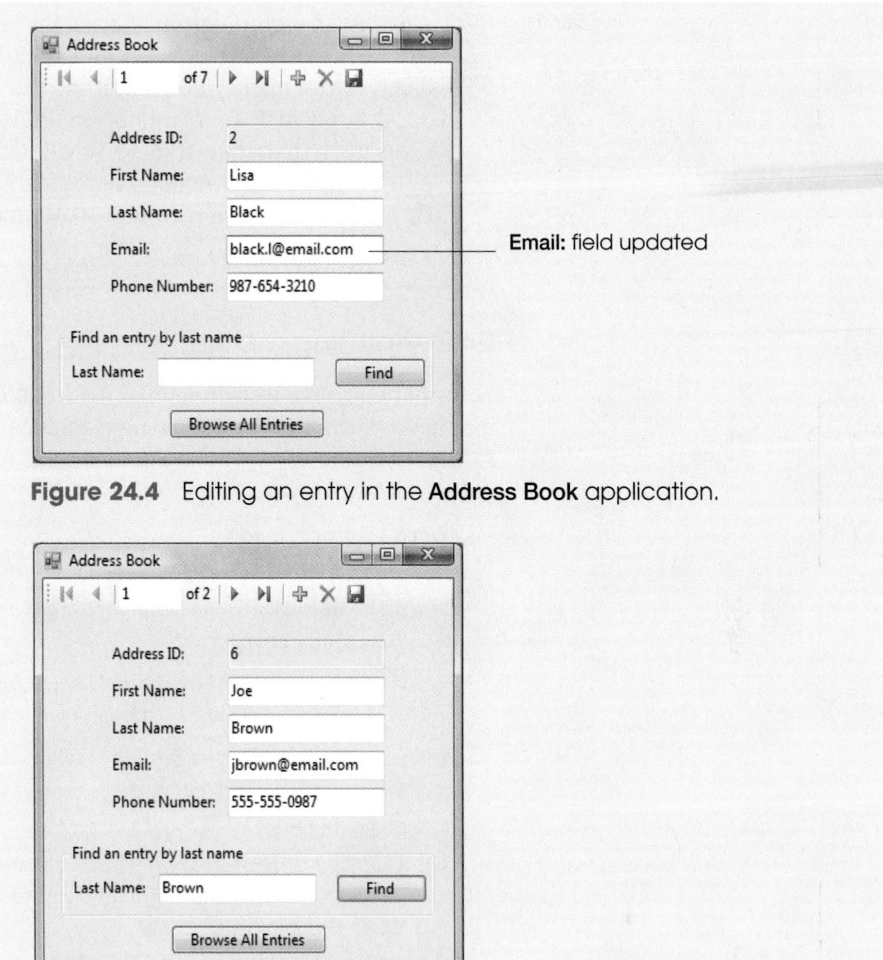

Figure 24.4 Editing an entry in the **Address Book** application.

Figure 24.5 Browsing entries by last name.

7. ***Browsing all entries.*** Click the **Browse All Entries** `Button` at the bottom of the `Form` to return to the full listing of address entries. The `BindingNavigator` now allows you to navigate through all the entries.

8. ***Deleting an entry.*** Navigate to the entry you added for `Beth Green`. Click the **Delete** `Button` × in the `BindingNavigator` (Fig. 24.6). Notice that the `BindingNavigator` now displays `4 of 6` instead of `4 of 7`. Click the **Save Data** `Button` to save your changes. Browse the entries to confirm that the `Beth Green` entry was deleted.

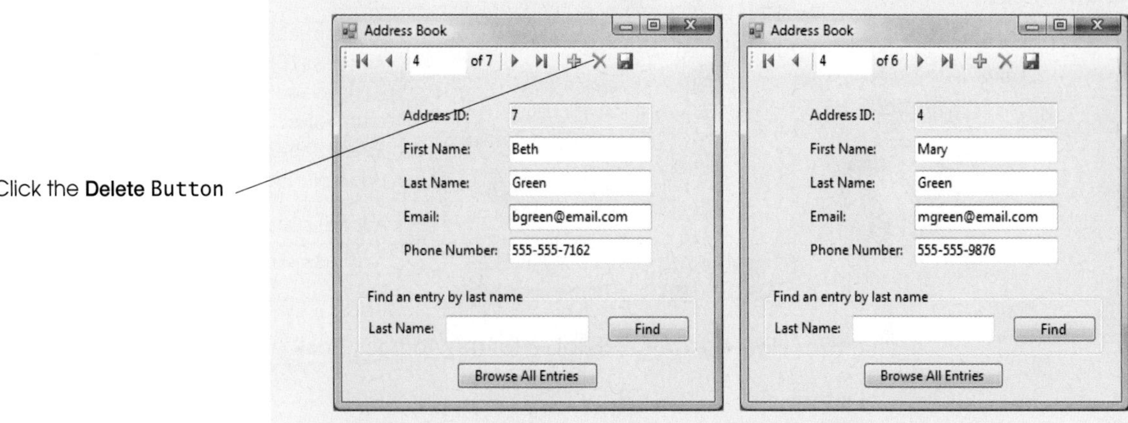

Figure 24.6 Deleting an entry in the **Address Book** application.

(cont.)

9. ***Closing the application.*** Close the application by clicking its close box. [*Note:* When you close the application, then run it again, notice that any changes you made to the database were not stored. Every time you start the application in **Debug** mode, the IDE copies the original database in the project's `bin\Debug` folder. To allow your database changes to be stored permanently, select `AddressBook.mdf` in the **Solution Explorer**, then set its **Copy To Output Directory** property to `Copy if newer`.]
10. ***Closing the IDE.*** Close the Visual Basic IDE by clicking its close box.

24.2 Planning the Address Book Application

Now that you have test-driven the **Address Book** application, you begin by analyzing the application. The following pseudocode describes the basic operation of the **Address Book** application. Some of the features described here are generated automatically for you.

```
When the Form loads
    Display the first entry in the AddressBook database

When the user clicks the BindingNavigator's auto-generated Add new Button
    Add a new entry

When the user clicks the BindingNavigator's auto-generated Save Data Button
    Update the database with any new, deleted or updated entries

When the user clicks the BindingNavigator's auto-generated Delete Button
    Delete the current entry displayed in the Form

When the user clicks the Browse All Entries Button
    Display the first entry in the database and allow the user to browse all
        entries with the BindingNavigator
    Clear the search text box

When the user clicks the Find Button
    If no entries have a last name that matches the input string,
        then display empty TextBoxes
    Otherwise, display the first entry with the specified last name and allow the
        user to browse through all matching entries with the BindingNavigator
```

Now that you've studied the application's pseudocode representation, you use an ACE table to help you convert the pseudocode to Visual Basic. Figure 24.7 lists the actions, controls and events that help you complete your own version of this application.

Action/Control/Event (ACE) Table for the Address Book Application

Action	Control	Event
Label the application's controls	`searchLabel`, `AddressIDLabel`, `FirstNameLabel`, `LastNameLabel`, `EmailLabel`, `PhoneNumberLabel`	
	`AddressBookForm`	Load
Display the first entry in the AddressBook database	`AddressBindingSource`	

Figure 24.7 ACE table for the **Address Book** application. (Part 1 of 2.)

Action	Control	Event
	AddressBindingNavigator-AddNewItem	Click
Add a new entry	AddressIDTextBox, FirstNameTextBox, LastNameTextBox, EmailTextBox, PhoneNumberTextBox	
	AddressBindingNavigatorSaveItem	Click
Update the database with any new, deleted or updated entries	AddressBindingSource, database (object of class Address-BookDataClassesDataContext)	
	AddressBindingNavigator-DeleteItem	Click
Delete the current entry displayed in the Form	AddressBindingSource	
	browseAllButton	Click
Display the first entry in the database and allow the user to browse all entries with the BindingNavigator	AddressBindingSource	
Clear the search text box	searchTextBox	
	findButton	Click
If no entries have a last name that matches the input string, then display empty TextBoxes	searchTextBox, AddressBindingSource	
Otherwise, display the first entry with the specified last name and allow the user to browse through all matching entries with the BindingNavigator	searchTextBox, AddressBindingSource	

Figure 24.7 ACE table for the **Address Book** application. (Part 2 of 2.)

24.3 Creating Database Connections

In this tutorial, you use LINQ to SQL and the IDE's **Data Sources** window to create an application that interacts with a database. A **database** is an organized collection of data. Many different strategies exist for organizing data in databases to allow easy access to and manipulation of the data. A **database management system** (**DBMS**) enables you to access and store data without worrying about how it is organized. In this tutorial, you use a SQL Server Express DBMS. You connect to the database in the following box.

Adding a Database Connection to the Address Book Application

1. ***Creating the project.*** Create a new **Windows Forms Application** named `AddressBook`. Change the name of the source file to `AddressBook.vb` and change the `Form`'s `Name` to `AddressBookForm`. Change the `Form`'s `Font` to 9pt **Segoe UI**. Then set the `Form`'s `Text` property to `Address Book`.

(cont.)

2. ***Adding a database to the project.*** To interact with a database you must connect to it in the project. Select **Tools > Connect to Database....** The **Choose Data Source** dialog (Fig. 24.8) opens the first time you add a database to an application. Select **Microsoft SQL Server Database File** from the **Data source:** `ListBox`. If you check the **Always use this selection** `CheckBox`, Visual Basic will use this type of database file by default. Click **Continue** to open the **Add Connection** dialog. Notice that the **Data source:** `TextBox` reflects your selection in the **Choose Data Source** dialog. You can click the **Change...** `Button` to select different type of database. Next, click **Browse...**, locate the `AddressBook.mdf` database file in the `C:\Examples\Tutorial24` directory, select it and click **Open**. You can click **Test Connection** to verify that the IDE can connect to the database through SQL Server Express. Click **OK** to create the connection.

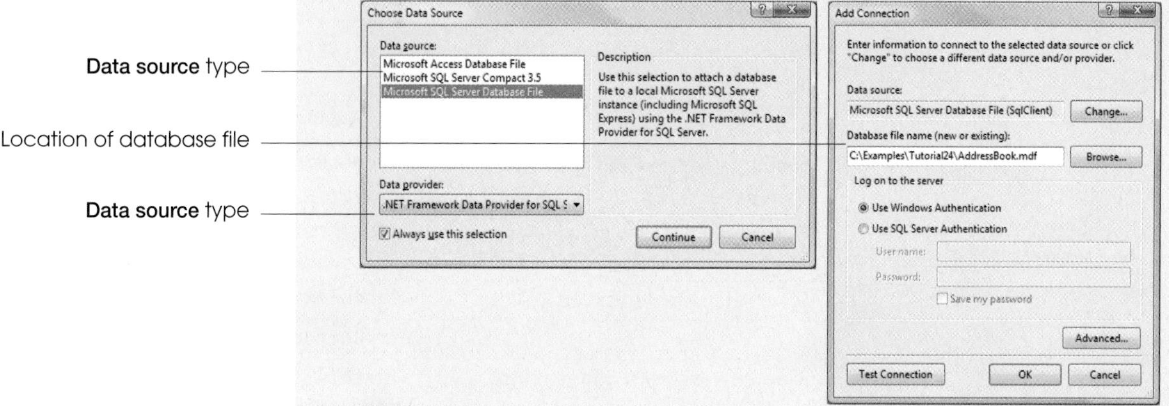

Figure 24.8 Adding a database with the **Add Connection** dialog.

3. ***Opening the Database Explorer.*** If the **Database Explorer** is not open in the Visual Basic IDE, select **View > Database Explorer**. The **Database Explorer** displays the database connections available to your project.

4. ***Viewing the `Addresses` table of the `AddressBook.mdf` database.*** A database **table** stores related information in rows and columns. Relational databases, such as those managed by SQL Server Express, consist of one or more tables. The `AddressBook.mdf` database contains only one table, `Addresses`. To view the contents of the `Addresses` table, first expand the **AddressBook.mdf** node in the **Database Explorer**, then expand the **Tables** node. Right click **Addresses**, and select **Show Table Data** (Fig. 24.9).

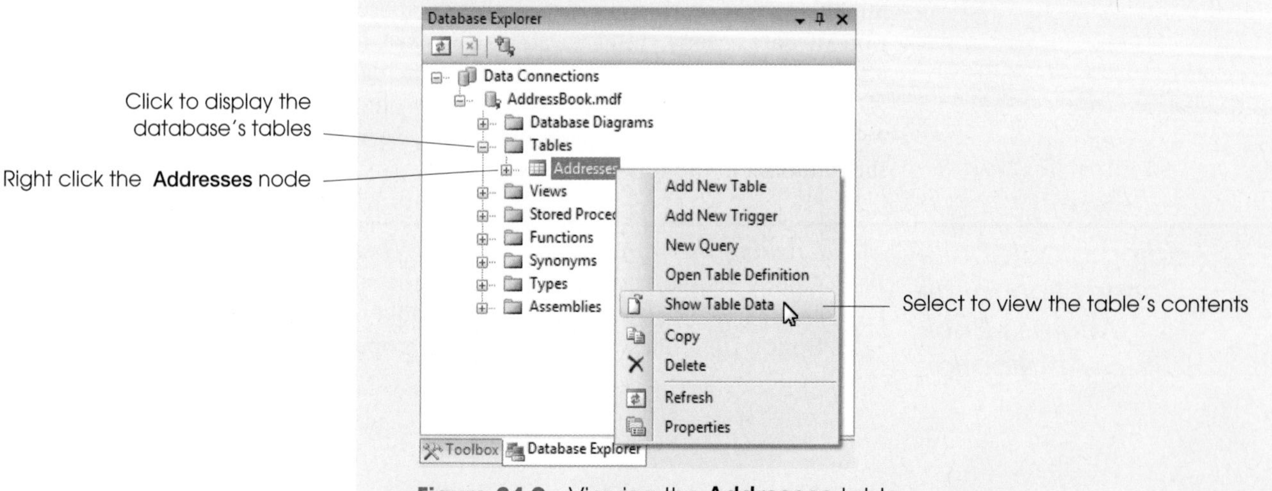

Figure 24.9 Viewing the **Addresses** table.

(cont.)

5. ***Understanding the database.*** Figure 24.10 displays the contents of the `Addresses` table used in the **Address Book** application. This table contains six records and five fields. A **record** is a table row, and a **field** is a table column. For example, in this table, the **AddressID**, **FirstName**, **LastName**, **Email** and **PhoneNumber** columns are fields that represent the data in each record.

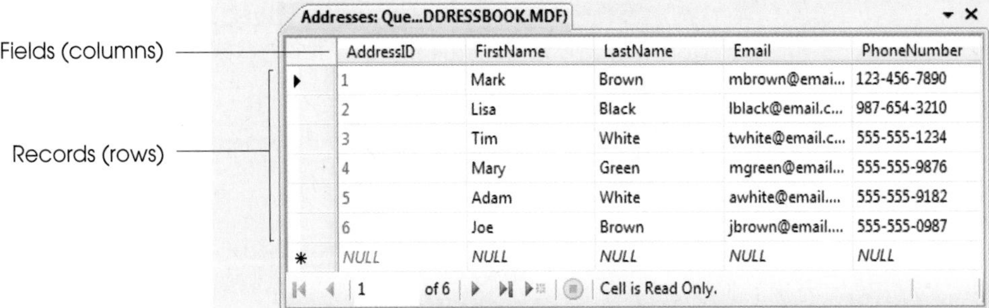

	AddressID	FirstName	LastName	Email	PhoneNumber
▶	1	Mark	Brown	mbrown@emai...	123-456-7890
	2	Lisa	Black	lblack@email.c...	987-654-3210
	3	Tim	White	twhite@email.c...	555-555-1234
	4	Mary	Green	mgreen@email...	555-555-9876
	5	Adam	White	awhite@email....	555-555-9182
	6	Joe	Brown	jbrown@email....	555-555-0987
*	*NULL*	*NULL*	*NULL*	*NULL*	*NULL*

Figure 24.10 **Addresses** table data.

In addition to records and fields, a table should contain a **primary key**, which is a field (or combination of fields) containing unique values that are used to distinguish records from one another. In this table, the **AddressID** field is the primary key for referencing the data. The **AddressID** field can act as the primary key because the **AddressID** is configured in the database's definition to be set automatically to a unique value. [*Note:* Creating databases is beyond the scope of this book, so we provide you with preconfigured databases for this tutorial's example and exercises. For more information on databases and SQL check out our SQL Server 2008 (`www.deitel.com/SQLServer2008/`) and MySQL (`www.deitel.com/MySQL/`) Resource Centers.]

6. ***Closing the Addresses window.*** Right click the **Addresses** tab in the IDE and select **Close**.

Now that you've established a connection the `AddressBook.mdf` database, you create a set of LINQ to SQL classes to allow your application to access and manipulate the data in the database. You learn how to create these classes in the following box.

Modeling the Database with LINQ to SQL Classes

1. ***Adding LINQ to SQL classes.*** **LINQ to SQL classes** create an in-memory model of your application's database. These classes use ADO.NET technologies to retrieve information from and send information to the database. **ADO.NET** is a part of the .NET Framework used to interact with databases. The LINQ to SQL classes manage all the ADO.NET code behind the scenes—you do not have to write any ADO.NET code. You use these classes to access the database and manipulate the information it contains. Right click the **AddressBook** project in the **Solution Explorer** and select **Add > New Item...**. In the **Add New Item** dialog, select **LINQ to SQL Classes** and enter `AddressBookDataClasses.dbml` in the **Name:** `TextBox` (Fig. 24.11). Click the **Add** `Button`. The `AddressBookDataClasses.dbml` (representing the LINQ to SQL classes) file now appears in the **Solution Explorer**.

(cont.)

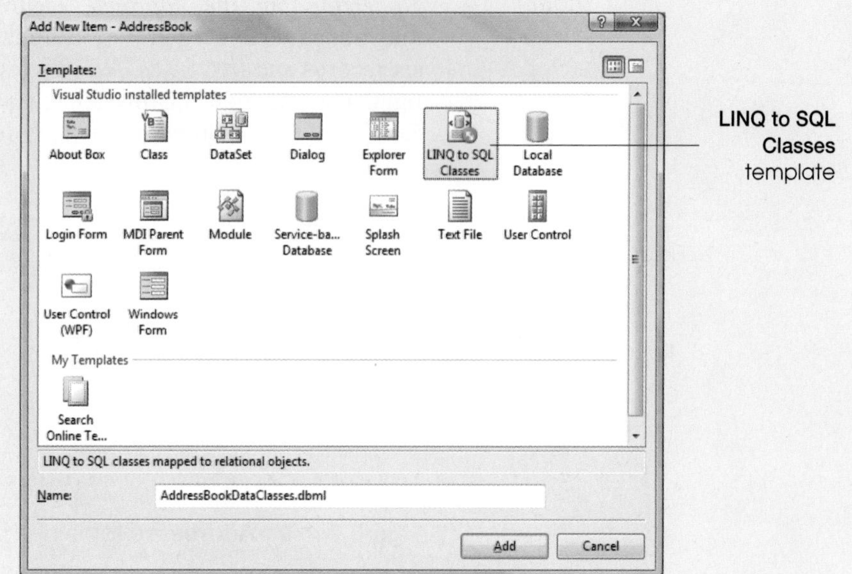

Figure 24.11 Adding LINQ to SQL classes.

2. ***Adding a database table to the LINQ to SQL classes.*** After adding the LINQ to SQL classes to your project, the IDE opens the Object Relational Designer (Fig. 24.12) to allow you to specify which tables in the database should be accessible through your LINQ to SQL classes. If the **Object Relational Designer** is not open, double click `AddressBookDataClasses.dbml` in the **Solution Explorer**. The right side of the **Object Relational Designer**—the **Methods Pane** (Fig. 24.12)—allows you to add stored procedures from the database to your application. We do not use stored procedures in this book. You can hide the **Methods Pane** by right clicking it and selecting **Hide Methods Pane**.

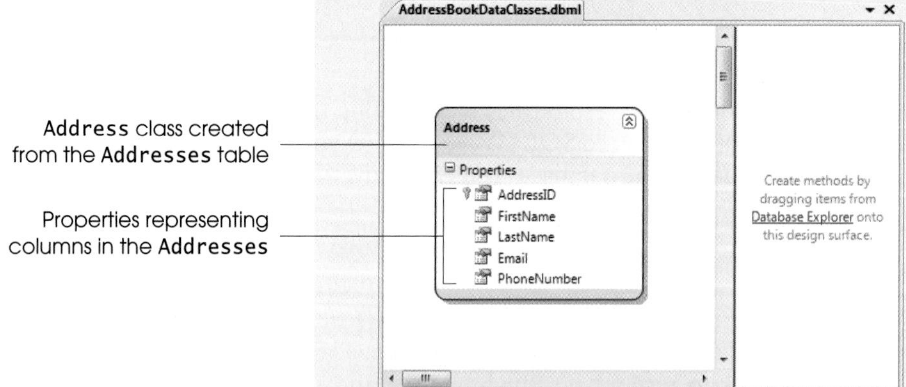

Figure 24.12 Adding a table from the **Database Explorer** to the **Object Relational Designer**.

To enable access to a database table, you drag the table from the **Database Explorer** onto the left pane of the **Object Relational Designer**. Expand the **AddressBook.mdf** node in the **Database Explorer**, then expand the **Tables** node. Drag the `Addresses` table onto the **Object Relational Designer** (Fig. 24.12). A dialog appears prompting you to copy the database file to your project, click **Yes**.

(cont.)

When you drag the `Addresses` table onto the **Object Relational Designer**, the IDE creates classes that represent the `Addresses` table and an `Address` entry. These classes are part of the LINQ to SQL classes. The `Address` class—representing a single address—is displayed in the **Object Relational Designer** (Fig. 24.12). The properties defined in class `Address` match the columns in the `Addresses` table. The IDE also creates class `AddressBookDataClassesDataContext`, which manages the connection to the database and the objects representing the database in your application.

3. ***Saving the project.*** Select **File > Save All** to save your modified code. Save the project in the `C:\SimplyVB2008` directory.

The LINQ to SQL classes you just created provide everything you need to connect to and manipulate the database. You can retrieve, edit, add and delete addresses in the `AddressBook.mdf` database. The IDE provides a way to automatically add GUI elements to your application that allow the user to browse through the database contents and to edit, update or delete data. To use these auto-generated GUI controls, you must first create a data source object based on your LINQ to SQL classes. You learn to create a data source in the following box.

Adding a Data Source to the Address Book Application

1. ***Adding a data source to the project.*** A data source helps you create and manage data-bound GUI controls. A **data-bound control** displays information contained in a data source. When the information in the data source changes, the control updates to display the new information. The `Binding-Navigator` and `TextBoxes` in the completed application are data-bound controls—the information they display is updated when you browse to a different entry in the `Addresses` table. Open the **Data Sources window** (Fig. 24.13) by selecting **Data > Show Data Sources**. In the **Data Sources** window, click the link **Add New Data Source...** or click the **Add New Data Source** `Button`. This opens the **Data Source Configuration Wizard**, which guides you through creating a data source. Select **Object** in the wizard (Fig. 24.14) and click **Next >**.

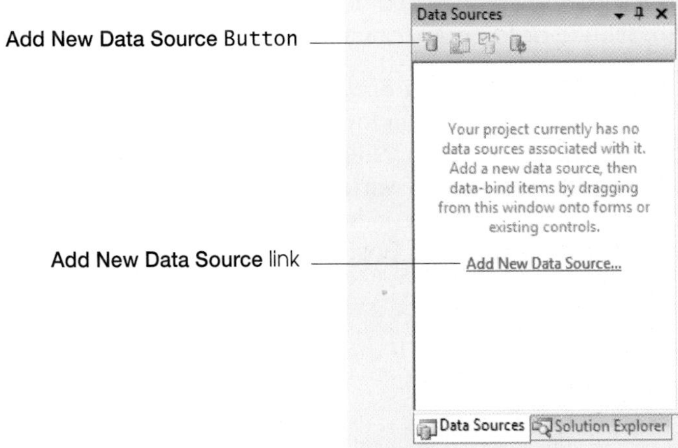

Figure 24.13 **Data Sources** window.

2. ***Selecting the object to manage data-bound controls.*** The **Data Source Configuration Wizard** prompts you to select the object whose information is displayed in the data-bound controls. Expand the `AddressBook` node and select the `Address` class as in Fig. 24.15 and click **Finish**. If the `Address` class is not displayed as in Fig. 24.15, select **File > Save All** to save your modified files. Then repeat these steps.

(cont.)

Select **Object** as the data source type

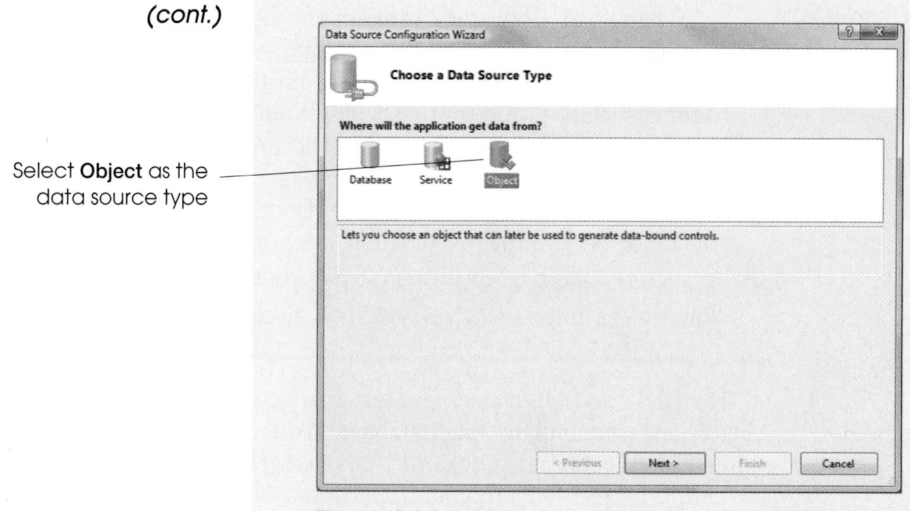

Figure 24.14 **Data Source Configuration Wizard** dialog.

Select the `Address` class as the object data source

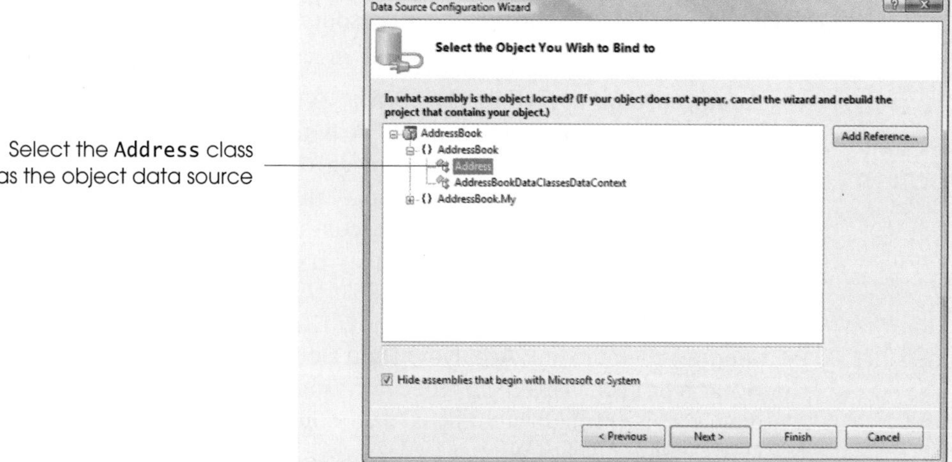

Figure 24.15 Select **Address** to add a data source that can bind `Address` information to data-bound controls.

3. ***Viewing the data source in the Data Sources window.*** An **Address** node now appears in the **Data Sources** window with child nodes for each property in the `Address` class (Fig. 24.16). Note that the appearance of the data source in the **Data Sources** window varies slightly depending on whether you are in **Design** view or **Code** view. Figure 24.16 shows the **Data Sources** window when the IDE is in **Design** view.

Data source name

`Addresses` table's fields represented in the data source

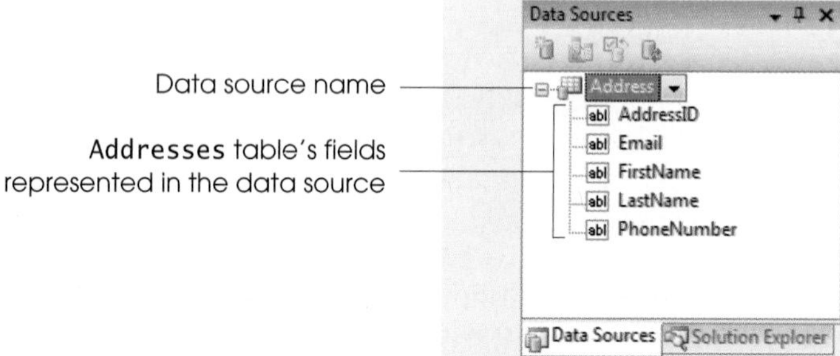

Figure 24.16 Updated **Data Sources** window.

4. ***Saving the project.*** Select **File > Save All** to save your modified code.

Now that you've added the `AddressBook.mdf` database, the LINQ to SQL classes and a data source, you can display the data from the database's `Addresses` table in your program. The IDE provides design tools that generate GUI controls to display data from a data source on the `Form`. Simply drag and drop items from the **Data Sources** window onto a `Form`, and the IDE generates appropriate GUI controls. In the following box, you learn how to do this in the **Address Book** application.

Displaying the Address Fields on the Form

1. ***Specifying the controls used to display the fields in each row of data.*** The IDE allows you to specify the type of control(s) that it creates when you drag and drop a data source onto a `Form` in **Design** view. Open `AddressBookForm` in **Design** view, then click the **Address** node in the **Data Sources** window (Fig. 24.17). This node becomes a drop-down list when you select it. [*Note:* This does not occur if you are not in a `Form`'s **Design** view.] Click the down arrow to view the items in the list. The icon to the left of **DataGridView** is initially highlighted, because a `DataGridView` is the default control used to display data as a table. Select the **Details** option in the drop-down list to indicate that the IDE should create a set of `Label–TextBox` pairs for each field name and value when you add the **Address** data source to the `Form`. (You'll see what this looks like in Fig. 24.18.) You can also choose the **Customize...** option to select other controls that are capable of being bound to the data.

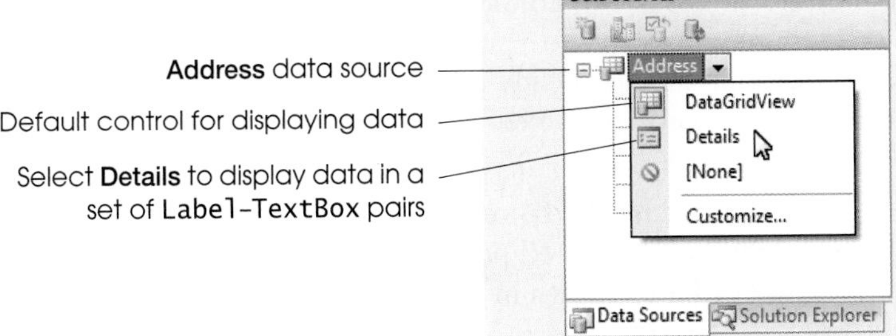

Figure 24.17 Selecting a display format for the data.

2. ***Dragging the Address data source node onto the Form.*** Drag the **Address** node from the **Data Sources** window to the `Form`. The IDE creates a series of `Labels` and `TextBoxes` (Fig. 24.18) because you selected **Details** in the preceding step. The IDE sets the text of each `Label` based on the corresponding property name in the data source, and inserts spaces into multiword names to make the `Labels` more readable (e.g., `FirstName` becomes `First Name`).

   The IDE also creates a `BindingNavigator` and a `BindingSource`. A `BindingNavigator`'s `Buttons` resemble the controls on a CD or DVD player and allow you to move to the first record of data, the preceding record, the next record and the last record. The control also displays the currently selected record number in a `TextBox`. You can use this `TextBox` to enter the number of a record that you want to select. A `BindingNavigator` also has `Buttons` that allow you to add a new record, delete a record and save changes to the underlying data source (that is, the `Addresses` table of the `AddressBook.mdf` database). The `BindingSource` manages the interaction between the data source and the data-bound controls on the `Form`.

(cont.)

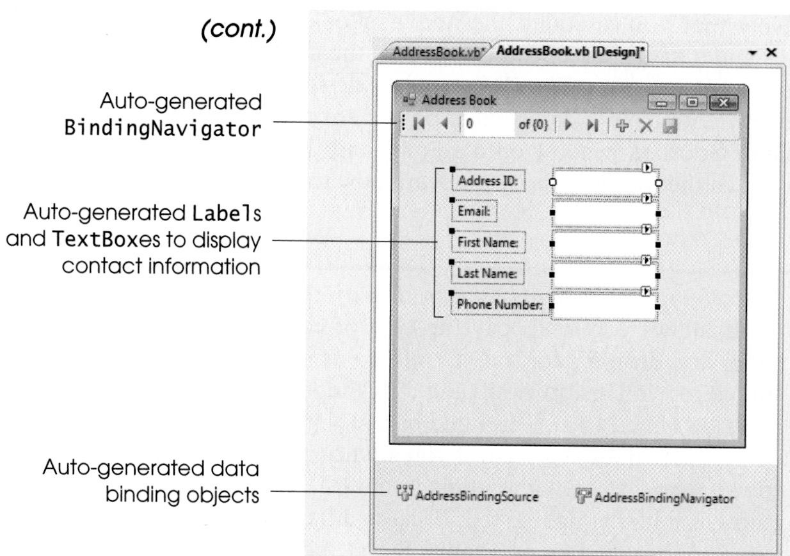

Figure 24.18 Displaying a table on a Form using a series of Labels and TextBoxes.

3. ***Making the AddressID TextBox Read Only.*** The AddressID column of the Addresses table is an auto-incremented column that is used to uniquely identify each record in the Addresses table, so users should not be allowed to edit the values of this column. Select the **Address ID:** TextBox and set its ReadOnly property to True. Also set its TabStop property to False. [*Note:* You may need to click in an empty part of the Form to deselect the other Labels and TextBoxes before selecting the **Address ID:** TextBox.]

4. ***Repositioning the Labels and TextBoxes.*** The IDE creates the Label/TextBox pairs in alphabetical order. Reposition the GUI controls to place them in a more natural order as shown in Fig. 24.19, then modify the application's tab order.

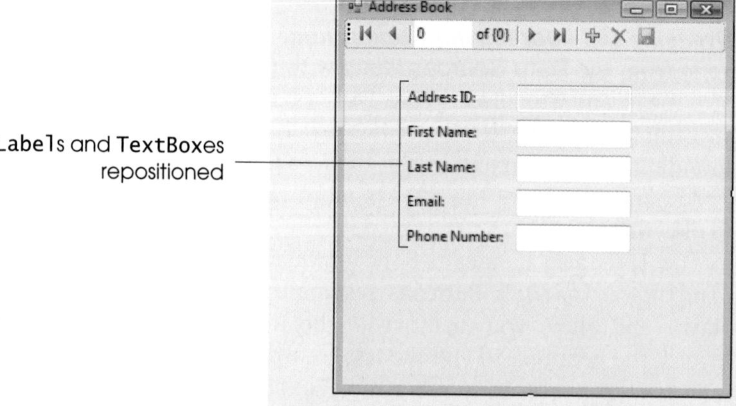

Figure 24.19 GUI controls repositioned.

5. ***Saving the project.*** Select **File > Save All** to save your modified code.

SELF-REVIEW

1. A database connection is added to an application with the ________ menu item.

a) **Data > Add New Data Source...**
b) **View > Database Explorer**
c) **Tools > Connect to Database...**
d) None of the above

2. The _________ allow(s) you to connect to the database and manipulate the information it contains.
   a) LINQ to SQL classes
   b) data source
   c) database table
   d) None of the above

3. The _________ provide(s) GUI controls to navigate through the entries in a database.
   a) LINQ to SQL classes
   b) `BindingNavigator`
   c) `BindingSource`
   d) database

Answers: 1) c. 2) a. 3) b.

24.4 Programming the Address Book Application

You've now created everything you need to connect to the `AddressBook.mdf` database and manipulate its information. The IDE generated additional code, such as the code that defines the LINQ to SQL classes, as well as the designer code that declares the auto-generated GUI controls and objects in the component tray. To view the auto-generated code for the LINQ to SQL classes, click the **Show All Files** `Button` in the **Solution Explorer**, then expand the `AddressBookDataClasses.dbml` node. The `AddressBookDataClasses.designer.vb` file contains the LINQ to SQL class definitions. Next, you write the code that enables your application to display address book data.

Coding the Form's Load Event Handler

1. ***Creating a `DataContext` instance variable.*** Switch to **Code** view, then add lines 2–3 of Fig. 24.20. Line 3 creates an instance variable refers to an `AddressBookDataClassesDataContext`—this class was defined as part of the LINQ to SQL classes you created earlier in this tutorial. The `AddressBookDataClassesDataContext` object connects to the database and interacts with it on the application's behalf. This object has properties representing each table you added to the `AddressBookDataClasses` LINQ to SQL classes in the **Object Relational Designer** (i.e., `Addresses`). You use this object in your LINQ statements to query the database.

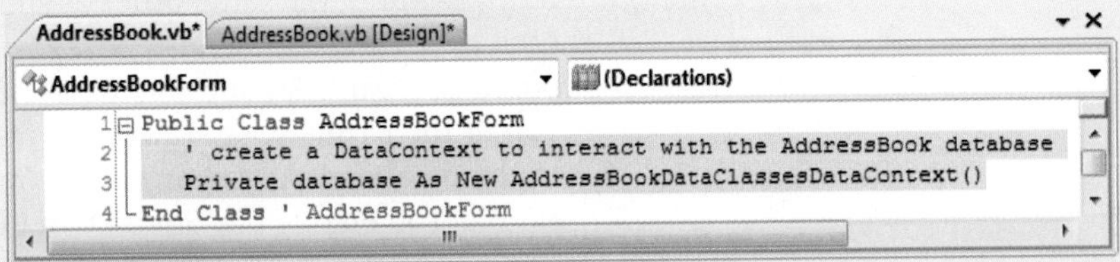

Figure 24.20 Creating a `DataContext` object.

2. ***Retrieving data from the database.*** Add lines 5–12 of Fig. 24.21 to define the `FillAll` method. Lines 9–11 define a LINQ query that retrieves each entry in the `Addresses` table. The `From` clause (line 9) specifies the data source for the query as `database.Addresses`—an object in the `AddressBookDataClassesDataContext` that represents the `Addresses` table. When this query executes, the `AddressBookDataClassesDataContext` object handles all the details of querying the database. Line 10 uses the LINQ clause `Order By` to sort the query results according to the property specified after the `Order By` keywords. This query sorts the results by the `LastName` property.

   Line 8 assigns the result of the query to the `AddressBindingSource`'s `DataSource` property, which specifies the data source used for binding purposes. This assignment fills the `AddressBindingSource`'s `DataSource` with `Address` objects containing data from the `Addresses` table in the `AddressBook.mdf` database.

(cont.)

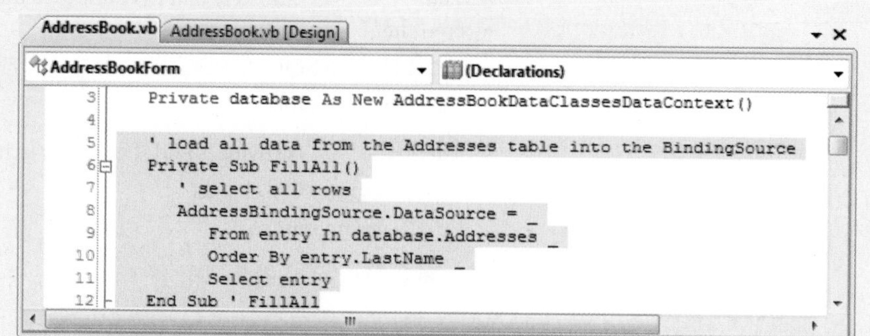

Figure 24.21 Retrieving data from the database using LINQ.

3. ***Creating the Form's Load event handler.*** Double click the `Form` in **Design** view to generate its `Load` event handler. Add lines 18–19 of Fig. 24.22 to the event handler. Line 19 calls method `FillAll` to retrieve the information from the database and display it on the `Form`.

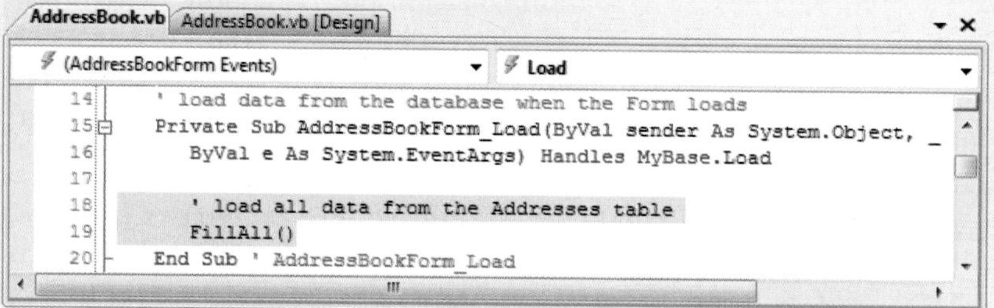

AddressBook.vb
AddressBook.vb [Design]
(AddressBookForm Events)
Load
14 ' load data from the database when the Form loads
15 Private Sub AddressBookForm_Load(ByVal sender As System.Object, _
16 ByVal e As System.EventArgs) Handles MyBase.Load
17
18 ' load all data from the Addresses table
19 FillAll()
20 End Sub ' AddressBookForm_Load

Figure 24.22 Retrieving data from the database when the `Form` loads.

4. ***Running the application.*** Select **Debug > Start Debugging** to run the application (Fig. 24.23). You can browse through the entries using the `BindingNavigator`. [*Note:* You must increase the width of the `TextBoxes` to accommodate the information.] As you browse the entries, notice that they are not in the same order as shown in the `Addresses` table in the database (Fig. 24.10)—they are now sorted alphabetically by last name. At this point, you can also add and delete entries. However, the **Save Data** `Button` in the `BindingNavigator` is disabled—you cannot save your changes to the database. Any changes you make are lost when you close the application. You enable the **Save Data** `Button` in the next box.

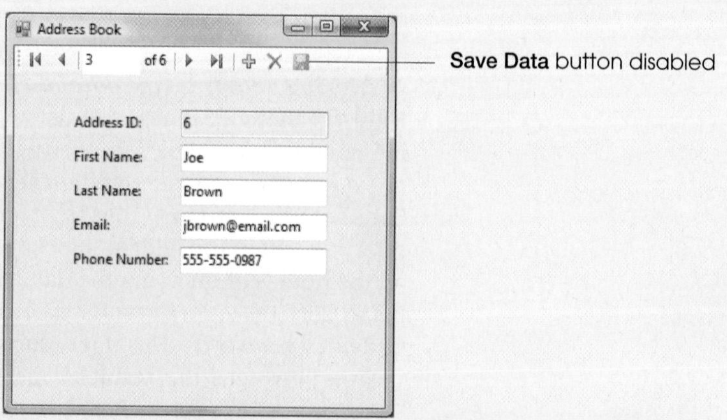

Figure 24.23 Browsing entries in the **Address Book** application.

5. ***Closing the application.*** Close your running application by clicking its close box.

Your **Address Book** application now allows the user to browse the entries stored in the `AddressBook.mdf` database. The user can also add, delete and edit entries, but the user cannot save the changes because the **Save Data** `Button` is disabled. In the next box, you learn how to enable the user to save their changes using the `BindingNavigator`'s **Save Data** `Button`.

Enabling the *`BindingNavigator`'s* *Save Data Button*

1. ***Coding the Save Data Button's `Click` event.*** Select the `BindingNavigator`'s **Save Data** `Button` and set its `Enabled` property to `True`. Double click the **Save Data** `Button` to create its `Click` event handler. Add lines 27–34 of Fig. 24.24. Saving the changes to the database is a two-step process. First, the data source associated with the data-bound controls (the `BindingSource`) must be updated to include any changes made by the user. Second, the database on disk must be updated to match the new contents of the data source.

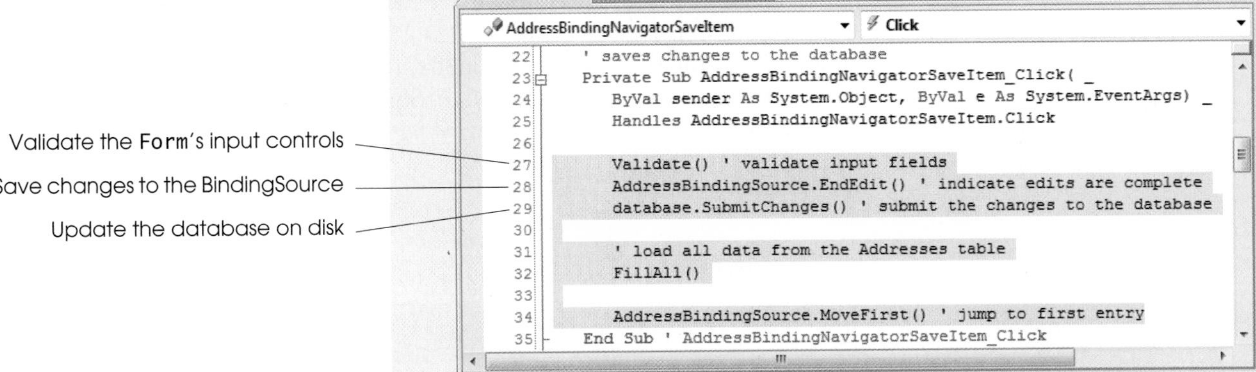
AddressBook.vb
AddressBook.vb [Design]
AddressBindingNavigatorSaveItem
Click
22 ' saves changes to the database
23 Private Sub AddressBindingNavigatorSaveItem_Click(_
24 ByVal sender As System.Object, ByVal e As System.EventArgs) _
25 Handles AddressBindingNavigatorSaveItem.Click
26
27 Validate() ' validate input fields
28 AddressBindingSource.EndEdit() ' indicate edits are complete
29 database.SubmitChanges() ' submit the changes to the database
30
31 ' load all data from the Addresses table
32 FillAll()
33
34 AddressBindingSource.MoveFirst() ' jump to first entry
35 End Sub ' AddressBindingNavigatorSaveItem_Click
Validate the Form's input controls
Save changes to the BindingSource
Update the database on disk

Figure 24.24 `Click` event handler for the **Save Data** `Button`.

Before the event handler saves any changes, line 27 calls the `Form`'s `Validate` method to validate any of the controls on the `Form` that implement `Validating` or `Validated` events. These events enable you to validate user input and indicate errors for invalid data. Line 28 invokes `AddressBindingSource`'s `EndEdit` method to ensure that the object's associated data source is updated with any changes made by the user to the currently selected row (for example, adding a row or changing a column value). Any changes to other rows were applied when you selected another row. Note that the application assumes the user has entered data in each input control.

Line 29 invokes `AddressBookDataClassesDataContext`'s `SubmitChanges` method to write the changes to the SQL Server database on disk—making the changes persistent after the application terminates. The LINQ to SQL classes you created use ADO.NET to manage the interaction with the database required to update the data and save the changes.

When you add a new entry it is added to the end of the data source's items, so the entries are likely no longer be in alphabetical order. Line 32 calls method `FillAll` to reload and sort the entries when the user clicks the **Save Data** `Button`. Line 34 calls the `BindingSource`'s `MoveFirst` method to move to the first entry.

2. ***Saving changes to the database.*** Select **Debug > Start Debugging** to run the application. Add an entry and click the **Save Data** `Button` to save the new entry. Close the running application by clicking its close box. Select **Debug > Start Debugging** to run the application again. Notice that the entry you added still exists. Recall that you must set the **Copy to Ouput** property of `AddressBook.mdf` to **Copy if newer** to retain your changes.

(cont.)

3. ***Closing the running application.*** Close the running application by clicking its close box.

While the `BindingNavigator` allows you to browse the address book entries, it would be more convenient to be able to find a specific entry by last name. In the next box, you add GUI controls to the `Form` that allow the user to search for an entry by last name. Then you create a LINQ query that searches the `AddressBook.mdf` database for entries with the specified last name.

Searching the Last-Name Field in the `AddressBook.mdf` Database

1. ***Adding controls to allow users to specify a last name to locate.*** Add controls to allow the user to enter a last name for which to search. Add to the `Form` a `Label` named `searchLabel`, a `TextBox` named `searchTextBox` and a `Button` named `findButton` (Fig. 24.25). Place these controls in a `GroupBox` named `findByLastNameGroupBox`, then set the `GroupBox`'s `Text` property to `Find an entry by last name`. Set the `Text` properties of the `Label` and `Button` as shown in Fig. 24.25.

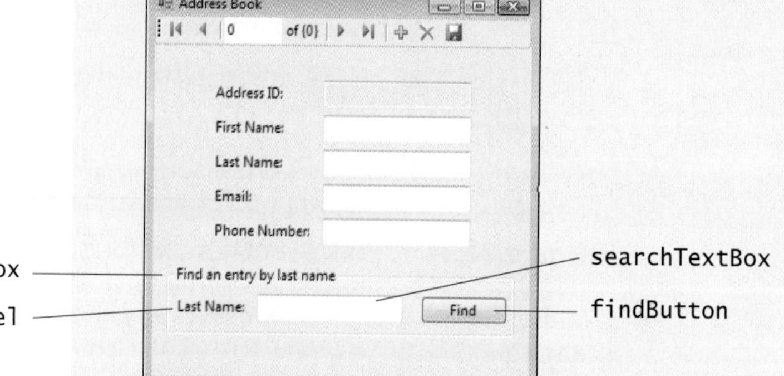

Figure 24.25 Add controls to search data by last name.

2. ***Creating the `findButton_Click` event handler.*** Double click the **Find** `Button` in **Design** view to create its `Click` event handler.

3. ***Retrieving and displaying entries with the specified last names.*** Add lines 41–48 of Fig. 24.26 to the `findButton_Click` event handler. Lines 43–46 define a LINQ query that retrieves from the `Addresses` table (line 43) entries where the last name matches the name specified in `searchTextBox` (line 44). Because all entries returned by this query have the same last name, it makes no sense to order the results by last name as you did in the `FillAll` method's query. Instead, line 45 orders the results by first name. Line 42 assigns the result of the query to the `AddressBindingSource`'s `DataSource` property to allow the user to browse only the entries with the specified last name. Line 48 jumps to the first entry in the result.

4. ***Saving the project.*** Select **File > Save All** to save your modified code.

(cont.)

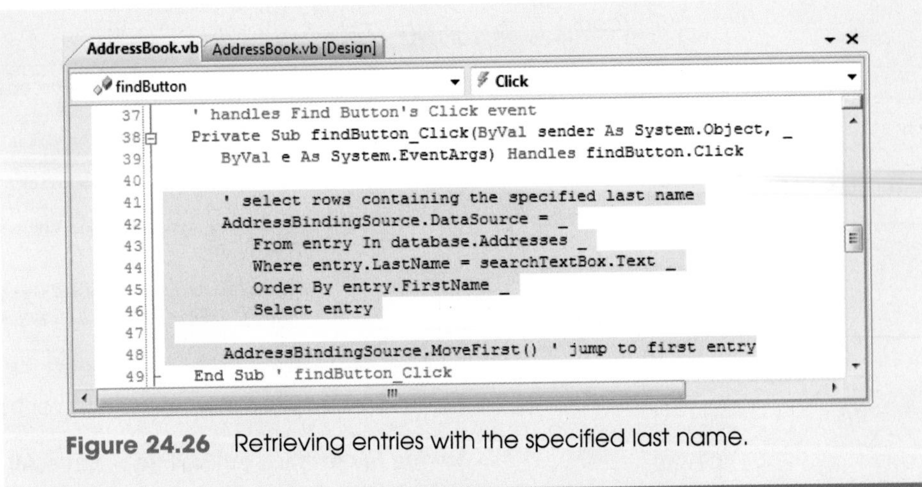

AddressBook.vb
AddressBook.vb [Design]
findButton
Click
' handles Find Button's Click event
Private Sub findButton_Click(ByVal sender As System.Object, _
ByVal e As System.EventArgs) Handles findButton.Click
' select rows containing the specified last name
AddressBindingSource.DataSource = _
From entry In database.Addresses _
Where entry.LastName = searchTextBox.Text _
Order By entry.FirstName _
Select entry
AddressBindingSource.MoveFirst() ' jump to first entry
End Sub ' findButton_Click

Figure 24.26 Retrieving entries with the specified last name.

Now you are ready to add the **Browse All Entries** `Button` and create the `browseAllButton_Click` event handler, which allows users to return to browsing all the rows after searching for specific rows. You add this `Button` and create its `Click` event handler in the following box.

Adding the Browse All Entries `Button` and Its `Click` Event Handler

1. ***Adding the `browseAllButton` to the Form.*** Add a `Button` named `browseAllButton` and set its `Text` property to `Browse All Entries`. The completed `Form` in **Design** view is shown in Fig. 24.27.

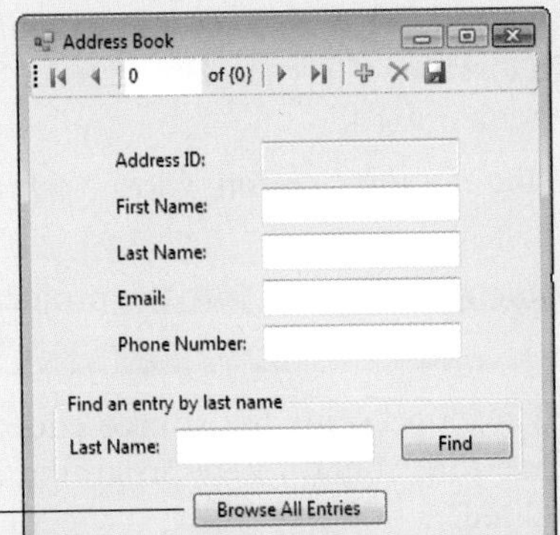

Figure 24.27 Adding the **Browse All Entries** `Button` to the `Form`.

2. ***Creating the `browseAllButton_Click` event handler.*** Double click the **Browse All Entries** `Button` in **Design** view to create its `Click` event handler.

3. ***Refilling Address `BindingSource` with all the rows in the database table.*** Add lines 56–60 of Fig. 24.28 to the `browseAllButton_Click` event handler. Line 57 calls method `FillAll` to refill the `AddressBindingSource` with all entries from the database. Line 59 jumps to the first entry. Line 60 clears the `searchTextBox`.

(cont.)

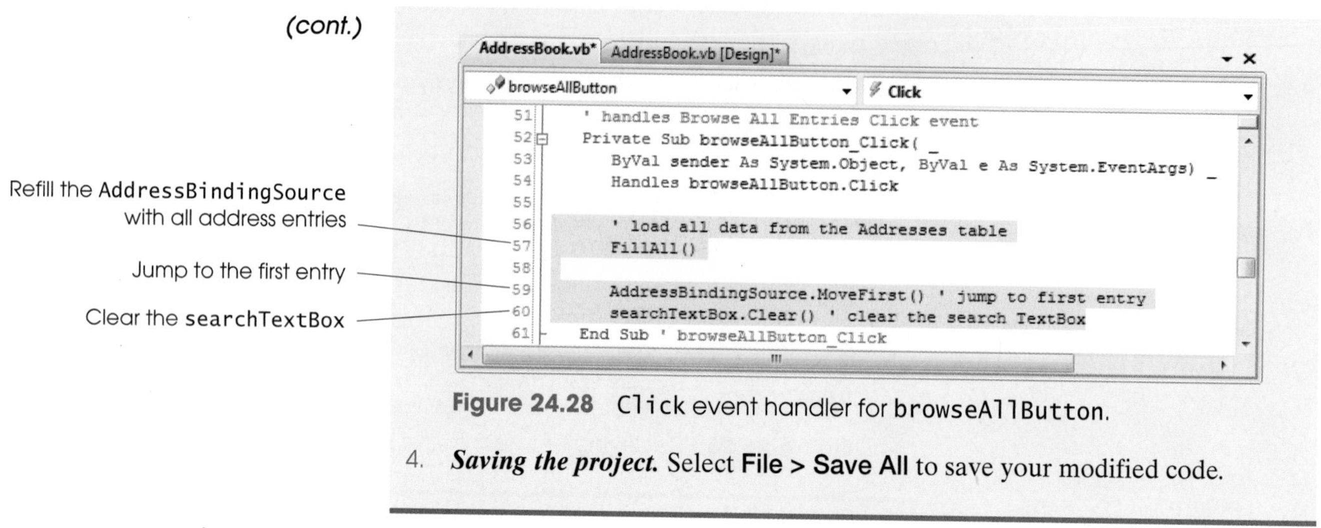

Figure 24.28 `Click` event handler for `browseAllButton`.

4. ***Saving the project.*** Select **File > Save All** to save your modified code.

Now that you've completed the **Address Book** application, you test it in the following box to ensure that it is functioning properly.

Testing Your Completed Address Book Application

1. ***Running the application.*** Select **Debug > Start Debugging** to run your application. Enter a new contact by clicking the **Add new** `Button` of the `BindingNavigator`, filling in the fields then clicking the **Save Data** `Button`. Next, search for the last name of the contact that you entered, using `searchTextBox` and `findButton`. Now click the **Browse All Entries** `Button`. Test the delete function by deleting an entry and then clicking the **Save Data** `Button`. Click the **Browse All Entries** `Button` again to see if the entry has been erased.
2. ***Closing the application.*** Close your running application by clicking its close box.
3. ***Closing the project.*** Close the project by selecting **File > Close Project**.

Figure 24.29 presents the source code for the **Address Book** application. The lines of code that contain new programming concepts you learned in this tutorial are highlighted.

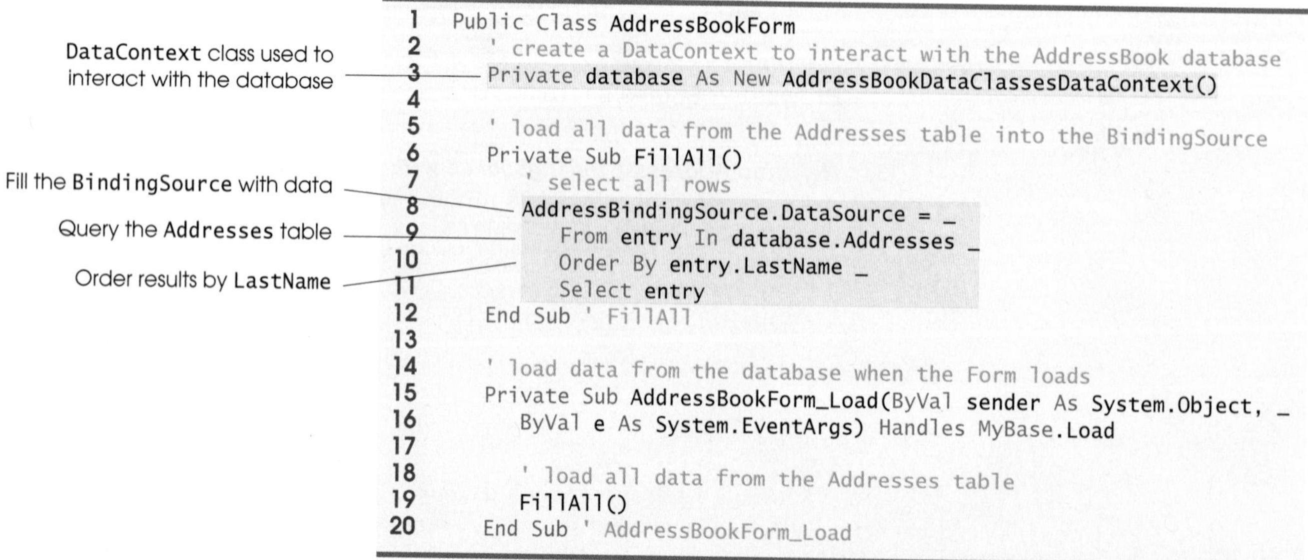


```
Public Class AddressBookForm
   ' create a DataContext to interact with the AddressBook database
   Private database As New AddressBookDataClassesDataContext()

   ' load all data from the Addresses table into the BindingSource
   Private Sub FillAll()
      ' select all rows
      AddressBindingSource.DataSource = _
         From entry In database.Addresses _
         Order By entry.LastName _
         Select entry
   End Sub ' FillAll

   ' load data from the database when the Form loads
   Private Sub AddressBookForm_Load(ByVal sender As System.Object, _
      ByVal e As System.EventArgs) Handles MyBase.Load

      ' load all data from the Addresses table
      FillAll()
   End Sub ' AddressBookForm_Load
```

Figure 24.29 **Address Book** application code. (Part 1 of 2.)

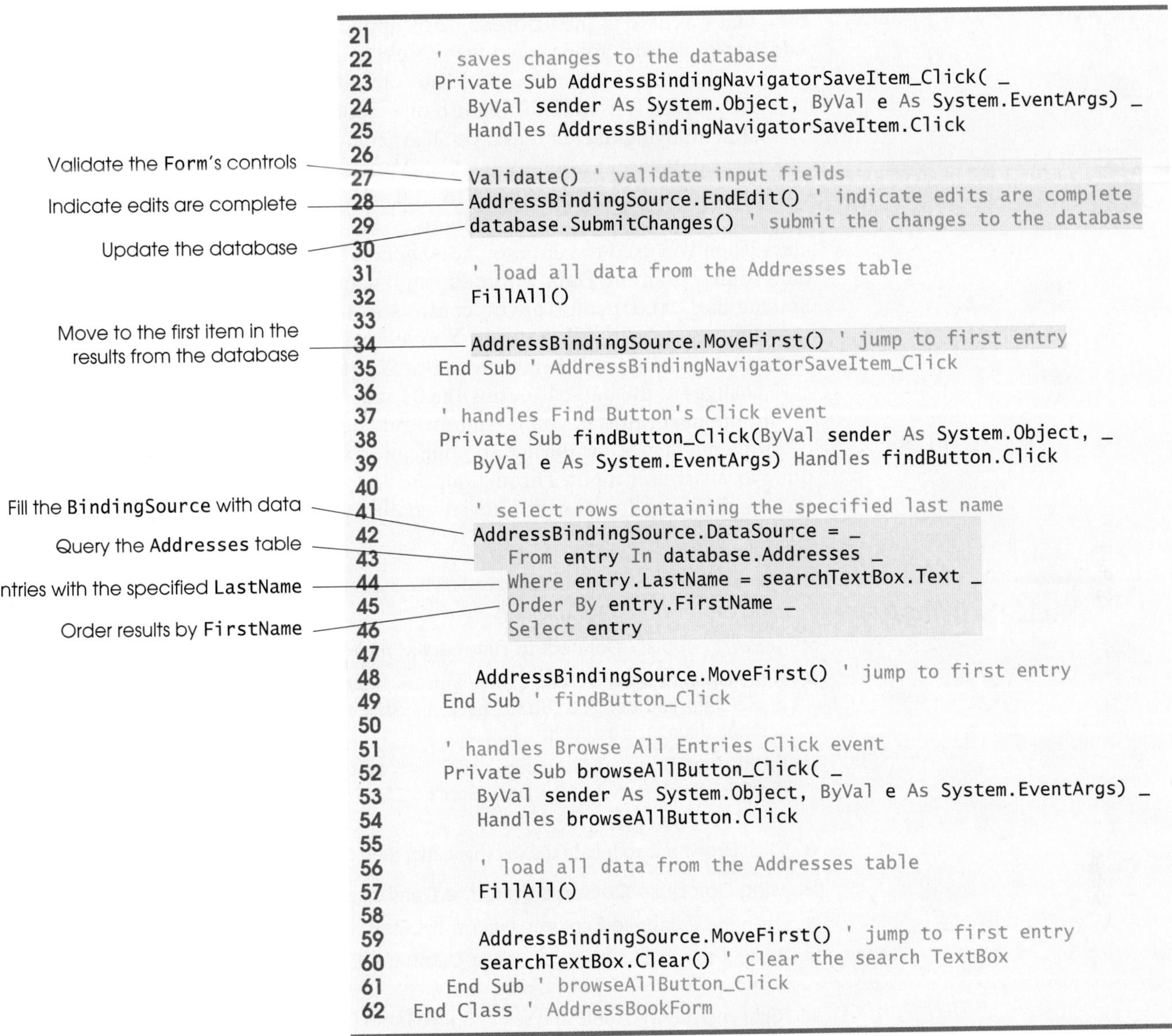
Validate the Form's controls
Indicate edits are complete
Update the database
Move to the first item in the results from the database
Fill the BindingSource with data
Query the Addresses table
Entries with the specified LastName
Order results by FirstName

```

   ' saves changes to the database
   Private Sub AddressBindingNavigatorSaveItem_Click( _
      ByVal sender As System.Object, ByVal e As System.EventArgs) _
      Handles AddressBindingNavigatorSaveItem.Click

      Validate() ' validate input fields
      AddressBindingSource.EndEdit() ' indicate edits are complete
      database.SubmitChanges() ' submit the changes to the database

      ' load all data from the Addresses table
      FillAll()

      AddressBindingSource.MoveFirst() ' jump to first entry
   End Sub ' AddressBindingNavigatorSaveItem_Click

   ' handles Find Button's Click event
   Private Sub findButton_Click(ByVal sender As System.Object, _
      ByVal e As System.EventArgs) Handles findButton.Click

      ' select rows containing the specified last name
      AddressBindingSource.DataSource = _
         From entry In database.Addresses _
         Where entry.LastName = searchTextBox.Text _
         Order By entry.FirstName _
         Select entry

      AddressBindingSource.MoveFirst() ' jump to first entry
   End Sub ' findButton_Click

   ' handles Browse All Entries Click event
   Private Sub browseAllButton_Click( _
      ByVal sender As System.Object, ByVal e As System.EventArgs) _
      Handles browseAllButton.Click

      ' load all data from the Addresses table
      FillAll()

      AddressBindingSource.MoveFirst() ' jump to first entry
      searchTextBox.Clear() ' clear the search TextBox
   End Sub ' browseAllButton_Click
End Class ' AddressBookForm
```

Figure 24.29 **Address Book** application code. (Part 2 of 2.)

SELF-REVIEW

1. The `DataContext`'s _________ method writes the modified version of a table (in memory) to the database on disk.

   a) `Update` b) `Fill`
   c) `SubmitChanges` d) None of the above

2. When creating a LINQ query to retrieve information from the database, use properties of the _________ class in the `From` clause to access the database's tables.

   a) `Database` b) `Table`
   c) `Addresses` d) `DataContext`

Answers: 1) c. 2) d.

24.5 Wrap-Up

In this tutorial, you learned that a database is an organized collection of data and that database management systems provide mechanisms for storing and organizing data. You then examined the contents of the Microsoft SQL Server Express database that was used in the **Address Book** application. While examining the database `AddressBook.mdf`, you learned that a field in a database table is a column and that a record is an entire table row. You also learned that each record must contain a primary key, which is used to distinguish one record from another.

After studying the database, you learned how to create LINQ to SQL classes to model the database in your application. You used the LINQ to SQL classes to interact with the database. The LINQ to SQL classes use ADO.NET to communicate with the database. You learned how to create a data source from a LINQ to SQL class. Then you used the data source to generate data-bound controls by dragging a data source from the **Data Sources** window onto a `Form`. You used the `BindingSource` and `BindingNavigator` controls to update the information displayed in the auto-generated GUI controls. You learned how to access and manipulate the database's content using LINQ and a `DataContext` object. You also learned how to save changes to the database using the `DataContext`.

In the next tutorial, you learn how to handle exceptions, which are indications of problems that occur during an application's execution. You use exception handling to verify user input. Throughout the text, you have been using `Val` to perform this functionality. In the next tutorial, you learn a more sophisticated technique for handling invalid user input.

SKILLS SUMMARY

Adding a Database Connection

- Select the **Tools > Connect to Database...** menu item.
- If the **Choose Data Source** dialog appears, select **Microsoft SQL Server Database File** in the **Data source:** `ListBox`. Check the **Always use this selection** `CheckBox` to prevent the dialog from appearing again.
- In the **Add Connection** dialog, make sure that **Microsoft SQL Server Database File (SqlClient)** is selected as the **Data Source**. If it is not, click **Change...** `Button` to select a new data source type.
- Click **Browse...** to locate the database file, then click **OK** to create the connection.

Viewing Database Contents Using the Database Explorer Window

- Open the **Database Explorer** window by selecting **View > Database Explorer**.
- Expand the database's node in the **Database Explorer** window node, then expand the **Tables** node.
- Right click desired table and select **Show Table Data**.

Creating LINQ to SQL Classes

- Right click the project in the **Solution Explorer** and select **Add > New Item...**.
- Select the **LINQ to SQL Classes** template in the **Add New Item** dialog.
- Enter a name in the **Name:** `TextBox` and click **Add**.
- If necessary, open the **Object Relational Designer** by double clicking the LINQ to SQL classes file (`.dbml`) in the **Solution Explorer**.
- Drag tables from the **Database Explorer** onto the **Object Relational Designer** to create classes that represent the tables in your database.

Adding a Data Source Using the Data Sources Window

- Open the **Data Sources** window by selecting **Data > Show Data Sources**.
- In the **Data Sources** window, click **Add New Data Source...** to open the **Data Source Configuration Wizard**.
- Select **Object** and click **Next >** in the first screen of the **Data Source Configuration Wizard**.
- Choose the object that contains the data to bind to your controls.
- Click **Finish** to create the data source and close the **Data Source Configuration Wizard**.

Displaying Database Data on a Form Using Drag-and-Drop

- While in **Design** view, open the **Data Sources** window by selecting **Data > Show Data Sources**.
- Click the node of the data source you want to display in the **Data Sources** window, thereby causing this node to become a drop-down list.
- Select the format in which you want to display the data from the node's drop-down list.
- Drag and drop the data source onto the `Form`.
- Fill the data source with information from the database in the `Form`'s `Load` event.

Specifying the Data Viewed in the GUI Controls

- Create a LINQ query to retrieve the desired information from the database.
- Assign the result of the LINQ query to `BindingSource`'s `DataSource` property.

Using LINQ to Query the Database

- Create a `DataContext` object.
- Use the `DataContext` object's properties to specify in the `From` clause the table to query.

Updating the Database

- Call the `Form`'s `Validate` method to perform any required validation.
- Call the `BindingSource`'s `EndEdit` method to indicate that the changes are complete.
- Use the `DataContext` object's `SubmitChanges` method to write the changes to the database.

KEY TERMS

ADO.NET—Part of .NET Framework that is used to interact with databases.

`BindingNavigator`—A set of controls that allow you to manipulate and navigate through data in a data source.

`BindingSource`—A component that manages the data used by a `BindingNavigator`.

database—Organized collection of data.

database management system (DBMS)—Provides mechanisms for storing and organizing data.

data-bound control—A control that displays information contained in a data source. When the information in the data source changes, the control updates to display the new information.

Database Explorer window—Window used to view and manipulate database information in the Visual Basic 2008 Express IDE.

`DataContext` class—LINQ to SQL classes representation of a database in the application. Manages interactions between the application and the database.

`DataSource` property of class `BindingSource`—Specifies the data managed by the `BindingSource`.

Data Sources window—Window used to connect an application to a data source and create data-bound controls.

Data Source Configuration Wizard—Wizard used to add a data source to the application.

`EndEdit` method of class `BindingSource`—Saves all edits made to the `BindingSource`'s data.

field—Column in a database table.

instant-access application—Application that immediately locates a particular record of information.

LINQ to SQL classes—Creates a model of a database in an application. These classes are used to manipulate the database's contents.

`.mdf` file—A SQL Server Express database file.

`MoveFirst` method of class `BindingSource`—Moves to the first item in the `BindingSource`.

Object Relational Designer—Allows you to specify which tables in a database are accessible through an application's LINQ to SQL classes.

Order By clause of a LINQ query—Orders the result of a LINQ query by the specified property.

primary key—Field (or combination of fields) in a database table that contains unique values used to distinguish records from one another.

query—Request information that satisfies given criteria.

record—An entire table row in a database.

SQL Server Express—A database management system built by Microsoft.

Structured Query Language (SQL)—Language often used by relational databases to perform queries and manipulate data in relational databases.

SubmitChanges method of class DataContext—Updates the database on disk with any changes made in the application.

table—Used to store related information in rows and columns. (Represented in the application by the LINQ to SQL classes.)

CONTROLS, EVENTS, PROPERTIES & METHODS

BindingNavigator BindingNavigator This control allows the user to navigate through records in a data source. BindingNavigator also has Buttons that allow you to add a new row, delete a row and save changes to the underlying data source. An object of this type is created automatically when you drag a data source onto a Form in **Design** view to create the auto-generated GUI controls.

BindingSource BindingSource This control manages the information used by the BindingNavigator.

- ***Property***

  DataSource—Specifies the data managed by the BindingSource.

- ***Methods***

  EndEdit—Saves all edits made to the BindingSource's data.

  MoveFirst—Moves to the first item in the BindingSource.

DataContext A class generated when you create a set of LINQ to SQL classes. An object of this class manages the connection to the database, provides properties representing the tables in the database and enables you to use LINQ to perform database queries, inserts, updates and deletes.

- ***Method***

  SubmitChanges—Saves changes in the LINQ to SQL objects back to the corresponding database.

MULTIPLE-CHOICE QUESTIONS

24.1 A ________ provides mechanisms for storing and organizing data.

a) relational database
b) connection object
c) data command
d) database management system

24.2 An entire row in a database table is known as a ________.

a) record
b) field
c) column
d) primary key

24.3 A primary key is used to ________.

a) create rows in a database
b) identify fields in a database
c) distinguish between records in a table
d) read information from a database

24.4 In a LINQ query, the ________ clause sorts the results according to the specified property.

a) Sort By
b) By
c) Order By
d) Sort

24.5 The `DataContext` class allows you to ________.

a) specify a database table to use in a LINQ query
b) create a new database
c) update the contents of a database
d) Both a and c

24.6 The ________ method of the `DataContext` class modifies information in a database.

a) `Update` b) `Modify`
c) `Edit` d) `SubmitChanges`

24.7 A ________ is an organized collection of data.

a) record b) database
c) data reader d) primary key

24.8 The ________ property of a `BindingSource` specifies the data managed by the `BindingSource`.

a) `Data` b) `DataSource`
c) `SourceData` d) `Source`

24.9 A ________ allows the user to navigate through information stored in a data source.

a) `SourceNavigator` b) `BindingNavigator`
c) `BindingSource` d) None of the above

EXERCISES

24.10 ***(Stock Portfolio Application)*** A stock broker wants an application that displays a client's stock portfolio (Fig. 24.30). All the companies that the user holds stock in should be displayed in a `ComboBox` when the application is loaded. When the user selects a company from the `ComboBox`, the stock information for that company automatically displays in `Label`–`TextBox` pairs.

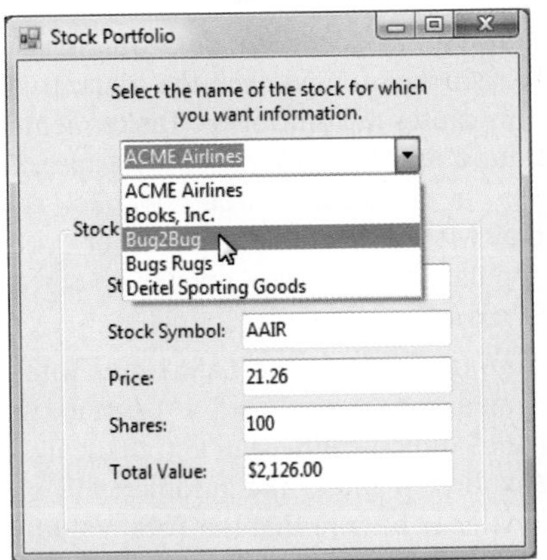

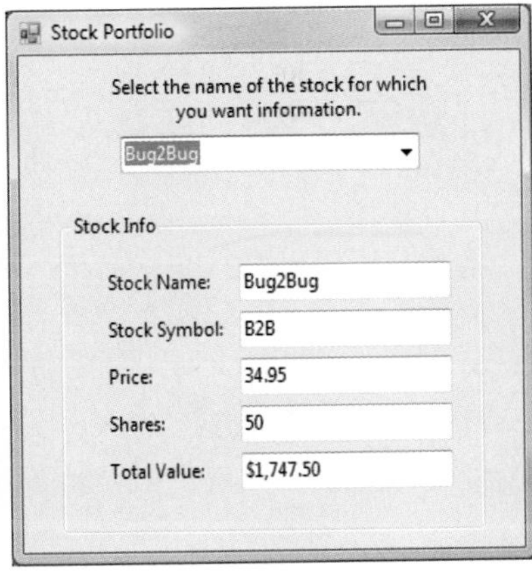

Figure 24.30 **Stock Portfolio** application.

a) ***Creating a Windows Forms Application.*** Select **File > New Project...** and create a new **Windows Forms Application** named `StockPortfolio`. In the **Solution Explorer**, rename the `Form1.vb` file to `StockPortfolio.vb`.

b) ***Configuring the Form's properties.*** Change the `Form`'s `Name` property to `StockPortfolioForm` then change the `Text` property to `Stock Portfolio`. Change the `Form`'s `Font` property 9pt **Segoe UI**.

c) ***Adding a display `Label` to the `Form`.*** Add a `Label` named `displayLabel`. Set its `Text` property to `Select the name of the stock for which you want information` and center the text in the `Label`. Set the `Label`'s `AutoSize` property to `False` and resize it to fit the text on two lines. Position the `Label` on the `Form` as shown in Fig. 24.30.

d) ***Adding a database to the project.*** Select **Tools > Connect to Database...** to open the **Add Connection** dialog. Check that the **Data Source:** is set to **Microsoft SQL Server Database File (SqlClient)**. Click **Browse...** to select the `Stocks.mdf` database file in the `C:\Examples\Tutorial24\Exercises\Databases` directory. Click **OK** to add the connection.

e) ***Creating LINQ to SQL classes.*** Right click the project in the **Solution Explorer** and select **Add > New Item...**. In the **Add New Item** dialog, select **LINQ to SQL Classes** and enter `StocksDataClasses.dbml` in the **Name:** `TextBox`, then click **Add**. Drag the **Stocks** table from the **Database Explorer** onto the **Object Relational Designer** to create the `Stock` class. Click **Yes** when asked if you want to copy the database file to your project.

f) ***Adding a data source to the project.*** Open the **Data Sources** window and click the **Add New Data Source...** link. Choose the **Object** data source type, then click **Next >**. Select the `Stock` class—created in the LINQ to SQL classes when you dragged the **Stocks** table onto the **Object Relational Designer**—and click **Finish**. [*Note:* If the `Stock` class does not appear under the **StockPortfolio** node in the **Data Source Configuration Wizard**, save your project and try again.]

g) ***Adding a display `GroupBox` to the `Form`.*** Add a `GroupBox` named `stockInfoGroupBox` to the `Form`. Position the `GroupBox` as shown in Fig. 24.30.

h) ***Adding controls that display stock portfolio data on the `Form`.*** Choose `Details` from the **Stock** drop-down list in the **Data Sources** window and drag-and-drop the **Stock** node onto the `Form`. Expand the `TextBox`es to accommodate the display data. Move the automatically generated `Label`s and `TextBox`es so that they are centered in `stockInfoGroupBox`. Reorder the `Label`–`TextBox` pairs as **Stock Name**, **Stock Symbol**, **Price** then **Shares**.

i) ***Deleting `BindingNavigator`.*** You navigate through the data with the `stockNameComboBox`, so you do not need the `BindingNavigator` control in this application. To delete it, just click the `BindingNavigator` in the `Form` and press *Delete*.

j) ***Adding a `ComboBox` to the `Form` that displays all the stock names.*** Add a `ComboBox` named `stockNameComboBox` below the `displayLabel`.

k) ***Making the `ComboBox` data-bound to retrieve all the stock names.*** Select `stockNameComboBox` and click the black triangle in the upper-right corner of the control. This causes a **ComboBox Tasks** menu to appear. In this menu, check the **Use data bound items** `CheckBox`, which causes four `ComboBox`es to appear below the `CheckBox`. In the **Data Source** `ComboBox` select `StockBindingSource`. Then, in the **Display Member** and **Value Member** `ComboBox`es, select `StockName`. This automatically populates `stockNameComboBox` with the names of all the `Stock`s in the `StocksBindingSource`.

l) ***Adding a* Total Value *`Label` and* Total Value *`TextBox` onto the `Form`.*** Add a `Label` named `totalLabel` and a `TextBox` named `totalTextBox` to the `Form`. Place the `Label` directly under the automatically generated `Label`s from *Step h*, and the `TextBox` directly under the automatically generated `TextBox`es. To make the application look neat, be sure that the **Total Value:** `Label` and **Total Value:** `TextBox` are the same size as the automatically generated controls.

m) ***Retrieving information from the database when the `Form` loads.*** Double click the `Form` in **Design** view to create its `Load` event handler. Create a `StocksDataClassesDataContext` object as an instance variable above the `Load` event handler. In the `Load` event handler, use a LINQ query to retrieve all the stocks from the `Stocks` table in the database (ordered by name) and assign the result to the `StockBindingSource`'s `DataSource` property.

n) ***Updating `totalTextBox` in `StockBindingSource`'s `PositionChanged` event and the `Form`'s `Load` event.*** In the `Form`'s `Load` event handler, create a local variable of type `Stock` and assign it the currently displayed `Stock` using the `Current` property of class `StockBindingSource` (you need to cast the `Object` returned by property `Current` to a `Stock` object). Pass this `Stock` object to the `CalculateStockValue` method—which you define in the next step—and display the result, formatted as currency, in `totalTextBox`.

Select `StockBindingSource` in the **Class Name** `ComboBox`, then select `PositionChanged` in the **Method Name** `ComboBox` to create the `StockBinding-Source`'s `PositionChanged` event handler. Write code to access the currently displayed `Stock` object and pass it to method `CalculateStockValue`. Display the result, formatted as currency, in `totalTextBox`.

o) ***Defining the `CalculateStockValue` method.*** Create a `Function` procedure named `CalculateStockValue`. This method takes as an argument a `Stock` object and returns the product of the `Stock`'s price and the number of shares as a `Decimal`.

p) ***Running the application.*** Select **Debug > Start Debugging** to run your application. Select different stocks from the `ComboBox`. Verify that the `TextBoxes` that display the stock information are modified appropriately when a new stock is chosen.

q) ***Closing the application.*** Close your running application by clicking its close box.

24.11 ***(Airline Reservation Application)*** An airline company wants you to develop an application that displays flight information (Fig. 24.31). The database contains two tables, one containing information about the flights, the other containing passenger information. The user should be able to choose a flight number from a `ComboBox`. When a flight number is chosen, the application should display the date of the flight, the flight's departure and arrival cities and the names of the passengers scheduled to take the flight.

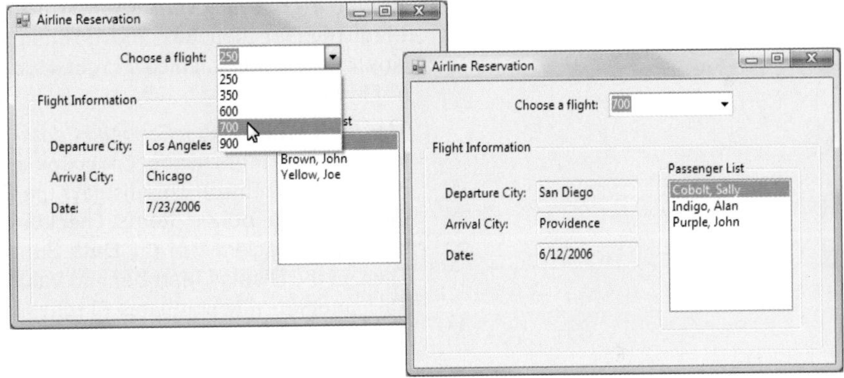

Figure 24.31 **Airline Reservation** application.

a) ***Creating a Windows Forms Application.*** Select **File > New Project...** and create a new **Windows Forms Application** named `AirlineReservation`. In the **Solution Explorer**, rename the `Form1.vb` file to `AirlineReservation.vb`.

b) ***Configuring the Form's properties.*** Change the `Form`'s `Name` property to `Airline-ReservationForm`, then change the `Text` property to `Airline Reservation`. Change the `Form`'s `Font` property 9pt **Segoe UI**.

c) ***Adding a database to the project.*** Select **Tools > Connect to Database...** to open the **Add Connection** dialog. Check that the **Data Source:** is set to **Microsoft SQL Server Database File (SqlClient)**. Click the **Browse...** `Button` to select the `Reservations.mdf` database in the `C:\Examples\Tutorial24\Exercises\Databases` directory. Click **OK** to add the connection.

d) ***Creating LINQ to SQL classes.*** Right click the project in the **Solution Explorer** and select **Add > New Item...**. In the **Add New Item** dialog, select **LINQ to SQL Classes** and enter `ReservationsDataClasses.dbml` in the **Name:** `TextBox`, then click **Add**. Drag the **Flights** and **Reservations** tables from the **Database Explorer** onto the **Object Relational Designer** to create the `Flight` and `Reservation` classes. Click **Yes** when asked if you want to copy the database file to your project.

e) ***Adding a data source to the project.*** Open the **Data Sources** window and click **Add New Data Source...**, then choose the **Object** data source type and click **Next >**. Select the `Flight` class—created by the LINQ to SQL classes when you dragged the **Flights** table onto the **Object Relational Designer**—and click **Finish**. [*Note:* If the `Flight` class does not appear under the **AirlineReservation** node in the **Data Source Configuration Wizard**, save your project and try again.] Repeat this process to add the `Reservation` class as a data source.

f) ***Adding two GroupBoxes to the Form.*** Add a GroupBox named flightInformation-GroupBox and one named passengerListGroupBox as seen in Fig. 24.31. Set the Text property of flightGroupBox to Flight Information. Then, set the Text property of passengerGroupBox to Passenger List. Add a ListBox named passenger-ListBox to the passengerGroupBox.

g) ***Adding controls that display flight and passenger information on the Form.*** Choose **Details** from the **Flight** drop-down list in the **Data Sources** window and drag-and-drop the **Flight** node onto the flightGroupBox. Delete the **Flight Number:** Label and TextBox. Reorder the Label–TextBox pairs as **Departure City**, **Arrival City** and **Date**. Make all the TextBoxes ReadOnly. Expand the TextBoxes to accommodate the display data. Move the automatically generated Labels and TextBoxes so that they are positioned as in Fig. 24.31.

Drag-and-drop the **Reservation** data source onto the passengerListBox in the **Passenger List** GroupBox. Click the black triangle in the upper-right corner of the ListBox to open the **ListBox Tasks** menu. Verify that the **Data Source** is set to ReservationBindingSource and the **Display Member** is set to Name.

h) ***Deleting BindingNavigator control.*** You navigate through the data with the flightNumberComboBox, so you do not need the BindingNavigator control. To delete it, just click the BindingNavigator in the Form and press *Delete*.

i) ***Adding a ComboBox that displays all the flight numbers.*** Add a ComboBox named flightNumberComboBox and position it above the **Flight Information** GroupBox. Now create a label named flightNumberLabel and set its Text property to Choose a flight:.

j) ***Making flightNumberComboBox data-bound so that it displays all the flight numbers.*** Select flightNumberComboBox and click the black triangle in the upper-right corner of the control. This displays the **ComboBox Tasks** menu. In this menu, check the **Use data bound items** CheckBox, which causes four ComboBoxes to appear below the CheckBox. In the **Data Source** ComboBox, select FlightBindingSource. Then, in the **Display Member** and **Value Member** ComboBoxes, select FlightNumber. This automatically populates flightNumberComboBox with the flight numbers of all the Flights in the FlightBindingSource.

k) ***Programming the AirlineReservationForm_Load event handler.*** Double click the Form in **Design** view to create its Load event handler. Create a ReservationsData-ClassesDataContext object as an instance variable above the Load event handler. In the Load event handler, use a LINQ query to retrieve all the flights from the Flights table in the database (ordered by flight number) and assign the result to FlightBind-ingSource's DataSource property. Below the LINQ query, write code that retrieves the currently displayed Flight from the FlightBindingSource and passes the Flight's FlightNumber to method DisplayPassengers (which you define in a later step).

l) ***Creating an event handler for the FlightBindingSource's PositionChanged event.*** Select FlightBindingSource in the **Class Name** ComboBox, then select Position-Changed in the **Method Name** ComboBox to create the FlightBindingSource's PositionChanged event handler. Write code to access the currently displayed Flight object and pass its FlightNumber to method DisplayPassengers as a Decimal.

m) ***Defining the DisplayPassengers method.*** Create a Sub procedure named Display-Passengers. This method takes as an argument a Decimal representing a flight number. Write a LINQ query that retrieves from the database all Reservations containing the given flight number ordered by the passenger's name. Assign the result to ReservationBindingSource's DataSource property.

n) ***Running the application.*** Select **Debug > Start Debugging** to run your application. Select a flight from the **Choose a Flight:** ComboBox. Verify that the flight information is correct. Repeat this process for the other flights.

o) ***Closing the application.*** Close your running application by clicking its close box.

TUTORIAL 25

Enhanced Car Payment Calculator Application

Introducing Exception Handling

Objectives

In this tutorial, you learn to:

- Use exception handling.
- Use the `Try`, `Catch` and `Finally` blocks to handle exceptions.
- Use the `Throw` statement to indicate an exception and to specify that an existing exception needs further processing.

Outline

In this tutorial, you learn about **exception handling**. An **exception** is an indication of a problem that occurs during an application's execution. The name "exception" comes from the fact that such problems occur *infrequently*—if the "rule" is that a statement normally executes correctly, then the "exception to the rule" is that a problem occurs. Exception handling enables you to create applications that can resolve (or handle) exceptions while an application executes. In many cases, handling an exception allows an application to continue executing as if no problem had been encountered.

The tutorial begins with a test-drive of the **Enhanced Car Payment Calculator** application, then overviews exception handling concepts and demonstrates basic exception-handling techniques. You learn the specifics of exception handling with the `Try`, `Catch` and `Finally` blocks.

25.1 Test-Driving the Enhanced Car Payment Calculator Application

In this tutorial, you enhance the **Car Payment Calculator** application from Tutorial 9 by adding exception-handling statements. This application must meet the following requirements:

Application Requirements

A bank wishes to accept only valid data from users on their car loans. Although the application you developed in Tutorial 9 calculates a result when incorrect data is entered, this result does not correctly represent the user's input. Alter the **Car Payment Calculator** *application to allow users to enter only* `Integer`*s in the* **Price:** `TextBox` *and* **Down payment:** `TextBox`*. Similarly, allow users to enter only* `Double` *values in the* **Annual interest rate:** `TextBox`*. If the user enters anything besides an* `Integer` *for the price or down payment, or a* `Double` *for the interest rate, a message dialog should be displayed instructing the user to input proper data. The interest rate should be entered such that an input of 5 is equal to 5%.*

The original **Car Payment Calculator** application used the `Val` function to set the value of the variables used in the application. This ensured that the payment calculation was always performed using numeric values. However, as discussed in Tutorial 5, the value returned by `Val` is not always the value the user intended to input. For example, if the user accidently inputs a character in the middle of the down payment (e.g., `54a7`), `Val` returns the numeric value up until it reaches the character (e.g., `54`)—any number after the character is lost, and the calculation is incorrect. Also, `Val` does not prevent the user from entering a `Double` value for the price or down payment, for which `Integer` values are expected. You add exception handling to the **Car Payment Calculator** application so that when invalid input is entered, the application does not calculate monthly payments and the user is asked to enter valid input. If the user provides valid input, the application calculates the monthly payments for a car when financed for 24, 36, 48 and 60 months. Users input the car price, the down payment and the annual interest rate. You begin by test-driving the completed application. Then you learn the additional Visual Basic capabilities needed to create your own version of this application

Test-Driving the Enhanced Car Payment Calculator Application

1. ***Opening the completed application.*** Open the directory `C:\Examples\Tutorial25\CompletedApplication\EnhancedCarPaymentCalculator` to locate the **Car Payment Calculator** application. Double click `EnhancedCarPaymentCalculator.sln` to open the application in the IDE.

2. ***Running the* Enhanced Car Payment Calculator *application.*** Select **Debug > Start Debugging** to run the application (Fig. 25.1).

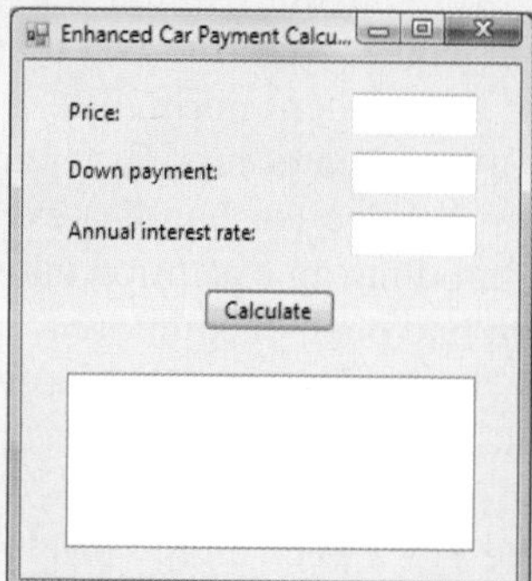

Figure 25.1 Running the completed **Enhanced Car Payment Calculator** application.

3. ***Entering an invalid value in the* Down payment: *`TextBox`.*** Enter `16900` in the **Price:** `TextBox`, `6000.50` in the **Down payment:** `TextBox` and `7.5` in the **Annual interest rate:** `TextBox` (Fig. 25.2).

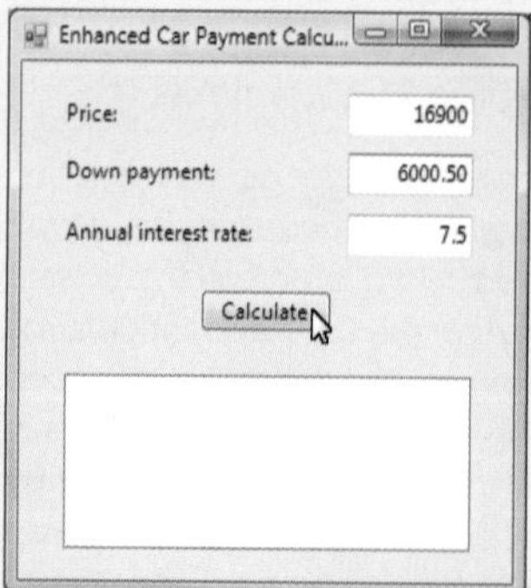

Figure 25.2 Entering an invalid value in the **Down payment:** `TextBox`.

(cont.) 4. ***Attempting to calculate the monthly payment amounts.*** Click the **Calculate** `Button` to attempt to calculate the monthly payment. Note that an error message dialog (Fig. 25.3) appears.

Displaying a message when an exception is thrown

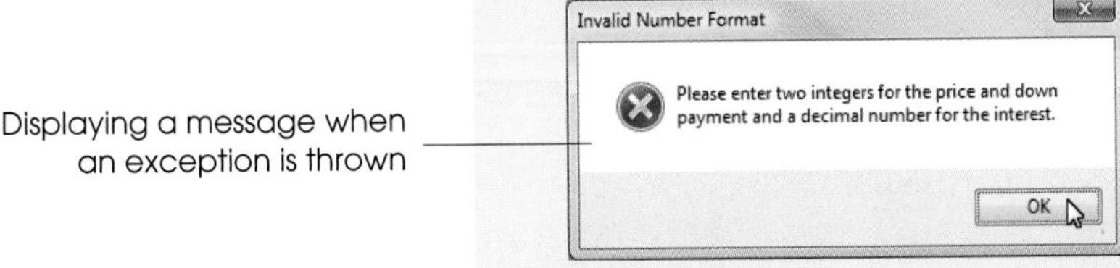

Figure 25.3 Message dialog displayed when incorrect input is entered.

5. ***Entering non-numeric data in the Down payment: TextBox.*** Change the value `6000.50` in the **Down payment:** `TextBox` to `600p` (Fig. 25.4). Click the **Calculate** `Button` to attempt to display the monthly payment in the `TextBox`. The message dialog shown in Fig. 25.3 appears again (a non-numeric character like `p` cannot be entered when an `Integer` is expected). The same problem occurs when the user mistakenly includes a dollar sign in the input (e.g., `$6000`).

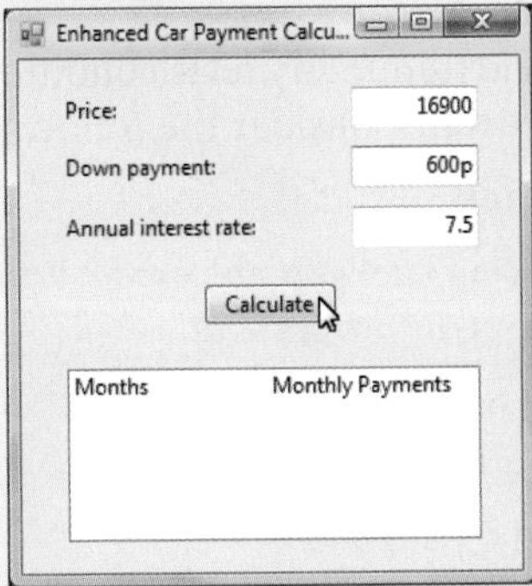

Figure 25.4 Entering non-numeric data in the **Down Payment:** `TextBox`.

6. ***Entering non-numeric data in the Annual interest rate: TextBox.*** Change the value `600p` in the **Down payment:** `TextBox` to `6000`. Enter `7.5%` in the **Annual interest rate:** `TextBox` (Fig. 25.5). Click the **Calculate** `Button` to attempt to calculate the monthly payment. The message dialog shown in Fig. 25.3 appears again (`7.5` is the correct input; entering the `%` character is incorrect).

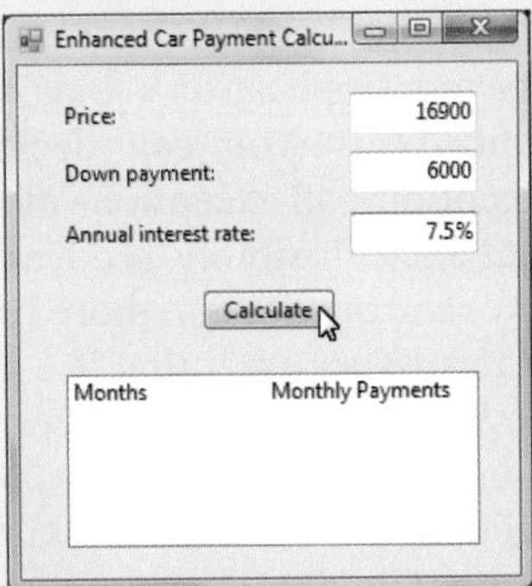

Figure 25.5 Entering non-numeric data in the **Annual interest rate:** `TextBox`.

7. ***Correcting the input.*** Change the value `7.5%` in the **Annual interest rate:** `TextBox` to `7.5`, and click the **Calculate** `Button` to display the monthly payments (Fig. 25.6).

(cont.)

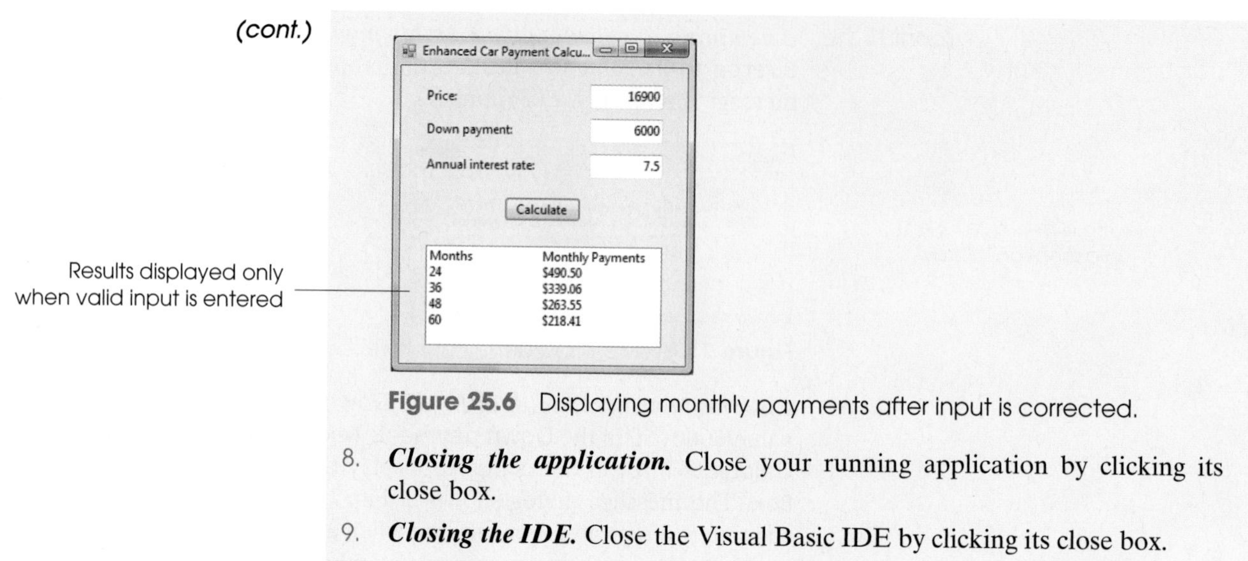

Figure 25.6 Displaying monthly payments after input is corrected.

8. ***Closing the application.*** Close your running application by clicking its close box.
9. ***Closing the IDE.*** Close the Visual Basic IDE by clicking its close box.

25.2 Introduction to Exception Handling

Application logic frequently tests conditions that determine how application execution should proceed. Consider the following pseudocode:

```
Perform a task

If the preceding task did not execute correctly
    Perform error processing

Perform the next task

If the preceding task did not execute correctly
    Perform error processing

...
```

In this pseudocode, you begin by performing a task. Then you test whether the task executed correctly. If not, you perform error processing. Otherwise, you continue with the next task. Although this form of error checking works, intermixing application logic with error-handling logic can make the application difficult to read, modify, maintain and debug—especially in large applications. In fact, if problems occur infrequently, intermixing application and error-handling logic can degrade an application's performance, because the application must explicitly test for errors after each task to determine whether the next task can be performed.

Exception handling enables you to remove error-handling code from the code that implements your application's logic, thereby improving application clarity and enhancing modifiability. You can decide to handle only the exceptions you choose— all exceptions, all exceptions of a certain type or all exceptions in a group of related types. Such flexibility reduces the likelihood that errors will be overlooked and makes the application more robust.

A method **throws an exception** if a problem occurs during the method execution but the method is unable to correct the problem. There is no guarantee that there will be an **exception handler**—code that executes when the application detects an exception—to process that kind of exception. If there is, the exception handler catches and handles the exception. If there is not, the exception is sent to the calling method, which may or may not handle it. An **uncaught** (or **unhandled**) **exception**—an exception that does not have an exception handler—likely causes application execution to terminate. This can actually help you locate problems in your code.

SELF-REVIEW

1. An ________ executes when the application detects an exception.
   a) exception code
   b) exception processor
   c) exception handler
   d) None of the above

2. A method ________ an exception if a problem occurs during the method execution but the method is unable to correct the problem.
   a) throws
   b) catches
   c) returns
   d) None of the above

Answers: 1) c. 2) a.

25.3 Exception Handling in Visual Basic

Visual Basic provides **Try statements** to enable exception handling. A `Try` statement consists of a `Try` block followed by at least one `Catch` block (or a `Finally` block, as you'll learn later) and is terminated with keywords **`End Try`**. A **`Try` block** consists of the `Try` keyword followed by a block of code in which exceptions might occur. The `Try` block encloses statements that might cause exceptions and statements that should not execute if an exception occurs. Many of the methods in the .NET Framework Class Library throw exceptions when passed invalid input. An exception is thrown using the **`Throw`** keyword followed by the exception object to be thrown, as in:

```
Throw New Exception()
```

When a statement such as this executes, it creates an `Exception` object and passes it to the calling method.

Generally, at least one `Catch` block (also called an exception handler) appears after the `Try` block, before the `End Try` keywords. A **`Catch` block** contains code that handles an exception and allows the application to continue executing correctly. A `Catch` block can specify a parameter that identifies the type of exception the exception handler can process. A `Catch` block that does not specify a parameter catches all exceptions. A parameterless `Catch` block, if present, should be placed after all other `Catch` blocks.

If an exception occurs in a `Try` block, the `Try` block terminates immediately. As with any other block of code, when a `Try` block terminates, local variables declared in the block go out of scope. Next, the application searches for the first `Catch` block (immediately following the `Try` block) that can process the exception type that occurred. The application locates the matching `Catch` block by comparing the thrown exception's type with each `Catch` block's parameter type. A match occurs if the exception type matches the `Catch` block's parameter type. When a match occurs, the code in `Catch` block executes. When a `Catch` block finishes processing the exception, local variables declared in the `Catch` block (and the `Catch` block's parameter) go out of scope. The `Try` statement's remaining `Catch` blocks are ignored, and execution resumes at the first line of code after the `End Try` keywords. (You'll learn another possibility when we introduce `Finally` blocks later in this tutorial.)

If there is no `Catch` block that matches the exception thrown in the corresponding `Try` block, the exception is passed to the method that called the current method, which then attempts to handle the exception. If the calling method does not handle the exception, the exception is again passed to the previous method in the call chain. If the exception goes unhandled, Visual Basic displays a dialog providing the user with information about the exception. The user can then choose to exit or continue running the application, although the application likely will not execute correctly due to the exception.

If no exceptions occur in a `Try` block, the application ignores the `Catch` block(s) for that `Try` block. Application execution resumes with the next statement after the `End Try` keywords.

SELF-REVIEW

1. A `Try` statement typically contains a ________ block and at least one ________ block.
   a) `Catch`, `Try` b) `Try`, `Catch`
   c) `Throw`, `Catch` d) None of the above

2. If no exceptions occur in a `Try` block, the application ignores the ________ for that block.
   a) `Catch` block(s) b) `Return` statement
   c) Both of the above d) None of the above

Answers: 1) b. 2) a.

25.4 Constructing the Enhanced Car Payment Calculator Application

Now that you've been introduced to exception handling, you construct your **Enhanced Car Payment Calculator** application. The following pseudocode describes the basic operation of the application:

```
When the user clicks the Calculate Button:
    Clear the ListBox of any previous text

    Try
        Get the car price from the Price: TextBox
        Get the down payment from the Down payment: TextBox
        Get the annual interest rate from the Annual interest rate: TextBox
        Calculate the loan amount (price minus down payment)
        Calculate the monthly interest rate (annual interest rate divided by 12)
        Calculate and display the monthly payments for 2, 3, 4 and 5 years
    Catch
        Display the error message dialog
```

Now that you've test-driven the **Enhanced Car Payment Calculator** application and studied its pseudocode representation, you use an ACE table to help you convert the pseudocode to Visual Basic. Figure 25.7 lists the actions, controls and events that help you complete your own version of this application.

Action/Control/Event (ACE) Table for the Enhanced Car Payment Calculator Application

Action	Control/Class/Object	Event
Label all the application's components	`priceLabel`, `downPaymentLabel`, `interestLabel`	Application is run
	`calculateButton`	`Click`
Clear the ListBox of any previous text	`paymentsListBox`	
Try Get the car price from the Price: TextBox	`priceTextBox`	
Get the down payment from the Down payment: TextBox	`downPayment-TextBox`	
Get the annual interest rate from the Annual interest rate: TextBox	`interestTextBox`	
Calculate the loan amount		
Calculate the monthly interest rate		
Calculate and display the monthly payments for 2, 3, 4 and 5 years	`paymentsListBox`	
Catch Display the error message dialog	`MessageBox`	

Figure 25.7 **Enhanced Car Payment Calculator** application ACE table.

Now that you've analyzed the **Enhanced Car Payment Calculator** application's components, you learn how to use exception handling in your application.

Handling a Format `Exception`

1. ***Copying the template to your working directory.*** Copy the `C:\Examples\Tutorial25\TemplateApplication\EnhancedCarPaymentCalculator` directory to your `C:\SimplyVB2008` directory.

2. ***Opening the* Enhanced Car Payment Calculator *application's template file.*** Double click `EnhancedCarPaymentCalculator.sln` in the `EnhancedCarPaymentCalculator` directory to open the application in the IDE.

3. ***Studying the code.*** View lines 25–27 of Fig. 25.8. Lines 25–26 read the `Integer` values from the **Down payment:** and **Price:** `TextBoxes`, respectively. Line 27 reads a `Double` value from the **Annual interest rate:** `TextBox`. These lines are different from the ones in the **Car Payment Calculator** application that you developed in Tutorial 9. These three statements now must explicitly convert the data in the `TextBoxes` to `Integer` and `Double` values, using the methods of the `Convert` class, because **Option Strict** is set to `On`. However, these statements still use the `Val` function, which could cause the application to use incorrect data in its calculation, producing invalid results.

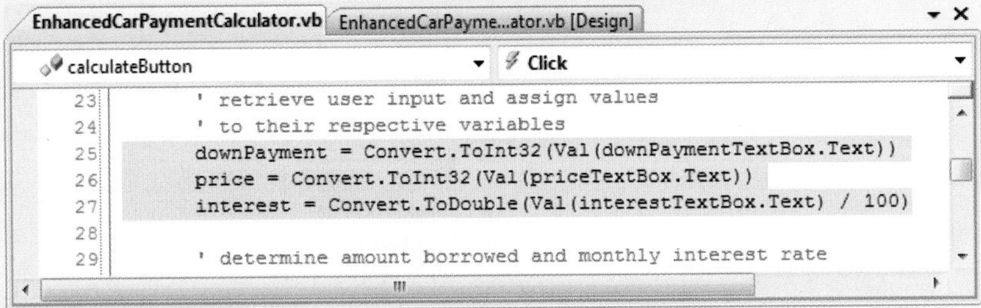

Figure 25.8 `Val` ensures data is in numeric format.

Before using a method, read its online documentation to determine whether it throws exceptions. If so, use the exception-handling techniques of this chapter to help make your code more robust. To access the online documentation for a method in the .NET Framework Class Library, you can click its name in the source-code editor and press *F1*.

Method `Convert.ToInt32` throws a `FormatException` if it cannot convert its argument to an `Integer`. The `FormatException` class represents exceptions that occur when a method is passed an argument that is not in the expected format (e.g., an object of the wrong type, or a `String` containing non-numeric characters when only numeric characters are allowed). The call to the `Convert.ToInt32` method does not currently throw an exception when the application is run because `Val` converts its argument to a numeric value. This numeric value is the argument passed to `Convert.ToInt32`, so an `Integer` value is always created. The `Convert.ToDouble` method performs in a similar manner by throwing a `FormatException` if it cannot convert its argument to a `Double`.

4. ***Changing the existing code.*** Change lines 25–27 of your template application to match lines 25–27 of Fig. 25.9 by removing the `Val` function call and the parentheses that designate its argument. Removing the `Val` function call causes `Convert.ToInt32` and `Convert.ToDouble` to throw an exception if invalid input is entered into one of the `TextBoxes`. This allows you to add code later in this box to catch the exception and ask the user to enter correct data.

(cont.)

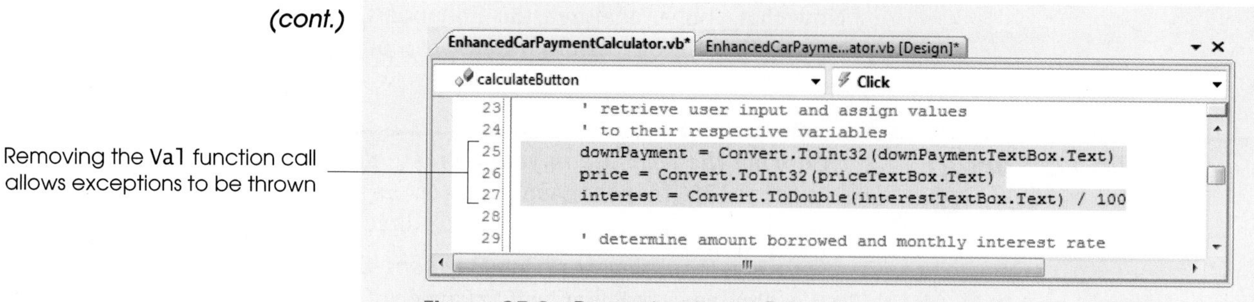

Figure 25.9 Removing the `Val` function call from the application.

5. ***Causing a `FormatException`.*** Select **Debug > Start Debugging** to run your application. Enter invalid input as in Fig. 25.4 and click the **Calculate `Button`**. The **Exception Assistant** shown in Fig. 25.10 appears, informing you that an exception has occurred. Note that the exception assistant indicates where the exception occurred and the type of the exception, and provides links to helpful information on handling the exception. Close the Exception Assistant by clicking its close box. Then, stop debugging by selecting **Debug > Stop Debugging**.

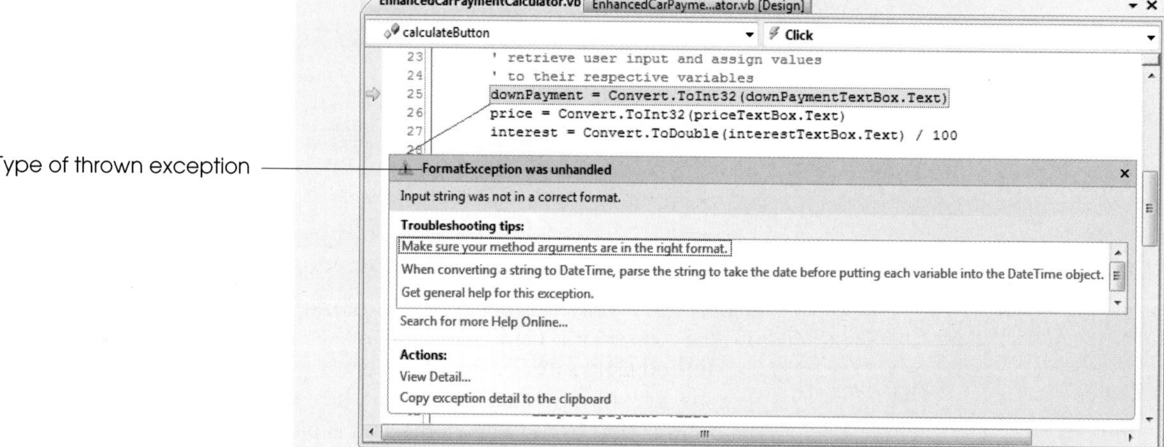

Figure 25.10 Exception Assistant reveals a `FormatException`.

6. ***Adding a `Try` block to your application.*** Add lines 23–24 of Fig. 25.11 to your application; however, do not press *Enter* when you are done typing line 24; instead, add line 51 of Fig. 25.12 to your application. The code currently contained between these two lines is the code that might throw an exception and code that you do not want to execute if an exception occurs. Note that the `Try` keyword in line 24 is underlined, indicating a syntax error. Adding the `Try` keyword to your application creates a syntax error until a corresponding `Catch` (or `Finally`) block is added to the application. In the next step, you add a `Catch` block to fix the error in line 24.

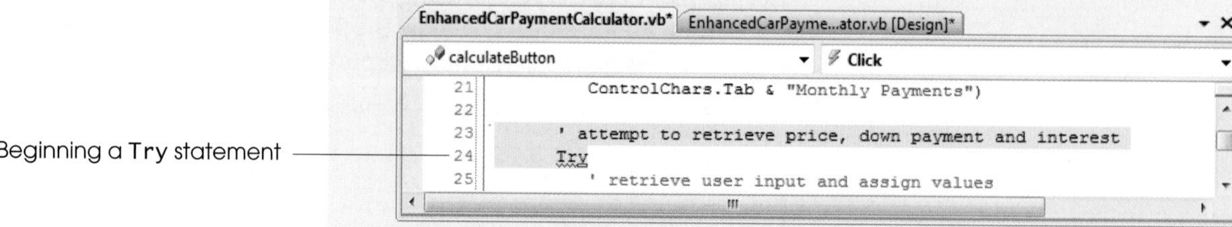

Figure 25.11 Enabling exception handling using a `Try` block.

(cont.)

Ending a Try statement

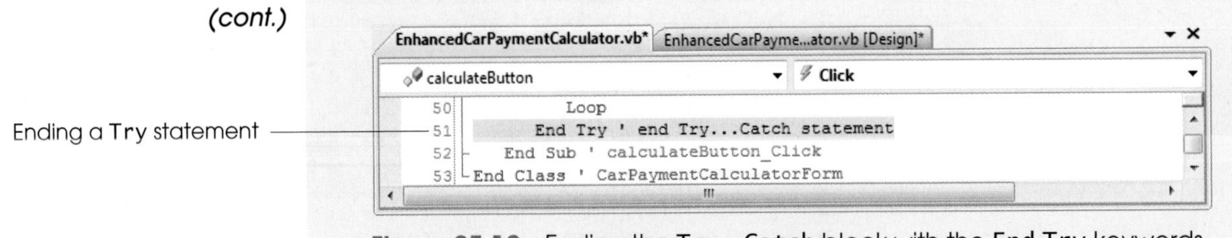

Figure 25.12 Ending the Try...Catch block with the End Try keywords.

7. ***Adding a Catch block to your application.*** Insert a blank line before End Try, then add lines 52–53 of Fig. 25.13. Keyword Catch begins a Catch block. A Catch block ends when either another Catch block, a Finally block or the End Try keywords are reached. Line 53 specifies that this Catch block executes if a FormatException occurs. When an exception is caught here, it is assigned to variable formatExceptionParameter. This code executes if the user enters invalid input in a TextBox. Note that adding a Catch block fixed the error in line 24.

Catching a FormatException

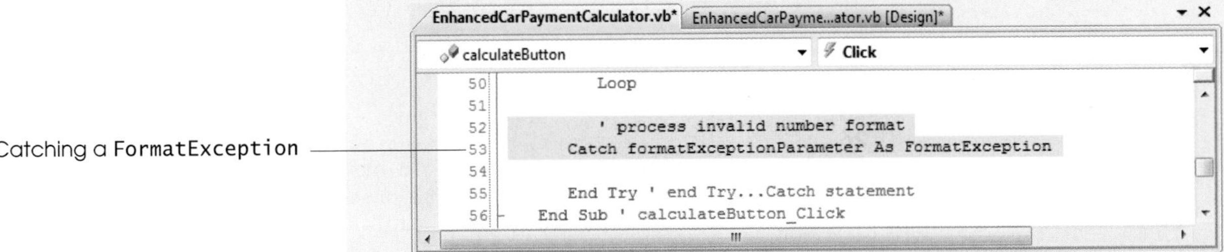

Figure 25.13 Handling a FormatException.

8. ***Displaying an error message to the user.*** Add lines 54–59 of Fig. 25.14 to the Catch handler to display a MessageBox instructing the user to enter valid input. Note that the MessageBoxIcon.Error icon is used because an exception is an error that occurs during the execution of the application. If you would like to access the error message in the exception object, you can access its Message property.

Displaying a message when the Catch block executes

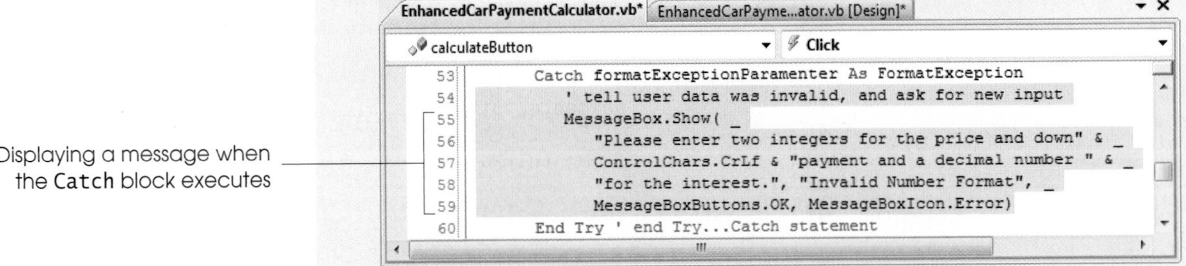

Figure 25.14 Displaying a message dialog to the user.

9. ***Running the application.*** Select **Debug > Start Debugging** to run your application. Enter valid input, and verify that the output contains the correct payment amounts. Enter invalid input to ensure that the MessageBox is displayed. Test the application with invalid values in each TextBox.

10. ***Closing the application.*** Click your running application's close box.

11. ***Closing the IDE.*** Close the Visual Basic IDE by clicking its close box.

Figure 25.15 presents the source code for the **Enhanced Car Payment Calculator** application. The lines of code that contain new programming concepts you learned in this tutorial are highlighted.

```
Public Class EnhancedCarPaymentCalculatorForm

   ' handles Calculate Button's Click event
   Private Sub calculateButton_Click(ByVal sender As System.Object, _
      ByVal e As System.EventArgs) Handles calculateButton.Click

      Dim years As Integer = 2 ' repetition counter
      Dim months As Integer = 0 ' payment period
      Dim price As Integer = 0 ' car price
      Dim downPayment As Integer = 0 ' down payment
      Dim interest As Double = 0 ' interest rate
      Dim monthlyPayment As Decimal = 0 ' monthly payment
      Dim loanAmount As Integer = 0 ' cost after down payment
      Dim monthlyInterest As Double = 0 ' monthly interest rate

      ' remove text displayed in ListBox
      paymentsListBox.Items.Clear()

      ' add header to ListBox
      paymentsListBox.Items.Add("Months" & ControlChars.Tab & _
         ControlChars.Tab & "Monthly Payments")

      ' attempt to retrieve price, down payment and interest
      Try
         ' retrieve user input and assign values
         ' to their respective variables
         downPayment = Convert.ToInt32(downPaymentTextBox.Text)
         price = Convert.ToInt32(priceTextBox.Text)
         interest = Convert.ToDouble(interestTextBox.Text) / 100

         ' determine amount borrowed and monthly interest rate
         loanAmount = price - downPayment
         monthlyInterest = interest / 12

         ' calculate for two, three, four and five year loans
         Do While years <= 5
            ' calculate payment period
            months = 12 * years

            ' calculate monthly payment using Pmt
            monthlyPayment = Convert.ToDecimal( _
               Pmt(monthlyInterest, months, -loanAmount))

            ' display payment value
            paymentsListBox.Items.Add(months & ControlChars.Tab & _
               ControlChars.Tab & String.Format("{0:C}", _
               monthlyPayment))

            years += 1 ' increment counter
         Loop

         ' process invalid number format
      Catch formatExceptionParameter As FormatException
         ' tell user data was invalid, and ask for new input
         MessageBox.Show( _
            "Please enter two integers for the price and down" & _
            ControlChars.CrLf & "payment and a decimal number " & _
            "for the interest", "Invalid Number Format", _
            MessageBoxButtons.OK, MessageBoxIcon.Error)
      End Try ' end Try statement
   End Sub ' calculateButton_Click
End Class ' EnhancedCarPaymentCalculatorForm
```


Figure 25.15 **Enhanced Car Payment Calculator** Application.

SELF-REVIEW

1. If you are attempting to catch multiple errors, you may use several ________ blocks after the ________ block.

   a) `Try`, `Catch` b) `Catch`, `Try`
   c) `Throw`, `Try` d) None of the above

2. The exception you wish to handle should be declared as a parameter of the ________ block.

   a) `Try` b) `Catch`
   c) `Throw` d) None of the above

Answers: 1) b. 2) b.

25.5 Additional Exception Handling Capabilities

Visual Basic provides several additional exception handling capabilities not used in this book. An optional `Finally` **block** can be placed before the `End Try` keywords in a `Try` statement and allows you to specify code that always executes, whether or not an exception occurs in the corresponding `Try` block. This is particularly useful when working with resources that require explicit action to release them (e.g., calling the `Close` method on a `StreamReader` or `StreamWriter` object when finished processing a file or database connection). A `Try` statement containing a `Finally` block is not required to also contain a `Catch` block.

If an exception occurs in a `Try` block, the `Try` block terminates immediately. When a `Catch` block finishes processing the exception, execution resumes at the first line of code in the `Finally` block. If the `Try` block finishes executing *without* throwing an exception, the `Catch` blocks are ignored and execution resumes at the first line of code in the `Finally` block. When the end of the `Finally` block is reached, execution resumes at the first line of code after the `End Try` keywords.

If there is no `Catch` block that matches the exception thrown in the corresponding `Try` block (or if there is no `Catch` block what so ever), execution resumes at the first line of code in the `Finally` block. After the `Finally` block executes, the exception is passed to the method that called the current method, which then attempts to handle the exception.

Sometimes a `Catch` block may decide either that it cannot process a certain exception or that it can only partially process the exception. In such cases, the exception handler can defer the handling (or perhaps a portion of it) to another `Catch` block. The exception handler achieves this by **rethrowing the exception** using the `Throw` statement

`Throw` *exceptionReference*

where *exceptionReference* is the parameter for the exception in the `Catch` block. You can also do this without specifying *exceptionReference* in the preceding statement. When a rethrow occurs, the next enclosing `Try` statement (if any)—normally in the calling method—detects the rethrown exception and attempts to catch it.

Another feature in Visual Basic 2008 related to exception handling is the `Using` statement, which concisely represents a `Try...Finally` that automatically deallocates a resource after it is used in the `Try` block. The `Using` statement is beyond the scope of this book. For information on `Using`, visit `msdn2.microsoft.com/en-us/library/htd05whh.aspx`. Also, you should investigate the `IDisposable` interface (`msdn2.microsoft.com/en-us/library/system.idisposable.aspx`), which is a required part of implementing code with the `Using` statement.

SELF-REVIEW

1. The ________ (if any) is/are always executed regardless of whether an exception occurs.

   a) `Catch` block b) `Finally` block
   c) both `Catch` and `Finally` blocks d) None of the above

2. If an exception occurs in a `Try` block, the `Finally` block is executed _________.
   a) before the `Catch` block executes
   b) instead of the `Catch` block
   c) after the `Catch` block executes
   d) None of the above

Answers: 1) b. 2) c.

25.6 Wrap-Up

In this tutorial, you learned exception-handling concepts and when to use exception handling in Visual Basic. You learned how to use a `Try` statement with `Catch` blocks to handle exceptions in your applications. You applied your knowledge of exception handling in Visual Basic to enhance your **Car Payment Calculator** application to check for input errors. You used a `Try` block to enclose the statements that might throw `FormatExceptions` and a `Catch` block to handle the `FormatExceptions`. This allows your application to recover from otherwise fatal errors.

Next, you learned about additional exception handling capabilites. You learned that a Finally block contains code that is always executed, regardless of whether or not an exception was thrown. You also learned that the `Throw` statement can be used to rethrow an exception that cannot be handled in the `Catch` block.

In the next tutorial, you learn about mouse events and Windows Presentation Foundation (WPF), Microsoft's new framework for graphics, GUI and multimedia. You create an application that allows users to paint pictures on the screen using the mouse.

SKILLS SUMMARY

Handling an Exception

- Enclose in a `Try` block any code that might generate an exception and any code that should not execute if an exception occurs.
- Follow the `Try` block with one or more `Catch` blocks. Each `Catch` block is an exception handler that specifies the type of exception it can handle.
- Follow the `Catch` blocks with an optional `Finally` block that contains code that should always execute, regardless of whether or not an exception was thrown.

KEY TERMS

`Catch` block—Also called an exception handler, this block executes when the corresponding `Try` block in the application detects an exceptional situation and throws an exception of the type the `Catch` block declares.

`End Try` keywords—Indicates the end of a sequence of blocks containing a `Try` block, followed by zero or more `Catch` blocks and an optional `Finally` block. At least one `Catch` or `Finally` block must precede the `End Try` keywords

exception—An indication of a problem that occurs during an application's execution.

Exception Assistant—A window that appears in the IDE indicating where an exception has occurred, the type of exception, and information on handling the exception.

exception handler—A block that executes when the application detects an exceptional situation and throws an exception.

exception handling—Processing problems that occur during application execution.

`Finally` block—An optional block of code that follows the last `Catch` block in a sequence of `Catch` blocks or the `Try` block if there are no `Catch`es. The `Finally` block provides code that always executes, whether or not an exception occurs.

`FormatException` class—An exception of this type is thrown when a method cannot convert its argument to a desired numeric type, such as `Integer` or `Double`.

`Message` property of an exception object—Provides access to the error message in an exception object.

rethrow an exception—The `Catch` block can defer the exception handling (or perhaps a portion of it) to another `Catch` block by using the `Throw` statement.

`Throw` statement—The statement used to throw an exception.

throws an exception—A method throws an exception if a problem occurs while the method is executing.

`Try` block—A block of statements that might cause exceptions and statements that should not execute if an exception occurs.

uncaught (unhandled) exception—An exception that does not have an exception handler. Uncaught exceptions might terminate application execution.

MULTIPLE-CHOICE QUESTIONS

25.1 Dealing with exceptional situations as an application executes is called ________.

a) exception detection
b) exception handling
c) exception resolution
d) exception debugging

25.2 A(n) ________ is always followed by at least one `Catch` block or a `Finally` block.

a) `if` statement
b) event handler
c) `Try` block
d) None of the above

25.3 The method call `Convert.ToInt32("123.4a")` will throw a ________.

a) `FormatException`
b) `ParsingException`
c) `DivideByZeroException`
d) None of the above

25.4 If no exceptions are thrown in a `Try` block, ________.

a) the `Catch` block(s) are skipped
b) all `Catch` blocks are executed
c) an error occurs
d) the default exception is thrown

25.5 A(n) ________ is an exception that does not have an exception handler, and therefore might cause the application to terminate execution.

a) uncaught block
b) uncaught exception
c) error handler
d) thrower

25.6 A `Try` block can have ________ associated with it.

a) only one `Catch` block
b) several `Finally` blocks
c) one or more `Catch` blocks
d) None of the above

25.7 The ________ statement is used to rethrow an exception from inside a `Catch` block.

a) `Rethrow`
b) `Throw`
c) `Try`
d) `Catch`

25.8 ________ marks the end of a `Try` block and its corresponding `Catch` and `Finally` blocks.

a) `End Try`
b) `End Finally`
c) `End Catch`
d) `End Exception`

25.9 A `Finally` block is located ________.

a) after the `Try` block, but before each `Catch` block
b) before the `Try` block
c) after the `Try` block and the `Try` block's corresponding `Catch` blocks
d) Either b or c

25.10 A(n) ________ is executed if an exception is thrown from a `Try` block or if no exception is thrown.

a) `Catch` block
b) `Finally` block
c) exception handler
d) All of the above

EXERCISES

25.11 (***Enhanced Miles Per Gallon Application***) Modify the **Miles Per Gallon** application (Exercise 13.13) to use exception handling to process the `FormatExceptions` that occur when converting the `Strings` in the `TextBoxes` to `Doubles` (Fig. 25.16). The original application allowed the user to input the number of miles driven and the number of gallons used for a tank of gas to determine the number of miles the user was able to drive on one gallon of gas.

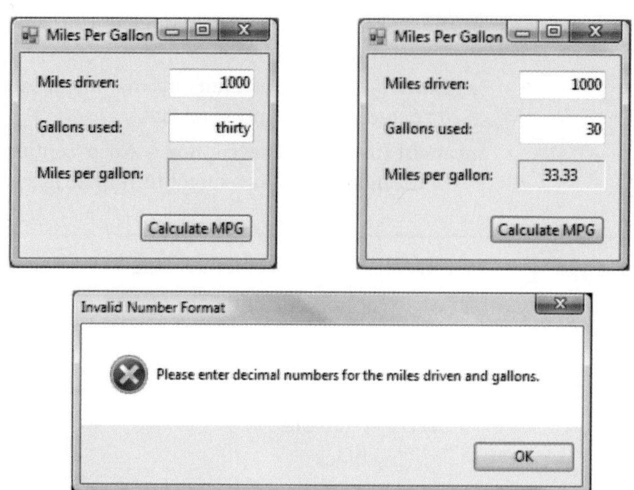

Figure 25.16 Enhanced **Miles Per Gallon** application's GUI.

a) ***Copying the template to your working directory.*** Copy the directory `C:\Examples\Tutorial25\Exercises\EnhancedMilesPerGallon` to your `C:\SimplyVB2008` directory.

b) ***Opening the application's template file.*** Double click `EnhancedMilesPerGallon.sln` in the `EnhancedMilesPerGallon` directory to open the application.

c) ***Adding a*** **`Try`** ***block.*** Find the `calculateMPGButton_Click` event handler. Enclose all of the code in this event handler in a `Try` block.

d) ***Adding a*** **`Catch`** ***block.*** After the `Try` block you added in *Step c*, add a `Catch` block to handle any `FormatExceptions` that may occur in the `Try` block. Inside the `Catch` block, add code to display an error message dialog.

e) ***Running the application.*** Select **Debug > Start Debugging** to run your application. Enter invalid data, as shown in Fig. 25.16, and click the **Calculate MPG** `Button`. A `MessageBox` will appear asking you to enter valid input. Enter valid input and click the **Calculate MPG** `Button` again. Verify that the correct output is displayed.

f) ***Closing the application.*** Close your running application by clicking its close box.

g) ***Closing the IDE.*** Close the Visual Basic IDE by clicking its close box.

25.12 (***Enhanced Prime Numbers Application***) Modify the **Prime Numbers** application (Exercise 13.17) to use exception handling to process the `FormatExceptions` that occur when converting the `Strings` in the `TextBoxes` to `Integers` (Fig. 25.17). The original application took two numbers (representing a lower bound and an upper bound) and determined all of the prime numbers within the specified bounds, inclusive. An `Integer` greater than 1 is said to be prime if it is divisible by only 1 and itself. For example, 2, 3, 5 and 7 are prime numbers, but 4, 6, 8 and 9 are not.

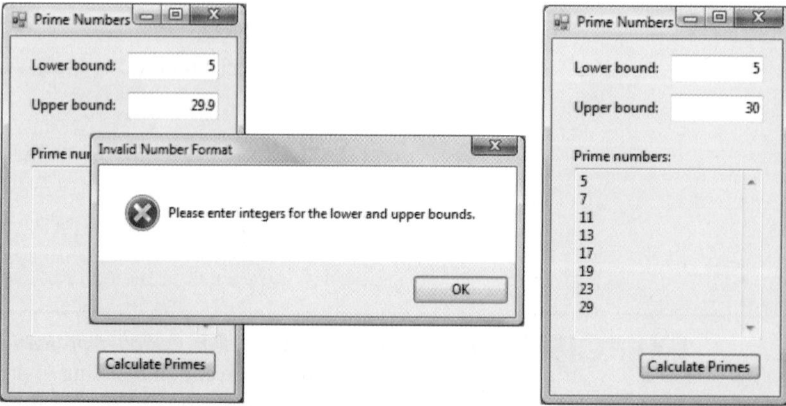

Figure 25.17 Enhanced **Prime Numbers** application's GUI.

a) ***Copying the template to your working directory.*** Copy the directory `C:\Examples\Tutorial25\Exercises\EnhancedPrimeNumbers` to your `C:\SimplyVB2008` directory.

b) ***Opening the application's template file.*** Double click `EnhancedPrimeNumbers.sln` in the `EnhancedPrimeNumbers` directory to open the application.

c) ***Adding a `Try` block.*** Find the `calculatePrimesButton_Click` event handler. Enclose all the code following the variable declarations in a `Try` block.

d) ***Adding a `Catch` block.*** Add a `Catch` block that catches any `FormatExceptions` that may occur in the `Try` block you added to `calculatePrimesButton_Click` in *Step c*. Inside the `Catch` block, add code to display an error message dialog.

e) ***Running the application.*** Select **Debug > Start Debugging** to run your application. Enter invalid data, as shown in Fig. 25.17, and click the **Calculate Primes** `Button`. A `MessageBox` should appear asking you to enter valid input. Enter valid input and click the **Calculate Primes** `Button` again. Verify that the correct output is displayed.

f) ***Closing the application.*** Close your running application by clicking its close box.

g) ***Closing the IDE.*** Close the Visual Basic IDE by clicking its close box.

25.13 (***Enhanced Simple Calculator Application***) Modify the **Simple Calculator** application (Exercise 6.13) to use exception handling to process the `FormatExceptions` that occur when converting the `Strings` in the `TextBoxes` to `Integers` and the `DivideByZeroException` that occurs when performing the division (Fig. 25.18). We define what a `DivideByZeroException` is shortly. The application should still perform simple addition, subtraction, multiplication and division.

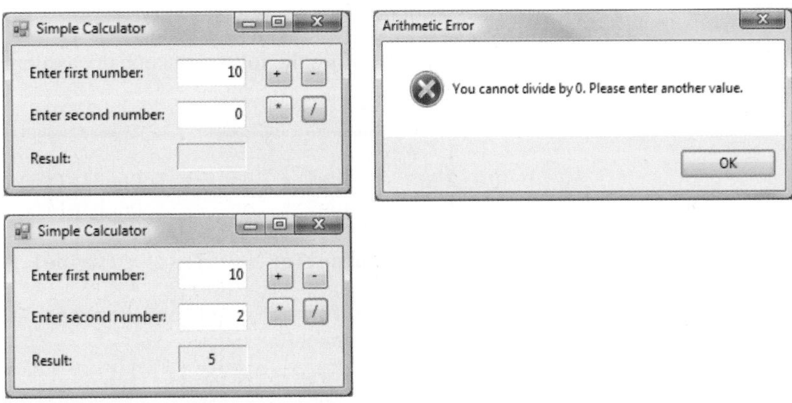

Figure 25.18 Enhanced **Simple Calculator** application.

a) ***Copying the template to your working directory.*** Copy the directory `C:\Examples\Tutorial25\Exercises\EnhancedSimpleCalculator` to your `C:\SimplyVB2008` directory.

b) ***Opening the application's template file.*** Double click `EnhancedSimpleCalculator.sln` in the `EnhancedSimpleCalculator` directory to open the application.

c) ***Adding a `Try` block to the `addButton_Click` event handler.*** Find the `addButton_Click` event handler. Enclose the body of `addButton_Click` in a `Try` block.

d) ***Adding a `Catch` block to the `addButton_Click` event handler.*** Add a `Catch` block that catches any `FormatExceptions` that may occur in the `Try` block that you added in *Step c*. Inside the `Catch` block, add code to display an error message dialog.

e) ***Adding a `Try` block to the `subtractButton_Click` event handler.*** Find the `subtractButton_Click` event handler, which immediately follows `addButton_Click`. Enclose the body of the `subtractButton_Click` in a `Try` block.

f) ***Adding a `Catch` block to the `subtractButton_Click` event handler.*** Add a `Catch` block that catches any `FormatExceptions` that may occur in the `Try` block that you added in *Step e*. Inside the `Catch` block, add code to display an error message dialog.

g) ***Adding a `Try` block to the `multiplyButton_Click` event handler.*** Find the `mulitplyButton_Click` event handler, which immediately follows `subtractButton_Click`. Enclose the body of the `multiplyButton_Click` in a `Try` block.

h) ***Adding a Catch block to the multiplyButton_Click event handler.*** Add a Catch block that catches any FormatExceptions that may occur in the Try block that you added in *Step g*. Inside the Catch block, add code to display an error message dialog.

i) ***Adding a Try block to the divideButton_Click event handler.*** Find the divideButton_Click event handler, which immediately follows multiplyButton_Click. Enclose the body of the divideButton_Click in a Try block.

j) ***Adding a Catch block to the divideButton_Click event handler.*** Add a Catch block that catches any FormatExceptions that may occur in the Try block that you added in *Step i*. Inside the Catch block, add code to display an error message dialog.

k) ***Adding a second Catch block to the divideButton_Click event handler.*** Immediately following the first Catch block inside the divideButton_Click event handler, add a Catch block to catch any DivideByZeroExceptions. A **DivideByZeroException** is thrown when division by zero in integer arithmetic occurs. Inside the Catch block, add code to display an error message dialog.

l) ***Running the application.*** Select **Debug > Start Debugging** to run your application. Enter valid input for the first number and 0 for the second number, then click the Button for division. A MessageBox should appear asking you not to divide by 0. Enter invalid input (such as letters) for the first and second numbers, then click each of the Buttons provided. This time a MessageBox should appear asking you to enter valid input. Enter valid input and click each of the Buttons provided. Verify that the correct output is displayed.

m) ***Closing the application.*** Close your running application by clicking its close box.

n) ***Closing the IDE.*** Close the Visual Basic IDE by clicking its close box.

What does this code do?

25.14 What does the following code do, assuming that value1 and value2 are both declared as Doubles?

```
Try
   value1 = Convert.ToDouble(input1TextBox.Text)
   value2 = Convert.ToDouble(input2TextBox.Text)

   outputTextBox.Text = (value1 * value2).ToString()

Catch formatExceptionParameter As FormatException
   MessageBox.Show( _
      "Please enter floating-point values.", _
      "Invalid Number Format", _
      MessageBoxButtons.OK, MessageBoxIcon.Error)
End Try
```

What's wrong with this code?

25.15 The following code should add integers from two TextBoxes and display the result in resultTextBox. Assume that value1 and value2 are declared as Integers. Find the error(s) in the following code:

```
Try
   value1 = Convert.ToInt32(input1TextBox.Text)
   value2 = Convert.ToInt32(input2TextBox.Text)

   outputTextBox.Text = (value1 + value2).ToString()
End Try

Catch formatExceptionParameter As FormatException
   MessageBox.Show( _
      "Please enter valid Integers.", _
      "Invalid Number Format", _
      MessageBoxButtons.OK, MessageBoxIcon.Error)
End Catch
```

TUTORIAL 26

CheckWriter Application

Introducing Graphics and Printing

Objectives

In this tutorial, you learn to:

- Print.
- Draw two-dimensional shapes.
- Use type `Single`.
- Use keyword `Me`.
- Control the colors and patterns of filled shapes.
- Use `Graphics` objects.
- Draw shapes on an object.
- Create an application to write checks.

Outline

Graphics allow you to visually enhance Windows applications. In this tutorial, you learn about tools for drawing two-dimensional shapes, and for controlling colors and fonts. To build the **CheckWriter** application, you use the GDI+ **Application Programming Interface (API)**. An API is the interface used by an application to access the operating system and various services on a computer. **GDI+ (Graphics Device Interface)** is a graphics API for creating and manipulating two-dimensional vector graphics, fonts and images. A **vector graphic** is not represented as a grid of pixels, but is instead represented by a set of mathematical properties called vectors, which describe a graphic's dimensions, attributes and position. Using the GDI+ API, you can create robust graphics without worrying about the specific details of graphics hardware.

The .NET `System.Drawing` namespace and the other namespaces that comprise GDI+ contain many sophisticated drawing capabilities. The `System.Drawing.Printing` namespace is used in the **CheckWriter** application to specify how a check is printed on the page.

GDI+ graphics capabilities help you preview and print a check using the **CheckWriter** application. To complete the application, you learn how to draw shapes, change the styles of the lines used to draw shapes and control the colors of filled shapes. You also learn how to specify a text style using fonts.

26.1 Test-Driving the CheckWriter Application

This application must meet the following requirements:

Application Requirements

A local business is responsible for distributing paychecks to its employees. The human-resources department needs a way to generate and print the paychecks. You have been asked to create an application that allows the human-resources department to input all the information necessary for a valid check, which includes the employee's name, the date, the amount that the employee should be paid and the company's address information. Your application should graphically draw the check so that it can be printed.

This application prints a paycheck. The user inputs the check number, the date, the numeric amount of the check, the employee's name, the amount of the check written in words and the company's address information. The user can press the **Preview** `Button`, which displays the format of the check. The user can then press the **Print** `Button` if the format is acceptable, causing the check to print from the printer. You begin by test-driving the completed application. Then you learn the additional Visual Basic capabilities needed to create your own version of this application.

Test-Driving the CheckWriter Application

1. ***Opening the completed application.*** Open the directory `C:\Examples\Tutorial26\CompletedApplication\CheckWriter` to locate the **CheckWriter** application. Double click `CheckWriter.sln` to open the application in the Visual Basic IDE.

2. ***Running the CheckWriter application.*** Select **Debug > Start Debugging** to run the application (Fig. 26.1).

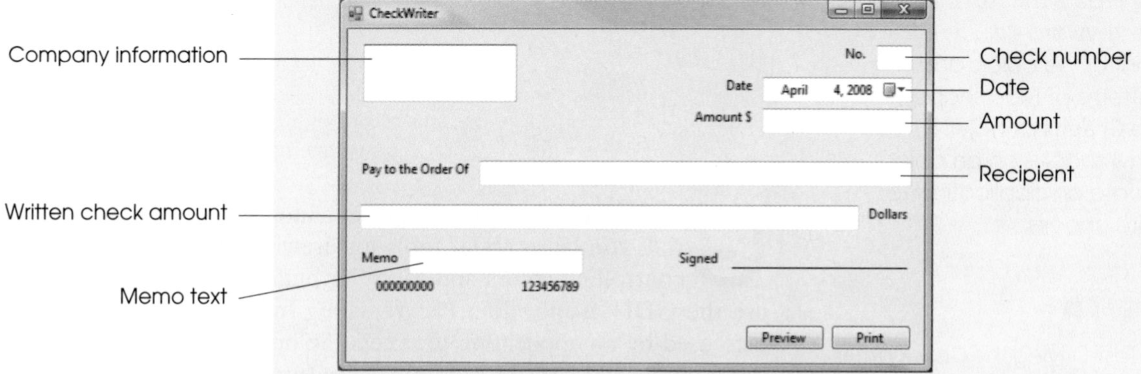

Figure 26.1 **CheckWriter** application displaying an empty check.

3. ***Providing inputs for the company information.*** In the company information `TextBox`, type `The Company`, then press *Enter* to proceed to the next line of the `TextBox`. Type `123 Fake Street`. Press *Enter* to proceed to the third line of the `TextBox`. Type `Any Town, MA 11111`.

4. ***Providing values for the remaining information.*** For the **No.** field, input the check number `100`. Leave the **Date** field (represented by a `DateTimePicker` control) as today's date, which is the default. Input `1,000.00` as the check amount. Enter `John Smith` as the recipient, and type `One Thousand and 00/100` in the `TextBox` to the left of **Dollars**. In the **Memo** field, type `Paycheck`. The check should appear as shown in Fig. 26.2.

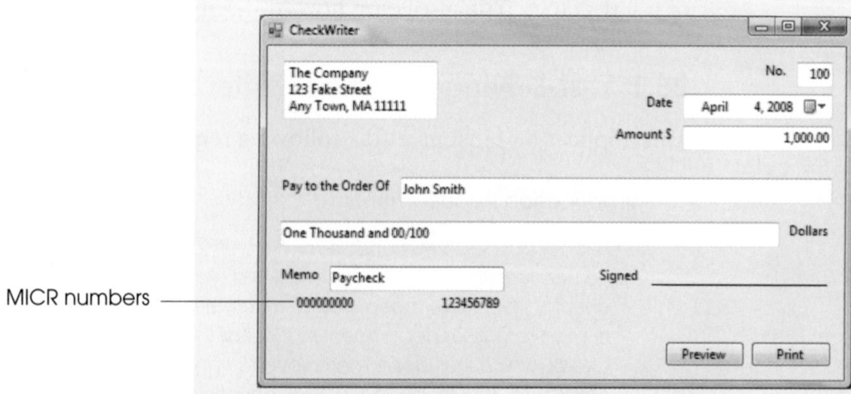

Figure 26.2 **CheckWriter** application displaying a completed check.

(cont.)

You may have noticed that at the bottom-left side of all bank checks is a string of numbers and symbols. These are called Magnetic Ink Character Recognition (MICR) numbers. MICR numbers are broken into three components. The first nine digits are the bank's routing number, followed by the account number and then the check number. Banks have special machines that read these numbers and route the check to the appropriate account. Using the MICR font, you can create MICR numbers in your check-writing application. (We did not use the MICR font in this application.) To download the MICR font, visit `www.newfreeware.com/graphics/696/`.

5. ***Previewing the check.*** Click the **Preview** `Button` to display the completed check in a **Print preview** (Fig. 26.3). This dialog is actually a control of type `PrintPreviewDialog`, which is used to display how a document appears before it is printed. [*Note:* Printing or previewing the document is not possible when there is no printer installed on your computer.]

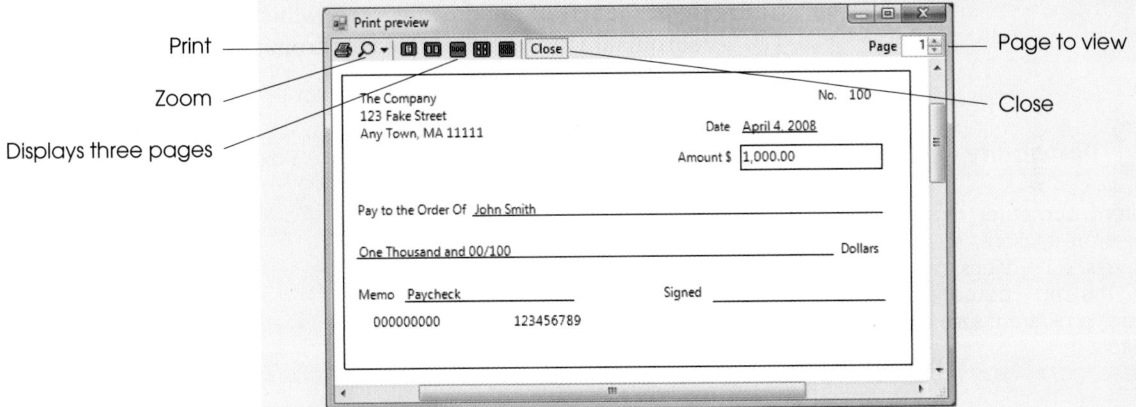

Figure 26.3 Preview of the completed check.

The **Print preview** dialog contains several toolbar `Buttons`. The first `Button` is the print `Button` (🖶), which allows the user to print the document. The next `Button` (🔍) zooms in and out, allowing the user to view the document at different sizes. The next five `Buttons` allow the user to specify the number of pages that can be displayed in the dialog at one time. The user can view one, two, three, four or six pages at a time in the dialog box. The **Close** `Button` closes the dialog box. Finally, the right-most control in the dialog box allows the user to specify which page of the document to view. The `PrintPreviewDialog` control is discussed in detail later in this tutorial. The document that displays in this dialog box is the `PrintDocument`, an object that you create when coding the application.

6. ***Closing the Print Preview dialog.*** Click **Close** to close the **Print preview** dialog.

7. ***Printing the check.*** To print the check, your computer must be connected to a printer. Click the **Print** `Button`. The check prints from the default printer of your computer.

8. ***Closing the application.*** Close your application by clicking its close box.

9. ***Closing the IDE.*** Close the Visual Basic IDE by clicking its close box.

26.2 GDI+ Introduction

This section introduces the graphics classes and structures used in this tutorial and discusses GDI+ graphics programming. Graphics typically consist of lines, shapes, colors and text drawn on the background of a control.

You use the methods of class **Graphics** to draw on the Form. Class Graphics contains methods used for drawing text, lines, rectangles and other shapes. Objects of the Pen and Brush classes affect the appearance of the lines and shapes you draw. A **Pen** specifies the line style used to draw a shape (for example, line thickness, solid lines, dashed lines, etc.). A **Brush** specifies how to fill a shape (for example, solid color or pattern). The drawing methods of class Graphics usually require a Pen or Brush object to render a specified shape.

The Color structure contains pre-defined colors and methods that allow you to create new colors. Objects of the Font class affect the appearance of text. The **Font** class contains properties (such as Bold, Italic and Size) that describe font characteristics. The **FontFamily** class contains methods for obtaining font information (such as **GetName**).

GDI+ uses a **coordinate system** (Fig. 26.4) to identify every point on the screen. A coordinate pair has both an ***x*-coordinate** (the horizontal coordinate) and a ***y*-coordinate** (the vertical coordinate). The *x*-coordinate is the horizontal distance from zero at the left of the drawing area, which increases as you move to the right. The *y*-coordinate is the vertical distance from zero at the top of the drawing area, which increases as you move down.

Portability Tip

Different computer monitors have different resolutions, so the density of pixels on various monitors will vary. This may cause graphics to appear in different sizes on different monitors.

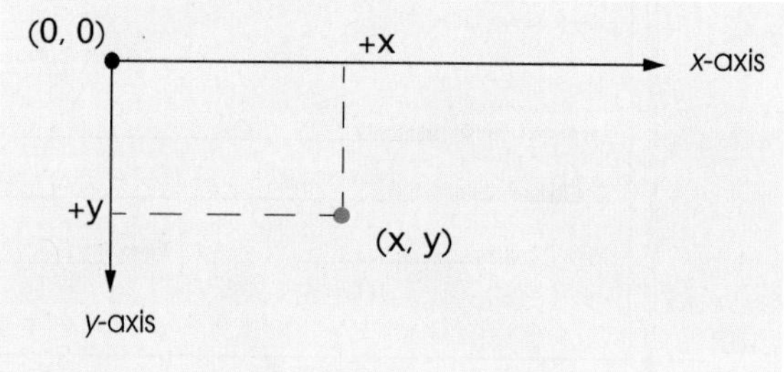

Figure 26.4 GDI+ coordinate system.

The ***x*-axis** defines every horizontal coordinate, and the ***y*-axis** defines every vertical coordinate. You position text and shapes on the screen by specifying their (*x*, *y*) coordinates. The upper-left corner of a GUI component (such as a Panel or the Form) has the coordinates (0, 0). In the diagram in Fig. 26.4, the red point at position (*x*, *y*) is *x* pixels to the right of position (0, 0) along the *x*-axis and *y* pixels below position (0, 0) along the *y*-axis. Coordinate units are measured in pixels, which are the smallest units of resolution on a computer monitor.

SELF-REVIEW

1. The ________ class contains properties that describe font characteristics.

   a) Font b) GDIFont
   c) SystemFont d) FontStyle

2. The ________ corner of a GUI component has the coordinate (0, 0).

   a) lower-left b) upper-right
   c) upper-left d) lower-right

Answers: 1) a. 2) c.

26.3 Constructing the CheckWriter Application

Now that you've learned about the features that you'll use in your **CheckWriter** application, you need to analyze the application. The following pseudocode describes the basic operation of the **CheckWriter** application:

When the user clicks the Preview Button
  Retrieve check information from the user
  Display the check in a Print Preview dialog

When the user clicks the Print Button
  Retrieve check information from the user
  Print the check on the printer

Now that you've test-driven the **CheckWriter** application and studied its pseudocode representation, you use an ACE table to help you convert the pseudocode to Visual Basic. Figure 26.5 lists the actions, controls and events that help you complete your own version of this application.

Action/Control/Event (ACE) Table for the CheckWriter Application

Action	Control/Object	Event
Label the application's controls	`checkNumberLabel`, `dateLabel`, `amountLabel`, `payeeLabel`, `dollarsLabel`, `memoLabel`, `signedLabel`, `underlineLabel`, `abaLabel`, `accountLabel`	
	`previewButton`	`Click`
Retrieve check information from the user	`checkNumberTextBox`, `dateTimePicker`, `amountTextBox`, `payeeTextBox`, `dollarTextBox`, `memoTextBox`, `payerTextBox`	
Display the check in a Print preview dialog	`previewObject`	
	`printButton`	`Click`
Retrieve check information from the user	`checkNumberTextBox`, `dateTimePicker`, `amountTextBox`, `payeeTextBox`, `dollarTextBox`, `memoTextBox`, `payerTextBox`	
Print the check on the printer	`document`	

Figure 26.5 ACE table for the **CheckWriter** application.

Now that you have an understanding of the **CheckWriter** application, you can begin to create it. A template application is provided that contains many of the GUI's controls. You begin by creating a `PrintPreviewDialog` object in the following box.

Adding a `PrintPreviewDialog` in the CheckWriter Application

1. ***Copying the template to your working directory.*** Copy the `C:\Examples\Tutorial26\TemplateApplication\CheckWriter` directory to your `C:\SimplyVB2008` directory.
2. ***Opening the* CheckWriter *application's template file.*** Double click `CheckWriter.sln` in the `CheckWriter` directory to open the application in the Visual Basic IDE.

(cont.)

3. ***Adding the `PrintPreviewDialog`.*** In the **Toolbox**, locate the **PrintPreview-Dialog** control

PrintPreviewDialog

in the **All Windows Forms** group, and drag and drop it onto the `Form`. The control appears in the component tray as shown in Fig. 26.6.

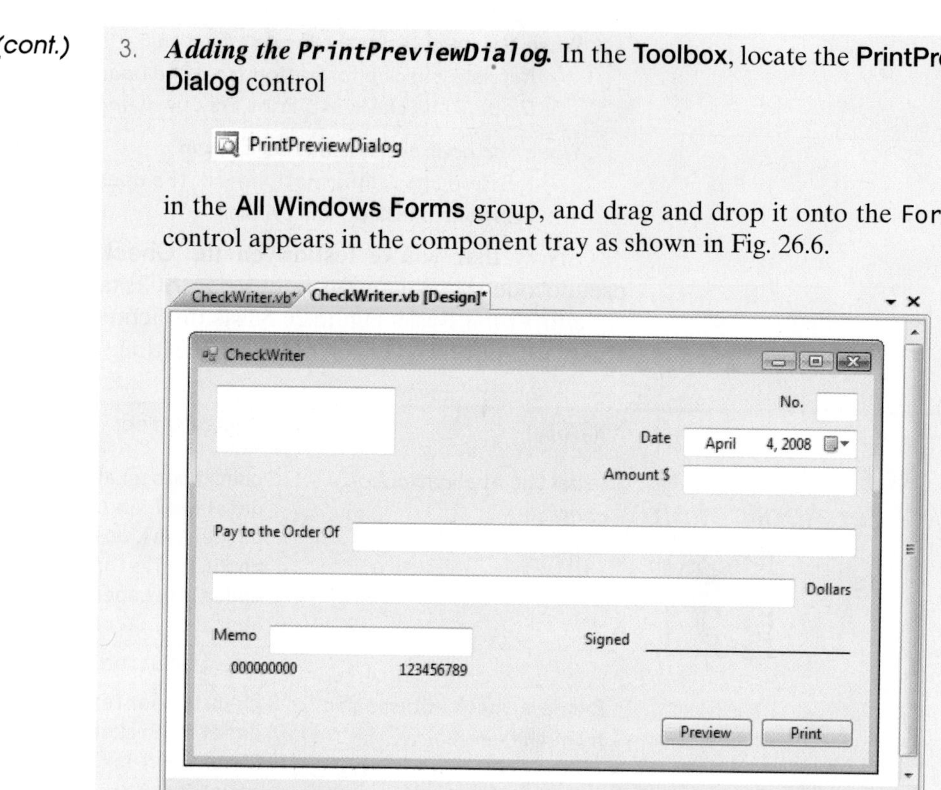

`PrintPreviewDialog` in the component tray

Figure 26.6 **CheckWriter** application in **Design** view with `PrintPreviewDialog`.

The `PrintPreviewDialog` control displays a dialog that allows users to view a document at different sizes, print a document and display multiple pages of a document before printing. Make sure the `PrintPreviewDialog` object that you just created is selected, and change its `Name` property to `previewObject`. This object has a `Document` property that specifies the document to preview. The document must be a `PrintDocument` object, as will be discussed later in the tutorial. For now, do not specify the document.

4. ***Setting the `UseAntiAlias` property to `True`.*** The `PrintPreviewDialog` also contains the `UseAntiAlias` property, which makes the text in the dialog appear smoother on the screen. To accomplish this, set the `UseAntiAlias` property to `True`.

5. ***Saving the project.*** Select **File > Save All** to save your modified code.

SELF-REVIEW

1. Use a ________ control to preview a document before it is printed.

   a) `PrintDialog` b) `PrintPreviewDialog`
   c) `PrintPreviewControl` d) `PrintDocument`

2. A `PrintPreviewDialog` object has a ________ property that specifies the document to preview.

   a) `Preview` b) `PreviewDocument`
   c) `View` d) `Document`

Answers: 1) b. 2) d.

26.4 PrintPreviewDialogs and PrintDocuments

In the **CheckWriter** application, you use an object of the PrintPreviewDialog class. As previously mentioned, this object displays a dialog that shows a document as it appears when it is printed. Recall that the dialog object contains the **Document** property, which allows you to specify the document to preview, and that the object specified in the Document property must be of type PrintDocument. The PrintPreviewDialog's ShowDialog method displays the preview dialog. You use this method later in the application.

The **PrintDocument** object allows you to specify how to print a specified document. The object raises a **PrintPage** event when the data required to print the current page is needed (that is, when the document is printed or a print preview is generated). You can define this object's PrintPage event handler to specify what you want to print. The PrintDocument also contains a **Print** method that uses a Graphics object to print the document. You use method Print later in this tutorial.

SELF-REVIEW

1. The object assigned to the Document property must be of type ________.

   a) PrintPreviewDialog b) PrintDocument
   c) PrintPreviewControl d) PrintDialog

2. The ________ event handler of object PrintDocument uses a Graphics object to print the document.

   a) Graphics b) Document
   c) PrintPage d) None of the above

Answers: 1) b. 2) c.

26.5 Creating an Event Handler for the CheckWriter Application

Now that you've created the PrintPreviewDialog object in the **CheckWriter** application, you can begin to add functionality to the application. Before you can use print features, you must import the System.Drawing.Printing namespace. You implement these features in the following box.

Importing a Namespace

1. ***Switching to Code view.*** Select **View > Code** to view the CheckWriter.vb code.

2. ***Importing namespaces.*** Add line 1 before the class CheckWriterForm definition, as shown in Fig. 26.7 to import the **System.Drawing.Printing** namespace. This statement allows your application to access Windows services related to printing. After you import the namespace, the application can use PrintDocument objects. The namespace also enables access to the **PrintPageEventArgs** class. This class's Graphics property provides a Graphics object used to draw the graphics that appear on the printed page.

   Importing namespace System.Drawing.Printing

   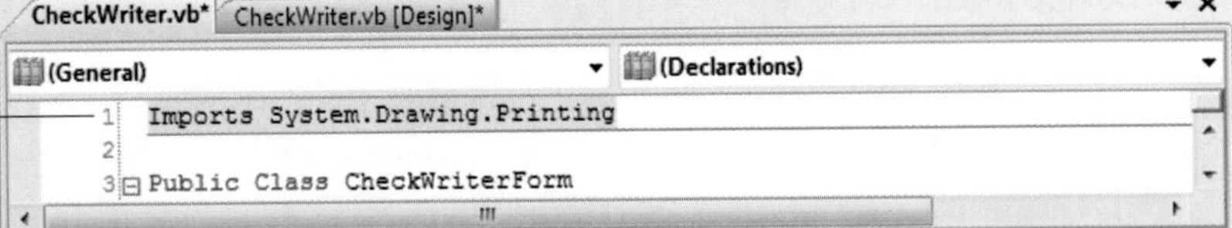

   Figure 26.7 Import System.Drawing.Printing namespace.

3. ***Saving the project.*** Select **File > Save All** to save your modified code.

Now that you've imported namespace `System.Drawing.Printing`, you can write code to enable printing and previewing. You begin by defining the `document_PrintPage` method, which specifies what to print. When printing the check, you want the printed document to resemble the application's `Form`. This can be accomplished using a `For Each...Next` statement that draws in a `Graphics` object the contents of each control. You can then print the check using this `Graphics` object. You begin writing code to perform these actions in the following box.

Defining an Event Handler to Print Pages

1. ***Creating the `document_PrintPage` method.*** Add lines 5–9 into the application code, as in Fig. 26.8. These lines create the event handler for the `PrintPage` event. You need to type these lines to create the event handler because the `PrintDocument` object has not yet been created. You create this object later in the tutorial.

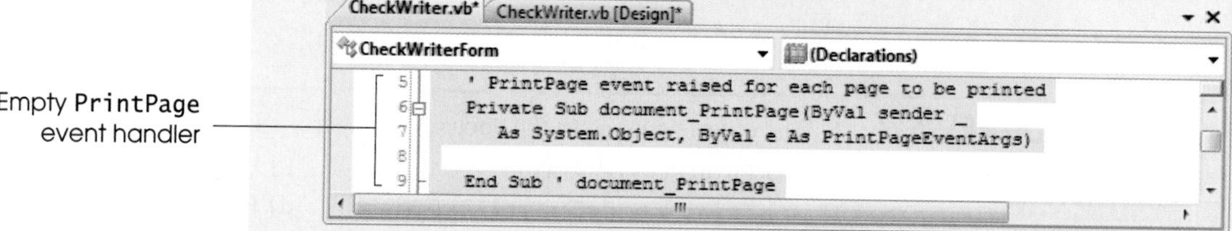
CheckWriter.vb*
CheckWriter.vb [Design]*
CheckWriterForm
(Declarations)
5 ' PrintPage event raised for each page to be printed
6 Private Sub document_PrintPage(ByVal sender _
7 As System.Object, ByVal e As PrintPageEventArgs)
8
9 End Sub ' document_PrintPage
Empty PrintPage event handler

Figure 26.8 `document_PrintPage` event handler.

2. ***Declaring the variables.*** Add lines 9–22 of Fig. 26.9 to the event handler. Line 9 declares a `Font` variable named `fontObject` that is used to specify the text font. Lines 12–13 declare `Single` variables that represent the *x*- and *y*-coordinates where controls appear on the `Form`. `Single` is a type that stores floating-point values. `Single` is similar to `Double`, but is less precise and requires less memory. Lines 16 and 19 declare `Single` variables, which specify the coordinates of the left and top margins of the page to be printed. These values are determined by using the `MarginBounds.Left` and `MarginBounds.Top` properties of the `PrintPageEventArgs` object (`e` from line 7) that is passed when the `PrintPage` event is raised. Line 22 declares the `String` variable `controlText`, which is used to store text from the controls.

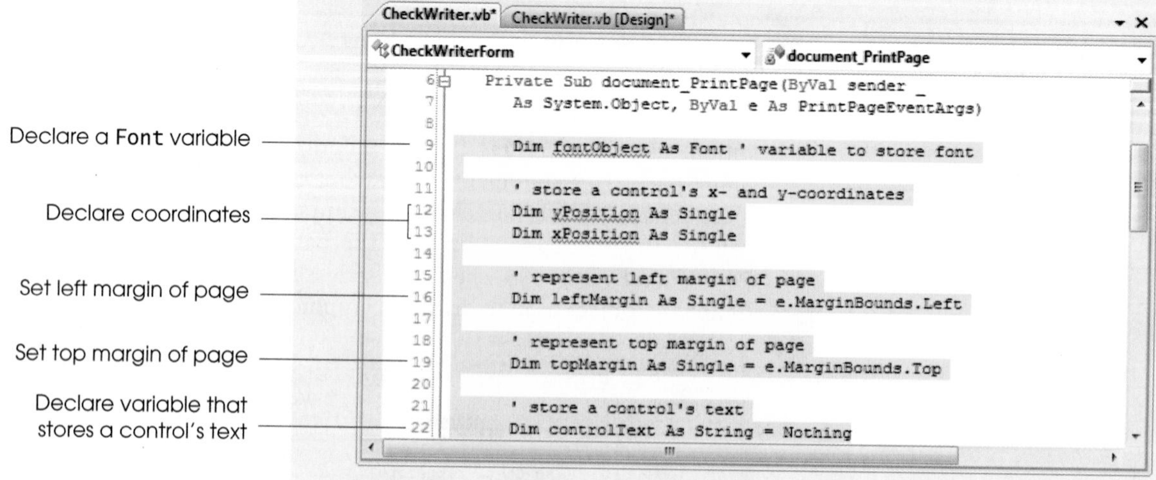
CheckWriter.vb*
CheckWriter.vb [Design]*
CheckWriterForm
document_PrintPage
6 Private Sub document_PrintPage(ByVal sender _
7 As System.Object, ByVal e As PrintPageEventArgs)
8
9 Dim fontObject As Font ' variable to store font
10
11 ' store a control's x- and y-coordinates
12 Dim yPosition As Single
13 Dim xPosition As Single
14
15 ' represent left margin of page
16 Dim leftMargin As Single = e.MarginBounds.Left
17
18 ' represent top margin of page
19 Dim topMargin As Single = e.MarginBounds.Top
20
21 ' store a control's text
22 Dim controlText As String = Nothing
Declare a Font variable
Declare coordinates
Set left margin of page
Set top margin of page
Declare variable that stores a control's text

Figure 26.9 Variables created for `document_PrintPage`.

(cont.)

3. ***Iterating through the controls on the Form.*** Add lines 24–28 of Fig. 26.10 to the `PrintPage` event handler. This `For Each...Next` statement iterates through the controls on the `Form` to print the check. You define this statement's body in the next box.

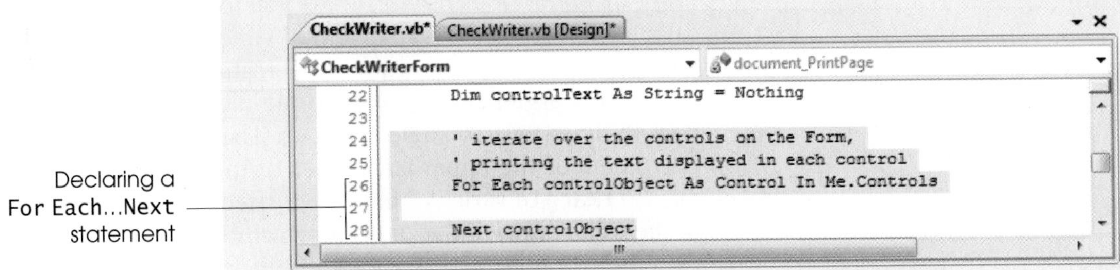

Figure 26.10 `For Each...Next` statement used for iteration.

4. ***Adding formatting lines and drawing the check's border.*** Add lines 30–54 of Fig. 26.11 into the event handler. Checks contain lines for payee, payment amount, and memo information. To draw these lines, call the **`DrawLine`** method on the `Graphics` object (which is received by this event handler as part of the `PrintPageEventArgs` parameter). Method `DrawLine` takes five arguments, the first of which specifies the `Pen` to use to draw the line. A **`Pen`** specifies the characteristics of the line that is drawn. Lines 31, 38, 46 and 53 each use a value from the **`Pens`** enumeration (`Pens.Black`) to specify that a solid black line should be drawn. The next four arguments consist of the coordinates of the line's endpoints in the following order: x1, y1, x2, y2. Lines 31–35 draw the payee line, using the `Location` property of the `payeeTextBox` control as arguments in the method call. Note that you add `15` to the *y*-coordinates for the line because the control's *y*-coordinate represents the *top* of the control—the line is now drawn at the bottom of the control. Lines 38–43 and lines 46–50 similarly use their respective control location properties to draw a line in the appropriate place on the check.

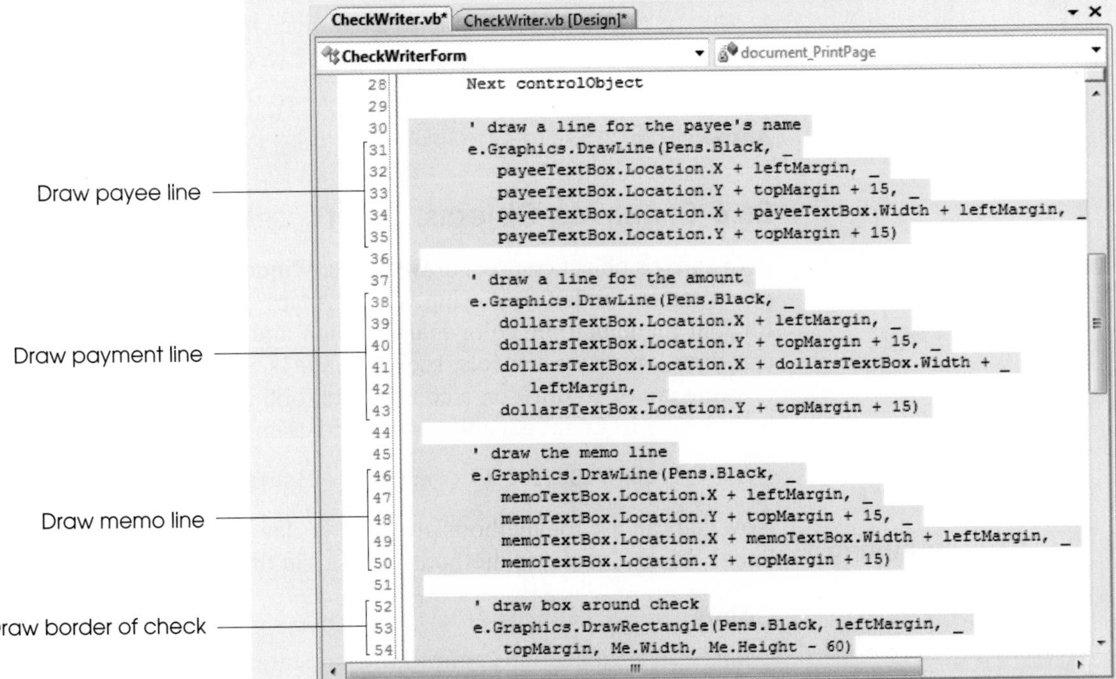

Figure 26.11 Event handler `document_PrintPage` modified to draw formatting lines on the check.

(cont.)

The `Form`'s border is not contained in a control—you must use a `Graphics` object to draw a rectangle around the check to be printed. To draw the rectangle around the check, use the `PrintPageEventArgs` object (`e` from line 7) that is passed when the `PrintPage` event is raised. The `Graphics` property of this object again allows you to specify what you want to print. By calling the `DrawRectangle` method (lines 53–54) on the `Graphics` object, you can specify the properties of the rectangle to draw.

The first argument you pass to the method is a `Pen` object that specifies how to draw the rectangle's border. The second argument specifies the *x*-coordinate of the upper-left corner of the rectangle you wish to draw. Use the `leftMargin` variable that you created in *Step 2* to represent the position of the left margin of the page on which the check prints. This value ensures that the rectangle aligns with the left margin. The third argument in the method specifies the *y*-coordinate of the upper-left corner of the rectangle. Use the `topMargin` variable that you created in *Step 2* to represent the position of the top margin of the page on which the check prints.

The fourth and fifth arguments specify the width and height of the rectangle. The width is set to `Me.Width`, which returns the width of the `Form`. Keyword `Me` references the current object—in this case, the `Form`. The height, on the other hand, is set to `Me.Height - 60`. This value is the height of the `Form` minus 60 pixels. You subtract 60 pixels because you do not want to print the space for the `Buttons` on the bottom of the `Form`. These `Buttons` were created to allow users to print and preview the checks. (They were not intended to be printed on the checks.)

5. ***Saving the project***. Select **File > Save All** to save your modified code.

SELF-REVIEW

1. Importing the `System.`________ namespace gives you access to print-related functions.

   a) `Windows` b) `Printing`
   c) `Drawing.Printing` d) `Drawing`

2. The ________ keyword references the current object.

   a) `Me` b) `Current`
   c) `Form` d) None of the above

Answers: 1) c. 2) a.

26.6 Graphics Objects: Colors, Lines and Shapes

A `Graphics` object controls drawing in a Windows `Forms` application. In addition to providing methods for drawing various shapes, `Graphics` objects contain methods for font manipulation, color manipulation and other graphics-related actions. You can draw on many controls, such as `Labels` and `Buttons`, which have their own drawing areas. To draw on a control, first obtain a `Graphics` object for the control by invoking its `CreateGraphics` method, as in

```
Dim graphicsObject As Graphics = displayPanel.CreateGraphics()
```

Now you can use the methods provided in class `Graphics` to draw on the `displayPanel`. Many `Graphics` methods are used in this tutorial.

Good Programming Practice

When working with color, keep in mind that many people are color blind or have difficulty perceiving and distinguishing colors. So, use colors that can be distinguished easily.

Colors

Colors can enhance an application's appearance and help convey meaning. For example, a red traffic light indicates stop, yellow indicates caution and green indicates go. The `Color` structure defines methods and constants used to manipulate colors.

Every color can be created from a combination of alpha, red, green and blue components. The alpha value determines the **opacity** (amount of transparency) of the color. For example, the alpha value 0 specifies a transparent color, and the value 255 specifies an opaque color. Alpha values between 0 and 255 (inclusive) result in a blending of the color's RGB value with that of any background color, causing a semi-transparent effect. All three RGB components are Bytes that represent integer values in the range 0–255. The first number in the RGB value defines the amount of red in the color, the second defines the amount of green and the third defines the amount of blue. The larger the value for a particular color, the greater the amount of that color. Visual Basic enables you to choose from almost 17 million colors. If a screen can't display all of these colors, it displays the color closest to the one specified, or it attempts to imitate the color using **dithering** (using small dots of existing colors to form a pattern that simulates the desired color). Figure 26.12 summarizes some predefined Color constants. You can also find a list of various RGB values and their corresponding colors at http://en.wikipedia.org/wiki/List_of_colors.

Constant	RGB value	Constant	RGB value
Color.Orange	255, 200, 0	Color.White	255, 255, 255
Color.Pink	255, 175, 175	Color.Gray	128, 128, 128
Color.Cyan	0, 255, 255	Color.DarkGray	64, 64, 64
Color.Magenta	255, 0, 255	Color.Red	255, 0, 0
Color.Yellow	255, 255, 0	Color.Green	0, 255, 0
Color.Black	0, 0, 0	Color.Blue	0, 0, 255

Figure 26.12 Color structure constants and their RGB values.

You can use pre-existing colors, or you can create your own by using the **FromArgb** method. The statement

```
Dim colorSilver As Color = Color.FromArgb(192, 192, 192)
```

creates a silver color and assigns it to variable colorSilver. Now you can use colorSilver whenever you need a silver color. The Color method FromArgb is used to create this color and other colors by specifying the RGB values as arguments. The method sets the alpha value to 255 (that is, opaque) by default.

Drawing Lines, Rectangles and Ovals

This section presents several Graphics methods for drawing lines, rectangles and ovals. To draw shapes and Strings, you must specify the type of Brushes and Pens to use. A Pen, which functions much like an ordinary pen, is used to specify such characteristics as the color and width of the shape's lines. Most drawing methods require a Pen object. To fill the interior of objects, you must specify a Brush. All classes derived from the abstract class Brush define objects that fill the interiors of shapes with color patterns or images. For example, a SolidBrush specifies the Color that fills the interior of a shape. The following statement creates a SolidBrush with the color orange:

```
Dim brush As New SolidBrush(Color.Orange)
```

Many drawing methods have multiple versions. When employing methods that draw outlined hollow shapes, use versions that take a Pen argument. When employing methods that draw shapes filled with colors, patterns or images, use versions that take a Brush argument. Many of these methods require x, y, width and height arguments. The x and y arguments represent the shape's upper-left corner coordinate. The width and height arguments represent the width and height of the shape in pixels, respectively. Figure 26.13 summarizes several `Graphics` methods and their parameters.

`Graphics` Drawing Methods and Descriptions

Note: Many of these methods have multiple overloaded versions.

```
DrawLine(ByVal p As Pen, ByVal x1 As Single, ByVal y1 As Single,
   ByVal x2 As Single, ByVal y2 As Single)
```
Draws a line from the point `(x1, y1)` to the point `(x2, y2)`. The `Pen` determines the color, style and width of the line.

```
DrawRectangle(ByVal p As Pen, ByVal x As Single, ByVal y As Single,
   ByVal width As Single, ByVal height As Single)
```
Draws a rectangle of the specified `width` and `height`. The top-left corner of the rectangle is at the point `(x, y)`. The `Pen` determines the rectangle's color, style and border width.

```
FillRectangle(ByVal b As Brush, ByVal x As Single, ByVal y As Single,
   ByVal width As Single, ByVal height As Single)
```
Draws a solid rectangle of the specified `width` and `height`. The top-left corner of the rectangle is at the point `(x, y)`. The `Brush` determines the fill pattern inside the rectangle.

```
DrawEllipse(ByVal p As Pen, ByVal x As Single, ByVal y As Single,
   ByVal width As Single, ByVal height As Single)
```
Draws an ellipse inside a rectangular area of the specified `width` and `height`. The top-left corner of the rectangular area is at the point `(x, y)`. The `Pen` determines the color, style and border width of the ellipse.

```
FillEllipse(ByVal b As Brush, ByVal x As Single, ByVal y As Single,
   ByVal width As Single, ByVal height As Single)
```
Draws a filled ellipse inside a rectangular area of the specified `width` and `height`. The top-left corner of the rectangular area is at the point `(x, y)`. The `Brush` determines the pattern inside the ellipse.

Figure 26.13 `Graphics` methods that draw lines, rectangles and ovals.

SELF-REVIEW

1. The RGB value of a `Color` represents ________.
   a) the index number of a color
   b) the amount of red, green and blue in a color
   c) the thickness of the drawing object
   d) the type of shape to draw

2. The ________ method is used to draw solid rectangles.
   a) `DrawRectangle` b) `FillRectangle`
   c) `SolidRectangle` d) `OpaqueRectangle`

Answers: 1) b. 2) b.

26.7 Printing Each Control of the CheckWriter Application

Earlier, you created an empty `For Each...Next` statement to iterate through all the controls on the `Form`. Now you write code for the body of the `For Each...Next` statement to print all the controls on the `Form`, except for the `Buttons`.

Iterating through All the Objects of the Form to Print Each Control

1. ***Checking for `Buttons`.*** In the body of the `For Each...Next` statement of `document_PrintPage`, add lines 27–30 of Fig. 26.14. Adding this `If...Then` statement determines whether the current control is a `Button`. If the control is not a `Button`, then the body of the `If...Then` statement executes. However, if the control is a `Button`, the `For Each...Next` statement continues to the next control on the `Form`.

(cont.)

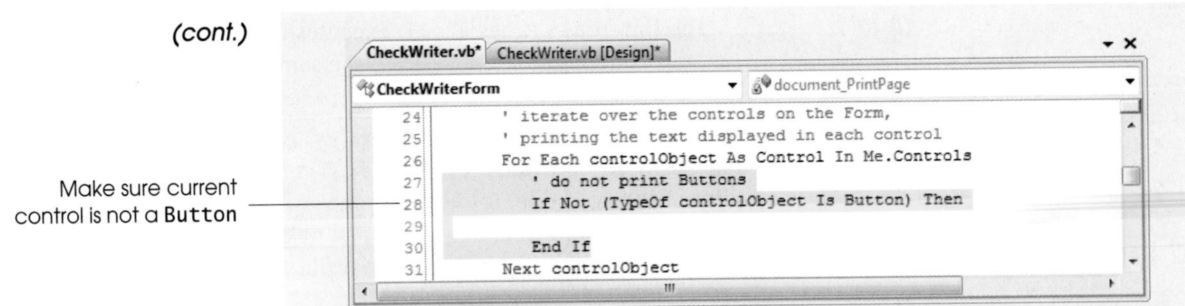

Figure 26.14 Code to determine whether the current control is a `Button`.

2. ***Defining the body of the If...Then statement.*** Now you add code that properly prints the value that appears in each control on the check. Add lines 29–44 of Fig. 26.15 into the body of the `If...Then` statement.

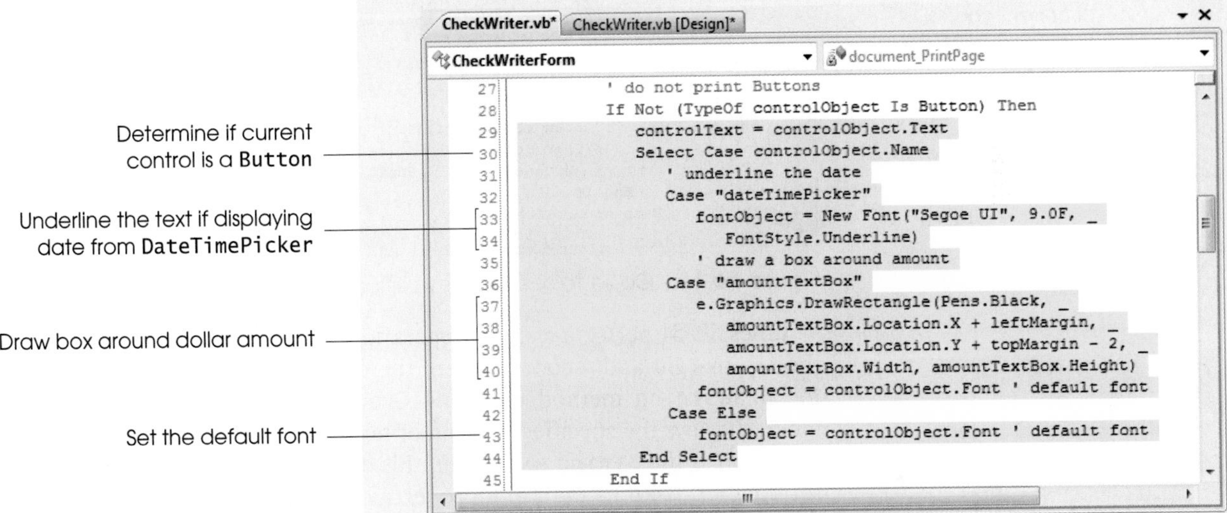

Figure 26.15 `Select Case` statement to print controls.

Line 29 sets the `controlText` variable that you created earlier to `controlObject.Text`. This contains the value of the control's `Text` property (text displayed to the user or entered by the user). The `Select Case` statement (lines 30–44) specifies how each control prints. The controlling expression is set to the value `controlObject.Name`. This is the `Name` property of the control. You can use the `Name` property to select specific controls that need to be treated differently when printed.

The first `Case` (lines 32–34) handles the `dateTimePicker` control. It sets `fontObject` to the date's font style—underlined 9pt `Segoe UI` font (the same as the control's text). The date is underlined and appears in 9pt in `Segoe UI` font. Fonts are discussed in detail later in this tutorial.

The second `Case` (lines 36–41) executes if the control is `amountTextBox`. This `Case` draws the box that around the decimal check amount. `Graphics` method `DrawRectangle` is invoked via the `e.Graphics` property. The rectangle's outline prints in black as indicated by `Pens.Black`. The *x*- and *y*-coordinates are specified by adding the `TextBox`'s *x*-*y* location on the `Form` to variables `leftMargin` and `topMargin`, respectively. Recall that you begin printing the check at the corner of the top and left margins. Adding the margin values to the `Location` properties ensures that `amountTextBox` prints in the same position as it appears on the `Form`. (Line 36 subtracts two points of space to center the box on the text.) Line 38 sets the font of the text to draw to the same value as the font used to display text in the control.

(cont.)

The third `Case` (lines 42–43) executes for all the other controls. This `Case` sets the `fontObject` font style to the same value as the font used to display text in the control. Line 44 ends the `Select Case` statement.

3. ***Setting the positions of the text of each control.*** Add lines 46–55 of Fig. 26.16 to the body of the `If...Then` statement. Lines 47–48 set the `xPosition` variable to `leftMargin + controlObject.Location.X`. By adding the *x*-coordinate of the current control (represented by `controlObject.Location.X`) to the left margin, you ensure that the check will not draw outside the margins of the page.

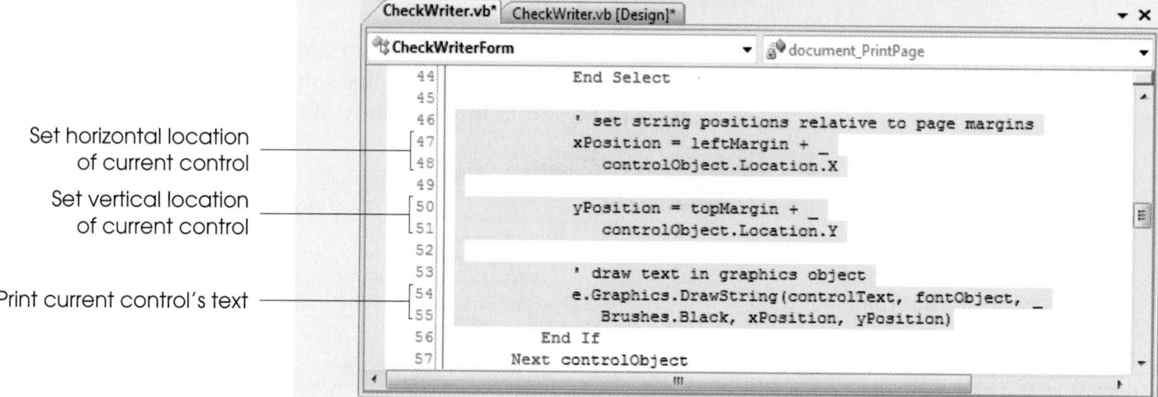

Figure 26.16 Code to set `String` positions of the controls.

Lines 50–51 perform a similar operation, setting `yPosition` to the sum of the top margin and *y*-coordinate of the control's location. Lines 54–55 call the `DrawString` method on the `e.Graphics` property. The **`DrawString`** method draws the specified `String` of text in the `Graphics` object. The first argument is the `String` to draw, in this case `controlText`. Recall that you set `controlText` to the `Text` property of the current control. The second argument is the font, which is specified by `fontObject`. The third argument specifies a `Brush`. You pass the value `Brushes.Black`, which creates a black brush object to draw the text. The **`Brushes`** class provides properties to access `Brush` objects of any standard color. The fourth and fifth arguments are the *x*- and *y*-coordinates where the first character of the `String` prints. Use the `xPosition` and `yPosition` variables that you set in lines 47–51 to print the text at the correct location on the page.

4. ***Saving the project.*** Select **File > Save All** to save your modified code.

SELF-REVIEW

1. The ________ method draws a specified `String` of text.
   a) `String`
   b) `PrintString`
   c) `DrawString`
   d) `Draw`

2. Typing `Brushes.Black` ________.
   a) obtains a black `Brush` object
   b) retrieves the color of a brush
   c) paints the screen black
   d) creates a `Pen` object

Answers: 1) c. 2) a.

26.8 Font Class

In the **CheckWriter** application, you used a `Font` object to specify the style of the text printed on a page. This section introduces the methods and constants contained in the `Font` class. Note that `Font`s are immutable—once a `Font` has been created, its properties cannot be modified. That means that if you require a different Font, you must create a new Font object with the appropriate settings. That's the reason you created a new Font in lines 33–34 of Fig. 26.15 for the DateTimePicker control. There are many versions of the Font constructor for creating custom Fonts. Some properties of the Font class are summarized in Fig. 26.17.

Property	Description
Bold	Sets a font to a bold font style if value is set to True.
FontFamily	Represents the FontFamily of the Font (a grouping structure to organize fonts with similar properties).
Height	Represents the height of the font.
Italic	Sets a font to an italic font style if value is set to True.
Name	Sets the font's name to the specified String.
Size	Represents a Single value indicating the current font size measured in design units. (Design units are any specified units of measurement for the font.)
SizeInPoints	Represents a Single value indicating the current font size measured in points.
Strikeout	Sets a font to the strikeout font style if value is set to True (for example, ~~Strikeout~~).
Underline	Sets a font to the underline font style if the value is set to True.

Figure 26.17 Font class read-only properties.

Common Programming Error

Specifying a font that is not available on a system is a logic error. If this occurs, the system's default font is used instead.

Note that the Size property returns the font size as measured in **design units**, whereas SizeInPoints returns the font size as measured in points (a more common measurement). The Size property can be specified in a variety of ways, such as inches or millimeters. Some versions of the Font constructor accept a GraphicsUnit argument—an enumeration that allows users to specify the unit of measurement used to describe the font size. Members of the GraphicsUnit enumeration include Point (1/72 inch), Display (1/100 inch), Document (1/300 inch), Millimeter, Inch and Pixel. If this argument is provided, the Size property contains the size of the font as measured in the specified design unit, and the SizeInPoints property contains the size of the font in points. For example, if you create a Font having size 1 and specify that GraphicsUnit.Inch will be used to measure the font, the Size property will be 1, and the SizeInPoints property will be 72 because there are 72 points in an inch. If you create a new Font object without specifying a GraphicsUnit, the default measurement for the font size is GraphicsUnit.Point (thus, the Size and SizeInPoints properties will be equal).

The Font class has several overloaded constructors. Many of which require a font name, which is a String representing a font currently supported by the system. Common fonts include *Arial* and *Times New Roman*. Constructors also require the font size as an argument. Last, Font constructors usually require a font style, specified by an element of the **FontStyle** enumeration: FontStyle.Bold, FontStyle.Italic, FontStyle.Regular, FontStyle.Strikeout and FontStyle.Underline. You can specify multiple FontStyle elements by combining them using the Or operator (e.g., FontStyle.Bold Or FontStyle.Italic uses a bold italic font).

SELF-REVIEW

1. The most common measurement of font size is ________.

a) points
b) inches
c) pixels
d) millimeters

2. ________ is an example of a font style.

   a) `Bold`
   b) `Italic`
   c) `StrikeOut`
   d) All of the above

Answers: 1) a. 2) d.

26.9 Previewing and Printing the Check

After defining how objects are printed in the `document_PrintPage` event handler, you must define what occurs when each `Button` is clicked. You begin with the `printButton_Click` event handler to specify the functionality when clicking the **Print** `Button`. You write this event handler in the following box.

Defining the `printButton_Click` Event Handler

1. ***Creating the `printButton_Click` event handler.*** In the Windows `Form` Designer, double click the **Print** `Button`. The `printButton_Click` event handler appears in the `CheckWriter.vb` file.

2. ***Creating a `PrintDocument` object.*** Add lines 90–91 of Fig. 26.18 into the event handler. The `PrintDocument` object is used to help print the check. Be sure to add the comments and line-continuation characters as shown in Fig. 26.18 so that the line numbers in your code match those presented in this tutorial.

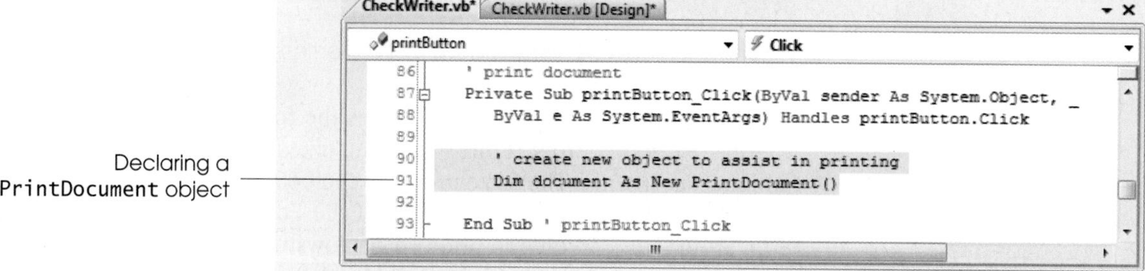

CheckWriter.vb*
CheckWriter.vb [Design]*
printButton
Click
86 ' print document
87 Private Sub printButton_Click(ByVal sender As System.Object, _
88 ByVal e As System.EventArgs) Handles printButton.Click
89
90 ' create new object to assist in printing
91 Dim document As New PrintDocument()
92
93 End Sub ' printButton_Click
Declaring a PrintDocument object

Figure 26.18 Code that creates the `PrintDocument` object.

3. ***Specifying the `PrintPage` event handler.*** Add lines 93–95 of Fig. 26.19 into the event handler. These lines specify the event handler called when the `PrintPage` event is raised. Lines 94–95 use the **`AddHandler`** statement to associate the `PrintPage` event of the `document` object with the event handler specified after the **`AddressOf`** operator (the `document_PrintPage` event handler that you created earlier in this tutorial). To execute the code in the event handler, you must provide the name of the event handler you created to handle the event after operator `AddressOf`.

Adding an event handler for the `PrintDocument` object

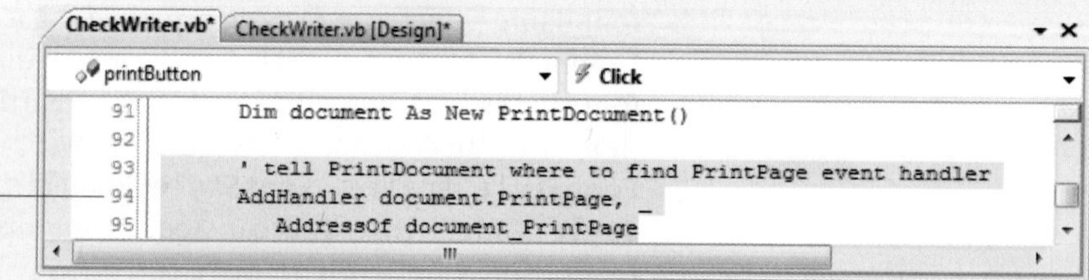

CheckWriter.vb*
CheckWriter.vb [Design]*
printButton
Click
91 Dim document As New PrintDocument()
92
93 ' tell PrintDocument where to find PrintPage event handler
94 AddHandler document.PrintPage, _
95 AddressOf document_PrintPage

Figure 26.19 Code that adds a `PrintPage` event handler to the `Print-Document` object.

(cont.)

4. ***Verifying that the user has a printer.*** Add lines 97–101 of Fig. 26.20 to the `printButton_Click` event handler. Line 98 uses the property `PrinterSettings.InstalledPrinters.Count` to determine how many printers are installed on the user's computer. This property is not limited to physical printers, it includes the Microsoft XPS Document Writer installed as part of .NET 3.5. If there are no printers (the `Count` property is `0`), the user cannot print or preview the document. Line 99 in the body of the `If...Then` statement displays an error message by calling procedure `ErrorMessage`, which you define in the next box. Line 100 exits the event handler using the `Return` keyword.

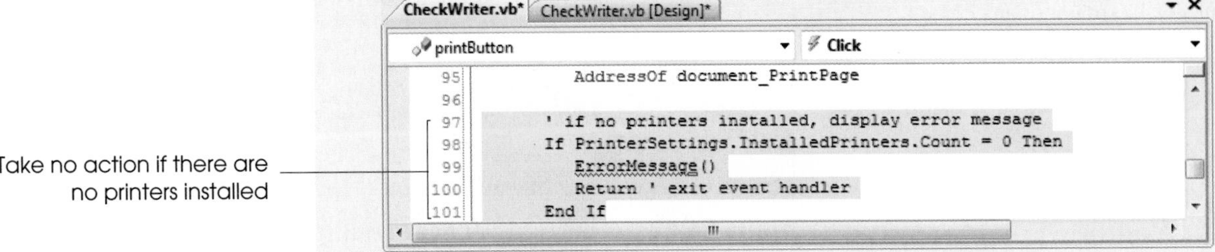
CheckWriter.vb*
CheckWriter.vb [Design]*
printButton
Click
95 AddressOf document_PrintPage
96
97 ' if no printers installed, display error message
98 If PrinterSettings.InstalledPrinters.Count = 0 Then
99 ErrorMessage()
100 Return ' exit event handler
101 End If
Take no action if there are no printers installed

Figure 26.20 Exiting the event handler if no printers are installed.

5. ***Printing the document.*** Add lines 103–104 of Fig. 26.21 to the `printButton_Click` event handler. Line 104 calls the `PrintDocument`'s `Print` method. The `Print` method, in turn, raises the `PrintPage` event each time it needs output for printing. Your `PrintPage` event handler then executes and uses a `Graphics` object to draw. The `Graphics` object is obtained from the `Graphics` property of the `PrintPageEventArgs` class. In this case, the `PrintPageEventArgs` object was passed as argument `e`. The method `document_PrintPage` uses this `PrintPageEventArgs`' `Graphics` object to call the `DrawRectangle`, `DrawLine` and `DrawString` methods.

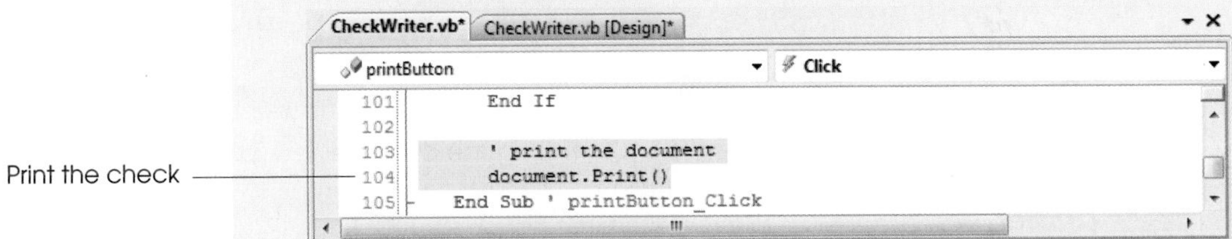
CheckWriter.vb*
CheckWriter.vb [Design]*
printButton
Click
101 End If
102
103 ' print the document
104 document.Print()
105 End Sub ' printButton_Click
Print the check

Figure 26.21 Event handler `printButton_Click` modified to print the document.

6. ***Saving the project.*** Select **File > Save All** to save your modified code.

Now that you've defined the `printButton_Click` method, you complete the application by coding the `Click` event handler for the **Preview** `Button`. When this `Button` is clicked, a dialog appears allowing the user to preview the check before printing it. You create the `previewButton_Click` event handler to enable this feature in the following box.

Defining the `previewButton_Click` Event Handler

1. ***Creating the `previewButton_Click` event handler.*** In the Windows `Form` Designer, double click the **Preview** `Button`. The `previewButton_Click` event handler appears in the `CheckWriter.vb` file.

(cont.)

2. ***Creating the* `PrintDocument` *object and adding the* `PrintPage` *handler.*** Add lines 111–116 of Fig. 26.22 into the event handler. As in the `printButton_Click` event handler, line 112 creates a new `PrintDocument` object named `document`. Lines 115–116 specify that the `PrintDocument` object's `PrintPage` event handler is method `document_PrintPage`.

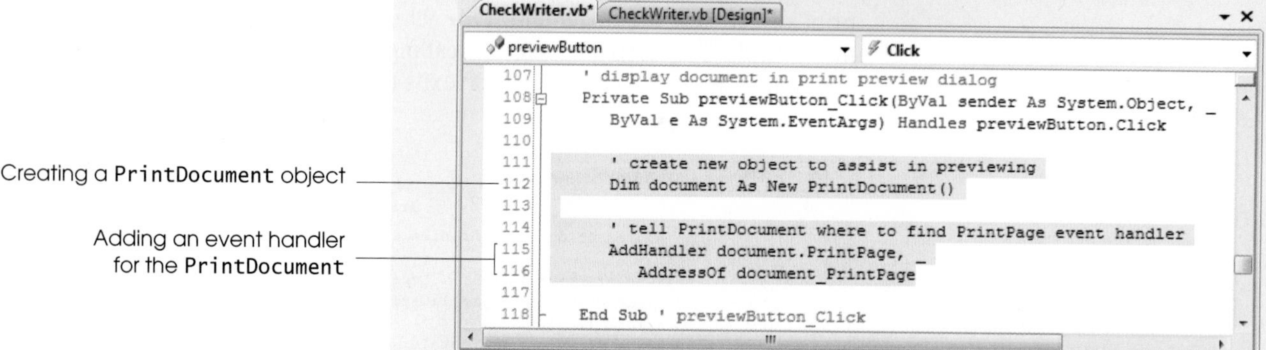
CheckWriter.vb*
CheckWriter.vb [Design]*
previewButton
Click
107 ' display document in print preview dialog
108 Private Sub previewButton_Click(ByVal sender As System.Object, _
109 ByVal e As System.EventArgs) Handles previewButton.Click
110
111 ' create new object to assist in previewing
112 Dim document As New PrintDocument()
113
114 ' tell PrintDocument where to find PrintPage event handler
115 AddHandler document.PrintPage, _
116 AddressOf document_PrintPage
117
118 End Sub ' previewButton_Click
Creating a PrintDocument object
Adding an event handler for the PrintDocument

Figure 26.22 Event handler `previewButton_Click` modified to create `PrintDocument` and add `PrintPage` event handler.

3. ***Verifying that the user has a printer.*** Add lines 118–122 of Fig. 26.23 to the `previewButton_Click` event handler. These lines of code are exactly the same as the code from *Step 4* of the previous box. An error message is displayed if there are no installed printers.

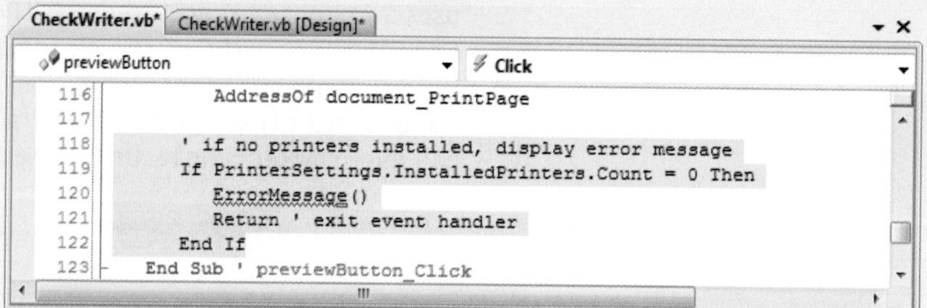
CheckWriter.vb*
CheckWriter.vb [Design]*
previewButton
Click
116 AddressOf document_PrintPage
117
118 ' if no printers installed, display error message
119 If PrinterSettings.InstalledPrinters.Count = 0 Then
120 ErrorMessage()
121 Return ' exit event handler
122 End If
123 End Sub ' previewButton_Click

Figure 26.23 Exiting the print preview event handler if no printers are installed.

4. ***Specifying the* `PrintPreviewDialog` *object's* `Document` *property.*** Add line 124 of Fig. 26.24 into the event handler. Recall that when you created the `PrintPreviewDialog` object, you learned that its `Document` property specifies the document to preview. This property requires that its value be of type `PrintDocument`, the same class you use to print the check. This line sets `previewObject`'s `Document` property to `document` (the `PrintDocument` you created at line 112).

Setting the document to preview

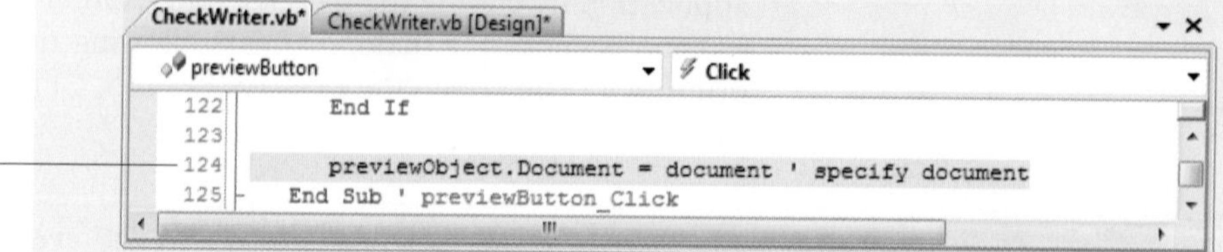
CheckWriter.vb*
CheckWriter.vb [Design]*
previewButton
Click
122 End If
123
124 previewObject.Document = document ' specify document
125 End Sub ' previewButton_Click

Figure 26.24 Event handler `previewButton_Click` modified to set the `PrintPreviewDialog` object's `Document` property.

(cont.)

5. ***Showing the Print preview dialog.*** Add line 125 into the event handler, as shown in Fig. 26.25. This line invokes the `PrintPreviewDialog` object's `ShowDialog` method to display the **Print preview** dialog that displays how the `PrintDocument` appears when printed. To display the document, the `PrintPreviewControl`—a member of the `PrintPreviewDialog`—raises the `PrintPage` event. Rather than using the `Graphics` object to print a page using your printer, the `PrintPreviewDialog` uses the `Graphics` object to display the page on the screen.

Displaying the preview dialog

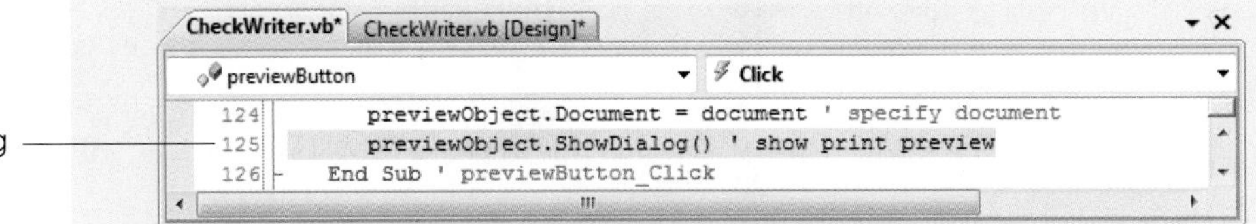
CheckWriter.vb*
CheckWriter.vb [Design]*
previewButton
Click
124 previewObject.Document = document ' specify document
125 previewObject.ShowDialog() ' show print preview
126 End Sub ' previewButton_Click

Figure 26.25 Event handler `previewButton_Click` modified to show preview dialog.

6. ***Defining the `ErrorMessage` procedure.*** Add lines 128–135 of Fig. 26.26 into your application. Lines 131–134 display an error message to the user indicating that printing and print previewing the check is not possible if there is no printer installed on the computer.

Method to display error message

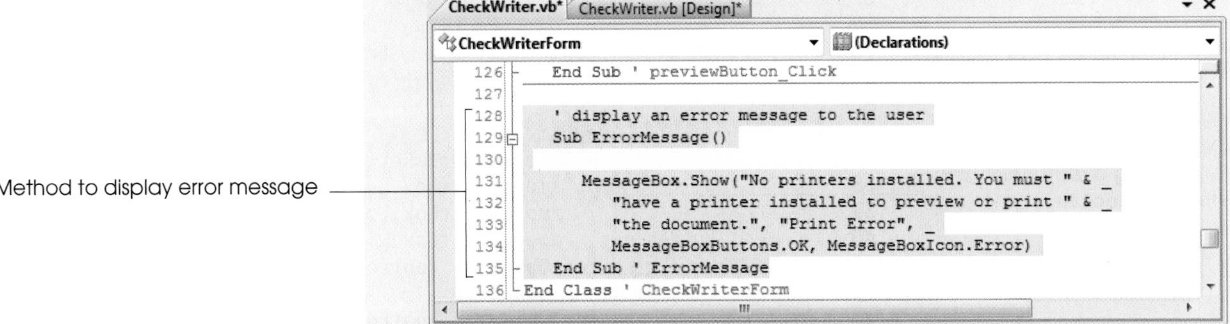
CheckWriter.vb*
CheckWriter.vb [Design]*
CheckWriterForm
(Declarations)
126 End Sub ' previewButton_Click
127
128 ' display an error message to the user
129 Sub ErrorMessage()
130
131 MessageBox.Show("No printers installed. You must " & _
132 "have a printer installed to preview or print " & _
133 "the document.", "Print Error", _
134 MessageBoxButtons.OK, MessageBoxIcon.Error)
135 End Sub ' ErrorMessage
136 End Class ' CheckWriterForm

Figure 26.26 Displaying an error message when no printer is installed.

7. ***Running the application.*** Select **Debug > Start Debugging** to run your application. Enter the information for the check, and click the **Preview** `Button`. The check is displayed in the print preview. Use the **Print** `Button` to print the check. Verify that the check prints out to your default printer (if you have a printer set up).

8. ***Closing the application.*** Close your running application by clicking its close box.

9. ***Closing the IDE.*** Close the Visual Basic IDE by clicking its close box.

Figure 26.27 presents the source code for the **CheckWriter** application. The lines of code that contain new programming concepts you learned in this tutorial are highlighted.

Importing the necessary namespace

```
Imports System.Drawing.Printing

Public Class CheckWriterForm

```

Figure 26.27 **CheckWriter** application code. (Part 1 of 4.)

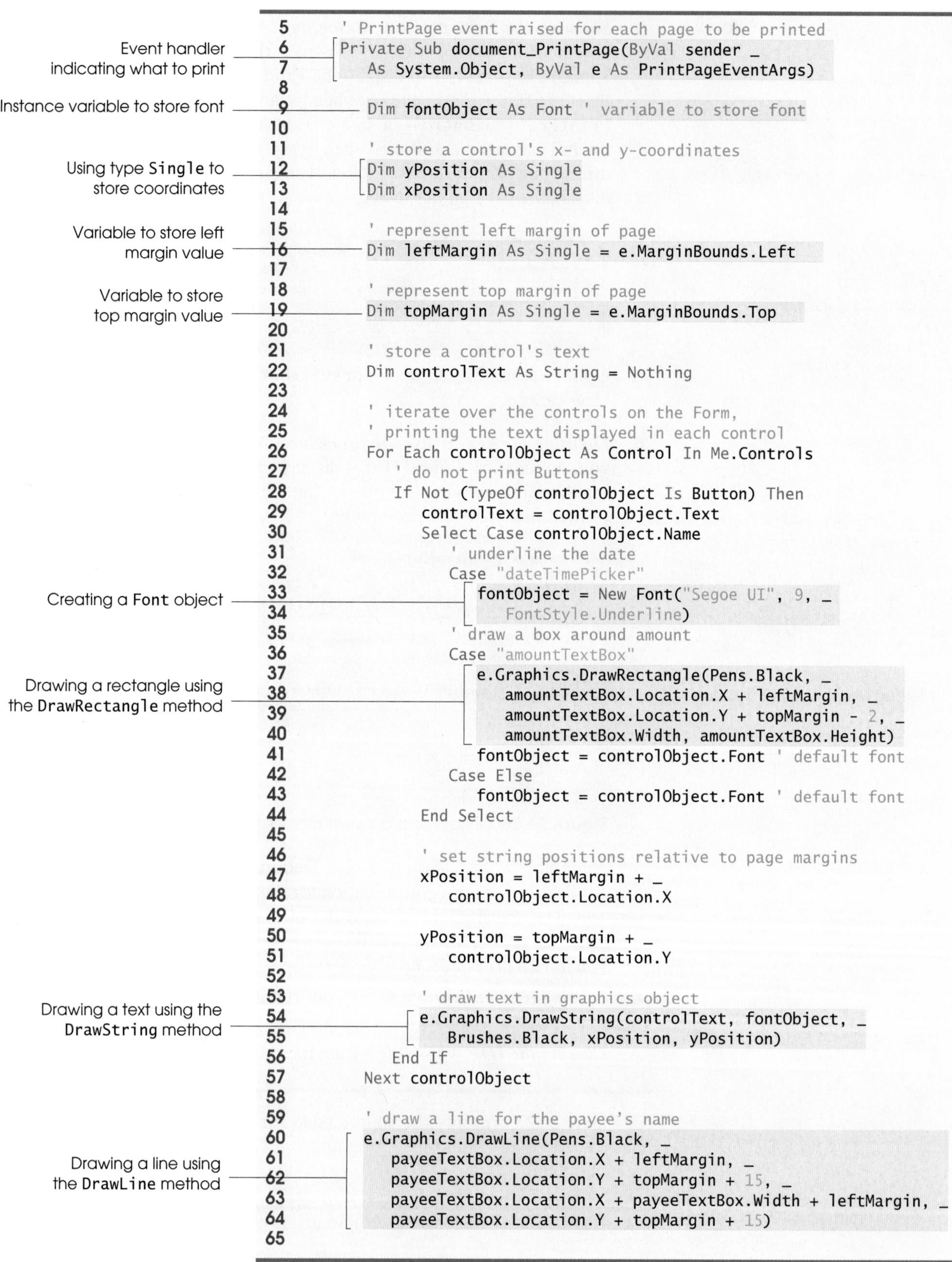

```
   ' PrintPage event raised for each page to be printed
   Private Sub document_PrintPage(ByVal sender _
      As System.Object, ByVal e As PrintPageEventArgs)

      Dim fontObject As Font ' variable to store font

      ' store a control's x- and y-coordinates
      Dim yPosition As Single
      Dim xPosition As Single

      ' represent left margin of page
      Dim leftMargin As Single = e.MarginBounds.Left

      ' represent top margin of page
      Dim topMargin As Single = e.MarginBounds.Top

      ' store a control's text
      Dim controlText As String = Nothing

      ' iterate over the controls on the Form,
      ' printing the text displayed in each control
      For Each controlObject As Control In Me.Controls
         ' do not print Buttons
         If Not (TypeOf controlObject Is Button) Then
            controlText = controlObject.Text
            Select Case controlObject.Name
               ' underline the date
               Case "dateTimePicker"
                  fontObject = New Font("Segoe UI", 9, _
                     FontStyle.Underline)
               ' draw a box around amount
               Case "amountTextBox"
                  e.Graphics.DrawRectangle(Pens.Black, _
                     amountTextBox.Location.X + leftMargin, _
                     amountTextBox.Location.Y + topMargin - 2, _
                     amountTextBox.Width, amountTextBox.Height)
                  fontObject = controlObject.Font ' default font
               Case Else
                  fontObject = controlObject.Font ' default font
            End Select

            ' set string positions relative to page margins
            xPosition = leftMargin + _
               controlObject.Location.X

            yPosition = topMargin + _
               controlObject.Location.Y

            ' draw text in graphics object
            e.Graphics.DrawString(controlText, fontObject, _
               Brushes.Black, xPosition, yPosition)
         End If
      Next controlObject

      ' draw a line for the payee's name
      e.Graphics.DrawLine(Pens.Black, _
         payeeTextBox.Location.X + leftMargin, _
         payeeTextBox.Location.Y + topMargin + 15, _
         payeeTextBox.Location.X + payeeTextBox.Width + leftMargin, _
         payeeTextBox.Location.Y + topMargin + 15)
```


Figure 26.27 **CheckWriter** application code. (Part 2 of 4.)

```
         ' draw a line for the amount
         e.Graphics.DrawLine(Pens.Black, _
            dollarsTextBox.Location.X + leftMargin, _
            dollarsTextBox.Location.Y + topMargin + 15, _
            dollarsTextBox.Location.X + dollarsTextBox.Width + _
               leftMargin, _
            dollarsTextBox.Location.Y + topMargin + 15)

         ' draw the memo line
         e.Graphics.DrawLine(Pens.Black, _
            memoTextBox.Location.X + leftMargin, _
            memoTextBox.Location.Y + topMargin + 15, _
            memoTextBox.Location.X + memoTextBox.Width + leftMargin, _
            memoTextBox.Location.Y + topMargin + 15)

         ' draw box around check
         e.Graphics.DrawRectangle(Pens.Black, leftMargin, _
            topMargin, Me.Width, Me.Height - 60)
      End Sub ' document_PrintPage

      ' print document
      Private Sub printButton_Click(ByVal sender As System.Object, _
         ByVal e As System.EventArgs) Handles printButton.Click

         ' create new object to assist in printing
         Dim document As New PrintDocument()

         ' tell PrintDocument where to find PrintPage event handler
         AddHandler document.PrintPage, _
            AddressOf document_PrintPage

         ' if no printers installed, display error message
         If PrinterSettings.InstalledPrinters.Count = 0 Then
            ErrorMessage()
            Return ' exit event handler
         End If

         ' print the document
         document.Print()
      End Sub ' printButton_Click

      ' display document in print preview dialog
      Private Sub previewButton_Click(ByVal sender As System.Object, _
         ByVal e As System.EventArgs) Handles previewButton.Click_

         ' create new object to assist in previewing
         Dim document As New PrintDocument()

         ' tell PrintDocument where to find PrintPage event handler
         AddHandler document.PrintPage, _
            AddressOf document_PrintPage

         ' if no printers installed, display error message
         If PrinterSettings.InstalledPrinters.Count = 0 Then
            ErrorMessage()
            Return ' exit event handler
         End If

         previewObject.Document = document ' specify document
         previewObject.ShowDialog() ' show print preview
      End Sub ' previewButton_Click
```

Drawing a box around the check

Create a PrintDocument object

Add an event handler for the PrintDocument object

Display an error message if no printers are installed

Printing the document

Create a PrintDocument object

Add an event handler for the PrintDocument object

Display error message if no printers are installed

Specifying the print document

Previewing the document to be printed

Figure 26.27 **CheckWriter** application code. (Part 3 of 4.)

```
    ' display an error message to the user
    Sub ErrorMessage()

        MessageBox.Show("No printers installed. You must " & _
           "have a printer installed to preview or print " & _
           "the document.", "Print Error", _
           MessageBoxButtons.OK, MessageBoxIcon.Error)
    End Sub ' ErrorMessage
End Class ' CheckWriterForm
```

Figure 26.27 **CheckWriter** application code. (Part 4 of 4.)

SELF-REVIEW

1. When you associate an event with an event handler, keyword ________ is used to specify the location of the event handler.
   a) `AddHandler` b) `AddressOf`
   c) `HandlerEvent` d) Both a and b

2. The ________ object contains the `PrintPage` event.
   a) `PrintDocument` b) `PrintPreviewDialog`
   c) `PrintPreviewControl` d) `PrintDialog`

Answers: 1) b. 2) a.

26.10 Wrap-Up

In this tutorial, you were introduced to the topic of graphics and printing. You created a **CheckWriter** application that allows you to enter data in a check and print it using the printer installed on your computer. You learned how to use the `Graphics` object and its members. While building the **CheckWriter** application, you used these concepts to draw shapes and `String`s using graphics objects such as `Pen`s and `Brushes`. You also learned how to use code to create fonts to apply to text you wish to display or print.

You studied several new classes, including `PrintPreviewDialog` and `PrintDocument`. You used the `PrintDocument` class to create a `PrintDocument` object. You then used its `PrintPage` event to execute code that draws and prints the check when the user clicks the **Print** `Button`. You also added a `PrintPreviewDialog` in your application, allowing the user to preview a check before printing it.

Microsoft has released a set of free Visual Basic Power Packs designed to make developing applications with Visual Basic even easier. The latest Power Pack includes several additional printing controls. You can download the Visual Basic Power Packs at `msdn.microsoft.com/en-us/vbasic/bb735936.aspx`.

In the next tutorial, you learn about mouse events and Windows Presentation Foundation (WPF), Microsoft's new framework for graphics, GUI and multimedia.

SKILLS SUMMARY

Printing a Line

- Use the `PrintPageEventArgs` object's `Graphics` property.
- Use the `Graphics` property to invoke the `DrawLine` method.
- Specify the five parameters—a `Pen` object, the first *x*-coordinate, the first *y*-coordinate, the second *x*-coordinate and the second *y*-coordinate.

Printing a Rectangle

- Use the `PrintPageEventArgs` object's `Graphics` property.
- Use the `Graphics` property to invoke the `DrawRectangle` method.
- Specify the five parameters—a `Pen` object, the *x*-coordinate, the *y*-coordinate, the width and the height.

Printing a `String`

- Use the `PrintPageEventArgs` object's `Graphics` property.
- Use the `Graphics` property to invoke the `DrawString` method.
- Specify the five parameters: the `String` to print, the font style, the `Brush` object, the *x*-coordinate and the *y*-coordinate of where to begin printing the `String`.

Associating an Event with a Defined Event Handler

- Follow the format `AddHandler` *objectName*`.`*eventName*`, AddressOf` *eventHandlerName*, where *objectName* represents the name of the object with which the event is associated, *eventName* represents the name of a valid event and *eventHandlerName* represents the name of the defined event handler to be associated with the specified event.

Printing a Document

- Create a new `PrintDocument` object.
- Define the `PrintDocument`'s `PrintPage` event handler to specify what to print.
- Use the `PrintDocument` to invoke the `Print` method.

Displaying a Print Preview Dialog

- Create a `PrintPreviewDialog` object.
- Specify the `PrintDocument` to preview in the `PrintPreviewDialog`'s `Document` property.
- Invoke the `PrintPreviewDialog`'s `ShowDialog` method.

KEY TERMS

`AddHandler` statement—Adds an event handler for a specific event.

`AddressOf` operator—Specifies the location of a method, which can be associated with an event.

API (application programming interface)—The interface used by a program to access the operating system and various services on the computer.

`Brush` object—An object used to specify drawing parameters when drawing solid shapes.

`Brushes` class—Provides easy access to `Brush` objects representing the standard colors.

`Color` structure—Represents a color and provides methods for creating custom colors.

`Control` class—A type that can be used to declare variables for referencing controls on the `Form`. Defines the common properties and methods of Windows Forms controls.

coordinate system—A scheme for identifying every possible point on the computer screen.

design units—Any specified units of measurement for the font.

dithering—Using small dots of existing colors to form a pattern that simulates a desired color.

`Document` property of class `PrintPreviewDialog`—Allows you to specify the document that is displayed in the dialog.

`DrawLine` method of class `Graphics`—Draws a line of a specified color between two specified points.

`DrawRectangle` method of class `Graphics`—Draws the outline of a rectangle of a specified size and color at a specified location.

`DrawString` method of class `Graphics`—Draws the specified `String` at the specified location.

`Font` class—Contains properties that define unique fonts.

`FontFamily` class—Represents the `FontFamily` of the `Font` (a grouping structure to organize fonts with similar properties).

`FontStyle` enumeration—Provides constants for specifying a font's style. These include `FontStyle.Bold`, `FontStyle.Italic`, `FontStyle.Regular`, `FontStyle.Strikeout` and `FontStyle.Underline`.

`FromArgb` method of `Color` structure—Creates a new `Color` object from RGB values and an alpha value.

GDI+ (Graphics Device Interface)—An application programming interface (API) that provides classes for creating two-dimensional vector graphics.

`GetName` method of class `FontFamily`—Returns the name of the `FontFamily` object.

`MarginBounds.Left` property of class `PrintPageEventArgs` —Specifies the left margin of a printed page.

`MarginBounds.Top` property of class `PrintPageEventArgs` —Specifies the top margin of a printed page.

`Me` keyword—References the current object.

opacity—Amount of transparency of the color.

`Pen` object—Specifies drawing parameters when drawing shape outlines.

`Print` method of class `PrintDocument`—Prints a document.

`PrintDocument` class—Allows the user to describe how to print a document.

`PrintPage` event—Occurs when the data required to print the current page is needed.

`PrintPageEventArgs` class—Contains data passed to a `PrintPage` event.

`PrintPreviewDialog` control—Previews a document in a dialog box before it prints.

`PrinterSettings.InstalledPrinters.Count` property—Determines how many printers are installed on the user's computer.

`Single` data type—Stores floating-point values. `Single` is similar to `Double`, but is less precise and requires less memory.

`System.Drawing.Printing` namespace—Allows your applications to access all services related to printing.

`UseAntiAlias` property of class `PrintPreviewDialog`—Makes the text in the `PrintPreviewDialog` appear smoother on the screen.

vector graphics —Graphics created by a set of mathematical properties called vectors, which include the graphics' dimensions, attributes and positions.

***x*-axis**—Describes every horizontal coordinate.

***x*-coordinate**—Horizontal distance (increasing to the right) from the left of the drawing area.

***y*-axis**—Describes every vertical coordinate.

***y*-coordinate**—Vertical distance (increasing downward) from the top of the drawing area.

CONTROLS, EVENTS, PROPERTIES & METHODS

`Font` Class used to define the font face, size and style of text throughout an application.

- ***Properties***

  `Bold`—Sets the weight of the text.

  `FontFamily`—Contains a `FontFamily` object, which is used to store font face information.

  `Italic`—Sets the angle of the text.

  `Size`—Sets the size of the text.

  `SizeInPoints`—Returns the size of the text measured in points.

`Graphics` The class that contains methods used to draw text, lines and shapes.

- ***Methods***

  `DrawLine`—Draws a line of a specified size and color.

  `DrawRectangle`—Draws the outline of a rectangle of a specified size and color at a specified location.

  `DrawString`—Draws a `String` in a specified font and color at a specified position.

`PrintDocument` This class allows you to specify how to print a document.

- ***Event***

  `PrintPage`—Raised when data required to print a page is needed.

- ***Method***

  `Print`—Uses a `Graphics` object to print a page.

You begin by test-driving the completed application. Then you learn the additional Visual Basic capabilities needed to create your own version of this application.

Test-Driving the Painter Application

1. ***Opening the completed application.*** Open the directory `C:\Examples\Tutorial27\CompletedApplication\Painter` to locate the **Painter** application. Double click `Painter.sln` to open the application in the Visual Basic IDE.
2. ***Running the Painter application.*** Select **Debug > Start Debugging** to run the application (Fig. 27.1).

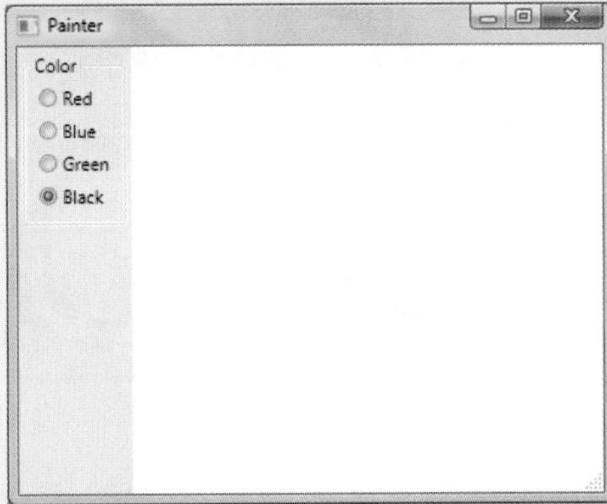

Figure 27.1 **Painter** application before drawing.

3. ***Drawing with the mouse.*** To draw using the **Painter** application, press and hold down the left mouse button while the mouse pointer is anywhere over the white area of the application (Fig. 27.2). To stop drawing, release the mouse button. Note that the application draws small black circles as you move the mouse while pressing the left mouse button.

Drawing lines composed of small, colored circles

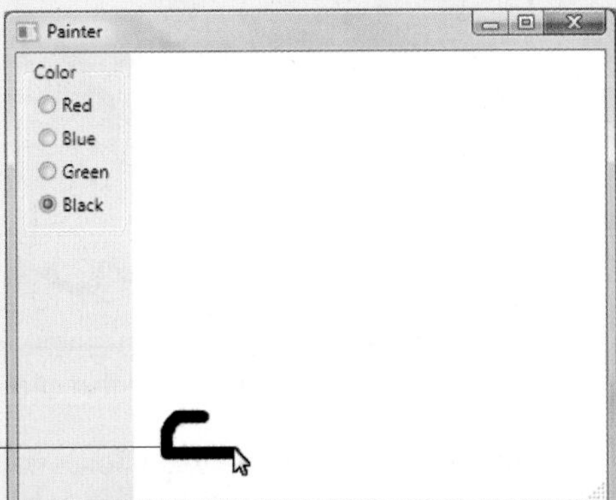

Figure 27.2 Drawing in the **Painter** application.

4. ***Changing the color.*** Use the `RadioButtons` in the **Color** `GroupBox` to change the color of the circles you draw (Fig. 27.3).
5. ***Being creative.*** Draw a cat and a computer mouse, as shown in Fig. 27.4. Be creative and have fun—your drawing need not look like the image shown.
6. ***Using the eraser.*** Hold down the right mouse button and move the mouse pointer over part of your drawing. This "erases" the drawing wherever the mouse pointer comes into contact with colored areas by displaying white circles (Fig. 27.5).

(cont.)

Use the `RadioButtons` to select a color

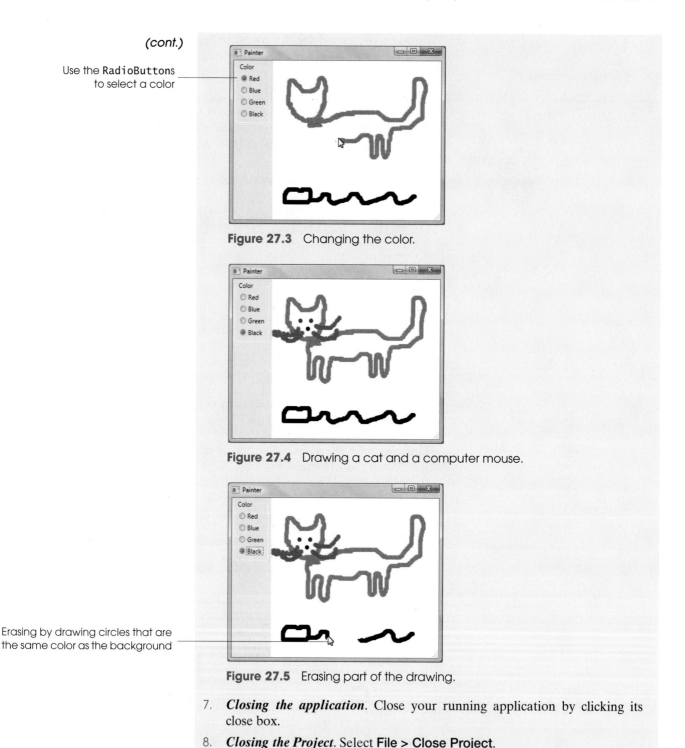

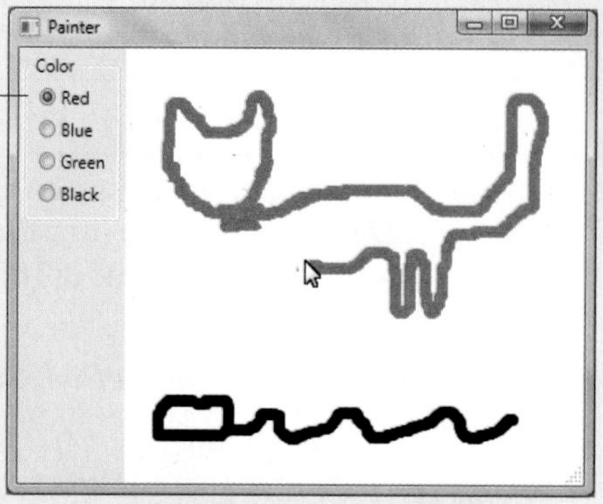

Figure 27.3 Changing the color.

Figure 27.4 Drawing a cat and a computer mouse.

Erasing by drawing circles that are the same color as the background

Figure 27.5 Erasing part of the drawing.

7. ***Closing the application***. Close your running application by clicking its close box.
8. ***Closing the Project***. Select **File > Close Project**.

27.2 Windows Presentation Foundation (WPF)

Windows Presentation Foundation (WPF) is Microsoft's new graphics framework, available on both Windows Vista and Windows XP as part of the .NET 3.5 framework. Originally introduced in .NET 3.0, WPF represents the biggest change in Windows GUI development since the introduction of Windows `Forms`. WPF allows you to create more powerful and flexible GUIs than Windows `Forms` and to create media-rich experiences with animations, audio, video and graphics. Silverlight, a subset of WPF, allows you to create equally stunning WPF web-based applications. We introduce Silverlight in Tutorial 32.

27.3 XAML (Extensible Application Markup Language)

WPF uses **XAML** (pronounced "zammel")—**Extensible Application Markup Language**—to describe the application's interface. XAML is a form of **XML** (**Extensible Markup Language**). XML permits document authors to create markup (i.e., a text-based notation for describing data) for virtually any type of information. Document authors to create entirely new markup languages for describing any type of data, such as mathematical formulas, software-configuration instructions, chemical molecular structures, music, news, recipes and financial reports. XML describes data in a way that both human beings and computers can understand.

Figure 27.6 is a simple XML document that describes information for a baseball player. We use this example to introduce basic XML syntax. Lines 1–2 are XML comments.

```
1  <!-- Fig. 27.6: player.xml -->
2  <!-- Baseball player structured with XML -->
3  <player>
4     <firstName>John</firstName>
5     <lastName>Doe</lastName>
6     <battingAverage>0.375</battingAverage>
7  </player>
```

Figure 27.6 XML that describes a baseball player's information.

XML documents contain text that represents content (i.e., data), such as John (line 4 of Fig. 27.6), and **elements** that specify the document's structure, such as `firstName` (line 4 of Fig. 27.6). XML documents delimit elements with **start tags** and **end tags**. A start tag consists of the element name in angle brackets (e.g., `<player>` and `<firstName>` in lines 3 and 4, respectively). An end tag consists of the element name preceded by a forward slash (/) in angle brackets (e.g., `</firstName>` and `</player>` in lines 4 and 7, respectively). An element's start and end tags enclose text that represents a piece of data (e.g., the player's `firstName`—John—in line 4, which is enclosed by the `<firstName>` start tag and `</firstName>` end tag). Every XML document must have exactly one root element that contains all the other elements. In Fig. 27.6, the root element is `player` (lines 3–7).

XML-based markup languages—called **XML vocabularies**—provide a means for describing particular types of data in standardized, structured ways. Some XML vocabularies include XHTML (Extensible HyperText Markup Language—for creating web pages), MathML (for mathematics), VoiceXML™ (for speech), CML (Chemical Markup Language—for chemistry), XBRL (Extensible Business Reporting Language—for financial data exchange) and XAML (for creating WPF GUIs).

When you compile your WPF application, the computer interprets the XAML markup to create and configure the user interface. Using XAML rather than Visual Basic code to describe the user interface allows it to be interpreted by applications other than Visual Studio. Microsoft has developed applications, such as Expression Blend, geared toward designers who specialize in creating GUIs. You can open the same solution in either Visual Studio or Expression Blend. This enables programmers to focus on the application's logic and enables designers to focus on the GUI's look-and-feel. It also allows designers and programmers to work together more efficiently. This is a big advantage of WPF over Windows `Forms`.

WPF provides many controls, some of which correspond directly to Windows `Forms` controls. In WPF, you can add `Buttons`, `CheckBoxes`, `GroupBoxes`, `RadioButtons`, `Labels` and `TextBoxes` among others, just as you would in a Windows `Forms` application. These basic WPF controls function much as their Windows `Forms` counterparts. WPF also includes controls for layout and multimedia. As you'll see in the next section, WPF takes a different approach to the layout of your user interface than Windows Forms.

WPF is an exciting new technology. It provides a new way to create visually stunning Windows applications. However, at the time of this writing, the WPF tools in Visual Studio are not as well developed as those for Windows Forms. For this reason, many application developers, especially those focused on business applications, continue to use Windows Forms. As WPF matures and better tools are created, WPF will become the standard technology for creating Windows GUI applications. In the following section you'll create the **Painter** application's GUI using WPF. We encourage you to visit our WPF Resource Center (www.deitel.com/WPF/) to learn more about WPF.

27.4 Creating the Painter Application's GUI in WPF

In this section, you create the **Painter** application's GUI using WPF. In Windows Forms, you place controls in specific locations on the Form using the Location property. By contrast, WPF discourages the use of absolute positioning. Instead, you use layout containers that automatically position the controls you place inside them. This allows WPF GUIs to adapt gracefully when the user resizes the window. Windows Forms applications can achieve this functionality through the use of more advanced controls not discussed in this book. The following box guides you through creating a WPF user interface.

Creating a WPF Application

1. ***Creating a WPF application.*** To create a WPF application, select **File > New Project...** to open the **New Project** dialog. Select the **WPF Application** template and name the project Painter (Fig. 27.7). Click **OK** to create the project.

Select the **WPF Application** template

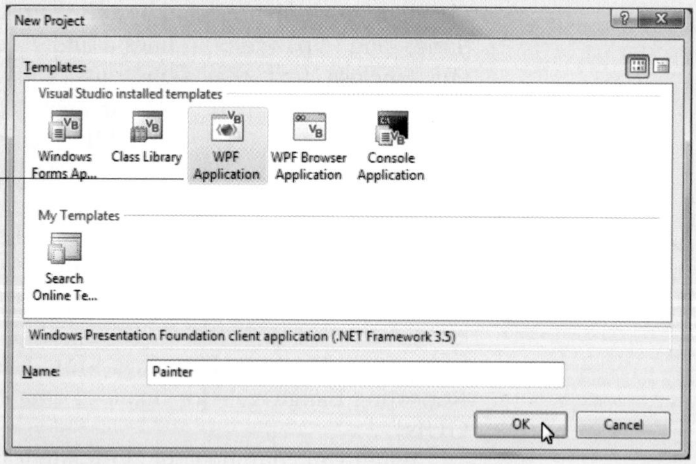

Figure 27.7 Creating a WPF application.

2. ***Examining the WPF Application project.*** Figure 27.8 shows your newly created WPF application in Visual Basic. You see the familiar **Solution Explorer** and **Properties** windows. The **Properties** window looks different from the Windows Forms **Properties** window, but it serves the same purpose. Click anywhere in the design space. At the top of the WPF **Properties** window, you can set the name of the selected control in the **Name:** TextBox. There is also a **Search:** TextBox that you can use to help locate properties faster. The **Toolbox** contains only the WPF controls by default. We'll discuss these windows in more detail later in this tutorial.

(cont.)

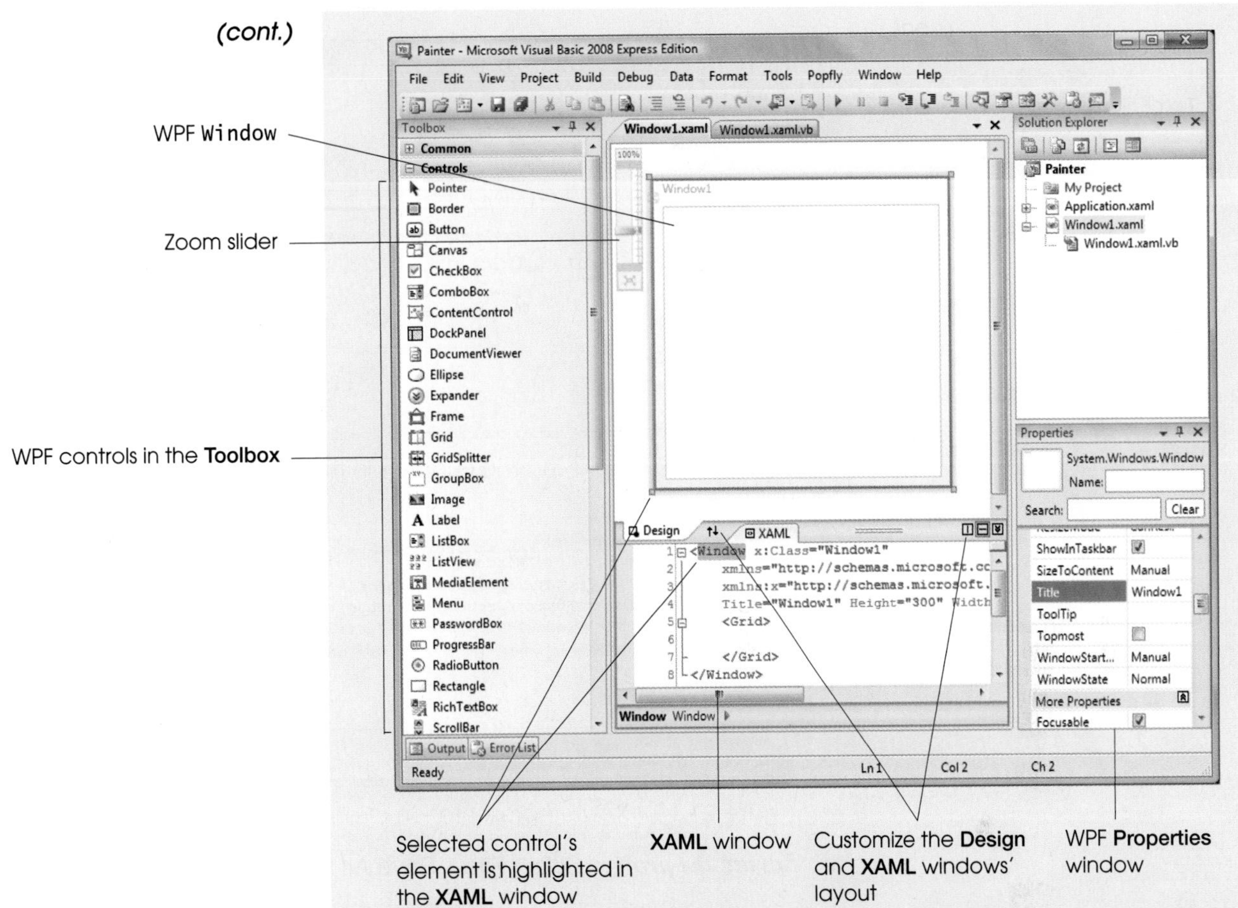

Figure 27.8 Newly created WPF application in the IDE.

The most notable difference from the Windows `Forms` designer is the division of the design space into two sections, **Design** and **XAML**. The **Design** portion is similar to the **Designer** view in Windows `Forms`. However, instead of a `Form`, WPF uses a **`Window`** to contain the controls which make up the user interface. The WPF **Design** space also allows you to view your `Window` at different zoom levels using the slider in the top left corner.

The **XAML** window contains the application's XAML markup. Recall that XAML describes the application's interface. The **XAML** window does not show line numbers by default. To display the line number, select **Tools > Options** to open the **Options** dialog (Fig. 27.9). Check the **Show all settings** `CheckBox`, then expand the **Text Editor** category. Select the **XAML** category and check the **Line numbers** `CheckBox`. Click **OK** to close the dialog and apply the new settings.

Every WPF control is represented by an element in XAML (e.g., `<Window>` in line 1 and `<Grid>` in line 5 of Fig. 27.10). When you select a control in the designer, its corresponding XAML element is highlighted (Fig. 27.8). You can also click inside an element in the XAML to select its corresponding control in the designer. An element is delimited with a start tag (e.g., `<Window>` and `<Grid>` in lines 1 and 5 of Fig. 27.10) and end tag (e.g., `</Grid>` and `</Window>` in lines 7–8). The start tag also specifies the element's **attributes** (e.g., `Title`, `Height` and `Width` in line 4) which set properties of the element. We'll explore these attributes in more detail shortly. Lines 2–3 define the XML namespaces used in the XAML document. Every WPF application you create in this book uses these namespaces, which provide access in the XAML to the WPF controls.

(cont.)

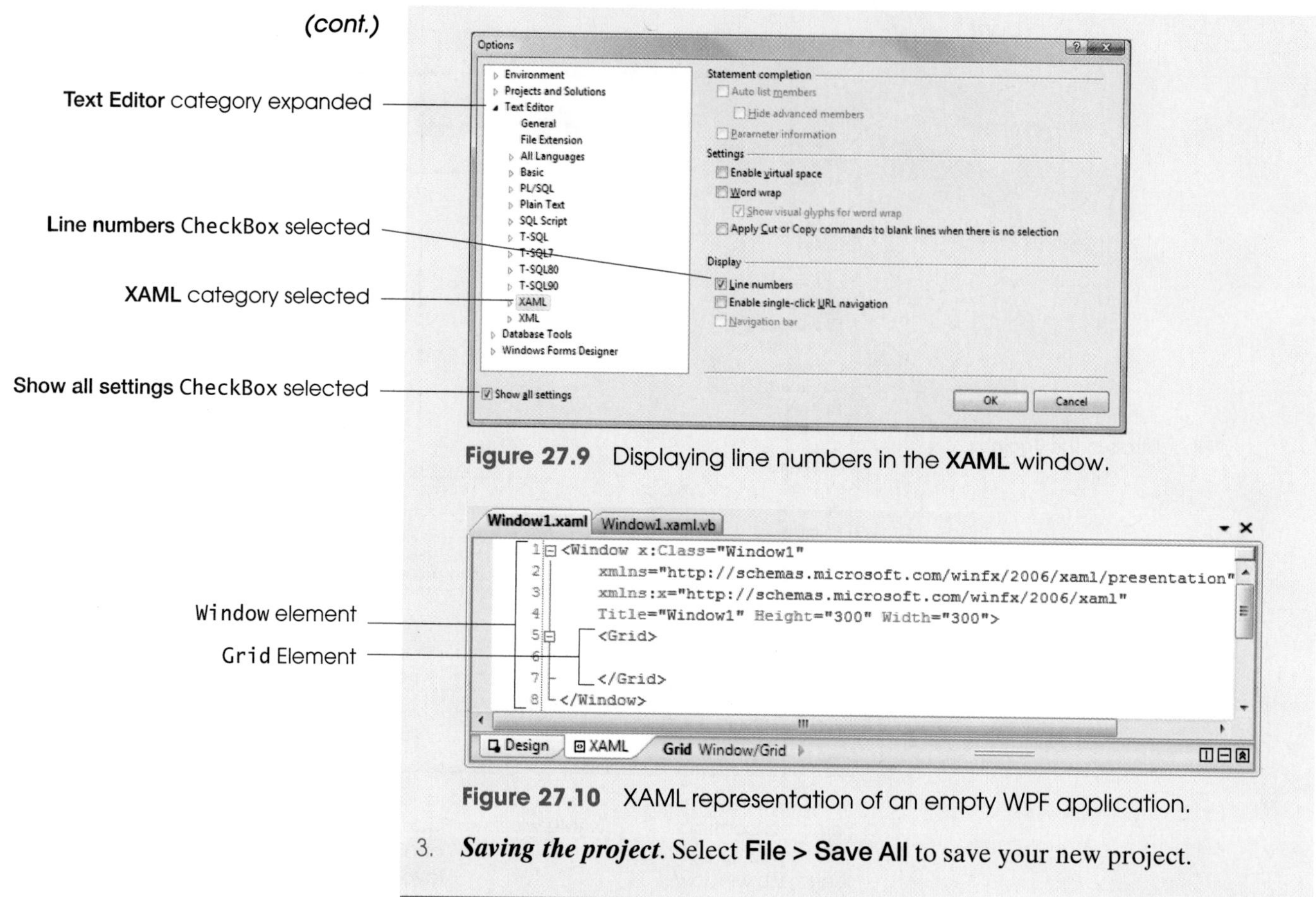

Figure 27.9 Displaying line numbers in the **XAML** window.

Figure 27.10 XAML representation of an empty WPF application.

3. ***Saving the project.*** Select **File > Save All** to save your new project.

In Windows Forms you placed a control on the `Form` and set the `Location` and `Size` properties (either manually or by using the mouse) to determine its position and size, respectively. When you run a typical Windows `Forms` application and resize the `Form`, the controls stay in place. Advanced controls and techniques are available that allow you to create resizable user interfaces with Windows `Forms`. In WPF, resizable controls and interfaces are the norm. You are discouraged from using fixed sizes and coordinates. Instead, controls are automatically sized based on their content. You place your controls in **layout containers** which position the controls based on their size and the amount of available space in the container.

The most flexible layout container is the `Grid`. Notice that a `Grid` is the default layout container in a WPF application (Fig. 27.10). The `Grid` control creates an invisible table of rows and columns to divide the `Window` into different regions. You place controls in these cells to determine where they appear on the screen. By default, the `Grid` consists of one row and one column.

Modifying the `Window` and `Grid` Controls

1. ***Changing the `Window`'s properties.*** Recall from the previous box that an element's start tag specifies its property values specified as attributes. You can modify a control's properties by editing the attributes in the XAML directly. Line 4 of the **Painter** application's XAML sets the `Window`'s `Title`, `Height` and `Width` attributes. Each attribute consists of a name (which corresponds to the property name in the control), an equal sign and a value in double quotes. Change the `Window`'s title by setting the `Title` property to `Painter` in the XAML. The text in the `Window`'s title bar updates accordingly (Fig. 27.11). You may also modify properties in the **Properties** window as you do for Windows `Forms`.

(cont.)

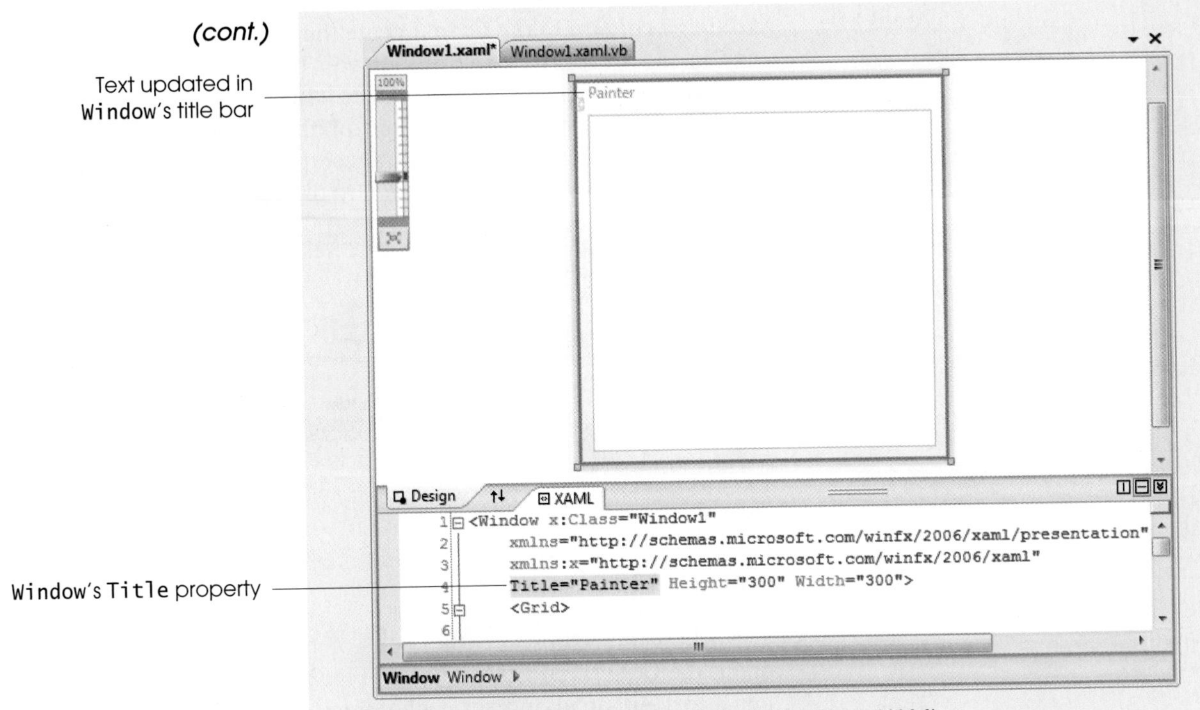

Figure 27.11 Changing the `Window`'s title in XAML.

2. ***Selecting the `Grid`.*** The default `Grid` contains a single row and column. The **Painter** application uses a `Grid` with two columns. To create the two columns, first select the `Grid` control by clicking in the center of the `Window` or anywhere within the `Grid`'s start and end tags in the XAML (Fig. 27.12). Note that when you select a control in the **Design** area, the control's start tag is highlighted.

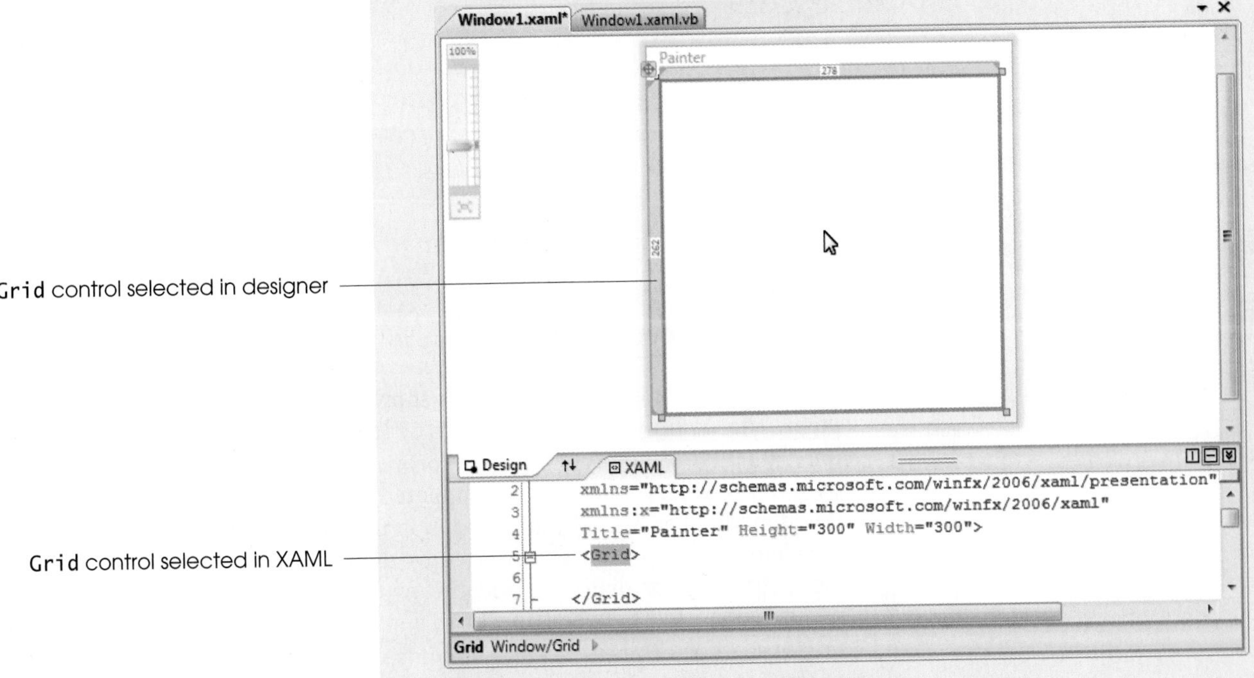

Figure 27.12 Selecting the `Grid` control.

(cont.)

3. ***Adding a column to the Grid.*** Locate the `Grid`'s `ColumnDefinitions` property in the **Properties** window. If you have trouble finding the `ColumnDefinitions` property, use the **Search:** box in the **Properties** window (Fig. 27.13). Start typing the name of the property you want to set. The **Properties** window displays only those properties that match what you've typed so far. Click the **Clear** `Button` to display the full list of properties.

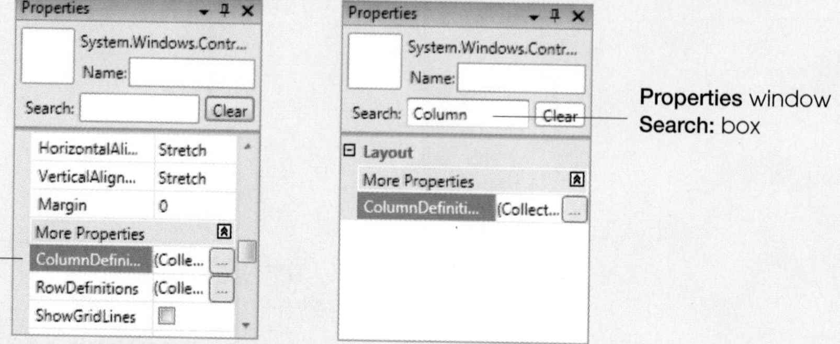

Figure 27.13 `Grid` properties.

Clicking the ellipsis to the right of the `ColumnDefinitions` property opens the **Collection Editor** dialog (Fig. 27.14), which allows you to add columns to your `Grid` and set each column's properties. Note that when this dialog opens, the `ListBox` on the left is empty. The default single column (not shown in the dialog's `ListBox`) is replaced by the first `ColumnDefinition` you add to the `Grid`. Click the **Add** `Button` twice to add two `ColumnDefinitions` to the `Grid`. For now, don't modify any other properties in this dialog. You'll edit them in a later step. Click **OK** to close the dialog.

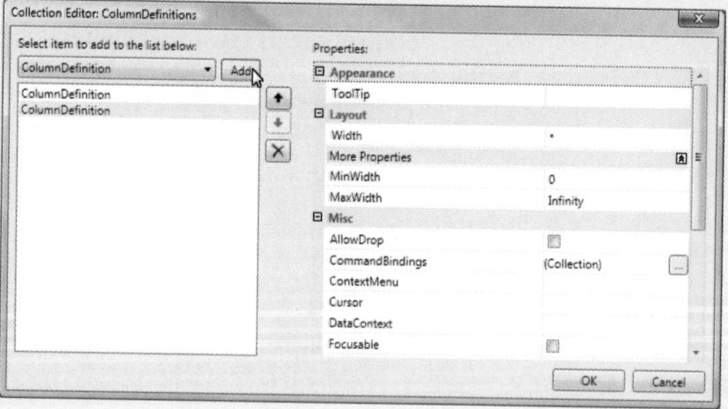

Figure 27.14 **Collection Editor** dialog for property `ColumnDefinitions`.

4. ***Examining the XAML.*** Figure 27.15 shows the effects of adding the two columns. The **Design** tab shows the two `Grid` columns separated by a thin blue line. When you modify a control's properties through the **Properties** window, the XAML is automatically updated to reflect those changes. Similarly, if you modify the XAML, the `Window` in the **Design** tab is updated to reflect the changes. Lines 6–9 were inserted by the IDE when you clicked **OK** in the **Collection Editor** dialog to add the two columns to the `Grid`. These elements are nested between the `Grid`'s start and end tags to show that the `ColumnDefinitions` are **child elements** of the `Grid` control—they are part of the `Grid`. Any element placed between the start and end tags of another element becomes a child of that element.

(cont.)

Notice that the `ColumnDefinition` elements (lines 7–8) do not have start and end tags—they are defined with a single tag that ends with />. These are called **empty elements** and are equivalent to the normal start and end tags with no content between them, as in:

```
<ColumnDefinition></ColumnDefinition>
```

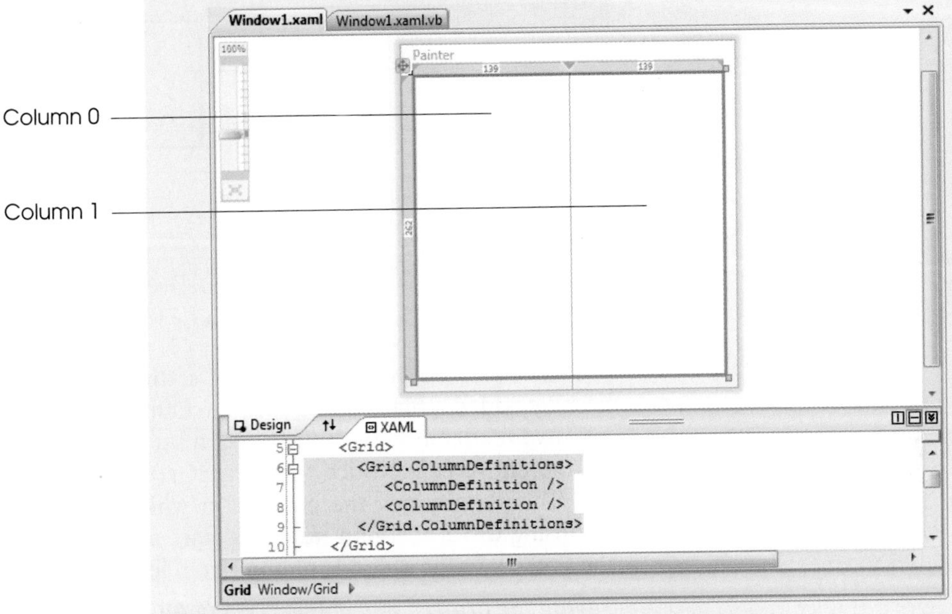

Column 0

Column 1

```
5   <Grid>
6       <Grid.ColumnDefinitions>
7           <ColumnDefinition />
8           <ColumnDefinition />
9       </Grid.ColumnDefinitions>
10  </Grid>
```

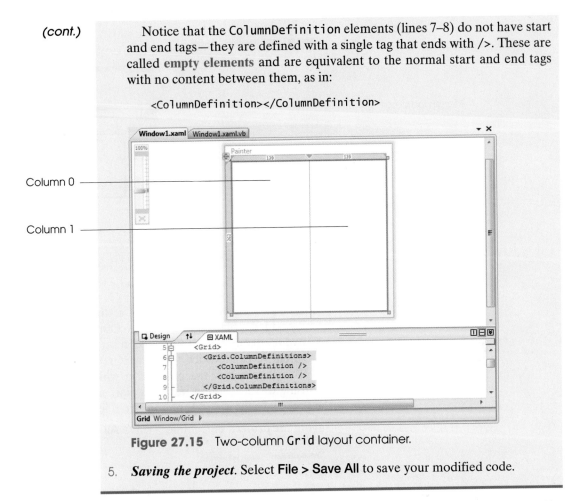

Figure 27.15 Two-column `Grid` layout container.

5. ***Saving the project.*** Select **File > Save All** to save your modified code.

In the next box you create the painting surface for the **Painter** application. The application allows the user to "paint" by drawing small circles at the mouse pointer's location. When drawing the circles, you must be able to place them in a specific location. WPF provides support for absolute positioning through the `Canvas` control. The **`Canvas`** is a layout container that allows you to position elements using absolute coordinates relative to the `Canvas`'s top-left corner. This is the same layout concept you've used in Windows `Forms`.

Adding the Painting Canvas

1. ***Adding a `Canvas` to the `Grid`.*** As in Windows `Forms` applications, you can drag and drop controls from the **Toolbox** onto a WPF `Window`. Drag the `Canvas` control from the **Toolbox** and drop it in the right column of the `Grid` (Fig. 27.16). When you add a control to the `Grid`, the IDE automatically sets its **`Name`** and `Margin` properties. The **`Margin`** property specifies the amount of space to leave between a control's edge and any adjacent controls or its container. You can set margin for each side individually by setting the `Margin` property to a comma-separated list of four values. These values determine the spacing around the left, top, right and bottom sides, respectively. You also can use a single value to set the same spacing on all sides. The IDE sets the initial `Margin` value for a control so the control appears exactly where you drop it and to match the default size of the control. This is contrary to WPF's layout philosophy and often yields unwanted results. Use the **Properties** window to set the `Margin` for the `Canvas` to `0` on all sides so the control fills the `Grid` cell. Set the `Canvas`'s `Name` to `paintCanvas` using the **Name:** `TextBox` at the top of the **Properties** window.

(cont.)

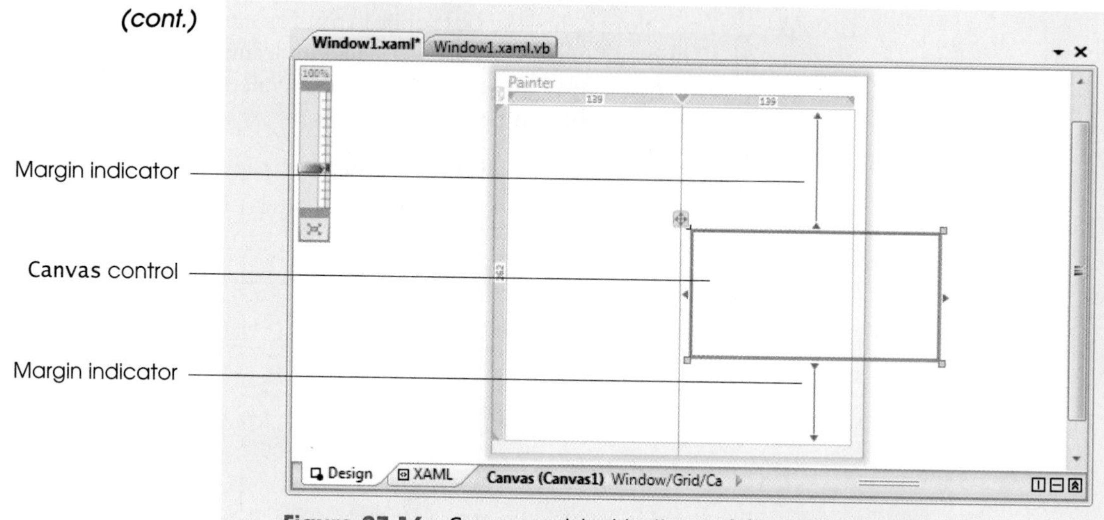

Figure 27.16 Canvas added to the Grid's right column.

Figure 27.17 shows the effects of setting the Margin and Name properties. We added a blank line above the Canvas tag in the XAML (line 11) to improve readability. With the Margin set to 0, the Canvas now expands to fill the entire cell. Notice the **Grid.Column** attribute set in the Canvas's tag. This determines the column in which the element is placed in the enclosing Grid. Column numbers start at 0, so Grid.Column="1" places the Canvas in the second column (from left to right).

2. ***Saving the project.*** Select **File > Save All** to save your modified code.

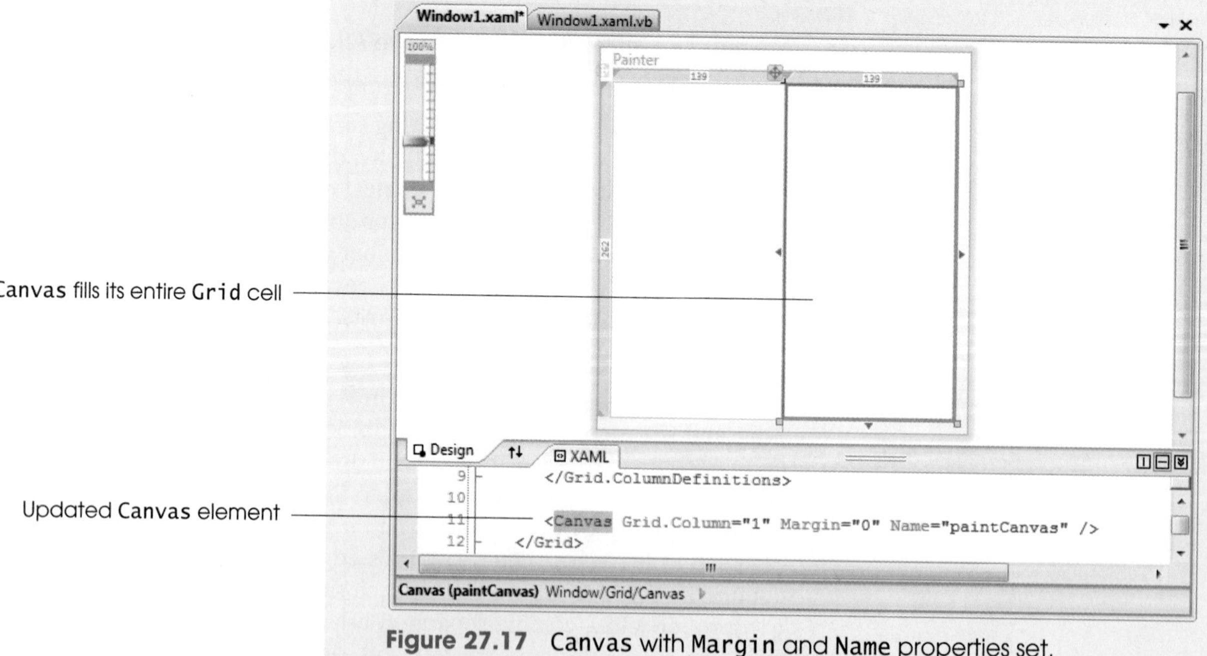

Figure 27.17 Canvas with Margin and Name properties set.

Next, you add the RadioButtons that allow the user to choose a color in which to paint. The RadioButtons are placed in a GroupBox. In Windows Forms, you added controls to a GroupBox by dragging them from the **Toolbox** and dropping them into the GroupBox on the Form. In WPF, a GroupBox functions differently. A GroupBox is a type of content control. A **content control** can hold *only* one piece of content, which can be of any type. To place more than one item in a content control, you must place a layout container in the content control, then place additional items in the layout container. This restriction may seem unnecessarily complicated. However, this approach allows content controls to contain any type of content without the addition of properties to support different types of content.

The `Window` control is another example of a content control. As such, the nested element in a `Window` is almost always a layout container. The `Window` has the additional restriction that it cannot be nested in another control—it must be the outermost element, also known as the **root element** in the XAML.

Adding the Color Options

1. ***Adding a GroupBox to the Grid.*** Drag a `GroupBox` control from the **Toolbox** and drop it in the left column of the `Grid`. Again, the IDE sets the `Margin` property, attempting to position the control at the coordinates where you placed it (Fig. 27.18). Set the `Margin` property to `3` to leave a small amount of whitespace around the control. Note that the `GroupBox` expands across *both* columns of the `Grid`. When you added the `GroupBox` to the `Grid`, the `Margin` values created by the IDE caused it to overlap both columns. To allow for this, the IDE also set the **`Grid.ColumnSpan`** property to `2`. To fix this, set the `GroupBox`'s `Grid.ColumnSpan` property to `1`. Also set the `Name` property to `colorGroupBox` and the `Header` property to `Color`. The **`Header`** property sets the text displayed at the top of the `GroupBox`. Figure 27.19 shows the `GroupBox` with the properties set correctly (lines 13–14). Note that we added a line break in the `GroupBox`'s XAML tag to improve readability.

GroupBox before setting its properties

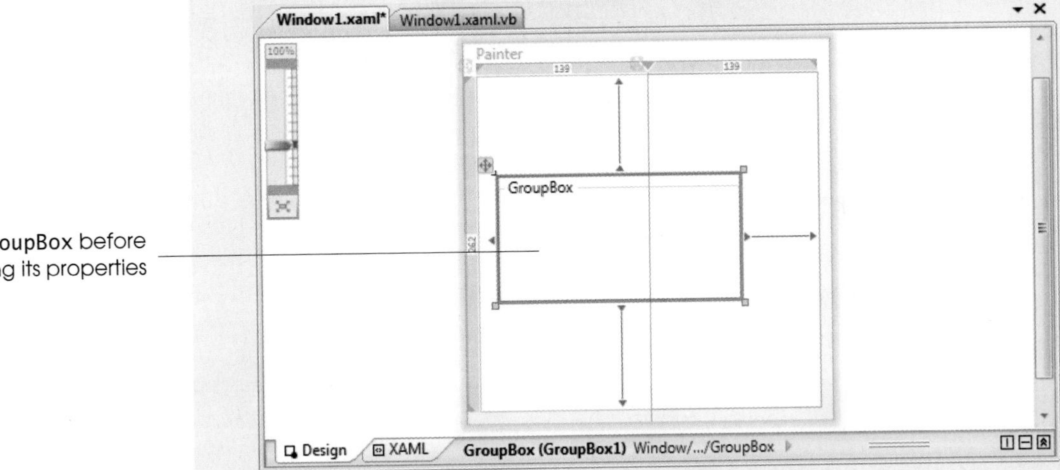

Figure 27.18 `GroupBox` added to the `Grid` spans both columns.

2. ***Adding a StackPanel to the GroupBox.*** Recall that the `GroupBox` is a content control and may contain only one element. To place the four `RadioButton`s in the `GroupBox`, you must first add a layout container. Drag a `StackPanel` control from the **Toolbox** and drop it into the `GroupBox`. A **`StackPanel`** arranges its child elements vertically (by default) or horizontally. The IDE sets the default size of a `StackPanel` to 200 by 100. Change the `StackPanel`'s `Width` and `Height` properties to `Auto`. Do this by deleting the values in the fields to the right of each property in the **Properties** window—or you can delete the `Width` and `Height` attributes from the `StackPanel`'s XAML tag. The `StackPanel` now fills the entire `GroupBox` (Fig. 27.20). Set the `StackPanel`'s `Name` property to `colorStackPanel` and its `Margin` property to `3`.

(cont.)

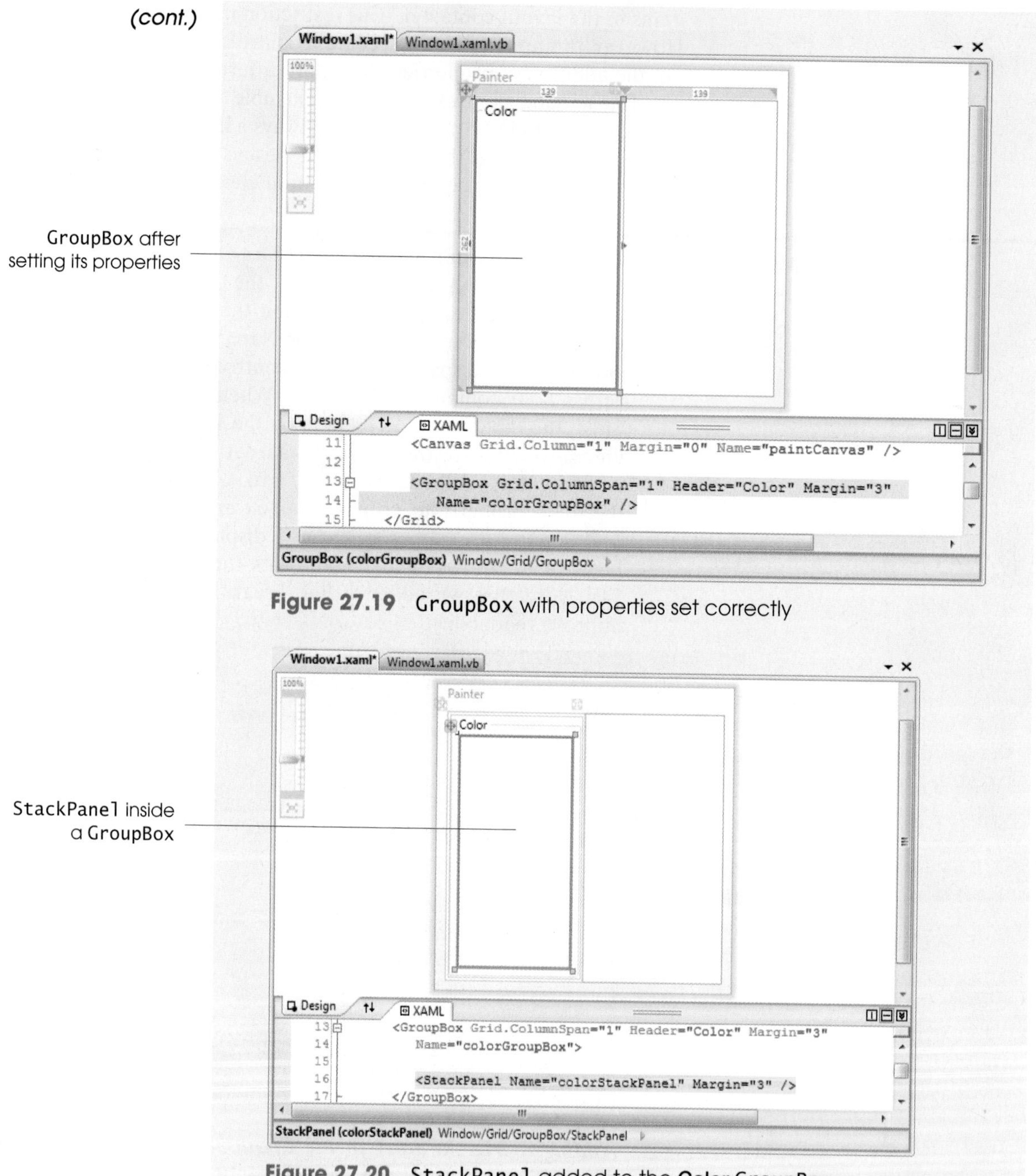

Figure 27.19 GroupBox with properties set correctly

Figure 27.20 StackPanel added to the **Color** GroupBox.

3. ***Adding the RadioButtons.*** Drag four RadioButton controls from the **Toolbox** and drop them into the StackPanel. Notice that no matter where on the StackPanel you drop the RadioButton, it is positioned directly below the RadioButtons previously added (Fig. 27.21). This demonstrates how a StackPanel controls the layout of its children.

   Set the Width and Height properties of each RadioButton to Auto and the Margin to 3. Set the Content properties to Red, Blue, Green and Black from top to bottom. Set their Name properties according to their colors (e.g., redRadioButton, blueRadioButton). Set the **Black** RadioButton's IsChecked property to True to make it the default selection.

(cont.)

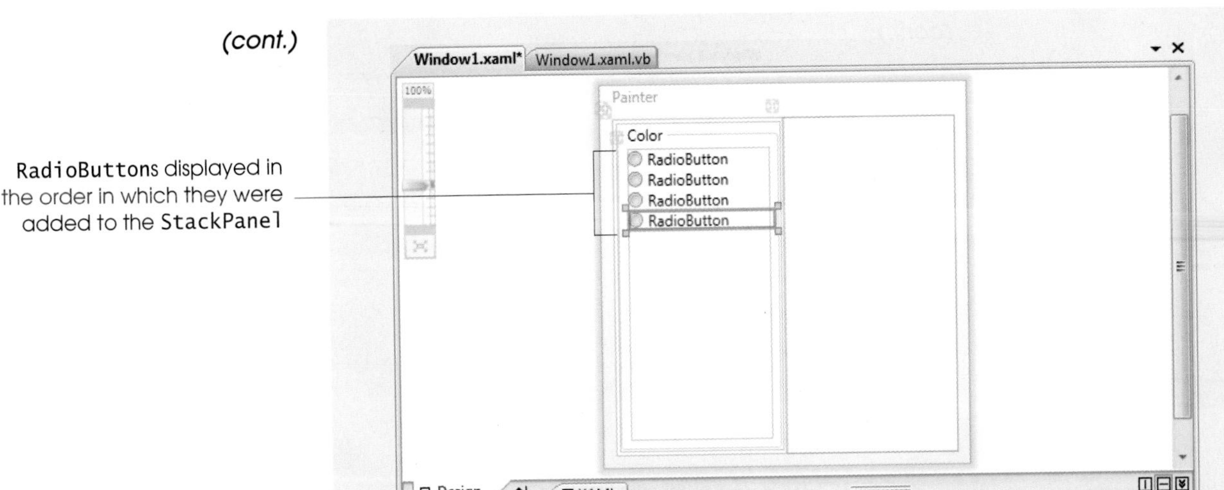

Figure 27.21 `RadioButtons` added to a `StackPanel`.

Notice that each `RadioButton` expands horizontally to fill the `StackPanel`. This provides more space than is needed. Select the `StackPanel` and change its `HorizontalAlignment` property to `Left`. The `StackPanel` shrinks to the width of its largest element and aligns itself to the left side of its container. Change the `StackPanel`'s `VerticalAlignment` to `Top`—it shrinks to the height required to fit its elements and aligns to the top of its container (Fig. 27.22).

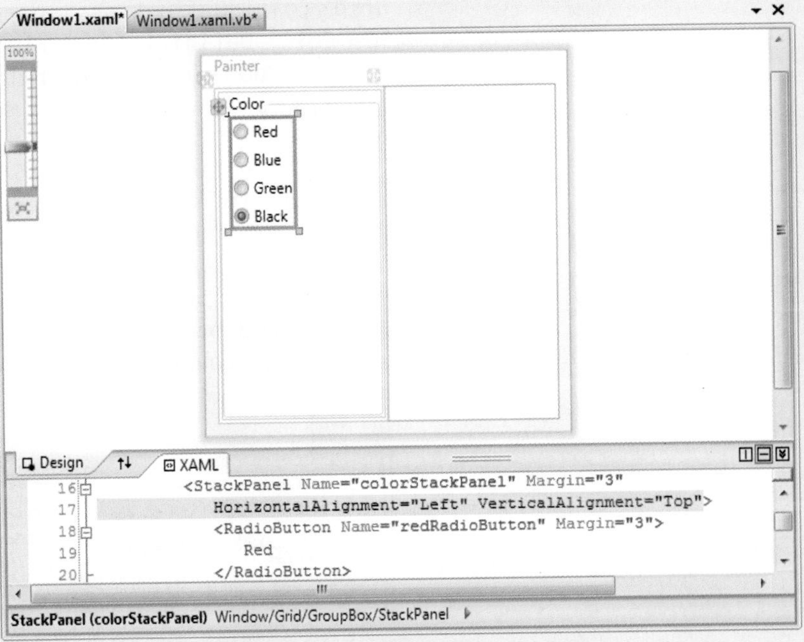

Figure 27.22 `StackPanel` resized to fit its elements.

4. ***Resizing the GroupBox***. Set the `GroupBox`'s `HorizontalAlignment` and `VerticalAlignment` properties to `Left` and `Top`, respectively. This causes the **Color** `GroupBox` to shrink to fit its content as the `StackPanel` did (Fig. 27.23).

(cont.)

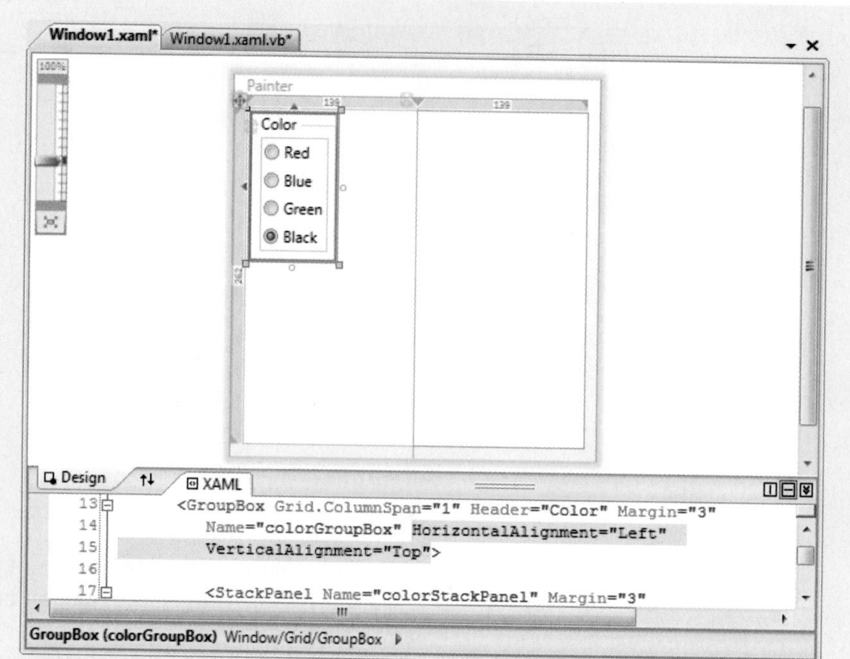

Figure 27.23 `GroupBox` resized to fit its elements.

5. ***Resizing the `Grid` column.*** Open the **Collection Editor** dialog for the `Grid`'s `ColumnDefinitions` property by clicking the ellipsis next to the `Grid`'s `ColumnDefinitions` property in the **Properties** window. Select the first `ColumnDefinition` in the `ListBox` on the left side of the dialog. In the **Properties** window on the right side of the dialog, set the `Width` property to `Auto` (Fig. 27.24)—this causes the column to resize automatically to fit its content. Note that you must type the value `Auto`. Select the second `ColumnDefinition` in the `ListBox`. By default, a `ColumnDefinition`'s `Width` property is set to *, causing the column to resize proportionally to the other column(s). This enables the second column to occupy all remaining space in the `Grid`. Click **OK** to close the dialog. Because the first column is set to extend only far enough to fit its elements, the second column expands to fill the remaining available space (Fig. 27.25). Select the `Canvas` in the second column and notice that it still expands to fill the entire column, as in Fig. 27.17.

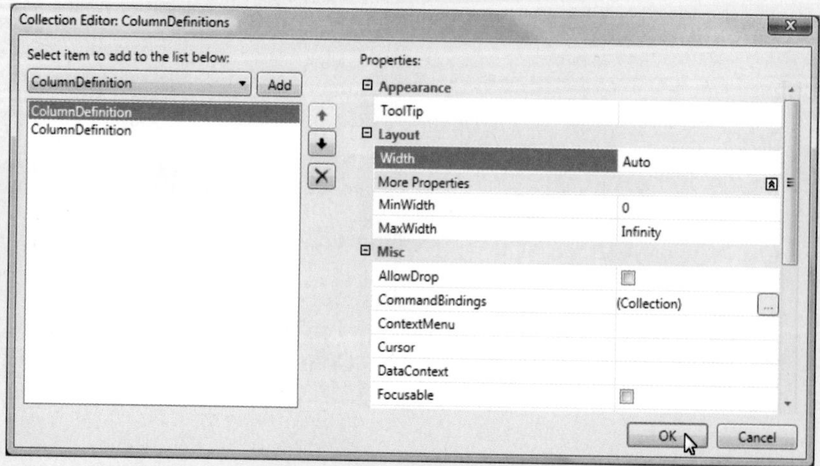

Figure 27.24 Setting column width with the **Collection Editor** dialog.

(cont.)

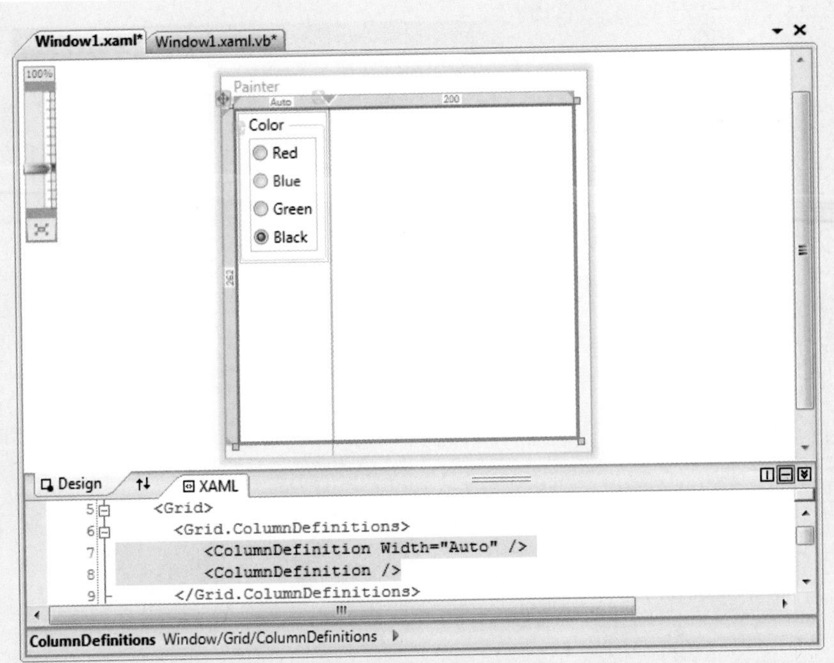

Figure 27.25 `Grid` columns resized to fit their content.

6. ***Saving the project.*** Select **File > Save All** to save your modified code.

An important advantage of WPF is the flexibility of the application's layout. Notice that you haven't set the size of any controls to a specific value—everything is sized relative to its content or the available space in the Window. This allows you to create GUIs which maintain their layout when content changes or the Window is resized. The next box demonstrates this flexibility.

Demonstrating Layout Flexibility in WPF

1. ***Setting background colors.*** Change the `Background` property of the `Window` to `Beige`. Set the `Background` property of the `Canvas` to `White`. This helps make the separate elements stand out and allows the user to clearly see the painting area.

2. ***Running the application.*** Select **Debug > Start Debugging** to run the **Painter** application. If you get an error regarding `Option Strict`, double click the error in the **Error List** window. Hover over the code underlined with the jagged blue line indicating the error. This error occurs because `Option Strict On` disallows such implicit conversions. Click the **Error Correction Options** icon ( ) and apply the suggested correction by clicking the blue text toward the top of the **Error Correction Options** window (Fig. 27.26). This correction uses function **CType** to explicitly convert the first argument to the type specified by the second argument. This error will be fixed in Service Pack 1 for Visual Studio 2008. Close the `MyWpf-Extension.vb` tab. Select **Debug > Start Debugging** to run the application.

3. ***Resizing the `Window`.*** Resize the running application's `Window`. Notice that the column containing the `GroupBox` expands and contracts in the vertical direction only—the width remains the same. The column containing the `Canvas`, as well as the `Canvas` itself, expands and contracts to fill the remaining available `Window` space (Fig. 27.27). To accomplish this flexibility with Windows `Forms` requires more advanced techniques and controls.

(cont.)

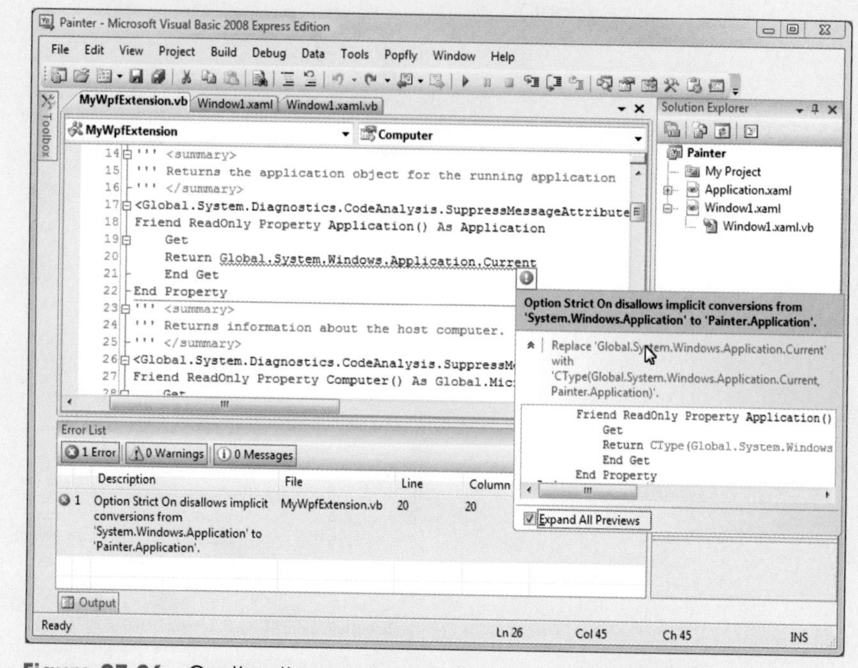

Figure 27.26 Casting the application type to comply with `Option Strict`.

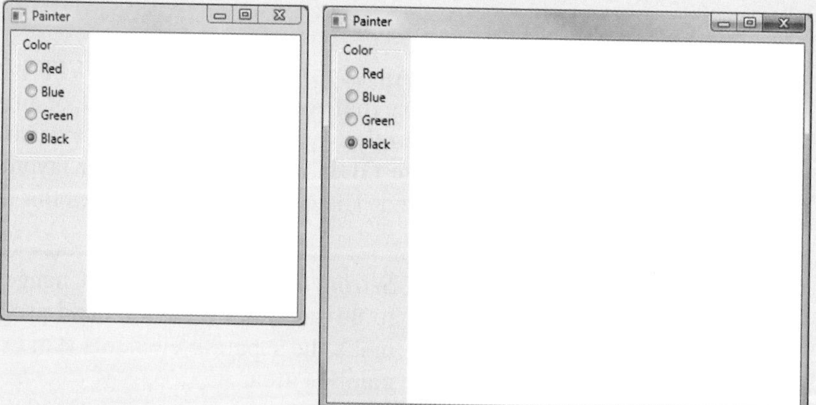

Figure 27.27 **Painter** application's GUI responding to `Window` resizing.

4. ***Closing the application.*** Close your running application by clicking its close box.

5. ***Saving the project.*** Select **File > Save All** to save your modified code.

1. The _________ is the most powerful and flexible layout container.
   a) `Canvas` b) `StackPanel`
   c) `Grid` d) `GroupBox`

2. A _________ can only contain one element.
   a) layout container b) content control
   c) `Canvas` d) flow container

Answers: 1) c. 2) b.

27.5 Constructing the Painter Application

Before you begin programming the **Painter** application, you should review the application's functionality. The following pseudocode describes the basic operation of the **Painter** application and what happens when the user moves the mouse pointer over the application's Canvas:

```
When the left mouse button is pressed:
    Enable drawing

When the right mouse button is pressed:
    Enable erasing

When the left mouse button is released:
    Disable drawing

When the right mouse button is released:
    Disable erasing

When the mouse is moved:
    If drawing is enabled
        Call method PaintCircle to draw a circle in the selected color at the
        position of the mouse pointer
    Else If erasing is enabled
        "Erase" by drawing a circle at the position of the mouse pointer in the
        Canvas's background color
```

Now that you've test-driven the **Painter** application and studied its pseudocode representation, you use an ACE table to help you convert the pseudocode to Visual Basic. Figure 27.28 lists the actions, controls and events that help you complete your own version of this application.

Action/Control/Event (ACE) Table for the Painter Application

Action	Control/Object/Class	Event
	paintCanvas	MouseLeft-ButtonDown
Enable drawing		
	paintCanvas	MouseRight-ButtonDown
Enable erasing		
	paintCanvas	MouseLeft-ButtonUp
Disable drawing		
	paintCanvas	MouseRight-ButtonUp
Disable erasing		
	paintCanvas	MouseMove
If drawing is enabled Draw a circle in the selected color at the position of mouse pointer	Ellipse	
Else If erasing is enabled "Erase" by drawing a circle at the position of the mouse in the Canvas's background color	Ellipse	

Figure 27.28 **Painter** application's ACE table.

The next sections show you how to respond to mouse events. At first, your **Painter** application draws a circle when the user presses or releases the left mouse button. Next, you modify the application so that it draws when the user moves the mouse with the left button pressed. If the user moves the mouse without pressing a mouse button, nothing is drawn. To complete the **Painter** application, you add the eraser capability, which requires you to determine when the user presses the right mouse button.

27.6 Handling the `MouseLeftButtonDown` Event

This section begins our discussion of handling **mouse events**, which occur when the user interacts with the `Window` or controls on the `Window` using the mouse. In the **Painter** application, the user interacts with the `Canvas` to draw.

A `Canvas`'s **`MouseLeftButtonDown`** event occurs when the left mouse button is pressed while the mouse pointer is over the `Canvas`. You add a `MouseLeftButton-Down` event handler to your application in the following box. When you run your application after following the steps in this box, you can press the left mouse button to draw a circle on the `Canvas`. When you add the eraser capability to the **Painter** application in Section 27.9, you learn how to process right mouse button events.

Handling the MouseDown Event

1. ***Renaming the projects files.*** Begin by renaming the **Painter** application's project files. Select the `Window1.xaml` file in the **Solution Explorer** and set its `File Name` property to `Painter.xaml`. This also renames the code-behind file to `Painter.xaml.vb`, similar to the code-behind file for a `Form`. You must also change the application's **Startup URI**, the file in which the application begins executing. Right click the `Painter` project file in the **Solution Explorer** and select **Properties** to open the project's properties tab. You can also double click the **My Project** folder. Select **Painter.xaml** from the **Startup URI:** `ComboBox` (Fig. 27.29). Close the projects properties tab.

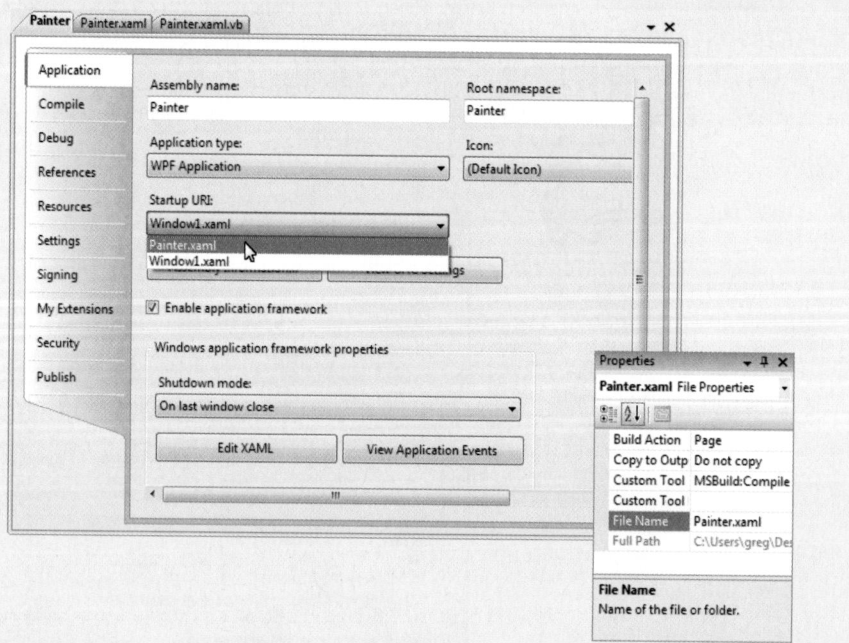

Figure 27.29 Renaming the project files.

2. ***Changing the `Window`'s `Class` attribute and opening the code-behind file.*** Change the `Window`'s `Class` attribute in the XAML to `PainterWindow` (Fig. 27.30). Select **View > Code** to open the `Painter.xaml.vb` code-behind file. Change the class name to `PainterWindow` to match the value set for the `Window`'s `Class` attribute (Fig. 27.31).

(cont.)

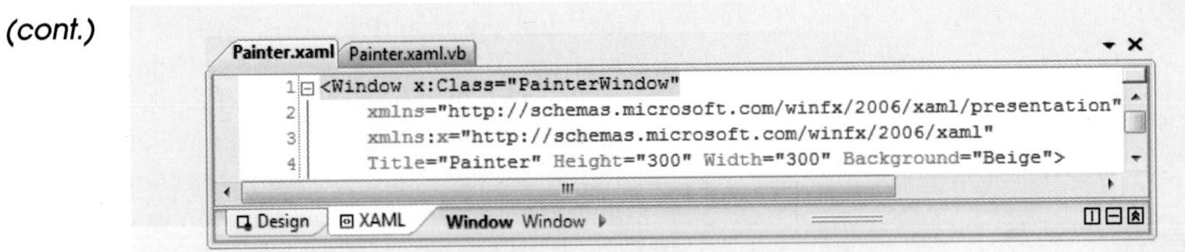

Figure 27.30 Setting the `Window`'s `Class` attribute.

3. ***Generating the `MouseLeftButtonDown` event handler.*** To generate the `MouseLeftButtonDown` event handler, select `paintCanvas` from the **Class Name** `ComboBox` (Fig. 27.31) in **Code** view. Then select `MouseLeftButtonDown` from the **Method Name** `ComboBox`.

Class Name `ComboBox` with `paintCanvas` selected

Method Name `ComboBox` with `MouseLeftButtonDown` selected

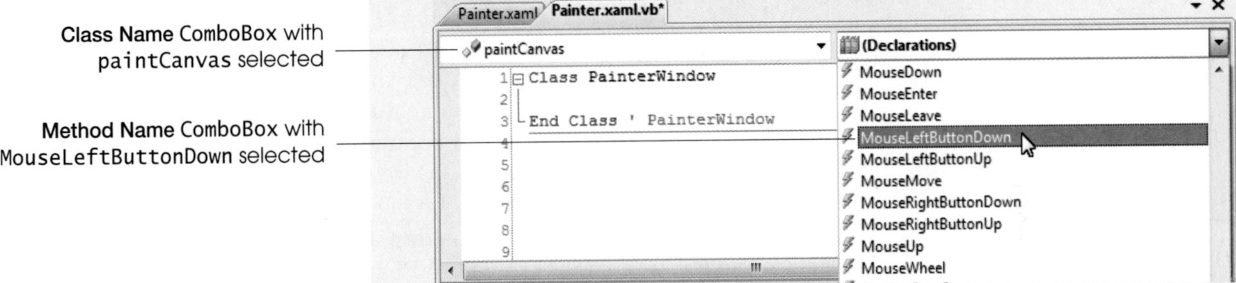

Figure 27.31 Creating a `MouseLeftButtonDown` event handler.

This generates the event handler `paintCanvas_MouseLeftButtonDown` (Fig. 27.32). As always, you should add a comment and format your code to improve readability (lines 3–9). The application invokes `paintCanvas_MouseLeftButtonDown` when the user generates the `Canvas`'s `MouseLeftButtonDown` event by pressing the left mouse button when the mouse pointer is over `paintCanvas`.

`MouseButtonEventArgs` argument

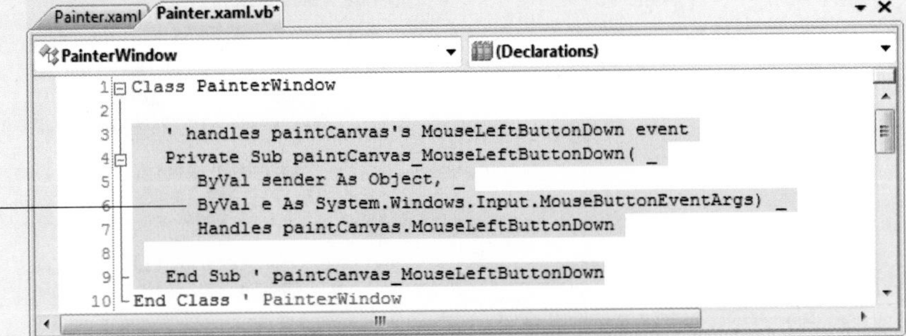

Figure 27.32 `MouseLeftButtonDown` event handler generated for `paintCanvas`.

The second argument passed to event handler `paintCanvas_MouseLeftButtonDown` is a variable of type **`MouseButtonEventArgs`** (line 6). This `MouseButtonEventArgs` object (referenced by `e`) contains information about the `MouseLeftButtonDown` event, including the coordinates of the mouse pointer when the left mouse button is pressed on the `Canvas`.

(cont.)

Note that the *x*- and *y*-coordinates of the `MouseButtonEventArgs` object are relative to the top-left corner of the `Window` or control that raises the event. Point *(0,0)* represents the upper-left corner of the `Window` or control. If you wish to access the *x*- and *y*-coordinates of the mouse, use method **`GetPosition`** of class `MouseButtonEventArgs` to obtain a **`Point`** object representing the position of the mouse pointer over the `Canvas`. Use property **`X`** of the `Point` to access the *x*-coordinate. Use property **`Y`** of the `Point` to access the *y*-coordinate of the mouse.

4. ***Drawing a circle on the Canvas.*** Add lines 2–23 of Fig. 27.33 above the `MouseLeftButtonDown` event handler. Line 3 declares the constant instance variable `DIAMETER` which is used to set the size of the circle drawn on the `Canvas`.

   Lines 6–23 define the `PaintCircle` method, which paints a circle on the `Canvas` in the color represented by the `Brush` passed as the first argument at the location passed as the second argument. A **`Brush`** is used to fill shapes with color. To see a list of available `Brush` colors, type the word `Brushes` followed by a dot, and the *IntelliSense* feature will provide a drop-down list of predefined `Brush` colors. Line 10 creates an object of class **`Ellipse`**—the WPF class used to draw an ellipse (a circle is an ellipse with equal width and height). Figure 27.34 shows a diagram of a general ellipse. The dotted rectangle—known as the ellipse's **bounding box**—specifies an ellipse's width, height and location on the `Canvas`. WPF provides several classes for drawing shapes other than ellipses.

   The **`Fill`** property of class `Ellipse` (line 13 of Fig. 27.33) sets the color of the `Ellipse`. The `Width` and `Height` properties (lines 14–15) set the width and height of the `Ellipse`, respectively. An `Ellipse` with equal width and height is a circle. Lines 18–19 set the `Ellipse`'s position on the `Canvas`. The **`SetTop`** and **`SetLeft`** methods of class `Canvas` set the top and left coordinates, respectively, of an element (the first argument) on the `Canvas` to a `Double` value (the second argument).

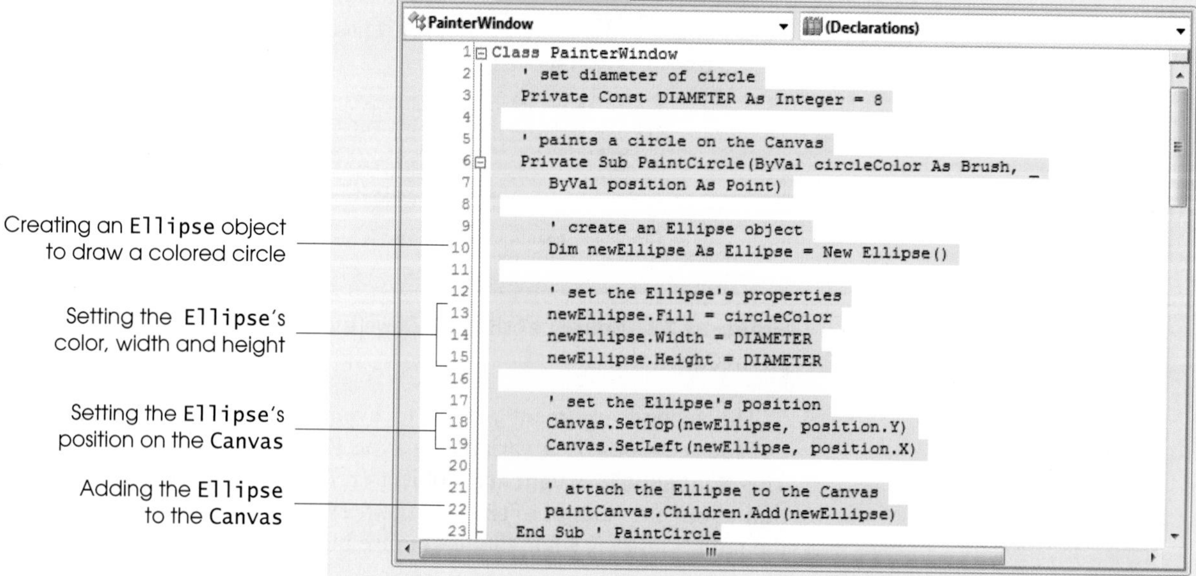


```
1  Class PainterWindow
2     ' set diameter of circle
3     Private Const DIAMETER As Integer = 8
4
5     ' paints a circle on the Canvas
6     Private Sub PaintCircle(ByVal circleColor As Brush, _
7        ByVal position As Point)
8
9        ' create an Ellipse object
10       Dim newEllipse As Ellipse = New Ellipse()
11
12       ' set the Ellipse's properties
13       newEllipse.Fill = circleColor
14       newEllipse.Width = DIAMETER
15       newEllipse.Height = DIAMETER
16
17       ' set the Ellipse's position
18       Canvas.SetTop(newEllipse, position.Y)
19       Canvas.SetLeft(newEllipse, position.X)
20
21       ' attach the Ellipse to the Canvas
22       paintCanvas.Children.Add(newEllipse)
23    End Sub ' PaintCircle
```

Figure 27.33 Drawing a circle on the `Canvas`.

(cont.)

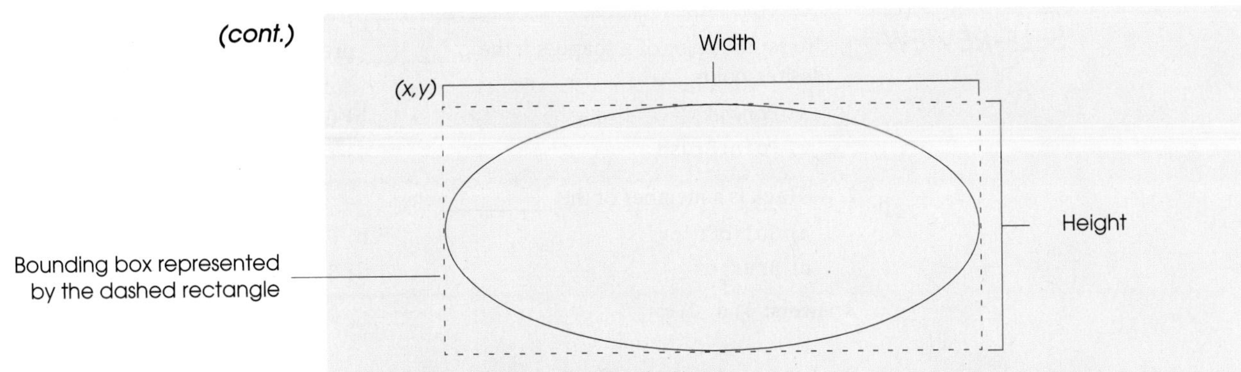

Figure 27.34 General ellipse.

Line 22 uses the `Add` method of the `paintCanvas`'s `Children` property to add the `Ellipse` to the `Canvas`. The **`Children`** property is a collection of all the child elements nested in the `Canvas`.

5. ***Modifying the `MouseLeftButtonDown` event handler.*** Add lines 31–33 to the `paintCanvas_MouseLeftButtonDown` event handler (Fig. 27.35). Line 32 retrieves the position of the mouse cursor relative to the control passed to the `GetPosition` method—the `paintCanvas`. Line 33 calls the `PaintCircle` procedure, passing a black `Brush` and the mouse cursor's position as the arguments.

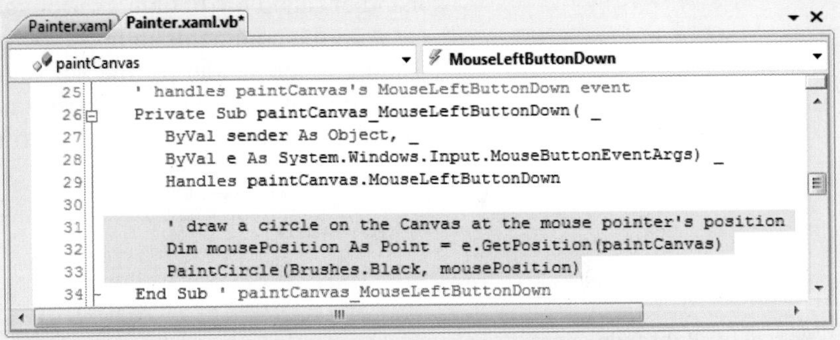

Figure 27.35 Adding code to the `MouseLeftButtonDown` event handler.

6. ***Running the application.*** Select **Debug > Start Debugging** to run your application. Notice that a small black circle is drawn when the left mouse button is pressed while the mouse pointer is over the `Canvas` (Fig. 27.36).

7. ***Closing the application.*** Close your running application by clicking its close box.

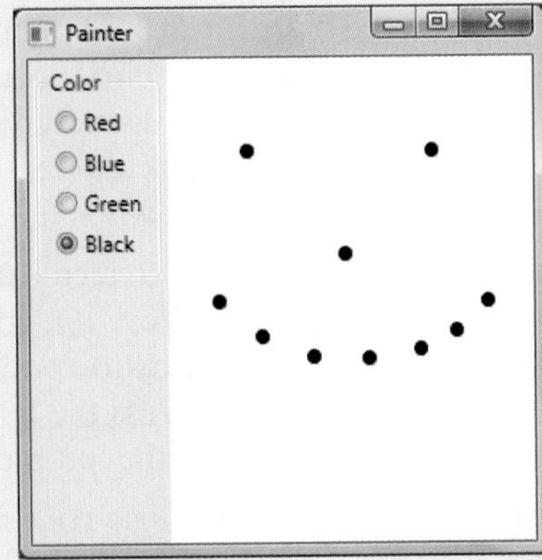

Figure 27.36 Running the application.

SELF-REVIEW

1. To set the color of a shape, set the ________ property of the shape to a `Brush` of the desired color.

   a) `Pencil` b) `Color`
   c) `PaintBrush` d) `Fill`

2. `Black` is a member of the ________ class.

   a) `SolidColor` b) `FillColor`
   c) `Brushes` d) `SystemColor`

Answers: 1) d. 2) c.

27.7 Handling the `MouseLeftButtonUp` Event

The application lets the user click anywhere on the `Canvas` and place a black circle. To enhance the application further, you'll have it place a green circle on the `Canvas` when the user releases the left mouse button. A `Canvas`'s `MouseLeftButtonUp` event occurs when the user releases the left mouse button while the mouse pointer is over the `Canvas`. You add this functionality in the following box.

Handling the MouseUp Event

1. ***Adding the `MouseLeftButtonUp` event handler.*** Select `paintCanvas` from the **Class Name** `ComboBox`, as you did in Fig. 27.31. Then select `MouseLeft-ButtonUp` from the **Method Name** `ComboBox`. This creates an empty event handler called `paintCanvas_MouseLeftButtonUp` (Fig. 27.37).

   Add the comments in lines 36 and 42 to your application. This header is similar to the header for the `MouseLeftButtonDown` event handler (the only difference is that the word `Down` is now `Up`). The `MouseLeftButtonUp` event handler executes only when the left mouse button is released.

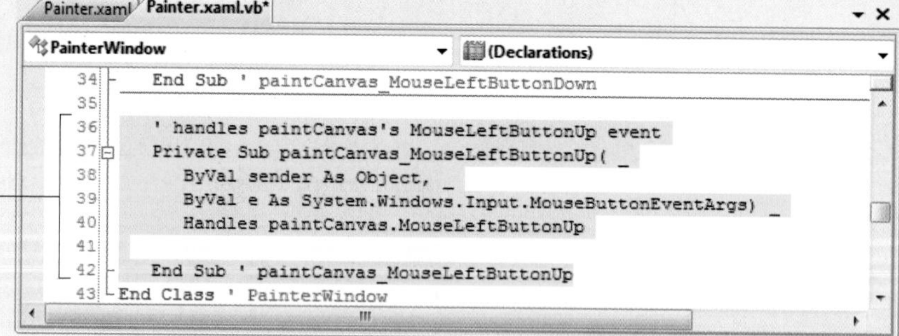

`MouseLeftButtonUp` event handler after commenting and formatting

Figure 27.37 `MouseLeftButtonUp` empty event handler.

2. ***Drawing a circle when the user releases a mouse button.*** Add lines 42–44 of Fig. 27.38 to the `MouseLeftButtonUp` event handler to draw a green circle at the position of the mouse pointer on the `Canvas` whenever the user releases the left mouse button. The diameter of each "mouse up" circle is the same as the diameter of the `Black` circles drawn by the `MouseLeftButtonDown` event handler that is called when left mouse button is pressed.

3. ***Running the application.*** Select **Debug > Start Debugging** to run your application (Fig. 27.39). Press and hold the left mouse button, move the mouse pointer to a new location and release the button. Note that a `Black` circle is drawn when you press the left mouse button and that a `Green` circle is drawn when you release the left mouse button.

4. ***Closing the application.*** Close your running application by clicking its close box.

(cont.)

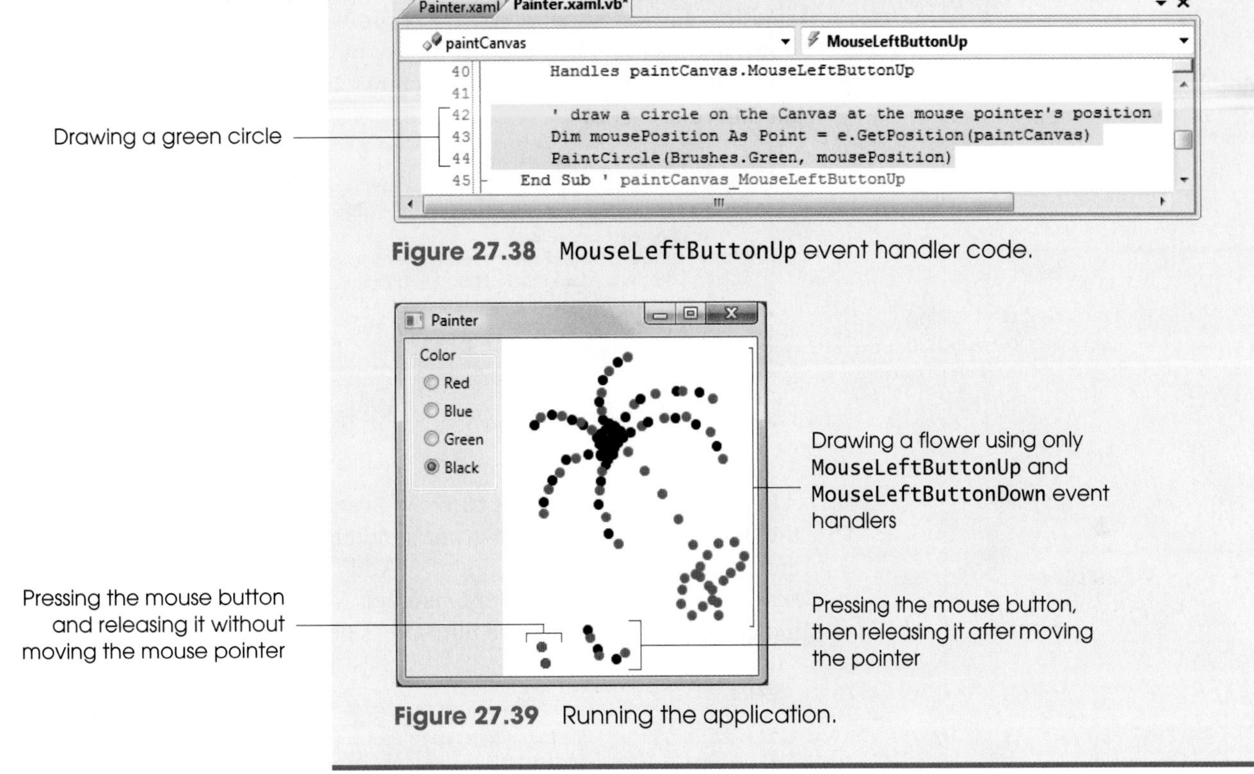

Figure 27.38 `MouseLeftButtonUp` event handler code.

Figure 27.39 Running the application.

SELF-REVIEW

1. Releasing the left mouse button generates a ________ event.
   a) `MouseLeftButtonRelease` b) `MouseLeftButtonUp`
   c) `MouseOff` d) `MouseClick`

2. The ________ and ________ methods set the `Ellipse`'s position on the `Canvas`.
   a) `Top`, `Left` b) `Upper`, `Left`
   c) `SetUpper`, `SetLeft` d) `SetTop`, `SetLeft`

Answers: 1) b. 2) d.

27.8 Handling the MouseMove Event

Currently, the application allows you to draw only isolated circles when the left mouse button is pressed or released. It does not yet allow you to draw more sophisticated shapes and designs. Next, you enhance your application to provide more drawing capabilities. The application will be able to continuously draw `Black` circles as long as the mouse is being moved across the `Canvas` with the left mouse button down. If the left mouse button is not pressed, moving the mouse across the `Canvas` does not draw anything. To add this functionality, you begin by modifying your two event handlers.

Modifying the Painter Application

1. ***Adding a `Boolean` variable to specify whether a mouse button is pressed.*** Add lines 5–6 of Fig. 27.40 to your application. Line 6 declares and initializes the `Boolean` instance variable `shouldPaint`. The application must be able to determine whether the left mouse button is pressed, because the application should draw on the `Canvas` only when the left mouse button is held down.

(cont.)

You alter the MouseLeftButtonDown and MouseLeftButtonUp event handlers so that shouldPaint is True when the left mouse button is held down and False when the left mouse button is released. When the application is first loaded, it should not "paint" anything, so this instance variable is initialized to False.

Declaring and setting an instance variable to control painting

```
Painter.xaml | Painter.xaml.vb*
PainterWindow | (Declarations)
Class PainterWindow
   ' set diameter of circle
   Private Const DIAMETER As Integer = 8

   ' specify whether moving the mouse should draw
   Private shouldPaint As Boolean = False
```

Figure 27.40 Boolean instance variable shouldPaint is declared and set to False.

2. ***Altering the MouseLeftButtonDown event handler.*** Remove the code inside the MouseLeftButtonDown event handler, leaving just the procedure header and the End Sub statement. Add line 34 of Fig. 27.41 to the MouseLeftButtonDown event handler to set shouldPaint to True. This indicates that the left mouse button has been pressed.

Allow drawing when left mouse button is pressed

```
Painter.xaml | Painter.xaml.vb*
paintCanvas | MouseLeftButtonDown
28    ' handles paintCanvas's MouseLeftButtonDown event
29    Private Sub paintCanvas_MouseLeftButtonDown( _
30       ByVal sender As Object, _
31       ByVal e As System.Windows.Input.MouseButtonEventArgs) _
32       Handles paintCanvas.MouseLeftButtonDown
33
34       shouldPaint = True ' OK to draw on the Canvas
35    End Sub ' paintCanvas_MouseLeftButtonDown
```

Figure 27.41 Setting shouldPaint to True.

3. ***Altering the MouseLeftButtonUp event handler.*** Remove the code inside the MouseLeftButtonUp event handler, leaving just the procedure header and the End Sub statement. Add line 43 of Fig. 27.42 to set shouldPaint to False. This indicates that the left mouse button has been released.

Disable drawing when left mouse button is released

```
Painter.xaml | Painter.xaml.vb*
paintCanvas | MouseLeftButtonUp
37    ' handles paintCanvas's MouseLeftButtonUp event
38    Private Sub paintCanvas_MouseLeftButtonUp( _
39       ByVal sender As Object, _
40       ByVal e As System.Windows.Input.MouseButtonEventArgs) _
41       Handles paintCanvas.MouseLeftButtonUp
42
43       shouldPaint = False ' do not draw on the Canvas
44    End Sub ' paintCanvas_MouseLeftButtonUp
```

Figure 27.42 Setting shouldPaint to False.

4. ***Saving the project.*** Select **File > Save All** to save your modified code.

You've altered the event handlers to set the value of the shouldPaint variable to indicate whether a mouse button is pressed. Next, you handle the **MouseMove** event, which is raised whenever you move the mouse over the **Painter** application's Canvas. You define the MouseMove event handler in the following box.

Adding the MouseMove Event Handler

1. ***Adding the MouseMove event handler.*** Select `paintCanvas` from the **Class Name** `ComboBox` as in Fig. 27.31. Then select `MouseMove` from the **Method Name** `ComboBox` to generate the empty `MouseMove` event handler `paintCanvas_MouseMove` (Fig. 27.43). Add comments to lines 46 and 52. Notice that the `MouseMove` event handler receives a `MouseEventArgs` parameter (line 49) rather than a `MouseButtonEventArgs` parameter.

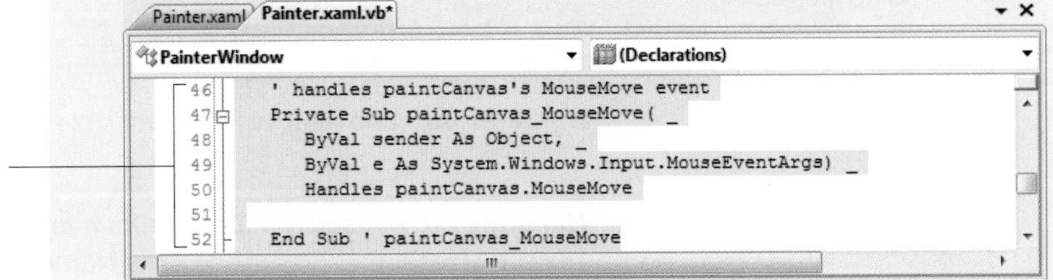

Figure 27.43 `MouseMove` empty event handler.

2. ***Adding code to the MouseMove event handler.*** Add lines 52–57 of Fig. 27.44 to the `MouseMove` event handler, which executes each time the user moves the mouse while it's over the `Canvas`. The `If...Then` statement tests the value of `shouldPaint`. If it's `True` (the left mouse button is pressed), the `PaintCircle` method draws a black circle on the `Canvas`. If it's `False` (left mouse button is not pressed), then nothing is drawn.

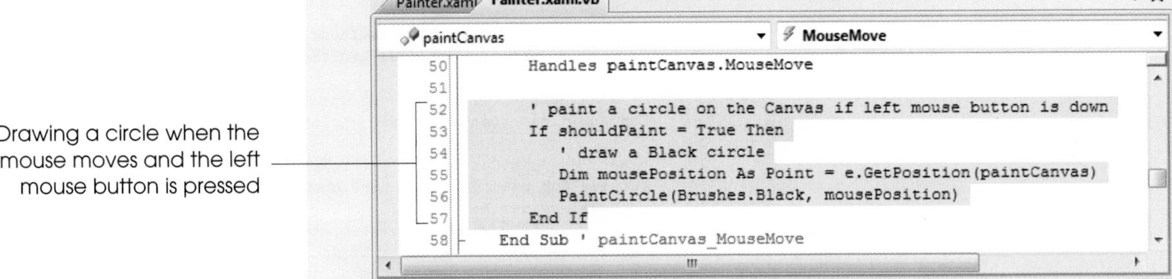

Figure 27.44 `MouseMove` event handler draws a circle on the `Canvas` if left mouse button is held down.

3. ***Running the application.*** Select **Debug > Start Debugging** to run your application. Try drawing various shapes and designs on the `Canvas`.
4. ***Closing the application.*** Close your running application by clicking its close box.
5. ***Saving the project.*** Select **File > Save All** to save your modified code.

27.9 Handling Right Mouse Button Events

Now that your application allows the user to draw using the mouse, you are going to add the code that allows the user to "erase" by moving the mouse over the drawing with the right mouse button pressed. You learn how to do this in the following box.

Erasing the Canvas

1. ***Adding a Boolean variable to specify whether the application should erase while the mouse pointer is moving.*** Add lines 5–6 of Fig. 27.45 to your application (above the initialization of `shouldPaint`). Instance variable `shouldErase` specifies whether moving the mouse pointer should act like an eraser.

(cont.)

Declaring and setting an instance variable to control erasing

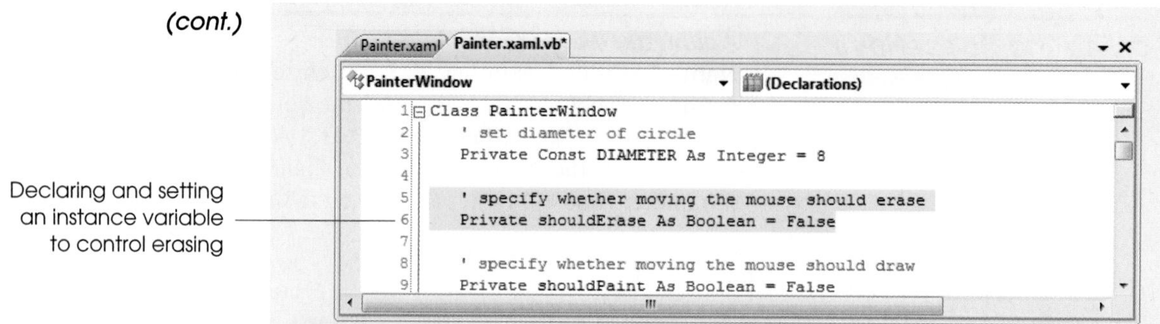

Figure 27.45 `Boolean` instance variable `shouldErase` is declared and set to `False`.

2. ***Handling the `MouseRightButtonDown` and `MouseRightButtonUp` events.*** Select `paintCanvas` from the **Class Name** `ComboBox`, then add event handlers for the `MouseRightButtonDown` and `MouseRightButtonUp` events (Fig. 27.46). Add line 69 to the `MouseRightButtonDown` event handler to set `shouldErase` to `True`. Add line 78 to the `MouseRightButtonUp` event handler to set `shouldErase` to `False`.

Enable erasing

Disable erasing

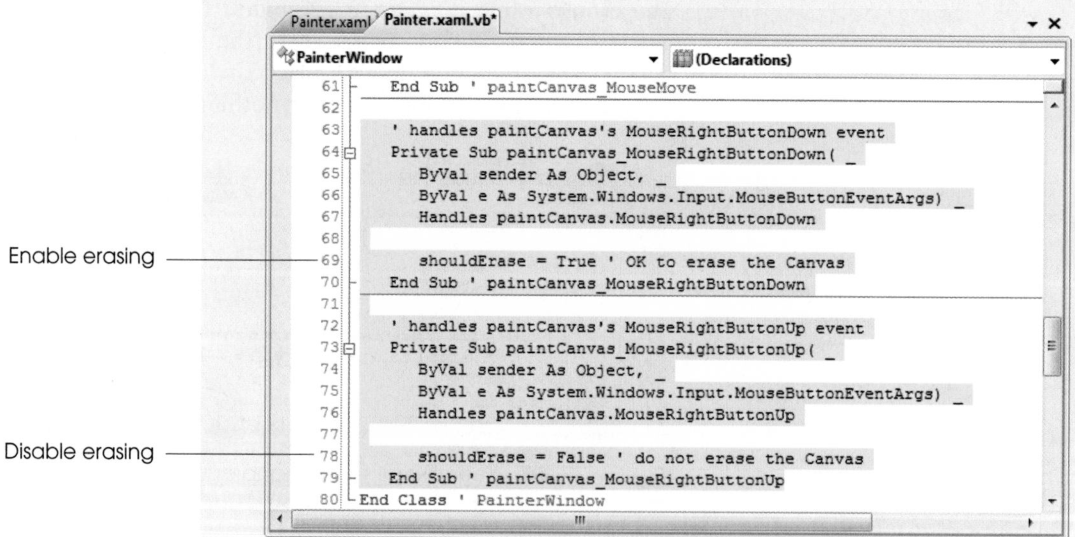

Figure 27.46 Enabling and disabling erasing.

3. ***Drawing when the left mouse button is pressed.*** Replace the code in event handler `paintCanvas_MouseMove` with lines 55–64 of Fig. 27.47. If `shouldPaint` is `True` (line 56), lines 58–59 draw a black circle—the left mouse button is pressed.

4. ***Erasing when the right mouse button is pressed.*** The `MouseMove` event handler does not actually erase anything. Instead, when `shouldErase` is `True` (line 60 of Fig. 27.47), the `PaintCircle` method (lines 62–63) draws a circle that is the same size as the black circle and has the same color as the `Canvas`'s background. This allows the mouse pointer to act like an eraser. Note that the first argument to `PaintCircle` is `paintCanvas.Background`. The **Background** property returns the `Canvas`'s background color as a `Brush`.

5. ***Running the application.*** Select **Debug > Start Debugging** to run your application. Try drawing various shapes and designs on the `Canvas`, then try to erase them.

(cont.)

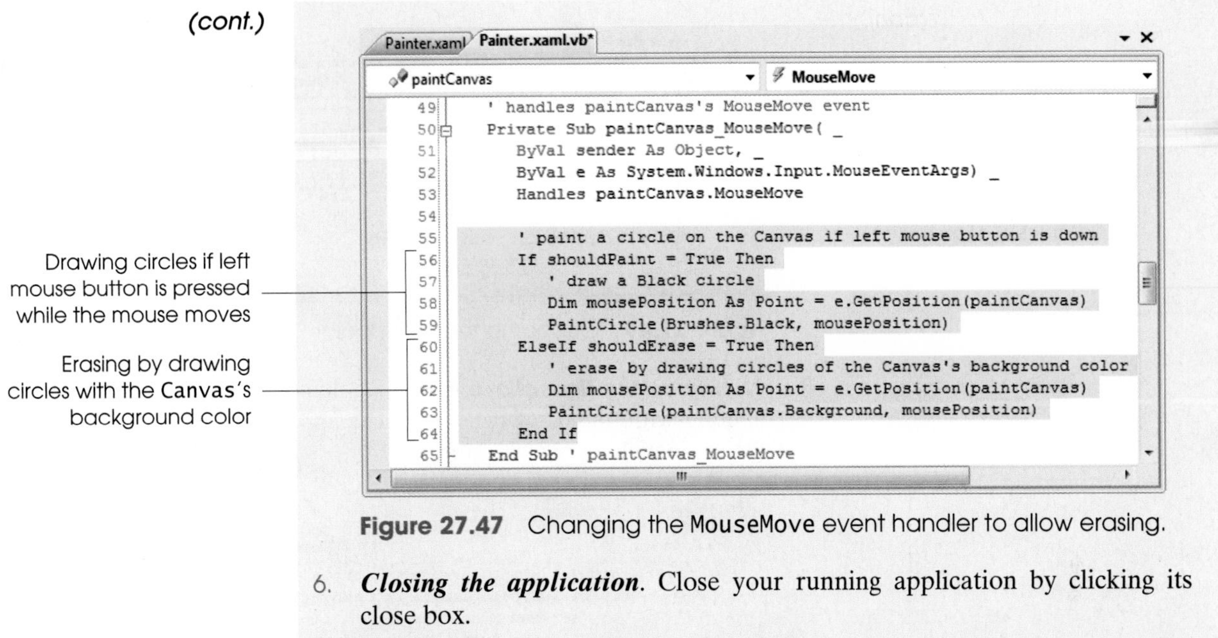

Figure 27.47 Changing the `MouseMove` event handler to allow erasing.

6. ***Closing the application.*** Close your running application by clicking its close box.
7. ***Saving the project.*** Select **File > Save All** to save your modified code.

27.10 Select Colors with `RadioButtons`

Your **Painter** application now allows the user to draw on the `Canvas` using the left mouse button and to erase parts of the `Canvas` using the right mouse button. In the next box you enhance the **Painter** application by allowing users to choose from several color options using `RadioButtons`.

Choosing Colors with `RadioButtons`

1. ***Adding a `Brush` variable to specify the selected color.*** Add lines 5–6 of Fig. 27.48 to your application (above the initialization of `shouldErase`). Instance variable `brushColor` specifies the color in which to draw circles.

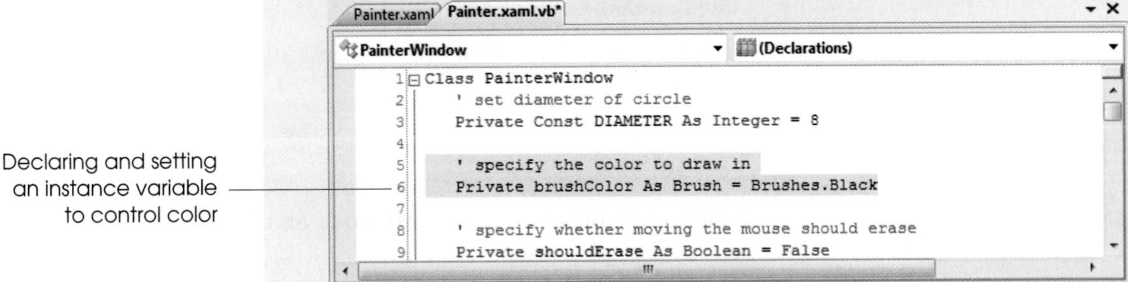

Figure 27.48 `Brush` instance variable `brushColor`.

2. ***Handling the `RadioButton Checked` events.*** Double click the **Red** `RadioButton` in **Design** view to generate its `Checked` event handler. The `Checked` event is raised when the `RadioButton` is selected. Note that this is different than a Windows `Forms RadioButton`, which raises a `CheckedChanged` event both when it is selected and deselected. Add line 94 to the **Red** `RadioButton`'s `Checked` event handler (Fig. 27.49). This line sets `brushColor` to `Red`. Add `Checked` event handlers for the remaining `RadioButtons`. Each `RadioButton`'s event handler should set `brushColor` to the color specified in its `Content`.

(cont.)

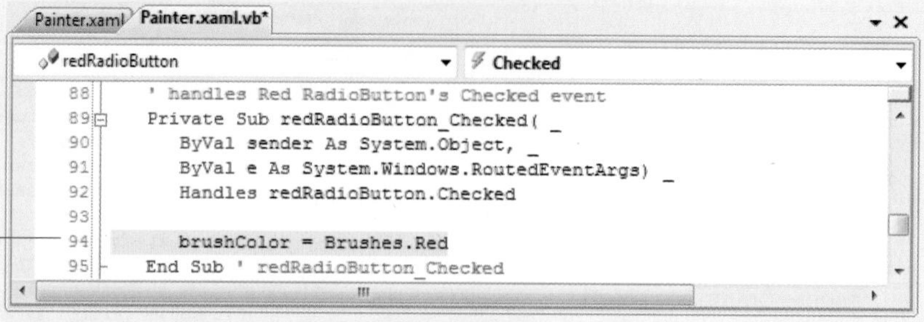

Painter.xaml
Painter.xaml.vb*
redRadioButton
Checked
88 ' handles Red RadioButton's Checked event
89 Private Sub redRadioButton_Checked(_
90 ByVal sender As System.Object, _
91 ByVal e As System.Windows.RoutedEventArgs) _
92 Handles redRadioButton.Checked
93
94 brushColor = Brushes.Red
95 End Sub ' redRadioButton_Checked
Set brushColor to Red

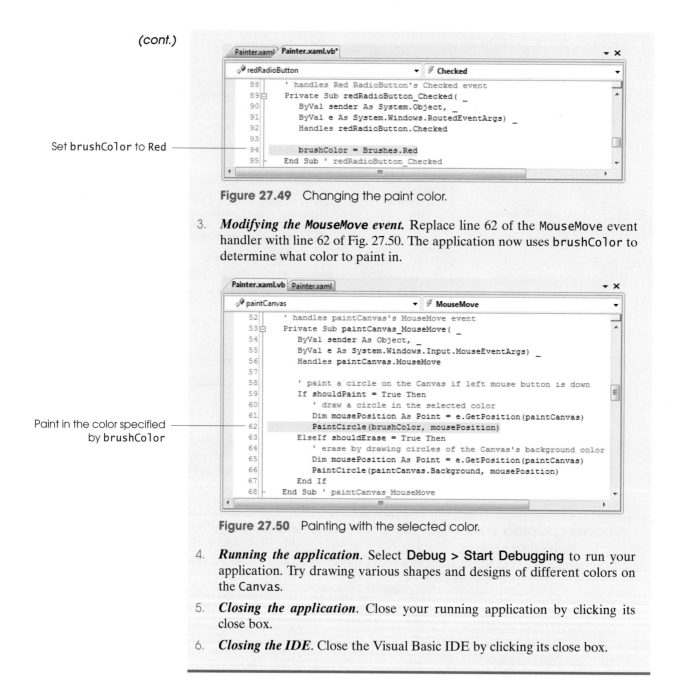

Figure 27.49 Changing the paint color.

3. ***Modifying the MouseMove event.*** Replace line 62 of the `MouseMove` event handler with line 62 of Fig. 27.50. The application now uses `brushColor` to determine what color to paint in.

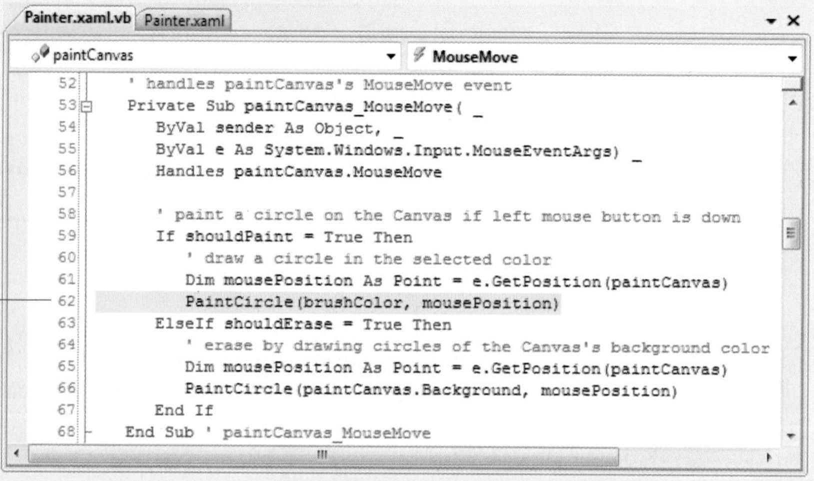

Painter.xaml.vb
Painter.xaml
paintCanvas
MouseMove
52 ' handles paintCanvas's MouseMove event
53 Private Sub paintCanvas_MouseMove(_
54 ByVal sender As Object, _
55 ByVal e As System.Windows.Input.MouseEventArgs) _
56 Handles paintCanvas.MouseMove
57
58 ' paint a circle on the Canvas if left mouse button is down
59 If shouldPaint = True Then
60 ' draw a circle in the selected color
61 Dim mousePosition As Point = e.GetPosition(paintCanvas)
62 PaintCircle(brushColor, mousePosition)
63 ElseIf shouldErase = True Then
64 ' erase by drawing circles of the Canvas's background color
65 Dim mousePosition As Point = e.GetPosition(paintCanvas)
66 PaintCircle(paintCanvas.Background, mousePosition)
67 End If
68 End Sub ' paintCanvas_MouseMove
Paint in the color specified by brushColor

Figure 27.50 Painting with the selected color.

4. ***Running the application.*** Select **Debug > Start Debugging** to run your application. Try drawing various shapes and designs of different colors on the `Canvas`.
5. ***Closing the application.*** Close your running application by clicking its close box.
6. ***Closing the IDE.*** Close the Visual Basic IDE by clicking its close box.

Figure 27.51 presents the XAML code and Fig. 27.52 presents the source code for the **Painter** application.

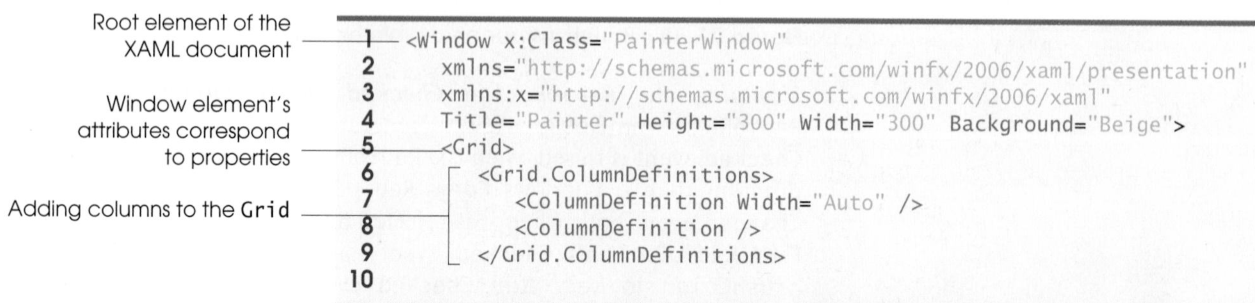

Root element of the XAML document

Window element's attributes correspond to properties

Adding columns to the `Grid`

```
<Window x:Class="PainterWindow"
    xmlns="http://schemas.microsoft.com/winfx/2006/xaml/presentation"
    xmlns:x="http://schemas.microsoft.com/winfx/2006/xaml"
    Title="Painter" Height="300" Width="300" Background="Beige">
    <Grid>
      <Grid.ColumnDefinitions>
        <ColumnDefinition Width="Auto" />
        <ColumnDefinition />
      </Grid.ColumnDefinitions>

```

Figure 27.51 **Painter** application's XAML markup. (Part 1 of 2.)

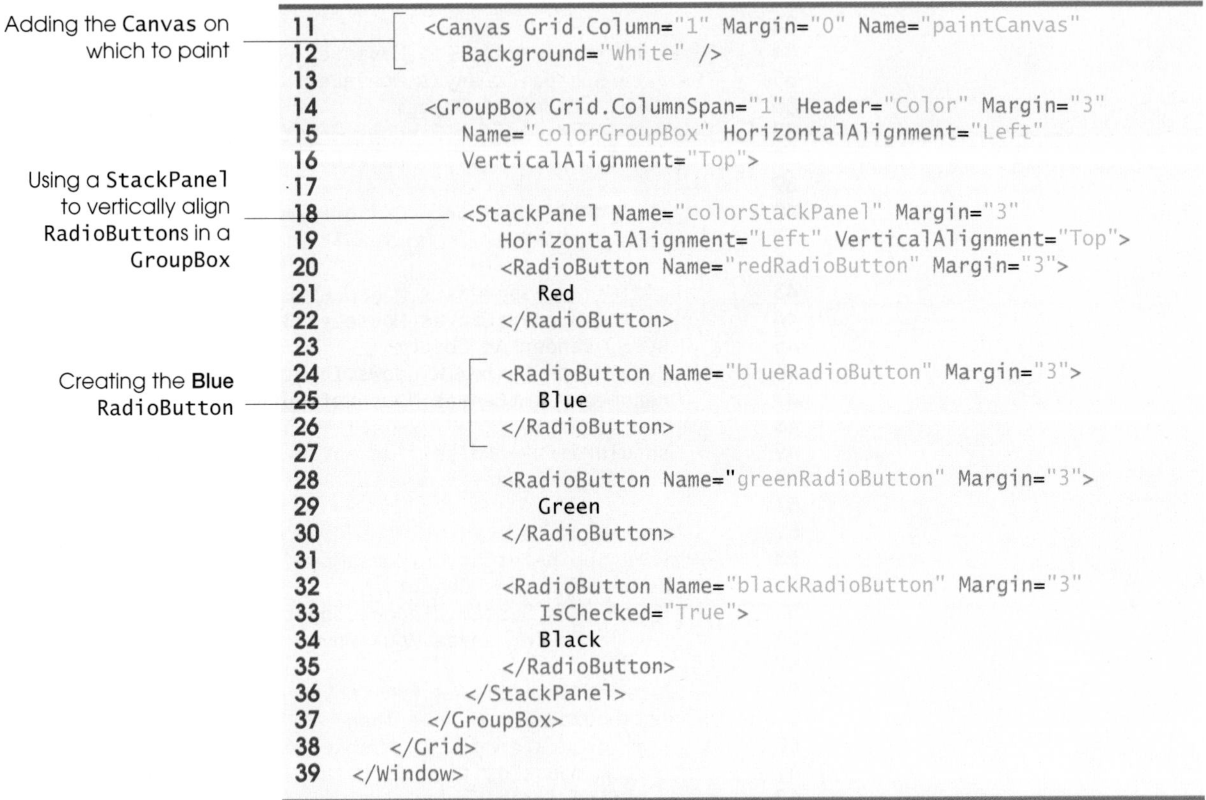

Adding the Canvas on which to paint

Using a StackPanel to vertically align RadioButtons in a GroupBox

Creating the **Blue** RadioButton

```
    <Canvas Grid.Column="1" Margin="0" Name="paintCanvas"
       Background="White" />

    <GroupBox Grid.ColumnSpan="1" Header="Color" Margin="3"
       Name="colorGroupBox" HorizontalAlignment="Left"
       VerticalAlignment="Top">

       <StackPanel Name="colorStackPanel" Margin="3"
          HorizontalAlignment="Left" VerticalAlignment="Top">
          <RadioButton Name="redRadioButton" Margin="3">
             Red
          </RadioButton>

          <RadioButton Name="blueRadioButton" Margin="3">
             Blue
          </RadioButton>

          <RadioButton Name="greenRadioButton" Margin="3">
             Green
          </RadioButton>

          <RadioButton Name="blackRadioButton" Margin="3"
             IsChecked="True">
             Black
          </RadioButton>
       </StackPanel>
    </GroupBox>
  </Grid>
</Window>
```

Figure 27.51 **Painter** application's XAML markup. (Part 2 of 2.)

Brush used to specify the color used later to paint an Ellipse

Create a new Ellipse object

Set the color and size of the Ellipse

Setting the Ellipse's position on the Canvas

Adding the Ellipse to the Canvas

```
Class PainterWindow
   ' set diameter of circle
   Private Const DIAMETER As Integer = 8

   ' specify the color to draw in
   Private brushColor As Brush = Brushes.Black

   ' specify whether moving the mouse should erase
   Private shouldErase As Boolean = False

   ' specify whether moving the mouse should draw
   Private shouldPaint As Boolean = False

   ' paints a circle on the Canvas
   Private Sub PaintCircle(ByVal circleColor As Brush, _
      ByVal position As Point)

      ' create an Ellipse object
      Dim newEllipse As Ellipse = New Ellipse()

      ' set the Ellipse's properties
      newEllipse.Fill = circleColor
      newEllipse.Width = DIAMETER
      newEllipse.Height = DIAMETER

      ' set the Ellipse's position
      Canvas.SetTop(newEllipse, position.Y)
      Canvas.SetLeft(newEllipse, position.X)

      ' attach the Ellipse to the Canvas
      paintCanvas.Children.Add(newEllipse)
   End Sub ' PaintCircle
```

Figure 27.52 **Painter** application's code. (Part 1 of 3.)

Handling the `Canvas`'s `MouseLeftButtonDown` event

Retrieve the mouse pointer's position relative to the `Canvas` at the time of the `MouseMove` event

Changing the `brushColor` to Red when the **Red** `RadioButton` is selected

```

   ' handles paintCanvas's MouseLeftButtonDown event
   Private Sub paintCanvas_MouseLeftButtonDown( _
      ByVal sender As Object, _
      ByVal e As System.Windows.Input.MouseButtonEventArgs) _
      Handles paintCanvas.MouseLeftButtonDown

      shouldPaint = True ' OK to draw on the Canvas
   End Sub ' paintCanvas_MouseLeftButtonDown

   ' handles paintCanvas's MouseLeftButtonUp event
   Private Sub paintCanvas_MouseLeftButtonUp( _
      ByVal sender As Object, _
      ByVal e As System.Windows.Input.MouseButtonEventArgs) _
      Handles paintCanvas.MouseLeftButtonUp

      shouldPaint = False ' do not draw on the Canvas
   End Sub ' paintCanvas_MouseLeftButtonUp

   ' handles paintCanvas's MouseMove event
   Private Sub paintCanvas_MouseMove( _
      ByVal sender As Object, _
      ByVal e As System.Windows.Input.MouseEventArgs) _
      Handles paintCanvas.MouseMove

      ' paint a circle on the Canvas if left mouse button is down
      If shouldPaint = True Then
         ' draw a circle in the selected color
         Dim mousePosition As Point = e.GetPosition(paintCanvas)
         PaintCircle(brushColor, mousePosition)
      ElseIf shouldErase = True Then
         ' erase by drawing circles of the Canvas's background color
         Dim mousePosition As Point = e.GetPosition(paintCanvas)
         PaintCircle(paintCanvas.Background, mousePosition)
      End If
   End Sub ' paintCanvas_MouseMove

   ' handles paintCanvas's MouseRightButtonDown event
   Private Sub paintCanvas_MouseRightButtonDown( _
      ByVal sender As Object, _
      ByVal e As System.Windows.Input.MouseButtonEventArgs) _
      Handles paintCanvas.MouseRightButtonDown

      shouldErase = True ' OK to erase the Canvas
   End Sub ' paintCanvas_MouseRightButtonDown

   ' handles paintCanvas's MouseRightButtonUp event
   Private Sub paintCanvas_MouseRightButtonUp( _
      ByVal sender As Object, _
      ByVal e As System.Windows.Input.MouseButtonEventArgs) _
      Handles paintCanvas.MouseRightButtonUp

      shouldErase = False ' do not erase the Canvas
   End Sub ' paintCanvas_MouseRightButtonUp

   ' handles Red RadioButton's Checked event
   Private Sub redRadioButton_Checked( _
      ByVal sender As System.Object, _
      ByVal e As System.Windows.RoutedEventArgs) _
      Handles redRadioButton.Checked

      brushColor = Brushes.Red
   End Sub ' redRadioButton_Checked

```

Figure 27.52 **Painter** application's code. (Part 2 of 3.)

```
   ' handles Blue RadioButton's Checked event
   Private Sub blueRadioButton_Checked( _
      ByVal sender As System.Object, _
      ByVal e As System.Windows.RoutedEventArgs) _
      Handles blueRadioButton.Checked

      brushColor = Brushes.Blue
   End Sub ' blueRadioButton_Checked

   ' handles Green RadioButton's Checked event
   Private Sub greenRadioButton_Checked( _
      ByVal sender As System.Object, _
      ByVal e As System.Windows.RoutedEventArgs) _
      Handles greenRadioButton.Checked

      brushColor = Brushes.Green
   End Sub ' greenRadioButton_Checked

   ' handles Black RadioButton's Checked event
   Private Sub blackRadioButton_Checked( _
      ByVal sender As System.Object, _
      ByVal e As System.Windows.RoutedEventArgs) _
      Handles blackRadioButton.Checked

      brushColor = Brushes.Black
   End Sub ' blackRadioButton_Checked
End Class ' PainterWindow
```

Figure 27.52 **Painter** application's code. (Part 3 of 3.)

1. Moving the mouse pointer generates a ________ event.
   a) `MouseMove` b) `MousePositionChanged`
   c) `MouseOver` d) `MouseChanged`

2. The ________ event is raised when a `RadioButton` is selected.
   a) `CheckedChanged` b) `IsChecked`
   c) `Checked` d) `CheckedEvent`

Answers: 1) a. 2) c.

27.11 Wrap-Up

In this tutorial, you learned the basics of Windows Presentation Foundation. You learned how to create a GUI using WPF layout containers and content controls. You saw the advantages to WPF's layout strategy. You created a basic GUI using the `Window`, `Grid`, `Canvas`, `StackPanel`, `GroupBox` and `RadioButton` controls.

Next, you learned the essentials of mouse event handling. You handled common mouse events—`MouseMove`, `MouseLeftButtonUp`, `MouseLeftButtonDown`, `MouseRightButtonUp` and `MouseRightButtonDown`—and how to create mouse event handlers associated with a `Canvas`. You generated these event handlers by selecting the appropriate mouse event from the **Method Name** `ComboBox` after selecting `paintCanvas` from the **Class Name** `ComboBox`. The skills you learned in this tutorial are similar to the skills needed to handle mouse events in Windows `Forms` application.

You used WPF class `Ellipse` to draw circles in the **Painter** application. You learned how to use a `Brush` object to draw a shape in a solid color specified by one of the predefined `Brush` objects in the `Brushes` class.

The **Painter** application uses mouse events to determine what the user wants to do. The user moves the mouse with the left mouse button held down to draw on the `Canvas`. Moving the mouse across the `Canvas` without pressing a button does not draw anything on the `Canvas`. You provided the **Painter** application with an eraser.

When users move the mouse with the right mouse button pressed, the **Painter** application draws circles with the Canvas's background color.

To build the **Painter** application, you used MouseButtonEventArgs and MouseEventArgs objects, which are passed to mouse event handlers and provide information about mouse events. Method GetPosition of the MouseButtonEventArgs and MouseEventArgs objects returned a Point object specifying the *x*- and *y*-coordinates where the mouse event occurred.

In the next tutorial, we begin our four-tutorial case study in which we develop a data-driven ASP.NET web application.

SKILLS SUMMARY

Creating a GUI with WPF

- Create a new project using the **WPF Application** template.
- Use a Grid layout container to divide your GUI into sections. Though we used only columns in this tutorial, you can also create rows.
- Use a Canvas layout container to position elements using coordinates.
- Use a StackPanel layout container to arrange elements either horizontally or vertically (the default).
- Use a GroupBox content control to group related elements visually.
- Use RadioButtons to enable users to select only one of several options.

Raising Events with a Mouse

- Pressing a mouse's buttons and moving the mouse raise events.

Handling Mouse Events

- The MouseButtonEventArgs and MouseEventArgs classes contain information about mouse events, such as the Point where the mouse event occurred. Each mouse event handler that involves a button receives an object of class MouseButtonEventArgs as an argument. The MouseMove event handler receives an object of class MouseEventArgs as an argument.
- Moving the mouse raises event MouseMove.
- Pressing the left mouse button raises event MouseLeftButtonDown.
- Pressing the right mouse button raises event MouseRightButtonDown.
- Releasing the left mouse button raises event MouseLeftButtonUp.
- Releasing the right mouse button raises event MouseRightButtonUp.

Creating an Event Handler for a Mouse Event Associated with a Canvas

- Select ***CanvasName*** from the **Class Name** ComboBox, where ***CanvasName*** is the name of the application's Canvas. Then select the appropriate event from the **Method Name** ComboBox.

Drawing on a Canvas

- Shape classes are used to draw shapes on a Canvas or other control.
- Create an instance of a shape class (by invoking the class's constructor) to access methods for drawing the shape.
- Display the shape using the Add method of the Canvas's Children property.

Drawing a Solid Ellipse

- Use the shape class Ellipse to draw an ellipse.
- Pass a Brush object to the Fill property to specify the shape's color.
- Specify the color, the coordinates of the bounding box's upper-left corner and the width and height of the bounding box. When the width and height of the bounding box are equal, a circle is drawn.

KEY TERMS

attribute in XAML—Can be used to set an object's property values. Represented in XAML by placing a property name, an equal sign (=) and a value in double quotes inside the opening tag of the object's XAML element.

Background property of class Canvas—Gets or sets the Brush value used as the background color of the Canvas.

bounding box of an ellipse—Specifies an ellipse's location, width and height.

Brush class—Used to fill shapes and controls with colors.

Canvas layout container—A WPF control that enables absolute positioning of its child elements.

child element—XAML element that is nested inside another element.

Children property of Canvas—Returns a collection of all the child elements nested in a Canvas.

ColumnDefinition element of a Grid—Specifies the attributes of a column in a Grid.

ColumnDefinitions property of a Grid—Provides access to the collection of ColumnDefinitions for a Grid.

content control—A WPF control that can hold one piece of content of any type.

CType function—Function that converts its first argument to the type specified in its second argument.

element in XML—Markup that describes a piece of data. Delimited by start and end tags.

Ellipse class—The shape class that draws an ellipse. This class contains properties including Fill, Width and Height. If the width and height are the same, a circle is drawn.

empty element in XML—Shorthand notation for an element with no content between its start and end tags.

end tag—Delimits the end of an XML element.

eXtensible Application Markup Language (XAML)—*See* XAML.

eXtensible Markup Language (XML)—*See* XML.

Fill property of an Ellipse—Specifies the Brush that is used to color the Ellipse.

GetPosition method of classes MouseButtonEventArgs and MouseEventArgs—Returns a Point object representing the position of the mouse pointer over a control.

Grid layout container—A WPF control that organizes its children in rows and columns.

GroupBox content control—A control that places a titled border around its content.

Header property of a GroupBox—Sets the text displayed in a GroupBox's border.

layout container—A control that positions its child controls based on their size and the amount of available space in the container.

mouse event—Generated when a user interacts with an application using the computer's mouse.

MouseButtonEventArgs class—Specifies information about a mouse event involving a button press or release.

MouseLeftButtonDown event—Generated when the left mouse button is pressed.

MouseRightButtonDown event—Generated when the right mouse button is pressed.

MouseEventArgs class—Specifies information about a MouseMove.

MouseMove event—Generated when a mouse pointer is moved.

MouseLeftButtonUp event—Generated when the left mouse button is released.

MouseRightButtonUp event—Generated when the right mouse button is released.

Point class—Contains an X and a Y property representing the coordinates of a point.

SetLeft method of Canvas—Sets the left coordinate of an element (the first argument) on the Canvas to a Double value (the second argument).

SetTop method of Canvas—Sets the top coordinate of an element (the first argument) on the Canvas to a Double value (the second argument).

StackPanel layout container—A WPF control that organizes its children horizontally or vertically (the default).

start tag—Delimits the beginning of an XML element.

Title property of a Window—Specifies the text that appears in the Window's title bar.

Window control—The root control in a WPF application. Analogous to a Form in a Windows Forms application.

Windows Presentation Foundation (WPF)—Microsoft's new graphics framework that allows you to create powerful and flexible GUIs and to create media-rich experiences with animations, audio, video and graphics.

`X` property of class `Point`—The property of class `Point` that specifies the *x*-coordinate.

XAML (eXtensible Application Markup Language)—An XML vocabulary for describing WPF user interfaces.

XML (eXtensible Markup Language)—Language for creating markup for describing data in a manner that both humans and computers can understand.

XML vocabulary—XML-based markup language that provides a means for describing a particular type of data in a standardized, structured manner. For example, XAML is an XML vocabulary that describes WPF user interface information.

`Y` property of class `Point`—The property of class `Point` that specifies the *y*-coordinate.

CONTROLS, EVENTS, PROPERTIES & METHODS

`Canvas` Canvas This control allows the user to place elements using coordinates.

- ***In action***

- ***Events***

`MouseLeftButtonDown`—Raised when the user presses the left mouse button over the `Canvas`.

`MouseLeftButtonUp`—Raised when the user releases the left mouse button over the `Canvas`.

`MouseRightButtonDown`—Raised when the user presses the right mouse button over the `Canvas`.

`MouseRightButtonUp`—Raised when the user releases the right mouse button over the `Canvas`.

- ***Properties***

`Background`—Specifies the background color of the `Canvas`.

`Children`—Specifies the elements contained in the `Canvas`.

`Grid.Column`—Specifies the `Grid` column in which the `Canvas` is contained.

`Height`—Specifies the height of the `Canvas`.

`HorizontalAlignment`—Specifies the horizontal alignment of the `Canvas`.

`Margin`—Specifies amount of space around the `Canvas`.

`Name`—Specifies the name used to access the `Canvas` programmatically. The name should be appended with the `Canvas` suffix.

`VerticalAlignment`—Specifies the vertical alignment of the `Canvas`.

`Width`—Specifies the width of the `Canvas`.

- ***Methods***

`Children.Add`—Adds the specified element to the `Canvas`.

`SetLeft`—Sets the left position of the specified element relative to the top-left corner of the `Canvas`.

`SetTop`—Sets the top position of the specified element relative to the top-left corner of the `Canvas`.

`Ellipse` The class that contains methods used to draw an ellipse.

- ***Properties***

`Fill`—Specifies the color of the ellipse.

`Width`—Specifies the width of the ellipse.

`Height`—Specifies the height of the ellipse.

Grid Grid This control allows the user to place elements into an invisible table which controls their positioning.

- ***Properties***

  `ColumnDefinition`—Specifies the properties of a column in a `Grid`, including width, height and positioning.

  `ColumnDefinitions`—A collection of the columns in a `Grid`.

GroupBox GroupBox This control groups related controls visually.

- ***In action***

- ***Properties***

  `Grid.Column`—Specifies the `Grid` column in which the `GroupBox` is contained.

  `Header`—Specifies the text displayed at the top of the `GroupBox`.

  `Height`—Specifies the height of the `GroupBox`.

  `HorizontalAlignment`—Specifies the horizontal alignment of the `GroupBox`.

  `Margin`—Specifies amount of space around the `GroupBox`.

  `Name`—Specifies the name used to access the `GroupBox` programmatically. The name should be appended with the `GroupBox` suffix.

  `VerticalAlignment`—Specifies the vertical alignment of the `GroupBox`.

  `Width`—Specifies the width of the `GroupBox`.

MouseButtonEventArgs The class that contains information about mouse events that involve a button press or release.

- ***Method***

  `GetPosition`—Returns a `Point` representing the position of the mouse pointer when the event occurred.

MouseEventArgs The class that contains information about mouse events.

- ***Method***

  `GetPosition`—Returns a `Point` representing the position of the mouse pointer when the event occurred.

Point The class that contains information representing a location in the application.

- ***Properties***

  `X`—Specifies the *x*-coordinate of the location.

  `Y`—Specifies the *y*-coordinate of the location.

RadioButton RadioButton This control allows enables users to select only one of several options.

- ***In action***

  Black

- ***Event***

  `Checked`—Raised when the user selects the `RadioButton`.

- ***Properties***

  `Content`—Specifies the text displayed to the right of the `RadioButton`.

`Height`—Specifies the height of the `RadioButton`.

`HorizontalAlignment`—Specifies the horizontal alignment of the `RadioButton`.

`IsChecked`—Specifies whether the `RadioButton` is selected.

`Margin`—Specifies amount of space around the `RadioButton`.

`Name`—Specifies the name used to access the `RadioButton` programmatically. The name should be appended with the `RadioButton` suffix.

`VerticalAlignment`—Specifies the vertical alignment of the `RadioButton`.

`Width`—Specifies the width of the `RadioButton`.

`StackPanel` StackPanel This control arranges its elements horizontally or vertically.

- ***Properties***

`Height`—Specifies the height of the `StackPanel`.

`HorizontalAlignment`—Specifies the horizontal alignment of the `StackPanel`.

`Margin`—Specifies amount of blank space around the `StackPanel`.

`Name`—Specifies the name used to access the `StackPanel` programmatically. The name should be appended with the `StackPanel` suffix.

`VerticalAlignment`—Specifies the vertical alignment of the `StackPanel`.

`Width`—Specifies the width of the `StackPanel`.

`Window` The class that represents an application's GUI.

- ***Properties***

`Class`—Specifies the Visual Basic class associated with the `Window`.

`Title`—Specifies the text displayed in the `Window`'s titlebar.

MULTIPLE-CHOICE QUESTIONS

27.1 The *x*- and *y*-coordinates of the `Point` object returned by the `GetPosition` method of class `MouseEventArgs` are relative to ________.

a) the screen
b) the application
c) the layout container that contains the control that raised the event
d) the control passed as an argument to `GetPosition`

27.2 The ________ property of the `Ellipse` class specifies the color of the ellipse.

a) `FillEllipse`
b) `Color`
c) `Brush`
d) `Fill`

27.3 The ________ object passed to a mouse event handler contains information about the mouse event that was raised.

a) `MouseArgs`
b) `MouseButtonEventArgs`
c) `MouseEventArgs`
d) Both b and c

27.4 The ________ event is raised when the right mouse button is pressed.

a) `MouseRightButtonDown`
b) `MouseRightClick`
c) `MouseRightDown`
d) `MouseRightPress`

27.5 A ________ object is used to fill a shape with color.

a) `Painter`
b) `Brush`
c) `FillColor`
d) `Marker`

27.6 A ________ event is raised every time the mouse interacts with a control.

a) control
b) mouse pointer
c) mouse
d) user

27.7 The ________ layout container arranges its elements either horizontally or vertically.

a) `Stack`
b) `Canvas`
c) `StackPanel`
d) `Grid`

27.8 The _________ is the default layout container in a WPF application.

a) `Canvas`
b) `Grid`
c) `StackPanel`
d) None of the above

27.9 The _________ layout container allows absolute positioning of its child elements.

a) `Grid`
b) `Canvas`
c) `StackPanel`
d) None of the above

27.10 The _________ content control may not be nested in any other control.

a) `GroupBox`
b) `Window`
c) Both of the above
d) Neither of the above

EXERCISES

27.11 ***(Line Length Application)*** The **Line Length** application will draw a straight black line on a `Canvas` and calculate the length of the line (Fig. 27.53). The line begins at the coordinates where the left mouse button is pressed and stops at the point where the left mouse button is released. The application displays the line's length (that is, the distance between the two endpoints) in the `Label` **Length =**. Use the following formula to calculate the line's length, where (x_1, y_1) is the first endpoint (the coordinates where the mouse button is pressed) and (x_2, y_2) is the second endpoint (the coordinates where the mouse button is released). To calculate the distance (or length) between the two points, use the equation:

$$d = \sqrt{(x_1 - x_2)^2 + (y_1 - y_2)^2}$$

To draw a straight line, you need to use the `Line` class. When drawing lines, use the `Stroke` property to specify the line's color rather than the `Fill` property. Use the `Line`'s `X1`, `Y1`, `X2` and `Y2` properties to specify its start point and end point. Then add it as a child of the `Canvas`.

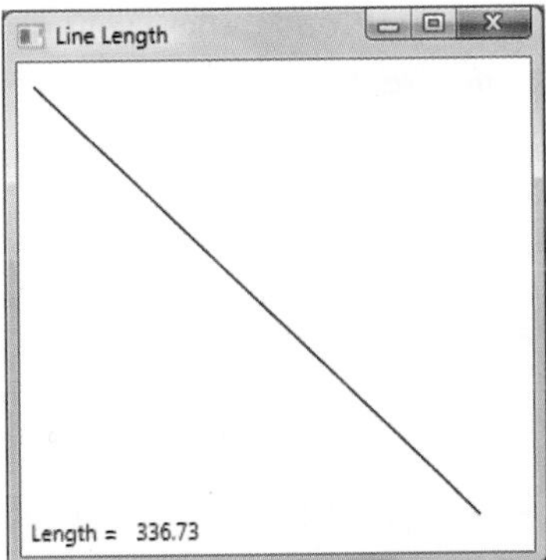

Figure 27.53 **Line Length** application's GUI.

a) ***Creating a new WPF application.*** Create a new WPF application and name it `LineLength`. Change the `Window`'s `Title` to `Line Length`.

b) ***Adding the layout containers.*** Add a `Canvas` to the WPF application's `Grid`. Name the `Canvas` `lineCanvas`. Add a `StackPanel` to the `Grid` and name it `outputStackPanel`—check the XAML to be sure the `StackPanel` is nested in the `Grid` element, not the `Canvas`.

c) ***Adding the output `Labels`.*** Add two `Labels` to the `StackPanel`. Name the first Label `lengthLabel` and set its `Content` property to `Length =`. Name the second `Label` `lengthOutputLabel` and delete the text in its `Content` property. Set the `Width` and `Height` properties of both `Labels` to `Auto`.

d) ***Setting properties of the layout containers.*** Set the `StackPanel`'s `Orientation` property to `Horizontal` to arrange its elements horizontally. Set the `Width` and `Height` properties to `Auto`. Set the `HorizontalAlignment` and `VerticalAlignment` properties to `Left` and `Bottom`, respectively. Set the `Margin` property to `0`. Set the

Canvas's `Width` and `Height` properties to `Auto`, and the `Margin` property to `0`. Set the Canvas's `Background` property to `White`.

e) ***Renaming the project files.*** Rename the `Window1.xaml` project file to `LineLength.xaml`. Change the startup URI to `LineLength.xaml`. Change the `Window`'s `Class` attribute to `LineLengthWindow`. Change the class name in the code-behind file to `LineLengthWindow`.

f) ***Declaring instance variables.*** Select **View > Code** to open the application's code-behind file. Change the class name to `LineLengthWindow`. Declare and initialize two `Point` variables in which you store the start points and end points of the `Line`.

g) ***Creating the `Length` method.*** Define a `Function` procedure named `Length` that uses the formula given in the exercise description to return the distance between two endpoints as a `Double`. The `Function` procedure should use the following statement to perform the line-length calculation, where `xDistance` is the difference between the two points' *x*-coordinates and `yDistance` is the difference between their *y*-coordinates:

```
Math.Sqrt((xDistance ^ 2) + (yDistance ^ 2))
```

h) ***Adding a `MouseLeftButtonDown` event handler.*** Create a `MouseLeftButtonDown` event handler for the `Canvas`. Add code to store the coordinates of the first endpoint of the line. Clear the `lengthOutputLabel` by setting its `Content` property to the empty `String`.

i) ***Adding a `MouseLeftButtonUp` event handler.*** Create a `MouseLeftButtonUp` event handler. First store the coordinates of the line's second endpoint. Then call the `Length` method to obtain the distance between the two endpoints (the line's length). Finally, display the line on the `Canvas` and the line's length in the **Length =** `Label`, as in Fig. 27.53.

j) ***Running the application.*** Select **Debug > Start Debugging** to run your application. Draw several lines and view their lengths. Verify that the length values are accurate.

k) ***Closing the application.*** Close your running application by clicking its close box.

l) ***Closing the IDE.*** Close the Visual Basic IDE by clicking its close box.

27.12 ***(Circle Painter Application)*** The **Circle Painter** application draws a blue circle of a randomly chosen size when the user presses the left mouse button anywhere over the `Canvas` (Fig. 27.54). The application randomly selects a circle diameter in the range from `5` to `199`, inclusive. Using the `Stroke` property rather than the `Fill` property of class `Ellipse` draws the outline of an ellipse. Recall that an ellipse is a circle if the height and width arguments are the same (in this case, the randomly selected `diameter`). Use the *x*- and *y*-coordinates of the `MouseLeftButtonDown` event as the *x*- and *y*-coordinates of the circle's bounding box.

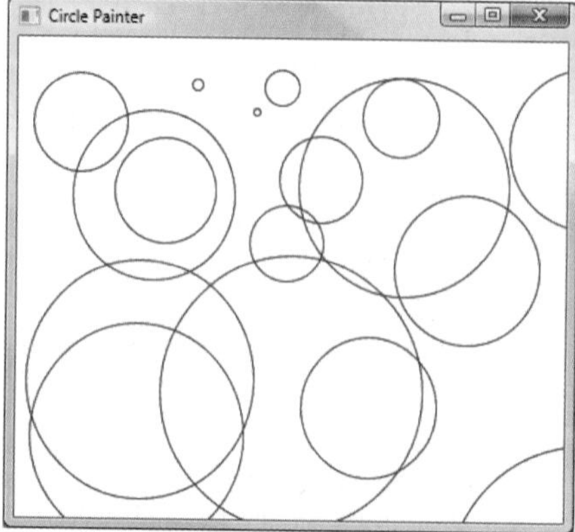

Figure 27.54 **Circle Painter** application's GUI.

a) ***Creating a new WPF application.*** Create a new WPF application and name it `CirclePainter`. Rename the `Window1.xaml` file to `CirclePainter.xaml`. Change the project's startup URI to `CirclePainter.xaml`. Change the `Window`'s `Title` to `Circle Painter` and its `Class` attribute to `CirclePainterWindow`. Change the class name in the code-behind file to `CirclePainterWindow`.

b) ***Adding a Canvas to the application.*** Add a `Canvas` to the application and name it `circleCanvas`. Set its `Margin` property to `0` so it fills the entire `Grid` cell in which it's contained. Set its `Background` property to `White`.

c) ***Creating the `PaintCircle` method.*** Create a `Sub` procedure called `PaintCircle` which takes as arguments a `Brush` and a `Point` object. The procedure paints a circle on the `Canvas` in the specified color at the specified location. Generate a random number to use as the circle's diameter, using a `Random` object, and store it in a variable. Create a new `Ellipse` object and set its `Width` and `Height` properties to the randomly generated diameter. Set its `Stroke` property to blue. Set its position using the coordinates of the `Point` passed as an argument.

d) ***Adding a `MouseLeftButtonDown` event handler.*** Create a `MouseLeftButtonDown` event handler. In the event handler, retrieve the *x*- and *y*-coordinates of the location of the mouse pointer when the left mouse button was pressed. Call method `PaintCircle` to paint a blue circle at the mouse pointer's position.

e) ***Running the application.*** Select **Debug > Start Debugging** to run your application. Draw several blue circles and make sure that they are of different sizes.

f) ***Closing the application.*** Close your running application by clicking its close box.

g) ***Closing the IDE.*** Close the Visual Basic IDE by clicking its close box.

27.13 ***(Advanced Circle Painter Application)*** In this exercise, you enhance the application you created in Exercise 27.12. The advanced **Circle Painter** application draws blue circles with randomly generated diameters when the user presses the left mouse button. When the user presses the right mouse button, the application draws a red circle with a randomly generated diameter (Fig. 27.55).

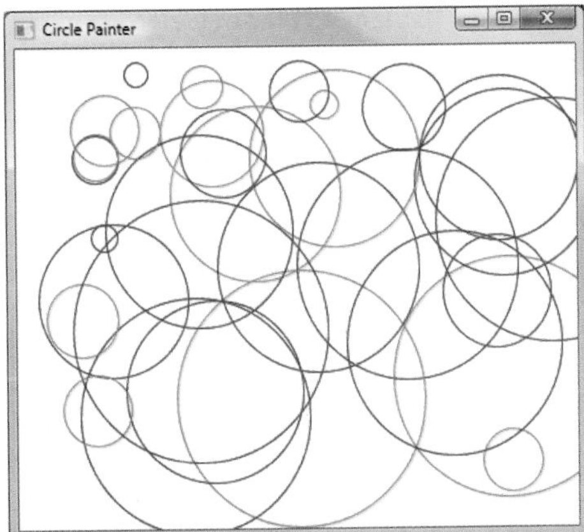

Figure 27.55 Advanced **Circle Painter** application's GUI.

a) ***Copying the template to your working directory.*** Make a copy of the `CirclePainter` directory from Exercise 27.12 in your `C:\SimplyVB2008` directory. Rename the copied directory `AdvancedCirclePainter`. If you have not completed Exercise 27.12, follow the steps in Exercise 27.12 to complete the application.

b) ***Opening the application's template file.*** Double click the `CirclePainter.sln` file in the `AdvancedCirclePainter` directory to open the application.

c) ***Drawing the appropriate circle.*** Create a `MouseRightButtonDown` event handler that draws a red circle at the mouse pointer's position when the right mouse button is pressed.

d) ***Running the application.*** Select **Debug > Start Debugging** to run your application. Draw several blue circles of different sizes using the left mouse button, then draw several red circles of different sizes using the right mouse button.

e) ***Closing the application.*** Close your running application by clicking its close box.

f) ***Closing the IDE.*** Close the Visual Basic IDE by clicking its close box.

What does this code do?

27.14 Consider the `MouseMove` event handler below. What happens when the user moves the mouse? Assume that `displayLabel` has been placed in the GUI.

```
Private Sub paintCanvas_MouseMove(ByVal sender As Object, _
   ByVal e As System.Windows.Input.MouseEventArgs)
   Handles paintCanvas.MouseMove

   Dim position As Point = e.GetPosition(paintCanvas)

   displayLabel.Content = "I'm at " & _
      position.X & ", " & position.Y & "."
End Sub ' paintCanvas_MouseMove
```

What's wrong with this code?

27.15 The following code should draw a solid `Blue` circle of diameter `5` that corresponds to the movement of the mouse. Find the error(s) in the code:

```
Private Sub paintCanvas_MouseMove(ByVal sender As Object, _
   ByVal e As System.Windows.Input.MouseEventArgs) _
   Handles paintCanvas.MouseMove

   Dim position As Point = e.GetPosition(paintCanvas)

   If shouldPaint = True Then
      ' create an Ellipse object
      Dim newEllipse As Ellipse = New Ellipse()

      ' set the Ellipse's properties
      newEllipse.Stroke = Brushes.Blue
      newEllipse.Width = 5
      newEllipse.Height = 10

      ' set the Ellipse's position
      Canvas.SetTop(newEllipse, position.X)
      Canvas.SetLeft(newEllipse, position.Y)

      ' attach the Ellipse to the Canvas
      paintCanvas.Children.Add(newEllipse)
   End If
End Sub ' PaintCanvas_MouseMove
```

Programming Challenge

27.16 ***(Advanced Painter Application)*** Extend the `Painter` application to enable a user to change the size of the circles drawn and to undo or clear the painting (Fig. 27.56).

Figure 27.56 **Advanced Painter** application's GUI.

a) ***Copying the template to your working directory.*** Copy the directory C:\Examples\Tutorial27\Exercises\AdvancedPainter to your C:\SimplyVB2008 directory.

b) ***Opening the application's template file.*** Double click AdvancedPainter.sln in the AdvancedPainter directory to open the application.

c) ***Adding the Size options.*** Add a GroupBox to the StackPanel in column 0 of the Grid. Change its Header property to **Size**, its Margin to 3 and its Width property to Auto. Add a StackPanel to the **Size** GroupBox and change its Width to Auto and its Margin to 3, then set the GroupBox's Height to Auto. Add three RadioButtons to the StackPanel, then set the StackPanel's Height property to Auto. Set the Width and Height of each RadioButton to Auto and the Margin to 3. Set the Content properties of the RadioButtons to Small, Medium and Large as in Fig. 27.56 and name each one accordingly. Set the IsChecked property of the **Medium** RadioButton to True.

d) ***Adding the Undo and Clear options.*** Add two Buttons to the StackPanel in column 0. Name the first Button undoButton and change its Content property to Undo. Set its Margin property to 3, 10, 3, 3 to add extra space between the **Undo** Button and the GroupBox above it. Name the second Button clearButton and change its Content property to Clear. Set its Margin to 3.

e) ***Declaring an enumeration to store the circle diameter sizes.*** Declare an enumeration Sizes to store the possible values of diameter. Set constant SMALL to 4, MEDIUM to 8 and LARGE to 10.

f) ***Adding event handlers for the Size RadioButtons.*** The **Size** RadioButton's event handlers should set instance variable diameter to Sizes.SMALL (for the **Small** RadioButton), Sizes.MEDIUM (for the **Medium** RadioButton) or Sizes.LARGE (for the **Large** RadioButton).

g) ***Coding the mouse event handlers.*** The MouseLeftButtonDown, MouseRightButtonDown, MouseLeftButtonUp and MouseRightButtonUp event handlers behave exactly as they do in the **Painter** application.

h) ***Coding the MouseMove event handler.*** The MouseMove event handler behaves the same way as the one in the **Painter** application. The color of the brush that draws the circle when shouldPaint is True is specified by brushColor. The eraser color is specified by the Canvas's Background property, and its size is specified by diameter.

i) ***Coding the Undo Button's event handler.*** The **Undo** Button's event handler removes the last circle added to the Canvas. Double click the **Undo** Button in **Design** view to generate its Click event handler. Use an If...Then statement to determine if there are any circles left on the Canvas. [*Hint:* The Canvas's Children property is a collection, so you can use the Count property to retrieve the number of items in Children.] Use the RemoveAt method of the Canvas's Children property to remove the last circle added.

j) ***Coding the Clear Button's event handler.*** The **Clear** Button's event handler should remove all the circles from the Canvas. Use the Clear method of the Canvas's Children property to remove all the circles from the Canvas.

k) ***Running the application.*** Select **Debug > Start Debugging** to run your application. Start drawing on the Canvas using different brush sizes and colors. Use the right mouse button to erase part of your drawing.

l) ***Closing the application.*** Close your running application by clicking its close box.

m) ***Closing the IDE.*** Close the Visual Basic IDE by clicking its close box.

28 TUTORIAL

Objectives

In this tutorial, you learn to:

- Understand the multitier architecture of data-driven web applications.
- Understand the process of requesting a resource from a web server and receiving a response from a web server.
- Use the ASP.NET Development Server that is built into Visual Web Developer 2008 Express to test web applications on your local computer.
- Use a web browser to interact with a web application.

Outline

Bookstore Web Application

Introducing Visual Web Developer 2008 Express and the ASP.NET Development Server

In previous tutorials, you used Visual Basic to develop Windows applications. Each application contained a GUI that enabled you interact with the application. With Visual Basic and Visual Web Developer 2008 Express (or a complete version of Visual Studio 2008) you can create **web applications** that use Microsoft's **ASP.NET 3.5** to create web content—data that can be viewed in a web browser such as Firefox or Internet Explorer. This web content includes HTML (HyperText Markup Language) documents and images.

In this tutorial and Tutorials 29–31, you learn important web-development concepts in the context of the **Bookstore** web application. This application consists of two web pages. The first page displays a list of books. The user selects a book, then clicks a `Button` to direct the browser to a second web page. In the second page, the server retrieves information about the selected book from a database then that information is displayed for the user in the web browser. The second web page also contains a `Button` that the user can click to return to the first web page, where the user can then select a different book. After learning the fundamental web-development concepts that are required to understand the **Bookstore** web application, you test-drive the application. In Tutorials 29–31, you analyze the pseudocode and ACE table and develop the **Bookstore** web application. At the end of Tutorial 31, we introduce Ajax programming with ASP.NET Ajax to help make the web application more responsive—Ajax helps make web applications feel more like desktop applications.

28.1 Multitier Architecture

Web applications are **multitier applications** that divide functionality into separate **tiers** (that is, logical groupings of functionality). Such applications are sometimes referred to as ***n*-tier applications**. The separate tiers of an application can be located on the same computer or on separate computers distributed across any computer network, including the Internet. Figure 28.1 illustrates the basic structure of a multitier application.

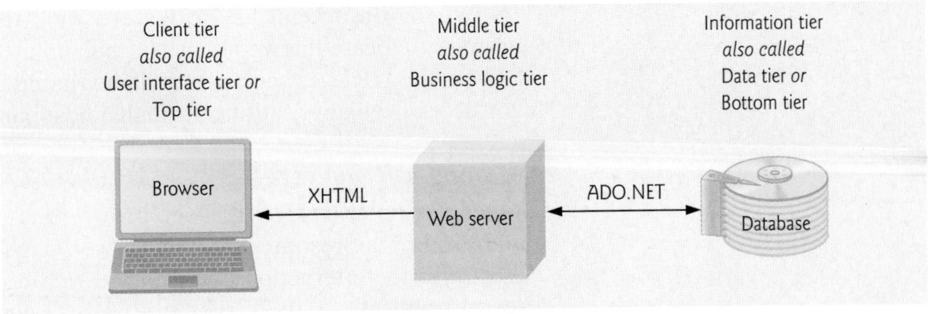

Figure 28.1 Three-tier application model.

The **information tier** (also called the **data tier** or the **bottom tier**) maintains data for the application. The information tier for the **Bookstore** web application is represented by a SQL Server Express database that contains book titles, author names, copyright dates, edition numbers, ISBN numbers, book descriptions and file names for each book's cover image.

The **middle tier**, also called the **business logic** tier, controls interactions between application clients (such as web browsers) and application data in the information tier. In the **Bookstore** web application, the middle-tier code determines which book was selected and which book's information is retrieved from the database. The middle-tier code also determines how the selected book's data is displayed. The middle tier processes client requests (for example, a request to view a book's information) from the top tier, which we define shortly, and retrieves data from the database (author names, prices, descriptions, etc.) in the information tier. The middle tier then processes data and presents the content to the client. In other words, the middle tier represents the functionality of the web application.

The **client tier**, or **top tier**, is the application's user interface, which is typically a web browser. In the **Bookstore** web application, the client tier is represented by the pages displayed in the web browser. The user interacts directly with the **Bookstore** web application through the client tier (browser) by selecting from a list and clicking `Button`s. The browser reports the user's actions to the middle tier, which processes the information. The middle tier can also make requests to and retrieve data from the information tier. The client tier then displays to the user the data retrieved by the middle tier from the information tier.

SELF-REVIEW

1. A database is located in the ________ tier.

   a) top
   b) middle
   c) information
   d) None of the above

2. The role of the middle tier is to ________.

   a) display the application's user interface
   b) provide a database for the application
   c) control the interaction between the client and information tiers
   d) control the interaction between the client and the user interface

Answers: 1) c. 2) c.

28.2 Web Servers

A **web server** is specialized software that responds to client (web browser) requests by providing requested resources (such as HTML documents). To request documents from web servers, users must know the locations at which those documents reside. A **URL (Uniform Resource Locator)** can be thought of as an address that directs a browser to a resource on the web. A URL contains a computer name (called a **host name**) or an **IP address** that identifies the computer on which the web server resides.

When you access the **Bookstore** web application, you provide a URL in a browser to locate the web pages of the application. In this tutorial, you use `localhost` in the URL—a special host name that identifies the local computer. Normally, you access web applications through a host name such as `www.deitel.com`.

Making a Request

When you enter a URL in a web browser, it interacts with a web server to retrieve and display the resource (such as a web page) specified by the URL. Figure 28.2 illustrates the interaction between the web browser (the client side) and the web-server application (the server side). The web browser uses the host name in the URL to locate the web server from which to request the resource. The remainder of the URL after the host name specifies the path to the resource. For example, in the URL `http://www.deitel.com/ResourceCenters.html`, `www.deitel.com` is the host name and `ResourceCenters.html` specifies the path to an HTML document on the web server—in this case, the document is located at the root level of the server. The web server uses the path information it receives as part of the request to locate the appropriate resource on the server.

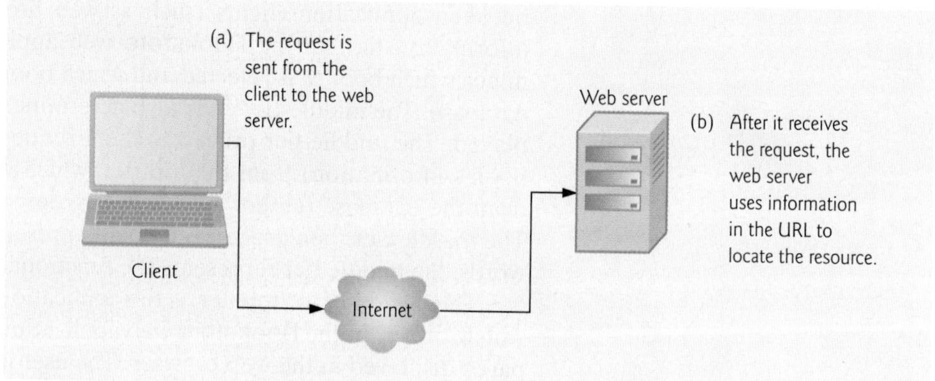
(a) The request is sent from the client to the web server.
Web server
(b) After it receives the request, the web server uses information in the URL to locate the resource.
Client
Internet

Figure 28.2 Client interacting with a web server. *Step 1:* The request.

Receiving a Response

Figure 28.3 depicts the server responding to a request. The server first sends a message to the client that includes a numeric code and a phrase describing the status of the request. If the request is successful, the server sends the contents of the requested resource to the client. The client-side browser then parses the content it receives and renders (or displays) the results in the browser window. Otherwise, the web browser typically displays a message indicating that the resource was not found.

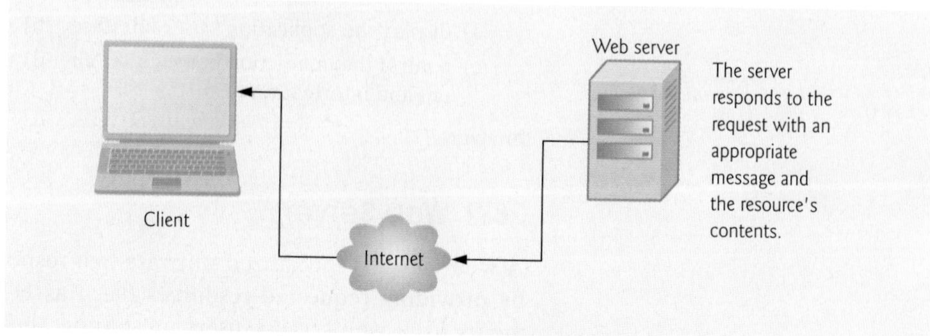
Web server
The server responds to the request with an appropriate message and the resource's contents.
Client
Internet

Figure 28.3 Client interacting with a web server. *Step 2:* The response.

SELF-REVIEW

1. A(n) ________ is software that responds to client requests.
   a) HTML document
   b) web browser
   c) host name
   d) web server

2. A(n) ________ specifies the computer on which the web server resides.
   a) HTML document
   b) web browser
   c) host name
   d) web server

Answers: 1) d. 2) c.

28.3 Visual Web Developer 2008 Express and the ASP.NET Development Server

In Tutorials 28–31, you use **Visual Web Developer 2008 Express** (which we refer to as Visual Web Developer from this point forward) to test-drive and build the **Bookstore** web application. Visual Web Developer (which is located on the DVD supplied with this book and can be downloaded from `www.microsoft.com/express/`) includes the **ASP.NET Development Server**—a web server you can use to test your ASP.NET web applications. Follow the instructions in the Before You Begin section of the book (just after the Preface) to ensure that you have Visual Web Developer installed. If you have a full Visual Studio 2008 product, you do not need to install Visual Web Developer.

The ASP.NET Development Server is designed for learning and testing purposes. It allows you to execute web applications on your computer and to respond to requests from browsers on the same computer. Thus, you do not need to be connected to a network to learn web-application-development techniques. Unfortunately, the ASP.NET Development Server cannot respond to requests from other computers. After successfully creating an ASP.NET web application, you can use Visual Web Developer's "Copy Web Site" capability to publish your application to a Microsoft **Internet Information Services (IIS)** web server so that your application can receive requests from any client on the web. Since the web application you build uses ASP.NET 3.5, the server must have the .NET Framework version 3.5 installed.

28.4 Test-Driving the Bookstore Web Application

In the next three tutorials, you build an application that displays book information to users upon request. Your **Bookstore** web application must meet the following requirements:

Application Requirements

A bookstore employee receives e-mails from customers asking for information pertaining to the books the store provides online. Responding to the numerous e-mails can be a tedious and time-consuming task. The employee has asked you to create a web application that allows users to view information about various books online. This information includes the book's cover image, author(s), ISBN number, edition number, copyright date and a brief description of the book.

The **Bookstore** web application uses ASP.NET and is designed to allow users to view information about the books offered by the store. You begin by test-driving the completed application. Then, you learn the additional ASP.NET technologies that you need to create your own version of this application.

Test-Driving the Completed Bookstore Web Application

1. ***Opening the Bookstore project.*** In Visual Web Developer, select **File > Open Web Site...** to display the **Open Web Site** dialog. In the dialog (Fig. 28.4), click the **File System** button, browse to `C:\Examples\Tutorial28\CompletedApplication` and select the `Bookstore` folder that contains the web application. Then click the **Open** button.

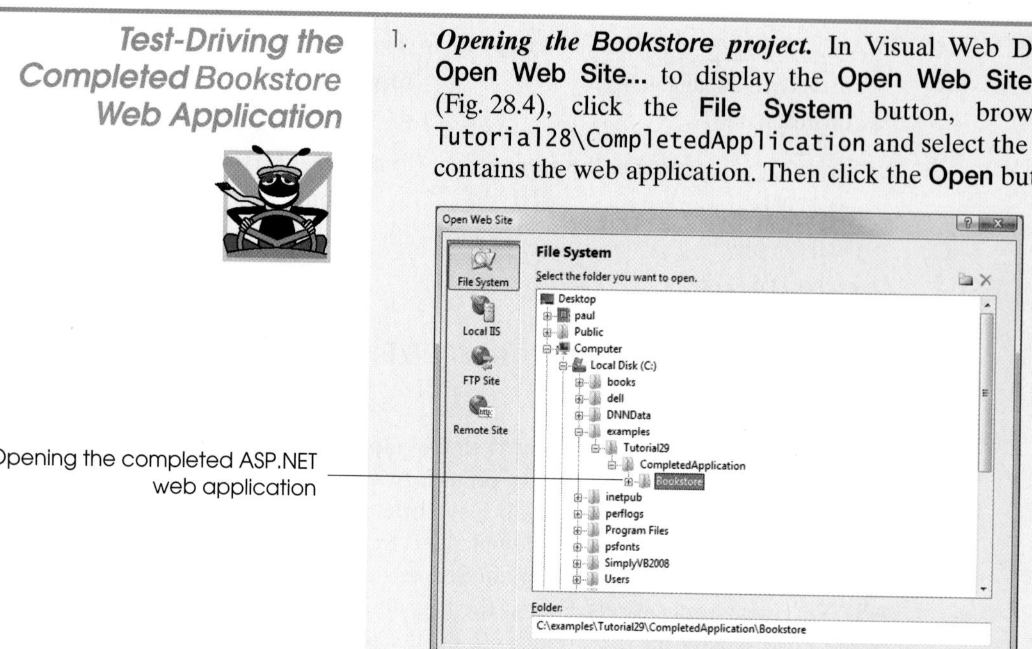
Opening the completed ASP.NET web application

Figure 28.4 Opening the `Bookstore` web application.

2. ***Setting the start page.*** The start page is the first page that loads when you execute the application. To specify the start page, right click the `Books.aspx` file in the **Solution Explorer** and select **Set As Start Page** (Fig. 28.5). Files with the extension `.aspx` (usually referred to as **Web Forms**, **Web Form Pages** or **ASPX pages**) contain the web page's GUI. The Web Form file represents the web page that is sent to the client browser. [*Note:* From this point onward, we refer to Web Form files as ASPX pages.] A web application can contain several ASPX pages. In this example, `Books.aspx` displays the available books to the user. The page `BookInformation.aspx` displays information about the selected book. You must set `Books.aspx` to appear first so the user can select a book.

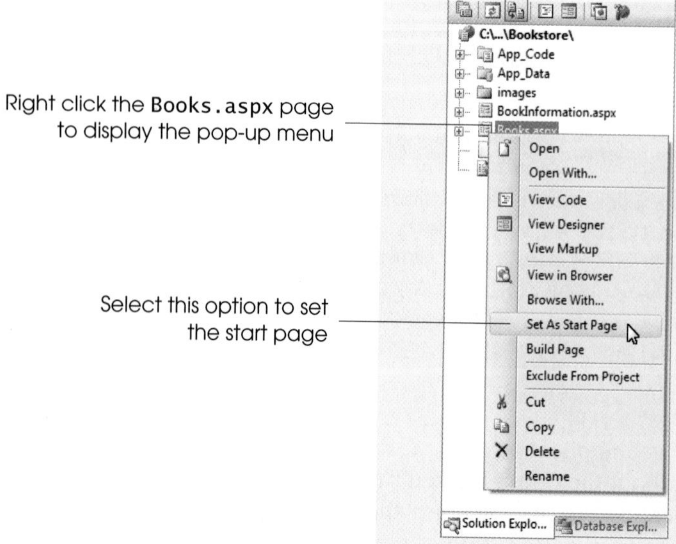
Right click the Books.aspx page to display the pop-up menu
Select this option to set the start page

Figure 28.5 Setting `Books.aspx` as the web application's start page.

(cont.)

3. ***Running the application.*** Select **Debug > Start Debugging** to run the application. The `Books.aspx` page appears in Internet Explorer, as shown in Fig. 28.6. This page displays a `ListBox` containing the available books. Although this `ListBox` looks similar to the `ListBox` control you've used in Windows applications, this `ListBox` is actually a **web control** (also called an **ASP.NET server control**). Programmers customize ASPX pages by adding web controls, such as `Label`s, `TextBox`es, `Button`s and others. Web controls look similar to their Windows Forms counterparts.

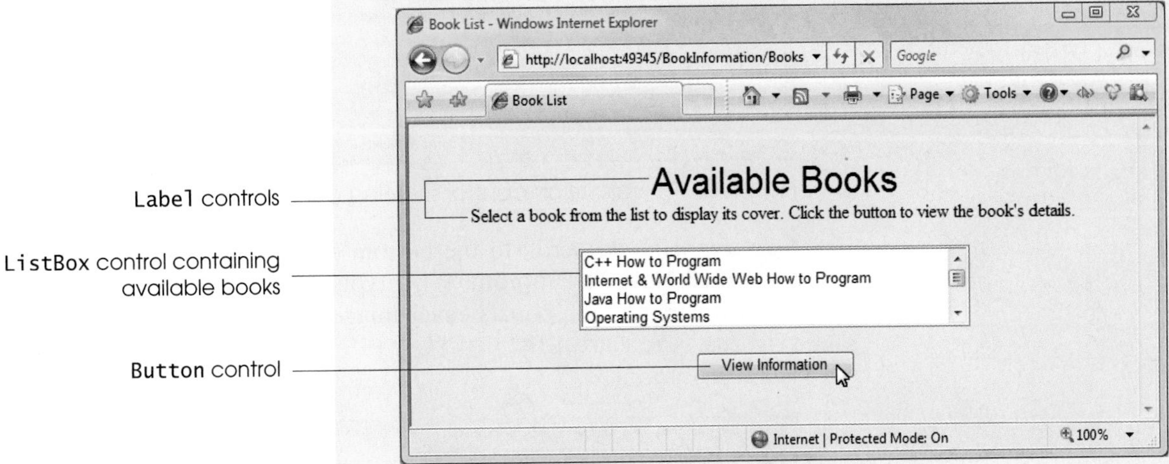

Figure 28.6 Page that displays a list of available books.

Internet Explorer and its HTML content represent the client tier. In Tutorial 29, you add web controls, such as `Label`s to display text, a `ListBox` to display the list of available books, `Button`s to load a different page and a `DetailsView` to display information on a particular book.

The books displayed in the `ListBox` are retrieved from a database using a LINQ to SQL data source. The database, named `Bookstore.mdf`, is the information tier of this three-tier application. Although only the book titles are displayed in the `ListBox`, the database includes other information. In Tutorial 30, you examine the application's information tier and learn how to connect to the database to access the data.

4. ***Attempting to press the View Information `Button` before selecting a book.*** Press the **View Information** `Button` without selecting a book. The page responds by indicating that you must select a book first (Fig. 28.7). This is an example of an ASP.NET **`RequiredFieldValidator`** control—one of several ASP.NET validation controls you can see in the **Validation** section of the **Toolbox**. A **validation control** determines whether the data in another web control exists, is in the proper format, has the proper value or is within the proper range of values. For example, validation controls could determine whether a user provided information in a required field or whether a zip-code field contains exactly five digits. Validation controls validate user input in the web browser before the user submits a Web Form to the server (in our case, by clicking the **View Information** `Button`). This gives this user immediate feedback on the data they input—they don't have to wait for the server to validate the data, then send a response indicating that the data is invalid. When the ASP.NET server creates a web page to send to the client, it converts each validation control into JavaScript that executes in the web browser. However, some clients do not support scripting or disable it. So, for security reasons, validation is always performed on the server, too—whether or not scripting is enabled on the client.

(cont.)

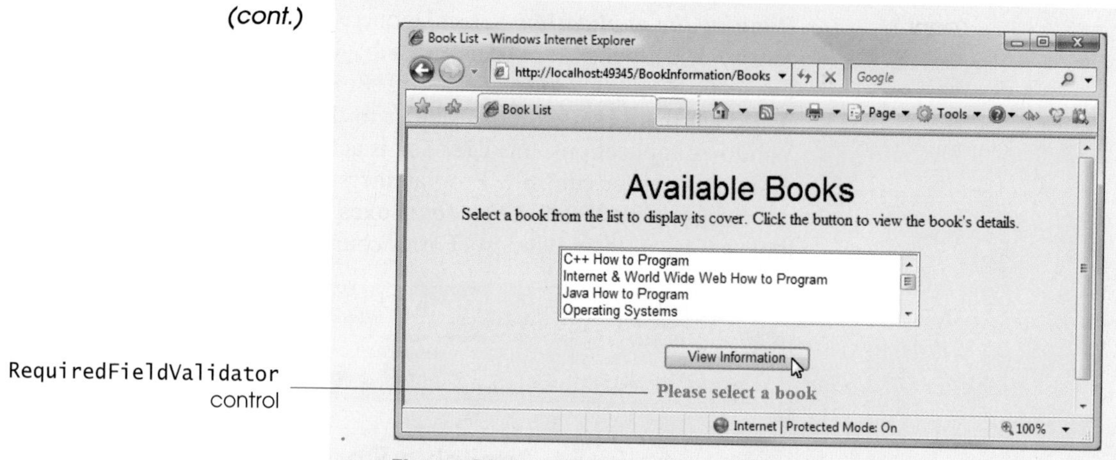

Figure 28.7 Validation control showing an error message.

5. ***Selecting a book.*** Scroll to the bottom of the `ListBox` and select **Visual C++ 2008 How To Program**. When you select a book an `ItemSelected` event occurs and the book's cover image is displayed below the `ListBox` (Fig. 28.8). You use LINQ to SQL to obtain the appropriate image file name in Tutorial 31.

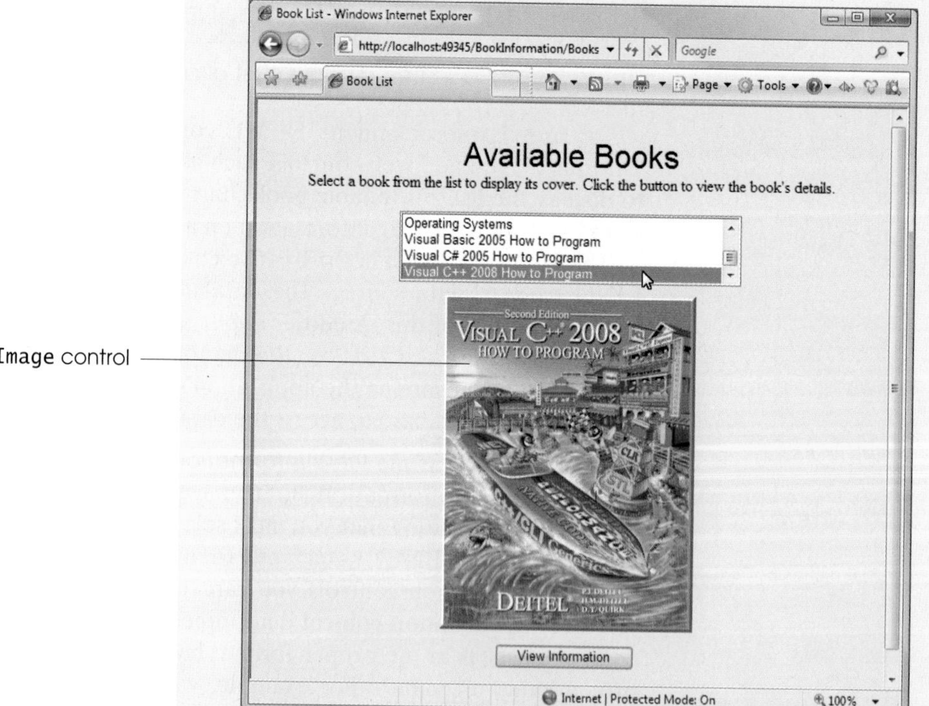

Figure 28.8 Displaying the selected book's cover image.

6. ***Viewing the book's details.*** Click the **View Information** `Button` to display the `BookInformation.aspx` page (Fig. 28.9), which displays the selected book's title, author and cover image. This page also contains a table that lists the selected book's copyright date, edition number, ISBN number and a description of the book. In Tutorial 31, you use a technique called session tracking to pass the product ID of the selected book from the `Books.aspx` page to the `BookInformation.aspx` page. You then obtain the product ID in the `BookInformation.aspx` page and use it with LINQ to SQL to obtain the detailed information about the book from the database.

(cont.)

When clicked, this **Button** returns user to **Books.aspx**

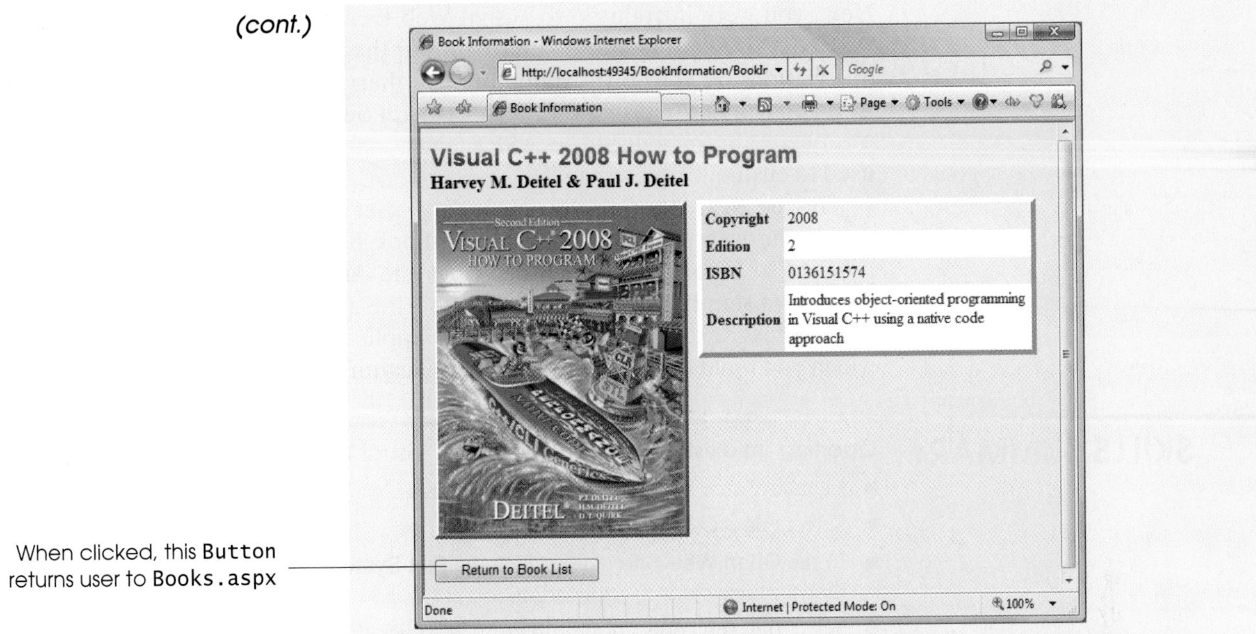

Figure 28.9 Page that displays the selected book's information.

7. ***Returning to Books.aspx.*** After viewing a book's information, you can decide whether you wish to view another book's information. The bottom of this page contains a **Return to Book List** `Button` that redirects the browser back to the `Books.aspx` page to redisplay the list of book titles.
8. ***Closing the browser.*** Click the browser's close box to close the browser window. This terminates debugging in Visual Web Developer.
9. ***Closing the IDE.*** Close the IDE by clicking its close box.

This example uses all three tiers of a three-tier application. The information tier is the database from which the application retrieves book information. The middle tier is the code that controls what happens when you interact with the application's web pages. The client tier is represented by the web pages in which you select a book and view its information.

SELF-REVIEW

1. Web controls also are called _________.
   a) ASP.NET server controls
   b) ASP controls
   c) HTML controls
   d) None of the above
2. In real-world ASP .NET applications, typically clients are _________ that request ASPX pages that reside on web servers.
   a) Web Form pages
   b) web controls
   c) web browsers
   d) None of the above

Answers: 1) a. 2) c.

28.5 Wrap-Up

In this tutorial, you learned about the components of a three-tier application. You were introduced to the information tier, which maintains the data for the application. You then learned about the client tier, which displays the application's user interface, and the middle tier, which provides the communication between the information and client tiers. You also learned how a web browser (the client) makes a request of a web server and how the web server responds to the web browser.

Next, you were introduced to Visual Web Developer 2008 Express and its built-in ASP.NET Development Server. Together, these enable you to build and test web applications on your own computer. You then test-drove the three-tier **Bookstore** web application. In doing this, you learned how to run ASP.NET web applications. You were also introduced to ASPX pages, and you learned that web controls are used to customize these pages.

In the next tutorial, you create the user interface for this application. You design the web pages that display the book list and book information. You then proceed to Tutorial 30, which describes the database used in the application and provides a step-by-step discussion of how the application connects to the database. Our discussion of the **Bookstore** web application concludes with Tutorial 31, in which you build the **Bookstore** web application's middle-tier logic.

SKILLS SUMMARY

Opening an existing web application in Visual Web Developer 2008 Express

- Launch Visual Web Developer 2008 Express.
- Select **File > Open Web Site...**.
- In the **Open Web Site** dialog, click the **File System** button, then browse to the directory that contains the web application.
- Select the web application's directory and click the **Open** button.

Setting the Start Page for a web application

- In Visual Web Developer, right click the start page in the **Solution Explorer** window.
- Select **Set As Start Page**.

Testing the web application, using the built-in ASP.NET Development Server

- Open the application in Visual Web Developer 2008 Express.
- Select **Debug > Start Debugging** to run the application and display the start page in Internet Explorer.

KEY TERMS

ASP.NET Development Server—A web server that you can use to test your ASP.NET web applications. It is specifically designed for learning and testing purposes to execute web applications on the local computer and to respond to browser requests from the local computer.

ASP.NET 3.5 technology—Can be combined with Visual Basic to create web applications.

ASP.NET server control—Another name for a web control.

`.aspx` extension—The file-name extension for ASP.NET Web Forms pages.

ASPX page—File that specifies the GUI of a web page using web controls. Also called Web Forms or Web Form Pages.

bottom tier—The tier (also known as the information tier, or the data tier) containing the application data of a multitier application—typically implemented as a database

business logic tier—The tier that controls interaction between the client and information tiers. Also called the middle tier.

client tier—The user interface of a multitier application (also called the top tier).

data tier—The tier (also known as the information tier, or the bottom tier) containing the application data of a multitier application, typically implemented as a database.

host name—Name of a computer where resources reside.

information tier—Tier containing the application data; typically implemented as a database. Also called the bottom tier or data tier.

Internet Information Services (IIS)—A Microsoft web server.

IP address—Unique address used to locate a computer on the Internet.

`localhost`—Host name that identifies the local computer.

middle tier—Tier that controls interaction between the client and information tiers (also called the business logic tier).

multitier application—Application (sometimes referred to as an *n*-tier application) whose functionality is divided into separate tiers, which can be on the same machine or can be distributed to separate machines across a network.

***n*-tier application**—Another name for a multitier application.

`RequiredFieldValidator` control—A validation control which ensures that a web control contains data before the user can submit a web form to a web server.

top tier—Tier containing the application's user interface. Also called the client tier.

uniform resource locator (URL)—Address that can be used to direct a browser to a resource on the web.

Visual Web Developer 2008 Express—A Microsoft tool for building ASP.NET 3.5 web applications.

web applications—Applications that create web content.

web controls—Controls, such as `TextBox`es and `Button`s, that are used to customize ASPX pages.

Web Form—Another name for an ASPX page.

Web Form page—Another name for an ASPX page.

web server—Specialized software that responds to client requests by providing resources.

MULTIPLE-CHOICE QUESTIONS

28.1 ASPX pages have the ________ extension.

a) `.html` b) `.wbform`
c) `.vbaspx` d) `.aspx`

28.2 ________ applications divide functionality into separate tiers.

a) *n*-tier b) Multitier
c) Both a and b d) None of the above

28.3 All tiers of a multitier application ________.

a) must be located on the same computer
b) must be located on different computers
c) can be located on the same computer or on different computers
d) must be arranged so that the client and middle tier are on the same computer and the information tier is on a different computer

28.4 The client tier interacts with the ________ tier to access information from the ________ tier.

a) middle; information b) information; middle
c) information; bottom d) bottom; information

28.5 A ________ is software that responds to client requests by providing resources.

a) web server b) host name
c) Both a and b d) None of the above

28.6 A(n) ________ can be thought of as an address that is used to direct a browser to a resource on the web.

a) middle tier b) ASPX page
c) URL d) query string

28.7 ________ is a web server.

a) IIS b) Visual Web Developer 2008 Express
c) Both a and b d) None of the above

28.8 The ________ tier is the application's user interface.

a) middle b) client
c) bottom d) information

28.9 The ________ tier contains the application's business logic.

a) middle
b) client
c) top
d) information

28.10 The ________ tier contains the application's data.

a) middle
b) client
c) top
d) information

EXERCISES

28.11 *(Phone Book Application)* Over the next three tutorials, you create a **PhoneBook** application. This application should consist of two ASPX pages, named `PhoneBook` and `PhoneNumber`. The `PhoneBook` page displays a `DropDownList` (a Web control similar to a `ComboBox` Windows `Form` control) that contains the names of several people. The names are retrieved from the `Phone.mdf` database. When a name is selected and the **Get Number** `Button` is clicked, the client browser is redirected to the `PhoneNumber` page. The telephone number of the selected name should be retrieved from the database and displayed in a `Label` on the `PhoneNumber` page. For this exercise, you need only organize the components (`PhoneBook` and `PhoneNumber` ASPX pages, `Phone.mdf` database and the code that performs the specified functionality) of this web application into separate tiers. Decide which components belong in which tiers. You will begin building the solution using Visual Web Developer in the next tutorial.

28.12 *(US State Facts Application)* Over the next three tutorials, you will create a **US State Facts** application. This application is designed to allow users to review their knowledge about specific U.S. states. This application should consist of two ASPX pages. The first page (named `States`) should display a `ListBox` containing 10 different state names. These state names are stored in the `StateFacts.mdf` database. The user should be allowed to select a state name and click a `Button` to retrieve information about the selected state from the database. The information should be displayed on a different ASPX page (named `StateFacts`). The `StateFacts` page should display an image of the state flag and list the state capital, state flower, state tree and state bird (retrieved from the database). You will be provided with images of the state flags. For this exercise, you need only organize the components (`States` and `StateFacts` ASPX pages, `StateFacts.mdf` database and the code that performs the specified functionality) of this web application into separate tiers. Decide which components belong in which tiers. You will begin building the solution using Visual Web Developer in the next tutorial.

TUTORIAL 29

Bookstore Web Application: Client Tier

Introducing Web Controls

Objectives

In this tutorial, you learn to:

- Create an **ASP.NET Web Site** project in Visual Web Developer 2008 Express.
- Create and design ASPX pages.
- Use Web Form controls.
- Specify the look-and-feel of controls, using the `CssStyle` attribute and control properties.

Outline

In this tutorial, you create the client tier (user interface) of your three-tier **Bookstore** web application, using visual-programming techniques. You begin by creating the application's **ASP.NET Web Site** project. You then learn about web controls by creating the application's GUI.

29.1 Analyzing the Bookstore Web Application

Now that you have taken the three-tier **Bookstore** web application (in Tutorial 28) for a test-drive, you need to analyze the application components. The following pseudocode describes the application's basic operation:

```
When the Books page is requested
    Retrieve the book titles from the database
    Display book titles in a ListBox

When the user selects a book title from the ListBox
    Display the book's cover image below the ListBox in an Image

When the user clicks the View Information Button
    If the user did not select a book from the ListBox
        Display an error message
    Otherwise
        Store the selected book's product ID
        Redirect the browser to the BookInformation page

When the BookInformation page is requested
    Retrieve the selected book's information from the database
    Display the book title in a Label
    Display the authors in a Label
    Display the cover art in an Image
    Display the remaining information in a DetailsView

When the user clicks the Return to Book List Button on the
BookInformation page
    Redirect the browser back to the Books page
```

The ACE table in Fig. 29.1 lists the actions, controls and events that help you complete your own version of this application.

Action/Control/Event (ACE) Table for the Bookstore Web Application

Action	Control/Object	Event
Label the Books page	`availableLabel`, `instructionsLabel`	
	`Page`	`Load` (for `Books.aspx`)
Retrieve the book titles from the database	`linqDataSource`	
Display book titles in a ListBox	`bookTitlesListBox`	
	`bookTitlesListBox`	`SelectedIndex-Changed`
Display the book's cover image below the ListBox in an Image	`bookTitlesListBox`, db (an object of class `BookInformationDB-DataContext`), `coverImage`	
	`informationButton`	`Click`
If the user did not select a book from the ListBox	`bookTitlesListBox`	
Display an error message	`bookRequiredField-Validator`	
Otherwise		
Store the selected book's product ID in a session variable	`bookTitlesListBox`, `Session`	
Redirect the browser to the BookInformation page	`Response`	
	`Page`	`Load` (for `Book-Information.aspx`)
Retrieve the selected book's information from the database	db (an object of class `BookInformationDB-DataContext`), `Session`	
Display the book title in a Label	`bookTitleLabel`	
Display the authors in a Label	`authorsLabel`	
Display the cover art in an Image	`bookImage`	
Display the remaining information in a DetailsView	`linqDataSource`, `bookDetailsView`	
	`bookListButton`	`Click`
Redirect the client browser back to the Books page	`Response`	

Figure 29.1 ACE table for the web-based **Bookstore** web application.

29.2 Creating ASPX Pages

Now that you've been introduced to Visual Web Developer, the ASP.NET Development Server and three-tier web-based application concepts, you begin creating the **Bookstore** web application that you test-drove in the last tutorial.

This web-based application allows users to view information about books they select. Users can then return to the page containing the list of books and select another book. You create the **ASP.NET Web Site project** for the **Bookstore** in the following box.

[*Note:* As you preceed through this case study, be sure to format your code as we show in the screen captures, so that your line numbers match up with the steps in the text.]

Creating an ASP.NET Web Site Project

1. ***Creating the project.*** In Visual Web Developer, select **File > New Web Site...** to display the **New Web Site** dialog (Fig. 29.2). In this dialog, select **ASP.NET Web Site** in the **Templates:** pane. Then select **File System** in the **Location:** drop-down list to create a web application on your local disk drive. We are using **File System** so you can run the web application on your local computer. You can specify the location of the project in the **Location:** `TextBox`. To create a **Bookstore** folder in the **C:\SimplyVB2008** directory to store your new website, type `C:\SimplyVB2008\Bookstore` in the **Location:** `TextBox`. Select **Visual Basic** in the **Language:** `TextBox` to use Visual Basic to program in the code-behind files that provide the ASPX page's functionality. Code-behind files will be discussed further in Tutorial 31. Click **OK** to create the project.

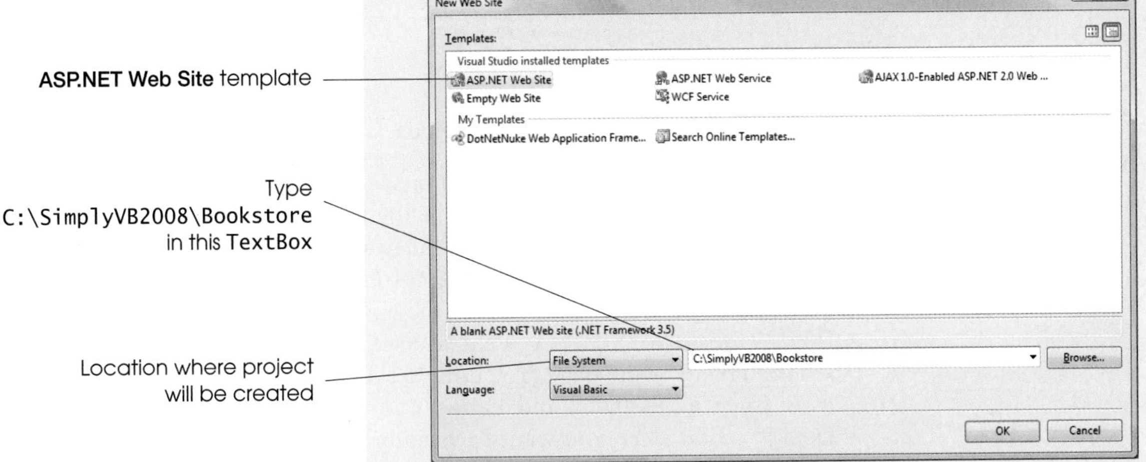

Figure 29.2 Creating an **ASP.NET Web Site** in Visual Web Developer.

2. ***Examining the project files.*** The **Solution Explorer** window for the **Bookstore** web application is shown in Fig. 29.3. As with Windows applications, Visual Web Developer creates several files for each new **ASP.NET Web Application** project. `Default.aspx` is the default name for the ASPX page and `web.config` specifies configuration options for the web application.

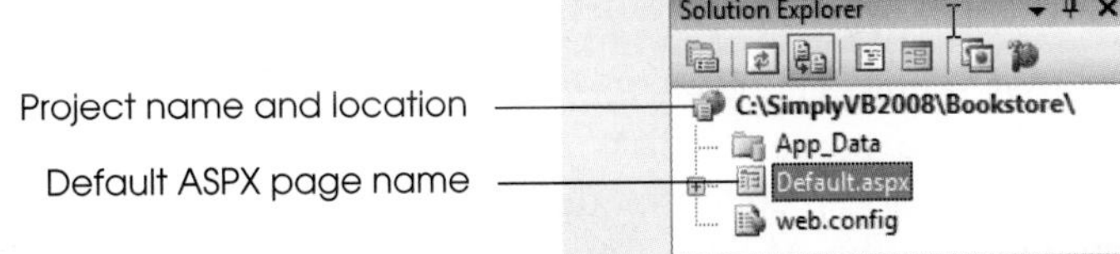

Figure 29.3 **Solution Explorer** window for the `Bookstore` project.

3. ***Viewing the Toolbox.*** ASPX pages can be customized by using **web controls**, which are used in ASPX pages in much the same way as Windows controls are used for Windows Forms. You use web controls to create the user interface of your **Bookstore** web application. Figure 29.4 shows the **Standard** controls listed in the **Toolbox**. If the **Toolbox** is not currently displayed, select **View > Toolbox**.

   The left part of the figure displays the beginning of the **Standard** controls list, and the right part of the figure displays the remaining web controls and other web control groups. Note that some controls, such as `Label`, `TextBox` and `Button`, have the same names as their Windows `Forms` counterparts. However, the functionality provided by web controls is different. Web controls can be used only with ASPX pages.

(cont.)

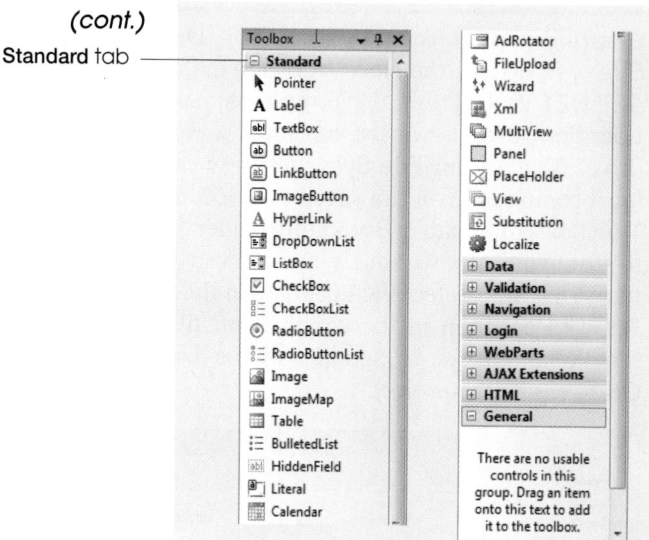

Figure 29.4 **Web Forms** tab in **Toolbox**.

4. ***Viewing the ASPX page in Design mode.*** When you create a web application, an ASPX page is displayed in the **Web Form Designer** (Fig. 29.5). [*Note:* We don't apply a `Lucida` font to the word "Form" in "Web Form Designer" because Web Forms are not instances of class `Form`.] The Web Form Designer contains three viewing modes. The **Design mode** (Fig. 29.5) is a WYSIWYG (what you see is what you get) editor that consists of a blank white page. You double click or drag and drop **Toolbox** controls (such as `Buttons` and `Labels`) to display them on the form. Use **Design** mode when you want to visually create the ASPX page's GUI by dragging and dropping web controls onto the ASPX page.

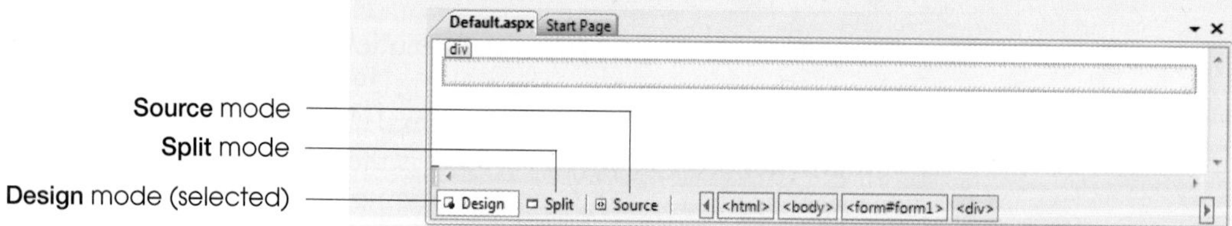

Figure 29.5 **Design** mode of Web Form Designer.

5. ***Switching to Split mode.*** The Web Form Designer also can display the ASPX page in **Source** mode or **Split** mode (Fig. 29.6). **Source mode** shows the ASP.NET markup code that defines the look-and-feel of a web page. **Split mode** shows the ASP.NET markup and the WYSIWYG design of the page. Click the **Split** button. **Split** mode is preferred by many developers. (We primarily use **Design** mode in this tutorial.) Unlike the Windows `Forms` Designer, you can also drag and drop controls from the **Toolbox** in **Source** mode.

   ASPX pages are defined using a combination of HTML and ASP.NET markup. (We reformatted lines 1–5 of the markup in Fig. 29.6 for readability.) The ASP.NET web controls that you add to your page are placed in the `div` element (lines 13–15 of Fig. 29.6), which appears in **Design** mode as a dotted rectangle. ASP.NET markup represents instructions processed on the web server. These instructions become part of your ASP.NET Web Forms page's class definition, which translates ASP.NET markup on the web server into HTML controls and content for rendering in a web browser. This content is sent to a browser client as part of a response to a client request.

(cont.)

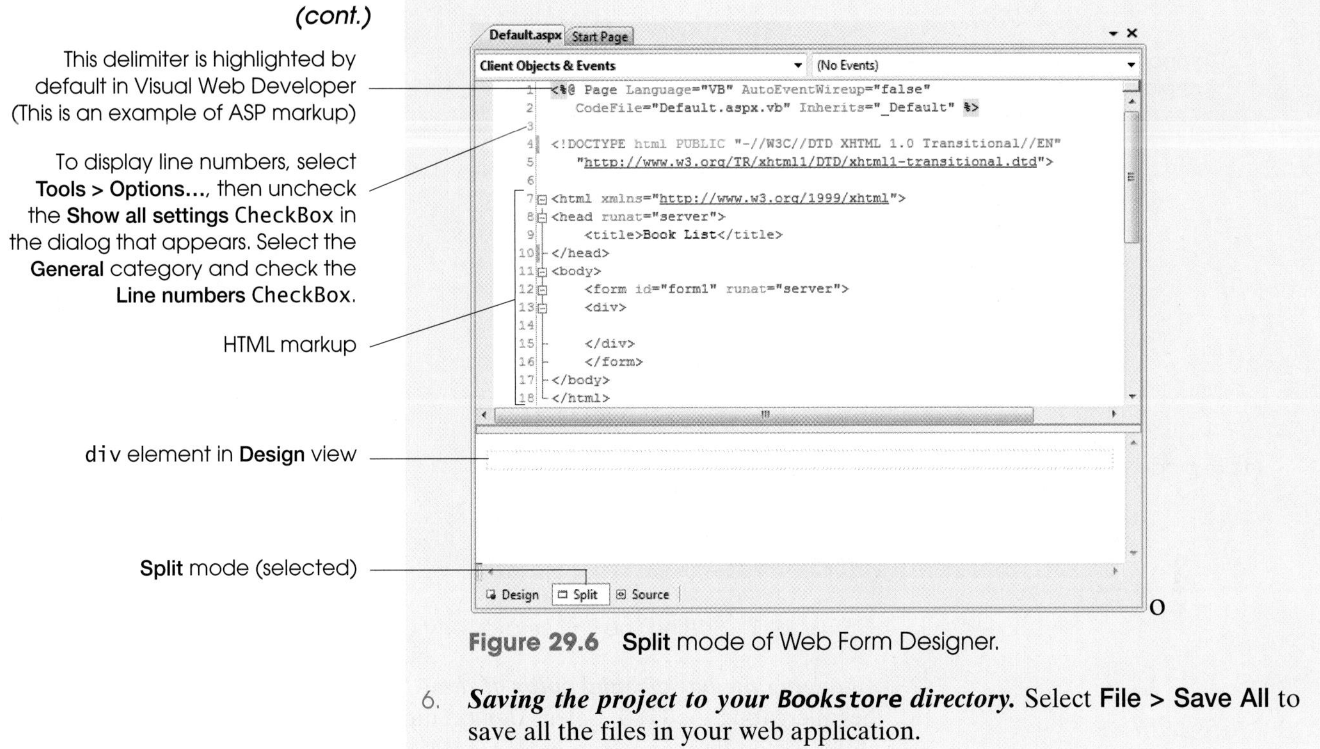
This delimiter is highlighted by default in Visual Web Developer (This is an example of ASP markup)
To display line numbers, select Tools > Options..., then uncheck the Show all settings CheckBox in the dialog that appears. Select the General category and check the Line numbers CheckBox.
HTML markup
div element in Design view
Split mode (selected)
Default.aspx
Start Page
Client Objects & Events
(No Events)
Design
Split
Source

Figure 29.6 **Split** mode of Web Form Designer.

6. ***Saving the project to your Bookstore directory.*** Select **File > Save All** to save all the files in your web application.

SELF-REVIEW

1. _________ mode allows you to view the ASPX page's markup.
   a) **Source** b) **Split**
   c) **Design** d) Both a and b

2. Some web control names are the same as Windows control names, _________.
   a) because their functionality is the same
   b) but the functionality provided by web controls is different
   c) because both web controls and Windows controls can be used in web applications
   d) None of the above

Answers: 1) d. 2) b.

29.3 Designing the Books.aspx Page

The **Bookstore** web application consists of two ASPX pages—`Books.aspx` and `BookInformation.aspx`—that display the list of available books and the information about the selected book, respectively. You design the `Books.aspx` page in the following box.

Creating the Books.aspx Page

Good Programming Practice

Change the ASPX page's name to a unique and meaningful name for easy identification.

1. ***Renaming the ASPX page.*** After you've viewed the contents of the default ASPX page (`Default.aspx`), you should give this ASPX page a meaningful name. Select the `Default.aspx` file in the **Solution Explorer** window and rename it to `Books.aspx`. In **Design** mode, click the Web Form Designer. The properties of the ASPX page should display in the **Properties** window. Note that ASPX pages are listed with the identifier **DOCUMENT** in the Component Object Box (Fig. 29.7). Select the **Title** property, and change `Untitled Page` to `Book List` to set the text that is displayed in the client browser's title bar.

(cont.)

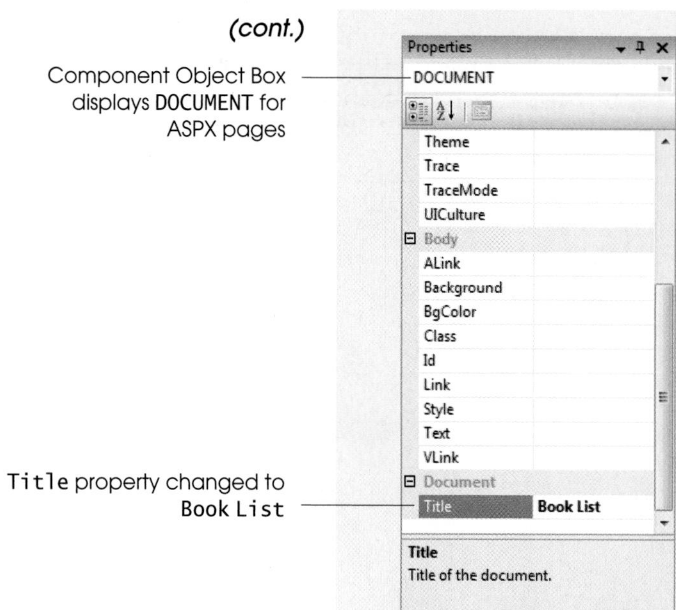

Figure 29.7 Setting the `Title` property of `Books.aspx`.

2. ***Changing the background color of the ASPX page.*** Now you are ready to begin creating the GUI. Select **Design** mode in the IDE. You use the **New Style** dialog to change the background color of the `Books.aspx` page to light blue. Select **Format > New Style...** to display the **New Style dialog**. In the dialog, select **body** from the **Selector** `ComboBox`, then click **Background** in the **Category** `ListBox`. Type `#CCFFFF` into the **background-color** `ComboBox` to specify a light blue color. Click **OK**. This creates a **`style` element** (lines 10–15) in the `head` element of the page and immediately changes the background color of the page (Fig. 29.8). The `style` element defines **CSS (Cascading Style Sheets)** styles that specify the look-and-feel of elements in the page. For more information on CSS, please visit our CSS Resource Center at `21www.deitel.com/CSS21/`. Note that when choosing a background color, you can also click the rectangle to the right of the **background-color** `ComboBox` in the **New Style** dialog to display the **More Colors dialog**. This dialog shows the so-called web-safe colors that should be able to display correctly across browsers and platforms. The color we used (`#CCFFFF`) is the hexadecimal value for one of the web-safe colors.

Portability Tip

When specifying colors for web applications, it is best to use a color from the web-safe colors shown in the **More Colors** dialog to ensure that colors display correctly in a web browser.

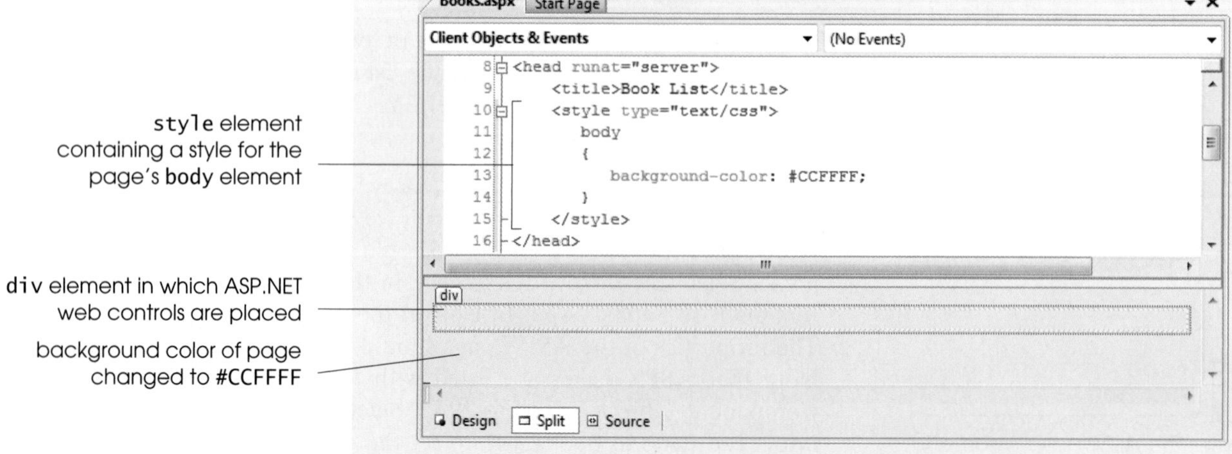

Figure 29.8 Setting the background color of the page.

(cont.)

Not checking the `CheckBox` **Apply new style to document selection** causes the style to be created but not applied to any controls.

3. ***Centering the content of the page.*** In **Design** mode, place the cursor in the dotted rectangle that represents the `div` element, then select **Format > New Style...** to display the **New Style** dialog. In the dialog, check the **Apply new style to document selection** `CheckBox`. Replace the default style name (`.newStyle1`) with `.mainDiv`. Click **Block** in the **Category** `ListBox`, then select `center` from the **text-align** `ComboBox`. Click **OK** to create the new style and apply it to the `div`. If you view the markup code in **Source** or **Split** mode, you'll see that applying the new style creates a `CssStyle` property for the control. Now, if you need to change the style of the control, you can simply modify its CSS style and the control will be updated automatically. The `div` now appears as shown in Fig. 29.9.

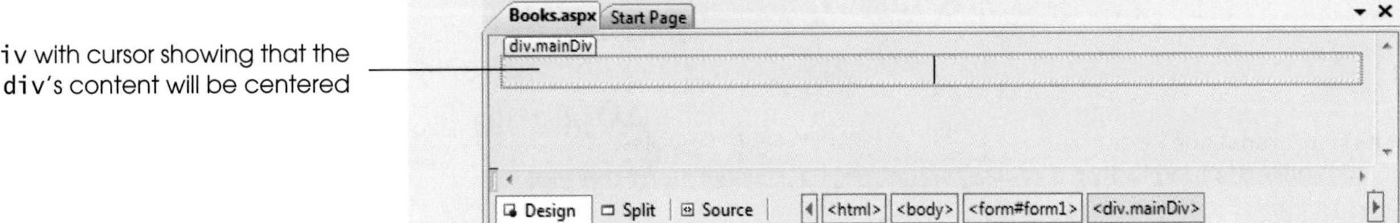

Figure 29.9 `div` element after applying a style.

4. ***Creating and styling a `Label`.*** Place the cursor in the dotted rectangle that represents the `div` element, then double click the **`Label` web control** **A** Label in the **Toolbox**'s **Standard** group. The `Label` initially appears as shown in Fig. 29.10. View its properties in the **Properties** window. Select the `ID` property, and change `Label1` to `availableLabel`. The **`ID` property** is used to identify controls, much like the `Name` property in Windows controls. Now change the `Label`'s `Text` property from `Label` to `Available Books`.

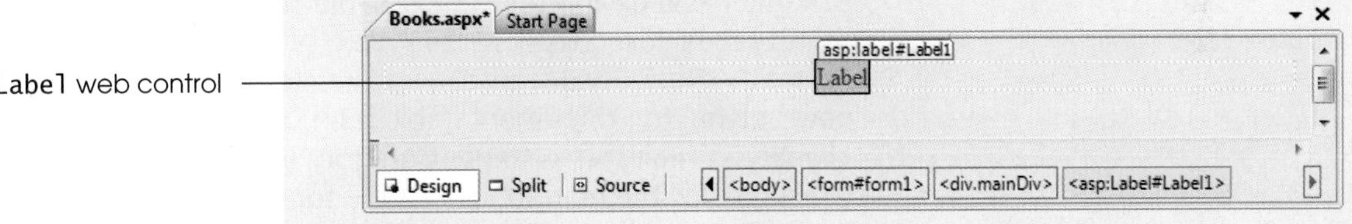

Figure 29.10 `Label` control displayed in the ASPX page.

Click the `Label`, then select **Format > New Style...** to display the **New Style** dialog. In the dialog, check the **Apply new style to document selection** `CheckBox` and name the style `.pageTitle`. Set the `Label`'s **font-family** to `Arial, Helvetica, sans-serif` and set its **font-size** to `XX-Large`. Click **OK** to create the new style and apply it to the `Label`. The `Label` now appears as shown in Fig. 29.11.

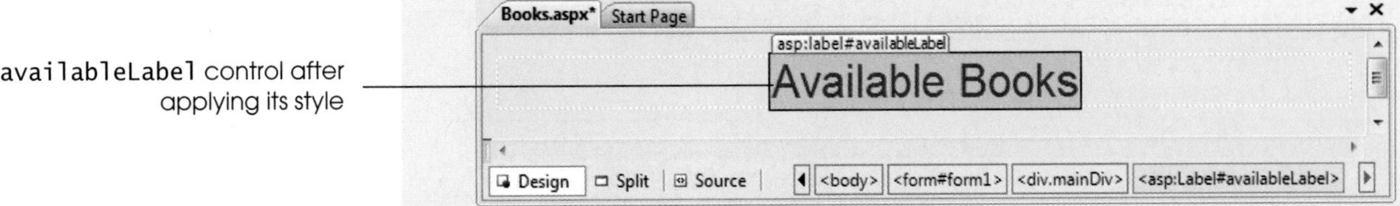

Figure 29.11 `availableLabel` control after applying its style.

(cont.)

5. ***Creating and styling another `Label`.*** Place the cursor to the right of the `availableLabel` and press *Enter*, then create another `Label` control. In the **Properties** window, change the `ID` of the `Label` to `instructionsLabel`, then change the `Text` property to "`Select a book from the list to display its cover. Click the button to view the book's details.`" Next, click the `Label` and select **Format > New Style...** to display the **New Style** dialog. Check the **Apply new style to document selection** `CheckBox` and name the style `.instructions`. Set the `Label`'s **font-size** to `Medium`. Select **Box** in the **Category** list, then uncheck the **Same for all** `CheckBox` for the **margin** and set the **top** and **bottom** margins to `10`. Click **OK** to create the new style and apply it to the `instructionsLabel`. It should now appear as shown in Fig. 29.12.

Figure 29.12 `instructionsLabel` control.

6. ***Creating and styling a `ListBox`.*** The next control you place on this page is a `ListBox`. The **`ListBox`** web control is similar to the `ListBox` Windows `Forms` control. In this application, it will contain a list of the available books offered by the bookstore. In the next tutorial, you retrieve information from the database to populate the `ListBox` with book titles. Position the cursor to the right of the `instructionsLabel` and press *Enter* twice. Then, double click the `ListBox` control ListBox in the **Toolbox**. Change the `ID` property of the `ListBox` to `bookTitlesListBox`. Next, click the `ListBox` and select **Format > New Style...** to display the **New Style** dialog. Check the **Apply new style to document selection** `CheckBox` and name the style `.bookList`. Select **Box** in the **Category** list, then uncheck the **Same for all** `CheckBox` for the **margin** and set the **top** and **bottom** margins to `10`. Next, Select **Position** in the **Category** list, and set the **width** to `350`. Click **OK** to create the new style and apply it to the `bookTitlesListBox`. It should now appear as shown in Fig. 29.13. [*Note:* `Unbound` appears in the `ListBox` because no items have been added to it.]

`bookTitlesListBox` control after applying its style

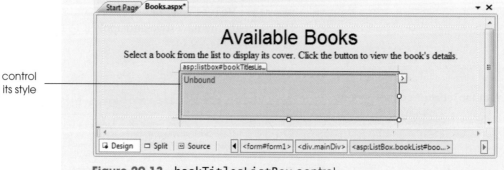

Figure 29.13 `bookTitlesListBox` control.

(cont.)

7. ***Adding an Image control.*** Position the cursor to the right of the ListBox and press *Enter*, then double click the **Image control** Image in the **Toolbox**. Change the Images's ID property to coverImage, its **BorderStyle** property to Outset and its **BorderWidth** property to 5 pixels. The BorderStyle property specifies the type of border that displays around the Image. Setting BorderStyle to Outset gives the Image a raised appearance. Property BorderWidth specifies the width of the Image's border. Set the Image's Visible property to False so that the Image is not displayed until the user makes a selection. The Books.aspx page should now appear as shown in Fig. 29.14. You'll choose the image to display based on the user's selection in Tutorial 31.

coverImage control with no image displayed

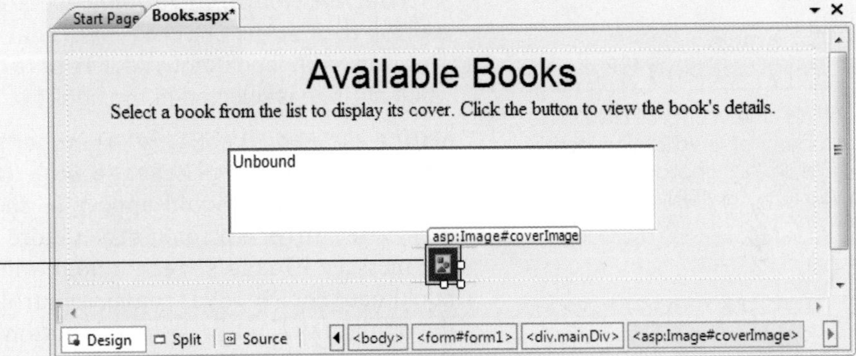

Figure 29.14 coverImage control.

8. ***Adding a Button control.*** Position the cursor to the right of the Image and press *Enter*, then double click the **Button control** Button in the **Toolbox**. Change the Button's ID to informationButton, and change its Text property to View Information. Next, click the Button and select **Format > New Style...** to display the **New Style** dialog. Check the **Apply new style to document selection** CheckBox and name the style .viewInfoButton. Select **Box** in the **Category** list, then uncheck the **Same for all** CheckBox for the **margin** and set the **top**, **right**, **bottom** and **left** margins to 10, 0, 10 and 0, respectively. Click **OK** to create the new style and apply it to the informationButton. It should now appear as shown in Fig. 29.15.

informationButton control after applying its style

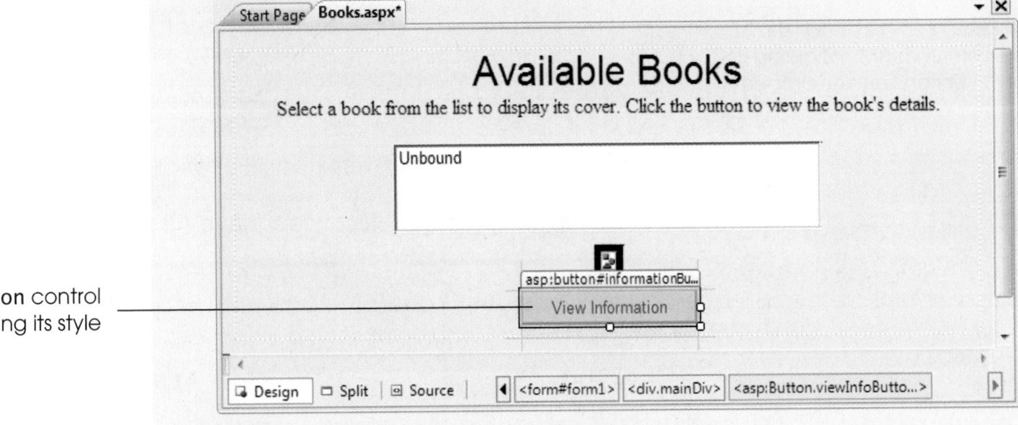

Figure 29.15 informationButton control.

9. ***Adding a RequireFieldValidator control.*** To make sure that a book in the bookTitlesListBox is selected when the informationButton is clicked, the application uses a RequiredFieldValidator control. You'll configure the RequiredFieldValidator to display an error message when no title is selected in the bookTitlesListBox.

(cont.)

The RequiredFieldValidator is located in the **Validation** group in the **Toolbox**. Position the cursor to the right of the informationButton and press *Enter*, then double click the RequiredFieldValidator control RequiredFieldValidator in the **Toolbox**. Change the RequiredFieldValidator's ID property to bookRequiredFieldValidator. Next, Click the RequiredFieldValidator, then select **Format > New Style...** to display the **New Style** dialog. In the dialog, check the **Apply new style to document selection** CheckBox and name the style .validatorText. Set the **font-size** to large and set the **font-weight** to bold. Click **OK** to create the new style and apply it to the RequiredFieldValidator.

10. ***Selecting the control to validate.*** Click the bookRequiredFieldValidator control, then set its **ControlToValidate property** to bookTitlesListBox. This causes the bookRequiredFieldValidator to display an error message when nothing is selected in the bookTitlesListBox.

Common Programming Error

Not setting the ControlToValidate property of a validation control results in an application error when you run your ASP.NET application.

11. ***Setting the RequiredFieldValidator's error message.*** In the **Properties** window, set the **ErrorMessage property** to Please select a book. The Books.aspx page should appear as shown in Fig. 29.16. Now if the user presses the informationButton before selecting a book from the ListBox, the message Please select a book will be displayed in the position of the bookRequiredFieldValidator control. You can confirm this by running the application and pressing the button in your browser window. [*Note:* A **Debugging not Enabled** dialog may pop up. Make sure the top RadioButton, **Modify the Web.config file to enable debugging**, is selected, then click **OK** so the application can be executed in debug mode.]

bookRequiredFieldValidator control after configuring its ErrorMessage property

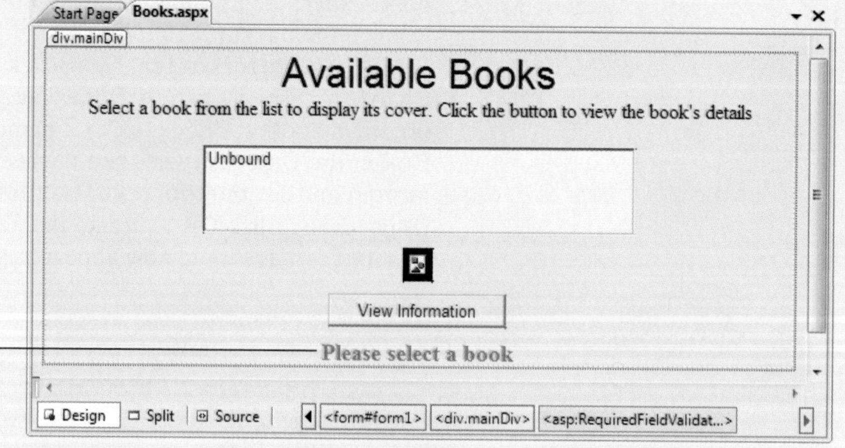

Figure 29.16 Books.aspx page after all controls have been added.

12. ***Saving the project.*** Select **File > Save All** to save your modified code.

SELF-REVIEW

1. Use the ________ property to change the name of a web control.
   a) Text
   b) Name
   c) ID
   d) Value

2. The ________ dialog enables you to create CSS styles for page elements.
   a) **New Style**
   b) **More Colors**
   c) **Format**
   d) None of the above

Answers: 1) c. 2) a.

29.4 Designing the BookInformation.aspx Page

Next, you design the `BookInformation.aspx` page, which displays the information about the book that was selected from the `ListBox` in `Books.aspx`.

Creating the BookInformation.aspx Page

1. ***Creating a new ASPX page.*** Select **Website > Add New Item...** (or right click the project name in the **Solution Explorer**, then select **Add > Add New Item...**), to display the **Add New Item** dialog (Fig. 29.17). Select **Web Form** in the **Templates:** pane, and rename the ASPX page to `BookInformation.aspx`, using the **Name:** `TextBox`. Make sure **Visual Basic** is selected in the **Language:** drop-down list, then click **Add**. `BookInformation.aspx` now appears in the **Solution Explorer** window.

Web Form template

Change the Name to `BookInformation.aspx`

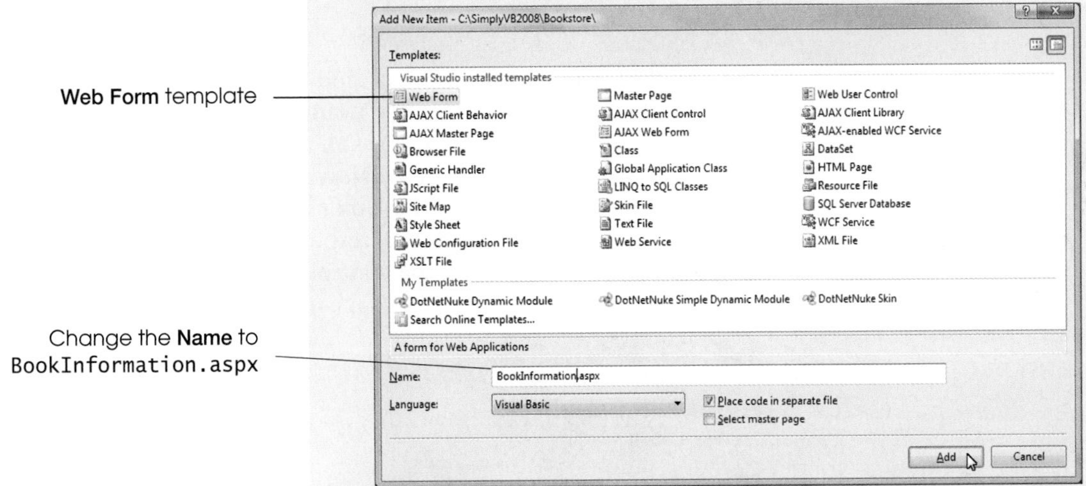

Figure 29.17 **Add New Item - Bookstore** dialog.

2. ***Changing the background color and page title.*** Switch to **Design** mode and change the background color of this page to light blue, as you did in *Step 2* of the box *Creating the `Books.aspx` Page*. Set the page's `Title` property to `Book List`.

3. ***Creating the `bookTitleLabel` `Label`.*** Use the techniques you learned in *Step 4* of the box *Creating the `Books.aspx` Page* to create a new `Label`. Change the `ID` property of the `Label` to `bookTitleLabel`. This `Label` displays the title of the book selected by the user. You do not yet know what book title will be selected, so clear the `Text` property of this `Label`. You'll set this property programmatically in Tutorial 31. Use the **New Style** dialog to create a style named `.bookTitle` for the `bookTitleLabel`. Set the **font-family** to `Arial, Helvetica, sans-serif`. Set the **font-size** to `x-large`, the **font-weight** to `bold` and the **color** to `#0000FF`. The `Label` should now appear as shown in Fig. 29.18.

`bookTitleLabel` control after applying its style

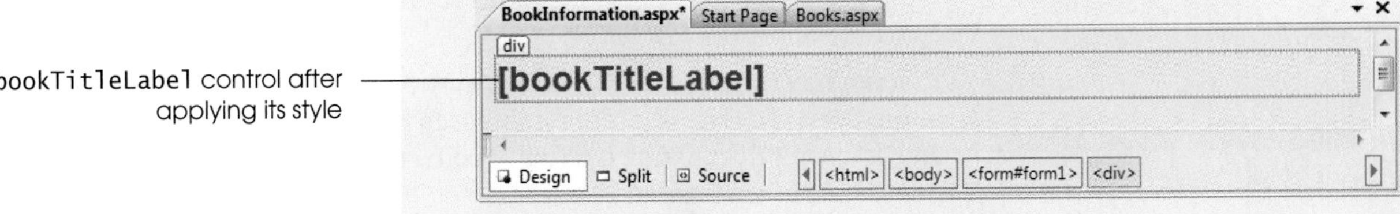

Figure 29.18 `bookTitleLabel` control.

(cont.)

4. ***Creating the `authorsLabel` `Label`.*** Add another `Label` control below the `bookTitleLabel`. Set the `Label`'s `ID` property to `authorsLabel` and clear its `Text` property. You'll set this property programmatically in Tutorial 31. Next, use the **New Style** dialog to create a style named `.authors` for the `authorsLabel`. Set the **font-size** to `large` and the **font-weight** to `bold`. The `Label` should now appear as shown in Fig. 29.19.

Figure 29.19 `authorsLabel` control.

5. ***Creating the `Image` control.*** Next, add an `Image` control to display the selected book's cover. Change the `Image` control's `ID` property to `book-Image`. Set the `BorderStyle` to `Outset` and the `BorderWidth` to 5 pixels. Next, select the `Image` and open the **New Style** dialog. Create a style named `.bookCover` for the `Image`. In the **Box** category, set the **top**, **right**, **bottom** and **left** margins to 10, 10, 10 and 0, respectively. In the **Layout** category, set the **float** to `left` (this enables the control in *Step 6* to appear to the right of the `Image`). The `Image` should now appear as shown in Fig. 29.20.

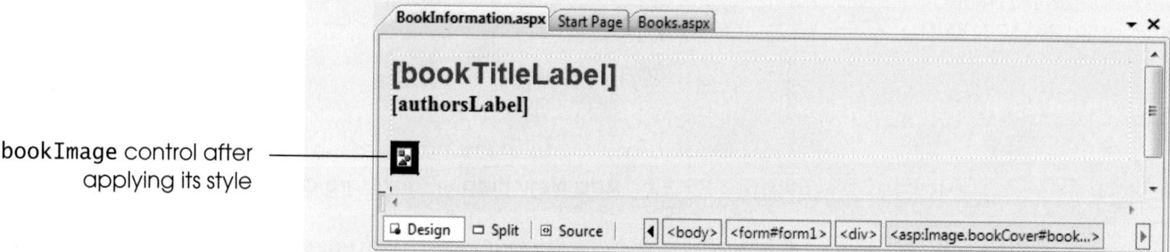

Figure 29.20 `bookImage` control.

6. ***Creating the `DetailsView` control.*** A `DetailsView` control displays property names and values for its data source in a tabular format. You'll populate this control programmatically later—we just designing the page here. Position the cursor to the right of the `bookImage`, then double click the `DetailsView` control DetailsView in the **Toolbox**'s **Data** group. Change the `ID` of the `DetailsView` to `bookDetailsView` and clear the values for the `Width` and `Height` properties. You'll set the width using a CSS style, and the height will be determined by the contents of the `DetailsView`. Next, select the `DetailsView` and open the **New Style** dialog. Create a style named `.detailsView` for the `bookDetailsView`. In the **Box** category, set the **top**, **right**, **bottom** and **left** margins to 10, 10, 10 and 0, respectively. In the **Border** category, set the **border-style** to `outset` and the **border-width** to 5. In the **Position** category, set the **width** to 350. The `DetailsView` should now appear as shown in Fig. 29.21.

7. ***Placing text into `DetailsView` cells.*** The information that will be displayed in the `DetailsView` is based on the user's selection in the `Books.aspx` page and is currently unknown. You specify the information to display in the `DetailsView` in Tutorial 31.

(cont.)

bookDetailsView control after applying its style

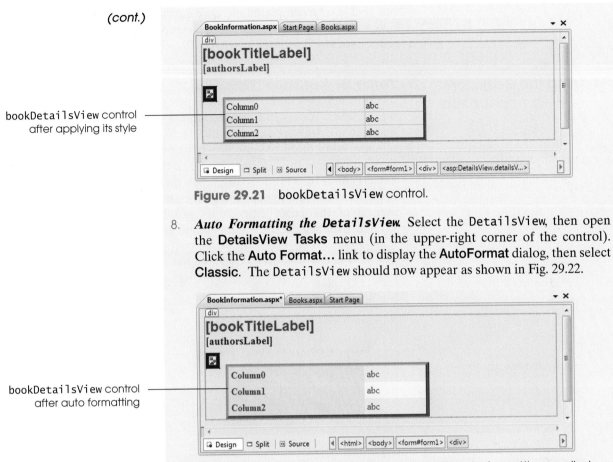

Figure 29.21 `bookDetailsView` control.

8. ***Auto Formatting the `DetailsView`.*** Select the `DetailsView`, then open the **DetailsView Tasks** menu (in the upper-right corner of the control). Click the **Auto Format...** link to display the **AutoFormat** dialog, then select **Classic**. The `DetailsView` should now appear as shown in Fig. 29.22.

bookDetailsView control after auto formatting

Figure 29.22 `bookDetailsView` control with auto formatting applied.

9. ***Creating the `bookListButton`.*** Add a `Button` below the `bookDetailsView`. Set the `Button`'s `ID` to `bookListButton`, and set its `Text` to `Return to Book List`. Next, select the `Button` and open the **New Style** dialog. Create a style named `.returnButton` for the `bookListButton`. In the **Box** category, set the **top** margin to `10`. In the **Layout** category, set **clear** to `both` (this ensures that the button is displayed on a line by itself in the web page). The `Button` should now appear as shown in Fig. 29.23.

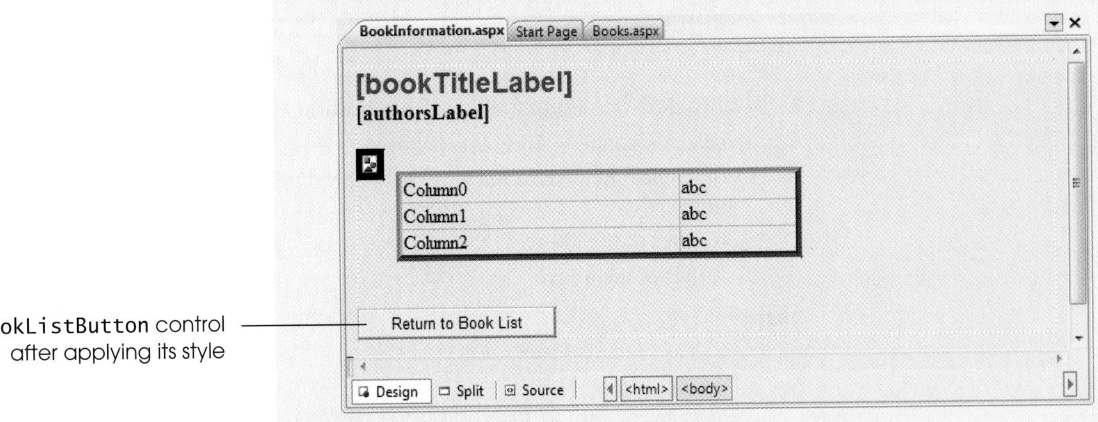

Figure 29.23 `bookListButton` control.

10. ***Saving the project.*** Select **File > Save All** to save your modified code.

Now that you've completed the user interface design, you run the application. You have specified only the **Bookstore** web application's user interface; therefore, it does not have any functionality.

Running the Bookstore Web Application

1. ***Testing the application.*** Ensure that the `Books.aspx` page is the start page by right clicking it in the **Solution Explorer** and selecting **Set As Start Page.** Next, select **Debug > Start Debugging** to run your application. The `Books.aspx` page appears (Fig. 29.24). Note that the `ListBox` does not contain any book titles, because you have not yet set up the database connections to retrieve the information. Click the **View Information** `Button`. The `RequiredFieldValidator` displays a message because you did not select a book, but nothing else happens. Currently, you have specified only the visual aspects of the page. Thus, users are not forwarded to `BookInformation.aspx` when the **View Information** `Button` is clicked.

Empty `ListBox` control

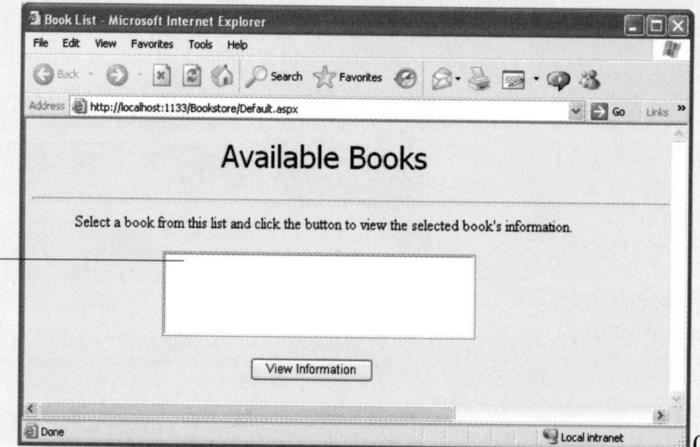

Figure 29.24 Empty `ListBox` of the `Books.aspx` page.

2. ***Closing the application.*** Close your running application by clicking the browser's close box.
3. ***Closing the IDE.*** Close Visual Web Developer by clicking its close box.

SELF-REVIEW

1. The ________ property is used to set the width of an `Image` control's border.
   a) `Width`
   b) `BorderStyle`
   c) `BorderWidth`
   d) None of the above.
2. To add a new Web Form to the web application ________.
   a) select **Website > Add New Item...**
   b) right click the project name in the **Solution Explorer**, then select **Add > Add New Item...**
   c) Neither of the above
   d) Either of the above

Answers: 1) c. 2) d.

29.5 Wrap-Up

In this tutorial, you created the ASPX pages for your three-tier **Bookstore** web application. You learned how to create an ASP.NET web application, how to add web controls to the ASPX pages and how to use the **New Style** dialog to create CSS styles. In doing so, you were introduced to Visual Web Developer's **Design**, **Split** and **Source** modes. You learned that **Design** mode is used to create the user interface, and **Source** mode allows you to view and edit the page's markup. You also learned that many programmers prefer **Split** mode because they can see both **Design** and **Source** modes at the same time.

The web controls you used in this tutorial included `Label`s, `Button`s, a `ListBox`, `Image`s and a `DetailsView`. You created a `RequiredFieldValidator` control to ensure that the user makes a selection from the `ListBox` in the `Books.aspx` page before the form can be submitted to the server. You also set the `Image` control's `BorderStyle` property to `Outset` and `BorderWidth` property to 5 pixels, which gave it a raised appearance.

In the next tutorial, you connect to and access the database, or information tier, of the application, which contains information about the books in the bookstore. You use LINQ to SQL classes and a `LinqDataSource` to bind the book titles to the `ListBox` control. After configuring the database access, you create the middle tier of the bookstore (Tutorial 31), which specifies the functionality of the ASPX pages.

SKILLS SUMMARY

Creating a local ASP.NET Web Application

- Select **File > New Web Site...**
- Select the **ASP.NET Web Site** icon from the **New Web Site** dialog's **Templates:** pane.
- Choose **File System** in the **Location:** drop-down list.
- Specify a location to store the file on your system.
- Choose **Visual Basic** in the **Language:** drop-down list and click **OK**.

Adding an ASPX Page to a Web Application

- Select **Website > Add New Item...** to display the **Add New Item** dialog, or right click the project name in the **Solution Explorer**, then select **Add > Add New Item...**.
- Select **Web Form** in the **Templates:** box, and rename the page in the **Name:** `TextBox`.
- Choose **Visual Basic** in the **Language:** drop-down list.
- Click **Add** to add the new ASPX page to the web application.

Creating a CSS style for a Web Control

- Select the web control.
- Select **Format > New Style...** to display the **New Style** dialog.
- Name the style and check the **Apply new style to document selection** `CheckBox`.
- Use the various categories and attributes to specify the look-and-feel of the control.

Changing to Design Mode

- Click the **Design** mode button beneath the ASPX page in the Web Form Designer.

Changing to Source Mode

- Click the **Source** mode button beneath the ASPX page in the Web Form Designer.

Changing to Split Mode

- Click the **Split** mode button beneath the ASPX page in the Web Form Designer.

KEY TERMS

ASP.NET Website project—The type of project you create with Visual Web Developer to build an ASP.NET application.

`BorderStyle` property of an `Image`—Defines the border (such as `outset`) around an image.

`BorderWidth` property of an `Image`—Defines the width of an `Image`'s border.

`Button` web control—Allows users to perform an action.

Cascading Style Sheets (CSS)—Used to define the look-and-feel of web page elements.

`ControlToValidate` property of a `RequiredFieldValidator`—Specifies the control that is validated by the `RequiredFieldValidator`.

Design mode—Displays the ASPX page's GUI at design time.

`DetailsView` control—A control in the **Data** group of the **Toolbox** that displays property names and values for its data source in a tabular format.

ErrorMessage property of a RequiredFieldValidator—Specifies the error message that appears when the user does not enter data in a required field of a web form.

ID property of a web control—Specifies the name of a web control for use in code.

Image web control—Displays an image in an ASPX page.

Label web control—Displays text on an ASPX page.

ListBox web control—Displays a list of items.

More Colors dialog—Displays the set of web-safe colors and enables you to create custom colors.

New Style dialog—Enables you to specify styles, such as position, for your web controls.

Source mode—Displays the ASPX page's markup at design time.

Split mode—Displays the ASPX page's **Source** and **Design** views at the same time.

style element—An element that is placed in the head element of a page. Contains CSS style definitions (such as those created with the **New Style** window).

Title property of an ASPX page—Specifies the page's title that displays in the title bar of the browser.

web control—Control that is used to construct web applications.

Web Form Designer—The design area in Visual Web Developer that enables you to visually build your ASPX pages.

CONTROLS, EVENTS, PROPERTIES & METHODS

Button Button This control allows the user to raise an action or event.

- ***In action***

- ***Properties***

CssStyle—Specifies the CSS style that defines the look-and-feel of the control.

ID—Specifies the name of the Button. The name should be suffixed with Button.

Text—Specifies the text displayed on the Button.

DetailsView DetailsView This control displays property names and values for its data source in a tabular format.

- ***In action***

- ***Properties***

CssStyle—Specifies the CSS style that defines the look-and-feel of the control.

ID—Specifies the name used to access the DetailsView control programmatically. The name should be suffixed with DetailsView.

Image Image This control displays an image on the ASPX page.

- ***In action***

- ***Properties***

  `BorderStyle`—Specifies the appearance of the `Image`'s border.

  `BorderWidth`—Specifies the width of the `Image`'s border.

  `ID`—Specifies the name used to access the `Image` control programmatically. The name should be suffixed with `Image`.

`Label` A Label This control displays text on the ASPX page that the user cannot modify.

- ***In action***

Available Books

- ***Properties***

  `CssStyle`—Specifies the CSS style that defines the look-and-feel of the control.

  `ID`—Specifies the name used to access the `Label` programmatically. The name should be suffixed with `Label`.

  `Text`—Specifies the text displayed on the `Label`.

`ListBox` ListBox This control allows the user to view and select from multiple items in a list.

- ***In action***

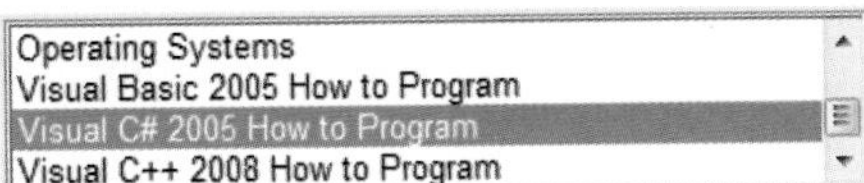

- ***Properties***

  `CssStyle`—Specifies the CSS style that defines the look-and-feel of the control.

  `ID`—Specifies the name used to access the `ListBox` control programmatically. The name should be suffixed with `ListBox`.

`RequiredFieldValidator` RequiredFieldValidator This control enables you to specify that an element in a Web Form is required before a form can be submitted.

- ***In action***

Please select a book

- ***Properties***

  `ControlToValidate`—Specifies the Web Form element that is required before the form can be submitted.

  `CssStyle`—Specifies the CSS style that defines the look-and-feel of the control.

  `ErrorMessage`—Specifies the text that will be displayed if the required Web Form element is not supplied when the Web Form is submitted.

  `ID`—Specifies the name used to access the `RequiredFieldValidator` control programmatically. The name should be suffixed with `RequiredFieldValidator`.

MULTIPLE-CHOICE QUESTIONS

29.1 You change the ________ style attribute of the ASPX page to specify the color that displays in the background of the page.

a) `back-color` b) `bg-color`
c) `background-color` d) `color`

29.2 `Button`, `Label` and `ListBox` web controls can be dragged onto a Web Form from the ________.

a) **Toolbox** b) **Properties** window
c) **Solution Explorer** d) None of the above

29.3 The _________ dialog can be used to specify the style of a web control on an ASPX page.

a) **Toolbox**
b) **Style**
c) **New Style**
d) None of the above

29.4 Which of the following is not a view mode in the Web Form Designer?

a) Dual mode
b) **Split** mode
c) **Source** mode
d) **Design** mode

29.5 The `BorderStyle` property of the `Image` control _________.

a) specifies the color of the border
b) specifies the type of border that displays around the `Image` control
c) specifies the width of the border
d) Both a and b

29.6 Setting the `BorderStyle` property to `Outset` makes an `Image` appear _________.

a) raised
b) with a bold border
c) with the specified border width
d) with the specified border color

29.7 The _________ mode allows you to create the ASPX page's GUI by dragging and dropping controls on the page.

a) **Source**
b) **Design**
c) **Split**
d) All of the above

29.8 To specify the spacing around a control, define a style containing the _________ style attribute.

a) `font-size`
b) `margin`
c) `border-style`
d) `border-width`

29.9 The _________ property specifies the number of pixels used to form an `Image`'s border.

a) `Border`
b) `Width`
c) `BorderWidth`
d) None of the above

29.10 The _________ control enables you to specify that an element in a Web Form is required before a form can be submitted.

a) `RequiredField`
b) `Validator`
c) `RequiredFieldValidator`
d) None of the above

EXERCISES

[*Note:* An ASPX page is the application's start page if that this page appears first when you run the application. You can set a page as the start page by right clicking the file in the **Solution Explorer** and selecting **Set As Start Page**.]

29.11 *(**Phone Book** Application: GUI)* Create the user interface for the **Phone Book** application. The design for the two pages for this application is displayed in Fig. 29.25.

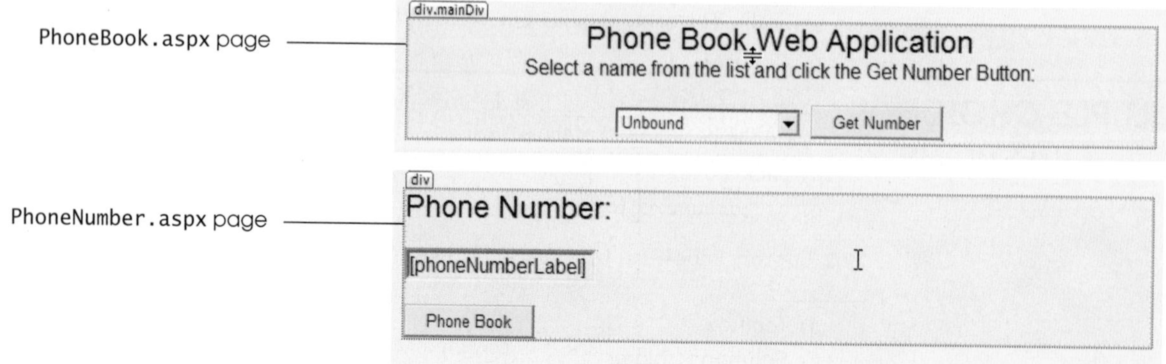

Figure 29.25 **Phone Book** application ASPX pages' design.

a) ***Creating an ASP.NET web application.*** Create an ASP.NET web application project in the `C:\SimplyVB2008` directory, and name it `PhoneBook`. Rename the ASPX page to `PhoneBook.aspx` and set `PhoneBook.aspx` as the start page. Also set the page's `Title` property to `Phone Book`.

b) ***Changing the font and background color of the page.*** Use the **New Style** dialog as demonstrated in this tutorial to change the `font-family` for the page to `Arial, Helvetica, sans-serif` and the `background-color` to `#FFFFCC`.

c) ***Centering the `div` element's contents.*** Select the `div` element in **Design** mode. Use the **New Style** dialog to create a new style named `.mainDiv` with its `text-align` style attribute set to `center`.

d) ***Adding a `Label`.*** Create a `Label` named `phoneBookLabel` and change its `Text` property to `Phone Book Web Application`. Use the **New Style** dialog to create a `.pageTitle` style and set the `font-size` to `X-Large`.

e) ***Adding another `Label`.*** Create another `Label` named `instructionsLabel` below the `phoneBookLabel`. Set the `Text` property to `Select a name from the list and click the Get Number Button:`.

f) ***Adding a `DropDownList`.*** Position the cursor to the right of the `instructionsLabel` and press *Enter* twice. Insert a `DropDownList` web control named `namesDropDownList`. The `DropDownList` web control looks similar to the `ComboBox` Windows `Form` control. Set the control's `Width` property to `150px`.

g) ***Adding a `Button`.*** Create a `Button` named `getNumberButton` to the right of the `namesDropDownList`. Change its `Text` property to `Get Number`.

h) ***Adding another ASPX page to the Phone Book application.*** Add another ASPX page to the **Phone Book** application and name it `PhoneNumber.aspx`. Change the `Title` property to `Phone Number`.

i) ***Changing the font and background color of the page.*** Use the **New Style** dialog as demonstrated in this tutorial to change the `font-family` for the page to `Arial, Helvetica, sans-serif` and the `background-color` to `#FFFFCC`.

j) ***Adding a `Label` to `PhoneNumber.aspx`.*** Create a `Label` named `numbersLabel`. Change its `Text` property to `Phone Number:`. Use the **New Style** dialog to create a `.pageTitle` style and set the `font-size` to `X-Large`.

k) ***Adding another `Label`.*** Position the cursor to the right of the `numbersLabel` and press *Enter* twice. Create another `Label` named `phoneNumberLabel`. Clear its Text property, set its `BorderStyle` property to `Inset`, and set its `Width` property to `150px`.

l) ***Adding a `Button` to the `PhoneNumber.aspx` page.*** Position the cursor to the right of the `phoneNumberLabel` and press *Enter* twice. Create a `Button` named `phoneBookButton`. Change its `Text` property to `Phone Book`.

m) ***Saving the project.*** Save all the files in your project.

29.12 *(US State Facts Application: GUI)* Create the user interface for the **US State Facts** application. The design for the two pages of this application is displayed in Fig. 29.26.

a) ***Creating an ASP.NET web application.*** Create a new ASP.NET web application project in the `C:\SimplyVB2008` directory and name it `USStateFacts`. Rename the first ASPX page to `States.aspx` and set `States.aspx` as the start page. Also set the page's `Title` property to `States`.

b) ***Changing the font and background color of the page.*** Use the **New Style** dialog as demonstrated in this tutorial to change the `font-family` for the page to `Arial, Helvetica, sans-serif` and the `background-color` to `#CCFFFF`.

c) ***Centering the `div` element's contents.*** Select the `div` element in **Design** mode. Use the **New Style** dialog to create a new style named `.mainDiv` with its `text-align` style attribute set to `center`.

d) ***Adding a `Label`.*** Create a `Label` named `statesLabel` and change its `Text` property to `States`. Use the **New Style** dialog to create a `.pageTitle` style and set the `font-size` to `XX-Large`.

e) ***Adding another `Label`.*** Create another `Label` named `instructionsLabel` below the `statesLabel`. Set the `Text` property to `Select a state from the list and click the button to view facts about that state:`.

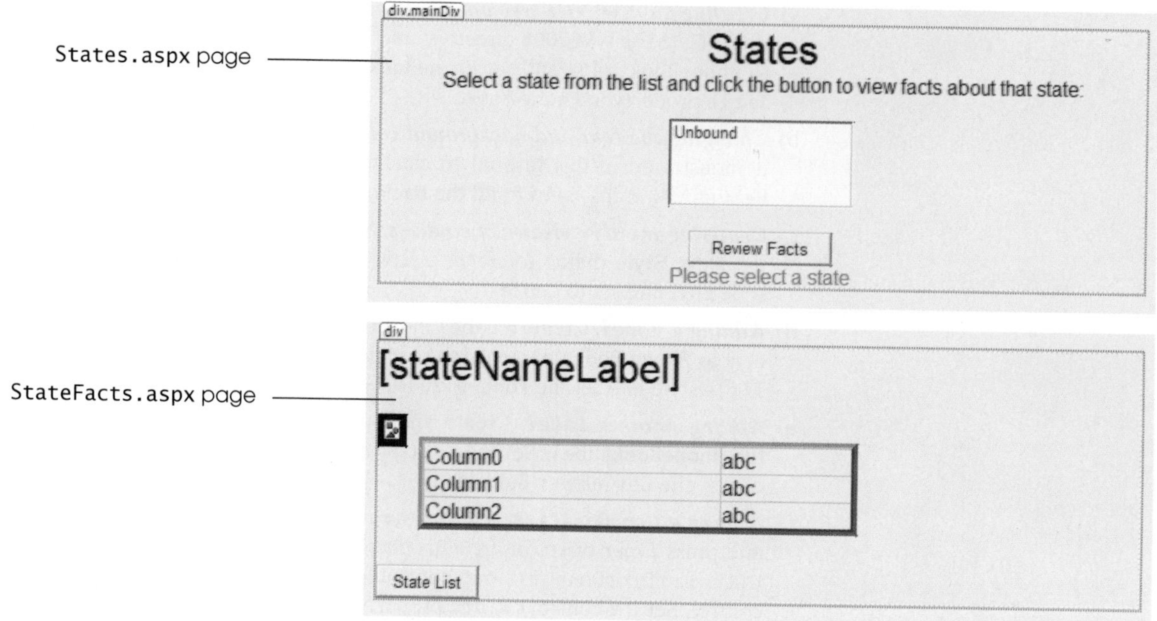

Figure 29.26 **US State Facts** application ASPX pages' design.

f) ***Adding a* `ListBox`.** Position the cursor to the right of the `instructionsLabel` and press *Enter* twice. Insert a `ListBox` web control named `statesListBox`. Set the control's `Width` property to `150px`.

g) ***Adding a* `Button`.** Position the cursor to the right of the `instructionsLabel` and press *Enter* twice. Create a `Button` named `factsButton`. Change its `Text` property to `Review Facts`.

h) ***Adding a* `RequireFieldValidator`.** Create a `RequiredFieldValidator` named `statesRequiredFieldValidator` below the `Button`. Set its `ErrorMessage` property to `Please select a state` and its `ControlToValidate` to `statesListBox`.

i) ***Adding another ASPX page to the US State Facts application*.** Add another ASPX page to the **US State Facts** application and name it `StateFacts.aspx`. Also set the page's `Title` property to `State Facts`.

j) ***Changing the font and background color of the page*.** Use the **New Style** dialog as demonstrated in this tutorial to change the `font-family` for the page to `Arial, Helvetica, sans-serif` and the `background-color` to `#CCFFFF`.

k) ***Adding a* `Label`.** Create a `Label` named `stateNameLabel` and clear its `Text` property. Use the **New Style** dialog to create a `.pageTitle` style and set the `font-size` to `XX-Large`.

l) ***Adding an* `Image` *control*.** Position the cursor to the right of the `instructionsLabel` and press *Enter*. Insert an `Image` control named `flagImage`. Set its `BorderStyle` to `Outset` and its `BorderWidth` to `5px`. Do not set its height and width to allow the `Image` control to automatically resize according to the loaded image. Use the **New Style** dialog to create a `.stateFlag` style and set the margins for the `top`, `right`, `bottom` and `left` to 10, 10, 10 and 0, respectively. Also set the float to `left`.

m) ***Adding a* `DetailsView`.** Position the cursor to the right of the `Image` and insert a `DetailsView` named `stateDetailsView`. Set its `Width` property to `355px`. Use the **New Style** dialog to create a `.detailsView` style and set the margins for the `top`, `right`, `bottom` and `left` to 10, 10, 10 and 0, respectively. Also set the style's `border-style` attribute to `outset` and the `border-width` attribute to `5`.

n) ***Adding a* `Button` *to* `StateFacts.aspx`.** Insert a `Button` named `stateListButton` below the `DetailsView`. Change its `Text` property to `State List`. Use the **New Style** dialog to create a `.stateButton` style that sets the `clear` attribute to `both`. This ensures that the control appears on a line by itself in the page.

o) ***Saving the project*.** Save all the files in your project.

TUTORIAL

Objectives

In this tutorial, you learn to:

- Connect to a database in Visual Web Developer.
- Create LINQ to SQL classes in a web application.
- Create a `LinqDataSource`.
- Create a data-bound `ListBox` using a `LinqDataSource`.

Outline

Bookstore Web Application: Information Tier

Examining the Database and Creating Database Components

This tutorial focuses on the web application's information tier, where the application's data resides. In your **Bookstore** web application, the information tier is represented by a Microsoft SQL Server Express database, `Bookstore.mdf`, that stores each book's information. Before you begin this tutorial, you should be familiar with the database concepts presented in Tutorial 24, **Address Book** Application.

Now, you create the database connection and define the LINQ to SQL classes that your application uses to manipulate the database's information. You also create a `LinqDataSource` used to display book titles in a data-bound `ListBox`. In fact, the information tier consists solely of the `Bookstore.mdf` database. The LINQ to SQL classes and the `LinqDataSource` created in this tutorial are actually part of the middle tier, because they perform the functionality of retrieving data from the database. You create these objects here because they interact with the information tier and do not require you to write any code. You complete the **Bookstore** web application by creating the middle tier in the next tutorial.

30.1 Reviewing the Bookstore Web Application

You took the three-tier **Bookstore** web application for a test-drive (Tutorial 28) and designed the GUI using web controls (Tutorial 29). Now you are ready to create the database components for the application. Before you begin, you should review the pseudocode and the ACE table (Fig. 30.1) for this application:

```
When the Books page is requested
    Retrieve the book titles from the database
    Display book titles in a ListBox

When the user selects a book title from the ListBox
    Display the book's cover image below the ListBox in an Image

When the user clicks the View Information Button
    If the user did not select a book from the ListBox
        Display an error message
    Otherwise
        Store the selected book's product ID
        Redirect the browser to the BookInformation page
```

When the BookInformation page is requested
Retrieve the selected book's information from the database
Display the book title in a Label
Display the authors in a Label
Display the cover art in an Image
Display the remaining information in a DetailsView

When the user clicks the Return to Book List Button on the BookInformation page
Redirect the browser back to the Books page

Action/Control/Event (ACE) Table for the Bookstore Web Application

Action	Control/Object	Event
Label the Books page	`availableLabel`, `instructionsLabel`	
	`Page`	Load (for `Books.aspx`)
Retrieve the book titles from the database	`linqDataSource`	
Display book titles in a ListBox	`bookTitlesListBox`	
	`bookTitlesListBox`	`SelectedIndex-Changed`
Display the book's cover image below the ListBox in an Image	`bookTitlesListBox`, db (an object of class `BookInformationDB-DataContext`), `coverImage`	
	`informationButton`	`Click`
If the user did not select a book from the ListBox	`bookTitlesListBox`	
Display an error message	`bookRequiredField-Validator`	
Otherwise		
Store the selected book's product ID in a session variable	`bookTitlesListBox`, `Session`	
Redirect the browser to the BookInformation page	`Response`	
	`Page`	Load (for `Book-Information.aspx`)
Retrieve the selected book's information from the database	db (an object of class `BookInformationDB-DataContext`), `Session`	
Display the book title in a Label	`bookTitleLabel`	
Display the authors in a Label	`authorsLabel`	
Display the cover art in an Image	`bookImage`	
Display the remaining information in a DetailsView	`linqDataSource`, `bookDetailsView`	
	`bookListButton`	`Click`
Redirect the client browser back to the Books page	`Response`	

Figure 30.1 ACE table for the **Bookstore** web application.

30.2 Information Tier: Database

The information tier maintains all the data needed for an application. The database that stores this information may contain product data, such as a description and quantity in stock, and customer data, such as a user name and shipping information.

The **Bookstore** web application stores book data in a Microsoft SQL Server Express database (`Bookstore.mdf`). This data is retrieved from the database using Visual Basic code and LINQ to SQL. The database contains one table (named `Products`) that stores each book's information.

The table contains eight fields (columns)—`ProductID`, `Title`, `Authors`, `Copyright`, `Edition`, `ISBN`, `Coverart` and `Description`. These fields contain an ID number, the title, authors, copyright date, edition number, ISBN number, image file name and description of each book, respectively. Figure 30.2 displays the `Products` table of `Bookstore.mdf`, using the **Database Explorer** window in Visual Web Developer 2008 Express.

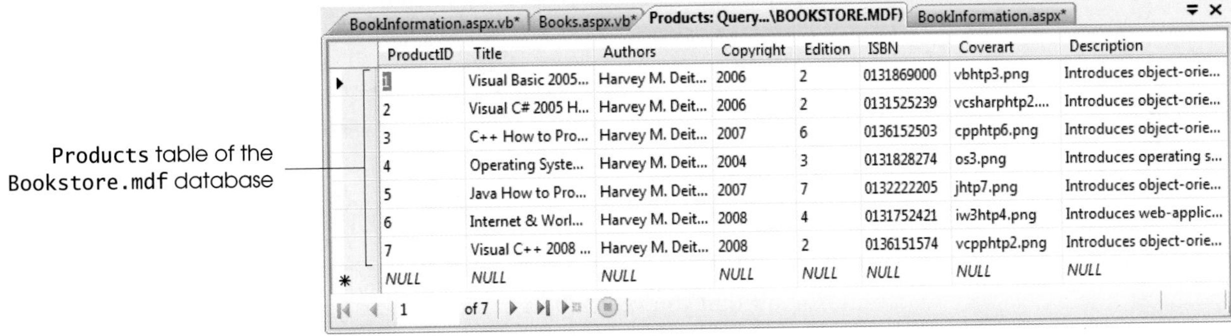

ProductID	Title	Authors	Copyright	Edition	ISBN	Coverart	Description
1	Visual Basic 2005...	Harvey M. Deit...	2006	2	0131869000	vbhtp3.png	Introduces object-orie...
2	Visual C# 2005 H...	Harvey M. Deit...	2006	2	0131525239	vcsharphtp2....	Introduces object-orie...
3	C++ How to Pro...	Harvey M. Deit...	2007	6	0136152503	cpphtp6.png	Introduces object-orie...
4	Operating Syste...	Harvey M. Deit...	2004	3	0131828274	os3.png	Introduces operating s...
5	Java How to Pro...	Harvey M. Deit...	2007	7	0132222205	jhtp7.png	Introduces object-orie...
6	Internet & Worl...	Harvey M. Deit...	2008	4	0131752421	iw3htp4.png	Introduces web-applic...
7	Visual C++ 2008 ...	Harvey M. Deit...	2008	2	0136151574	vcpphtp2.png	Introduces object-orie...
NULL	NULL	NULL	NULL	NULL	NULL	NULL	NULL

Figure 30.2 `Products` table of the `Bookstore.mdf` database.

30.3 Connecting to the Database and Retrieving Information

Before you begin programming this web application's middle tier, you must set up the database connection and define the classes that retrieve information from the database. First, you add the database to the web application. You then create a set of LINQ to SQL classes to model the database in your web application as you did in Tutorial 24. Finally, you use a `LinqDataSource` to display the book titles in the `bookTitlesListBox`. You add the database connection in the following box.

Adding the `Bookstore.mdf` Database to the Bookstore Web Application

1. ***Opening the Bookstore web application in Visual Web Developer.*** Open Visual Web Developer and select **File > Open Web Site...** to display the **Open Web Site** dialog. In this dialog, click **File System**, then select the **Bookstore** folder you created in the last tutorial (in `C:\SimplyVB2008`) and click the **Open** `Button` to open the **Bookstore** web application.

2. ***Adding a database to the web application.*** You must add the `Bookstore.mdf` database to the application before accessing its data. This connection allows you to return information about a specific book from the database to the application. To add a the `Bookstore.mdf` database, select **Tools > Connect to Database...** to open the **Add Connection** dialog. If the **Data source:** is not already set to **Microsoft SQL Server Database File (SqlClient)**, click the **Change...** `Button`, select **Microsoft SQL Server Database File** and click **OK**. Next, click **Browse...**, locate the `Bookstore.mdf` database file in the `C:\Examples\Tutorial31` directory, select it and click **Open**. You can test the connection to the database by clicking the **Test Connection** `Button`. Click **OK** to create the connection (Fig. 30.3).

(cont.)

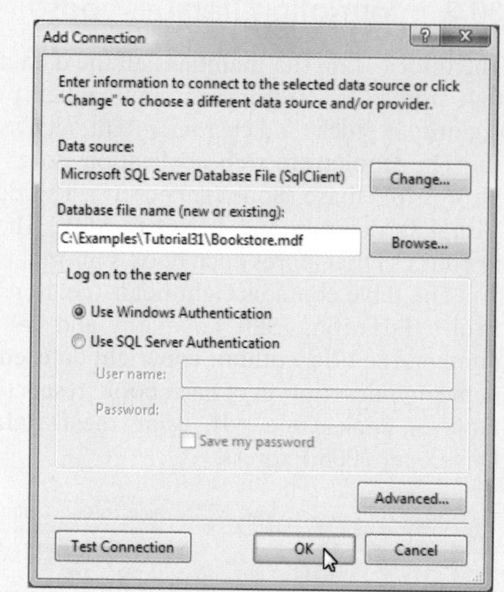

Figure 30.3 Adding the `Bookstore.mdf` database to the web application.

3. ***Saving the project.*** Select **File > Save All** to save your modified code.

Now that you've established the database connection, you create LINQ to SQL classes that allow your application to interact with the database.

Creating LINQ to SQL Classes from the `Bookstore.mdf` Database

1. ***Creating LINQ to SQL classes.*** Right click the project in the **Solution Explorer** and select **Add > New Item...**. In the **Add New Item** dialog, select **LINQ to SQL Classes** and enter `BookInformationDB.dbml` in the **Name:** `TextBox` (Fig. 30.4). Click the **Add** `Button`. A dialog appears asking if you would like to put `BookInformationDB.dbml` in the **App_Code** folder. Click **Yes** (Fig. 30.5). [*Note:* This may take a few seconds.] The `BookInformationDB.dbml` file now appears in the **App_Code** folder in the **Solution Explorer**. The App_Code folder is generally used to store your web application's code files (other than the `aspx.vb` code-behind files). This is a protected folder that can be accessed only by the server

Select **LINQ to SQL Classes** in **Templates:** pane

Rename the LINQ to SQL classes

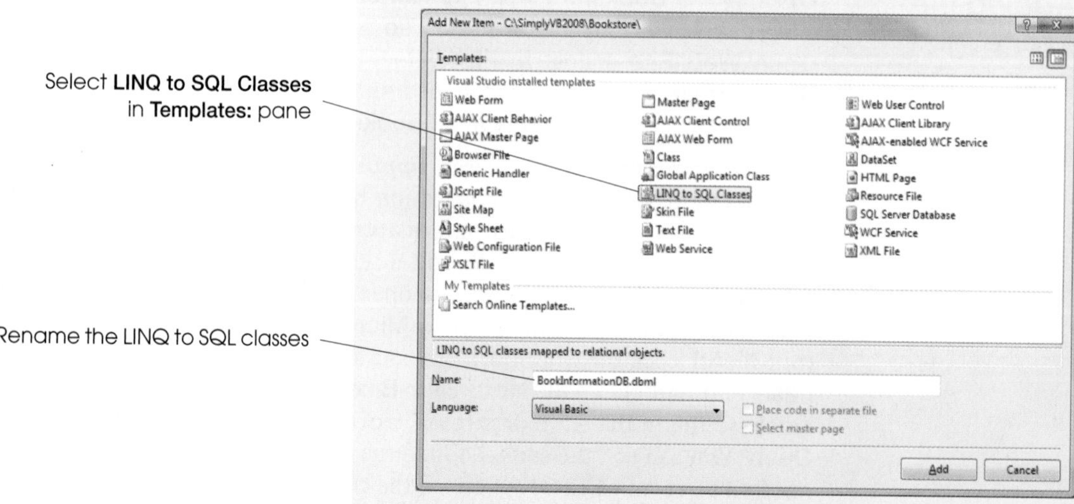

Figure 30.4 Adding LINQ to SQL classes.

(cont.)

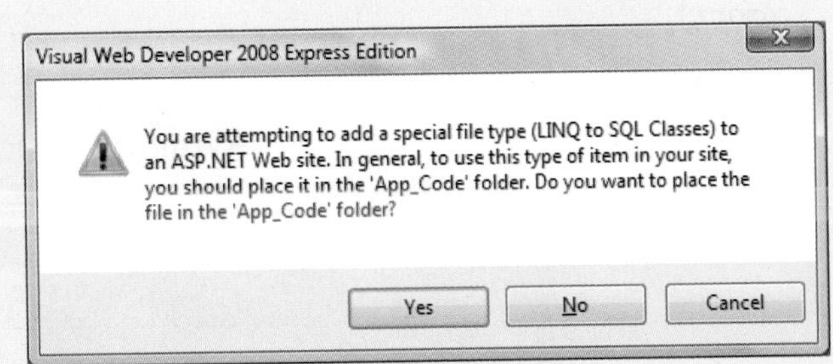

Figure 30.5 Confirming that the LINQ to SQL classes will be added to the **App_Code** folder.

2. ***Adding the Products table to the LINQ to SQL classes.*** If the **Object Relational Designer** is not open, double click `BookInformationDB.dbml` in the **Solution Explorer**. To enable access to a database table, you drag the table from the **Database Explorer** onto the **Object Relational Designer**. Expand the **Bookstore.mdf** node in the **Database Explorer**, then expand the **Tables** node. Drag the `Products` table onto the **Object Relational Designer** (Fig. 30.6). A dialog appears prompting you to copy the database file to your project, click **Yes**. The `Bookstore.mdf` database now appears in the **App_Data** folder in the **Solution Explorer**. The App_Data folder is generally used to store external sources of data used by the web application. This is another protected folder that can be accessed only by the server.

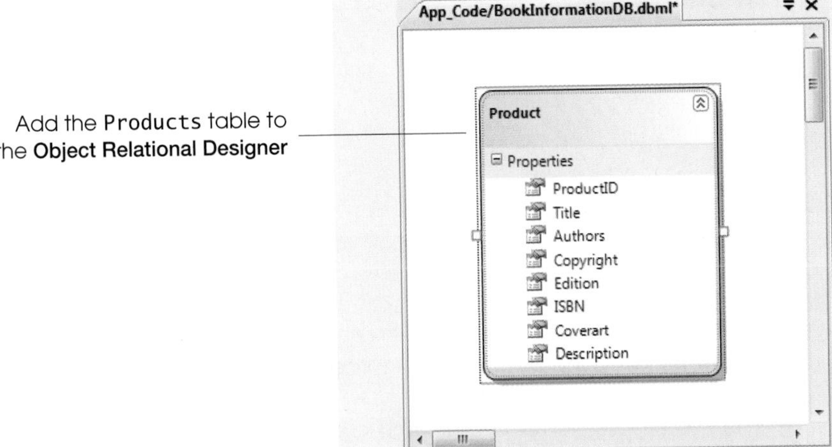

Figure 30.6 Adding the `Products` table to the LINQ to SQL classes.

3. ***Saving the project.*** Select **File > Save All** to save your modified code.

The LINQ to SQL classes create a model of the `Bookstore.mdf` database. You use this model to manipulate the information in the database. In the next box, you create a `LinqDataSource` that binds the book titles in the database to the `bookTitlesListBox` in the `Books.aspx` page. A `LinqDataSource` uses LINQ to retrieve information from a `DataContext` object.

Creating a `LinqDataSource`

1. ***Creating a `LinqDataSource`.*** Select the `bookTitlesListBox` in the `Books.aspx` page. Click the small black arrow in the upper-right corner of the control to open the **ListBox Tasks** menu (Fig. 30.7). Select **Choose Data Source...** to open the **Data Source Configuration Wizard**.

(cont.)

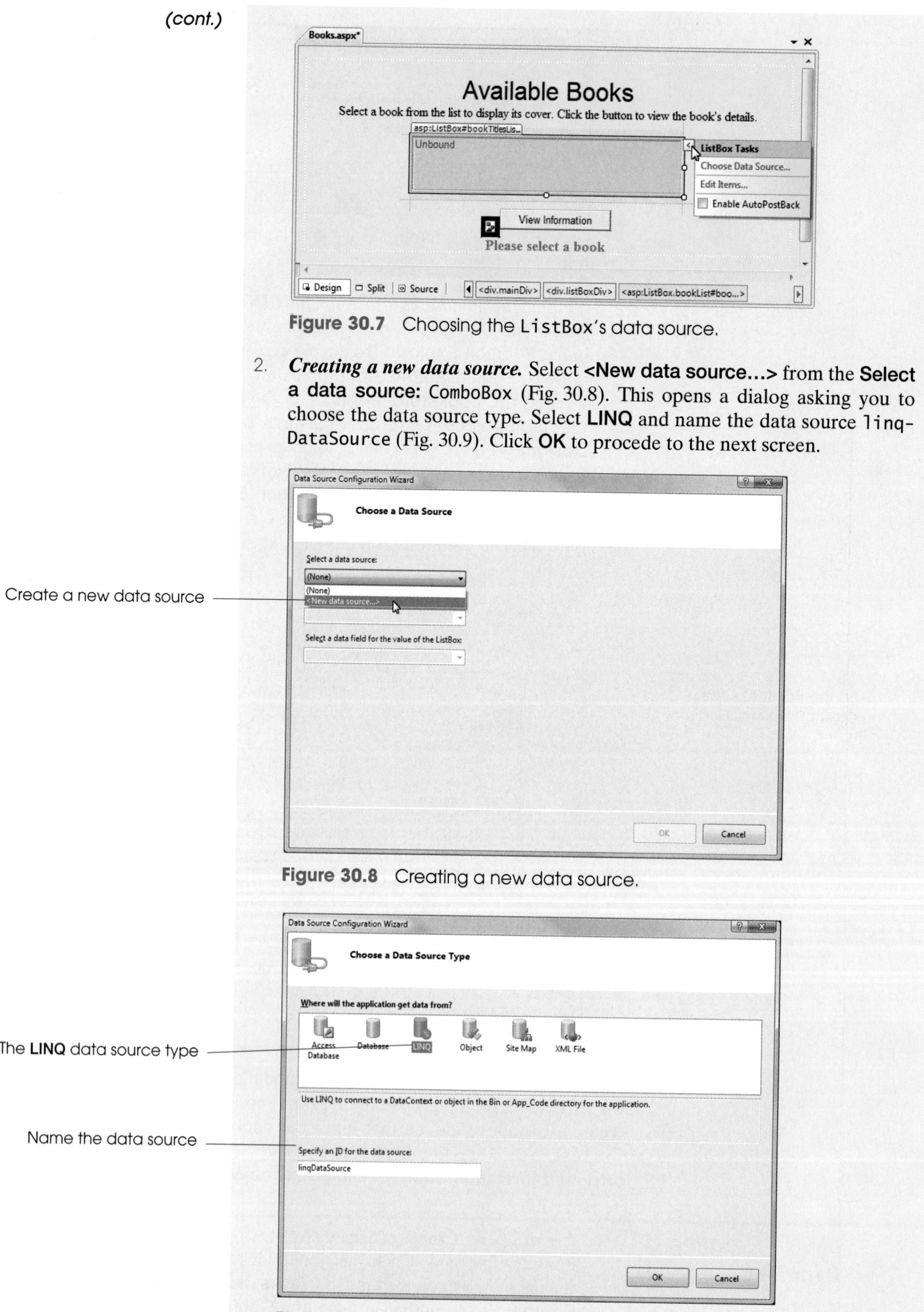

Figure 30.7 Choosing the `ListBox`'s data source.

2. ***Creating a new data source.*** Select **<New data source...>** from the **Select a data source:** `ComboBox` (Fig. 30.8). This opens a dialog asking you to choose the data source type. Select **LINQ** and name the data source `linqDataSource` (Fig. 30.9). Click **OK** to procede to the next screen.

Figure 30.8 Creating a new data source.

Figure 30.9 Creating a `LinqDataSource`.

(cont.)

3. ***Choosing the DataContext object.*** The next screen asks you to choose a context object. Recall from Tutorial 24 that the LINQ to SQL classes include a `DataContext` object used to access the database tables you added to the **Object Relational Designer**. Select the `BookInformationDBDataContext` object from the `ComboBox` and click **Next >** (Fig. 30.10).

`BookInformationDBDataContext` object selected as the data source's context

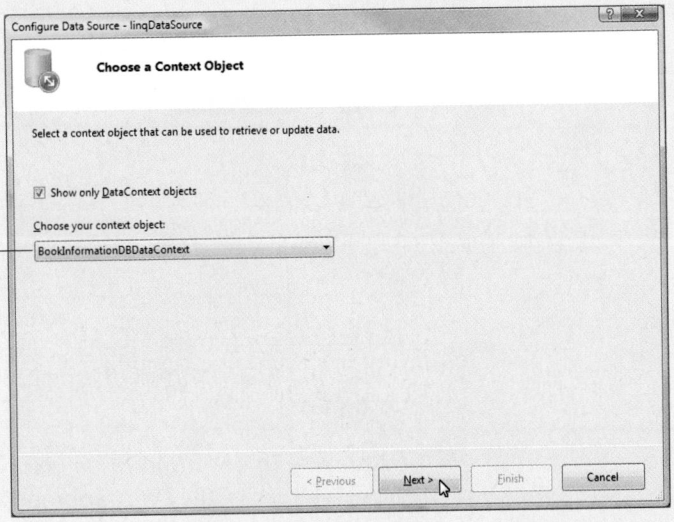

Configure Data Source - linqDataSource

Choose a Context Object

Select a context object that can be used to retrieve or update data.

Show only DataContext objects

Choose your context object:

BookInformationDBDataContext

< Previous Next > Finish Cancel

Figure 30.10 Selecting a `DataContext` object for the data source.

4. ***Configuring the data source.*** The next dialog allows you to configure the information contained in the data source (Fig. 30.11). You added only one table (`Products`) to the LINQ to SQL classes, so the IDE automatically selects it as the table which contains information for this data source. By default, the `LinqDataSource` retrieves all columns from the specified table—indicated by the * `CheckBox`. Leave this `CheckBox` selected. You can also order the information contained in the data source—click the **Order By...** `Button` to determine how the information in the data source is sorted. In the **Configure OrderBy Expression** dialog that opens, select **Title** from the `ComboBox` in the **Sort by** `GroupBox` (Fig. 30.12), then click **OK** to close the **Configure OrderBy Expression** dialog. The information in the `LinqDataSource` will be ordered alphabetically by book title. Click **Finish** to close the **Configure Data Source – linqDataSource** dialog.

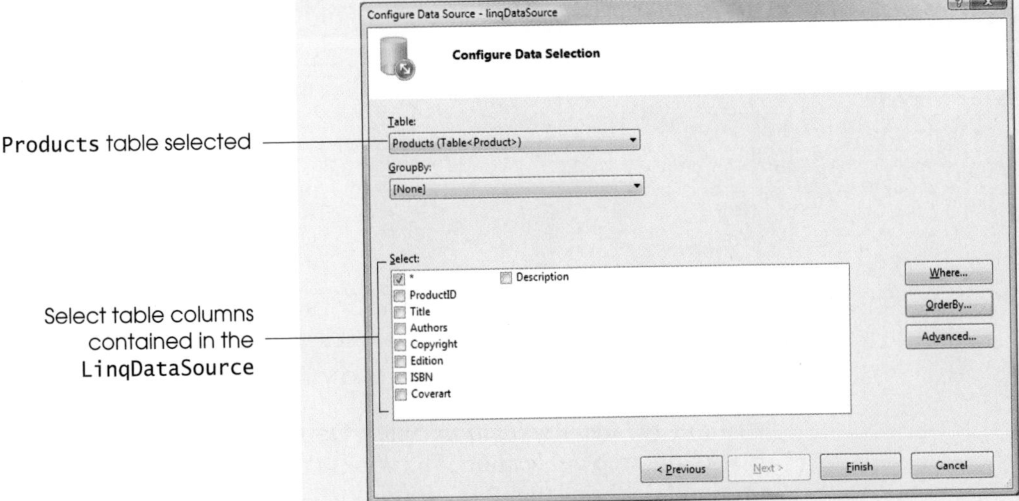

Figure 30.11 Configuring the information contained in the data source.

(cont.)

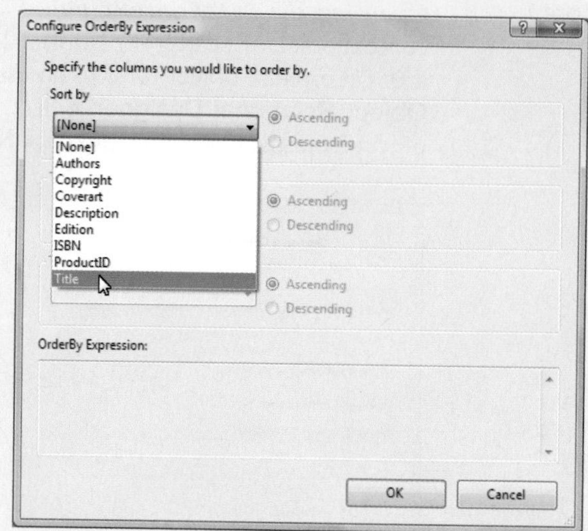

Figure 30.12 Determine the order in which information is stored in the data source.

5. ***Displaying information in the data-bound `ListBox`.*** You are now back to the first screen of the **Data Source Configuration Wizard**. Select **Title** from the **Select a data field to display in the ListBox:** `ComboBox`. This displays the book titles in the `ListBox`. Then select **ProductID** from the **Select a data field for the value of the ListBox:** `ComboBox` (Fig. 30.13). When you access the `ListBox`'s `SelectedValue` property, it will return the `ProductID` of the book whose `Title` is currently selected in the `ListBox`. This will be used uniquely identify the selected book. Click **OK** to close the **Data Source Configuration Wizard**. Notice that a `LinqDataSource` control now appears in the **Design** view of the `Books.aspx` page—this is the data source you just created. You can reconfigure the data source by selecting it and clicking the small black arrow in the upper-right corner of the control.

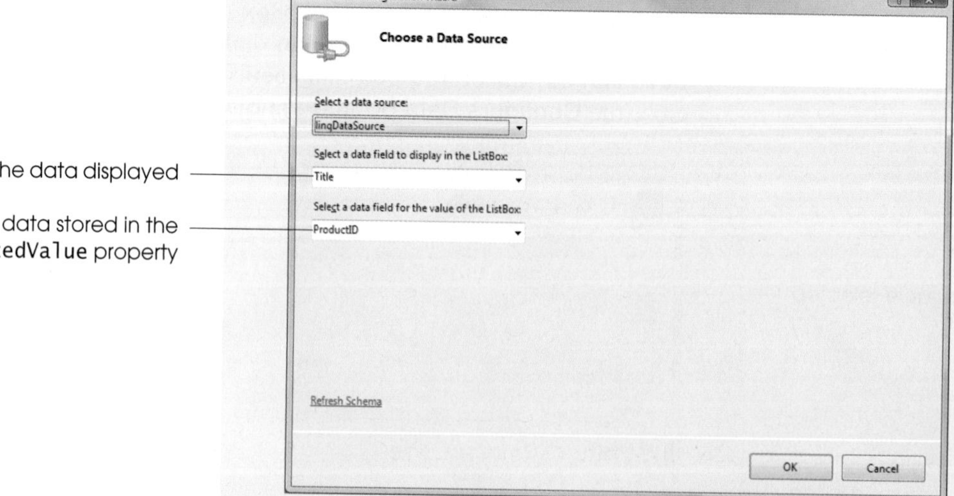

Figure 30.13 Setting the display and value fields for the `ListBox`.

6. ***Running the web application.*** Select **Debug > Start Debugging** to run the **Bookstore** web application. The `bookTitlesListBox` displays the `Titles` of the books in the `Bookstore.mdf` database in alphabetical order (Fig. 30.14).

(cont.)

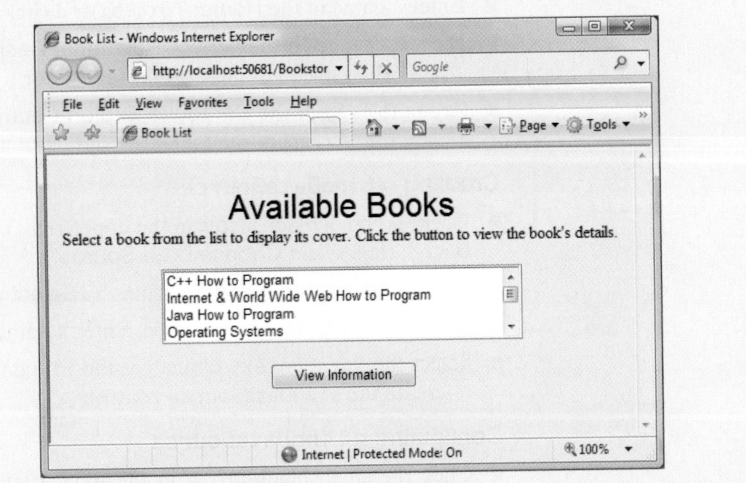

Figure 30.14 Books.aspx displaying book titles in data-bound ListBox.

7. ***Closing the running web application.*** Close the running web application by clicking the browser's close box.
8. ***Saving the project.*** Select **File > Save All** to save your modified code.

SELF-REVIEW

1. A ________ binds information in a LINQ to SQL class to a web control.
   a) LinqDataSource
   b) database
   c) ListBox
   d) None of the above
2. A LinqDataSource retrieves data using a ________.
   a) database
   b) table
   c) DataContext object
   d) data-bound control

Answers: 1) a. 2) c.

30.4 Wrap-Up

In this tutorial, you were introduced to the information tier of the three-tier, **Bookstore** web application. You examined the contents of the Bookstore.mdf database. You configured the information tier of the **Bookstore** web application by creating a database connection, LINQ to SQL classes and a LinqDataSource. You used the **Data Source Configuration Wizard** to determine the information retrieved by the data source. You then used the LinqDataSource to display book titles in the bookTitlesListBox when the Books.aspx page loads.

In the next tutorial, you create the middle tier of your **Bookstore** web application. You add code to your application to control what data from the database is displayed on the BookInformation.aspx page.

SKILLS SUMMARY

Adding a Database Connection

- Select the **Tools > Connect to Database...** menu item.
- In the **Add Connection** dialog, select **Microsoft SQL Server Database File (SqlClient)** as the **Data Source**.
- Click **Browse...** to locate the database file, then click **OK** to create the connection.

Creating LINQ to SQL Classes

- Right click the project in the **Solution Explorer** and select **Add > New Item...**.
- Select the **LINQ to SQL Classes** template in the **Add New Item** dialog.

- Enter a name in the **Name:** `TextBox` and click **Add**.
- If necessary, open the **Object Relational Designer** by double clicking the LINQ to SQL classes file (`.dbml`) in the **Solution Explorer**.
- Drag tables from the **Database Explorer** onto the **Object Relational Designer** to create classes that represent the tables in your database.

Creating a `LinqDataSource`

- Click the small black arrow in the upper-right corner of the control you want to make data bound, then select **Choose Data Source...**.
- Select **<new data source...>** from the **Select a data source:** `ComboBox`.
- Select the **LINQ** data source type. Enter a name for the data source and click **OK**.
- Select the `DataContext` object for the `LinqDataSource`, then click **Next >**. Click **Finish** to create the `LinqDataSource` control.

Configuring a `LinqDataSource`

- Click the small black arrow in the upper-right corner of the `LinqDataSource` control, then select **Configure Data Source...** from its **LinqDataSource Tasks** menu.
- Select a `DataContext` object for the `LinqDataSource`, then click **Next >**.
- Select the table from which to retrieve information.
- Select the fields contained in the data source.
- Click the **OrderBy...** `Button` to specify the ordering of the data source's items.
- Click **Finish**.

Displaying Data from the `LinqDataSource` in a `ListBox`

- Click the small black arrow in the upper-right corner of the `ListBox`.
- Select **Choose Data Source...** from the **ListBox Tasks** menu.
- Select a data source from the **Select a data source:** `ComboBox`.
- Select the field to be displayed in the `ListBox` from the **Select a data field to display in the ListBox:** `ComboBox`.
- Select the value contained in the `ListBox`'s `SelectedValue` property from the **Select a data field for the value of the ListBox:** `ComboBox`.
- Click **OK**.

KEY TERMS

App_Code folder—The project folder where the application-code files (other than the `aspx.vb` code-behind files) are stored. This is a protected folder that is accessible only to the server.

App_Data folder—The project folder where external sources of data (i.e., the `Bookstore.mdf` database file) are stored. This is a protected folder that is accessible only to the server.

`LinqDataSource`—A data source that uses LINQ to retrieve information from a `DataContext` object.

MULTIPLE-CHOICE QUESTIONS

30.1 The ________ binds a control to data retrieved from LINQ to SQL classes.

a) `DataContext` object b) database
c) `LinqDataSource` d) None of the above

30.2 LINQ to SQL classes are stored in the ________ folder of the application.

a) **App_Code** b) **App_Data**
c) **Default** d) None of the above

30.3 Another name for the database tier is ________.

a) the information tier b) the bottom tier
c) Both a and b d) None of the above

30.4 A SQL Server Express database file is placed in the ________ folder.

a) **App_Code** b) **App_Data**
c) **Default** d) None of the above

EXERCISES

30.5 *(**Phone Book** Web Application: Database)* Create the database connections and data sources for the **Phone Book** web application.

a) ***Opening the application.*** Open the **Phone Book** web application that you created in Tutorial 29.

b) ***Adding the `Phone.mdf` database to the Phone Book web application.*** Add the database `C:\Examples\Tutorial31\Exercises\Databases\Phone.mdf` as you did in the box *Adding the `Bookstore.mdf` Database to the **Bookstore** Web Application.*

c) ***Adding LINQ to SQL classes to the Phone Book web application.*** Create a set of LINQ to SQL classes named `PhoneBookDB.dbml`. Add the `Phone` table from the `Phone.mdf` database to the LINQ to SQL classes.

d) ***Adding a `LinqDataSource` to the `PhoneBook.aspx` page.*** Add a `LinqDataSource` to the `PhoneBook.aspx` page and name it `linqDataSource`. Use this data source to display the names from the database in the `namesDropDownList` in the `PhoneBook.aspx` page. Sort the names alphabetically. The `namesDropDownList`'s `SelectedValue` property should contain the `IDNumber` for the selected `Name`.

e) ***Saving the project.*** Select **File > Save All** to save your modified code.

30.6 *(**US State Facts** Web Application: Database)* Create the database connections and data sources for the **US State Facts** web application.

a) ***Opening the application.*** Open the **US State Facts** web application that you created in Tutorial 29.

b) ***Adding the `StateFacts.mdf` database to the US State Facts web application.*** Add the database `C:\Examples\Tutorial31\Exercises\Databases\StateFacts.mdf` as you did in the box *Adding the `Bookstore.mdf` Database to the **Bookstore** Web Application.*

c) ***Adding LINQ to SQL classes to the US State Facts web application.*** Create a set of LINQ to SQL classes named `StateFactsDB.dbml`. Add the `StateFacts` table from the `StateFacts.mdf` database to the LINQ to SQL classes.

d) ***Adding a `LinqDataSource` to the `States.aspx` page.*** Add a `LinqDataSource` to the `States.aspx` page and name it `linqDataSource`. Use this data source to display the state names from the database in the `statesListBox` in the `States.aspx` page. Sort the names alphabetically. The `statesListBox`'s `SelectedValue` property should contain the `StateID` for the selected `Name`.

e) ***Saving the project.*** Select **File > Save All** to save your modified code.

31 TUTORIAL

Objectives

In this tutorial, you learn to:

- Write the functionality for the middle tier, using Visual Basic code.
- Modify code-behind files in a web application.
- Pass information between ASPX pages using session handling.
- Use partial page updates.

Outline

Bookstore Application: Middle Tier

Introducing Code-Behind Files, Session State and ASP.NET Ajax

In earlier tutorials, you built the client tier and created connections to the information tier of the **Bookstore** web application. In this tutorial, you learn about the middle tier and complete the **Bookstore** web application by programming the middle tier's functionality. Recall that the middle tier is responsible for interacting with the client and information tiers. The middle tier accepts user requests for data from the client tier, retrieves the data from the information tier (that is, the database) and responds to the client's requests.

31.1 Reviewing the Bookstore Web Application

You've taken the three-tier **Bookstore** web application for a test-drive (in Tutorial 28), and created the web pages (Tutorial 29) and database components (Tutorial 30) for the application. Now you write code to specify the **Bookstore** web application's functionality. Before you begin to create the middle tier, you should review the application's pseudocode and the ACE table (Fig. 31.1):

```
When the Books page is requested
    Retrieve the book titles from the database
    Display book titles in a ListBox

When the user selects a book title from the ListBox
    Display the book's cover image below the ListBox in an Image

When the user clicks the View Information Button
    If the user did not select a book from the ListBox
        Display an error message
    Otherwise
        Store the selected book's product ID
        Redirect the browser to the BookInformation page

When the BookInformation page is requested
    Retrieve the selected book's information from the database
    Display the book title in a Label
    Display the authors in a Label
    Display the cover art in an Image
    Display the remaining information in a DetailsView
```

When the user clicks the Return to Book List Button on the BookInformation page
    Redirect the browser back to the Books page

Action/Control/Event (ACE) Table for the Bookstore Web Application

Action	Control/Object	Event
Label the Books page	`availableLabel`, `instructionsLabel`	
	`Page`	`Load` (for `Books.aspx`)
Retrieve the book titles from the database	`linqDataSource`	
Display book titles in a ListBox	`bookTitlesListBox`	
	`bookTitlesListBox`	`SelectedIndex-Changed`
Display the book's cover image below the ListBox in an Image	`bookTitlesListBox`, `db` (an object class `Book-InformationDBData-Context`), `coverImage`	
	`informationButton`	`Click`
If the user did not select a book from the ListBox	`bookTitlesListBox`	
Display an error message	`bookRequiredField-Validator`	
Otherwise		
Store the selected book's product ID in a session variable	`bookTitlesListBox`, `Session`	
Redirect the browser to the BookInformation page	`Response`	
	`Page`	`Load` (for `Book-Information.aspx`)
Retrieve the selected book's information from the database	`db` (an object of class `BookInformationDB-DataContext`), `Session`	
Display the book title in a Label	`bookTitleLabel`	
Display the authors in a Label	`authorsLabel`	
Display the cover art in an Image	`bookImage`	
Display the remaining information in a DetailsView	`linqDataSource`, `bookDetailsView`	
	`bookListButton`	`Click`
Redirect the client browser back to the Books page	`Response`	

Figure 31.1 ACE table for the **Bookstore** web application.

In this tutorial, you implement the interaction between the user interface and the database of the **Bookstore** web application. You write the code that determines which images are displayed by the `Image` controls and the code that redirects the client browser to another page when a `Button` is clicked. You also use a `LinqDataSource` to determine which information is retrieved from the database and displayed in the `DetailsView` control.

31.2 Programming the Books Page's Code-Behind File

At this point, you've created the **Bookstore** web application's GUI and added database connections. You also created a `LinqDataSource` to display book titles in a `ListBox`. You now begin programming the rest of the web application's functionality. You start with the `Books.aspx` page in the following box.

Changing the Class Name in `Books.aspx.vb`

1. ***Opening the Bookstore web application in Visual Web Developer.*** Open Visual Web Developer, and select **File > Open Web Site...** to display the **Open Web Site** dialog. In this dialog, click **File System**, then select the **Bookstore** folder in the `C:\SimplyVB2008` directory and click the **Open** `Button` to open the **Bookstore** web application.

2. ***Displaying the `Books.aspx` page's code-behind file in the Solution Explorer.*** Every ASPX page created in Visual Web Developer has a corresponding class written in a .NET language, such as Visual Basic. This class includes event handlers, initialization code, methods and other supporting code that represents the middle tier of this web application. The Visual Basic file that contains this class is called the **code-behind file** and defines the ASPX page's functionality. It has the file extension `.aspx.vb`. If it is not already selected, click the **Nest Related Files** `Button` (Fig. 31.2) in the **Solution Explorer** toolbar. Expand the `Books.aspx` node to display the code-behind file, `Books.aspx.vb` (Fig. 31.2).

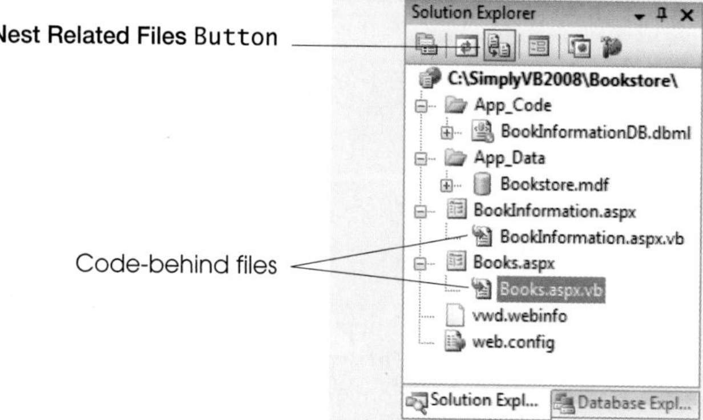

Figure 31.2 Code-behind files for the `Books.aspx` and `BookInformation.aspx` pages in the **Solution Explorer**.

3. ***Viewing the `Books.aspx.vb` code-behind file.*** Figure 31.3 displays `Books.aspx.vb`—the code-behind file for `Books.aspx`. Visual Web Developer generates this code-behind file when the project is created. To view this file, double click `Books.aspx.vb` in the **Solution Explorer** window. [*Note:* You also can right click `Books.aspx` and select **View Code** to view the code-behind file.] There are no commands in this file because you have not yet started to write event handlers.

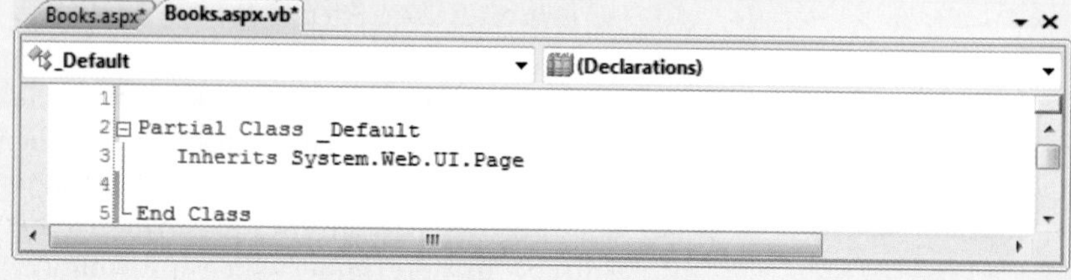

Figure 31.3 Code-behind file for `Books.aspx`.

(cont.)

4. ***Changing the class name in* `Books.aspx.vb`*.*** Delete the blank line above the class definition. Change the class name in line 1 of `Books.aspx.vb` from `_Default` to `Books` (Fig. 31.4). Line 2 of `Books.aspx.vb` indicates that this class inherits from the `Page` class. The **`Page`** class defines the basic functionality for an ASPX page, much as the `Form` class defines the basic functionality for a Windows `Form`. The `Page` class is located in the `System.Web.UI` namespace. The `Page` class provides properties, methods and events that are useful for creating web applications. Also add the comment in line 4 after the `End Class` keywords.

Good Programming Practice

For clarity, give an ASPX page's class the same name as the page (e.g., `Books` for `Books.aspx`).

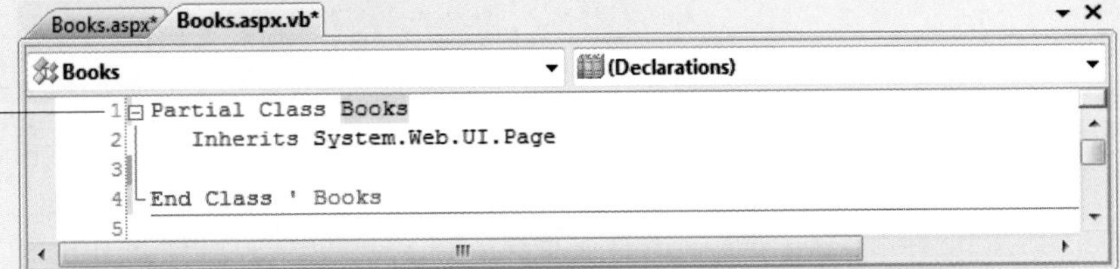

Figure 31.4 Changing the `Books.aspx` page's class name.

5. ***Modifying the* `Inherits` *attribute in* `Books.aspx`*.*** In **Source** view for `Books.aspx`, change the `Inherits` attribute in the `Page` directive in line 2 (we reformatted the first line to split over two lines) from `Inherits="_Default"` to `Inherits="Books"` (Fig. 31.5). This ensures that the code from the ASPX page markup will become part of the Books class in the code-behind file.

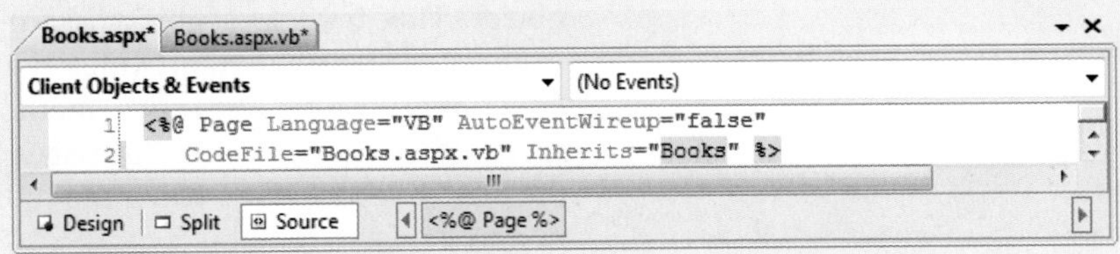

Figure 31.5 Changing the `Books.aspx` `Inherits` attribute.

6. ***Saving the project.*** Select **File > Save All** to save your modified code.

Next, you define the `informationButton_Click` event handler. This event handler is invoked when the user clicks the **View Information** `Button`. The event handler determines the selected book and redirects the client browser to the `BookInformation` page. You create the event handler in the following box.

Defining the `Click` Event Handler for the View Information `Button`

1. ***Creating the* `Click` *event handler.*** Switch to **Design** view for `Books.aspx`. Double click the **View Information** `Button` to create the event handler `informationButton_Click` in the file `Books.aspx.vb`.

2. ***Adding code to the* `Click` *event handler.*** Add lines 8–12 of Fig. 31.6 to the event handler. Normally, web applications are stateless—variable data associated with a particular user is not maintained across different ASPX pages. However, you can use ASP.NET's session tracking features to share data for a user across pages. To do so, you create **`Session` items**. Line 9 adds a **key-value pair** to the **`Session`** object. A key/value pair associates a value (of any type) with a corresponding name (key) which is used to identify the value—similar to the `Dictionary` collection you used in Tutorial 21. The `Session` object is defined for you to use in your ASP.NET pages. It is part of the Page class that defines the basic functionality of your page.

(cont.)

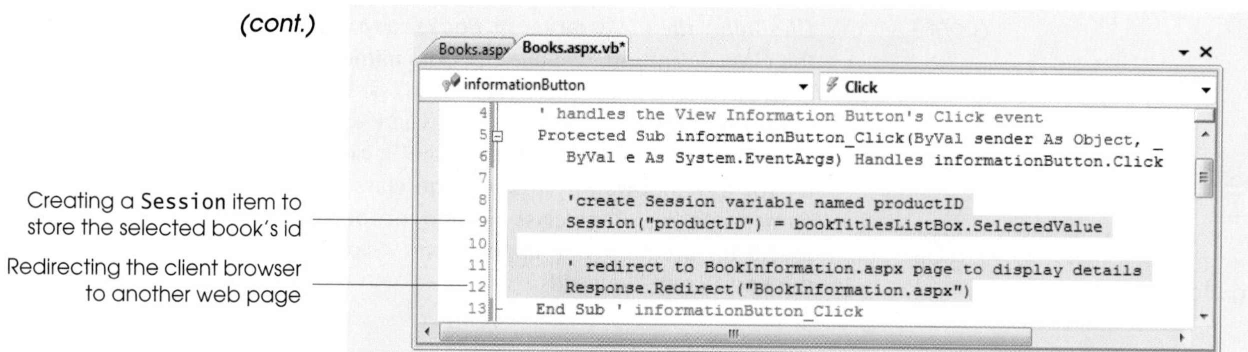

Figure 31.6 `informationButton_Click` event handler definition.

In this case, the key is the name `productID`, and the value is the selected book's `ProductID`, which is obtained from `bookTitlesListBox`'s property **`SelectedValue`**. The storage of key/value pairs across web pages is made possible by **session state**, which is ASP.NET's built-in support for tracking data. Session state enables the current user's information (including the book the user has selected) to be maintained throughout a browser session—that is, while the user is interacting with the website. Session state resides in the memory of the web server. By default, session state is maintained until the user closes the browser or until the user does not interact with the website for 20 minutes, whichever comes first.

After specifying the value for the `productID` key, the page redirects the client browser by calling the `Redirect` method (line 12) of the `Response` object. The **`Response`** object is a predefined ASP.NET object (inherited from class `Page`) that provides methods for responding to clients. The `Response` object's **`Redirect`** method redirects the browser to the URL specified as its argument. All pages in the web application have access to the `Session` object. So when the redirect occurs, the session-state information in the `Session` object can be used in the `BookInformation` page.

3. ***Saving the project.*** Select **File > Save All** to save your modified code.

Before you finish programming the `Books.aspx.vb` code-behind file, you need to place images of the book covers in the `Bookstore` directory so the application can access them. The `Books.aspx` page displays the cover image of the selected book below the `ListBox`. You finish programming the `Books.aspx.vb` code-behind file in the next box.

Displaying the Selected Book's Cover Image

1. ***Locating the images.*** Use Windows Explorer to locate the `C:\Examples\Tutorial31\images` directory, which contains the book cover images.
2. ***Placing the images in the* Bookstore *directory.*** Copy the `images` directory to the `C:\SimplyVB2008\Bookstore` directory. Click the **Refresh** `Button` in the **Solutions Explorer**'s toolbar. The `images` directory should now appear in the **Solution Explorer**. You can also drag the `images` folder directly from **Windows Explorer** into the `C:\SimplyVB2008\Bookstore` directory at the top of the **Solution Explorer** in Visual Web Developer.

(cont.)

3. ***Defining the `ListBox`'s `SelectedIndexChanged` event handler.*** Double click the `bookTitlesListBox` in **Design** view to create its `SelectedIndex-Changed` event handler, which executes when you select an item in the `ListBox`. Add lines 20–30 of Fig. 31.7 to the event handler. Line 21 creates a `DataContext` object used to retrieve information from the database. Lines 24–27 retrieve the selected book from the database and assign it to local variable `coverFile`. The LINQ query's `Where` clause (line 26) determines whether the book in the database contains the `ProductID` of the book selected in the `bookTitlesListBox`. The `Select` clause (line 27) returns the name of the book's cover image.

```
Books.aspx   Books.aspx.vb*
bookTitlesListBox   SelectedIndexChanged
15    ' display the cover image of the selected book
16    Protected Sub bookTitlesListBox_SelectedIndexChanged( _
17       ByVal sender As Object, ByVal e As System.EventArgs) _
18       Handles bookTitlesListBox.SelectedIndexChanged
19
20       ' create the DataContext for querying the database
21       Dim db As New BookInformationDBDataContext()
22
23       ' get the book cover's file name for the selected book
24       Dim coverFile = _
25          (From item In db.Products _
26           Where item.ProductID = bookTitlesListBox.SelectedValue _
27           Select item.Coverart).Single()
28
29       coverImage.ImageUrl = "images/" & coverFile ' specify filename
30       coverImage.Visible = True ' display image
31    End Sub ' bookTitlesListBox_SelectedIndexChanged
```

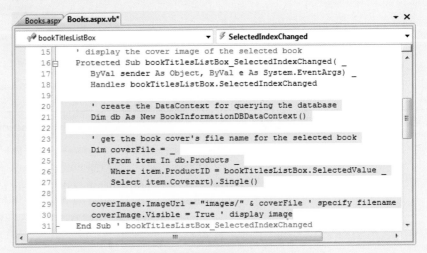

Figure 31.7 Displaying the selected book's cover image.

Note that the query is placed in parentheses and that we call method `Single` (line 27) on the result of the query. This returns *one* item in the query's result—an exception occurs if more than one item is returned. You use method `Single` because you want to return only one item—as opposed to a collection of items. In this case, the `Coverart` column in the database table is a `String` value, so `Single` returns a `String`. Since a single `String` is returned, you can use the `coverFile` variable (line 29) without retrieving it from a collection returned by the query, as is usually the case. Line 29 displays the image in the `Image` control by assigning it to the `Image` control's `ImageUrl` property. Line 30 makes the `Image` control visible.

4. ***Enabling `AutoPostBack` on the `ListBox`.*** To display the book's cover image, the server must receive the `SelectedIndexChanged` event from the `ListBox`. Switch to **Design** view and select the `bookTitlesListBox`. Click the small black triangle in the upper-right corner of the `ListBox` to open the **ListBox Tasks** menu. Click the **Enable AutoPostBack** `CheckBox` (Fig. 31.8). When the selected index changes, the browser rerequests the page automatically, rather than requiring the user to press a button. The server responds to the `SelectedIndexChanged` by determining the selected image, then resends the page back to the client. This process is sometimes called a "round trip." When the page reloads, the selected book's cover image is displayed below the `ListBox`. You can test this functionality by running the application. Click an item in the `ListBox` to see the corresponding book cover image.

5. ***Saving the project.*** Select **File > Save All** to save your modified code.

(cont.)

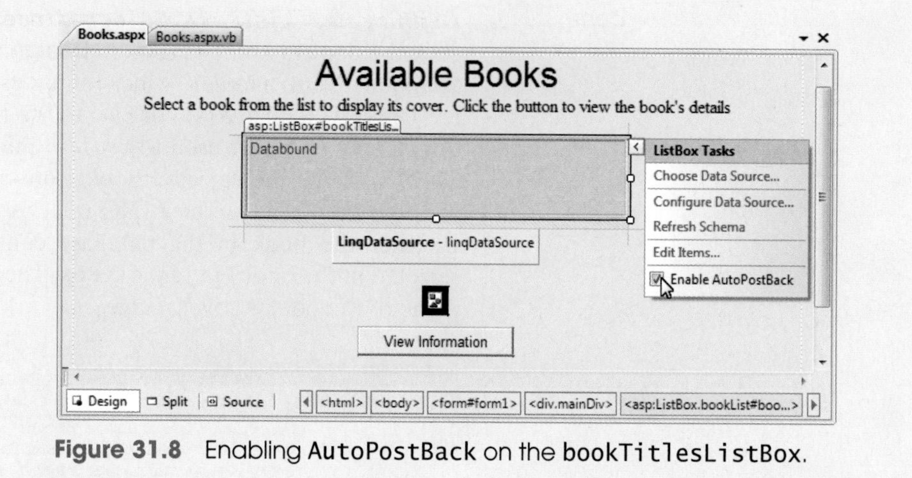

Figure 31.8 Enabling `AutoPostBack` on the `bookTitlesListBox`.

SELF-REVIEW

1. The ________ class defines the basic functionality for an ASPX page.
   a) `Form` b) `WebForm`
   c) `Page` d) None of the above

2. The ________ property forces the browser to reload the ASPX page automatically in response to a control's event
   a) `AutoPostBack` b) `Reload`
   c) `RePost` d) `ForcePostBack`

Answers: 1) c. 2) a.

31.3 Coding the `BookInformation` Page's Code-Behind File and Data Binding to the `DetailsView`

The `BookInformation.aspx` page displays information about the book the user selected. In the following box, you add the code to the `Page_Load` event handler of the `BookInformation.aspx` page that retrieves the requested book's information from the database.

Defining the Page_Load Event Handler for `BookInformation.aspx`

1. ***Viewing the Code-Behind File.*** Right click `BookInformation.aspx` in the **Solution Explorer**, and select **View Code** to view the code-behind file `Book-Information.aspx.vb`. Note that the class name is `BookInformation` (Fig. 31.9)—when you created this page by adding a new Web Form to the project, Visual Web Developer automatically named the class correctly. Delete the blank line above the class definition.

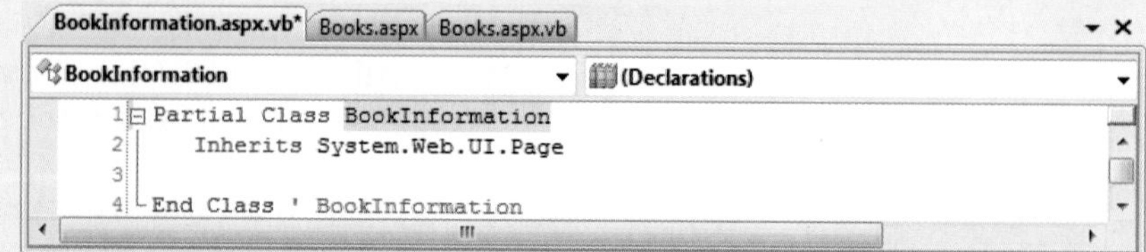

Figure 31.9 `BookInformation` class definition.

(cont.)

2. ***Inserting the Page_Load event handler.*** When the `BookInformation.aspx` page is loaded, you want the book's information to be displayed immediately. An ASPX page's **Page_Load** event handler is invoked when the page is loaded. To insert a `Page_Load` event handler into the `BookInformation` class, select **(Page Events)** from the **Class Name** drop-down list, then select **Load** from the **Method Name** drop-down list (Fig. 31.10).

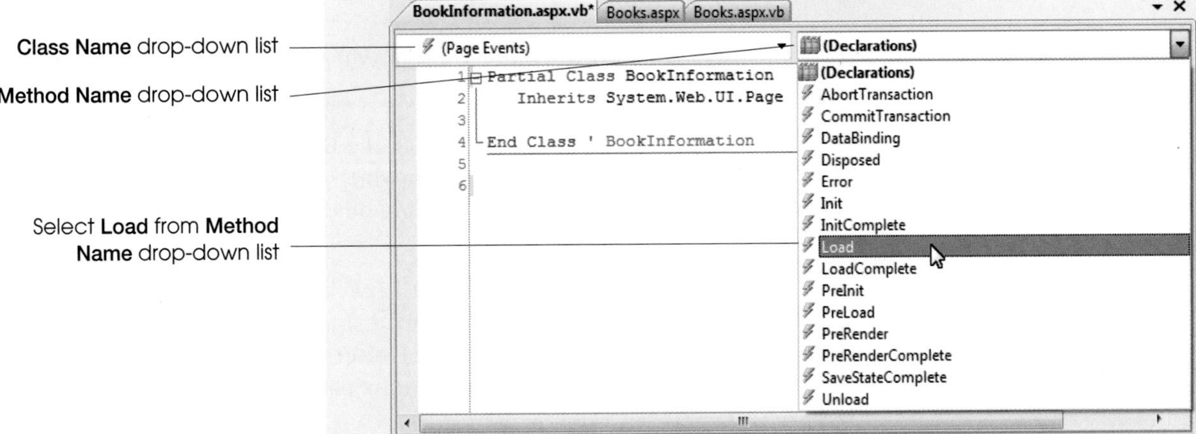

Figure 31.10 Creating the `BookInformation Page_Load` event.

3. ***Retrieving the selected book from the database.*** Add lines 8–25 of Fig. 31.11 to the `Page_Load` event handler for the `BookInformation.aspx` page. Line 9 creates a `DataContext` object used to retrieve information from the `Bookstore.mdf` database. Line 13 retrieves the value for the `productID Session` item created in the **View Information** `Button`'s `Click` event handler in the `Books.aspx` page. The `Session` item's value is returned as an `Object`—you convert it to an `Integer` and assign it to local variable `productID`.

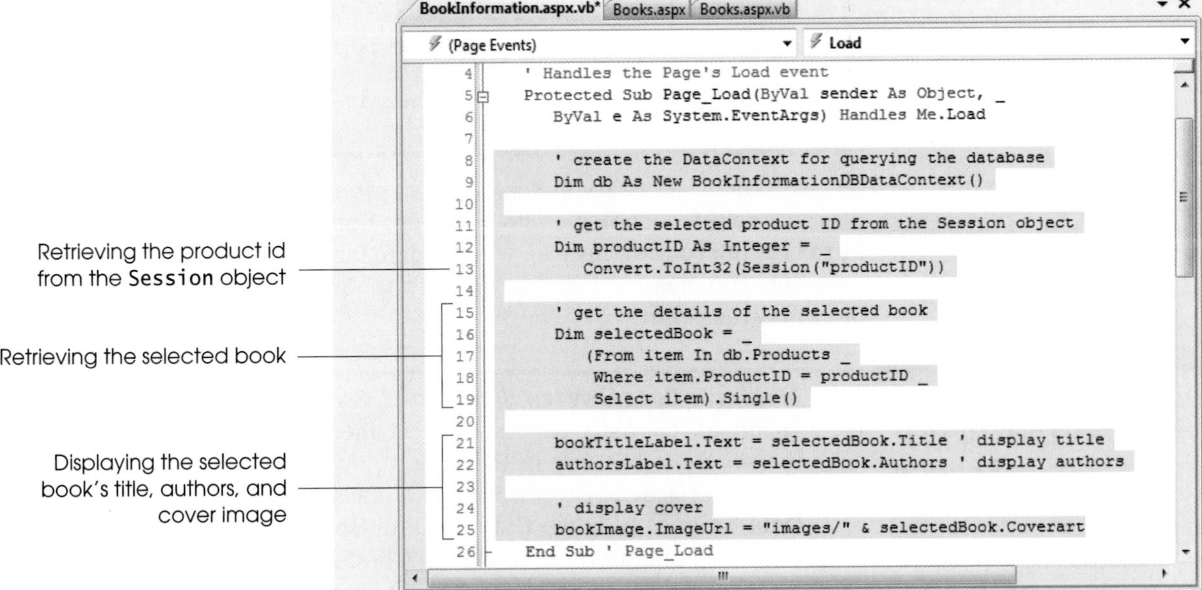

Figure 31.11 `Page_Load` event handler modified to set a parameter value and open a database connection.

(cont.)

Lines 16–19 use a LINQ query to retrieve from the database the book whose `ProductID` matches the value stored in the `productID Session` item. Once again, you use method `Single` to retrieve a single item from the database—in this case, a `Product` object representing the selected book. Recall that the LINQ to SQL classes create a `Product` class to represent one record in the `Products` table. Lines 21 –25 display the selected book's title, authors and cover image in their corresponding web controls on the `BookInformation.aspx` page.

4. ***Saving the project.*** Select **File > Save All** to save your modified code.

The final event handler you define in the `BookInformation.aspx` page is the `bookListButton_Click` event handler, which allows the user to return to the list of available books. You create this event handler in the following box.

Defining the `bookListButton_Click` Event Handler

1. ***Creating the `bookListButton_Click` event handler.*** Double click the **Return to Book List** `Button` in **Design** view to create the `bookListButton_Click` event handler. The **Return to Book List** `Button` redirects the client browser back to the `Books.aspx` page.

2. ***Adding code to the event handler.*** Add lines 32–33 of Fig. 31.12 to the `bookListButton_Click` event handler. Line 33 redirects the user to the `Books.aspx` page by calling the `Redirect` method of class `Response`.

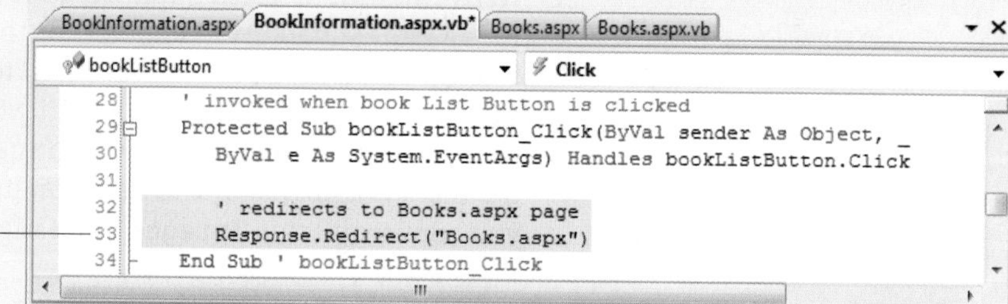
BookInformation.aspx
BookInformation.aspx.vb*
Books.aspx
Books.aspx.vb
bookListButton
Click
28 ' invoked when book List Button is clicked
29 Protected Sub bookListButton_Click(ByVal sender As Object, _
30 ByVal e As System.EventArgs) Handles bookListButton.Click
31
32 ' redirects to Books.aspx page
33 Response.Redirect("Books.aspx")
34 End Sub ' bookListButton_Click
Redirecting to the Books.aspx page

Figure 31.12 Definition of the `bookListButton_Click` event handler.

3. ***Saving the project.*** Select **File > Save All** to save your modified code.

No code is necessary in `BookInformation.aspx.vb`'s code-behind file to display the selected book's `ISBN`, `Edition`, `Copyright`, and `Description` in the `DetailsView` control. Instead, you use data binding to do this automatically. In the next box, you create a `LinqDataSource` to display the book's information in the `DetailsView` control.

Creating a Data-Bound `DetailsView` Using a `LinqDataSource`

1. ***Making a `DetailsView` data bound.*** Switch to **Design** view of the `BookInformation.aspx` page and select the `bookDetailsView` control. Click the small black arrow in the upper-right corner of the `bookDetailsView` control (Fig. 31.13) to display its **DetailsView Tasks** menu. Select **<New Data Source...>** in the **Choose Data Source:** `ComboBox` to open the **Data Source Configuration Wizard**'s **Choose a Data Source Type** dialog. Choose the **LINQ** data source type and name it `linqDataSource`. Click **OK**.

(cont.)

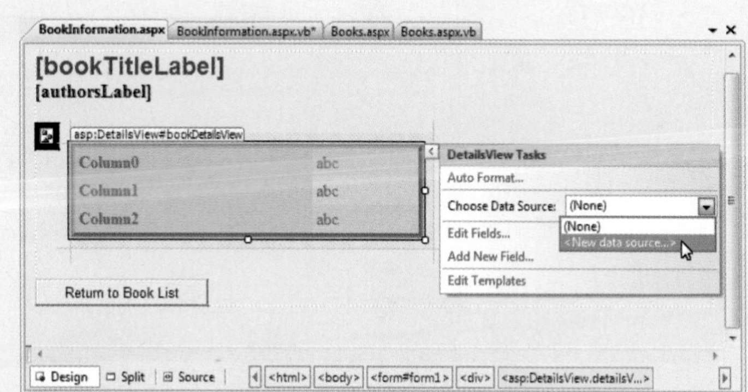

Figure 31.13 Select `<New Data Source...>` in the **Choose Data Source:** `ComboBox`.

2. ***Configuring the `LinqDataSource`'s data fields.*** In the **Configure Data Selection** dialog that appears, select the `BookInformationDBDataContext` object you created in Tutorial 31, then click **Next >**. In the next screen, ensure that the **Products** table is selected in the **Table:** `ComboBox`. Check the **Copyright**, **Edition**, **ISBN** and **Description** `CheckBoxes` (Fig. 31.14). The `LinqDataSource` will contain information for each selected field of the `Products` table.

Selecting table fields retrieved by the `LinqDataSource`

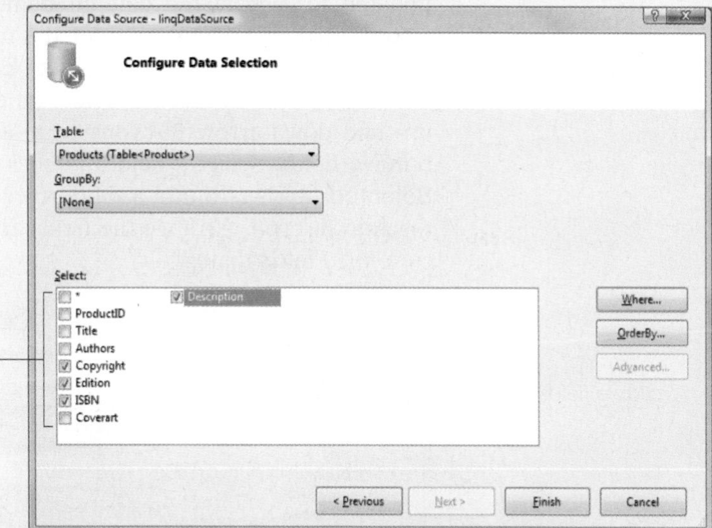

Figure 31.14 Configuring the `LinqDataSource`'s fields.

3. ***Configuring the `LinqDataSource`'s `Where` expression.*** Click the **Where...** `Button` to configure the `LinqDataSource`'s `Where` expression. This allows you to specify constraints on the data retrieved by the data source—like defining a `Where` clause in a LINQ query. In the **Configure Where Expression** dialog, select `ProductID` from the **Column:** `ComboBox`. Select == from the **Operator:** `ComboBox`. Select `Session` from the **Source:** `ComboBox` (Fig. 31.15). These values indicate the database column to check, the relational operator and the source of the value the column is checked against, respectively. In the **Parameter properties** `GroupBox` enter `productID` in the **Session field:** `TextBox`. Click the **Add** `Button`. This expression indicates that the `LinqDataSource` is to retrieve from the database only the entry containing a `ProductID` that matches the value in the `productID` `Session` item. Click **OK** to close the **Configure Where Expression** dialog. Click **Finish** to close the **Configure Data Source** dialog.

(cont.)

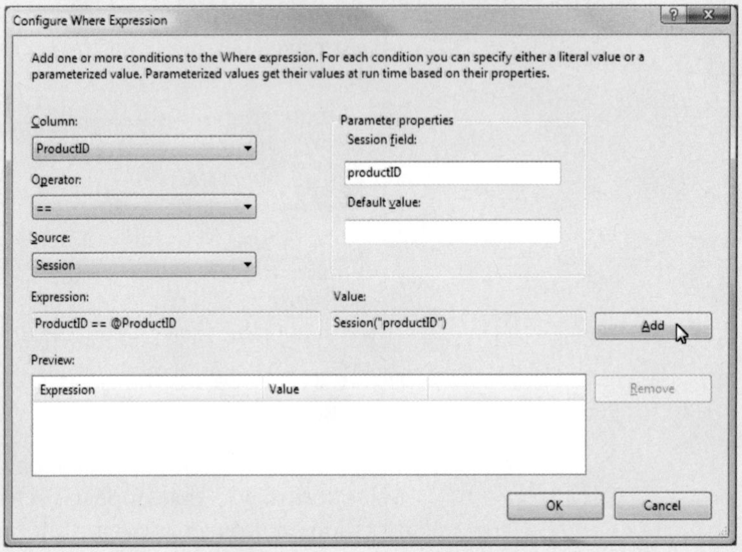

Figure 31.15 Configuring the `LinqDataSource`'s `Where` expression.

4. ***Examining the data-bound `DetailsView`.*** The `bookDetailsView` is now bound to the information in `linqDataSource`. The fields have been updated to display the column names selected in the **Configure Data Source** dialog. You can reorder the fields in the `DetailsView`. Open the **DetailsView Tasks** menu and select **Edit Fields...** to open the **Fields** dialog (Fig. 31.16). To reorder, select a field in **Selected fields:** and click the up- and down-arrow `Buttons` to move the field. You can also add and remove fields. Select a field and click the [X] `Button` to remove it from **Selected fields:**. To add a field, select it from **Available fields:** and click the **Add** `Button`. Arrange the fields as shown in Fig. 31.16 and click **OK** to close the **Fields** dialog.

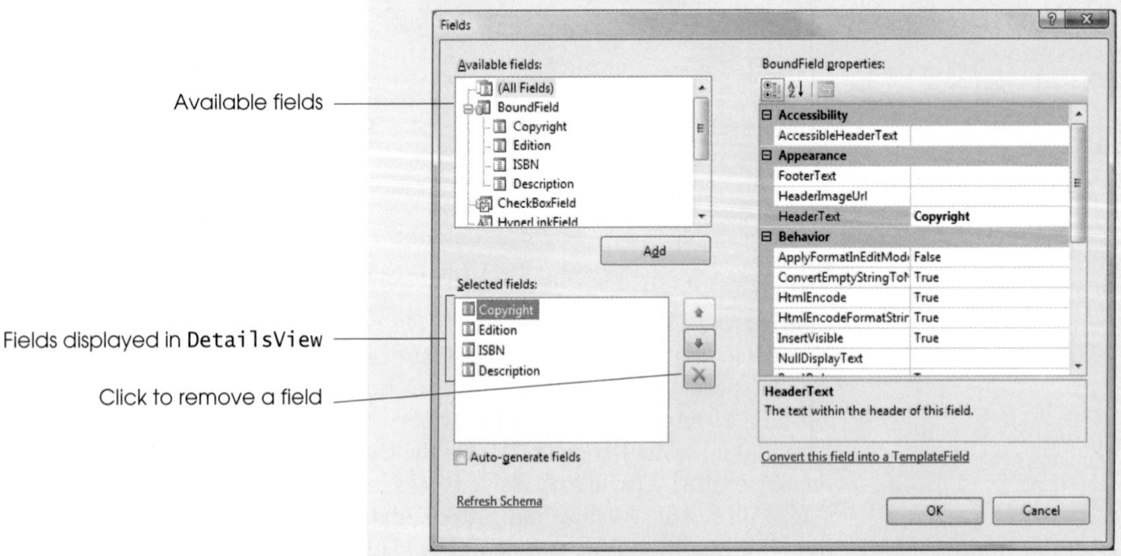

Figure 31.16 Modifying the displayed fields in the `DetailsView`.

5. ***Saving the project.*** Select **File > Save All** to save your modified code.

Now that you have completed the **Bookstore** web application, you test it to ensure that it is functioning properly in the following box.

Testing Your Completed Bookstore Web Application

1. ***Running the application.*** Select **Debug > Start Debugging** to run your web application. Select a book title from the `ListBox`—the page reloads with the book's cover image displayed below the `ListBox`. Click the **View Information** `Button`. The `BookInformation.aspx` page loads and displays the books information. This web application performs the same functions as the completed **Bookstore** web application that you test-drove in Tutorial 28. If no book title is selected when the **View Information** `Button` is clicked, the `RequiredFieldValidator` tells the user to `Please select a book`.

   As you interact with the application, notice that the browser reloads the `Books.aspx` page every time you select a book from the `bookTitlesListBox`. Such a simple page can usually be loaded with limited wait time. However, an ASPX page often contains a significant amount of content that can take time to download and render in the browser. In the next section, you learn how to use ASP.NET Ajax to improve the page's performance by loading only the portion of the page that has changed (that is, the book cover image displayed when the user makes a selection in the `ListBox`).

2. ***Closing the application.*** Close your running application by clicking the browser's close box.

31.4 ASP.NET Ajax

In this section, you learn the difference between a traditional web application and an Ajax web application. You also learn how to use **ASP.NET Ajax** to quickly and easily improve the user experience for your web applications. To demonstrate ASP.NET Ajax capabilities, you enhance the **Bookstore** web application by displaying the selected book's cover art on the `Books.aspx` page *without* reloading the entire page. The only modifications to this web application appear in `Books.aspx` file. You use Ajax-enabled controls to add this feature.

Traditional Web Applications

Figure 31.17 presents the typical interactions between the client and the server in a traditional web application, such as one that uses a user registration form. First, the user fills in the form's fields, then submits the form (Fig. 31.17, *Step 1*). The browser generates a request to the server, which receives the request and processes it (*Step 2*). The server generates and sends a response containing the exact page that the browser renders (*Step 3*), which causes the browser to load the new page (*Step 4*) and temporarily makes the browser window blank. Note that the client *waits* for the server to respond and *reloads the entire page* with the data from the response (*Step 4*). While such a **synchronous request** is being processed on the server, the user cannot interact with the web page. Frequent long periods of waiting, due perhaps to Internet congestion, have led some users to refer to the World Wide Web as the "World Wide Wait." If the user interacts with and submits another form, the process begins again (*Steps 5–8*).

This model was originally designed for a web of hypertext documents—what some people call the "brochure web." As the web evolved into a full-scale applications platform, the model shown in Fig. 31.17 yielded "choppy" application performance. Every full-page refresh required users to reload the full page. Users began to demand a more responsive model.

Ajax Web Applications

Ajax web applications add a layer between the client and the server to manage communication between the two (Fig. 31.18). When the user interacts with the page, the client requests information from the server (*Step 1*). The request is intercepted by the ASP.NET Ajax controls and sent to the server as an **asynchronous**

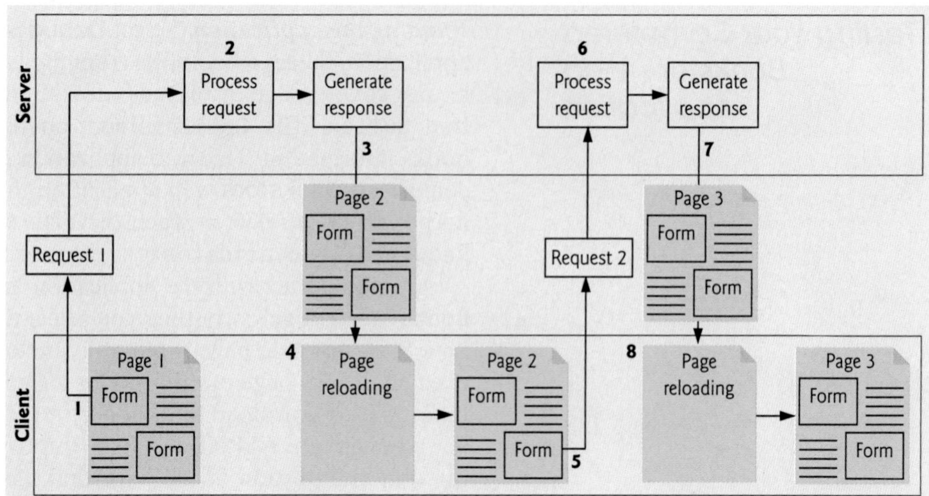

Figure 31.17 Classic web application reloading the page for every user interaction.

request (*Step 2*)—the user can continue interacting with the application in the client browser while the server processes the request. Other user interactions could result in additional requests to the server (*Steps 3* and *4*). Once the server responds to the original request (*Step 5*), the ASP.NET Ajax control that issued the request calls a client-side function to process the data returned by the server. This function—known as a **callback function**—uses **partial page updates** (*Step 6*) to display the data in the existing web page *without reloading the entire page.* At the same time, the server may be responding to the second request (*Step 7*) and the client browser may be starting another partial page update (*Step 8*). The callback function updates only a designated part of the page. Such partial page updates help make web applications more responsive, making them feel more like desktop applications. The web application does not load a new page while the user interacts with it. In the following box, you use ASP.NET Ajax controls to enhance the `Books.aspx` page.

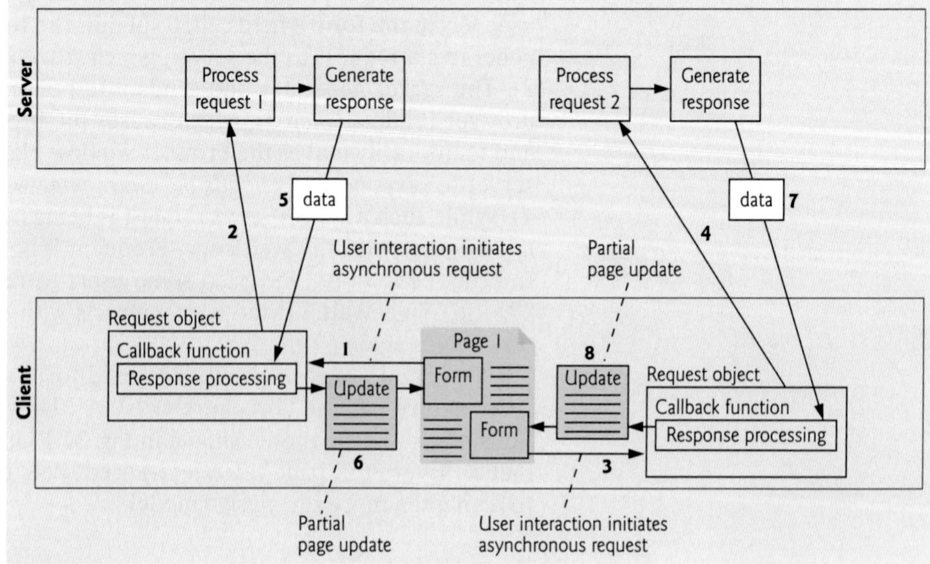

Figure 31.18 Ajax-enabled web application interacting with the server asynchronously.

Using ASP.NET Ajax to Enhance the `Books.aspx` Page

Common Programming Error

Putting more than one instance of the `ScriptManager` control on an ASPX page results in an `InvalidOperationException` when the page is initialized.

1. ***Adding a `ScriptManager` control to `Books.aspx`.*** The key control in every ASP.NET Ajax-enabled web application is the `ScriptManager`, which manages the client-side scripts that enable asynchronous Ajax functionality. There can be only one `ScriptManager` per page. Drag the `ScriptManager` from the **AJAX Extensions** tab in the **Toolbox** and place it before any controls that use the scripts it manages (i.e., before any ASP.NET Ajax controls on the page). This generates lines 48–49 (Fig. 31.19) in to create the `ScriptManager` control.

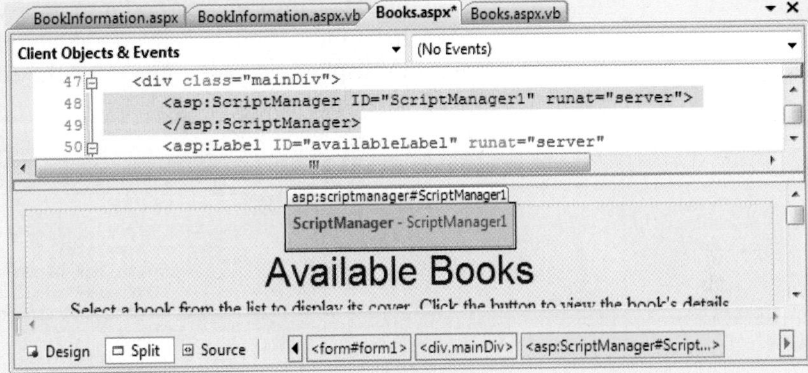

Figure 31.19 Adding a `ScriptManager` to the `Books.aspx` page.

2. ***Adding an `UpdatePanel` control.*** The `UpdatePanel` control eliminates full-page refreshes by isolating a section of a page for a partial page update. To implement a partial page update, drag the `UpdatePanel` control from the **AJAX Extensions** tab in the **Toolbox** and place it to the left of the `bookTitlesListBox`. Add lines 60–61 of Fig. 31.20 into the `UpdatePanel` element to create the `UpdatePanel`'s `ContentTemplate`, which encloses the control that initiates an asynchronous request to the server and the controls that should be updated when the `UpdatePanel` performs a partial page update.

Common Programming Error

A `ScriptManager` must appear before any controls that use the scripts it manages.

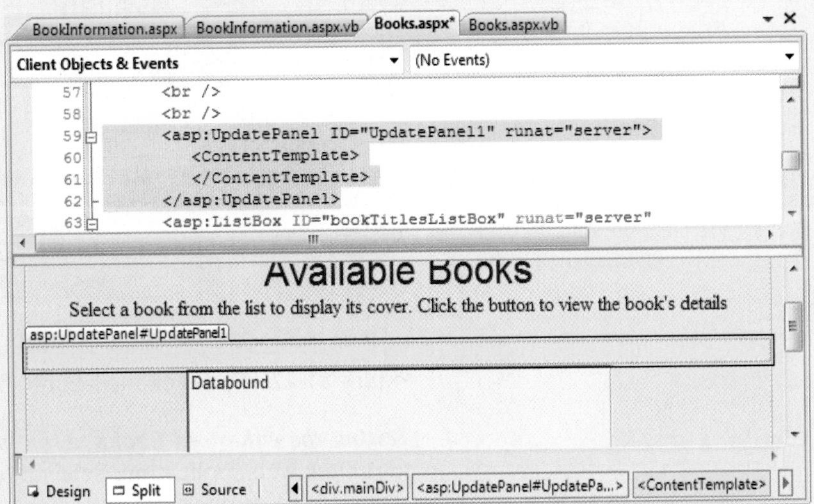

Figure 31.20 Adding an `UpdatePanel` to the `Books.aspx` page.

(cont.)

3. ***Placing page content in the `UpdatePanel`.*** Cut and paste the tags for the `bookTitlesListBox`, `linqDataSource` and `coverImage` controls (lines 63–72 of `Books.aspx`) into the `UpdatePanel`'s `ContentTemplate` tag (lines 61–70 of Fig. 31.21). The `bookTitlesListBox` initiates the asynchronous request and the `coverImage` control is updated when the `UpdatePanel` performs a partial page update. Figure 31.22 shows the `UpdatePanel` in **Design** view. You can see that the `UpdatePanel` now contains the `bookTitlesListBox`, `linqDataSource` and `coverImage` controls. When the user selects an item in the `ListBox`, the request is intercepted by the `UpdatePanel` and turned into an asynchronous request. When the response from the server is received, the `UpdatePanel` performs a partial page update to display the cover image of the selected book. Select **File > Save All** to save your changes.

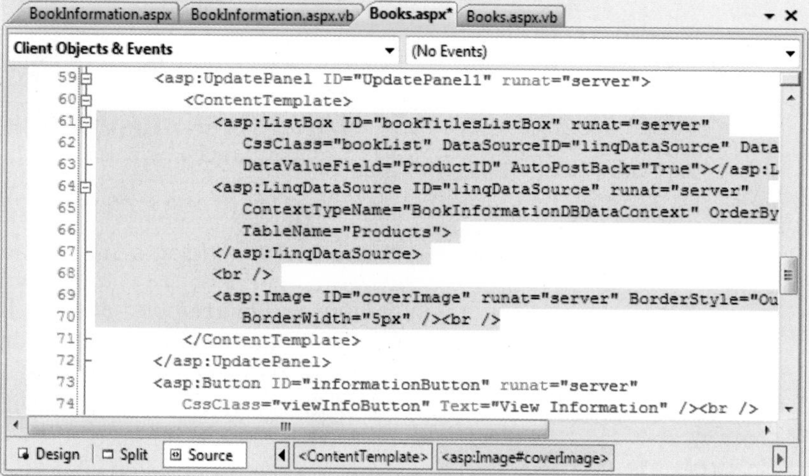

Figure 31.21 Pasting controls into the `UpdatePanel`'s `ContentTemplate`.

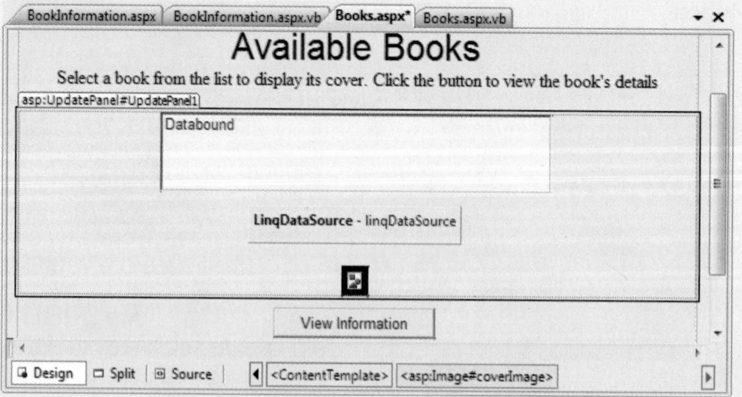

Figure 31.22 `UpdatePanel` containing the controls to be updated.

4. ***Testing the enhanced `Books.aspx` page.*** Select **Debug > Start Debugging** to run the web application. Select a book title from the `ListBox`. The book's cover image displays below the `ListBox` as it did before. However, notice that only the area of the browser containing the `ListBox`, `LinqDataSource` and `Image` is refreshed—the rest of the page is unaffected.

5. ***Closing the application.*** Close your running application by clicking the browser's close box.

6. ***Closing the project.*** Close the project by selecting **File > Close Project**.

Figures 31.23 and 31.24 display the complete code for the `Books.aspx.vb` and `BookInformation.aspx.vb` code-behind files of the **Bookstore** web application, respectively. The lines of code that contain new programming concepts you learned in this tutorial are highlighted.

Creating a `Session` item

Redirecting client browsers to `BookInformation.aspx` page

Returning a single element from a LINQ query

```
Partial Class Books
   Inherits System.Web.UI.Page

   ' handles the View Information Button's Click event
   Protected Sub informationButton_Click(ByVal sender As Object, _
      ByVal e As System.EventArgs) Handles informationButton.Click

      'create Session variable named productID
      Session("productID") = bookTitlesListBox.SelectedValue

      ' redirect to BookInformation.aspx page to display details
      Response.Redirect("BookInformation.aspx")
   End Sub ' informationButton_Click

   ' display the cover image of the selected book
   Protected Sub bookTitlesListBox_SelectedIndexChanged( _
      ByVal sender As Object, ByVal e As System.EventArgs) _
      Handles bookTitlesListBox.SelectedIndexChanged

      ' create the DataContext for querying the database
      Dim db As New BookInformationDBDataContext()

      ' get the book cover's file name for the selected book
      Dim coverFile = _
         (From item In db.Products _
          Where item.ProductID = bookTitlesListBox.SelectedValue _
          Select item.Coverart).Single()

      coverImage.ImageUrl = "images/" & coverFile ' specify file name
      coverImage.Visible = True ' display image
   End Sub ' bookTitlesListBox_SelectedIndexChanged
End Class ' Books
```

Figure 31.23 `Books.aspx.vb` code listing.

Using a `Session` item to determine the `ProductID` of the selected book.

Returning a single element from a LINQ query

```
Partial Class BookInformation
   Inherits System.Web.UI.Page

   ' Handles the Page's Load event
   Protected Sub Page_Load(ByVal sender As Object, _
      ByVal e As System.EventArgs) Handles Me.Load

      ' create the DataContext for querying the database
      Dim db As New BookInformationDBDataContext()

      ' get the selected product ID from the Session object
      Dim productID As Integer = _
         Convert.ToInt32(Session("productID"))

      ' get the details of the selected book
      Dim selectedBook = _
         (From item In db.Products _
          Where item.ProductID = productID _
          Select item).Single()

      bookTitleLabel.Text = selectedBook.Title ' display title
      authorsLabel.Text = selectedBook.Authors ' display authors

```

Figure 31.24 `BookInformation.aspx.vb` code listing. (Part 1 of 2.)

```
         ' display cover
         bookImage.ImageUrl = "images/" & selectedBook.Coverart
      End Sub ' Page_Load

      ' invoked when book List Button is clicked
      Protected Sub bookListButton_Click(ByVal sender As Object, _
         ByVal e As System.EventArgs) Handles bookListButton.Click

         ' redirects to Books.aspx page
         Response.Redirect("Books.aspx")
      End Sub ' bookListButton_Click
   End Class ' BookInformation
```

Figure 31.24 `BookInformation.aspx.vb` code listing. (Part 2 of 2.)

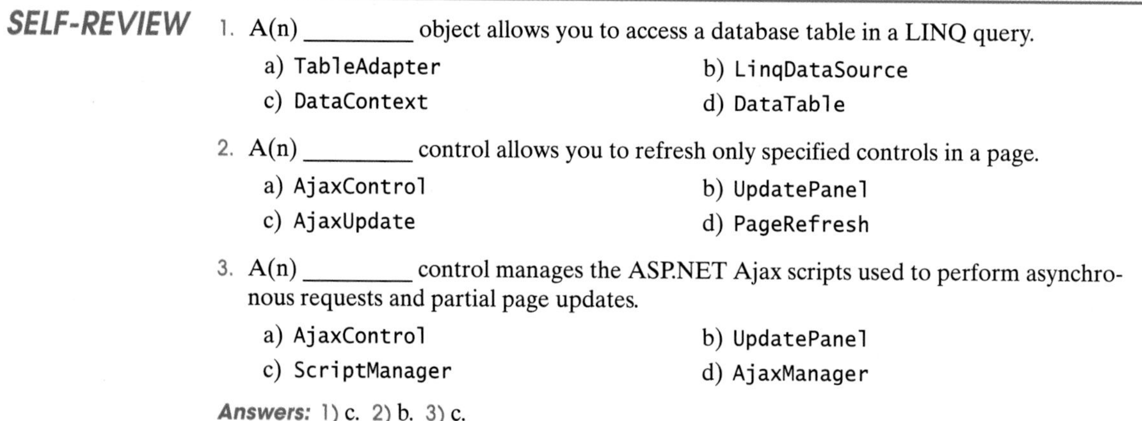

SELF-REVIEW

1. A(n) ________ object allows you to access a database table in a LINQ query.
   a) `TableAdapter` b) `LinqDataSource`
   c) `DataContext` d) `DataTable`

2. A(n) ________ control allows you to refresh only specified controls in a page.
   a) `AjaxControl` b) `UpdatePanel`
   c) `AjaxUpdate` d) `PageRefresh`

3. A(n) ________ control manages the ASP.NET Ajax scripts used to perform asynchronous requests and partial page updates.
   a) `AjaxControl` b) `UpdatePanel`
   c) `ScriptManager` d) `AjaxManager`

Answers: 1) c. 2) b. 3) c.

31.5 Internet and Web Resources

For more information on ASP.NET Ajax, please visit our ASP.NET Resource Center at `www.deitel.com/aspdotnet3.5` and our ASP.NET Ajax Resource Center at `www.deitel.com/aspdotnetajax`.

31.6 Wrap-Up

In this tutorial, you programmed the middle tier of your three-tier **Bookstore** web application. By defining methods and event handlers, you specified the actions that execute when the user interacts with ASPX pages. You learned about `Session` items and how they are used to maintain session state between ASPX pages. You also learned about the `Redirect` method of class `Response`—used to redirect the client browser to other web pages.

You learned about `Session` items and the `Redirect` method, and used them in the **Bookstore** web application. You began with the first ASPX page of the web application, `Books.aspx`. This page retrieves the book titles from the database and displays the titles in a `ListBox` control when the ASPX page loads. You defined the actions that occur when the user clicks the **View Information** `Button`. In the `Click` event handler, you created a `Session` item to store the product ID of the book selected by the user. You also used the `Redirect` method to direct users to the `BookInformation.aspx` page. You then added code that displays the selected book's cover image below the `ListBox`.

Then, you defined the `BookInformation.aspx` page's `Page_Load` event handler to display the title, authors and cover image of the selected book. Recall that you used the value stored in the `Session` object to determine the product ID of book selected by the user. You also used a data-bound `DetailsView` control to display the copyright date, ISBN number, edition, and description of the selected book. With a small amount of code, you were able to control the flow of data from the information tier to the client tier, completing the three-tier **Bookstore** web application. Finally, you learned how to use the ASP.NET Ajax `UpatePanel` to perform a partial page update and enhance your web application's user experience.

SKILLS SUMMARY

Accessing the Code-Behind File

- Click the **Nest Related Files** `Button` in the **Solution Explorer** window.
- Click the plus box next to the desired ASPX page to display the corresponding code-behind file name.
- Double click the code-behind file's name to view the code-behind file.

Configuring the Information Retrieved by a `LinqDataSource`

- In the **Configure Data Selection** dialog of the **Data Source Configuration Wizard**, select the `CheckBoxes` corresponding to the table fields that should be included in the `LinqDataSource`.
- If necessary, click the **Where...** `Button` to open the **Configure Where Expression** dialog. Use the `ComboBoxes` and `TextBoxes` to specify the conditions an item must satisfy to be included in the `LinqDataSource`.

Creating and Using a `Session` Item

- Assign a value to `Session("`*nameOfKey*`")`, where *nameOfKey* represents the key in a key/value pair and the value assigned is associated with *nameOfKey*.
- Use `Session("`*nameOfKey*`")` to retrieve the item's value. Cast the value to the appropriate type.

Redirecting the Client Browser to Another Web Page

- Type `Response.Redirect("`*URLOfPage*`")`, where *URLOfPage* represents the URL of the page to which the client browser redirects.

Using Partial Page Updates With ASP.NET Ajax Controls

- Add a `ScriptManager` at the top of the ASPX page, before any ASP.NET Ajax controls.
- Add an `UpdatePanel` to the ASPX page and create its `ContentTemplate` tag.
- Place the control that initiates an asynchronous request and the controls to be updated by the `UpdatePanel` between the `ContentTemplate` start and end tags.

KEY TERMS

ASP.NET Ajax—ASP.NET web controls that enable Ajax functionality.

asynchronous request—A request that is performed in the background. The user can continue interacting with the web application while the server processes the request.

callback function—Client-side function that processes the response to an asynchronous request.

code-behind file—File that contains a class which provides an ASPX page's functionality.

`ContentTemplate` element of the `UpdatePanel` control—Contains the control that initiates an asynchronous request and the controls updated when the `UpdatePanel` performs a partial page update.

key/value pair—Associates a value with a corresponding key, which is used to identify the value. The `Session` object stores key/value pairs.

`Page` class—Defines the basic functionality for an ASPX page.

`Page_Load` event handler—Executes when an ASPX page is loaded.

partial page update—Refreshes a section of the page *without* reloading the entire page.

`Redirect` method of class `Response`—Redirects the client browser to another web page.

`Response` object—An object that provides methods for responding to a client request.

`ScriptManager` control—Manages the client-side scripts that enable asynchronous Ajax functionality.

`SelectedValue` property of class `ListBox`—Returns the value of the selected item.

session state—ASP.NET's built-in support for tracking data throughout a browser session.

`Session` object—Object that is maintained across several web pages containing a collection of key/value pairs that are specific to a given user.

`Single` method of a LINQ query—Returns a single object from a LINQ query rather than a collection.

synchronous request—The user must wait until the server processes the request and returns the resulting page.

`UpdatePanel` control—ASP.NET Ajax control that performs a partial page update of the controls contained in its `ContentTemplate`.

CONTROLS, EVENTS, PROPERTIES & METHODS

ASPX page Page on which controls are dropped to design the GUI.

- ***Event***

  `Load`—Raised when the ASPX page is created.

`Image` Image This control displays an image on the ASPX page.

- ***In action***

- ***Properties***

  `BorderStyle`—Specifies the appearance of the `Image`'s border.

  `BorderWidth`—Specifies the width of the `Image`'s border.

  `ID`—Specifies the name used to access the `Image` control programmatically. The name should be suffixed with `Image`.

  `ImageUrl`—Specifies the location of the image file.

`ListBox` ListBox This control allows the user to view and select from multiple items in a list.

- ***In action***

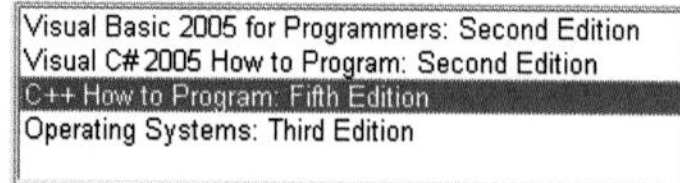

- ***Event***

  `SelectedIndexChanged`—Raised when a different item in the `ListBox` is selected

- ***Properties***

  `CssStyle`—Specifies the CSS style that defines the look-and-feel of the control.

  `ID`—Specifies the name used to access the `ListBox` control programmatically. The name should be suffixed with `ListBox`.

  `SelectedValue`—Returns the value of the selected item in the `ListBox`.

`Response` This class provides methods for responding to clients.

- ***Method***

  `Redirect`—Redirects the client browser to the specified location.

`ScriptManager` ScriptManager This control manages the client-side scripts that enable asynchronous Ajax functionality.

UpdatePanel UpdatePanel This control allows you perform a partial page update.

- *Property*

  ContentTemplate—Contains the control that initiates an asynchronous request and the the controls that are updated when the UpdatePanel performs a partial page update.

MULTIPLE-CHOICE QUESTIONS

31.1 The Page_Load event handler ________.

a) redirects the client browser to different web pages
b) defines the functionality when a Button is clicked
c) executes when an ASPX page loads
d) defines the functionality when a web control is selected

31.2 The Redirect method of class Response ________.

a) refreshes the current web page
b) sends the client browser to a specified web page
c) responds to user input
d) responds to the click of a Button

31.3 Session items are used in the **Bookstore** web application because ________.

a) variables in ASP.NET web applications must be created as Session items
b) values need to be shared among web pages
c) Session items are simpler to create than instance variables
d) Both a and b

31.4 Session state is used for ________ in ASP.NET.

a) tracking user-specific data
b) running an application
c) using a database
d) None of the above

31.5 The file extension for an ASPX code-behind file is ________.

a) .asp
b) .aspx
c) .aspx.vb
d) .code

31.6 The Response object is a predefined ASP.NET object that ________.

a) connects to a database
b) retrieves information from a database
c) creates web controls
d) provides methods for responding to client requests

31.7 The Redirect method of class Response takes a(n) ________ as an argument.

a) URL
b) Integer value
c) Boolean value
d) DataContext object

31.8 The ________ property specifies the image that an Image control displays.

a) ImageGIF
b) ImageURL
c) Image
d) Display

31.9 The Visual Basic file that contains the AgSPX page's corresponding class is called the ________.

a) ASPX file
b) code-behind file
c) class file
d) None of the above

31.10 Information can be maintained across web pages by adding a ________ to the Session object.

a) key/value pair
b) number
c) database connection object
d) None of the above

EXERCISES

31.11 ***(Phone Book Web Application: Functionality)*** Define the middle tier for the **Phone Book** web application. The running web application is shown in Fig. 31.25.

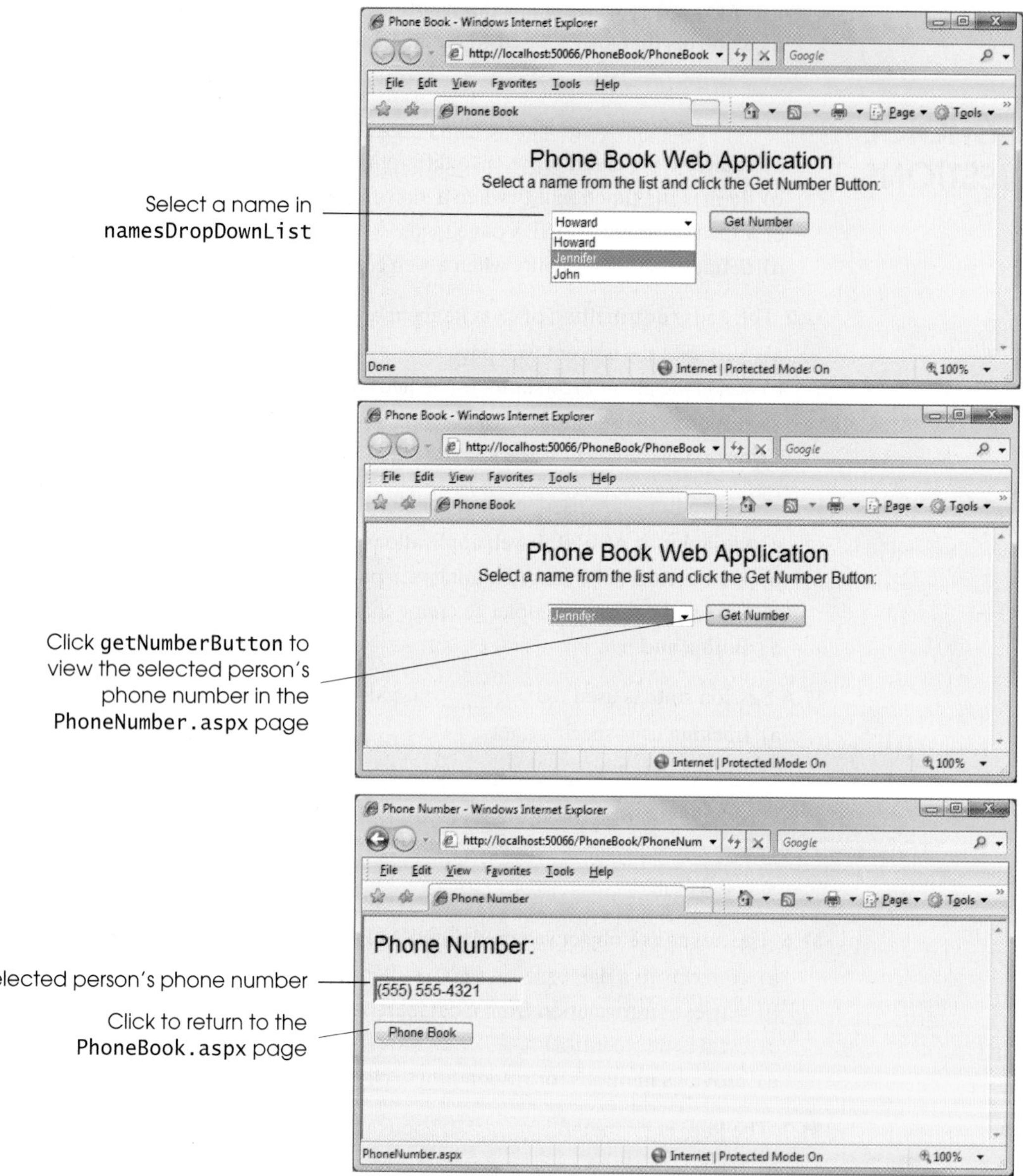

Figure 31.25 Running the **Phone Book** web application.

a) ***Opening the web application.*** Open the **Phone Book** web application that you created in Tutorial 29 and continued to develop in Tutorial 30.

b) ***Creating the Get Number `Button`'s `Click` event handler.*** Double click the **Get Number** `Button` to create its `Click` event handler.

c) ***Creating a `Session` item.*** In the `Click` event handler, create a `Session` item with the key `IDNumber` to store the `IDNumber` of the selected entry.

d) ***Redirecting to the `PhoneNumber.aspx` page.*** In the `Click` event handler, use the `Redirect` method to redirect the client browser to the `PhoneNumber.aspx` page.

e) ***Defining the `Page_Load` event handler for the `PhoneNumber.aspx` page.*** As you did in *Step 3* in the box, *Defining the `Page_Load` Event Handler for the `BookInformation.aspx` Page*, create a `PhoneBookDBDataContext` object named `db`. Then create a LINQ query that selects a single item from the database—the entry containing the `IDNumber` in the `IDNumber` `Session` item. Retrieve the appropriate phone number and assign it to `phoneNumberLabel`'s `Text` property.

f) ***Creating the* Phone Book *Button's* Click *event handler.*** Double click the **Phone Book** Button to create its Click event handler.

g) ***Redirecting to the* PhoneBook.aspx *page.*** In the Click event handler, use method Redirect to redirect the client browser to the PhoneBook.aspx page.

h) ***Running the web application.*** Select **Debug > Start Debugging** to run your web application. Select an entry and click the **Get Number** Button. Verify that the correct number is displayed on the PhoneNumber.aspx page. Click the **Phone Book** Button to return to the PhoneBook.aspx page.

i) ***Closing the web application.*** Close your running web application by clicking the browser's close box.

j) ***Closing the IDE.*** Close the Visual Web Developer IDE by clicking its close box.

31.12 *(US State Facts **Web Application: Functionality**)* Define the middle tier for the **US State Facts** web application. The running web application is shown in Fig. 31.26.

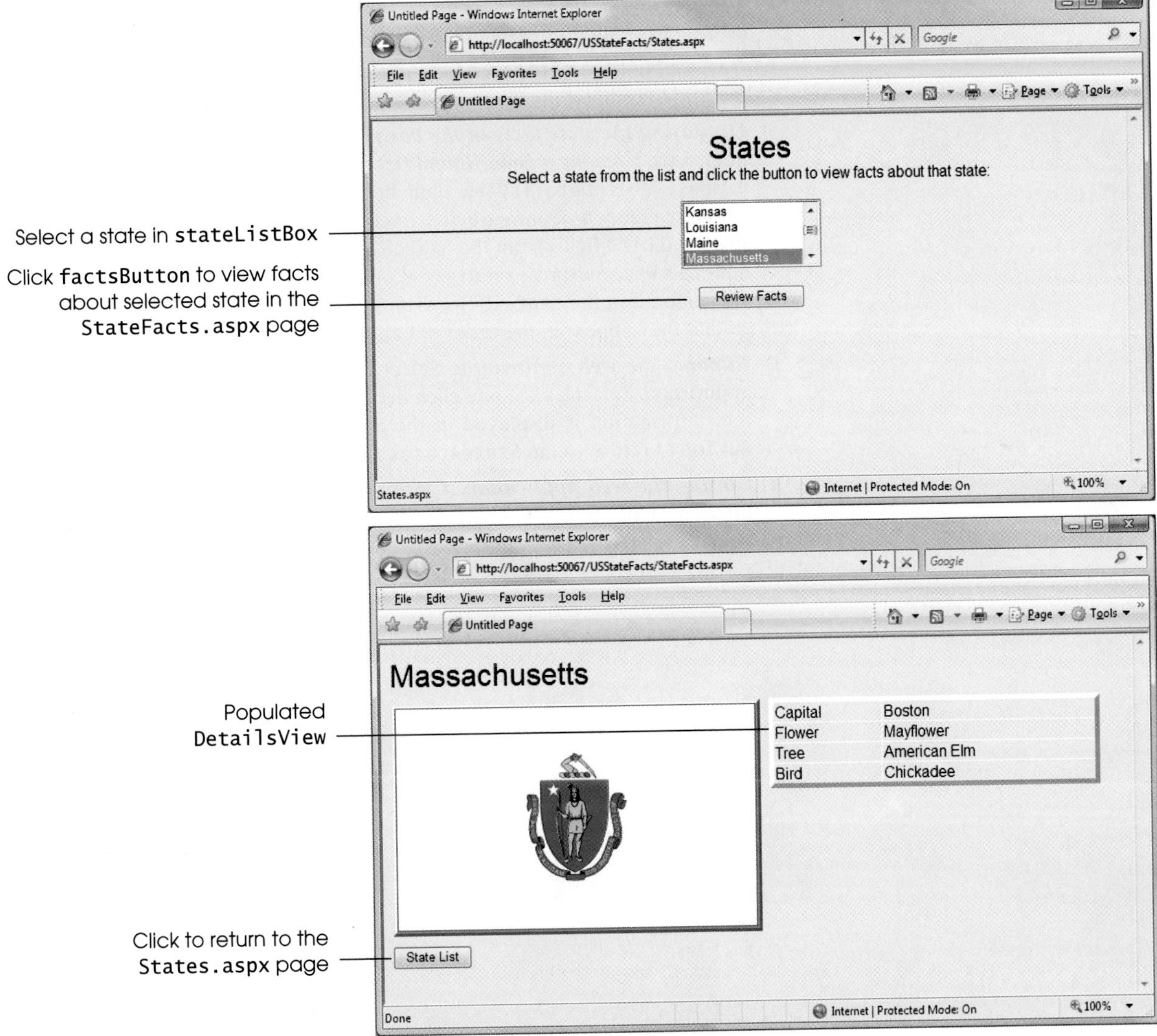

Figure 31.26 Running the **State Facts** application.

a) ***Opening the web application.*** Open the **US State Facts** web application that you created in Tutorial 29 and continued to develop in Tutorial 30.

b) ***Copying the* FlagImages *directory to your project directory.*** Copy the directory C:\Examples\Tutorial31\Exercises\FlagImages to the USStateFacts directory.

c) ***Creating the* Review Facts *Button's* Click *event handler*.** Double click the **Review Facts** Button to create its Click event handler.

d) ***Creating a* Session *item*.** Create a Session item named StateID in the Click event handler and assign it the StateID for the selected state.

e) ***Redirecting to the* StateFacts.aspx *page*.** In the Click event handler, use the Redirect method to redirect the client browser to the StateFacts.aspx page.

f) ***Defining the* Page_Load *event handler of the* StateFacts.aspx *page*.** As you did in *Step 3* in the box, *Defining the Page_Load Event Handler for the BookInformation.aspx Page*, create a StateFactsDBDataContext object named db. Then create a LINQ query that selects a single item from the database—the entry containing the StateID in the StateID Session item. Retrieve the appropriate state Name and assign it to stateNameLabel's Text property. Also retrieve the file name for the appropriate flag image and assign it to flagImage's ImageURL property. [*Note:* You need to prefix the file name of the image with FlagImages\.]

g) ***Creating the* State List *Button's* Click *event handler*.** Double click the **State List** Button to create its Click event handler.

h) ***Redirecting to the* States.aspx *page*.** In the Click event handler use the Redirect method to redirect the client browser to the States.aspx page.

i) ***Displaying the state facts in the* DetailsView.** Similar to the process demonstrated in the box, *Creating a Data-Bound DetailsView Using a LinqDataSource*, you need to make stateDetailsView data bound. Connect stateDetailsView to a new LinqDataSource. Configure the LinqDataSource to select the Capital, Flower Tree and Bird fields from the StateFacts database table. Configure the LinqDataSource's Where expression to select only the database entry containing the StateID value stored in the StateID Session item. Now, like *Step 4*, edit the displayed fields so that they appear in the order of Capital, Flower, Tree and Bird.

j) ***Running the web application.*** Select **Debug > Start Debugging** to run your web application. Select a state and click the **Review Facts** Button and verify that the correct information is displayed in the StateFacts.aspx page. Click the **State List** Button to return to the States.aspx page.

k) ***Closing the web application.*** Close your running web application by clicking the browser's close box.

l) ***Closing the* IDE.** Close the Visual Web Developer IDE by clicking its close box.

TUTORIAL

Weather Viewer Application

Introducing Microsoft Silverlight, XML, LINQ to XML and Web Services

Objectives

In this tutorial, you learn to:

- Use Silverlight to create a rich Internet application.
- Create Silverlight user interfaces in XAML.
- Use LINQ to XML to convert XML into a collection of Visual Basic objects.
- Use XML Axis properties to manipulate XML content in Visual Basic.
- Customize the appearance of existing Silverlight controls.
- Create a custom Silverlight control.

Outline

Silverlight™, formerly code-named "Windows Presentation Foundation Everywhere (WPF/E)," is Microsoft's platform for **Rich Internet Applications (RIAs)**—web applications that offer the responsiveness and rich GUI features of desktop applications. Silverlight is designed to complement RIA technologies, such as Adobe Flash and Flex, Sun's JavaFX and Microsoft's own ASP.NET Ajax. Silverlight currently runs as a browser plug-in for Internet Explorer, Firefox and Safari on recent versions of Microsoft Windows and Mac OS X. Silverlight is also available on Linux systems via the Mono Project's Moonlight (`mono-project.com/Moonlight`).

Microsoft announced Silverlight 1.0 Beta and 1.1 Alpha at the 2007 MIX conference (`www.visitmix.com`), Microsoft's annual conference for web developers and designers. The demos were compelling, and many technology bloggers who attended the conference blogged about Silverlight's excitement and potential. Since then, Microsoft has continued developing and enhancing Silverlight. At the time of this writing, Silverlight is currently available in version 2.0 Beta.

For information on the latest version(s) of Silverlight and to find additional Silverlight web resources, please visit our Silverlight Resource Center at `www.deitel.com/silverlight/`.

32.1 Platform Overview

Silverlight applications consist of a user interface described in Extensible Application Markup Language (XAML) and a code-behind file (or files) containing the program logic. As you learned in Tutorial 27, XAML is Microsoft's XML vocabulary for describing user interfaces in Microsoft's Windows Presentation Foundation (WPF). In fact, the XAML used in Silverlight is a subset of that used in WPF.

Silverlight 1.0 focused primarily on media and supported programming only in JavaScript. Its primary purpose was to take advantage of the increasing popularity of web-based video to drive user adoption—it is well known that users are willing to install software to watch video. Microsoft also provides a service called Silverlight Streaming (`streaming.live.com`) that allows users to distribute media-based Silverlight applications for free.

Silverlight 2's .NET Platform Subset

Silverlight 2 is a robust, cross-platform, cross-browser subset of the .NET platform that runs on Windows and Mac OS X as a plug-in (approximately a 4 megabyte download) for several popular web browsers, including Internet Explorer, Safari and Firefox. Silverlight 2 is also available on Linux systems via the Mono Project's Moonlight—visit the web site `mono-project.com/Moonlight` for more information.

When Silverlight 2 is released, computers running the Silverlight 1.0 browser plug-in will automatically be upgraded to Silverlight 2. This should immediately make Silverlight 2 a widespread platform for RIAs.

The subset of the .NET Framework available in Silverlight 2 includes APIs for collections, input/output, generics, multithreading, globalization, XML and LINQ. It also includes APIs for interacting with JavaScript and the elements in a web page, and APIs for local storage of web-application data to help you create more robust web-based applications.

Because Silverlight 2 is an implementation of the .NET Platform, developers can create Silverlight applications in .NET languages such as Visual Basic, Visual C#, IronRuby and IronPython. This makes it easy for developers familiar with .NET programming for Windows to create applications that run in a web browser. It also provides a substantial performance improvement over Silverlight 1.0 because you compile Silverlight 2's .NET code and then the compiled code is executed on the client—unlike JavaScript, which is interpreted and executed on the client at runtime. For a detailed feature comparison of Silverlight 1.0 and Silverlight 2 Beta, visit `silverlight.net/GetStarted/overview.aspx`.

Graphics and GUI Capabilities

Silverlight 2's graphics and GUI capabilities are a subset of the Windows Presentation Foundation (WPF) framework (introduced in Tutorial 27). Some capabilities supported in Silverlight include GUI controls, layout management, graphics, animation and multimedia. There are also styles and template-based skinning capabilities to manage the look-and-feel of a Silverlight 2 user interface. Figure 32.1 shows the default list of controls that you can use today in Silverlight applications. More controls will be made available over time.

Silverlight 2 controls			
`Border`	`Button`	`Calendar`	`Canvas`
`CheckBox`	`ContentControl`	`DataGrid`	`DatePicker`
`Ellipse`	`Grid`	`GridSplitter`	`HyperlinkButton`
`Image`	`Line`	`ListBox`	`MediaElement`
`MultiScaleImage`	`RadioButton`	`Rectangle`	`RepeatButton`
`ScrollBar`	`ScrollViewer`	`Slider`	`StackPanel`
`TextBlock`	`TextBox`	`ToggleButton`	`ToolTip`

Figure 32.1 Default controls listed in the IDE's **Toolbox** for Silverlight applications.

Data Binding

Like WPF, Silverlight provides a powerful data-binding model that makes it easy for you to display data from objects, collections, databases, XML and even other controls in your GUIs.

Networking

Silverlight 2 also provides rich networking support, enabling you to write browser-based applications that invoke web services and use other networking technologies.

32.2 Silverlight 2 Runtime and Tools Installation

To build and execute the examples in this tutorial, you'll need to download and install the following software.

Silverlight 2 Runtime

You can download the Silverlight 2 Runtime plug-in from

`www.microsoft.com/silverlight/resources/installationFiles.aspx?v=2.0`

After installing the plug-in, go to

`silverlight.net/themes/silverlight/community/gallerydetail.aspx?cat=2`

and try some of the sample applications. We list many other demo websites in our Silverlight Resource Center (`www.deitel.com/Silverlight/`).

Silverlight Tools Beta 1 for Visual Studio 2008

At the time of this writing, Silverlight 2 development is not yet supported in Microsoft's Visual Studio Express editions. For this reason, you'll need a complete version of Visual Studio 2008 to build this tutorial's applications. You'll also need the Silverlight Tools Beta 1 for Visual Studio 2008 from

`go.microsoft.com/fwlink/?LinkID=112029`

Download and execute the file `silverlight_chainer.exe`, then follow the on-screen instructions to install the tools for developing Silverlight 2 applications in Visual Studio 2008.

Silverlight 2 SDK (Software Development Kit) Beta 1

If you don't have access to a complete version of Visual Studio 2008, Microsoft also provides the Silverlight 2 SDK Beta 1, which you can get at

`go.microsoft.com/fwlink/?LinkID=111096&clcid=0x409`

The SDK provides documentation, sample code and tools to help you build applications for the Silverlight 2 beta. We do not cover the SDK in this book.

32.3 Test-Driving the Weather Viewer Application

In this tutorial, you create a **Weather Viewer** application. This application must meet the following requirements:

Application Requirements

You have been asked to create a web-based application that allows the user to enter a zip code and displays the weather forecast for the corresponding United States city. To obtain the weather forecast, you must use the `GetWeatherByZipCode` *web service provided by* `www.webservicex.net`*. (You can learn about the web service at* `www.webservicex.net/WCF/ServiceDetails.aspx?SID=44`*.) The application should display the days of the week returned by the web service and the image that represents the weather for each day. The user should then be able to click the appropriate day to see the high and low temperatures for that day in both Fahrenheit and Celsius.*

You begin by test-driving the completed application. [*Note:* You must be connected to the Internet for this example to work as it interacts with a web service provided by the website `www.webservicex.net`.] Then you learn the additional Visual Basic techniques needed to create your own version of this application.

Test-Driving the WeatherViewer Application

1. ***Opening the completed application.*** Open the directory `C:\Examples\Tutorial32\CompletedApplication\WeatherViewer` to locate the **Weather Viewer** application. Double click `WeatherViewer.sln` to open the application in the Visual Studio IDE. [*Note:* Recall that you must use a full version of Visual Studio 2008 with the Silverlight tools installed to perform the steps in this tutorial, because the Silverlight development tools are not yet available for the Visual Studio Express editions.]

2. ***Running the Weather Viewer application.*** Select **Debug > Start Without Debugging** or type *Ctrl* + *F5* to run the application (Fig. 32.2).

Note that the screen captures in this tutorial were taken in Internet Explorer 8 beta, but the application runs in any browser with the Silverlight 2 runtime installed

`TextBox` in which the user enters the zip code

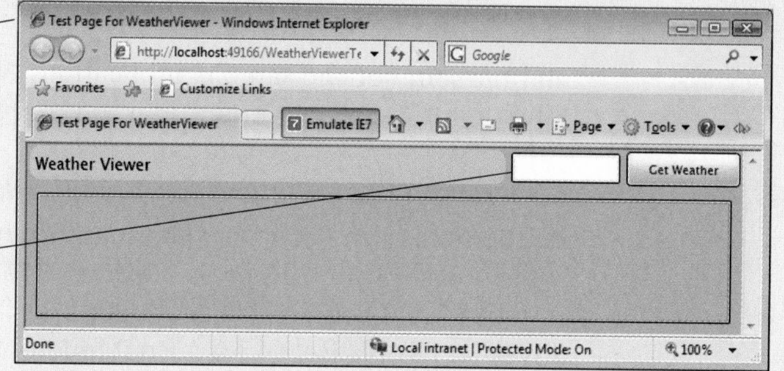

Figure 32.2 **Weather Viewer** application before the user enters a zip code.

3. ***Entering a US Zip Code.*** Enter a US zip code in the `TextBox` (Fig. 32.3), then press the **Get Weather** `Button` to obtain the weather forecast for the specified zip code. (A list of US zipcodes can be found at the site `zip4.usps.com/zip4/`.)

User selects a day to see the detailed forecast for that day

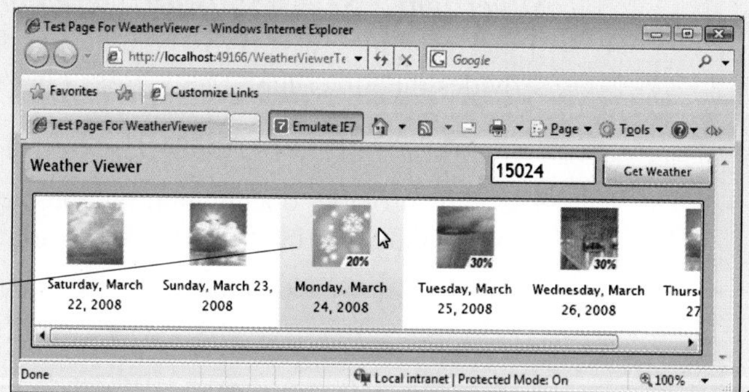

Figure 32.3 Displaying the weather forecast for the specified zip code.

4. ***Displaying the Forecast Details.*** Click one of the days in the forecast to see the complete details for that day (Fig. 32.4). Notice that you must click the **Close** `Button` to return to the forecast.

Customized control displays the detailed forecast and blocks the user from accessing the rest of the GUI until the **Close** `Button` is clicked

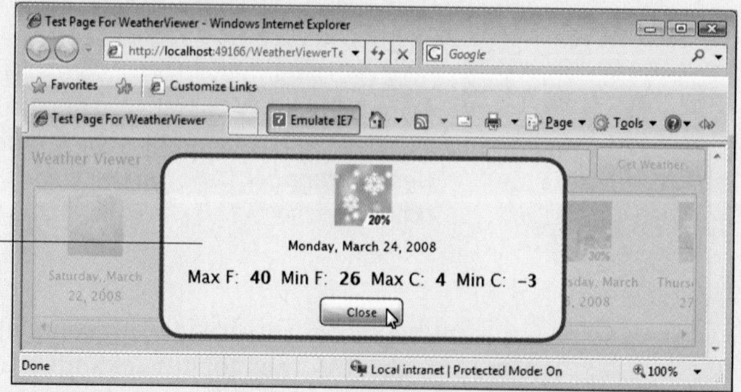

Figure 32.4 Complete weather details for the selected day.

(cont.)

5. ***Closing the application.*** Close your running application by clicking the browser's close box.
6. ***Closing the IDE.*** Close the IDE by clicking its close box.

32.4 Overviewing the Weather Viewer Application

Before you begin building the **Weather Viewer** application, you should review its functionality. The following pseudocode describes the application's basic operation:

```
When the user presses the Get Weather Button:
    Obtain the US zip code from the TextBox
    Use a WebClient object to invoke the WeatherForecast web service from
        www.webservicex.net

When the response data is received from the web service:
    Convert the XML weather forecast into WeatherData objects
    Use data binding to display the Weather Data objects in a ListBox

When the user selects a particular day in the weather forecast:
    Display the complete details of the forecast for that day

When the user clicks the Close Button in details view:
    Close the details view

When the user changes the text TextBox:
    Clear the contents of the ListBox
```

Now that you've test-driven the **Weather Viewer** application and studied its pseudocode representation, you will use an ACE table to help you convert the pseudocode to Visual Basic. Figure 32.5 lists the actions, controls and events that help you complete your own version of this application.

Action/Control/Event (ACE) Table for the Weather Viewer Application

Action	Control/Object/Class	Event
	submitButton	Click
Obtain the zip code from the TextBox	inputTextBox	
Use a WebClient object to invoke the GetWeatherByZipCode web service from www.webservicex.net	weatherService	
	weatherService	DownloadString-Completed
Convert the XML weather forecast into WeatherData objects	XDocument, WeatherData	
Use data binding to display the Weather Data objects in a ListBox	forecastList	
	forecastList	SelectionChanged
Display the complete details of the forecast for that day	forecastList, completeDetails	
	closeButton	Click
Close the details view	completeDetails	
	inputTextBox	TextChanged
Clear the contents of the ListBox		

Figure 32.5 **Weather Viewer** application's ACE table.

In this tutorial, you'll build the **Weather Viewer** application in stages:

- In Section 32.5, Creating the **Weather Viewer** Application, you build a new Silverlight application, then build a portion of the application's GUI.
- In Section 32.6, Calling a Web Service and Using LINQ to XML to Process the Results, you invoke a web service from a Silverlight application. You then learn how to convert the XML returned from the web service used in this application into objects of our own class named `WeatherData`. Finally, you'll display the text representation of the weather forecast in a Silverlight `DataGrid` control.
- In Section 32.7, Customizing the Data Presentation, you display a portion of the weather forecast in a customized `ListBox` that renders its elements horizontally, rather than vertically.
- In Section 32.8, Creating a Customized Silverlight Control, you build a custom control to display the detailed weather forecast for a particular day.

32.5 Creating the Weather Viewer Application

In this section, you build a Silverlight application containing the basic layout and a portion of the GUI for the **Weather Viewer** application.

Creating a Silverlight Application

1. ***Creating a Silverlight Application project.*** In Visual Studio, select **File > New Project...** to display the **New Project** dialog (Fig 28.6). In the dialog, under the Visual Basic Silverlight project types, select **Silverlight Application** and name your project `WeatherViewer`, then click **OK**.

Silverlight Applcation project template

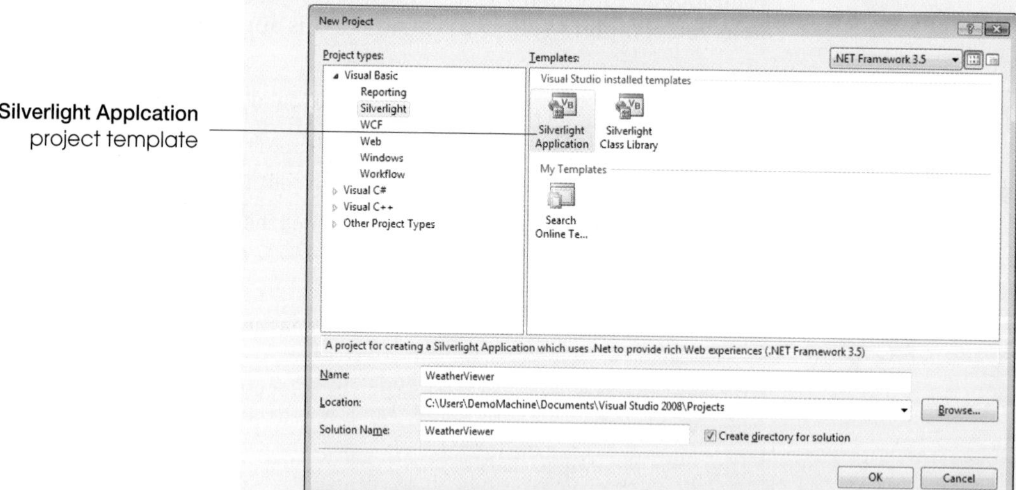

Figure 32.6 Creating a new **Silverlight Application** project.

2. ***Adding a test web site for the Silverlight application.*** In the **Add Silverlight Application** dialog that appears after you click **OK** in *Step 1*, select the `RadioButton` **Add a new Web to the solution for hosting the control** and choose **Web Application Project** from the **Project Type** `ComboBox`. A Silverlight application must be hosted in a web page. The **Web Application Project** will be used to test the Silverlight application in a web browser. Building the solution automatically copies the compiled Silverlight application into the **Web Application Project**. You can then test the application using the built-in web server in Visual Studio. Click **OK** to dismiss the dialog and create the Silverlight application.

(cont.) Your IDE should now appear similar to Fig. 32.7. We also expanded the `App.xaml` and `Page.xaml` nodes in the **Solution Explorer** and collapsed the node for the **Web Application Project**.

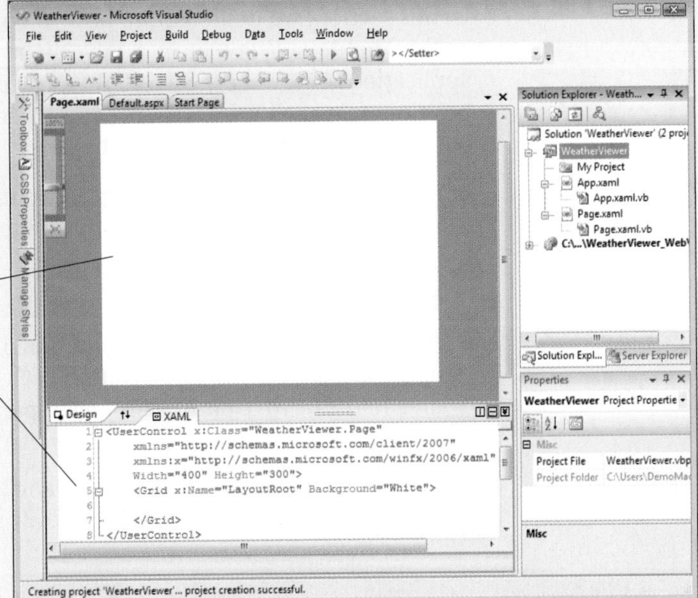

Figure 32.7 New Silverlight application in Visual Studio.

At the time of this writing the **Design** view is read-only and the **Properties** window is not yet enabled for Silverlight development with the Silverlight Tools Beta 1 for Visual Studio 2008. For this reason, much of the code you write in this tutorial will be in the context of the XAML files. According to Microsoft, by late summer 2008, you'll be able to use the **Design** view and the **Properties** window just as you did for the applications in Tutorial 27.

Basics of a Silverlight Application Project

A basic Silverlight application has two XAML files—`Page.xaml` and `App.xaml`. **`Page.xaml`** defines the application's GUI, and its code-behind file **`Page.xaml.vb`** declares the GUI event handlers (and other methods required by the application). **`App.xaml`** declares your application's shared resources, such as styles that can be applied to various GUI elements. The code-behind file **`App.xaml.vb`** defines application-level event handlers, such as an event handler for unhandled exceptions. We don't use `App.xaml` in this tutorial.

The `Page.xaml` file shown in the **XAML** tab of Fig. 32.7 is similar to the default XAML for a WPF application. In WPF, the main element in the XAML is a `Window`. In Silverlight, the main element is a **`UserControl`**. The default `UserControl` has a class name specified with the `x:Class` attribute (line 1), specifies the namespaces in lines 2 and 3 to provide access to the Silverlight controls throughout the XAML, and has a `Width` and `Height` of `400` and `300`, respectively. These numbers are system-independent pixel measurements, where each pixel is actually measured as 1/96 of an inch. Lines 5–7 are the default `Grid` layout container. Unlike a WPF application, the `x:Name` (the name used in code that manipulates the control) and `Background` attributes are set by default in a Silverlight application.

A compiled Silverlight application is packaged by the IDE as a **`.xap` file** containing the application and its supporting resources (such as images or other files used by the application). The web page in which the Silverlight application will be hosted references the application's `.xap` file to launch the Silverlight Runtime, which then executes the application. The test web application that was created for you contains the file `WeatherViewerTestPage.aspx`, which loads and executes the Silverlight application.

Laying Out and Building the GUI

In this section, we demonstrate how to control layout using `Grid`s of rows and columns. The default layout in a Silverlight application uses a `Grid` (just as in WPF applications); however, Silverlight provides both fixed positioning and dynamic positioning capabilities. There are three types of layout containers in Silverlight—`Canvas`, `StackPanel` and `Grid`.

- A `Canvas` enables you to precisely control the positioning of each control. If the `Canvas` is resized, the controls on the `Canvas` do not move.
- A `StackPanel` enables you to place a set of controls horizontally or vertically (the default). This is often used to organize subsets of your GUI.
- A `Grid` is the most flexible layout panel in Silverlight. It enables you to specify rows and columns and position each control in a particular row and column in the `Grid`. Controls may also span multiple rows or columns. The rows and columns can have fixed sizes or can be auto-sized.

In the next box, you use `StackPanel`s and `Grid`s to define the layout of this application. You also add several controls to the GUI.

Defining the Layout Using `Grid`s

1. ***Changing the background color and showing the gridlines.*** Change the background color of the `Grid` to `LightSkyBlue`. You can do this by removing `White` from the `Background` attribute on line 5, then typing *Ctrl + Space* displays the IntelliSense window containing the predefined color names from which you can select a value. You can also specify any color you wish as a hexadecimal value of the form #RRGGBB, where RR, GG and BB are hexadecimal values for the red, green and blue portions of a color, respectively. Next, press *Enter* before the closing right angle bracket (>) and insert the **`ShowGridLines`** attribute as shown on line 6 (Fig. 32.8). This displays the grid lines so you can see the grid layout better as you design and build your GUI. [*Note:* Once the tools for Silverlight development are complete, you'll be able to set property values like this through the **Properties** window as you did for WPF applications.]

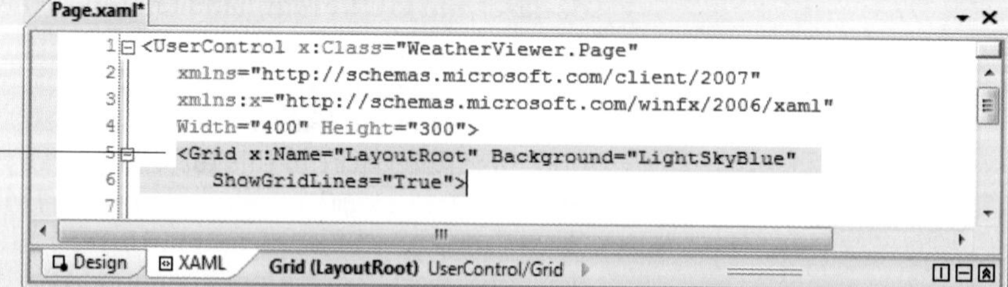

`Grid` layout container with `Background` of `LightSkyBlue` and gridlines displayed

Figure 32.8 Changing the background color of the `Grid` and displaying grid lines.

2. ***Defining rows and a column in the main `Grid`.*** By default, a `Grid` contains one row and one column. We'd like to split the `Grid` into two rows and one column. Insert lines 7–14 (Fig. 32.9) to define two rows and one column in the `Grid`. Lines 7–10 create a **`Grid.RowDefinitions`** element that contains two **`RowDefinition`** elements. The first `RowDefinition` indicates that the height of that row should be 35 pixels—again, one pixel in WPF is 1/96th of an inch. The asterisk (*) in the second `RowDefinition` (line 9) indicates that the second row should occupy all remaining space in the `Grid`.

(cont.)

Note that when you type a `RowDefinition` element, the IDE inserts it as

```
<RowDefinition></RowDefinition>
```

When nothing is placed between the tags of an element, you can shorthand the element as

```
<RowDefinition />
```

a so-called empty element. You can still define attributes in the empty element as we did with the `Height` in lines 8–9.

Lines 12–14 create a `Grid.ColumnDefinitions` element containing one `ColumnDefinition` for a column that occupies the entire width of the `Grid`—as indicated by the asterisk (*) in line 13.

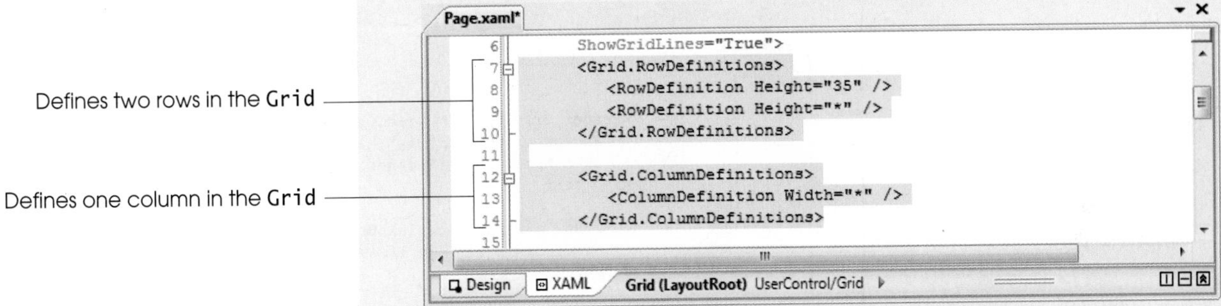

Figure 32.9 Defining the rows and column in the main `Grid`.

3. ***Creating another Grid to place in the first row of the main Grid.*** The first row of the GUI contains three elements. You use a `Grid` to specify the width of each control in this row. Insert lines 16–26 (Fig. 32.10) before the main `Grid`'s ending `</Grid>` tag. Lines 16–26 define the `Grid` element that manages the GUI controls in the first row. Lines 17–19 create a `Grid.RowDefinitions` element that contains one `RowDefinition` element for a row that has the maximum height allowed by the first row of the main `Grid` (that is, 35 pixels). Lines 21–25 create a `Grid.ColumnDefinitions` element containing three `ColumnDefinitions`. The second and third columns are each 110 pixels wide (lines 23–24). The first column uses all the remaining space in the width of the main `Grid`—as indicated by the asterisk (*) at line 22.

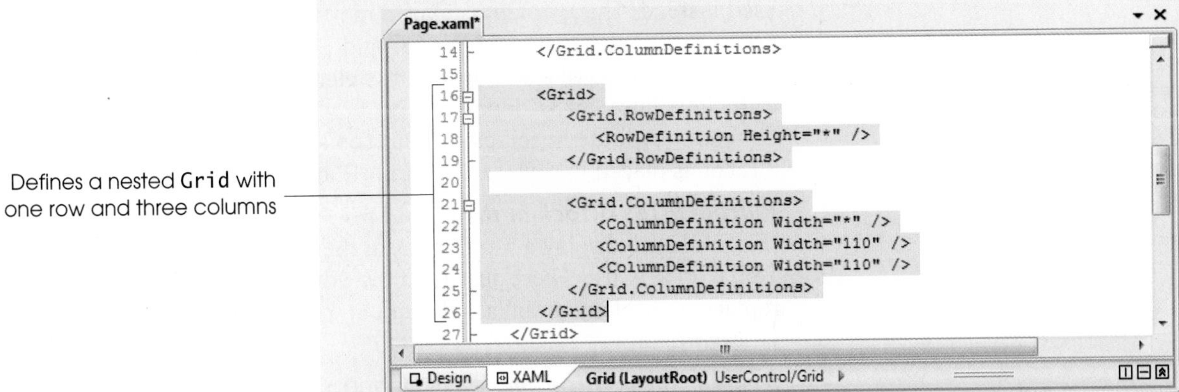

Figure 32.10 Defining a `Grid` that will contain the first row of elements in the GUI.

(cont.)

4. ***Inserting controls in the first row of the GUI.*** Next, insert lines 27–37 (Fig. 32.11) into the nested `Grid` element to create the first row of the GUI. Lines 27–30 create a **`Border`** element that contains a **`TextBlock`** element (line 29). In this case, the `Border` element has several attributes. The **`Grid.Row`** and **`Grid.Column`** attributes indicate the row and column in which the `Border` is placed in its enclosing `Grid`. Rows and columns start from `0`, so the `Border` element is placed in row `0` (the only row in this `Grid`) and column `0` (the first column in this `Grid`). The `Border` has a **`CornerRadius`** of `10` (which rounds its corners), a `Background` color of `LightGray` and a `Margin` of `2` (which adds 2 pixels of space around the outside edges of the `Border`). Note that you can drag and drop Silverlight controls from the **Toolbox** into the XAML code. [*Note:* A control can span multiple rows or columns by specifying the **`Grid.RowSpan`** or **`Grid.ColSpan`** attributes.]

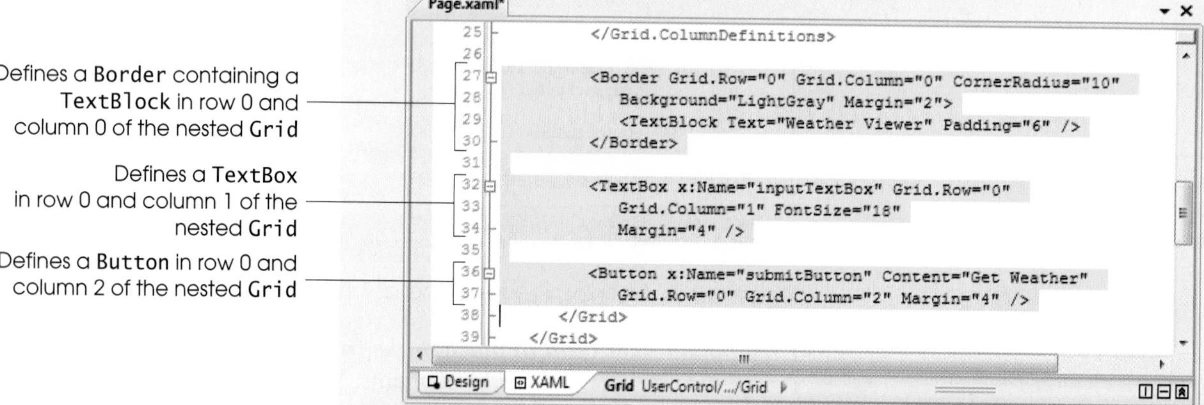
Page.xaml*
25 </Grid.ColumnDefinitions>
26
27 <Border Grid.Row="0" Grid.Column="0" CornerRadius="10"
28 Background="LightGray" Margin="2">
29 <TextBlock Text="Weather Viewer" Padding="6" />
30 </Border>
31
32 <TextBox x:Name="inputTextBox" Grid.Row="0"
33 Grid.Column="1" FontSize="18"
34 Margin="4" />
35
36 <Button x:Name="submitButton" Content="Get Weather"
37 Grid.Row="0" Grid.Column="2" Margin="4" />
38 </Grid>
39 </Grid>
Design
XAML
Grid UserControl/.../Grid
Defines a Border containing a TextBlock in row 0 and column 0 of the nested Grid
Defines a TextBox in row 0 and column 1 of the nested Grid
Defines a Button in row 0 and column 2 of the nested Grid

Figure 32.11 Inserting controls into the nested `Grid`.

The `TextBlock` element is used to place text in the GUI. Its **`Text`** attribute indicates that `Weather Viewer` should be displayed inside the `Border`, and its `Padding` attribute indicates that there are `6` pixels of space around the text on the inside of the `Border`.

Lines 32–34 define a **`TextBox`** element. The **`x:Name`** attribute specifies the name that is used in Visual Basic code to access this control programmatically. Some Silverlight controls don't have a `Name` property, so `x:Name` can be used instead. This element is placed in row `0` and column `1` of the `Grid`. The **`FontSize`** of the text is `18` pixels, and the **`Margin`** attribute indicates that there are `4` pixels of space around the element.

Finally, lines 36–37 define a **`Button`** with the `x:Name` `submitButton`. Its `Content` attribute specifies the `Button`'s caption (i.e., `Get Weather`). This `Button` is placed in row `0` and column `2` and has a `Margin` of `4` pixels.

5. ***Placing a `TextBlock` in the second row of the main `Grid`.*** Add lines 40–41 (Fig. 32.12) to display a `TextBlock` in the second row of the main `Grid`. The `TextBlock` is used here just to show you that there is a second row. You replace this element in a subsequent box with a control to display the weather data.

6. ***Running the application.*** Select **Debug > Start Debugging** to run the application (Fig. 32.13). Try resizing the browser window. Notice that the application does not resize automatically. [*Note:* If the **Debugging Not Enabled** dialog appears, leave the first `RadioButton` checked and click **OK** to enable debugging.]

(cont.)

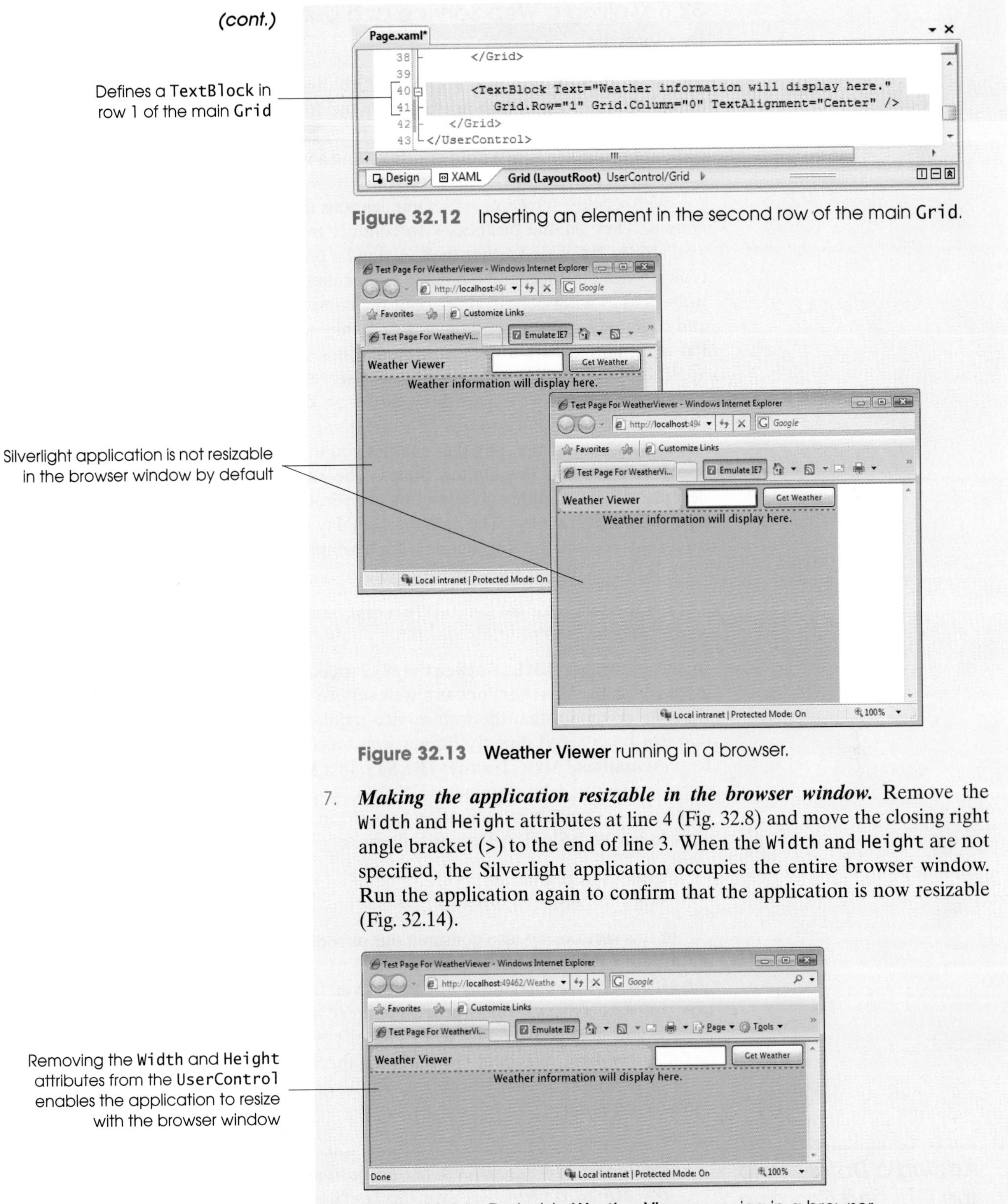

Figure 32.12 Inserting an element in the second row of the main `Grid`.

Figure 32.13 **Weather Viewer** running in a browser.

7. ***Making the application resizable in the browser window.*** Remove the `Width` and `Height` attributes at line 4 (Fig. 32.8) and move the closing right angle bracket (>) to the end of line 3. When the `Width` and `Height` are not specified, the Silverlight application occupies the entire browser window. Run the application again to confirm that the application is now resizable (Fig. 32.14).

Figure 32.14 Resizable **Weather Viewer** running in a browser.

32.6 Calling a Web Service and Using LINQ to XML to Process the Results

This section introduces web services, which promote software portability and reusability in applications that operate over the Internet. A **web service** is a software component stored on one computer that can be accessed via method calls through standard protocols over a network. Invoking a web service's methods to obtain data is known as **consuming the web service**.

Web services have important implications for business-to-business (B2B) transactions. They enable businesses to conduct transactions via standardized, widely available web services rather than relying on proprietary applications. Web services typically are platform and language independent, so companies can collaborate via web services without worrying about the compatibility of their hardware, software and communications technologies. Companies such as Amazon, Google, eBay, PayPal and many others are using web services to their advantage by making their applications available to partners via web services.

In this section, you learn how to use an object of class **`WebClient`** from the `System.Net` namespace to invoke a weather-forecast web service provided by the site `www.webservicex.net` that enables you to obtain a weather forecast for a particular zip code in the United States. The web service returns XML data that describes the maximum and minimum temperatures for the corresponding city over a period of several days. The data for each day also contains a link to an image that represents the weather for that day. For a sample of the XML that is returned, enter the following URL in your web browser:

```
www.webservicex.net/WeatherForecast.asmx/GetWeatherByZipCode?ZipCode=
   01754
```

In the preceding URL, `GetWeatherByZipCode` is the name of a method being invoked on the `WeatherForcast` web service and `?ZipCode=01754` specifies the zip-code argument that the web service requires to perform its task. Web services that can be invoked directly from a web browser like this use a technique called **Representational State Transfer (REST)**. In a REST-based web service, each operation is identified by a unique URL. So, when the server receives a request, it immediately knows what operation to perform. You can learn more about web services in our Web Services Resource Centers:

```
www.deitel.com/WebServices/
www.deitel.com/RESTWebServices/
```

In this section, we also continue our introduction to LINQ by presenting some features of LINQ to XML, enabling you to use LINQ to process XML data quickly and efficiently. As part of this discussion, you learn about Visual Basic's new XML axis property syntax, which provides direct access to XML data in your code. Finally, you use data binding to display the weather information in a Silverlight `DataGrid` control. You begin by replacing the `TextBlock` in the bottom row of the main `Grid` with a `DataGrid` control. You then add an event handler for the `Button`'s `Click` event.

Adding a DataGrid to the GUI and Creating the `submitButton`'s `Click` Event Handler

1. ***Replacing the `TextBlock` in the bottom row of the main `Grid` with a `DataGrid` control.*** Remove the `TextBlock` at lines 40–41, then place the cursor in line 39 and double click the **`DataGrid`** control in the **Toolbox** to insert a `DataGrid` control (Fig. 32.15).

(cont.)

Defines a `DataGrid` control

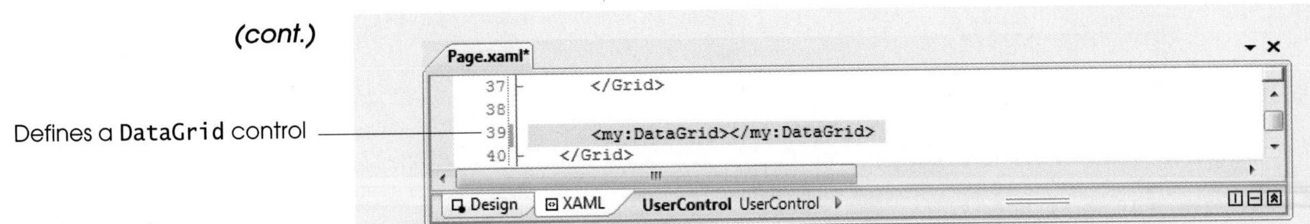

Figure 32.15 Inserted `DataGrid` element.

The `DataGrid` control is in a separate library (known as an assembly) from the other Silverlight controls. An **assembly** (represented as a `.dll` file) is the mechanism used to package compiled .NET code for reuse. When you insert a `DataGrid`, note that the IDE uses the XML namespace `my:` to qualify the element's name. The IDE also adds a new `xmlns` attribute to the `UserControl`'s opening tag. For readability, reformat the `UserControl`'s opening tag as shown in Fig. 32.16. Line 2 specifies the namespace in which the `DataGrid` class resides and the assembly file that contains its code.

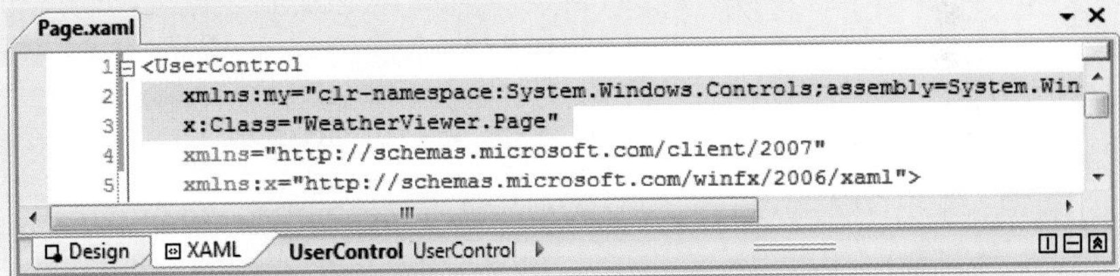

Figure 32.16 Reformatting the `UserControl` start tag for readability.

2. ***Configuring the DataGrid.*** Edit the `DataGrid` control (now in line 41) to appear as shown in Fig. 32.17. The `DataGrid`'s `x:Name` attribute indicates the control's name for use in Visual Basic code (i.e., `forecastList`). The control is placed in the second row of its enclosing `Grid` (that is, the main `Grid`). The attribute **`AutoGenerateColumns`**, when set to `True`, indicates that the `DataGrid` should determine its columns from the source of its data. (We discuss this again shortly.) The `DataGrid` has a `Margin` of 10 pixels around its edges.

`DataGrid` control configured to appear in row 1 of the main `Grid`

Page.xaml*

```
39         </Grid>
40
41         <my:DataGrid x:Name="forecastList" Grid.Row="1"
42            AutoGenerateColumns="True" Margin="10" />
43     </Grid>
```

Design XAML Grid (LayoutRoot) UserControl/Grid

Figure 32.17 Configuring the `DataGrid`.

3. ***Adding the Get Weather Button's `Click` event handler.*** Open the code-behind file for `Page.xaml` by right clicking `Page.xaml` in the **Solution Explorer** and selecting **View Code**. At the top of the **Code** view window are two `ComboBox`es. The **Class Name** `ComboBox` (on the left; Fig. 32.18) lists classes and objects in your `Page.xaml` file. Select `submitButton` from the **Class Name** `ComboBox`, then select `Click` from the **Method Name** `ComboBox` (on the right; Fig. 32.19) to insert a **`Click`** event handler for the `Button`. [*Note:* You'll eventually be able to do this by double clicking the `Button` in **Design** view as you do with Windows `Forms` and WPF applications now.] Be sure to add the comment before the constructor at line 4 in Fig. 32.19 so your line numbers match ours.

(cont.)

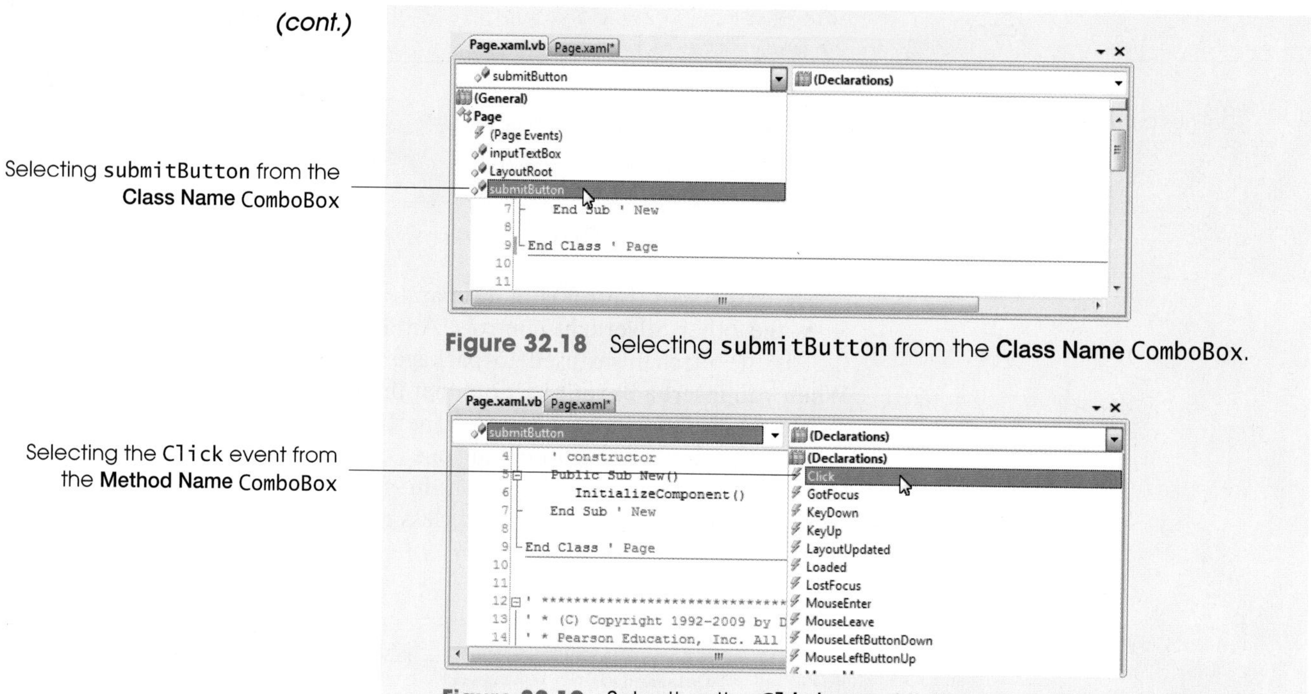

Figure 32.18 Selecting `submitButton` from the **Class Name** `ComboBox`.

Figure 32.19 Selecting the `Click` event in the **Method Name** `ComboBox`.

4. ***Inserting the Get Weather `Button`'s event-handling code.*** When the user presses the **Get Weather** `Button`, the application should obtain the zip code and use it to invoke the web service. Insert the code shown in Fig. 32.20. Reformat the `submitButton_Click` event handler as shown in lines 10–12 and insert the comment before it in line 9. Line 14 obtains the zip code from the `inputTextBox`. Line 15 sets the `Cursor` for the application to the `Wait` cursor. We do this because invoking a web service could incur network delays (e.g., the server may be busy) and we want the application's user to know that the application is performing a task. Lines 18–20 format the `forecastURL` that is used to access the web service. Line 23 uses an object named `weatherService` of type `WebClient` to invoke the web service asynchronously. This enables the user to continue interacting with the application while the web service responds to the request. We define this object in the next box, then discuss line 23 in more detail.

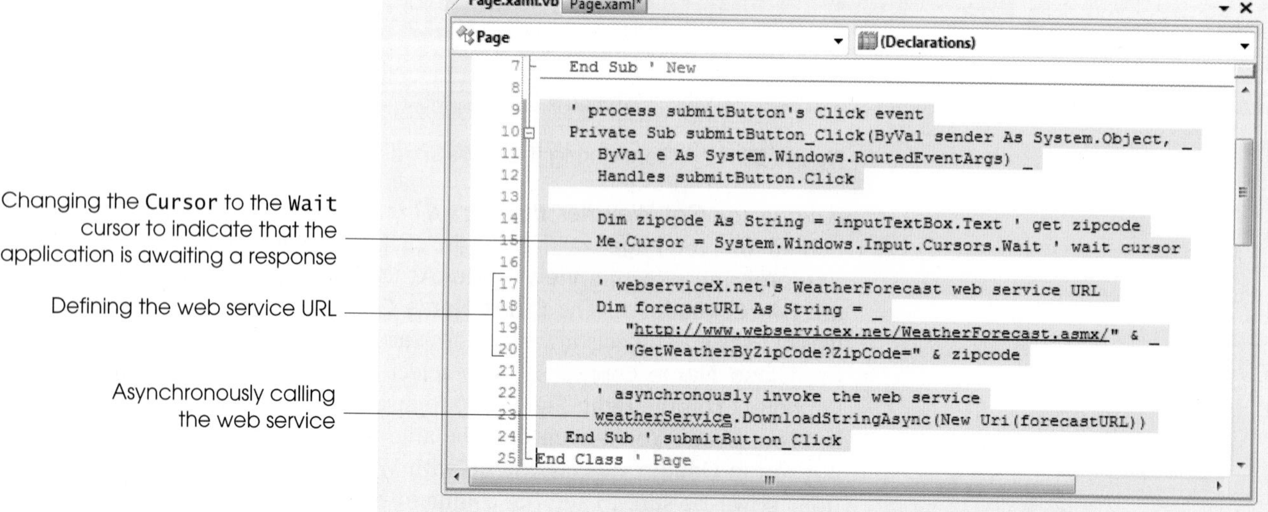

Figure 32.20 **Get Weather** `Button`'s event handling code.

In the next box, you add the `WebClient` object used to invoke the web service and you create an event handler to process the web service's response.

Creating a WebClient Object and Using It to Invoke a Web Service

1. ***Importing the `System.Net` namespace and defining a `WebClient` object.*** To remove the error in line 23 of Fig. 32.20, you must import the `System.Net` namespace and define a `WebClient` object as an instance variable in your `Page` class. Insert lines 1–2 of Fig. 32.21. Then insert lines 6–8 of Fig. 32.22 to create a `WebClient` object as an instance variable. The keyword `WithEvents` on line 7 indicates that the `WebClient` object has events associated with it and enables you to write code that can respond to those events. If you examine the code in the `Designer.vb` file of a Windows `Forms` application, you'll see that your GUI controls are declared with this keyword to enable event handling.

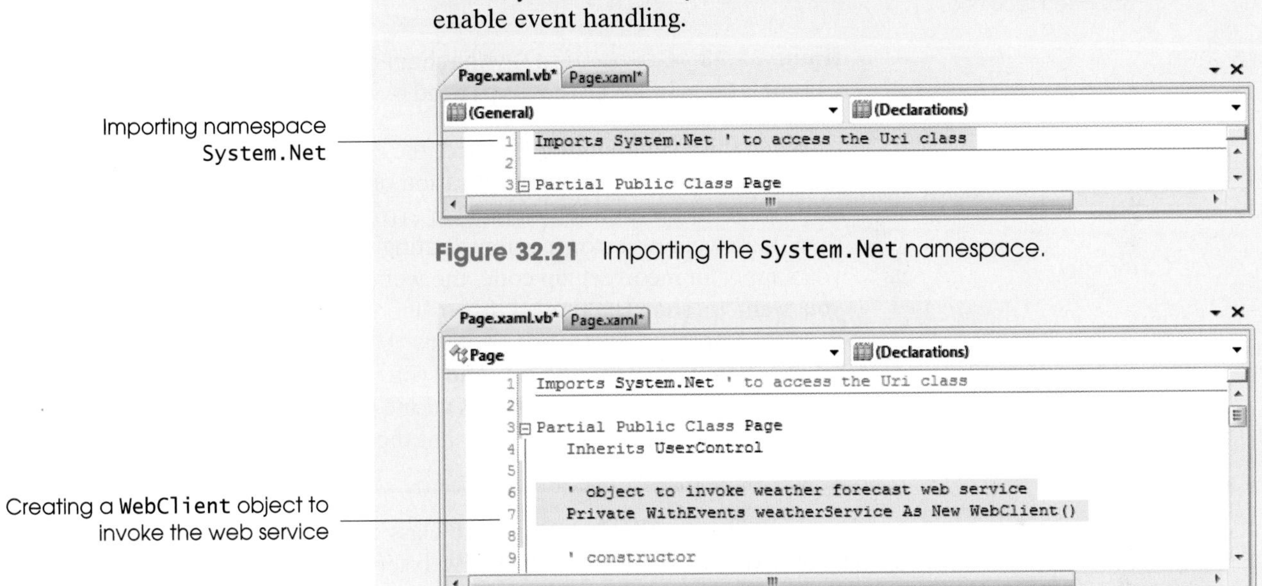
Importing namespace System.Net
Page.xaml.vb* Page.xaml*
(General)
(Declarations)
1 Imports System.Net ' to access the Uri class
2
3 Partial Public Class Page
Creating a WebClient object to invoke the web service
Page.xaml.vb* Page.xaml*
Page
(Declarations)
1 Imports System.Net ' to access the Uri class
2
3 Partial Public Class Page
4 Inherits UserControl
5
6 ' object to invoke weather forecast web service
7 Private WithEvents weatherService As New WebClient()
8
9 ' constructor

Figure 32.21 Importing the `System.Net` namespace.

Figure 32.22 Creating a `WebClient` object.

The most important event for the `WebClient` object in this example is the `DownloadStringCompleted` event. When this event occurs, we'd like the application to process and display the weather information. Line 23 in Fig. 32.20 (which is now line 28 after this step), calls the `weatherService` object's `DownloadStringAsync` method to invoke the web service. The web service's location must be specified as an object of class `Uri` (also from the `System.Net` namespace). Class `Uri`'s constructor receives a `String` representing a uniform resource identifier, such as the `http` address of a web service. In this example, the web service is invoked asynchronously—this means the application can continue executing and the user can continue interacting with it while waiting for a response from the web service. When the response is received, the `DownloadStringCompleted` event handler is called to process the results.

2. ***Inserting the event handler for the `DownloadStringCompleted` event.*** In **Code** view, select the `weatherService` object from the **Class Name** `ComboBox`, then select `DownloadStringCompleted` from the **Method Name** `ComboBox`, to insert an event handler for the `DownloadStringCompleted` event. Format the event handler and insert the code as shown in Fig. 32.23, lines 31–42.

(cont.)

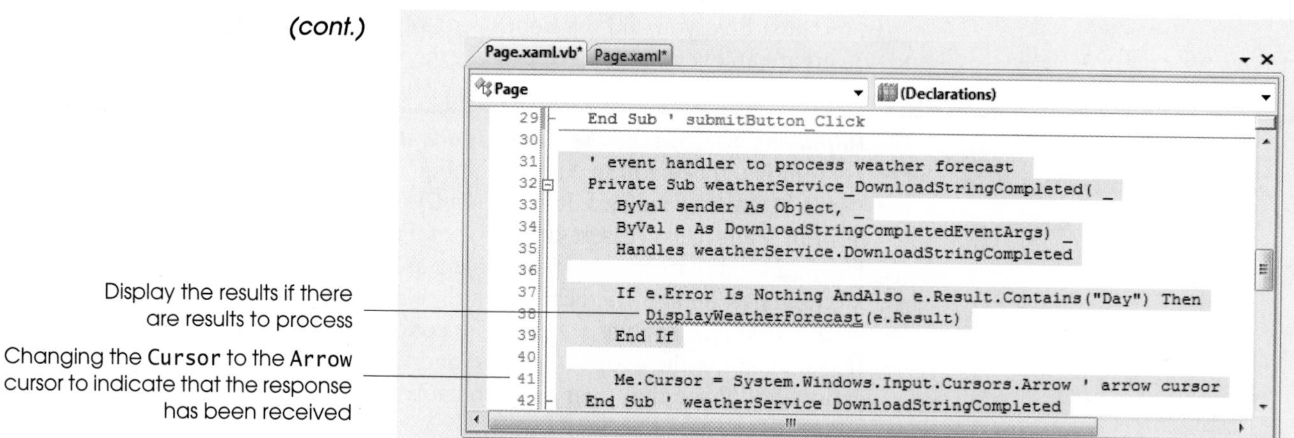

Figure 32.23 Calling `DisplayWeatherForecast` in response to the `WebClient`'s `DownloadStringCompleted` event.

When this event handler is called, the parameter `e` (line 34) contains the web service's response (or an indication of an error). Line 37 uses the property **`Error`** to determine whether an error occurred. If `Error` is `Nothing`, then there were no errors communicating with the web service. However, if you supply an incorrect zip code, the web service does not return data that you want to show in the GUI. So line 37 also determines whether the **`Result`** property (a `String`) contains the substring `"Day"`. If so, there is information you can display, and you call method `DisplayWeatherForecast` (defined in the next box). Line 41 resets the mouse cursor to the standard `Arrow` cursor to indicate that the web-service request is complete.

Next, you'll use .NET's `XDocument` class and **LINQ to XML** to process the `String` of XML results returned by the web service and convert the XML data into a collection of `WeatherData` objects. We've provided class `WeatherData` for you. It consists of instance variables and properties to represent the data for one day in a weather forecast. The properties are named `DayOfWeek`, `WeatherImage`, `MaxTemperatureF`, `MinTemperatureF`, `MaxTemperatureC` and `MinTemperatureC`. The text representations of these properties will be displayed in the `DataGrid`.

Previously you used LINQ to Objects to access and manipulate the elements of a collection. As shown in the next box, LINQ can be applied to other types of data, such as XML, as well.

Using LINQ to XML to Convert XML Data into a Collection of Objects

1. ***Adding the `WeatherData` class to the project.*** Right click the `WeatherViewer` project in the **Solution Explorer** and select **Add > Existing Item....** Next, navigate to `C:\Examples\Tutorial32\` and double click `WeatherData.vb` to add the file to the project.

2. ***Importing namespace `System.Xml.Linq`.*** Add line 2 (Fig. 32.24) to the `Page.xaml.vb` code-behind file. Notice that the IDE reports an error, indicating that the namespace cannot be found. `System.Xml.Linq` is not part of the Silverlight Runtime and, by default, is not available in a Silverlight project. In the next step, you add a reference to this namespace's assembly so you can use the namespace's members in your Silverlight application.

(cont.)

Importing namespace `System.Xml.Linq`

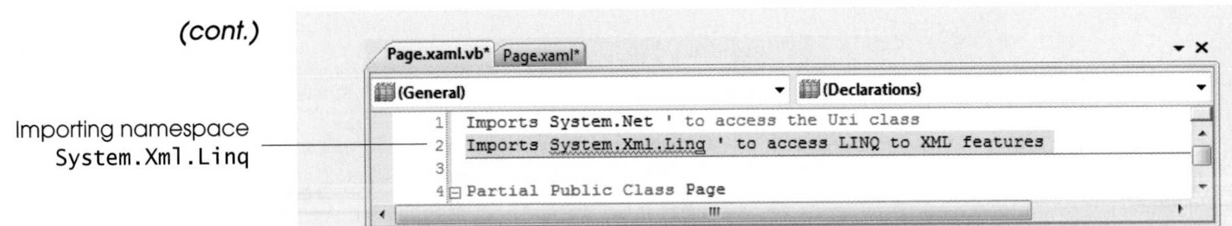

Figure 32.24 Importing the `System.Xml.Linq` namespace.

3. ***Adding a reference to the*** **`System.Xml.Linq`** ***assembly.*** To use LINQ to XML in a Silverlight application, you must first add a reference to its assembly into your project. Right click the `WeatherViewer` project in the **Solution Explorer** and select **Add Reference...** to display the **Add Reference** dialog. In the **.NET** tab, scroll down and select the assembly `System.Xml.Linq` (Fig. 32.25) and click **OK** to add the LINQ to XML assembly to your project.

Selecting the `System.Xml.Linq` assembly to add to your project

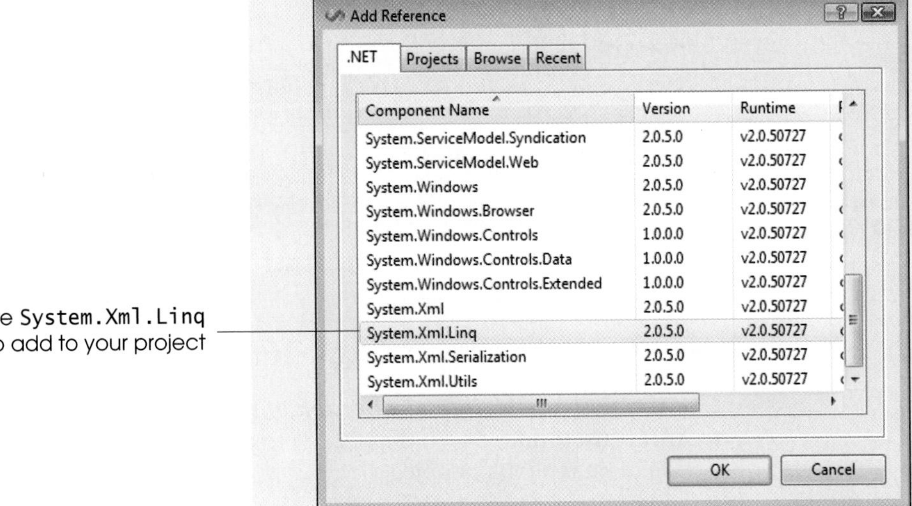

Figure 32.25 Adding a reference to the `System.Xml.Linq` assembly.

4. ***Importing the XML namespace for the XML returned by the web service.*** XML uses namespaces in a manner similar to Visual Basic applications to uniquely identify XML vocabularies. To enable this application to process the XML data in the weather forecast correctly, you must import the namespace contained in the XML. Depending on your browser, if you enter the URL

```
http://www.webservicex.net/WeatherForecast.asmx/
   GetWeatherByZipCode?ZipCode=01754
```

you may be able to see that the `WeatherForecast` XML element contains the `xmlns` attribute

```
xmlns="http://www.webservicex.net"
```

To provide access to the elements in this XML namespace add lines 4–6 (Fig. 32.26). The angle brackets in line 6 are a new Visual Basic 2008 syntax that enables you to import an XML namespace into Visual Basic code so you can access elements of the XML directly using XML properties, which you'll do in *Step 6*.

(cont.)

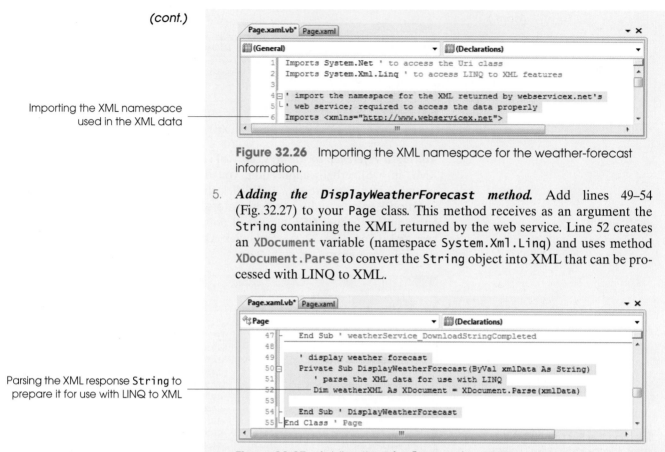

Importing the XML namespace used in the XML data

```
Page.xaml.vb* | Page.xaml
(General) | (Declarations)
1  Imports System.Net ' to access the Uri class
2  Imports System.Xml.Linq ' to access LINQ to XML features
3
4  ' import the namespace for the XML returned by webservicex.net's
5  ' web service; required to access the data properly
6  Imports <xmlns="http://www.webservicex.net">
```

Figure 32.26 Importing the XML namespace for the weather-forecast information.

5. ***Adding the `DisplayWeatherForecast` method.*** Add lines 49–54 (Fig. 32.27) to your `Page` class. This method receives as an argument the `String` containing the XML returned by the web service. Line 52 creates an `XDocument` variable (namespace `System.Xml.Linq`) and uses method `XDocument.Parse` to convert the `String` object into XML that can be processed with LINQ to XML.

Parsing the XML response `String` to prepare it for use with LINQ to XML

```
Page.xaml.vb* | Page.xaml
Page | (Declarations)
47     End Sub ' weatherService_DownloadStringCompleted
48
49     ' display weather forecast
50     Private Sub DisplayWeatherForecast(ByVal xmlData As String)
51        ' parse the XML data for use with LINQ
52        Dim weatherXML As XDocument = XDocument.Parse(xmlData)
53
54     End Sub ' DisplayWeatherForecast
55  End Class ' Page
```

Figure 32.27 Adding the `DisplayWeatherForecast` method.

6. ***Converting the XML into a collection of `WeatherData` objects with LINQ to XML.*** Insert lines 54–70 (Fig. 32.28) to convert the XML data into a collection of `WeatherData` objects.

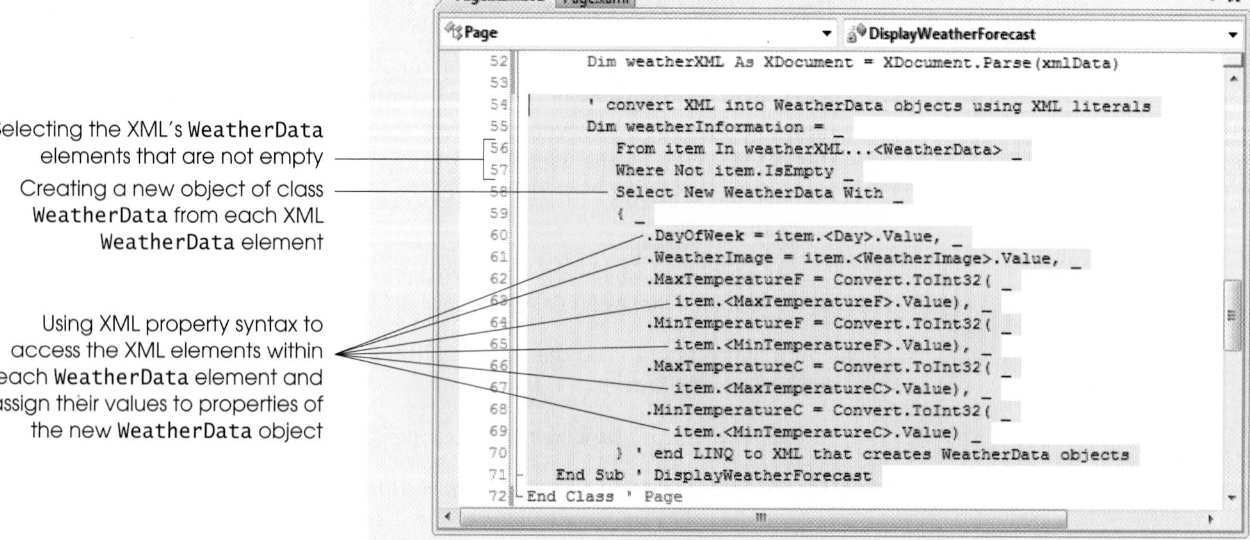

Selecting the XML's `WeatherData` elements that are not empty

Creating a new object of class `WeatherData` from each XML `WeatherData` element

Using XML property syntax to access the XML elements within each `WeatherData` element and assign their values to properties of the new `WeatherData` object

```
Page.xaml.vb* | Page.xaml
Page | DisplayWeatherForecast
52        Dim weatherXML As XDocument = XDocument.Parse(xmlData)
53
54        ' convert XML into WeatherData objects using XML literals
55        Dim weatherInformation = _
56           From item In weatherXML...<WeatherData> _
57           Where Not item.IsEmpty _
58           Select New WeatherData With _
59           { _
60              .DayOfWeek = item.<Day>.Value, _
61              .WeatherImage = item.<WeatherImage>.Value, _
62              .MaxTemperatureF = Convert.ToInt32( _
63                 item.<MaxTemperatureF>.Value), _
64              .MinTemperatureF = Convert.ToInt32( _
65                 item.<MinTemperatureF>.Value), _
66              .MaxTemperatureC = Convert.ToInt32( _
67                 item.<MaxTemperatureC>.Value), _
68              .MinTemperatureC = Convert.ToInt32( _
69                 item.<MinTemperatureC>.Value) _
70           } ' end LINQ to XML that creates WeatherData objects
71     End Sub ' DisplayWeatherForecast
72  End Class ' Page
```

Figure 32.28 Converting XML to `WeatherData` objects with LINQ to XML.

(cont.)

Line 55 declares variable `weatherInformation` without a data type—the compiler will infer this variable's type from the object that we assign to it, as it did when you used LINQ to Objects and LINQ to SQL. Lines 56–70 are LINQ to XML code that performs the conversion. Notice that the LINQ to XML code uses the same basic syntax (`From`, `Where` and `Select` clauses) as in LINQ to Objects and LINQ to SQL. This demonstrates a key feature of LINQ—the ability to query many types of data sources using the same syntax.

The `From` clause (line 56) indicates that we are selecting items from the `weatherXML` `XDocument` object. The ellipsis notation (`...`) to the right of `weatherXML` represents Visual Basic 2008's new **XML descendants property** that is used to select XML elements from the document. The elements you wish to select are specified in angle brackets (< and >) after the `...` notation. In this case, `<WeatherData>` indicates that all the `WeatherData` elements in the XML document should be selected. The XML descendants property syntax is one of several new features for accessing XML in Visual Basic. These features are known as **XML axis properties**.

The `Where` clause (line 57) ensures that the selected item is not empty—that is, if the element does not contain child elements that represent the forecast for a given day, then you do not want to process that element.

The `Select` clause (lines 58–70) creates a new `WeatherData` object for each `WeatherData` element that is not empty in the XML. The **`With`** keyword indicates that the new `WeatherData` object should be used implicitly to access the object's properties on the left side of each assignment in lines 60–69. Line 60 assigns the new object's `DayOfWeek` property the `Value` of the currently selected `item`'s `<Day>` element. The notation `<Day>` uses Visual Basic 2008's new **XML child property** syntax to access the `Day` child element of the currently selected `WeatherData` XML element. Note that you use the actual element name, just as it appears in the XML. (Recall from the beginning of this section that you can view a sample of the weather service's XML directly in your web browser.) Similarly, lines 61, 63, 65, 67 and 69 use the XML property syntax to access the XML child elements `WeatherImage`, `MaxTemperatureF`, `MinTemperatureF`, `MaxTemperatureC` and `MinTemperatureC`, respectively. In each case, you then use the `Value` property of the XML element to obtain the `String` representing its value. For the temperature values, which are represented as `Integers` in a `WeatherData` object, you convert these `Strings` to `Integers` using method `Convert.ToInt32`.

7. ***Displaying the collection of `WeatherData` objects in the `DataGrid`.*** Save your files (**File > Save All**) to ensure that the forecastList is recognized by *IntelliSense* then insert lines 72–73 (Fig. 32.29). WPF's powerful data-binding capabilities make it easy for you to display the weather data in the `DataGrid`. Recall that you set the attribute `AutoGenerateColumns` to `True` for the `DataGrid`. This enables the `DataGrid` to create columns based on the properties of the objects in a collection. You specify the collection with the `DataGrid`'s `ItemsSource` property (line 73).

Specifying the `DataGrid`'s `ItemsSource` from which it will extract data to display

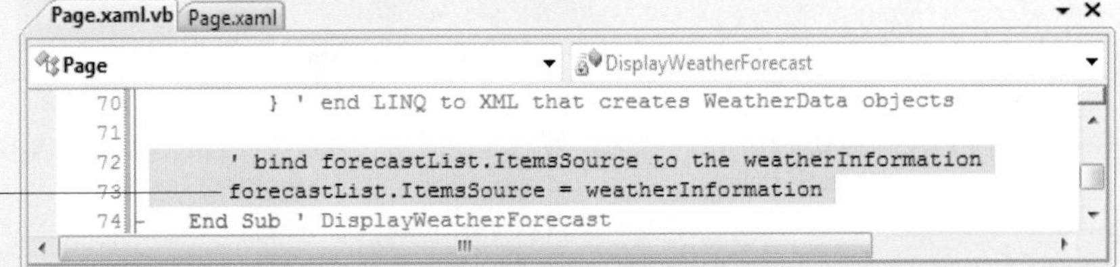

Figure 32.29 Binding the `DataGrid`'s `ItemsSource` property to the collection of `WeatherData` objects.

(cont.)

8. ***Running the Weather Viewer application***. Select **Debug > Start Debugging** to run the application (Fig. 32.30). Enter a zip code and press the **Get Weather** `Button` to invoke the web service. Your output should appear similar to the one shown here. [*Note:* It may take several seconds for the results to be returned.]

DataGrid showing the data from a collection of WeatherData objects

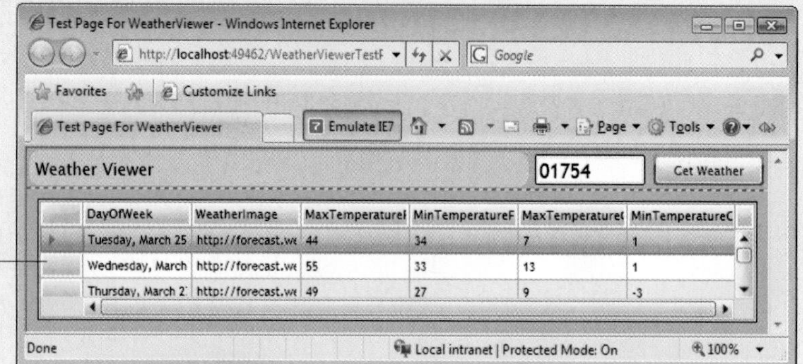

Figure 32.30 Displaying the weather forecast in a `DataGrid`.

9. ***Closing the application***. Close your running application by clicking the browser window's close box.

32.7 Customizing the Data Presentation

In this section, you customize the presentation of the weather data. In particular, the data returned by the web service includes links to images that represent the weather forecast for each day. These images should be displayed in the GUI. You begin by replacing the `DataGrid` used in Section 32.6 with a **`ListBox`** control, which displays a vertical list of items with a vertical scrollbar if there are too many items to display in the control. Each item in a `ListBox` is rendered using the `ListBox`'s default **`ItemTemplate`**, which displays a string representation of the item. A powerful feature of WPF and Silverlight is the ability to customize the `ListBox`'s `ItemTemplate` to specify how the data should be rendered—in this case, you display the weather image and the date. You can also replace the `ListBox`'s default **`ItemsPanel`** (which arranges the items in the `ListBox` vertically), so that the `ListBox`'s items appear horizontally instead.

For now, you show just the weather image and the day of the week. In Section 32.8, you display the complete details for a given day using a custom Silverlight control.

Replacing the `DataGrid` with a `ListBox`

1. ***Replacing the `DataGrid` with a `ListBox`***. Replace lines 41–42 in the file `Page.xaml` with lines 41–42 of Fig. 32.31. Name the `ListBox` the same as the `DataGrid` (`forecastList`) so that no changes are required in the code-behind file. Once you've added the `ListBox`, remove the `xmlns:my` declaration in line 2—it was for the `DataGrid` control and is no longer needed.

Replacing the DataGrid with a ListBox

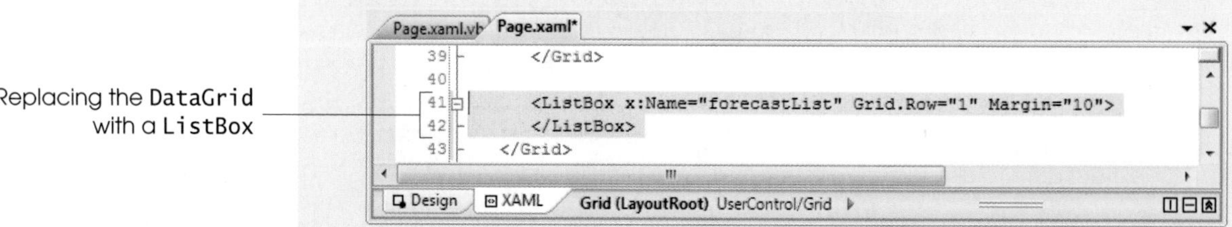

Figure 32.31 Replacing the `DataGrid` with a `ListBox`.

(cont.)

2. ***Running the Weather Viewer application.*** Select **Debug > Start Debugging** to run the application (Fig. 32.32). Enter a zip code and press the **Get Weather** button to invoke the web service. Your output should appear similar to the one shown here. [*Note:* It may take several seconds for the results to be returned.] By default, a `ListBox` shows the `String` representation of each item in its `ItemsSource`. Since we did not define a `ToString` method for the `WeatherData` class, the `ListBox` shows the name of the class (the default `ToString` representation for an object).

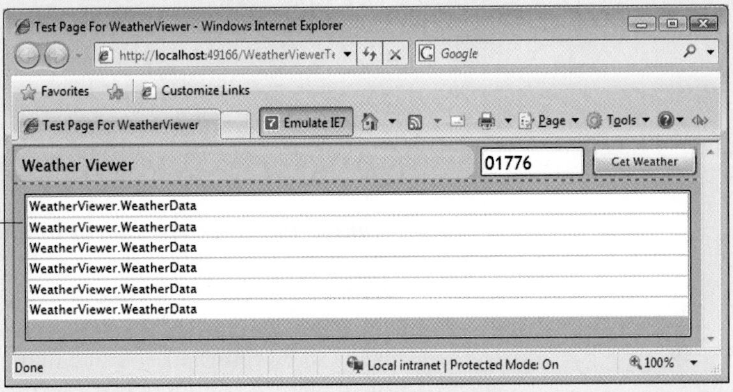

`ListBox` rendering its items as `Strings`

Figure 32.32 Showing the `String` representation of `WeatherData` objects in the `ListBox`.

3. ***Closing the application.*** Close your running application by clicking the browser window's close box.

Obviously, this is not how the weather data should be displayed in the `ListBox`. In the next box, you customize the `ListBox`'s `ItemTemplate` to specify the precise data you wish to display in each item—the weather image and the date. In Section 32.8, you'll create a custom Silverlight control to display the complete weather details for a given day.

Changing the `ListBox`'s `ItemTemplate` to Display the Date and the Weather Image

1. ***Changing the `ListBox`'s `ItemTemplate`.*** Insert lines 41–52 in the `ListBox` element of `Page.xaml` (Fig. 28.33). The **`ListBox.ItemTemplate`** element replaces the default `ItemTemplate` for the `ListBox`, enabling you to customize its appearance. The `ListBox.ItemTemplate` element contains a **`DataTemplate`** element (lines 42–51), which enables you to bind data from a data source (such as a collection) to the `ListBox`'s items. Lines 43–50 define a `StackPanel` that contains an **`Image`** control and a `TextBlock` control. The `Image` control's **`Source`** attribute specifies the location of the image to display. This attribute's value—`{Binding WeatherImage}`—uses the **`Binding` markup extension** to obtain the attribute's value from the `WeatherImage` property of an object in this `ListBox`'s `ItemsSource` (i.e., the collection of `WeatherData` objects you created in Section 32.6).

   The `Image` control also specifies the `Margin`, `Width` and `Height` attributes (55 and 58 are the width and height of the images provided by `webservicex.net`). Line 47 uses the `Binding` markup extension to set the `TextBlock` control's `Text` attribute to the value of a `WeatherData` object's `DayOfWeek` property. You also specify several other attributes for the `TextBlock` (lines 48–49). The text in this `TextBlock` is centered, 12 pixels in size, with a margin of 5 pixels around the edges of the text. If necessary, the text wraps to multiple lines.

(cont.)

Creating a custom `ListBox` `ItemTemplate` that displays the weather image and date for each `WeatherData` object

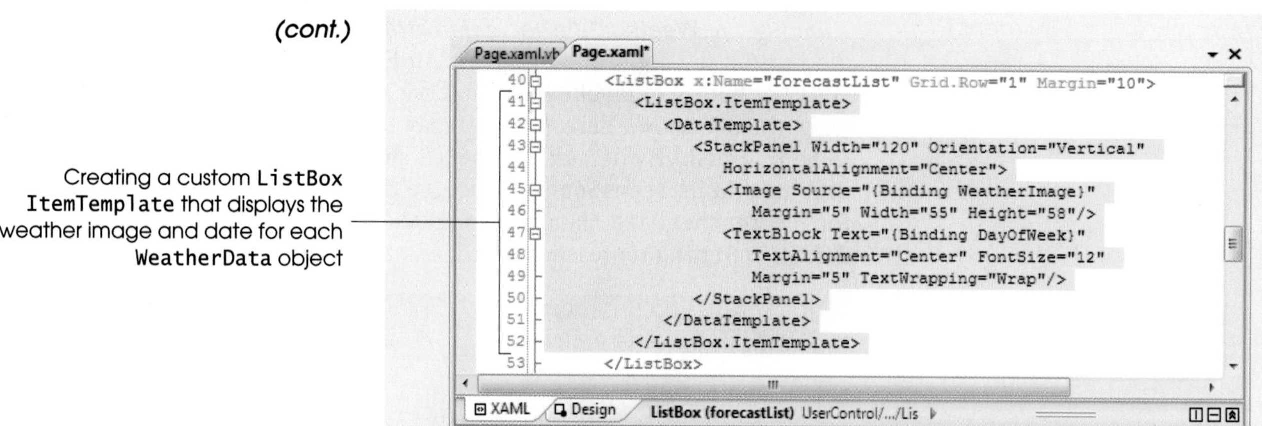

Figure 32.33 Changing the `ListBox`'s `ItemTemplate`.

2. ***Running the Weather Viewer application.*** Select **Debug > Start Debugging** to run the application (Fig. 32.34). Enter a zip code and press the **Get Weather** `Button` to invoke the web service. Your output should appear similar to the one shown here. [*Note:* It may take several seconds for the results to be returned.] Notice that each element in the list now consists of both a picture and some text representing the day of the week. You can use the scrollbar at the right of the `ListBox` to scroll through the complete weather forecast.

`ListBox` items rendered with a custom `ItemTemplate`

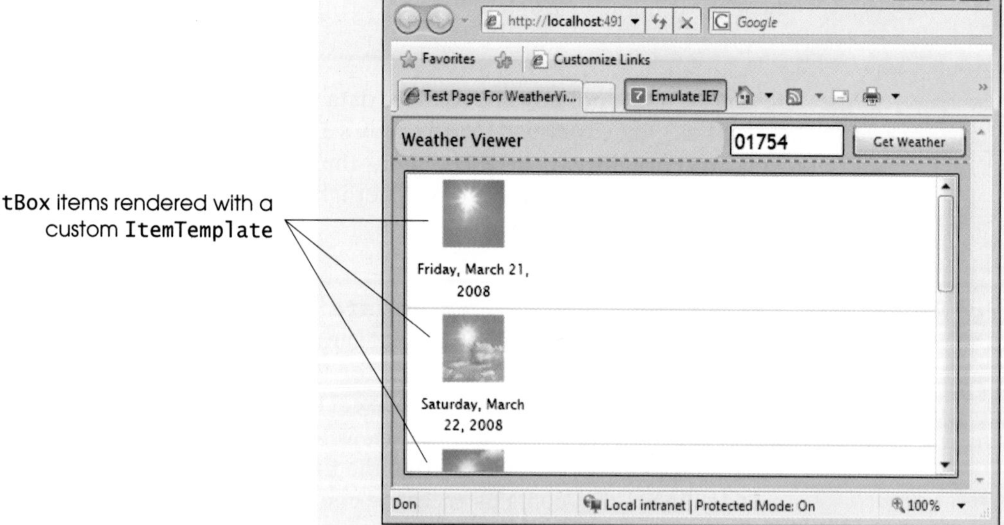

Figure 32.34 Displaying an image and the day of the week for each day in the weather forecast.

3. ***Closing the application.*** Close your running application by clicking the browser window's close box.

In the test drive of the **Weather Viewer** application, the weather forecast was displayed horizontally. This effect can be achieved easily in WPF and Silverlight by replacing the `ListBox`'s default `ItemsPanel`, which arranges a `ListBox`'s items vertically, with an `ItemsPanel` that arranges them horizontally. You create this effect in the next box.

Changing the `ListBox's` `ItemsPanel` to Arrange the Items Horizontally

1. ***Changing the `ListBox's ItemsPanel`.*** Insert lines 41–45 in the `ListBox` element and before the `ListBox.ItemTemplate` element (Fig. 28.35). The `ListBox.ItemsPanel` element replaces the default `ItemsPanel` for the `ListBox`, enabling you to specify how the items in the `ListBox` should be organized. The `ListBox.ItemsPanel` element contains an `ItemsPanelTemplate` element (lines 42–44), which specifies the orientation of the `ListBox`'s elements. Line 43 defines a `StackPanel` with its `Orientation` attribute set to `Horizontal`.

Creating a custom `ListBox` `ItemsPanel` that arranges the `ListBox` items horizontally in a `StackPanel`

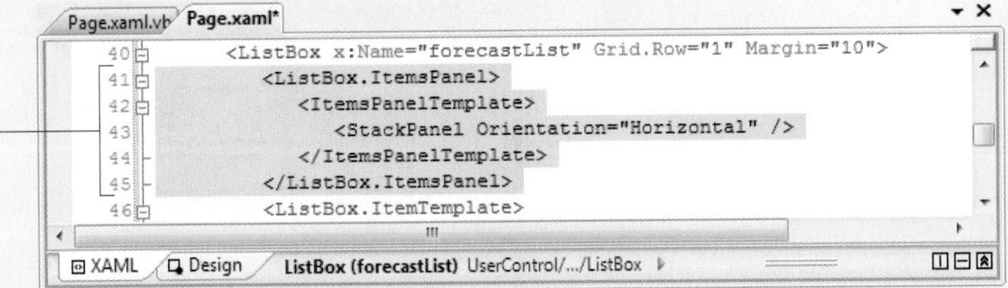

Figure 32.35 Changing the `ListBox's ItemsPanel`.

2. ***Running the Weather Viewer application.*** Select **Debug > Start Debugging** to run the application (Fig. 32.36). Enter a zip code and press the **Get Weather** `Button` to invoke the web service. Your output should appear similar to the one shown here. [*Note:* It may take several seconds for the results to be returned.] Notice that the `ListBox` items are now arranged horizontally. Also, notice that the `ListBox` still provides a scrollbar automatically when the items cannot all be shown at once. You've completely changed the look-and-feel of this `ListBox`, yet it still functions just as a default `ListBox` does.

`ListBox` items rendered horizontally with a custom `ItemsPanel`

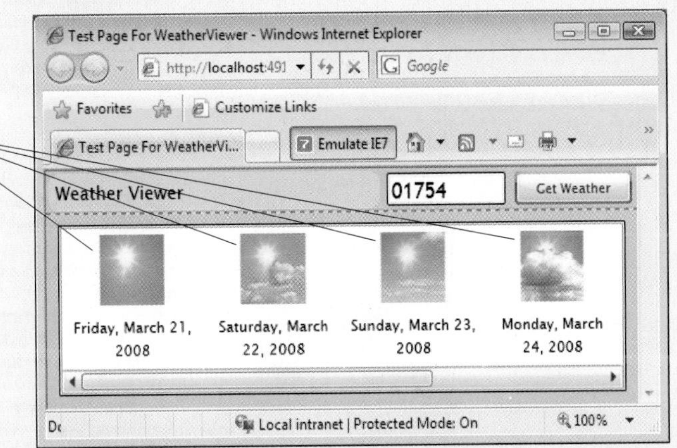

Figure 32.36 Displaying the `ListBox` items horizontally.

3. ***Closing the application.*** Close your running application by clicking the browser window's close box.

32.8 Creating a Customized Silverlight Control

The final piece of the **Weather Viewer** application is to create a custom Silverlight control that displays the weather details for a specific day the user selects in the `ListBox`. You'll also add an event handler that clears the weather forecast if the user changes the text `TextBox`.

Adding a UserControl to the Application

1. ***Adding a new*** `UserControl` ***to the application.*** Right click the `WeatherViewer` project in the **Solution Explorer** and select **Add > New Item....** Select the **Silverlight User Control** template and name the file `WeatherDetailsView.xaml` (Fig. 32.37).

Silverlight User Control template

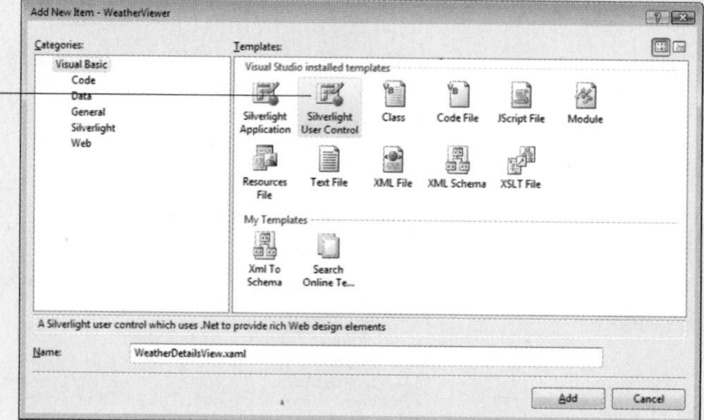

Figure 32.37 Adding a new `UserControl` to a Silverlight application.

2. ***Building the custom control.*** Remove the new `UserControl`'s `Width` and `Height` attributes so that the control scales to fit the layout container in which you place it. Next, replace the `Grid` element in the XAML with the one shown in lines 4–34 of Fig. 32.38.

Figure 32.38 Adding controls to a new `UserControl`.

(cont.)

The `Grid` uses the default one row and one column, so no row or column definitions are needed. Lines 5–6 create a **`Rectangle`** control with its `HorizontalAlignment` and `VerticalAlignment` attributes set to `Stretch`, so the `Rectangle` fills the entire `Grid` cell. The `Rectangle`'s **`Fill`** attribute specifies its fill color (`"Aquamarine"`) and its **`Opacity`** attribute specifies that the `Rectangle` should be semitransparent. This value is a number from `0` to `1`, where `0` is completely transparent and `1` is completely opaque.

The `Border` element (lines 7–33) encloses all the other elements in the custom control. Line 8 introduces the **`BorderBrush`** attribute, which specifies the color of the `Border`, and the **`BorderThickness`** attribute, which controls the thickness of the `Border` in pixels.

Lines 10–32 define a vertical `StackPanel` that consists of an `Image` (lines 11–12), a `TextBlock` (lines 13–15), a horizontal `StackPanel` (lines 16–30) and a `Button` (line 31). The `Image` and `TextBlock` elements use the same settings as in `Page.xaml`. The horizontal `StackPanel` contains `TextBlocks` that display the temperature information for a particular day. Lines 18, 21, 24 and 27 display labels for the temperature values. Lines 19–20, 22–23, 25–26 and 28–29 display the temperature values. In each of these `TextBlocks`, a `Binding` markup extension is used to specify the `WeatherData` property that is bound to the control. The actual `WeatherData` object that is the source of this data is specified by setting this custom control's `DataContext` property later.

Finally, the `Button` object (line 31) is provided to allow the user to close the custom control and return to the main application. Be sure to save your project before continuing with the next step.

3. ***Adding a `Click` event handler for the Close `Button`.*** Right click in the XAML for the `WeatherDetailsView` and select **View Code**. In the **Class Name** ComboBox, select `closeButton`, then select `Click` from the **Method Name** ComboBox to insert the event handler. Format the code as shown in Fig. 32.39. Next, insert line 13, which uses the custom control's **`Visibility`** property to hide the custom control when the user clicks the **Close** `Button`.

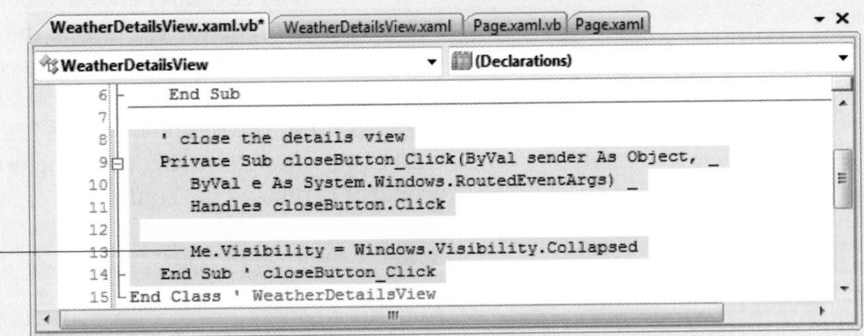
WeatherDetailsView.xaml.vb*
WeatherDetailsView.xaml
Page.xaml.vb
Page.xaml
WeatherDetailsView
(Declarations)
6 End Sub
7
8 ' close the details view
9 Private Sub closeButton_Click(ByVal sender As Object, _
10 ByVal e As System.Windows.RoutedEventArgs) _
11 Handles closeButton.Click
12
13 Me.Visibility = Windows.Visibility.Collapsed
14 End Sub ' closeButton_Click
15 End Class ' WeatherDetailsView
Hides the custom control when the user clicks the Close Button

Figure 32.39 `Click` event handler for the **Close** `Button`.

At this point, you are ready to create the code that displays the complete weather details when the user selects a day from the `forecastListBox`.

Displaying the Complete Weather Details for the Selected Day

1. ***Adding a `WeatherDetailsView` control to the GUI.*** To use the new control, you must first add line 2 (Fig. 32.40) to `Page.xaml`. This enables you to use the new control in your application. In this case, you are creating an XML namespace called `Weather` and indicating that it represents the `WeatherViewer` namespace in the project (your project's name is the default namespace for the project's classes). Save your project so that it becomes aware of the new namespace.

(cont.)

XML namespace that enables you to use the new `WeatherDetailsView` in the GUI

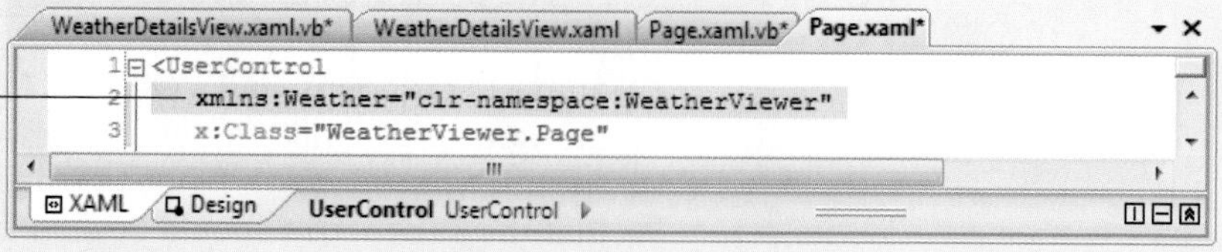

WeatherDetailsView.xaml.vb* | WeatherDetailsView.xaml | Page.xaml.vb* | Page.xaml*

```
1 <UserControl
2     xmlns:Weather="clr-namespace:WeatherViewer"
3     x:Class="WeatherViewer.Page"
```

XAML | Design | UserControl UserControl

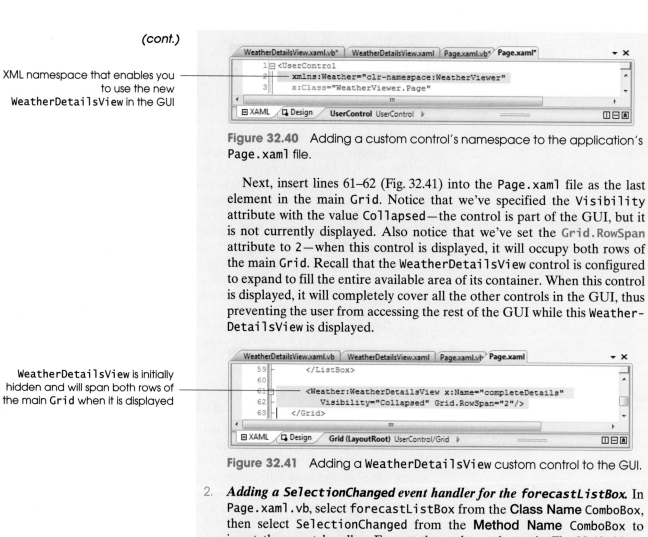

Figure 32.40 Adding a custom control's namespace to the application's `Page.xaml` file.

Next, insert lines 61–62 (Fig. 32.41) into the `Page.xaml` file as the last element in the main `Grid`. Notice that we've specified the `Visibility` attribute with the value `Collapsed`—the control is part of the GUI, but it is not currently displayed. Also notice that we've set the `Grid.RowSpan` attribute to `2`—when this control is displayed, it will occupy both rows of the main `Grid`. Recall that the `WeatherDetailsView` control is configured to expand to fill the entire available area of its container. When this control is displayed, it will completely cover all the other controls in the GUI, thus preventing the user from accessing the rest of the GUI while this `WeatherDetailsView` is displayed.

`WeatherDetailsView` is initially hidden and will span both rows of the main `Grid` when it is displayed

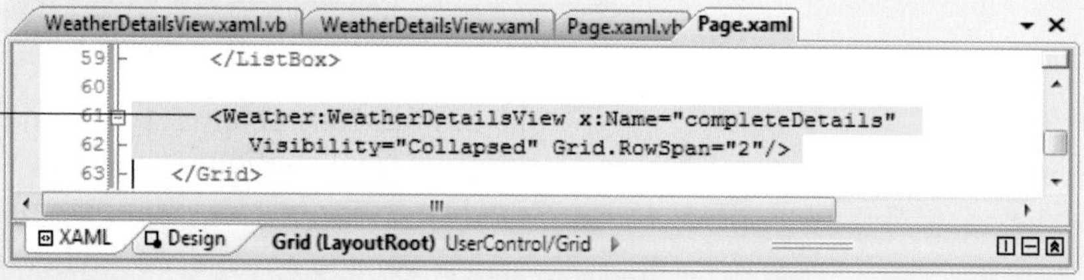

WeatherDetailsView.xaml.vb | WeatherDetailsView.xaml | Page.xaml.vb | Page.xaml

```
59         </ListBox>
60
61         <Weather:WeatherDetailsView x:Name="completeDetails"
62             Visibility="Collapsed" Grid.RowSpan="2"/>
63     </Grid>
```

XAML | Design | Grid (LayoutRoot) UserControl/Grid

Figure 32.41 Adding a `WeatherDetailsView` custom control to the GUI.

2. ***Adding a `SelectionChanged` event handler for the `forecastListBox`.*** In `Page.xaml.vb`, select `forecastListBox` from the **Class Name** ComboBox, then select `SelectionChanged` from the **Method Name** ComboBox to insert the event handler. Format the code as shown in Fig. 32.42. Next, insert lines 82–88. Line 82 determines whether there is a selected item in the `ListBox`. If so, line 84 sets the `DataContext` property for the `WeatherDetailsView` (`completeDetails`) to the selected item in the `forecastList`. Then line 87 uses the `WeatherDetailsView`'s `Visibility` property to display the control.

Specifies that the currently selected `ListBox` item will supply the data for the `WeatherDetailsView`

Shows the `WeatherDetailsView`

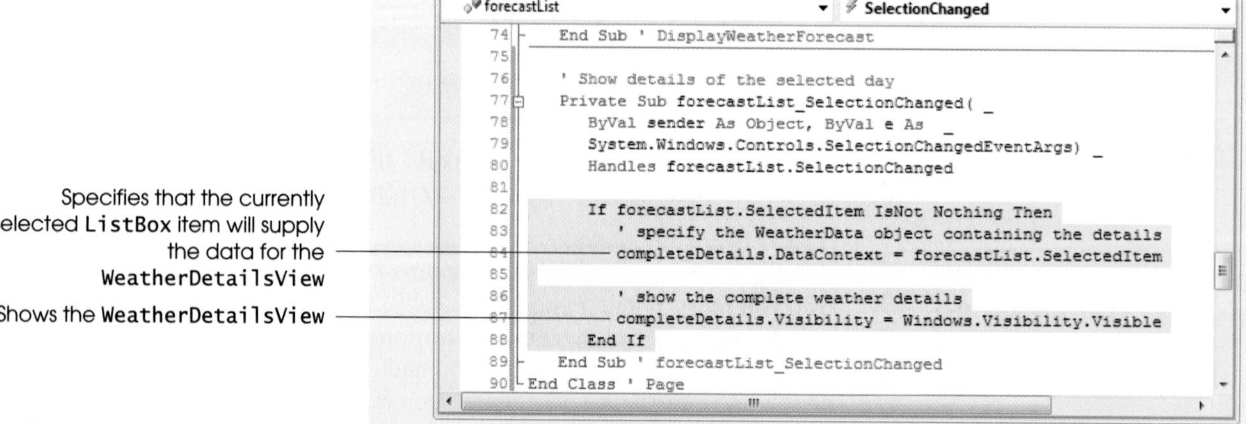

Figure 32.42 `forecastListBox`'s `SelectionChanged` event handler.

(cont.)

3. ***Adding a TextChanged event handler for the TextBox.*** In `Page.xaml.vb`, select `inputTextBox` from the **Class Name** ComboBox, then select TextChanged from the **Method Name** ComboBox to insert the event handler. Format the code as shown in Fig. 32.43. Next, insert line 96, which clears the `ListBox` when the user begins typing another zip code. When a `ListBox`'s `ItemsSource` property is set to `Nothing`, no items will display in the `ListBox`.

WeatherDetailsView.xaml.vb | WeatherDetailsView.xaml | Page.xaml.vb* | Page.xaml

Page | (Declarations)

```
89    End Sub ' forecastList_SelectionChanged
90
91    ' clear the Grid when the text in inputTextBox changes
92    Private Sub inputTextBox_TextChanged(ByVal sender As Object, _
93       ByVal e As System.Windows.Controls.TextChangedEventArgs) _
94       Handles inputTextBox.TextChanged
95
96       forecastList.ItemsSource = Nothing ' clear the ListBox
97    End Sub ' inputTextBox_TextChanged
98 End Class ' Page
```

Clears the `ListBox` when the user changes the text in the `TextBox`

Figure 32.43 `TextChanged` event handler for the `inputTextBox`.

4. ***Running the Weather Viewer application.*** Select **Debug > Start Debugging** to run the application. Enter a zip code and press the **Get Weather** `Button` to invoke the web service. Once the weather forecast displays, click a day in the forecast to see the details view. Your browser window should appear similar to Fig. 32.44. [*Note:* You can eliminate the dotted line across the user interface by removing the `ShowGridLines` attribute from the opening tag of the main `Grid` element in `Page.xaml` (line 7).]

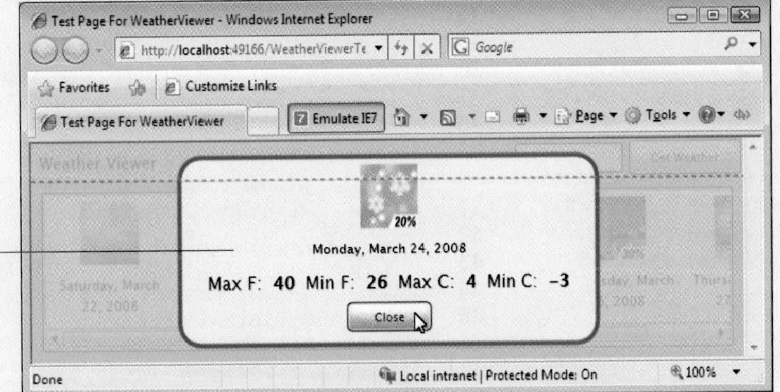

`WeatherDetailsView` displayed after the user selected a specific day from the `ListBox`

Figure 32.44 Displaying the `WeatherDetailsView` for a specific day.

5. ***Closing the application.*** Close your running application by clicking the browser window's close box.

6. ***Closing the IDE.*** Close the IDE by clicking its close box.

32.9 Final Weather Viewer Application Code

Figures 32.45–32.48 present the complete source code for the **Weather Viewer** application. The lines of code containing new programming concepts that you learned in this tutorial are highlighted.

XML namespace for custom `WeatherDetailsView` control

Defining rows in the main `Grid`

Defining rows in the nested `Grid`

Defining a `Border` containing a `TextBlock`

Defining a `TextBox` for user input

Defining a `Button` to invoke the web service

Defining a `ListBox` with a custom look-and-feel to display the weather forecast

Defining a `WeatherDetailsView` to display the complete details view for a selected day

```
<UserControl
    xmlns:Weather="clr-namespace:WeatherViewer"
    x:Class="WeatherViewer.Page"
    xmlns="http://schemas.microsoft.com/client/2007"
    xmlns:x="http://schemas.microsoft.com/winfx/2006/xaml">
    <Grid x:Name="LayoutRoot" Background="LightSkyBlue">
       <Grid.RowDefinitions>
          <RowDefinition Height="35" />
          <RowDefinition Height="*" />
       </Grid.RowDefinitions>

       <Grid.ColumnDefinitions>
          <ColumnDefinition Width="*" />
       </Grid.ColumnDefinitions>

       <Grid>
          <Grid.RowDefinitions>
             <RowDefinition Height="*" />
          </Grid.RowDefinitions>

          <Grid.ColumnDefinitions>
             <ColumnDefinition Width="*" />
             <ColumnDefinition Width="110" />
             <ColumnDefinition Width="110" />
          </Grid.ColumnDefinitions>

          <Border Grid.Row="0" Grid.Column="0" CornerRadius="10"
             Background="LightGray" Margin="2">
             <TextBlock Text="Weather Viewer" Padding="6" />
          </Border>

          <TextBox x:Name="inputTextBox" Grid.Row="0"
             Grid.Column="1" FontSize="18"
             Margin="4"/>

          <Button x:Name="submitButton" Content="Get Weather"
             Grid.Row="0" Grid.Column="2" Margin="4" />
       </Grid>

       <ListBox x:Name="forecastList" Grid.Row="1" Margin="10">
          <ListBox.ItemsPanel>
             <ItemsPanelTemplate>
                <StackPanel Orientation="Horizontal" />
             </ItemsPanelTemplate>
          </ListBox.ItemsPanel>
          <ListBox.ItemTemplate>
             <DataTemplate>
                <StackPanel Width="120" Orientation="Vertical"
                   HorizontalAlignment="Center">
                   <Image Source="{Binding WeatherImage}"
                      Margin="5" Width="55" Height="58"/>
                   <TextBlock Text="{Binding DayOfWeek}"
                      TextAlignment="Center" FontSize="12"
                      Margin="5" TextWrapping="Wrap"/>
                </StackPanel>
             </DataTemplate>
          </ListBox.ItemTemplate>
       </ListBox>

       <Weather:WeatherDetailsView x:Name="completeDetails"
          Visibility="Collapsed" Grid.RowSpan="2"/>
    </Grid>
</UserControl>
```

Figure 32.45 `Page.xaml`—Main page of the Silverlight application defines the user interface.

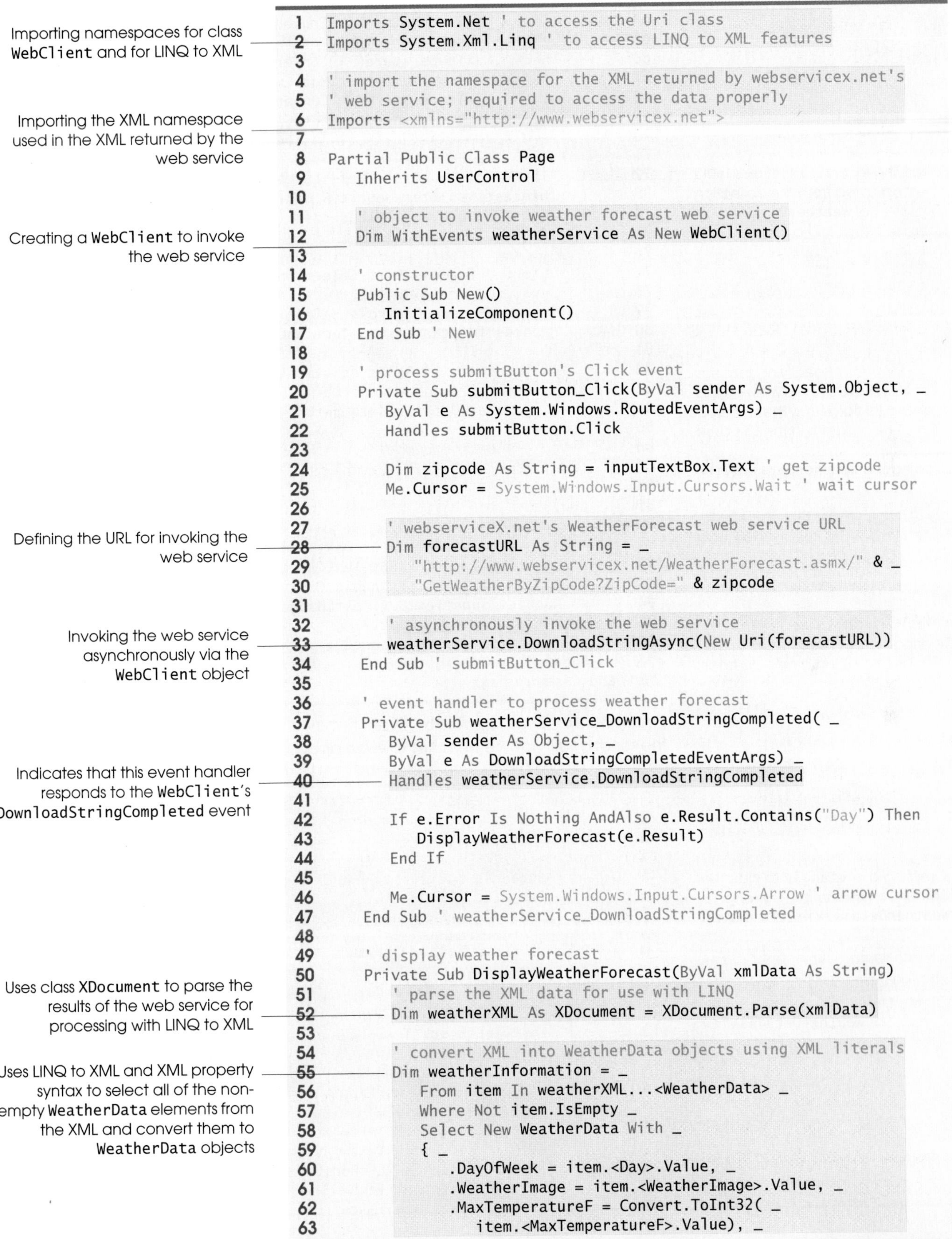
Importing namespaces for class WebClient and for LINQ to XML
Importing the XML namespace used in the XML returned by the web service
Creating a WebClient to invoke the web service
Defining the URL for invoking the web service
Invoking the web service asynchronously via the WebClient object
Indicates that this event handler responds to the WebClient's DownloadStringCompleted event
Uses class XDocument to parse the results of the web service for processing with LINQ to XML
Uses LINQ to XML and XML property syntax to select all of the non-empty WeatherData elements from the XML and convert them to WeatherData objects

```
Imports System.Net ' to access the Uri class
Imports System.Xml.Linq ' to access LINQ to XML features

' import the namespace for the XML returned by webservicex.net's
' web service; required to access the data properly
Imports <xmlns="http://www.webservicex.net">

Partial Public Class Page
   Inherits UserControl

   ' object to invoke weather forecast web service
   Dim WithEvents weatherService As New WebClient()

   ' constructor
   Public Sub New()
      InitializeComponent()
   End Sub ' New

   ' process submitButton's Click event
   Private Sub submitButton_Click(ByVal sender As System.Object, _
      ByVal e As System.Windows.RoutedEventArgs) _
      Handles submitButton.Click

      Dim zipcode As String = inputTextBox.Text ' get zipcode
      Me.Cursor = System.Windows.Input.Cursors.Wait ' wait cursor

      ' webserviceX.net's WeatherForecast web service URL
      Dim forecastURL As String = _
         "http://www.webservicex.net/WeatherForecast.asmx/" & _
         "GetWeatherByZipCode?ZipCode=" & zipcode

      ' asynchronously invoke the web service
      weatherService.DownloadStringAsync(New Uri(forecastURL))
   End Sub ' submitButton_Click

   ' event handler to process weather forecast
   Private Sub weatherService_DownloadStringCompleted( _
      ByVal sender As Object, _
      ByVal e As DownloadStringCompletedEventArgs) _
      Handles weatherService.DownloadStringCompleted

      If e.Error Is Nothing AndAlso e.Result.Contains("Day") Then
         DisplayWeatherForecast(e.Result)
      End If

      Me.Cursor = System.Windows.Input.Cursors.Arrow ' arrow cursor
   End Sub ' weatherService_DownloadStringCompleted

   ' display weather forecast
   Private Sub DisplayWeatherForecast(ByVal xmlData As String)
      ' parse the XML data for use with LINQ
      Dim weatherXML As XDocument = XDocument.Parse(xmlData)

      ' convert XML into WeatherData objects using XML literals
      Dim weatherInformation = _
         From item In weatherXML...<WeatherData> _
         Where Not item.IsEmpty _
         Select New WeatherData With _
         { _
            .DayOfWeek = item.<Day>.Value, _
            .WeatherImage = item.<WeatherImage>.Value, _
            .MaxTemperatureF = Convert.ToInt32( _
               item.<MaxTemperatureF>.Value), _
```

Figure 32.46 Page.xaml.vb—Event handlers and other methods that implement the functionality of the WeatherViewer application's main GUI. (Part 1 of 2.)

```
                .MinTemperatureF = Convert.ToInt32( _
                   item.<MinTemperatureF>.Value), _
                .MaxTemperatureC = Convert.ToInt32( _
                   item.<MaxTemperatureC>.Value), _
                .MinTemperatureC = Convert.ToInt32( _
                   item.<MinTemperatureC>.Value) _
             } ' end LINQ to XML that creates WeatherData objects

         ' bind forecastList.ItemsSource to the weatherInformation
         forecastList.ItemsSource = weatherInformation
      End Sub ' DisplayWeatherForecast

      ' Show details of the selected day
      Private Sub forecastList_SelectionChanged( _
         ByVal sender As Object, ByVal e As _
         System.Windows.Controls.SelectionChangedEventArgs) _
         Handles forecastList.SelectionChanged

         If forecastList.SelectedItem IsNot Nothing Then
            ' specify the WeatherData object containing the details
            completeDetails.DataContext = forecastList.SelectedItem

            ' show the complete weather details
            completeDetails.Visibility = Windows.Visibility.Visible
         End If
      End Sub ' forecastList_SelectionChanged

      ' clear the Grid when the text in inputTextBox changes
      Private Sub inputTextBox_TextChanged(ByVal sender As Object, _
         ByVal e As System.Windows.Controls.TextChangedEventArgs) _
         Handles inputTextBox.TextChanged

         forecastList.ItemsSource = Nothing ' clear the ListBox
      End Sub ' inputTextBox_TextChanged
   End Class ' Page
```

Specifying that the `ListBox` should be populated from the collection of `WeatherData` objects

Specifying that the `WeatherDetailsView` should obtain its data from the selected item in the `ListBox`

Showing the `WeatherDetailsView`

Clearing the `ListBox` when the user begins typing a new zip code

Figure 32.46 `Page.xaml.vb`—Event handlers and other methods that implement the functionality of the `WeatherViewer` application's main GUI. (Part 2 of 2.)

```
<UserControl x:Class="WeatherViewer.WeatherDetailsView"
   xmlns="http://schemas.microsoft.com/client/2007"
   xmlns:x="http://schemas.microsoft.com/winfx/2006/xaml">
   <Grid>
      <Rectangle HorizontalAlignment="Stretch" Fill="Aquamarine"
         VerticalAlignment="Stretch" Opacity="0.8" />
      <Border CornerRadius="20" Background="AliceBlue"
         BorderBrush="Blue" BorderThickness="4"
         Width="400" Height="175">
         <StackPanel>
            <Image Source="{Binding WeatherImage}"
               Margin="5" Width="55" Height="58" />
            <TextBlock Text="{Binding DayOfWeek}" Margin="5"
               TextAlignment="Center" FontSize="12"
               TextWrapping="Wrap" />
            <StackPanel HorizontalAlignment="Center"
               Orientation="Horizontal">
               <TextBlock Text="Max F:" Margin="5" FontSize="16"/>
               <TextBlock Text="{Binding MaxTemperatureF}"
                  Margin="5" FontSize="16" FontWeight="Bold"/>
               <TextBlock Text="Min F:" Margin="5" FontSize="16"/>
               <TextBlock Text="{Binding MinTemperatureF}"
                  Margin="5" FontSize="16" FontWeight="Bold"/>
```

Creating a `Rectangle` to hide the other controls on the GUI when a `WeatherDetailsView` is displayed

Using data binding to display `WeatherData` properties in the `WeatherDetailsView`

Figure 32.47 `WeatherDetailsView.xaml`—Custom `UserControl` that displays the complete details of the weather forecast for a given day. (Part 1 of 2.)

```
                <TextBlock Text="Max C:" Margin="5" FontSize="16"/>
                <TextBlock Text="{Binding MaxTemperatureC}"
                    Margin="5" FontSize="16" FontWeight="Bold"/>
                <TextBlock Text="Min C:" Margin="5" FontSize="16"/>
                <TextBlock Text="{Binding MinTemperatureC}"
                    Margin="5" FontSize="16" FontWeight="Bold"/>
            </StackPanel>
            <Button x:Name="closeButton" Content="Close" Width="80"/>
        </StackPanel>
    </Border>
  </Grid>
</UserControl>
```

Figure 32.47 `WeatherDetailsView.xaml`—Custom `UserControl` that displays the complete details of the weather forecast for a given day. (Part 2 of 2.)

```
Partial Public Class WeatherDetailsView
   Inherits UserControl

   Public Sub New()
      InitializeComponent()
   End Sub ' New

   ' close the details view
   Private Sub closeButton_Click(ByVal sender As Object, _
      ByVal e As System.Windows.RoutedEventArgs) _
      Handles closeButton.Click

      Me.Visibility = Windows.Visibility.Collapsed
   End Sub ' closeButton_Click
End Class ' WeatherDetailsView
```

Hiding the `WeatherDetailsView` when its **Close** `Button` is pressed

Figure 32.48 `WeatherDetailsView.xaml.vb`—Code-behind file for the custom `UserControl` named `WeatherDetailsView`.

32.10 Wrap-Up

In this tutorial, you learned how to build Silverlight applications in Visual Studio 2008. You learned that Silverlight is a robust, cross-platform, cross-browser subset of the .NET platform. You used XAML markup to build a Silverlight user interface. You specified the layout of the GUI using a combination of `Grid` and `StackPanel` layout containers. You learned how to use the **Class Name** and **Method Name** `ComboBox`es in **Code** view to create event handlers for Silverlight controls. You used a `WebClient` object to invoke a web service, then used class `XDocument` and LINQ to XML to process the XML results returned by the web service. You learned about Visual Basic's XML axis properties for accessing XML elements directly in code. You used data binding and the `Binding` markup extension to associate data with GUI controls. You learned how to customize the look-and-feel of a `ListBox` control by replacing its `ItemTemplate` and `ItemsPanel`. Finally, you created a custom Silverlight control.

SKILLS SUMMARY

Creating a Silverlight Application Project

- In Visual Studio, select **File > New Project...** to display the **New Project** dialog. In the dialog, under the Visual Basic Silverlight project types, select **Silverlight Application**, name your project, then click **OK**.
- In the **Add Silverlight Application** dialog that appears after you click **OK**, select the `RadioButton` **Add a new Web** to the solution for hosting this control and choose **Web Application Project** from the **Project Type** `ComboBox`.

Changing the Background Color of a Grid

- Change the background color by removing White from the Background attribute, then press *Ctrl + Space* to display a menu of the predefined color names from which to select a value. You can also specify any color you wish as a hexadecimal value of the form #RRGGBB.

Showing Grid Lines in a Grid

- Insert the ShowGridLines attribute in the Grid element's opening tag.

Defining Rows and Columns in a Grid

- To define rows, create a Grid.RowDefinitions element in the Grid. Within that element, define RowDefinition elements for each row of the Grid.
- To define rows, create a Grid.ColumnDefinitions element in the Grid. Within that element, define ColumnDefinition elements for each column of the Grid.

Placing a Control in a Particular Grid Location

- In the control's start tag, specify the Grid.Row and Grid.Column attributes.
- Use Grid.RowSpan or Grid.ColSpan to make a control span multiple rows or columns.

Placing a Border Around a Control

- Place the control inside a Border element and use the Border's attributes (such as Background and CornerRadius) to configure its style.

Displaying Text

- Define a TextBlock element and set its Text attribute.

Specifying the FontSize of a Control

- Set the control's FontSize attribute to a value in WPF pixels (recall that each pixel is 1/96 of an inch).

Accessing a Control Programmatically

- Define the control's x:Name attribute.

Placing a Button on the GUI

- Define a Button element and set its Content attribute.
- Use the Button's Click event to respond when the user presses the Button.

Making a Silverlight Application Resizable in the Browser Window

- Remove the Width and Height attributes of the application's UserControl element.

Using a DataGrid Element

- Double click the DataGrid control in the **Toolbox**.
- Set attribute AutoGenerateColumns to True if you want the DataGrid to determine its columns from the source of its data.
- Set the DataGrid's ItemsSource property to specify the collection of data to display in the DataGrid

Invoking a Web Service Asynchronously

- Import the System.Net namespace and define a WebClient object using the WithEvents keyword to indicate that the object can generate events.
- Create a DownloadStringCompleted event handler for the WebClient.

- Invoke the web service asynchronously by calling the WebClient object's DownloadStringAsync method with the web service Uri as an argument.
- When the DownloadStringCompleted event handler is called, the parameter's Result property contains the web service's response as a String.

Parsing XML Data Returned from a Web Service

- Add a reference to the System.Linq.Xml assembly. Right click the project name in the **Solution Explorer** and select **Add Reference...** to display the **Add Reference** dialog. In the **.NET** tab, scroll down and select the assembly System.Xml.Linq and click **OK**.
- Import namespace System.Xml.Linq.
- Import the XML namespace for the XML returned by the web service.
- Create an XDocument variable and use method XDocument.Parse to convert the String object into XML that can be processed with LINQ to XML.

Converting XML into a Collection of Objects Using LINQ to XML

- Use a LINQ From clause to select items from the XDocument object. Use an XML descendants property to specify which elements to select.
- Use a Where clause to specify the selection criteria.
- Use a Select to convert each selected element into a new object. Use the With keyword to indicate that the new object should be used implicitly to access its properties.
- Use Visual Basic 2008's new XML property syntax to access the child elements of the selected element and use the Value property to get the value of the child element. Note that you use the actual element name, just as it appears in the XML.

Using a ListBox Control to Display a Collection of Objects

- Set the ListBox's ItemsSource property to specify the collection of data to display in the ListBox.

Changing the ListBox Control's ItemTemplate

- Use the ListBox.ItemTemplate element to replace the default ItemTemplate for the ListBox.
- In the ListBox.ItemTemplate element, place a DataTemplate element to enable you to bind data from a data source (such as a collection) to the ListBox's items.
- In the DataTemplate element define a layout container with nested elements that represent the new way to render an item.
- Use the Binding markup extension to select properties of an object that should be bound to controls.

Changing the ListBox Control's ItemsPanel

- Use the ListBox.ItemsPanel element to replace the default ItemsPanel for the ListBox.
- Nest an ItemsPanelTemplate element in the ListBox.ItemsPanel element to specify the orientation of the ListBox's elements.
- Define the new way to arrange ListBox items as a nested element in the ItemsPanelTemplate element.

Adding a Custom Control to a Silverlight Application

- Right click the project name in the **Solution Explorer** and select **Add > New Item...**. Select the **Silverlight User Control** template and name the file.

- Define controls and layouts as you do for the main GUI of your application.

Using Data Binding with a Custom Control

- Set the `DataContext` property of the custom control to the object that provides the data for binding.
- Use `Binding` markup extensions to select the properties to bind to controls in the custom control.

KEY TERMS

assembly—The mechanism used to package compiled .NET code for reuse.

`AutoGenerateColumns` attribute of a `DataGrid`—When set to `True`, indicates that a `DataGrid` should determine its columns from the source of its data.

`App.xaml`—XAML file that declares a Silverlight application's shared resources, such as styles that can be applied to various GUI elements.

`App.xaml.vb`—Code-behind file that defines application-level event handlers, such as an event handler for unhandled exceptions.

`Binding` markup extension—Binds a property of an object to an attribute of a control.

`Border` element—Used to place a border around any Silverlight control.

`Button` element—Displays a button in a Silverlight GUI.

`Click` event of a `Button`—Raised when the user presses the `Button`.

consuming a web service—The process of invoking a web service and manipulating its results.

`Content` attribute of a `Button`—Specifies the text on the `Button`.

`CornerRadius` attribute of a `Border`—Specifies the rounding of the corners of a `Border`.

`DataContext` property of a Silverlight control—Specifies the object from which the control can obtain data via `Binding` markup extensions.

`DataGrid` control—Displays data in rows and columns. Can bind a collection of objects to this control via its `ItemsSource` property.

`DownloadStringAsync` method of class `WebClient`—Asynchronously invokes a web service so the application can continue executing.

`DownloadStringCompleted` event of class `WebClient`—Raised when a web service responds to an asynchronous invocation.

`Error` property of class `DownloadStringCompletedEventArgs`—Specifies the error that occurred, if any, during a web-service invocation.

`Fill` attribute of `Rectangle` element—Specifies a `Rectangle`'s fill color.

`FontSize` attribute of a Silverlight control—Specifies the size in pixels of the font used by a control.

`Grid.Column` attribute of a Silverlight control—Specifies the column in which a control should be placed in the enclosing `Grid` layout container.

`Grid.ColumnDefinitions` element—A nested element of a `Grid` layout container. Contains a set of `ColumnDefinition` elements that define the columns of the `Grid` and their characteristics.

`Grid.ColSpan` attribute of a Silverlight control—Specifies how many columns a control should occupy in its enclosing `Grid` layout container.

`Grid.Row` attribute of a Silverlight control—Specifies the row in which a control should be placed in the enclosing `Grid` layout container.

`Grid.RowDefinitions` element—A nested element of a `Grid` layout container. Contains a set of `RowDefinition` elements that define the rows of the `Grid` and their characteristics.

`Grid.RowSpan` attribute of a Silverlight control—Specifies how many rows a control should occupy in its enclosing `Grid` layout container.

`Image` control—Displays an image in a Silverlight GUI.

`ItemsPanel` of a `ListBox`—*See* `ListBox.ItemsPanel` element.

`ItemsPanelTemplate` element—Used to redefine the `ItemsPanel` of a `ListBox` to change how `ListBox` items are arranged.

`ItemTemplate` of a `ListBox`—*See* `ListBox.ItemTemplate` element.

LINQ to XML—LINQ capabilities that enable manipulation of XML data.

ListBox control—Displays a list of items in a Silverlight GUI.

ListBox.ItemsPanel element—Defines how the items in a ListBox are arranged in the GUI (e.g., vertically, horizontally, etc.).

ListBox.ItemTemplate element—Defines the look-and-feel of each ListBox item. The default ItemTemplate displays the String representation of each item.

Margin attribute of a Silverlight control—Specifies the amount of space around the edges of a control.

Opacity attribute of Rectangle element—Specifies a Rectangle's transparency—a number from 0 to 1, where 0 is completely transparent and 1 is completely opaque.

Orientation attribute of a StackPanel layout container—Determines whether a StackPanel arranges its child elements vertically (the default) or horizontally.

Page.xaml—XAML file that defines a Silverlight application's GUI.

Page.xaml.vb—Code-behind file that declares GUI event handlers (and other methods required by a Silverlight application).

Rectangle element—Displays a rectangle in a Silverlight GUI.

Representational State Transfer (REST)—A way to invoke a web service in which each operation is identified by a unique URL.

Result property of class DownloadStringCompletedEventArgs—A String representing the results returned by the invoked web service.

Rich Internet Applications (RIAs)—Web applications that offer the responsiveness and rich GUI features of desktop applications.

RowDefinition element—Nested in a Grid.RowDefinitions element to specify the characteristics of a row in a Grid layout container.

ShowGridLines attribute of Grid layout container—Displays grid lines so you can see the grid layout as you design and build your GUI.

Silverlight—Microsoft's platform for Rich Internet Applications (RIAs).

Silverlight Application project template—Visual Studio 2008 project template for building Silverlight applications. To use this, you must have Silverlight Tools for Visual Studio 2008 installed.

Source attribute of an Image—Specifies the URL from which to obtain the image for display in the control.

Text attribute of a TextBlock—Specifies the text in a TextBlock.

TextBlock element—Displays text in a Silverlight GUI.

TextChanged event of a TextBox—Raised when the user changes the text in a TextBox.

UserControl—The main element in a Silverlight application. Contains all other elements in the GUI.

Visibility attribute of a Silverlight control—Specifies whether a control is Visible or Collapsed (not visible) in the GUI.

Web Application Project—A project that can be used to test a Silverlight application in a web browser. One of these can be created for you when you create a new Silverlight application.

web service—A software component stored on one computer that can be accessed via method calls by an application (or other software component) on another computer over a network.

WebClient class—An object of this class can be used to invoke a web service.

WithEvents keyword—Used in the declaration of an object that can generate events. Enables you to create event handlers for such an object.

.xap file—File-name extension for a compiled Silverlight application that is packaged by the IDE into a file containing the application and its supporting resources (such as images or other files used by the application).

`x:Name` attribute of a Silverlight control—Used to specify the name of the control so that you can access it programmatically from Visual Basic.

`XDocument` class—Class that enables you to process XML data programmatically.

`XDocument.Parse` method—Method that parses XML into a form that can be accessed programmatically.

XML descendants property—New Visual Basic 2008 syntax that enables you to specify the elements to select from an XML document for processing in a LINQ to XML expression.

XML axis properties—New Visual Basic 2008 syntax for accessing XML elements directly from Visual Basic code.

CONTROLS, EVENTS, PROPERTIES & METHODS

`Border` Border This control allows the user to place a visual border around any element or elements.

- ***In action***

- ***Properties***

`Background`—Specifies the background color of the `Border`.

`BorderBrush`—Specifies the color of the `Border`.

`BorderThickness`—Specifies the thickness of the `Border`.

`CornerRadius`—Rounds the corners of the `Border`. A higher value creates a more dramatic curve.

`Grid.Column`—Specifies the column of the enclosing `Grid` in which the `Border` is placed.

`Grid.Row`—Specifies the row of the enclosing `Grid` in which the `Border` is placed.

`Margin`—Specifies amount of space around the `Border`.

`Button` Button This control allows the user to raise an action or event.

- ***In action***

- ***Properties***

`Content`—Specifies the text displayed on the `Button`.

`Grid.Column`—Specifies the column of the enclosing `Grid` in which the `Button` is placed.

`Grid.Row`—Specifies the row of the enclosing `Grid` in which the `Button` is placed.

`Margin`—Specifies amount of space around the `Button`.

`x:Name`—Specifies the name used to access the `Button` programmatically in Silverlight. The name should be appended with the `Button` suffix.

`DataGrid` DataGrid Definition

- ***In action***

	DayOfWeek	WeatherImage	MaxTemperatureF	MinTemperatureF	MaxTemperatureC	MinTemperatureC
▸	Thursday, March 2	http://forecast.we	46	28	8	-2
	Friday, March 21,	http://forecast.we	42	22	6	-6
	Saturday, March 2	http://forecast.we	44	20	7	-7
	Sunday, March 23,	http://forecast.we	42	19	6	-7
	Monday, March 24,	http://forecast.we	39	22	4	-6
	Tuesday, March 25	http://forecast.we	41	25	5	-4

■ *Properties*

`AutoGenerateColumns`—When set to `True`, indicates that a `DataGrid` should determine its columns from the source of its data

`Grid.Row`—Specifies the row of the enclosing `Grid` in which the `DataGrid` is placed.

`Margin`—Specifies amount of space around the `DataGrid`.

`x:Name`—Specifies the name used to access the `DataGrid` programmatically in Silverlight. The name should be appended with the `DataGrid` suffix.

`Grid` Grid This control allows the user to place elements into an invisible table which controls their positioning.

■ *Properties*

`Background`—Specifies the background color of the `Grid`.

`ColumnDefinition`—Specifies the properties of a column in a `Grid`, including width, height and positioning.

`ColumnDefinitions`—A collection of the columns in a `Grid`.

`RowDefinition`—Specifies the properties of a row in a `Grid`, including width, height and positioning.

`RowDefinitions`—A collection of the rows in a `Grid`.

`ShowGridLines`—When `True`, disaplays the grid lines so you can see the grid layout.

`x:Name`—Specifies the name used to access the `Grid` programmatically in Silverlight. The name should be appended with the `Grid` suffix.

`Image` Image This control loads and displays an image.

■ *In action*

■ *Properties*

`Height`—Specifies the height of the `Image`.

`Margin`—Specifies the amount of space around the `Image`.

`Source`—Specifies the location of the image and its file name.

`Width`—Specifies the width of the `Image`.

`ListBox` ListBox This control displays a list of items from which the user can select.

■ *In action*

■ *Properties*

`DataTemplate`—Enables you to bind data from a data source (such as a collection) to the `ListBox`'s items.

`Grid.Row`—Specifies the row of the enclosing `Grid` in which the `ListBox` is placed.

`ItemsPanel`—Specifies how the items in a `ListBox` are arranged.

`ItemsPanelTemplate`—Used to redefine how the items in a `ListBox` are arranged.

`ItemTemplate`—Specifies the look-and-feel of each item in a `ListBox`.

`Margin`—Specifies the amount of space around the `ListBox`.

`x:Name`—Specifies the name used to access the `ListBox` programmatically. The name should be appended with the `ListBox` suffix.

`StackPanel` StackPanel This control arranges its elements horizontally or vertically.

- ***In action***

Saturday, March 22, 2008

- ***Properties***

`Height`—Specifies the height of the `StackPanel`.

`HorizontalAlignment`—Specifies the horizontal alignment of the `StackPanel`.

`Margin`—Specifies amount of blank space around the `StackPanel`.

`Name`—Specifies the name used to access the `StackPanel` programmatically. The name should be appended with the `StackPanel` suffix.

`Orientation`—Specifies whether the child elements should be arranged horizontally or vertically (the default).

`VerticalAlignment`—Specifies the vertical alignment of the `StackPanel`.

`Width`—Specifies the width of the `StackPanel`.

`TextBlock` TextBlock This control displays text in a GUI.

- ***In action***

Weather Viewer

- ***Properties***

`FontSize`—The size in pixels of the font in the `TextBlock`.

`Margin`—Specifies the amount of blank space around the `TextBlock`.

`Text`—Specifies the text displayed in the `TextBlock`.

`TextAlignment`—Specifies the alignment of the text in the control.

`TextWrapping`—Specifies whether or not the text in the control should wrap to multiple lines if the text is too wide for the control.

`x:Name`—Specifies the name used to access the `TextBlock` programmatically. The name should be appended with the `TextBlock` suffix.

`UserControl` This is the main control in a Silverlight application and can be used to create custom controls as well.

- ***Properties***

`Height`—Specifies the height of the `Image`.

`Width`—Specifies the width of the `Image`.

`x:Class`—Specifies the name of the class that defines the control.

`xmlns`—Used to specify XML namespaces for elements used in the `UserControl`.

`TextBox` TextBox A control in which the user can enter data.

- ***In action***

- ***Properties***

`FontSize`—The size in pixels of the font in the `TextBox`.

`Grid.Column`—Specifies the column of the enclosing `Grid` in which the `TextBox` is placed.

`Grid.Row`—Specifies the row of the enclosing `Grid` in which the `TextBox` is placed.

`Margin`—Specifies the amount of space around the `TextBox`.

`x:Name`—Specifies the name used to access the `TextBox` programmatically. The name should be appended with the `TextBox` suffix.

MULTIPLE-CHOICE QUESTIONS

32.1 The _________ property of a `DataGrid` specifies the collection of objects to display in the control.

a) `DataSource` b) `DataContext`
c) `ItemsSource` d) None of the above

32.2 An object of class _________ can be used to invoke a web service.

a) `WebClient` b) `WebService`
c) `CallService` d) None of the above

32.3 The `ListBox` control's _________ can be used to customize the look-and-feel of the `ListBox`'s items.

a) `ItemsPanel` b) `ItemTemplate`
c) `ItemsSource` d) None of the above

32.4 The `ListBox` control's _________ specifies how a `ListBox`'s items are arranged.

a) `ItemsPanel` b) `ItemTemplate`
c) `ItemsSource` d) None of the above

32.5 Namespace _________ is required to use LINQ to XML in your application.

a) `System.Linq` b) `System.Xml`
c) `System.Xml.Linq` d) None of the above

32.6 The _________ element defines rows in a `Grid` layout container.

a) `Grid.Rows` b) `Grid.RowDefinitions`
c) `GridRowDefinitions` d) None of the above

32.7 Which of the following are layout containers in Silverlight?

a) `Canvas` b) `StackPanel`
c) `Grid` d) All of the above

32.8 The _________ layout container allows absolute positioning of its child elements.

a) `Canvas` b) `StackPanel`
c) `Grid` d) All of the above

32.9 The Visual Basic XML property syntax for the XML element `Employee` would be _________.

a) `Employee` b) `<Employee>`
c) `"Employee"` d) None of the above

32.10 XDocument method _________ converts a `String` containing XML into an object that can be used with LINQ to XML.

a) `Convert` b) `CreateXML`
c) `Parse` d) None of the above

EXERCISES

32.11 ***(Enhanced Weather Viewer Application)*** Modify the **Weather Viewer** application you built in this tutorial to display the name of the city and state for the zip code input by the user. These are specified by elements named `PlaceName` and `StateCode` in the XML returned by the web service. The new GUI should appear as shown in Fig. 32.49.

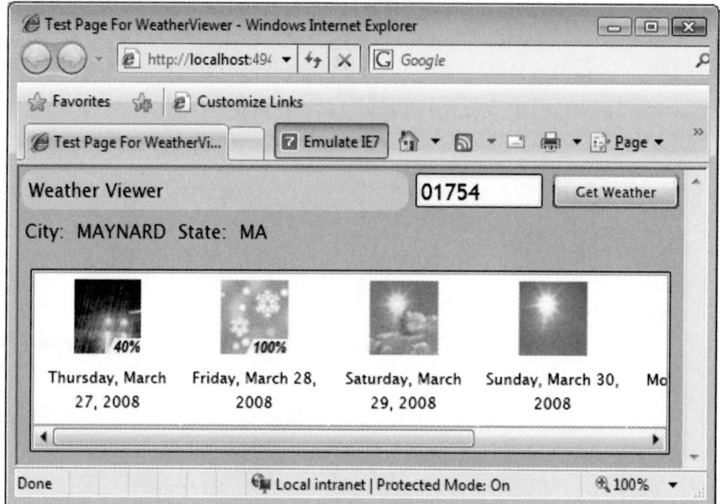

Figure 32.49 Displaying the city and state information in the **Weather Viewer**.

a) ***Copying the template to your working directory.*** Copy the directory `C:\Examples\Tutorial32\Exercises\WeatherViewer_Enhanced` to your `C:\SimplyVB2008` directory.

b) ***Opening the application's template file.*** Double click `WeatherViewer.sln` in the `WeatherViewer` directory to open the application.

c) ***Adding a new `RowDefinition`.*** Add a new `RowDefinition` between lines 8 and 9 of `Page.xaml` and set its `Height` attribute to `35` pixels. [*Note:* You'll need to update the `RowSpan` of the `WeatherDetailsView` from 2 to 3.]

d) ***Changing the `ListBox`'s row in the `Grid`.*** In line 41 of `Page.xaml`, change the `ListBox`'s `Grid.Row` attribute from `1` to `2`, so that it appears in the bottom row of the main `Grid`.

e) ***Adding a horizontal `StackPanel` to the middle row of the main `Grid`.*** Before the `ListBox` at line 41, insert a `StackPanel` and set its `Orientation` property to `Horizontal` and its `Grid.Row` column to `1`. Set this control's `x:Name` attribute to `cityStateStackPanel`.

f) ***Adding `TextBlock`s to the `StackPanel`.*** Add four `TextBlock`s to the `StackPanel`. Set the `Text` attribute of the first `TextBlock` to `City:` and that of the third `TextBlock` to `State:`. These will be used as labels for the other two `TextBlock`s. Set the `Margin` attribute of all four `TextBlock`s to `5`.

g) ***Adding class `CityState` to the project.*** Right click the `WeatherViewer` project in the **Solution Explorer** and select **Add > Existing Item...**. Next, navigate to `C:\Examples\Tutorial32\Exercises\` and double click `CityState.vb` to add the file to the project. This class consists of `String` properties `City` and `State`.

h) ***Creating an object of class `CityState` containing the city and state information.*** Insert the following lines after line 52 in the `DisplayWeatherForecast` method of the file `Page.xaml.vb`. The variable `cityStateObject` is assigned a new `CityState` object with its `City` property initialized with the `PlaceName` element from the XML response and its `State` property initialized with the `StateCode` element from the XML response.

```
' new object containing City and State properties
Dim cityStateObject = New CityState With _
{ _
   .City = weatherXML...<PlaceName>.Value, _
   .State = weatherXML...<StateCode>.Value _
} ' end creation of new object
```

i) ***Setting the `DataContext` of the `cityStateStackPanel`.*** Insert the following lines immediately after the code you inserted in *Step h*. This code enables the `cityStateStackPanel` to use the data in the `cityStateObject`.

```
' bind object to cityStateStackPanel
cityStateStackPanel.DataContext = cityStateObject
```

j) ***Binding the city and state information to `TextBlocks` in the `cityStateStackPanel`.*** In the second and fourth `TextBlocks` from *Step f*, set the `Text` attributes using `Binding` markup extensions. The `Text` property of the second `TextBlock` should be set to the `City` property. The `Text` property of the fourth `TextBlock` should be set to the `State` property.

k) ***Running the application.*** Select **Debug > Start Debugging** to run your application. Enter a zip code and confirm that the city and state are displayed properly.

l) ***Closing the application.*** Close your running application by clicking the browser's close box.

m) ***Closing the IDE.*** Close the IDE by clicking its close box.

Programming Challenge

32.12 ***(Length/Distance Converter)*** The website `www.webservicex.net` provides several other useful web services. One of these is their length/distance converter. Use this web service and the techniques you learned in this chapter to create a Silverlight length/distance converter.

You can invoke the web service with a URL of the form:

```
http://www.webservicex.net/length.asmx/ChangeLengthUnit?LengthValue=
100&fromLengthUnit=Inches&toLengthUnit=Centimeters
```

If you try the preceding URL in your web browser, you'll see that 100 inches converts to 254 centimeters. The XML returned by the web service appears as follows:

```
<?xml version="1.0" encoding="utf-8" ?>
<double xmlns="http://www.webserviceX.NET/">254</double>
```

The element `double` contains the result. The web-service method `ChangeLengthUnit` requires three parameters named `LengthValue`, `fromLengthUnit` and `toLengthUnit`, each of type `String`. The complete list of values you can supply for the `fromLengthUnit` and `toLengthUnit` parameters can be found by looking at the bottom of the following web page in its section **WSDL Schema**:

```
http://www.webservicex.net/WCF/ServiceDetails.aspx?SID=71
```

The user should be able to enter a number in a TextBox, then select the two units of measurement from `ListBoxes` and click a `Button` to invoke the web service. You can bind each `ListBox`'s `ItemsSource` property to an array of `Strings` containing the complete list of measurement names.

APPENDIX

Operator Precedence Chart

Operators are shown in decreasing order of precedence from top to bottom, with levels of precedence separated by horizontal lines. Visual Basic operators associate from left to right.

Operator	Type
`TypeOf`	type comparison
`^`	exponentiation
`+`	unary plus
`-`	unary minus
`*`	multiplication
`/`	division
`\`	integer division
`Mod`	modulus
`+`	addition
`-`	subtraction
`&`	concatenation
`<<`	bitwise left shift
`>>`	bitwise right shift
`=`	relational is equal to
`<>`	relational is not equal to
`<`	relational less than
`<=`	relational less than or equal to
`>`	relational greater than
`>=`	relational greater than or equal to
`Like`	pattern matching
`Is`	reference comparison
`IsNot`	reference comparison
`Not`	logical negation
`And`	logical AND without short-circuit evaluation
`AndAlso`	logical AND with short-circuit evaluation
`Or`	logical inclusive OR without short-circuit evaluation
`OrElse`	logical inclusive OR with short-circuit evaluation
`Xor`	logical exclusive OR

Figure A.1 Operator list (in order of operator precedence).

A P P E N D I X

ASCII Character Set

The digits in the left column of Fig. B.1 are the left digits of the decimal equivalent (0–127) of the character code, and the digits in the top row of Fig. B.1 are the right digits of the character code. For example, the character code for "F" is 70, and the character code for "&" is 38.

Most users of this book are interested in the ASCII character set used to represent English characters on many computers. The ASCII character set is a subset of the Unicode character set used by Visual Basic .NET to represent characters from most of the world's languages.

	0	1	2	3	4	5	6	7	8	9
0	nul	soh	stx	etx	eot	enq	ack	bel	bs	ht
1	nl	vt	ff	cr	so	si	dle	dc1	dc2	dc3
2	dc4	nak	syn	etb	can	em	sub	esc	fs	gs
3	rs	us	sp	!	"	#	$	%	&	‘
4	(	)	*	+	,	-	.	/	0	1
5	2	3	4	5	6	7	8	9	:	;
6	<	=	>	?	@	A	B	C	D	E
7	F	G	H	I	J	K	L	M	N	O
8	P	Q	R	S	T	U	V	W	X	Y
9	Z	[	\	]	^	_	’	a	b	c
10	d	e	f	g	h	i	j	k	l	m
11	n	o	p	q	r	s	t	u	v	w
12	x	y	z	{	|	}	~	del		

Figure B.1 ASCII character set.

APPENDIX

GUI Design Guidelines

This appendix contains a complete list of the GUI design guidelines presented at the end of each tutorial. The guidelines are organized by tutorial; within each tutorial section, they are organized by control.

Tutorial 3: Welcome Application (Introduction to Visual Programming)

Overall Design

- Use colors in your applications, but not to the point of distracting the user.

Form

- Choose short, descriptive `Form` titles. Capitalize words that are not articles, prepositions or conjunctions. Do not use punctuation.
- Use 9pt `Segoe UI` font to improve readability for controls that display text.

Label

- Use `Label`s to display text that users cannot change.
- Ensure that all `Label` controls are large enough to display their text. You can do this by setting `AutoSize` to `True`, or by setting `AutoSize` to `False` and resizing the `Label` manually.

PictureBox

- Use `PictureBox`es to enhance GUIs with graphics that users cannot change.
- Images should fit inside their `PictureBox`es. This can be achieved by setting `PictureBox` property `SizeMode` to `StretchImage`.

Tutorial 4: Designing the Inventory Application (Introducing TextBoxes and Buttons)

Overall Design

- Leave space between the edges of the `Form` and its controls.
- Although you can drag a `Label` control to a location on the `Form`, the `Location` property can be used to specify a precise position.
- Place an application's output below and/or to the right of the `Form`'s input controls.

- As you drag controls, the IDE displays blue and purple lines called snaplines. The blue lines help you position controls relative to one another. The purple lines help you position controls relative to the control text.

Button

- Buttons are labeled using their Text property. These labels should use book-title capitalization and be as short as possible while still being meaningful to the user.
- Buttons should be stacked downward from the top right of a Form or arranged on the same line starting from the bottom right of a Form.

Form

- Changing the Form's title allows users to identify the Form's purpose.
- Form titles should use book-title capitalization.
- Change the Form font to 9pt Segoe UI to be consistent with Microsoft's recommended font for Windows Vista.

Label

- A Label used to describe the purpose of a control should use sentence-style capitalization and end with a colon. These types of Labels are called descriptive Labels.
- The TextAlign property of a descriptive Label should be set to MiddleLeft. This ensures that text within groups of Labels aligns.
- Place each descriptive Label above or to the left of the control (for instance, a TextBox) that it identifies.
- Align the left or right sides of a group of descriptive Labels if the Labels are arranged vertically.
- Use a descriptive Label to identify an output Label.
- Output Labels should be distinguishable from descriptive Labels. This can be done by setting the BorderStyle property of an output Label to Fixed3D.
- If several output Labels are arranged vertically to display numbers used in a mathematical calculation (such as in an invoice), use the MiddleRight value for the TextAlign property.
- A descriptive Label and the control it identifies should be aligned on the left if they are arranged vertically.
- The text in a descriptive Label and the text in the control it identifies should be aligned if they are arranged horizontally.

TextBox

- Use TextBoxes to input data from the keyboard.
- Each TextBox should have a descriptive Label indicating the input expected from the user.
- Make TextBoxes wide enough for their expected inputs.

Tutorial 7: Wage Calculator Application (Introducing Algorithms, Pseudocode and Program Control)

Overall Design

- Format all monetary amounts using the C (currency) format specifier.

TextBox

- When using multiple TextBoxes vertically, align the TextBoxes on their right sides, and where possible make the TextBoxes the same size. Left-align the descriptive Labels for such TextBoxes.

Tutorial 8: Dental Payment Application (Introducing CheckBoxes and Message Dialogs)

CheckBox

- A CheckBox's label should be descriptive and as short as possible. When a CheckBox label contains more than one word, use book-title capitalization.
- Align groups of CheckBoxes either horizontally or vertically.

Message Dialog

- Text displayed in a dialog should be descriptive and as short as possible.

Tutorial 9: Car Payment Calculator Application (Introducing the Do While...Loop and Do Until...Loop Repetition Statements)

ListBox

- A ListBox should be large enough to display all of its content or large enough that scrollbars may be used easily.
- Use headers in a ListBox when you are displaying tabular data. Adding headers improves readability by describing the information that is displayed in the ListBox.

Tutorial 10: Class Average Application (Introducing the Do...Loop While and Do...Loop Until Repetition Statements)

Overall Design

- Transfer the focus to the control that should be used next.

Button

- Disable a Button when its function should not be available to users.
- Enable a disabled Button when its function once again should be available to users.

Tutorial 11: Interest Calculator Application (Introducing the For...Next Repetition Statement)

NumericUpDown

- A NumericUpDown control should follow the same GUI Design Guidelines as a TextBox.
- Use a NumericUpDown control to limit the range of numeric user input.

TextBox

- If a TextBox will display multiple lines of output, set the Multiline property to True and left align the output by setting the TextAlign property to Left.
- If a TextBox is used to display output, set the ReadOnly property to True to ensure that the user cannot change the output.
- If a multiline TextBox will display many lines of output, limit the TextBox height and use a vertical scrollbar to allow users to view additional lines of output.

Tutorial 12: Security Panel Application (Introducing the Select Case Multiple Selection Statement)

Overall Design

- If your GUI is modeling a real-world object, its design should mimic the physical appearance of the object.

TextBox

- Mask passwords or other sensitive pieces of information in TextBoxes.

Tutorial 14: Shipping Time Application (Using Dates and Timers)

DateTimePicker

- Use a DateTimePicker to retrieve date and time information from the user.
- Each DateTimePicker should have a corresponding descriptive Label.
- If the user is to specify a time of day or a date and time, set the DateTimePicker's ShowUpDown property to True. If the user is to specify only a date, set the DateTimePicker's ShowUpDown property to False to allow the user to select a day from the month calendar.

GroupBox

- GroupBox titles should be concise and should use book-title capitalization.
- Use GroupBoxes to group related controls in a box with a title.

Tutorial 17: Flag Quiz Application (Introducing One-Dimensional Arrays and ComboBoxes)

ComboBox

- Each ComboBox should have a descriptive Label that describes the ComboBox's contents.
- If a ComboBox's content should not be editable, set its DropDownStyle property to DropDownList.

Tutorial 18: Sales Data Application (Introducing Two-Dimensional Arrays, RadioButtons and the MSChart Control)

RadioButton

- Use RadioButtons when the user must choose only one option from a group.
- Always place each group of RadioButtons in a separate container (such as a GroupBox).
- Align groups of RadioButtons either horizontally or vertically.

Tutorial 19: Microwave Oven Application (Building Your Own Classes and Objects)

Panel

- Use Panels to organize groups of related controls where the purpose of the controls is obvious. If the purpose of the controls is not obvious, use a GroupBox rather than a Panel, because GroupBoxes can contain captions.
- Although it is possible to have a Panel without a border (by setting the BorderStyle property to None), use borders on your Panels to improve user interface readability and organization.
- A Panel can display scrollbars when it is not large enough to display all of its controls. To increase usability, we suggest avoiding the use of scrollbars on Panels. If a Panel is not large enough to display all of its contents, increase the size of the Panel.

Tutorial 20: Shipping Hub Application (Introducing Collections, the For Each...Next Statement and Access Keys)

Overall Design

- Set a control's TabStop property to True only if the control is used to receive user input.
- Use the TabIndex property to define the logical order in which the user should enter data. Usually the order transfers the focus of the application from top to bottom and left to right.
- Use access keys to allow users to "click" a control using the keyboard.

Tutorial 21: Typing Application (Introducing Keyboard Events, Menus, Dialogs and the `Dictionary` Collection)

`MenuStrip`

- Use book-title capitalization in menu-item text.
- Use separator bars in a menu to group related menu items.
- If clicking a menu item opens a dialog, an ellipsis (...) should follow the menu item's text.

APPENDIX

Visual Basic 2008 Express Windows Form Designer Tools

This book presents many controls that are available in Visual Basic 2008 Express. In all, there are 67 items available to you by default in the **Toolbox**. This appendix contains a chart (Fig. D.1) indicating the purpose and usage of most of these. A list of web resources can be found after the chart.

Icon	Item	Purpose	Usage
	`Pointer`	Allows you to select and modify elements in the IDE. The pointer is not a control.	Allow the user to navigate a GUI.
	`Background-Worker`	Performs tasks asynchronously to the thread of the main application.	Used to execute time consuming tasks in the background.
	`Binding-Navigator`	Creates a `ToolStrip` to access and modify data.	Used to add, delete, update and navigate through data.
	`BindingSource`	Simplifies the process of binding controls to a data source.	Acts as data source to which components can bind to access data.
	`Button`	Allows users to indicate that an action should be performed.	Most commonly used to execute code when clicked.
	`CheckBox`	Allows the user to select or deselect an option.	Becomes checked when selected and unchecked when deselected.
	`Checked-ListBox`	Provides the user with a checkable list of items.	Much like a `CheckBox`, but all options are contained in a format similar to that of a `ListBox`.

Figure D.1 Visual Basic 2008 Express Windows `Form` Designer Tools. (Part 1 of 5.)

Icon	Item	Purpose	Usage
	`ColorDialog`	Allows the user to display the Windows **Color** dialog.	Used to retrieve a user's color selection in an application.
	`ComboBox`	Provides a short list of items in a drop-down menu.	Allow the user to view, enter new text in or search with a search `String` from multiple items in a list.
	`ContextMenu-Strip`	Displays a menu of programmer-defined options when the user right-clicks an object.	Provide additional options or features as a shortcut.
	`DataGridView`	Displays data within a chart.	Represent ADO.NET data in a scrollable chart.
	`DataSet`	Allows users to create a dataset.	Used to interact with data (typically from a database).
	`Date-TimePicker`	Allows users to choose the date and time.	Display or allow the selection of a time and date.
	`DomainUpDown`	Displays string values, using the up and down arrows.	Select strings from an `Object` collection.
	`ErrorProvider`	Displays errors regarding a control to the user.	Inform the user if there is an error associated with the control.
	`EventLog`	Allows interaction with Windows event logs.	Read, write, update and delete event log entries and entire logs.
	`FileSystem-Watcher`	Listens to the file system change notifications.	Raise events when a directory or a file in a directory changes.
	`FlowLayout-Panel`	Arranges its contents in a horizontal or vertical flow direction.	Used to specify flow direction, wrapping or clipping.
	`Folder-BrowserDialog`	Used to browse, select and create new folders.	Used when the application user should not be allowed to select files.
	`FontDialog`	Displays a font dialog that includes all available fonts installed on the computer.	Used to retrieve a user-specified font format and size in an application.
	`GroupBox`	Allows controls to be grouped together.	Organize related controls separately from the rest of the `Form`.
	`HelpProvider`	Provides additional help features for a specific control.	Create additional help features for a control.
	`HScrollBar`	A horizontal scrollbar.	Allow users to view text or graphics that may be too large to display horizontally in a control.

Figure D.1 Visual Basic 2008 Express Windows `Form` Designer Tools. (Part 2 of 5.)

Icon	Item	Purpose	Usage
	`ImageList`	A manageable list of images.	Store a list of images for use in other controls, such as a `ListView` or menu.
	`Label`	Displays text to the user.	Identify specific items on the `Form` or display general-purpose text.
	`LinkLabel`	Similar to a `Label` control but can include hyperlinks.	Display a hyperlink label that, when clicked, will open a file or Web page.
	`ListBox`	Provides a list of items.	Allow the user to view and select from multiple items in a list.
	`ListView`	Displays a group of items with identifiable icons.	Display a list of items (such as files) much like Windows Explorer.
	`MaskedTextBox`	Distinguishes between proper and improper user input.	Enable programmers to specify the format of text input.
	`MenuStrip`	Creates a menu object on a `Form`.	Allow users to select options from menus, adding functionality to the application.
	`MonthCalendar`	Allows the user to select the date and time from a calendar that displays one month at a time.	Retrieve a user's date selection from a calendar.
	`NotifyIcon`	Creates icons that are displayed in a status area, usually while an action is performed in the background.	Remind the user that a certain process is running in the background of the application.
	`NumericUpDown`	Contains a number that is increased or decreased by clicking the up or down arrows.	Allow the user to specify a number in programmer-defined increments.
	`OpenFileDialog`	Displays a dialog to assist the user in selecting a file.	Retrieve user's file-name selection.
	`PageSetupDialog`	Displays a dialog to allow the user to change a document's page properties.	Allow users to modify the page settings and printer options.
	`Panel`	Similar to a `GroupBox`, but can include a scrollbar.	Group controls separately on the `Form`.
	`PictureBox`	Displays images.	Allow users to view graphics in an application.
	`PrintDialog`	Allows the user to select a printer and printing options.	Shown to retrieve user selection for printing options.
	`PrintDocument`	Executes the printing process.	Accessed to print documents.

Figure D.1 Visual Basic 2008 Express Windows `Form` Designer Tools. (Part 3 of 5.)

Icon	Item	Purpose	Usage
	PrintPreview-Control	Allows the user to preview a document before printing it.	Display a preview of the document.
	PrintPreview-Dialog	A dialog used to display a PrintPreviewControl.	Display a print-preview dialog.
	Process	Provides access to local and remote processes.	Enable the programmer to start and stop local system processes.
	ProgressBar	Displays a visual representation of the progress of an action or set of actions.	Inform the user of the completeness of an operation.
	PropertyGrid	Provides a user interface for browsing an object's properties.	Display the properties of another GUI control.
	RadioButton	Provides the user with a list of options from which only one or none can be selected.	Allow users to select at most one option from several.
	RichTextBox	Creates a TextBox control with advanced text-editing capabilities.	Allow users to perform more sophisticated editing beyond the features of a TextBox.
	SaveFile-Dialog	Assists the user in selecting a location in which to save a file.	Allow files to be saved.
	SerialPort	Provides access to serial ports.	Interact with a device that is connected to a serial port.
	Split-Container	Two panels, separated by a movable bar.	Group controls separately on the Form in resizable areas.
	Splitter	Allows the user to resize a docked control within an application.	Give the users the ability to change the size of a control.
	StatusStrip	Display useful information regarding the Form or objects in the application.	Notify the user of information not intended for the body of a Form.
	TabControl	Displays available tab pages in which you can place other controls.	Allow multiple tab pages on a Form.
	TableLayout-Panel	A panel that dynamically lays out its controls in a grid.	Allow controls to dynamically resize based on the current set of controls displayed.
abl	TextBox	Accepts user input from the keyboard. Can also be used to display text.	Used to retrieve user input from the keyboard.
	Timer	Performs an action at programmer-specified intervals. A Timer is not visible to the user.	Allow the action of an event through a specific amount of time.

Figure D.1 Visual Basic 2008 Express Windows Form Designer Tools. (Part 4 of 5.)

Icon	Item	Purpose	Usage
	ToolStrip	Contains icons representing specific commands.	Provide the user with options in a toolbar.
	ToolStrip-Container	Provides panels for managing other controls.	Used to organize one or more ToolStrip, StatusStrip, and MenuStrip controls.
	ToolTip	Displays text information about an object when the mouse cursor is over it.	Display additional information to the user.
	TrackBar	Allows the user to set a value from a specified range.	Similar to the scrollbar, but includes a range of values.
	TreeView	Displays a tree structure of objects, using nodes.	Display a hierarchical representation of a collection of objects.
	VScrollBar	Allows users to view text or graphics that may be too large to display vertically in a control.	Enable a vertical scrollbar in the control.
	WebBrowser	Provides a managed wrapper for the WebBrowser ActiveX control.	Used to embed web browsing capabilities in an application.

Figure D.1 Visual Basic 2008 Express Windows Form Designer Tools. (Part 5 of 5.)

D.1 Internet and Web Resources

A great way to learn about controls not covered in this book is to use them. Several web sites provide information to help you get started. The following sites should help you as you explore new features of Visual Basic 2008 Express:

msdn2.microsoft.com/en-us/library/xfak08ea.aspx
This site provides documentation for the most commonly used Windows Form controls, grouped by function.

www.exforsys.com/content/view/1515/350/
This site provides articles describing features and usage of common controls in Visual Basic 2008. You will also find links to discussions of more advanced topics in other languages.

msdn2.microsoft.com/en-us/library/3xdhey7w.aspx
This web page provides a more technical description of controls you can use on a Windows Form.

APPENDIX

Keyword Chart

The table of Fig. E.1 contains a complete listing of Visual Basic keywords. Many of these keywords are discussed throughout the text.

Visual Basic Keywords			
AddHandler	AddressOf	Alias	And
AndAlso	As	Boolean	ByRef
Byte	ByVal	Call	Case
Catch	CBool	CByte	CChar
CDate	CDbl	CDec	Char
CInt	Class	CLng	CObj
Const	Continue	CSByte	CShort
CSng	CStr	CType	CUInt
CULng	CUShort	Date	Decimal
Declare	Default	Delegate	Dim
DirectCast	Do	Double	Each
Else	ElseIf	End	EndIf
Enum	Erase	Error	Event
Exit	False	Finally	For
Friend	Function	Get	GetType
GetXmlNamespace	Global	GoSub	GoTo
Handles	If	Implements	Imports
In	Inherits	Integer	Interface
Is	IsNot	Let	Lib
Like	Long	Loop	Me
Mod	Module	MustInherit	MustOverride
MyBase	MyClass	Namespace	Narrowing

Figure E.1 Visual Basic keywords. (Part 1 of 2.)

Visual Basic Keywords			
New	Next	Not	Nothing
NotInheritable	NotOverridable	Object	Of
On	Operator	Option	Optional
Or	OrElse	Overloads	Overridable
Overrides	ParamArray	Partial	Private
Property	Protected	Public	RaiseEvent
ReadOnly	ReDim	REM	RemoveHandler
Resume	Return	SByte	Select
Set	Shadows	Shared	Short
Single	Static	Step	Stop
String	Structure	Sub	SyncLock
Then	Throw	To	True
Try	TryCast	TypeOf	UInteger
ULong	UShort	Using	Varint
Went	When	While	Widening
With	WithEvents	WriteOnly	Xor

The following are keywords, although they are not used in Visual Basic:

EndIf GoSub Let Variant Wend

Figure E.1 Visual Basic keywords. (Part 2 of 2.)

APPENDIX

Primitive Data Types

The table of Fig. F.1 contains the Visual Basic primitive data types, the number of bytes that a value of each type occupies in memory and the range of values that each type supports.

Type	Size in bytes	Value range
SByte	1	–128 to 127, inclusive
Byte	1	0 to 255, inclusive
Boolean	2	True or False
Char	2	0 to 65,535, inclusive (representing the Unicode character set)
Short	2	–32,768 to 32,767, inclusive
UShort	2	0 to 65,535, inclusive
Integer	4	–2,147,483,648 to 2,147,483,647, inclusive
UInteger	4	0 to 4,294,967,295, inclusive
Single	4	negative range: –3.4028235E+38 to –1.401298E-45 positive range: 1.401298E–45 to 3.4028235E+38
Long	8	–9,223,372,036,854,775,808 to 9,223,372,036,854,775,807, inclusive
ULong	8	0 to 18,446,744,073,709,551,615, inclusive
Double	8	negative range: –1.79769313486231570E+308 to –4.94065645841246544E–324 positive range: 4.94065645841246544E–324 to 1.79769313486231570E+308
Date	8	0:00:00 on 1 January 0001 to 23:59:59 on 31 December 9999

Figure F.1 Visual Basic primitive types. (Part 1 of 2.)

Type	Size in bytes	Value range
`Decimal`	16	Range with no decimal point: ±79,228,162,514,264,337,593,543,950,335 Range with 28 places to the right of the decimal point: ±7.9228162514264337593543950335 The smallest nonzero number is ±0.0000000000000000000000000001 (±1E–28)
`String`	Depends on platform	Up to approximately 2 billion Unicode characters

Figure F.1 Visual Basic primitive types. (Part 2 of 2.)

Additional Primitive Type Information

This appendix is based on information from Section 7.3 of The Microsoft Visual Basic Language Specification (available at `msdn2.microsoft.com/en-us/library/ms234437.aspx`).

A

access key—Keyboard shortcut that allows the user to perform an action on a control using the keyboard.

access modifier—Keywords used to specify what members of a class a client may access. Includes keywords `Public` and `Private`.

accessors—Methodlike code units that handle the details of modifying and returning data.

action expression (in the UML)—Used in an action state within a UML activity diagram to specify a particular action to perform.

action state—An action to perform in a UML activity diagram that is represented by an action-state symbol.

action-state symbol—A rectangle with its left and right sides replaced with arcs curving outward that represents an action to perform in a UML activity diagram.

action/decision model of programming—Representing control statements as UML activity diagrams with rounded rectangles indicating *actions* to be performed and diamond symbols indicating *decisions* to be made.

active tab—The tab of the document displayed in the IDE.

active window—The window that is currently being used—sometimes referred to as the window that has the focus.

activity diagram—A UML diagram that models the activity (also called the workflow) of a portion of a software system.

Ada—A programming language, named after Lady Ada Lovelace, that was developed under the sponsorship of the U.S. Department of Defense (DOD) in the 1970s and early 1980s.

Add method of class `Dictionary`—Adds a key/value pair to a `Dictionary` collection.

Add method of class `List`—Adds a specified object to the end of a `List`.

Add method of `Items`—Adds an item to a `ListBox` control.

`AddHandler` statement—Adds an event handler for a specific event.

`AddressOf` operator—Specifies the location of a method, which can be associated with an event.

ADO.NET—Part of the .NET Framework that is used to interact with databases.

algorithm—A procedure for solving a problem, specifying the actions to be executed and the order in which they are to be executed.

Alphabetical icon—The icon in the **Properties** window that, when clicked, sorts properties alphabetically.

And operator—A logical operator used to ensure that two conditions are *both* true before choosing a certain path of execution. Does not perform short-circuit evaluation.

`AndAlso` operator—A logical operator used to ensure that two conditions are *both* true before choosing a certain path of execution. Performs short-circuit evaluation.

API (application programming interface)—The interface used by a program to access the operating system and various services on the computer.

App_Code folder—The project folder where the application-code files (other than the `aspx.vb` code-behind files) are stored. This is a protected folder that is accessible only to the server.

App_Data folder—The project folder where external sources of data (i.e., the `Bookstore.mdf` database file) are stored. This is a protected folder that is accessible only to the server.

`App.xaml`—XAML file that declares a Silverlight application's shared resources, such as styles that can be applied to various GUI elements.

`App.xaml.vb`—Code-behind file that defines application-level event handlers, such as an event handler for unhandled exceptions.

argument—Inputs to a procedure call that provide information needed to perform the procedure's task.

arithmetic and logic unit (ALU)—The "manufacturing" section of the computer. The ALU performs calculations and makes decisions.

arithmetic operators—The operators `+`, `-`, `*`, `/`, `\`, `^` and `Mod`.

ARPAnet—The grandfather of today's Internet.

array—A data structure containing data items of the same type.

array bounds—Integers that determine what indices can be used to access an element in an array. The lower bound is 0; the upper bound is the length of the array minus one.

`Array.Sort` method—Sorts the values of an array into ascending order.

`As` keyword—Used in variable declarations. Indicates that the following word (such as `Integer`) is the variable type.

ASP.NET—.NET software that helps you create web applications.

ASP.NET 3.5 technology—Can be combined with Visual Basic to create web applications.

ASP.NET Ajax—ASP.NET web controls that enable Ajax functionality.

ASP.NET Development Server—A web server that you can use to test your ASP.NET web applications. It is specifically designed for learning and testing purposes to execute web applications on the local computer and to respond to browser requests from the local computer.

ASP.NET server control—Another name for a web control.

ASP.NET Website project—The type of project you create with Visual Web Developer to build an ASP.NET application.

.aspx extension—The file-name extension for ASP.NET Web Forms pages.

ASPX page—File that specifies the GUI of a web page using web controls. Also called Web Forms or Web Form Pages.

assembler—A translator program that converts assembly-language programs to machine language at computer speeds.

assembly—The mechanism used to package compiled .NET code for reuse.

assembly language—A type of programming language that uses English-like abbreviations to represent the fundamental operations on the computer.

assignment operator—The "=" symbol used to assign values in an assignment statement.

assignment statement—A statement that copies one value to another. An assignment statement contains an "equals" sign (=) operator that causes the value of its right operand to be copied to its left operand.

asterisk (*)—Multiplication operator. The operator's left and right operands are multiplied together.

asynchronous request—A request that is performed in the background. The user can continue interacting with the web application while the server processes the request.

attribute—Another name for a property of an object.

attribute in XAML—Can be used to set an object's property values. Represented in XAML by placing a property name, an equal sign (=) and a value in double quotes inside the opening tag of the object's XAML element.

auto-hide—A space-saving IDE feature used for windows such as **Toolbox**, **Properties** and **Solution Explorer** that hides a window until the mouse pointer is placed on the hidden window's tab.

`AutoGenerateColumns` attribute of a `DataGrid`—When set to `True`, indicates that a `DataGrid` should determine its columns from the source of its data.

`AutoSize` property of a `Label`—Determines whether a `Label` is automatically sized based on its content.

B

`BackColor` property—Specifies the background color of the `Form` or a control.

Background property of class Canvas—Gets or sets the `Brush` value used as the background color of the `Canvas`.

backslash (\)—Integer division operator. The operator divides its left operand by its right and returns an `Integer` result.

bandwidth—The information-carrying capacity of communications lines.

BASIC (Beginner's All-purpose Symbolic Instruction Code)—A programming language for writing simple programs. Developed in the mid-1960s by Professors John Kemeny and Thomas Kurtz of Dartmouth College. Its primary purpose was to familiarize novices with programming techniques.

`Beep`—Causes your computer to make a beep sound.

binary digit—A digit that can assume one of two values.

binary operators—An operator that takes two operands.

`Binding` markup extension—Binds a property of an object to an attribute of a control.

`BindingNavigator`—A set of controls that allow you to manipulate and navigate through data in a data source.

`BindingSource`—A component that manages the data used by a `BindingNavigator`.

bit—Short for "binary digit"—a digit that can assume one of two values.

block—A group of code statements.

block scope—Variables declared inside control statements, such as an `If...Then` statement, have block scope. Block scope begins at the identifier's declaration and ends at the block's final statement (for example, `Else` or `End If`).

body of a control statement—The set of statements that are enclosed in a control statement.

book-title capitalization—A style that capitalizes the first letter of the each word in the text (for example, **Calculate Total**).

`Boolean` data type—A data type whose variable can have the value `True` or `False`.

`Border` element—Used to place a border around any Silverlight control.

`BorderStyle` property—Specifies the appearance of a `Label`'s border, which allows you to distinguish one control from another visually. The `BorderStyle` property can be set to `None` (no border), `FixedSingle` (a single dark line as a border), or `Fixed3D` (giving the `Label` a "sunken" appearance).

`BorderStyle` property of an `Image`—Defines the border (such as `outset`) around an image.

`BorderWidth` property of an `Image`—Defines the width of an `Image`'s border.

bottom tier—The tier (also known as the information tier, or the data tier) containing the application data of a multitier application—typically implemented as a database

bounding box of an ellipse—Specifies an ellipse's location, width and height.

break mode—The IDE mode when application execution is suspended. This mode is entered through the debugger.

breakpoint—A location where execution is to suspend, indicated by a solid maroon circle.

`Brush` class—Used to fill shapes and controls with colors.

`Brush` object—An object used to specify drawing parameters when drawing solid shapes.

`Brushes` class—Provides easy access to `Brush` objects representing the standard colors.

bug—A flaw in a program that prevents it from executing correctly.

built-in data type—A data type already defined in Visual Basic, such as an `Integer`.

business logic tier—The tier that controls interaction between the client and information tiers. Also called the middle tier.

`Button` control—When clicked, commands the application to perform an action.

Button element—Displays a button in a Silverlight GUI.

Button web control—Allows users to perform an action.

ByRef keyword—Used to pass an argument by reference.

byte—Eight bits.

ByVal keyword—The keyword specifying that the calling procedure should pass a copy of its argument's value to the called procedure.

C

C#—A programming language that was designed specifically for the .NET platform. It has roots in C, C++ and Java, adapting the best features of each. Like Visual Basic, C# is object oriented and has access to .NET's powerful library of prebuilt components, enabling you to develop applications quickly.

callback function—Client-side function that processes the response to an asynchronous request.

callee—The procedure being called.

caller—The procedure that calls another procedure. Also known as the calling procedure.

Cancel value of DialogResult enumeration—Used to determine whether the user clicked the **Cancel** Button of a dialog.

Canvas layout container—A WPF control that enables absolute positioning of its child elements.

caret (^)—Exponentiation operator. This operator raises its left operand to a power specified by the right operand.

Cascading Style Sheets (CSS)—Used to define the look-and-feel of web page elements.

Case Else statement—Optional statement whose body executes if the Select Case's test expression does not match an expression of any Case.

case sensitive—The instance where two words that are spelled identically are treated differently if the capitalization of the two words differs.

Case statement—Statement whose body executes if the Select Case's test expression matches the Case's expression.

Catch block—Also called an exception handler, this block executes when the corresponding Try block in the application detects an exceptional situation and throws an exception of the type the Catch block declares.

Categorized icon—The icon in the **Properties** window that, when clicked, sorts properties categorically.

Central Processing Unit (CPU)—The part of the computer's hardware that is responsible for supervising the operation of the other sections of the computer.

Char data type—Primitive type that represents a character.

Char structure—Stores characters (such as letters and symbols).

character literal—A single character represented as a value of type Char. Create a character literal by placing a single character in double quotes followed by the letter c (e.g., "0"c).

character set—The set of all characters used to write applications and represent data items on a particular computer. Visual Basic uses the Unicode character set.

Chars property of class String—Returns the character located at a specific index in a String.

CheckBox control—A small square GUI element that either is empty or contains a check mark.

CheckBox label—The text that appears next to a CheckBox.

Checked property of the RadioButton control—Displays a small dot in the control when True. When False, the control displays an empty white circle.

Checked property of the CheckBox control—Specifies whether the CheckBox is checked (True) or unchecked (False).

CheckedChanged event—Raised when a RadioButton's state changes.

CheckFileExists property of class OpenFileDialog—Enables the user to display a warning if a specified file does not exist.

child element—XAML element that is nested inside another element.

Children property of Canvas—Returns a collection of all the child elements nested in a Canvas.

class—The type of a group of related objects. A class specifies the general format of its objects; the properties and actions available to an object depend on its class. An object is to its class much as a house is to the blueprint from which a house is constructed.

class definition—The code that belongs to a class, beginning with keywords Public Class and ending with keywords End Class.

Class keyword—The keyword that begins a class definition.

Class Keyword—Reserved word required to begin a class definition.

class name—The identifier used to identify the name of a class in code.

Clear method of Items—Deletes all the values in a ListBox control.

Click event—An event raised when a user clicks a control.

Click event of a Button—Raised when the user presses the Button.

client—When an application creates and uses an object of a class, the application is known as a client of the class.

client tier—The user interface of a multitier application (also called the top tier).

Close method of class StreamWriter or StreamReader—Used to close the stream.

COBOL (COmmon Business Oriented Language)—A programming language that was developed in the late 1950s by a group of computer manufacturers in conjunction with government and industrial computer users. This language is used primarily for business applications that manipulate large amounts of data.

code editor—A window where a user can create, view or edit an application's code.

Code view—A mode of the Visual Basic IDE where the application's code is displayed in an editor window.

code-behind file—Visual Basic file that contains a class which provides an ASPX page's functionality.

collection—A class used to store groups of related objects.

Color structure—Represents a color and provides methods for creating custom colors. Also contains several predefined colors as properties.

ColorDialog class—Used to display a dialog from which the user can select colors.

column—The second dimension of a two-dimensional array.

ColumnDefinition element of a Grid—Specifies the attributes of a column in a Grid.

ColumnDefinitions property of a Grid—Provides access to the collection of ColumnDefinitions for a Grid.

ComboBox control—Combines a TextBox with a ListBox.

comment—Text that follows a single-quote character (') and is inserted to improve an application's readability.

compilation error—An error that occurs when program statements violate the grammatical rules of a programming language or when statements are simply incorrect in the current context.

compiler—A translator program that converts high-level-language programs into machine language.

component object box—The ComboBox at the top of the **Properties** window that allows you to select the Form or control object whose properties you want set.

component tray—The area below the Windows Form Designer that contains controls, such as Timers, that are not part of the graphical user interface.

componentization—*See* divide-and-conquer technique.

computer—A device capable that can perform computations and make logical decisions millions, billions and even trillions of times faster than human beings can carry out the same tasks.

computer program—A set of instructions that guides a computer through an orderly series of actions.

computer programmer—A person who writes computer programs.

condition—An expression with a True or False value that is used to make a decision.

conditional If expression—A shorthand representation of an If...Then...Else statement.

consistent state—A way to maintain the values of an object's instance variables such that the values are always valid.

Const keyword—Used to declare a named constant.

constant—An identifier whose value cannot be changed after its initial declaration.

constructor—A special class method that initializes a class's variables when an object of that class is created.

consuming a web service—The process of invoking a web service and manipulating its results.

container—An object, such as a GroupBox or Form, that contains other controls.

ContainsKey method of class Dictionary—Determines whether the Dictionary contains the key specified as an argument.

Content attribute of a Button—Specifies the text on the Button.

content control—A WPF control that can hold one piece of content of any type.

Contents command—The command that displays a categorized table of contents in which help articles are organized by topic.

ContentTemplate element of the UpdatePanel control—Contains the control that initiates an asynchronous request and the controls updated when the UpdatePanel performs a partial page update.

context-sensitive help—A help option (launched by pressing *F1*) that provides links to articles that apply to the current content (that is, the item selected with the mouse pointer).

control—A reusable GUI component, such as a GroupBox, RadioButton, Button or Label.

Control class—A type that can be used to declare variables for referencing controls on the Form. Defines the common properties and methods of Windows Forms controls.

control structure (control statement)—An application component that specifies the order in which statements execute (also known as the flow of control).

control structure (statement) nesting—Placing one control statement in the body of another control statement.

control structure (statement) stacking—A set of control statements in sequence. The exit point of one control statement is connected to the entry point of the next control statement in sequence.

ControlChars.Tab constant—Represents a tab character.

controlling expression—Value compared sequentially with each Case until either a match occurs or the End Select statement is reached. Also known as a test expression.

ControlToValidate property of a RequiredFieldValidator—Specifies the control that is validated by the RequiredFieldValidator.

Convert class—Provides methods for converting data types.

coordinate system—A scheme for identifying every possible point on the computer screen.

CornerRadius attribute of a Border—Specifies the rounding of the corners of a Border.

Count property of Items—Returns the number of ListBox items.

Count property of List—Returns the number of objects in the List.

counter—A variable used to determine the number of times the body of a repetition statement executes.

counter-controlled repetition—A technique that uses a counter variable to determine the number of times that the body of a repetition statement executes. Also called definite repetition.

CType function—Function that converts its first argument to the type specified in its second argument.

CType operator—Converts the object passed as the first argument to the type passed as the second argument.

currency format—Used to display values as monetary amounts.

CustomFormat property of a DateTimePicker control—The DateTimePicker property that contains your format string with which to display the date and/or time when DateTimePicker Format property is set to Custom.

D

data hierarchy—Collection of data items processed by computers that become larger and more complex in structure as you progress from bits, to characters, to fields and up to larger data structures.

Data menu—The menu of the IDE that contains commands for interacting with databases.

Data Source Configuration Wizard—Wizard used to add a data source to the application.

Data Sources window—Window used to connect an application to a data source and create data-bound controls.

data structure—Groups and organizes related data.

data tier—The tier (also known as the information tier, or the bottom tier) containing the application data of a multitier application, typically implemented as a database.

data-bound control—A control that displays information contained in a data source. When the information in the data source changes, the control updates to display the new information.

database—An organized collection of data used to store information for access by applications.

Database Explorer window—Window used to view and manipulate database information in the Visual Basic 2008 Express IDE.

database management system (DBMS)—Collection of programs that provide mechanisms for storing and organizing data in a database.

database management system (DBMS)—Provides mechanisms for storing and organizing data.

`DataContext` class—LINQ to SQL classes representation of a database in the application. Manages interactions between the application and the database.

`DataContext` property of a Silverlight control—Specifies the object from which the control can obtain data via `Binding` markup extensions.

`DataGrid` control—Displays data in rows and columns. Can bind a collection of objects to this control via its `ItemSource` property.

`DataSource` property of class `BindingSource`—Specifies the data managed by the `BindingSource`.

`DataSource` property of class `ComboBox`—Specifies the source of items listed in a `ComboBox`.

`Date` type—A type whose properties can be used to store and display date and time information.

`Date` variable—A variable of type `Date`, capable of storing date and time data.

`DateChanged` event of `MonthCalendar` control—Raised when a new date (or a range of dates) is selected.

`DateTime` primitive type—The .NET Framework Class Library type that corresponds to the `Date` keyword.

`DateTimePicker` control—Retrieves date and time information from the user.

Debug menu—The menu of the IDE that contains commands for debugging and running an application.

debugger—A tool that allows you to analyze the behavior of your application to determine whether it is executing correctly.

debugging—The process of fixing errors in an application.

`Decimal` data type—Used to store monetary amounts.

decimal digits—The digits 0, 1, 2, 3, 4, 5, 6, 7, 8 and 9.

decision symbol—The diamond-shaped symbol in a UML activity diagram that indicates that a decision is to be made.

declaration—The reporting of a new variable to the compiler. The variable can then be used in the Visual Basic code.

declare a variable—Report the name and type of a variable to the compiler.

`DefaultBackColor` property—Contains the default background color for a control.

deferred execution—A LINQ query is not executed until you begin to iterate over its results.

definite repetition—*See* counter-controlled repetition.

delimiter—Marks the boundaries between fields in a record of a text file.

descriptive `Label`—A `Label` used to describe another control on the `Form`. This helps users understand a control's purpose.

design mode—IDE mode that allows you to create applications using Visual Studio 2008's windows, toolbars and menu bar.

Design mode—Displays the ASPX page's GUI at design time.

design units—Any specified units of measurement for the font.

Design view—The IDE view that contains the Windows Forms designer to allow you to layout controls in a Windows Forms application.

`Designer.vb` file—The file containing the declarations and statements that build an application's GUI.

`DetailsView` control—A control in the **Data** group of the **Toolbox** that displays property names and values for its data source in a tabular format.

dialog—A window that can display and gather information.

`DialogResult` enumeration—An enumeration that contains values corresponding to standard dialog `Button` names.

diamond symbol—A symbol (also known as the decision symbol) in a UML activity diagram; this symbol indicates that a decision is to be made.

`Dictionary` collection—A collection of key/value pairs.

`Dim` keyword—Indicates the declaration of a variable.

dismiss a dialog—Synonym for closing a dialog.

dithering—Using small dots of existing colors to form a pattern that simulates a desired color.

divide-and-conquer technique—Constructing large applications from small, manageable pieces to make development and maintenance of large applications easier.

`Do Until...Loop` repetition statement—A control statement that executes a set of body statements *until* its loop-termination condition becomes `True`.

`Do While...Loop` repetition statement—A control statement that executes a set of body statements *while* its loop-continuation condition is `True`.

`Do...Loop Until` repetition statement—A control statement that executes a set of statements at least once until the loop-termination condition becomes `True` after the loop executes.

`Do...Loop While` repetition statement—A control statement that executes a set of statements at least once while the loop-continuation condition is `True` after the loop executes.

`Document` property of class `PrintPreviewDialog`—Allows you to specify the document that is displayed in the dialog.

dot operator—*See* member-access operator.

dotted line—A UML activity diagram symbol that connects each UML-style note with the element that the note describes.

Double data type—Stores both whole and fractional numbers. Normally, Doubles store floating-point numbers.

double-selection statement—A control statement that selects between two different actions or sequences of actions (e.g., an If...Then...Else statement).

double-subscripted array—*See* two-dimensional array.

DownloadStringAsync method of class WebClient—Asynchronously invokes a web service so the application can continue executing.

DownloadStringCompleted event of class WebClient—Raised when a web service responds to an asynchronous invocation.

DrawLine method of class Graphics—Draws a line of a specified color between two specified points.

DrawRectangle method of class Graphics—Draws the outline of a rectangle of a specified size and color at a specified location.

DrawString method of class Graphics—Draws the specified String at the specified location.

DropDownList value of DropDownStyle property —Specifies that a ComboBox is not editable.

DropDownStyle property of class ComboBox—Property of the ComboBox control that specifies the appearance of the ComboBox.

dynamic resizing—A capability that allows certain objects (such as Lists) to increase or decrease in size based on the addition or removal of elements from that object. Enables the List object to increase its size to accommodate new elements and to decrease its size when elements are removed.

E

element—An item in an array.

element in XML—Markup that describes a piece of data. Delimited by start and end tags.

element of a For Each...Next statement—Used to store a reference to the current value of the collection being iterated.

Ellipse class—The shape class that draws an ellipse. This class contains properties including Fill, Width and Height. If the width and height are the same, a circle is drawn.

Else keyword—Indicates the statements to be executed if the condition of the If...Then...Else statement is false.

ElseIf keyword—Keyword used for the nested conditions in nested If...Then...Else statements.

embedded parentheses—Another term for nested parentheses.

empty element in XML—Shorthand notation for an element with no content between its start and end tags.

empty string—A string that does not contain any characters.

Enabled property—Specifies whether a control such as a Button appears enabled (True) or disabled (False).

Enabled property of a TextBox—When False, specifies that the TextBox does not responds to user input.

Enabled property of class ComboBox—Specifies whether a user can select an item from a ComboBox.

Enabled property of GroupBox control—When False, disables all controls contained in the GroupBox.

End Class keywords—Keywords that indicate the end of a class definition.

End Enum keywords—Ends an enumeration.

End Function keywords—Indicates the end of a Function procedure.

End Select keywords—Terminates the Select Case statement.

End Sub keywords—Indicates the end of a Sub procedure.

end tag—Delimits the end of an XML element.

End Try keywords—Indicates the end of a sequence of blocks containing a Try block, followed by zero or more Catch blocks and an optional Finally block. At least one Catch or Finally block must precede the End Try keywords

EndEdit method of class BindingSource—Saves all edits made to the BindingSource's data.

EndOfStream property of class StreamReader—Returns a Boolean value indicating whether the end of the file has been reached.

EndsWith method of class String—Determines whether a String ends with a particular substring.

Enum keyword—Begins an enumeration.

enumeration—A group of related, named constants.

equality operators—Operators = (is equal to) and <> (is not equal to) that compare two values.

Error List window—A window which displays compilation errors in your code.

Error property of class DownloadStringCompletedEventArgs —Specifies the error that occurred, if any, during a web-service invocation.

ErrorMessage property of a RequiredFieldValidator—Specifies the error message that appears when the user does not enter data in a required field of a web form.

event—A user action that can trigger an event handler.

event handler—A section of code that is executed (called) when a certain event is raised (occurs).

event-driven program—A program that responds to user-initiated events, such as mouse clicks and keystrokes.

exception—An indication of a problem that occurs during an application's execution.

Exception Assistant—A window that appears in the IDE indicating where an exception has occurred, the type of exception, and information on handling the exception.

exception handler—A block that executes when the application detects an exceptional situation and throws an exception.

exception handling—Processing problems that occur during application execution.

executable statements—Actions that are performed when the corresponding Visual Basic application is run.

explicit conversion—An operation that converts a value of one type to another type using code to (explicitly) tell the application to do the conversion. An example of an explicit conversion is to convert a value of type Double to type Decimal using a Convert method.

exponentiation operator (^)—This operator raises its left operand to a power specified by the right operand.

expression list—Multiple expressions separated by commas. Used for Cases in Select Case statements, when certain statements should execute based on more than one condition.

eXtensible Application Markup Language (XAML)—*See* XAML.

extensible language—A language that can be "extended" with new data types. Visual Basic is an extensible language.

eXtensible Markup Language (XML)—*See* XML.

F

field—Group of characters that conveys some meaning. For example, a field consisting of uppercase and lowercase letters can represent a person's name.

file—Collection of data that is assigned a name. Used for long-term persistence of large amounts of data, even after the application that created the data terminates.

File class—Provides methods for file manipulations including creating, copying and deleting files.

File Name property—Specifies the name of a source code file.

FileName property of class OpenFileDialog—Specifies the file name selected in the dialog.

Fill attribute of Rectangle element—Specifies a Rectangle's fill color.

Fill property of an Ellipse—Specifies the Brush that is used to color the Ellipse.

final state—Represented by a solid circle surrounded by a hollow circle in a UML activity diagram; the end of the workflow after an application performs its activities.

Finally block—An optional block of code that follows the last Catch block in a sequence of Catch blocks or the Try block if there are no Catches. The Finally block provides code that always executes, whether or not an exception occurs.

FixedSingle value of the BorderStyle property of a Label—Specifies that the Label will display a thin, black border.

Flat value of the FlatStyle property of a Button—Specifies that a Button will appear flat.

FlatStyle property of a Button—Determines whether the Button will appear flat or three-dimensional.

floating-point division—Divides two numbers (whole or fractional) and returns a floating-point number.

focus—Designates the window currently in use.

Focus method—Transfers the focus of the application to the control on which the method is called.

Font class—Contains properties that define unique fonts.

Font property—Specifies the font name, style and size of any displayed text in the Form or one of its controls.

FontDialog class—Used to display a dialog from which the user can choose a font and its style.

FontFamily class—Represents the FontFamily of the Font (a grouping structure to organize fonts with similar properties).

FontSize attribute of a Silverlight control—Specifies the size in pixels of the font used by a control.

FontStyle enumeration—Provides constants for specifying a font's style, including FontStyle.Bold, FontStyle.Italic, FontStyle.Regular, FontStyle.Strikeout and FontStyle.Underline.

For Each...Next repetition statement—Repetition statment that iterates over each element in an array or collection.

For keyword—Begins the For...Next statement.

For...Next header—The first line of a For...Next repetition statement. The For...Next header specifies all four essential elements for counter-controlled repetition.

For...Next repetition statement—Repetition statement that handles the details of counter-controlled repetition. The For...Next statement uses all four elements essential to counter-controlled repetition in one line of code (the name of a control variable, the initial value, the increment or decrement value and the final value).

Form—The object that represents the Windows application's graphical user interface (GUI).

format control string—A string that specifies how data should be formatted.

Format property of a DateTimePicker control—The property of the DateTimePicker control that allows you to specify a predefined or custom format with which to display the date and/or time.

format specifier—Code that specifies the type of format that should be applied to a string for output.

FormatException class—An exception of this type is thrown when a method cannot convert its argument to a desired numeric type, such as Integer or Double.

formatting text—Modifying the appearance of text for display purposes.

Fortran (Formula Translator)—A programming language developed by IBM Corporation in the mid-1950s (and still widely used) to create scientific and engineering applications that require complex mathematical computations.

Framework Class Library—.NET's collection of "prepackaged" classes and methods for performing mathematical calculations, string manipulations, character manipulations, input/output operations, error checking and many other useful operations.

From clause (of a LINQ query)—Specifies a range variable and the data source to query.

FromArgb method of Color structure—A method that creates a new Color object from RGB values and an alpha value.

FullOpen property of class ColorDialog—Property that, when True, enables the ColorDialog to provide a full range of color options when displayed.

Function keyword—Begins the definition of a Function procedure.

Function procedure—A procedure similar to a Sub procedure, with one important difference: Function procedures return a value to the caller, whereas Sub procedures do not.

functionality—The actions an application can execute.

G

GDI+ (Graphics Device Interface)—An application programming interface (API) that provides classes for creating two-dimensional vector graphics.

Get accessor—Used to retrieve a value of a property.

Get/End Get keywords—Reserved words that define a property's Get accessor.

GetName method of class FontFamily—Returns the name of the FontFamily object.

GetPosition method of classes MouseButtonEventArgs and MouseEventArgs—Returns a Point object representing the position of the mouse pointer over a control.

GetUpperBound method of class Array—Returns an array's highest index.

graphical user interface (GUI)—The visual part of an application with which users interact.

Grid layout container—A WPF control that organizes its children in rows and columns.

Grid.Row attribute of a Silverlight control—Specifies the row in which a control should be placed in the enclosing Grid layout container.

Grid.RowDefinitions element—A nested element of a Grid layout container. Contains a set of RowDefinition elements that define the rows of the Grid and their characteristics.

Grid.RowSpan attribute of a Silverlight control—Specifies how many rows a control should occupy in its enclosing Grid layout container. There is also a Grid.ColSpan attribute.

group (of a For Each...Next statement)—Specifies the array or collection through which you wish to iterate.

GroupBox content control—A control that places a titled border around its content.

GroupBox control—Groups related controls visually.

guard condition—An expression contained in square brackets above or next to the arrows leading from a decision symbol in a UML activity diagram that determines whether workflow continues along a path.

H

Handles clause—Specifies the event handled by an event handler and the object to which the event corresponds.

hardware—The various devices that make up a computer, including the keyboard, screen, mouse, hard drive, memory, CD-ROM, DVD, printer and processing units.

header—A line of text at the top of a ListBox that clarifies the information being displayed.

Header property of a GroupBox—Sets the text displayed in a GroupBox's border.

Height property—This property, a member of property Size, indicates the height of the Form or one of its controls in pixels.

high-level language—A type of programming language in which a single program statement accomplishes a substantial task. High-level languages use instructions that look almost like everyday English and contain common mathematical notations.

Horizontal value of ScrollBars property—Used to display a horizontal scrollbar on the bottom of a TextBox.

host name—Name of a computer where resources reside.

HTML (HyperText Markup Language)—A technology used to describe how a browser should display a web page.

HyperText Transfer Protocol (HTTP)—The protocol used to transmit HTML files over the web.

icon—The graphical representation of commands in the Visual Studio 2008 IDE.

I

icon—The graphical representation of commands in the Visual Studio 2008 IDE.

ID property of a web control—Specifies the name of a web control for use in code.

identifier—A series of characters consisting of letters, digits and underscores used to name program units such as classes, controls and variables.

IEnumerable interface—Provides methods to iterate through a set of objects, such as an array or a collection.

If...Then statement—Selection statement that performs an action (or sequence of actions) based on a condition. This is also called the single-selection statement.

If...Then...Else statement—Selection statement that performs an action (or sequence of actions) if a condition is true and performs a different action (or sequence of actions) if the condition is false. This is also called the double-selection statement.

Image control—Displays an image in a Silverlight GUI.

Image property—Indicates the file name of the image displayed in a PictureBox.

Image web control—Displays an image in an ASPX page.

Image.FromFile—A method of class Image that returns an Image object containing the image located at the path you specify.

immutable—Describes an object that cannot be changed after it is created. In Visual Basic, Strings are immutable.

implicit conversion—An operation that converts a value of one type to another type without writing code to (explicitly) tell the application to do the conversion.

Increment property of a NumericUpDown control—Specifies by how much the current number in the NumericUpDown control changes when the user clicks the control's up (for incrementing) or down (for decrementing) arrow.

index—An array element's position number, also called a subscript. An index must be zero, a positive integer or an integer expression that yields a non-negative result. If an application uses an expression as an index, the expression is evaluated first, to determine the index.

index of a List—The value with which you can refer to a specific element in an List, based on the element's location in the List.

indexed array name—The array name followed by an index enclosed in parentheses. The indexed array name can be used on the left side of an assignment statement to place a new value into an array element. The indexed array name can be used in the right side of an assignment to retrieve the value of that array element.

`IndexOf` method of class `String`—Returns the index of the first occurrence of a substring in a `String`. Returns `-1` if the substring is not found.

infinite loop—An error in which a repetition statement never terminates.

information tier—Tier containing the application data; typically implemented as a database. Also called the bottom tier or data tier.

initial state—Represented by a solid circle in a UML activity diagram; the beginning of the workflow before the application performs the modeled activities.

initializer list—The required braces ({ and }) surrounding the initial values of the elements in an array. When the initializer list is empty, the elements in the array are initialized to the default value for the array's data type.

input—Data that the user enters into an application.

input device—Devices that are used to interact with a computer, such as keyboards, mice, microphones, scanners and digital cameras.

input unit—The "receiving" section of the computer that obtains information (data and computer programs) from various input devices, such as keyboards, mice, microphones, scanners and digital cameras.

`Insert` method of a `ListBox`'s `Items` property—Inserts an item in a `ListBox` at the location specified by its first argument.

`Insert` method of class `List`—Inserts a specified object into the specified location of a `List`.

`Insert` method of class `String`—Returns a new `String` object with the specified substring inserted at the given index of the original `String`.

instance variable—Declared inside a class but outside any procedure of that class. Instance variables have module scope.

instant-access application—Application that immediately locates a particular record of information.

instantiate an object—Create an object (or instance) of a class.

`Int32.MaxValue` constant—The largest possible 32-bit `Integer` (2,147,483,647).

integer—A whole number, such as `919`, `-11`, `0` and `138624`.

`Integer` data type—Stores integer values.

integer division—Integer division takes two `Integer` operands and yields an `Integer` result. The fractional portion of the result is discarded.

Integrated Development Environment (IDE)—A software tool that enables you to write, run, test and debug programs quickly and conveniently.

IntelliSense—Visual Basic IDE feature that aids you during development by providing windows that list program items that are available in the current context.

interface—Specifies a set of methods that can be called on an object which implements the interface to perform certain tasks.

internal web browser—The web browser (Internet Explorer) included in Visual Basic 2008 Express, with which you can browse the web.

Internet—A worldwide computer network. Most people today access the Internet through the web.

Internet Information Services (IIS)—A Microsoft web server.

`Interval` property of a `Timer` control—The `Timer` property that specifies the number of milliseconds between `Tick` events.

invoking a procedure—Causing a procedure to perform its designated task.

IP address—Unique address used to locate a computer on the Internet.

`Is` keyword—A keyword that, when followed by a comparison operator, can be used to compare the controlling expression of a `Select Case` statement and a value.

`IsControl` method of structure `Char`—Determines whether the `Char` passed as an argument represents a control key.

`IsNot` operator—Determines whether two reference variables contain references to different objects or whether a single reference variable refers to an object.

`Items` property of `ComboBox`—Collection containing the values displayed in a `ComboBox`.

`Items` property of the `ListBox` control—Returns an object containing all the values in the `ListBox`.

`ItemsPanel` of a `ListBox`—See `ListBox.ItemsPanel` element.

`ItemsPanelTemplate` element—Used to redefine the `ItemsPanel` of a `ListBox` to change how `ListBox` items are arranged.

`ItemTemplate` of a `ListBox`—See `ListBox.ItemTemplate` element.

J

Java—A popular programming language that is used to create web pages with dynamic content , to build large-scale enterprise applications, to enhance the functionality of web servers, to provide applications for consumer devices and for many other purposes.

`Join` method of class `String`—Concatenates the elements in a `String` array, separated by the first argument. A new `String` containing the concatenated elements is returned.

K

key/value pair—Associates a value with a corresponding key, which is used to identify the value. The `Session` object stores key/value pairs.

keyboard event—Raised when a key on the keyboard is pressed or released.

`KeyChar` property of class `KeyPressEventArgs`—Contains data about the key that raised the `KeyPress` event.

`KeyCode` property of class `KeyEventArgs`—Contains data about the key that raised the `KeyDown` event.

`KeyDown` event—Generated when a key is initially pressed. Used to handle the event raised when a key that is not a letter or number key is pressed.

`KeyEventArgs` class—Stores information about special modifier keys.

`KeyPress` event—Generated when a key is pressed. Used to handle the event raised when a letter or number key is pressed.

KeyPressEventArgs class—Stores information about character keys.

Keys enumeration—Contains values representing keyboard keys.

KeyUp event—Generated when a key is released.

keyword—A word in code reserved by the compiler for a specific purpose. By default, these words appear in blue in the IDE and cannot be used as identifiers.

L

Label—Control that displays text the user can't modify.

Label web control—Displays text on an ASPX page.

Language-Integrated Query (LINQ)—Provides support for writing queries in Visual Basic.

LastIndexOf method of class String—Returns the index of the last occurrence of a substring in a String. Returns -1 if the substring is not found.

layout container—A control that positions its child controls based on their size and the amount of available space in the container.

left operand—The expression on the left side of a binary operator.

length of an array—The number of elements in an array.

Length property of class Array—Contains the length of (or number of elements in) an array.

Length property of class String—Returns the number of characters in a String.

Length property of class String—Returns the number of characters in the String for which it is called.

line-continuation character—An underscore character (_) preceded by one or more space characters, used to continue a statement to the next line of code.

LINQ to SQL classes—Creates a model of a database in an application. These classes are used to manipulate the database's contents.

LINQ to XML—LINQ capabilities that enable manipulation of XML data.

LinqDataSource—A data source that uses LINQ to retrieve information from a DataContext object.

List(Of T) class—Has the same capabilities as an array, as well as dynamic resizing.

ListBox control—Allows the user to view items in a list. Items can be added to or removed from the list programmatically.

ListBox control—Displays a list of items in a Silverlight GUI.

ListBox web control—Displays a list of items.

ListBox.ItemsPanel element—Defines how the items in a ListBox are arranged in the GUI (e.g., vertically, horizontally, etc.).

ListBox.ItemTemplate element—Defines the look-and-feel of each ListBox item. The default ItemTemplate displays the String representation of each item.

literal String object—A String constant written as a sequence of characters in double quotation marks (also called a string literal).

Load event of a Form—Raised when an application initially executes.

local type inference—Visual Basic 2008 compiler feature that enables it to infer a local variable's type based on the context in which the variable is initialized.

local variable—Declared inside a procedure or block, such as the body of an If...Then statement. Local variables have either procedure scope or block scope.

localhost—Host name that identifies the local computer.

Locals window—Allows you to view the state of the variables and properties in the current scope during debugging.

location bar—The ComboBox in Visual Basic's internal web browser where you can enter the name of a web site to visit.

Location property—Specifies the location (*x*- and *y*-coordinates) of the upper-left corner of a control. This property is used to place a control on the Form precisely.

Locked property—Prevents a control from being moved or resized.

logic error—An error that does not prevent the application from compiling successfully, but does cause the application to produce erroneous results.

logical exclusive OR (Xor) operator—A logical operator that is True if and only if one of its operands is True and the other is False.

logical operators—The operators (for example, AndAlso, OrElse, Xor and Not) that can be used to form complex conditions by combining simple ones.

loop—Another name for a repetition statement.

loop-continuation condition—The condition used in a repetition statement (such as a Do While...Loop) that enables repetition to continue while the condition is True and that causes repetition to terminate when the condition becomes False.

loop-termination condition—The condition used in a repetition statement (such as a Do Until...Loop) that enables repetition to continue while the condition is False and that causes repetition to terminate when the condition becomes True.

M

***m*-by-*n* array**—A two-dimensional array with *m* rows and *n* columns.

machine language—A computer's natural language, generally consisting of streams of numbers that instruct the computer how to perform its most elementary operations.

Margin attribute of a Silverlight control—Specifies the amount of space around the edges of a control.

margin indicator bar—A margin in the IDE where breakpoints are displayed.

MarginBounds.Left property of class PrintPageEventArgs—Specifies the left margin of a printed page.

MarginBounds.Top property of class PrintPageEventArgs—Specifies the top margin of a printed page.

masking—Hiding text such as passwords or other sensitive pieces of information that should not be observed by other people as they are typed. Masking is achieved by using the PasswordChar property of the TextBox for which you would like to hide data. The actual data entered is retained in the TextBox's Text property.

masking character—Used to replace each character displayed in a TextBox when the TextBox's data is masked for privacy.

Max method of class Math—A method of class Math which returns the greater of its two arguments.

MaxDate property of a DateTimePicker control—The DateTimePicker property that specifies the latest value that the DateTimePicker allows the user to enter.

MaxDropDownItems property of class ComboBox—Property of the ComboBox control that specifies how many items can be displayed in the drop-down list. If the ComboBox has more elements than this, it provides a scrollbar to access all of them.

Maximum property of a NumericUpDown control—Determines the maximum input value in a particular NumericUpDown control.

MaxLength property of TextBox— Specifies the maximum number of characters that can be input into a TextBox.

.mdf file—A SQL Server Express database file.

Me keyword—References the current object.

member-access operator—Also known as the dot operator (.). Allows you to access a control's properties using code.

members of a class—Methods, variables and properties declared within the body of a class.

memory—Another name for the memory unit.

memory unit—The rapid-access, relatively low-capacity "warehouse" section of the computer, which stores data temporarily while an application is running.

menu—Design element that groups related commands for Windows applications. Although these commands depend on the application, some—such as Open and Save—are common to many applications. Menus are an integral part of GUIs, because they organize commands without cluttering the GUI.

menu bar—Contains the menus for a window.

Menu Designer mode in the Visual Basic IDE—Design mode in the IDE that allows you to create and edit menus and menu items.

menu item (or command)—A command located in a menu that, when selected, causes an application to perform a specific action.

MenuStrip control—Allows you to add menus to your application.

merge symbol (in the UML)—A diamond symbol in the UML that joins two flows of activity into one flow of activity.

message dialog—A window that displays messages to users or gathers input from users.

Message property of an exception object—Provides access to the error message in an exception object.

MessageBox class—Provides a method for displaying message dialogs.

MessageBox.Show method—Displays a message dialog.

MessageBoxButtons constants—The identifiers that specify the Buttons that can be displayed in a MessageBox dialog.

MessageBoxIcon constants—Identifiers that specify the icons that can be displayed in a MessageBox dialog.

method—A portion of a class that performs a task and possibly returns information when it completes the task.

method overloading—Allows you to create multiple methods with the same name but different signatures.

microprocessor—The chip that makes a computer work (that is, the "brain" of the computer).

Microsoft Developer Network (MSDN)—An online library that contains articles, downloads and tutorials on technologies of interest to Visual Basic developers.

middle tier—Tier that controls interaction between the client and information tiers (also called the business logic tier).

Min method of class Math—A method of class Math which returns the lesser of its two arguments.

MinDate property of a DateTimePicker control—Specifies the earliest value that the control allows the user to enter.

Minimum property of a NumericUpDown control—Determines the minimum input value in a particular NumericUpDown control.

minus box—An icon that, when clicked, collapses a node.

Mod (modulus operator)—The modulus operator yields the remainder after division.

modifier key—Key such as *Shift*, *Alt* or *Control* that modifies the way that an application responds to a keyboard event.

module scope—Variable declared inside a class definition but outside any of the classes procedures have module scope. Module scope begins at the identifier after keyword Class and terminates at the End Class statement, enables all procedures in the same class to access all instance variables defined in that class.

MonthCalendar control—Displays a calendar from which a user can select a range of dates.

More Colors dialog—Displays the set of web-safe colors and enables you to create custom colors.

mouse event—Generated when a user interacts with an application using the computer's mouse.

MouseButtonEventArgs class—Specifies information about a mouse event involving a button press or release.

MouseEventArgs class—Specifies information about a MouseMove.

MouseLeftButtonDown event—Generated when the left mouse button is pressed.

MouseLeftButtonUp event—Generated when the left mouse button is released.

MouseMove event—Generated when a mouse pointer is moved.

MouseRightButtonDown event—Generated when the right mouse button is pressed.

MouseRightButtonUp event—Generated when the right mouse button is released.

MoveFirst method of class BindingSource—Moves to the first item in the BindingSource.

Multiline property of a TextBox control—Specifies whether the TextBox is capable of displaying multiple lines of text. If the property value is True, the TextBox may contain multiple lines of text; if the value of the property is False, the TextBox can contain only one line of text.

multiple-selection statement—Performs one of many actions (or sequences of actions) depending on the value of the controlling expression.

multiplication operator—The asterisk (*) used to multiply two operands, producing their product as a result.

multitier application—Application (sometimes referred to as an *n*-tier application) whose functionality is divided into separate tiers, which can be on the same machine or can be distributed to separate machines across a network.

mutually exclusive options—A set of options of which only one can be selected at a time.

N

***n*-tier application**—Another name for a multitier application.

name of a variable—The identifier used in an application to access or modify a variable's value.

`Name` property—Assigns a unique and meaningful name to a control for easy identification.

namespace—Classes in the .NET Framework Class Library are organized by functionality into these directory-like entities.

narrowing conversion—A conversion where the value of a "larger" type is being assigned to a variable of a "smaller" type, where the larger type can store more data than the smaller type. Narrowing conversions can result in loss of data, which can cause subtle logic errors.

nested `For...Next` statements—A `For...Next` statement defined in the body of another `For...Next` statement. Commonly used to iterate over the elements of a two-dimensional array.

nested parentheses—These occur when an expression in parentheses is found within another expression surrounded by parentheses. With nested parentheses, the operators contained in the innermost pair of parentheses are applied first.

nested statement—A statement that is placed inside another control statement.

NET Framework—Microsoft-provided software that executes applications, provides the Framework Class Library and supplies many other programming capabilities.

.NET Framework Class Library—.NET's collection of "prepackaged" classes and methods for performing mathematical calculations, string manipulations, character manipulations, input/output operations, error checking and many other useful operations.

.NET Initiative—Microsoft's vision for using the Internet and the web in the development, engineering, distribution and use of software.

.NET Platform—The set of software components that enables .NET programs to run—allows applications to be distributed to a variety of devices as well as to desktop computers. Offers a programming model that allows software components created in different programming languages (such as Visual Basic and C#) to communicate with one another.

`New` keyword—Used to call a constructor when creating an object.

New Project dialog—A dialog that allows you to choose what type of application you wish to create.

New Style dialog—Enables you to specify styles, such as position, for your web controls.

`Next` method of class `Random`—A method of class `Random` that, when called with no arguments, generates a positive `Integer` value between zero and the constant `Int32.MaxValue`. When called with arguments, the method generates an `Integer` value in a range constrained by those arguments.

`NextDouble` method of class `Random`—A method of class `Random` that generates a positive `Double` value that is greater than or equal to 0.0 and less than 1.0.

nondestructive memory operation—A process that does not overwrite a value in memory.

`None` value of `ScrollBars` property—Used to display no scrollbars on a `TextBox`.

`Not` (logical negation) operator—A logical operator that enables you to reverse the meaning of a condition: A `True` condition, when logically negated, becomes `False`, and a `False` condition, when logically negated, becomes `True`.

note—An explanatory remark (represented by a rectangle with a folded upper-right corner) describing the purpose of a symbol in a UML activity diagram.

`Nothing` keyword—Used to clear a reference's value.

`Now` property of `Date` type—Returns the current system time and date.

`Now` property of type `Date`—The `Date` property that retrieves your computer's current time.

`NumericUpDown` control—Allows you to specify maximum and minimum numeric input values. Also allows you to specify an increment (or decrement) when the user clicks the up (or down) arrow.

O

object initializer—Uses keyword `With` to assign property values to a newly created object.

Object Relational Designer—Allows you to specify which tables in a database are accessible through an application's LINQ to SQL classes.

object technology—A packaging scheme for creating meaningful software units. The units are large and are focused on particular application areas. There are date objects, time objects, paycheck objects, file objects and the like.

object-oriented programming (OOP)—Models real-world objects with software counterparts.

objects—Software components that model items in the real world.

off-by-one error—The kind of logic error that occurs, for example, when a loop executes for one more or one less iteration than is intended.

one-dimensional array—An array that uses only one index.

opacity—Amount of transparency of the color.

`Opacity` attribute of `Rectangle` element—Specifies a `Rectangle`'s transparency—a number from 0 to 1, where 0 is completely transparent and 1 is completely opaque.

`OpenFileDialog` component—Enables an application to use the **Open** dialog, which allows users to specify a file to be opened

operand—An expression on which an operator performs its task.

`Option Strict`—When set to `On`, disallows implicit narrowing conversions (for example, conversion from `Double` to `Deci-`

mal). If you attempt an implicit narrowing conversion, the compiler issues a compilation error.

Optional parameter—A parameter that is specified with a default value. If the corresponding argument is omitted in the procedure call, the default value is supplied by the compiler.

Or operator—A logical operator used to ensure that either *or* both of two conditions are true in an application before a certain path of execution is chosen.

Order By clause of a LINQ query—Orders the result of a LINQ query by the specified property.

OrElse operator—A logical operator used to ensure that either *or* both of two conditions are true in an application before a certain path of execution is chosen. Performs short-circuit evaluation.

Orientation attribute of a StackPanel layout container—Determines whether a StackPanel arranges its child elements vertically (the default) or horizontally.

output—The results of an application.

output device—A device to which information that is processed by the computer can be sent.

output Label—A Label used to display results.

output unit—The section of the computer that takes information the computer has processed and places it on various output devices, making the information available for use outside the computer.

Output window—A window which displays the result of the compilation.

P

PadLeft method of class String—Adds characters to the beginning of a string until the length of the string equals the specified length.

PadRight method of class String—Adds characters to the end of a string until the length of the string equals the specified length.

Page class—Defines the basic functionality for an ASPX page.

Page_Load event handler—Executes when an ASPX page is loaded.

Page.xaml—XAML file that defines a Silverlight application's GUI.

Page.xaml.vb—Code-behind file that declares GUI event handlers (and other methods required by a Silverlight application).

palette—A set of colors.

Panel control—Used to group controls. Unlike GroupBoxes, Panels do not have captions.

parameter—A variable declared in a procedure's parameter list that can be used in the body of the procedure.

***Parameter Info* feature of the IDE**—Provides information about procedures and their arguments.

parameter list—A comma-separated list in which the procedure declares each parameter's name and type.

partial page update—Refreshes a section of the page *without* reloading the entire page.

Pascal—A programming language designed for teaching structured programming, named after the 17th-century mathematician and philosopher Blaise Pascal.

pass-by-reference—When an argument is passed by reference, the called procedure can access and modify the caller's argument value directly. Keyword ByRef indicates pass-by-reference (also called call-by-reference).

pass-by-value—When an argument is passed by value, the application makes a copy of the argument's value and passes the copy to the called procedure. With pass-by-value, changes to the called procedure's copy do not affect the caller's argument value. Keyword ByVal indicates pass-by-value (also called call-by-value).

PasswordChar property of a TextBox—Specifies the masking character for a TextBox.

Pen object—Specifies drawing parameters when drawing shape outlines.

persistent data—Data maintained in files which exists after the application that created the data terminates.

PictureBox—Control that displays an image.

pin (or pushpin) icon—An icon that enables or disables the auto-hide feature.

pixel—A tiny point on your computer screen that displays a color.

plus box—An icon that, when clicked, expands a node.

Pmt function—A built-in Visual Basic function that, given an interest rate, the total number of payments and a monetary loan amount, returns a Double value specifying the amount per payment.

Point class—Contains an X and a Y property representing the coordinates of a point.

position number—A value that indicates a specific location within an array. Position numbers begin at 0 (zero).

precision—Specifies the number of digits to the right of the decimal point in a formatted floating-point value.

primary key—Field (or combination of fields) in a database table that contains unique values used to distinguish records from one another.

primary memory—Another name for the memory unit.

primitive data type—A data type already defined in Visual Basic, such as Integer.

Print method of class PrintDocument—Prints a document.

PrintDocument class—Allows the user to describe how to print a document.

PrinterSettings.InstalledPrinters.Count property—Determines how many printers are installed on the user's computer.

PrintPage event—Occurs when the data required to print the current page is needed.

PrintPageEventArgs class—Contains data passed to a PrintPage event.

PrintPreviewDialog control—Previews a document in a dialog box before it prints.

Private keyword—Member-access modifier that makes members accessible only to the class that defines the members.

procedural programming language—A programming language (such as Fortran, Pascal, BASIC and C) that focuses on actions (verbs) rather than things or objects (nouns).

procedure—A set of instructions for performing a particular task.

procedure body—The declarations and statements that appear after the procedure header but before the keywords `End Sub` or `End Function`. The procedure body contains Visual Basic code that performs actions, generally by manipulating or interacting with the parameters from the parameter list.

procedure call—Invokes a procedure, specifies the procedure name and provides arguments that the callee (the procedure being called) requires to perform its task.

procedure definition—The procedure header, body and ending statement.

procedure header—The first line of a procedure (including the keyword `Sub` or `Function`, the procedure name, the parameter list and the `Function` procedure return type).

procedure name—Follows the keyword `Sub` or `Function` and distinguishes one procedure from another. A procedure name can be any valid identifier.

procedure scope—Variables declared inside a procedure but outside a control statement have procedure scope. Variables with procedure scope cannot be referenced outside the procedure in which they are declared.

program control—The task of ordering an application's statements in the correct order.

programmer-defined class (programmer-defined type)—A class defined by a programmer, as opposed to classes predefined in the Framework Class Library.

programmer-defined procedure—A procedure created by a programmer to meet the unique needs of a particular application.

project—A group of related files that compose an application.

properties—Object attributes, such as size, color and weight.

Properties window—The window that displays the properties for a `Form` or control object.

property—Specifies a control or `Form` object's attributes, such as size, color and position.

property definition—Contains accessors—portions of code that handle the details of modifying and returning data.

property definition—Defines the accessors for a property.

`Property`/`End Property` keywords—Reserved words indicating the definition of a class property.

pseudocode—An informal language that helps you develop algorithms.

pseudorandom numbers—A sequence of values produced by a complex mathematical calculation that simulates random-number generation.

`Public` keyword—Member-access modifier that makes instance variables or methods accessible wherever the application has a reference to that object.

Q

query—Request information that satisfies given criteria.

query (LINQ)—Retrieves specific information from a data source, such as a collection.

***Quick Info* box**—Displays the value of a variable during debugging.

R

`RadioButton` control—Appears as a small circle that is either blank (unchecked) or contains a smaller dot (checked). Usually these controls appear in groups of two or more. Exactly one `RadioButton` in a group is selected at one time.

`Random` class—Contains methods to generate pseudorandom numbers.

random-access memory (RAM)—An example of primary memory.

range variable (LINQ)—The control variable for a LINQ query.

`ReadAllLines` method of class `File`—Returns an array of `Strings` containing each line of the file.

`ReadLine` method of class `StreamReader`—Reads a line from a file and returns it as a `String`.

`ReadOnly` property of a `TextBox` control—Determines whether the user can change the value of a `TextBox`.

real-time error checking—Feature of the Visual Basic IDE that provides immediate notification of possible errors in your code. For example, unrecognized identifier errors are indicated by blue, jagged underlines in code.

record—A collection of related fields. Usually a `Class` in Visual Basic composed of several fields (called member variables in Visual Basic).

record key—Identifies a record and distinguishes it from all other records.

`Rectangle` element—Displays a rectangle in a Silverlight GUI.

rectangular array—A type of two-dimensional array that can represent tables of values consisting of information arranged in rows and columns. Each row contains the same number of columns.

`Redirect` method of class `Response`—Redirects the client browser to another web page.

redundant parentheses—Unnecessary parentheses used in an expression to make it easier to read.

reference—Keyword `New` creates a new object in memory and returns a reference to that object. You typically store an object's reference in a reference-type variable so you can interact with the object.

reference type—A type that stores the location of an object. Any type that is not a value type is a reference type. Primitive type `String` is a reference type.

relational operators—Operators < (less than), > (greater than), <= (less than or equal to) and >= (greater than or equal to) that compare two values (also known as comparison operators).

`RemoveAt` method of class `List`—Removes the object located at a specified location of a `List`.

repetition statement—Allows you to specify that an action or actions should be repeated, depending on the value of a condition.

repetition structure (or repetition statement)—Allows the programmer to specify that an action or sequence of actions should be repeated, depending on the value of a condition.

Replace method of class String—Returns a copy of the String for which it is called. Replaces all occurrences of the characters in its first String argument with the characters in its second String argument.

Representational State Transfer (REST)—A way to invoke a web service in which each operation is identified by a unique URL.

RequiredFieldValidator control—A validation control which ensures that a web control contains data before the user can submit a web form to a web server.

reserved words (keywords)—Words that are reserved by the Visual Basic compiler.

Response class—Provides methods for responding to a client request.

Result property of class DownloadStringCompletedEventArgs—A String representing the results returned by the invoked web service.

rethrow an exception—The Catch block can defer the exception handling (or perhaps a portion of it) to another Catch block by using the Throw statement.

Return keyword—Signifies the return statement that sends a value back to the procedure's caller.

Return statement—Used to return a value from a procedure.

return type—Data type of the result returned from a Function procedure.

reusing code—The practice of using existing code to build new code. Reusing code saves time, effort and money.

RGB value—The amount of red, green and blue needed to create a color.

Rich Internet Applications (RIAs)—Web applications that offer the responsiveness and rich GUI features of desktop applications.

right operand—The expression on the right side of a binary operator.

row—The first dimension of a two-dimensional array.

RowDefinition element—Nested in a Grid.RowDefinitions element to specify the characteristics of a row in a Grid layout container.

rules of operator precedence—Rules that determine the precise order in which operators are applied in an expression.

run mode—IDE mode indicating that the application is executing.

runtime error—An error that has its effect at execution time.

S

scope—The portion of an application in which an identifier (such as a variable name) can be referenced. Some identifiers can be referenced throughout an application—others can be referenced only from limited portions of an application (such as within a single procedure or block).

screen scraping—The process of extracting desired information from the HTML that composes a web page.

ScriptManager control—Manages the client-side scripts that enable asynchronous Ajax functionality.

scroll arrows—Arrows at the ends of a scrollbar that enable you to scroll through items.

ScrollBars property of a TextBox control—Specifies whether a TextBox has a scrollbar and, if so, of what type. By default, property ScrollBars is set to None.

secondary storage media—Devices such as magnetic disks, optical disks and magnetic tapes on which computers store files.

secondary storage unit—The long-term, high-capacity "warehouse" section of the computer.

Segoe UI font—The Microsoft-recommended font for use in Windows Vista applications.

Select Case statement—The multiple-selection statement used to make a decision by comparing an expression to a series of conditions. The algorithm then takes different actions based on those values.

Select clause (of a LINQ query)—Specifies the value(s) placed in the results of the query.

Select Resource dialog—Used to import files, such as images, to any application.

SelectedIndex property of class ComboBox—Specifies the index of the selected item. Returns -1 if no item is selected.

SelectedIndexChanged event of ComboBox—Raised when a new value is selected in a ComboBox.

SelectedValue property of class ListBox—Returns the value of the selected item.

selection structure (or selection statement)—Selects among alternative courses of action.

SelectionStart property of MonthCalendar control—Returns the first (or only) date selected.

sender event argument—Event argument that contains a reference to the object that raised the event (also called the source of the event).

sentence-style capitalization—A style that capitalizes the first letter of the first word in the text. Every other letter in the text is lowercase, unless it is the first letter of a proper noun (for example, Cartons per shipment).

separator bar—Bar placed in a menu to separate related menu items.

sequence structure (or sequence statement)—Built into Visual Basic—unless directed to act otherwise, the computer executes Visual Basic statements sequentially.

sequential execution—Statements in an application are executed one after another in the order in which they are written.

sequential-access file—File containing data that is read in the order in which it was written to the file.

Session object—Object that is maintained across several web pages containing a collection of key/value pairs that are specific to a given user.

session state—ASP.NET's built-in support for tracking data throughout a browser session.

Set accessor—Provides data-validation capabilities to ensure that the value is set properly.

Set/End Set keywords—Reserved words that define a property's Set accessor.

SetLeft method of Canvas—Sets the left coordinate of an element (the first argument) on the Canvas to a Double value (the second argument).

SetTop method of Canvas—Sets the top coordinate of an element (the first argument) on the Canvas to a Double value (the second argument).

short-circuit evaluation—The evaluation of the right operand in AndAlso and OrElse expressions occurs only if the first condition meets the criteria for the condition.

ShowDialog method of class FontDialog or ColorDialog—The method that displays the dialog on which it is called.

ShowDialog method of class OpenFileDialog—Displays the Open dialog and returns the result of the user interaction with the dialog.

ShowGridLines attribute of Grid layout container—Displays grid lines so you can see the grid layout as you design and build your GUI.

ShowUpDown property of a DateTimePicker control—The DateTimePicker property that, when True, allows the user to specify the time using up and down arrows, and, when False, allows the user to specify the date using a calendar.

signature—Specifies a procedure's parameters and their types.

Silverlight—Microsoft's platform for Rich Internet Applications (RIAs).

Silverlight Application project template—Visual Studio 2008 project template for building Silverlight applications. Must have Silverlight Tools for Visual Studio 2008 installed.

simple condition—Contains one expression that evaluates to True or False.

Single data type—Stores floating-point values. Single is similar to Double, but is less precise and requires less memory.

Single method of a LINQ query—Returns a single object from a LINQ query rather than a a collection.

single-entry/single-exit control structure (or statement)—A control statement that has one entry point and one exit point. All Visual Basic control statements are single-entry/single-exit control statements.

single-quote character(')—Indicates the beginning of a code comment.

single-selection statement—The If...Then statement, which selects or ignores a single action or sequence of actions.

size of a variable—The number of bytes required to store a value of the variable's type.

Size property—Property that specifies the height and width, in pixels, of the Form or one of its controls.

SizeMode property—Property that specifies how an image is displayed in a PictureBox.

sizing handle—Square that, when enabled, can be used to resize the Form or one of its controls.

small circles (in the UML)—The solid circle in an activity diagram represents the activity's initial state, and the solid circle surrounded by a hollow circle represents the activity's final state.

software—The set of applications that run on computers.

software reuse—The reuse of existing pieces of software, an approach that enables you to avoid "reinventing the wheel," helping you to develop applications faster.

solid circle (in the UML)—A UML activity diagram symbol that represents the activity's initial state.

solution—Contains one or more projects.

Solution Explorer—A window that provides access to all the projects and their files in a solution.

Sorted property of class ComboBox—When set to True, sorts the items in a ComboBox alphabetically.

Source attribute of an Image—Specifies the URL from which to obtain the image for display in the control.

Source mode—Displays the ASPX page's markup at design time.

special characters—Characters that are neither digits nor letters.

special symbols—$, @, %, &, *, (,), -, +, ", :, ?, / and the like.

Split method of class String—Splits the words in a String whenever a space is reached.

Split mode—Displays the ASPX page's Source and Design views at the same time.

SQL Server Express—A database management system built by Microsoft.

Sqrt method of class Math—A method of class Math which returns the square root of its argument.

StackPanel layout container—A WPF control that organizes its children horizontally or vertically (the default).

Start Page—The initial page displayed when Visual Studio 2008 is opened.

start tag—Delimits the beginning of an XML element.

StartsWith method of class String—Determines whether a String starts with a particular substring.

state button—A button that can be in the on/off (true/false) state.

statement—A unit of code that, when compiled and executed, performs an action.

Step keyword—Optional component of the For...Next header that specifies the increment or decrement (that is, the amount added to or subtracted from the control variable each time the loop is executed).

straight-line form—The manner in which arithmetic expressions must be written to be represented in Visual Basic code.

stream—A sequence of characters.

StreamReader class—Provides methods for reading information from a file.

StreamWriter class—Provides methods for writing information to a file.

StretchImage—Value of PictureBox property SizeMode that scales an image to fill the PictureBox.

string constant—A String constant written as a sequence of characters in double quotation marks (also called a string literal).

String data type—Stores a series of characters.

string literal—A String constant written as a sequence of characters in double quotation marks (also called a literal String object).

string-concatenation operator (&)—This operator combines its two operands into one string value.

String.Format method—Formats a string.

structured programming—A technique for organizing program control using sequence, selection and repetition structures to help you develop applications that are easy to understand, debug and modify.

Structured Query Language (SQL)—Language often used by relational databases to perform queries and manipulate data in relational databases.

`style` element—An element that is placed in the `head` element of a page. Contains CSS style definitions (such as those created with the **New Style** window).

`Sub` keyword—Begins the definition of a `Sub` procedure.

`Sub` procedure—A procedure similar to a `Function` procedure, with one important difference: `Sub` procedures do not return a value to the caller, whereas `Function` procedures do.

submenu—Menu within another menu.

`SubmitChanges` method of class `DataContext`—Updates the database on disk with any changes made in the application.

subscript—*See* index.

substring—A sequence of characters in a `String`.

`Substring` method of class `String`—Returns characters from a string, corresponding to the arguments passed by the user, that indicate the start position within a `String` and the number of characters to return.

`Substring` method of class `String`—Creates a new `String` object by copying part of an existing `String` object.

synchronous request—The user must wait until the server processes the request and returns the resulting page.

syntax—Specifies how a statement must be formed to compile without syntax errors.

syntax error—An error that occurs when program statements violate the grammatical rules of a programming language. Syntax errors are a subset of compilation errors.

`System.Collections.Generic` namespace—Contains collection classes such as `List`.

`System.Drawing.Printing` namespace—Allows your applications to access all services related to printing.

T

`TabIndex` property—A control property that specifies the order in which focus is transferred to controls on the `Form` when the *Tab* key is pressed.

table—A two-dimensional array used to contain information arranged in rows and columns.

table in a database—Used to store related information in rows and columns. (Represented in the application by the LINQ to SQL classes.)

`TabStop` property—A control property that specifies whether a control can receive the focus when the *Tab* key is pressed.

templates—Starting points for the projects you create in Visual Basic.

temporary variable—Used to store data when swapping values.

`Text` attribute of a `TextBlock`—Specifies the text in a `TextBlock`.

text file—A file containing human-readable characters.

`Text` property—Sets the text displayed on a control.

`Text` property of class `ComboBox`—Returns the currently selected `String` in the `ComboBox`.

`TextAlign` property—Specifies how text is aligned within a `Label`.

`TextBlock` element—Displays text in a Silverlight GUI.

`TextBox` control—Retrieves user input from the keyboard.

`TextChanged` event—Occurs when the text in a `TextBox` changes.

`Throw` statement—The statement used to throw an exception.

throws an exception—A method throws an exception if a problem occurs while the method is executing.

`Tick` event of a `Timer` control—Raised after the number of milliseconds specified in the `Timer` control's `Interval` property has elapsed (if `Enabled` is `True`).

`Timer` control—Generates `Tick` events to run code at specified intervals.

title bar—The top of a window in which the title of the window is displayed.

`Title` property of a `Window`—Specifies the text that appears in the `Window`'s title bar.

`Title` property of an ASPX page—Specifies the page's title that displays in the title bar of the browser.

`To` keyword—Used to specify a range of values. Commonly used in `For...Next` headers to specify the initial and final values of the statement's control variable.

`Today` property of type `Date`—Returns the current date with the time set to midnight.

`ToList` method of interface `IEnumerable`—Returns a `List` of the items contained in an `IEnumerable` object.

`ToLongDateString` method of type `Date`—Returns a `String` containing the date in the format "Wednesday, October 30, 2002."

toolbar—A bar that contains buttons that, when clicked, execute commands.

toolbar icon—A picture on a toolbar button.

Toolbox—A window that contains controls used to build and customize `Forms`.

Tools menu—A menu of the IDE that contains commands for accessing additional IDE tools and options that enable customization of the IDE.

`ToolStripMenuItem` class—Class which represents an individual menu item in a `MenuStrip`.

tooltip—The description of an icon that appears when the mouse pointer is held over that icon for a few seconds.

top tier—Tier containing the application's user interface. Also called the client tier.

`ToShortTimeString` method of type `Date`—Returns a `String` containing the time in the format "4:00 PM."

`ToString` method—Returns a `String` representation of the object or data type on which the method is called.

`ToUpper` method of class `String`—Returns the uppercase representation of a `String`. Similarly, `ToLower` returns the lowercase representation of a `String`.

transfer of control—Occurs when an executed statement does not directly follow the previously executed statement in a running application.

transferring the focus—Selecting a control in an application.

transition—A change from one action state to another that is represented by transition arrows in a UML activity diagram.

translator program—Converts assembly-language programs to machine languag.

Transmission Control Protocol/Internet Protocol (TCP/IP) —The combined set of communications protocols for the Internet.

`Trim` method of class `String`—Removes all whitespace characters from the beginning and end of a `String`.

truth table—A table that displays the `Boolean` result of a logical operator for all possible combinations of `True` and `False` values for its operands.

`Try` block—A block of statements that might cause exceptions and statements that should not execute if an exception occurs.

two-dimensional array—An array that contains multiple rows of values.

type of a variable—Specifies the kind of data that can be stored in a variable and the range of values that can be stored.

`TypeOf...Is` expression—Returns True if the object referenced by the variable is of the specified type.

U

UML (Unified Modeling Language)—An industry standard for modeling software systems graphically.

unary operator—An operator that takes only one operand.

uncaught (unhandled) exception—An exception that does not have an exception handler. Uncaught exceptions might terminate application execution.

Unicode—A character set containing characters that are composed of two bytes. Characters are represented in Visual Basic using the Unicode character set.

uniform resource locator (URL)—Address that can be used to direct a browser to a resource on the web.

`UpdatePanel` control—ASP.NET Ajax control that performs a partial page update of the controls contained in its `ContentTemplate`.

`UseAntiAlias` property of class `PrintPreviewDialog`—Makes the text in the `PrintPreviewDialog` appear smoother on the screen.

`UserControl`—The main element in a Silverlight application. Contains all other elements in the GUI.

V

`Val` function—Filters a number from its argument if possible. This avoids errors introduced by entering nonnumeric data when only numbers are expected. However, the result of the `Val` function is not always what you intended.

value of a variable—The piece of data that is stored in a variable's location in memory.

`Value` property of a `DateTimePicker` control—Stores the value (such as a time) in a `DateTimePicker` control.

value type—A type that is defined as a `Structure` in Visual Basic. A variable of a value type contains a value of that type. The primitive types (other than `String`) are value types.

`ValueChanged` event of a `DateTimePicker` control—Raised when a user selects a new day or time in the `DateTimePicker` control.

variable—A location in the computer's memory where a value can be stored.

vector graphics—Graphics created by a set of mathematical properties called vectors, which include the graphics' dimensions, attributes and positions.

`Vertical` value of `ScrollBars` property—Used to display a vertical scrollbar on the right side of a `TextBox`.

`Visibility` attribute of a Silverlight control—Specifies whether a control is `Visible` or `Collapsed` (not visible) in the GUI.

Visual Basic—Programming language introduced by Microsoft in 1991 to make programming Windows applications easier.

visual programming—Technique in which Visual Basic processes your actions (such as clicking, dragging and dropping controls) and writes code for you.

visual programming with Visual Basic—You use Visual Studio's graphical user interface to conveniently drag and drop predefined controls into place on the screen, and to label and resize them. Visual Studio writes much of the Visual Basic code, saving you considerable effort.

Visual Studio—Microsoft's integrated development environment (IDE), which allows developers to create applications in a variety of .NET programming languages.

Visual Web Developer 2008 Express—A Microsoft tool for building ASP.NET 3.5 web applications.

volatile memory—Memory that is erased when the machine is powered off.

W

Watch window—A Visual Basic IDE window that allows you to view and modify variable values while an application is being debugged.

Web Application Project—A project that can be used to test a Silverlight application in a web browser. One of these can be created for you when you create a new Silverlight application.

web applications—Applications that create web content.

web controls—Controls, such as `TextBoxes` and `Buttons`, that are used to customize ASPX pages.

Web Form—Another name for an ASPX page.

Web Form Designer—The design area in Visual Web Developer that enables you to visually build your ASPX pages.

Web Form page—Another name for an ASPX page.

web server—Specialized software that responds to client requests by providing resources.

web service—A software component stored on one computer that can be accessed via method calls by an application (or other software component) on another computer over a network.

web-safe colors—Colors that display the same on different computers.

`WebClient` class—An object of this class can be used to invoke a web service.

`Where` clause (of a LINQ query)—Specifies the conditions that must be met for an item to be included in the results.

whitespace character—A space, tab or newline character.

widening conversion—A conversion in which the value of a "smaller" type is assigned to a variable of a "larger" type—that is, a type that can store more data than the smaller type.

`Width` property—This setting, a member of property `Size`, indicates the width of the `Form` or one of its controls, in pixels.

`Window` control—The root control in a WPF application. Analogous to a `Form` in a Windows `Forms` application.

Windows Form Designer—Used to design the GUI of a Windows Forms application.

Windows Forms application—An application that executes on a Windows operating system (e.g., Windows XP or Vista) and has a graphical user interface (GUI)—the visual part of the application with which the user interacts.

Windows Presentation Foundation (WPF)—Microsoft's new graphics framework that allows you to create powerful and flexible GUIs and to create media-rich experiences with animations, audio, video and graphics.

`With` keyword—Specifies that the subsequent property assignment statements contained between curly braces refer to the newly created object in an object initializer.

`WithEvents` keyword—Used in the declaration of an object that can generate events. Enables you to create event handlers for such an object.

workflow—The activity of a portion of a software system.

World Wide Web (WWW)—A communications system that allows computer users to locate and view multimedia documents (such as documents with text, graphics, animations, audios and videos).

World Wide Web Consortium (W3C)—A forum through which qualified individuals and companies cooperate to develop and standardize technologies for the web.

`Write` method of class `StreamWriter`—Writes a `String` to a file.

`WriteLine` method of class `StreamWriter`—Writes a `String` and a line terminator to a file.

X

`X` property of class `Point`—The property of class `Point` that specifies the *x*-coordinate.

`.xap` file —File-name extension for a compiled Silverlight application that is packaged by the IDE into a file containing the application and its supporting resources (such as images or other files used by the application).

***x*-axis**—Describes every horizontal coordinate.

***x*-coordinate**—Horizontal distance (increasing to the right) from the left of the drawing area.

`x:Name` attribute of a Silverlight control—Used to specify the name of the control so that you can access it programmatically from Visual Basic.

XAML (eXtensible Application Markup Language)—An XML vocabulary for describing WPF user interfaces.

`XDocument` class—Class that enables you to process XML data programmatically.

`XDocument.Parse` method—Method that parses XML into a form that can be accessed programmatically.

XML (eXtensible Markup Language)—Language for creating markup for describing data in a manner that both humans and computers can understand.

XML descendants property—New Visual Basic 2008 syntax that enables you to specify the elements to select from an XML document for processing in a LINQ to XML expression.

XML axis properties—New Visual Basic 2008 syntax for accessing XML elements directly from Visual Basic code.

XML vocabulary—XML-based markup language that provides a means for describing a particular type of data in a standardized, structured manner. For example, XAML is an XML vocabulary that describes WPF user interface information.

`Xor` (logical exclusive OR) operator—A logical operator that is `True` if and only if one of its operands is `True` and the other is `False`.

Y

`Y` property of class `Point`—The property of class `Point` that specifies the *y*-coordinate.

***y*-axis**—Describes every vertical coordinate.

***y*-coordinate**—Vertical distance (increasing downward) from the top of the drawing area.

INDEX

C

D

J

K

L

M

P

X

Y

The DEITEL® Suite of Products...

HOW TO PROGRAM BOOKS

C++ How to Program Sixth Edition

BOOK / CD-ROM

©2008, 1504 pp., paper (0-13-615250-3)

The complete authoritative DEITEL® *LIVE-CODE* introduction to programming with C++! The Sixth Edition takes an easy-to-follow, carefully developed early classes and objects approach to programming in C++. The text includes comprehensive coverage of the fundamentals of object-oriented programming in C++. It includes an optional automated teller machine (ATM) case study that teaches the fundamentals of software engineering and object-oriented design with the UML 2.0 in Chapters 1-7, 9 and 13. Additional integrated case studies appear throughout the text, including the `Time` class (Chapter 9), the `Employee` class (Chapters 12 and 13) and the `GradeBook` class (Chapters 3-7). This new edition includes a chapter on C++ game programming with the OGRE and OpenAL libraries, and a chapter on the Boost C++ Libraries, Technical Report 1 (TR1) and the forthcoming C++0X standard.

Small C++ How to Program Fifth Edition

BOOK / CD-ROM

©2005, 848 pp., paper (0-13-185758-4)

Based on chapters 1-13 (except the optional OOD/UML case study) and appendices of *C++ How to Program, Fifth Edition*, *Small C++* features a new early classes and objects approach and comprehensive coverage of the fundamentals of object-oriented programming in C++. Key topics include applications, variables, memory concepts, data types, control statements, functions, arrays, pointers and strings, inheritance and polymorphism.

Now available for both *C++ How to Program, 6/e* and *Small C++ How to Program, 5/e:* C++ Web-based *Cyber Classroom* included with the purchase of a new textbook. The *Cyber Classroom* includes a complete e-book, audio walkthroughs of the code examples, a Lab Manual and selected student solutions. See the *Cyber Classroom* section of this advertorial for more information.

Java™ How to Program Seventh Edition

BOOK / CD-ROM

©2007, 1500 pp., paper (0-13-222220-5)

The complete authoritative DEITEL® *LIVE-CODE* introduction to programming with the new Java™ Standard Edition 6! *Java How to Program, Seventh Edition* is up-to-date with Java™ SE 6 and includes comprehensive coverage of the fundamentals of object-oriented programming in Java; an early classes and objects approach; and an optional automated teller machine (ATM) case study that teaches the fundamentals of software engineering and object oriented design with the UML 2.0 in Chapters 1-8 and 10. Additional integrated case studies appear throughout the text, including GUI and graphics (Chapters 3-12), the `Time` class (Chapter 8), the `Employee` class (Chapters 9 and 10) and the `GradeBook` class (Chapters 3-8). New topics covered include Java Desktop Integration Components, Ajax Web application development with JavaServer Faces, web services and more.

Small Java™ How to Program Sixth Edition

BOOK / CD-ROM

©2005, 624 pp., paper (0-13-148660-8)

Based on chapters 1-10 of *Java™ How to Program, Sixth Edition*, *Small Java* is for use with J2SE™ 5.0, features an early classes and objects approach and comprehensive coverage of the fundamentals of object-oriented programming in Java. Key topics include applications, variables, data types, control statements, methods, arrays, object-based programming, inheritance and polymorphism.

Now available for both *Java How to Program, 7/e* and *Small Java How to Program, 6/e:* Java Web-based *Cyber Classroom* included with the purchase of a new textbook. The *Cyber Classroom* includes a complete e-book, audio walkthroughs of the code examples, a Lab Manual and selected student solutions. See the *Cyber Classroom* section of this advertorial for more information.

Sign up now for the FREE ***DEITEL® Buzz Online*** newsletter at:
`www.deitel.com/newsletter/subscribe.html`

Visual Basic® 2005 How to Program Third Edition

BOOK / CD-ROM

©2006, 1513 pp., paper (0-13-186900-0)

The complete authoritative DEITEL® *LIVE-CODE* introduction to Visual Basic programming. *Visual Basic® 2005 How to Program, Third Edition* is up-to-date with Microsoft's Visual Basic 2005. The text includes comprehensive coverage of the fundamentals of object-oriented programming in Visual Basic including a new early classes and objects approach and a new optional automated teller machine (ATM) case study that teaches the fundamentals of software engineering and object-oriented design with the UML 2.0 in Chapters 1,3–9 and 11. Additional integrated case studies appear throughout the text, including the `Time` class (Chapter 9), the `Employee` class (Chapters 10 and 11) and the `Gradebook` class (Chapters 4–9). This book also includes discussions of more advanced topics such as XML, ASP.NET, ADO.NET and Web services. New Visual Basic 2005 topics covered include partial classes, generics, the `My` namespace and Visual Studio's updated debugger features. *Visual Basic® 2008 How to Program, 4/e* coming Summer 2008.

Visual C++® 2008 How to Program, Second Edition

BOOK / CD-ROM

©2008, 1500 pp., paper (0-13-615157-4)

This Second Edition is based on our C++-standard-compliant textbook, *C++ How to Program, Sixth Edition*, and is intended for courses that offer a Microsoft-specific C++ programming focus using Visual C++ 2008. Microsoft has determined that most Visual C++ developers primarily use native C++. As a result, the book now focuses on native C++ and presents examples of .NET managed code programming with C++/CLI, where appropriate. The book takes an easy-to-follow, carefully developed early classes and objects approach, with comprehensive coverage of object-oriented programming. The optional automated teller machine (ATM) case study teaches the fundamentals of software engineering and object-oriented design with the UML 2.0. Additional integrated case studies appear throughout the text. This edition includes new coverage of .NET generics, collections and regular expressions.

Visual C#® 2005 How to Program Second Edition

BOOK / CD-ROM

©2006, 1591 pp., paper (0-13-152523-9)

The complete authoritative DEITEL® *LIVE-CODE* introduction to C# programming. *Visual C#® 2005 How to Program, Second Edition* is up-to-date with Microsoft's Visual C# 2005. The text includes comprehensive coverage of the fundamentals of object-oriented programming in C#, including a new early classes and objects approach and a new optional automated teller machine (ATM) case study that teaches the fundamentals of software engineering and object-oriented design with the UML 2.0 in Chapters 1, 3–9 and 11. Additional integrated case studies appear throughout the text, including the `Time` class (Chapter 9), the `Employee` class (Chapters 10 and 11) and the `Gradebook` class (Chapters 4–9). This book also includes discussions of more advanced topics such as XML, ASP.NET, ADO.NET and Web services. New Visual C# 2005 topics covered include partial classes, generics, the `My` namespace, .NET remoting and Visual Studio's updated debugger features. *Visual C#® 2008 How to Program, 3/e* coming Summer 2008.

C How to Program Fifth Edition

BOOK / CD-ROM

©2007, 1130 pp., paper (0-13-240416-8)

C How to Program, Fifth Edition—the world's best-selling C text—is designed for introductory through intermediate courses and programming languages survey courses. This comprehensive text is aimed at readers with little or no programming experience through intermediate audiences. Highly practical in approach, it introduces fundamental notions of structured programming and software engineering and gets up to speed quickly. The Fifth Edition features new chapters on the C99 standard and an introduction to game programming with the Allegro C Library.

www.deitel.com www.prenhall.com/deitel
Check out our Resource Centers at www.deitel.com/resourcecenters.html

Advanced Java™ 2 Platform How to Program

BOOK / CD-ROM

©2002, 1568 pp., paper (0-13-089560-1)

Expanding on the world's best-selling Java textbook—*Java™ How to Program—Advanced Java™ 2 Platform How To Program* presents advanced Java topics for developing sophisticated, user-friendly GUIs; significant, scalable enterprise applications; wireless applications and distributed systems. Primarily based on Java 2 Enterprise Edition (J2EE) 1.2.1, this textbook integrates technologies such as XML, JavaBeans, security, JDBC™, JavaServer Pages (JSP™), servlets, Remote Method Invocation (RMI), Enterprise JavaBeans™ (EJB), design patterns, Swing, J2ME™, Java 2D and 3D, XML, design patterns, CORBA, Jini™, JavaSpaces™, Jiro™, Java Management Extensions (JMX) and Peer-to-Peer networking with an introduction to JXTA.

Internet & World Wide Web How to Program Fourth Edition

BOOK / CD-ROM

©2008, 1552 pp., paper (0-13-175242-1)

This book introduces students with little or no programming experience to the exciting world of Web-based applications. It has been substantially reworked to reflect today's Web 2.0 rich Internet application-development methodologies. The book teaches the skills and tools for creating dynamic Web applications. Topics include introductory programming principles, markup languages (XHTML/XML), scripting languages (JavaScript, PHP and Ruby/Ruby on Rails), Ajax, web services, web servers (IIS/Apache), relational databases (MySQL/SQL Server 2005 Express/Apache Derby/Java DB), ASP .NET 2.0 and JavaServer™ Faces (JSF). You'll build Ajax-enabled rich Internet applications (RIAs)—using Ajax frameworks, Adobe® Flex™ and Microsoft® Silverlight—with the look-and-feel of desktop applications. The Dive Into® Web 2.0 chapter exposes readers to many other topics associated with Web 2.0 applications and businesses. After mastering the material in this book, students will be well prepared to build real-world, industrial-strength, Web-based applications.

> "As always, I am impressed with the Deitel organization and its books. I love teaching from them not only because the content is so sound, but also because of the competent and timely expertise and support provided."
>
> — Robert A. Long, Indiana University

Python How to Program

BOOK / CD-ROM

©2002, 1648 pp., paper (0-13-092361-3)

This exciting textbook provides a comprehensive introduction to Python—a powerful object-oriented programming language with clear syntax and the ability to bring together various technologies quickly and easily. This book covers introductory programming techniques and more advanced topics such as graphical user interfaces, databases, wireless Internet programming, networking, security, process management, multithreading, XHTML, CSS, PSP and multimedia. Readers will learn principles that are applicable to both systems development and Web programming.

XML How to Program

BOOK / CD-ROM

©2001, 1112 pp., paper (0-13-028417-3)

This book is a comprehensive guide to programming in XML. It teaches how to use XML to create customized tags and includes chapters that address markup languages for science and technology, multimedia, commerce and many other fields. Concise introductions to Java, JavaServer Pages, VBScript, Active Server Pages and Perl/CGI provide readers with the essentials of these programming languages and server-side development technologies to enable them to work effectively with XML. The book also covers topics such as XSL, DOM™, SAX, a real-world e-commerce case study and a complete chapter on Web accessibility that addresses Voice XML. Other topics covered include XHTML, CSS, DTD, schema, parsers, XPath, XLink, namespaces, XBase, XInclude, XPointer, XSLT, XSL Formatting Objects, JavaServer Pages, XForms, topic maps, X3D, MathML, OpenMath, CML, BML, CDF, RDF, SVG, Cocoon, WML, XBRL and BizTalk™ and SOAP™ Web resources.

Perl How to Program

©2001, 1057 pp., paper (0-13-028418-1)

This comprehensive guide to Perl programming emphasizes the use of the Common Gateway Interface (CGI) with Perl to create powerful, dynamic multi-tier Web-based client/server applications. The book begins with a clear and careful introduction to programming concepts at a level suitable for beginners, and proceeds through advanced topics such as references and complex data structures. Key Perl topics such as regular expressions and string manipulation are covered in detail. The authors address important and topical issues such as object-oriented programming, the Perl database interface (DBI), graphics and security. Also included is a treatment of XML, a bonus chapter introducing the Python programming language, supplemental material on career resources and a complete chapter on Web accessibility.

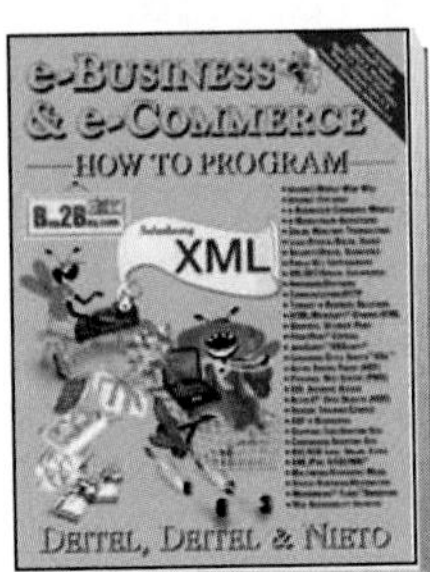

e-Business & e-Commerce How to Program

BOOK / CD-ROM

©2001, 1254 pp., paper (0-13-028419-X)

This book explores programming technologies for developing Web-based e-business and e-commerce solutions, and covers e-business and e-commerce models and business issues. Readers learn a full range of options, from "build-your-own" to turnkey solutions. The book examines scores of the top e-businesses (examples include Amazon, eBay, Priceline, Travelocity, etc.), explaining the technical details of building successful e-business and e-commerce sites and their underlying business premises. Learn how to implement the dominant e-commerce models—shopping carts, auctions, name-your-own-price, comparison shopping and bots/intelligent agents—by using markup languages (HTML, Dynamic HTML and XML), scripting languages (JavaScript, VBScript and Perl), server-side technologies (Active Server Pages and Perl/CGI) and database (SQL and ADO), security and online payment technologies.

"In my courses, I've read several Deitel books. I really enjoy reading and learning from them because they're written in a fashion that's very easy to follow. It's almost like someone is speaking to you, and you don't get lost in a lot of unnecessarily complicated paragraphs. There are sections that have some humor and the real world examples they use help you understand why some things that are good in theory don't work as well in practice. I think Paul and Harvey Deitel have done an amazing job researching the latest technologies and then presenting them in a very understandable way. Whenever I take a new class and find out that we are to use a Deitel book, I'm very happy about that because they're my favorite. I know I can rely upon the book to explain the subject clearly."

— Christine Spencer, Graduate of MIT

For ordering information,
visit us on the Web at www.prenhall.com.

INTERNATIONAL ORDERING INFORMATION

CANADA:
Pearson Education Canada
26 Prince Andrew Place
PO Box 580
Don Mills, Ontario M3C 2T8 Canada
Tel.: 416-925-2249; Fax: 416-925-0068
e-mail: phcinfo.pubcanada@pearsoned.com

EUROPE, MIDDLE EAST, AND AFRICA:
Pearson Education
Edinburgh Gate
Harlow, Essex CM20 2JE UK
Tel: 01279 623928; Fax: 01279 414130
e-mail: enq.orders@pearsoned-ema.com

BENELUX REGION:
Pearson Education
Concertgebouwplein 25
1071 LM Amsterdam
The Netherlands
Tel: 31 20 5755 800; Fax: 31 20 664 5334
e-mail: amsterdam@pearsoned-ema.com

ASIA:
Pearson Education Asia Pte. Ltd.
23/25 First Lok Yang Road
Jurong, 629733 Singapore
Tel: 65 476 4688; Fax: 65 378 0370

JAPAN:
Pearson Education Japan
Ogikubo TM Bldg. 6F. 5-26-13 Ogikubo
Suginami-ku, Tokyo 167-0051 Japan
Tel: 81 3 3365 9001; Fax: 81 3 3365 9009

INDIA:
Pearson Education
Indian Branch
482 FIE, Patparganj
Delhi – 110092 India
Tel: 91 11 2059850 & 2059851
Fax: 91 11 2059852

AUSTRALIA:
Pearson Education Australia
Unit 4, Level 2, 14 Aquatic Drive
Frenchs Forest, NSW 2086, Australia
Tel: 61 2 9454 2200; Fax: 61 2 9453 0089
e-mail: marketing@pearsoned.com.au

NEW ZEALAND/FIJI:
Pearson Education
46 Hillside Road
Auckland 10, New Zealand
Tel: 649 444 4968; Fax: 649 444 4957
E-mail: sales@pearsoned.co.nz

SOUTH AFRICA:
Maskew Miller Longman
Central Park Block H
16th Street Midrand 1685
South Africa
Tel: 27 21 686 6356; Fax: 27 21 686 4590

LATIN AMERICA:
Pearson Education Latin America
Attn: Tina Sheldon
1 Lake Street
Upper Saddle River, NJ 07458

The SIMPLY SERIES!

The Deitels' *Simply Series* takes an engaging new approach to teaching programming languages from the ground up. The pedagogy of this series combines the DEITEL® signature *LIVE-CODE Approach* with an *APPLICATION-DRIVEN Tutorial Approach* to teach programming with outstanding pedagogical features that help students learn. They have merged the notion of a lab manual with that of a conventional textbook, creating a book in which readers build and execute complete applications from start to finish, while learning the fundamental concepts of programming!

Simply Visual Basic® 2008 An APPLICATION-DRIVEN Tutorial Approach, Third Edition

©2009, 848 pp., paper (0-13-605303-3)

Simply Visual Basic® 2008 An APPLICATION-DRIVEN Tutorial Approach, 3/e, guides readers through building real-world applications that incorporate Visual Basic 2008 programming fundamentals. Learn GUI design, controls, methods, functions, data types, control statements, procedures, arrays, object-oriented programming, exception-handling, collections, strings and characters, sequential files and more in this comprehensive introduction to Visual Basic 2008. Higher-end topics include LINQ, ASP .NET 3.5, ASP.NET AJAX, Visual Web Developer 2008 Express, database programming, multimedia and graphics, Silverlight and Web applications development.

Simply C# An APPLICATION-DRIVEN Tutorial Approach

©2004, 992 pp., paper (0-13-142641-9)

Simply C# An APPLICATION-DRIVEN Tutorial Approach guides readers through building real-world applications that incorporate C# programming fundamentals. Learn GUI design, controls, methods, functions, data types, control statements, procedures, arrays, object-oriented programming, strings and characters, sequential files and more in this comprehensive introduction to C#. We also include higher-end topics such as database programming, multimedia and graphics and Web applications development.

Simply Java™ Programming An APPLICATION-DRIVEN Tutorial Approach

©2004, 1300 pp., paper (0-13-142648-6)

Simply Java™ Programming An APPLICATION-DRIVEN Tutorial Approach guides readers through building real-world applications that incorporate Java programming fundamentals. Learn GUI design, components, methods, event-handling, types, control statements, arrays, object-oriented programming, exception-handling, strings and characters, sequential files and more in this comprehensive introduction to Java. We also include higher-end topics such as database programming, multimedia, graphics and Web applications development.

Simply C++ An APPLICATION-DRIVEN Tutorial Approach

©2005, 704 pp., paper (0-13-142660-5)

Simply C++ An APPLICATION-DRIVEN Tutorial Approach guides readers through building real-world applications that incorporate C++ programming fundamentals. Learn methods, functions, data types, control statements, procedures, arrays, object-oriented programming, strings and characters, pointers, references, templates, operator overloading and more in this comprehensive introduction to C++.

THE BUZZ ABOUT THE DEITEL® SUITE OF PRODUCTS!

Deitel & Associates garners worldwide praise for its best-selling *How to Program Series* of books and its signature *Live-Code Approach*. See for yourself what our readers have to say:

"I'm glad to see the early treatment of objects done so well. This is perhaps the most comprehensive Visual Basic .NET text accessible to the beginner."

— Gavin Osborne, Saskatchewan Institute of Applied Science and Technology

"A great book for the novice programmer for learning VB. NET quickly and writing programs with significantly improved performance, and vastly improved readability."

— Sujay Ghuge, Verizon Information Technology

"The book is comprehensive, correct and crystal clear. No other textbook comes close in carefully explaining the intricacies of this powerful language."

— James Huddleston, Independent Contractor

"This book is one of the best of its kind. It is an excellent 'objects first' coverage of C++ that remains accessible to beginners. The example-driven presentation is enriched by the optional OOD/UML ATM cases study that contextualizes the material in an ongoing software engineering project."

— Gavin Osborne, Saskatchewan Institute of Applied Science and Technology

"I am continually impressed with the Deitels' ability to clearly explain concepts and ideas, which allows the student to gain a well-rounded understanding of the language and software development."

— Karen Arlien, Bismarck State College

"Great early introduction to classes and objects. The combination of live-code examples and detailed figures provides a unique visualization of C++ concepts."

— Earl LaBatt, University of New Hampshire

"Probably the most complete coverage of learning through examples in published material today. This material is such high quality—it is unbelievable. The ATM is super."

— Anne Horton, AT&T Bell Laboratories

"*Java How to Program, 6/e* is an excellent book to learn how to program in Java. The book does an excellent job describing the new features included in the JDK 5.0, including generics and formatted output. The book is easy to read with numerous, simple-to-follow code examples."

— Doug Kohlert, Sun Microsystems

"An excellent combination of C#, UML and pseudocode that leads the reader to create good applications and well designed algorithms, using the best practices! Few books mix all of this so well. Great idea and great work!"

— Jose Antonio Seco, Andalucia's Parlamient, Spain

"The writing style is comprehensive, systematic and clear. Nothing is either skipped or glossed over. Of particular note is the authors' attention to good software engineering concepts, and the wide selection of code examples provides excellent reinforcement for the practical application of developing Java skills."

— Dean Mellas, Computer and information Sciences, Cerritos College

"Good job! Introduces OOP without burying the reader in complexity. I think the level of conceptual detail is perfect. This will be a great help the next time I teach 101."

— Walt Bunch, Chapman University

"The new edition... is by far the best student-oriented textbook on programming in the C language—the Deitels have set the standard-again! A thorough, careful, student-oriented treatment of not just the langauge, but more importantly, the ideas, concepts, and techniques of programming! The addition of 'live code' is also a big plus—encouraging active participation by the student. A great text!"

— Richard Albright, Goldey-Beacom College

"Once again the Deitel team has produced another academic winner. From start to finish they have the novice programmer in mind...They give enough theory so the students can learn the "why" and not just the "how." The book is an interesting text with practical examples to tie together the theory and the practice. I strongly recommend it as a VB 2005 book for beginning VB students regardless of their academic major."

— Harlan Brewer, Select Engineering Services, Inc.

"Bravo for a wonderful learning experience! I have seen (and bought) lots of programming books (Basic, C, C++) over the years, yours is number one on my list. Wow... it is a joy to work with. Thanks."

— Thomas J. McGrail, Longs, SC

MULTIMEDIA CYBER CLASSROOMS

Premium content available with *Java™ How to Program, Seventh Edition* and *C++ How to Program, Sixth Edition!*

Java How to Program, 7/e and *C++ How to Program, 6/e* are now available with 12-month access to the web-based *Multimedia Cyber Classroom* for students who purchase new copies of these books! The *Cyber Classroom* is an interactive, multimedia, tutorial version of DEITEL textbooks. *Cyber Classrooms* are a great value, giving students additional hands-on experience and study aids.

NOW AVAILABLE
for Java How to Program, 7/e and C++ How to Program, 6/e
(with purchase of a new book)

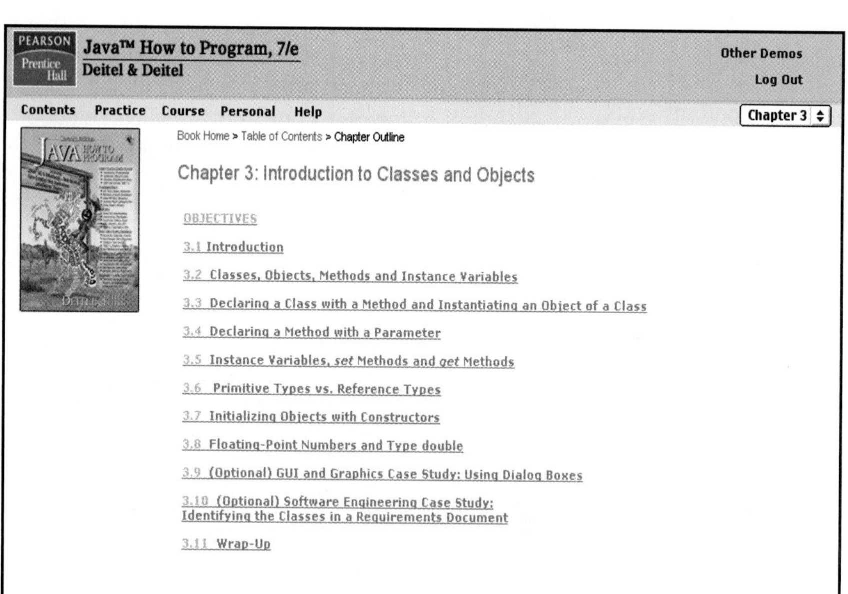

PEARSON Prentice Hall
Java™ How to Program, 7/e
Deitel & Deitel
Other Demos
Log Out
Contents Practice Course Personal Help
Chapter 3
Book Home > Table of Contents > Chapter Outline
Chapter 3: Introduction to Classes and Objects
OBJECTIVES
3.1 Introduction
3.2 Classes, Objects, Methods and Instance Variables
3.3 Declaring a Class with a Method and Instantiating an Object of a Class
3.4 Declaring a Method with a Parameter
3.5 Instance Variables, set Methods and get Methods
3.6 Primitive Types vs. Reference Types
3.7 Initializing Objects with Constructors
3.8 Floating-Point Numbers and Type double
3.9 (Optional) GUI and Graphics Case Study: Using Dialog Boxes
3.10 (Optional) Software Engineering Case Study: Identifying the Classes in a Requirements Document
3.11 Wrap-Up

DEITEL® Multimedia Cyber Classrooms *feature an e-book with the complete text of their corresponding* How to Program *titles.*

active figure

Click here to listen.

Not working? Get QuickTime.

```
// Fig. 3.1: GradeBook.java
// Class declaration with one method.

public class GradeBook
{
   // display a welcome message to the GradeBook user
   public void displayMessage()
   {
      System.out.println( "Welcome to the Grade Book!" );
   } // end method displayMessage

} // end class GradeBook
```

Fig. 3.1	Class declaration with one method.

Close

© 2007 Pearson Prentice Hall, Inc. | A Pearson Education Company | Upper Saddle River, New Jersey 07458
Activebook Technology Developed by Active Learning Technologies, Inc.
Legal Notice | Privacy Statement
PEARSON Prentice Hall

Unique audio "walkthroughs" of code examples reinforce key concepts.

Sign up now for the FREE ***DEITEL® Buzz Online*** newsletter at:
www.deitel.com/newsletter/subscribe.html

MULTIMEDIA CYBER CLASSROOMS

DEITEL® *Multimedia Cyber Classrooms* include:

- The full text, illustrations and program listings of its corresponding *How to Program* book.
- Hours of detailed, expert audio descriptions of hundreds of lines of code that help to reinforce important concepts.
- An abundance of self-assessment material, including practice exams, hundreds of programming exercises and self-review questions and answers.

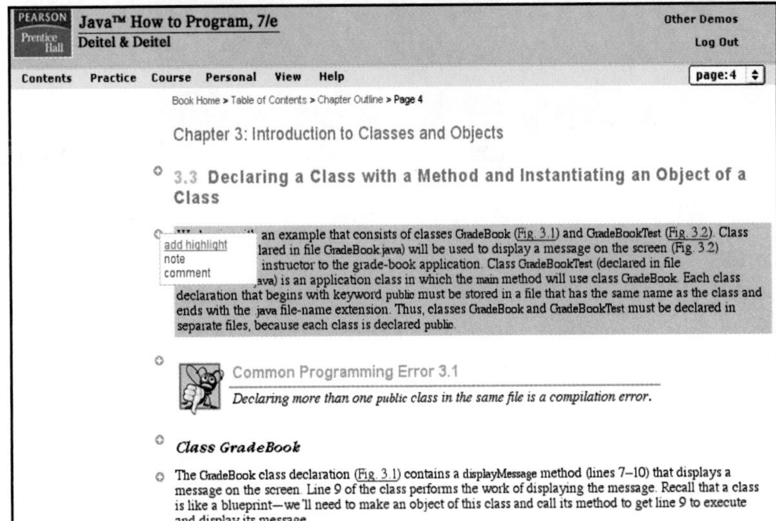

DEITEL® Multimedia Cyber Classrooms *offer a host of interactive features, such as highlighting of key sections of the text...*

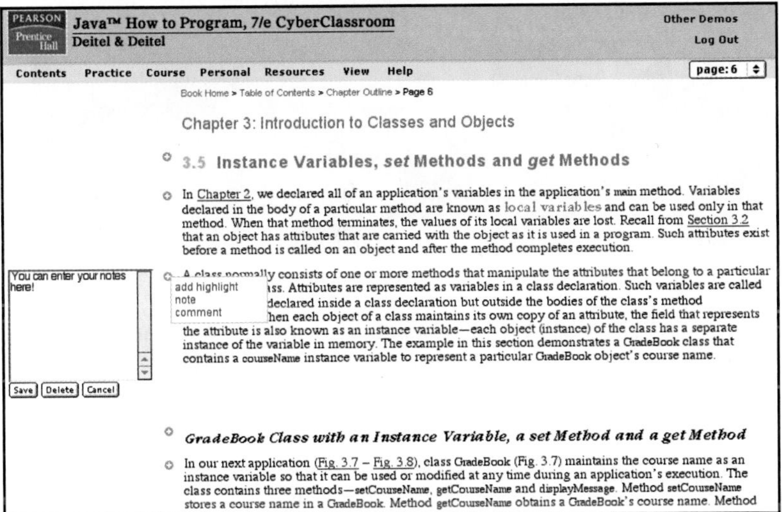

...and the ability to write notes in the margin of a given page for future reference.

- Intuitive browser-based interface designed to be easy and accessible.
- A Lab Manual featuring lab exercises as well as pre- and post-lab activities.
- Student Solutions to approximately one-half of the exercises in the textbook.

Students receive 12-month access to a protected web site via access code cards packaged with these new textbooks. (Simply tear the strip on the inside of the Cyber Classroom package to reveal access code.)

For more information, please visit:
www.prenhall.com/deitel/cyberclassroom

www.deitel.com www.prenhall.com/deitel
Check out our Resource Centers at www.deitel.com/resourcecenters.html

DEITEL® BUZZ ONLINE NEWSLETTER

Each issue of our free, e-mail newsletter, the *DEITEL® BUZZ ONLINE*, is now sent to about 50,000 opt-in subscribers. This weekly newsletter provides updates on our publishing program, our instructor-led professional training courses, timely industry topics and the continuing stream of innovations and new Web 2.0 business ventures emerging from Deitel.

The DEITEL® Buzz Online includes:

- Resource centers on programming, Web 2.0 and more.
- Updates on all Deitel publications of interest to students, instructors and professionals.
- Free tutorials and guest articles (part of the Deitel Free Content Initiative).
- Information on our instructor-led professional training courses taught worldwide.
- Detailed ordering information, additional book resources, code downloads and more.
- Available in both HTML or plain-text format.
- Previous issues are archived at: `www.deitel.com/newsletter/backissues.html`.
- Check out the complete list of Resource Centers at `www.deitel.com/ResourceCenters.html`.

Please add the domain **deitel.com** to your list of allowed senders.
If you are unable to read this newsletter in your e-mail client, please click here to view it in a Web browser.

Deitel® Buzz Online

Your Information Resource for Building Web 2.0 Businesses

Cutting-Edge Textbooks, E-Learning and Media Solutions Published by Pearson/Prentice Hall!
Cutting-Edge Programming Languages Training Delivered at Organizations Worldwide!

Welcome to the April 27, 2008 issue of the *Deitel Buzz Online Newsletter!* In this issue we introduce our new ADO.NET Resource Center. You can also visit our complete Resource Center list.

Be sure to check out the 35% discounts that Informit.com is offering on our *Java Fundamentals I and II* LiveLessons video course and on our new book *AJAX, Rich Internet Applications, and Web Development for Programmers* (the *Deitel Developer Series* version of *Internet & World Wide Web How to Program, 4/e*).

In upcoming newsletters we'll preview our new books *Simply Visual Basic 2008, 3/e* (coming this May), *Visual Basic 2008 How to Program, 4/e* (coming this summer) and *Visual C# 2008 How to Program, 3/e* (coming this summer).

New! ADO.NET Resource Center

To sponsor Deitel Resource Centers or to commission custom Resource Centers, contact Abbey Deitel.

Welcome to the ADO.NET Resource Center. ADO.NET, part of Microsoft's .NET Framework class library, allows programmers to access and modify data in relational database systems, such as Microsoft SQL Server. Start your search here for ADO.NET tutorials, articles, sample chapters, books, blogs, videos, eBooks, FAQs and more. In the ADO.NET Resource Center, you'll find links to:

- The article, "What's New in ADO.NET?" from Microsoft's ".NET Developers Guide."
- "Overview of ADO.NET," from the Microsoft .NET Framework Developer's Guide.
- The tutorial, "Introduction to ADO.NET," by Dimitrios Markatos.
- "ADO.NET Definitions and Examples," from Data Direct.
- The sample chapter, "An Introduction to Database Programming," from *Murach's ADO.NET 2.0 Database Programming with VB 2005*, by Anne Boehm.
- The Microsoft ADO.NET Solution Center.
- The article, "Roadmap for ADO.NET DataSet, DataView, and DataViewManager Objects," from Microsoft.
- The three-part article, "Implementing a Generic Data Access Layer in ADO.NET," by Joydip Kanjilal.
- The presentation, "Developers Overview of the ADO.NET Entity Framework for Visual Studio 2008," from Microsoft.
- The tutorial, "SQL Anywhere ADO.NET Entity Framework," from Sybase.
- Microsoft ADO.NET Team Blog.
- The article, "ADO.NET Tech Preview: Entity Data Model," from Microsoft.
- The ADO.NET Entity Framework & liNQ to Relational Data web site.
- The article, "Migrating Database Applications from JDBC to ADO.NET," by Andrew J. Bradfield.
- The article, "How to Connect to a Database and Run a Command by Using ADO.NET and Visual Basic.NET," from Microsoft.
- The webcast, "Microsoft ADO.NET Concurrency Using Visual Basic Windows Forms," from Microsoft.
- The white papers, "Overview ADO.NET: Data Services ("Project Astoria")," and "Using ADO.NET Data Services," from Microsoft.
- The article, "Code Access Security and ADO.NET," from Microsoft.
- The article, "ADO.NET Data Service (Astoria) in Silverlight 2 (Beta 1)," by Michael Sync.
- The tutorial, "Calling Stored Procedures with ADO.NET," by Paul Kimmell.
- The video, "ADO.NET Data Services—Querying with URL's," from Microsoft.
- The webcast, "Microsoft ADO.NET: Programming ADO.NET DataSets," presented by Vijaya Byri and Manisha Gupta of Microsoft.
- ADO.NET books, conferences, blogs, eBooks, videos, webcasts, sample chapters, FAQs and tutorials.
- And more...

Check out the following related Deitel Resource Centers:

- Ajax
- ASP.NET
- ASP.NET Ajax
- ASP.NET 3.5
- C#
- DotNetNuke (DNN)
- Internet Explorer 7 (IE7)
- Microsoft liNQ
- Microsoft Popfly
- .NET
- .NET 3.0
- .NET 3.5
- SharePoint
- Silverlight
- Silverlight 2.0
- SQL Server 2008
- Visual Basic
- Visual Basic 2008
- Visual C++
- Visual C# 2008 and C# 3.0
- Visual Studio Team System
- Windows Communication Foundation
- Windows Presentation Foundation
- Windows Vista

Now Available! *Visual C++ 2008 How to Program*

Now Available! *Internet and World Wide Web How to Program, 4/e*

35% Discount at Informit.com! *AJAX, Rich Internet Applications, and Web Development for Programmers*

35% Discount at Informit.com! *Java Fundamentals I and II (LiveLessons Video Training)*

Check it Out! The Free 81-Page *Dive Into Web 2.0* e-Book

Last Week's Newsletter

Complete Resource Center List

Internships Honors Internship Program Summer 2008

Instructor Resources Information for Instructors Teaching from our Books

Corporate Training On-Site Programming-Languages Training

Recent Publications *AJAX, Rich Internet Applications, and Web Development for Programmers (Deitel Developer Series professional book based on Internet and World Wide Web How to Program, 4/e)*

Visual C++ 2008 How to Program, 2/e

Internet and World Wide Web How to Program, 4/e

C++ How to Program, 6/e

C How to Program, 5/e

C# for Programmers, 2/e (Deitel Developer Series professional book based on *Visual C# 2005 How to Program*)

Java How to Program, 7/e

Simply C++

Simply C#

Simply Java Programming

Simply Visual Basic 2005, 2/e

Small C++ How to Program, 5/e

Small Java How to Program, 5/e

Visual Basic 2005 How to Program, 3/e (college textbook)

Visual Basic 2005 for Programmers, 2/e (Deitel Developer Series professional book)

Visual C# 2005 How to Program, 2/e (college textbook)

Operating Systems, 3/e

All Deitel Publications

Tutorials from the Deitel Free Content Library

Customer Service

Turn the page to find out more about Deitel & Associates!

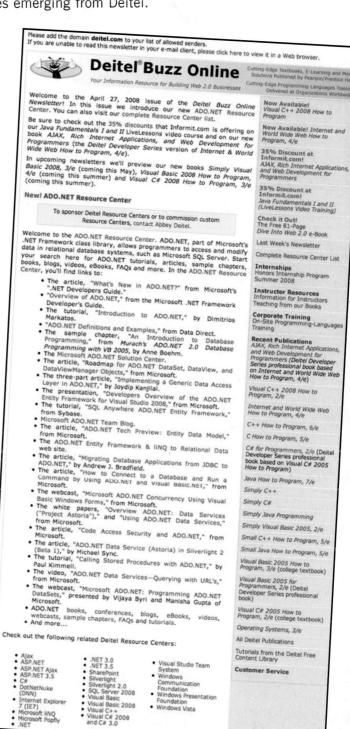

To sign up for the *DEITEL® BUZZ ONLINE* newsletter, visit `www.deitel.com/newsletter/subscribe.html`.

DIVE INTO® SERIES CORPORATE TRAINING DELIVERED WORLDWIDE

Deitel & Associates, Inc. provides intensive, lecture-and-laboratory courses to organizations worldwide. The programming courses use our signature *Live-Code Approach*, presenting complete working programs.

Deitel & Associates, Inc. has trained over one million students and professionals worldwide through Dive Into® Series corporate training courses, public seminars, university teaching, *How to Program Series* textbooks, *Deitel® Developer Series* books, *Simply Series* textbooks, *Cyber Classroom Series and Live Lessons* multimedia packages, *Complete Training Course Series* textbook and multimedia packages, broadcast-satellite courses and Web-based training.

Educational Consulting

Deitel & Associates, Inc. offers complete educational consulting services for corporate training programs and professional schools including:

- Curriculum design and development
- Preparation of Instructor Guides
- Customized courses and course materials
- Design and implementation of professional training certificate programs
- Instructor certification
- Train-the-trainers programs
- Delivery of software-related corporate training programs

Visit our Web site for more information on our Dive Into® Series corporate training curriculum and to purchase our training products.

Would you like to review upcoming publications?

If you are a professor or senior industry professional interested in being a reviewer of our forthcoming publications, please contact us by email at `deitel@deitel.com`. Insert "Content Reviewer" in the subject heading.

Are you interested in a career in computer education, publishing and training?

We offer a limited number of full-time positions available for college graduates in computer science, information systems, information technology, management information systems, advertising and marketing. Please check our Web site for the latest job postings or contact us by email at `deitel@deitel.com`. Insert "Full-time Job" in the subject heading.

Are you a Boston-area college student looking for an internship or co-op?

We have a limited number of competitive summer positions and 15-20-hr./week school-year opportunities for computer science, IT/IS, MIS and marketing majors. Students work at our headquarters west of Boston. We also offer full-time co-ops for students taking a semester off from school. This is an excellent opportunity for students looking to gain industry experience and earn money to pay for school. Please contact us by email at `deitel@deitel.com`. Insert "Internship" in the subject heading.

Would you like to explore contract training opportunities with us?

Deitel & Associates, Inc. is looking for contract instructors to teach software-related topics at our clients' sites in the United States and worldwide. Applicants should be experienced professional trainers or college professors. For more information, please visit `www.deitel.com` and send your resume to Abbey Deitel at `deitel@deitel.com`.

Are you a training company in need of quality course materials?

Corporate training companies worldwide use our *How to Program Series* textbooks, *Complete Training Course Series* book and multimedia packages, *Simply Series* textbooks and our *Deitel® Developer Series* books in their classes. We have extensive ancillary instructor materials for many of our products. For more details, please visit `www.deitel.com` or contact us by email at `deitel@deitel.com`.